STAY TUNED

A CONCISE HISTORY OF AMERICAN BROADCASTING

SECOND EDITION

Christopher H.
Sterling

*The George Washington
University*

John M.
Kittross

*Emerson
College*

Wadsworth
Publishing Company
*Belmont
California*

Dedication

*to our parents–who were there
and thus listened to many things
we missed*

Communications Editor
Rebecca Hayden

Editorial Assistant
Tamiko Verkler

Production
Greg Hubit Bookworks

Designer
Dare Porter

Cover Designer
Frances Hasegawa and Vargas/Williams/Design

Copy Editor
Patricia Harris

Library of Congress Cataloging in Publication Data

Sterling, Christopher H., 1943–
  Stay tuned.

  Includes bibliographical references
  1. Broadcasting—United States—History.
I. Kittross, John M., 1929–
II. Title.
HE8689.8.S73   1990   384.54′0973
                                89-16675

ISBN 0-534-11905-0

Printed in the United States of America

 2 3 4 5 6 7 8 9 10

94 93 92 91 90

Chapter Opening Photo Credits

Chapter 1: *Courtesy of AT&T Photo Center* • Chapter 2: *Smithsonian Institution Photo 76–14662* • Chapter 3: *Courtesy of Group W and Broadcast Pioneers Library (WJZ, Newark, in 1923)* • Chapter 4: *Smithsonian Institution Photo 76–14658* • Chapter 5: *Culver Pictures, Inc. (George Burns and Gracie Allen in the 1930s)* • Chapter 6: *Culver Pictures, Inc. (Edward R. Murrow during World War II)* • Chapter 7: *Indelible, Inc. (Milton Berle)* • Chapter 8: *Courtesy of National Broadcasting Company, Inc. (Chet Huntley and David Brinkley at 1956 Democratic Convention)* • Chapter 9: *Courtesy of KQED (from Sesame Street)* • Chapter 10: *Photo courtesy of The National Broadcasting Company, Inc. (The Cosby Show)* • Chapter 11: *Courtesy of NASA (30/20 GHz satellite concept)*

Cover Photo Credit:
Culver Pictures, Inc.

ings books; nobody talked about LPTV or HDTV; the FCC was still a force to be reckoned with; "indecency" was left to the pulpit and the pamphlet; and nobody ever dreamed that all three networks, the most stable part of the industry, would be sold.

There are those who now say that the "gee-whiz" or "glamorous something special" hallmark of broadcasting has dissipated. They say that broadcasting is only one small but inseparable part of our current culture and economy. By 1980, it was clear that the new breed of MBAs were in control of broadcasting, as they were in many other industries, and were treating broadcasting as "just another business" that could be manipulated for improvement of the short-term "bottom line" according to the gospel of the graduate business schools. Additionally, the Reagan administration had the political clout to expand the "marketplace ideology" policies supporting arbitrary deregulation that had surfaced late in the Carter administration. These views are held by many outside of broadcasting and, due to the influence of the present crop of business managers who do not think of broadcasting as a calling, by many now in positions of leadership in radio and television. The authors of *Stay Tuned*, however, are not convinced that we should dismiss the special nature of broadcasting that easily. We believe that it *is* special, even if its shape has changed.

We have tried to cover the turbulent first decade of this new shape of the industry in an all-new chapter 10, while retaining those portions of earlier chapters that have withstood the test of time and the slings and arrows of our colleagues and students. Rewritten chapters 9 and 11 benefit from what we have learned since the first edition. Corrections and minor updatings have been made in chapters 1 through 8,

Preface to the Second Edition

In the decade since publication of the first edition of *Stay Tuned*, the world has not stood still. Indeed, the jury is out as to whether this period has not seen more changes in broadcasting than any other decade since broadcasting became an industry in the 1920s.

It may be argued that the late 1970s were the period of highest complexity, even achievement, of the broadcasting industry, as described in chapters 3 through 9. It was a period of real scarcity of outlets, with limited opportunity for entry. But it also was the last period when the people running the industry had come up through the ranks and perhaps still believed in broadcasting as a public interest, convenience, and/or necessity.

Actually, 1978 marked the start of a new ball game. At that time, only three-quarters of today's full-power stations were on the air; cable served only half the number of homes it serves today—and pay-cable was only starting; home VCRs were virtually unknown; PBS rarely made the ratings books;

and the greatly expanded glossary and bibliography include the results of current knowledge and scholarship. Tables in Appendix C have been updated, a difficult task since the FCC, in the name of "deregulation," no longer collects much of the data we had access to earlier.

To do all this required help. Frank Kahn voluntarily supplied a surgical overview of the first edition; George Shiers brought his technical knowledge to bear, as did Paul Beck; Amy Vossen gleefully unlimbered her blue pencil on the new sections; Donald G. Godfrey, Harry Sova, and Michael J. Stanton provided useful feedback as they reviewed chapters 10 and 11; the ever-patient Becky Hayden had every excuse to stop being patient; those who called upon us for information (and the settling of bets) found themselves pumped for information; those who complained about our subtitling the book "American," ignoring the other nations of this hemisphere, received apologies; and several classes of guinea pigs suffered good-humoredly.

As individuals, we have noted some changes that are not explicitly included in *Stay Tuned.* Our children are not children any more; there are new pets to feed; only one of the parents to whom we have dedicated this volume is still alive; we have both dabbled in academic administration; we have both moved to new locations (the George Washington University and Emerson College, respectively) and owe thanks to new presidents and chairpersons. We have both subscribed to cable and acquired VCRs. But the important things remain the same: the steadfast support of our wives, and our belief in—and excitement over—the importance of the history of broadcasting.

The ambiguous mirrors of radio and television, reflecting the world about us and projecting our interests and concerns upon themselves, are a major part of all our lives. In fact, most of us spend more time listening to and watching radio and television in an average week than doing anything else except perhaps sleeping.

But we feel, in addition, that any institution—such as broadcasting—must recognize its roots and learn from its history in order to compete with other institutions and to grow in a constantly changing environment. Even though the past never exactly repeats itself, our knowledge of it will shape our future course.

Our goal is to tell how American broadcasting got where it is today and, by analyzing principles, events, and trends, suggest what directions it may take in the future. We emphasize trends rather than incidents and trivia, key individuals rather than random examples, and basic principles rather than isolated facts. Instead of just listing events, we try to explain them, interrelating developments in technology, organization and structure of the industry, economics, news and entertainment programming, audience research, and public policy and regulation.

We have arranged our material both chronologically and topically. The chapters are built around well-defined, consecutive periods of broadcasting's development. The topical arrangement of sections within chapters is consistent throughout the book except for the first two chapters. Tables of contents for both approaches are provided.

Within each chapter describing an era, we start with technology—the conditions, inventions, and innovations of that period relating to broadcasting. Man-made laws are more easily changed than are natural laws governing the electromagnetic spec-

Preface to the First Edition

"... it might be advantageous to 'shout' the message, spreading it broadcast to receivers in all directions, and for which the wireless system is well adapted, seeing that it is so inexpensive and so easily and rapidly installed—such as for army manoeuvres, for reporting races and other sporting events, and, generally, for all important matters . . ."—J. J. Fahie, *A History of Wireless Telegraphy* (1901), p. 259

"In 1928 we were watching it grow.

"And in 1950 the radio art will have influenced this whole people for more than thirty years, breaking down their distance barriers, making all the world their neighbor, carrying the electric word from coast to coast and nation to nation . . . promoting understanding, sympathy, peace . . .

"It will have played its part in the development of music . . . in education, and in business, and in happiness . . ."—Paul Schubert, *The Electric Word* (1928), p. 311

We think that the history of broadcasting is important.

trum. Allocations of spectrum space trigger political attention because broadcasting is important to the public. Allocations of time and money are important to other technologically based media and industries. Technological innovation involves economic antecedents and consequences, from the acquisition and control of patents, the unwillingness to discard investment in obsolescent studio equipment and receivers, to the entire range of relationships between government, industry, and the public, as the financial stakes grow over the years. These relationships are often far more important than the individual inventors, innovators, or electronic devices they develop.

Within each chapter beyond the earliest, we then discuss the basic unit of broadcasting—the individual station, originally thought of as the outlet for local expression and regulated by Congress accordingly.

Stations soon found it more profitable to establish affiliation with a national network, helping create the power of nationwide broadcasting organizations, to which we turn our attention in the third section of most chapters. We see the changing cast of haves and have-nots among stations and networks constantly jockeying for position and often creating or coloring important trends in the not-so-monolithic broadcasting industry.

In the fourth section of chapter 3 and later chapters, we examine the checkered development of educational, later public, broadcasting and the often precarious fortunes of noncommercial broadcasters, supported by donations, schools, government, and, more recently, corporate underwriting.

However, radio and television in the United States have become overwhelmingly commercial in respect to overall investment, audience interest, or nearly any other criterion. By the late 1920s advertising agencies had assumed a dominant position in network programming policy-making, a position they held for nearly three decades. Also discussed in the fifth section of most chapters are the changing roles of different media as new broadcast advertising competitors arrived on the scene.

Certainly listeners value broadcasting almost exclusively for its programming. In the sixth part of all but the first two chapters we review the development of program types, the apparent cycles of their invention-imitation-decline over the years, and the borrowing by one medium of another's content. We explore reasons for television's rapid development of program diversity compared with radio; we see why entertainment programming has been most popular while specific news broadcasts are often most memorable. Broadcast programming helps us maintain our surveillance of the world, to integrate what we see and hear, and transmits our culture—whether we like it or not—from person to person, country to country, and generation to generation. At the same time, its entertainment is a counterbalance to the stresses of our increasingly complex society.

One cannot discuss programming without looking at the audiences, of which we are all a part. The seventh part of chapters 3 through 10 [11 in the second edition] covers various aspects of the audience for radio and television—how it evolved, its reflection in the development and sale of receivers, ways of measuring its size, needs, and desires, and the effects that broadcasting is believed to have on people.

Because the radio spectrum is considered to be a national natural resource, it is administered by the federal government. We devote the eighth section to the roles of the legislative, judicial, and executive branches of government as well as to that creature with characteristics of all three, the Federal Communications Commission and its predecessors. Communications policy in this country is an intricate combination of politics, economics, technology, and sometimes logic, formed in a crucible of opposing public and private interests. Because the regulatory policies and judicial doctrines form slowly, many problems in broadcasting continue without apparent solution for years or even decades.

Finally, each chapter ends with a very brief account of the parallel events in broadcasting elsewhere in the world and notes some relationships of American radio and television to other social expressions of the period, such as wars, fads, the Depression, and Watergate.

Within this topical structure, we follow not only trends and continuing problems but the contributions of individual persons. Problems often return in other guises with other casts of characters. Personnel changes create policy changes in or among networks, stations, advertisers, the FCC, Congress, and citizen groups that can affect the entire institution of broadcasting. In reviewing the lives of radio and television's pioneers, we are reminded that broadcasting has been a part of American life for little more than a lifetime.

The authors of this book are, quite frankly, fascinated with the subject of broadcasting. We have tried to share our enthusiasm and show why broadcasting history is interesting as well as important. Our method lacks some of the trappings of serious historiography (footnotes) but does include a detailed glossary in unusual format, a lengthy bibliography of sources for further reading, supplementary tables, a chronology, and an index. In *Stay Tuned* we have tried to note the important events and themes in American broadcasting's story through careful selection of items to

include in this single volume and subjects to analyze at length.

To find what we included, we suggest that you pay particular attention to the two tables of contents (chronological and topical), skim through the appendixes to get a sense of their contents, and then dig in where the book seems most relevant or interesting. No matter where you start or how you use the book, we hope you will obtain a better understanding of how broadcasting became the industry/art/babysitter/hero/villain/advertising medium/entertainer/news communicator and everything else it is today.

In the research, writing, and editing of this volume, we have had the help of many people. Among those who deserve our warmest thanks are (alphabetically): Joseph E. Baudino, of the Westinghouse Broadcasting Company and the Broadcast Pioneers, for his unparalleled knowledge of radio's early days; Joseph Berman, of Ohio University, for helpful criticism and encouragement; Gordon Greb, of San Jose State University, for his expert knowledge of early radio pioneer "Doc" Herrold; Kenneth Harwood, Dean of Temple University's School of Communications and Theater; the ever-patient Becky Hayden, of Wadsworth, who more than any other person is responsible for keeping us going for half a decade and hence for many of the strengths of this book; Temple colleague Sydney Head for his page-by-page criticism; Cathie Heinz and her staff at the Broadcast Pioneers Library in Washington; the *Journal of Broadcasting*'s many contributors during the long years when one or the other of us was editing it (1960–1976); collector of broadcast data *par excellence* Lawrence W. Lichty; consummate manuscript editor Jean Schuyler, who overcame the turgid prose of early drafts; Elliot Sivowitch of the Smithsonian's division of electricity and nuclear energy, who set us straight on many occasions; Robert R. Smith of Boston University, who offered valuable and constructive criticism at several stages of the book's gestation; Dallas W. Smythe of Simon Fraser University, who showed how to look behind the scenes; and Nathan B. Stubblefield, for obvious reasons.

We also owe gratitude to our many sources, among which are the books listed in the bibliography, many that are not so listed, several different libraries, countless secondhand bookshops, various Temple University departmental chairmen—one a former Iowa radio station manager and network operations supervisor, the second a former Philadelphia weekend television anchorman, and the third the son-in-law of radio's *The Whistler*—who ignored the mounting quantity of xerography requisitions, and many others.

As with most such volumes, our families gave far beyond the call of duty, without even the inner spur of scholarship or the outer spur of academic politics, and we hope that this recognition of the Sterling (Ellen, Jennifer, and Robin), and Kittross (Sally, David, Julie, and Serendipity) clans will be an aid to them during the transition of becoming reacquainted with husbands and fathers.

And, of course, for several years we have had each other to fight with, leading us to adopt the cheerful injunction in Backstrom and Hursh's *Survey Research* that "the authors will attribute any errors to each other."

C.H.S. & J.M.K.

Contents (Chronological)

Alternate Contents (Topical)

List of Boxed Features, Illustrations, and Tables

About the Authors

Christopher H. Sterling is a professor of communications and directs the graduate program in telecommunications at George Washington University, having joined that faculty in 1982. In 1980–1982, he served as a special assistant to FCC commissioner Anne Jones. Before that, he served for a decade on the faculty of Temple University's School of Communications and Theater. Sterling founded *Communication Booknotes* in 1969 and still edits the bi-monthly review service, edited *Journal of Broadcasting* for five years, and was chairman of the Broadcast Education Association in 1985–1987. Among his other books, he is co-author, with Sydney Head, of *Broadcasting in America* (6th ed., 1990) and authored *Electronic Media: Trends in Broadcasting and Newer Technologies, 1920–1983*. He has lectured on American communications policy in the United States, Europe, and South America and edits a bi-weekly newsletter on American electronic media published by the U.S. Information Agency for readers overseas. His hobbies include collecting material on the history of telecommunications, passenger air and sea travel, and medieval castles. He and his wife have two daughters and live in the Virginia suburbs of Washington, D.C.

John M. Kittross is professor of mass communication at Emerson College. After nine years on the faculty of the University of Southern California and more than 16 on the faculty of Temple University (where he was associate dean for graduate matters in the School of Communications and Theater), he moved to Emerson in January 1985 as an administrator, returning to teaching in the fall of 1987. His interest in radio was kindled in high school, and his first full-time job in broadcasting was in the newsroom of WNYC at the side of his Antioch College classmate, Rod Serling. Other jobs in the media followed before Kittross earned his doctorate in communications at the University of Illinois. Among other scholarly publication efforts, he wrote *Television Frequency Allocation Policy in the United States*, was editor of the *Journal of Broadcasting* for more than 12 years, edited *Administration of American Telecommunications Policy, Documents in American Telecommunications Policy*, and *Free & Fair: Courtroom Access and the Fairness Doctrine* (with Kenneth Harwood), and compiled *A Bibliography of Theses and Dissertations in Broadcasting, 1920–1973*. He considers himself a jack of all trades and a gadfly, appreciates and uses gadgets, holds an amateur radio license, is thrilled by the experience of learning something new, enjoys consulting on a variety of topics, and is inordinately proud of his personal library. With their two grown children now located elsewhere, Kittross and his wife live with his dog and books in the western suburbs of Boston.

The Context
of
Broadcasting

"What Hath God Wrought?"—first official words over the initial (1844) American telegraph line

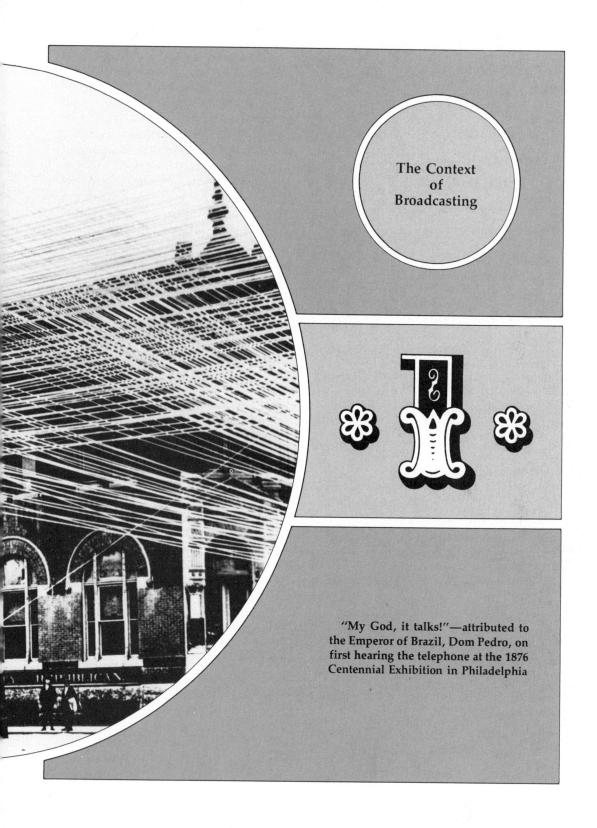

The Context
of
Broadcasting

"My God, it talks!"—attributed to
the Emperor of Brazil, Dom Pedro, on
first hearing the telephone at the 1876
Centennial Exhibition in Philadelphia

Many people living today can remember a time before radio broadcasting. A much larger number can remember what the world was like before television. Most Americans may spend more time with radio and television than they do at any other activity, including working and sleeping, and most Americans get most of their news from television. Obviously, we are dealing here with a phenomenon that is not only recent but extremely important, one whose cultural impact is almost inestimable. Why, then, do we know so little about its development?

Unfortunately, most early broadcasters and inventors were too busy creating an industry, and surviving in what they had created, to think of recording its development for those who followed. Now the time is growing short to capture this history from those who lived it. At the same time, more and more pragmatic reasons for knowing it are cropping up, and more people are becoming interested in it.

For example, regulation of space communications satellites follows principles established in international agreements in 1906, and even some from 1865. The American Telephone and Telegraph Company's decisions to avoid unrestrained competition in 1926 and 1976 are wholly consistent with their decisions of the 1880s to stay out of that hurly-burly. Early television programming of the late 1940s and early 1950s resembles the development of radio programming in the 1920s and 1930s. The beginnings of both cable television and pay-TV are discernible in a telephonic system in Budapest nearly 100 years ago that distributed music and information for a fee. Videodisc recording is a descendant of Baird's television experimentation in England during the 1920s. As early as 1945, Arthur C. Clarke wrote a full description of space communications satellites.

In addition to basic principles, cur-

Outline:
The Context of Broadcasting

rent problems have their roots in the past. For instance, placing the international distress ("SOS") frequency at 500 kHz in 1912 led some years later to placing standard (AM) broadcasting on a portion of the spectrum utterly unsuited to competitive local broadcasting. Television has been affected by earlier spectrum decisions: New Jersey's 1970s fight for a VHF channel is really an attempt to overturn a 1945 political decision by the FCC that is a cornerstone of the United States television system. The perennially controversial Fairness Doctrine stems from specific statutory language in 1959, a 1949 FCC policy decision, a 1941 licensing case, the "public interest, convenience and necessity" language in the Communications Act of 1934, and interstate commerce regulation right back to the Constitution in 1789. Indeed, there is hardly an argument on any aspect of modern broadcasting that does not leave one with a feeling of having heard all this before!

1·1   The Concept of Mass Communication

The concept of *mass communication* that distinguishes radio and television broadcasting from the telephone or even closed-circuit television refers to the effort to share information or entertainment with varied and probably large numbers of people through a technological intermediary. We can trace this concept along the path of direct human communication all the way from primitive spoken language and cave drawing to the telegraph and telephone, and we can follow the development of modern mass communication from the introduction of print five hundred years ago to the increasingly elaborate technologies of the motion picture, radio, and television.

When one imparts ideas and information "to whom it may concern" through some mechanical or electromechanical means, usually rapidly, over considerable distance, to a large and essentially undifferentiated audience, and when there are many copies of the message (duplicates of a newspaper or individual television sets tuned in)—then we have *mass* communication.

A *mass medium* is (1) the means—a printing press or a radio transmitter—by which the communicator produces and distributes copies of the message to the mass audience or (2) the industry that operates the means. A *mass audience*, usually large but sometimes only a handful, consists of people who typically are associated only by their attention to the same message. The distance between the medium and the audience can usually be measured in miles, but a newspaper restricted to a campus is still a mass medium. The audience may be highly specialized rather than undifferentiated—an abstruse scientific journal may reach only specialists in that field. Although Letters to the Editor and call-in programs on radio involve some person-to-person communication, they can still be considered mass communication to the rest of the audience. Circulation or coverage may be small. Unit cost to the consumer, typically low, may be high, as it was with early-day television. Messages usually are transmitted and received at or about the same time—but many books are timeless in appeal.

1·2   Early Communication

Mass communication began when a cave dweller first shouted a warning to all the tribe within earshot or, closer to modern methods, used a technological device such as a horn, bells, a hollow-tree drum, a signal fire, a flag of cloth or wood, or a piece of reflecting metal to maintain surveillance of his or her surroundings and improve his or her chances of survival. Slowly people became capable of using more complex ways to transmit their culture to the next generation. The realistic paintings of animals and animal hunts on cave walls probably served as hunting lessons for younger members of the tribe, and possibly also as religious symbols intended to ensure good fortune on future hunts. In this way the tribe could refresh their memories and build on the lessons already learned without each generation having to start all over again.

Slowly, over thousands of years, pictures of people, places, animals, and things became conventionalized and stylized into symbols. Although the mass of the people still learned through oral tradition or storytelling, small ruling classes and religious elites developed a system of pictographs and hieroglyphics—the printed, stamped, inscribed, painted, or carved "word." Written language was a code that only a tiny fraction of society could understand.

Communication typically depended upon human senses and abilities. When *speed* was uppermost—a prearranged code of signal fires carried news of the fall of Troy across most of Greece in a single night—the *amount* of information transmitted had to be small. Sending a long or complicated message took a longer time— as with the Romans' semaphore and flashing light devices—and sometimes involved a human carrier using whatever means of travel was available, whether it was a horseman using a Roman road or a Royal Incan messenger using a high-speed foot trail in the Andes.

After the fall of Rome in the fourth century A.D., the Roman Catholic church preserved much of the knowledge of the past in its monasteries. By painstakingly reproducing books by hand, the monks managed to preserve some of the culture of the past that was not being transmitted by word of mouth among the illiterate masses.

The first real change in mass communication came with the introduction of the printing press and movable type. People in the Far East learned to construct wood block and then tin letters and form a page that would print many copies. The first use of movable type—whereby separate wood or metal letters could be temporarily combined into desired words—in the Western world is ascribed to Johann Gutenberg of Mainz, Germany, who either developed his own press, type, and ink, or applied the Eastern system in 1456. The new process soon spread across Europe and reached Mexico in 1539, although its use was sometimes held up by the Church, which objected strongly both to losing its monopoly of recorded communications and to the increase of secular publishing that the Renaissance had stimulated.

Although tremendously faster than hand copying, printing was restricted to the relatively slow speeds of hand-operated presses until the 1800s, when larger, motor-driven presses became practical and common. Low-cost printing made books available to many more people, was a stimulus to literacy, standardized the appearance of alphabets, and enhanced the idea of the utility of books, reducing their artistic and increasing their social importance.

1·3   The Rise of Mass Society

Significant changes were taking place in Western society in Gutenberg's day. A new class of traders and merchants, between the rich and the poor, kept themselves informed of foreign developments in technology, commerce, and politics. Reformation within the Catholic church and revolt from without brought new patterns of societal control to Europe. The spread of secular news and knowledge brought a loosening of religious control over everyday life. In addition, the long-lasting feudal system began to give way to parliamentary government as the population, spear-headed by the growing merchant middle class, began to question the spending practices of monarchs.

At the same time, a renaissance of learning and art was taking place. Starting in southern Europe, the fine arts flourished, science and technology advanced, knowledge was acquired from the East, and new ideas once again became acceptable. Versatile men appeared, like Leonardo da Vinci, who could work in medicine, science, military technology, art, and music. Sometimes the noble families, who still held most of the money, and consequently power, acted as patrons of a *high culture* of artists, musicians, architects, and some scientists—all of whom produced their work for this small elite or for the church.

In many civilizations, millions of common people who provided the economic base for high culture had their own thematically and technically simple *folk culture* from which the high culture often borrowed. Folk culture of the Middle Ages took the form of fairs, circuses, traveling minstrels, song and story sessions, and morality plays, providing some religious instruction and a great deal of diverting entertainment.

In the 1700s the Industrial Revolution spread from England to the continent. Machines, driven by water and steam instead of human and animal power, supplied an increasing amount of manufactured goods that the home couldn't produce, at prices that individual craftsmen couldn't match. By the 1800s, manpower needs of industry, expansion of international commerce, and the start of mechanized agriculture led people toward city living.

The growing cities furnished an industrial base, great amounts of information and people who wanted it, and a market for mass-produced entertainment and information. The density of population made distribution easy. The local tavern continued to serve as a center of communications as it had for hundreds of years, but information now came as posted broadside advertisements or printed newspapers in addition to the traditional word of mouth from travelers. This situation was analogous to the "first color TV set in town" in the local bar or the cluster of men around the transistor radio in the Arabian coffee house.

Although literacy was increasing, thanks to the rise of public and private schooling toward the end of the nineteenth century, improvements in transportation and technology were more important to communication in the increasingly urbanized society. Steam power permitted the mechanization of printing presses, made transportation by water faster and more reliable, and allowed the railroad (supplemented by improved carriage and wagon roads) to knit all parts of a country together. Greater occupational specialization, particularly in cities, led to an increased use of money instead of barter and to an increased need for news and entertainment—mass communication.

And, most important, in the nineteenth century the first electrical communication devices (the telegraph and then the telephone) decisively overcame the problem of speed without dependence upon unaided senses or transportation. By the mid-1800s, both the socioeconomic systems of the more developed countries and their emerging technologies were ready for invention and later introduction of the components of the mass electronic media we know today: radio and television broadcasting.

1•4 Early Electrical Communication

For centuries the technological development of communication revolved around distance, speed, number of copies, and quantity of content. Each new technology was a balance of these demands. The Pony Express could deliver mail faster than any other method, but it could carry only a few pounds at a time. If many copies of a communication were required, or if each copy contained many pages, production might take much more time and space than for a limited output.

While the development of print media answered the fundamental question of quantity, it did so at the expense of speed—the time needed for gathering information, setting it in type, and printing, binding, and distributing newspapers, magazines, or books. Improving routes and methods of transportation shortened distances, but the speed with which news could travel still was limited by how fast man, animal, train, or ship could go.

Combining distance with speed became possible with development of telegraph systems. The first of these was the mechanical semaphore originated by the Romans and forgotten during the Middle Ages. Rediscovered, the semaphore systems of several European countries reached a high degree of efficiency in the late 1700s. Semaphores were fast and simple for *short* messages, but the equipment was expensive to build and operate, and many towers would be needed to relay signals over

long distances. Their inefficiency for long messages and their high personnel costs limited use to the most urgent needs. Although lights could be used at night, the semaphore was essentially a daytime, good-weather system that, like all telegraphs, achieved point-to-point rather than broadcast communication.

1•41 The Electrical Telegraph

However useful the semaphore was, it was quickly rendered obsolete by invention of the electrical telegraph. Electricity could travel through a wire at almost the speed of light, and it could surmount fog or bad weather. Wherever a wire could be strung, there the electrical telegraph could go; nor did operators have to be within sight of each other. All that was needed was a source of electricity, a switch or key to manipulate the current, a wire to conduct electricity, and a mechanism—the element inventors changed most frequently—to "read" the transmitted message visually or audibly.

In the United States, the first practical telegraph was invented by Samuel Finley Breese Morse, then well-known as an artist. In 1832 he learned from a fellow passenger on board ship returning from Europe about the electromagnet and work being done on electrical signaling for railways in England. Morse worked on electrical telegraphy over much of the next three years. His first instrument, in 1835, used pulses of current to deflect an electromagnet, which moved a marker to produce a written code on a strip of paper. A year later he modified the device to emboss the paper with dots and dashes. These were elements in what is now called "Morse code," even though it probably was actually developed by Morse's financial partner Alfred Vail. This code was carefully constructed, in keeping with what we now call Information Theory, with the most common letter, *e*, coded in the easiest form, one dot. With such a code, the inventor needed only one wire circuit to send sequentially even the longest messages. Some earlier devices had needed a separate wire circuit for each letter of the alphabet!

In 1840, Morse secured a patent on the system and set out to obtain financial backing for a demonstration. His ultimate source of funds, as with so many later inventions, was the United States government. In 1843 Congress appropriated $30,000, and Morse used the money to construct a demonstration line that spanned the 40 miles between Washington and Baltimore. First he had to solve many technological problems—particularly those involving insulating the wires so that the electricity wouldn't leak into the ground —as is often the case when scaling up from a laboratory model. The official first message, "What hath God wrought," was sent May 24, 1844.

In 1847 Congress sold the demonstration line to Morse interests, and the United States opted out of governmental control of telecommunications for the time being. Morse soon found that it was extremely hard to defend his patent because the technology was so simple. As a result, more than 50 telegraph companies were operating by 1851, and many more followed. But the number of important companies shrank steadily after the creation of the Western Union Telegraph Company in 1856, as uneconomical duplications and poorly engineered lines led to mergers and absorptions. By the early 1900s only Western Union and Postal Telegraph remained strong—and, at the start of World War II, after Congress passed a special antitrust law exemption, Western Union took over Postal Telegraph.

The telegraph was so efficient that it quickly eliminated competing forms of communication, such as the Pony Express, which died as soon as the first transcontinental telegraph line opened in 1861. While the telegraph naturally had important wartime applications, major emphasis in the United States was on commercial development. In the late 1840s five New York newspapers organized the Associated Press to get pooled telegraphic reports of the Mexican War. In England, Julius Reuter, who began a "pigeon post" in the 1850s to provide market prices to businessmen, adopted telegraphy and expanded his reports into a general news service for newspapers.

In Europe, development of land telegraphy followed a different path. Governments retained controlling interest in telegraphy and subsequent means of telecommunication. They placed military and political uses first and often postponed commercial telegraphy for years. Some countries continued to use the old optical telegraph and semaphore systems, which had been so fully developed, until the late 1850s.

The telegraph and the railroads intertwined to spearhead the economic development of the United States. The telegraph needed a right-of-way between centers of population while the railroads needed some means of dispatching trains; both needed agents or operators. Their problems were solved by combining the jobs of station agent and telegraph operator in one person who handled railroad service messages and public messages alike. This system almost doubled the freight-handling capacity of the railroad and substantially reduced the cost of maintaining telegraph operators. As the number of competing railroad companies declined, mostly through merger and purchase, so did the number of potential telegraph lines running between the same pairs of cities.

1•42   Submarine Cables

Although the telegraph could deliver a message almost instantaneously, in transmission its capability stopped at the ocean's edge. The first underwater cable, laid in 1850 across the English Channel, lasted only a short time, since its wire bundles were highly susceptible to damage from fishermen, dragging anchors, and corrosion and short-circuiting by sea water. In 1858, after several short cables had been installed successfully, wealthy American businessman Cyrus W. Field organized the first of several transatlantic cable layings. The first, between England and the United States, lasted about six months and was unreliable. In 1866, Field and his associates laid a new cable from Ireland to Newfoundland that worked. Although the transmission speed was only six words a minute, the success of this transatlantic cable inspired installation of cables between other continents, and spurred commercial and diplomatic communication.

Although pairs of nations had previously reached bilateral agreements, by 1865 there was enough general need and basis for agreement on operational techniques and finances for an International Telegraph Convention to meet in Paris. The convention agreed on priority of messages (governmental, then telegraph administration, and then commercial or private), uniformity of rates (set by distance), methods for settling accounts between countries, and meetings scheduled to update regulations. This gathering was the genesis of the International Telegraph Union—now the International Telecommunication Union (ITU), a world organization under the United Nations that allocates radio spectrum space and sets standards for international telegraph and telephone.

1•43   The Telephone

The electrical telegraph had several drawbacks: it could transmit only a few words per minute, it required trained operators, it conveyed emotion or emphasis poorly, it required a new alphabet (Morse code), and it was one-way. If the human voice could be transmitted in a two-way system, all of these problems would be overcome.

On February 14, 1876, Alexander Graham Bell, a successful teacher of the deaf, filed for a patent on such a device. He demonstrated his invention at the Philadelphia Centennial Exhibition of 1876 and attracted considerable attention. The first telephone system, with 21 subscribers, was established two years later in New Haven, Connecticut. Although Bell benefited financially from his invention, his financial backer and father-in-law Gardner Hubbard, and his excellent business manager Theodore Vail, a distant cousin of Morse's backer, had control.

After an unsuccessful attempt to sell the invention outright for $100,000 to Western Union in 1877, Bell and his associates redoubled their efforts to fight patent infringements and conflicts, purchase improvements on the telephone, and put systems into the most populated portions of city after city. Competition came from numerous small companies, many with a cavalier attitude toward the patent system, and from Western Union. This immensely wealthy and powerful company, realizing its earlier mistake, had set out to establish a rival telephone company based on other patents.

However, when financial baron Jay

Gould threatened to establish a rival tele-graph company in association with Bell's company in an effort to depress Western Union's stock and then buy it cheaply, Western Union hurriedly made peace with the Bell interests in 1879, giving up all ideas about competing in the telephone field in exchange for the Bell interests stay-ing out of the telegraph industry. By 1909 the Bell system was so successful that the American Telephone and Telegraph Com-pany (as it had been named in 1885) was able to purchase Western Union—only to have to resell it in 1914 because of the antitrust laws.

In its first ten years, AT&T made some of the corporate decisions that guided it until it was split into several parts in 1984. Since it could expect rival companies to appear in 1894 when Bell's basic patents expired, AT&T decided to initiate research to improve the telephone in small but patentable steps, to purchase successive developments by independent inventors—such as Michael Pupin's loading coil, which made long-distance telephony practical—and to concentrate on a part of the industry that only one company could feasibly oper-ate—long distance communication. While an estimated six thousand firms battled in the late 1890s for local telephone business, AT&T worked to create transcontinental telephone service, which they accom-plished in 1915. Until stopped by a threat-ened antitrust action just before World War I, AT&T also bought many competing local firms.

This philosophy is still evident. AT&T has made large concessions to the antitrust laws—relinquishing royalties in 1956 on all patents, including the transis-tor—in order to keep control of its manu-facturing subsidiary, Western Electric. Even when the court-approved 1984 "divesti-ture" led to the end of the integrated "Bell System" consisting of research, manufac-turing, and long-distance and local tele-phone service facilities owned by AT&T, the parent company tried to carve out a niche for itself (in information transmission, combining long-distance communication and computers), leaving the aging local systems to the seven spun-off regional Bell operating companies and telephones to be made and sold by anyone. Although the local Bell companies serve only about 85 percent of the nation's telephones, keeping them reasonably safe from the antitrust laws, it is in the long-distance business that competition is most fierce. Fighting hard are such giants as AT&T, MCI, Sprint, and Allnet and a host of small companies that lease facilities in bulk, then resell them at a discount.

AT&T also searched for a "natural monopoly" in broadcasting. During the 1920s, when it could not maintain a mon-opoly of commercial "radio telephony for hire" or "toll broadcasting," it sold its sta-tions to competitors; in the 1950s when it no longer sold the lion's share of certain transmitters and speech-input equipment, AT&T dropped that business completely. While AT&T still supplies some intercon-nections for the networks, domestic com-munications satellites have taken over this activity too, forcing AT&T into the com-petitive mode it avoided for more than a century.

Although most European coun-tries placed telephone operations, like the telegraph, within a government depart-ment, usually the postal service, in the United States private ownership of the tel-ephone was challenged only once. This occurred during World War I, when the federal government took over telephone, telegraph, and railroad companies to as-sure the priority of military operations and war production during a time of commu-nication and transportation shortages. Some earlier proposals for government ownership of electrical communication, notably by Postmaster General Burleson in 1914 and an earlier postmaster general in 1872, got nowhere. The actual wartime takeover did not hamper the operations of the Bell System, however, since all details and virtually all policy were left to Bell executives, who inaugurated federal policies, including installation service charges, that state regulatory agencies previously had blocked. After the war, although the navy still wished to control wireless, AT&T easily retrieved its facilities.

1•44   The Electrical Manufacturing Industry

The successful development of telegraph and telephone in the United States led to near-monopolies by Western Union (telegraph) and AT&T (telephone). At the same time, as electricity was used more after 1880, companies appeared that manufactured electric lights, electric motors, and the like. The most important electrical manufacturing firms were Westinghouse, started in 1886, which brought the alternating current power system to the United States, and General Electric, formed in 1892 as an amalgamation of two older firms, including Thomas Edison's. After several years of competition and patent arguments, GE and Westinghouse agreed in 1896 that GE should receive two-thirds of the business growing from their shared patents. This early patent "pool" agreement was an important precedent for the radio manufacturing industry. Another important firm was Western Electric, which specialized in telephone communications equipment and was taken over by AT&T in 1881.

All these firms were interrelated, not necessarily through ownership but because the manufacturing companies provided equipment and services to the communications organizations while the latter, fed by increasing public use of their facilities, provided a demand on the electrical manufacturing companies. Each one was so wrapped up in its own business that research was limited to perfecting the products that were already selling and little time, personnel, or money was spent on new systems such as wireless—which will be discussed fully in chapter 2.

1•5   Broadcasting: A New Mass Communication Medium

Radio *broadcasting* was a new electrical communications concept. Telegraph, telephone, and early radio were only faster means of point-to-point or interpersonal communication. It took time to overcome this mental barrier that made any other course seem unknowable. History tells us that nothing could beat the speed of the royal Incan messengers, until the horse was introduced to the Western Hemisphere. Similarly, the Pony Express lasted 16 months, until the transcontinental telegraph was completed. The limits of the telegraph—its low words-per-minute capacity and need for trained operators—were "impassable," until the innovation of the telephone permitted rapid two-way conversation by distant laymen. Radio removed our dependence on wires, and finally "broadcasting" presented a new concept, just as movable type had when it bypassed the barrier—slow production of copies—of hand-lettering, and made widespread literacy worthwhile. Americans living when radio was new felt that it was a miracle—a cheap and pervasive national mass medium.

Although radio seemed to spring full-blown upon America in the early 1920s, amateur operators had been transmitting and listening to speech and music since 1906. After commercial broadcasting started in 1922 and networks were fully established in 1926, everyone agreed that radio was truly a mass medium: a few programming sources (networks) geared to reach as large an undifferentiated audience as possible, for the purpose of purveying goods and services through advertisements. Even when, in the late 1950s and in the 1960s, radio networks virtually disappeared, and radio became a local medium serving specialized groups while television took over the national business, radio remained a mass medium.

But just what is *broadcasting*? It clearly has a different method of delivery from the other media of mass communication—and often a different message to deliver. According to Section 3(o) of the Communications Act of 1934, broadcasting is "the dissemination of radio communications intended to be received by ·the public, directly or by means of intermediary relay stations." The three essential elements here are "radio communication" (meaning use of wireless electromagnetic radiation—see Appendix B); "intended for" (meaning that everyone "whom it may concern or interest" is welcome to listen in, distinguishing a broadcast from the private interchange of telephone, telegraph, postal service, or even Citizens Band [CB] radio); and "the public" (laymen, who may merely be curious). Although *broadcasting* and *broadcasting station* (radio and television) are discussed in 3.21, we should establish here that broadcasting signifies transmission of music, speech, and/or pictures in forms that the general public can understand, on a regular and announced schedule, on a frequency band for which the general public has receivers, by a station licensed by the government for that purpose (if licensing was then required).

Broadcasting is an industry, an in-stitution, and a process, and we intend to examine all three. The system of broadcasting in the United States is virtually unique in the world (not necessarily better; simply different), and this book explores how the system is unique, how it got that way, and why.

As recently as 35 years ago, for example, the number of radio stations supposedly was limited by "technology" (the more stations, the more interference), or, more likely, by economics (only networks could finance expensive programming, by spreading costs over many stations), and politics (rural areas need clear-channel stations, and rural areas elect more than their share of legislators). We ignored the technological barriers—who cares about long-distance interference if the audience lives within a score of miles of the transmitter? The economic "necessity" of networks disappeared with the development of less expensive but still effective local program formats. The political "imperatives" of radio allocation shifted significantly as a result of "one man, one vote" Supreme Court decisions.

Television might some day travel the same road—but it also might follow a different path. VCRs, color, portable television sets, and cable are already part of the industry. The barriers that still face television are the speed of light, the ranges over which our senses operate, and the number of hours in the day. But can these be any more impassable than the walls that used to hamper older forms of communication? For instance, although propagation speeds may be limited, research indicates that "compression" of the television picture and sound is possible without loss of comprehension; a form of "fast motion." All of the strictly-entertainment media might be replaced in an Orwellian future by direct electrical stimulation of the brain, rather than by the slower and more imperfect use of sensory inputs. Telepathy is now a science-fiction concept, as were television and the atomic bomb; but we all know how many hours of subjective time our minds can cover in a few seconds of dreaming. More likely, but still in the science-fiction category, is the possibility of completely random access to nearly unlimited amounts of television programming through the use of computer scheduling, multiplexed additional channels (wired or broadcast), multiple-pickup playback video disc recorders in the stations, and inexpensive home VCRs.

The limits we live with are in our own minds. By learning how previous limits were breached, perhaps we can look more wisely at the problems of today, such as fairness, access, more cable channels and fewer system operators, limits on the number of on-air channels, deregulation, direct broadcast satellites, audience fragmentation, high-definition television, pay-TV, indecency and violence, automation, and advertising and programming standards. In order to affect the future wisely, we *must* become aware of past principles, trends, decisions, and events.

New ways of applying or modifying old solutions may change the ground rules of broadcasting as completely as the vacuum tube supplanted the old rotary-generator transmitters or the iconoscope removed the mechanical limitations of the television scanning disc. It may take time —3-D color TV was first shown in 1926— but technology, structure, function, and regulation will adapt when and if the will, desire, and imagination are ready for another chapter in the unfinished story of broadcasting.

Further Reading

Of the many books providing a useful context of American history against which media development can be placed, two stand out. Boorstin (1973) has become a classic social history of the United States, with graceful writing, good insight, and extensive annotated reading lists. Beniger (1986) argues that the present "information age" can be traced back to technological and economic patterns set in manufacturing and consumer life by the early twentieth century.

Focusing on development of popular culture and communication development are Hogben (1949), which traces graphic communication from the Stone Age, and Nye (1970), which is a pioneering attempt at an integrated single-volume history of American culture, concentrating on the written form, as in novels and poetry. The three-volume set of extensive research essays and annotated bibliographies edited by Inge (1979–1981) is the definitive reference to date on virtually all manifestations of American popular culture. A pictorial history of popular show business is found in Csida (1978), which deals mainly with this century as reported in *Billboard*. Toll (1982) offers a brief assessment of twentieth-century show business, with chapters on film, recordings, the stage, popular music, and types of content: westerns, musicals, crime, sexuality, and comedy.

Print media development is highlighted in Tebbel (1975), which covers books, magazines, and newspapers and includes a bit on broadcasting. A classic work on the newspaper as a social instrument, with a wealth of statistical information, is Lee (1937), while Emery and Emery (1988) is the standard college journalism history text, covering print and broadcast services. For magazines, see Peterson (1964). Desmond's four-volume (1978–1984) history of world news reporting is the most extensive analysis of the topic through 1945. The rise and role of the news agencies is the focus of several useful studies. One of the earliest, Rosewater (1930), remains the best scholarly analysis. The first century of the British agency Reuters is told in Storey (1951), while Gramling (1940) provides a popularized narrative of The Associated Press, showing how important stories were covered. Morris (1957) does a comparable job for United Press. All of these relate to some degree the impact of the telegraph, and later of the telephone, on news reporting.

Turning to electrical and electronic media, the best historical bibliography is Shiers and Shiers (1972), while a good chronological reference is in Davis's three volumes (1981–1985). Dummer (1977) provides an annotated guide to patents and inventions in electronics over two centuries. McMahon (1984) provides a short history of electrical engineering in America.

Two books attempt an assessment of the role of electronic communication. Winston (1986) argues that the telephone, the computer, television, and satellite communication have had a more limited impact than many assume because of society's often unintended means of limiting radical change. Czitrom (1982), on the other hand, reviews the rise of telegraph to 1900, film to World War I, and radio to World War II to background three chapters on important theorists of communications' role. The best integrated histories of telegraph-telephone-cables and wireless are Harlow (1936) from a technological point of view and Herring and Gross (1936) and Brock (1981) from legal and economic viewpoints.

Telegraph history appears to be enjoying a revival of interest in the 1980s, but the best references are still years old. The definitive discussion of preelectric telegraph (or semaphore) systems is found in Wilson (1976). Fahie (1884) remains an excellent overall history of the pretelephone telegraph industry. The best biographies of Morse are Prime (1875), and Mabee (1943). The most detailed analyses of various American telegraph companies and the

people who ran them are in Reid (1879) and Thompson (1947). More detail of the various patent fights and claims in early telegraphy and telephony is found in both Marland (1964) and the King monograph (1962). Collins (1977) provides an integrated history of Canadian telecommunications.

The first century of submarine cables is reviewed briefly in Clarke (1975), while a more technical discussion based on original sources is in Dibner (1964). The most detailed history and technical description of cable technology at the end of the nineteenth century is in Bright (1898). Cyrus Field is discussed in many books—the best biography is that by Carter (1968). A fascinating discussion of the many impacts of the first successful Atlantic cable is found in the "retrospective technology assessment" by Coates and Finn (1979).

Given its century-long importance in our lives, there is amazingly little historical material published on the telephone. Its technical history is best told by Rhodes (1929), while the definitive biography of Bell is by Bruce (1973). A good study of the development of the American telephone industry, drawn from research done for the trial that led to the 1984 breakup of AT&T, is in Smith (1985). For discussions of the growth and role of AT&T in the nineteenth and twentieth centuries, see Danielian and the related FCC telephone investigation report (both 1939), the more recent popular narrative (also more favorable to AT&T) in Brooks (1976), or the handsomely illustrated album by Boettinger (1983). Pool (1977) collects original essays on the social impact of the telephone through history. The more recent regulatory upheaval in the telecommunications business is related in Henck and Strassburg (1988), and, for a detailed study based directly on AT&T records and written with company support, Temin and Galambos (1987).

The Prehistory
of
Broadcasting
(to 1919)

2

". . . Signor Marconi gave a practical demonstration which showed that even in its present state the instruments can be made useful in signaling between ships and shore, and there is a certainty of working under all conditions of weather which is not common to any other mode of communication at sea."—Lt. G. W. Denfield, U.S. Navy, in report to Secretary of the Navy, 1899

The Prehistory
of
Broadcasting
(to 1919)

2

"... a company incorporated for $2,000,000, whose only assets were de Forest's patents chiefly directed to a strange device like an incandescent lamp which he called an Audion and which device had proven worthless."
—government prosecutor in 1912 mail fraud stock case

This chapter describes the many technological problems that slowed broadcasting's development and relates the fundamental wireless discoveries and their initial applications. Although thirty years passed between the first theorizing about wireless in 1865 and Marconi's first practical system experiments, our concern is mostly with the subsequent rise of wireless communication from an isolated invention to a widespread, practical innovation. Even as it was already in use, researchers in many nations who were working to perfect wireless saw it only as a point-to-point medium that could straddle natural barriers and operate more cheaply than the wire telegraph or telephone. Few then thought that the absence of privacy protection from listeners-in would one day become one of radio's strongest advantages.

As radio's military and commercial values became obvious after 1895, major countries tried to develop their own systems so as not to have to depend upon others in emergencies. This competition increased the importance of patents, for by controlling essential patents one country or firm could dominate broadcasting's development for years. The many different systems that succeeded have subtle and complicated distinctions, but in this chapter we concentrate more on the impact and application of wireless, or radio, than on its technical intricacies. Other technical material is in the glossary (Appendix B), to which readers (of this chapter in particular) should refer.

Outline:
The Prehistory of Broadcasting (to 1919)

2·1   Fundamental Wireless Discoveries

As with many other nineteenth-century inventions, radio developed in widely separated places when the conditions were right. Also typical of that perio was the importance of the individual inventor or innovator who—unlike the twentieth-century research team working in industrial laboratories—borrowed one element, added another, and was frequently ignorant of work done elsewhere. The invention or innovation (an invention introduced commercially as a new or improved product or process) was often the result of luck or curiosity rather than systematic scientific research applied to a specific problem.

In retrospect, wireless, or radio, is a logical extension of wired telegraphy and telephony. Wires were physical in nature, easily broken, and hard to string between distant communities or over physical obstacles. With wireless techniques, communication could take place as rapidly as with wired devices but did not require a physical connection. Distant locations could be contacted quickly; relaying might be unnecessary; and ships could keep in touch with land. The penalty for this was that a radio message would go out in all directions at once and could be picked up by anyone who cared to listen. A wired circuit, on the other hand, was relatively private and would normally reach the desired party.

2•11   Conduction and Induction

There are three important kinds of electrical transmission: conduction, induction, and radiation. *Conduction* means the sending of impulses through a medium capable of transmitting electricity—a wire, salt water, the earth. *Induction* refers to the appearance of a current in one circuit when it is placed near another, already charged circuit, without a physical connection. Induction can cause cross talk on a telephone circuit, and induction coils permit the recording of telephone conversations without wire hookups. *Radiation* means the generation of electromagnetic waves, generally from an antenna. The radio transmissions of today use this last method, which became practical just before 1900.

A Spaniard, Salvá, proposed using sea water as a conductor in 1795, 50 years before the first practical wired electrical telegraph system was built. In 1838 Carl August Steinheil, a Munich physics professor, proposed using railway rails as conductors and then experimented with the bare earth, sending messages for 50 feet. Morse, after constructing his wired system, suggested using water to extend land lines. Some of his assistants succeeded in receiving water-borne electrical signals over a distance of two miles.

Many other experimenters contributed to our knowledge of transmitting electricity. One of the most resourceful was Mahlon Loomis, a Washington, D.C., dentist who succeeded in 1866 in sending signals between mountains nearly 20 miles apart in Virginia. In 1872 Loomis received the first patent for wireless in America and the next year persuaded Congress to grant his company a federal charter. However, the financial panic of 1872 dried up potential sources of investment, and the Chicago fire of 1871 helped bankrupt some of his backers. Although no commercial system using the Loomis technique was successful, as late as 1924 the U.S. Signal Corps still recommended as a "field expedient" receiver his remarkably simple apparatus involving kite-flown aerials with a galvanometer in series with the aerial and ground. Another early experimenter, William Henry Ward of Auburn, New York, patented a "telegraphic tower"—looking remarkably like the early commercial space satellite communications receiving station at Andover, Maine—in 1872, which reportedly could send signals to many receiving antennas if all were "connected to the earth."

Flow Chart on Invention of Radio and Television / This chart traces the development of radio and television and shows how broadcasting was the result of experimentation and research by many scientists and inventors. The chart was drawn by Max Gschwind for Fortune Magazine (December 1954) and is reproduced here by permission.

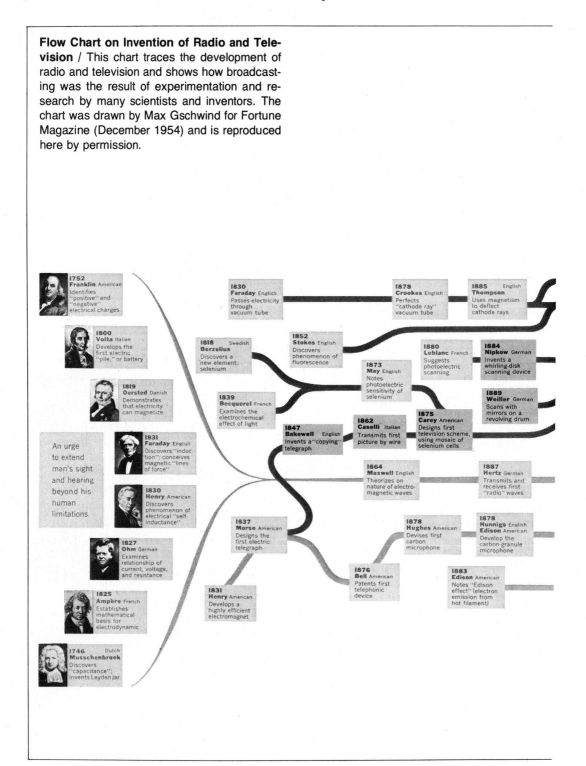

Photo credits: Volta, Oersted, Henry, Ampère (Culver Service); Faraday (Associated Press); Ohm (Brown Brothers); Musschenbroek (from *Grote Nederlanders* by Dr. G. C. Gerrits, E. J. Brill, Leiden, 1948); photo on right page (Andreas Feininger-*Life*).

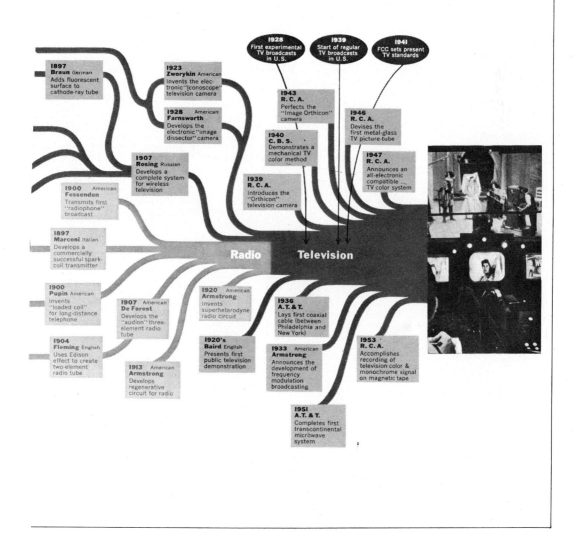

Two Early American Radio Inventors / Reproduced from the patent records are the Loomis patent of 1872 (see 2.11), the first wireless patent granted in the United States, and a diagram from a 1908 patent of Nathan Stubblefield showing how his system would work near a waterway (other diagrams applied to railroads and roadways).

UNITED STATES PATENT OFFICE.

MAHLON LOOMIS, OF WASHINGTON, DISTRICT OF COLUMBIA.

IMPROVEMENT IN TELEGRAPHING.

Specification forming part of Letters Patent No. **129,971**, dated July 30, 1872.

To all whom it may concern:

Be it known that I, MAHLON LOOMIS, dentist, of Washington, District of Columbia, have invented or discovered a new and Improved Mode of Telegraphing and of Generating Light, Heat, and Motive-Power; and I do hereby declare that the following is a full description thereof.

The nature of my invention or discovery consists, in general terms, of utilizing natural electricity and establishing an electrical current or circuit for telegraphic and other purposes without the aid of wires, artificial batteries, or cables to form such electrical circuit, and yet communicate from one continent of the globe to another.

To enable others skilled in electrical science to make use of my discovery, I will proceed to describe the arrangements and mode of operation.

As in dispensing with the double wire, (which was first used in telegraphing,) and making use of but one, substituting the earth instead of a wire to form one-half the circuit, so I now dispense with both wires, using the earth as one-half the circuit and the continuous electrical element far above the earth's surface for the other part of the circuit. I also dispense with all artificial batteries, but use the free electricity of the atmosphere, co-operating with that of the earth, to supply the electrical dynamic force or current for telegraphing and for other useful purposes, such as light, heat, and motive power.

As atmospheric electricity is found more and more abundant when moisture, clouds, heated currents of air, and other dissipating influences are left below and a greater altitude attained, my plan is to seek as high an elevation as practicable on the tops of high mountains, and thus penetrate or establish electrical connection with the atmospheric stratum or ocean overlying local disturbances. Upon these mountain-tops I erect suitable towers and apparatus to attract the electricity, or, in other words, to disturb the electrical equilibrium, and thus obtain a current of electricity, or shocks or pulsations, which traverse or disturb the positive electrical body of the atmosphere above and between two given points by communicating it to the negative electrical body in the earth below, to form the electrical circuit.

I deem it expedient to use an insulated wire or conductor as forming a part of the local apparatus and for conducting the electricity down to the foot of the mountain, or as far away as may be convenient for a telegraph-office, or to utilize it for other purposes.

I do not claim any new key-board nor any new alphabet or signals; I do not claim any new register or recording instrument; but

What I claim as my invention or discovery, and desire to secure by Letters Patent, is—

The utilization of natural electricity from elevated points by connecting the opposite polarity of the celestial and terrestrial bodies of electricity at different points by suitable conductors, and, for telegraphic purposes, relying upon the disturbance produced in the two electro-opposite bodies (of the earth and atmosphere) by an interruption of the continuity of one of the conductors from the electrical body being indicated upon its opposite or corresponding terminus, and thus producing a circuit or communication between the two without an artificial battery or the further use of wires or cables to connect the co-operating stations.

MAHLON LOOMIS.

Witnesses:
BOYD ELIOT,
C. C. WILSON.

No. 887,357.

PATENTED MAY 12, 1908.

N. B. STUBBLEFIELD.
WIRELESS TELEPHONE.
APPLICATION FILED APR. 5, 1907.

3 SHEETS—SHEET 1.

Fig.3

Fig.2

Fig.1

Witnesses

Jas. K. M⁻Cathran

B.G. Fretes

Nathan B. Stubblefield, Inventor

By

E.G. Siggers

Attorney

Most early experimenters believed in the concept of "ether" or "aether" as a medium (thought to be part of the atmosphere, hence "airwaves") that existed specifically to transmit electrical impulses. They thought that if they could successfully tap it and insert an impulse, the ether would carry the impulse for great distances. The idea of the ether, defined later as "that which carries radio waves," apparently served as mental crutch, because it hung on in physics and radio engineering literature until the end of the 1930s.

In the early 1870s, Elihu Thompson and Thomas A. Edison individually began to detect sparks created by generators some distance from the measurement point. Edison in 1885 took out his only patent in wireless for an induction system that used antennas to get above the earth's curvature and its conduction. A year later, Professor Amos Dolbear of Tufts College in Massachusetts took out a patent for his "electrostatic telephone," a system of telephonic (voice) induction communication using a tin roof or a wire hanging from a kite to induce current into the "ether." Some energy may have been radiated from his antenna as well, but Dolbear had no good means of detecting the weaker radiated waves, even though they could reach a greater distance. A contemporary Harvard physicist, John Trowbridge, proposed inductive methods to reach ships at sea.

Another American inventor who attempted commercial application of his discoveries was Nathan B. Stubblefield of Kentucky. Having read about recent electrical radiation experiments in popular science magazines, he started experimenting with a system in the late 1880s. In 1892 he demonstrated ground conduction voice signals over several hundred yards. Later, although possibly never realizing the three distinct types of transmission, he switched to induction and communicated from the shore to ship stations on lakes or rivers. Stubblefield was particularly interested in communicating to and from moving vehicles over relatively short distances. Like Loomis, he got caught in a commercial scheme that, in this case, was in the nationwide-publicity and funding stage before Stubblefield pulled out, claiming that his business partners were making crooked deals using him as a scapegoat and cheating him. Although he was a prolific inventor, even patenting the tin-cans-connected-by-string telephone, Stubblefield eventually died of starvation.

It is not surprising that commercial attempts at harnessing both induction and nonmetallic earth and water conduction failed. There were variations in conductivity, losses caused by the signal going in all directions at once, and limits to the amount of power that a sending coil of reasonable size could hold. So far, induction and nonmetallic conduction could not hope to compete with the wire telegraph and telephone except possibly for short distances to moving vessels or vehicles. Researchers also had difficulty in demonstrating reliability of their signals, or even any results at all. Typically, they used galvanometers to register that a signal had been sent or received, but these meters could easily confuse interpreters, react to other electrical impulses, like lightning flashes, or fail to register adequately the minute amounts of current transmitted. Furthermore, a radiation component in many of the inductive experiments may have accounted for much of whatever success they had.

2•12   Radiation

The development of radiation for wireless communication rested upon a firm theoretical framework. The major findings of a Scottish mathematician and physicist James Clerk Maxwell, published in 1864, suggested that a signal could be sent out electromagnetically that would be completely detached from the point of origin. Using mathematical equations, he demonstrated that electricity, light, and heat are essentially the same and that all radiate at the same speed in free space.

German physicist Heinrich Hertz demonstrated the correctness of Clerk Maxwell's theories in a series of experiments in 1887–1888. The fundamental unit of frequency, the Hertz (Hz), is named for him. Hertz measured the speed of electromagnetic radiation—the speed of light—the length of various waves, and similar parameters but did not promote the use of wireless for communication. His crude but reasonably effective detector of radiated waves was a device that allowed an electric spark to jump a small gap between two charged steel balls when the receiving coil was placed facing a nearby transmitting spark coil. Hertz never achieved much range, and this device was superseded by the much more efficient invention of French physicist Édouard Branly, in the early 1890s. His *coherer* consisted of a glass tube filled with metal filings that cohered or packed together and permitted an electrical current to pass whenever a wireless signal was being received. Although the coherer permitted reception of very weak radiated currents, it had to be tapped mechanically after each pulse in order to restore the filings to their prereception looseness. In the late 1890s, English physicist and author Sir Oliver Lodge worked out the principle of resonance *tuning* so that both receiver and transmitter would operate on the same wavelength or frequency without dissipating the signal over a broad portion of the spectrum.

In addition to Hertz, Branly, and Lodge, we find numerous persons whose work, while not universally recognized, either led or could have led to a practical wireless system. Among the most prominent was Alexander Popoff. This Russian professor at the University of Kronstadt developed a better coherer and vertical antenna around 1895 and noted the connection between Hertzian waves and static, but he was intent upon developing a detection-prediction system for thunderstorms rather than a system of communication. (An analogous system for the purpose of detecting tornados by their *noise signature* on television channel 2 was tested in the United States in the early 1970s.) Popoff, whom the Soviet Union considers the inventor of radio, worked extensively in wireless and made equipment for the Russian navy.

2•121 Marconi The most widely known inventor-innovator in the field of wireless, the man most historians credit with inventing radiotelegraphy, is the Italian Guglielmo Marconi. Marconi was interested in making radio work and only secondarily in *how* it worked. In 1894, age twenty, he read of Hertz's experiments and aimed to apply this knowledge to communication. Supported by a wealthy father, Marconi was able during the next year to improve the Hertz transmitter, to note that a signal sent from an elevated antenna would go farther, to use a ground connection as well as an antenna, to make the Branly-Lodge coherer more sensitive, and to add a telegraph key and batteries. By 1896 he could transmit and receive two miles or more on his father's estate near Bologna.

It was obvious to his family that the young man would shortly have developed a commercially valuable, wireless telegraphy system. After the Italian government expressed no interest, the family decided to send him to England, which,

Marconi and the Transatlantic "S": 1901 / Winds, as much as or more than distance, nearly undid Marconi's hopes of sending a wireless signal across the Atlantic Ocean late in 1901. First, a gale nearly wrecked the large Poldhu station in Cornwall. Then, just two months later, a similar storm demolished the new Marconi station on Cape Cod, threatening a long postponement of the tests. Then, with the Poldhu apparatus jury-rigged, Marconi and his assistants sailed for Newfoundland, which was somewhat closer, in the dead of winter. Marconi described what happened in a speech given a year later:

R 7502 Marconi's Wireless Telgraph Experimental Station, South Wellfleet, Mass.

The first experiments were carried out in Newfoundland last December, and every assistance and encouragement was given me by the Newfoundland Government. As it was impossible at that time of the year to set up a permanent installation with poles, I carried out experiments with receivers joined to a vertical wire about 400 ft. long, elevated by a kite. This gave a very great deal of trouble, as in consequence of the variations of the wind constant variations in the electrical capacity of the wire were caused. My assistants in Cornwall had received instructions to send a succession of "S's," followed by a short message at a certain pre-arranged speed, every ten minutes, alternating with five minutes' rest during certain hours every day. Owing to the constant variations in the capacity of the aerial wire it was soon found out that an ordinary syntonic receiver was not suitable, although a number of doubtful signals were at one time recorded. I, therefore, tried various microphonic self-restoring coherers placed in the secondary circuit of a transformer, the signals being read on a telephone. With several of these coherers, signals were distinctly and accurately received, and only at the pre-arranged times, in many cases a succession of "S's," being heard distinctly although, probably in consequence of the weakness of the signals and the unreliability of the detector, no ac-

tual message could be deciphered. The coherers which gave the signals were one containing loose carbon filings, another, designed by myself, containing a mixture of carbon dust and cobalt filings, and thirdly, the "Italian Navy Coherer," containing a globule of mercury between two plugs. . . .

The result of these tests was sufficient to convince myself and my assistants that, with permanent stations at both sides of the Atlantic, and by the employment of a little more power, messages could be sent across the ocean with the same facility as across much shorter distances.

Source: G. Marconi, "The Progress of Electric Space Telegraphy," delivered Friday, June 13, 1902, before the Royal Institution, London. Reprinted in Eric Eastwood (ed.) *Wireless Telegraphy* (New York: John Wiley, 1974), pages 72–88, at page 86. Courtesy of Applied Science Publishers Ltd., England.

as the most important maritime power with its empire and control of most of the world's cables, was the country most concerned with development of long-range communication. At age twenty-two, Marconi arrived in London. His Irish-born mother's contacts carried him to the head of the telegraph system of the British Post Office, William Preece, who had done some wireless experimentation himself. Preece took the young Italian under his wing and helped him to improve his system and show it to important persons in British finance and government.

Marconi's work progressed rapidly. Soon, his signals reached eight miles or more; in 1899 he spanned the English Channel, and two years later he transmitted the letter S in Morse code across the Atlantic to Newfoundland. However, wire telegraph interests in Newfoundland invoked their monopoly franchise and forced Marconi to dismantle his station. Then, incorporating Lodge's tuning principle into his apparatus, Marconi achieved a standard of reliability that overcame the skepticism his "miraculous" invention had provoked. Actually, Marconi may not have invented anything, as Hertz or others had, but he assembled the fruits of many lines of development into a working apparatus.

Marconi managed to attract excellent business and technical managers and advisers, who put together the first wireless firm that could cultivate a profitable market. His company, formed in 1897, was first called the Wireless Telegraph and Signal Company but was changed in 1900 to Marconi's Wireless Telegraph Co., Ltd., or simply "British Marconi." Together with an American subsidiary formed two years later, it quickly became dominant in both marine and transatlantic communication, remaining so until after World War I. Marconi, although something of a showman, was primarily interested in experimenta-

tion, winning the Nobel Prize for physics in 1909, and let his well-qualified advisers and staff run the business. The companies concentrated on commercial applications of wireless telegraphy, as well as the British Empire's worldwide communications needs. Although the Marconi companies had some difficulty persuading land-line telegraph companies and government administrations to relay messages from wireless receiving stations to their final destinations, the marine business was profitable—at lower rates than the telegraph cable—as early as 1910.

2•122 *Fessenden* The first major experimenter in the United States to work with wireless was Reginald A. Fessenden, a Canadian with far less business acumen than Marconi and a temper that repeatedly alienated his backers. He became a professor of electrical engineering at the University of Pittsburgh after having worked for Edison and with the U.S. Weather Bureau on a system of wireless transmission of forecasts. He wanted to develop a workable system of transoceanic wireless using continuous waves rather than Marconi's spark gap technique. Fessenden believed that this method would provide the power necessary to obtain more effective Morse code transmissions and simultaneously create the quieter carrier wave required for voice transmission.

In 1900, Fessenden asked GE to make him a high-speed generator of alternating currents, or alternator, to use as a transmitter. The electrical manufacturing firms accepted special orders for machinery from communications inventors and organizations, and this was the first major request for wireless apparatus. The customer received the essential equipment and service, and the manufacturing company kept the business, profit, and ideas.

It took three years for GE to design

and deliver the first alternator to Fessenden, who worked for a full decade with GE engineers. One of these, E. F. W. Alexanderson, later perfected the alternator for GE, working along different lines from Fessenden. To fund his experimentation, Fessenden found financial backing to form the National Electric Signaling Company in 1902. When the financial panic of 1907 wiped out an opportunity to sell the company to AT&T, Fessenden founded a company in which his original backers had no part. This led to lengthy law suits between backers and inventor and the eventual sale of assets—primarily patents—to Westinghouse after World War I. This firm failed chiefly because of the backers' lack of technical knowledge and understanding and the inventor's difficult personality.

Fessenden continued to contribute important technological developments for many years. He is most remembered for transmitting probably the first publicly announced broadcast of radio telephony, from his station at Brant Rock, Massachusetts, on Christmas Eve 1906. Following a private demonstration a month before, Fessenden alerted ships up and down the East Coast of the United States by wireless telegraphy and arranged for newspaper reporters to listen in in New York to the Christmas Eve broadcast, followed by one on New Year's Eve. If one considers the "general public" of the day as those few who owned and used receiving equipment, mainly ships at sea, and the newspapers as representatives of the public, then the 1906 transmissions were the first

Site of the World's First Voice and Music Broadcast: 1906 / This is a postcard view of Fessenden's Brant Rock station, showing the tall tubular tower with its adjustable antenna at the top, and the two summer cottages that were converted into living quarters and station headquarters. The tower was demolished in 1912 or 1913. This particular card was mailed in July of 1907, just six months after the Christmas Eve broadcast discussed in the text—and bears the handwritten comment on the back "Did you get my wireless?"

The Wireless Station-Brant Rock, Mass.
No. 1691 Moore & Gibson Co., New-York. Germany

broadcasts. They were scheduled, they were for the general public, and listening required no special knowledge of code since they consisted of voice and music. The publicity they received included apocryphal stories of shipboard radio operators hearing angels' voices. However, since Fessenden's purpose was to make money from his inventions of long- and medium-range radio apparatus, he meant these broadcasts as publicity and not as a program service to the public.

2•123 *de Forest*   Another very important American inventor-innovator of radio was Lee de Forest. After earning a Ph.D. from Yale in 1899 with a dissertation on wireless telegraphy, de Forest worked briefly for Western Electric. In 1900–1901 he developed his own wireless telegraphy system as competition for Marconi, who was then getting established. De Forest's system was a technical failure but a publicity bonanza. He had arranged to wireless the results of a 1901 yacht race from a boat to one of the smaller press associations, but a Marconi set on another boat created such interference that neither signal could get through. The newspaper publicity about the attempt, however, reached stock promoter Abraham White, who decided to back de Forest.

The De Forest Wireless Telephone Company was established in 1902, with de Forest concentrating on research and White promoting heavy sales of stock. Customers included the army, the navy, and the United Fruit Company, which needed radio to communicate with its plantations in Central America, but sales were limited compared to stock sold and expectations engendered. As a result, in what was to become a common tale, the backers dissolved the company in 1907 and sold its assets to the United Wireless Telegraph Company, in an effort to remove the inventor from any benefits.

Fortunately de Forest retained the rights to his most important invention, the Audion or triode vacuum tube (see 2.22), and immediately set up his own firm, the De Forest Radio Telephone Company. During the next few years, de Forest accomplished some spectacular publicity events: in 1907 he offered occasional telephonic, classical music broadcasts; in the summer of 1908, he broadcast a long phonograph record concert from the Eiffel Tower, with reception reported 500 miles away, although it was more reliable at 25 miles; in 1910 he broadcast Enrico Caruso in two operas from the Metropolitan Opera House in New York to perhaps fifty people. Financial problems, law suits, and criminal stock fraud charges forced de Forest to sell some of the Audion rights to an undisclosed agent of AT&T at a low price. Even so, the de Forest company went bankrupt in 1911, the first of his several business catastrophes. Clearly, de Forest was a better inventor than he was businessman or scientist, and his reputation as the "father of radio" is based largely and deservedly on the Audion, which played a key role in electronics for several decades.

2•2   Improvements in Wireless

With basic wireless principles known, attention turned—over the next several years—to perfecting both transmission and reception of radio signals.

2•21   *Transmission*

Marconi's early experiments and initial commercial installations used the spark gap transmission pioneered by Heinrich Hertz in the 1880s. Although simple to construct, the spark gap transmitter required a large amount of power, radiated energy over a broad band, was bulky, and produced a thunderous and disagreeable crash. Furthermore, it was either "on" or "off," and it could not be modulated for speech and music.

An early improvement on the spark gap transmitter was the *arc*. Danish inventor Valdemar Poulsen patented an arc generator in 1902 that, by using a much narrower gap, could give a nearly continuous series of sparks, or arc. Because this system, called *CW* or *continuous wave*, was inherently more efficient for communication than was the spark gap, it could be used over longer distances. The Poulsen

arc was normally a huge, expensive, water-cooled device, but it could be applied to smaller shipboard installations. In 1909 Cyril F. Elwell purchased United States rights to it and set up the Federal Telegraph Company of California to exploit its potential. In the years around the beginning of World War I, the U.S. Navy's enthusiasm for this device resulted in contracts for several shore stations capable of long-distance communication with the fleet. The largest Poulsen arc station, started during the war but not finished until 1920, was at Bordeaux, France. This 1,000 kw station was perhaps the high point of trying to span the Atlantic with brute power. The Poulsen patents controlled by Federal were important in the years immediately after World War I (see 3.1), and the Poulsen arc remained in shipboard installations until the start of World War II.

The next major system, also developed before World War I, was the alternator, originated by Fessenden and built to his specifications by GE. The first was delivered in 1906 and soon others followed. By 1911, after Fessenden had ended his association with his financial backers, GE engineer E. F. W. Alexanderson rapidly perfected ideas of his own.

The Alexanderson alternator was a huge piece of machinery, very much like a power-plant generator but rotating much faster. Such high-speed rotation created complex mechanical problems, but by 1909 Alexanderson had developed a 100,000-cycle alternator that produced smooth, continuous waves. Although the first successful unit produced only 2,000 watts, higher power soon followed, and, by 1915, 50 kw units were being built. After long negotiations, GE and British Marconi agreed that Marconi would have exclusive rights to use the alternator, and GE would have exclusive rights to make it. The first

---

Typical Early Wireless Transmitter / Taken from a typical book of the time intended for radio experimenters, this is both a drawing and an electrical schematic of a spark-gap transmitter—the standard wireless transmitter from the time of Hertz in the 1880s to the time of World War I. That it was used for wireless telegraphy (code) and not telephony (voice and music) is evident by the telegraph key—the spark jumping the gap made far too much noise for successful voice transmission. Working with a battery, the system was self-contained, thus not requiring plug-in sources of current. The receiving end might consist of a coherer (in the earliest days), and after 1900 a crystal detector as is shown in the box on page 80.

Source: Yates and Pacent (1920), page 61.

The Alexanderson Alternator / Alternator developer E. F. W. Alexanderson is seen watching one of the 50 kw alternators in action. These huge machines were the first effective means of long-distance and transatlantic communication by wireless. Photo courtesy of General Electric.

50 kw unit was installed in New Jersey in 1917, and the following year a 200 kw unit, the most powerful and efficient transmitter in the world, was installed at New Brunswick, New Jersey. Using the government call letters NFF, the powerful unit announced President Wilson's Fourteen Points to the world in 1918. The agreement between Marconi and GE was set aside during the war but was to become instrumental in structuring American radio immediately afterward (see 3.12).

The next means of transmission, still in use today, involved vacuum tubes. Although experimentation began around 1912, high-powered vacuum-tube transmitters did not become common for more than a decade. Thomas Edison first noted that a heated filament gave off electrons —the blackening of a light bulb, or "Edison effect." In 1904 John Ambrose Fleming, working for British Marconi, discovered that, since electrons were negative, a positively charged plate could collect them. Therefore, electricity would flow whenever the plate was positively charged. When the plate was negatively charged, no current would flow. This made the tube a perfect one-way gate or *valve* that could be used to change alternating current, such as a radio wave, to pulsating direct current. This one-way flow, in a process known as *detection*, enabled one to hear an audible signal of dots and dashes or speech no matter how high above audible range the radio wave frequency was. Detection was essential to radio reception (see 2.22). De Forest inserted into the Fleming valve a third element, a grid carrying a slight charge that could be varied from neutral, which offered no hindrance to current, to slightly negative, which would block current. This invention made a vacuum tube function as an amplifier, since the larger current flowing from filament to plate

would vary in step with a much smaller control current placing a charge on the grid. De Forest first used his triode, or Audion, as an amplifier as well as a detector early in the century. AT&T engineers (see 2.123), improved the device—by using a high rather than partial vacuum, for instance—and put it to work as an amplifier on long-distance telephone lines, including the first transcontinental one in 1915.

Because of their lighter weight and low current demand, vacuum tubes were used during World War I for specialized receivers and transmitters—after the navy had agreed to indemnify manufacturers for patent infringement suits. This was necessary since de Forest controlled the use of the third element and Marconi owned the rights to the first two elements, which together formed the diode, or Fleming valve. As early as October 1915, speech and music traveled across the Atlantic from the U.S. Navy station at Arlington, Virginia (NAA), to the Eiffel Tower in Paris —through several hundred triodes connected in parallel. Even though this experiment showed the advantages of the vacuum-tube transmitter, including its freedom from problems of moving machinery and its small bulk and weight in relation to distance covered—an even greater relative saving than the transistor offered in recent years—the alternator still worked well for code transmissions for many years. It was for the transmission of music and speech, and broadcasting in particular, that the vacuum-tube transmitter became essential.

2• 22   *Reception*

In 1900 the only device generally available for detecting radio waves was the Branly-Lodge coherer, as modified slightly by Marconi. It was very delicate, permitted only slow message speeds because of its need to be tapped regularly between incoming pulses, occasionally gave false indications, and was not readily adaptable to tuning. Marconi's 1902 magnetic detector was more sensitive, permitted reception over 500 miles by day and 1,500 by night, but was hard to construct. During the period from 1903 to 1908, Fessenden developed an electrolytic detector that was used extensively until about 1913. This silent and automatic device needed no "tapper" since it used liquid rather than particles.

A completely different approach led to the development of the crystal detector around 1906 by Greenleaf W. Pickard and H. H. C. Dunwoody. Pickard had found that a crystal of silicon would allow electricity to flow in one direction. Using a small metal point, called a *cat's whisker,* to find the most effective spot on the crystal, he constructed a detector of radio waves far less expensive than previous models and just as effective. Dunwoody discovered that carborundum, an extremely hard, electrical furnace by-product, also would work well. By allowing electricity to flow in one direction only, it converted the very rapidly alternating *radio-frequency* wave into a series of pulses whose variations in strength (amplitude) were in the audio-frequency range to which earphones and the human ear could respond. These detectors were the first *solid state* devices and, for several decades, the only ones. The crystal detector permitted hundreds of thousands of hobbyists and the general public to pick up radio signals—for the price of a pair of earphones and a few cents' worth of wire, crystal, and cat's whisker. The major drawbacks of the crystal set— which was in general use for decades, and which hobbyists still use—were the dif-

ficulty of finding the right spot with the cat's whisker—solved by permanently affixing the whisker at the factory and sealing the crystal in a case—and the inability of such a simple receiver to amplify the weak incoming signals.

In its original form, the Fleming valve (see 2.21), which permitted electricity to flow in only one direction, could function as a detector. Although the 3-element de Forest Audion, patented in 1906–1907, also could be used as a detector, it did not improve detection per se. Its greatest value was in amplifying weak incoming radio waves. A radio-frequency amplification stage or two before the detector and an audio-frequency amplification stage or two afterward would permit reliable reception of exceedingly weak radio signals —and this eventually led to the use of loudspeakers instead of earphones. Manufacturing tolerances were at first loose, permitting inconsistent results that kept de Forest tied up in patent suits for many years. Although associated circuitry was not well understood at the time, the invention of the amplifying triode proved critical to the future development of radio.

At about the time de Forest sold telephonic rights to the Audion to AT&T, Edwin Howard Armstrong, best known later as the inventor of FM, was working on circuitry that would use the Audion as a transmitter, as well as an amplifier and detector in a radio receiver of unsurpassed sensitivity and selectivity. Within a few months of each other in 1914, de Forest and Armstrong individually applied for patents on what became known as the regenerative or *feedback* circuit. One of the longest and bitterest fights in radio history resulted from this conflict over patent priority, leading in 1928 and again in 1934 to the United States Supreme Court. Although the engineering community generally believed that Armstrong had a sounder grasp of the principles behind the circuit than de Forest had, the court held in favor of de Forest. Today, engineering texts and organizations generally give Armstrong credit for this crucial invention, but the law gave it to de Forest. The struggle embittered both men.

The regenerative and superregenerative receivers were very sensitive, but required extremely delicate tuning to keep them from oscillating so that no intelligible sounds could get through and interference would disrupt reception elsewhere in the vicinity. The solution lay in the heterodyne receiver, patented by Fessenden as early as 1905, and in the superheterodyne receiver, invented by Armstrong in 1918 and still in use today. These circuits were not practical until the development of the Audion.

Besides detecting and amplifying incoming signals, it was necessary at the turn of the century to find a means of *tuning* to a single station so that stations on nearby frequencies could operate without interference. Techniques were being explored: Sir Oliver Lodge had patented a system he called *syntonic tuning* as early as 1897, and, shortly afterward, both Marconi in England and John Stone Stone in America developed ways of selecting desired frequencies and rejecting unwanted ones through the principle of resonance. When a singer sings a note that hits the resonant frequency of a glass, acoustical energy is transferred so efficiently that it shatters the glass. In the same way, proper adjustment of the inductance or capacitance in a tuning circuit of a receiver—or transmitter, for that matter—can set up a condition whereby only the desired or resonant frequency is picked up. As usual, a patent fight ensued, but both patents—and the lives of the two inventors—expired before the case was settled.

2·3   Maritime Applications

Radio equipment for more than experimental purposes was first installed on oceangoing ships and in the shore stations that were built to communicate with them. Much as the telegraph had nearly doubled the railroad's freight-carrying capacity through more efficient scheduling and routing, so radio enabled ships to improve their cargo pickup schedules, to inform owners of their approach, and to learn of weather and other conditions en route. Over and above these commercial benefits, however, at least in the public mind, was the safety of lives and property at sea.

2·31   Wireless and Commercial Shipping (to 1914)

As early as 1899 ships in distress were calling for help by radio. Marconi's reputation in Great Britain grew after the crew of a coastal lightship was saved from a severe storm in this way. In 1909 when the liner *Republic* collided with the *Florida* in a fog off the East Coast of the United States, the radio operator on the sinking liner stayed at his post and issued a call for help that resulted in saving almost all those aboard. In that same year, passengers and crew on 18 other ships with radio installations were saved, thanks to radio, but those on many more ships without radio were not. One of the biggest peacetime maritime disasters was the sinking of the liner *Titanic* on her maiden voyage in April 1912. The ship rammed an iceberg and three hours later went to the bottom off the Newfoundland Banks together with 1,500 passengers and crew. Some 700 were saved by a ship that picked up the *Titanic*'s wireless call for help 58 miles away, but a much nearer ship did not assist because its only radio operator, after many hours on duty, was sound asleep when the messages came over the radio.

This disaster pointed up the necessity not only for radio installations but enough qualified operators to man the apparatus, and led to tighter regulation of radio equipment on passenger and larger ocean-going cargo ships. While later research throws doubt that it ever happened, David Sarnoff (years later president, then chairman of the board, of RCA) encouraged the story that, as a young Marconi operator assigned to the New York station atop the John Wanamaker department store, with the airwaves cleared by government order, he stayed at his post for many hours during the *Titanic* disaster, sending messages to coordinate rescue traffic and compile a list of survivors. Sarnoff soon was named commercial manager of American Marconi.

When Marconi first started installing wireless in ships, his was the best equipment available. Other apparatus could be used, but Marconi and his business associates found ways to keep Marconi apparatus most in demand. A 1901 agreement with the Lloyds of London insurance pool to equip Lloyds' signal stations served to gain acceptance and prestige for Marconi equipment early on; and Marconi allowed its shore stations to communicate only with ships that rented Marconi equipment and trained operators. As various nations began passing laws regulating radio to save lives at sea, and as ship-owners became more aware of its commercial benefits, more and more vessels acquired Marconi apparatus. To support their own manufacturers, nations other than England permitted or suggested other brands of wireless apparatus, but ships equipped with them could not —until after 1903 (see 2.4)—then communicate with Marconi shore stations.

By the start of World War I, British Marconi stood preeminent in the field.

It controlled wireless communications throughout the British Empire and had taken over the assets of de Forest's United Wireless, thus controlling—through its subsidiary, the American Marconi Company—90 percent of all American ship-to-shore commercial communication.

Some specialized radio operations did not need interconnection with Marconi installations. As early as 1904, the United Fruit Company used de Forest apparatus to make ships available for loading fruit as soon as it was ready to pick. In 1907, switching to Fessenden equipment, United Fruit constructed the first radio-transmitting facilities in most of the Central American republics. It established an operating subsidiary, Tropical Radio Telegraph Company, in 1913 and was among the leaders in upgrading transmitting and receiving equipment—sometimes because a hurricane had conveniently blown away the obsolete gear. By the early 1920s, United Fruit had invested nearly $4 million dollars in establishing radio in the region, equipping its ships, and even acquiring patents on a crystal receiver.

For dispatching of ships, radio had no equal. For point-to-point messages, however, undersea cable offered strong competition. In 1907 British Marconi offered transatlantic wireless telegraphy at only 18 cents a word, as compared to the cable companies' 25-cent rate. The greater reliability of cable evened the odds and helped to prolong this commercial war for many years. Radio had more luck in the Pacific, where fewer cables meant less competition and less interference meant greater reliability.

2•32   Wireless and the U.S. Navy

The first important armed-forces tests of radio were conducted independently by the United States Navy and the British Royal Navy in 1899. The American tests were made of Marconi apparatus aboard the U.S. battleships *New York* and *Massachusetts*. Although radio signals bridged distances of up to 40 miles, it was clear that the lack of suitable tuning devices led to unacceptable interference. Furthermore, the just adopted Marconi policy of renting rather than selling equipment and services was politically unacceptable. Obviously, the navy could not accept being dependent upon a foreign power, no matter how friendly.

For the next few years, the navy searched for a different, reliable radio system, in the meantime not using any wireless at sea. Neither the de Forest nor the Fessenden systems seemed to do the trick, nor did various European systems. In 1903 the navy installed some German (Slaby-Arco) apparatus on ships of the North Atlantic Fleet, which gave them a clear advantage in war games over another part of the fleet without any radio communications. At the same time, the navy started to build powerful shore stations, and by 1904, 20 of these were in operation. One of these, in Arlington, Virginia, broadcast precise time signals, a useful aid to navigation.

As early as 1905, after further comparative tests, the navy began a conscious swing to American-made equipment. In 1907–1908 it gave de Forest a scant month to install radiotelephone transmitters on the ships of the Great White Fleet, being readied for an around-the-world "show the flag" mission. Partly because of hasty installation, these devices worked poorly, except for the one on the U.S.S. *Ohio*, which transmitted voice and music to the crew, to other ships in the fleet, and to listeners in ports of call. However, these unreliable radio telephones were removed when the fleet returned in 1909, and in-

terest in naval wireless telephony languished for nearly a decade until the United States entered World War I in 1917.

During this period, the navy concentrated on expanding shore stations and shipboard wireless telegraphy installations. In 1912 it began building a chain of stations to connect American bases in the Pacific, including Hawaii and the Philippines, at the same time that British Marconi was constructing the "Empire system" for use of the Royal Navy and to eliminate the British Empire's dependence on easily severed cables. After contracting with the Federal Telegraph Company for a Poulsen arc installation at the Arlington station in 1913, the U.S. Navy installed similar transmitters in the Pacific, including one of 500 kw in Manila. Coastal shore stations in the United States were located a few hundred miles apart so that, if one station was out of operation, another could reach naval units at sea. Unfortunately, most of this equipment could function over only a few hundred miles to two thousand or so miles—a serious drawback if the navy expected the fleet to be in action across the Atlantic or Pacific.

Another drawback to the navy's use of radio was the resistance of personnel to innovation. Most shipboard installations were primitive, hand-built affairs. Few men were adequately trained to get the most from them, and fewer still cared to learn. Doubtful senior officers discouraged diversion of scarce navy funds for wireless, and field commanders disliked being tied to headquarters by an electronic umbilical cord. The telegraph had already limited the freedom of army commanders to "fight their own war," but, until the advent of wireless, naval commanders retained independence due to the nature of their forces and battleground. Nevertheless, foresighted naval officers realized that wireless would be useful in wartime—

if its problems and drawbacks could be overcome.

2·4   First Attempts at Regulation

Radio clearly was such a potential saver of lives and property in peril at sea that otherwise acceptable practices that interfered with its operation there had to be overcome. British Marconi's policy not to communicate with users of other companies' facilities, even sometimes in an emergency, was seen as a blatant attempt to establish a monopoly. Interference was increasing as more stations went on the air and receivers became more sensitive. It occurred not only between ship stations but between ships, land stations, and a growing number of amateur stations.

Other factors helped to sway public opinion in the direction of government control of radio. Business scandals involved de Forest in this country and Marconi stock in the United Kingdom. The growing militant nationalism in most technologically developed countries worsened the confusion over rates, equipment standards, and interconnection procedures. How could radio achieve full stature when each nation rallied around its own radio equipment manufacturers, and based industry standards on political policy rather than technology? Some international solution to these problems was indicated.

As early as 1903, the government of Imperial Germany called the first international convention on radio. This Berlin Conference stemmed partly from the refusal of the Marconi Company to relay signals from a yacht belonging to a German prince on a visit to North America. The eight nations attending—except for the United Kingdom and Italy, which not surprisingly supported the Marconi position

—issued a protocol calling for all wireless systems to communicate under all conditions with all other wireless systems. With the requirement that each country would have to pass the enabling laws, the meeting adjourned with plans to reconvene the following year.

The subsequent meeting was postponed once—Great Britain and Italy still were not ready—and then again—the Russo-Japanese War of 1905—and finally took place in Berlin in 1906. Delegates from 27 nations—including the U.S. with a naval officer delegation—worked out two protocols, one for ship-to-ship and the other for ship-to-shore communication, both calling for communication without regard for the type of equipment used. Also the international distress call was changed from CQD (roughly, "calling all stations, disaster") to an arbitrary three dots, three dashes, and three dots all run together: the famous SOS still in use.

These agreements were to take effect on July 1, 1908, but there were many delays and complications. Countries with Marconi contracts asked for time to work them out. In the United States, Congress initially refused to ratify the agreements, accepting the testimony of American wireless-manufacturing firms that they would stifle development of radio and place it under international rather than national control. It was not until the planners of a third conference, to be held in London in 1912, quietly withdrew the invitation to the United States that Congress passed the first radio law in this country, the Wireless Ship Act of 1910.

The absence of a specific law did not mean that Americans were not trying to settle the problem of interference between stations, which was caused largely by the uncoordinated use of radio by private commercial and experimental stations, the army, the navy, the Weather

The Beginnings of Radio Regulation / (excerpts from three key acts)

An Act to Require Apparatus and Operators for Radio Communication on Certain Ocean Steamers, approved June 24, 1910 . . . it shall be unlawful for any ocean-going steamer of the United States or of any foreign country, carrying passengers and carrying fifty or more persons, including passengers and crew, to leave or attempt to leave any port of the United States unless such steamer shall be equipped with an efficient apparatus for radio-communication, in good working order, in charge of a person skilled in the use of such apparatus, which apparatus shall be capable of transmitting and receiving messages over a distance of at least one hundred miles. . . .

. . . That for the purpose of this act apparatus for radio communications shall not be deemed to be efficient unless the company installing it shall contract in writing to exchange, and shall, in fact, exchange, as far as may be physically practicable, to be determined by the master of the vessel, messages with shore or ship stations using other systems of radio-communication.

An Act to Amend the Act of 1910, approved July 23, 1912 . . . an auxiliary power supply, independent of the vessel's main electric power plant, must be provided which will enable the sending set for at least four hours to send messages over a distance of at least one hundred miles day or night, and efficient communication between the operator in the radio room and the bridge shall be maintained at all times. The radio equipment must be in charge of two or more persons skilled in the use of such apparatus, one or the other of whom shall be on duty at all times while the vessel is being navigated . . .

An Act to Regulate Radio Communication, approved August 13, 1912 . . . That a person, company, or corporation within the jurisdiction of the United States shall not use or operate any apparatus for radio communication as a means of commercial intercourse among the several States . . . except under and in accordance with a license, revocable for cause, in that behalf granted by the Secretary of Commerce and Labor upon application therefore . . .

That every such license shall be in such form as the Secretary . . . shall determine and shall contain restrictions . . . on and subject to which the license is granted; . . . that every such license shall be issued only to citizens of the United States . . . shall specify the ownership and location of the station . . . and other particulars for its identification and to enable its range to be estimated; shall state the purpose of the station . . . shall state the wavelength or the wavelengths authorized for use by the station for the prevention of interference and the hours for which the station is licensed for work . . .

Bureau, and the Department of Agriculture. A board set up in 1904 by President Theodore Roosevelt to resolve these difficulties recommended navy control of most radio, especially in wartime; legislation to prevent commercial interests from controlling radio; peacetime direction of radio by the Department of Commerce and Labor; and installation of government stations in all United States territories. Although none of these suggestions was formally adopted, one could trace their basic outline in American radio regulation for nearly two decades.

The Wireless Ship Act of 1910, which Congress passed after several attempts, contained in one page nearly all called for in the 1906 Berlin protocol: ocean-going vessels with 50 or more passengers traveling between ports 200 or more miles apart had to carry radio apparatus capable of reaching 100 miles day or night and an operator to run it. Partly because of the lesson learned from the *Republic* disaster, and partly because the law created a market for more sales, the manufacturers accepted this act. It met the demands of the 1903 and 1906 conferences indirectly, calling for "an efficient apparatus for radio-communication" and then defining "efficient" by stating that "apparatus for radio-communication shall not be deemed to be efficient unless the company installing it shall contract in writing to exchange, and shall, in fact, exchange . . . messages with shore or ship stations using other systems of radio-communication." This approach, together with similar laws passed in other countries (one in the United Kingdom as early as 1904 called for trained radio operators), solved the problem. It is interesting to note that the 1910 act was not cited as a precedent when television was faced with the problem of sets that could not pick up UHF channels in the late 1950s and early 1960s.

In 1912 some 29 nations met in London and agreed to strengthen the 1906 protocol, particularly, as a result of the *Titanic* disaster that year, in recommending that two operators be available on most vessels. The United States amended the 1910 act to provide that any ship with 50 or more passengers, regardless of distance between customary ports and including the Great Lakes for the first time, had to have radio, an auxiliary power supply capable of operating it, two or more operators, and good communication between the radio operator and the bridge. A month later, in August, Congress passed the Radio Act of 1912, which took seven pages to spell out public policy (stations had to be licensed by the Secretary of Commerce and Labor, government stations had priority, etc.) and standards of operation (messages were to be secret, wavelengths and transmitter power were to be selected for minimal interference, etc.). This law governed the regulation of radio, including the as yet little-known concept of broadcasting, until 1927.

2·5   The First Broadcasters

In selecting the most important early broadcasters, one has to use a detailed definition of broadcasting. For example, although Stubblefield transmitted speech successfully (see 2.11), he hardly intended to reach the general public, a major criterion in our definition, and his transmissions apparently relied on induction, which is inherently short-range, rather than on radiation. In another example, Théodore and François Puskás linked telephone subscribers in Budapest to a central unit that provided a news and music service. However, this "Telephonic Newspaper," which ran from 1893 until at least the middle 1930s, used wire or cable, not radio—in a process called *rediffusion* still used in a number of countries. This might be thought of as the precursor of cable television (CATV), but it was not broadcasting by radio to the general public. Early in the century an ingenious operator at the Mare Island navy base in California had produced musical tones by rapidly changing the speed of rotary generators of radio waves so that the musical pitch of the signal changed—similar to the musical games played today with "touch tone" telephone equipment.

However, there were numerous examples of true broadcasting before its commonly accepted inauguration on KDKA late in 1920 (see 3.21). Fessenden's Christmas Eve 1906 broadcast was one. Fessenden had tried to ensure a maximum audience, and, although some ship operators and a smattering of reporters in New York had to act as surrogates for the general public, this transmission was intended for a general audience; it was telephony, speech and music; it required no special knowledge for decoding; and anyone with a receiver could pick it up.

But neither Fessenden nor de Forest, who made a number of broadcasts in 1907 and 1908, had incentive to establish a regular public series of broadcasts. Their stations were experimental and promotional, and the service they provided to listeners was incidental. Except that they were better known and that their equipment was more powerful than most, they were amateur radio operators, or hams. By 1912 there were more than a thousand such hobbyists, most of them interested primarily in communicating with fellow amateurs, almost exclusively by Morse code, and not in broadcasting. However, by 1915, having formed a national organization, the American Radio Relay League, and established a magazine, *QST*, they had become a potential political

power, a source of trained operators for wartime, and an important group of listeners, as well as tinkerers whose curiosity and work led to many important advances of the technical radio art.

Perhaps the strongest claimant to being first to broadcast intentionally to a general audience, using electromagnetic waves, on a schedule, and with voice rather than code transmissions, was Charles D. "Doc" Herrold, who operated a College of Engineering and Wireless in San Jose, California. He was not the first to broadcast speech and music, not even in California, but early in 1909, as an adjunct to his school, Herrold presented regularly scheduled news reports and musical programs. Starting with a spark gap transmitter, he soon developed an arc that transmitted better quality voice and music. At first he broadcast only on Wednesday nights for an hour or so but soon changed to every day. Herrold built some receivers and made them available for public use in hotel lobbies. In 1915, during the San Francisco Exposition, the station broadcast six to eight hours a day with de Forest apparatus receiving its transmissions at the convention site. De Forest later said that Herrold's station "can rightfully claim to be the oldest broadcasting station of the entire world. . . ." When the Radio Act of 1912 was passed, Herrold's station was licensed and operated until World War I, when all amateur stations were closed down. Herrold resurrected the station in December 1921 or January 1922 under the call letters KQW, using more conventional apparatus than the "Herrold System of Radio Telephony," which would not work on the wavelengths the Secretary of Commerce then assigned for broadcasting. KQW, later sold and moved to San Francisco, still broadcasts as 50,000 watt KCBS, with a legitimate claim as the descendant of the *first* broadcasting station in the

Herrold's KQW: The First Real Station?

WIRELESS TELEGRAPH
TO BE DEMONSTRATED

PROF. HERROLD, FORMER SAN JOSEAN, HAS MADE MANY INTERESTING EXPERIMENTS

WILL PERFORM FEAT OF FIRING MINIATURE POWDER MINE BY WIRELESS

Public interest is focusing on a novel form of entertainment to be given in the Y.M.C.A. Hall, Friday evening July 16th. Chas. D. Herrold, a former San Josean will appear here for the first time in a lecture "The Story of Wireless." He has devoted a number of years to a careful experimental study of wireless telegraphy and telephony. For several months past he has had a system installed on board the sloop Dorothy on the San Joaquin River and a permanent station at Stockton. A portable outfit was also sent to Vernalis, Cal. and his assistant in charge kept in touch with him by ether waves. In the Friday evening entertainment he will show the public how it is possible to time two stations so that other stations cannot get the messages. He will perform the feat of firing a miniature powder mine by wireless and will have installed on the stage a complete wireless station. The equipment includes two large Rumkoeff Tesia [sic] coils capable of producing 400,000 volts of electricity. A feature of the entertainment will be a perfect imitation of lightning. A series of long, zig-zag discharges will be led over a plate 12 feet long under the enormous tension of nearly 500,000 volts.

"Doc" Herrold stands at the doorway of his second station, about 1913. The large circular cones on the table are part of Herrold's own system of wireless telephony, which he used until World War I. Photo courtesy of KCBS Radio.

Source: San Jose *Daily Mercury* news item Thursday morning, July 15, 1909. Courtesy of San Jose *Mercury*.

United States—even though the delay in returning to the air after World War I had destroyed its claim as the *oldest* station now operating (see 3.2).

Herrold was but one of a growing number of experimental broadcasters. From 1912 to 1914, Alfred Goldsmith operated station 2XN at City College of New York. In 1916, G. C. Conner and C. V. Logwood broadcast music over 2ZK in New Rochelle, New York, for an hour each evening. In East Pittsburgh, Pennsylvania, Westinghouse engineer Frank Conrad began that same year to send voice and music programs from his home to the Westinghouse plant five miles away. Soon he was scheduling music broadcasts for friends—a humble beginning for an enter-

prise we will discuss in the next chapter (see 3.21). At the University of Wisconsin, Professor E. M. Terry set up 9XM (later WHA) for telegraphic weather forecasts and market reports for mariners on the Great Lakes and farmers. Allowed to stay on the air during World War I, Terry also experimented with voice broadcasts, the genesis of WHA's claim to be the first station. Some experimenters of this period reached great distances with their low-power transmitters because there were few stations to offer interference.

Even as experimentation in broadcasting progressed, most radio people believed that the future of radio lay with *narrowcasting* or point-to-point communication, particularly between mobile stations

Conrad's "Home" Station / Equipment used by Dr. Frank Conrad, assistant chief engineer of Westinghouse, in the years before KDKA was established in 1920. Conrad transmitted radio telephone programs from his garage, using the call letters 8XK. Photo courtesy of Westinghouse and Joseph E. Baudino.

or over difficult terrain. "Radio people" in this instance included the major electrical and wireless firms, who would have to support any new use of radio. One exception was David Sarnoff, who, some years after his outstanding service at the Marconi station in New York during the *Titanic* disaster, had been promoted to commercial manager of American Marconi. In a 1916 memo to Edward J. Nally, general manager of the firm, he proposed:

> . . . a plan of development which would make radio a "household utility" in the same sense as the piano or phonograph. The idea is to bring music into the house by wireless. . . . The problem of transmitting music has already been solved in principle and therefore all the receivers attuned to the transmitting wavelength should be capable of receiving such music. The receiver can be designed in the form of a simple "Radio Music Box" and arranged for several different wavelengths, which should be changeable with the throwing of a single switch or pressing of a single button. . . . The box can be placed on a table in the parlor or living room, the switch set accordingly and the transmitted music received. There should be no difficulty in receiving music perfectly when transmitted within a radius of 25 to 50 miles. . . . The same principle can be extended to numerous other fields as, for example, receiving of lectures at home which can be made perfectly audible; also events of national importance can be simultaneously announced and received.

Although Sarnoff's memo was filed and forgotten for years, public interest in radio was exhibited by more than 8,500 licensed amateurs, some of whom transmitted voice and music, and most of whom listened. However, the complexity and unreliability of equipment, the necessity for earphones, and the limited programming tended to restrict radio to the engineering-minded. Neither engineers nor businessmen had much interest in visionary schemes.

2•6   Radio at War

Armies had used the telegraph for 50 years, and World War I added all the newer devices that could be converted to warfare—the automobile, the airplane, the radio—and stimulated their development as well. Although the war halted most private experimentation and closed amateur stations, the army and navy's need for reliable, efficient apparatus for communication hastened the introduction of wireless in all forms.

2•61   Radio in World War I

In the Gulf of Mexico, the U.S. Navy was able to intercept some Mexican ships during an incident prior to America's entry into World War I, thanks to radio. In Europe, Germany had had to turn to radio when Britain cut Germany's cable connections early in the war. Germany used radio sometimes for propaganda but usually for scheduling and dispatching commercial and naval vessels. Its "broadcast" nature, however, permitted the British to intercept German messages and decipher them with the aid of a captured code book. One message, sent by the German Foreign Ministry to their ambassador in Mexico City, proposed offering the Mexicans large chunks of United States territory if Mexico would join Germany in the event of war with the United States —the famous "Zimmermann Telegram." The British were delighted to inform the United States government, and the world, about the perfidy of the Germans and provided Washington with the key to the German code. What made this more infuriating to the Americans was that a German-owned but American-navy-operated station in New Jersey had relayed the original message, still in code, as a diplomatic courtesy.

The navy was operating the German-owned transmitter because the government had taken over all high-power stations—even American Marconi's—as a national security measure. All amateur stations, including broadcast experimenters, were closed down in 1917. The navy's own 35 coastal stations, its high-power chain across the Pacific, and radio telegraph apparatus on nearly all major vessels had cost about $20 million by April 6, 1917, when the United States entered the war. After that date, the navy also acted as censor on all wireless and cable communication channels and the government took over the railroad and telephone industries, the latter assigned to the Post Office Department. The navy communicated with the fleet in European waters from major shore stations including the American Marconi installation at New Brunswick, New Jersey. This station was particularly important, since it used a 200 kw Alexanderson alternator, which had replaced the 50 kw one and could be heard all over Europe.

With its great interest in rapid and efficient communication, the navy was in an excellent position to use wireless. However, it suffered from two shortages: trained personnel and top-flight equipment. The first shortage was solved through recruiting amateur operators and establishing radio schools around the country, including one at Harvard University. By the Armistice, November 11, 1918, some 7,000 men had been trained and 3,400 were under instruction. This group, added to the thousands of hams who managed

to keep up their interest in wireless during the war, strongly influenced postwar radio developments.

Technologically, radio advanced during the war. Lightweight vacuum-tube transmitters and receivers were developed. Even airplanes carried them, including one set designed by Major Edwin Armstrong. Low-power, tactical radio sets were not nearly so prevalent as they are today. In World War I, an army division of 20,000 men rarely would have more than six radio sets—one for each of four regiments, one for the artillery, and one at headquarters. (By the early 1950s, one transmitter served every 6.3 men in an army division, and today some units have even more.) Although radio added greatly to the flexibility of ground communication during World War I, the demands of reliability, secrecy, and relatively immobile trench warfare made telephone and telegraph service more common than wireless.

2•62   The First Patents Pool

The navy could requisition high-power stations from private companies, train operators for them, and close down domestic stations to prevent the transmittal of espionage, but obtaining efficient and modern shipboard radio equipment was another story.

Vacuum-tube equipment was obviously the best, but nobody could legally make triode vacuum tubes when de Forest controlled the patent on the third electrode and Marconi controlled the Fleming patents on the first two electrodes. Furthermore, some of the navy's earlier sources were busy making equipment for either the Germans or the Allies. Litigation on the de Forest and Fleming patents had continued for years, and court decisions in 1916 tied most companies into knots. Years

Use of Radio by the U.S. Army and Navy in 1917–1918

The Army Signal Corps   Although a transatlantic radio station was built near Bordeaux, the War Department in Washington had no radio contact with its commanders in the field, and these commanders had no very dependable wireless systems among themselves. Radio carried little of the war's communications load. In the first place, the tactical situation again and again brought the Western Front into small areas and mired it there. For another reason, although nearly 10,000 radio sets, chiefly airborne radiotelegraph, were produced for the Signal Corps and Air Service, the conflict was over too soon for the combat signalman or aviator to use them much. Finally, radio was too new to have passed the awkward age. Spark-type equipment did have the advantage of not requiring a skilled man to tune it or mend it, but was so heavy it could scarcely be moved, was often unintelligible, and was frequently out of commission. Tube equipment generally replaced it. Radio's chief use was for intelligence work. At goniometric stations it took what were later called "fixes" upon enemy transmitters and identified their location by the intersection of the angles. It intercepted German ground telegraph, telephone, aircraft, and artillery signals. . . . The most interesting aspect of Signal Corps radio in World War I was the consolidation of the hitherto scattered efforts in scientific research . . . [but] for the most part, none of the laboratory improvements got into production before the Armistice. Had any been developed before the war, radio history would have been made, for the critical inadequacy of equipment necessitated remarkable advances in the field.

Source: Dulany Terrett, *The Signal Corps: The Emergency* (Washington: Government Printing Office, 1956), pages 18–19.

Naval Radio   In the operating field the Navy became the sole agency, with the exception of U.S. Army field communications, for providing U.S. radio communications, both military and commercial, from the date we entered the war until 1 March 1920. Much was done during the period to increase the reliability of long-range communications by encouraging the development of higher powered arcs and alternators and by the Navy's own design of heterodyne and neutrodyne receivers, multiple-stage amplifiers, and other ancillary apparatus. By the end of the war, sufficient progress had been made in the development of static-reducing balanced antenna systems, together with improvements to transmitters and receiving equipments, to insure reliable transatlantic radio communications.

Source: Captain L. S. Howeth, *History of Communications-Electronics in the United States Navy* (Washington: Government Printing Office, 1963), page 209.

Iconographic Collection, State Historical Society of Wisconsin.

before, Western Electric (AT&T) had purchased some rights to the triode from de Forest, but not enough. If tube equipment was to become available, the patent situation would have to be resolved.

The wartime solution was an emergency pool of patents set up under navy protection. This offer of indemnification, in effect, said: "Use what you need to give us the best equipment, and if you are sued for patent infringement, we'll pay the bill." As the result, the navy could get the equipment, mostly from civilian plants.

At the end of the war, all the temporarily shelved problems came back, together with some caused by the war itself. Should the navy relinquish control over transoceanic wireless? What about the telephone industry, and the amateurs? How could the triode legally be manufactured and used? The patents pool had worked well; could it or should it continue? What about jobs for the returned radio operators? What about factories that had been turning out war-related radio apparatus? Should the government allow Marconi to expand its monopoly, particularly with respect to messages from America to Europe and the Pacific? Should Marconi alone have the Alexanderson alternator? The next chapter tells how these questions were answered.

2•7   The Stage Is Set

We can think of developments up to 1895 as background, for it was only with Marconi's active experimentation in that year that wireless began to move from theory to practice. The key people include Clerk-Maxwell, who first theorized about wireless communication; Hertz, who experimentally proved Clerk-Maxwell correct; Marconi, who took wireless from experiment to practical reality; Fleming, who developed the first vacuum tube with

two elements; Fessenden, the first important American experimenter and the first broadcaster; de Forest, who made amplification possible with his three-element vacuum tube; Alexanderson, who achieved the first reliable means of long-range wireless communication and unwittingly Americanized broadcast development; and Armstrong, who invented receiver circuits that greatly improved reception.

We can divide this era into the wireless experimental period (up to about 1900), practical maritime application (1900–1914), and radio in World War I (1914–1919). We see in these years first attempts at international and American regulation of wireless; intense nationalism in wireless development, with British interests dominating; and the first broadcasts and broadcasting stations both here and abroad. Of overriding importance was the control of key patents, determining which countries, business firms, and individuals would play leading roles. The most important concept, generally held, was that wireless was essentially a means of rapid, long-distance, point-to-point—narrowcast—communications, for international and maritime message transmission. Only a handful of experimenters grasped its potential for *broad*casting to the public.

Further Reading

For an annotated guide to the many books, journals, and articles on all aspects of electrical communications, including companies and inventors, see Shiers and Shiers (1972). For early wired electrical communications, see the books noted in chapter 1.

The standard early histories of wireless development are Fahie (1901) and Lodge (1900), both written from original sources by men active in the field. See also the historical chapters in Fleming (1906 and 1908 editions) and the Sivowitch article (1971). Though undocumented, an accurate narrative of the experimental and World War I periods is found in Schubert (1928). More recent treatments of these early years are found in Dalton (1975), which in three volumes carries the technical story to 1930 in clear text and diagrams; Aitken (1976 and 1985), a scholarly analysis of the origins and development of radio (to about 1932) that is definitive; and two brief narrative overviews, Wedlake (1973) and Leinwoll (1979), that bring the technical story closer to the present. Douglas (1987) offers a fine mix of technical, social, and political analysis of the invention of American broadcasting in the first two decades of the century.

There are three good histories of radio detection, two concentrating on the vacuum tube. The definitive and detailed story in all countries up to about 1930 is Tyne (1977), while an illustrated approach, designed for collectors of old tubes and covering 70 years, is found in Stokes (1982). Phillips (1980) describes in considerable detail the pretube era of coherers and other detectors.

For more detail on specific inventors and inventions, see the narrative histories by Appleyard (1930) and Hawks (1972) and the capsule biographies in Dunlap (1944). Exhaustive in detail is Blake (1928), while McNicol (1946) describes clearly how early inventions built on one another. O'Hara and Pricha (1987) explores the relationship of Hertz's work to Maxwell's theories. Howeth (1963) is crucial to an understanding of the U.S. Navy's important role in the early years. Maclaurin (1949) is a fascinating and valuable analysis of radio's technical rise, the role patent fights had in the process of invention, and the success or failure of innovation. A useful British view of this period stressing the role of the Marconi company is found in Sturmey (1958).

The development and role of early amateur radio operators is discussed in DeSoto (1936) and in *Fifty Years of A.R.R.L.* (1965).

Biographies of Marconi include those by Dunlap (1937), Marconi (his daughter, 1962), and Jolly (1972). Other biographies include Fessenden (1940), a memoir by the inventor's wife; de Forest's autobiography (1950); the life of Armstrong by Lessing (1956 or 1969 edition); and the several lives of Sarnoff: Lyons's fawning portrait (1966); Dreyer's more balanced view (1977); and Bilby's (1986) sometimes critical life although the author worked with the RCA chief. The best history of the Marconi companies is in Baker (1972), while the role of radio at sea is related in the Marconi-published history by Hancock (1950). Histories of specific American firms are almost nonexistent outside of company-produced booklets. An exception is Sobel (1986), telling the history of RCA from formation to reabsorption by General Electric.

The earliest days of broadcasting, covered in more detail in the books noted in chapter 3, are discussed in the first volumes of the histories by Archer (1938) and Barnouw (1966), while Briggs (1961) provides a parallel discussion of early British radio broadcasting. Early regulation of wireless is reviewed best in Howeth (1963). Worldwide technical, application, and legal developments are reviewed in the annual *Year Book of Wireless Telegraphy and Telephony* (1913–1923).

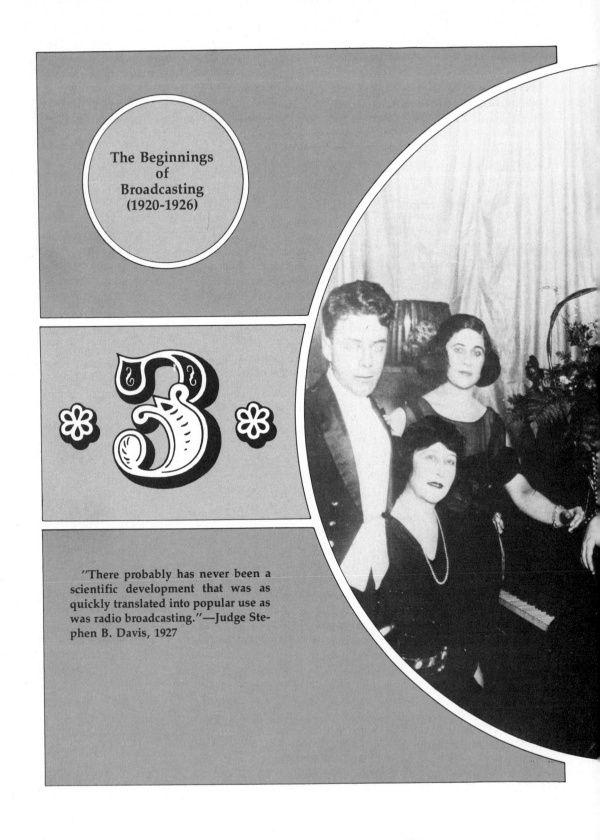

The Beginnings of Broadcasting (1920-1926)

3

"There probably has never been a scientific development that was as quickly translated into popular use as was radio broadcasting."—Judge Stephen B. Davis, 1927

The Beginnings
of
Broadcasting
(1920-1926)

3

"I believe that the quickest way to kill broadcasting would be to use it for direct advertising. The reader of the newspaper has an option whether he will read an ad or not, but if a speech by the President is to be used as the meat in a sandwich of two patent medicine advertisements there will be no radio left."—Herbert Hoover, Secretary of Commerce, at the Third National Radio Conference, October 6-10, 1924

The war was over. America began to emerge from its isolation from the world, although the failure of the U.S. Senate to ratify the League of Nations Covenant showed we had a long way to go. Politically, the country drifted until the "normalcy" of the Harding administration starting in 1921. While many rural areas endured economic hardship, the corporate world in the cities faced the pent-up demand for all the goods and services unavailable since early 1917. Migration from countryside to city accelerated, while restrictive legislation slowed immigration from abroad. The new mobility of the automobile, adding congestion to the cities and creating the suburbs, expanded the

Outline:
The Beginnings of Broadcasting (1920–1926)

immediate horizons of Americans. It took them to where things were happening. At the same time, the motion picture shattered barriers of time and distance and showed ordinary audiences a new, faster life outside their immediate surroundings. The changes in American attitudes that accompanied both these developments were ready targets for men and women who preferred a rigid, traditional, moral climate—such as the reformers who were flushed with Prohibition, their victory over Demon Rum.

The period became known as the Roaring Twenties. Radio would play a big part in communication of that frenzied lifestyle. The country's literary life was prolific, with young writers here and abroad turning out essays, novels, poetry, and plays that depicted the age. The first tabloid newspaper, the *New York Daily News*, appeared in 1919, followed by such untraditional magazines as *Reader's Digest* (1922), *Time* (1923), and *The New Yorker* (1925). Magazines generally used more photographs than print media had in the past and covered a greater variety of events and developments—not just the effects of the car and motion pictures, not just political scandals, but sports events, sensational crimes and trials, the rise in aviation, trends in science, and the latest fads. Behind this surge of activity in the media was the expanding role of business and the prosperity that business brought to many Americans who suddenly had more leisure and money than ever before.

It was against this background of national change that radio broadcasting began. Starting slowly, it quickly gathered pace to become one of the biggest and longest lasting fads. But before broadcasting could become an industry, several important economic, technological, and social developments had to occur both here and abroad. While foreign countries faced the same problems, the American solution was unique.

3·1   Important Precedents

Though often forgotten today, several developments in the 1918–1922 period helped to set the pattern of American broadcasting. They received little public attention at the time but were far more important in the long run than later widely publicized occurrences on or about radio.

3·11   What Almost Happened: Government Control

The sometimes destructive competition between rival telegraph and telephone companies, the monopolistic trend in each field of communications due largely to economies of scale, the advantages of governmental control of wireless, the navy experiences during the war (see 2.61–2.62), and the example of many European countries—all led to a strong push for a government-owned-and-operated wireless system. In Europe, almost all telegraph and telephone systems were part of the postal service. In the United States, at the end of World War I, the belief recurred that Congress had made a wrong turn in the late 1840s when, after providing capital for Morse, it allowed the telegraph to revert to private hands (see 1.41 and 1.43).

Before the United States entered the war, an effort to establish government control reached Congress. An interdepartmental radio committee proposed, on November 21, 1916, revision of the Radio Act of 1912 to allow, among other changes, government stations to compete with commercial interests for purchase of private stations. The Marconi interests fought virtually every section of this proposed legislation, but it was finally introduced into the House as the Alexander bill, after the representative who introduced it. Secretary of the Navy Josephus Daniels strongly urged its adoption as did, to the surprise of other amateur organizations, Hiram Percy Maxim, head of the American Radio Relay League and a noted inventor. Spirited debate arose over the provisions for limiting foreign ownership of any operating commercial company, with the Marconi interests objecting particularly. Their concern raised suspicions that Marconi *was* bent on establishing postwar dominance in the field.

Our entrance into the war, and the navy's assumption of operational control of all stations on April 7, 1917, lifted the pressure on Congress. However, one month after the Armistice, Secretary Daniels, still strongly favoring government ownership, helped to revive hearings on the Alexander bill before the House Merchant Marine Committee. But the navy had run into criticism for using wartime emergency powers to purchase the stations of the Federal Telegraph Company, some of the coastal Marconi stations, and installations in all seagoing vessels of American registry—through the Shipping Board. This criticism and the Republican congressional sweep in the 1918 elections sounded the death knell of the Alexander bill. Until he left office in 1920, Secretary Daniels continued to press for commercial use of navy-controlled stations or, failing that, at least making overseas radiocommunication from the United States a private monopoly in American hands, but the bill was tabled on January 16, 1919.

Furthermore, after the war, the navy not only suffered from a lack of trained operators and funds, but faced a strong and growing clamor for return of government-operated stations to their owners. This outcry, joined by amateurs,

as well as AT&T and Marconi, led President Wilson, on July 11, 1919, to order all seized stations returned to their owners as of March 1, 1920. The amateurs were allowed back on the air on October 1, 1919.

3•12   The Birth of RCA

The trigger that led to establishment of the Radio Corporation of America was the renewal of negotiations between British Marconi and GE over the Alexanderson alternator in March 1919, a bare four months after the end of World War I (see 2.21). It was the second round in a series of discussions that had begun in 1915. Marconi now offered to buy 24 large alternators, 14 of which American Marconi would use, for $127,000 each—a vast sum for that day. This represented more than $3 million worth of business to GE, which, like other firms, was then painfully adjusting to the end of wartime government spending. At that time GE had no interest in the communications business itself. The following month Marconi offered to pay an additional million dollars to compensate GE for development costs *if* GE, which would retain manufacturing rights, granted Marconi the exclusive right to buy the Alexanderson alternator. Because this machine was the best and most reliable transatlantic radio communication device known at that time, acceptance of the offer would give Marconi a monopoly on American radio communications with Europe.

Most Americans, whether or not they favored government control, deplored the idea of allowing a foreign company to control American communications facilities (see 3.11). When Owen D. Young, then head of GE's legal department, approached Acting Secretary of the Navy Franklin D. Roosevelt for the navy's view of the proposed Marconi contract, he found strong opposition to the potential monopoly of any foreign firm.

Documentation of what happened next is sparse. Two American naval officers, Admiral William H. G. Bullard and Commander Stanley C. Hooper, known as the "father of naval radio," played a part in organizing governmental support for a "chosen instrument"; but their role apparently was insufficient to justify RCA's claim that the firm was organized in response to a government request. The architect of the scheme that finally resolved the Marconi contract and many other postwar problems (see 2.62) was Owen D. Young, later to become chairman of the board of GE. A genius at negotiation, Young persuaded GE's directors to buy a controlling interest in American Marconi. British Marconi sold its holdings without much fuss, since it was clear that Congress *would not* accept foreign control of communications and *would* accept an American "chosen instrument" in international radio communication, and since the navy still held the American Marconi stations. GE then bought out the holdings of American stockholders of American Marconi. This first block in the Young edifice gave GE control of most United States–based ship-to-shore and international radio stations as well as rights under existing Marconi contracts with ship operators. Marconi, in return, could now use the Alexanderson alternator for its own stations in the British Empire.

Since GE preferred the manufacturing business, it established the Radio Corporation of America in October 1919 to operate these stations. RCA's Delaware charter required that at least 80 percent of its stock be in American hands, that all officers be American citizens, and that the government have a representative on the board of directors to "present and discuss informally" the government's views. Ad-

miral Bullard, whom President Wilson appointed to the post, had little influence on corporate decisions, however. The unilateral placing of this provision in RCA's by-laws did not carry the same weight as it would have with a public corporation or quasi-official arm of the government organized or chartered by Congress. Young was named chairman of the board, and two former American Marconi officers, Edward J. Nally and David Sarnoff, became respectively president and commercial manager of the new firm. On the day of RCA's formation, GE and RCA signed a cross-licensing agreement calling for mutual use of each other's radio patents. A month later, GE transferred to RCA the tangible assets of what had been American Marconi, and the navy promptly turned over the former American Marconi stations.

RCA's primary role was to be an instrument of American policy in the international communications field. Some of its other roles did not come to light for several years, and the most important of these was the resolution of a decade-old conflict over patent rights for technology that included the triode vacuum tube.

3•13   *Patents Pooling: Westinghouse versus RCA*

At the end of the war, it looked as though the design and manufacture of radio apparatus would be set back several years as the navy program of indemnifying manufacturers against patent infringement suits came to an end and the advanced designs that had come from this period could no longer be used. Radio required the use of many patents, which were held by many individuals and companies. Amateur operators, however, could pirate these designs and techniques—with the exception of vacuum tubes and high-powered transmitters—and build their own equipment fairly easily. They could get the few items that were hard to produce at home from small manufacturers, many of whom were rather lax about paying royalties. The greatest hindrance to the manufacture of advanced radio receivers was the unavailability of the triode, de Forest's Audion. De Forest controlled some rights to the third element, and he had sold some to Western Electric (AT&T) years before, but British Marconi still controlled the basic two-element tube, the diode or Fleming valve (see 2.21).

The pieces of this jigsaw puzzle fell into place when GE, RCA, and AT&T signed a further patents pooling agreement on July 1, 1920. Since AT&T, through its subsidiary Western Electric, had the right to use the third element of the triode, and since GE and RCA, through their purchase of Marconi assets, could use and license the patents for the diode, the cross-licensing agreement made the commercial sale of triodes legal for the first time.

What was Westinghouse doing all this time? GE's role was clear; it was the patron of RCA and the busy manufacturer of electrical and electronic apparatus. RCA not only operated overseas radio communications—primarily to Europe as the result of agreements with Marconi and various foreign post and telegraph administrations—but also managed a large and growing pool of important radio patents. AT&T retained the rights to use all patents necessary for the rental of radio and wire telephony service. Among other small companies, United Fruit had joined the patents pool, bringing in its crystal receiver and loop antenna patents in March 1921. But where was Westinghouse, one of the largest and most energetic electrical manufacturing firms in the world?

Although RCA–GE–AT&T had all the elements necessary to construct and operate a profitable communications system, their patent situation did not give them a monopoly. At the end of the war there was still room for a communications system that did not rely on the RCA–GE–AT&T patents pool. Westinghouse, as a major competitor of GE, decided to fill that space in radio. The company had done considerable radio research and manufacturing during the war, and it owned many important patents. Westinghouse wanted to get into the international communications market, which, together with maritime radio, was considered the future profit center of wireless. It acquired control of the International Radio Telegraph Company, which had Fessenden's heterodyne and continuous-wave transmitter patents (see 2.2), as well as some useful foreign contacts, in May 1920, a few months after RCA's establishment. That summer, Westinghouse president Samuel M. Kintner traveled to various countries in an attempt to line up traffic agreements. He met great difficulties because of RCA's iron-clad agreement with British Marconi, and received cooperation only from a war-cowed Germany. Not yet discouraged, Westinghouse purchased the Armstrong regenerative and superheterodyne receiver patents in October 1920 for $335,000 and arranged with the U.S. Navy for the non-exclusive use of a large block of important patents.

These patents included some German patents, which the navy had acquired from the custody of the Alien Enemy Property Custodian, and the very important patents for the Poulsen arc transmitter, which the navy had bought from the Federal Telegraph Company in 1917, when it looked as though Federal was going to sell to Marconi. This sale had some questionable aspects, with at least one historian pointing out its "suspicious circumstances," the subsequent suicide of one of the chief actors and the resignations of several officials. The $1.6 million purchase of May 15, 1918, gave the navy not only the Poulsen and other patents but a chain of high-power stations on the Pacific Coast.

Therefore, by late 1920, Westinghouse was in an excellent position to challenge RCA and its associates. It had an operating company, the Armstrong and Pupin patents, the Fessenden patents, rights to use the Poulsen arc and many other devices, the glimmer of a profitable receiving-set manufacturing business in conjunction with broadcasting stations (more on this in 3.2), and the possibility of beating RCA to a lucrative communications circuit or two. Yet, within nine months, Westinghouse gave up its independent course and joined the patents pool. Why?

The story may never be clear, but it appears that Westinghouse was neatly mousetrapped by RCA. On January 8, 1921, the Federal Telegraph Company, (which still existed as a corporation), entered into a contract with the Chinese government to build stations in China to communicate with a high-power California station. By some means, Federal persuaded the navy to return the Poulsen patents on March 19, 1921—with no exchange of money—so that it could construct these stations. Apparently, the government considered $1.6 million a worthwhile price for three years' use of Federal's stations and patents, without concomitant infringement suits, and for the retained right to use the patents in question and any later ones developed by Federal. But once it had returned the patents to Federal, the navy could no longer grant Westinghouse a license to use them. Perhaps by coincidence, only a few months later, in December 1921, David Sarnoff wrote the government that RCA was "ready to cooperate with and assist" Federal in its project. This move led to the establishment, in September 1922, of the Federal Telegraph Company of Delaware, which was organized so that RCA could take over the contract with China and, as a matter of fact, control the Federal Telegraph Company of California—and the Poulsen patents.

A major corporation such as Westinghouse does not survive by making mistakes or moving slowly. Then again, the entire gambit by Westinghouse may have been nothing more than a strategem devised by its patent chief Otto Schairer, later to hold the same post at RCA, to ensure that Westinghouse would enter the patents pool on as favorable terms as the original members. Within six months after Federal's repossession of the Poulsen patents and long before RCA overtly took charge of Federal's activities, Westinghouse quietly joined RCA, AT&T, and GE in a patents pooling agreement. The International Radio Telegraph Company's business was absorbed into RCA on June 30, 1921, the same day that RCA concluded its cross-licensing agreement with Westinghouse.

Who won? The infant radio manufacturing industry did. The American people, tired of waiting for the squabbling over patent rights to subside, probably won as well. RCA finally fitted together the last sections of "Owen D. Young's famed jigsaw puzzle." GE could now manufacture, and RCA sell, radio receiving sets for the general public, using Westinghouse's Armstrong patents and demonstration of a market for them. AT&T could manufacture transmitters and use radio telephony in its domestic business. The navy could breathe more easily and deal with one company instead of several. Westinghouse, in 1922 the second largest participant after GE, controlled 20.6 percent of RCA's common and preferred stock com-

The Origins of the Patents Pool: 1919–1922 / See the text for discussion of the motivations of the participants. In essence, GE bought American Marconi at the instigation of naval officers, in April 1919, in order to found RCA as a "chosen instrument" of American overseas communications. GE, RCA, and AT&T formed a patents pool, bringing in United Fruit and others not shown on the accompanying chart. Westinghouse attempted to compete head on with RCA using purchased patents and other patents obtained nonexclusively from the navy. The navy had acquired some of these from the Alien Enemy Property Custodian during World War I, and some, the Poulsen arc patents, purchased along with several stations from Federal Telegraph of California. In returning the stations and the patents to Federal without payment shortly after Federal contracted to establish radio links between the United States and China, the navy automatically restricted Westinghouse from using them. RCA agreed to "cooperate" with Federal, later establishing Federal Telegraph of Delaware as a subsidiary. Westinghouse, now without transmitter patents and prevented by RCA–British Marconi relationships from establishing competing traffic agreements with many countries, joined the patents pool in June 1921, in a relatively strong position thanks to its ownership of the Armstrong patents and its early commitment to domestic radio broadcasting.

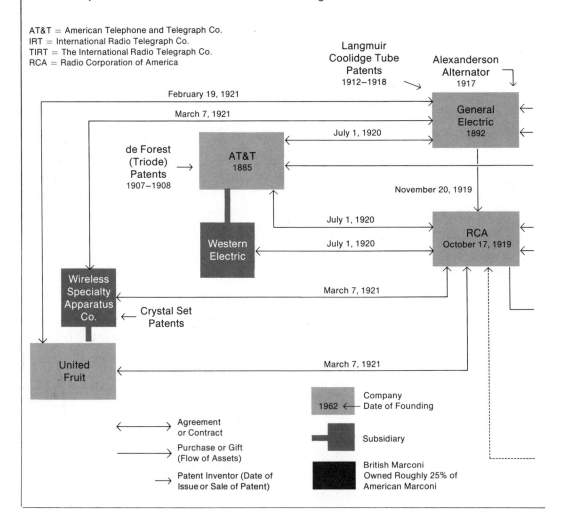

AT&T = American Telephone and Telegraph Co.
IRT = International Radio Telegraph Co.
TIRT = The International Radio Telegraph Co.
RCA = Radio Corporation of America

The patents pool agreements established the following division of functions, among others, until the participating companies modified or abrogated the agreements in the mid-1920s:

a. Each of the major participants (RCA, GE, AT&T, Westinghouse) could build equipment for its own use, including broadcasting transmitters.

b. AT&T could sell broadcast transmitters to outsiders, and reserved the right to use radiotelephony for hire.

c. GE and Westinghouse could manufacture radio receivers and supply them to RCA, which acted as sales agent (GE built approximately 60 percent, Westinghouse 40 percent).

d. RCA would administer the patents pool, collecting royalties from outsiders.

e. RCA would also operate all maritime and transoceanic radio communication for hire.

(It was not until several years later that RCA was allowed to manufacture receivers and engage in broadcasting and networking in its own name.)

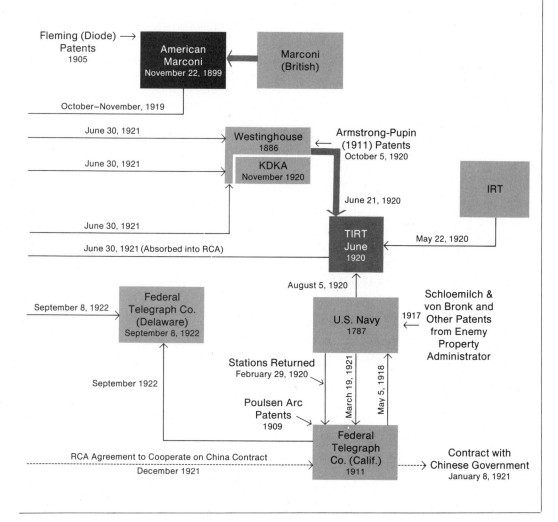

pared to 25.8 percent for GE, 4.1 percent for AT&T, 3.7 percent for United Fruit, and 45.8 percent for other owners including the general public and former American Marconi shareholders. According to agreements with both GE and Westinghouse, RCA would be the sole selling agent for the manufacturing firms' radio receivers and would take approximately 60 percent from GE and 40 percent from Westinghouse. Nearly two thousand patents were pooled. Everyone was to have a piece of the action in the field of radio as it was then understood—the field of international, maritime, and amateur radio. The signers did not realize that the development of radio *broadcasting* to the general public would make the patent agreements uncomfortably binding within only a few months.

3·2   The Pioneer Stations

In 2.5 we tentatively honored Fessenden for delivering the *first broadcast* in America and Herrold for maintaining the *first broadcasting station* with a regular schedule of programs. However, a controversy remains as to which is the *oldest* broadcasting station in America; depending upon the definitions and the data accepted, there are several legitimate candidates. Our criteria for making this determination are that a broadcasting station must (1) utilize radio waves, (2) to send noncoded sounds by speech or music, (3) in the form of a continuous program service, (4) intended to be received by the public, and (5) if after 1912, be licensed by the government. The *first* station is the one that had all these characteristics at the earliest date, although the *first broadcast* needn't meet the third criterion. The *oldest* radio station is the one *presently operating* that met all five criteria at the earliest date.

3·21   The Oldest Stations

Fessenden's 1906 transmissions fit our definition of the first true broadcasts but did not meet the third criterion. It was Herrold's continuous service of music and voice to the general public—at least to the extent of supplying receivers for hotel lobbies—that earned the distinction of "first station." Determining the oldest station is more difficult.

A lack of data and a question of definition place Herrold's station KQW in San Jose, now KCBS in San Francisco, in an ambiguous position. Although "Doc" Herrold started in 1909 and was broadcasting one night a week regularly by 1912, his station had a substantial gap in service during *and after* World War I. Our criteria should tolerate a short-term suspension of service, technical failures, "acts of God," and other matters outside the station operator's control; and the wartime closing of amateur stations in 1917 could be considered in this light. However, despite the present operators' claim that the station returned to the air "very shortly" after the war (amateurs were on the air as early as October 1, 1919, and stations seized by the navy were returned on March 1, 1920), their documentation is not adequate. Licenses for experimental stations 6XE and 6XF were issued to Herrold in mid-1920, but there is no evidence that he *broadcast* anything over these stations, and, indeed, although KQW received a regular broadcast license on December 9, 1921, there is no record of the station having gone on the air until a month later than that.

Professors Earle M. Terry and Edward Bennett, and others, were issued licenses for 9XM to operate at the University of Wisconsin at Madison before World War I. After 1915, this station (now WHA) was licensed to the university. Providing radio-*telegraphed* weather reports and communicating with the navy's Great Lakes Training Station, 9XM was one of the few to stay on the air during much of the war. Although it may have transmitted by radiotelephone as early as February 1919 to Great Lakes, broadcast service apparently started between September 29, 1920, and January 19, 1921—almost certainly toward the end of this period, since Professor Terry wrote the Federal Radio Commission in 1928 that KDKA (see below) antedated 9XM "by a few months."

There are numerous other claims to the title of "oldest station in the United States," each with its supporters. Some are little known: KQV, Pittsburgh, overshadowed by KDKA, has never pushed for recognition. WRUC, Union College, according to a 1970 article, signed on on October 14, 1920; however, it no longer uses radiation to serve its campus-limited audience. Some claims are for foreign stations: CFCF in Montreal, Canada, and PCGG in the Netherlands both claim November 1919 as their starting date. Some rely upon variations in the definition of broadcasting: WEAF, New York, did not go on the air until 1922 but was the first broadcasting station to go *commercial* by selling time (see 3.5). WBZ, Boston, which took to the air in September 1921, was erroneously listed as the first station to receive a "broadcasting" license from the Department of Commerce—evidently because its licensing coincided with the adoption of a new classification system.

KDKA, Pittsburgh, and WWJ, Detroit, both backed by large corporations, have jousted for years over the primacy title. Since both stations apparently went on the air in 1920, they antedate most other claimants as continuing broadcasting services as such and not as adjuncts to wireless experimentation.

KDKA started as a prewar, 1916 amateur experimental station licensed to Dr. Frank Conrad, a Westinghouse engineer. When the war ended, Conrad was able to reopen station 8XK quickly—probably between June 15 and August 1, 1919 —since during the war he had operated a station from his home in connection with designing equipment for the navy. On October 17, 1919, Conrad delighted and amazed hams for miles around when he placed his microphone before a phonograph—an act that not only spared his voice but apparently initiated postwar broadcasting. Amateurs and war veterans trained to build and operate radio receivers wrote him so many requests for musical selections that Conrad decided to broadcast a program of records for two hours each Wednesday and Sunday evening instead of trying to comply with single requests. He sometimes added talks, sports scores, and live vocal and instrumental renditions by his young sons.

Late in the summer of 1920, growing interest in these broadcasts led the Joseph Horne Company, a Pittsburgh department store, to advertise amateur wireless sets for $10 and up on which to listen to Conrad's station. This ad struck the eye of H. P. Davis, Westinghouse vice president, who was eager to establish a postwar market for the company's radio manufacturing capability. At an executive meeting on September 30, 1920, Davis suggested that Westinghouse build a station and advertise and broadcast a program every night so that people would acquire the habit of listening. He observed that if there were sufficient interest to justify a department store in speculatively advertising radio sets for sale, there would probably be sufficient public interest to justify the expense of rendering a regular broadcasting service, looking both to the further sale of receivers and promotion of the Westinghouse Company name as return for the costs of broadcasting. An application to this effect was filed with the Department of Commerce on October 16, and the license for KDKA was issued 11 days later.

The first broadcast, held on election night, November 2, 1920, came from a 100 watt transmitter in a tiny makeshift shack atop a Westinghouse manufacturing building at East Pittsburgh. Conrad was not there; he was at home, standing by with 8XK in case KDKA's new transmitter failed to work properly. The election returns, courtesy of a telephone connection with the *Pittsburgh Post*, were broadcast to an estimated few thousand listeners, including some people at a Pittsburgh country club, over Westinghouse-supplied loudspeakers. The broadcast started at 6 P.M. and continued until the following noon, even though Governor James M. Cox had earlier conceded the presidential election to Senator Warren G. Harding. The next evening KDKA broadcast only from 8:30 until 9:30. The transmitter soon was relocated and increased in power, but the studio remained on the roof for months in somewhat more spacious, airy, and sound-controlled quarters: a tent. When the tent blew down in a gale, it was re-erected inside, providing the necessary acoustic control.

In Detroit, amateur station 8MK went on the air on August 20, 1920, with voice and phonograph music, from a makeshift "radio phone room" on the second floor of the *Detroit News* building. The Radio News and Music Company, formed by associates of de Forest to sell his radio equipment, held the license. Although the *News*, a Scripps paper, apparently financed the broadcasts, it gave them no mention for days. On October 15, 1921, a broadcasting license with the call letters WBL, changed to WWJ on March 3, 1922, was issued to the *Detroit News*.

The preceding accounts suggest

the great difficulty of comparing and adjudicating conflicting claims. As to *broadcasting* licenses, KDKA led WBL (WWJ) by nearly a year. Conrad's *amateur* station, 8XK, successor to the prewar station, went on the air more than a year before 8MK and was broadcasting music ten months earlier. As to license-holding, in either case Westinghouse or one of its officers held a license before the *Detroit News* did. Only by maintaining that 8XK is *not* the precursor of KDKA, *and* that 8MK *is* the precursor of WWJ, can one uphold WWJ's claim —and both Conrad's status as a Westinghouse employee and the *News's* delay in applying for a broadcasting license belie that position.

Radio broadcasting appeared to grow slowly for the first year or so after

Early Radio Announcer / One of the first full-time radio announcers was Harold W. Arlin of station KDKA, shown here as he broadcast in the early 1920s—complete with tuxedo, then almost mandatory for evening announcing duties. He did the first play-by-play sports and introduced many noted personalities in their radio debuts. Photo courtesy of Group W and Broadcast Pioneers Library.

KDKA went on the air. By January 1, 1922, the Department of Commerce had authorized only 30 broadcasting stations; and only 100,000 receivers were sold during 1922. However, the statistics are misleading. Hobbyists made many thousands of receivers, since a crystal set was inexpensive and could be put together easily, while thousands of war-trained radio experts produced advanced equipment. Some stations with amateur licenses broadcast regular programs of speech and music. By May 1, 1922, the *Radio Service Bulletin* of the Bureau of Navigation, Department of Commerce, listed 218 stations "broadcasting market or weather reports, and music, concerts, lectures, etc," many of them on the air only a few hours a week. By March 1, 1923, the number had climbed to 556, and in that year 550,000 radio receivers were produced commercially, with an average retail value of $55 each. The boom was on.

*Westinghouse was the first company to move decisively into radio broadcasting, characterized up till then by the haphazard operations and unreliable equipment of hobbyists and amateurs. In September 1921, when KDKA was on its feet, Westinghouse opened WBZ, Springfield, Massachusetts, and WJZ, Newark, New Jersey, although they were licensed on different dates. In keeping with KDKA's makeshift quarters, WJZ started out in a curtained-off section of the ladies' lounge at the Westinghouse plant in Newark. This first station in the New York area later became the key station of the Blue Network. WBZ moved to Boston in later years and for some time operated station WBZA in Springfield *synchronized* on the same frequency. Westinghouse also established KYW in Chicago, which after several shifts now is located in Philadelphia, and stations in Hastings, Nebraska (a remote-controlled *repeater* station duplicating the

KDKA signals), and Cleveland. Many Westinghouse officials enjoyed being associated with broadcasting, but the company backed these ventures chiefly to spark public interest in receiver sales. But by 1972, little less than sixty years after H. P. Davis had noticed that advertisement for a radio receiver in a Pittsburgh newspaper, Westinghouse was no longer making radio receivers domestically. On the other hand, its broadcast operations—known as "Group W" and including KDKA (AM, TV, Pittsburgh), KYW (AM, TV, Philadelphia), WBZ (AM, TV, Boston), WINS (AM, New York), WMAQ (AM, Chicago), KPIX (TV, San Francisco), WJZ (TV, Baltimore), WOWO (AM, Fort Wayne), KFWB (AM, Los Angeles), and FM stations in Sacramento, San Diego, Phoenix, Houston, San Antonio, and Dallas—are still going strong.

*RCA delayed entering domestic radio broadcasting until it had set up the international communication links for which it had been established. The company's first broadcasting facility, WDY, went on the air on December 14, 1921, from the General Electric factory in Roselle Park, New Jersey. Its transmitter was one that RCA had installed, under the call letters WJY, for one night for a blow-by-blow account of the Dempsey-Carpentier heavyweight boxing championship match on July 2, 1921 (see 3.64). The estimated 200,000 listeners were lucky, for the transmitter burned out only a minute or so after the end of the fight. Even with 500 watts of power, a high output for the day, WDY was too far—approximately 16 miles—from New York City to attract live talent of any stature. Also, music from records played at home on an acoustic, spring-powered phonograph would have been probably cheaper and certainly more enjoyable than WDY's static-ridden transmission through earphones. WDY lasted

only until February 24, 1922, when RCA agreed to share half the operating expense of Westinghouse's better-located and better-engineered WJZ.

General Electric also entered the broadcasting business, a bit behind its partners in the patents pool. Like Westinghouse, its original purpose was to encourage the sale of radio receivers. Its first station, WGY, operated from the GE plant at Schenectady, New York, with 1,500 watts of power when it first went on the air on February 22, 1922. With favorable atmospheric conditions, the well-engineered station was able to reach the Pacific Coast and England. Such ranges were not uncommon, even with relatively low power, when there were few stations on the air to cause degradation of the signal;

even WDY could be heard as far west as Omaha. GE also founded KOA in Denver and KGO in Oakland. In 1986, GE bought RCA/NBC. After selling some of its own and NBC's, GE now operates 13 stations (1 AM, 5 FM, and 7 TV) around the country.

3·22   Boom (1922–1925)

By 1922 the country was afire with radio fever. More than 600 stations went on the air that year, but many went off again in a few months, weeks, or even days. Of the survivors we can identify many by their three-letter call signs (KYW, WHN), although some of the earliest had four letters (KDKA). The initial letters of call signs had been assigned by international agreement in 1912, with W, K, A,

---

Who Were the Early Broadcasters? / As noted in 3.22, a radio station was seldom the primary concern of early broadcasters. It was nearly always an arm of some other business or activity, often promotional but mostly noncommercial. The best tabulation was done by the Department of Commerce as of February 1, 1923.

Type of Owner	Number of Stations	Percentage of Total
Radio and electrical manufacturers and dealers	222	39%
Educational institutions	72	13
Newspapers and other publications	69	12
Department stores	29	5
Automobile, battery, and cycle dealers	18	3
Music, musical instrument, and jewelry stores	13	2
Churches and YMCAs	12	2
Police and fire departments, and cities	7	1
Hardware stores	6	1
Railroad, power, and telephone companies	9	1
Other commercial businesses	19	3
Other and unknown	100	17
	576	100%

Source: U.S. Department of Commerce, *Radio Service Bulletin* (February 1, 1923), as reprinted in Banning (1946), pages 132–133, and adapted herein.

and N going to the United States. By custom, and later by rule, W belonged to broadcasting stations east of the Mississippi and K west, although there are a handful of exceptions (see Appendix B). Radio and electrical manufacturers and dealers, ranging from giants like GE and Westinghouse to one-man repair shops in small towns, owned by far the largest number of stations.

Most station licensees spent little money on broadcasting and could expect little direct return. The manufacturing companies, and many dealers, provided the program service to encourage people to buy sets. Department stores owned a station as a publicity investment; although it wasn't advertising, the simple announcement of ownership or location was worth the cost. Virtually all the stations that went on in 1921 and 1922 were operated as a side line. Licensees were seeking publicity, fun, or prestige in the community. Educational institutions used radio as an extension service or a physics department laboratory. Churches and other crusading organizations were early operators of radio. Newspapers built stations so as to keep up with new entertainment and news technology, for publicity, and as a symbol of their perceived public service role.

These early stations were primitive. Many operated from hotels, trading publicity for free room; but, since the hotel often was the tallest building in town, at least it was thought then to be an excellent location for antenna towers. Most studios had little equipment. A piano was a must, as was a microphone. Burlap served as sound control for years. Volume control and mixing were not yet available and phonograph records were played on a conventional acoustic phonograph with a microphone stationed before the open doors. At first, almost all transmitters were hand-made, with indifferent results. Lack of volume controls and limiting devices made it possible for an opera singer to blow out a tube and throw the station off the air. Carbon telephone-type microphones tended to "freeze up" when very loud sibilant sounds were spoken into them.

Many transmitters of the early 1920s usually radiated less wattage than one studio light. Within a few years, most stations were rated from 100 to 500 watts, although about 15 were as high as 1,000 watts and five or six were "high power," running 5,000 watts. Such amounts of transmitter power were satisfactory when only a few hundred stations were on the air. A 100 watt station of the middle 1920s would send a reliable signal out 20 to 50 miles, a feat that today—with approximately 5,000 transmitters on the standard (AM) broadcast band in the United States—would take many times as much radiated power. Because receivers had low sensitivity and often poor quality, broadcasters kept asking the Secretary of Commerce, the licensing authority, for *superpower* that would enable them to deliver a clearer signal to more people. Late in 1925, WGY experimentally broadcast with 50,000 watts. Of course, if *everyone* had higher power, interference would remain—and at a higher level.

As broadcasting stations went on the air in large numbers, they also went off. For example, in just five months of mid-1923, 150 stations left the air. Their failure was financial rather than technical. When a station had been on the air for some time, and its novelty had worn off, the licensee became more concerned about its cost. Although electrical current for low-power stations was not very expensive, transmission tubes and other parts were. The station needed consistent sources of programming, and record stores soon tired of lending or giving records in exchange

Early Radio Studios / Early radio studios reflected their times: chintz furniture, plants, the almost required piano—and draped walls to improve acoustics. The announcer and piano player appear in KDKA's inside studio at Christmas of 1922; the second draped studio is Westinghouse's WBZ in Springfield, Massachusetts, in 1922 (note the record player, used for music to fill between live presentations); and the third picture shows a large-station prestige studio from sometime in the 1926–1928 period. In all cases the studios are fairly large and have many chairs for performers to sit on while waiting to broadcast.

Courtesy of Group W and Broadcast Pioneers Library

Smithsonian Institution Photo No. 76-14663

Smithsonian Institution Photo No. 76-14657

for an occasional plug. Talent began demanding payment for their time or effort. It became clear that, if broadcasting were to become more than an adjunct to another enterprise, it had to have a direct source of income. In June 1922, RCA's David Sarnoff proposed a nonprofit broadcasting company supported by a 2 percent tax on receiver sales, but his idea got nowhere.

Nevertheless, people were starting to listen to radio for its content and not for its novelty. Although homemade receivers, typically crystal sets requiring minimal construction skill and no power, were still common, more and more persons purchased ready-made receivers. For example, in the summer of 1923, Gimbel Brothers department store in New York purchased from RCA 20,000 Westinghouse receiving sets with a retail value of at least $3 million. The total value of sets sold in 1923—excluding tubes, which were sold separately—was between $30 and $45 million, a figure that increased to approximately $100 million in 1924. The average retail value of sets climbed steadily from $50 in 1922 to over $135 in 1929. More than 4.1 million sets were manufactured commercially between 1922 and 1925.

By 1925 the growth of radio began to create problems. In major cities there were too many stations on a limited band for good reception (see 3.8)—for instance, 23 in Los Angeles and 40 in Chicago. Receivers were unselective; transmitters tended to drift. With the limited spectrum space and equipment available, the typical large city could accommodate only seven stations without resorting to *share-time* operations. In Los Angeles and Chicago, share-time might allow a single station as little as one hour or two of air time daily, divided into widely separated parts of the day. With four or five stations using the same channel, no one of them could build an audience. Because many of their listeners were DX fans, who listened for distant stations, some cities designated "silent nights," when local stations signed off early to improve distance reception.

3•23   Conflict: Radio Group versus Telephone Group

Although interference between stations was the conflict most apparent to listeners, it became less important in the early 1920s than the issue of financial support. Broadcasting was not considered when the original patents pool agreements were signed. Since no money was expected at first from broadcasting operations, Westinghouse, GE, and RCA all built stations without worrying about the agreements. After assuming control of WJZ in 1923, RCA opened another New York station, WJY, and moved them both to Aeolian Hall—WJZ with a light, popular format and WJY with a "quality" program of talks, music, and education. By this time, RCA was spending approximately $100,000 a year to maintain its three stations, now including WRC in Washington, without any direct income from them. Westinghouse was not far behind in outlay.

It remained for AT&T to find a way to make radio broadcasting pay. In the original patent agreements, AT&T had reserved the right—the sole right, it claimed—to use radio telephony for hire. In July 1922 it built station WBAY in New York, only to discover through error that the location of a transmitter in a large steel-frame-building-lined city negatively affects reception decisively, and that this kind of engineering is an art, not a science. AT&T's second attempt was successful. WEAF, equipped with the best studio apparatus and an excellent transmitter, received much praise after it went on the air on August 16, 1922.

AT&T was now ready to move. Under the 1919–1921 patent agreements, what became known as the Telephone Group—essentially, AT&T and its manufacturing subsidiary Western Electric—held that it had the *exclusive* right to (1) manufacture and sell radio transmitters for broadcasting, (2) sell time for advertising, named *toll broadcasting* in a parallel to toll or long-distance telephone calls, and (3) interconnect stations by wire for network or chain broadcasting. In each of these matters it had to contend with the opposed corporate goals of the Radio Group —GE, RCA, and Westinghouse.

Although AT&T's legal grounds with respect to the first point were excellent, the company actually lost in the court of public opinion. When station WHN (New York) settled out of court in the winter of 1924, agreeing to pay AT&T $4 per watt of power over the life of the patents, whether or not Western Electric had made the transmitter, it was merely acknowledging a hopeless legal position. But to the public, already disturbed at the growth and power of trusts and cartels, AT&T seemed to be jumping with hobnailed boots all over the little fellow.

The second point burst like a sky-rocket over the radio scene when WEAF, shortly after going on the air, offered to sell time by the minute to whoever wished to use it (see 3.5).

The third point became increasingly important between 1923 and 1926 as the Telephone Group interconnected its affiliated stations with Bell System wires, engineered to carry music as well as voice, while the Radio Group had to make do with inferior Western Union circuits. Of course, AT&T received no revenue from the Radio Group when they used other circuits, but the poor voice quality over Western Union telegraph wires caused the Radio Group to lose much public favor.

Throughout the history of American broadcasting, AT&T's role in interconnecting stations has been an important one. When broadcasters objected to high AT&T video connection rates in the late 1940s and boycotted Bell System facilities, they found themselves turning again to Western Union lines for local loops if not for intercity circuits. One program was involved both times: the six-day bicycle races from Madison Square Garden in New York (see 7.32).

Stations that took out transmitter licenses from AT&T were generally able to sell advertising time and afford interconnections by telephone lines. Few stations, however, were willing to pay a high price for what might be an unprofitable business. After the WHN case, many stations capitulated, but others went off the air or hoped that they were small enough for AT&T to overlook.

The Radio Group maintained (1) that only the firms in the patents pool (see 3.12 and 3.13) had the right to make and sell radio receivers to the public, (2) that any station could at least recoup program costs from sponsors, and (3) that stations could be interconnected by any means available. RCA sued the A.H. Grebe radio company in support of the first point and won an important legal precedent: manufacturers had to take out licenses from RCA in order to make many receiver parts. The royalties ran high—in 1927, for example, at $7\frac{1}{2}$ percent of the net selling price, including cabinets. RCA granted licenses solely to larger customers and even limited these purchases to relatively inefficient circuits—for which, of course, they had to buy RCA tubes. The royalty situation—as well as poor management, inadequate sales promotion, and rapid development of newer and better designs—drove many manufacturers out of business. Of the 748 radio manufacturing companies established between 1923 and 1926, only 72 lasted until 1927, and only 18 of these survived the Depression into 1934. As for the second and third points, a certain degree of fuzziness existed in application. Although some stations were able to sell advertising time for cash, most simply traded air time for products or services. As noted above, the Radio Group tried to meet the question of interconnection head-on.

Throughout the period from 1922 to 1924, attempts were made to reconcile the differences between the two groups. As the fight grew hotter, AT&T sold its RCA stock, although it remained a member of the patents pool. In 1923, Congress, concerned over RCA actions against Grebe and others, ordered the Federal Trade Commission to investigate RCA for violation of the antitrust laws. Clearly, RCA no longer had the image it had had in 1919. The FTC report of 1924, which examined manufacturing, international communications, and the role of radio, resulted in complaints against seven companies besides RCA. This proceeding dragged on for six more years (see introduction to Chapter 4).

In 1925 the Radio Group and the Telephone Group agreed to binding arbitration. After months of hearings, the arbitrator decided nearly all issues in favor of the Radio Group position. As a result, the telephone company's lawyers announced that since the 1920–1921 agreements must have been illegal to have given RCA such a monopoly, AT&T would have to withdraw from them. With the prospect of putting the patent hassle back six years, both sides tried again to agree on what the words written in 1920 meant in the radically changed world of 1925.

Early in 1926 the stalemate was broken with an involved, three-part agreement that clearly settled the functions of the telephone and radio interests. First,

the license or patents pool agreement was redefined in light of the realities of the broadcasting industry of 1926. Second, AT&T received a monopoly of providing wire interconnections between stations. Third, AT&T sold WEAF to RCA for $1 million and agreed not to re-enter broadcasting as a station owner for eight years, under penalty of having to refund part of the price.

Not only had AT&T wearied of the battle, but such a competitive business did not fit its longstanding corporate philosophy. This philosophy favored monopoly, such as it had in long-distance telephony, over head-to-head competition—which it really didn't have to face until the 1970s. AT&T also favored the cautious introduction of technological innovations (see 1.13). In addition, many Bell executives were disturbed to see time, effort, and money going into entertainment and other broadcasting instead of the point-to-point communications business on which the firm was based.

3·3   The Start of Networking

The idea of connecting two or more stations for simultaneous broadcast of a program probably existed from the start of broadcasting. In this way a given message could reach a far larger audience, at reasonable cost, than from a single station. The earliest known efforts at relaying a program were *remote* reports from sports events sent back over telephone lines, sometimes from a distant city. True chain or network broadcasting started on January 4, 1923, when telephone circuits connected WNAC in Boston and WEAF in New York for a five-minute saxophone solo originating at WEAF. Although generally satisfied with the experiment, AT&T engineers knew that substantial improvements in their lines would be necessary for the regular transmission of music.

In June 1923, WEAF (New York), WGY (Schenectady), KDKA (Pittsburgh), and KYW (then in Chicago) were connected for a special program on the anniversary of the electric light. A month later, the first "permanent"—more than one program—chain was established when WEAF piped programs to WMAF, a South Dartmouth, Massachusetts, station owned and supported as a public service by eccentric millionaire E. H. R. Green, who picked up the bill for three or four hours a day of New York programming.

The WEAF group made ambitious plans for nationwide broadcasting of Warren G. Harding's speeches during the summer of 1923, but the President's illness and death abbreviated the effort. President Coolidge's first message to Congress, on December 4, was heard over a number of stations as far away as Missouri and Texas. Radio covered both political conventions of 1924, and AT&T was building a permanent hookup connecting Washington, New York, Providence, Buffalo, Pittsburgh, and Chicago. On October 24, 1924, President Coolidge spoke to the U.S. Chamber of Commerce in Washington—and to the United States through 22 stations from coast to coast. When Coolidge was inaugurated the following March, 15 million people heard the ceremony over 24 stations. By this time, WEAF (AT&T) had an operating network of more than 20 stations, and the WJZ (Radio Group) network, concentrated in the East, was much smaller. Advertisers were interested in these networks, but they were more engineering and programming devices than sales organizations.

Although telephone lines were the best medium for interconnecting stations, other techniques were tried. Westinghouse used shortwave transmissions in 1923–1924 to connect KDKA with satellite stations KFXX in Hastings, Nebraska, and KDPM in Cleveland. Amateur radio operators had opened up the shortwave spectrum, earlier thought useless, and had even sent a signal across the Atlantic in 1921. With higher shortwave power, KDKA relayed programs in the winter of 1923–1924 to a station in Manchester, England, for rebroadcast. This followed an ambitious experiment during the last week of November 1923, when stations in Great Britain picked up about fifteen American stations using their regular medium-wave transmitters.

Another interesting network experiment was a precursor of cable television. Early in 1923, a company in Dundee, Michigan, offered subscribers a wired radio system, providing programs from several stations for $1.50 a month. In Europe and the Soviet Union, earlier rediffusion systems such as the Puskás brothers' Telephonic Newspaper in Budapest (see 2.5) were a major technique for aural dissemination, but they never caught on in America.

3·4   Early Educational Broadcasting

The prospect of educating larger numbers of people attracted universities and colleges to the radio fad in 1921 and 1922. They first established stations as informal laboratories for engineering schools and physics departments or strictly for publicity. Even before World War I, radio telegraph and some radio telephone experimentation had taken place at colleges and universities such as Arkansas, Cornell, Dartmouth, Iowa, Loyola, Nebraska, Ohio State, Penn State, Purdue, Tulane, Villanova, and Wisconsin. Afterward, many of these stations and many new ones went on the air: New York University,

Nebraska, and Tufts were among the schools that offered extension courses by radio in the early 1920s. A few others tried to use radio for fund raising without much success; land-grant colleges, in particular, offered adult education, primarily in home economics and agriculture. Of the more than 200 stations licensed to educational institutions in the early and middle 1920s, 72 were on the air in 1923 and 128 in 1925.

Noncollege broadcasters also scheduled educational programs in the form of "radio schools of the air," lectures, and even courses for credit. WJZ began such broadcasts in 1923. WEAF followed, and WLS in Chicago began its *Little Red Schoolhouse* series in 1924.

3·5   The Problem of Financial Support

The primary problem that broadcasters faced in the early 1920s was how to pay for programming. Stations struggled along as adjuncts to other enterprises or as hobbies. David Sarnoff, whose proposal for a "radio music box" was so prescient, suggested having a 2 percent tax on receiver sales. In 1924, New York businessmen formed a committee to solicit funds from the radio audience for the hiring of high-class talent for WEAF. This effort failed partly because the fractionated radio audience distrusted such a benefit to the AT&T station. The idea of voluntary audience contributions to a common fund controlled by an elected or appointed board also failed. Another gimmick was for a station to establish an "invisible theater of the air," in which the audience could "buy seats." One New York station tried to gather $20,000 in this way but gave up and returned the contributions when it could collect only $1,000. This idea still survives: some stations sell printed program schedules to augment income, and many public

television stations and many noncommercial radio stations, such as the Pacifica Foundation group, depend largely upon audience donations.

One approach that was not tried in this country became the standard practice abroad: levying an annual tax on radio receivers for the support of broadcasting authorities or companies. In this way, the audience supported the programming by buying and using sets, and the government, as collector and distributor of fees, had a say in the programming. In America a few municipalities and states have used general tax revenues to support broadcasting stations such as New York City's WNYC, but the national approach never took hold—perhaps for fear of governmental control of content, belief that free enterprise should determine radio operation, or dislike of taxation in general. (Current discussions over the financing of public television reflect these discussions and debates of the 1920s.)

The financial technique that eventually succeeded was direct advertising—the purchase of time from a station for the presentation of commercial messages. The first *commercial*—so named from AT&T accounting practices—lasted for 10 or 15 minutes on WEAF in the early evening of August 28, 1922. It was a pitch by the Queensboro Corporation for a cooperative (similar to a condominium) apartment house complex in Jackson Heights, a section of New York City recently opened up by a new rapid transit line. A salesman for the company, which owned most of Jackson Heights, referred briefly to author Nathaniel Hawthorne, namesake of the apartment house, and devoted the rest of the broadcast to a sales talk very much like today's offerings of land in Florida or Arizona. This broadcast, which probably took up less than the allotted time, cost $100; it was repeated for five days, and then again a month later. Several thousand dollars in sales were reported.

Tidewater Oil and American Express also bought time in those first weeks, but after two months WEAF had sold only three hours and collected $550. As with television two decades later, only a few far-sighted firms—including a department store, a political organization, and a motion picture producer—saw the great potential of radio as an advertising medium in those first four months when the station realized a net income of only about $5,000. By 1923 Gimbel's department store and other advertisers had begun sponsoring entertainment programs.

Some other stations, adopting this means of recouping expenses, ran afoul of AT&T's policy of exacting additional royalties for the use of radio telephony for hire. By the end of 1925, about half the stations on the air paid these royalties, which were part of the transmitter royalty payment and ranged from $500 to $3,000 in a lump sum.

These stations soon developed pricing policies geared to the market. Important stations in major markets, such as WEAF, could charge $500 for an hour of time. Boston stations might charge $250, Cincinnati and Detroit around $200, and Washington, D.C., $150. An advertiser might "buy" the 13-station WEAF chain for $2,600, a saving of $300 over the individual station rates.

The advertising heard in the early 1920s was what we would call *institutional*, with no mention of price or sometimes even place of sale. Announcers described their products glowingly but generally, often postponing mention of the sponsor's name until the end. Increasingly, the sponsor attached its name to the program, such as the *A & P* (food store) *Gypsies*, the *Cliquot Club* (soft drink) *Eskimos*, and the *Lucky Strike* (cigarette) *Hour*.

As soon as the Radio Group and the Telephone Group had signed the 1926 agreements, all stations could accept advertising. However, *direct advertising*, mentioning product, place, and price, was still frowned upon (see quote at start of this chapter). The president of AT&T, trying to protect its "monopoly" of broadcast advertising, expressed doubt as to the feasibility of the listener's having to buy or lease receivers from the broadcasting company. Sarnoff was still calling for outright philanthropic endowment. A GE spokesman opined that broadcasting eventually would be supported by voluntary contributions or by licensing individual receivers, another scheme doubted by AT&T. It was not until 1928 that broadcast advertising clearly became the breadwinner for American radio broadcasting—even though many persons objected to the mixing of programming and advertising.

3•6   Early Radio Programming

Early radio programs, resembling vaudeville in that there were several acts, usually musical, were presented with awesome seriousness. Announcers wore tuxedos, at least at the larger stations, and studios were decorated with potted palms. The tuxedos and palms lasted for decades in Great Britain but were soon discarded in the United States for everyday use. The earliest announcers were selected for their ability to speak with dignity, to sing or play an instrument in a pinch, and, until volume controls were developed, to push singers in and out from the carbon microphones. Instead of using names, announcers were known by certain initials: Thomas H. Cowan, apparently the first so identified in New York radio, was ACN (Announcer Cowan, Newark) when he started broadcasting over WJZ in October 1922.

An announcer for more than 30 years, Cowan became chief announcer of WNYC when it went on the air in 1924. Milton Cross, whose career spanned more than half a century (to his death in 1974), closely followed Cowan over WJZ, as AJN, using his middle initial since C was already taken. Cross became best known for his broadcasts from the Metropolitan Opera. Perhaps the most famous announcer of this period was Graham McNamee, who went to work for WEAF in 1923 and quickly created a following for his sports broadcasts.

Many stations tried to broadcast on a schedule, but luck played a large part in a given night's actual content. Major programs were announced and publicized, but poor weather or slow transportation often prevented a guest artist from appearing. When stations arranged to broadcast special talent or dance bands— usually from the studio but sometimes by remote telephone line from a hotel ballroom—they might run the program as long as the individual or group had something to offer. Although phonograph records sometimes were used, they were considered a low-class source of programming. There were few planned programs at first, only short segments like stories and articles in a magazine. Often, the programs of several stations that shared time on a single channel sounded so much alike that none of the stations could build an individual audience. Stations with only a few hours' air time on occasional nights early in the 1920s realized the desirability of regular hours—even on a shared channel. The addition of daytime programming advanced station recognition in the larger markets. However, regardless of the quantity of a station's production, program elements were similar. By 1925, the percentages of time devoted to various types of programs on five stations in major cities was as shown in the boxed table.

3•61   Music

Because familiarity often makes it more enjoyable, music has been an entertainment staple for centuries; it is not "used up" in the same way as comedy or dramatic material. However, because music production frequently requires a large ensemble, it is not cheap. Phonograph records were initially the answer, but their imperfect quality meant poor sound reproduction; in fact, in 1922 the Secretary of Commerce prohibited large stations from using records and giving the public nothing more than what it could enjoy without a radio (see 3.8). The networks (see 4.3) refused as a matter of pride to air records, even battlefield recordings during World War II, until the late 1940s, and only in the early 1950s did records become the mainstay of radio programming (see 7.61).

In the 1920s, many artists were glad to appear for publicity value alone. Dance bands provided "potted palm" music, named for the decor of the hotel ballrooms in which they played. One of the first to be broadcast by remote pickup was the Vincent Lopez group, which had a weekly 90-minute program on WJZ in 1921. For years the radio audience instantly recognized the salutation "Lopez speaking." The same year, a group known as "Coon Sanders' Nighthawks" became so popular over WDAF in Kansas City, especially with DX-ers all over the country, that the group moved to Chicago.

Local stations imitated the larger ones, frequently nurturing talent up to the big time. The WLS (Chicago) *Barn Dance* country and western music program began in 1924 and lasted for many years. Of the big bands that were becoming popular, many had begun as small groups and built their reputations over radio, such as Lawrence Welk's, which had started in the 1920s in Yankton, South Dakota.

Types of Programs Broadcast in 1925 / This chart shows the kind of program broadcast in a period in February 1925 on three stations in New York, one in Chicago, and one in Kansas City. These powerful outlets in major cities were the stations most listened to at night but were not typical of local radio. Compare to table on page 120 for comparable data for 1932, and to table on page 276 for postwar radio in 1946.

Program Type and Subtypes	Percentage of Time
Music	**71.5%**
Dance	22.9%
Vocal	8.1
Combination	14.1
Concert orchestras	4.3
Soloists	7.6
Phonograph records	—
String ensembles	10.1
Sacred	1.0
Miscellaneous	3.4
Drama	**.1**
Continued plays, reading, etc.	.1
Sketches	—
Onetime plays	—
Other Entertainment	**6.8**
Women's	2.4
Children's	3.7
Feature	.7
Star (other than music)	.0
Information	**11.5**
Education	4.9
News	.7
Political	1.8
Market reports	3.6
Weather	.3
Sports	.2
Other	**10.1**
Foreign-originated	—
Health exercises	1.8
Church services	3.1
Miscellaneous	5.2
Total	**100.0%**

Source: William Albig, *Modern Public Opinion* (New York: McGraw-Hill, 1956), Table 20, page 447. By permission.

Classical music was also a staple on radio in the 1920s. In 1921, when Westinghouse put KYW on the air in Chicago, it programmed little more than the Chicago Opera, using a sophisticated ten-microphone system on the stage. In March 1922, WJZ brought orchestra and singers into the studio for a one-and-one-quarter-hour presentation of Mozart's *The Impresario*. The New York Philharmonic began weekly broadcasts over WEAF that November. The prestige associated with classical music appealed to several advertisers, sponsors of such programs as the National Carbon Company's *Eveready Hour*, which started in February 1924 as the first sponsored network program.

3•62   Variety and Vaudeville

Vaudeville—or traveling stage musical, comedy, and acrobatic acts—inspired several kinds of programs: professional acts, typically touring from theater to theater, local talent nights, and song-and-patter teams. The motion picture already had damaged the profitability of organized stage vaudeville circuits, and radio pushed it into its grave as talented performers gave up the nomadic life for broadcasting. Some of these gave more to radio than they got in return; some were one-man programming departments. Singer Wendell Woods Hall, a red-haired ukulele player with some stage and records following, worked a 3 P.M. to 3 A.M. shift on KYW at $25 a week in 1922, after several months' work for nothing but excellent publicity. Although his late-night program made him one of the first well-known radio performers, the station carried him on a *sustaining* (no advertising) basis. In 1924, Hall was married over the air (WEAF), one of the earliest radio news

stunts. In New York, movie-theater owner Samuel S. Rothafel, known as "Roxy," joined the radio bandwagon as an impresario and master of ceremonies by putting his Capitol Theater show *Roxy's Gang* on WEAF almost intact in January 1923. The program, a happy mixture of music, comedy routines, and other things, lasted for 15 years. Al Jolson and Eddie Cantor were two of the vaudeville and variety people who had switched to radio by the end of the 1920s, although "big name" comedy-variety programming didn't start on the networks until 1933 (see 4.61). For those who were not headliners, performing on radio became more attractive than making one-night stands and more secure because radio was a dangerous competitor to the vaudeville circuits.

Although *talent night* could produce a sure-fire audience of the performers' friends and relatives, there was not enough talent in smaller towns, not enough local identification, not enough audience interest in this free entertainment to attract the kind of audience that the broadcaster desired.

Both local talent shows and vaudeville, but primarily vaudeville, produced the song-and-patter teams. These two-man (most women then on radio were singers only) teams would travel from station to station, offering songs and light chatter, often in dialect, for several weeks before moving on. Some stayed with one station and became well known, like Billy Jones and Ernie Hare, who began broadcasting on WEAF in mid-1923 and became known over the first few years as the Happiness Boys (Happiness Candy), the Interwoven Pair (Interwoven socks), and the Tastee Loafers (a baking company). Called radio's first real comedy team, they appealed through a combination of light comedy, music, and topical comment.

3•63   *Politics and News*

Music and variety made up more than three-fourths of the average station's programming in the early and mid-1920s. They were relatively easy to provide, were flexible to program, and could be accomplished with available talent. However, even in the infancy of broadcasting, stations were experimenting with ways of providing information to their listeners.

From the 1920 election returns over KDKA—and, indeed, a 1916 election-night broadcast by Lee de Forest—to the Iran-Contra hearings of the 1980s, broadcasting and politics have been linked. Radio's first major political project was the 1924 election. From President Coolidge's December 1923 speech to Congress, through the nominating conventions, and to the election returns, radio was an ever fascinating source of firsthand information for millions of Americans. Chains of stations carried major speeches and comment. Coolidge's renomination by the Republicans was cut and dried; the Democratic convention went through 103 ballots before deciding on compromise candidate John W. Davis. For years afterward, radio listeners remembered or were reminded by comedians of the sound of a leather-lunged Alabama delegate starting off each roll call with "Alabama casts 24 votes for Oscar W. Underwood"—a favorite son candidate. After a few ballots, the convention began to echo the call, and radio made it a catch-line all over the country. The night before the election, the President addressed the nation over 26 stations hooked up coast-to-coast by AT&T, reaching an estimated 20 to 30 million people of a total population of roughly 110 million. Several big-city stations started the now traditional practice of interrupting regular programming to carry returns and some crude analysis. KDKA was on the air from 7 P.M. until 4 A.M. the next morning, and many other stations stayed on past midnight. Between reports, stations offered musical interludes. For the first time, the whole nation was able to hear election returns virtually as soon as they were known. To their annoyance, newspapers had been scooped by radio.

Other kinds of news programs were less common. There were no daily newscasts at first. Many people felt that radio should provide entertainment and occasional special presentations and that newspapers could carry the news. Newspaper-owned stations sometimes used news bulletins as teasers to stimulate newspaper sales, and other stations sometimes read news as a filler, without bothering to pay or, often, to identify the source. Lecturers or commentators often discussed current news events. Perhaps the best-known commentator was H. V. Kaltenborn, an assistant editor of the *Brooklyn Eagle*, which sponsored him for a weekly news commentary over WEAF starting in October 1923. His clipped pronunciation and incisive comment later distinguished him as network news reporter-commentator.

Many stations *did* carry special events, or "emergency" news where speed was important. Since all stations in the early 1920s were required to listen periodically to the maritime distress frequency of 500 kHz, reports of shipwrecks were prominent in news broadcasting, and the nearest powerful stations could, and indeed were required to, relay the SOS messages themselves.

Probably the best-known special news coverage of the mid-1920s was WGN's (Chicago) broadcasts from the 1925 Scopes "monkey" (teaching of Darwin's theory of evolution) trial in Dayton, Ten-

An Early Station Schedule: 1922 / This form letter was sent to letter writers who reported reception of the Westinghouse Chicago station KYW and requested a schedule. Between programmed reports, the station either played light studio music or simply went off the air.

Westinghouse Electric & Manufacturing Company

To....Chicago.................   From......Chicago.................

For Mr...W. C. Evans, Chief............ Department..Radio Station KYW
                    Operator

Subject: Date: April 21,1922.

> The attached is a copy of our present schedule
> for broadcasting, with the exception of the evening
> performance, which has in no wise been changed,
> namely:
>
> > 7:30 - - Bedtime story
> > 7:40 - - Special feature
> > 8:00 to 9:00 - - Musical Program.
>
> If for any reason it is not possible to broadcast on
> this schedule, please let me have a memorandum to
> that effect for each case, with the exception of the
> present 3:00 o'clock period, with which, as you
> know, I am familiar.
>
> For your information, it is also possible that the
> 7:30 to 9:00 period may be changed shortly, but
> at present we will maintain that schedule.

RADIO PUBLICITY DEPARTMENT.

G.H.Jaspert-MR

Westinghouse Electric & Manufacturing Company

General Offices and Main Works
East Pittsburgh, Pa.

N. G. SYMONDS
~~DISTRICT MANAGER~~
DISTRICT MANAGER
MALCOLM CARRINGTON,
ASST. DISTRICT MANAGER

(W)

IN REPLY PLEASE ADDRESS THE COMPANY
AND REFER TO _____

III WEST WASHINGTON STREET, CHICAGO, ILL.

Your letter commenting on the reception of our broadcasting of Chicago Board of Trade quotations, U. S. Bureau of Markets reports, financial summary, and baseball news, is indeed appreciated.

Our schedule is:

9:25 A.M.   Opening Market Quotations, Chicago Board of Trade.

10:00 A.M.   Market Quotations, Chicago Board of Trade; Quotations every half hour thereafter until 1:00 P.M.

1:20 P.M.   Closing Market Quotations, Chicago Board of Trade.

2:15 P.M.   News and Market Reports

3:00 P.M.   American and National League baseball team line-ups; progress of games every half hour thereafter until close of all games.

4:15 P.M.   News, Markets, and Stock Reports

6:30 P.M.   News, Final Market, Financial, and summaries of principal games played in American and National League.

9:00 P.M.   Summaries of principal games played in American and National League.

It is our purpose to make this service as completely satisfactory to you as possible. We are pleased to have your comments concerning the reception of our broadcasting.

Yours very truly,

[signature]

G.H.Jaspert-MR   RADIO PUBLICITY DEPARTMENT.

nessee. The famous confrontations between Clarence Darrow for the defense
and William Jennings Bryan for the prosecution were carried live to Chicago audiences, reputedly costing the station
$1,000 a day in personnel, telephone line,
and other items. There was little concern
then over radio's presence in the courtroom; the microphone stood squarely in
front of the bench, and all parties accepted
the wider forum it provided. This was a far
cry from the furor over coverage of the
Hauptmann (Lindbergh kidnaping) trial a
decade later (see 5.63).

3•64   Other Talk Programs

Many program types familiar to-
day were first tried in the 1920s, including
religion, education, and sports. Educational programming has been discussed
(see 3.4). Religious programming started
when the U.S. Army Signal Corps (apparently unconcerned about separation of
church and state) broadcast a church service in Washington, D.C., in August 1919.
KDKA was probably the first private station to broadcast religious services when,
on January 2, 1921, it transmitted an Epis-
copalian service, with microphones for organ, choir, and clergyman and with two
technicians (a Jew and a Catholic) dressed
in choir robes, on standby in case anything
went wrong. As the years went by, stations traditionally broadcast a religious
service or talk each week, usually on
Sunday.

Considering their later popularity,
it is odd that sports programs were seldom
scheduled in the early 1920s. In April 1921,
KDKA gave a blow-by-blow account of a
boxing match. In July RCA broadcast the
Dempsey-Carpentier heavyweight fight
(see 3.21), with Major J. Andrew White, an
early radio promoter and founder of Wire-

less Age, managing the broadcast. Later
that summer KDKA covered a tennis tournament and a baseball game. Although
few teams liked the idea of letting radio
siphon off their attendance, the World Series was carried as early as 1922 over WJZ
and other stations of the Radio Group,
using Western Union lines, and noncommercial events such as sailing regattas were
commonly described over the air.

During the mid-1920s, radio aired
almost any subject discussed in public from
astrology to politics; it programmed academic and popular lectures, cooking lessons, exercise programs. Programs for
farmers—first market and weather reports, and then how-to talks—began to
appear on Midwest stations in 1921–1922,
particularly those operated by land-grant
colleges with strong departments of agriculture. The battery-powered radio found
a tremendous audience among rural
Americans, nearly half the population (48.8
percent in 1920), who lived days away
from the news at the end of poor roads
and without telephones.

The *public service* program or announcement was an early feature. A marathon broadcast by WLS in March 1925,
which raised $200,000 for tornado relief in
Illinois, set a standard for other disasters:
first news or warnings of a flood or storm
and then appeals for help and funds for its
victims.

3•65   Drama

Radio drama did not become very
popular until the 1930s and 1940s. When
it first was thought of, producers had the
fortunately erroneous impression that the
action of a drama would have to take place
in a tunnel or cave so that the audience
could identify with something they
couldn't see. Probably the first play broad-

cast on radio was "The Perfect Fool," which was having a successful run on Broadway with Ed Wynn in the lead. Wynn, starring also in the WJZ version on February 19, 1922, "froze" before the microphone and later complained that only with an audience to react against could he correctly time his delivery. When he became a regular radio performer, using the "perfect fool" character, Wynn insisted on a studio audience.

In the fall of 1922, GE's station WGY offered the first dramatic series, the weekly *WGY Players*, and in 1925 established a contest for audience-submitted scripts. Other stations, particularly in major cities with access to acting troupes, began to offer plays adapted from the stage or films. Probably the first play designed for radio was called "When Love Wakens" (note the "W–L–W"), written and directed by Fred Smith, program director of WLW (Cincinnati) in April 1923. Although original drama was tried elsewhere, it often lacked the audience-pulling power of a proven story and required enormous talent to produce successfully.

3•7   Creation of the Radio Audience

The increase in radio listening was both spontaneous and created: spontaneous in that experimenters and early program listeners were motivated to build or buy receivers, and created in that many more Americans had to be persuaded that the sizable investment of time and money was worthwhile—that radio was more than a fad.

3•71   *Development of the Receiver*

Until late 1920, just before KDKA's first broadcast, all receivers were home-made. Some, like the crystal set, were cheap and simple—all it took was some wire and an oatmeal box to wind it on, a purchased piece of galena or other crystal and cat's whisker to probe it with, and a pair of earphones. More complicated sets were more expensive—the price of tubes, like many weekly wages, started at $6—though not beyond the capabilities of experienced amateurs or the thousands of ex-servicemen trained in radio. Early sets varied in cost, looks, and effectiveness, until more advanced superregenerative or superheterodyne circuits became available and design more standard. Almost all had limited sensitivity—ability to pick up weak signals—and very limited selectivity—ability to tune sharply and pick up only one frequency at a time; and tube sets required not only expensive tubes but several types of expensive batteries, including cumbersome and heavy automobile storage batteries. Virtually all sets needed earphones for listening, making radio a solitary pastime, although several sets of phones could be hooked up at one time. Even when loudspeakers were developed, the additional amplification they demanded was so expensive—in both components and batteries—that they were not widely used. Early receivers were hard to tune, their many controls requiring an artist's touch, and their audio quality left much to be desired.

In fall 1920, commercially manufactured radios became available, principally in large department stores. The Westinghouse "Aeriola Jr." was a crystal set that cost $25, and the "Aeriola Sr." was a tube set for $60. By 1922 there were hundreds of manufacturing companies varying considerably in size. Many smaller companies assembled parts supplied by other companies. RCA, as sales agent for sets made by Westinghouse and GE, was the foremost distributor, but Crosley,

Grebe, and Atwater Kent also became familiar brands. Fortunately for the companies competing with RCA, the RCA–GE –Westinghouse agreements (see 3.12, 3.13) that required RCA to market GE and Westinghouse receivers worked against RCA because the long lead-time needed for this intercompany ordering made its "Radiola" sets obsolete by the time they hit the market. The public soon realized that inexpensive sets were no bargain due to their lack of quality and performance, and the average price per set climbed well above $100.

After 1923 advertising and merchandising of radio receivers stressed brand name and product dependability. A National Radio Chamber of Commerce, later the Radio Manufacturers Association and now the Electronic Industries Association, was established to improve quality standards, collect sales data, and speak for the industry in forums or before government and private bodies. After Westinghouse brought the Armstrong superheterodyne patent into the patents pool, RCA gained recognition with the first superheterodyne receivers, which were expensive but sold well because they improved reception. Crosley, hoping to reverse the trend toward expensive sets, marketed the $10 Crosley "Pup" in 1924, a small metal box with a single tube on top that could receive stations up to around fifteen miles away.

By 1924 radio manufacturers were incorporating by the hundreds but were

---

The Early Radio Receiver: Homemade Variety / This is from one of many published instructions for a do-it-yourself radio receiver which could be assembled at a fraction of the cost of a commercially manufactured set.

FIG. 4. ASSEMBLED RECEIVING SET

Source: Department of Commerce, Bureau of Standards. *Construction and Operation of a Simple Homemade Receiving Outfit.* Washington: Government Printing Office, 1922. Pages 12 and 16.

8. APPROXIMATE COST OF PARTS

The following list shows the approximate cost of the parts used in the construction of the receiving station. The total cost will depend largely on the kind of apparatus purchased and on the number of parts constructed at home.

Antenna:

Wire, copper, bare or insulated, No. 14 or 16, 100 to 150 feet	$0.75
Rope, ¼ or ⅜ inch, 2 cents per foot.	
2 insulators, porcelain	.20
1 pulley	.15
Lightning switch, 30-ampere battery switch	.30
1 porcelain tube	.10

Ground connections:

Wire (same kind as antenna wire).	
2 clamps	.30
1 iron pipe or rod	.25

Receiving set:

3 ounces No. 24 copper wire, double cotton covered	.75
1 round cardboard box	
2 switch knobs and blades complete	1.00
18 switch contacts and nuts	.75
3 binding posts, set screw type	.45
2 binding posts, any type	.30
1 crystal, tested	.25
3 wood screws, brass, ¾ inch long	.03
2 wood screws for fastening panel to base	.02
Wood for panels (from packing box).	
2 pounds paraffin	.30
Lamp cord, 2 to 3 cents per foot.	
Test buzzer	.50
Dry battery	.30
Telephone receivers	4.00

Total	10.70

If the switches are constructed as directed and a single telephone receiver be used, the cost may be kept well below $10.

If a head set consisting of a pair of telephone receivers instead of a single telephone receiver is used, the cost of this item may be about $8 instead of $4. Still more efficient and expensive telephone receivers are available at prices ranging up to about $20.

WASHINGTON, March 27, 1922.

going bankrupt at nearly the same rate. In 1925, in spite of fall "radio shows" in major cities when set makers released next year's models just like automobiles, more manufacturers went out of business than started. The survivors usually were the larger and stronger companies—including several thousand that made components, in addition to the manufacturers and assemblers of complete sets—but virtually every year saw fewer of them.

Radio receiver manufacture became big business as the 1920s wore on (see Appendix C, table 8). Circuit designs were changed annually, with emphasis on easier operation by nontechnically minded listeners, especially women. The public bought sets enthusiastically—a half million in 1923, a million and a half in 1924, two million in 1925, one and three-quarters million in 1926. For example, when Gimbel's department store had a sale in May 1925 of Freed-Eisemann Neutrodyne five-tube receivers—including one "Prest-O-Lite" A battery of 90 amperes, two 45-volt B batteries, one phone plug, a complete antenna outfit, vacuum tubes, and a choice of loudspeakers—it took 240 clerks to sell the 5,300 receivers, at $98.75, $15 down—even though this price represented as much as several months of a workingman's wages. These 5,300 sets joined the 2.5 million already in use at the end of 1924.

In 1926 "battery-eliminator" or plug-in models reached the market to the delight of everyone except the battery manufacturers and households with no electricity, a rapidly shrinking proportion. A simple connection to house current eliminated 40 to 50 pounds of batteries and a maze of wiring. Common in the later 1920s were improvements in appearance —a mahogany box was more acceptable in the living room than a homemade *breadboard* receiver without a cabinet; in conven-

ience—John V. L. Hogan's *uni-tuning* reduced controls to one tuning knob and a volume control; and in economy—the plug-in model was cheaper. As listeners assiduously updated their installations, older sets went to the attic to provide parts for future experimenters, or out to rural areas without electricity and with less esthetic sensibility.

3•72   A National Craze

By the end of 1921 about one in every 500 American households had a radio receiver; by 1926 one radio receiver had been sold for every six households. Considering that some high-income households probably had purchased more than one receiver in this period and that home-built sets, not included in the statistics, counteracted any bias in the figures, it was estimated that one family in six had a radio. All over the country, newspapers, magazines, clubs, and classes fed the urge for more information about this marvel. Prearranged groups listened around sets in hotel lobbies or stores. Because of Prohibition, there were no legal saloons where people could enjoy radio on the house. (This was not the situation when television came in, however; then the local tavern typically was the earliest location for television.) Frequently radio retailers installed a mobile receiver in the back of a car to promote sales. Radio basically was an urban medium in its early years. Cost and poor reception kept farm families from owning sets, although buying increased rapidly when stations offered market and weather reports and when county extension agents explained radio's technicalities and expense and its potential benefits to the farmer.

During the early and middle-1920s audience research and listener feedback

The Early Radio Receiver: Commercial Models

Illustration shows Type R-D-5 Regenerative Receiver and Detector —$60.00

Type A-2 Two-Stage Amplifier—$40.00 (Licensed under Armstrong Patents)

ATWATER KENT
R A D I O

FOR the owner of Radio there is more and better broadcasting than ever before. Concerts, operas, lectures, sermons, educational courses, market, weather and special reports, and always the thrill of unexpected announcements of important happenings.

ATWATER KENT Radio in your home will assure you countless evenings filled with joy.

You will find Atwater Kent Receiving Sets and Loud Speakers well within your means. To fully appreciate their many advantages, see the new Models at any radio dealer's.

Note the materials used in their construction; the best that money can buy. Feel how smoothly the dials turn; that's but one example of their master workmanship. And then listen to the remarkable reception. Note the ease with which you can bring in stations, with ample volume, even from a distance.

For selectivity, distance, volume, clear reception, simplicity of operation and beauty of design, ATWATER KENT Radio is unexcelled.

These qualities your radio must have to give you perfect satisfaction. Be sure of getting them all by buying ATWATER KENT.

Instructive literature on request

ATWATER KENT MANUFACTURING CO., 4709 Wissahickon Ave., Philadelphia, Pa.

THINK OF WHAT IS BACK OF IT

Pacific Coast prices slightly higher

MU-RAD RECEIVERS

The Ultimate in Radio Reception

The New Star in the Radio World

"WHEN KNIGHTHOOD WAS IN FLOWER," Crusaders in distant lands communicated with their own countries by carrier pigeon. The system, learned from the Saracens, was greatly perfected by the Crusaders. *Today*, ordinary radio reception has been excelled by a new perfection of the art—MU-RAD RECEIVERS. Swift as thought, clear as the voice, sensitive beyond belief! Cities, 4,300 miles and more away, send their news and entertainment to the MU-RAD owner. Conservatively guaranteed for 1000 miles, using only a two-foot loop aerial.

WRITE FOR LITERATURE

MU-RAD LABORATORIES, INC.

808 FIFTH AVE. ASBURY PARK, NEW JERSEY

were slight. Broadcasters programmed to suit their own desires since they knew little about the audience's makeup, listening habits, or preferences, other than what they picked up in social and business conversations. The station could determine its area coverage from the postmarks on listener requests for DX cards, which it sent to verify long-range reception; and could get additional feedback through comment cards—supplied by radio shops to enable listeners to relate where they heard a certain broadcast, what they thought of it, and what receiving equipment was used; signal coverage maps prepared by engineers to show the potential audience; receiver sales records kept by retail outlets; and station mail counts of listener response, often to a *giveaway* offer. At best, these data enabled station owners to make an educated guess as to audience size and potential size. Most did not bother to guess, at least not until advertising became their main support. Then, the audience became the station's most valuable asset, and knowledge of it made the difference between success and failure.

3·8 Further Attempts at Regulation

All these developments took place within the inadequate regulatory pattern of the Radio Act of 1912, which was passed long before broadcasting was conceived (see 2.4). It empowered the Secretary of Commerce to license all stations and operators for commercial or amateur radio transmissions; indeed, it gave him no discretion, but required him to license all applicants meeting the minimal standards—essentially United States citizenship—and assign call letters (see Appendix B). Upon President Warren G. Harding's election in 1920, the Secretary of Commerce appointment went to Herbert Hoover, fresh from

an active engineering and public service career, most recently providing food relief to war-torn Europe. Until 1921 the Bureau of Navigation of the Department of Commerce kept track of amateur and commercial (maritime) radio operations.

When broadcasting to the public started, the department allocated a single wavelength for it, although experimentation frequently took place elsewhere on the spectrum. This wavelength of 360 meters, or 833.3 kHz, was not far from the international distress and calling frequency of 600 meters (500 kHz), a range familiar to experimenters and amateur hobbyists. (The 600-meter wavelength had been selected partly because it was the longest for which an antenna could be strung between the masts of a typical ship.) In December 1921, before the number of broadcasting stations began to climb sharply, a second wavelength of 485 meters (618.6 kHz) was added, primarily for crop reports and weather forecasts. To broadcast such "government services," stations would switch easily from 360 meters up to 485 meters, since the transmitters were tuned, like a radio receiver, rather than fixed by crystal control on a particular frequency.

During spring 1922, there were so many stations on the air that the department *had* to provide a third wavelength that summer of 400 meters (750 kHz) for Class B stations. These typically better stations were required to operate with at least 500–1,000 watts and could not use phonograph records. The new rule tended to create a privileged class on 400 meters, with most stations still crowded on the 360-meter wavelength. Although those who ran the powerful stations, and the typical listener, liked this move, it did not relieve the increased crowding on the airwaves. In a way, it was surprising that this system worked at all for its short life, until

May 1923, since the Radio Act of 1912 gave the Secretary of Commerce very little administrative power beyond that of persuasion.

3•81 Hoover and the National Radio Conferences

As the number of broadcasting stations grew from 30 to more than 500 in a single year, government, as well as commercial and amateur operators, faced new problems. Complaints of interference were filed; pressure mounted for greater coordination. Secretary Hoover, in need of constructive advice, convened a conference of civilian and government experts, at the direction of the President, to discuss radio's problems and suggest legislative solutions. Fifteen official delegates—ten representing governmental interests and five nongovernmental interests, particularly in science and engineering—gathered in Washington on February 27, 1922. (Members of the American Radio Relay League, meeting a little earlier in the same city, were very unhappy at the prospect of additional regulation!) Disagreement marked the conference when AT&T, GE, Westinghouse, and RCA favored keeping the Commerce Department in control of broadcasting rather than giving that role to the army or the navy, and the navy and the post office had different ideas. The conference agreed, however, on some recommendations: (1) that the government regulate technical aspects of broadcasting by assigning stations to specific frequencies, with specific power and hours of operation; (2) that more channels be added to reduce interference; (3) that radio be considered a public utility, operating in the public interest; (4) that advertising be limited to naming the sponsor; and (5) that four classes of station be recognized, government, private (educational), private (others), and toll (paid service). These recommendations, as introduced into the House of Representatives by Congressman Wallace H. White, Jr., (R-Maine) called for administration by the Secretary of Commerce with no provision for court review, while his opponents called for an independent commission. The bill passed the House on the second try early in 1923 but died in the Senate Interstate Commerce Committee.

While waiting for congressional action, Hoover opened up the new Class B 400-meter frequency, as the number of stations increased from 60 to nearly 600. Three channels were clearly insufficient for satisfactory nationwide broadcast service, and Hoover called the second National Radio Committee conference. It convened on March 20, 1923, with 20 delegates. Its report reiterated the need for congressional action and called for various holding actions: (1) establishment of three classes of stations; (2) division of the country into five regions, with stations assigned accordingly to provide more equal service—an obvious political need; (3) giving the Secretary of Commerce discretion to choose among applicants for the same facilities, instead of prolonging the voluntary allotment of segments of time on a single wavelength to several stations; and (4) discussion of station financing and copyright, suggested by the American Society of Composers, Authors, and Publishers (ASCAP), a performing rights licensing organization.

As a result of the conference, Secretary Hoover announced a new system of frequency assignments on May 15, 1923. There would be, eventually, two classes of stations occupying the band from 550 kHz to 1,350 kHz (see diagrams on page 86). Stations originally operating on 833.3 kHz were designated Class C until they could be reclassified into A or B. Class A stations, transmitting with less that 500 watts, were assigned to the top and bottom of this band: 550–800 kHz and 1,000–1,350 kHz. Class B stations, using 500 watts or more, were assigned to 870–1,000 kHz, leaving 833.3 kHz unmolested with "guard band" of nearly 35 kHz on either side. This vast increase in spectrum space made many receivers out of date but established AM radio broadcasting firmly in the heart of its current band and made adequate regulation possible.

But adequate regulation was not to come from the Department of Commerce, at least not under the 1912 Radio Act. In summer 1923, the U.S. Court of Appeals for the District of Columbia ruled in *Hoover* v. *Intercity Radio* that the Secretary of Commerce could not regulate radio other than assign wavelengths and that his license-issuing function was purely clerical. A 1912 opinion of the attorney general had come to essentially the same conclusion, and a later opinion and the 1925 *Zenith-WJAZ* case (see 3.82) concurred.

During 1923 and 1924, Congress still couldn't pass a new radio bill. Hoover called the Third National Radio Conference in October 1924 and told the 90-odd delegates that the country needed a broadcasting system controlled largely by self-regulatory bodies rather than government. President Coolidge echoed some of Hoover's philosophy when he advised the conference that the government should not operate stations in competition with private broadcasters and that there should be no monopoly in broadcasting. David Sarnoff's announcement that RCA was planning a chain of superpower, 50,000 watt, stations, starting with one in New York, led to objections from smaller broadcasters and study by a conference committee. The conference concluded that: (1) it strongly opposed monopolistic practices; (2) the power of the Department of Commerce should be extended in technical areas only; (3) national broadcasting through wired interconnection of stations, rather than shortwave, should be encouraged; (4) experimentation with superpower should have strict supervision; (5) power of existing stations should be increased, particularly where rural listeners would benefit; (6) the top of the broadcasting band should be extended to 1,500 kHz, and the regional zoning system should be revised to increase the number of channels by 30, to 96, and (7) the classifying and labeling of stations should be changed. The third conference made no call for congressional action; in fact, Hoover asked Congressman White not to introduce a bill until some of the problems raised at the conference could be corrected or put into more specific recommendations for legislative action.

A year later, the fourth and largest National Radio Conference was held in Washington on November 9, 1925. Its 400 delegates considered three topics: limiting the number of stations, granting licenses on the basis of "public interest" service to the listener, and appointing local committees, familiar with their own areas, to help the Secretary of Commerce select recipients of broadcast franchises. The conference strongly supported limiting the number of stations, even if it meant allowing the secretary to remove some of the 80 stations still on 833.3 kHz. The principle agreed to was that having a few stations broadcasting high quality programs was more desirable than having many stations offering mediocre programs, and that adding new channels would be irrelevant to this problem and unfair to other radio services. The conference found it difficult to define "public service" but supported the suggestion that a prospective licensee offer more than desire and money in order to procure a license. The idea of local com-

Growth of the Standard (AM) Broadcast Band / In the diagrams below, each bar represents the standard (AM) broadcast band (medium-wave) frequency allocation in the United States in the mid-1970s. Superimposed on those bars are earlier allocations for AM stations (see 3.22 and 3.81). Small circled numbers refer to notes at end of diagrams. Actual allocations extend 5 kHz above and below the numbers shown on each line. Expansion to 1,605 kHz is expected in the 1990s.

August 1912 (amateur operators only)

833 kHz ⋮ 360 meters

December 1921 (about 30 broadcast stations on the air)

① ②

619 kHz ⋮ 485 meters

August 1922 (about 400 broadcast stations)

③

400 meters ‒ 750 kHz

May 1923 (about 560 broadcast stations) ④

"A"   "B"   "A"   1,350 kHz

550 kHz   800 kHz ‒ "C" ‒ 870 kHz ‒ 1,000 kHz

April 1927 (about 680 broadcast stations)

(Experimental) ⑤

550 kHz   1,500 kHz   2,000 kHz

August 1933 (about 600 broadcast stations)   1,500 kHz ‒   ‒ 1,550 kHz

⑥

550 kHz   1,530 kHz ‒   ‒ 1,570 kHz

March 1941 (862 broadcast stations)

⑦

550 kHz   1,600 kHz

(*Note:* for clarity, repeated assignments in the 1912–1923 period are noted by arrows rather than kHz and meter duplications.)

Legend

Present-day (post-1952) AM broadcast band (535–1605 kHz).

Regular single channel (vertical line) or series of channels assigned.

Experimental single channel (vertical line) or series of experimental channels assigned.

Notes

1. Used only for government reports (weather, crops, etc.).

2. Used for all other program types: entertainment, lectures, etc.

3. Called Class B with more stringent technical and some programming requirements. By October 1922, six months after this allocation, congestion was so great that time-sharing was necessary for stations on this wavelength in larger cities.

4. For this allocation, the following restrictions were in force: Class A— less than 500 watts, located on top and bottom of band; Class B—500 or more watts in middle of the band; Class C—temporary for stations on 360 meters (833 kHz) until they were reassigned to Class A or B. Because such stations, often the older ones, were seldom equipped to stay exactly on frequency, space was left on either side of the single channel; Class D—(not shown) for developmental work, with frequencies assigned to radio equipment manufacturers.

5. For experimental use only, including AM and visual (TV) experimentation. Most 1,500–2,000 kHz assignments were temporary.

6. Specific 20 kHz-wide channels (twice the normal AM channel width) were set aside on 1,530, 1,550 and 1,570 kHz for high-fidelity AM experimental broadcasting. Only a few stations were assigned here.

7. The 540 kHz channel was added to the U.S. AM band in December 1952, the last expansion to date.

mittees was rejected. The conference decided that advertising was a proper means of support for broadcasting if it was indirect or institutional—apparently an acknowledgment that advertising was the best support option available. Matters discussed at earlier conferences were again raised. As to copyright, since the courts had made it plain that broadcasting constituted a public performance, it was decided that stations needed permission of the originator to rebroadcast programs. Public utility status as advocated by the first conference was rejected. Superpower experiments had proved that smaller stations need not be as worried about being "blanketed" by larger stations. Congressional action was again urged, specifically

for administrative flexibility for the secretary, a commission or some other administering body, and renewable and revocable, for cause, five-year license terms. A baker's dozen of formal recommendations were introduced as H.R. 5589 by Congressman White in December 1925, and an amended version became the Radio Act of 1927 (see 4.81).

3•82   Chaos

The already tenuous authority of the Secretary of Commerce disintegrated shortly after the Fourth National Radio Conference. Late in 1924 the Zenith Radio Corporation, a receiver manufacturer, ap-

---

An FRC Commissioner Describes the Chaos of 1926–1927 / In a June 1927 speech in Chicago, newly appointed FRC Commissioner Orestes H. Caldwell looked back on the post-Zenith case confusion that precipitated the Radio Act of 1927 (see 4.81):

...many stations jumped without restraint to new wave lengths which suited them better, regardless of the interference which they might thus be causing to other stations. Proper separation between established stations was destroyed by other stations coming in and camping in the middle of any open spaces they could find, each interloper thus impairing reception of three stations—his own and two others. Instead of the necessary 50-kilocycle separation between stations in the same community, the condition soon developed where separations of 20 and 10 kilocycles, and even 8, 5, and 2 kilocycles, existed. Under such separations, of course, stations were soon wildly blanketing each other while distracted listeners were assailed

with scrambled programs.... Some of the older stations also jumped their power ...and heterodyne interference between broadcasters on the same wave length became so bad at many points on the dial that the listener might suppose instead of a receiving set he had a peanut roaster with assorted whistles. Indeed, every human ingenuity and selfish impulse seemed to have been exerted to complicate the tangle in the ether.

Source: Federal Radio Commission. *First Annual Report: 1927.* (Washington Government Printing Office, 1927) pages 10–11.

plied for a permit, built a station, and in due course received a license for 930 kHz, which it had to share with several other stations. Zenith soon outgrew the two hours a week it had originally requested and asked for permission to broadcast longer hours on an unused wavelength at 910 kHz, which the United States had agreed to reserve for Canadian stations. Permission was refused. When Zenith defiantly "jumped" to 910 kHz, other stations announced their intention to jump. The Commerce Department took Zenith to court, but an Illinois Federal District Court decided on April 26, 1926, that there was "no express grant of power in the Act to the Secretary of Commerce to establish regulations." Finally, the Commerce Department tried to get the pending Dill-White radio bill through Congress, but it was too late in the session. The attorney general, in a requested opinion issued on July 8, 1926, supported the position that the secretary did not have adequate legal power to deal with the situation. The department then had no choice but to continue processing applications, and, in a period of seven months in 1926, more than 200 new stations went on the air, creating intolerable interference in major urban areas.

3•83   Initial Self-Regulation

Secretary Hoover had preached that industry could avoid governmental control through self-regulation. The cacophony on the air after mid-1926 was ample proof that broadcasters could not cooperate sufficiently to function without outside regulatory force. Indeed, what self-regulation there was resulted mostly from external threat rather than internal conviction. In the earliest years, self-regulation meant little other than "silent nights."

Time-sharing was mostly voluntary, but, except for the period after the Zenith decision, there was always the threat of government action. In technical matters, broadcasting clearly needed a governmental traffic cop; in programming, broadcasting managed alone, typically exercising its freedom by censoring many dissenting points of view and presenting a conservative, business-oriented middle-class viewpoint. The avoidance of controversy became almost a fetish in later years.

Although a matter more of self-interest than self-regulation, the broadcasters' fight with ASCAP (American Society of Composers, Authors, and Publishers) in the early 1920s led the way toward organizing the broadcasting industry, a necessary step toward self-regulation. ASCAP—a performing rights, copyright-licensing agency founded in 1914 —was concerned that record sales and, increasingly, broadcasting were the cause of declining revenues from sheet music sales. In 1922–1923, ASCAP demanded royalties from several selected stations for playing ASCAP-licensed music. Although AT&T's WEAF agreed to pay a few hundred dollars a year for a blanket license, possibly because of AT&T's own stance on patent rights, most stations balked because they had no income and relatively large expenses already. Broadcasters contended not only that they ran a nonprofit business but that the publicity they gave to the music probably boosted record and sheet music sales. When ASCAP threatened to bring suit, as the Copyright Act of 1909 clearly allowed, a few stations capitulated but others dropped ASCAP-controlled popular music from their repertoires.

On April 25 and 26, 1923, a small group of broadcasters met in Chicago to establish a common front against ASCAP, leading to, in later years, its own music-licensing organization. This group, calling itself the National Association of Broadcasters, picked the head of Zenith, Commander Eugene F. McDonald, Jr., as its first president. Representatives from about 20 stations attending NAB's initial convention in New York that fall discussed politicians on the air, the need for technical cooperation and control, and possible revisions in the copyright law. The new group was small and largely ineffective at first—ASCAP got its royalties—but the groundwork had been laid for a powerful organization that would face ASCAP again with somewhat different results (see 5.85).

3·9   Radio's Early Impact

There were indicators of the roles of radio in this country and abroad beyond its impact on the American home of the 1920s that we have already noted (see 3.72).

3·91   Domestic Effects

The radio craze or fad of 1921–1922 perhaps is best seen in the popular literature that grew up to feed and support, and be supported by, the national interest in wireless. Technical magazines about wireless had been around for some time, but they catered to the experimenter and not to the general public. Shortly after the first broadcasting stations went on the air, some general interest radio periodicals appeared. *Radio Broadcast*, which began in May 1922, concentrated on programming and industry economics, but in 1924 it began a column of radio criticism, particularly of musical programs. Then other popular radio periodicals, mixtures of fan and how-to-do-it technical magazines, lured an avid public. Almost all general magazines of information, opinion, and entertainment featured articles about broadcasting.

In the early years, newspapers devoted considerable attention to radio. In 1922 the *New York Times* started a regular radio section with the late Orrin E. Dunlap, Jr.—now better known for his many books on radio and television—as columnist-critic; in 1924 the *Christian Science Monitor* started a radio section; in 1925 Ben Gross began his forty-five-year career with the *New York Daily News* and a writer signing himself "Pioneer" offered technical tips and brief reviews in the *New York Tribune*. Books appeared in increasing numbers, many on "how to build your own radio set," a few of the "gee whiz!" school covering all aspects of radio, and no less than four different series of boys' thrillers with the same title of "The Radio Boys."

Broadcasting to the public had by no means killed the amateur radio service. The American Radio Relay League became active again after World War I, and its publication *QST* reached an expanding membership. In 1925, a 23-nation conference created an International Amateur Radio Union to combat restrictive laws around the world. Ham operators and experimenters deserved credit for the development of new operating techniques, efficient equipment and circuits, and the opening up of the higher reaches of the electromagnetic spectrum.

Radio had a telling effect on other industries. Hardest hit was the phonograph record industry, which suddenly faced competition from "free" music sent over the air. As radio-transmitted sound improved and as the amount of broadcast music increased, demand for expensive but low-fidelity phonographs lessened and the companies that made them suffered. Radio also undermined vaudeville, although the traveling shows, some of which survived into the 1930s, were also a victim of the motion picture. Many of the acoustic and electronic principles that produced radio were applied to the sound motion picture, which made its appearance in the late 1920s. Without the Audion, sound motion pictures would have been impossible. The weekly bible of show business, *Variety*, started a special radio section in 1924 in testimony to the growing importance of the medium.

All in all, radio was a common household device by 1926. Although serious technical interference and economic problems existed, its potential for supplying entertainment to the American public was evident. Fortuitously but fortunately, the leisure time of most Americans was expanding just as radio was developing. Effects from the rapid spread of news and the loss or reduction of regional speech dialects and patterns were more subtle or more gradual.

3•92   Radio Abroad

Although much attention was diverted to broadcasting, a strong interest in the market for point-to-point international communications remained. With the end of navy control of radio facilities in March 1920, commercial transatlantic wireless service returned, with RCA, the "chosen instrument" of American communications policy, profiting from traffic agreements with British Marconi and with other administrations.

Interestingly enough, the alternator that led to the birth of RCA was quickly superseded by high-power vacuum-tube transmitters. Discovery of the propagation characteristics of shortwaves suddenly made much-prized longwave frequencies less desirable. Shortwaves had been discarded commercially, with the belief that nothing below 200 meters (1,500 kHz) would work except for very short distances, but amateur operators had found

ways to use them for long-range transmissions. Ham operators bridged the Atlantic with shortwave as early as December 1921 but did not know how to overcome a high level of interference. However, after the major manufacturing and operating companies, including Marconi, had been shown the possibilities of long-range skywave transmissions on shortwave frequencies, it did not take long to make it practical. By the late 1920s, shortwave was used for long-distance telephone as well as the "Empire Chain" of stations connecting all the British Empire. The amateurs were "kicked upstairs" again, to yet higher frequencies, when their playground just below 200 meters was taken over by commercial and governmental radio services.

Radio broadcasting developed in many other countries at the same time it developed in the United States. Less developed nations did not establish indigenous radio broadcasting for some years, although some colonies had a radio system modeled on the mother country's. The first broadcasting station in Great Britain began in February 1920, near London. When a few other stations began experimental voice and music transmissions, interference and political and financial considerations caused the General Post Office, the licensing authority, to step in. This led to the establishment of the single British Broadcasting Company, owned and operated by a consortium of major manufacturing firms. It began operations in 1922, with eight stations, and received income in the form of royalties on receiver sales—discontinued in 1924—and yearly license fees for sets. In return for the risks taken by the manufacturers, the post office agreed to have imported receivers banned from the market. For a number of reasons the private company was politically disturbing and did not work very well. When the House of

Commons called for an investigation in 1923, the Sykes Committee recommended governmental control, but it was not accomplished until 1927. Just as Sarnoff was to rise from obscurity to dominate the development of RCA, so did John C. W. Reith, the managing director of the privately owned British Broadcasting Company, advance to develop the publicly owned British Broadcasting Corporation. In his 15 years leading the BBC ending in mid-1938, he imposed his personal values upon an entire system, which pays at least lip service to them today, half a century later. For his service he was knighted and later made a peer.

Broadcasting also got underway in other parts of the world. In Europe, a Netherlands station claims a starting date of 1919 (see 3.21), Spain started by 1921, France and the Soviet Union in 1922, Germany in 1923, Italy in 1924. By 1926 there were 170 stations in Europe, 5 in Africa, 40 in Latin America, 10 in Asia—mainly in Japan, which had begun the government-owned NHK in 1925—and 20 scattered about Oceania, chiefly in Australia, New Zealand, and the Philippines. Broadcasting in Canada began in 1919 over a Marconi-operated transmitter in Montreal. There were 34 privately owned Canadian stations by 1922–1923, and roughly 75 by 1926. The first Mexican station was established in 1921, the second opened in 1923, and by 1926 there were about 10 privately owned stations and one government-owned educational operation, started in 1924. Few sets were manufactured domestically, and few sets were imported until Mexico issued its first radio law in 1926.

In 1926, an estimated 12½ million homes had radio; half of them were in the United States, which also had half the broadcast transmitters then operating—and the real growth was just around the corner.

3•93 Period Overview

Surprisingly, only one important precedent emerged as radio spread over the country: broadcasting in the United States essentially was to be privately owned and commercially supported. This was a time of both program and technical experimentation. The way was paved for permanent networks, educational broadcasting had its brief fling with AM stations, the radio receiver developed from an ugly battery-powered apparatus to a handsome piece of plug-in furniture, which became more sensitive, selective, and reliable each year. Regulation, however, was a patchwork based on the 1912 Radio Act, which was never intended to cover broadcasting, and the era ended with chaos and federal helplessness.

Radio's product was new and free —once you had a receiver—and that was enough to create a tremendous nationwide boom. A similar period of excitement would occur three decades later with the initial spread of television. Radio was both a hobby for searchers for distant stations and a pastime for listeners, and program types showed that duality. Led by a few big stations, radio quickly settled into a pattern of quarter-hour and half-hour programs offered at set times. It began as an evening medium and slowly spread into daytime hours as the audience increased and program material and advertising support became available for music, variety, and talk.

The early 1920s were a period of widespread experimentation where successful trials sometimes became precedents for newer stations. It was an exciting time for workers in broadcasting and often a frustrating one for an audience that could not hear clearly or hear all it wanted. By 1926 some wondered whether the industry's lack of financial and organizational stability was bringing the radio fad to an end.

Further Reading

The best social history overview of this era is found in Barnouw (1966). Stressing behind-the-scenes business maneuvering, but of lesser value because of its RCA bias, is Archer (1938). Views of the radio industry by contemporaries responsible for major decisions can be found in the interesting collection of talks titled *The Radio Industry* (1928). Schubert (1928) offers an undocumented but highly accurate and exciting account of these early years, while Banning (1946) provides the best history of an early station, AT&T's WEAF. The most detailed review of the "oldest station" controversy is Baudino and Kittross (1977). The development of early broadcast advertising and program formats is best told in Hettinger (1933). Recent research on radio in the 1920s and

---

Key Broadcasting Indicators: 1925 / This is the first of 12 tables that provide comparable data for a 60-year period (to 1985) at five-year intervals, the tables being found toward the end of chapters 3–10. Sources for 1–3 and 11 are the tables in Appendix C, while other information comes from sources indicated below. Most data are for January 1.

Indicators	AM Station Data
1. Number of commercial stations	445
2. Number of noncommercial stations	125
3. Total broadcasting stations on the air	570
4. Number of network-affiliated stations	12
5. Percentage of commercial stations affiliated with networks	2.7%
6. Total industry income	na
7. One-hour station rate (New York)	$500
8. One-minute station rate (New York)	na
9. One-hour network rate evening	$4,080
10. Number of broadcasting employees	na
11. Percentage of families with sets	10.1%
12. Broadcasting regulatory budget (Dept. of Commerce)	na

Notes (see Appendix D for full citations):

na = not available or not applicable.

4. and 5. refers for this year to AT&T-owned and WEAF-centered Broadcasting Company of America with 12 affiliates and some alternates.

6. Hettinger (1933) says no reliable data is available before 1931.

7. Evening rate for WEAF according to Archer (1938) page 360.

8. Few if any stations sold time in this small amount.

9. See note on 4–5. This figure, however, includes 17 stations.

While in later tables most data are for a specific month, usually January, data shown here cover several different months of 1925 due to a lack of standard sources.

some contemporary reports are presented in Lichty and Topping (1975).

Contemporary views include a book by radio's first lasting personality (McNamee, 1926); articles in the monthly *Radio Broadcast* (1922–1930), then the most important periodical regularly discussing the industry; the first popular overview of radio broadcasting, programming, and likely effects and potential (Rothafel and Yates, 1925); a slightly more technical predecessor (Yates and Pacent, 1922); and the first scholarly book-length treatment of the economics of radio—indeed, the first doctoral dissertation on radio broadcasting—(Jome, 1925).

Legal aspects of radio in this confusing era can be found in the various reports of the National Radio Conferences (U.S. Dept. of Commerce 1923, 1924, 1926) and in the annual reports of the Department of Commerce, Bureau of Navigation, and later the Radio Bureau (U.S. Dept. of Commerce 1921–1926, 1927–1932). The detailed results of the first government investigation of the fledgling radio industry, concentrating on patents and economics, are found in the FTC report (1924). Rosen (1980) provides a good historical study of the changing roles of the federal government and the radio broadcasters in this period. Kittross (1977) includes many key documents.

Histories of broadcasting in other countries are just beginning to appear. Briggs (1961) provides a thorough and documented discussion of early radio broadcasting in Britain, a major model for other countries. Two very early books on radio in Britain are Burrows (1924), probably the first broadcasting history ever published, and Lewis (1924), which relates life at the early, commercial BBC. Pawley (1972) is a fine technical history of BBC radio, and later, television, engineering. McNeil and Wolfe (1982) is an album of interviews and illustrations from the earliest days of Canadian radio broadcasting. Early radio in Japan is reviewed in two official publications fron NHK (1967 and 1977). Finally, Unesco (1947–1951), in seven volumes, provides a wealth of detail on mass communication systems in virtually every country of the world, including how they started.

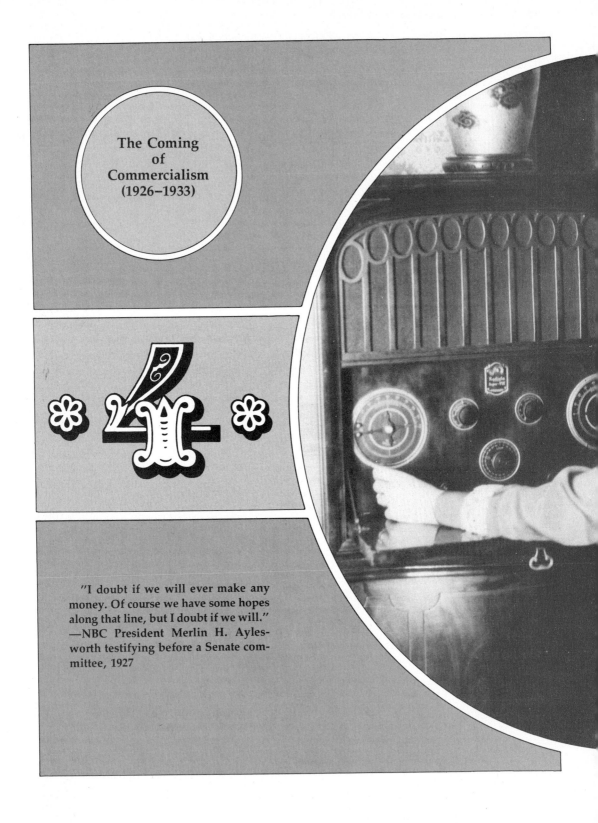

The Coming
of
Commercialism
(1926–1933)

"I doubt if we will ever make any money. Of course we have some hopes along that line, but I doubt if we will."
—NBC President Merlin H. Aylesworth testifying before a Senate committee, 1927

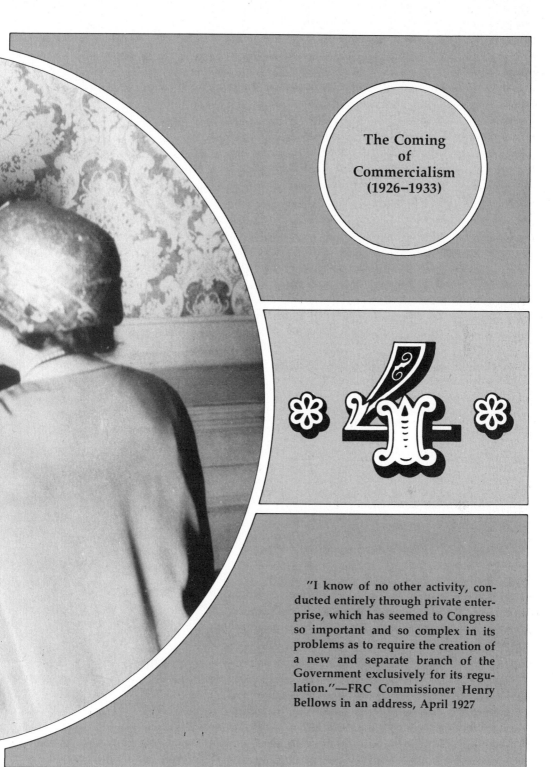

The Coming
of
Commercialism
(1926–1933)

"I know of no other activity, conducted entirely through private enterprise, which has seemed to Congress
so important and so complex in its
problems as to require the creation of
a new and separate branch of the
Government exclusively for its regulation."—FRC Commissioner Henry
Bellows in an address, April 1927

The late 1920s were a frenzied time in America—perhaps best epitomized by one man and one trend. The man was Charles A. Lindbergh, whose May 1927 solo flight from New York to Paris made him the greatest hero of modern times. This country and others pressed parades and awards upon him for months, and his subsequent flying exploits and personal life were always front-page news, as were more tragic events (see 4.64 and 5.63).

The continuing trend was the rising stock market, which epitomized and encouraged the spirit of progress that pervaded the country. Nearly everyone, so it seemed, was "in the market," usually buying stock on margin. In 1928, when Herbert Hoover won the presidency, films

Outline:
The Coming of Commercialism (1926–1933)

were beginning to talk, Prohibition was a national joke, automobiles were competing with railroad transportation, and airmail pilots were attempting national airline service. Navy officer Richard E. Byrd explored the Arctic and then the Antarctic, and in 1929–1930 the nation could hear his broadcasts from "Little America" near the South Pole. Rumors were abroad of something called television—radio programs you could see as well as hear.

Then, in late 1929, the stock market crash brought this period of expansion and excitement to a sudden stop. In a few weeks, many investors were wiped out and, more important, the nation's spirit also sank into psychological depression. In late 1930, when millions were unemployed and breadlines formed in all major cities, the Hoover administration kept saying that the economy would soon turn for the better. But 1931 and election year 1932 were even worse. On a warm night in 1932, army troops with tear gas routed World War I veteran "Bonus marchers" from their tarpaper shacks in Washington, D.C. New York Governor Franklin D. Roosevelt won the November election and swept into the White House in March, brandishing a combination of skills—including his frequent use of radio—that would help move the country out of the Depression.

The present pattern of American broadcasting was set in the years between 1926 and 1933. Modernizing of federal regulation, the rise of national networks, acceptance and success of radio advertising, and a phenomenal increase in the radio audience—all took place in that short period. Only the years just after World War II saw changes of similar magnitude, and these were superimposed on the existing pattern rather than basically altering it. The 1926–1933 developments were more than evolutionary; they were basic directional decisions. Made by a wide variety

of people, they removed broadcasting from the role of experimental novelty and made it an industry. The rapid shift from boom to crash of the economy had important effects on radio's growth and role. Most of the changes in broadcasting that took place during this period were begun before 1930, and were merely consolidated after that year, paralleling the changes in the nation's social fabric.

A good example of this consolidation was the major change in character and function of the Radio Corporation of America, then the most important single voice in the radio manufacturing and broadcasting industries. In 1930 the radio-receiver manufacturing divisions of GE and Westinghouse were unified within RCA, and facilities and key personnel, like television experimenter Vladimir Zworykin (see 5.14) and patent chief Otto Schairer (see 3.13), were transferred from Westinghouse to RCA. However, a few months later, the federal government began to pursue antitrust prosecution recommendations made as early as 1923 in the FTC investigation of radio (see 3.23). In May 1930, a Justice Department antitrust suit sought to undo RCA's newly unified ownership, contending that it was an unfair monopoly in restraint of trade in the field of radio apparatus. AT&T, by then divested of RCA stock, pulled out of the arrangements with little trouble (see 4.31). Over the next two and one-half years, lawyers tried to figure out ways for GE and Westinghouse to ease out of RCA control and manufacturing agreements without harming any of the firms irreparably. Finally, on November 13, 1932, they worked out a compromise acceptable to the Justice Department, and a consent decree was issued on November 21. GE and Westinghouse had a short transition period in which to divest themselves of RCA stock and get their representatives off the RCA board. Exclusive license agreements made from 1919 to 1921 (see 3.13) became non-exclusive. GE and Westinghouse could not compete with RCA for two years, after which they could manufacture and sell their own radio receivers. RCA had to program radio stations owned by the two other firms for a decade, a boon to its subsidiary, NBC. RCA became a totally independent manufacturing, selling, international communications, and broadcasting concern, separate for the first time since its formation from GE (but see 10.33), Westinghouse, AT&T, and other firms. As a convience, it also continued to administer the patents pool, now nonexclusive. Although the newspapers gave the compromise minor coverage, it had major effects on the radio industry in the 1930s.

4•1   Technology: Better Sound and Early Television

By the late 1920s, technical changes in radio broadcasting were evolutionary rather than basic. They had to do mostly with improving the poor quality of transmitted sound and the elimination or lessening of over-the-air static. At the same time, reports began to reach the public of laboratory developments that were to eventuate in television. Breathless accounts of "television around the corner" began to show up regularly in the press.

4•11   Improvement of Sound

By the late 1920s, radio transmitters could send out a clean signal that would stay on its assigned frequency, and directional antennae that would limit interference with nearby stations were to be designed in later years. At the *studio* there was much room for better sound repro-

duction. The earlier standard of the telephone, capable of adequate voice but very poor music reproduction, was no longer acceptable.

In planning studios, new stations were beginning to rely on architects to improve sound quality instead of using cut-and-try burlap-covered walls still common in smaller stations. The carbon microphone, with its narrow-frequency response and habit of freezing up for sibilant sounds, began to give way in the 1930s to the condenser microphone, which had survived ten years of testing, and the dynamic microphone—still the most common type—both of which made radio talk and music sound more real because of their better frequency response.

Throughout the 1920s, radio stations generally presented music "live," or used regular, home-variety 78-rpm records, which had very poor frequency response and played for only three or four minutes a side. In 1929, WOR became one of the first stations to use electrical transcriptions: 33⅓-rpm discs, made with particular care, which were as large as 16 inches in diameter and played for 15 minutes a side. (Modern *microgroove* LPs have higher quality and play for a longer time.) These first transcriptions were substantially the same as those used for the earliest sound motion pictures, when silent films were synchronized to disc recordings in the projection booth. This new kind of recording made programming more flexible and improved sound, and more than one hundred stations began to use transcriptions regularly.

All attempts to broadcast better sound were limited by what the station could produce and transmit, the network carry on its lines, and the home set receive and reproduce. By 1933 the typical station transmitter could transmit an audio-frequency bandwidth of at least 3,750 cycles per second—the equivalent radio-frequency bandwidth is exactly twice as much, or 7,500 Hz—and the best transmitters were capable of 5,000 Hz audio (10 kHz radio bandwidth). Low-frequency limits on transmission were in the 30–50 Hz range. Essentially the same bandwidth (30–5,000 Hz) is used today in standard (AM) broadcasting, although (1) a number of stations take advantage of a provision in the Federal Communications Commission regulations that permits them to use a wider bandwidth if they do not adversely affect other stations and (2) at one time a number of "high-fidelity" stations in the 1,500–1,600 kHz band were allowed to transmit 10,000 Hz audio. Although all these figures and standards seem inadequate, considering that the young human ear can hear up to 20,000 cycles or higher, 5,000 Hz sounds quite real compared to the 2,500 Hz bandwidth of a regular telephone instrument and circuit. Indeed, the main limitation on good network sound was the inability of AT&T lines to carry more than 4,000 Hz tones. The use of specially engineered lines overcame this difficulty but at considerable expense to the broadcaster. The home receiver typically lagged behind the studio and transmission facilities. Its audio had a tinny sound and rarely reproduced the higher and the lower portions of the audio spectrum. Unfortunately for the innovators of FM radio (see 5.11) and true high-fidelity music reproduction systems, the public became very used to this "radio sound," which was, in all fairness, better than the hand-wound acoustic Victrola phonograph or the telephone.

4•12 Technological Prehistory of Television

Although television in the form of mechanical scanning systems (see Appendix B) developed at full speed in the 1920s, it had a long history. One popular history of television (Hubbell) claims that the story goes back 4,000 years, but modern development started with the 1873 discovery by Joseph May and Willoughby Smith that the element selenium was capable of conducting small amounts of electricity in direct response to the amount of light falling on it. Later inventors, such as George R. Carey in 1877, found that banks of selenium cells, placed in a mosaic analogous to the human eye and wired individually, could send the elements of a picture as electrical signals from each cell simultaneously to a bank of lamps that lit in response to the electricity. In 1880, Maurice Leblanc and others developed the principle of scanning, or viewing picture elements successively, rather than all at once as in a mosaic device, and transmitting them sequentially over a single circuit. This approach was analogous to the solution of the similar problem faced by the telegraph industry at its start (see 1.41). A major refinement was the mechanical device—the mirror drum and, in 1883, Paul Nipkow's scanning disc—capable of scanning and transmitting even a moving picture. These devices are briefly discussed in Appendix B under "Television's Early Technological Development."

4•13 Development of Mechanical Television

Of the many inventors and experimenters who worked on mechanical television in the 1920s, three made outstanding progress: Herbert E. Ives of Bell Telephone Laboratories, who worked with all the resources of a major corporation; John Logie Baird, a self-taught Scottish inventor whose system almost became the British standard; and Charles Francis Jenkins, an American whose "radio movies" ran neck and neck with Baird but did not come close to the prize.

Ives was assigned, with the help of substantial funds and staff, to keep AT&T "abreast of the general advances in the art of television." From research on wire-photo transmission in 1923–1924, his work culminated in 1927 with wire transmissions of still and moving pictures over hundreds of miles. In one example, Secretary of Commerce Herbert Hoover spoke and was viewed on a $2 \times 2\frac{1}{2}$–foot neon-tube screen over a circuit from Washington to New York. In this April 7, 1927, demonstration, the picture was low definition —50 lines—but synchronized sound accompanied it. By the next year, outdoor scenes could be picked up and a three-channel color system was demonstrated. Bell Labs never promoted its system commercially, being content to keep "abreast of the art" with an eye eventually to servicing the interconnection of television stations. These experiments also generated Picturephone service, which AT&T has trotted out of the lab at intervals from 1927 to the present.

Baird (not to be confused with Hollis S. Baird, an American television experimenter) generally is credited with establishing television in Great Britain. In 1923, using a mechanical scanning system of his own design, he transmitted the first silhouette television picture by wire— almost simultaneously with Jenkins (see below). In 1925 both men transmitted moving silhouettes, and in 1926 Baird succeeded in producing shades of gray. Turning next to live action scenes as a source, in February 1928 he televised a woman's image from London to Hartsdale, New York, using the shortwave band to achieve that distance. Later that year he transmitted to the liner *Berengaria* a thousand miles at sea, and in 1932, foreshad-

owing today's large-scale closed-circuit transmissions of sports events, he transmitted the English Derby to a large screen in a London movie theater where 4,000 persons watched the race. Alexanderson had conducted a similar demonstration in Schenectady in 1930 and later at a Brooklyn theater. Many individuals and small firms constructed Baird "Televisors," as the television receivers were called.

In 1935, when the Television Committee of the British government had to choose television standards for the United Kingdom, comparative tests were held of the Baird mechanical system and an electronic system controlled by the giant EMI (Electric and Musical Industries Ltd.) company based partly on Zworykin's work in the United States (see 5.14). The committee decided in favor of the latter because they believed that Baird's system, although it tested well, was near the end of its potential development, while the electronic system could be improved considerably. Although greatly disappointed, Baird stayed in the field. In December 1941 he demonstrated improved color and stereoscopic three-dimensional television, areas he had worked in since 1928.

Jenkins, who invented a variety of devices based on drum and disc scanners, gave the first public demonstration of mechanical picture transmission in the U.S. in 1923 when he transmitted, by wireless, a photograph of President Harding from Washington to Philadelphia. From still silhouettes in 1923, Jenkins went to moving silhouettes, and then motion pictures, over navy station NOF in Washington, in 1925. His equipment was not as well engineered as Ives's, but he was a good publicist and aroused interest among amateurs and other experimenters. His system could transmit limited motion, achieving about sixty lines resolution at its best, compared to Ives's 48 lines and the 525 lines currently used

Eyewitness Accounts of the First Television / The first public demonstration of television was conducted in January 1926 in London by John Logie Baird (see 4.13).

The proof of Baird's achievement came on Tuesday, January 26. During the evening some forty members of the Royal Institution and other guests gathered at 22 Frith Street to see what the inventor had to offer. Besides Baird and Hutchinson, the only other "official" host was W. C. Fox, a Press Association journalist and friend of Baird. Fox greeted the visitors, who were allowed to enter the cluttered rooms in small groups after they signed a register. He recalls the event:

It was a cold January night and the members of the Royal Institution arrived in twos and threes. When they came out after the demonstration their remarks, such as I overheard, were much as one would expect. Some thought it was nothing worth consideration; others considered it the work of a young man who did not know what he was doing, while a few, a very few, thought there was something there capable of development. There was no realisation of the fact that they had been present at the birth of a new science.

Fox was at the head of the stairs on this occasion, but Baird had given him a personal demonstration a few days earlier:

The received image was admittedly crude, but it was recognisable as—whatever it might be— a face, a vase of flowers, a book opened and shut, or some simple article of every day life. The image received was pinkish in colour and tended to swing up and down. It was not possible to see much of the apparatus as it was covered by screens of one sort and another—extraneous light was not wanted and would interfere with the image.

A short, factual account of the demonstration appeared in *The Times* two days later. The reporter described the transmitting machine and the results:

. . . consisting of a large wooden revolving disk containing lenses, behind which was a revolving shutter and a light sensitive cell. The head of a ventriloquist's doll was manipulated as the image to be transmitted, though the human face was also reproduced. First on a receiver in the same room as the transmitter and then on a portable receiver in another room, the visitors were shown recognizable reception of the movements of the dummy and of a person speaking. The image as transmitted was faint and often blurred, but substantiated a claim that through the "Televisor," as Mr. Baird has named his apparatus, it is possible to transmit and reproduce instantly the details of movement, and such things as the play of expression on the face.

Source: George Shiers, "Television 50 Years Ago," *Journal of Broadcasting* 19:387–400, at pages 393–394 (Fall 1975). By permission.

in the United States. Claiming an amateur viewing audience of thousands, Jenkins organized a company in 1929 to manufacture both transmitting and receiving apparatus. The Jenkins Television Company announced commercial programs for 1930 and licensed a number of other manufacturers to use its patents, but it could not make a profit selling expensive novelties during a depression and quickly went into receivership. The De Forest Company purchased its assets, selling them in turn to RCA. Allen B. Dumont, chief engineer of the de Forest firm, became interested in television as a result, and later became a manufacturer of cathode-ray tubes and other television equipment and a televi-

sion broadcasting entrepreneur (see 7.32).

The scanning disc in many different forms held sway for roughly 50 years of television experimentation. Although many improvements could be achieved in mechanical scanning, mechanical problems increased with every increase in picture definition. However, many techniques investigated led to useful and practical results. Arthur Korn's 1902 facsimile experiments led to developments in television. In the late 1940s, CBS used the spinning disc principle for a system of color television (see 6.82 and 7.821). More recently, that system was modified to send the first color transmissions from the moon to earth in 1970.

Vaudeville Faces Television / Famous producer Flo Ziegfeld (right) looks into a Charles Francis Jenkins mechanical television receiver in 1928. From his expression, it may be that he did not think television was the show business medium of the future. Smithsonian Institution Photo No. 76-14655.

4•14   *Television Goes Public*

The television that promoters earnestly touted around 1930 was a collection of uncoordinated and incompatible systems. The Federal Radio Commission did little from 1927 to 1933 to establish television standards; perhaps it preferred to imitate the development of AM radio's equipment standards, which had evolved with a minimum of government supervision. To provide for orderly progression in television, the Radio Manufacturers Association in 1931 set nonmandatory standards at 48 lines and 15 pictures a second, with a secondary standard of 60 lines for more advanced research efforts. These standards were set somewhat below the most advanced state of the art, presumably for the benefit of promoters, inventors, and manufacturers who were impatient to introduce television commercially. Pressure for equipment standards in the 1920s and early 1930s might have been heavier had it not been possible, with a little adjustment, to receive signals from a station using one mechanical scanning system on a receiver designed for a different system. However, with the advent of rival electronic camera and complex synchronization systems in the mid-1930s (see 5.14) the lock-and-key aspect of television standards became operative; no electronic commercial television system would succeed until the government determined, or the whole industry adopted, common standards.

When early television experimenters were trying signal transmission by radio, they had little trouble obtaining frequencies. Nearly the entire spectrum above the standard broadcast (AM) band, then ending at 1,500 kHz, was available, although techniques for transmitting at these high frequencies generally were not then known. An associate of one experimenter complained that during the 1920s "there were no usable radio channels broad enough to carry the television signal required for adequate detail in the received image." Accordingly, in 1928, the FRC made the first provisions for television—*within* the standard broadcast band. Since these 10 kHz–wide channels were of no practical use to television, the allocation was changed to five 100 kHz–wide channels in the 2–3 MHz band. Despite the wider channels, some promoters agitated in 1929 for the return of visual broadcasting to the AM band, where transmission characteristics and equipment were familiar. This move was successfully opposed by radio broadcasters, networks, and manufacturers. Although transmissions on the 2 MHz band could travel thousands of miles, the FRC maintained at a 1930 television conference (1) that the pressure of other services and the need for a wider band-width for all-electronic scanning and higher definition would soon force television from the 2 MHz band and (2) that, to expand successfully, television would have to take over the largely uncharted spectrum above 30 MHz. The logical position that television would have to find its home in the VHF band was taken seriously, and many experimenters and manufacturers started to investigate the properties and the implications of use of the higher frequencies.

The willingness of financiers to back television in the late 1920s and the 1929 pleading with the FRC for television space on AM channels were not altruistic. Promoters saw television as the next great get-rich-quick opportunity. Pamphlets and magazines carried flamboyant articles urging the general public to "get on the bandwagon" and exaggerated claims of television's spread. They implied that experimental television stations (18 of them in cities such as Chicago, Boston, New

York, and Detroit by 1931) were broadcast stations serving the public and quoted often questionable surveys indicating far more television receiving sets in homes than other sources estimated. Jenkins alone claimed an audience of "some 25,000 lookers-in scattered throughout the States."

Programming was sketchy. A New York newspaper carried weekly program listings of four New York stations and one in Boston that largely presented test patterns and inexpensive or free motion picture short subjects for irregular brief periods. But attempts at more imaginative programming began early with a production of *The Queen's Messenger*, an old melodrama, over the GE station in Schenectady, New York, on September 11, 1928.

Although television seemed to be imminent, opposition by larger radio broadcasters and manufacturers delayed its arrival and then the Depression dried up capital. The Depression also gave radio broadcasting a chance to expand its audience and profits, accumulating funds for later investment in television, and gave manufacturers time to learn more about electronic television.

4·2   Stations: Structure and Stagnation

The number of radio broadcasting stations on the air declined in the late 1920s and early 1930s, from a high of 681 in 1927 to a low of 599 in 1933. While the Depression was a major factor beginning in 1932–1933, as business generally slowed down and advertising-based radio followed, a glance at the numbers (see Appendix C, table 1) shows that the major decline took place in 1928 and 1929 *before* the Depression began. The number of educational stations also declined from the 1927 total of 100 as schools could no longer afford them.

This precipitate decline was due not so much to economic factors as to the establishment of the Federal Radio Commission (FRC) early in 1927 (see 4.81). The FRC's first accomplishment was to lessen interference, which had become acute after the 1926 *Zenith* decision (see 3.82) by setting up a classification system that distinguished stations by type and service, reassigned many stations, and eliminated portable, low-power fringe operations. By late 1928 interference was greatly lowered and the quality of the remaining stations was improved by requirements for 100 percent modulation, crystal frequency control, and the like. Nighttime interference (see Appendix B, under Allocation, Assignments, Licensing) was cleaned up largely by forcing stations to curtail hours on the air and use lower power at night. All these decisions now had the force of law, and the FRC could revoke a broadcasting license—a power that Secretary of Commerce Hoover lacked earlier in the decade. The elimination of channel jumping and unauthorized power changes by early 1928 brought stability. The Federal courts consistently upheld the FRC, establishing a firm legal base for its subsequent actions.

Another development of this period was a steady increase in station transmitting power. Not only was higher power seen as a way of overcoming natural static, but also, as more stations came on the air, it became necessary just for a station to be heard. Where, in 1927, 28 percent of all stations used less than 100 watts, six years later only 3 percent were as low as 100 watts. Where in 1927 only three stations were using the 30,000-watt maximum, by 1933 22 stations were using 50,000 watts, the limit for AM stations established in 1928 and still in effect today (see 5.22). Stations WGY in Schenectady (General Electric), WEAF, New York (RCA–NBC), and

KDKA, Pittsburgh (Westinghouse), were among the first stations to transmit at the new power limit in 1928. In smaller communities, however, power ratings of 250 and 500 watts were the norm, with some of 100 watts or even less. Some man-made interference, often caused by oscillating receivers, and lots of natural static still plagued radio, but FRC regulatory actions had lessened it.

Both regulation and the trend toward more power and better equipment led to higher operating costs for nearly all stations. This increased economic burden, coming just before and during the Depression, brought about important changes in station ownership. The typical small operators of the 1920s, in some instances running five- and ten-watt stations in their homes or garages for a couple of hours a week, could not meet the costs of keeping a license, improving equipment, and paying for programming as well as other increasing demands on time, energy, and money. Many hobbyists and other shakily financed operators were forced off the air; many educational stations crumbled. In their places came the commercial broadcasting companies, groups of people in business solely to operate radio stations. Not gone, but declining numerically, were the laundries, hotels, department stores, and restaurants that operated broadcasting stations as a sideline. Only in the smaller cities and towns did radio bring the carefree aspect of its first years into the 1930s. In bigger cities, business methods and operators were converting it into an advertising-based, money-making industry.

Newspaper ownership of radio stations grew from approximately 5 percent of all stations in the mid-1920s to 13 percent by 1933, demonstrating that other media were recognizing radio's importance as a means of communication.

Newspapers were both hedging their bets in the news communications competition and seeking prestige in their communities by having a hand in the new enterprise. Typical examples were the *Milwaukee Journal*, which had reported on the growth of radio in the early 1920s, purchased station KWAF in 1927 for its frequency assignment, junked its equipment, and gone on the air with new equipment and higher power in mid-1927 as WTMJ (*The Milwaukee Journal*); and the *Chicago Tribune*, which in 1924 took over a station that had had three owners in two years and renamed it WGN (World's Greatest Newspaper).

4·3   The Rise of National Networks

The national networks as we know them developed in the late 1920s from the temporary and experimental networks put together earlier in the decade (see 3.3). They were to affect radio development more than any other organization besides the federal government.

4·31   Creation of NBC

The network of stations based on AT&T-owned WEAF in New York operated successfully while the Telephone Group and Radio Group were negotiating in 1925–1926 (see 3.23). In May 1926, AT&T made its broadcast properties a semi-independent subsidiary, the Broadcasting Company of America, both to pressure the Radio Group into granting more concessions to AT&T on matters other than broadcasting and to prepare for the expected purchase of their stations by RCA. Announcement of initial agreement in July 1926 caused consternation among the closely knit staff at WEAF, and numerous problems developed in merging the oper-

An Era Begins (1926)

Announcing the

National Broadcasting Company, Inc.

National radio broadcasting with better programs permanently assured by this important action of the Radio Corporation of America in the interest of the listening public

THE RADIO CORPORATION OF AMERICA is the largest distributor of radio receiving sets in the world. It handles the entire output in this field of the Westinghouse and General Electric factories.

It does not say this boastfully. It does not say it with apology. It says it for the purpose of making clear the fact that it is more largely interested, more selfishly interested, if you please, in the best possible broadcasting in the United States than anyone else.

Radio for 26,000,000 Homes

The market for receiving sets in the future will be determined largely by the quantity and quality of the programs broadcast.

We say quantity because they must be diversified enough so that some of them will appeal to all possible listeners.

We say quality because each program must be the best of its kind. If that ideal were to be reached, no home in the United States could afford to be without a radio receiving set.

Today the best available statistics indicate that 5,000,000 homes are equipped, and 21,000,000 homes remain to be supplied.

Radio receiving sets of the best reproductive quality should be made available for all, and we hope to make them cheap enough so that all may buy.

The day has gone by when the radio receiving set is a plaything. It must now be an instrument of service.

WEAF Purchased for $1,000,000

The Radio Corporation of America, therefore, is interested, just as the public is, in having the most adequate programs broadcast. It is interested, as the public is, in having them comprehensive and free from discrimination.

Any act of radio transmission which causes the public to feel that the quality of the programs is not the highest, that the use of radio is not the broadest and best use in the public interest, that it is used for political advantage or selfish power, will be detrimental to the public interest in radio, and therefore to the Radio Corporation of America.

To insure, therefore, the development of this great service, the Radio Corporation of America has purchased for one million dollars station WEAF from the American Telephone and Telegraph Company, that company having decided to retire from the broadcasting business.

The Radio Corporation of America will assume active control of that station on November 15.

National Broadcasting Company Organized

The Radio Corporation of America has decided to incorporate that station, which has achieved such a deservedly high reputation for the quality and character of its programs, under the name of the National Broadcasting Company, Inc.

The Purpose of the New Company

The purpose of that company will be to provide the best program available for broadcasting in the United States.

The National Broadcasting Company will not only broadcast these programs through station WEAF, but it will make them available to other broadcasting stations throughout the country so far as it may be practicable to do so, and they may desire to take them.

It is hoped that arrangements may be made so that every event of national importance may be broadcast widely throughout the United States.

No Monopoly of the Air

The Radio Corporation of America is not in any sense seeking a monopoly of the air. That would be a liability rather than an asset. It is seeking, however, to provide machinery which will insure a national distribution of national programs, and a wider distribution of programs of the highest quality.

If others will engage in this business the Radio Corporation of America will welcome their action, whether it be cooperative or competitive.

If other radio manufacturing companies, competitors of the Radio Corporation of America, wish to use the facilities of the National Broadcasting Company for the purpose of making known to the public their receiving sets, they may do so on the same terms as accorded to other clients.

The necessity of providing adequate broadcasting is apparent. The problem of finding the best means of doing it is yet experimental. The Radio Corporation of America is making this experiment in the interest of the art and the furtherance of the industry.

A Public Advisory Council

In order that the National Broadcasting Company may be advised as to the best type of program, that discrimination may be avoided, that the public may be assured that the broadcasting is being done in the fairest and best way, always allowing for human frailties and human performance, it has created an Advisory Council, composed of twelve members, to be chosen as representative of various shades of public opinion, which will from time to time give it the benefit of their judgment and suggestion. The members of this Council will be announced as soon as their acceptance shall have been obtained.

M. H. Aylesworth to be President

The President of the new National Broadcasting Company will be M. H. Aylesworth, for many years Managing Director of the National Electric Light Association. He will perform the executive and administrative duties of the corporation.

Mr. Aylesworth, while not hitherto identified with the radio industry or broadcasting, has had public experience as Chairman of the Colorado Public Utilities Commission, and, through his work with the association which represents the electrical industry, has a broad understanding of the technical problems which measure the pace of broadcasting.

One of his major responsibilities will be to see that the operations of the National Broadcasting Company reflect enlightened public opinion, which expresses itself so promptly the morning after any error of taste or judgment or departure from fair play.

We have no hesitation in recommending the National Broadcasting Company to the people of the United States.

It will need the help of all listeners. It will make mistakes. If the public will make known its views to the officials of the company from time to time, we are confident that the new broadcasting company will be an instrument of great public service.

RADIO CORPORATION OF AMERICA

OWEN D. YOUNG, *Chairman of the Board*   JAMES G. HARBORD, *President* ations and personnel of Radio Group station WJZ and Telephone Group station WEAF. The following month, RCA absorbed WCAP, Washington, which had been sharing time with RCA's WRC. On September 9, RCA formed a new corporation, the National Broadcasting Company (NBC), with ownership held by RCA (50 percent), GE (30 percent), and Westinghouse (20 percent), naming as president Merlin H. Aylesworth, former managing director of the National Electric Light Association—who did not even own a radio at the time. On November 1, NBC turned over to the Broadcasting Company of America a check for $1,000,000, which consummated the purchase of WEAF, took AT&T out of the broadcasting business, and firmly established NBC. Partly to broaden public interest plans for the network-to-be, and partly for public relations, NBC appointed an advisory council of 12—later 19—distinguished Americans to advise it on programming. This committee, proving to be more valuable for its public relations and publicity contributions than for its real effect on network operations, was disbanded a decade later, without fanfare.

The "permanent" network era of radio broadcasting was inaugurated the night of November 15, 1926, with a program presented live—as were all network programs until the late 1940s— before 1,000 guests in the Grand Ballroom of the Waldorf-Astoria Hotel in New York. Aylesworth was master of ceremonies for the four-hour program, which originated in the ballroom—singers, orchestras, comedy teams—and from *remote* pickups in other cities—a singer in Chicago, Will Rogers from Kansas City. Newspapers reported that this extravaganza cost $50,000 to produce, half for talent and the rest mostly for technical arrangements, but Aylesworth later admitted that most of the talent appeared free in return for the publicity. Twenty-one affiliates and four other stations carried the program, which originated at WEAF and was heard as far west as Kansas City. The stations, most of them independently owned but formerly affiliated with the old AT&T network, were connected by 3,600 miles of special telephone cable.

In the same period, NBC took over operation of RCA's WJZ in New York as the base for a second network, which would incorporate the old Radio Group network. In December the second network was announced, and, on January 1, 1927, it joined the WEAF-based network in a broadcast of Graham McNamee's play-by-play coverage of the Rose Bowl game between Stanford and Alabama (a 7–7 tie). The WJZ-based network's first coast-to-coast hookup had only six affiliates. The WEAF-based chain became known as the Red network, and the WJZ-based chain as the Blue. How this came about is not clear, but some say that AT&T engineers kept the network routings straight on a map by coloring the circuits for one red and the other blue.

A third NBC network was begun in April 1927. The Pacific Coast Network, stretching from Los Angeles to Seattle, was based on stations KGO and KPO in San Francisco, and was primarily organized for sales rather than programming. It lasted only until late 1928, when NBC began fulltime coast-to-coast programming on both Red and Blue, eliminating the need for separate West Coast programming.

In October 1927 headquarters of NBC and operations for both WEAF-Red and WJZ-Blue were moved to new quarters at 711 Fifth Avenue. Eight studios, four of them two stories high, with elaborate sound-proofing, allowed simultaneous broadcasting, recording, and rehearsal. Since the studios were tightly sealed from one another and from their own control rooms, special air conditioning had to be installed.

In May 1930, with the short-lived unification of GE–Westinghouse–RCA interests, RCA took over full control of NBC operations. Two years later RCA gained complete ownership when NBC became one of the corporate entities that it retained after a 1932 antitrust consent decree separated the radio manufacturers' operations. Within five years of its establishment, NBC was planning to move its operations into Radio City, a central building in the new Rockefeller Center complex in midtown New York City. Indeed, this expression of confidence, in the middle of the Depression, caused the name Radio City frequently to be applied to the entire center. The new headquarters in the 70-story RCA Building were occupied late in 1933, combining almost all New York operational facilities of NBC, except the transmitters of the New York stations, using the most up-to-date equipment.

By 1933, NBC owned 10 stations outright, seven using 50,000 watts and all but one licensed for unlimited time operation. There were two stations each in the cities of New York (WEAF, later known as WRCA and now WNBC; and WJZ, later WABC), Chicago (WMAQ and WENR), San Francisco (KPO and KGO), and Washington (WRC and WMAL) plus one station each in Denver (KOA, later sold) and Cleveland (WTAM, later WKYC). In a city with two owned-and-operated (O & O) stations, one would be affiliated with the Red Network, the other with the Blue. Besides their O & O stations, the networks had affiliations with many independently owned stations, some of which contracted (affiliated) with one of the two networks and some of which joined either network for a particular broadcast depending on

demand from the advertisers, the network, or the station. In 1927, 22 stations were affiliated with the Red Network, and 6 with the Blue, for a total of nearly 7 percent of all stations. By 1933, Red had 28, Blue had 24, and 36 were supplemental; these 88 stations constituted nearly 15 percent of all stations at that time. Although the two networks were of similar size in 1933, NBC-Red had the pick of stations and programs, and far more advertising income (see Appendix C, table 2). Having two affiliates in each of most large cities also gave NBC an advantage over independent stations and competitive networks. By programming one affiliate against the other and by engaging in competitive price cutting that few independent stations could afford, NBC developed a strong lead in the industry—a role that became the focus of an important investigation a few years later (see 5.3 and 5.83).

4•32   CBS Develops

The birth of NBC's major competitor, the Columbia Broadcasting System, Inc., was far more complicated and drawn out. It probably began at the fourth convention of the National Association of Broadcasters in September 1926 when promoter George A. Coats, speaking before 25 to 30 delegates, called for a broadcasting program bureau as a way of lessening the industry's reliance on ASCAP music (see 3.83). Within a month—which also saw the announcement of NBC—one of the audience, Arthur Judson (who died at ninety-three early in 1975) had organized the Judson Radio Program Corporation in New York. As business manager of the Philadelphia Orchestra, and with good contacts throughout the entertainment field, he hoped to sell cooperative booking of talent to the NBC networks. But NBC turned him down, and Judson considered establishing a rival radio network.

Late in January 1927, when both NBC networks were operating, Judson and three other stockholders, including Coats, formed the rival United Independent Broadcasters, Inc. Like NBC, the company's purpose was to purchase time on radio stations, sell time to advertisers, and provide programming. Coats and another stockholder accomplished the first aim when they negotiated with Dr. Leon Levy, owner of WCAU in Philadelphia, a weekly price of $500 for 10 hours of station time. Soon, they had 12 prospective affiliates—with WOR, which covered the New York area from its Newark, New Jersey, location, as the key station—at a total commitment of $6,000 a week in time charges alone. The network had no income as yet, and no figures for the costs of AT&T-supplied wire connections and programming material. The shaky condition of this "paper network" led AT&T to deny line service to UIB for fear that it would be unable to pay its bills.

Now came a series of providential rescues. A rumor was flying in the phonograph industry that RCA was going to merge with the major recording firm Victor Talking Machine Company, then in desperate straits because of obsolescent technology and radio competition. (The two firms did merge early in 1929.) Hearing the rumor, Victor's chief competitor, the Columbia Phonograph Corporation, became interested in a possible merger with UIB. This situation was analogous to the financial "raid" on Western Union in the late 1870s involving the National Bell Telephone Company (now AT&T) as a means of exerting pressure (see 1.43). The scenario in 1927 was different. UIB, with 16 signed-up stations, now had commitments of $8,000 a week just for time. On April 5, 1927, the record company and UIB

merged their resources, while retaining separate corporate identities, and created the Columbia Phonograph Broadcasting System, Inc. The agreement gave the network $163,000 in cash to start operations. In return, the record firm gained some operational control over the radio network, stealing a march on its rival, and the station-network identification title, which it hoped would sell phonographs and records.

During the summer, CPBS secured AT&T line service and finally, after nearly a year of gestation and several postponed opening dates, went on the air September 25, 1927, with a broadcast from the Metropolitan Opera of *The King's Henchman*, with the composer-critic Deems Taylor as narrator. The network's problems were reflected in the debut program, which, besides its postponements, was afflicted halfway through by a violent thunderstorm, adding electrical static to financial concern. The Judson Radio Program Corporation, which had retained that part of the business, was supposed to provide programs, and UIB had to pay stations for time, whether or not there was a sponsor to cover costs. After losing $100,000 in the first month, the record company opted out of the merger, and again the fledgling network seemed to have reached the end of its string.

Arthur Judson went to WCAU owner Levy to seek a way out. Levy and his brother, in turn, while purchasing some shares, persuaded millionaire sportsman Jerome H. Louchheim to buy control of UIB, in spite of a negative reaction from Louchheim's lawyer. With the added funds, UIB was able to guarantee payments to the telephone company for several months. On November 19, Columbia Phonograph Broadcasting System became plain Columbia Broadcasting System, with UIB and CBS briefly existing side-by-side for the purpose of operating a radio network. One of UIB's key officials, pioneer announcer J. Andrew White, even persuaded the affiliate stations to take a lower weekly guarantee for their 10 hours in order to give CBS a chance.

However, CBS losses continued as advertisers flocked to the increasingly successful NBC. Louchheim and the Levys advanced money as it was needed for operation, and more shares of stock were issued to Louchheim and the Levys to cover their advances. After a couple of months with the network, the new backers got cold feet and offered the controlling interest in CBS-UIB for sale.

A purchaser was already on the scene. In one of its first time sales, CBS had contracted with the Congress Cigar Company of Philadelphia, through the latter's young vice president, William S. Paley, son of the firm's owner, for a series of 26 programs to advertise La Palina cigars. The show started in 1928, and in short order there were highly satisfactory results. On September 28, 1928, Paley, with his own money and money from his family, bought a controlling interest in CBS for approximately $300,000. He planned to take a six-month leave of absence from the cigar company, get CBS-UIB in better shape, and then go back to selling cigars. He changed his mind in only three weeks —and ran CBS for nearly half a century, stepping down as chief executive only in the spring of 1977. Additional family investments, including $400,000 for flagship station WABC (now WCBS) in New York in December 1929, brought the total to $1.5 million, but Paley created a business worth hundreds of times what his family paid for it, largely through his ability as a negotiator, first with affiliates and then with the stars that made CBS programming famous (see 5.3 and 7.61).

Paley's first change was to merge the two existing networks into one—Columbia Broadcasting System, Inc. He increased the amount of outstanding stock and sold it to get badly needed liquid reserves. Station contracts were changed in March 1929 so that the network paid stations $50 for each hour actually used rather than $500 a week for ten hours regardless of the time used, and the stations paid the network for sustaining (nonsponsored) programs provided—which they often sold to local sponsors. This way, it was felt, both stations and network would be lowering their financial sights until the operation was on its feet. Paley retained Judson and White as program advisers.

CBS achieved permanent status in September 1929, just a year after Paley had taken over, when it moved into the top ten floors of 485 Madison Avenue, where it remained until the mid-1960s. Another sure sign of success was the increasing number of its affiliated stations from 17 (4 percent of all stations) in 1928 to 91 (nearly 16 percent of all stations) in 1933 (see Appendix C, table 2).

The CBS network, like both NBC networks, depended on its stable of O & O stations for major and predictable income. By 1933 CBS owned seven stations, one each in New York (WABC, later named WCBS), Washington (WJSV, later sold), Cincinnati (WKRC, later sold), Chicago (WBBM), Charlotte, North Carolina (WBT, later sold), Minneapolis (WCCO, later sold), and St. Louis (KMOX). All these stations operated unlimited time and were broadcasting with 50,000 watts of power by the early 1930s.

4·4   The Decline of Educational AM Radio

Although educational AM stations had proliferated in the early 1920s to more than 200, almost all of them had left the air by the end of the decade. Their problems began in 1925, mainly because of financial pressures on the schools, increasing greatly during the Depression, school administrators' indecision and lack of purpose and interest, and share-time commercial broadcasters' efforts to gain air time and stifle competition for listeners. Under this load, educational stations dropped out at an increasing rate after 1926. An added factor was the cost of providing programming and making major technical improvements in order to meet the FRC requirements of 1927–1928 (see 4.81). Some educational stations were sold to commercial interests that promised to air educational programs, a few converted to commercial operation, and most simply went off the air. Even with a handful of new stations in the 1926–1933 period, particularly in 1927 and 1928, the number of operating educational standard broadcast stations dropped steadily from 98 in 1927 (approximately 13 percent of all stations) to 43 in 1933 (about 7 percent).

Since the possible benefits from using radio as a teacher were not recognized at first, preference being given to traditional teaching methods, money went in other budgetary directions, particularly because there were not enough trained and interested personnel and support from college and university administrations. Besides the high costs of revising facilities to meet FRC technical standards, the FRC's 1927–1929 reallocations and elimination of marginal stations (see 4.82) often gave channels to commercial operators at the expense of educational institutions. Commercial stations had more lobbying clout and, in many cases, appeared to be more stable. Commercial stations sometimes promised regular free time to educational institutions if the school's educational station would go off the air—and then

dropped the educational programming once they were in control.

Concern for their dwindling numbers and interest in new ways of using radio effectively led radio educators to the formation of national groups. In mid-1929, the Advisory Committee on Education by Radio was formed with backing from the Payne Fund, the Carnegie Endowment, and J.C. Penney, but it died before 1930 without having had much effect. In 1930, two rival organizations appeared that would represent educational radio for ten years: the National Advisory Council on Radio in Education and the National Committee on Education by Radio. The *Council* worked with grants from the Rockefeller Foundation and Carnegie Endowment and called for time on commercial stations to meet educators' needs. The *Committee,* with support from the Payne Fund, asked that nonprofit educational operations fill 15 percent of all station assignments—more than twice the number then on the air—attacked "commercial monopolies," and disagreed with the "halfway" measures of the Council.

The controversy over educational radio's predicament led, in 1932, to a Senate-mandated survey of educational programs on both commercial and noncommercial stations. Having carefully timed their survey for National Education Week, when commercial stations typically scheduled educational programs, the FRC found that commercial stations were adequately filling educational needs. Congress was not yet convinced (see 5.4), and 12 of the few remaining educational stations began in 1933 to take advertising to meet costs and cover ASCAP music licensing fees.

Although the future for educational stations looked bleak, radio still performed a number of educational functions. Beginning in early 1929, the Payne Fund supported daily *Ohio School of the Air* broadcasts on commercial station WLW for in-school listening. The Ohio state legislature appropriated money for some production—in the studios of WOSU, Ohio State University's station—of this series of instructional programs with related teacher guides and pupil materials, which was later carried over WOSU. Another early educational series for below-college classroom listening was the *Wisconsin School of the Air*, which began on university-owned WHA in fall 1931. WHA started a *College of the Air* two years later. The national commercial networks also regularly scheduled some educational programs.

During the years 1927–1933, the heyday of educational radio ended and the few remaining stations began a period of limited experimentation. Many educators, acutely aware of their lost opportunities, searched for other broadcast outlets, debated the issue nationally, and scrambled for local funds and facilities. Despite problems of money and policy, educational radio's champions kept a foothold in American broadcasting.

4·5   Depression Radio Advertising

In the Depression, and partly because of it, advertising became the accepted means of support for radio stations and the expanding networks. Advertisers turned to radio even while retrenching in other media purchases, because radio's audience grew larger and more loyal as it had less money for other leisure-time pursuits. Large stations and the networks began to make appreciable profits, paving the way for new programs and more promotion.

4·51   *Advertising Becomes King*

Radio became an accepted medium of mass advertising in 1928 because:

(1) coast-to-coast network coverage made programs available to 80 percent of the nation's homes, although only 30 percent of them had receivers; (2) far less mutual interference and reduced time-sharing made listening more enjoyable; (3) better and less expensive radio receivers led to larger audiences; (4) the first scientific radio listener research was underway; (5) potential advertisers recognized radio's commercial role and value as a result of successful campaigns; (6) major national advertising agencies showed increasing interest in radio; and (7) the public accepted advertising on networks in 1927–1928. NBC had nearly forty sponsors that year, as CBS was struggling with four, but the following year their combined total was sixty-five. Many stations were still losing money, but the pattern was set and favorable.

The Depression pushed down many of the last barriers to *direct* advertising. Advertising had begun on radio as a genteel sales message broadcast in "business" (daytime) hours, with no hard sell or mention of price. Under the pressures of a Depression economy stations began to accept more and longer ads—including some fifteen- and thirty-minute "programs" of advertising content—harder selling ads, and even barter ads, whereby stations traded time for hard goods they could use. Advertising spread to all hours of the broadcast day, and evening *prime time* hours with the most listeners commanded the highest prices.

Broadcast advertising, both on and off the networks, became so complex that a number of middleman institutions evolved for the mutual benefit of sponsors and radio stations or networks. First were advertising agencies, which typically had considered radio a fad in the early 1920s before radio carried much advertising. One 998-page book on advertising published in 1923 dismissed radio broadcasting in two sentences: "The development of radio broadcasting is presenting another possibility of mass communication which probably will be utilized for advertising purposes. It is too early to predict what its possibilities may be or how successfully it may be used."* With national programs on major networks becoming more complicated to produce, and more expensive, the axiom of "he who pays the piper calls the tune" came into full operation. First, agencies merely purchased air time for their sponsor clients, and stations or networks continued to develop programs. Soon, however, some agencies engaged in production in an attempt to create a profitable *package* of program and advertising pleasing to the sponsor. The networks concurred. Without having to worry about either production or pleasing the sponsor, they reaped their normal income by simply providing air time for the finished product. By 1931–1932, the agencies had taken on program selection, casting, direction, and other production aspects on networks and a few larger stations, frequently renting studios from the former. In smaller markets and stations, apart from the influence of network programs supplied to affiliates, the agency role was restricted pretty much to purchase of time and placing of sponsor ads.

Except for network advertising, purchasing time on stations across the nation was difficult and time-consuming. Few local stations could afford to have full-time representatives in New York and other big cities where advertisers and advertising agencies were located. Hence, they took to hiring a firm to represent them and paid it a commission—nominally 15 percent of the involved time sales, after the 15 percent advertising agency commission

had been deducted—on national advertiser time or spot sales. The first true station representative (rep) firm, Edward Petry & Co., was formed early in 1932 to help local stations sell time in the major cities. Before that, most rep firms were brokers for sponsors, by playing off one station against another. (Advertising agencies also originally were brokers, which accounts for their income typically coming from commissions paid by the media rather than fees paid by the sponsor.) The new type of rep firm would represent only one station in a market and "sell" it to a sponsor through its agency. Station reps existed to serve their media clients, not the sponsor. This practice gave important individual stations more national and regional advertising business, since sponsors' agencies and stations' reps bought and sold station time with the idea of getting the widest coverage for a product message—sometimes with programs, sometimes with spot advertising—without having to concern themselves with programs. Of little importance at first, station reps had an increasing financial impact later in the decade.

Broadcast advertising was becoming more sophisticated. By the early 1930s, an advertiser could prerecord messages on electrical transcriptions and mail them to many stations, often for simultaneous use. Even though the networks stuck to their ban on recordings in either program or advertising material, the volume of broadcast advertising increased. Advertising copy became more versatile as agency copywriters vied with one another for the best approach for a given client. Sometimes agencies turned to research for ideas and answers, but other times the sponsor—or his wife—made decisions by intuition.

According to McCann-Erickson data, radio advertising volume climbed from about 2 percent ($20 million) of ad-

*Daniel Starch, *Principles of Advertising*. Chicago: A. W. Shaw, 1923, p. 866.

vertising expenditures in 1928 to nearly 11 percent ($75 million) in 1932 (see Appendix C, table 4). Even though the deepening Depression caused an advertising decline of $10 million a year later, this reduced the volume by only half a percentage point. Radio had obviously become an important element of the advertising "mix," and much of this gain was at the expense of newspapers and magazines.

In 1932, an FRC study of advertising time found that, overall, 36 percent of air time had commercial sponsorship—and 78 percent of that was local advertising—leaving 64 percent unsponsored or *sustaining*; that is, the station or network sustained the program's production and time costs. This pattern varied little by station

size or power. Sustaining time was slightly more prevalent before 6 P.M., mainly because radio was only just beginning to offer regular daytime programs.

4·52   Network-Station Economics

The table below indicates that network broadcast advertising expanded sharply in the 1927–1930 period. By 1932, the Depression was causing the networks either to hold their own or decline in most categories of advertising. Since less commercial time was supporting a larger number of sustaining hours, the amount of time sold was crucial to the entire medium.

Network management originally

The Economics of Network Advertising: The First Six Years / The following figures show the expansion of national advertising on CBS and the NBC-Red and -Blue networks combined.

Year	Money Expended for Time on All Networks		Commercial Time as Percentage Total Hours Broadcast		Net Pretax Income of All Networks	
	$	% Increase	%	% Increase	NBC Red and Blue	CBS
1927	$ 3,832,150	—	20.5	—	$(464,400)	$(220,100)
1928	10,252,497	167.5	27.7	35.1	427,200	(179,400)
1929	19,729,571	80.6	24.7	(10.8)	798,200	474,200
1930	26,819,156	43.2	29.2	18.2	2,167,500	985,400
1931	35,787,299	33.5	36.5	25.0	2,663,200	2,674,200
1932	39,106,776	9.3	25.5	(30.1)	1,163,300	1,888,100

Sources: First four columns from Herman S. Hettinger, *A Decade of Radio Advertising* (Chicago: University of Chicago Press, 1933), Tables 19, 20, and 23 on pages 113–118; last two columns from FCC, *Report on Chain Broadcasting* (Washington: Government Printing Office, 1941), pages 17, 24. Data for 1927 in last two columns includes two months of 1926 for NBC but only eight months of 1927 for CBS. Figures in last two columns rounded to nearest 100. Data in parenthesis indicates loss.

thought—or at least said—that they would not make money. NBC President Aylesworth expressed this belief to a Senate committee in 1927, but one year later the network made a half-million-dollar net profit. CBS had a rockier start, offering no effective competition for nearly two years to the two NBC chains, with their 75 stations. As shown in the table, however, all three chains, especially because of their O & O stations, soon began to make healthy profits.

In 1932 and 1933 the newer CBS surpassed NBC, in number of stations and income, before they resumed a rough parity. RCA and NBC officials claimed that this income discrepancy was due partly to NBC's providing public service programs, which were typically sustaining, while CBS made money on sponsored entertainment programming. This position was not supported by the facts; all three networks produced many public service programs. The networks' Depression-caused income decline after 1931 occurred when businesses that were losing money pared advertising expenditures as an initial economy. Surprisingly enough, radio increased its income during the first two years of the Depression. The fact that it was "free" once the set was bought created a large audience. This audience, supplied to advertisers at a small price per thousand, created such a tempting market that they stuck with radio as long as they could, particularly for high volume–low unit cost merchandise or services.

Local stations suffered more. Many faced business communities buttoning down for the Depression and showing little interest in a new advertising medium. Potential advertisers often waited to see results and gain experience from network advertising, agencies were just starting to get interested in radio, and reps were a new business. At the same time, though,

an increasing flow of books, articles, and talks on how best to advertise on radio persuaded many advertisers to take the initial plunge during this period.

Gross receipts varied from a few hundred dollars per station to more than $1.5 million, for an industry total of $18.5 million. Networks earned another $37.5 million, giving radio broadcasting a total income of nearly $56 million in 1931. However, the industry spent more than it earned by several hundred thousand dollars. Of the 513 stations reporting to the FRC for 1931, 333 reported a profit ranging from $14 to $376,000 while the remaining 180 stations were in the red, with losses ranging from $22.50 to $178,000 for a firm operating two stations. Radio was making and spending a lot of money; networks and their O & O stations accounted for half and all other stations for the other half. Income had risen rapidly from less than $5 million in 1927 to nearly $56 million just four years later, thanks to the formation of three networks and acceptance of advertising by the business community and the listening audience. More than six thousand persons worked in radio stations and networks in 1930–1931.

4·6 Developing Program Diversity

In 1928, radio offered more features, less education, more plays (up to 4.2 percent), and fewer children's programs than in 1925 (see 3.6), but generally the time devoted to particular types of programs remained proportionately similar for years. A 1928 study of 100 stations in the western United States by Federal Radio Commissioner Harold Lafount showed that the average station was on the air 54 hours a week, with 1 hour of network programs, 25 hours of studio programs, 7 hours— only 13 percent—of "mechanical" (records and electrical transcriptions) programs, 4 hours of orchestras from remote locations, 8 hours of religion, 5 hours of education and lectures other than on farm subjects, 3 hours of farm reports, talks, and so forth, and 1 hour of weather and stock reports.

Although music remained the mainstay of both networks and independent stations, programming on radio after 1927 developed two distinct types: network, usually more lavish and diversified, and local, mainly music and sometimes recorded. The majority of programs were sustaining throughout the 1927–1933 period. In 1926–1927, the first season of formally organized networks, more minutes of a sample January 1927 week were devoted to concert music (585) than to musical variety and light music (570). All other programming together—general variety, news and commentary, religious, homemaker and miscellaneous talk programs—occupied only 420 minutes a week. In other words, the two NBC networks—CBS was not yet on the air (see 4.32)—programmed only 26 hours a week, or about three and one-half hours per day.

Like individual stations before them, networks programmed at first only in the evening hours. As the supply of sets, programming, the interest of advertisers, and the demands of affiliated stations increased, they added daytime hours, pretty much filling them by 1933. In the process of expansion, most major network program types made their appearance (see Appendix C, table 6).

4•61   *Variety*

Heavily sponsored from the start, radio variety programs grew in number and importance throughout the 1926–1933 period. The so-called *general variety* show, a sort of magazine of entertainment, was

first programmed in 1926–1927 and reached daytime schedules as early as 1929–1930. "Radio's first really professional variety show," which started in October 1929, was the Fleischmann Yeast program, featuring the young crooner Rudy Vallee. Popular from the start, it remained with the same sponsor for a decade. Hillbilly and country-western variety also started early, with *Dutch Masters Minstrels* appearing in 1928–1929 and the even more famous *National Barn Dance* reaching a national audience late in 1933. This type of programming, which had begun earlier on local stations in the South, soon became popular all over the country through network distribution. Combination orchestra and talk formats, or *semivariety*, appeared in the 1930–1931 season. Newspaper entertainment columnist Ed Sullivan, whose subsequent television variety program ran for more than two decades, made his first broadcast series appearance in the 1931–1932 season.

Also popular were *comedy variety* programs, usually composed of a comedian or comedy team with a backup orchestra. On NBC's first season, Smith Brothers cough drops made use of their famous two faces trademark with a comedy team named "Trade and Mark," backed by an orchestra. Reflecting the social standards of that period, *Majestic Theater: Two Black Crows* featured two white actors playing Negroes and was very popular in the 1928–1929 season and for several years thereafter. In 1931–1932, one of the early big stars, "Banjo Eyes" Eddie Cantor, began a comedy-variety series that drew high ratings for more than ten years. The next season saw a parade to the network microphones of soon-to-be-famous radio comedians, many of whom were former vaudevillians. Al Jolson, famous as the singer in the early Hollywood talkie *The Jazz Singer*; George Burns and Gracie Allen, a husband and wife team; Ed Wynn, fresh from *The Perfect Fool* on Broadway; Jack Benny; Fred Allen, who was to maintain a fake feud with Benny for years; the Marx Brothers, best known for their movies; and Jack Pearl, who created on radio the German tall-tale teller, Baron Munchausen—all appeared in their own network shows for the first time that year. Most of these comedians lasted on radio for a decade or more, Burns and Allen and Benny each for more than thirty years on radio and then television. Each added his or her own bit to radio's traditions; Wynn's program, for instance, introduced studio audiences to provide reaction to liven the program (see 3.65) and distract Wynn from the frightening microphone. Comedy shows all had orchestras and typically used "second bananas" (a burlesque term) or "sidekick" foils (or "straight men") but relied most heavily on comedy sketches and monologues.

Local stations also depended on variety programming, although it was usually sustaining. As vaudeville tours played to dwindling paying audiences and stalled all over the country, many troupes turned to local radio for short-term employment. Some performers left the traveling circuit altogether and began to work in radio, full time if possible, although pay often was only food and shelter. On many stations local talent was even cheaper, as anyone with any musical or comedy accomplishment was invited on the air just to fill time. One such early starter was

---

An Evening's Network Programming: 1930 /
These are evening schedules for WEAF (NBC-Red's flagship station) and WABC (the key CBS station), both in New York. Blank time periods indicate that the previous program continues. Programs with an asterisk are sustaining (not sponsored). Naturally, programs would vary from night to night.

Tuesday, November 4, 1930

	WEAF	WABC
6:00	*Black and Gold Room Orchestra	*Harry Tucker and his Barclay Orchestra
6:30	*Who's Behind the Name?	*Crockett Mountaineers
6:45	*Black and Gold Room Orchestra	*Tony's Scrap Book
7:00	Air Scoops with Elinor Smith (Daggett & Ramsdell Co.)	*Columbia Educational Features
7:15	*Laws that Safeguard Society	Westchester County Salon Orchestra (Westchester Realty Board)
7:30	Soconyland Sketches (Standard Oil Co. of New York)	Wise Shoe Program (Wise Shoes, Inc.)
7:45		*The Early Book Worm— (Alexander Woolcott)
8:00	*Troika Bells	Blackstone Program (Waitt & Bond, Inc.)
8:15	*Snoop & Peep	
8:30	Florsheim Frolic (Florsheim Shoe Co.)	Kaltenborn Edits the News (S. W. Straus & Co.)
8:45		Premier Salad Dressers (Francis H. Leggett & Co.)
9:00	Eveready Program (National Carbon Co., Inc.)	Henry and George (Consolidated Cigar Co.)
9:30	Happy Wonder Bakers (Continental Baking Corp.)	Philco Symphony Concert (Philadelphia Storage Battery Co.)
10:00	Enna Jettick Songbird (Dunn & McCarthy Go.)	Graybar's Mr. and Mrs. (Graybar Electric Co.)
10:15	B. A. Rolfe and his Lucky Strike Dance Orchestra (American Tobacco Co.)	Paramount-Publix Radio Playhouse (Paramount-Publix Corp.)
11:00	*Mystery House	*Will Osborne and his Orchestra
11:15		*Columbia's Radio Column
11:30	*Vincent Lopez and his Hotel St. Regis Orchestra	*Mickey Alpert and his Orchestra from Boston
12:00	*Duke Ellington and his Cotton Club Orchestra	*Asbury Park Casino Orchestra
12:30	Jack Albin and his Hotel Pennsylvania Orchestra	*Nocturne—Ann Leaf at the Organ

Sustaining program

Source: "Radio Advertising," *Fortune* (December 1930), page 113. Courtesy of Fortune Magazine.

(Arthur) "Red" Godfrey, known in Baltimore radio as the "warbling banjoist," who was later to find great success in radio and television. Formats generally were informal, although some stations tried to create low-cost versions of well-known network shows.

4•62   Music

Music programs were the most important content of networks and local stations in respect to hours aired per week. As with variety programs, there were several types, but the usual program was built around an orchestra or a singer specializing in popular or light classical music. These programs usually had sponsors from the start and, as early as 1926–1927, many bore the sponsor's name in the title as in *Cliquot Club Eskimos* and *Michelin Tiremen*. Some performers sang under "house names," but the audience soon recognized such voices as that of the mysterious "Silver Masked Tenor," Joseph M. White, of the Goodrich Silvertown Orchestra, who never sang without his mask.

At first, orchestras alone were most popular in network music programming, but after 1930 the audience apparently began to prefer light musical variety programs. These were variety shows built around singers or orchestras rather than masters of ceremony or comedians. Most ran 15 or 30 minutes, and some were used as sustaining filler between sponsored shows. Falling in this category were the vaudeville-derived song and patter teams discussed in 3.62 and the early radio appearances of famous crooner Bing Crosby in 1931.

Sponsors sought and gained prestige through broadcast concert music. The Atwater Kent Sunday evening music hours began on the old AT&T network in 1925 and stayed with NBC for several years. The Boston Symphony Orchestra, Chicago Civic Opera, and National Symphony Orchestra joined another half-dozen concert orchestras in the first (1926–1927) network season. The New York Philharmonic, conducted by Arturo Toscanini, who later conducted NBC's own symphony orchestra, made its first radio broadcasts in fall 1927—a year that saw some 20 "concert music" programs. Until the late 1940s the networks always scheduled at least 20 such programs, usually sponsored by prestigious firms. (As television came in during the early 1950s, the number of concert music programs dropped slightly but rose again later, although mostly for sustaining programs, until network radio essentially ceased to exist.) One program that still goes on is the Saturday afternoon broadcast of the Metropolitan Opera, which started in the fall of 1931. Announcer Milton Cross (see 3.6) gave the commentary on these broadcasts from their start until his death in 1974. Many other concert music programs had large audiences and long life: NBC's *Music Appreciation Hour*, with noted conductor Walter Damrosch as host, became an educational hit over the Blue network during Friday morning school hours after 1928; and the Mormon Tabernacle Choir broadcast live from Salt Lake City weekly for more than 50 years.

As local station schedules expanded to 12- and 18-hour broadcast days in larger cities, music became increasingly important. Music of all kinds comprised 50 to 60 percent of most schedules, with popular and semiclassical works predominating. The specific sound varied tremendously, depending on local talent, audience composition, competition on the air, and network affiliation, if any. Musical programs were nearly always live, with orchestras and soloists playing in studios or at remote pickup locations. The still strong anti-record stigma on the networks some-times filtered down to local stations (see 3.8).

Although announcers of musical programs sometimes performed so well that they became radio personalities, some listeners found commercials and talk annoying. In 1928–1929 a Chicago firm attempted to overcome these drawbacks to radio music, which most listeners preferred to the home phonograph, by providing a musical service over telephone lines for a fee—a throwback to the Puskás brothers' service in Budapest (see 2.5).

4•63   Drama

Of all radio program types, drama had the slowest start; broadcasting theater to an unseeing audience was difficult for both actors and audience. The initial efforts were light "homey or love interest" half-hour shows, leading in a few years to the women's serial. The first of these, in late 1929, was the ethnic, immensely popular *Rise of the Goldbergs*, written by Gertrude Berg, who also starred as "Molly," as even her friends came to call her over the years. This program, built around the doings of an urban Jewish family, helped establish the idea of a continuing cast in a different situation each week. *Vic and Sade* was another superbly written popular program, lasting from 1932 to 1945. An increasing number of these light programs originated from Chicago. The first program from the West Coast was the supremely popular *One Man's Family*, which originated in San Francisco in April 1932. Serial drama established a daytime standard of several 15-minute programs—three at first, five later—a week in 1932–1933. By spring 1933, daytime *soap opera*—so called because of the soap company sponsorship common to the genre—included long-lived

The Romance of Helen Trent and *Ma Perkins*. All these, written by a handful of writers, would have long runs, *Ma Perkins* until 1960, and were the prelude to a flood. The soap opera was a true serial, with stories slowly unfolding day after day, over years.

Comedy drama usually presented standard characters getting into and out of various situations week after week, each episode being complete in itself. The first and most famous, however, began as a two-character dialogue. Freeman F. Gosden and Charles J. Correll, who had started together in vaudeville, created a blackface routine in return for free meals from a small station in a Chicago hotel. The *Chicago Tribune*'s station, WGN, then hired the pair for nearly 600 episodes of their *Sam 'n' Henry* act over the next two years. With success came an unsuccessful demand by the performers for more money, and Gosden and Correll moved to WMAQ. When WGN refused to release the program name to a competitor, the performers had to come up with a new one. Thus, *Amos 'n' Andy* came into being, with the two vaudevillians playing all the parts in an increasingly complicated series built around the Freshair Taxicab Company and the fraternal lodge Mystic Knights of the Sea. Although the program was carefully scripted, with even the pronunciation written in, it usually was aired without rehearsal in order to maintain spontaneity. Five-minute bits on 78-rpm records were both officially and unofficially syndicated to smaller stations. The whole show went to NBC-Blue in summer 1929 for a reputed $100,000 a year for the team. It was well worth it. *Amos 'n' Andy* quickly became a craze and then an institution. Almost everyone tuned in five, and later six, nights a week, and movie theaters were known to interrupt films for 15 minutes so that the audience could hear the evening's episode. While blacks would find the dia-

Types of Programs Broadcast in 1932 / Shown below are the program types broadcast by nine major-market radio stations (four in New York, four in Chicago, and one in Kansas City) in a two-week period in February. When compared to 1925 data, there have been declines in music and "other" categories and an increase in drama and other entertainment (see table on page 73). Compare this also with Appendix C, table 6, to see what the networks were programming in 1932, and with p. 276 for 1946 station programming.

Program Type and Subtypes	Percentage of Time
Music	**64.1%**
Dance	23.5%
Vocal	13.0
Combination	3.6
Concert orchestras	8.4
Soloists	4.5
Phonograph records	3.2
String ensembles	3.3
Sacred	.6
Miscellaneous	4.0
Drama	**6.5**
Continued plays, reading, etc.	2.0
Sketches	3.3
Onetime plays	1.2
Other Entertainment	**13.3**
Women's	4.9
Children's	3.5
Feature	4.0
Star (other than music)	.9
Information	**12.1**
Education	7.2
News	1.2
Political	1.4
Market reports	.5
Weather	.1
Sports	1.7
Other	**4.0**
Foreign-originated	.5
Health exercises	.6
Church services	2.2
Miscellaneous	.7
Total	**100.0%**

Source: William Albig, *Modern Public Opinion* (New York: McGraw-Hill, 1956), Table 20, page 447. By permission.

logue insulting today, a large number, as well as the country's white majority, enjoyed it in its time. Many suggest that this program helped more than any other to sell radio to advertisers and the public alike. Other comedy programs came and went, but *Amos 'n' Andy* remained popular for many years.

Thriller drama—action, western, crime, and suspense—began about the same time. The first was *Empire Builders*, a semi-informative show sponsored by a railroad and heard only in the Midwest in its first (1928–1929) season. In 1930, the western came to radio with *Death Valley Days*, an anthology of tales introduced by a host, which retained its format in television a quarter-century later. In 1931, the crime program began with *Sherlock Holmes*, which remained on network radio for many years with different casts, straying far from the Arthur Conan Doyle original. The classic crime drama was *The Shadow*, whose chief character, Lamont Cranston—played at one time by Orson Welles—was a "wealthy young man-about-town" who had a "hypnotic power to cloud men's minds so they cannot see him." The invisible effect was created aurally and psychologically by putting Cranston's voice through a filter that made it sound like a telephone conversation. For two decades a bloodcurdling laugh and the slogan "Crime does not pay . . . the Shadow knows!" identified the Shadow. *Little Orphan Annie*, based on the comic strip, took

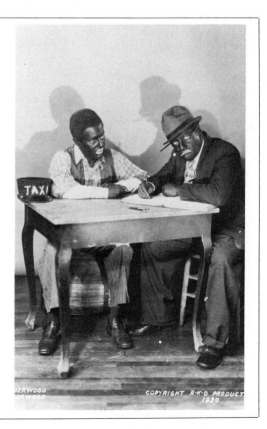

Amos 'n' Andy / Though racist in today's view, this comedy helped to propel network radio into faster and wider acceptance in the late 1920s and early 1930s, with the comic misadventures of two taxi drivers and their friends and relations. Freeman F. Gosden and Charles J. Correll, originators of *Amos 'n' Andy*, were white—but are shown here in blackface. Photo courtesy of National Broadcasting Company, Inc.

to the air in fall 1931, the first of many children's adventure serial programs.

A very different kind of drama began in 1931 when the weekly newsmagazine *Time* created a radio program. Whether the *March of Time* should be classified as drama or news has been a source of argument. Each program contained the three or four most easily dramatized events of the week before, with actors selected to sound as much as possible like the personages they portrayed. In the late 1930s, pressure from the White House forced the removal of a sound-alike for President Roosevelt. The program's signature, announcer Westbrook Van Voorhis's impressive vocal "Time . . . marches on!" became a catch phrase.

Drama was rare on local stations, because of the costs of good talent and production, but some stations tried amateur dramatic presentations and a few became known nationally for their dramatic programs. For example, WXYZ in Detroit rapidly built a following with *The Lone Ranger*, a western program mainly for children, which started in 1933. The program soon became a factor in the formation of the Mutual network (see 5.3). Local stations offered other dramatic programs by means of *syndication*, whereby one station or studio produced a program series and then sold or rented recordings of it to local stations elsewhere. This procedure permitted stations in smaller and more remote towns to have professional drama without network dependency. The opposite also occurred, with local acts eventually receiving national exposure through syndication. For example, a comedy team known as "Smackouts" began with small bits on the air in Chicago, graduated to the network level *National Farm and Home Hour*, and later achieved national success with a family show of their own as *Fibber McGee and Molly*.

4·64   News

Prior to 1930, the public could hear Frederick William Wile, David Lawrence, and H. V. Kaltenborn in separate once-a-week news commentaries and expect radio to inform it in times of high public interest or tension. This was demonstrated by the attention listeners gave to bulletins that were issued on Charles Lindbergh's solo airplane flight across the Atlantic. But regular *hard news* broadcasting, as it is known today, did not exist until Lowell Thomas began a 15-minute newscast five times a week on NBC-Blue in fall 1930—which was aired until early in 1976. Kaltenborn soon switched to three times a week, and in 1932 Boake Carter and Edwin C. Hill adopted similar 15-minute formats. The networks had no daytime newscasts during this period.

In its coverage of the Lindbergh baby kidnaping in 1932, radio showed a new responsibility. The networks scrapped evening schedules for several days to bring details—although NBC had waited a day, thinking the news too sensational for even brief bulletins. The positive audience reaction to such occasional reporting and the regular newscasts made network planners realize that news could be a powerful ingredient in programming. Coverage of the 1932 presidential campaign (see below) strengthened this feeling.

During this period, radio received its hard news mostly from the wire services, Associated Press, United Press, and International News Service, which were controlled by the newspaper industry. The nation's press, already feeling the competition for advertising revenues, became alarmed over radio's small incursions into news reporting. When newspaper pressure made the wire services unavailable to radio, CBS began its own newsgathering, frequently ignoring the copyright law with a copy of a newspaper, scissors, and paste, in mid-1933. Rival NBC tried telephone inquiries, but both the Blue and the Red networks relied primarily on the wire services —when they could get them.

Late in 1933, tension between print and broadcasting came to a head, with the newspapers holding the high hand. Many papers stopped free listings of radio programs, demanding payment for such "advertisements." In a major agreement signed in December at New York's Biltmore Hotel between the newspaper industry and the networks, radio stations were restricted to (1) issuing only two five-minute newscasts per day, at 9:30 A.M. and 9 P.M. or later, to protect both morning and afternoon papers; (2) broadcasting interpretation and comment as opposed to hard news reporting; (3) using news provided by the Press-Radio Bureau, a new service to which the wire services would funnel copy for rewriting in radio style; (4) depending *only* on the new Press-Radio Bureau, stopping their own newsgathering activities, and (5) broadcasting only unsponsored news. Radio had to accept the agreement, since it was a relatively new business supposedly dependent on the wire services controlled by newspapers for hard news and since newspaper ownership of many stations divided the radio industry.

The Press-Radio Bureau came into existence on March 1, 1934, and immediately ran into competition. As only the networks had signed the Biltmore Agreement for radio, many independent stations and affiliates decided to set up separate newsgathering operations not bound by the agreement. Of those established, Transradio Press Service, headed by the former director of the CBS News Service, quickly became the largest.

Within a year, with less than half the radio stations subscribing to the Press-Radio Bureau and its restrictions, the news-paper industry realized it was losing. The directors of commercially based INS and UP—AP was a cooperative, owned by member papers—decided to sell news to radio stations without restriction, if the competition warranted. It did; thus, after about a year, the Biltmore Agreement was effectively dead. Few local stations broadcast hard news programs during the 1926–1933 period although some newspaper-owned outlets gave brief headlines. Radio was primarily for entertainment rather than information, and except for local highlights, most stations let newspapers handle news.

4·65   Election Broadcasting

Radio's election coverage, which dated back at least to 1916, continued to expand. In the 1928 campaign between Republican Herbert Hoover and Democrat Alfred E. Smith, governor of New York, approximately $2 million was spent on radio for national and local candidates, with the Democrats outspending the GOP for national candidates by more than $200,000. The new practice of charging candidates for time—remember, few stations sold time for any purpose in 1924—accounted for much of the rising cost, and the increased use of radio time—especially the one-minute spot announcements pioneered by the Republicans—for the rest. Neither candidate was an ideal radio speaker, but Smith's constantly mispronounced "raddio" was probably most noticeable. On election eve both candidates made one-hour nationwide broadcasts, Hoover from his home in Palo Alto and Smith from New York City. Election night was a network affair, with both NBC and CBS interjecting news reports into special entertainment programming. Most national and local election reports were sustaining.

Four years later, in the midst of the Depression, the incumbent Hoover took on another New York governor, Franklin D. Roosevelt. Although the GOP used nearly twice as much time on national radio as in 1928, the new medium could not change political reality, and F.D.R. soundly beat Hoover. It is estimated that the two parties spent upwards of $5 million on the radio campaigns, with 25 percent going for national hookups. Election night broadcasts resembled those four years earlier, but they began earlier —6 P.M. instead of 8 P.M.—and included analysis as well as returns.

4•66   Other Talk Programs

Various kinds of talk shows filled many hours a week, especially during the day, as network schedules expanded. In these years, only special sports events were covered in play-by-play detail, and some local stations broadcast more than others. From the beginning of network programming, religious programs were prominent, especially multidenominational services and talks. Harry Emerson Fosdick began a long-running Prostestant program, which became *National Vespers* on NBC-Blue in 1929. The *Catholic Hour* appeared a year later. Of a different order, though still professing to be a religious program, were the CBS commentaries of Catholic priest Charles E. Coughlin. Broadcasting from his Shrine of the Little Flower in Royal Oak near Detroit, Michigan, beginning late in 1930, the program grew out of a regional broadcast first aired in 1926. Discussing economics and politics as well as his religious views, the "radio priest" backed Roosevelt fervently until F.D.R. was elected and his policies had crystallized. Then Father Coughlin turned against F.D.R. and became a notorious "rabblerouser" (see 5.64).

Talk programs led the way into daytime programming, with cooking, beauty hints, gossip, and other shows designed for the housewife. The long-running *National Farm and Home Hour*, produced with U.S. Department of Agriculture help, began in fall 1928. *Cheerio*, an inspirational talk show, began a long career the same season. Walter Winchell started his celebrated gossip show on NBC-Blue in 1932.

Both major networks offered educational programs. NBC introduced its *Music Appreciation Hour* (see 4.62) in 1928, and CBS followed in February 1930 with its *American School of the Air*, a sustaining program except for the first three months. Both of these programs aimed at classroom listeners. In 1932 the *American School of the Air* reached some twenty thousand schools with a number of different course offerings each week. The *National Farm and Home Hour* and the *March of Time* were typical of generally educational programs.

Most local stations placed talk programs between musical presentations. Astrologers, children's storytellers, cooking teachers, gossipers, advisers—all found their way to the air. More than 1½ percent of air time was devoted to health exercise programs until 1932. Some stations became famous for a particular talk program —such as the Kansas station that broadcast a "medical question box" (see 4.83) —and some stations offered a particular type of program—such as local sports coverage in towns with college or professional teams, even though there was some fear of radio's effect on gate receipts.

4•7   Audience: Craze to Consequence

Radio's real impact in the 1926–1933 period occurred in the growing radio audience. By 1928–1929 the home radio tinkerer had given way numerically to the family that purchased a ready-made receiver, plugged it in, and listened. By 1933 about two-thirds of the nation's homes had radios (see Appendix C, table 8). Once a mystery and a novelty, radio listening had become the habit of millions.

4•71   The Changing Receiver Market

By 1928 there were about sixty makers of radio broadcast receivers in the country, two of which had one-third of the market, and four of which had two-thirds. In addition to GE and Westinghouse, important independent producers included Atwater Kent, which turned from making automobile ignition systems to building radios in a huge factory in Philadelphia, and Grigsby-Grunow, which built a reputation on its console "Majestic" model, turning out 5,000 sets a day in its Chicago plant in 1929. Stromberg-Carlson turned from telephone equipment to fine, expensive receivers, and Crosley, owner of WLW, Cincinnati, began at the other extreme, making inexpensive receivers that most could afford.

In 1927–1928 the heavy, large, expensive to operate, and inconvenient battery-operated receiver became obsolete, as alternating-current (plug-in) sets became available except in places without power lines. By May 1928 it was estimated that 7½ million of the nearly 12 million radio receivers in use were the "standard" type, with loudspeakers—the others being crystal sets or obsolete one-tube models. The radio audience was reportedly nearly forty million out of a total population of 120 million. Receivers became furniture, the larger loudspeakers sounded better, and prices went up in a boom market, peaking in 1929 at $136 for an average set. The result was overproduction by perhaps a million units. Manufacturers, faced with unloading these sets in the Depression,

dropped prices to below $90 in 1930 and to an average of $47 by 1932. Many makers and retailers went out of business, and others began to produce smaller and cheaper sets including table models.

Competition grew as the Philadelphia Storage Battery Company (Philco), driven out of most of its radio battery business by plug-in circuits, converted quickly to making radio sets and tubes. Tube production was very important, as tubes—costing at least a dollar or two apiece—were sold separately from receivers until the mid-1930s. RCA, because of its patent position, sold perhaps 60 percent of all radio tubes until 1931, when Philco stopped buying from RCA in a fight over specifications and price, and started to make its own. In 1934 Philco had attracted 20 percent of the tube market compared to RCA's 40 percent. But Philco already outshone other radio manufacturers by producing fully one-third of *all* receivers manufactured in the country, having completely converted to the superheterodyne circuit in home and automobile radios. Though the new circuits were more expensive, volume production drove prices down and markets up. In 1933, when the Depression caused lower sales of expensive radios, many makers, notably Crosley and Emerson, made small tube radios to sell for less than $15—an unheard-of price for anything but a crystal set a year or so earlier. Quality suffered, but the audience grew nonetheless. To. a great extent, radio circuits became standardized, and experimentation with new or expensive models decreased. Consoles still were made, but smaller table receivers predominated.

4•72   Development of Audience Research

Little was known about the radio audience except that it was growing. The 1930 U.S. Decennial Census collected information about radio ownership, showing that, while half the urban families in the country had receivers, only 21 percent of rural farm and 34 percent of rural nonfarm families had. Receivers were concentrated in the Northeast, in midwestern cities, and in the Far West. Penetration of radio ranged from New Jersey's high of 63 percent to Mississippi's low of 5 percent of families. Of special interest was the increase in farm listeners, as the spread of electricity to rural areas made fast, direct communication possible for the first time —especially important in a national crisis like the Depression.

The first system of program ratings appeared in 1929, when Archibald M. Crossley (no relation to Powel Crosley, Jr., the WLW owner and set maker) formed the Cooperative Analysis of Broadcasting (CAB) to find out how many persons listened to NBC and CBS programs. This service, which benefited advertising agencies but was paid for largely by networks and stations, was the standard for five years. Crossley researchers would call a preselected sample of homes the morning following the program(s) to be rated and ask whoever answered "who had listened to what" the night before. The rating produced by this technique—a percentage of set-using families listening to one program or network—was applied only to sponsored shows, as the service was established for the Association of National Advertisers. Noting that ratings were costing about forty cents a call, CAB tried a postcard system but got only a 3 to 5 percent response rate. Dividing each day into four parts, CAB then investigated which program was turned on. It found that most people listened to radio at night: fully half the sets were in use at 9 P.M. and 10 P.M., with perhaps a third at 7 P.M. and 11 P.M. —establishing the concept of *prime time*.

Local stations began to conduct audience research under pressure from advertisers who demanded such information before they would purchase time. Most stations were content to solicit reactions to programs and read incoming mail. Others, using FRC-required engineering surveys of their coverage area, simply thought of the population residing within the coverage area as their audience. Under increasing sponsor pressure, they acknowledged that such figures did not reflect actual listenership, and turned to active methods of discovering audience loyalty and interest. Stations variously made free premium offers, to boost audiences and to gauge their size; analyzed set sales figures, to establish the size and approximate location of the potential audience; and mailed questionnaires that sought data on audience size, preferences, and basic demographic characteristics. A few larger stations sent out interviewers to collect the same data. Although costly, personal interviews avoided a sampling bias of telephone interviews: only about half the American homes had telephones in the early 1930s. The stations that interviewed by telephone started using both recall and coincidental—calling when the program was on the air—methods around 1930.

Most broadcasters, however, had too few sponsors and too little money for this kind of effort. Thus, throughout the 1927–1933 period, little was known about radio listeners' reactions. While ratings were affecting network programs, local stations still made programming decisions and placed advertising without much knowledge of their audience.

4•8   Regulating Order out of Chaos

After the 1926 Zenith decision (see 3.82), Secretary of Commerce Hoover figuratively threw up his hands over the worsening interference situation. His call for industry self-regulation apparently fell on deaf ears. Congress made sporadic attempts to replace the obsolete 1912 Radio Act. In 1926 both houses of Congress finally passed radio bills, but major differences had to be resolved by a joint conference committee. The House bill called for the Secretary of Commerce to have strong licensing authority, with a new Federal Radio Commission (FRC) to serve as a board of appeal from the secretary's decisions. The Senate bill called for the FRC to have the licensing authority. Facing the delay of the joint conference committee, and the Christmas recess, Congress passed a stopgap bill giving all broadcast stations ninety-day licenses, which could be renewed only if the station waived all rights to a specific frequency. But the new Christmas radios of 1926 still received a vast amount of unchecked interference from nearly seven hundred stations.

4•81   The Federal Radio Commission

The Radio Act of 1927 was passed on February 18 and sent to President Coolidge, who signed it into law on February 23. It created a Federal Radio Commission of five members, appointed to overlapping six-year terms and representing five geographical regions of the country. The FRC was to have licensing authority for only one year, in order to straighten out the interference and regulatory chaos, and then the Secretary of Commerce was to regain it as the FRC became an appellate body (but see 4.82).

The House-Senate compromise is clearly reflected in this scheme. The FRC would have initial control over all interstate and foreign radio communications that originated in the United States. Specifically, it would have the power to clas-

sify stations, prescribe the nature of service to be provided, assign frequencies, determine power and location of transmitters, regulate apparatus used, make regulations to prevent interference, set up zones of service (coverage areas), and make special regulations concerning chain broadcasting when necessary; but it would have no power to censor broadcasts. The act established a maximum period of three years for a license, renewable only to those stations adhering to FRC regulations and the law, and revokable for cause. The FRC was to keep radio service relatively equal throughout the country. Its decisions were not absolute but could be appealed to the U.S. Court of Appeals for the District of Columbia.

There were several key assumptions underlying the Radio Act of 1927. Equality of transmission facilities, reception, and service was a political goal. The public at large owned the radio spectrum, but individuals could be licensed to use frequencies. Because the number of channels that could be used without interference was limited, and because the number of applicants was larger than the number of channels, some criterion for choosing licensees had to be devised. Congress labeled this criterion the "public interest, convenience, and/or necessity" but did not define it in the 1927 act. Indeed, it remains undefined in statute to this day. It was the basis, however, on which discretionary control could be built, and it would be defined, however loosely, in the body of case law that was sure to develop. Essential to the operation of this principle was the concept that the broadcaster was ultimately responsible for his operation and that the government would step in only if the licensee did not adequately perform service to the listeners. This was a recognition that earlier self- and governmental-regulation had not worked and that broadcasting was a unique service requiring unique regulation. Although channels were scarce, radio as a form of expression was covered by the First Amendment and the Radio Act of 1927, thus precluding heavyhanded censorship.

Armed with these powers and restraints, the FRC began to function in March 1927. President Coolidge nominated five commissioners, but Congress approved only three before it adjourned. Two of these, including the chairman, died before the year was out, leaving the FRC with only one salaried appointee for much of its first year. In addition, since Congress had neglected to allocate specific funds for the FRC, the new agency camped out for many months in Hoover's Department of Commerce with a very small staff, much of it lent by the Commerce and Navy departments.

4•82   Clearing the Interference

Because the immediate job of reducing interference between stations was primarily technical, many of the original commission members were experts in radio. They included a naval officer—former RCA board member Admiral Bullard, an engineer and editor, a station manager, a radio inspector for the Department of Commerce, and a lawyer; and the earliest replacements were a former educational broadcaster and a set manufacturer. Their work was cut out for them because, in passing the Radio Act, Congress had stipulated that all licenses would expire two months after the act became law. Faced with an April 24 deadline, the FRC first extended amateur and ship licenses indefinitely in order to concentrate on the broadcasting situation. It sent a questionnaire to all stations to determine who was broadcasting where, when, and with what

power. It "summarily removed" some forty stations operating on six frequencies reserved for Canada. It granted temporary extensions—initially for 60 days, later for 90—to most broadcasting stations after April 24, specifying power and times of operation on particular frequencies with minimum 50 kHz separations between stations in the same city. This action went a long way toward moving or eliminating the nearly 130 stations that had been off-frequency when the Radio Act of 1927 was passed (see 3.82).

It soon became clear that merely moving stations around was not going to reduce interference permanently. A classification system similar to that developed by Hoover in the mid-1920s would be necessary. The first step in this direction was a series of FRC general orders, which progressively widened the broadcast band to the entire spectrum between 550 kHz and 1,500 kHz (General Order No. 4); notified portable stations that they would be eliminated by fall but allowed temporary service with up to 100 watts on 1,470 kHz and 1,490 kHz (General Order No. 6); tightened allowable frequency deviations (General Order No. 7); and designated, in preparation for hearings, 600–1,000 kHz as a band to be kept free from heterodynes or other interference (General Order No. 19). Although these steps were constructive, the job was only partly done. The FRC, empowered to act in this way for only a year, had almost run out of time when Congress extended its licensing authority in March 1928 for another year.

Congress added a provision intended to promote equality of service throughout the country and stop the trend toward more stations in the larger eastern cities. Named the Davis Amendment after the Tennessee representative who introduced it, the new law required the licensing authority—the FRC for another year, and then, presumably, the Secretary of Commerce—to work out means for assigning equal numbers of stations and equal amounts of power and air time to each of the country's five zones. In addition, all commissioners were to be legislated out of office by early 1929, thus putting them in effect on probation to clean up the remaining interference problems. Heedful of the Davis Amendment as well as their basic charge, the FRC, in May 1928, issued General Order No. 32, which was aimed at 164 stations believed to be causing the most interference. After a series of hearings requested by most of the affected stations, the commission removed 109 stations from the air, reducing the total number to around 590 by July 1. Portable

stations were completely eliminated, since they caused traveling interference and insurmountable regulatory problems under the Davis Amendment.

In July and August, the FRC issued the outline of its station classification plan, particularly General Order No. 40. The 96 available frequencies, each 10 kHz wide, were classified. There were to be 40 "cleared" stations, eight per zone, on which only one station would be placed anywhere in the country during evening hours, thus allowing better skywave reception in rural areas. These stations would operate with high power: 25,000 and later 50,000 watts. An additional 35 channels, seven per zone, would provide regional service with only two or three stations on

---

The FRC Establishes the Basic AM Allocation: 1928

General Order No. 40, issued yesterday by the Federal Radio Commission, supplies the official basis for an adjustment in the assignment of the country's broadcasting facilities, under a plan which it is believed will provide an improved standard of radio reception generally.... The plan calls for full-time assignments for 100-watt stations equalling in number the total of all other classes of broadcasters put together. Of the 74 channels made available for high-grade reception, 34 will be assigned for regional service, permitting 125 full-time positions for this type of station, and 40 channels will be assigned to stations with minimum power of 5,000 watts and a maximum to be determined.... On these 40 channels only one station will be permitted to operate at any time during night hours, thus insuring clear reception of the sta-

Source: Statement to Accompany General Order No. 40, FRC, August 30, 1928 as reprinted in 1928 *Annual Report* of FRC, pages 49–50.

tion's program up to the extreme limit of its service range.

A majority of the commission believes that this plan is the best which could be devised with due regard to existing conditions. It provides, or at least makes possible, excellent radio reception on 80 per cent of the channels. The few other channels will suffer from heterodyne interference except in a small area close to each station.

Source: FRC *Annual Report* (1928), page 17.

The basic plan of allocation of regular broadcast facilities placed into effect by the Federal Radio Commission has been continued unchanged insofar as concerns the general plan of allocation of stations by frequencies, power, and hours of operation.

Source: FCC *Annual Report* (1935), page 23 (first report of the FCC).

each regional frequency using no more than 1,000 watts. The remaining 21 channels were either for low-power (100 to 5,000 watts) local stations, with many stations per frequency, or reserved by international agreement for Canada or Mexico. Claiming that this plan, which although modified still governs AM station assignment, would allow "excellent reception on 80 percent of the channels," the FRC reassigned existing stations in November 1928.

Once again, just as the FRC was beginning to have some'major effect, its licensing authority was about to expire. Once again Congress extended it, this time to the end of 1929. A shift from technical to legal problems was apparent in congressional approval of an FRC general counsel and legal staff. By mid-1929, the FRC staff of nearly one hundred persons had more than tripled in one year. Since it was also clear that some of the FRC's functions were less temporary than originally conceived, the FRC licensing authority was extended at the end of 1929 "until such time as is otherwise provided by law." To handle broadcasting's complexities, the country needed a body able to put congressional policy determinations into regulations, administer those regulations, and adjudicate disagreements.

Even with license extensions and reduced interference and number of stations, the FRC still had to equalize radio service in the country's five zones as called for by the Davis Amendment. When it tried quota systems, given states usually ended up with portions of stations, an obvious impossibility. In 1930, it devised a system whereby every broadcast station received a number of points reflecting its power and time on the air; but even with some station changes, radio service remained "under quota" in the South and Far West and "over quota" in the Midwest and Northeast. It became obvious to many

that the FRC was spending an inordinate amount of time trying to overcome financial, political, and technical problems in order to meet Congress's arbitrary and politically stimulated requirements. Except for the equalization issue, however, the FRC had effectively dealt with interference by the early 1930s and was ready to pursue legal and programming issues.

4•83 Improving Content

An early FRC programming concern had been the airing of phonograph records, which were considered to be inferior to live music and hence "deceptive" to the audience (see 3.8) as well as generally available in stores and thus wasteful of air time. General Order No. 16 of August 1927 required clear identification of such "mechanical reproductions" with the exception of electrical transcriptions, which were of better technical quality and could not be purchased by the public. The point was both to improve the sound quality of what was on the air and to avoid wasteful broadcast duplication of commercial records people could play on phonographs.

Between 1927 and 1934, the federal courts—particularly the U.S. Court of Appeals for the District of Columbia—handled some sixty broadcast-related cases, 41 of which involved the FRC's basic role and the constitutionality of all or parts of the 1927 Radio Act. The courts generally were sympathetic to the FRC claim of special expertise and its position that the overriding criterion was to be the "public interest, convenience, or necessity"—general and undefined as that standard was. Unless the FRC ignored evidence or procedural requirements, the court usually upheld it, even if the case involved some aspect of programming.

The appellate courts quickly sup-

ported the right of the FRC to make regulations, and the constitutionality of the
law, the commission's right to refuse to
grant a license, the public interest standard, power to prevent transfer of ownership, congressional authority to regulate
broadcasting, and FRC discretionary powers. Numerous cases touched on programming matters—using a station for personal
editorializing and defamatory attacks, ov-
ercommercialization, lack of programming
balance—and some of the most interesting
dealt centrally with programming and the
public interest standard.

Four early programming cases
stand out. One was that of Dr. John R.
Brinkley, who used his Milford, Kansas,
station KFKB for a "medical question box"
program in which he prescribed his own
patent medicines—by number, to be dispensed by his own or friendly pharmacies
—for unseen patients and promoted a
questionable goat gland male sexual reju-
venation operation. The American Medical
Association was particularly displeased,
and the FRC eventually failed to renew
Brinkley's license—with the reviewing
court pointing out in 1931 that consideration of past behavior was not censorship.
Brinkley moved to the border town of Del
Rio, Texas, and continued broadcasting
from Mexico, beyond the writ of the FRC.
He was finally forced off the air in 1940 in
a frequency reallocation. A similar case
was that of Norman Baker, whose license
in Muscatine, Iowa, was not renewed in
1931 because he used station KTNT to make
"bitter attacks" on persons with whom he
disagreed, as well as to exploit his medical
theories and practices, and to promote his
cancer hospital and merchandise. The
Brinkley case figured as a precedent in the
Baker decision. In the 1930 case, William
B. Schaeffer was denied renewal for his
Portland, Oregon, station KVEP because
he allowed former political candidate Rob-

ert Duncan to attack his former opponent
and backers over the air with "indecent
and obscene" language. Schaeffer contended that, once having sold the time to
Duncan, he was no longer responsible, but
the commission insisted that the licensee
has to maintain control over material aired
over the station. The Court of Appeals determined that this FRC dictum did not
constitute censorship, and Schaeffer went
off the air. Another case involving content
was that of the Reverend Robert P. Schuler
of the Trinity Methodist Church in Los
Angeles, licensee of KGEF. Schuler had
been convicted of attempting to use radio
to "obstruct orderly administration of public justice" in "sensational rather than instructive" broadcasts, as he attacked religious organizations, public officials, the
courts, institutions, and individuals in violent language. Citing the Brinkley case,
the Court of Appeals upheld the FRC, and
the Supreme Court refused to review.

The FRC established important
technical, procedural, and legal precedents which still stand today. In 1932 it
stopped issuing general orders and codified a set of rules and regulations, some of
which provided precedent for its successor
organization. In its seven years, the FRC
cleared away the worst of the growth period's interference, established detailed
regulations and standards, and made them
stick in a series of important court cases.
Broadcasting gained the solid regulatory
underpinning even broadcasters agreed
was needed.

4•84   Development of Self-Regulation

The fledgling National Association
of Broadcasters (see 3.83), which had
fought for creation of the FRC, because
established stations had most to lose from
unrestrained competition, worked with it

throughout the FRC's seven years of life. Up to the late 1920s the NAB had primarily fought ASCAP demands (not very successfully), sought technical regulation, and acted as an information exchange and trade organization to promote radio. Now it added lobbying for commercial broadcasting's interests before Congress and the FCC, and pushing self-regulation of the industry to disarm rising governmental and public concern. The NAB feared that a Pandora's box had been opened now that the government had, and intended to use, the power to regulate *all* radio stations closely. On March 25, 1929, the NAB convention approved NAB's first Code of Ethics, a brief statement of general dos and don'ts relating to programming and advertising practices. The major aim of the code was to prevent the broadcast of fraudulent, deceptive, or indecent programs or advertising material that might offend any group of listeners. Distributed to NAB members only was a Code of Commercial Practice, which called for most advertising to be aired before 6 P.M. and for only "goodwill" or institutional advertising to be broadcast in prime time hours.

4•85   Music Licensing

As in the 1920s, however, NAB's major concern was ASCAP's demand for higher royalties; in early 1932 the increase asked was an estimated 300 percent. Though it tried to establish a solid broadcaster front, NAB was undermined when ASCAP offered a lower rate to newspaper-owned stations—a successful attempt to divide and conquer as well as ingratiate the press. After many newspaper-owned stations took this bait, other broadcasters had to sign and pay greatly increased rates for music. NAB again tried to set up a competitive music licensing agency, but its

Radio Program Foundation soon died of broadcaster disinterest.

4•9   A Growing Social Impact

Radio was becoming a major institution. In 1933, high school and college students nationwide debated the question "Resolved: that the United States should adopt the essential features of the British system of radio operation and control," informing many people about the good points and the shortcomings of both systems. During the latter part of the 1926–1933 period, a large radio trade press developed. The most important advertising/business-oriented journal, *Broadcasting*, began as a twice-monthly periodical in 1931 and today is the weekly bible for much of the industry. *Variety* moved its radio section to second-place importance in space and location, right behind films, forcing vaudeville to third place. Fan magazines came and went, with one of the best, *Radio Broadcast*, dying during the Depression.

The potential of radio as material for a university course of study was realized in several schools during the late 1920s. Among the first was the University of Southern California in 1929. Most such early courses were in English or speech departments and aimed particularly at basic training for on-the-air announcing. The earliest textbooks on radio also appeared in these years, including books on radio advertising for agencies and advertisers, announcing techniques, and even dramatic scripts.

4•91   Effects on Other Media

The Depression, together with radio's grip on people's leisure and money, nearly killed off phonographs and the recording industry. Many smaller companies disappeared because they couldn't afford to switch from mechanical to electronic recording methods even though they would improve sound quality. The scarcity of capital caused many record firms to merge with stronger companies. Victor merged with RCA in 1929; Columbia Phonograph, weakened by losses during its fling at owning a broadcast network, became part of the American Record Corporation and later CBS, which had achieved strength and size since their previous association. Victor, building on work done for films and radio stations, introduced the 33⅓-rpm disc in 1931, but the absence of high quality records and a good inexpensive player kept this experiment from catching on. Radio stations used the slower-speed discs, which provided more content per side, but the public had to make do with 78-rpm records for another 17 years.

Broadcast music affected musicians too. Some, like orchestra leader Fred Waring, complained that playing songs on radio hurt record sales; others that radio didn't play or pay them enough. In Chicago, the American Federation of Musicians called a strike to express its concern over radio's effects on musicians' employment (see 6.83).

The print media also felt radio's encroachment. During the "Press-Radio War" (see 4.64), most newspapers dropped free radio program listings and cut radio-related news. Radio's share of advertising placed in the five major media increased from less than 2 percent in 1928 to more than 10 percent by 1933—and much of this increase was at the direct expense of newspapers. Magazines, too, felt the pinch, some of them losing ads to radio as early as 1928.

The motion picture industry was changing over from silent to sound movies. Warner's introduction of sound-on-disc pictures late in the 1920s had thrown Hollywood into chaos. Picture companies faced not only the immense costs of sound-conversion for the studios and thousands of theaters across the country but also techniques for silencing noisy cameras and protecting fragile microphones and hiding them from view. While radio receivers were shown in a few films, motion picture studios limited the appearance of their contract actors on radio for fear of both overexposure and competition. Like radio, the movie industry did well during the Depression, although it had to endure flurries of cost reduction, give away free dishes, and often lower admission prices. To a great extent, film and radio complemented one another in the 1930s—fulfilling related but not duplicated interests and needs of their audiences.

4•92   Growth of Radio Abroad

The series of international radio conferences begun in 1903 (see 2.4) continued. The fourth meeting, postponed from 1917 due to wartime and postwar technical and political changes, was held in Washington in October 1927 with 300 or so delegates from nearly 80 countries. Its job was to minimize the interference caused by the rise in number and power of radio broadcasting and amateur stations. The conference (1) allocated for amateurs specific bands with minimal technical limitations, allowing for flexibility and change; (2) issued new general regulations covering radio in all countries and more detailed supplemental regulations that referred only to nations with government-run radio systems, thus excluding the United States with its commercial system; and (3) set up a technical committee to work on a frequency allocation table for the world. The fifth radio conference, held in Madrid in 1932, was the least important of the series since the 1927 regulations and the worldwide Depression had limited technical progress and financial investment. However, the conference decided to combine telegraph and radio regulations and to change the name of the International Telegraph Union to International Telecommunications Union.

To the north, Canada had some seventy-five stations by 1927, which provided service to every province although most of the stations, with half the total power, were concentrated in such major cities as Montreal and Toronto. Canada was principally concerned with two problems familiar to American broadcasting—the amount of advertising carried by stations and the lack of radio in rural areas—and one unique to that country—the cultural and social impact of increasing amounts of programming from another country, the United States. In 1928 the Canadian government appointed a study commission to recommend a new system of broadcasting, which was to have far-reaching consequences for the privately owned stations in Canada. An operating body, the Canadian Radio Broadcasting Commission, was established in 1932 to set up a national system of broadcasting and to regulate radio.

To the south, Mexican broadcasting expanded. A limited number of stations in the larger cities were using increasing amounts of power to reach rural listeners. Government agencies placed receivers in schools and workingmen's centers to receive the government-supported educational station. License periods up to 20 years, weak enforcement of the 1926 basic law, and unlimited transmitter power all helped to make Mexico a haven for shady border station operations aimed at United States audiences but free from FRC control. By 1934, 12 such high-powered border stations, including John Brinkley's XER, were operating or under construction.

Radio grew apace in Europe as well as in North America. In Great Britain, the British Broadcasting Company owned by manufacturing companies gave way to the British Broadcasting Corporation on January 1, 1927. This government-chartered monopoly, supported by post office–collected license fees on receivers, set an enduring standard for public service broadcasting. By 1932 United Kingdom radio operations were centralized in the handsome new Broadcasting House in London, although lip service was paid to broadcasting in outlying regions such as Scotland and Wales. Germany and France were advanced in radio, both technically and in station growth. International broadcasting became common in the early 1930s, with Radio Moscow initiating one of the first shortwave broadcasting stations in 1929. In late 1932, England began its BBC Empire Service to the Commonwealth, and France broadcast extensively to its many colonies. The League of Nations opened a shortwave station in 1932. In most European countries, the government either directly operated or chartered and controlled the broadcasting establishment, and supported it by collecting annual taxes on receiving sets in the same way the British government supported the BBC. Advertising rarely was used for support. Short- and longwave frequencies augmented medium-wave ones in Europe because the medium-wave broadcast band used in the United States could not adequately contain and separate the many broadcasting stations and languages of the many countries on the closely packed European continent.

4·93   *Period Overview*

The 1926–1933 period is one of the two most important in the history of broadcasting; only 1946–1952 (Chapter 7) exceeds its importance in setting present-day patterns of radio and television. Laboratories were experimenting with television, but television broadcasting had not yet been innovated. National radio networks and the FRC developed, creating more than anything else the structural and regulatory basis for broadcasting in the 1970s. Of nearly equal importance, the stabilizing effects of networks and the FRC helped bring on increasing dominance by major advertisers, especially in network broadcasting.

Each of these factors helped bring permanence and standards to what had been a day-to-day fad. Radio now could compete with other media for advertising dollars and audience. The FRC's clearing of technical interference and the wider diversity of programs secured a lasting association of radio with its audience. News and drama made their first appearances on network and major station program schedules.

The importance of this period is underscored when we realize that the 1933

Key Broadcasting Indicators: 1930 / This is the second of 12 tables providing comparable information for a 60-year period (to 1985) at five year intervals. Sources for items 1–5 and 11 are the tables in Appendix C, while other information comes from sources indicated below. Most data are for January 1.

Indicators	Am Station Data
1. Number of commercial stations	569
2. Number of noncommercial stations	49*
3. Total stations on the air	618
4. Number of network-affiliated stations	131
5. Percentage of commercial stations affiliated with networks	23%
6. Total industry income (add 000,000)	$77*
7. One-hour station rate (New York)	$750*
8. One-minute station rate (New York)	na
9. One-hour network rate evening,	$4,890*
10. Number of broadcasting employees	6,000
11. Percentage of families with sets	46%
12. Broadcasting regulatory budget (FRC)	$295,440

Notes (See Appendix D for full citations):
* = data are for 1931.
na = not available or not applicable.
6. Hettinger (1933), page 109, giving FRC-gathered information for 1931, said to be the first year for which reliable data are available.
7. WEAF, key station of NBC-Red; from Dunlap (1931), page 304.
8. Few stations then sold such brief amounts of time.
9. Basic NBC-Red Network of 20 stations. Blue with 13 stations went for $1,000 less. Total Red network (54 stations): $11,350; total Blue network (47 stations): $10,250. Source as in note 7.
10. Lichty and Topping (1975), table 23, page 290.

broadcast industry was very much like to-day's in structure, while the industry of 1926—only seven years earlier—was only roughly formed. In this short space of time, broadcasting had been molded to a pattern that would hold for decades to come and to which newer broadcast media, like FM, television, and even cable, would have to adapt.

Further Reading

The classic background reading on the 1920s and the 1930s is the pair of social histories by Allen (1931 and 1940). A useful assessment of media in the interwar period is found in the papers collected by Covert and Stevens (1984).

The best overview of this period, replete with social history and anecdote, is Barnouw (1966), with Archer's two volumes (1938, 1939) providing an RCA-biased view of the big business aspects of radio's organizing years. Good contemporary reviews are found in Goldsmith and Lescaboura (1930), Codel's collection (1930), the first *Annals* compilation (1929), and the National Association of Broadcasters' industry view of itself (1933).

The best discussions of mechanical television developments are found in Dinsdale (1932), Felix (1931), Moseley's 1952 biography of Baird, Dunlap's 1932 popular work reprinted from his *New York Times* columns, and Sheldon and Grisewood's volume, the first general-interest American book on television (1929). General technological overviews of television can be found in Maclaurin (1949). For a British point of view, see Pawley (1972).

Early potential and subsequent decline of educational radio are the subjects of Perry (1929), Tyler's national survey (1933), Lingel's bibliography (1932), and Frost's station-by-station history of educational AM licensees (1937a). A short historical review of educational radio is found in Wood and Wylie (1977).

For background on the development of advertising generally, see the annotated bibliography by Pollay (1979), the old but still valuable and detailed history of prebroadcast advertising found in Presbrey (1929), and two more recent histories bringing the story up to date: Fox (1984) and Pope (1983). The most useful social analyses of the milieu within which advertising developed, and the impact that advertising had, are two volumes by Ewen (1976 and 1982).

The role and process of radio advertising are the focus of Felix (1927), the first book-length treatment of the subject; the FRC (1932), which compares American and foreign practice; Arnold (1933), the first to discuss television's potential in detail; and Hettinger (1933), the first scholarly analysis of the early years of radio advertising. Spalding's article (1964) is also of value.

A detailed and interesting discussion of network radio programs, listed in alphabetical fashion, is in Dunning (1976). Network radio content is listed in Summers (1958), and the programs are described and casts listed in Buxton and Owen (1972). Husing (1935) offers an interesting first-person account by a well-known sports announcing personality. Chase (1942) presents a narrative history of radio content, and Settel (1967) does the same thing with pictures and text. The effects of content on the audience are analyzed in Cantril and Allport's pioneering analysis (1935), while methods of audience analysis are reviewed in Lumley (1934).

An interesting assessment of this period of regulatory transition is Rosen (1980). A good contemporary view is the legal analysis in Davis (1927), the first book devoted to radio law in the United States.

The FRC's annual reports (1927–1933—no report was issued for 1934) and Schmeckebier (1932) offer the best and most detailed review of this short span of years. Kahn (1984) includes some cases mentioned in the text as well as the key laws, and other documents, while Kittross (1977) includes other important documents.

To understand the impact of radio, read the radio columns or sections of major newspapers or magazines, plus specialized periodicals including *Broadcasting*. See also Buehler (1933) and Aly and Shively (1933) for debate handbooks on that year's comparison between American and British broadcasting. Batson (1930) analyzes broadcast developments in other countries, while Briggs (1965) details developments in Great Britain and Peers (1969) discusses Canadian radio.

5

Radio's Golden Age (1934–1941)

Anncr: "Ladies and gentlemen, I have a grave announcement to make. Incredible as it may seem, both the observations of science and the evidence of our eyes lead to the inescapable assumption that those strange beings who landed in the Jersey farmlands tonight are the vanguard of an invading army from the planet Mars." —Orson Welles's "War of the Worlds" broadcast, October 30, 1938, on CBS

Radio's
Golden
Age
(1934–1941)

5

"The country has as many stations as it can support. Additional facilities will necessitate the commercialization of stations to the exclusion of public service."—former FRC Commissioner H. A. Lafount, 1936

In September 1934 tourists swarmed to
Asbury Park, New Jersey, to view the
blackened hulk of the cruise liner *Morro
Castle* lying off the beach, a grisly remnant
of the disaster in which 134 passengers
and crew had burned to death or drowned.
On the beach a horde of salesmen hawk-
ing souvenir postcards and candy bars gave
shape to former President Coolidge's stand
that "the business of America is business."
For most Americans, the *Morro Castle* was
a distraction from worry over jobs and
paychecks. Franklin Roosevelt's New Deal
fight to bring the nation out of the Depression had just begun—and the still smoking ship was less depressing and more interesting than the bread lines of the
unemployed.

Outline:
Radio's Golden Age (1934–1941)

But with money still tight and unemployment high, radio came into its own. Once you had a set, radio was free, unlike newspapers, magazines, books, the movies, or the stage. While Americans turned to radio primarily for entertainment, they also absorbed news of conditions in other parts of the country, social upheaval in other parts of the world. They became both politically aware and dependent on radio for information.

Radio reported the sudden disasters—the *Morro Castle,* floods, the assassination of Louisiana populist Senator Huey P. Long in 1935—and slow political change—Hitler rearming Germany, war clouds gathering in the Far East, then in Spain, and finally throughout Europe as Germany lit the match of World War II. In 1936 the king of England used radio to tell the world directly that he was giving up the throne for the "woman I love."

The radio voice of Franklin Roosevelt carried his plans for the country into the American home, aided by the REA (Rural Electrification Administration), which brought centrally generated electricity, and thus batteryless radio, to most farm dwellers for the first time. He talked about the many federal agencies created to conquer the Depression. Citizens began to turn to Washington for leadership instead of to state capitals—and the federal government responded with new agencies, including the Federal Communications Commission (FCC).

Radio reflected a country that was drinking legally again, with the lifting of Prohibition, and traveling farther—DC-3s were flying coast-to-coast overnight, transatlantic air service was promised, and Pennsylvania was building an unlimited-speed, multilane turnpike. Listeners in Maine knew that duststorms on the Great Plains were blowing away the rich Midwest topsoil, that floods on the Mississippi and Ohio were threatening river towns, and that persons dispossessed by the duststorms and economic conditions wandered across the country by car or freight train—Okies migrating to California to find a new beginning. John Steinbeck immortalized this saga in his 1939 novel *The Grapes of Wrath*, later made into a movie.

To most Americans, the 1930s brought new leisure. The five-day work week and the eight-hour day were becoming common. More people flocked to the movies every week. Walt Disney's first all-cartoon feature film *Snow White* appeared in 1937, and the highly creative *Fantasia* followed in 1940. The movie version of Margaret Mitchell's *Gone With the Wind* even permitted a spoken "damn"! Such big dance bands as Benny Goodman, Glenn Miller, and the Dorsey Brothers brought swing music to college proms and roadhouses alike, thanks to radio and juke boxes. People also read books. A generation of novelists came to maturity, including Sinclair Lewis, Edna Ferber, Ernest Hemingway, and John Steinbeck. The new picture magazines *Life* and *Look* quickly achieved high circulations.

But perhaps the most popular pastime was radio. This was truly radio's golden age, before competition from television or World War II battlefield reports diverted listeners from the fine entertainers who were starting their broadcasting careers. Radio audiences grew steadily and broadcasting pioneers of the 1920s reaped a considerable profit. Although radio was still innovative and experimental, the medium was no longer novel—it was not only accepted but welcomed.

5·1   Innovations around the Corner

Even during a period of relative stability in the broadcasting industry, seeds of drastic change were germinating in laboratories across the country. Books and periodicals dwelled on technological improvements that were "just around the corner," and would change people's lives as AM radio had in the 1920s—in particular, static-free radio—FM; still pictures by wireless—facsimile; and perhaps most interesting to the public, moving pictures sent to the home by wireless—television (see 5.14). Their respective backers believed that FM radio, facsimile, or television was *the* future of broadcasting, while the AM radio broadcasters feared that confusion and costly innovation would endanger their industry. This conflict was clear by the time this country entered World War II, when the battle in broadcasting had to defer to the battles against Germany and Japan.

5•11   Invention of FM Radio

Throughout most of radio's development, static had interfered with reception, especially during summer thunderstorms and in the semitropical American South. Since the rasping "jamble" caused by lightning was amplitude modulated, a possible solution was to use frequency modulation for radio. Although the concept of FM dated back to the Poulsen Arc (see 2.21) in the early 1900s, experimentation had stopped in the early 1920s because most radio engineers thought that FM's drawbacks, such as distortion, outweighed its benefits and that the only solution was to overpower static by forcing a huge amount of transmitter power through as narrow a channel as possible. AM stations based their drive for additional power in the 1930s on the same idea (see 5.22).

An important radio engineer who disagreed with this conclusion was Edwin

Armstrong, inventor of the feedback circuit (see 2.22) and other devices. Following his Signal Corps service in World War I, Armstrong began his own search for a way to eliminate static, working at first with his former teacher, Professor Michael Pupin, at Columbia University and later alone. After devoting two years to frequency-modulated radio waves, Armstrong arrived in late 1930 at the key to successful FM broadcasting: the FM broadcast channel had to be many times *wider* than the standard AM channel of 10 kHz. Using a channel 200 kHz wide, with low power, Armstrong got excellent audio frequency response with FM—and virtually no static, even in electrical storms. (Actually, the swing of the modulated FM signal occupied only 75 kHz, but the additional bandwidth protected against interference from adjacent channels due to the instability of receiving equipment on the very high frequencies employed). Armstrong applied for the first four patents on his FM system in 1930 and received them just after Christmas in 1933.

With the basic FM patents secure, Armstrong gave his first demonstration to an outsider. He and David Sarnoff of RCA had known each other for nearly 20 years. RCA had used Armstrong's earlier inventions, to their mutual profit, and had an option to purchase his new inventions; Armstrong was the largest individual stockholder in RCA, and his wife had been Sarnoff's secretary. Sarnoff was impressed with FM's results but also was worried because Armstrong touted his system not as a means of solving the static interference problems of the existing AM radio system but rather as a total replacement for AM. RCA, with its huge investment in AM broadcasting, would not readily undertake the heavy costs of developing a totally new system, especially one that was patented and promoted by someone else.

The First Public Demonstration of FM: 1935 / Edwin Armstrong's biographer Lawrence Lessing provides a gripping account of the first public demonstration of what FM could do. Remember, thunderstorms and other disturbances could ruin AM station reception—and many then felt the only answer was greater power. Armstrong's audience was made up of fellow engineers, who listened to the inventor's highly technical paper with no hint of the demonstration to come. Meanwhile, 17 miles north of the Manhattan meeting site, Armstrong's friend C. R. Runyon was making last-minute adjustments to the world's first FM radio station—and in the process was burning out a generator halfway into Armstrong's talk. Armstrong continued the technical talk until he received word that Runyon was ready. An FM receiver—hand-made, and one of the few then in existence—was set up near the lectern in the lecture hall.

For a moment the receiver groped . . . until the new station was tuned in with a dead unearthly silence, as the whole apparatus had been abruptly turned off. Suddenly out of the silence came Runyon's supernaturally clear voice: "This is amateur station W2AG in Yonkers, New York, operating on frequency modulation at two and a half meters." A hush fell over the large audience. Waves of two and a half meters ([approx.] 110 megacycles) were waves so short that up until then they had been regarded as too weak to carry a message across a street. Moreover, W2AG's announced transmitter power [100 watts] was barely enough to light one good-sized electric bulb. Yet these shortwaves and weak power were not only carrying a message over the seventeen miles from Yonkers, but carrying it by a method of modulation which the textbooks still held to be of no value. And doing it with a life-like clarity never heard on even the best clear-channel stations in the regular broadcast band. . . . A glass of water was poured before the microphone in Yonkers; it sounded like a glass of water being poured and not, as in the "sound effects" on ordinary radio, like a waterfall. A paper was crumpled and torn; it sounded like paper and not like a crackling forest fire. An oriental gong was softly struck and its overtones hung shimmering in the meeting halls' arrested air. . . . The absence of background noise and the lack of distortion in FM circuits made music stand out against the velvety silence with a presence that was something new in auditory experiences. The secret lay in the achievement of a signal-to-noise ratio of 100-to-1 or better, as against 30-to-1 on the best AM stations.

Source: Lawrence Lessing, *Man of High Fidelity: Edwin Howard Armstrong*. (Philadelphia: Lippincott, 1956), pages 209–210. By permission.

Still, Sarnoff sent some top RCA scientists to Columbia to observe more demonstrations and, on their advice, invited Armstrong to install equipment in RCA space atop the Empire State Building to test FM under broadcast conditions. RCA engineers, working with Armstrong for several months in 1934, made comparative broadcasts of music and other material using both AM and FM transmissions picked up by a receiving station 70 miles away. In November they transmitted by a single multiplexed FM carrier wave both the NBC-Red and -Blue programs of that day, a facsimile copy of part of the front page of the *New York Times*, and a telegraph message—all at the same time.

The parting of the ways came in spring 1935. On April 26, Armstrong publicly announced his new radio system and made plans for demonstrations for other engineers and the press. Just ten days later, RCA announced its decision to spend $1 million developing television (see 5.14). RCA had decided to go with television, a totally new medium already exciting the public, rather than what it considered only an improvement on an existing system. The potential profits of television were clearly more attractive. Late in 1935 Armstrong was asked to remove his FM apparatus from the Empire State Building so that room could be made for expanded RCA television experimentation.

5•12 Early Innovation of FM

Edwin Armstrong believed that FM was bound to replace AM so that static-free and better quality sound would prevail. With the end of RCA cooperation, he moved to promote his system by using his own substantial fortune—from the sale of earlier inventions, mostly to RCA—and by persuading influential broadcasters to back

him. In November 1935 Armstrong demonstrated FM to an engineering society meeting in New York, publishing the key parts of that paper a few months later. Despite continuing skepticism of Federal Communications Commission (FCC; see 5.8) engineers, Armstrong received permission to build his own experimental FM station at Alpine, New Jersey, on the Hudson River Palisades, within range of New York City. That fall the FCC held frequency allocation hearings (see 5.14) and provided the experimental radio service with space for 13 of Armstrong's 200 kHz channels but in three widely separated places in the spectrum. Only five channels were suitable for the existing transmitting and receiving technology. (See allocation chart in 6.81).

However, Armstrong plowed ahead. Support for FM came from the Yankee Network, a large New England AM network developed in the 1930s by John Shepard III, with ten stations in 1933 and twice as many a decade later. In spring 1937, Yankee applied for permission to build a 50 kw FM station in Paxton, Massachusetts, to experiment with long-range and relay broadcasting. Armstrong's own station, W2XMN in Alpine, became the first lasting FM station when it began low-power tests in April 1938. The first Yankee Network FM station started in 1939, followed by a second a few months later. General Electric established stations in Albany and Schenectady, New York, to test FM reception and made plans to manufacture receivers. Before the year was out, stations were on the air from Washington, D.C., New York City, several places in Connecticut, and Massachusetts. Three experimental stations, including one owned by NBC—RCA liked to hedge its bets—and two in Wisconsin, opened in early 1940, broadcasting special engineering test programs, a lot of music, and no commercials. Several New England stations experimented with relay broadcasting, whereby one station broadcast a program and others picked it up with sensitive antennas and rebroadcast it. In this way, they could avoid AT&T line connection expense and achieve better sound quality. Without static, and with an audio-frequency response up to 15 kHz, such relaying was possible on FM but not on AM (though experimentation with wide-band high audio fidelity AM also was ongoing).

The success of these experiments led to demand for receivers, and firms started making FM sets. Several stations attempted to promote interest among listeners in the better sound of the new system, although FM table model receivers cost at least $60. Supporters demonstrated FM reception to engineering, political, and social groups, and early in 1940 formed an FM trade association to persuade the FCC to allow commercial operation of FM stations.

More than 20 experimental FM stations were on the air, with more being built, when the FCC began eight days of hearings on FM's status in mid-March 1940. A wide variety of views was heard, and to most observers' surprise, RCA, then deep in television promotion, presented no objections to FM. The commission announced its approval of commercial FM on May 20 to begin January 1, 1941, on 40 channels provided in a new and wider band of 42–50 MHz with the lowest five channels reserved for educational stations. To accommodate FM, experimental television lost an existing channel and government services seven MHz of spectrum space, but they both gained even more space in other parts of the spectrum. Engineering rules released in June called for three classes of FM stations, defined by area served rather than power and frequency as with AM. The first construction

permits for commercial FM stations were issued to 15 applicants in October, and in December the FCC issued an FM call-letter plan, which used numbers and letters in a code signifying station geographic and frequency locations.

A number of factors held up FM's initial growth. Construction permits were frozen during the FCC investigation of newspaper control of radio stations (see 5.83). While about 40 stations were on the air by December, only half were operating commercially. Of the rest, operating with experimental licenses, few had full power. Nearly all FM stations were affiliated with an AM station in the same city or town and thus lacked impetus for a rapid push to full-fledged commercial operation. Preparations for national defense put increasing demands on construction materials. By the time the United States entered the war in December 1941, FM was a commercial service, but just barely. Fewer than four hundred thousand receivers were in the hands of the public, and few of the 50 or so stations were in the West or South.

5·13   Facsimile

The notion of sending print and still pictures by wire or wireless was not new. The newspaper industry used a process called *wirephoto*, by which a photograph was scanned and sent by wire. By the late 1930s, interest developed in the idea of sending entire newspapers by radio rather than having them hand-delivered to the home. Receivers were designed and some FM stations experimented with *fax*, but facsimile never got off the ground as a broadcast medium. There were several reasons: the greater interest in the *moving* pictures of television, competition with new FM and older but still expanding AM radio services, high costs of facsimile paper, and inability of the system to transmit quickly. Facsimile seemed to have more applications for industry than for the home. Only in the late 1960s did industrial and public safety uses of fax systems become important, but by then there were few proponents of home systems.

5·14   *Electronic Television*

Although many early television experimenters used mechanical devices for both transmitting and receiving (see 4.12), later experimenters realized that the cathode-ray tube, which had been developed by Sir William Crookes and others in the 1870s, could better display the televised image. In 1897, Professor Karl Ferdinand Braun of the Physical Institute of Strassburg produced the cathode-ray oscilloscope, which used the tube for the visual observation of electrical signals. A decade later, Professor Boris Rosing of the St. Petersburg Technological Institute modified a Braun tube to display very faint images from a mechanical scanner that fed into a photoelectric cell connected to the Braun tube.

This development made clear the outlines of a practical home-television system. Lee de Forest's Audion (see 2.22) would amplify the weak video current; the cathode-ray tube would need further development; and methods of transmitting by wireless and synchronizing transmitting and receiving apparatus would still have to be devised—but the basic idea was there. True, a television camera had to be designed that would break the picture down into very small elements and make sharp distinctions between light and shadow. Developing present technical standards took several decades.

The two paths of development of electronic scanning, which were merged

in the late 1930s, are associated with the names of Zworykin and Farnsworth. Vladimir K. Zworykin had been a student of Rosing's just before World War I and had started extensive work on television as early as 1917 as an employee of the Russian Wireless Telegraph and Telephone Company. The principles of the system that he later developed were in his mind by 1919 when he came to the United States. Joining the Westinghouse research staff in 1920, he spent several frustrating years, including a year and a half at another company, due to lack of interest in television at Westinghouse. He eventually received approval to work on television, photoelectric cells, and sound motion picture reproduction. Although Westinghouse took out the first patent on Zworykin's camera tube in 1923, a practical demonstration of what he called the *iconoscope*—from the Greek words *eikon* (image) and *skopein* (to view) —could not be made until 1928. This device used a storage-discharge effect to achieve sensitivity to lower light levels, and magnetic deflection to aim a beam of electrons across a target that had been charged by light impinging on it. Unbeknownst to Zworykin, the British physicist A. A. Campbell Swinton had anticipated the iconoscope in 1908 independently of Rosing's need for an electronic scanner, but Campbell Swinton had never developed it. David Sarnoff, then vice president and general manager of RCA, became interested in Zworykin's invention and offered him support, which increased in 1930 when RCA took over research in radio from GE and Westinghouse.

The other major inventor of electronic television was Philo T. Farnsworth, who worked under conditions very different from Zworykin's association with RCA's large industrial laboratory. As a boy in Rigby, Idaho, Farnsworth read popular electrical and radio magazines. In 1921, at age fifteen, he started studying photoelectricity and the cathode-ray tube. His high school notebooks later became crucially important in a major patent fight. While a student at Brigham Young University, he met San Francisco businessman George Everson, who arranged financial backing for the young inventor and later wrote a book about him. Farnsworth consistently had difficulty in working within an organization and in pressing an idea through to commercial success, although his scientific and engineering skills were exceptionally high. By 1927 he had transmitted his first picture—a 60-line image of a dollar sign! By 1930 he had developed an image dissector and a new television scanning and synchronizing system that he hoped to refine for commercial use. The Depression and increasing expenditures led him to accept financing from Philco—the Philadelphia Storage Battery Company, soon to be an important radio manufacturer—and move to Philadelphia, where he worked from 1931 to 1933. But the Philco management, which wanted to get in on the ground floor of television independently of RCA, decided that they could not wait for Farnsworth, despite his ability, to develop a a commercial system of television. Continuing his work in Philadelphia with the support of his California backers, Farnsworth steadily improved his system.

By 1938 more than $1 million dollars had been spent on Farnsworth's research, development, and legal fees—with only about 7 percent of that sum recovered from license fees and royalties. However, working with a series of excellent patent attorneys, the Farnsworth interests had 73 patents and 60 applications, approximately three-quarters of which represented the inventor's work on the image dissector, the image amplifier, and other devices. The strength of Farnsworth's patent position was proven by his winning in a number of important patent interference proceedings. In two of these, the Patent Office, concluding that the image dissector operated on different principles from the iconoscope, gave basic patents to both Farnsworth and Zworykin. In 1941 Farnsworth won a patent interference case against RCA that secured basic patents on synchronization and other important aspects of his television system. As a result, both RCA and AT&T decided to take out television licenses as early as 1939. For the first time RCA had to pay royalties to another concern; RCA patent manager Otto Schairer reportedly signing the royalty agreement with "tears in his eyes." The Farnsworth company went into manufacturing, but in 1940 Farnsworth—partly because of ill health, which plagued him until his death in 1971—resigned as research director.

Even more than Edwin Armstrong, Farnsworth typified the lone inventor in technological development. Uncomfortable when he had to work with the public or within a large group, he was obviously happier working in a small laboratory than as vice president of a manufacturing company. Television is an especially complex field, and the lone inventor or innovator is at a disadvantage compared to the research team whose work receives continuity and support from large corporation, government, or university funds.

Picture definition had been very limited at first, but both Farnsworth and Zworykin soon produced more detailed pictures with their delicate and expensive electronic gear than mechanical systems could produce (see 4.13). As early as 1927 Farnsworth demonstrated an electronic system with a resolution around 100 lines at 30 pictures per second, compared with the 30- to 60-line definition of the best mechanical systems of that time. RCA transmitted 120-line pictures electronically in 1931 and 343-line pictures four years later. Although mechanical systems eventually exceeded 200 lines, they had clearly approached the limits of their technology, while electronic television was capable of much improvement.

Continuing experimentation led to an increasing demand for spectrum space. Stations at Purdue University in Indiana and GE in Schenectady, New York, were sending recognizable images thousands of miles on the shortwave 2 MHz band, but the experimenters needed more and much wider channels and hoped for commercial operation on higher bands. Under pressure from conflicting FM and television in-terests, the FCC held a series of allocations hearings and decided in 1937 (1) to accept applications for experimental television stations in the band from 20 to 300 MHz, already rapidly filling with other services, and (2) to allocate seven channels, each 6 MHz wide, in the band between 54 and 108 MHz, with an additional 12 channels in the 156–294 MHz band set aside for ex-perimentation and expansion. Only the lower seven channels were put to use, however, as receivers of the period could not pick up the higher band transmissions, and transmitting devices at these frequen-cies were then not very efficient.

By the end of the 1936–1937 Infor-mal Engineering Conference, the FCC concluded that "television is not yet ready

The Rise of Electronic Television: 1930s / An experimental model television receiver (with a mirror to reflect the picture tube, which faces straight up) is tried out by RCA's Vladimir Zworykin—inventor of the iconoscope tube and one of the key figures in the development of electronic television. Courtesy of Group W and Broadcast Pioneers Library.

The First Television Sets Go on Sale: 1938–1939 / Television sets were probably first offered for public sale in the United States in April 1938 (England had beaten us by nearly two years) at Piser's Furniture Store in the Bronx, New York. About four thousand customers jammed the store for the first showing of a 3-inch ($125) and a 5-inch ($250) set offered by Communications System, Inc. The first table below shows what was available by Christmas 1938. Macy's department store had four different brands on sale in May 1939, and by July, as seen in the second table, 14 manufacturers were in production or planning for same. By December 1939, 8 set-makers had produced 5,000 television receivers—all before final FCC approval of standards. Prices ranged from $200 for 5-inch screens up to $600 for 9-inch sets. Most of these sets were used as demonstrators and very few were sold. *Note:* The dollar in those days was worth more than eight times what it is today.

TV Sets Available in December 1938

Company	Size of Screen (in inches)	Price Range (in dollars)
American Television Corp.	3, 5	$125–395
Andrea Radio Corp.	na	175–595
Dumont	14	395–445
General Electric	5, 9, 12	175–600
RCA	5, 9, 12	175–600

TV Sets Available in July 1939

Company	No. of Models	Size of Tube (in inches)	Retail Price (in dollars)
American Television Corp.	3	5	$185–395
Andrea Radio Corp.	2	5-12	190–350
Crosley	2-4	Announced for August	
Dumont	2	5	190–600
Farnsworth	2-4	Announced for the Fall	
General Electric	5	5-12	195–1,000
International Television	1-3	Announced for December	
Majestic	1	5	na
Majestic (kit)	1	5	125
Philco	6	5-9	200–425
Pilot	3	9-12	250–425
RCA	4	5-12	150–600
Stewart-Warner	1	9	600
Stromberg-Carlson	1	9	575
Westinghouse	3	5-12	200–600
Zenith	None for sale, but some for loan		

na = not available

Source: Alfred R. Oxenfeldt, *Marketing Practices in the TV Set Industry* (New York: Columbia University Press, 1964), pages 9–11. By permission.

for public service on a national scale," but that "the rate of [television] progress is rapid and the energies of the laboratories of the country are being concentrated on the technical development of television." Still, the FCC warned the public, "There does not appear to be any immediate outlook for the recognition of television service on a commercial basis," and it prohibited sponsorship of programs. It also required that licensees must conduct research and report on the result of that research to the FCC.

In 1938 RCA proceeded toward standardizing television for commercial use. It had spent millions of dollars on research and acquired competing and secondary patents. After negotiating an agreement on patents with Farnsworth in 1939 largely on Farnsworth's terms, it was ready to innovate television on its own standards and terms. Despite the displeasure of other experimenters and manufacturers, RCA persuaded the Radio Manufacturers Association (RMA) to consider adopting new television standards. When an RMA committee found that the only other practical system, Farnsworth's, was being merged with RCA's in a patents pool, the RMA adopted the RCA system. Before RCA could begin regular programming and sell receivers to the public, the FCC had to accept the proposed standards and then approve commercial operation. Several months after the RMA presented the proposed new standards on September 10, 1938, the FCC appointed a committee of three commissioners to investigate the status of television preparatory to recommending a course of action. The RMA request had aroused considerable public interest about television's future. Newspaper columnist Walter Winchell predicted on September 18 that "the local stores will be selling television sets for as

little as $3.95 by October 1." Things did not move quite that fast.

5·15   Television's False Dawn

The FCC television advisory committee moved cautiously. Its initial report of May 22, 1939, recommended that further delay in setting standards would best serve the public interest and straddled the fence by condemning premature standards while praising the proposed RMA-RCA standards as adequate.

In its second report, on November 15, 1939, the television advisory committee reversed itself and proposed standards of 441 lines, 30 pictures per second, which were, of course, supported by their author, RCA. Relying heavily on "the thoughts of the present leaders of the industry"—rather than upon such nonmanufacturing outsiders as Armstrong and CBS—the committee concluded that more rapid progress could be expected by "allowing commercial operation to recoup some developmental expense."

Opposition to the RCA proposals crystallized at FCC hearings starting January 15, 1940. Many sources—including Dumont, Zenith, which particularly disliked the weak synchronization technique, and Edwin Armstrong, who wanted additional frequencies for FM radio (see 5.22) —objected to certain technical standards and allocations. Some called for higher definition through a variety of ingenious means. In fact, virtually the entire manufacturing industry objected to being "frozen out" by the adoption of RCA's standards. RCA had the support of only its engineers and Farnsworth.

In the face of this controversy, the FCC reached a typical compromise: some television stations would be permitted "limited" commercial operation—to give program developers a chance to recoup some costs—starting September 1, 1940. At the same time, no standards of transmission would be fixed, since "crystallization of standards at the current level of the art, by whatever means accomplished, would inevitably stifle research in basic phases of the art in which improvement appeared promising." This decision meant that, despite the dangers of equipment obsolescence, the public was to have the "opportunity" to buy various types of receivers to determine which system it preferred.

Throughout this period, the FCC was preoccupied with the anticipated public investment in receivers. Even in its order of March 23, 1940, granting RCA limited commercial television, the FCC pointed out that "public participation in television experimentation at this time is desirable only if the public understands that it is experimenting in reception and not necessarily investing in receiving equipment with a guarantee of its continued usefulness." Despite this, RCA emphasized the sale of receivers to the public in its publicity for a broadcast on April 30, 1939, from the New York World's Fair.

Notwithstanding the commission's admonition against encouraging "a large public investment in receivers which may become obsolete in a relatively short time," RCA took the approval for "limited commercial broadcasting" as a green light to manufacture and sell television receivers. It launched an intensive promotion and advertising campaign on March 20, 1940, that said, in essence, television is here, the commission has approved it, and a new commercial service to the American home will start—in the New York area, at least—on September 1, 1940. This publicity campaign was preceded by a bitter fight

within the RMA when RCA's chief television engineer presented the company's position to an RMA committee as if it were a *fait accompli*, and when president David Sarnoff threatened to pull RCA out of the RMA, refusing to discuss "any program the purpose of which is to delay the commercialization of television"—a far cry from its January FCC testimony. Philco withdrew from the RMA television standards committee, saying that the committee could serve no further purpose, since widespread sale of RCA equipment would make consideration of any other standard futile. All other members of the committee except RCA and Farnsworth voted to consider new proposals, but none was forthcoming.

However, the FCC reacted strongly to RCA's strategy. It issued a vigorous order only two days after the RCA publicity campaign started, and Chairman James Lawrence Fly delivered his opinion of RCA, and a description of the issues, in a nationwide broadcast on April 2. The FCC order called for a new series of hearings, to start April 8, reopening the question of standards and starting date for commercial broadcasting. The hearings lasted five days, with the same cast of characters. President Roosevelt announced on April 12 that the administration would exert every effort to prevent television from coming under monopolistic control. The FCC stated that it would have acted sooner if it had known about the RCA statement and hostilities at the RMA February meetings. (Ten years later General Sarnoff claimed that he had "personally" shown FCC Chairman Fly the objectionable RCA advertisement *before* it was published.)

Put on the defensive at the hearings, RCA stimulated a Senate investigation of the FCC's television policy in mid-April. This tactic failed to soften Chairman Fly's determination, and the

The First Television Rate Card: 1941 / Here is a partial reproduction of the first of a long series of television rate cards for NBC's New York outlet (now WNBC-TV), dated for the beginning of U.S. commercial television. Compare these rates with those reported in the "Key Indicators" tables for later chapters.

NBC *Television* RATES
Station WNBT
EFFECTIVE JULY 1, 1941

I TRANSMISSION RATE

GROSS

	60 Min.	30 Min.	15 Min.
6:00 PM to 11:00 PM Daily	$120.00	$60.00	$30.00
8:00 AM to 12 Noon Daily	60.00	30.00	15.00
12 Noon to 6:00 PM Daily, exclusive of Saturday and Sunday	60.00	30.00	15.00
12 Noon to 6:00 PM Saturday and Sunday	90.00	45.00	22.50
11:00 PM to Sign Off Daily	90.00	45.00	22.50

{ Rates for other units of time in exact proportion to corresponding one-hour rate. No periods less than 5 minutes sold except for Service Spots.

SERVICE SPOTS *(News, Weather, Time, Etc.)*

Evening (6:00 PM to Sign Off)—$8.00 for maximum of 1 minute.
Day (8:00 AM to 6:00 PM)   —$4.00 for maximum of 1 minute.

II PROGRAM FACILITIES RATE

TYPE OF FACILITIES *(Based on time on the air to nearest 5 minutes.)*

	60 Min.	30 Min.	15 Min.	10 Min.	5 Min.
Main Studio	$150.00	$90.00	$60.00	$53.00	$45.00
Small Studio	75.00	45.00	30.00	26.00	22.00
Film Studio	75.00	45.00	30.00	26.00	22.00
Field Pickups	75.00	(Minimum Charge—$75.00)			

{ Rates for units of time longer than one hour in exact proportion to corresponding one-hour rate.

Service Spots—Facilities and Handling—$5.00 per spot.
(Must originate in small or film studio.)

FCC issued a scathing report on May 28 which condemned RCA, reviewed past developments, fostered research and development by other companies, limited station owning, and rescinded permission for commercial broadcasting until the entire industry could agree upon standards. A brief fight centered on the right of the FCC to regulate the manufacture and sale of, and public "right" to buy, television receivers; but Fly was able to give as good as he got, and RCA clearly lost this fray.

Political and legal arguments did not stop engineering developments. In July the RMA established a National Television System Committee (NTSC), chaired by W. R. G. Baker of GE. By January 27, 1941, after 5,000 man-hours of work, the industry was able to present a united front to the commission, which the next day called for a public hearing. At these hearings, starting March 20, 1941, the FCC found that the NTSC standards had virtually unanimous industry approval, and that the 525-line, 30-picture standards were far superior to those of 1940. In addition, the new standards substituted FM for AM sound in television and greatly strengthened the synchronization system. In its report of May 3, 1941, the FCC accepted the NTSC recommendations and approved commercial television operation using the new standards starting July 1, 1941. These basic standards are still in use today.

The FCC's decisions did give television a green light, although they took away one of its 19 channels, deferred action on CBS's suggestion that color television be considered, created a very minor problem of receiver obsolescence—affecting only a few thousand sets, which the manufacturer could convert—and, in general, reflected the salutary effects of knocking together the heads of engineers and manufacturers to achieve cooperation.

5•2   Station Expansion

As the country slowly emerged from the Depression, radio broadcasting began to expand again. In the 1935–1941 period, more than 200 new AM stations took to the air, while few went off (see Appendix C, table 1). By the late 1930s, cumulative investment in tangible broadcast property, in addition to receivers, was in the order of $65 million. Many communities got their first radio station, while most large cities added one or more stations. This expansion, however, was not uniform throughout the country. In 1936, 43 percent of *all* stations were in markets of 100,000 people or more, as were 60 percent of the regional and 90 percent of the clear-channel operations. Smaller communities usually had to make do with low-power (100–250 watts) local stations, 75 percent of which were located in such communities; most places under 10,000 population, and many under 50,000, had *no* local station. Thus radio was still a large-town or city service, and many listeners in rural areas had only secondary service (see 5.7).

The major reasons for urban bias in coverage were economic and technical. In a country still in a depression with restricted advertising budgets, placing a station in a market too small to support it adequately was economically foolish. Many cities without radio stations were served by numerous outlets in nearby metropolitan areas. Advertisers and their agencies, to avoid splitting up one audience with many stations, usually favored the larger operations.

The technical problems were more involved. For one thing, radio station power continued to increase. Whereas only 37 stations broadcast with from 5 to 10 kw in 1935, 140 stations broadcast with such power in 1940. Stations with 50 kw of power had increased from 29 to 39, but low-power (100 watts or less) stations had dropped from 179 to 98. Since new stations of the Depression years typically were established in areas with limited radio service, they created few interference problems. But the Davis Amendment (see 4.82) allowed the Federal Radio—and Federal Communications—Commission little flexibility in approving construction permit applications, as equality of facilities in the five zones had to be maintained. On June 5, 1936, the Davis Amendment was repealed, allowing more radio growth in highly populated areas by removing this artificial lid on radio expansion. A rush of applications followed for areas with the most population, again shortchanging rural areas and suburbs. The clear-channel stations in large cities were expected to provide service to thousands of square miles of rural areas at night, when sky-wave propagation allows radio waves to travel longer distances.

5•21   Minimizing Interference

A number of ways to reduce interference were proposed. One, first tried by the FRC, was to reduce nighttime power and number of stations on the air. By the late 1930s, about 10 percent of the stations were licensed to operate during daytime hours only and another 30 percent reduced power at night. A small proportion —4 percent in 1937—could broadcast only during specific, usually daytime, hours, and another 18 percent shared operations on the same frequency with another station in the same community. Another, more important means of limiting interference was the *directional antenna* (DA), which sent a station's signal out more strongly in one direction than another,

protecting other stations in the suppressed directions from much man-made interference. This engineering technique was used by only 12 stations in 1934 but by more than 200—roughly one-quarter of all stations—by 1941. When adjacent or co-channel stations in different communities used it, they normally could stay on the air with ordinary power serving their audiences, without overlapping. Sometimes the directional pattern—often a figure 8 or more complicated shape—required two to four expensive towers and great engineering skill.

However, something more was needed. Late in 1939 the Federal Communications Commission modified the 1928 FRC broadcast station classification system to allow four types of stations: Class I, high-power stations operating on the 25 clear channels; Class II, secondary stations operating on clear channels (but using less power at night, using DAs or, most often, going off the air at night to protect a dominant clear station); Class III, regional stations; and Class IV, low-power local operations on the few channels set aside for them. The major change was the establishment of Class II.

There was, and is, a continuing debate on the role of clear-channel stations, those 50 kw operations in major cities. Some observers consider them to be the first at the spigot, skimming off the best advertising dollars. Others, including rural spokesmen and their many defenders in government, see them as the only effective means of reaching most of the country at night. More than one-third of the nation's voters got their only reliable night radio service in the 1930s from clear-channel stations. The conflict between this kind of coverage and the equally important need for more stations on the air, especially local stations in areas with no primary service, led to major debates in the late 1930s.

5•22   *Superpower*

The licensees of clear-channel stations fueled the debate by forming a pressure group that pushed the commission for more power. *Superpower* was not a new term, but whereas it once had meant 1,000 or 5,000 or even 20,000 watts, 50,000 watts was now the limit for AM stations. Clear-channel operators said that yet greater power would allow better service to a wider coverage area, which usually meant more nighttime coverage for the rural areas. Opponents of superpower saw this demand as another ploy to get more power and economic clout for stations already too powerful.

Superpower was put to the test in Cincinnati. In 1934 Powel Crosley, Jr.'s clear-channel station WLW was allowed to broadcast with 500,000 watts from 1 A.M. to 6 A.M. as an experiment. On April 17, 1934, Crosley secured a short-term license for 500,000 watts around the clock to experiment with audience and advertiser reaction to the increase, as well as to measure day and night interference. The power increase somewhat extended the station's already wide coverage, but its main effect was to improve the signal substantially in areas already reached. It also caused immediate interference to CFRB in Toronto, and the Canadians complained. To protect CFRB, the FCC required WLW to install a directional antenna in February 1935, and the experiment continued. Listener surveys showed WLW as "first" in preference polls in 13 states, and "second" in six additional states—all of the Midwest and a chunk of the South and East. WLW acquired a national focus, dubbed itself the "Nation's Station," and soon subsisted completely on national and regional advertising. Local advertising disappeared partly because the station raised its rates by 20 percent—WLW explaining to the

commission that additional use of electricity and some expensive rewiring had helped push operating costs up 68 percent ($25 more per operating hour). With the rate card increase, WLW's income was soon three times that of other 50 kw stations, although additional operating costs kept its net profit about the same. But more important, WLW did not want to relinquish the national prestige that the higher power rating had brought.

Others, however, distrusted one station's having such a wide audience. United States senators expressed concern that regional and local stations might find it harder to serve local interests. Fifteen other 50 kw clear-channel stations filed applications with the FCC to operate with the higher power. Networks fretted that wide-coverage competition might affect their business, and smaller regional and local stations in WLW's coverage area complained about the station's domination. A 1938 "Sense of the Senate" resolution (not a law, but a consensus of the Senate's thinking) stated that 50 kw was plenty for any AM station within the American broadcasting structure—a limit still in effect. In March 1939 the FCC rescinded the 500 kw fulltime authorization for WLW, allowing only early morning experimentation once again. The station appealed, but the decision stuck. An attempt by some broadcasters to obtain 500 kw operation in 1940 because of the defense buildup also failed. WLW's early morning experiments continued until early 1942, when wartime restrictions ended them. The 500 kw transmitter eventually was broken up into smaller units and used for shortwave broadcasting.

In some ways, this superpower debate and experiment can be seen as the high-water mark of AM broadcasting facilities. Wartime problems soon hobbled AM radio expansion; and, after the war, although there were many new stations, attention was diverted to FM and television development. Most clear channels were nibbled away over the next decades (see 9.21).

By 1941 radio broadcasting was a fulltime business, and most station owners were fulltime broadcasters. The commission increased the stability of the industry in 1939 when it extended the license period from six months—which it had been since 1928—to one year, although the Communications Act permitted and the FCC later adopted a three-year period. Of all stations on the air in 1939, networks owned 4 percent and newspapers 28 percent. Such figures conceal the true concentration of power, however. With respect to clear-channel and high-power regional stations, networks owned 25 percent, newspapers 27 percent, and radio/electrical manufacturers about 13 percent—roughly two-thirds of the total. Broadcasting was to a great extent individually and locally owned, but the big-audience and big-profit stations were concentrated in fewer hands.

Another sign of growth amid relatively stable conditions was the near doubling of broadcast employees—stations and networks, full- and part-time—from 14,000 in 1935 to 27,000 in 1941. The National Association of Broadcasters estimated in 1940 that approximately 350,000 persons were employed because of radio in advertising agencies, radio manufacturing companies, and as talent as well as in stations and networks.

5·3   Network Domination

With a few exceptions, success in radio station operation in the 1930s required having a network affiliation—preferably NBC-Red or CBS. By late 1938 the four national networks (see below) had affiliated all the 52 clear-channel stations but two (and they had ties with Mutual), half the regional stations, and even some low-power local stations. In all, almost half the unlimited-time stations were network affiliates. These stations took in the lion's share of broadcast revenues, because the big audiences that popular network programs drew attracted local advertisers.

By 1941 there were four national networks—NBC-Red, NBC-Blue, CBS, and Mutual—and some 20 regional networks. Of the latter, 14 operated in only one state, while six had wider coverage, including the Don Lee Network on the West Coast and the Yankee Network in New England. Many regional networks offered special programming to their affiliates, others merely facilitated program exchange, but all networks made time-buying easier for the advertising agencies by offering a block of stations and wide coverage with one order.

NBC was, and is, totally controlled by RCA—then a publicly held corporation, now owned by GE. In 1941, after government antitrust action a decade earlier, no one individual or firm held more than one-half of 1 percent of its stock. During the 1930s NBC operated two separate networks: the more important Red Network with larger stations as affiliates, and far more advertising income and popular programs than the Blue Network with its less powerful stations and more public service and sustaining programming. In 1935, 14 percent of the country's stations were affiliated with one or the other of the NBC networks, a figure that went up to 25 percent by 1941, not including 100 stations listed as optional—at the sponsor's request—affiliates for either network. NBC owned ten stations and, from 1932 to 1940, was responsible for operating five others owned by Westinghouse—an agreement that ended when the FCC required licensees to program their own stations. Of the ten owned-and-operated (O & O) outlets, all but three were unlimited-time 50 kw stations. As broadcasting became more complicated in the 1930s, so did NBC. In 1930 it opened a short-lived talent agency. In 1934 it began a transcription service, first for its affiliates and then for other stations, which provided a regularly supplemented and renewed library of prerecorded music on large discs.

In the late 1930s CBS was about one-third owned and controlled by its president, William S. Paley, and his family. It affiliated with some 15–16 percent of all the stations on the air and from 1936 to 1939 owned nine stations outright. In 1939 CBS sold its Cincinnati outlet and, unlike NBC, settled for a large minority interest in two other stations. All but one of its O & Os were unlimited-time 50 kw operations. Like NBC, CBS operated an "artist's bureau"—a talent agency, which actually did more business with NBC than with CBS—and, starting in 1940, a transcription service. That CBS was not in the phonograph record business until the end of 1938, when it bought the American Record Corporation—which then had Columbia Phonograph Company as a subsidiary—and changed its name to Columbia Record Corp., can partly explain the six-year lag behind NBC. CBS was devoted to broadcasting and other program-related services, while NBC was only a small part of a large electrical manufacturing and communications firm.

In summer 1934, four major eastern and midwestern stations decided to make themselves available to advertisers at a group rate by interconnecting themselves by wire lines. The four stations were WGN (Chicago), owned by the *Chicago Tribune;* WOR (Newark, New Jersey), owned by the Bamberger department store; WLW (Cincinnati), owned by Powel Crosley, Jr., and just starting its 500 kw experiments; and WXYZ (Detroit), owned by George W. Trendle. The first three were 50 kw clear-channel stations trying to improve their economic condition outside the established networks, while WXYZ brought an especially popular new program, *The Lone Ranger,* to the new network. On September 29, 1934, the group changed its name from the provisional Quality Network to the Mutual Broadcasting System, a name that stressed its unique organizational structure.

Unlike CBS and NBC, Mutual did not have a central ownership with O & O stations and contractual affiliates. From the beginning it was a cooperative venture, more or less equally operated by its four partners, although only WGN and WOR technically owned the firm's nominal amount of stock. For two years Mutual remained limited to its original four stations but was heard in most of the eastern United States. When WXYZ left Mutual for NBC in late 1935, its place was taken by CKLW in Windsor, Ontario, which served the same region. In 1936 the 13 affiliates of the New England–based Colonial Network and the 10 affiliates of the West Coast–based Don Lee Network affiliated as well with Mutual, making it a true national network. The addition of other independent stations and networks, including a 23-affiliate Texas network, brought Mutual from less than half of 1 percent of all stations in 1935 to more than 19 percent by 1940, and brought the first network service to many communities. However, many of its new stations were primarily affiliated with NBC or CBS and used Mutual programs only as fillers; most of Mutual's affiliates were regional and local outlets with low power and relatively small audiences. Not surprisingly, therefore, this network lagged behind NBC and CBS in audience size and in advertising income. Because Mutual was a cooperative venture, most programs came from the founding or affiliate stations, although it did operate a small central news service in New York.

Perhaps the clearest indication of the importance of networks in the late 1930s—and the reason for the FCC investigation discussed in 5.83—was the increasing control that CBS and NBC exerted over their affiliates. Stations were bound to these networks for five-year periods, although the networks could end a contract after any single year. Mutual's one-year term for both sides was an exception. Affiliations were tightly exclusive: networks would provide programs only to their affiliates, and affiliates could provide time to other national chains only on occasions when their primary network did not care. Contracts assigned option periods each day to the network for its national commercial programming. CBS had the right to take all day, NBC most of the day, but it gave 28-day notice, and Mutual averaged four hours a day. Finally, stations legally could reject sustaining programs from the networks in order to air local shows, but rejecting commercially sponsored programs could jeopardize their affiliation.

The one-sided nature of network contracts was a result of relative strength. Local stations gave networks and national advertisers access to audiences in their communities. But networks had the advertising money to produce programs that stations needed to attract audiences. No single station could afford to put together programs that would be as popular as those of the networks. Networks also supplied sustaining programs that the stations could use as free "fill." Hence, the affiliated stations, even with regional coverage, needed the networks more than vice versa, and other stations always were waiting for a chance to affiliate. Networks could de-

mand and get major concessions, although powerful clear-channel stations could sometimes get better terms than smaller stations. In Mutual's cooperative arrangements, contracts tended at first to treat the two parties as equals. But when the proposed Transcontinental Network, which never materialized, threatened Mutual in 1938, MBS tightened its contracts in order to hold onto its affiliates. Clearly broadcasting in the 1930s was centrally controlled by the networks, and this concentration of programming authority brought government attention (see 5.83).

5•4   Educational Radio: Talk but Little Progress

The 38 AM educational stations on the air in 1936 had dropped to 35 by mid-1941 and today number no more than 25. About half the survivors in 1941 had been on the air more than 15 years, 12 were commercially supported, and 7 of these were affiliated with a network as well, airing educational programs only a few hours a day. One was operated by a high school, 2 were operated by church-affiliated educational groups, 9 by agriculture schools or state agricultural departments, and 11 by land-grant universities, mainly in the Midwest. Only 11 stations were licensed for unlimited broadcast time, about half of them in the 250–5,000 watt category.

Educational radio consisted of a few hardy survivors of the 200 educational stations that had started in the 1920s. Although they provided solid in-school instructional and at-home educational and cultural programs to supplement educational offerings of the networks and a few independent commercial stations, their dwindling numbers made educational radio a shadow of what its adherents wanted.

Seemingly, more organizations were

interested in educational radio than there were stations on the air during the late 1930s. Two of them (see 4.4), the National Advisory Council on Radio in Education and the National Committee on Education by Radio, continued their separate approaches to the problem. The council sponsored a series of useful publications and continued to push for cooperation with commercial broadcasters—although one of its experiments, using many commercial stations, was constantly rescheduled at less and less valuable air times. The committee worked for allocation of educational channels (see 4.4) and sponsored annual conferences from 1931 until 1938, when its Rockefeller Foundation support ended. One of the committee's more lasting influences was to help local groups establish listening councils: groups of critical listeners who worked with local broadcasters to improve existing programs and plan new ones.

The Institute for Education by Radio was established at Ohio State University in 1930 and ran an annual conference on educational radio until 1960. The Federal Radio Education Committee, officially sponsored by the Federal Communications Commission, had 39 members under the chairmanship of the U.S. Commissioner of Education and existed to eliminate conflicts and promote cooperation between commercial and educational licensees. Like the other groups, it sponsored conferences and studies and promoted educational radio but did little of substance to expand the service.

The National Association of Educational Broadcasters (NAEB), developed in 1934 from the Association of College and University Broadcasting Stations, which had been established in 1925 amid the rush to get education on the air. The NAEB, the only one of the educational radio groups to survive until the 1980s, op-

erated throughout the 1934–1941 period with about 25 member stations and little money. Acting primarily as a program idea exchange, it also sponsored off-the-air rebroadcast experiments.

The notion of reserving spectrum space for the exclusive use of education was developed during the 1930s. The National Committee on Education by Radio deserved much of the credit for lobbying through this proposal. Educators had lost interest when they realized that stations assigned to the part of the spectrum originally sought (1,500–1,600 kHz, just above the standard broadcast band of that time) typically would have less range than other stations, that they would have equipment expenses, and that few receivers could receive signals on those frequencies. When the Senate was considering the 1934 Communications Act, Senators Wagner and Hatfield sponsored an amendment allocating 25 percent of broadcast facilities (essentially, spectrum space) to nonprofit organizations. However, dissension among educators and solid commercial broadcaster opposition led to the proposal's defeat. In response to a congressional order for investigation contained in the Communications Act, the commission recommended in 1935 against reservation of special frequencies and for educator cooperation with commercial stations and networks. Hearings brought forth testimony that networks and big stations were much more cooperative with educators than were small and independent stations.

Early in 1938, however, the FCC reversed itself and provided the first specific spectrum reservations for noncommercial broadcast use, selecting channels in the 41–42 MHz band, far above the standard broadcasting band. On January 26, it set aside 25 channels in this band for in-school broadcasting. The first station licensed was the Cleveland Board of Education's WBOE, in November 1938. In 1939 the educational broadcasting allocation was shifted to 42–43 MHz, and stations were required to change from AM to the newer FM mode. Since FM required a wider bandwidth, this allocation provide only five channels, on which seven stations were transmitting to radio-equipped class-rooms by late 1941. When commercial FM went into operation, the educational allo-cation was for channels at the bottom of the band, which were fractionally easier for listeners to receive than higher ones.

Although the potential for educa-tional radio was considered good, financial realities restricted most FM broadcasts to in-school use. The 35 or so surviving ed-ucational stations on the standard AM band supplied a little adult education program-ming in evening hours. Most important, the precedent of setting aside channels for education had been established.

5·5   The Advertising Agencies Take Over

Just as the radio business reflected the Depression (see the drop in overall advertising income for 1933 shown in Ap-pendix C, table 4) so it reflected the coun-try's recovery in the second half of the dec-ade. Total revenues of $112 million in 1935 grew to more than twice that figure just six years later. In the same period, radio in-creased its portion of the advertising dollar from 7 percent to 11 percent—not a bad showing for a medium supported by ad-vertising for little more than a decade. Much of this growth, of course, was due to the peculiar economic relationship be-tween broadcasting and its audience. Once a person owned a radio receiver, he or she paid nothing for professional entertain-ment of high quality, but the advertiser paid dearly for the privilege of entertain-

ing potential customers among the lis-teners. Every year set owners had more time for radio because of household labor-saving devices, shorter work weeks, and Depression-caused unemployment.

Another factor in radio's success was the growing role of middlemen. The station time broker, active in radio's early advertising years, was replaced in the late 1930s by the station representative (see 4.51) who promoted to advertising agencies a single station in a given market, thus avoiding the time broker's conflict of in-terest in dealing with several stations in one market. The station rep received 10–15 percent of the station's advertising rate, after deducting the advertising agency commission of 15 percent. Rep firms grew from 28 in 1935 to about 40 five years later. The reps began to have a standardizing effect on their client stations, often sug-gesting which programming or advertising policies would appeal most to potential sponsors.

Representing the advertisers in all but the smallest markets were the adver-tising agencies, which as early as 1935 were placing three-quarters of the radio adver-tising orders. While many smaller agencies around the country were content to pur-chase time on existing programs through station reps in New York, in a few other big markets, and with the networks, large agencies worked closely with their clients and the radio networks, or big stations, to develop compatible program and advertis-ing packages. The agency created not only the ads but also the programs, contracted for talent and studio facilities—often from the networks—to produce programs, and then presented the finished program, with integrated commercials, to the network. In effect, the agencies bought time in large chunks from the networks and a few of the largest independent stations. Stations got the popular show, networks provided the facilities and collected the money—and Madison Avenue had all but total control over network prime-time and daytime programming.

Another example of the trend toward centralized program control was the musical program package recorded by transcription companies and sold to individual local stations in ready-to-air form, including advertising. Stations that had created their own programs in the 1920s now recognized the economy of centralized programming and the accessibility of the limited amount of popular talent through networks with which they were affiliated. In turn, the networks were glad to hand over their programming worries to the advertising agencies, which welcomed the opportunity to tie together program and commercial. Since the networks economically served the agencies, they felt free to let the agencies do the work and take the rap from the sponsors if anything went wrong.

Agency control of network programming continued until the advent of television in the late 1940s and early 1950s, with its enormous programming costs, discouraged agencies from making programming investments. At this stage, the television networks took over programming and, later, high prices virtually eliminated single sponsorship of programs with integrated commercials. In the 1970s, ironically, agitation grew for divorcing the networks from program production—a few people even suggesting that the agencies again take over that function.

By the mid-1930s, radio's advertising pattern for the next 15 years, and television's thereafter, was clearly established. Sixty percent of time sale revenues went to the networks and their handful of O & O stations, leaving 700 other radio stations to share the remaining 40 percent. Since most network O & Os were 50,000

watt clear-channel stations in the country's biggest markets, they naturally attracted advertising. National and regional advertisers turned first to the networks and spent relatively little on local station sponsorship or spot advertising (see Appendix C, table 4). Most small and medium-size stations had to rely on local advertising revenues.

The networks differed greatly. NBC-Red and CBS had the most popular programs, the highest charges for time, and the largest incomes. NBC-Blue was a distant third. Although it had about as many affiliates as NBC-Red, its usually lower-powered stations could not get the same advertiser support as the Red network's clear-channel and powerful regional affiliates. Also, the Blue network presented many sustaining programs—not just because they could not attract sponsors but also to counterbalance, in a public relations sense, the culturally lower but popular sponsored shows on the Red network. The fourth national network, Mutual, had little national advertising impact, since most of its stations arranged their own time sales outside Mutual's limited program exchanges. Some regional networks made a profit but were handling only a fraction as much business as any one of the national networks.

By the mid-1930s, the advertising agencies could recommend two time periods during the day as most desirable for their clients. Many food and soap manufacturing companies purchased daily time on agency-packaged serial *soap opera* programs in the late morning and early afternoon. These programs (see 5.62), named after their typical sponsors, dominated daytime scheduling and acquired large and loyal housewife audiences. The other key time, *prime time*, generally was 7 P.M. to 11 P.M. on the East and West coasts and 6 P.M. to 10 P.M. in the Central and Mountain time zones. Prime time cost the most because it had the most listeners, and was thus the most desirable.

Agencies and sponsors considered the best combination a high-power station operating on a channel toward the low-numbered end of the broadcast band in a large and prosperous market, and attracting a large audience, typically as a network affiliate. For example, in the late 1930s more than half of the revenue went to stations in markets of more than 400,000 population, and one-quarter of the revenue went to the 50 or so 50 kw stations. In 1938 the average station in a market of over a million population had a net income of $60,000 before taxes, while a station in a market of fewer than a half-million population might earn $20,000. In the same year, according to FCC data, about one-third of all radio stations lost money.

A station's expenditures, like its revenues, varied with market size and station type. Powerful stations in large markets would spend about 19 percent of the average expense dollar on technical items, 43 percent on programming, and 38 percent for sales and administration. A small station in a small market would spend about the same proportion on technical items, about half as much on programming, and maybe twice as much on sales and administration. With less revenue and fewer national advertisers, local stations often offered simpler programming; recorded music cost much less than live orchestras and other talent.

A 1938 FCC survey of 633 stations showed that fully two-thirds of their programs carried advertising, compared to one-third at the start of the decade. About three-quarters of the musical programs were sponsored, about two-thirds of drama, talks and dialogues, and news were sponsored, and half of the variety programs were sponsored and half sustaining. Most other programs, like religion and special events, were sustaining.

While the radio industry's income varied with the country's economic condition, radio advertising was clearly accepted. Of the many trade publications and books on radio advertising in the late 1930s, nearly all were optimistic about radio's value.

5·6   The Golden Age of Programming

In the last half of the 1930s, most full time radio stations broadcast at least 12 hours a day, and many for 18 hours or more. Generally stations filled the expanded air time with variations of program types already developed. Three departures from this pattern were news and commentary, the daytime serial drama, and quiz and audience-participation programs.

The FCC's March 1938 survey of programming showed that 53 percent was devoted to music, 11 percent to talks and dialogues, 9 percent to drama, 9 percent to variety, 9 percent to news (which would not have been measurable a few years earlier), 5 percent to religion and devotion, 2 percent to special events, and 2 percent to miscellaneous. While network affiliates got from 50 percent to 70 percent of programming from their network, they also increased the time devoted to local and live programming. Of all radio programming in the survey period, 64 percent was live —roughly half network and half local— while 21 percent was from electrical transcriptions and 12 percent was from phonograph records—a definite increase in nonlive programming on the typical station. (See box on the opposite page for a schedule of one major station in 1937.)

A Radio Station's Programs: 1937 / This is a typical weekday schedule for WTMJ, the *Milwaukee Journal* AM station, as taken from a telephone audience report. The listing does not show programs on the air before 8 A.M. or after 10 P.M. as calls were not made earlier or later than that. Actually, WTMJ went on the air around 6 A.M. and did not go off until about midnight—hours since extended, as is the case with most large city radio stations. Programs followed by # originate at the network level— in this case, NBC-Red.

A.M.

8:00	Winter Wonderland	10:00	Household Hints
8:15	Your Home Town	10:15	Backstage Wife #
8:30	Party Line	10:30	How to Be Charming
8:45	Bandmaster	10:45	Hello Peggy
9:00	What's New in Milwaukee	11:00	Helen Gahagan
9:30	Morning Melodies	11:15	Blue Room
9:45	Today's Children	11:30	Behind the Mike
		11:45	Heinie [German band music]

P.M.

12:30	Rhythm Rascals	3:45	Road of Life #
12:45	Sidewalk Reporter	4:00	Friendship Circle
1:00	Livestock Reports, News	4:30	Kitty Keene #
1:15	Remote Control	4:45	News
2:00	Pepper Young's Family #	5:00	Jack Armstrong [children's action-adventure] #
2:15	Ma Perkins #		
2:30	Vic & Sade #	5:15	Heinie
2:45	The O'Neills #	5:45	Sports Flash
3:00	Around the Town	6:00	Dairy Council
3:15	Guiding Light #	6:15	Uncle Ezra [country music] #
3:30	Paul Skinner	6:30	Easy Aces [comedy] #
		6:45	Kilowatt Hour

(Here is the Monday schedule for the evening "prime time")

7:00	Burns & Allen [comedy] #
7:30	Firestone Program [music] #
8:00	Fibber McGee & Molly [comedy] #
8:30	Hour of Charm [female orchestra] #
9:00	Contented Hour [music] #
9:30	Glen Gray and his Casa Loma Orchestra #

Source: Milwaukee Journal radio station audience research report information for November 1937, based on 49,100 completed telephone calls comparing WTMJ with six other area stations. Material now on file with, and supplied through the courtesy of, the Mass Communication History Center of the State Historical Society of Wisconsin.

5•61   Music and Variety

Music remained the staple of most radio schedules. Several transcription companies, operated both by networks and some independents, offered local stations prerecorded music, sometimes assembled into programs. By early 1939 more than 575 stations subscribed to at least one transcription service, and nearly half of them used two or more. RCA's transcription operation probably accounted for 35 percent of the industry's business, although 25 or 30 companies had combined annual revenues of $5 million in the late 1930s.

A station usually signed a contract with a transcription firm to deliver several hundred recorded musical selections— usually on 16-inch discs, running at 33⅓ rpm, with approximately 15 minutes per side—to start, and then perhaps 50 additional selections a month. The transcription firm usually dealt with only one station in a particular market to avoid program duplication, and payment by the station was either a percentage of its gross revenues or a flat sum. While such material averaged only 10–15 percent of time on network-affiliated stations, nonaffiliated local stations used it much more, some for 80 percent of their schedules. Popular songs and instrumentals predominated, but all kinds of music were offered.

Although the use of music increased locally, classical musical programs declined in importance on the networks after the early 1930s. A notable exception was the NBC Symphony Orchestra, one of the outstanding cultural creations of radio in America. The orchestra was founded when David Sarnoff helped persuade Arturo Toscanini, the just retired conductor of the New York Philharmonic, to return from Italy to conduct ten concerts, the first one on Christmas night 1937. NBC hired the best musicians possible to work in the new symphony orchestra. Three months later the network announced that Toscanini would lead the orchestra for another three years; but, as it turned out, the NBC Symphony continued for nearly 17 years until Toscanini's final retirement, well into his eighties, in 1954. The broadcasts normally originated from specially built Studio 8H, then the largest in the world, in the RCA Building in Rockefeller Center, and were broadcast on NBC-Blue on a sustaining basis, at the conductor's insistence. From 1948 the NBC Symphony was seen on television as well. After the NBC Symphony formally disbanded, the orchestra continued to play independently as the "Symphony of the Air."

Large dance bands were increasingly heard on both national and local programs. The 1930s were the "big band era," and many famous orchestras were heard first locally and then on the networks. Both industries benefited from such broadcasts, since the publicity of a major radio appearance attracted more people to the band's concerts. By 1937 the bands of Benny Goodman, Ozzie Nelson, Russ Morgan, Sammy Kaye, and Tommy Dorsey had played on network radio. *Your Hit Parade*, one of the top long-running radio programs, presented the most popular songs of the previous week, as determined by a national "survey" of record and sheet music sales, performed live by major singers and orchestras. The show began in fall 1935 and was sponsored on radio until 1953, and from 1951 until 1959 on television, by the American Tobacco Company's Lucky Strike (and, toward the very end, Hit Parade) cigarettes.

Local stations presented a wide range of live music, some stations supporting a full orchestra, and an increasing amount of recorded music. The conflict between broadcasters and ASCAP (see 5.85) had a substantial effect on radio music in 1940–1941.

Compared to the highly professional variety programs, local or national *amateur hour* broadcasts presented unknowns who would sing, tap dance, or do imitations in the hope of making a career. Such programs were used as fillers for years. Although the quality was uneven, the audiences that had cheered hometown talent supported contestants from all over the country. The most famous amateur variety show, *Major Bowes and His Original Amateur Hour,* began on New York station WHN in 1934 and moved to NBC-Red in March 1935. Within a few months, it was the most popular program on radio—at one time reaching a near-unbelievable rating of 45 when 20 was more typical! It presented amateurs who went on to fame—including Frank Sinatra, who made his radio debut in this program's first year—and others who went down to defeat and anonymity. Bowes became known by his catch-phrases and for his abrupt, even brutal manner with a gong as an aural equivalent of the "hook" used to remove inept or stage-frightened performers. The program continued on radio until 1952 and went on television from 1949 to the late 1960s, with Ted Mack serving as MC after Bowes's death—and bears a family resemblance to the *Gong Show* of the mid-1970s.

Many other national and local programs were built around a single performer, almost always a male singer or comic, usually backed by a musical group and supplemented by weekly guest performers. Most of these variety stars were products of vaudeville, burlesque, legitimate theater, or music halls. One was Bob Hope, who began his weekly show on CBS in 1935.

Such variety programming re-mained a network favorite, with little change, until inauguration of the army draft just before World War II gave a military slant to programs of the early 1940s. The *Army Show* (later the *Army Hour*), on NBC-Blue, *This Is Fort Dix* over Mutual, the Navy Band hour, and *Wings over America* were typical. The formats resembled earlier radio variety shows, with bits of song, humor, and chatter, but the participants frequently were military personnel, and the programs often originated from military camps and bases.

5•62   Drama

By far the most important network dramatic programming, in hours broadcast per week, was the woman's serial drama, or soap opera. Starting in 1935, the weekly hours of such fare increased sharply until, in 1940, the four networks combined devoted 75 hours a week to such programs, nine of every ten sponsored daytime network hours. These programs lasted 15 minutes, came on at the same time each weekday, and had soap and food manufacturers as sponsors. Typical of the longer running programs were *Back Stage Wife* ("what it means to be the wife of a famous Broadway star—dream sweetheart of a million other women"), which began in 1935; *The Guiding Light* (about a kindly cleric); *Lorenzo Jones* (inventor of useless gadgets); *Our Gal Sunday* ("Can this girl from a mining town in the West find happiness as the wife of a wealthy and titled Englishman?"); and *Road of Life* (doctors and nurses, although it began as the tale of an Irish-American mother's attempt to raise her children). In each case, domestic life was emphasized with its ups, and more usually, downs. Many of the actors and actresses played the same parts for decades. For a portion of each day, they performed a live, convincing, emotion-filled episode with little rehearsal, but their evenings were free for the stage or other professional activities. Behind many of the serials was the husband and wife team of Frank and Anne Hummert, who originally wrote all their own work but eventually employed dialogue writers to work within their character development and story lines. Elaine Carrington and Irna Phillips also wrote "soapers"—sometimes several at the same time.

The typical serial format was wonderfully simple: a brief musical introduction played on the studio organ, a narrator opening the day's episode with a recap of what had happened before, two segments of action separated by a commercial break, and a closing word from the narrator suggesting the problems ahead. Dialogue and organ music were somber and simple; story progress was very slow, giving time for character development and allowing a listener to miss an episode or two painlessly. Audiences were loyal, and many programs lasted 15 or more seasons, until radio's programming character changed in the 1950s. Listeners to soap operas were among the first studied by social psychologists, and much criticism was levied at the genre in 1940 and 1941, as it was nearly impossible to schedule anything else between 10 A.M. and 5 P.M. These complaints dropped off as the number of serials decreased during the war years.

"Prestige" drama increased in the 1930s. These programs usually were "anthologies" offering different stories with new casts each week, sometimes adaptations from other media, but often original radio plays. Writers such as poet Archibald MacLeish, later Librarian of Congress, and unknown authors such as Nor-

man Corwin and Arch Oboler gained recognition almost overnight. Prestige series included the *Columbia Workshop* of experimental drama on CBS, started late in 1936, and the more conventional *Lux Radio Theater*, which presented such stars as Helen Hayes, Leslie Howard, and an unknown player named Orson Welles in hour-long versions of current films.

Welles at twenty-three was the guiding light behind a new CBS series in fall 1938, the *Mercury Theater on the Air*. As writer, director, and star, he built up a company of actors whose names were famous for decades: Joseph Cotton, Agnes Moorehead, Everett Sloane, Ray Collins. His Sunday evening, October 30, 1938, Halloween program probably ranks as the most famous single radio show ever presented. It was an adaptation by Welles and Howard Koch of H. G. Wells's science fiction story "War of the Worlds." The location was changed to northern New Jersey, the time was moved to the present, and, even more important, the narrative was changed to reflect radio's format. Listeners who tuned in to the program's beginning, or who listened carefully to the between-acts announcements, understood these circumstances. But those who tuned in late—and many had a habit of listening to the first few minutes of ventriloquist Edgar Bergen and his dummy Charlie McCarthy on NBC before tuning over to CBS for the play—were due for a surprise. The program in progress seemed to feature a band performing in a hotel. A few moments later, an announcer broke in with a "news bulletin" saying that a gas cloud had been observed on the planet Mars. Then back to the music; another interruption, asking observatories to keep watch; more music; an interview with a "noted astronomer" on the possibility of life on Mars (unlikely); more music—and, suddenly, a bulletin saying that a large meteorite had fallen in the vicinity of Grovers Mill, New Jersey. The pace built in a series of news bulletins and on-the-spot reports of the opening of the cylindrical "meteorite," the emergence of the Martians, the assembly of Martian war machines, the rout of U.S. military forces, and government reaction. Reports of casualties, traffic jams, transmissions from hapless military pilots, ominous breaking off of on-the-spot reports, the later report of the "death" of the field reporter, and use of familiar names and places—all gave it reality. As the Martian war machines headed toward New York to discharge their poison gas over the city—to the sounds of fleeing ocean liners, the last gasps of a newsman atop the broadcasting studio, and the cracked voice of a solitary ham radio operator calling "Isn't anybody there? Isn't anybody?"—many listeners did not wait to hear the mid-program announcement that it was all a hoax. By 8:30, thousands of people were praying, preparing for the end, and fleeing the Martians.

These reactions were not silly, although it may look that way today. The pacing of the program undermined critical faculties. It convinced the listener that a reporter had traveled the miles from Grovers Mill "in ten minutes," when less than three minutes actually had elapsed. Already sure that mobs were fleeing, listeners who looked out their windows and saw lots of people going about normal pursuits assumed that everyone was trying to get away from the Martians, just as the radio said. If no one was in sight, they assumed that everyone else had fled and left them behind. Few heard the three announcements of the program's fictional nature or the last half-hour, which was mostly a monologue by Welles, as a scientist who believes that he is one of the few survivors and who observes the demise of the Martians from the effects of earthly germs and bacteria. If they had heard this obviously dramatic material, many persons might have caught on. In the East, especially near the "landing site," thousands of people—a small proportion of the population but a large number nevertheless—called police, fled their homes, or otherwise reacted as though the invasion were real.

This panic had a number of causes, notably the way the program's "Halloween prank" nature was glossed over in the introduction. Afterwards researchers learned that many listeners did not try to double check the "news" on another station or telephone friends; and that others, who found normal programming elsewhere on the dial, decided that these stations had not yet received the word. The panic was also a reaction to the "Munich Crisis" just one month before, when Americans had been glued to their radios expecting the world to go to war (see 5.63).

Welles was amazed but only slightly abashed at the program's impact. The FCC let it be known that it would not consider such "scare" programs and formats as broadcasting in the public interest. Although "War of the Worlds" was rebroadcast recently in the United States as a "period piece" without much effect, its original adaptation broadcast in other countries brought the same sort of panic. Several persons were killed in a riot in South America, when resentment over having been fooled boiled over. This drama showed better than any other program or episode the impact of radio on society— "if it was on the radio, then it must be true."

Thrillers and situation comedies filled more network time per week than any other form of drama. Adventure programs, starting in the early 1930s (see 4.63), were heard both in the evenings, as crime-detective shows for adults, and in the late

Orson Welles's Halloween Broadcast: 1938 / Orson Welles narrated the famous "War of the Worlds" broadcast on October 30, 1938—creating the kind of panic reported in the *New York Times* the following day. Photo credit: Culver Pictures, Inc.

NEW YORK, MONDAY, OCTOBER 31, 1938.

Radio Listeners in Panic, Taking War Drama as Fact

Many Flee Homes to Escape 'Gas Raid From Mars'—Phone Calls Swamp Police at Broadcast of Wells Fantasy

A wave of mass hysteria seized thousands of radio listeners throughout the nation between 8:15 and 9:30 o'clock last night when a broadcast of a dramatization of H. G. Wells's fantasy, "The War of the Worlds," led thousands to believe that an interplanetary conflict had started with invading Martians spreading wide death and destruction in New Jersey and New York.

The broadcast, which disrupted households, interrupted religious services, created traffic jams and clogged communications systems, was made by Orson Welles, who as the radio character, "The Shadow," used to give "the creeps" to countless child listeners. This time at least a score of adults required medical treatment for shock and hysteria.

In Newark, in a single block at Heddon Terrace and Hawthorne Avenue, more than twenty families rushed out of their houses with wet handkerchiefs and towels over their faces to flee from what they believed was to be a gas raid. Some began moving household furniture.

Throughout New York families left their homes, some to flee to near-by parks. Thousands of persons called the police, newspapers and radio stations here and in other cities of the United States and Canada seeking advice on protective measures against the raids.

The program was produced by Mr. Welles and the Mercury Theatre on the Air over station WABC and the Columbia Broadcasting System's coast-to-coast network, from 8 to 9 o'clock.

The radio play, as presented, was to simulate a regular radio program with a "break-in" for the material of the play. The radio listeners, apparently, missed or did not listen to the introduction, which was: "The Columbia Broadcasting System and its affiliated stations present Orson Welles and the Mercury Theatre on the Air in 'The War of the Worlds' by H. G. Wells."

They also failed to associate the program with the newspaper listing of the program, announced as "Today: 8:00-9:00—Play: H. G. Wells's 'War of the Worlds'— WABC." They ignored three additional announcements made during the broadcast emphasizing its fictional nature.

Mr. Welles opened the program with a description of the series of

Continued on Page Four

afternoons, as action-adventure serials for children. These live, mostly network shows could be technically complicated, with large casts, sound effects, and split-second timing. Programs included the true story–recreating *Gangbusters* starting in 1935, whose loud opening of sirens, machine-gun fire, and marching feet gave rise to the phrase "coming on like Gangbusters"; *Mr. Keen, Tracer of Lost Persons*; and *I Love a Mystery*, which had one of radio's most loyal audiences. The last was written by Carlton E. Morse, writer of the enduringly popular *One Man's Family*. *Mr. District Attorney*, a program starting in 1939 which opened with the DA reciting his oath of office, provided a generation with the concept of the law as protector as well as prosecutor.

Programs aimed at children included *Jack Armstrong—The All-American Boy*; *Tom Mix*, a cowboy-adventure program; *Captain Midnight* and *Hop Harrigan*, both with pilot-heroes; *Terry and the Pirates*, based on the Milton Caniff comic strip; and a number of other serials that made the American "children's hour" far different from the period of silence that the British offered for several decades. Two of the most important children's adventure programs were not serials. *The Lone Ranger* and *The Green Hornet*, which began over Mutual in 1938, were written and acted by the team at WXYZ, Detroit (see 4.63). Indeed, the publisher-hero Green Hornet was identified as the Lone Ranger's grandnephew! *The Green Hornet* used a classical

Radio's Comedy Stars of the 1930s / Two of radio's longest running comedians were Jack Benny (shown here—in the left photo—with his wife and comedy partner, Mary Livingstone) and Fred Allen (with his wife Portland Hoffa, in the right photo). The two—who actually admired each other—had a running on-air "feud," based on their very different approaches to radio comedy. Another ex-vaudevillian was George Burns, who supplied straight lines to his zany and confused wife, Gracie Allen (see picture at the beginning of this chapter). With the exception of Fred Allen, who appeared only sporadically on television, all of these stars made the transition from radio to television in the late 1940s and thus had broadcast careers of more than three decades. Photos courtesy of National Broadcasting Company, Inc.

music theme and a hard-punching opening: "He hunts the biggest of all game! Public enemies who try to destroy our America. . . . With his faithful valet, Kato, Britt Reid, daring young publisher, matches wits with the underworld, risking his life that criminals and racketeers, within the law, may feel its weight by the sting of— the Green Hornet!" Until FBI chief Hoover objected, the Green Hornet's targets were "public enemies that even the G-Men cannot catch." When the United States entered World War II, the faithful valet-chauffeur Kato was quickly changed from Japanese to Filipino.

Radio's half-hour situation comedies were a staple for years. *Li'l Abner* began over NBC in 1939, originating in

Chicago as many programs then did; Fanny Brice, about whom the musical *Funny Girl* was written, created her immortal *Baby Snooks*, the child demon who created crisis after crisis for her father and her baby brother Robespierre; *Blondie*, a 1939 CBS entry based on the Chic Young comic strip, featured the tribulations of Dagwood and Blondie Bumstead—another example of broadcasting's penchant for weak father figures; and *Henry Aldrich*—the misadventures of a crack-voiced adolescent—after appearing for some years as a segment on other programs, aired on its own over NBC-Blue in 1939.

Except for daytime serials and thriller programs, most network drama— anthology, or serial like *One Man's Family*

Oddly popular on radio, where the visual trick of ventriloquism could not be seen, were Edgar Bergen and his wooden dummy, Charlie McCarthy—though the wise-cracking dummy clearly walked away with the show. Famed comedy star W. C. Fields is about to perform a frontal lobotomy on McCarthy— the two traded barbs on the air for years. Photo credit: Culver Pictures, Inc.

Suggestions for Hopeful Radio Playwrights / This copy, reproduced exactly as the Aubrey, Moore and Wallace agency of Chicago sent it out to those requesting it, shows some of the limitations and problems of writing for a prime-time radio network drama program. Note some of the period taboos, such as women smoking. Similar, though usually much longer, guidelines exist for current television programs—but the price paid to authors has increased sharply from the $100 of 1938.

Suggestions for
Radio Playwrights
Campana's "First Nighter"(Friday NBC)
and "Grand Hotel" (Sunday NBC)

Regarding BOTH Programs

Both of these programs are very successful. They have
a large audience. During the years they have been on the
air we have received hundreds of thousands of letters all
of which have aided us in knowing what our audiences like.
Please keep this in mind as you read these suggestions.

Our radio listeners are primarily the family type of audience.
Consequently, we are interested in

Comedy and Farce
Melodrama
Light and Heavy Romances
Mystery
Adventure

that will provide wholesome entertainment for all members
of an average family. This means there are certain restrictions. As a suggestion, we offer a few taboos:

Sex
Profanity
Drunkenness or even drinking
Smoking by Women
Glorification of crime of
criminals
Anything that will offend
members of racial, political
or religious groups.

On the other hand, there is a wide range of possibilities
with real live characters, with plenty of action and dramatic conflict.

A few pointers:

1. Plays which have a definite love interest or a
mystery with an original "twist" before the ending are particularly desirable. While the conventional happy ending is not essential, it is
generally conceded to be better box-office.

2. "Plant" your characters -- i.e., tell us who they
are and where they are in the fewest possible words
as soon as possible after their entrance. Do not
use an announcer, narrator, or interpretor to describe scene or play. Characters must do all this
by their lines.

-2-

3. Do not shift scene unnecessarily. On the other hand,
    do not allow the whole play to become static.

4. If you have any good ideas on sound effects, write
    them in -- otherwise leave it alone. This part of
    the production is quite efficiently handled during
    rehearsals.

5. Radio drama is of necessity a natural and intimate
    form of entertainment, dialogue should not be stiff,
    or stagy. Make your characters real people.

6. Motivate all your characters and situations. Also
    remember that action is more entertaining than talk.
    Long conversations, unbroken by action, do not make
    good shows.

7. There is an efficient orchestra included in these
    programs, so that if you understand something about
    music and would like to use a little in your story,
    do so. The leading man, Don Ameche, has a pleasant
    and appealing singing voice and has successfully put
    over several roles in which he worked as a night club
    entertainer or a song writer, etc., etc.

8. When you have completed the first draft of your play
    -- read it over to yourself and then to someone of
    average intelligence and carefully note the reaction
    ... do they grasp the essentials of the plot?... does
    it sustain their undivided interest and attention?
    The most important requirement of a play is that it
    provide good entertainment. It must not be obvious,
    dull, trite, "draggy", etc.

9. Put plenty of color, action and motivation into your
    plot but keep the whole structure clear and well fo-
    cused. Brevity is the soul of wit and simplicity is
    the essence of good showmanship.

10. Suspense is important in order to carry the audience
    over the intermissions and make them await eagerly the
    climax of the play.

-3-

FIRST NIGHTER (Three Acts)   This is the "opening night" in the
    "Little Theatre Off Times Square"

Dramatic construction should be on an ascending line with
the "Big Scene", if possible, for the third act. As musical interludes occur between each act, in this series, it is
essential to build up the endings of Acts 1 and 2 in such a
manner as to leave a good carry-over. Usually suspense is
the best method.

Each act should average between five and six minutes actual
playing time, totaling 16 or 17$\frac{1}{2}$ minutes for three acts.
A manuscript of 2500 or 2600 words, averaging from 825 to
900 words per act makes the best play.

    Players

        Don Ameche -- leading man
        June Meredith -- leading lady
        Clifford Soubier -- an experienced heavy, villain
                            or "character" actor. Very
                            good in negro dialect also.

        Other actors vary according to the requirements of the
        script. It is desirable to have no more than four or
        five characters in order to keep the plot clear and
        understandable by the audience. Odd voices, taxi
        drivers, doormen, etc. may be used at your discretion.

GRAND HOTEL (Two Acts.)

Often the scenes are associated with or start in "Grand Hotel"
anywhere.
A musical interlude occurs between the acts and it is essential that the ending of Act I be built up to leave a good
carry-over.
The acts should be evenly divided with roughly 21 or 22
minutes for the total length, figuring about 150 words to
the minute.

    Players

        Don Ameche -- leading man
        Anne Seymour -- leading lady
        Other actors vary according to the requirements of
        the script. It is desirable to have no more than
        four or five as more than that number may become
        confusing to the audience.

                    - - x - -

Note: Authors are required to furnish only the play. Do not worry
       about the "Shell" or "Framework" of the program.

       For plays produced the author is remunerated on the day
       following the broadcast. Price $100 each.

       Please type your name and address clearly on the manuscript.
                        Address scripts to
                        L. T. Wallace, Vice President
                        AUBREY, MOORE & WALLACE, INC.
                            410 North Michigan Avenue
                                Chicago, Illinois.

and *Those We Love*—occurred in the evening. Only the largest stations produced their own dramatic programs regularly, most being content with network offerings, although many stations supplied dramatic or sound effects for commercials and special programs.

To an audience reared largely on movies, amateur theatricals, and traveling companies, radio provided something new and fascinating. The resulting loyal audience was very attractive to advertisers. Since it could perceive radio only by ear, the audience had to use its imagination to fill in the setting and the action. This it did well with the help of numerous musical and sound-effect conventions. Everyone understood transitions of time and space; the absence of carpet in radioland homes told the listener when somebody was entering or leaving a room. A filter that removed some of the audio frequencies placed a voice on the telephone; a bit more filter and some reverberation or "echo" would transport a ghost to fantasyland. But without the audience's imagination, radio drama never would have succeeded.

5•63   News

By the late 1930s, the providing of news broadcasts and commentary programs had become a recognized radio function, as the Press-Radio war ended and tensions in Europe and the Far East mounted.

The Biltmore Agreement of late 1933, which was intended to end the Press-Radio war (see 4.64), proved short-lived. As soon as the networks stopped gathering and reporting news, local stations or groups of stations took over. Transradio Press Service, Inc., a news agency whose news could be sponsored, served more stations in early 1935 than the Press-Radio

wire authorized by the Biltmore Agreement. Both UP and INS copied this service in 1935, leaving only AP, closely controlled by the newspaper industry, as a holdout. To save wire line costs, Transradio, UP, and INS sent short, telegraphic dispatches that required rewriting at the station. In July 1936 UP became the first news service to offer a special radio wire transmitting news summaries written and edited for radio delivery. By 1938 UP and INS had many more subscribers than Transradio, and many stations subscribed to more than one service. The Press-Radio wire, restrictive in news coverage and prohibiting sponsorship, withered and died in 1938 in the face of such competition—and the "war" ended with it. AP began to let newspaper-owned stations use its news on the air in 1939, opened up its news service and permitted sponsorship on all stations a year later, and began a special radio wire in early 1941. The attempts of the press to limit radio news failed because most people saw them correctly as limiting news dissemination on a competing medium. As real war drew nearer, people wanted more news. Print media groups tried repeatedly in the late 1930s to regain control of radio news, but they had lost the issue already.

In the late 1930s, individual radio stations across the country began to offer news programs varying in length and depth. Most stations had local news service, sometimes no more than headlines, often in cooperation with a local newspaper supplemented by one or more of the wire service radio wires. The FCC's 1938 programming survey showed that one-tenth of broadcast programming was news; with special events coverage added, radio devoted one-sixth of its programming to news and public affairs; and more news and special events programs originated locally than were supplied by national networks. Compared to newspapers, radio carried more international and crime-related news but fewer social events and stock and commodity market reports. Radio's ability to report natural and man-made disasters faster than the press doomed the newspaper "extra."

In the networks, the end of the Press-Radio war brought expansion of both domestic and foreign news reporting. NBC news director A. A. Schechter earned a reputation for getting stories through skillful use of the long-distance telephone and producing color or human interest stories rather than *hard news*. Both networks covered sports events, talks from famous people beamed from abroad by shortwave and then rebroadcast, a singing mouse contest, launching of ocean liners; both networks were establishing the personnel and technical means for regular international reporting. CBS news director Paul White directed César Saerchinger to cover the 1936 abdication of Great Britain's King Edward VIII and the 1937 coronation of King George VI. This latter broadcast may have been the first heard around the world, thanks to the British Broadcasting Corporation. In another memorable CBS broadcast, H. V. Kaltenborn reported on a 1936 skirmish in the Spanish Civil War while hiding in a haystack between the two armies; listeners in America could hear bullets hitting the hay above him while he spoke. In 1937 twenty-eight-year-old Edward R. Murrow took Saerchinger's place as CBS European director, arranging educational talks and other broadcasts from his base in London.

News reporting from abroad naturally picked up in quantity as diplomatic tensions increased. Radio reported the latest actions of dictators Hitler and Mussolini, and the often weak ripostes from Britain and France. Upon Germany's March 1938 annexation of Austria, CBS news di-

rector White devised a new broadcasting technique. Reporters in four or five European nations would stand by microphones connected to shortwave transmitters and discuss events of the day from their various vantage points, frequently being able to hear and comment on their colleagues' reports, coordinated by transatlantic radio and telephone from New York. Because this was done live in the evening on the East Coast of the United States, the reporters had to broadcast in the wee hours of the morning. CBS presented sixteen such roundups in the six days of the Austrian crisis. The techniques developed and personnel trained became vitally important when Hitler threatened Czechoslovakia in September 1938. NBC provided more than 460 broadcasts in those 18 days of the Munich crisis, including Max Jordan's scoop—a broadcast of the complete text of the four-power agreement just minutes after it was signed. At CBS, H. V. Kaltenborn—who could readily translate into English several languages used during the crisis—won acclaim by doing 85 broadcasts over the 18 days. He virtually lived in Studio 9, having food brought in and sleeping on a cot. News Director White orchestrated the coverage, pulling in as needed wire reports, CBS reporters abroad, and commentary from New York or Washington. In those 18 days of speeches, threats, and communiqués, Americans grew used to news bulletins cutting into their entertainment programs at any hour. Kaltenborn later said that he felt the crisis passed—only for a year as it turned out—because radio had mobilized public opinion against war. However, the audience's new faith in radio reporting was tested a month later when the Welles broadcast (see 5.62) scared millions.

The networks' news organizations were put to the test in 1939–1941 as war came to Europe and spread. By late 1939

CBS had 14 fulltime employees in European capitals, headed by Murrow in London, Eric Sevareid in Paris, and William L. Shirer in Berlin. NBC had a similar staffing pattern. When war came, both networks were able to provide a running commentary: Murrow from London on the beginning of the war . . . NBC providing eye-witness live coverage of the bleak winter on the Russo-Finnish front . . . NBC's scoop live from Montevideo harbor in December when the Germans scuttled their pocket battleship *Graf Spee* . . . conflicting reports from all over as Hitler invaded the low countries, Scandinavia, and France in 1940 . . . the combined broadcast by NBC's William Kerker and CBS's William L. Shirer in the forest of Compiègne in June 1940 when France surrendered to Hitler (most other correspondents were waiting for the news in Berlin) . . . a *London after Dark* broadcast over CBS in August 1940 in the midst of a German air raid at the height of the Battle of Britain. . . .

Wartime censorship restrictions forced many on-the-spot reports to be recorded originally, but most were live—a tribute to the newsmen's professionalism and the combatants' trust in their good faith. Edward R. Murrow led the way by proving to British censors, through trial broadcasts for several nights in a row, that he could broadcast without giving away military information. In his nightly "This . . . is London" reports to CBS, Murrow, from 1939 to 1941, probably gave Americans their best feel for the war in England. Night after night, he told how the war affected typical Londoners—in their homes, hiding from bombs in the London subway system, or working in factories turning out goods for the war.

Not only did radio report the news faster than competing media, it often reported directly from the scene, with the added color and interest of interviews and background sounds. Perhaps radio's outstanding performance in a domestic crisis was its cooperative coverage of the disastrous Ohio and Mississippi Valley floods of early 1937. Stations that were flooded out provided their personnel to stations still on the air. The latter scrapped program schedules and stayed on the air day and night directing flood victims to food and shelter. Many stations conducted fund-raising efforts to alleviate suffering. Some stations became arms of official agencies and provided a message service that normally might have been illegal point-to-point use of a broadcasting station. Reporters fanned out over the entire area, reporting news to local stations and networks alike. Radio's immediacy and portability were amply demonstrated.

In May 1937 Herb Morrison of Chicago station WLS, making a disc recording for archival purposes, watched the German airship *Hindenburg* come in for a routine landing at Lakehurst, New Jersey. As those on the ground watched in horror, the giant hydrogen-filled dirigible caught fire and, in less than a minute, burned to a mass of twisted girders on the ground, with the death of 30 passengers and crew. New York station WHN carried the news first, some eight minutes after the fire, and CBS and NBC followed within a half-hour. Morrison's recording was one of the dramatic events in radio's history. As the shock of this unexpected catastrophe overwhelmed him, he sobbed, "This is one of the worst catastrophes in the world . . . oh, the humanity" but stayed at his post and recorded some thirty minutes of the aftermath—between stints of helping in the rescue work. The recording, rushed back to Chicago and aired on WLS the next morning, was so newsworthy that the three networks temporarily suspended their no-recordings rule to play portions of it.

To cover foreign and domestic

news adequately, all the networks and many larger stations began to hire newsmen-commentators to report and analyze the rapid and bewildering events around the world. News commentary had been exempted from the short-lived Biltmore Agreement ban on sponsored news programs, and Lowell Thomas had broadcast on NBC-Blue since 1930 (continuing until June of 1976). Boake Carter and H. V. Kaltenborn had been on CBS for several seasons. Other commentators broadcasting between 1935 and 1939 were Gabriel Heatter, famous for his coverage of the Lindbergh kidnaping trial (see box below) in the early 1930s; newspaper columnist Drew Pearson; Dorothy Thompson, the first important woman commentator; Raymond Gram Swing; conservative Fulton Lewis, Jr.; veteran broadcaster Norman Brokenshire; and respected newspaperman Elmer Davis.

The war increased news broadcasting in America. From some 850 hours of news and on-the-spot news specials broadcast by all networks in 1937, the yearly total went up to 1,250 hours in 1939 and nearly tripled two years later to 3,450 hours. Evening commercial network time devoted to commentators, news, and talks went from 6.7 percent in winter 1938–1939 to 12.3 percent in winter 1940–1941. CBS consistently provided the most news programming in 1937–1941, with NBC-Red and -Blue jockeying for second position and Mutual a distant third. Nearly all radio

The Lindbergh Kidnaping Case: Trial by Circus?

Early in 1932, the nineteen-month-old son of aviation hero Charles Lindbergh was kidnaped from the Lindbergh estate near Hopewell, New Jersey. The crime attracted the attention of the country for over ten weeks as the police and a weird variety of hangers-on attempted to recover the child by making payment to the kidnaper. They all failed, and the child's long-dead body was found on May 12. The kidnaper had not been found, and newspaper, newsreel, and radio reporters withdrew from the story.

Two-and-one-half years later, however, Bruno Richard Hauptmann was arrested in New York in the act of passing one of the ransom bills. That event, and the trial of Hauptmann for the kidnaping early in 1935 brought back the press in droves to focus the nation's concentration on the small town of Flemington, New Jersey, where the trial took place. Hundreds of reporters and photographers squeezed into the courtroom and surrounding rooms in an attempt to bring every event of the trial to the country's newspaper readers and radio listeners. Photographers—many of whom were free-lance and aggressive—were all over and the scene was pandemonium. Near the front rail with the press was Gabriel Heatter, a reporter for the new Mutual radio network, given this special place because the judge's wife enjoyed his broadcasts! The trial lasted for six weeks and was front-page news for most of that time.

Late on the evening of February 13, 1935, the verdict came in and was soon flashed across the country—Hauptmann was found guilty and sentenced to die. (An Associated Press employee using a secret radio transmitter in the courtroom to get a scoop on rivals got the verdict wrong, and about ten minutes later AP had to send out a correction. The employee was fired.) Heatter's most famous moment came in early 1936 stations scheduled regular news programs by 1940-1941, with a few providing summaries every hour.

5•64   Political Broadcasting

Radio as a political instrument in the United States came into its own with the first administration of Franklin D. Roosevelt. Taking with him a habit from his New York governorship, F.D.R. began a series of "Fireside Chats" with the American public on the problems of Depression-hit America. There were 28 such broadcasts—8 in each of his first two terms, and 12 in the third, wartime term, nearly all of them half-hour programs

broadcast in prime time—and they generally received ratings near the top. Roosevelt had a natural approach to radio, and his words came across more as a conversation between friends than a political speech. In the third "chat," when he stopped for a moment and drank from a glass of water, it seemed perfectly natural and correct.

In the 1936 presidential election campaign, a desperate Republican party tried a number of innovative uses of radio. The GOP nominee, Kansas governor Alfred Landon, submitted to a lengthy radio interview just prior to his nomination. More than 200 stations carried the convention in Cleveland, and the convention floor bristled with microphones. Once the cam-

when Hauptmann finally went to the electric chair. Holding scripts to cover four eventualities—escape, suicide, reprieve, or delay—Heatter had to ad-lib for three-quarters of an hour when the execution was delayed—all this live on a coast-to-coast hookup.

The trial was important not only for its titillating effect on American lives in 1935 but for what came out of it—severe restrictions on reporting of courtroom events by radio and photographers (after 1952, such rules included television). Developed by the American Bar Association as a canon or rule of judicial procedure, Canon 35 limited radio access to the courtroom ostensibly to alleviate the circus-like atmosphere prevalent during the Hauptmann trial. Canon 35, now Canon 3A(7), is still hotly debated as a conflict of the First (free speech) and Sixth (fair trial) amendments to the Constitution. And it all dates back to that overcrowded courtroom.

The heavy media coverage of the Lindbergh trial is evident in the massed photographers facing the jury. United Press International Photo.

paign got underway, frequent spot radio commercials emphasized aspects of the GOP platform. In October, Senator Arthur Vandenberg presented a "debate" on CBS in which he asked questions of an absent President Roosevelt and then played carefully selected recordings of earlier F.D.R. speeches and promises. The program violated CBS policy against recordings, and many of the network's affiliates either refused to carry it or cut out during the program when they realized its unfair approach. Finally, when the networks refused to sell the Republicans time after the convention, the GOP used Chicago station WGN to present an allegorical play depicting its campaign promises.

On the other hand, the Democrats used nothing special—only F.D.R. That consummate political speaker had huge audiences listening to his broadcast speeches. On election night, the networks initially interrupted regular programs with ballot bulletins from time to time, supplementing with commentary. CBS went fulltime to election results at 10:30 P.M., while Mutual reported its first election that year.

The second Roosevelt administration showed increasing use of radio, not just by the President and his cabinet but by numerous federal agencies as well. The Office of Education, for example, produced 11 educational network programs; the Federal Theater Program—part of the Depression-spawned Works Progress Administration—produced more radio programming in its short life than any other agency; the departments of Agriculture and Interior supplied recorded programs to individual stations. Many local stations also benefited from the forecasting services of the U. S. Weather Bureau, and produced local programs featuring county agricultural agents.

The 1940 election campaign saw F.D.R. run again, this time against Repub-

lican Wendell Willkie, a little-known utilities executive before a whirlwind public relations campaign had propelled him into the limelight. Willkie pushed himself so hard that his voice weakened during the campaign—perhaps one of the reasons why Roosevelt consistently got higher ratings. Surveys conducted during this campaign suggested that most voters now considered radio more important than newspapers as a source of political news and tended to listen most to the candidate they favored; in other words, radio strengthened voters' predispositions. On election eve the Democrats mounted a special radio program of speeches, party propaganda, and entertainment by stage, screen, and radio stars. Fulltime election coverage, as in 1936, came after the regular prime-time entertainment, although bulletins were provided throughout the evening. Human interest pieces and voter interviews were more common than in previous years.

Political broadcasting was not limited to the presidential campaign. Louisiana Senator Huey Long made anti-F.D.R. populist speeches until his 1935 assassination. Like Roosevelt, he had an informal approach, inviting listeners to call a friend or two and tell them Huey Long was on the air, and then delaying the meat of his address for the next several minutes. Catholic radio priest Coughlin (see 4.66), after promising to leave the air in 1936 if his third-party candidate got less than nine million votes—he got less than one million —came back to rail against the New Deal. He became increasingly rightist, criticizing Jews and defending many of the tenets of Nazism, until pressure from the Church hierarchy and other sources forced him off the air.

Common on local stations were talks and discussions of local and national topics of interest. Such programs were inexpensive and easy to produce, particularly in college towns where professors were willingly drafted into occasional radio commentary. One of the better-known national programs, *The University of Chicago Roundtable*, began in 1931, went network (NBC) in 1933, and lasted for nearly 25 years. The surprisingly popular format consisted of faculty members and, occasionally, distinguished guests discussing a current topic. This program often outrated commercial programs and drew substantial mail from listeners seeking transcripts of programs. Another program of this type, NBC's *America's Town Meeting of the Air*, first aired in 1935 and involved members of the studio audience expressing their opinions on important issues.

5•65   Other Programs

Popular local station programs included man-on-the-street interviews and call-in interview programs, during which listeners could request a favorite musical selection or converse on an announced topic with a program host. People listened and participated because they enjoyed hearing themselves and other ordinary people on the radio.

Common both to local and network schedules were the nearly obligatory Sunday morning religious services, typically a live remote broadcast from a community church.

Some children's programs had large audiences. Featuring storytelling and

Remote Broadcasts Become Truly Portable / This hand-held transmitter, touted by NBC in 1936 as the "smallest practical radio broadcasting station ever devised" was used in covering the national political conventions (including the Socialist) of that year. It liberated the reporter from wires connected to a companion staggering under the weight of a "portable" backpack transmitter, and permitted the announcer to "wander freely about." Forty years later, however, all of the components— microphone, amplifiers, batteries, transmitter, antenna—in the 1936 device—and additional cueing circuits from the director back to the reporter—were contained in a lightweight telephone operator-type headset, with the transmitter itself a small box somewhat smaller than a cigarette pack sticking above the earphone with a tiny antenna waving jauntily above. Photo courtesy of Broadcast Pioneers Library and National Broadcasting Company, Inc.

music interspersed with commercial announcements, they made ingenious use of radio's aural qualities and their ability to stimulate the imagination.

On the networks, quiz and human-interest programs grew on prime time from two to ten hours a week from 1935 to 1941 but were less important during daytime hours. Some quiz programs used audience members as participants and others used professional panels, but each offered human interest, drama, and an opportunity for the listener to test himself and occasionally outguess the participant. Major growth of this genre came in 1938 with the arrival of *Kay Kyser's Kollege of Musical Knowledge*, a combination musical-variety and quiz format; the urbane *Information, Please!*, whose professional panel tried to answer questions sent in by the audience; *Dr. I.Q.*, whose host, broadcasting from theaters around the country, offered "ten silver dollars for that lady in the balcony if she can tell me. . . ." In *Truth or Consequences*, which aired in 1940, willing contestants from the audience who answered silly questions incorrectly had to perform silly stunts as a consequence.

5•7   Systematic Audience Research

In the late 1930s, the radio audience continued to grow, such that radio was readily accepted in most rooms in the house (and increasingly in the car). That growth in size led to higher rates to advertisers—who demanded more refined research about the audience to justify their increased expenditures. As the number of listeners increased, so did information about who listened—and why.

5•71   The Radio Receiver

The years 1935–1941 saw the radio audience grow by seven million homes to a total of 28.5 million, or 81 percent of American homes as compared with 67 percent at the start of the period. At the same time, a previously insignificant element of the radio audience grew even more rapidly: by 1941, 7.5 million automobiles, more than 27 percent, were equipped with radio—as compared with 9 percent in 1935. By 1938 the United States housed half the world's radio receivers, and more homes had radios than telephones, vacuum cleaners, or electric irons. The number of sets had grown by more than 100 percent since 1930.

Philco (see 4.71) remained behind RCA as a seller of radios until 1940, when it sold an equal volume of sets. Heavy promotion, pioneering battery-operated portable (but heavy!) radios and automobile radios, and aiming a line of efficient battery radios at rural listeners—all helped make Philco the growing giant of the period. Next in importance was Zenith, whose dynamic president Commander Eugene F. McDonald preferred aggressive selling and concentration on the home radio market to diversification. Here, too, innovations brought success—large, round, and easily read dials on radios starting in 1935, a simple radio antenna to improve reception, and an inexpensive shortwave-AM portable radio. Another relatively new firm, Emerson Radio, was primarily responsible for introducing the small, inexpensive table radio in 1933, a type which had almost four-fifths of the home radio market by 1941. Prices kept getting lower until, by 1939 and 1940, Emerson was marketing small sets at under $10—a price that naturally encouraged many families to have more than one set. Another aggressive firm, Motorola, moved into the automobile market and by 1941 was selling about one-third of all car radios, offering push-button sets tailored for specific car instrument panels. The hallmark of all these firms was aggressive salesmanship and price cutting rather than major technical development.

The onetime leader in the radio receiver field, RCA, was losing out in other fields as well. While it remained the largest maker of radio tubes in 1941, Sylvania and Raytheon were moving in on this market; Magnavox and other firms were taking part of RCA's loudspeaker business. Mail order firms frequently cut prices and traded for profit rather than loyalty to a given manufacturer. Part of RCA's problem was the long antitrust litigation of the early 1930s, which resulted in GE and Westinghouse starting to manufacture radio sets independently in 1935. Other firms once important in radio set manufacture, such as Grigsby-Grunow and Atwater Kent, disappeared during the Depression. Crosley declined sharply. Increasingly tight competition among the surviving firms led to narrow profit margins and little basic research. Radio circuits became standardized; parts were frequently interchangeable, and manufacturing techniques were streamlined and simplified. Many firms sold similar small table models, chairside radios, large floor consoles—some with phonographs—and automobile radios. The major results: more reliable radios at low prices and a growing multi-set radio audience.

5•72   Audience Patterns

By 1938 more than 91 percent of urban homes, and nearly 70 percent of rural homes, had radio. Half the homes in the country had at least two radios, and there were few differences in regional distribution. Radio was nearly universal in higher income homes, but even 57 percent of homes with income of less than $1,000 a year had at least one set. Radio was played in the average household more than five hours a day.

Urban and rural audiences used radio differently. Although fewer rural homes had sets, those with receivers tended to listen a few minutes more each day than urban homes. However, because of the dawn-to-dusk working schedules of farmers, rural audiences listened less than urban audiences in the evening—a pattern reflected today in scheduling of network programs an hour earlier in the Central and Mountain time zones (than on either Coast) because of line costs for separate feeds and presumed early-to-bed habits in the Midwest. As might be expected, rural homes (76 percent) preferred clear-channel stations to regional (21 percent) or local (2 percent) stations, because they represented the only reliable service in many rural areas. The problems of radio coverage were well known to station owners and engineers and the FCC; large areas of the country got no decent service at night, and some lacked reception around the clock. In June 1938 the FCC reported that 8 percent of the population had no reception in daytime and more than 17 percent were without it at night. This neglected segment of more than 20 million people was concentrated in rural areas where 16 percent had no daytime radio and fully one-third had no reception at night. Examination of popularity of network evening programs by basic program type in 1938 revealed other urban-rural differences. Urban listeners had less interest in news—it ranked fifth in urban areas but third in rural areas—perhaps because other means of news communication were more accessible in cities, and because rural families had a stronger need for weather and market information. Urban listeners had more interest in drama—it ranked third in urban areas but fifth in rural areas. All other program types were ranked the

The Radio Receiver Market in the Late 1930s / These two advertisements, from Motorola and RCA, show the variety of radio sets available in the prewar years.

1939 *Motorola* TABLE MODELS   BEAUTIFUL STYLING ★ PERFECT RECEPTION

← MODEL 59T-1

Genuine Solid American Walnut Cabinet : 5 Tubes (including ballast tube) : Superheterodyne : 5" Speaker : Top Tuning : Illuminated Dial : Plays on any 110 volt current : Tuning Range 540-1720 kc., includes 1st Police Band : Compact size : 11½" wide, 7½" high, 6½" deep : Unusual sensitivity, selectivity and freedom from interference.

Model 59T-11 as above in Ivory Finish

MODEL 59T-2 →

Genuine Solid American Walnut Cabinet : 5 Tubes : AC Superheterodyne : 5" Electro Dynamic Speaker : Illuminated Dial : 3.0 Watts Power Output : Tuning Range 540-1720 kc., includes 1st Police Band : Compact size : 11½" wide, 7½" high, 6½" deep : Outstanding sensitivity, sharp selectivity and marvelously good tone.

Model 59T-12 as above in Ivory Finish

← MODEL 59T-3

Solid Walnut Cabinet : 5 Tubes (including ballast tube) : Superheterodyne : 5" Speaker : Automatic Top Tuning with 4 Full-Range Push Buttons—each button easily set for any station : Illuminated Dial : Plays on any 110 volt current : Tuning Range 540-1720 kc., includes 1st Police Band : Heat-Treated Trimmers and Temperature Compensation to overcome drift : 10⅝x7⅝x6⅜".

Model 59T-13 as above in Ivory Finish

MODEL 59T-4 →

Solid Walnut Cabinet : 5 Tubes : AC Superheterodyne : 5" Electro Dynamic Speaker : Automatic Top Tuning with 4 Motorola Full-Range Push-Buttons—each button easily set for any station : Illuminated Dial : 3.0 Watts Power Output : Tuning Range 540-1720 kc., includes 1st Police Band : Heat-Treated Trimmer Condensers and Temperature Compensation : 11½x7⅝x6⅛" deep.

Model 59T-14 as above in Ivory Finish

← MODEL 59T-5

Glo-Wood Cabinet : 5 Tubes : 2 Bands—AC Superhet. : 6" Electro Dynamic Speaker : 6-Station Automatic Full Range Push Button Tuning—each button easily set for any station : Illuminated Straight Line Dial : Tuning Range 540-1720 kc., 5650-18,000 kc. : Includes 49, 31, 25, 19 and 16 meters short wave programs : 4.5 watts Output : Continuously Variable *Dual* Tone Control : Size 17" x 9⅜" x 8½" deep.

59F-1 PHONOGRAPH-RADIO SOLID MAHOGANY CABINET →

Crystal Pickup : Plays all 10" and 12" records with lid closed : self-starting constant speed motor : 3.0 watts power output : Tone control for phonograph and radio : 5 Tubes : 5" Speaker : AC Superheterodyne : Tuning Range 540-1720 kc., includes 1st Police Band : Beautiful cabinet of solid mahogany with 4 grille openings for better tone diffusion : Size 15" wide, 10½" deep, 10½" high : illuminated dial.

MODEL 89K-1 TIME-TUNING

The Radio that Tunes Itself! TIME-TUNING combined with 6-Button "Feather-Touch" Electric Automatic Tuning : continuously variable *Dual* Tone Control : Push-Pull : 10 watts power output : 8 Tubes : 10" Speaker : Tuning Range 540-1720 kc., includes 1st Police Band : Heat Treated Trimmer Condensers and Temperature Compensation to overcome drift : Hand rubbed Walnut finish lowboy cabinet : 31x13½x39" high.

69K-1 SIX TUBE PUSH-PULL

6 Tubes : 10" Speaker : 2 Bands—540-1720; 5650-18,000 kc. : Includes 49, 31, 25, 19 and 16 meters short-wave programs : 6-station *full-range* automatic tuning—each button easily set for any station : continuously variable *Dual* Tone Control : Push-Pull : 10 watts power output : Heat Treated Trimmers and Temperature Compensation : Beautiful Walnut finish lowboy cabinet. 28¼ x 12" x 39" high.

MODEL 89K-3 ELECTRIC TUNING

6-Button "Feather-Touch" Electric Automatic Tuning : continuously variable *Dual* Tone Control : 10 watts power output : 8 Tubes : 10" Speaker : Standard and short-wave bands—540-1720; 5600-18,000 kc., includes 49, 31, 25, 19 and 16 meter programs : Heat Treated Trimmer Condensers and Temperature Compensation to overcome drift : Hand rubbed Walnut finish lowboy cabinet : 25¾" x 13¼" x 43" high.

MODEL 6A-2 ARM CHAIR RADIO

6 Tubes : 10" Speaker : Acoustic Amplification and phasing : AC Superheterodyne : Electric Tuning Eye : 3 Bands—540-1720; 2200-7000; 7000-22,000 kc. : illuminated Dial : Individual Band Framing : continuously variable Tone Control : 4.5 watts power output : AVC : exquisite hand rubbed Walnut finish cabinet, 15⅝" x 22½" x 22" high.

MODEL 109K-1 TIME-TUNING

The Radio that Tunes Itself! TIME-TUNING combined with 6-Button "Feather-Touch" Electric Automatic Tuning : Tone-Color Control : Push-Pull : 14 watts power output : 10 Tubes : 12" Speaker : 3 Bands—540-1720; 2200-7000; 7000-22,000 kc. : Heat Treated Trimmers and Temperature Compensation to overcome drift : special sensitivity control link : Exquisite period design hand rubbed Walnut finish cabinet : 27"x13"x43".

59K-1 SIX PUSH-BUTTON Automatic

5 Tubes : 2 Bands—540-1720; 5650-18,000 kc. : Includes 49, 31, 25, 19 and 16 meters short-wave programs : 6-station *full-range* automatic tuning—each button easily set for any station : illuminated straight line dial : continuously variable *Dual* Tone Control : 4.5 watts power output : Heat-Treated Trimmers and Temperature Compensation : Beautiful Walnut finish lowboy cabinet : 25"x10⅝"x39" hi.

AMERICA'S FINEST RADIO ★ 1939 *Motorola* HOME RADIO ★

same: amateur (1), variety (2), serial drama (4), dance band music (6) and classical music (7).

Early research into listening habits found that, as income and education went up, the amount of radio listening (and later television watching) went down. Advertisers and networks applied the concept of *audience flow*, which describes a program's ability not only to attract an audience but to increase the audience for the shows before and after it. This led stations and networks to schedule *blocks* of compatible programs—such as one serial drama following another all afternoon—so as to build ever larger audiences throughout the evening.

5•73   Increased Research

In the late 1930s and early 1940s, there were two competing broadcast rating organizations. The Cooperative Analysis of Broadcasting (CAB, see 4.72), based in 33 cities, 14 on the East Coast, was a nonprofit organization run by advertisers and advertising agencies for the benefit of radio time buyers. Using a modified recall telephone interview system, CAB called numbers at random from a sample four times a day and asked the respondents what they had heard on the radio during the previous two or three hours. Ratings, processed and published every other week, were based on a total of 3,000 calls a day nationwide. Any single program's rating was based on at least 1,500 calls over the two-week period.

In the fall of 1934, Clark-Hooper, Inc., began to sell advertisers audience research on magazines and radio. The radio portion split off in 1938, becoming C. E. Hooper, Inc., which provided monthly ratings of network-sponsored, not sustaining, programs. Hooper pioneered national

use of the coincidental telephone method —which avoided the limitations of the listener's memory by asking what he or she was listening to *at that moment*. However, the coincidental technique required nearly ten times as many calls as the recall method in order to report data at 15-minute intervals. Both techniques suffered from the difficulties of telephoning in sparsely settled areas and discounting the radio homes without telephones.

Radio rating service reports were prepared both for broadcast time buyers (advertisers and their agencies) and sellers (networks and stations). Although they were expensive, particularly for the sellers, they soon gained a reputation for detail and accuracy. Both firms—Hooper and CAB, whose service was called the "Crossley rating" after Archibald M. Crossley, its founder—reported ratings or percentages of radio receivers tuned to a given station, network, or program in relation to total receivers whether in use or not. This raw quantitative data satisfied most advertisers until CAB started to supply qualitative information by breaking down program rating data by income groups and geographic areas—an innovation of great value to alert advertisers. As an index to listening behavior in a small sample of homes, marketing research company A.C. Nielsen was developing, but did not commercially introduce until 1942, an automatic "Audimeter" that recorded whether a set was on and to which channel it was tuned. More reliable and to some extent more valid for measuring *tuning* if not *listening* behavior than the telephone techniques, this device was also expensive and dependent on the audience member's returning the data. This technique became much more important for television than for radio research (see 6.72).

In addition to the ratings, which merely gave size-of-audience estimates, the first serious research analyses of radio's effect on its audience began to appear. In 1934 Frederick Lumley's *Measurement in Radio* supplied detailed information on the use of audience research. The size of his bibliography suggests that advertiser pressure had made management look seriously at the size and particulars of their prime and only "product"—their audience. In 1935 the first report of in-depth audience research, Hadley Cantril and Gordon W. Allport's *The Psychology of Radio*, examined the mental setting of radio—how listeners perceived music and speakers—and potential uses of this experimentally derived data. The first extensive study of a program, Cantril's 1940 *The Invasion from Mars: A Study in the Psychology of Panic*, which investigated listener reaction to Orson Welles's famous 1938 program (see 5.62), still is considered basic to the study of group panic and the mass media.

Founded late in 1937 by a Rockefeller Foundation grant to Princeton University, the Office of Radio Research was established there with Paul F. Lazarsfeld as director. He was assisted by two young researchers, Frank Stanton, who had worked in audience studies at CBS since 1935, and Hadley Cantril. The organization's first major publication was H. M. Beville's *Social Stratification of the Radio Audience* (1939), which is the earliest detailed description of audience ratings and the fruits of their first eight or nine years. Beville later became head of research for NBC, and Stanton started a three-decade tenure as president of CBS in 1946. In 1940 the Office of Radio Research moved to Columbia University in New York and issued its first commercial publication, Lazarsfeld's *Radio and the Printed Page*, a report on several studies comparing newspapers and radio. A year later it published the first of an intended annual series, Lazarsfeld and Stanton's *Radio Research 1941*,

which contained reports on research into radio music, radio in rural life, foreign language broadcasting, and use of radio and the press by young people. Only two other volumes, 1942–1943 and 1948–1949, followed in this series. Lazarsfeld and Stanton also developed the *program analyzer*, still in use at CBS and elsewhere, to obtain minute-by-minute reactions of a test audience to new programs.

The output of the Columbia-based project, which lasted well past the war years, is perhaps the clearest indication of academic concern for and interest in radio's influence. Other colleges and universities mounted similar but smaller projects, focusing mostly on audience effects but also on programming control and regulation. By 1939 at least 28 doctoral dissertations and 159 masters theses that dealt with broadcasting had been completed.

5·8 Formative Years of the FCC

Major changes in federal regulatory structure and approach after 1933 were built on the precedents of the Federal Radio Commission. Several problems had hindered the governmental role in electrical communications: regulation of closely related means of electrical communication was spread among various agencies, which frequently had little to do with one another. The Interstate Commerce Commission (ICC) controlled interstate telegraph and telephone traffic as little as possible; the FRC controlled most aspects of radio, including broadcasting; and the Department of Commerce had some regulatory voice in the wire and wireless common carrier industries. Members of Congress had attempted over the years to amend the Radio Act of 1927 to make the FRC a permanent administrative agency, since it had not been able to become the part-time adjudicatory body envisioned by the 1927 act. Because President Hoover did not favor these bills, they were killed by pocket veto.

5·81 Creation of the FCC

Soon after becoming President, Franklin D. Roosevelt appointed an inter-departmental committee on communications to examine the role of the nine governmental agencies involved with public, private, and governmental use of radio. In December 1933, this committee recommended creation of a Federal Communications Commission that would contain nearly all these functions, serving as an enlarged version of the FRC and regulating interstate telegraph and telephone as well. In February 1934, bills were introduced into Congress to establish such a commission, the "services affected to be all of those which rely on wires, cables, or radio as a means of transmission." The President specifically called for broad and non-restrictive legislation so that the new organization would have utmost flexibility. Representative, later Speaker, Sam Rayburn (D-Texas) introduced the House bill, which would replace the FRC with the FCC and modify the Radio Act of 1927 without abolishing it. Senator Clarence C. Dill (D-Washington) sponsored the Senate bill. It would replace the 1927 act and combine the duties of the different agencies in the new FCC, with rigidly defined radio and telegraph divisions, but would add more power to the new agency. FRC members generally backed the proposed changes, while the broadcasting industry, with the National Association of Broadcasters acting as spokesman, opposed them because the NAB feared any stronger governmental role in radio broadcasting. Both houses passed their bills, and the Presi-

dent signed a Senate-House compromise bill to go into effect July 1, 1934.

The Communications Act of 1934 incorporated in its Title III most of the provisions of the Radio Act of 1927, retaining the three-year broadcast license term, although the FRC was then restricting licenses to six months and the Senate had toyed with a one-year period. Title I set up the new commission with seven commissioners—two more than the old FRC—appointed to staggered terms of seven years each, providing that no more than four members could have the same political affiliation. Charged with designating internal operations and divisions, the commissioners initially established broadcast, telegraph, and telephone divisions but abolished them late in 1937. From then on they acted as a committee of the whole, occasionally appointing *ad hoc* subgroups to prepare investigative reports into specific subjects. Commissioners were to be nominated, and the chairman appointed, by the U. S. President, with the advice and consent of the Senate, and could not have a financial interest in the industry. The commission was to report annually to Congress. Title II dealt with common carriers and generally followed existing ICC regulations. Title IV was concerned with procedural and administrative matters, Title V with penal provisions and forfeitures, and Title VI with miscellaneous matters including the presidential emergency power to take over electrical and electronic communications in time of war or other emergency.

Most of the men appointed to the FCC in the 1930s were lawyers with public utility experience or governmental service. Although one engineer usually served on the commission, the need for technical expertise was less now that basic interference-reducing decisions had been made by the FRC and upheld by the courts.

5•82 Program Cleanup

The first FCC regulatory project was a concern of the old FRC—changing substandard program and advertising policies in broadcasting. Although the act forbade the FCC to censor, it could decide whether a station's policies and programs were in the public interest. This concern was apparent in a variety of hearings in the thirties: on renewal of a 1935 Missouri station for carrying broadcasts by an astrologer (this was frowned on by the FCC not only because such individual messages were not broadcasting but because they took advantage of listeners' credulity); on a New York licensee for showing poor taste in accepting contraceptive advertising; on New Jersey and New York stations for broadcasting horse race information, using a code that only subscribers to a certain racing newspaper could decipher (held to be unfair, since the broadcast excluded some listeners); on a New York station for relinquishing responsibility as well as authority when it sold blocks of time for others to program; on several stations for promoting fraudulent products, especially patent medicines; and on several southern and western stations for airing misleading personal advice programs. Perhaps the most publicized case involved an episode of the popular Chase and Sanborn–sponsored *Edgar Bergen and Charlie McCarthy Show* in December 1937, in which guest star Mae West added some racy inflections in an "Adam and Eve" sketch. Many listeners were offended, and the FCC was inundated with complaints. Other than reprimanding NBC and its affiliated stations, the commission took no action.

In very few cases did stations actually lose licenses or fail to get a renewal or a construction permit. In fact, only two licenses were revoked and eight weren't renewed between 1934 and 1941. But FCC "raised eyebrow" displeasure was sufficient to change operating policy at an offending station. In a 1939 memo, the FCC listed 14 kinds of program material or practices deemed not to be in the public interest: (1) defamation, (2) racial or religious intolerance, (3) fortune-telling or similar programs, (4) favorable reference to hard liquor, (5) obscenity, (6) programs depicting torture, (7) excessive suspense on children's programs, (8) excessive playing of recorded music to fill air time, (9) obvious solicitation of funds, (10) lengthy and frequent advertisements, (11) interruption of "artistic programs" by advertising, (12) false or fraudulent or otherwise misleading advertising, (13) presentation of only one side of a controversial issue —an early statement of the Fairness Doctrine (see 9.82), and (14) refusal to give equal treatment to both sides in a controversial discussion. The commission, until the deregulation of the 1980s, considered all but the last five to be poor programming practice at all times, and it even questioned some of the last five under some circumstances.

The Federal Trade Commission took over the major portion of advertising regulation, thanks to the Wheeler-Lea Act of early 1938. This act amended the FTC's original mandate to allow it to seek out and stop unfair and deceptive advertising in any medium, specifically for drugs, cosmetics, foods, means of product distribution, and marketing practices.

5•83 Investigations of Monopoly

The FCC also looked at monopoly practice in several communications industries. Under the strong guidance of Commissioner Paul Walker, it undertook a massive investigation of American Telephone and Telegraph's rate structure between 1936 and 1939, resulting in a limited rate reduction. Congress added pressure to this investigation and also, questioning FCC apparent unconcern about monopoly control of radio, considered several bills calling for FCC examination of the entire industry.

Under this pressure from its funding source, in March 1938 the FCC issued Order No. 37, an inquiry into "all phases of chain broadcasting and into the broadcasting industry generally" to see whether rules were needed to control network tendencies to monopoly. From November 1938 through May 1939, a subcommittee of four commissioners heard 73 days of testimony from 94 witnesses, resulting in thousands of pages of testimony and hundreds of exhibits on all aspects of network operation and its effect on the broadcasting industry. On June 12, 1940, the subcommittee issued a tentative, 1,300-page, mimeographed report of summarized testimony and recommended rule changes. Following hearing on these findings, the full commission, on May 2, 1941, released its *Report on Chain Broadcasting* containing specific regulations "designed to eliminate the abuses uncovered."

Of these regulations, the following were most important: (1) network affiliation contracts would be limited to a single year for both parties—previously, stations had been bound to networks for five years, but the networks were bound for only one year; (2) affiliations could no longer be exclusive—an affiliate could use programs

---

One Network Reacts to the Chain Broadcasting Report: 1941 / Seldom had the broadcast industry been as aroused as when the FCC issued its Chain Broadcasting Report and new rules in spring 1941. Here are some of the reactions to the report, which, although it survived a Supreme Court test (see 6.85), did not have the dire effects the broadcasters anticipated.

Columbia Broadcasting System here states . . . that, instead of benefiting the public, instead of promoting sound competition, instead of improving radio broadcasting, what the Commission proposes to do will have these effects: (1) It will threaten the very existence of present network broadcasting service, bring confusion to radio listeners, to radio stations, and to the users of radio [advertisers], and deprive business of an orderly and stable method of presenting sponsored programs to the public. (2) It will threaten the continuance to radio listeners of their favorite sustaining programs sent out by the networks, such as . . . symphony broadcasts, educational and religious programs, world news service. We do not see how, under these "regulations," Columbia or anyone else can afford to, or has any real inducement to, produce and improve the character of its public service. (3) It will establish radio monopolies in many sections of the country. . . . (4) In weakening the ability of the radio industry to give the kind of broadcasting service that people have come to demand, it may, in the end, encourage the government to take over broadcasting altogether. Meantime it opens the door to the complete domination of radio by whatever government happens to be in power. (5) It will cripple, if it does not paralyze, broadcasting as a national service at a time when radio should be encouraged to continue and enlarge its contribution to national unity and morale.

(NBC reacted as strongly. See Appendix C, tables 2 and 4, to see how "badly" radio was "harmed," how the networks "all but disappeared," and how radio profits "plunged.")

Source: "What the New Radio Rules Mean" (New York: CBS, May 1941) page 4.

from other networks or sources; (3) networks could no longer demand options on large amounts of station time, since the FCC believed that stations—that is, licensees—should be in charge of and responsible for their own program content and arrangement; (4) an affiliate could reject any network program which in its view did not meet the public interest, convenience, or necessity, and could not sign away that right in its affiliation contract; (5) networks would have no control over a station's rates for other than network programs; and (6) "no license shall be issued to a standard broadcast [AM] station affiliated with a network organization which maintains more than one network" except where such networks operated at different times or covered substantially different territory. These rules, and a seventh rule (not part of the chain broadcasting regulations) prohibiting duopoly, or the owning of two stations in the same service area by one licensee, would drastically affect the industry.

Immediate network reaction was generally sharply antagonistic. CBS and NBC both published booklets claiming that the proposed rules could destroy the American system of broadcasting. NBC stood to lose the most, as the sixth rule would force it to drop either the Red or the Blue chain, and the seventh would force it to sell one of the two stations it owned in New York, Chicago, Washington, and San Francisco—one affiliated with the Red and the other with the Blue network. Only Mutual applauded the new rules and had supported them in the hearings in the belief that they would make it more competitive with the other networks.

In October 1941, NBC and CBS brought suit in the Federal District Court in New York to set aside the regulations; Mutual entered the case on the other side. The FCC had twice postponed implemen-

tation of the new rules and now postponed them again. As the country entered World War II, the network rules were one of the hottest topics in the broadcasting industry. The commission, many local broadcasters, and many critics of broadcasting in Congress contended that by removing their dependence on network fare, the new rules would enable stations to develop better programming. (Two decades later, program syndicators also employed this reasoning in an effort to get FCC backing for more local television programming in prime time theretofore considered "network" time—see 9.3). The networks and their defenders claimed that the rules would weaken network operating flexibility and lower the quality of network programs.

The commission also began to move on the issue of co-ownership of newspapers and broadcast stations in the same market. In spite of congressional hearings and some FCC action by 1936, the proportion of newspaper-owned stations increased through the decade, until by 1940 more than 30 percent were in this category, many located in the same market as their owners. The FCC finally took action early in 1941, aware perhaps that the Democratic administration would be concerned about Republican newspapers' controlling of *all* news media and certainly that nearly one-quarter of the FM construction permits had gone to newspaper-connected applicants. FCC Chairman James Lawrence Fly announced in March 1941 FCC Order No. 79, which called for . . . an immediate investigation to determine what statement of policy or rules, if any, should be issued concerning applications for high frequency [stations] with which are associated persons also associated with the publication of one or more newspapers. . . ." While press ownership of AM stations also would be examined, issuance of construction permits to newspaper-controlled FM stations was frozen for the duration of the hearings, which lasted from July through October 1941 and then recessed. There was dissension within the industry and even within the FCC over the hearings. Two commissioners thought that the FCC was overstepping its authority and the First Amendment by in any way considering the newspaper business. Station owners claimed that anyone or any group should be allowed to own radio stations, and that newspapers were no exception. Critics of co-ownership argued that to have both media under single control could limit expression of different viewpoints and might encourage combined advertising practices that would squelch the establishment of new stations or newspapers in such a market (see 6.85).

5•84   Self-Regulation

The story of industry self-control in the late 1930s essentially is a review of the reorganization of the National Association of Broadcasters, the revision of its radio code, and the long fight with ASCAP over music rights (see 5.85). While the period left broadcasters with a stronger trade organization and more unified clout, fundamental problems obviously remained unsolved.

Members of the NAB had begun to realize its limitations, as battles with unions, music copyright organizations, Congress, and private groups came and went with little broadcaster input or impact. Until 1938 the association, operating on $80,000 a year, with a salaried managing director and an unpaid broadcaster as ceremonial president, lacked personnel and funds to function effectively as a trade and lobby group. Representation of broadcaster interests had to come mostly from the networks and larger stations and reflected their views. Realizing the need to centralize, coordinate, and concert its efforts in the face of government investigations and other problems, the 1938 NAB convention voted to increase the budget threefold, to support a paid president and staff with dues proportional to a member station's earning, and to form operating subdivisions focusing on law, labor questions, management problems, engineering issues, and the role of education on the air. In this way, it was hoped that NAB—and therefore most broadcasters—would keep up to date on issues, and the broadcasting industry's position on issues, and communicate unified views to Congress and the FCC.

Under the National Recovery Administration (NRA) ruling of 1933, the broadcasting industry's 1929 code became law for all stations including earlier non-subscribers. When the Supreme Court declared the NRA unconstitutional in 1935, the mandatory code went by the boards. Because of the antibroadcasting industry sentiment at the 1934 Communications Act hearings, the NAB hastily assembled a ten-point, unenforceable ethical code in 1935. After the NAB reorganization of 1938 and during the FCC investigation of chain broadcasting, the NAB implemented in July 1939 a greatly expanded and revised radio code—a later edition of which is still in use. The new code allowed only six to ten minutes of commercials per evening hour, with a bit more during the day. It permitted no separate scheduling of controversial issues; they were to be covered in news and special programs for the expression of opinions. It dealt with other issues in generalities and platitudes that had little effect on existing practices. Advertising agencies had helped to assure flexibility in the code, and a Code Compliance Committee supervised implementation. One effect of the code was a reduction of Father Coughlin's access to the air after code-subscribing stations learned that they would have to provide opportunity for other points of view. Many stations also thought labor union news to be controversial. In practice, the requirements for controversial issues or fund raising appeals served to limit access to radio drastically for all but commercial advertisers. Backers of the code claimed that selling time for controversial issues would overload the air with fractious arguments that would bore the listener seeking relaxation and entertainment. Critics of the code agreed that controversy might annoy some listeners and most certainly would not appeal to advertisers but argued that it was a necessary aspect of public interest broadcasting—an anticipation of the Fairness Doctrine. Despite these differences, broadcasters widely publicized the code as a symbol of their acceptance of responsibility to serve public needs (see 10.8).

5 • 85   The Music Licensing Battle

In the meantime, the original nemesis of NAB was flexing its muscles again. The American Society of Composers, Authors and Publishers (ASCAP), whose demands had led to formation of the NAB (see 3.83), had collected more than $800,000 (40 percent of its income) from radio music performance fees in 1930, $2.7 million in 1937 (60 percent), and $4.15 million (about two-thirds) in 1939. Many ASCAP members approved of such fees because they thought that radio was helping to kill the sheet-music and record businesses.

In 1937 ASCAP went too far—in the broadcasters' eyes—and announced an increase of 70 percent or more in its license rates. This demand forced broadcasters late in 1939 to create a fund to establish a temporary music licensing agency to compete with ASCAP: Broadcast Music, Incorporated (BMI). The $1.5 million fund was about half what stations had paid ASCAP in 1937, but BMI used it to advantage and immediately set out to build an alternative library of music. When ASCAP increased its rates again in 1940, broadcasters decided to make BMI permanent and not to renew ASCAP contracts ending that year.

For ten months beginning January 1, 1941, listeners heard BMI's few selections and a good deal of public domain music—music on which copyright had expired. Stephen Foster's "Jeannie with the Light Brown Hair" found sudden new popularity, and programs had new theme music. Although the networks and many stations stuck to their guns, some broadcasters chose to pay for ASCAP licenses rather than face checking each tune used or risk paying a fine of $250 for each performance of music without a license. The battle became more confusing early in 1941 when the Justice Department filed antitrust suits against not only ASCAP but the networks as principal backers of BMI. Some musicians and publishers switched from ASCAP to BMI and vice versa, but ASCAP music still was not played over most stations. In May 1941 Mutual defected and signed with ASCAP, and in October the industry and ASCAP compromised on payments much closer to the old rates than to the new demands. The standoff had cost ASCAP some $4 million in revenue, the need to operate under a consent decree signed with the Justice Department, and the permanent addition of BMI as a competitor. But by late October and early November, ASCAP music again was playing on networks and local stations, under new contracts which would last until 1950.

5·9   Radio's Role Here and Abroad

As a medium of entertainment and news, radio really came into its own both here and abroad during the late 1930s. Radio was not only accepted and enjoyed—it had rapidly become an essential element of government and business as well.

5·91   Here . . .

By the time the United States entered World War II in December 1941, radio had become a part of American life. Three events showed its impact clearly: the 1938 Orson Welles "War of the Worlds" broadcast, which created panic because listeners had learned to believe what they heard on radio (see 5.62); the ASCAP hassle, which limited popular music in early 1941 at the height of the big band craze (see 5.85); and the FCC investigation of the networks (see 5.83), by which the 10-year-old networks were shown to have attained the importance of much older businesses.

Politically, radio brought the government home to the average American, who hung onto President Roosevelt's words during the first 100 days of the New Deal, in the heart of the Depression. More people heard more candidates and political opinions than had been heard throughout the country's history. Some commentators claimed that radio caused the 87 percent increase in votes cast in national presidential elections from 1920 to 1940, while the population grew only by 25 percent.

Furthermore, by its coverage of domestic and international news events, radio became the news medium to which people turned first, replacing the century-old dominance of the newspaper.

Radio's increasing importance to the listener can be indexed in other ways: newspaper attempts to build or buy AM and FM stations as a hedge against the future; the use of motion picture stars and stories to promote films, as on *Lux Radio Theater*; the inclusion of radio-related questions on national polls and surveys, including the 1940 census; increased use of radio by public office seekers or, like Huey Long and Father Coughlin, opinion molders; ASCAP's reliance on revenue from radio above that from records, sheet music, or nightclub performance; the increase in car radios; and refinement of radio audience research, primarily to serve hard-nosed advertisers.

Another indication of radio's impact was the sharp rise in criticism of its programs and organization. Books, pamphlets, and articles charged that big business interests had taken over radio, particularly the networks, to the detriment of the average listener. Special interest groups bemoaned the lack of religious programming, the paucity of educational programs, the increasing flood of advertisements. Many critics believed that radio's chief problems were no longer technical, as they had been through the mid-1930s, but social, and that programming aimed at the lowest common denominator would make radio a societal liability.

In the late 1930s, Americans were both struggling up from the Depression and preparing against a war that by 1941 seemed inevitable. Radio broadcasting prospered accordingly: its increasing popularity filled a major marketing function when other media were suffering from lower revenues; it provided news and other information to the public; and it filled pleasurably the leisure hours that the Depression and then the shorter work week provided. Radio also prepared itself for service in the war that was to come.

5•92   . . . and Abroad

Radio broadcasting also was developing in Canada, Mexico, and Cuba. As the stations in these neighboring nations multiplied, they used greater power, spent longer hours on the air, and consequently produced greater interference. Both Canada and Mexico complained that the United States was hogging most of North America's clear channels and was ignoring their needs. This dissension led to a meeting early in 1937 to plan a fair division of the broadcast spectrum among the four countries, and a November 1937 conference in Havana, where representatives of the United States, Canada, Mexico, Cuba, Haiti, and the Dominican Republic drew up a North American Regional Broadcasting Agreement (NARBA). After ratification by the various legislatures, NARBA went into effect in late March 1941. This agreement forced many stations to change frequency in this country, Mexico, and Canada. In the United States, the FCC's moving 777 of the 862 stations on the air—only one to four channels for most of them—caused a minor technical expense rather than a major audience loss. About 100 Canadian stations were changed, and Mexico closed down many border stations that had long broadcast to the United States immune from FCC controls. In the end, Mexico and Canada gained better frequency allocations, and interference for all six countries was substantially reduced.

The story of radio abroad in the years 1934–1941 is essentially one of "haves" and "have-nots." While this country had fully half the world's radios, one for every 3.5 people, and Europe had one radio for every eight people, vast areas had little or no radio service or facilities. For example, rapidly industrializing Japan had but one receiver for every 28 people.

Mexico, importing most sets from the United States, had only one radio for every 64 persons, concentrated in major cities.

Patterns of control and organization were evident overseas. In most European countries, government controlled radio, sometimes indirectly, usually with annual license fees on receivers for support. Under Hitler, radio became a part of the German Propaganda Ministry. In the United Kingdom, the British Broadcasting Corporation was a government-chartered monopoly, a kind of public utility, supported by license revenue. Director-general until 1938 was the strong-minded Sir John Reith, who during his 15-year tenure put a philosophical stamp of "public service" on both commercial and noncommercial British broadcasting that has lasted to this day. Since broadcasting in the many colonies of European nations copied the mother country's, the majority of African and Asian systems—where radio existed at all—had central government control of facilities, finances, and programming. Countries of the Western Hemisphere, except for Canada and some of the West Indies and Latin America, tended to follow the commercially based system of the United States.

The use of shortwave for international broadcasting increased sharply during the 1930s as world tension rose. In this hemisphere, both commercial—primarily CBS and NBC—and governmental transmitters beamed broadcasts to Latin America by shortwave for rebroadcast over either medium- or shortwave domestic stations. By 1935 the Soviet Union, Germany, Italy, and Great Britain were sending out regular shortwave broadcasts to North America and the rest of the world, in appropriate languages. Since many floor-model console radios and some table radios sold here were equipped for shortwave listening, Americans frequently listened to shortwave in a time of crisis in Europe. Although much European shortwave propaganda was intended for other European nations—Germany, in particular, used radio to soften up enemy resolve before starting a diplomatic or military move—even after World War II began, some was directed at other parts of the world.

5•93   Period Overview

In these years prior to our entry into World War II, there were few departures from the trends established in the 1926–1933 period. Major technological changes were brewing for FM in the Armstrong laboratory and for television in the RCA and Farnsworth laboratories. While these new media already were competing for spectrum space, attention, and backing, only in the last months before Pearl Harbor would the public become aware of them. Their real impact would come after the war. After the initial shocks of FRC regulation and the Depression, broadcasting stations increased in number and power, and brought many communities their first local service. Radio carried news of political and economic changes and also took people's minds off their troubles.

Radio's winners and losers were easily identified in this period: networks and their supporting advertisers, influenced by the increasingly powerful advertising agencies, determined program content. What the networks presented, local stations carried, and copied in local programming. Commercial support, determined largely by audience ratings, was the substance of program and station survival. Many young entertainers began long careers on radio, and later on television. On the other hand, educational radio languished almost into nonexistence. Until Americans acknowledged the worldwide

threat of events in Europe, news and public affairs were limited in both national and local programming. Once war came, however, such previously unknown reporters as Edward R. Murrow became household names through their coverage of radio's first war.

Other than program domination by networks and advertising agencies, the most important development of the late 1930s was the growth of federal regulation. The FCC, established in 1934, completed the major technical receiver-interference reduction started by the FRC and turned to program content and media economics—areas that would demand increasing attention. Questionable program practices were brought to light and eliminated. Broadcast ownership and control, particularly as affected by the networks, was the subject of serious studies, numerous FCC hearings, and decisions. The general public neither knew nor cared about the behind-the-scenes battles—with the exception of the ASCAP-broadcasters fight that removed most popular music from the air for several months.

Radio as an increasing force in tying the nation together was illustrated in the first significant academic research into broadcasting. Radio's potential as both a positive and a negative propagandistic tool emerged in its early coverage of both the New Deal and the war in Europe. But the most important test for American radio was yet to come.

Further Reading

The blossoming of radio's impact is clearly seen in the great increase in number of books and other literature about radio in this period, making the following list much more selective than that for earlier chapters. Again, a good impression of radio's social role is found in Barnouw's second volume (1968), while a contemporary view with the ever-present RCA bias is in Archer (1939). The major trade periodical, *Broadcasting,* began to publish in 1931, so its pages are a mirror of history in this period. See *The First 50 Years of Broadcasting* (1982) for a book based on articles and photos from the 1931–1981 period; and see the 50th-anniversary issue of the magazine (October 12, 1981) for a chronology and special articles. Excellent readings on the period, many from the *Journal of Broadcasting,* are in Lichty and Topping (1975). Analyses of the industry, with a focus on the increasing importance of networks, are found in Robinson (1943) and in the FCC's *Report on Chain Broadcasting* (1941), one of the most important FCC documents on radio. An industry view of those same issues is in Sarnoff (1939).

The first practical guides to network-dominated radio advertising are Hettinger and Neff (1938) and Dygert

---

Key Broadcasting Indicators: 1935 and 1940 / This is the third of 12 tables offering comparable selected information for a 60-year period (to 1985) at five-year intervals. Sources for items 1–6 and 11 are the tables in Appendix C, while other information comes from sources indicated in the notes below. Most data are for January 1.

Indicators	AM Station Data	
	1935	1940
1. Number of commercial stations	543	± 730
2. Number of noncommercial stations	42	± 35
3. Total stations on the air	585	765
4. Number of network-affiliated stations	188	454
5. Percentage of commercial stations affiliated with networks	32%	59%
6. Total industry income (add 000,000)	$113	$216
7. One-hour station rate (New York)	$950	$1,200
8. One-minute station rate (New York)	na	na
9. One-hour network rate, evening	$14,250	$18,500
10. Number of broadcasting employees	14,600	25,700
11. Percentage of families with sets	67%	81%
12. Broadcasting regulatory budget (FCC)	$1,125,599	$1,838,175
13. Total FCC personnel	442	625

Notes (see Appendix D for full citations)

na = not available or not applicable

7. Station is WEAF, flagship of NBC-Red.

9. Network is NBC-Red with 68 stations in 1935 and 121 in 1940 (full network service).

10. Lichty and Topping (1975), table 23, page 290.

12. and 13. FCC Annual Reports, data for fiscal years 1935 and 1940.

(1939), which are interesting to compare with current textbooks. Eoyang (1936) examines industry economics in a broader context not readily found elsewhere. A good FCC study of economic and political regulatory discision making is in the *Report on Social and Economic Data* (1938). An overview of the difficult times for educational radio is found in Blakely (1979) and in a chapter in Gibson (1977) that focuses on the slight role then played by the federal government. Atkinson (1941, 1942a–d) and Frost (1937a and b) provide contemporary views of the steady decline of noncommercial stations, while Cooper (1942) offers the best annotated bibliography of the period.

An increasing amount of reference and historical material is appearing on the golden years of network radio. The standard sources are Summers (1958) for annual listings and Buxton and Owen (1972), Dunning (1976), and Terrace (1981) for details on all major programs. For an indexed catalog of program recordings in the Library of Congress from this period, see Smart (1982). A good narrative history of radio that covers this period is MacDonald (1979), which offers a general review followed by chapters on program content types.

Entertainment programming is covered in a variety of sources—fan magazines from the period are especially useful. Two short books by Harmon (1967 and 1970) provide nostalgic feeling for comedy and drama programs. Stedman (1977) offers a fine discussion of radio serials and their relationship to movie and television content of the same genre. Settel's pictorial history (1967) and Slide's collection of personality photos (1982) give a visual aspect to an aural period. The best assessment of radio comedy is the book by Wertheim (1979).

Music in radio is discussed in both DeLong (1980) and Eberly (1982), while the key role of the voice is assessed in Poindexter (1978), who reviews the "golden throats and silver tongues" of announcers of the era. Prestige radio drama as seen through the life of Norman Corwin is related in the biography by Bannerman (1986).

Radio's news and service roles are related in Baker's history of the first 60 years of farm broadcasting (1981) and in several books on radio news. Culbert's fine analysis of radio news in the late 1930s (1976), Fang's brief biographies of the top commentators of the era (1977), and Hosley's discussion of early foreign correspondents on American radio (1984) all indicate how radio news and commentary developed in the years up to World War II. More anecdotal are Schechter and Anthony's (1941) book on NBC news operations and the early wartime books by reporters Shirer (1941) and Murrow (1941). The varied roles of Father Coughlin appear in Marcus (1973).

The best history of radio audience research is in the first chapter of Beville (1988), while Connah (1938) reviews audience information of importance to advertisers. See also the books mentioned on page 187. The first book on radio esthetics was Arnheim (1936).

Other than the material on network regulation already mentioned, the best sources on the increasing federal role in regulating radio are Rose (1940), probably the best single book on public policy issues in the pretelevision industry; Frost (1937b); Herring and Gross (1936); Edelman's 1950 history of FRC and FCC administration of broadcast licensing; and the annual reports of the FCC beginning in 1935. For insight on contemporary legal thinking, see the approach taken by the senator largely responsible for the 1934 act (Dill, 1938) and the detailed study in the two volumes of Socolow (1939).

The beginnings of FM broadcasting are found in Lessing (1956) and Erickson (1973), both of which, especially the latter, are overly emotional and biased toward Armstrong. The development of U.S. television in the prewar period is best told in Abramson (1987) and Udelson (1982), while important contemporary studies of electronic television, both stressing the work of Farnworth, are Eckhardt (1936) and Everson (1949). Hubbell (1942) is a popular history of prewar television, and Waldrop and Borkin (1938) studies the economic empire-building behind the laboratory development of the video medium. Other useful contemporary views include Lohr (1940), in which the NBC president reviews RCA practice and expectations, and Porterfield and Reynolds (1940), which provides 11 papers from var-

ied points of view on television's likely future. Maclaurin (1949) discusses prewar patent battles in television, while Abramson (1955) is still the best overall technical history of television developments. A compendium of engineering, descriptive, and comparative papers on the finally approved NTSC standards is found in Fink (1943).

The pioneering British work in television is told in breezy, illustrated fashion in Norman (1984); in detailed, technical fashion in Burns (1986) and in Pawley's fine BBC technical history (1972); and in Swift (1950). Other analyses of broadcasting overseas appear in Briggs (1965), for the Reith years at the BBC, and in Huth (1937), for a French-language, country-by-country discussion of radio's status. Two British studies of radio's impact are Pegg (1983) and Maine's (1939) study of the BBC's audience. For studies of radio at war, see pages 244–245.

**Radio Goes
to War
(1941–1945)**

𝕮 ❀ **6** ❀

"Seems like free men have done it
again!"—On a Note of Triumph, Norman Corwin, 1945

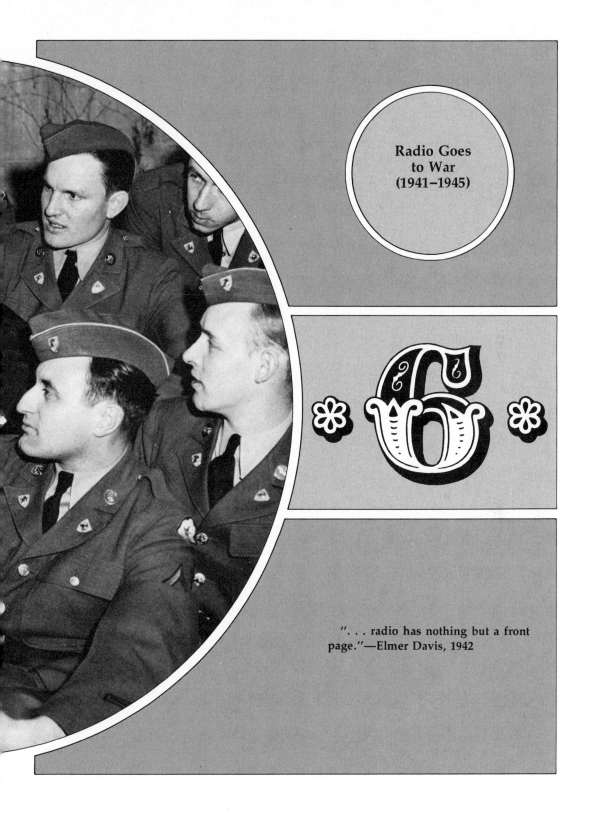

**Radio Goes
to War
(1941–1945)**

6

". . . radio has nothing but a front page."—Elmer Davis, 1942

The tension between the United States and Japan had been building weekly. While members of the America First Committee and others thundered against participating in a foreign war, the U.S. government was selling arms to the Allies in Europe, the navy had orders to shoot back if fired upon, and the army was priming itself with the draft and extensive maneuvers in Louisiana. Overseas, Hitler neared Moscow after his midsummer invasion of Russia; and General Douglas MacArthur, an American officer technically working for the government of the Philippines, said that he had what it took to resist Japanese invasion of "up to five million men." At home, war-related industries were humming as the

Outline:
Radio Goes to War (1941–1945)

country geared for the war that seemed to be coming.

December 7, 1941, was a Sunday, and across the country people were wading through the newspaper, going for a day's outing or Christmas window shopping, or just relaxing. In Washington, Secretary of State Cordell Hull expected two Japanese emissaries in the latest of many attempts to reduce the danger of war between the two countries.

Radio in those years devoted Sunday afternoon largely to public affairs and classical music. Audiences were not large, but they were loyal—and such programming was thought probably to please the FCC. At 2:30 P.M., eastern standard time, NBC-Red was about to broadcast a *University of Chicago Roundtable* program while NBC-Blue was in the middle of a Foreign Policy Association talk. A labor talk sponsored by the CIO had just finished on CBS, and the weekly New York Philharmonic broadcast would begin at 3 P.M. Listeners tuned in for the interim program were startled to hear newsman John Daly cut in at 2:31 with "The Japanese have attacked Pearl Harbor, Hawaii, by air, President Roosevelt has just announced. The attack was also made on naval and military activities on the principal island of Oahu." In his haste, Daly stumbled on the pronunciation of Oahu before repeating the incredible announcement. The other networks soon delivered similar bulletins, and Americans began to realize that war had come. For an hour or so, bulletins broke into regular programming, adding new details as military or Hawaiian authorities released them.

As afternoon wore on to evening on the East Coast, military censorship clamped down, leaving radio with limited information and unlimited demand for news. Hence, more and more analysis and commentary—much of it badly informed—filled networks' programming that Sunday evening. Military personnel were ordered, by radio, to report for duty in uniform immediately—including headquarters officers and technical personnel who had not worn uniforms for years. Stations and networks tossed aside program schedules, canceling some shows and delaying others to make room for news bulletins. Even commercials gave way to news.

On the West Coast, people were worried about possible air raids or naval bombardment of major cities or southern California airfields. Some antiaircraft guns were fired at nonexistent enemy airplanes. The federal government took emergency measures. Because enemy ships or planes could make use of radio broadcasts to "home in" on targets, and because spies might use amateur radio, the FCC ordered all amateurs to get off the air and dismantle their equipment. It also shut down many West Coast broadcast stations for several days to a week until initial fears of attack had died down. While some stations were silent for a few days, others broadcast only important news flashes. Taking amateurs off the air in wartime followed World War I precedent, while the silencing of regular radio broadcasting in California, Oregon, Washington, and the Territory of Hawaii was an isolated episode in this country's World War II procedures.

Personnel at all stations were confused as to what they should or should not transmit. The Naval Observatory stopped transmitting weather forecasts almost immediately, and station operators soon learned that, with a few exceptions, weather forecasts from other sources would be banned as well. The army prohibited the broadcast of any information on troop movements outside the country. In New York, the networks began to limit visitors

How United Press Covered the Pearl Harbor Story / Reprinted by permission of United Press International.

United Press Associations

INCORPORATED IN NEW YORK
GENERAL OFFICES
NEWS BUILDING NEW YORK CITY

FRANK H. BARTHOLOMEW
VICE PRESIDENT   December 11, 1941
814 MISSION STREET
SAN FRANCISCO, CAL.

United Press Pacific Division Clients:

  So many of you wired or wrote your thanks for the beat we gave you last Sunday forenoon from Honolulu on the Japanese attack that we are using this blanket method of answering your inquiries as to how it was done.

  Several days earlier, we had issued advance orders to the telephone company to put all leased wires into operation at a moment's notice. San Francisco bureau -- focal point of news from the Pacific -- was ready.

  James A. Sullivan, San Francisco bureau manager, was on duty Sunday, Dec. 7.

  At 11:24 a.m. the telephone rang. It was Mrs. Frank Tremaine, wife of our Hawaii manager in Honolulu.

  "Fifty unidentified planes attacked Honolulu this morning," she began, relaying the information coming into our Honolulu bureau from Tremaine at Fort Shafter, from Night Manager William F. Tyree at another post, and from staff members on other assignments.

  Ringing of the flash signal on our leased wire in San Francisco bureau, with the White House announcement of the attack, came at 11:26, while Mrs. Tremaine continued to dictate:

  "Several of the planes were shot down. Their attack seemed to center on Pearl Harbor and Hickam Field. Some bombs fell in the city.

  "Just a minute -- there's an explosion or something outside. I'll run to the window and see what it was....There's a lot of excitement outside. I'll call you back later."

  (The excitement was when an incendiary bomb landed 25 feet from The Advertiser building, home of the United Press bureau.)

  Sullivan, in San Francisco, telephoned the story to United Press in New York, from whence the first direct account of the attack was placed on United Press wires.

  Advance arrangements perfected several days earlier went into operation. Leased wires were opened to clients. United Press men in San Francisco telephoned you by long-distance to go to your office and turn on your teletypes. Cable re-write men and operators bulletined onto the wires the steady flood of urgent cables pouring in from Honolulu.

United Press Pacific Division Clients -- Page 2

In Honolulu, United Press was well prepared for the Japanese attack.

As Staffer Francis McCarthy said in the last story telephoned from Honolulu before all press communications were halted for nearly two days: "Now it is possible to reveal that the attack was not entirely unexpected."

McCarthy himself had arrived in Honolulu via Pan-American Clipper only four days before the attack, further augmenting the staff of the largest bureau operated in Hawaii by any news service.

Only United Press serves both morning and evening newspapers in Hawaii. Only United Press operates both day and night bureaus there.

United Press owns and operates the only news transmission system in Hawaii, including a full leased wire on the Island of Oahu and its own wireless-telegraphy plant for reception of news from the mainland. Other news services utilize the commercial routes and must yield priority to governmental traffic. With its own private system, handling press exclusively, United Press has no traffic-priority problem and has a clear channel at all times.

In Manila -- news center #2 in the War of the Pacific -- United Press similarly operates around the clock and owns and operates its own communications system for instantaneous and exclusive transmission of news.

Your news service has its own men at the places where news is going to originate in the next few days and weeks.

They include Harold Guard at Singapore; Francis M. Fisher at Chungking; Robert P. Martin at Shanghai; Jack Raleigh at Batavia; Darrell Berrigan at Bangkok; George Baxter at Hongkong.

History's biggest news story is breaking in territory strongly staffed by the largest world-wide press association.

                              Sincerely yours,

                              Frank H. Bartholomew

                              Manager, Pacific Division.

and station extra guards over control centers and transmitters—security precautions that quickly spread to stations in other regions.

On Monday, December 8, President Roosevelt went to Congress to request a declaration of war on Japan. As he was driven to the Capitol, the wire services and networks kept stations supplied with bulletins on Japanese attacks throughout French Indochina and the Philippines. At 12:40 P.M., Speaker Sam Rayburn introduced the President, who delivered his famous "Yesterday, December 7, 1941, a date which will live in infamy . . ." speech as millions of Americans listened on radio. That evening Roosevelt spoke to more than 62 million listeners, the largest audience for a single radio program up to that time.

American broadcasting rapidly switched to a wartime footing. The government established an Office of Censorship, which, within a month of the Pearl Harbor attack, published a voluntary code of censorship for broadcasting and other media. The chief censor was highly respected news commentator Elmer Davis. In January 1942 the FCC limited new station construction, and in April the War Production Board froze new receiver manufacture—both steps taken to preserve war-needed materials and labor supply. The government declared radio an essential industry to maintain its manpower strength, but the draft and enlistments shrank the work force anyway and equipment shortages hindered production and repairs. Broadcasting could not expand in number of stations or receivers, but programming services, news staffs, and time on the air increased sharply. Patriotic wartime elements became more common in regular and special programs on networks and local stations. Songs like "Remember Pearl Harbor" and "Praise the Lord and Pass the Ammunition" had brief popularity, and tension-relaxing humor and entertainment went into high gear.

6·1   Innovations: Recording Methods

An important technical trend was toward miniaturization of components. By 1943 and 1944 military units carried two-way radio sets, the famous *walkie-talkies*, a new kind of radio transceiver (transmitter/receiver) construction that made equipment smaller, lighter, and more rugged. FM radio's great value in ground tactical communications was facilitated by FM inventor Armstrong's waiving his rights to royalties on FM military applications.

Military research also produced knowledge about efficient use of very high and ultra high frequencies. Information on interference and propagation at those frequencies proved crucial in the 1944–1945 FCC hearings on spectrum allocations for FM and television services (see 6.2).

Destined to have great postwar applicability was an innovation begun before the war and refined during wartime both here and abroad: the tape recorder. Until the mid-1930s, recordings of broadcast or musical selections could be made with a disc recorder that made either the common 78-rpm musical recordings or 33⅓-rpm broadcast transcriptions, or on 35mm film. But the equipment needed for stability was too bulky and heavy for carrying or easy operation. Besides, war demand for shellac, then the primary ingredient in records, reduced the amount available for civilian use. Original transcription making switched from metal to very fragile glass bases.

In the late 1930s, several devices were under development as supplements or replacements for discs. In this country, magnetic wire and steel tape recorders received what little attention there was. By 1935 Bell Telephone Laboratories was operating an experimental system for which the high-grade steel tape cost $1.50 per foot. By 1938 the Brush Development Company had a steel tape dictating machine for sale. Overseas, the Germans used a steel tape magnetic recording machine to give time signals over various telephone systems and the BBC used a similar machine for recording its half-hour Empire Service programs. The sound fidelity was not very high, but such recorders would be adapted to record conferences or radio programs during the war. Since their manufacture had low priority, however, they were constructed by hand or adapted from existing units.

Another American firm, the Armour Research Foundation, developed a magnetic wire recorder when steel tape became scarce. This very thin—1/100 inch or so—wire could hold up to an hour of material per reel, although its quality was even poorer than steel tape and it often broke. One could repair a break by melting both ends with a lighted cigarette or by tying a square knot, but the resulting bumps could damage the delicate recording and playback heads. In 1943 Armour and its licensee Webster-Chicago (Webcor) began to manufacture a limited number of "portable"—50 pounds or more!—wire recorders for the military.

Various other techniques were explored. One used a base similar to motion picture film, on which grooves were magnetically etched. The Recordgraph, weighing 75 pounds, was so rugged it could be operated upside down. Although a number of war correspondents used these machines—including George Hicks in his famous D-Day reports—portable film recorders could be used only for low-quality voice recordings. These could be stored for a long time and were very cheap, but the

film wore out after it had been played 20 or 30 times.

The eventual winner was the paper or plastic base magnetic tape, which provided excellent sound quality with little or no surface noise. In 1941 the Germans programmed Radio Luxembourg, which they had captured in 1940, with prerecorded tapes operating at 30 inches per second (ips), four times the present broadcast standard. They provided such good sound that American forces moving across Europe in 1944 were surprised to capture radio stations operating only with large reels of tape and not live performers. By 1945 communications men had brought a number of German Magnetophones, including portable ones, to the United States for evaluation. The implications for postwar broadcasting were not overlooked (see 7.12).

6·2   Stations: Status Quo for the Duration

During the war, from 1942 through 1945, only 34 new AM and 28 FM stations took to the air, whereas earlier the number of stations had increased by 30 to 50 each year. This reduction was due not to economics but to government policy.

6·21   The AM Industry

On February 23, 1942, the FCC announced that, to preserve construction and electronic equipment for war needs, it would issue no permits for new station construction. In April, the War Production Board strengthened the FCC order when it limited construction of any kind to applicants who had all the needed materials in hand, or to builders of noncommercial educational stations. The FCC also froze major alterations to existing stations "for the duration" and, to conserve electrical power, tubes, and components, reduced requirements for minimum number of hours of broadcast service, and required stations to lower their power output by a rarely noticeable 20 percent. It ordered a massive inventory of tubes and unused transmitters in the hands of licensees and distributed the information to military and commercial broadcasters so that available supplies could be fully used. As trained engineers and other technical personnel became scarcer beginning in 1943, the FCC reduced requirements and restrictions so that other persons could read meters and do minor maintenance.

By early 1944, electronic production had improved enough for the FCC to authorize a limited number of new Class IV 250 watt local stations and allow facilities changes when matériel seemed to be available. Conditions tightened up again early in 1945, and new construction was limited to towns lacking primary service and to situations requiring minimal construction materials. Full wartime restrictions remained until August 1945 (see 7.21).

A strong indication of the FCC's faith in broadcasting's stability and ability to function in the public interest was the announcement on December 14, 1943, that for the first time it would license stations for the full statutory three years. Although both the 1927 and the 1934 acts had authorized three-year terms, for many years license renewal had been required every six months, then one year, and later two years. The full license period, of course, meant less paperwork for stations and commission, both of which were operating with severe manpower shortages.

6•22   FM Pioneering

When construction of new stations was frozen during the war, there were more than 900 AM stations. FM service, however, was just getting started. Many applications for construction permits were withdrawn because of lack of building and electronic materials, and the FCC eased its rules to allow FM stations that provided some public service to operate with whatever equipment they could gather. Philadelphia stations kept FM going in the face of replacement equipment shortages by rotating time on the air so that no station was broadcasting more than two days a week. They pooled all spare parts, programming material, and personnel.

In August 1943, the FCC dropped the cumbersome system of FM call letters using letter and number combinations, and many FM stations owned by AMs in the same market now took their sister station's call letters with an -FM suffix.

6•23   Television during the War Years

When the FCC gave television a green light for commercial development in spring 1941 (see 5.15), it also deleted one of television's 19 channels and deferred action on CBS's suggestion to consider color television. This decision created a problem of receiver obsolescence, but only a few thousand sets were affected, and the manufacturer could convert them (see box, page 229).

On July 1, 1941, both CBS and NBC New York stations converted from experimental to commercial status, becoming WCBW (CBS) and WNBT (NBC). By FCC regulation, both stations were on the air about 15 hours a week. Most programs —discussions, game shows, musical programs, and wrestling and boxing matches —were produced within the studio. Some sports events were covered live on a remote basis. Films, particularly free ones, were widely used; indeed, program schedules were divided into 20-minute multiples—just right for two reels of film (18 minutes in 35mm) and some commercials. Newscasts resembled motion picture newsreels in content. The first television commercial reportedly was a picture of a Bulova watch showing the correct time, and Lever Brothers, Procter & Gamble, and Sun Oil also were early sponsors of television programs. According to the first television rate card, WNBT's, one hour of prime time in New York cost $120, compared to $10,700 in 1975 and the 1941 radio rate of $1,200. (See box on page 152.)

A handful of other stations converted to commercial operation in later 1941 and early 1942: WPTZ (Philco) in Philadelphia, what would become KTLA in Los Angeles, WRGB (named after GE engineer W. R. G. Baker) in Schenectady, what would become WBBM-TV in Chicago, and a Zenith-owned station in the same city. But the audience grew very slowly, since very few sets—90 a month in New York early in 1942—were for sale, and their price was very high—several hundred dollars for a five- or eight-inch picture when minimum wage was 25¢ an hour. By the time we entered World War II, between 10,000 and 20,000 sets were in use, half in New York and the rest in Philadelphia, Chicago, Schenectady, and Los Angeles.

In December 1941, WCBW produced a 90-minute documentary on the Pearl Harbor attack, only hours after it happened. It included the latest news bulletins as well as analysis backed up by maps, charts, and models of affected areas in Hawaii and the Philippines. Later both New York stations presented War Bond drives and other patriotic material. NBC's television outlet carried a series of training programs for air raid wardens in New York, which many of them viewed on sets that individual owners loaned to firehouses and other posts.

The green light given to television in mid-1941 changed to red on May 12, 1942, when a War Production Board order, implemented by the FCC, forbade further building of stations so that materials could go to the war effort. Ten commercial stations, mostly converted from experimental ones, were then on the air, together with some remaining experimental transmitters. The commission allowed licensees that had construction permits and the necessary equipment to finish building in order to "keep alive this new art during the war." The FCC had previously dropped the minimum telecast hours from 15 to four a week in order to stretch matériel and manpower. Six stations throughout the country continued regular program service throughout the war. In New York, only the Dumont station, started in June 1942, maintained regular although limited service. Both NBC and CBS cut down to skeleton organizations and dropped television broadcasting altogether until summer 1944, after Dumont had begun a full commercial schedule.

Everyone was learning during the 1942–1945 wartime hiatus. The military learned how to use many of the higher-band television frequencies. Of the few thousand people with sets, many learned how to keep them working; about three-quarters of the sets survived the war, although many were in poor condition. While viewers enjoyed increased entertainment programming on the few stations, it was still in the era of monochrome (shades of gray) makeup and extremely strong—and hot—lighting that caused perspiration to fall from actors and then literally to boil off tabletops. A young man hired off the street as a cable puller one day could become a cameraman the next and a director shortly thereafter; for a brief interval cameramen were considered artists rather than technicians, and ingenuity compensated for small budgets and limited manpower. Program innovations were legion. GE presented the first complete televised opera in 1943; three stations interconnected to show an original short film a year later; and a New York station, with a commercial sponsor, offered the first musical program specially written for television. The presidential election of 1944 was sketchily covered, with local coverage in the convention city of Chicago sent on film to New York, since there was no direct coaxial cable or microwave link between East and Midwest.

The first trade association, the Television Broadcasters Association, was formed early in 1944, and both NBC and CBS announced plans for postwar television networks. The new image orthicon camera tube could get excellent pictures with only a small fraction of the light needed by the older iconoscope. Experiments with lighting, makeup, UHF transmissions, and film projection were conducted. On V-E and V-J days in 1945, WNBT telecast 15 hours of special programming about the ending of the shooting in Europe and Asia which was carried live on stations in Schenectady and Philadelphia as well as New York. Baseball broadcasts on one New York station could cause workers at another station to desert their posts and flock around a receiver (behind closed doors). But, it must be remembered, few people saw any of this, and television in effect marked time behind the scenes during the war—planning for the day when the light would turn green again.

6·3   The Splitup of NBC and Formation of ABC

With the limited growth in AM stations, the proportion of network radio affiliates rose from 60 percent of all stations in 1940–1941 to 95 percent in 1945.

Never before or since would network programming so dominate radio. Almost all the approximately 950 stations on the air had affiliations with one network, and many with more than one, especially if they were the only station in a smaller community. An increasingly large proportion—more than 40 percent at war's end—was affiliated with Mutual, usually smaller and less important stations. The NBC-Red and -Blue networks combined affiliated with about 35 percent of all stations and CBS affiliated with another 16 percent.

The major development during the war years was the appearance of two new networks. The Keystone Broadcasting System, established in 1940 and grown substantially by 1945, was a network in name only, as it existed to supply programs by transcription to secondary market affiliates—some 200 by the end of the war. It provided up to 28 hours a week in scripted and transcribed programs to stations that were apt also to be affiliated with Mutual or another major network.

An important aftermath of the FCC chain broadcasting rules and extended litigation over their implementation (see 5.83) was RCA's splitting its Red and Blue NBC networks into separate but wholly owned divisions. Red was called "NBC" over the air, and Blue "the Blue Network." When the Supreme Court upheld the FCC chain broadcasting rules in 1943, NBC had to divest itself of one of its networks (see 6.85). NBC sought a cash buyer for Blue, which had always had less important affiliated stations and had carried more sustaining programs than the powerful and popular Red network. At the end of July, just two months after the Supreme Court decision, RCA announced that the Blue network had been sold to WMCA (New York) owner Edward J. Noble, a candy manufacturer who had earned his fortune with Life Savers, for $8 million. The FCC approved the sale in mid-October, changing the ownership of New York flagship station WJZ and several others, and divorcing the Blue Network, Inc. from RCA. In 1945 the network became the American Broadcasting Company (ABC).

The war killed another attempt to establish a broadcast network. In 1940, just as the FCC announced commercial FM authorization effective for the coming year, some 15 FM station owners led by John Shepard III announced plans for an FM-only commercial network. They obtained a construction permit for a New York station, to be the "American Network" flagship, with the idea of relaying FM programs directly off the air, since FM was static-free, instead of leasing telephone circuits from AT&T as AM networks had to do. The first program was so relayed by seven northeastern stations in December 1941, but when the war froze FM station construction, the American Network was left with a bunch of paper affiliates unable to get on the air. This delay, plus pressure by the AM chains, led to the plan's demise and sale of its name to the Blue Network in mid-1944.

6·4   Education Struggles On

While educational broadcasting on AM remained limited in size and scope through the war years, a new hope had appeared when the FCC reserved FM channels for potential educational broadcasting licensees (see 5.4). By the end of 1941, however, only two educational FM stations had gone on the air. Although the construction freeze of 1942 exempted educational stations, the scarcity of construction materials and broadcast equipment coupled with the slow decision-making processes of educational institutions com-

bined to limit educational FM growth during the war to 12 authorizations and 6 stations on the air when the war ended in mid-1945.

Still, educational institutions made known their plans to apply for construction permits at the end of the war. Some states, notably Wisconsin, envisioned statewide educational networks of FM stations to broadcast school, college, and adult education programming. Educators realized that, after more than a decade of talking about educational radio, they finally had means to accomplish it—after the war.

6·5   Advertising: Ten-Cent Dollars

While it may not be politic to say so, World War II was one of the best things to happen to radio advertising. The impetus for AM radio's gravy years was the government imposition of a 90 percent excess-profits tax on American industry to discourage profiteering on war contracts. However, the tax bill had a provision that made excess profits used in advertising taxable at only the normal rates—if at all. Business directors soon realized they could buy a dollar's worth of advertising time or space for what was, in effect, ten cents. As paper rationing in 1943–1945 and shortages of newsprint led to smaller newspaper editions and often less advertising space, a number of advertisers switched to radio, which faced no such problem. Radio's share of advertising dollars increased from 12 percent in 1941 to 18 percent of a much larger base in 1945. Radio broadcasting passed newspapers as a national advertising medium in 1943. By 1945 more than 37 percent of national—but not local or regional—advertising dollars went to radio, with magazines a close second and newspapers third (see Appendix C, table 4).

From 1940 to 1945, gross revenues

for the networks and their owned-and-operated stations rose from $56.4 million to $100.9 million. Before-tax income, however, remained proportionately static—25 percent to 23 percent of revenues over the years covered—partially due to greatly increased expenses in covering war news around the world. The overall network advertising pattern was concentrated. Three advertising agencies, J. Walter Thompson, Young & Rubicam—both of which are still important—and Dancer-Fitzgerald-Sample, purchased about 25 percent of the time on the Red, Blue, and CBS networks. In 1945 CBS had 13 sponsors each of which bought more than $1 million worth of time, and three that bought more than $4 million worth, General Foods, Lever Brothers, and Procter & Gamble—still among the largest advertisers in the 1970s. Just seven sponsors and six agencies accounted for half of CBS's billings. The NBC-Red network had 11 purchasers of more than $1 million in time, ABC had 9, and Mutual had 3. Twelve sponsors and 5 agencies accounted for 40 percent of ABC's 1945 billings, while 6 sponsors and 5 agencies accounted for one-third of Mutual's. This concentration was not a wartime creation, but the high rate of income and profit was, thanks to the ten-cent dollars and the wartime rationing of paper.

While the networks and their 30 or so stations skimmed off the cream of revenue, more than one-third throughout these war years, the remaining 800 or so stations prospered as well. Gross revenues of the non-network-owned operations more than doubled from 1940, when 734 stations collected $90.6 million, to 1945, when 873 stations earned $198.3 million; but their net before-tax profit increased even more, from 21 to 30.5 percent of revenues in the same years. Some stations either had no income or did not report it

to the FCC, for Appendix C, table 1, shows about 30 to 50 more stations on the air each year than reported financial data. While one-third of all stations reported losses in 1939, less than 6 percent were in the red six years later—probably the lowest such figure in the history of radio. The entire radio industry, and especially the local stations, were profiting. While all radio stations increased their return on investment twofold, local stations enjoyed an 800 percent increase from 1939 to 1945.

Most radio advertising in these years was for insurance and for processed foods, drugs, toiletries, and tobacco—items which were often rationed but never unattainable during the war. Regional and national firms whose normal consumer manufacturing was halted for the duration turned to institutional advertising. For example, the major auto makers advertised mainly to keep the corporate name in the public's mind; the slogan "when better cars are built, Buick will build them" could be used even while the automobile firm was making tanks for the army. Since companies seeking to enhance their corporate name rather than sell a specific product often chose to sponsor prestige drama or musical programs on the larger stations or the networks, such programming became more common. Advertising agencies remained in control of most radio advertising and much of the programming.

The few commercial FM stations carried little or no advertising, not because they did not want to or try to sell time but because their audiences were too small and their broadcasting hours too few to attract sponsors. FM survived the war either on the profits of co-owned AM stations or out of the pockets of their respective owners. Stations kept expenses down by duplicating network shows or by programming recorded music.

6•6   Programming Patriotism

Like virtually all other aspects of American life, American radio reflected the war. There had been no overall radio industry planning for wartime operation, though individuals undoubtedly had given thought to it, particularly newsmen. Thus, when war came, radio took a while to adjust. With the exception of news broadcasts, radio in the first weeks after Pearl Harbor sounded much like prewar broadcasting. An indication of what was to come aired on December 15, when Norman Corwin's *We Hold These Truths* reminded Americans that the Bill of Rights was worth fighting for. The program was a combination of documentary, inspiration, news reporting, and patriotic fervor, but it elicited favorable comments.

Essentially, radio programs took three related approaches to the war. Getting most attention were special programs —usually appeals for scrap materials, the sale of War Bonds, and the like—built around major screen and radio stars. Probably the best-known effort of this kind was singer Kate Smith's 57 appearances during one day, February 1, 1944, in a War Bond appeal. She was later credited with having helped sell $112 million worth.

The second and most common approach was to insert war-related material into existing program series. Drama programs included references to rationing or to a son in the service; variety shows made increasing use of servicemen or took place at military camps, and musical programs featured war-related songs. Although "Coming in on a Wing and a Prayer" and "He Wears a Pair of Silver Wings" did well on *Your Hit Parade*, so did a woman's complaint, "They're Either Too Young or Too Old." Most songs as usual dealt with romance rather than warfare.

The third approach was to introduce a new program series devoted to the war or heavily reflecting its impact on the home front. An early example was *This Is War!*, a 13-week series of hour-long programs aired on 700 stations, counting those that aired it by transcription rather than live, on all four networks. The series was developed by and supported with funds of the government and the networks. Norman Corwin was the director and wrote half of the programs. The first went on the air on Valentine's Day 1942 while American eyes were focused on the worsening situation in the Philippines. Each succeeding Saturday evening for the next 12 weeks a different program attracted an estimated 20 million listeners while focusing on some aspect of the war—the White House role in this and past wars; the navy; the army; the air corps; our allies, now being referred to as the United Nations; the enemy and his propaganda. Famed writers Norman Corwin, Maxwell Anderson, Philip Wylie, and Stephen Vincent Benét and many Hollywood and radio stars contributed their efforts. According to the prospectus for the series, the producer's aim was to inspire, frighten, and inform all at the same time. Reaction to the series was generally positive, except for the complaint that the series aired simultaneously on all four networks and gave listeners no alternatives. This first all-network production also gave rise to a fear that government might dominate programming.

6•61   *Office of War Information*

Section 606 of the Communications Act of 1934 gives the President power to control operations of broadcast stations and other telecommunications facilities in time of war or other national emergency.

Many broadcasters feared that the government would take over radio completely, as it had in World War I, thus silencing commercial broadcasting for the duration. As it happened, Section 606 was not invoked for broadcasting; but two government agencies were set up to handle issues of vital communication on the one hand and censorship on the other (see 6.84).

In June 1942, President Roosevelt established the Office of War Information (OWI) and named veteran and highly respected *New York Times* and CBS news commentator Elmer Davis to head it. OWI, combining the operations and functions of four older and overlapping agencies, was intended to meet three needs of audiences in the United States and abroad: the need for news; the need for information as to what the public should do and when and how to do it; and the need for truthful explanations of war issues, the enemy and our allies, and, especially, the role of work and war production at home as well as the sacrifices war forced on everyone. Roughly two-thirds of OWI's budget went for overseas operations (see 6.92), leaving only one-third for the domestic branch. A section of the latter, the Radio Bureau, headed by a radio industry executive, was created to deliver important war-related messages efficiently to radio listeners.

In its first weeks of frenzied activity, the Radio Bureau established a general policy: the role of government was to steer —with "suggestions" for voluntary compliance—rather than direct or command the flow of information through privately owned communication media. It devoted a great deal of effort to involving station managers and respecting their views. In line with this policy, the Radio Bureau decided to tailor war messages for specific publics and to insert war messages into regular popular entertainment programs instead of creating special programs. It would emphasize quality rather than saturation quantity, and it would help broadcasters superimpose the war and its needs on existing programming rather than force major changes in content. In that way, popular radio programs would help maintain morale while delivering their large audiences to OWI for its war-related messages. OWI was behind a number of special program series, however. *This Is Our Enemy* appeared on the networks to enlighten listeners as to what the Axis powers stood for and had done. *You Can't Do Business With Hitler* ran by transcription on hundreds of stations, describing the broken promises of Nazi Germany.

Perhaps OWI's key job was to *limit* the flood of material that hit broadcasters in early 1942 as the country switched to a war footing. The problem was epitomized by the station that received a 20-inch stack, 16 pounds, of messages, scripts, and transcriptions for free-time and urgent broadcast in a single month! OWI had the task of coordinating and clearing all government messages, including those of the military services, and establishing priorities as to their importance at any given time. By OWI's limiting the number of government war messages and setting up specific ways of allocating them across the broadcast schedule, both advertisers and broadcasters could bear the costs as part of the war effort. At the same time, the reduction in number of messages kept the public from being saturated with government information and exhortation on top of the war news and consequently ignoring the whole issue.

6·62   News

The major role of radio during the war was, of course, to report the war's progress. The amount of radio news, including specials and on-the-spot coverage, increased by more than 1,000 hours a year to 1943, when it began to taper off. A look at the last column in the table on this page indicates that scheduled newscasts, at least, dropped off in the final year of the war. Although specific data are lacking, overall time devoted to news probably dropped off that year too, since the war ended in Europe in May and in the Pacific in August, and since audiences were tiring of constant war news by early 1945, when the final result of the fighting seemed clear.

Within that trend, other changes were noticeable. Network news increased mainly in evening hours, and by 1944 news specials and newscasts made up 16–20 percent of network program schedules. In many cases, fewer commercials were given during newscasts, CBS considering jingles and other "undue gaiety" unfitting for serious wartime news.

At first, because of technological limitations and censorship, war reporting was an after-the-fact recitation of events. The networks still adhered to their ban against recordings except under most unusual conditions. But military censors distrusted live reports for the same reason that they eliminated or severely restricted weather reports: the danger that apparently innocuous phrases or events—a station going off the air during an air raid, the absence of a reporter who might be expected to accompany an invasion force—would give information to the enemy.

The Growth of Network Wartime News: 1940–1945/That the war increased the amount of radio network time devoted to news seems obvious—but here are figures that demonstrate how great that increase was. See text for other comment on these figures.

Year	Total Yearly Hours of News*					Scheduled Newscasts (quarter hours per week) All Four Networks Combined
	NBC(Red)	CBS	Blue(ABC)	Mutual	Total	
1940	636	769	681	310	2,396	70
1941	983	829	796	840	3,448	66
1942	1,280	1,385	836	1,131	4,632	108
1943	1,641	1,454	909	1,370	5,274	123
1944	1,726	1,497	1,062	1,237	5,522	145
1945	#	#	#	#	#	135

* = includes regularly scheduled newscasts, specials, on-the spot broadcasts
\# = indicates figures not available

Source: First five columns from *Broadcasting* (April 23, 1945), page 23; last column figured from data in H. Summers. *A Thirty Year History of Programs Carried on National Radio Networks in the United States: 1926–1956* (Columbus: Ohio State University, 1958; reprinted by Arno Press, 1971).

But slowly censors were convinced that radio would not harm the war effort, as long as broadcasters took precautions against unauthorized persons using their facilities (see 6.84). Technicians were able to transmit usable shortwave signals to the United States. When reporters were allowed in the war zones or even neutral foreign capitals, they began filing live, on-the-scene stories such as Edward R. Murrow's 1940–1941 evening reports to CBS (see 5.63).

Radio reporters with the invasion fleet off North Africa in November 1942 provided a blow-by-blow account of the troops landing against the Vichy (collaborationist) French. By 1944 reporters for the radio networks were covering commando raids against the coast of France, going on air raids with bomber fleets, reporting on England at war, and covering early U.S. island invasions in the South Pacific. Reporters unknown before the war became identified with the area from which they spoke. The American radio audience associated ex-newspaperman Eric Sevareid with the fall of France in 1940 and later, reporting his survival of a plane crash deep in the jungle, in the China-Burma-India theater. Howard K. Smith reported for CBS from Europe. Charles Collingwood, also with CBS, reported the North African war and, later, D-Day and troop movements through France and into Germany. Webley Edwards and others reported Pacific naval battles and island-hopping inva-

A Great Reporter: World War II / Edward R. Murrow's reports about World War II in Europe, particularly his "This . . . is London" signature on early CBS broadcasts from Britain, made the war—and our future allies—familiar to millions of Americans. Photo credit: Culver Pictures, Inc.

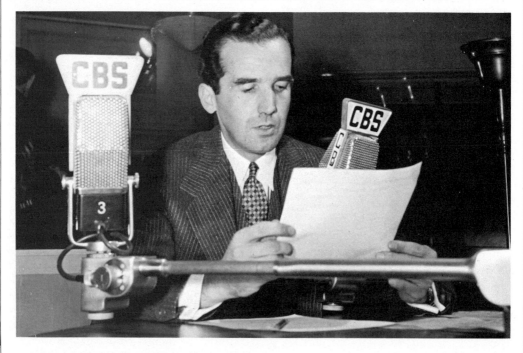

sions that first stopped and then turned the tide against the Japanese. Edwards reported live from a B-29 during an air raid against Japan. Earlier, one of Murrow's most memorable broadcasts came after he flew on an air-raid mission over Berlin, against the orders of his CBS superiors.

Some famous reporters and commentators worked at home: H. V. Kaltenborn, an anchorman for NBC; Lowell Thomas, continuing his evening CBS newscasts begun in 1930; John Daly; Robert Trout; and others. Pioneer announcer Graham MacNamee, only six months before his death, was on hand in New York when the giant French liner *Normandie,* being converted to a troopship, burned and capsized.

Of many notable broadcasts, D-Day—June 6, 1944, when the Allies invaded France—was particularly important. As George Hicks of CBS recorded troops going ashore from a navy ship, listeners could hear aircraft and antiaircraft guns in the background. The recording was sent to the United States by shortwave for later broadcast. Radio's role on D-Day was both tactical, calling upon resistance groups to hamper the German army, and morale-boosting here and in Europe—although the BBC lost some of its tremendous credibility when it broadcast, under orders, some false reports to mislead the Germans.

Radio's first intensive reporting of a President's death in office came on April 12, 1945, when Franklin D. Roosevelt, just starting his fourth term, died of a stroke in Georgia. First reports from network reporters around 5:45 P.M. produced stunned confusion. The deaths of other public figures were reported erroneously. In the middle of a children's adventure program, one character departed from the script to say "Just a minute, kids—President Roosevelt just died"—followed by a few

seconds that seemed like minutes until the news announcer confirmed the report. Within two hours of the first radio flash of the President's death, stations were reporting national and international reaction. Radio listeners heard four days of repeated news, reviews of the President's career, overviews of the war, predictions of the effect of F.D.R.'s death on the war effort, and somber music. The networks and many local stations deleted all commercials for the four days between his death and burial in Hyde Park, New York. Broadcasters themselves were strongly affected. When Arthur Godfrey reported the funeral procession moving down Washington's Pennsylvania Avenue over CBS, listeners heard him break into tears at the

The Show Must Go On versus Circumstances beyond Control

The tradition that the show must go on in spite of disasters received a severe test from World War II. Many individuals and stations managed to give recognition to the tradition, even when normal programming was impossible. Among them was the reporter speaking from Manila who was cut off in mid-sentence when a Japanese bombing attack knocked the station off the air shortly after Pearl Harbor. At the end of the war, he returned to the station and went on the air with "Hello, NBC—as I was saying before being so rudely interrupted . . ." followed by his four-year-old report! A similar story is told about BBC television, which was ordered to leave the air immediately after mobilization in 1939 so that its transmitters and towers could be used for the first crude radar aircraft warning system. Without even signing off, it "went to black" after a Walt Disney cartoon, "Mickey's Gala Premiere." When the service returned to the air approximately eight years later, the same cartoon was included in the inaugural broadcast.

Radio Brings the War to the Home Front / In mid-April 1945, reporters followed the advancing allied armies into what was left of Nazi Germany. On April 15, 1945, CBS radio correspondent Edward R. Murrow broadcast his impressions of the liberation of a large concentration camp.

. . . Permit me to tell you what you would have seen, and heard, had you been with me on Thursday. It will not be pleasant listening. If you are at lunch, or if you have no appetite to hear what Germans have done, now is a good time to switch off the radio, for I propose to tell you of Buchenwald. It is on a small hill about four miles outside Weimar, and it was one of the largest concentration camps in Germany, and it was built to last. As we approached it, we saw about a hundred men in civilian clothes with rifles advancing in open order across the fields. There were a few shots; we stopped to inquire. We were told that some of the prisoners had a couple of SS men cornered in there. We drove on, reached the main gate. The prisoners crowded up behind the wire. We entered.

And now, let me tell this in the first person, for I was the least important person there, as you shall hear. There surged around me an evil-smelling horde. Men and boys reached out to touch me; they were in rags and the remnants of uniform. Death had already marked many of them, but they were smiling with their eyes. I looked out over that mass of men to the green fields beyond where well-fed Germans were ploughing.

A German, Fritz Kercheimer, came up and said, "May I show you round the camp? I've been here ten years." An Englishman stood to attention, saying, "May I introduce myself, delighted to see you, and can you tell me when some of our blokes will be along?" I told him soon and asked to see one of the barracks. It happened to be occupied by Czechoslovakians. When I entered, men crowded around, tried to lift me to their shoulders. They were too weak. Many of them could not get out of bed. I was told that this building had once stabled eighty horses. There were twelve hundred men in it, five to a bunk. The stink was beyond all description.

When I reached the center of the barracks, a man came up and said, "You remember me. I'm Peter Zenkl, one-time mayor of Prague." I remembered him, but did not recognize him. He asked about Benes and Jan Masaryk. I asked how many men had died in that building during the last month. They called the doctor; we inspected his records. There were only names in the little black book, nothing more—nothing of who these men were, what they had done, or hoped. Behind the names of those who had died there was a cross. I counted them. They totalled 242. Two hundred and forty-two out of twelve hundred in one month.

As I walked down to the end of the barracks, there was applause from the men too weak to get out of bed. It sounded like the hand clapping of babies; they were so weak. The doctor's name was Paul Heller. He had been there since 1938.

As we walked out into the courtyard, a man fell dead. Two others—they must have been over sixty—were crawling toward the latrine. I saw it but will not describe it.

In another part of the camp they showed me the children, hundreds of them. Some were only six. One rolled up his sleeve, showed me his number. It was tattooed on his arm. B-6030, it was. The others showed me their numbers; they will carry them till they die.

An elderly man standing beside me said, "The children, enemies of the state." I could see their ribs through their thin shirts. The old man said, "I am Professor Charles Richer of the Sorbonne." The children clung to my hands and stared. We crossed to the courtyard. Men kept coming up to speak to me and to touch me, professors from Poland, doctors from Vienna, men from all Europe. Men from the countries that made America.

. . . Murder had been done at Buchenwald. God alone knows how many men and boys have died there during the last twelve years. Thursday I was told that there were more than twenty thousand in the camp. There had been as many as sixty thousand. Where are they now?

As I left that camp, a Frenchman who used to work for Havas in Paris came up to me and said, "You will write something about this, perhaps?" And he added, "To write about this you must have been here at least two years, and after that—you don't want to write any more."

I pray you to believe what I have said about Buchenwald. I have reported what I saw and heard, but only part of it. For most of it I have no words. Dead men are plentiful in war, but the living dead, more than twenty thousand of them in one camp. And the country round about was pleasing to the eye, and the Germans were well fed and well dressed. American trucks were rolling toward the rear filled with prisoners. Soon they would be eating American rations, as much for a meal as the men at Buchenwald received in four days.

If I've offended you by this rather mild account of Buchenwald, I'm not in the least sorry. I was there on Thursday, and many men in many tongues blessed the name of Roosevelt. For long years his name had meant the full measure of their hope. These men who had kept close company with death for many years did not know that Mr. Roosevelt would, within hours, join their comrades who had laid their lives on the scales of freedom.

From Murrow broadcast of April 15, 1945, from Buchenwald. Reprinted courtesy of the Estate of Edward R. Murrow.

end as he quickly turned the program over to a studio announcer. Although the Republicans bitterly opposed Roosevelt at election time, most Americans considered him the architect of the victory that was only a few weeks off; and the suddenness and irony of his death, after more than a dozen years in office, disturbed them deeply.

After a false alarm, radio finally reported the end of the war in Europe in early May 1945. Microphones stuck out of studio windows over the next several hours brought the sounds of celebrating America to listeners beyond the celebration sites. Three months later, radio reported the awesome and almost unbelievable effects of the first, Hiroshima, atomic bomb. Shortly after the dropping of the second, Nagasaki, atomic bomb came the report of V-J (Victory over Japan) day, and in September the moving broadcast of the surrender ceremonies on the battleship *Missouri* in Tokyo harbor.

For the true flavor of what radio sounded like during four years of war, one must listen to the many recordings that have survived. Reading about a broadcast, or even reading the original script, cannot convey the excitement of that spoken report. Besides, the unscarred American listener could hear the first three short notes and one long note of Beethoven's Fifth Symphony, signifying the Morse code three dots and a dash of "V for Victory," with a different reaction from the impact the underground guerrilla fighters felt when they heard those notes broadcast in Nazi-occupied Europe.

Radio and television news today —despite all our experiences since World War II—reflects the traditions that developed in the 1941–1945 period, when broadcast journalism came of age. The newscasters of World War II became the anchormen of the 1950s and 1960s.

6·63   Political Broadcasting

In 1944, because of his carefully concealed deteriorating health and his understandable preoccupation with the war effort, Roosevelt carried his fourth presidential campaign almost exclusively on radio. Although the Republican nominee, the articulate and respected Governor Thomas E. Dewey of New York, was the most effective radio speaker to run against Roosevelt, the Republicans proposed a series of half-hour dramatizations of campaign issues rather than long, dry speeches. The networks refused to air them, however, fearing that listeners, used to drama as entertainment, would confuse entertainment with news. Dewey and his supporters had to resort to conventional speeches, which they did in the heaviest use of radio in a campaign up to that time. On the Democratic side, a committee of Hollywood personalities made effective one-minute spot announcements to point out Republican problems and limitations. After the campaign, more than half of those asked in a national poll identified radio as their most accurate source of political information, while just over one-quarter chose newspapers and only 6 percent chose magazines. Political radio perhaps came of age on election night 1944 when, for the first time, all the networks dropped their regular programs in favor of continuous election returns and analysis. This was to become the standard format in later elections. Reports also were beamed overseas to the armed forces by OWI and other shortwave facilities (see also 6.61).

6·64   Music and Variety

Despite the increase in war-related news programming, music remained the staple of radio. The networks scheduled about one-third of their hours to popular music, with some classical music and opera on weekends. Popular music was still synonymous with the big bands of Glenn Miller, Benny Goodman, Harry James, and others. Of the new stars coming up Frank Sinatra was most notable. The young singer created a sensation among the "bobby-soxers," and vast crowds of teenage girls crammed New York's Paramount Theater on Times Square to hear him and squeal their delight. Sinatra soon had his own radio show and also appeared on United Service Organization (USO) tours which entertained the armed forces. Many musical groups kept up their home front programs and commitments while touring domestically and overseas before military audiences, but some joined the armed forces and served in the "Special Services."

The prime listening periods for classical music were Saturday and Sunday. On Saturday afternoons Milton Cross narrated the broadcasts of the Metropolitan Opera from New York for the Blue Network; Arturo Toscanini conducted the NBC Symphony Orchestra, first for NBC-Blue on Tuesday and Saturday evenings on a sustaining basis and then as a sponsored program for NBC-Red on Sunday evenings. On Sunday afternoons CBS offered the New York Philharmonic, first sustaining and then sponsored.

Many local stations used a similar pattern. Besides airing most of the network musical programs, affiliates added some of their own. Many large stations employed an orchestra and popular music groups. At smaller stations and nonaffiliates, where music averaged about half their total schedule, recorded music became more common. During the protracted American Federation of Musicians (AFM) dispute (see 6.83), more live orchestras played than otherwise might have been the case.

Almost all programs during the war had at least a thin veneer of wartime topicality, especially the variety shows. Musical programs often included war songs, but the variety programs featured soldiers as participants, originated in military camps and naval bases, and nearly always tried to build up patriotic fervor. New programs built around the military included NBC's *Army Hour*, beginning in April 1942, an army-produced drama-news feature-music combination that gave the civilian an image of army life, and *Command Performance*, produced by the OWI Radio Branch starting in March 1942, a collection of music and variety acts requested by servicemen. The show was broadcast on networks here and by Armed Forces Radio stations overseas.

Many stars got their radio start in the war years. Arthur Godfrey, after some years in Washington, went to the New York big time for CBS in 1941. Two years later Perry Como and Ed Sullivan began their own radio programs. Sullivan, a veteran Broadway newspaper columnist, was no smooth "personality" on the air, as audiences were to see for two decades on television, but he and his staff put together a well-balanced and audience-attracting program.

Some variety programs might have been classified also as situation comedies, especially those starring Jack Benny, ventriloquist Edgar Bergen and his dummy Charlie McCarthy—an unlikely but very popular gimmick on a sound medium—and Bob Hope. These were among the ten most popular network shows during the war, perhaps because they helped audiences forget the serious world outside.

Variety was somewhat harder for local stations to produce, but many middle- or large-size stations tried. Their shows usually reflected local culture and background—"country" dominated in the

South and West, Scandinavian farm life in the upper Middle West—and centered on a local orchestra, vocalist, or station-created talent agent. Amateur hours still were popular, and stations near military installations were likely to inject more military flavor into their programs than stations further removed.

6•65   Drama

There were two trends in wartime network drama: daytime serial soap opera declined by one-third, and serious drama increased noticeably, fueled by the advertisers' ten-cent dollars (see 6.5). While soap operas had been at their peak in 1940–1941 with nearly 75 hours a week, in the early 1940s they gave way somewhat to quiz programs and other variety daytime programming. The *soaps* suffered from overcrowding and similarity, and at first they ignored wartime events except for an occasional "son lost in action" or suitor "gone off to a war industry job," when an actor left for war. New soapers went on the air, but more went off, while the popular standards like *Helen Trent* and *Ma Perkins* plodded quietly on.

Wartime action-adventure programs also showed slight effects of war. The children's serial hero Jack Armstrong was on the Philippine island of Mindanao looking for uranium-235—three and one half years prior to announcement of the atomic bomb—when war came, and script writers moved fast to remove him from uncertainty and danger. Other thriller heroes went to war against the Axis, and stereotypical Japanese and German villains soon were common in *Suspense*, *Inner Sanctum*, and, starting in 1944, *The FBI in Peace and War* as well as in children's adventure serials. These action-adventure

and crime detective programs were building to a postwar peak of popularity.

Favorite situation comedies that started in the 1941–1945 period included *The Great Gildersleeve*, which grew out of a character on *Fibber McGee and Molly*—a *spin-off*, the way many later radio and television programs originated—*The Life of Riley*, and *Ozzie and Harriet*. The last, a long-running radio and later television series, began in 1945 after Ozzie Nelson gave up his band and married his lead vocalist Harriet Hilliard.

The serious drama programs that advertiser ten-cent dollars made possible were both dramatic and documentary, the latter dealing almost always with military affairs. Some programs, like *First Line of Defense*, *Service to the Front*, and *Pacific Story*, the networks offered to stations on a sustaining basis, with production help from various government agencies. Of the dramatic type, U.S. Steel sponsored the *Theater Guild on the Air* and Revlon backed the *Gertrude Lawrence Theater*. Although such prestige shows had fairly low ratings, their appeal to audiences in the higher socioeconomic brackets assured the advertiser of keeping the company name before prospective postwar purchasers and decision-makers.

6•66   Other Programs

The program darling of the late 1930s, the audience participation show, also grew in popularity during the war, because of its human interest—the entertainment value inherent in the way people behave in often-amusing situations. Art Linkletter's long-running *People Are Funny*, *Blind Date* (a program catering to soldiers and somewhat like television's *Dating Game*), a backwards quiz called *It Pays to*

Be Ignorant, and a gambler-appealing *Double or Nothing* quiz show—all began network runs. Some ran in prime time, and others began to encroach on daytime soap opera hours.

The 40 or so FM stations on the air during the war programmed orchestral music or duplicated co-owned AM station programming. FM operations generally broadcast from noon to 10 P.M. until equipment and personnel shortages led the FCC to allow a shorter schedule (see 6.22). AM-FM program duplication was very limited until the networks announced early in 1944 that an FM station could duplicate programs of its AM affiliate only if it carried *all* network programs, since the networks considered it unfair to network sponsors if only selected programs were carried. Although this cut down the amount of independent FM programming, networks, AM stations, and many FM proponents publicly argued further that only by carrying popular AM programs would FM attract and build a large audience. This argument was to be tested in the postwar years.

6•7 The Audience Tunes to Radio's War

World War II was broadcasting's first major war, and reporting the conflict made radio indispensable to the home front from 1941 to 1945. With a multicampaign war cutting across time zones, often half a world away, radio nearly always brought the first news of major events to increasing numbers of listening Americans. Newspapers provided depth and illustration, but radio nearly always delivered the scoops—frequently directly from the battlefield.

6•71 The Freeze on Receivers

The coming of war brought shortages and the meaning of "priorities" home to Americans. Within a month of Pearl Harbor, the Office of Price Administration (OPA) set price ceilings on radios and other consumer products, as a hint of stronger measures—such as rationing—yet to come. In the early months of 1942 governmental agencies examining army and navy needs for raw materials and production facilities discovered that nearly all consumer product production would have to be reduced drastically or stopped for the duration of the war. Advertisements began warning consumers of shortages ahead. Permits for new broadcast station construction were canceled in February (see 6.21), and in April the War Production Board ordered manufacturers to cease making civilian radio receivers immediately and turn full time to military communication needs. This ban originally affected only producers of AM sets but quickly spread to the fledgling FM and television receiver industries as well.

The freeze did not completely halt expansion of the radio audience at early 1942 levels. As seen in Appendix C, table 8, 31 million homes and more than 9 million automobiles had radios. More homes had radios than electricity, bathtubs, telephones, or cars. Because households with more than one receiver loaned, gave, or sold extra sets to persons without, the radio audience actually expanded during the next two years even with no new receiver construction. While car radios declined by three million during the war—most of them were junked along with the car—the number of radio homes increased by nearly four million.

Still, the overall number of receivers in service declined as older sets wore

The Attraction of the Daytime Serial

In size, the audience numbered approximately half of the women who were home during the daytime hours. In composition it included women of all cultural, economic and social levels. Among the faithful audience were many individuals whose relationship to the programs exceeded passive entertainment. For these listeners, the line between illusion and reality was too finely drawn to remain in view for an extended period of time. Whatever the level of rationalization employed, this segment of the audience did not regard the serial characters wholly as fiction. If one of the episodes involved the birth of a child the program could expect to receive not only notes of congratulations but baby gifts from all over the country. The same phenomenon occurred on the occasion of birthdays and anniversaries mentioned in any script. There were offers to loan money or to extend other assistance to destitute characters.

The primary reasons for listening, while often interrelated, can be distinguished as: (a) emotional escape from monotony, personal disappointment and difficulty; (b) provision of moral values and guidance in family and interpersonal problems; (c) bolstering of the female ego; (d) companionship and, lastly, (e) entertainment.

The housewife increasingly has been free to indulge in whatever diversion, real or imaginary, might lighten the drudgery of her workload and brighten her glamourless life. The convenience and accessibility of radio served for many either to create heroic fantasies or to channel existing reveries at little or no cost in time or work accomplished. At the same time the listener was exposed to a generally consistent sequence of problem-solution case studies designed as entertainment but from which, if she so desired, the modern woman could derive sufficient strength and conviction to meet her share of personal grief. Whether or not the serials expected to function as educational or therapeutic instruments, the fact remains that nearly half of the listeners placed heavy emphasis on the guidance, inspiration and practical assistance thus afforded.

The listener's sense of security was enhanced by emphasis placed in the serials upon such matters of special interest as marriage ties, the problems encountered by career women (a role the listener had avoided), the importance attached to the role of the wife and homemaker and, in all things, the ultimate triumph of good over evil. It was not by chance that nearly all of the moral, emotional and spiritual strength was invested in the female characters.

At a more widely shared level of appreciation, the serials were enjoyed simply for the companionship provided by characters who became familiar to the listener over a period of months and years. The punctuality and dependability of the daily visits doubtlessly lent a sense of order to many a pointless day.

Source: George A. Willey, "End of an Era: The Daytime Radio Serial," *Journal of Broadcasting* 5:97–115 (Spring 1961), pages 109–110. By permission.

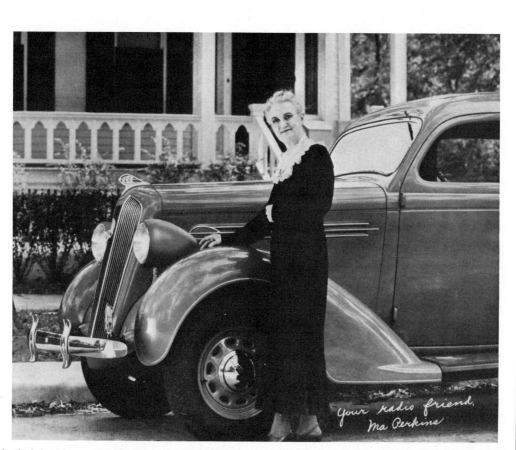

In their heyday, networks and advertisers sent out thousands of pictures to fans, showing the stars in costume—which, unfortunately, rarely matched listeners' imaginative expectations. This one, from the long-running soap opera *Ma Perkins* stresses the tie of serial to listener with its printed salutation, "Your radio friend . . ." Photo courtesy of the State Historical Society of Wisconsin.

out and were junked or gutted for spare parts. This trend jumped after April 1943 when the War Production Board ruled that a replacement part could be obtained only in return for the equivalent old part, which was rebuilt and recycled when possible. Even more important, radio repair became virtually impossible in 1943–1945 as the best technical personnel were in the service or working in war plants. As a result, set manufacturers by 1943–1944 were predicting a massive postwar radio replacement market.

During the war there probably were 400,000 FM receivers in use plus 10,000 television sets. It was estimated in 1945 that, while possibly 4,400 television sets existed in New York, one-quarter of them did not work. Nearly all FM and television sets were located in New England, New York, Philadelphia, Chicago, and Los Angeles but there was little for them to tune to (see 6.22 and 6.23). FM was able to provide minimal service in a few regions, but television practically closed up shop from 1942 until 1944. The war had cut off both FM and television just as their growth began.

6•72   *Wartime Radio Usage and Research*

Apart from the predictable increase in listening to news and other war-related programs, audience listening patterns did not change much during the war, even though many people's lives changed drastically, with more than 16,000,000 persons, including 200,000 women, in service during some part of the war. Restrictions on travel and other activities caused a slight increase in radio listening that had practically disappeared by 1945. With the motion picture industry producing several hundred films a year, people exhibited no

overwhelming need to turn more to radio for entertainment. There were nearly always more women tuned in than men, more lower than upper income listeners, everything else being equal, and more urban than rural listeners.

Initial research into specific types of programs and listeners disclosed, among other things, that different kinds of programs had varying amounts of *holding power*—the ability of a program to keep its initial audience for the entire show. Women's serial drama managed an 85 percent holding rating (in other words, only 15 percent tuned out before the show ended) and wartime news reports 79 percent. Drama usually held three-quarters of its audience, and variety shows did nearly as well. Rated typically lower were the new audience participation and quiz shows, popular music, and, lowest of all with only 59 percent holding power, concert music programs.

Audience research developments in 1941–1945 fell into three categories: audience ratings, in-depth program research, and propaganda analysis—the last done mainly by or for the military. In 1943 the Cooperative Analysis of Broadcasting (CAB, see 4.72) was dissolved, mainly in recognition of C.E. Hooper's "Hooperratings" as the final arbiter of network radio program success. Hooper continued using his coincidental telephone technique, even though some American homes had unlisted numbers and many had no telephone. He published the best description of his research technique in 1944 with Matthew Chappell in *Radio Audience Measurement*. However, other organizations had other techniques. In New York City, The Pulse used a roster-recall method, by which a selected audience member reviewed a list (roster) of programs for a prior period of time, usually a day, and indicated those he or she had listened to. This aided recall system could be done in person or by telephone. In the eastern states, A. C. Nielsen introduced its Nielsen Radio Index, using mechanical meters attached to radio sets, in fall 1942 (see 5.73). The meter produced a small length of film every week or so which showed to what station that radio had been tuned at a given time. The meter required no human service or interaction other than mailing the film to Nielsen, in exchange for a few quarters that came out of a slot in the meter, and inserting the new film that arrived in the mail. It worked at all hours as no other audience research technique could. The Nielsen equipment was expensive to install, the sample could not easily be changed, and people with meters might exhibit different listening habits from people without them, but the technique had promise. By the end of the war, the Nielsen Radio Index had become the first serious national competition to Hooper.

CBS backed a great deal of intensive research on programs and their audiences. Their electromechanical program-audience analyzer allowed intensive study of minute-by-minute reactions of 30 to 100 subjects to a specific program. Respondents sat in a room equipped with hand-held devices that allowed them to indicate their opinion of what they were hearing whenever a light signaled for a pro or con response. The hand devices were connected to a graphic recorder that told the researchers what moments in the program and its supporting commercials most appealed to or appalled the listeners. In this way, researchers learned what kinds of characters, language, situations, and events to put into programs and commercials to increase their appeal and audience holding power.

Researchers thoroughly examined the appeal and effects of serial soap operas, analyzing their educational aspects, the typical program formula's ability to attract and hold listeners, and characteristics of daily serial listeners. This was the first in-depth study of a segment of the radio audience since the "War of the Worlds" research of 1938–1940. It was learned that serial listeners felt tremendously loyal to the programs, their key characters, and often the sponsors' products (a fact of considerable interest to advertisers), and believed that they learned how to solve everyday problems from what they heard, and responded differently to different serials. Most serial listeners were from lower socioeconomic groups, and most listened to several serials each day. Ironically, this companionship role of soap operas was adequately understood only as the serial form began to slip in daytime radio schedules (see 6.65).

Finally, researchers looked into the presumed effect of propaganda on military and civilian subjects. The study of German radio programs and films, and some Allied efforts in the same media, gave clues as to how persuasion took place under various audience conditions. Findings bore fruit in Allied propaganda in both Europe and the Pacific—and domestic advertisers applied many of the basic results when the research findings became available after the war.

6•8 Postwar Planning and Wartime Control

Four major regulatory developments occurred in the early 1940s: a lengthy allocation process; governmental wartime censorship; the FCC attempt to control ownership of broadcast networks and stations, with a resulting congressional investigation of the commission; and an incredible wrangle between radio broadcasters, the American Federation of

Musicians, and the federal government. Oddly enough, censorship, which one might expect to be the most controversial and sticky, became an example of successful voluntary cooperation between government and broadcasters. Real sparks flew only over other developments.

6•81 *Allocations Conflict:*
      Television versus FM

As the war neared its end, in addition to hundreds of new AM station applications and requests for changes in existing stations, some 600 FM and 158 television applications to construct new facilities were piling up in the FCC's Washington offices. Some applications were frivolous, some were "insurance policies" filed by older media concerned about television competition, many were withdrawn, but most reflected a belief that radio and television broadcasting were headed for a postwar bonanza—tapping of the pent-up consumer demand of the war years. For the next decade, the struggle between services over spectrum space and channel allotments to various communities was to absorb the attentions of broadcasters, regulators, manufacturers, and politicians. The decisions of the 1944–1953 period (see also 7.8) shaped broadcasting, especially television, down to the present day.

During the 1930s, as new uses for radio developed, the usable, assigned part of the spectrum was continually moved upward. By the start of World War II, the practical limit for radio use was in the neighborhood of 100 MHz. Wartime research quickly opened the region above 100 MHz to tactical communication, radar, and many other uses. As in World War I, a constant interchange of ideas and technology went on between civilian and military engineers. Early in World War II larger manufacturing concerns realized that overcoming technical drawbacks to use of the VHF and UHF portions of the spectrum would probably be easier than overcoming political and economic objections to their use for television broadcasting and other civilian services. Some frequency bands were better than others for certain applications; for example, frequencies above 30 MHz generally were restricted to little more than the "line of sight" distance from the antenna to the horizon—50–90 miles, depending on antenna height—with the lower frequencies being somewhat better. The enormous inertia of investment in equipment, particularly home receivers, designed to operate in a particular band was another limiting factor. Technical aspects of the propagational characteristics of a given band were uppermost in the minds of engineers, but economic "realities" were uppermost in the minds of those who hired the engineers.

The complexity of these economic realities must be understood to perceive why certain decisions were made. At least four separate but related factors led to the 1944–1945 allocations decision climax: (1) the wartime freeze, which led to a pent-up consumer demand for new goods and services and made feasible the planning of changes long in advance of production; (2) the new international responsibilities of the United States, requiring a tremendous amount of spectrum space for the armed forces, and leadership and cooperation with the ITU and other world agencies in reestablishing allocations guidelines after the war; (3) the fight between FM radio and television for essentially the same spectrum space, since the VHF band was believed best suited to both; and (4) the television feud between those industry forces that wanted immediate postwar television and those that argued for further

The Changing Allocations for Television: 1937–1952/Though this chart covers a greater period than the chapter, the major allocation decision was made in 1945 (the third bar of the chart). Note the changing interrelationship of TV channels and FM channels. See notes.

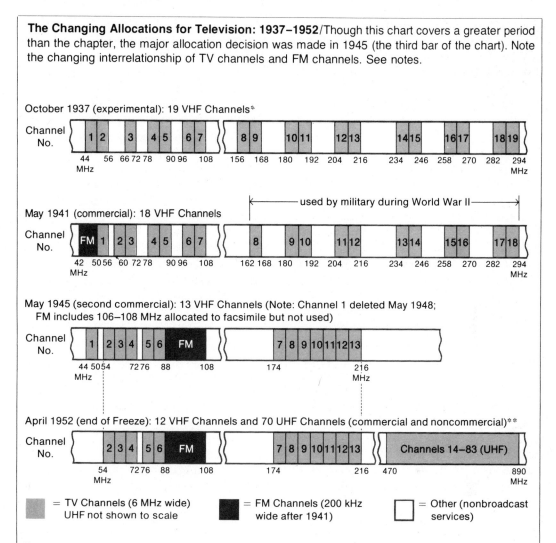

October 1937 (experimental): 19 VHF Channels*

May 1941 (commercial): 18 VHF Channels

used by military during World War II

May 1945 (second commercial): 13 VHF Channels (Note: Channel 1 deleted May 1948; FM includes 106–108 MHz allocated to facsimile but not used)

April 1952 (end of Freeze): 12 VHF Channels and 70 UHF Channels (commercial and noncommercial)**

Channels 14–83 (UHF)

= TV Channels (6 MHz wide) UHF not shown to scale

= FM Channels (200 kHz wide after 1941)

= Other (nonbroadcast services)

Notes:

*Earlier allocations: There were two allocations for visual broadcasting (television) prior to those shown on the charts, but both were short-lived and little used. The first came in the October–December 1928 period, and called for 10 kHz-wide channels at the upper end of the standard (AM) broadcast band. Such channels were too narrow to work, but their nearness to existing stations and receivers on the spectrum placed them technically in familiar territory. The second allocation, issued late in 1928 and actually used for several years, was in effect until the October 1937 allocation shown on the chart. This allocation provided for five 100 kHz-wide channels at 2.0–2.2 MHz and 2.7–2.9 MHz. They were for experimental work only and, partly because of the Depression, saw little use.

**Later changes: On May 20, 1970, the FCC removed television channels 70–83 from potential television broadcast use, applying them to land mobile needs. No on-air stations were affected, though several translators and other station assignments had to be moved. Sixty-eight television channels were left, although channel 37 (608–614 MHz) has been reserved for radio astronomy since 1963.

Source: FRC and FCC Annual Reports, and "Background of Frequency Modulation," in Milton B. Sleeper (ed.) FM Radio Handbook: 1946 Edition (Great Barrington, Mass.: FM Company, 1946), pages 3–7.

changes and improvements in standards and allocations before the postwar boom began. These economic and social problems complicated technical hearings already confused by military research findings on spectrum propagation characteristics. In addition, all parties recognized that the FRC and FCC allocation practice of the 1920s and 1930s merely to regularize existing uses and allow a service to spread out, as exemplified by AM radio (see 3.81 and 4.82), was inefficient and impractical.

The allocations hearings where all this came to a head were instigated by the international situation. The FCC had long been a member of the Interdepartmental Radio Advisory Committee (IRAC), the U.S. government body composed of major federal government *users* of the radio spectrum—the military services, FBI, Forest Service, and so forth. The FCC represented both its own limited needs and the far more important and large-scale needs of civilians, including common carrier, safety and special services, amateur, and radio and television broadcasting. In June 1943 an IRAC committee began to plan for postwar use of the spectrum, for not only had military needs mushroomed, but a plan would be needed to replace the prewar worldwide Cairo agreement of 1938. IRAC submitted a tentative plan to the FCC in the latter's capacity as a member, for the FCC has no control over federal governmental usage. The FCC, seeing the military's proposals as a naked spectrum grab, balked at approving anything until a public hearing on the issues had been held, as required by the Communications Act of 1934, since many allocation changes affected nongovernmental users. Although the Department of State announced it would use the IRAC proposals in postwar international meetings, the FCC stood ground and effectively won after not participating in the State Department's government-industry meetings.

Late in 1943, to make use of the rapidly increasing military spectrum and propagation research findings, the FCC called on the manufacturing industry to establish a Radio Technical Planning Board (RTPB) of industry and government engineers and other technical people, to evaluate wartime data in relation to prospective postwar changes in broadcasting and other allocations. Faced by the IRAC situation, the FCC urged the RTPB to present its case or cases at an extensive public hearing in fall 1944. RTPB was divided into several panels, each of which would consider a major topic—FM, television, facsimile, allocations in general—and make recommendations at the hearings.

The hearings lasted from September 28 to November 2, 1944, the most extensive conducted by the FCC up to that time. More than 230 witnesses testified, 4,559 pages of testimony were gathered, and 543 exhibits were submitted for the record. The presentation of still-secret military data required that some sessions be held behind closed doors. One of the first issues considered was the fight between FM and television interests (see 5.1).

In 1943, during Senate Commerce Committee hearings, Edwin Armstrong pleaded in favor of allocating additional frequencies for relaying FM broadcasts around the country. By this time there were more applications than available FM channels in New York and New England, and it was apparent that this region at least would need additional channels for FM broadcasting.

By 1944, however, Armstrong was fighting to retain the channels FM already had. His fight for additional space succumbed to the pressures of the wartime spectrum propagation research and the 1944 allocations hearings. During those hearings, the 1945 decisions, and ensuing appeals and suits, FM and television struggled for the mutually exclusive right to occupy various parts of the VHF spectrum, especially the 42–50 MHz band then occupied by 55 pioneer FM stations. This fight, lasting from 1944 through 1947, grew more and more bitter as RCA used all its large-corporation force to back television against FM and its solitary inventor. Since Armstrong, out of fairness to earlier small licensees, would not give RCA a special license to use and resell rights under Armstrong's patents, RCA resorted to other techniques, including refusal to pay Armstrong royalties due him from RCA production of television sets with FM sound. Careful review of the evidence indicates that RCA did not care much one way or the other about FM, but it was not going to let anything stand in the way of television!

Some of the 1944 testimony, concerning military advances in uses of frequencies as high as 300 MHz, was classified. Participants in the hearings had access to the data, but they could not utilize it or communicate it to their backers or the press. Consultants had to be members of the RTPB. This became important when the recommendation was made to move FM from its 42–50 MHz allocation "upstairs" to a position closer to 100 or even 120 MHz. The recommendation was based largely upon flawed classified information provided by former FCC engineer Kenneth Norton, who predicted that FM would experience serious interference on the 40–50 MHz band when the 11-year sunspot cycle reached its peak in 1947–1948. Although RTPB's Panel 5 (FM) recommended an expanded band in the 50 MHz area, the FCC, after announcing most other allocations, decided on June 27, 1945, to move FM to 88–106 MHz. A few months later it added the 106–108 MHz band pre-

viously reserved for facsimile. This new allocation for 100 channels provided 60 more than on the old band and reserved 20 of them for educational uses. The FCC never explained how television, whose picture transmissions were especially susceptible to interference, would avoid the hypothetical sunspot problem. On the other hand, Armstrong never explained how he could have a nationwide FM system with only 40 channels.

The move "upstairs" gave Armstrong more channels but at the unacceptable, to him, cost of starting over, since it made existing transmitters and receivers (perhaps 400,000) obsolete. Armstrong initiated several futile appeals to the courts, the legislative branch, and public opinion. He tried without success to make the FCC rescind its order and retain a couple of the old channels for relay purposes. His case sparked hearings in both the House and the Senate into FM and FCC allocation policies, but much recrimination failed to topple the FCC's decision. FM was trapped. The newer television service had won primary attention, and war-end demand for radio receivers was satisfied by the manufacture of AM sets. The manufacturing industry was afraid to confuse the buying public or divide the industry's priorities. Resolving the situation by ignoring FM took care of part of the problem, but the television manufacturing industry was split as well.

6•82 Allocations Hearings and Decision

The arguments over moving FM up to the 88–108 MHz band were but a sideshow to the main event between RCA, which wanted postwar television immediately, following "proved" standards, and CBS, which tried to delay full exploitation of television until it had completed research on color and high definition in the upper frequencies. (The situation was analogous to the Westinghouse decision at the end of World War I to use suddenly surplus manufacturing capacity for the production of broadcasting receivers.) If there were rival products, such as television *and* FM, or different television standards, the resulting public confusion might force manufacturers to divert facilities to less profitable lines of merchandise. Or, if one company controlled the patents and know-how, such as RCA with its television system, then other corporations might find themselves in the cold.

As a result, toward the end of World War II, the industry was divided. To RCA's great satisfaction and profit, almost the entire manufacturing industry favored RCA's position: the immediate establishment of postwar television using prewar standards, and the postponement of potential improvements in both standards and allocations to a vague future. CBS, lacking a strong patent position in black-and-white television, wanted to promote its system of color television and steal a march on RCA. It advocated further research on monochrome and color and an allocation system able to accommodate the foreseeable expansion of television—in particular, a large number of channels in the UHF band, with only temporary assignments on VHF. CBS asserted that delaying the innovation of higher-definition or color television would freeze the television system into the technical standards and allocation mold of 1941. The public had invested $2 million in receivers by 1944, but this was nothing compared to the hundreds of millions of dollars that it was expected to spend on television within two years of the war's end. CBS management and engineering witnesses called attention to the expensive military research

on the UHF band during the war and the possibility of its leading to a practical high-band color television system within a year —if everybody worked on it.

To gain manufacturing allies in its fight against RCA, as well as to show genuine interest in UHF, CBS ordered a UHF transmitter from General Electric and cooperated in the development of UHF receivers with Zenith, but it received little support before the FCC. The CBS system —which promised far better quality of both black-and-white and color picture than we now have—would require complete redesign of receivers to permit them to operate on the UHF band with a bandwidth of 16 MHz. Eventually, CBS managed to fit its color system, but not the proposed high-definition monochrome system, within a 6 MHz standard channel. Supporters of "television now" attacked CBS for trying to marshal public and industry support, while WCBS-TV (then WCBW) repeatedly announced that its broadcasts were not inducements to buy televisions sets "at this time." Resentful of its proposal to abandon the VHF band and all previous planning, they accused CBS of trying to hamstring television because of its investment in AM broadcasting and its lack of a manufacturing subsidiary to profit from the sale of television sets, and of trying to strengthen its own position while posing as a champion of science. Although many of these charges were valid, the opposition could not destroy the basic soundness of the CBS call for extensive serious planning for technical quality, the most logical allocations scheme, and the greatest amount of competition.

The lineup of opponents to CBS was formidable. As soon as the war ended, most electronics manufacturers would have excess plant capacity and some factories built with government money would be ready for purchase and conversion to television-receiver production based on pre-war technical standards. The introduction of new standards would require tooling up, and the delay might cause producers of black-and-white television to miss out on profits from the expected postwar surge of buying. In addition to RCA, manufacturers, broadcasters, and individuals who feared postwar unemployment and were looking for new industries to take up the slack all opposed these CBS proposals. They were joined by such bodies as the just formed Television Broadcasters Association.

Perhaps the greatest handicap of CBS was that it was moving counter to the demand for consumer goods. Its argument that postwar demand for radio and phonograph equipment could keep them busy while they engineered a new television system failed to convince an industry— and a country—impatient for glittering new services. People felt that the available television system should be exploited to the fullest, regardless of its shortcomings.

These shortcomings, generally recognized, included the psychological barrier that establishing television on VHF would create to changing the system later to UHF, and the existing allowance of too few channels for a nationwide, competitive television system. RCA, ignoring the lessons of television's false start in 1940, Dumont, and others believed that it was better to get started immediately on VHF and trust that future problems could be met with equanimity.

The most important support for the RCA position came from the RTPB Television Panel. It recommended at the hearings that television could and should be established in black-and-white, on 6 MHz channels on VHF frequencies. It suggested that 30 contiguous channels on the VHF band would be sufficient. On reviewing the latter proposal, the RTPB's Allocations Panel badly mangled it by recommending 26 channels, divided into seven segments rather than one continuous band. All were to be in VHF, with nine below 108 MHz. The three uppermost channels were for *local* or *community* station use, with low power and antenna, and would probably be needed only along the densely populated Atlantic seaboard. The RTPB Allocations Panel also suggested providing some 30 additional channels, each 20 MHz wide, for experimentation and future development.

Although the knowledge did not stop pressure for immediate activation of 15 or so channels, virtually all parties testifying at the FCC hearings agreed that at least 25 to 50 channels would be needed eventually and that their most logical location would be in the UHF. But, as a Philco executive put it, "There is no good reason why the public should not enjoy our present television while . . . research is going on." The rebuttal, by soon-to-resign FCC Chairman Fly, was disregarded: "I am rather regretful to see editorials talking about the necessity of freezing television at the prewar standards because there were 7,000 receivers in the market and in the hands of consumers. . . . If we are going to have that cry with 7,000 receivers we will never change [the system] basically . . . when the quantity of receivers may run into millions. . . ."

It would be hard to overemphasize the importance of the 1945 decisions that stemmed from these hearings. Much of their structure remains, and they are the source of many of today's problems. The January 15, 1945 report of the commission proposed assigning television only 12 VHF channels (six between 44 and 80 MHz, six between 180 and 216 MHz) as compared to the 25 or 30 proposed by the RTPB panels. Channels allocated to television in 1940 were permanently lost to military and other governmental uses. Spectrum space was so short that 11 of the 12 channels would have to be shared with government and nongovernment fixed and mobile services on a geographical mutual noninterference basis. The scheme did allow enough space for a maximum of seven stations in a given city but not enough for nationwide competitive service.

After further hearings and oral briefs early in 1945, including more classified testimony from military witnesses, the FCC issued its Final Reports on May 25 and June 27, 1945. Television received another channel near the high end of the VHF (174–180 MHz), and FM (see 6.81) was definitely moved up to 88–108 MHz, freeing the old FM band (44–50 MHz) for television's channel 1 as proposed earlier.

The June 27 report had four extremely serious drawbacks: (1) It required television to share channels with fixed and mobile services, a dangerous practice for a service highly susceptible to interference. (2) In discarding the engineering criterion of a continuous band of channels, it increased the cost of sets by requiring expensive switches that would cover four bands over a range of 172 MHz (from the bottom of Channel 1, at 44 MHz, to the highest part of Channel 13 at 216 MHz) rather than continuous tuning over only 78 MHz (13 channels at 6 MHz each). (3) It rendered the FM investment obsolete and delayed the start of postwar FM on a frequency band considered by many less suitable than its previous band. (4) And most important, it authorized full-fledged exploitation of television on an inadequate number of channels. The FCC decision to use the thirteen VHF channels was separate from its decision to reject CBS proposals for wide-band color television on the UHF band. Commission and industry unanimously agreed that thirteen channels were too few for nationwide, competitive service. No provision for alleviating the situation was made other than labeling some channels on the UHF band "experimental," although the FCC spoke of VHF as "temporary," with UHF the future "home" for television. In an ostensible effort to free television from its wartime fetters and speed its progress, the FCC actually bound the new service in a straightjacket.

Faced with the weight of opinion that RCA and its allies mustered, the FCC could not have done other than establish postwar television with prewar transmission and definition standards. RCA had worked *within* the industry to achieve its goals. As will be seen, RCA reaped the benefits from the tremendously rapid expansion of television service by selling sets and taking in huge patent royalties. Still working on its own color system, RCA fostered a "don't rock the boat" attitude in the industry with respect to color. The resulting FCC rejection of CBS's color and wide-band proposals encouraged expansion of black-and-white television service. The FCC, apparently eager to place its imprimatur on the winning side, approved.

6•83   The Petrillo Affair

In June 1940 James Caesar Petrillo, president of the Chicago local, was elected national president of the American Federation of Musicians. Soon afterward he demanded that broadcasters playing recorded music pay fees through the union, in addition to those paid to ASCAP and other performing rights societies (see 5.85) and "stand-by" fees paid to musicians by the networks since 1937, whenever they used recorded music more than once. When Petrillo's negotiations with the networks broke down in June 1942, he announced a complete ban on recording—

both for home use and broadcasting as of August, depending on public demand for music to pressure the record companies and networks to pay graduated fees directly to the union.

Petrillo struck what many considered a low blow in 1943 when he banned the traditional NBC broadcasts from the Interlochen, Michigan, Music Camp because the student musicians were not members of AFM, although many of their teachers were. The union barred the teachers from working at Interlochen, although the camp's director gave up his union membership in protest. Petrillo made the Interlochen ban stick under threat of a national AFM strike banning the performance of all kinds of music.

In summer 1943 Petrillo was asked to lift the recording ban on grounds of "national morale"—at least insofar as it affected music heard by the fighting forces. After Petrillo ignored these requests, the National War Labor Board ordered the AFM ban lifted in mid-1944, but the union stood fast. Even a plea from the President in October 1944 could not move Petrillo. The ban on recording broke down only when Decca Records and WOR in September 1943 and then Columbia and RCA in November 1944 gave in to AFM demands.

In spring 1944 Petrillo started a campaign to employ AFM members as *platter turners* (technicians who actually put records on turntables) in radio stations, and in February 1945 he ran out his next big gun, aimed at broadcasters alone. He ordered AFM musicians to refrain from playing for FM, which in the war years often rebroadcast AM programming, unless the parent AM stations hired duplicate stand-by orchestras of AFM members. No television work was permitted, pending further study. That battle would peak after the war, even though Petrillo successfully withstood outraged public opinion and

even a new law—the Lea Act, which forbade "featherbedding" and union "coercion"—designed to curb his power in 1946 (see 7.85).

Petrillo's muscle-flexing was a hint of rising union strength in the ranks of broadcast and broadcast-related employees. As the industry grew far beyond its wartime size after 1945, unionization became increasingly important (see 9.3). Foreshadowing jurisdictional disputes to come was a battle between the AFM and the National Association of Broadcast Engineers and Technicians (NABET) over control of the men who turned discs over on the turntables at radio stations. In Chicago, Petrillo's home town, the AFM won, but the technicians' unions won in other large markets while smaller towns were less unionized.

6•84   Office of Censorship

The first post–Pearl Harbor attempt to control what radio stations might say about the war effort came from the National Association of Broadcasters. Shortly after December 7, 1941, the NAB issued a list of 16 "do nots" to guide news reporters away from disseminating information of possible value to the enemy. Soon after, the government set up the Office of Censorship, under former newsman Byron Price, to oversee communications inside the United States. The office, operating under the premise that "what does not concern the war does not concern censorship," worked for voluntary cooperation of the various media. To secure industry cooperation and obtain the services of industry experts, it set up a broadcast division under direction of a radio station executive. Most NAB rules soon were made official. In its first version on January 15, 1942, the "Code of Wartime Practices for

American Broadcasters" noted that censorship was voluntary and that broadcast management was responsible for finding potentially dangerous material in news programming, other programs, and commercial copy. Broadcasters controlled most programs voluntarily by spot checking and submitted a few—news commentary by Drew Pearson and *The March of Time* on Blue, and *We, the People* on CBS—for formal prebroadcast censorship. This code, revised in May 1942 and again in December 1943, contained many "suggested" restrictions:

> *Broadcast no information on specific military units, installations, or disposition of enemy prisoners in the United States.*
>
> *In the event of an enemy attack, make no reports of damage inflicted—and no indication of an attack until it is over.*
>
> *Do not identify by name persons injured or killed in battle until the military authorities have indicated they have notified next of kin.*
>
> *Supervise musical request programs and "any program which permits the public accessibility to an open microphone is dangerous." This usually meant banning man-on-the-street interviews for fear that an agent could convey a message to the enemy through an innocent-sounding song or combination of words.*
>
> *Do not accept public service announcements by telephone; they must be in writing from a known source.*
>
> *Broadcast only foreign language programs that are accompanied by full English-language scripts for checking.*
>
> *Ban weather forecasts; knowledge of wind direction or barometric pressure would be vital to an enemy bombing attack.*

The 127 foreign language stations, broadcasting in 30 different foreign languages, offered a special problem. Stations broadcasting German or Italian programs were carefully investigated, and the Office of Censorship required them both to hire a linguist to check program content and to file translations of their programs. These expensive requirements forced many stations to drop foreign language broadcasts, just as World War I had helped diminish the foreign language newspaper in America.

Media people feared the tendency of bureaucracy to get too large and costly. They recalled the World War I efforts of the government to censor through the Creel Committee on Public Information, which many believed to have cut too deeply into film and the press. But the voluntary controls administered by the Office of Censorship seem to have worked well and with little controversy. There was common recognition of what was needed, and common resolve to accomplish it with the least conflict.

6•85   *The FCC Investigates . . .*

Cooperation is not a word to describe wartime activities of the FCC. The strongly held views of Chairman James Lawrence Fly—the first chairman to have the ear of the President—did not agree with those of most broadcasters and, as it turned out, many congressmen. Most of the commission's activities had little to do with the war, owing to the authority of the War Production Board, the Office of War Information, and the Office of Censorship. The FCC monitored enemy broadcasts, kept watch for unauthorized transmissions, and continued investigating station and network ownership.

The proposed chain broadcasting regulations of May 1941 (see 5.83) entailed the FCC in much legal wrangling. In January 1942, the Federal District Court for the Southern District of New York ruled that the court had no jurisdiction over the

NBC-CBS suit against promulgation of the proposed FCC rules. That same month, the Justice Department filed antitrust suits against CBS and NBC-RCA. That action, backed by the Mutual network, forced the major networks to appeal to the U.S. Supreme Court, which agreed in June 1942 to review the chain regulations. Its decision of May 10, 1943, was one of the legal landmarks in broadcasting history. In *NBC* v. *the United States*, the court, by a vote of 5-to-2, not only upheld the FCC's right to enforce the chain broadcasting regulations but also reinforced its rights under the Communications Act of 1934 to act in its best judgment under the "public interest, convenience, or necessity" rubric. The court held that regulation and selection of licensees was within the jurisdiction of the FCC as assigned by Congress, and that such regulations did not conflict, as the networks had claimed, with the First Amendment. This was the most important upholding to date of the FCC's powers. NBC reluctantly shed the Blue Network (see 6.3), and in October the government and Mutual withdrew the antitrust suits against NBC and CBS, having accomplished their purposes. The new FCC regulations went into effect in mid-1943, leading to the sale of some stations in cities where one licensee had owned more than one station, and to the long, difficult, physical and financial untangling of the Red and the Blue networks.

FCC investigation of newspaper

A Landmark Supreme Court Decision: 1943

The Act [of 1934] itself establishes that the Commission's powers are not limited to the engineering and technical aspects of regulation of radio communication. Yet we are asked to regard the Commission as a kind of traffic officer, policing the wave lengths to prevent stations from interfering with each other. But the Act does not restrict the Commission merely to supervision of the traffic. It puts upon the Commission the burden of determining the composition of that traffic.

———————

While Congress did not give the Commission unfettered discretion to regulate all phases of the radio industry, it did not frustrate the purposes for which the Communications Act of 1934 was brought into being by attempting an itemized catalogue of the specific manifestations of the general problems for the solution of which it was establishing a regulatory agency. That would have stereotyped the powers of the Commission to specific details in regulating a field of enterprise the dominant characteristic of which was the rapid pace of its unfolding.

———————

The question here is simply whether the Commission, by announcing that it will refuse licenses to persons who engage in specified network practices (a basis for choice which we hold is comprehended within the statutory criterion of "public interest"), is thereby denying such persons the constitutional right of free speech. . . . The licensing system established by Congress in the . . . Act of 1934 was a proper exercise of its power over commerce. The standard it provided for the licensing of stations was the "public interest, convenience, or necessity." Denial of a station license on that ground, if valid under the Act, is not a denial of free speech.

Source: National Broadcasting Co., Inc. et al. v. *United States et al.* 319 U.S. 190 at 215–216, 219, and 226–227 (May 10, 1943); the opinion written by Mr. Justice Felix Frankfurter.

ownership of radio stations also dragged on during the war. Begun in summer 1941, the hearings continued on and off until January 1944, when the commission "concluded, in the light of the record of this proceeding, and of the grave legal and policy questions involved, not to adopt any general rule with respect to newspaper ownership of radio stations." The commission submitted the results of its hearings to the interested congressional committees and decided to face the issue case by case instead of making rules. Nor did this end the matter; both the Justice Department and the FCC were still working on newspaper–broadcasting station joint ownership divestiture for decades.

6 • 86   . . . and Is Investigated

During the early 1940s the FCC was more the subject than the instigator of investigation. In 1940 RCA pushed a Senate investigation of the FCC after Chairman Fly forestalled RCA's plan to inaugurate commercial television with inadequate technical standards (see 5.15). For years disgruntled parts of the industry and critical members of the House and Senate had sought congressional investigation of the FCC, especially for alleged inaction on monopolistic control of broadcasting. While its chain broadcasting investigation helped allay some of the concern that the FCC did not go far enough in promoting the public interest, many thought that the commission had gone too far, including in 1942 congressmen, constituent broadcasters, and newspaper publishers. Leadership of the anti-FCC group fell, however, on Georgia Congressman Eugene E. Cox—ironically a former supporter of the commission—for reasons that were less savory than the economic conservatism of many senators

and representatives. The FCC had reported to the Department of Justice that Cox had illegally received payments from a Georgia station for representing that station's views before the FCC. Early in 1943 Cox pressured the House Speaker to appoint a five-man committee to investigate the FCC. Naturally, as proposer of the resolution, Cox became chairman of the committee!

The hearings, beginning in mid-1943, were not friendly. At the first session the FCC's general counsel was threatened with expulsion from the room for trying to speak to the committee. Cox and most of his fellow committeemen complained that the FCC had delved into programming and business aspects of broadcasting beyond its prerogatives, played political favorites in official actions, and entered wartime fields properly the army and navy's. They charged that Chairman Fly dominated the commission and helped his friends get station licenses. They said that the FCC was unpatriotic, in failing to implement a proposal to fingerprint radio operators; that it operated its monitoring service inadequately and drew manpower for it from military needs; and that it harbored potential subversives. They said that the FCC spent too much time and attention on broadcasting and neglected telephone and telegraph problems. The hearings dragged on for months, even with the resignation from the committee of chairman Cox, two general counsels (the second of whom, John J. Sirica, became the federal judge who presided over the Watergate break-in trial in the early 1970s), and most of the staff. With President Roosevelt's support of Fly and the personal nature of some of the charges, it was not surprising that the hearings had few results other than some FCC personnel changes, some specific findings that led to proposals to amend the 1934 Communications Act, and a mound of paper. Chairman Fly resigned early in 1944, Commissioner Payne was not reappointed, and Commissioner Craven declined renomination, although he returned to the FCC in the mid-1950s. In retrospect, the whole investigation may have been an exercise. But it made the commission even more cautious and responsive to congressional wishes and whims and taught Congress the publicity value of an FCC investigation, insuring that commissioners would be familiar with Capitol hearing rooms in years to come.

6·9   Radio in a World at War

Of all the wars of this century, radio had its greatest impact in World War II. Wireless had limited use in World War I, before broadcasting developed. Television was making strong inroads into radio's audience by the Korean War of the 1950s and had become dominant by the Vietnam War. Radio was effective in three ways during the 1939–1945 war: as a non-broadcasting aid to military tactics and strategy, enabling unprecedented coordination of air, sea, and ground forces; as a source of domestic information and entertainment (see 6.61); and as a medium for international propaganda (see 6.92).

6·91   Domestic Effects on Other Media

Radio helped tie the country together during the dark years of 1942–1943, when we "hung on" while our war machine geared for maximum effort, and the brighter 1944–1945 period, when we knew the enemy had to give in. Radio news reported the war at home and abroad, delivering more news to more citizens than any combination of print and film media. Radio's unique impact came from its mixture of programming-as-before combined with greatly increased news, news features, and commentary. Radio could entertain and inform the public faster and better than other means.

One reason for radio's success was the effect of the war on other media. Short supplies and poor quality of paper for newspapers and magazines helped push many advertisers to radio. Some newsprint went for comic books, which had their high point of readership in these years. Born in the mid-1930s, the comic book followed American fighting men around the world, often telling adventures of characters first heard on radio. The paperback book also bloomed during the war. If soldiers were not reading comics or listening to Armed Forces Radio, they were often reading paperback fiction, which took up less shipping space than hardbacks.

Hollywood went to war as much as radio. The stereotypical brutal German Nazi and sadistic "Jap" or "Nip" plied their evil ways on the screen even before we entered the war. Serial film characters turned their attention from fictional criminals to the Axis, in an orgy of entertainment propaganda. Perhaps more important to the morale of fighting men, many Hollywood stars went on the USO circuits, setting an example for radio and stage personalities. Military personnel around the world viewed Hollywood films, in a good example of distribution and exhibition under difficult conditions. As did radio creative personnel, many filmmakers lent their talents to the government for the duration; some, like Frank Capra, who directed the *Why We Fight* film series, worked in the service as professionals. Members of both industries, of course, joined the armed forces in other capacities and many saw combat.

The popular music business, at the height of the big band era when the war began, was hit hard in April 1942, when the War Production Board cut shellac supplies for records to 30 percent of 1941 consumption. The material was needed for wartime use, and its scarcity drastically reduced record output for several years. Not affected were most broadcast transcriptions, which already were recorded on vinyl, the plastic material from which all records soon would be made. The AFM recording ban discussed in 6.83 also reduced record industry output.

6•92   American Broadcasting Overseas

Overseas broadcasting by the United States took two forms: broadcasts intended for American troops abroad, and the fledgling propaganda efforts of the *Voice of America*. Troop broadcasting started out with a temporary, low-power unauthorized transmitter in Alaska, which tried to bring domestic radio fare to soldiers in one of the most physically demanding theaters of war. Army brass who discovered this operation recognized its potential value to morale. An attempt was made to meet this need through shortwave. However, because such facilities already were overtaxed, the Armed Forces Radio Service (AFRS) turned to regular medium-wave transmissions of two kinds: large, permanent stations at major bases and smaller, low-power temporary units that could follow an army on short notice. The military either climatized and issued receivers or, where troops were stationed in one location for a while, obtained some by purchase or, in occupied territory, by "moonlight requisition."

Frequently AFRS ran into difficul-

ties with technical matters, overly zealous censors, publicity-hungry senior officers, and the sensibilities of nations in which troops and AFRS might be stationed. AFRS stations primarily programmed domestic network radio fare: the programs minus the commercials, plus music recordings and a heavy dose of news. The Armed Forces Network (AFN) appeared in England in mid-1943 and soon operated more than 50 low-power stations on bases throughout the United Kingdom. After D-Day, shortwave relays delivered broadcast material to forces in France. The 20-hour AFN broadcast day contained regular AFRS fare, orientation programs, and public service announcements. AFN and AFRS programs had a minor propaganda effect on civilians around the bases, who trusted the news "that the Americans tell themselves" more than the output of overt psychological or political warfare outlets.

Our strategic overseas effort was the Voice of America (VOA). The government began production of radio programs in January 1942 and first applied the name "Voice of America" to the programming in February. From its start, VOA broadcast in a variety of languages to several parts of the world—broadcasts were carried on privately owned shortwave stations in this country, which the government took over for the duration late in 1942, or on new government-owned transmitters. After its formation in mid-1942 (see 6.61), OWI became responsible for VOA and rapidly built up a worldwide production and broadcast operation. By the end of the war, VOA had major production centers in New York and San Francisco, with more than 1,000 programs a week coming from New York alone. Programming consisted mainly of music, with news, commentary, entertainment programs from domestic radio, and programs specially designed for VOA broadcasts, often using well-known radio characters.

6•93   Axis Radio Propaganda

Starting in the late 1930s, the Rockefeller Foundation funded a short-wave listening project at Princeton University to monitor and translate German, Italian, Japanese, and other foreign broadcasts. In March 1941 the U.S. government assumed responsibility for the work when it created the Foreign Broadcast Intelligence Service (FBIS)—later the Foreign Broadcast Information Service—as a function of the FCC. The service regularly published summaries and digests of broadcasts, and recordings of some of the more important ones. In operation 24 hours a day, seven days a week, FBIS covered the world, receiving more than 1½ million words a day in late 1942 and 2½ million words a day by 1944. The FBIS continued after the war as part of the CIA and still issues respected summaries of Soviet, Chinese, and other foreign broadcasts.

The domestic audience for foreign broadcasting was quite small; perhaps 5 percent or 10 percent of the total population had and used shortwave listening equipment, typically as an "additional feature" on larger console and table model radios. It was estimated that 150,000 Americans tuned directly to generally English-language broadcasts from Germany, with fewer hearing Italian or Japanese transmissions.

German international radio broadcasting came under the Ministry of Enlightenment and Propaganda headed by Dr. Joseph Goebbels, a "natural" propagandist and one of Hitler's closest advisers. German radio transmitted to the world at large and to countries that were specific military targets. Broadcasts of the first type stressed the correctness of the German position on world issues, the fine life inside Nazi Germany, and the heroic exploits of German arms. The second kind created a climate of fear and fomented internal strife in the target country by stressing German military strength and supporting the rights of dissident or minority groups, particularly those of German origin. One of Goebbels' most famous, or infamous, radio personalities was "Lord Haw Haw," the microphone name for British turncoat William Joyce, who broadcast to the British Isles for the Nazis starting in 1939. His nickname came from his affected upperclass-English style. Joyce failed to sway his audience, however, for the British laughed at him even as he advised them of locations for upcoming bombing raids. Later in the war, Berlin transmitted "Axis Sally," an Ohio woman named Mildred Gillars, who tried to destroy the morale of the Allied forces by playing big band music and messages of impending doom. The soldiers usually listened to the music and ignored the message. At the end of the war, the British captured Joyce and hanged him as a traitor. American authorities tried Gillars and imprisoned her until 1961.

The Italians seemed to follow Germany's example, but without success. In addition to Mussolini's, the most famous voice used by Italy for overseas broadcasts to the United States belonged to American expatriate poet Ezra Pound. Pound declaimed the wonders of Fascist Italy and the damnation of the democracies fighting it. The Americans captured Pound, but committed him to a mental hospital for a number of years as unfit to stand trial.

The primary mission of Japanese overseas broadcasts during World War II was to convince fellow Asians of the inevitability and benefit of the "Greater East Asia Co-Prosperity Sphere" being built with the force of Japanese arms. For the American fighting men in the Pacific, Japanese broadcasting primarily meant Tokyo Rose (Iva Ikuko Toguri and others), who played band records and offered them a broadcast soft shoulder, telling them that, while they were fighting, other men were wooing their wives and sweethearts at home. Although the music was popular—one story claims that we parachuted new recordings on Tokyo to replace the old, scratchy ones (but the new batch all broke on landing)—the propaganda was largely ignored. The Americans captured and fined Toguri and sent her to prison. She later worked in Chicago while hoping for a pardon—finally granted in 1977.

Allied nations also broadcast beyond their borders, especially the British. The BBC was the main Allied voice heard in Europe for four long years, after Germany had conquered most of the continent early in 1940. It provided balanced news and comment and, increasingly, coded messages to specific resistance groups to coordinate guerrilla action with Allied military forces. The BBC's newscasts probably had the highest credibility of any nondomestic broadcasting service in the world. On D-Day it lost much of this credibility as it confused the Germans with false statements about the invasion.

To the listener, American broadcasting during World War II changed only in respect to increased war-related content and the freezing of physical growth. However, as in World War I, the prospect of change, particularly in television, was enormous. The demand for consumer goods, the possible postwar uses for electronic war matériel factories, the GIs' new skills in electronics and broadcasting, peacetime use of new leisure—all were crying for action. However, many key questions were put off until after the war even though, as will be seen in the following chapters, the answers turned out to be not readily available.

6•94   Period Overview

Although the war cramped radio, like the rest of the nation, with respect to personnel and material supplies, these were some of radio's best years in respect to economic success and public esteem. Radio's wartime news role was indispensable. The artificially low number of stations, held nearly constant due to the construction freeze, shared in a feast of wartime advertising income while other media suffered from paper shortages. With potential competition from FM and television also held back by the war, the AM network-dominated radio establishment reached its zenith.

Apart from that economic fact, the war years are important for the groundwork they contributed to postwar changes. A fourth national network, now ABC, resulted from the chain broadcasting rules and the 1943 Supreme Court case upholding the FCC. This court decision became a precedent for future FCC regulatory incursions into various aspects of the industry. While they achieved little public recognition and only limited discussion within much of the industry, the 1944 allocations hearings set the stage for television's postwar dominance (see 7.13, 7.8) and FM radio's birth and temporary decline (see 7.22). The issues, complicated in themselves, were made more so by wartime secrecy requirements. While the future was being set, the public took more notice of the less important Petrillo affair and the politically charged Cox hearings into the FCC.

The war years are best described as a profitable hiatus in the continuing development of American broadcasting. The war had global importance, and radio, apart from its important reportorial role, took a back seat for the duration together with most other civilian goods. But, as in the Depression, radio remained available to most of the public and served an important information and entertainment function.

Further Reading

Barnouw (1968) provides an overview of radio's domestic and foreign role during the war, while Lichty and Topping (1975) includes many useful contemporary accounts. Kirby and Harris (1947) offer an informal analysis of radio in the war effort. Severeid (1946), Kaltenborn (1950), and

---

Key Broadcasting Indicators: 1945 / This is the fourth of 12 tables offering comparable information for a 60-year period (to 1985), presented at five-year intervals. Sources for items 1-6 and 11 are the tables in Appendix C, while other information comes from sources indicated. This is the first table in the series to include information on FM and television, whose commercial operation was approved in 1941. Most data are for January 1.

Indicators	AM	FM	TV
1. Number of commercial stations	881	48	8
2. Number of noncommercial stations	38	8	—
3. Total stations on the air	919	52	8
4. Number of network-affiliated stations	874	na	na
5. Percentage of commercial stations affiliated with networks	95%	na	na
6. Total industry revenue (add 000,000)	$424.0	na	na
7. One-hour station rate (New York)	$1,200	na	na
8. One-minute station rate (New York)	na	na	na
9. One-hour network rate, evening	$18,500	na	na
10. Number of broadcasting employees	. . . . 37,800		
11. Percentage of families with sets	88%	na	.01%
12. Broadcasting regulatory budget (FCC)	. . . . $6,213,343		
13. Total FCC personnel	. . . . 1,513		

Notes (see Appendix D for full citations)

na = not applicable or not available.

2. Educational television allocations were not approved until 1952.

4. Many FM stations were network affiliates through their AM sister stations, but there are no clear records on this. Likewise, while many of the few television stations were network owned, the television networks had not yet been formed.

5. See note 4.

7. For WEAF, the NBC flagship station name in New York, call letters soon changed to WNBC.

9. NBC radio network with 150 affiliates.

10. The average weekly salary for those employees was $60.05; minimum wage was 25¢ an hour. Lichty and Topping (1975), page 290, table 23.

12–13. FCC budget for fiscal year 1945; of the total, $4.2 million was for war-related activities.

Kendrick (1969), Sperber (1986), and Persico (1988), all of which detail the life of Edward R. Murrow, and Smith (1978), which focuses on Murrow's wartime role; plus many other volumes by reporters detailing wartime experiences and radio's role in getting and reporting stories. Two paperbacks issued by CBS (1945a and b) provide transcripts of actual reports from war theaters and describe well how they sounded on the home front. A postwar textbook by CBS news director Paul White (1947) includes a fine chapter on radio's reporting of D-Day in Europe. For another network's role in the war, see NBC (1944). Bulman (1945) details the professional lives of the major wartime commentators—see also Fang (1977) and Culbert (1976). Dryer's collection (1942) is a contemporary view of radio in wartime, and Bannerman (1986) reviews Norman Corwin's wartime radio drama. Corwin's own book provides transcripts of one series (1942). Two general books of value for their discussion of wartime reporting are the fourth volume of Desmond's history of world reporting (1984), which covers the period leading to and during World War II, and Knightley's best-selling review of the wartime reporter in recent history (1975).

Studies of the audience add insight to this era. Kate Smith's 1944 War Bond drive and how and why it succeeded as radio mass persuasion is the subject of Merton's (1946) study. Chappell and Hooper (1944) is the best description of radio research immediately prior to the coming of television. See Lowery and De Fleur (1988) for an assessment of important wartime Army audience research. The 1941 *Annals* special issue on radio is full of contemporary insight.

For material on regulatory issues, see the sources noted in chapter 5, especially the hard-to-find wartime FCC annual reports, its *Report on Chain Broadcasting* (1941), and Robinson (1943). Good material on the Petrillo affair is in Warner (1953) and Llewellyn White (1947).

The literature on propaganda is large and growing. Invaluable background is in the three-volume anthology edited by Lasswell and others (1979–1980). A good study of the politics behind the operation of the Office of War Information is Winkler (1978). OWI as seen through the life of its director, Elmer Davis, is found in Burlingame (1961). A recent study of U.S. shortwave broadcasting to Latin America before and during World War II is in Fejes (1986). Four contemporary assessments of the radio war are Rolo (1942), Huth (1942), Childs and Whitton (1942), and Lean (1943), all of which cover Allied and Axis efforts. A fine study of the BBC during wartime is Briggs (1970), while a more focused assessment of BBC overseas broadcasts to Europe is in Bennett (1966). The BBC's *War Report* (1946) contains transcripts of the last year of war in Europe. A comparative study of British and German propaganda is in Balfour (1979). The material on German propaganda is extensive. Three studies focusing on Germany's radio applications are Delfiner (1974), which focuses on a specific 1938–1939 example; Kris and Speier (1944), which assesses German domestic radio; and Ettlinger (1943), a popularized narrative of the Axis use of international radio.

Era of
Great Change
(1945–1952)

7

"Television was already conducting itself provocatively, trying to get radio to pucker up for the kiss of death. Young men with crew cuts were dragging TV cameras into the studios and crowding the old radio actors out into the halls."—Comedian Fred Allen in Treadmill to Oblivion

Era of
Great Change
(1945–1952)

7

"In New York City, a considerable degree of specialization on the part of particular [radio] stations has already arisen—one station featuring a preponderance of classical music, another a preponderance of dance music, etc. With the larger number of stations which FM will make possible, such specialization may arise in other cities."—FCC, Public Service Responsibility of Broadcast Licensees (1946)

The seven years from late 1945 to early 1952 mark the transition of American broadcasting from a small radio system dominated by four networks to a far larger AM–FM radio and television system in which networks concentrated on television and left radio stations to their own programming resources. A reader only familiar with today's broadcasting would hardly recognize the limited system of 1945, while the 1952 system contained all the elements to be found a quarter-century later.

This same short period also marked a massive change in American life. By the fall of 1945, World War II was over and the United States had become the most prominent country in the world. Confusion

Outline:
Era of Great Change (1945–1952)

and expectation accompanied the end of wartime rationing and shortages and the implementing of plans for postwar consumption. Military personnel flooding home, though obviously welcome, clogged an overcrowded and changing employment market, and put an additional strain on inadequate amounts of housing. Millions of war-delayed marriages were celebrated and consummated, leading to the postwar baby boom and resulting demographic bulge down through the years. The G.I. Bill of Rights provided financing for hundreds of thousands of veterans to go to college. One industry after another endured union-management arguments and strikes. Every industry or service was in transition, particularly transportation.

Postwar inflation was fierce. The Hollywood motion picture industry almost succumbed to an important court case, a debilitating search for communist influences, and, finally, competition with an upstart: television.

The United States was also caught in international transition from 1945, when we dominated a world at relative peace, to 1952, when we were in a shooting war in Korea and a deepening cold war with the Soviet Union, a newly communist China, and a slowly expanding "third world" of newly independent nations attempting to maneuver between and manipulate both sides. The cold war almost reached the flash point in the 1948–1949 Berlin Airlift, by which the Western allies provided all of West Berlin's needs when the Russians cut off ground access. The war in Korea, which started in June 1950, found American troops fighting a major war in Asia, although the world was not plunged into total war and the participants limited the weaponry used. As will be seen, all of this affected broadcasting.

The important changes in radio and television resulted from the FCC technical investigations and rulemaking proceedings discussed in 6.8 and 7.8. A lengthy and at times bitter debate on broadcasting's public service responsibility in the FCC, both houses of Congress, and the courts indicated additional change. FM radio and television were being built on the profits of AM radio, which itself experienced a 59 percent growth in income and 156 percent growth in number of stations between 1944 and 1952 (see Appendix C, tables 1 and 4). The relatively small "club" was rapidly becoming a major industry employing many people and having a great variety of problems. The radio audience in any one locality listened to familiar programming but sensed the imminence of television, which only one person in ten had seen by mid-1948. And its coming hit people with the same feelings of expectation and excitement that the original radio audiences had felt in the early 1920s.

7·1   Technical Innovations: High Fidelity and Television

Generally speaking, the public has taken little notice of technical controversies. But, in the 1945–1952 period, large corporations vying for a vast potential market in improved phonograph records drew considerable public attention. At the same time, magnetic tape recordings entered the home entertainment market, several years after the professional broadcasting industry had adopted simpler models. More sophisticated technology—notably the transistor, invented in 1948—was still in the laboratory, as industry wrangled over standards for recording and television.

7·11   Battle of the Speeds

For nearly fifty years, the 78-rpm record had been a mainstay of home entertainment and broadcast music. Many stations also used 15-inch or 16-inch 33⅓-rpm electrical transcriptions for syndicated 15-minute programs but still had to depend on commercially available 78s for much of their daily musical programming. The 78 had many drawbacks: it was heavy and breakable; sound quality was mediocre; any musical selection that ran longer than four or five minutes took two, three, or more records; but most importantly, the constant need to change and turn records marred the appreciation of any extended piece of music. In an attempt to overcome

this problem, RCA had test-marketed a 33⅓-rpm standard-groove record for the home market in the early 1930s; but, because it would play only on a new-style record player, the project folded in the Depression economy within a few months.

In 1947–1948, however, engineers at CBS Laboratories, working under Peter C. Goldmark, devised a disc system with 33⅓-rpm speed and *microgroove* recording, which had many more recording grooves per inch of diameter. These two factors made it possible to put 20–25 minutes on each side of a 12-inch disc. CBS introduced this long-playing (LP) record in 1948 to an enthusiastic public in the form of a new system: slower recording speed, finer grooves, vinyl record base, a better stylus, higher quality microphones and recording amplifiers—all resulting in a vast improvement in the fidelity of sound and convenience of playing records. At last, the average music lover could hear superb reproductions of the finest music at his or her convenience. The LP—together with FM and interrupting of selections by commercials on AM stations—contributed to a drop in amount of classical music programming on low-fidelity AM radio. AM radio preferred serving a mass audience to a smaller class audience; but the public now expected higher sound quality on *all* radio, and that would require a considerable investment by stations.

A few months later RCA introduced its EP or "extended play" disc, intended primarily for popular music. A lightweight seven-inch disc with a 1½-inch hole in the middle—at first requiring another totally different reproduction system—revolved at 45 rpm and offered better sound quality than the 78-rpm record. Competition was tight for many months, with RCA even issuing symphonies and operas in the 45-rpm format, requiring a box of discs and killing the convenience of extended play. Eventually the public balked at having to invest in three separate systems in order to play available records. The RCA 45 became the standard format for popular single tunes, while classics and collections of popular music were recorded on the 33⅓-rpm disc. RCA later unhappily adopted the 33⅓-rpm LP for its fine catalogue of classical music. In short order, the 78 faded from the scene except for collectors, and record players capable of all three speeds came on the market. This standardization proved beneficial to all concerned and established a home music-reproduction pattern that lasted until cassette tape recording became popular in the 1960s.

7•12 The Coming of Tape and Hi-Fi

In the late 1940s, magnetic recording arrived on the domestic professional and consumer market. In 1947 Sears Roebuck sold a military-developed model with thin wire as the recording medium for $170 —a very high price considering that the minimum wage was slowly rising from 25 cents an hour. It was intended mainly for business use, as its fidelity was not good enough for musical recordings and recording wire was very difficult to repair or edit. The machines were heavy and cumbersome but far more portable than earlier devices of comparable sound quality. The first tape recorders went on sale about the same time, using a ¼-inch-wide paper base tape that allowed about 15 minutes of sound recording on a seven-inch reel.

If necessity is the mother of invention, then laziness may be the mother of necessity. The broadcast networks long had prohibited recordings because of their generally inferior quality, even refusing to bend the rules for on-the-scene news cov-

erage during the war. Popular radio singer Bing Crosby wanted to record his program rather than follow the usual network practice of doing two live shows in one night to cover different time zones. NBC's ban on recordings kept him from pursuing other interests, including golf. Crosby had seen tape recorders in use in Europe when he was entertaining troops during the war, and his Crosby Research Foundation, which eventually amassed many patents on magnetic tape recording, developed recording techniques and equipment of high quality. He took his program, and high ratings, to ABC, which welcomed him and his ideas. New techniques and devices, including plastic-based rather than paper-based tape, soon followed, and by the early 1950s reel-to-reel tape recorders were standard equipment at most broadcasting stations. Time zone differences could be handled by a simple replaying of a tape, and, in recording studios, networks, and stations, the Magnecord or later the Ampex recorder became a programming standby.

Development of the LP record and magnetic recording led to a new consumer industry. The term *hi-fi*—short for high fidelity sound reproduction—was used in England before the war for certain custom designs, but now small firms such as Fisher or H.H. Scott began applying it to limited and even mass-production equipment. Hi-fi addicts became sophisticated as to the size and location of loudspeakers, the power and distortion of amplifiers, and the specifications of radio tuners. Many hi-fi sets—actually collections of matched components—were designed to take advantage of the growing number of FM stations, many of which programmed classical music (see 7.62), the flood of LP records, and the promise of home tape recording. Where once only professional users of sound equipment purchased precision devices, now a groundswell of consumers bought high-priced components, mass-produced units that frequently promised more than they delivered, and even build-your-own kits.

7•13   . . . and Television

The technical standards for television had been adopted in 1941 (see 5.15), but a number of important refinements appeared after the war. Chief among them was the new and sensitive orthicon camera tube announced by RCA in October 1945 —and shortly afterwards the image orthicon still used today. This tube was a great improvement over the iconoscope and became the standard for years. Since the IO could work with much less light, television became more sensitive to minor light variations than most motion picture photography. Actors no longer had to swelter under hundreds of foot-candles of light, station owners no longer had to pay for enormous quantities of power and light, and engineers welcomed the stability of the new tube.

Another development was the use of motion picture film in television programming. There were many problems involved in matching a mechanical-optical medium (film) providing 24 pictures a second with an electronic medium (television) operating at 30 pictures a second. A workable means of telecasting films soon was developed, using a film projector with a special shutter aimed at a television camera. A *film chain,* as this combination was known, became the key piece of equipment for new stations as it could run feature or even free industrial or commercial films more cheaply than live programming. A mirror device even permitted *multiplexing* more than one projector into a single camera.

But preserving televised images was harder to do. For years, once a program was telecast, it was lost; there was no good way of recording both picture and sound from the television screen. Finally, in 1947–1948, a film camera was able to record pictures in synchronization off a specially bright television kinescope or picture tube—at a price: film, or *kinescope,* recordings of television programs were less clear, less well defined, had less contrast than the original television picture, and were far poorer than an original film. Thus, making *kines* was an art. The viewing public readily spotted even the best as a poor recording. Some programs were recorded in this way only for archival purposes, but the networks used kinescope recordings only to supply programs to affiliate stations not yet connected by wire or microwave relay for simultaneous transmission.

Kinescope recording was so unsatisfactory that several firms tried to develop an electronic system that would be more compatible with electronic television. Bing Crosby Enterprises conducted one of the first demonstrations of magnetic videotape recording in late 1951. Again, the singer was seeking a way to record his television musical variety program to avoid the inconvenience of doing it live. However, it took several years before videotape systems became commercially practical. By 1952 the tape still had to be moved at an almost fantastic 100 inches per second past the recording heads, but the picture was vastly better than existing kinescope standards. Videotape would also be cheaper than kinescopes because the tape could be reused many times, could be played back immediately without processing, and, most important, was electronic—probably equal in quality to live television. Broadcasters would have to wait until the late 1950s, but the end product—if RCA and Ampex were correct—would be worth waiting for.

7•2   Growth of AM, FM, and Television

The 1946–1952 period is characterized by an almost explosive growth in number of AM stations as well as the arrival of large numbers of both FM radio and television outlets. Although the new services were growing rapidly, AM radio outdistanced them in new stations and additional communities served by at least one station.

7•21   Postwar Expansion of AM

The pressure to open new AM radio stations was intense. The natural growth of radio had been held back for more than 15 years, first because of the economic depression and then because of the wartime freeze in priorities. In addition, many returning military personnel wanted to apply wartime radio training and experience to broadcasting—many to start their own stations. Businessmen were aware of the financial potential of radio, the capital was available for starting new stations, and prospects for the tried-and-true AM industry looked more favorable than the new services of FM and television (see 7.22 and 7.23), particularly since transmitting equipment and audiences were more readily available.

In addition, the FCC early in 1946 changed its technical standards for radio to allow more stations on the same or adjacent channels to be located in a given area. Since more stations on the same number of channels meant greater signal interference, the decision reduced the effective range of many stations and reversed the long-held policy of serving rural areas—overrepresented in Congress—through clear-channel stations. Under pressure from persons desiring licenses,

the FCC decided that local radio listeners would be better off with reception of one or two local stations serving local needs than with reception of one or two distant signals. After the rules were changed, even though existing stations were to have been protected, AM stations increased from about 930 in 1945 to more than 2,350 seven years later.

More than two-thirds of this growth was in smaller stations in smaller markets. Often the new station was the first in a town that previously had relied on distant stations. From 1945 to 1949 alone, more than 560 communities received their first local AM radio station, some received more than one new AM station and an FM station as well. From 1945 to 1950, additional stations on formerly clear (one station only) channels increased by 10, while regional stations rose by 68 and local stations by 453! But, as noted, this growth was achieved at the cost of greater interference. Whereas less than 10 percent of AM stations during the war had operated in daytime only, nearly one-third had to be so limited by 1950, and many more had to lower power at night or use directional antennas to protect existing stations. All of this made radio more complicated and expensive, and in some communities led to inferior reception. Where before the war there might have been several clear or high-power stations in a major city, after the war new lower power stations in many of that city's suburbs fragmented both the listening audience and the advertiser's dollars (see 8.5).

Not all AM operators were successful. A few went under and many remained marginally profitable in the late 1940s, partly because of the technical problems already described and partly because some officials and many broadcasters kept saying that AM was obsolete. They claimed that FM soon would replace AM and that

television would then reduce or even eliminate radio as a major force.

7•22   The FM Enigma

Expansion of postwar FM was
clouded by Edwin H. Armstrong's continuing and losing fight to regain the prewar
40 MHz band for either FM direct broadcast or interstation relay, and by continuing difficulty in obtaining transmitters and
other equipment designed for the new 88
–108 MHz band (see 6.81). From 1945 to
1948, the 50 or so FM stations that had
been on the air before the war could
broadcast on both the old band and the
new. At the end of 1948, low-band FM

transmissions were canceled, and some
400,000 prewar FM receivers became useless. Armstrong sparked two congressional investigations but could not dis-
lodge the FCC from its 1945 decision to
move FM to the new band nor lengthen
the time allowed for the changeover. Many
listeners, stuck with expensive but useless
receivers, were cautious about supporting
the new medium further.

To allay some of this concern, the
FCC consistently referred to FM as the
preferred radio service, even suggesting
that AM might eventually be phased out
in its favor and that television would have
limited importance for some time due to
its costs. On the surface, it looked as
though many people were taking the pro-

Postwar Patterns: Broadcasting Explodes / The substantial and sudden growth of radio and television right after World War II marked a period of activity unique in broadcasting—all three services
were growing together rapidly for the first time. That growth is apparent in this comparison showing
stations actually on the air, authorized but not yet on the air, and pending applications for new stations—all for June 30 of each year. The FCC had dismissed without prejudice all wartime applications
for AM and FM stations, explaining the "na" under "pending" for 1945 for both services.

Year	AM Radio			FM Radio			Television		
	On Air	Authorized (not on air)	Pending	On Air	Authorized (not on air)	Pending	On Air	Authorized (not on air)	Pending
1945	931	24	na	46	19	na	9	—	118
1946	961	254	680	55	401	250	6	24	40
1947	1,298	497	666	238	680	431	11	55	9
1948	1,693	331	575	587	433	90	29	80	294
1949	2,006	173	382	737	128	65	70	47	338
1950	2,144	159	277	691	61	17	105	4	351
1951	2,281	104	270	649	10	10	107	2	415
1952	2,355	65	323	629	19	9	108	—	716

Note: A freeze on new TV station authorizations was in effect from September 1948 until April 1952 (see 7.82).

Source: FCC *Annual Reports.* For summary data as of January 1, see Appendix C, table 1, which includes information for
educational stations, excluded here except for AM (about 25 on the air each year).

ferred advice. At the end of the war, more than 600 applications for new FM stations piled up and the commission allowed recipients a "conditional grant" to proceed with personnel, studio, and program planning prior to station construction. The initial screening allowed faster processing of the successful applicant's engineering submissions and got stations on the air in shorter time. Recognizing the demand for more channels, yet mindful that many potential licensees still in the military would be delayed in applying, the FCC held back some FM channels between 1946 and 1947, against strong industry opposition. By far the largest proportion of new FM licenses went to AM station operators; by 1949, for example, 85 percent of FM stations on the air were owned by AM licensees. Usually both stations were in the same town, with the FM outlet as insurance against possible AM demise—or protection against independent competition.

In its planning for FM, the FCC considered the lack of planning that had gone into AM assignments over the years. When AM stations applied for maximum power, the FCC had granted it as long as it did not cause major interference to an existing station, even though it might prevent smaller stations from getting started elsewhere and deny AM stations in the same market an equal technological chance to compete for advertising business. To avoid creating the same problem with FM, the FCC decided to assign all FM stations in a single area so that they were roughly equal in coverage, could compete for advertisers fairly, and would not cause interference elsewhere.

But the FM boom of the 1940s was short-lived. Total authorizations began to drop in 1949, and the stations-on-the-air count dropped the following year and kept dropping—as the number of AM and television stations continued to grow. FM's

fortunes declined because (1) FM equipment companies had to take time to reengineer to the new higher band at the same time that prewar equipment became obsolete; (2) the resulting confusion in the minds of broadcasters, potential advertisers (see 7.51), and the public made buyers suspicious; (3) FM receiver sales were erratic and only a fraction of the number promised were manufactured (see 7.71); (4) common AM-FM ownership for more than 80 percent of the FM outlets lessened aggressive pursuit of FM success, and the limited money, time, and personnel were frequently committed to television; (5) duplicated programming on many AM-FM stations (see 7.62) made the newer radio service pointless to most potential listeners; thus (6) few FM networks offered special programming; and (7) advertisers showed little interest and support. In addition to these problems, FM had to compete with both its sister media: established and growing AM and more exciting television. By 1952, FM's future looked bleak to all but a handful of independent station operators who programmed classical and other music for a small audience of hi-fi buffs. FM was a class service in what was supposed to be a mass medium. Two years later, frustrated by FM's decline and exhausted financially and mentally by constant patent royalty battles with RCA, Edwin Armstrong killed himself, ending his two-decade-long fight for "radio's second chance."

7•23   Establishment of Television

As the postwar period began, only six television stations were on the air, in New York, Washington, Schenectady, Chicago, Philadelphia, and Los Angeles, broadcasting a few hours a day. Due to

Early Television Studios

Most pre-Freeze television stations varied greatly in layout, construction, and equipment. In the largest cities, giant radio studios designed for large studio audiences—including NBC's famous 8H, the home of the NBC Symphony Orchestra—were converted to television, and downtown motion picture and stage theaters were used as well. Most stations established a makeshift studio—few could afford two—in a building designed for some other purpose, with too low a ceiling for proper lighting, inadequate or nonexistent air conditioning, poor soundproofing, and a rabbit's warren of offices and corridors. Two studio cameras and their control units, at least one film chain for showing motion pictures, slides, or stills, and a network connection were all that was needed. Some studios were also oddly shaped or had supporting columns that interrupted space, camera movement, and lighting; some were housed in war-surplus Quonset huts. When a building was specially built, it was usually of inexpensive cinderblock construction. Although engineers liked the even illumination of fluorescent lighting, creative production people used motion picture lighting techniques because fluorescents could not be dimmed and were inappropriate for dramatic lighting. Too often, in the earliest studios, cameras moving over irregular wooden floors produced bumps and wiggles on the air. Microphones designed for radio had to be positioned so close to the actors that they often appeared in the picture. Monochromatic (black, white, purple) makeup had—thankfully—been discarded, but few studios bothered with anything but shades of gray for their settings. Soundproofing followed radio practice, and absorbent materials were draped everywhere the fire inspectors would permit, to soak up echoes and camera noise and other movement. Since all programs were live, actors and other talent had to watch not only script, director, and clock but camera as well. The tremendous heat from the lighting—an actor could lose seven to ten pounds during a performance—made air conditioning essential for the sake of both people and equipment; but because of power demands, cost, and noise from air conditioners, many studios were uncomfortable hothouses even in the dead of winter. Even CBS had to use converted space for its New York studio; and if a camera broke down, as frequently happened with hand-made equipment, the show had to go on with only one camera.

Television stations operated by networks and large AM radio stations whose owners had been planning them for years still had too little space, even though the height in the studio may have appeared enormous to radio veterans; some studios had several cameras in each, and interconnected control facilities provided flexible operation. The needs for set construction and storage, repair space, and ready access for large and awkward equipment were usually overlooked by those without stage or feature film backgrounds, further reducing the number of "more than adequate" television studio installations. Television was new, experimental, in the red, and faced an uncertain future.

An early television drama takes place under the hot television lights (note the protective hat on the cameraman) and with boom mikes and theatrical sets. These programs were the training ground for the first generation of television technicians and on-air personnel. Courtesy of Wisconsin Center for Film and Theater Research.

some confusion on final allocations (see 6.82 and 7.81) and the high cost of station construction, television's postwar start was far slower than had been the case for either AM or FM. The additional investment, in the absence of public support, made investors wary. Television equipment was more complicated to manufacture, and equipment makers wanted first to meet the highly profitable demand for AM station equipment and receivers.

When the television Freeze began in September 1948 (see 7.82), only 34 stations were telecasting from 21 cities to about one million sets. The Freeze would artificially limit television to larger markets. Even if there had been no government-imposed moratorium, high capital and operating costs probably would have slowed television's establishment in smaller markets. Even in one-station markets with an audience monopoly, the great costs so reduced advertising income, determined essentially by audience size, that few stations could operate in the black in their first years. Yet, despite these limitations, the demand for television stations increased each year of the Freeze, as stations that had received construction permits got on the air. The major manufacturers of television transmitters—RCA, GE, and Dumont—were running six months late when the Freeze began, and were hard pressed to meet the demand when it ended. Pioneering would pay off handsomely. The 107 stations that got on the air before or during the Freeze became the major money earners of the industry for more than a decade afterwards.

Since in most cases pioneer television station operators also owned AM outlets, they had some broadcast experience and the AM operation was often the source of developmental money. But otherwise television was sufficiently new and different that owners had to feel their way through problems of construction, equipment, programming, and daily operation. With few television-experienced personnel, a young war veteran might become a director in a matter of months, weeks, or even days—and had to learn everything on the job. This led to mistakes but also to a feeling of teamwork that lasted until the industry grew to the point of being impersonal. In one respect early television pioneering was markedly different from radio in the 1920s. Television had the advantage of being able to recruit radio's managers, and the pattern was clearly set: as soon as possible network interconnections of stations would cross the country (see 7.32), bringing common programming to all.

7•24   The First Debate over Pay-Television

An emotional issue in this period was whether television should be supported by direct payments from the public instead of indirect advertising revenues. The idea was not new—there had been pay-radio and even pay-television proposals in the 1930s—but the great increase in television costs over those of radio revived it in the late 1940s. Zenith, the giant Chicago radio and later television manufacturer, under the direction of Commander Eugene F. McDonald, Jr., was the major proponent of pay-TV, but also working on specific proposals and techniques were New York–based Skiatron and, on the West Coast, Telemeter, owned primarily by Paramount Pictures. Each firm had its own system, but all involved sending a scrambled picture via a normal broadcast channel and making the unscrambling technique available to customers on a pay-per-viewing basis. This channel would be useless, of course, to persons who did not pay.

Zenith's "Phonevision" system initially sent signals over telephone wires to unscramble the television signal, which came over the air in scrambled form. This system was the first to receive a major test, when, early in 1951, some 300 families in Chicago were equipped with the telephone lines enabling them to purchase programs in addition to seeing regular "free" television. Many thousands of families had applied, and the sample was expected to be a cross section of urban population program interests. For three months the pay channel, an experimental station licensed to Zenith, supplied feature films and other special entertainment at least three times a day. Zenith maintained that the test was a major success, even though film distributors refused to supply first-run films for the venture. Early in 1952, armed with the test results, which could be interpreted in various ways, Zenith petitioned the FCC to allow regular pay-TV programming in major American cities. In the meantime, Skiatron tested its "Subscriber-vision" in New York, using the facilities of WOR-TV and another sample of 300. Telemeter conducted tests in Los Angeles and wealthy Palm Springs.

Backing for pay-TV came from major professional sports teams concerned about television inroads on their gate receipts (see 7.91) and from cultural organizations, such as symphony orchestras, seeking a new source of revenue. Violently opposed were movie makers and theater owners, although they accepted theater-shown pay-TV events, and commercial television broadcasters. Another group argued for pay-TV via cable, which did not occupy a scarce broadcast channel and was less susceptible to illegal unscrambling by ingenious technicians and tinkerers. Indeed, to prove that cable was the only practical method, one party had a standing offer to "decode" any unscrambling device

used with on-air pay-TV. All sides flooded the public with propaganda booklets and articles and appealed to the FCC for a clean-cut decision on pay-television, which the commission deferred until late 1968 (see 9.22).

7•25   *Effects of Growth
        on Ownership Patterns*

The drastic change and adjustment in postwar broadcasting is perhaps best seen in relation to station ownership. Between 1923 and 1945 only a limited infusion of new owners and ideas occurred because stations grew slowly in numbers and not many stations changed hands. From 1945 to 1952, however, the near tripling of AM stations and the arrival of FM and television produced a flood of new owners.

Prewar AM radio was controlled by companies or individuals concerned with station operation in major and medium-sized cities, where virtually all stations were on the air day and night and transmitting power increased steadily over the years. One of the largest ownership classes was newspapers, which owned some 30 percent of all stations by 1940. But by 1952 they dropped to just over 20 percent, as newspapers concentrated on the newer media (see below) and independent broadcasters, many of them war veterans, opened AM stations.

The new stations tended to be in smaller towns and suburbs, had less power —most were on regional or local channels —often were restricted by directional antennas or limited to daylight broadcast hours, and had to face competition from FM, television, and older AM stations. These variances led to far greater divergence at industry conventions than before. A large proportion of the new stations competed without network affiliation, which, prior to 1947 or 1948, had been considered almost essential to rapid success. This was due to two factors: the networks did not want or need affiliates to overlap in geographical coverage, and the role of radio networks was declining (see 7.31). The overall effect was to create greater diversity in AM operations.

Most FM stations were built by AM licensees. They not only possessed experience in broadcasting but often were first in line for the new services, wanting to protect their AM investment and possibly profit from new financial opportunities. AM licensees owned roughly four-fifths of FM stations, which usually only duplicated AM programming (see 7.62) and occupied channels that an independent (non-AM) owner might otherwise have used. This is not to suggest a conspiracy, but it helps explain FM's impending problems of survival. Newspaper owners moved into FM as they had earlier built or purchased AM stations. Throughout the 1945–1952 period, with minor fluctuations, newspapers controlled about one-third of the FM stations on the air.

Most early television stations also were operated by AM licensees. Television required some outside revenue to survive several years of massive losses, and, with the exception of stations that were supported by receiver sales—DuMont, GE, and RCA, for example—this came from AM income. Newspapers were bigger owners in television than they had been in either radio medium. By the beginning of the Freeze in 1948, they controlled nearly one-third of the television stations. More important, since they held a large number of approved applications, by 1952 they owned more than 45 percent of the television stations. Television costs tended to encourage multiple-station ownership, whereby an owner could apply economies

of scale to management even if it had only one station in a given region, since television owners often were larger corporations with nationwide interests, whereas radio was generally considered small local business.

The coming of FM and television raised a phenomenon that had disappeared from AM broadcasting with enforcement of the duopoly rule: a single owner possessing more than one station in the same market. AM-FM, AM-TV, and AM-FM-TV combinations lessened the diversity potential of new media and new owners, for now a single owner could run three stations—and sometimes the newspaper, too—under single direction in the same market. Some smaller communities had only one media owner. Critics became increasingly concerned about this concentration of media control (see 9.84).

7·3   Radio Networks Give Way to Television

At the end of the war in 1945, 95 percent of all radio stations were affiliated with one or more of the four national networks. Only seven years later, affiliation had dropped to just over half of all radio stations on the air. In the same period, television networks grew from vague proposals into powerful combinations having affiliation agreements with virtually all on-air television stations. Between these two developments, the industry saw radio as a *national* advertising and programming medium give way almost totally to television.

7·31   The Old Order Passes

Oddly enough, the radio networks ranked in number of affiliates in reverse order to their importance in broadcasting. CBS and NBC led in importance and impact, but ABC had about 50 more affiliates than either of them and Mutual had two and one-half times as many, although these usually were smaller rural stations lacking the audience pull of the major stations affiliated with NBC and CBS. Newest of the major networks was the American Broadcasting Company, as the Blue Network was known after 1945 (see 6.3).

CBS had named thirty-seven-year-old Dr. Frank Stanton as its president early in 1946, although William Paley retained ownership control. From this position Stanton became a spokesman for the broadcasting industry during the next 25 years, much as David Sarnoff spoke for most of the electronics industry. Both NBC

and CBS observed their twenty-fifth anniversaries in 1951–1952, with promotional hoopla about the great past days of radio and the wonderful coming days of television. Internetwork rivalry continued, with both ABC and CBS making major talent raids (see 7.61) on bigger NBC. Starting as early as 1947, ABC sought merger partners to bolster its financial position (see 7.32). A swap in call letters was arranged over several years to identify flagship stations more easily with their network; for example, CBS's WABC call letters went to the American Broadcasting Company's New York outlet, whose WJZ call letters went to Baltimore after a decent interval, while CBS obtained the call letters WCBS from a station in the South.

Even with the FCC chain broad-

The CBS Team/CBS radio in its most important days and CBS television for its first quarter-century was shaped primarily by two men: Since 1929 William S. Paley (left) served first as president and then as chairman; and Frank Stanton (right) served as president from 1946 to 1971. Both men are shown in the late 1960s. For the competing NBC executive team, see page 330. Photos courtesy of CBS Inc.

casting rules (see 6.85), the national networks exercised great power over individual affiliates. In several cases, when local radio stations wanted to substitute a local program for a network program, network officials threatened to reconsider the station's affiliation contract. Even though the station licensee, by law, had the responsibility for what went over the air, until 1948 or so such threats had great effect, for network affiliation was the key to success.

Later, however, as independent radio stations increased and television networks expanded, the radio network declined in importance almost as fast as it had risen, leaving a residue of news, brief features, special events, and well into the 1960s such die-hard entertainment programs as Arthur Godfrey on CBS and Don McNeill's *Breakfast Club* on ABC. With audience interest focusing on television, advertisers and popular programs soon left radio for television. By 1951–1952, large chunks of time previously network-programmed were coming back to the affiliate stations for local programming.

The change in role was not unexpected. Early in 1949, NBC President Niles Trammell predicted that "within three years, the broadcast of sound or ear radio over giant networks will be wiped out." But apparently most network executives did not agree. For various reasons, chiefly its much higher costs, they felt that television would grow slowly enough to make a gradual radio-to-television transition during the 1950s. But the public's interest in and advertiser fascination with television, as well as the impatience of radio executives to make a mark in television, left network radio a dying operation by 1950.

There were still attempts to introduce different types of radio networks. Several were limited, regional FM-only arrangements. But in late 1947, the exclusively FM Continental Radio Network

added eastern and midwestern stations by use of AT&T wire or off-air relays. Programs of music originating at several stations were picked up by other affiliates, with some distant stations receiving the material on tape or by wire lines. FM inventor Edwin Armstrong, whose own W2XMN in Alpine, New Jersey, was an important affiliate, secretly met nearly all the expenditures of the operation. Continental went out of business after Armstrong's death. For a time in the 1940s, both ABC and CBS proposed special networks for their FM affiliates, with high-fidelity duplication of AM network programs. This proposal was aimed at protecting the network organization should AM die off, but, in the end, a few FM stations simply affiliated with conventional low-fidelity AM-based networks.

More interesting, and generating considerably more publicity, was the establishment of the Liberty Broadcasting System. Begun as a single station in Texas by Gordon McLendon in 1948, LBS was based on skillful re-creation of baseball games by McLendon, who combined wire service reports of an ongoing game with sound effects records to make his listeners think they were hearing a play-by-play description. The legality of the method was questionable, because the ball clubs controlled the rights to game broadcasts. By 1949 McLendon's station was feeding the games to more than 80 others in the Southwest. Recreating both baseball and football games—and carrying many as direct play-by-play broadcasts—McLendon's operation had expanded to 200 stations by 1950 and was assuming network stature, with six hours of programming per day. McLendon announced plans for a nationwide network with 16 hours a day of varied programming, just when the established networks, except for Mutual, were letting their radio operations slide in favor of television. By June 1951, the Liberty network had 400 affiliated stations and boasted a strong news department with a growing reputation. Then the organization started to come apart. To obtain funds for continued expansion, Liberty brought in a Texas oilman whose role and conservative views soon decimated the news staff. At about the same time, several ball clubs brought suit against Liberty. The costs of litigation, plus natural advertiser and broadcaster aversion to legal controversy, led to suspension of network operations in mid-1952. A couple of revival attempts failed, and Liberty's former affiliates either signed with one of the big four or turned independent.

➤ Perhaps the radio networks assisted in their own demise when they provided the initial financial support for television stations and networks, an invaluable training ground for personnel, and models for television network organization, operations, and programming.

7•32 The New Television Networks

The expansion of television networks has to be examined in relation to (1) the technology and implications of coaxial cable and microwave relay, and (2) the actions of individual networks. The required technology for interconnection of television stations was understood by the early 1940s, but wartime priorities and the high cost of installation in relation to a very few stations and receiver owners delayed action. As with existing radio network interconnections, AT&T would provide the means of television networking and rental charges to stations and networks would pay for it—another direct outgrowth of the 1926 radio group–telephone company agreement (see 3.23). The first coaxial television cable (see Appendix B), between New York, Philadelphia, and Washington, D.C., was laid early in 1946. Television stations in the three cities were thus able to carry the Louis-Conn heavyweight championship boxing match by cable, and the Schenectady station received the telecast by relay and rebroadcast it to its small audience. The wide publicity given to that event helped convince many persons that television networks were not far off. By November 1947, the cable was extended from New York to Boston, interconnecting the major population centers of the coastal Northeast. Turning west, AT&T engineers interconnected stations in the East with those in the Midwest by late 1948 so that major cities in the northern and eastern half of the nation were receiving network programs simultaneously. Major interconnection links ran from Boston to Washington, from Philadelphia west to Chicago, from Milwaukee south to St. Louis, and from Detroit to Cincinnati. Expansion of network lines from this point took more time since population centers were farther apart.

In an almost direct parallel to the events of the early 1920s, the embryonic television networks clashed with AT&T over the rates to be charged for use of the coaxial cable. AT&T wished to establish a permanent tariff as soon as possible and discontinue experimental use of the line. When the broadcasters, judging the proposed rates far too high, refused to pay, AT&T cut off the service. Before a compromise was reached, a New York station used old Western Union twisted-pair telegraph lines to carry the video signal of the six-day bicycle races from Madison Square Garden to the studio—just as, more than 20 years earlier, the same licensee had used Western Union wires to carry the same races on radio during a similar battle.

Since the South and the West had

fewer stations and viewers—in spite of a north-south interconnection installed on the West Coast in 1950—AT&T's investment in coaxial cable would take much longer to be paid off. Of course, the cable also could carry thousands of simultaneous telephone conversations, but telephoning also was greatest between major centers of population. Construction began on the main trunk east-west line in 1950. On most of this route point-to-point microwave radio relay towers with the same signal-carrying capacity as the coaxial cable were built about 30 miles apart, so that each tower would receive the signal, beef it up, and retransmit it to the next tower. All this was done at electronic speeds, with only a fraction of a second elapsing from initiation of a television signal on one end of the line to its reception on the other. The line was finished in time for testing in late summer 1951, just 36 years after completion of the first transcontinental telephone line. AT&T had laid plans for an inaugural program on all four networks late in September, but when President Truman was scheduled to address the peace conference officially ending the war with Japan in San Francisco on September 4, that occasion was used to open the coast-to-coast link. Ninety-four stations carried the address to about 95 percent of the country's television sets, with a potential audience of a million viewers. The remaining stations got a delayed program by kinescope recording. A few weeks later, regular national network telecasting began, sharing the one line. One of the first broadcasts was CBS's new *See It Now* series with Edward R. Murrow (see 7.64). It opened with a shot of Murrow in a control room with television monitors showing *live* scenes from both the Atlantic and the Pacific oceans. Television had obliterated distance and opened a window on the world.

The development of television networks differed in several respects from the rise of the radio chains. First, the video webs grew directly and rapidly from radio organizations complete with personnel, funding, and expertise, and they led the television industry from the start rather than following individual stations as radio had done. This also speeded the industry's development. Second, virtually all stations were affiliated with one or more—frequently two or three—networks at a time; the only independent stations in those early years were in New York and Los Angeles. Third, networking developed on a broad front, with no fewer than four competitors throughout this period. As with radio but to a greater degree, the networks initially lost money, with even owned-and-operated stations earning too little to cover the massive capital expenditures, but were operated with the expectation of future profits. Fourth, although radio networks could use conventional AT&T or even Western Union wire lines, television networks depended on installation of coaxial cable or microwave circuits for intercity connections. Fifth, television offered more program variety from the start than radio did in its earliest years (see 7.63 and 4.6).

It was clear as early as 1941 that owners of the more profitable radio networks would undertake the formation of television networks. First into the ring after the war was NBC, which by February 1946 had an informal four-station network of flagship WNBT in New York and affiliates in Washington, Philadelphia, and Schenectady. Since new stations nearly all immediately assumed a primary or secondary affiliation with NBC, by fall 1948 NBC had nearly 25 affiliates throughout the Northeast and into the Middle West, plus some noninterconnected affiliates on the West Coast. This marked the start of the first network season. Before 1948 most stations programmed on their own, receiving only a few programs from the fledgling networks.

Because ABC was the newest radio network and a weak third in importance (see 6.3), it decided to move rapidly into television to attain equality with NBC and CBS. It signed an affiliate in Philadelphia even before opening its first owned-and-operated station. Expansion into television was a heavy investment for a network controlled largely by one man, Edward Noble, who had a majority ownership stemming from his purchase of the Blue Network from NBC in 1943. As a result, ABC floated a series of stock sales in the late 1940s to fund network expansion. Even by 1947 there were rumors that ABC was seeking either a merger partner or a purchaser to gather sufficient capital to compete with better-financed CBS and NBC. Early in 1951, ABC admitted that it was negotiating with International Telephone & Telegraph, CBS, and General Tire & Rubber. The latter two companies planned to split up the network if successful in their bids. But Noble decided against division of the network and turned to a new prospective partner, United Paramount Theaters (UPT), headed by Leonard Goldenson.

UPT was the exhibition side of the original Paramount motion picture company, divorced from the production side as a result of a court mandate following an antitrust consent decree (see 7.91). UPT had money to invest in broadcasting and, after intensive bargaining, ABC and UPT announced in May 1951 that they would exchange stock and merge, with Noble as chairman of the board, and Goldenson as president. The two firms' boards approved the deal that summer and asked for FCC approval, required because transfer of control of stations was involved. The FCC held long hearings on UPT's previous antitrust problems in the motion picture field and their potential influence on its operation of a broadcasting network, and also

weighed the basic question of such concentration of media control. Final approval of the merger in February 1953 gave ABC cash to continue television expansion, which almost had stopped in 1951 for want of capital. But this time ABC was still in a weak third position from which it took more than two decades to recover.

CBS was a relatively small company among American businesses, unable to command the financial leverage of RCA. It entered television strongly backing its own color system and holding back on network expansion until the color decision was in (see 7.821). As a result, unlike both NBC and ABC, CBS had to purchase rather than build most of its O & O stations in major markets. Its choices were fairly limited and the stations it bought could not contribute much to network startup costs.

A fourth television network was *without* radio connections. In 1944 Allen B. Dumont put WABD, named for himself, on the air in New York with announced plans for a postwar television network. After the war, Dumont started WTTG—named after his chief engineer, Thomas T. Goldsmith—in Washington, and pressed ahead with his network plans. His financial support came from a prosperous television manufacturing business. Dumont's plan was to expand along the Atlantic Coast and then pick up affiliates and other O & Os inland as receiver ownership increased and the AT&T coaxial cables expanded westward. Unfortunately, this plan did not succeed. New television stations typically took on a primary affiliation with a major network, usually NBC or CBS, and at best made a secondary or tertiary connection with ABC and Dumont—with Dumont often left out. To earn income, the Dumont network offered to sublease its AT&T-supplied network lines in daytime hours for closed-circuit use at $11,000 an hour, but there were no takers. The affil-

Network-Owned Television Stations: A Changing Cast / The following table shows network-constructed (C), -purchased (P), or -merged (M) owned-and-operated stations from 1941 to date. For multiple ownership rules, see 7.25, 9.84, and 10.85. The cities are listed by their market order as of 1988. For each station entry, the top line gives the current call letters (or the call used when network owned the station minus any "-TV" suffix) and the channel number, while the second line provides the date the station began operation under network control, with a letter indicating whether the network constructed, purchased, or acquired the station through merger. Termination dates are shown for stations no longer network owned. Current O & Os are boldfaced.

Market Rank/City	ABC	CBS	NBC
1. New York	**WABC (7)** **(1948, C)**	**WCBS (2)** **(1941, C)**	**WNBC (4)** **(1941, C)**
2. Los Angeles	**KABC (7)** **(1949, C)**	KTTV (11) (1948–1951, P) **KCBS (2)** **(1951, P)**	**KNBC (4)** **(1947, P)**
3. Chicago	**WLS (7)** **(1948, C)**	**WBBN (2)** **(1953, P)**	**WMAQ (5)** **(1948, C)**
4. Philadelphia	**WPVI (6)** **(1985, M)**	**WCAU (10)** **(1958, P)**	WRCV (3) (1955–1965, P)
5. San Francisco	**KGO (7)** **(1949, C)**	—	
7. Detroit	WXYZ (7) (1948–1985, P)	—	—
8. Dallas–Ft. Worth	—	—	—
9. Washington	—	WTOP (9) (1950–1954, P)	**WRC (4)** **(1947, C)**
10. Houston	**KTRK (13)** **(1985, M)**	—	—
11. Cleveland	—	—	**WKYC (3)** **(1948–1955, C)** **(1965, P)**
12. Atlanta	—	—	—
13. Minneapolis–St. Paul	—	WCCO (4) (1952–1954, P)	—
16. Miami	—	**WCIX (6)** **(1988, P)**	**WTVJ (4)** **(1987, P)**
18. St. Louis	—	KMOX (4) (1957–1986, P)	—
19. Denver	—	—	**KCNC (4)** **(1986, M)**
23. Hartford–New Haven	—	WHCT (18) (1956–1958, P)	WNBC (30) (1956–1958, P)
30. Milwaukee	—	WXIX (19) (1954–1959, P)	—
35. Raleigh-Durham	**WTVD (11)** **(1985, M)**	—	—
38. Buffalo	—	—	WBUF (17) (1955–1958, P)
63. Fresno	**KFSN (30)** **(1985, M)**	—	—

ABC: ABC built the first five stations it owned. Technically, the licenses did change hands when ABC merged with United Paramount Theaters in the 1950s and again when Capital Cities bought ABC in 1985, adding three stations.

CBS: CBS station interests in markets 2, 9, and 13 were minority interests, not controlling shares, ranging in each case from 45 percent to 49 percent. Its short-lived operations in markets 21 and 24 were the only CBS ventures into UHF operation. Of those, the Milwaukee station has since been deleted entirely. The present CBS station in market 2 is wholly owned.

NBC: For the story behind NBC ownerships in markets 4 and 8, see text 8.3. The Cleveland station is the only one owned by the same network at two separate times. NBC's short-lived experiments with UHF are found in markets 21 and 28. Its New York station has used a variety of call letters (WNBT, WRCA-TV, WNBC-TV). GE bought NBC's parent, RCA, in 1986.

Call letters and channels—particularly of stations that started as experimental stations—changed during the years.

All data from two sources: Network Study Staff, Federal Communications Commission, *Network Broadcasting.* 85th Cong., 2d Sess., House Report 1297 (1958), page 575, table 48, and *Broadcasting Yearbook.*

iated stations grew in number, but few took a substantial number of Dumont programs. As the Freeze on new stations (see 7.82) continued, it became obvious that Dumont's lack of network success had more than financial roots. There were too few channels in the major markets, only a handful with as many as four commercial stations on the air. As a result, he became an ardent proponent of providing an adequate number of competitive channels in most markets (see 7.82).

Within a short six years, television networks went from paper plans to operating coast-to-coast entities. The operating pattern of networking was quickly based on the radio model—except that the networks, rather than the advertising agencies, had to bankroll expensive program development (see 7.5)—and has changed little since. Virtually all on-air stations, other than those in the few cities with four or more commercial channels or in the hinterland beyond network service, were affiliated with one or more of the national networks.

7·4   Rebirth of Educational Broadcasting

The outlook for noncommercial educational broadcasting was brighter in 1945 than it had been for 15 years. First, there was a new radio service: noncommercial FM broadcasting. Second, pressures were building for similar channel reservations for educational television. Educational organizations that had nearly been squeezed out of the AM band since the mid-1920s would finally have opportunities and room to broadcast.

7·41   *Expansion into FM*

Placement of the educational allocation on the 88–92 MHz band in 1945 (see 6.82) made educators especially optimistic. The number of FM educational stations on the air grew steadily from six in 1946 to more than 90 in 1952—14 percent of all FM stations on the air. Particularly useful was the NAEB, which helped lay plans for a national FM network of stations, with an interim tape-recording program exchange to serve the many university-owned stations in the Midwest and community and educational institutions elsewhere. The concept of the NAEB Tape Network started when Seymour N. Siegel, manager of New York City's noncommercial AM-FM station WNYC, saw his first hand-made American magnetic tape recorder late in 1946. In 1951, the NAEB received a Kellogg Foundation grant to establish permanent headquarters at the University of Illinois and begin a tape duplication operation to facilitate a noninterconnected "bicycle network," in which one station's programs were delivered to other stations in succession. More than 40 stations soon were participating. Efforts to set up a national interconnected noncommercial FM network, however, lagged until the late 1960s. Some regional networks were established, especially in Wisconsin where by 1952 a state-supported eight-station network provided a full day's programming to most of the state.

Perhaps chastened by earlier experiences with educational AM radio, educational institutions, school districts, and municipalities applied for FM licenses very slowly. Apart from past disappointments and the problem of cost—especially for colleges and universities straining to serve millions of postwar students—potential educational FM station operators were wary of the continuing scarcity of FM receivers (see 7.71) and television's possible effect on radio. Late in 1948 the FCC, recognizing the burden of high cost and the limited or campus-only uses planned by some colleges, allowed educational FM licensees to broadcast with as few as 10 watts of power—enough for a two- to five-mile range—instead of the normal, more expensive lower limit of 250 watts. By requiring fewer technicians with high training, the low-power class added many new stations. Of the 92 educational FM stations on the air in 1952, more than one-third were 10 watt operations.

7•42   Hopes for Educational Television

More than anything else, the lobbying effort for educational reservations for television (see 7.825) forced a not yet completely mended split among educational broadcasters. Some concentrated quietly on radio and other traditional media, while others focused on high-pressure lobbying and fund-raising for educational television (ETV). The problems were immense; few schools or districts could afford television broadcasting, and commercial broadcasters, contending that they could meet educational needs, tried to defeat any reservation of channels for education. That claim had been voiced before, in the late 1920s and when Congress debated the Communications Act of 1934. It sparked educators to work together to convince their boards that ETV was worthwhile, and to maintain the right to seek their own station.

In October 1950, with the enthusiastic backing of FCC Commissioner Frieda Hennock, a successful lawyer who was the first woman commissioner, representatives of several organizations met to form the Joint Committee (later Council) on Educational Television (JCET). With foundation and other support, JCET mounted an intensive campaign before the FCC for educational television reserva-

tions. This organization first was seen as an ad hoc group which would cease operations as soon as the FCC provided the reserved channels, but its need for permanence soon became clear. For one thing, JCET had to fight a two-front battle—getting the needed allocation on the one hand and finding and encouraging potential educational broadcasters on the other. CBS, having to *buy* into top markets because of its late entry into television station ownership, and the National Association of Broadcasters were the chief opponents of reserved channels for education. They contended that educators were not ready for television and that, at most, some UHF channels, not allocated to television, would suffice. Also bothersome were conservative educators who only recently had grasped the potential benefits of radio, let alone far more expensive and complicated television. In addition to lobbying, JCET provided a public information program to mobilize public opinion in ETV's favor until a prestigious cooperating organization, the National Citizens Committee for Educational Television, took over this function.

Reasoning that proof of the lack of educational material on the air would influence FCC decision-makers, NAEB sponsored content analyses of the program fare of commercial stations in major cities. The first, covering a January 1951 week of New York television, found virtually no educational programming. Studies in other cities during 1951–1954 showed the same pattern (see table on page 282).

In spring 1948 at least five universities were active in ETV. The University of Iowa had applied for a station, Iowa State University had received a construction permit, the University of Michigan was providing educational programs over a Detroit station, American University was doing the same on a Washington, D.C., network outlet, and Kansas State University was continuing experimentation. To get coverage over a wide area at limited cost, educators took part in Westinghouse and Glenn L. Martin aircraft company experiments with "Stratovision" in the late 1940s (see 7.823) and provided regular airborne transmissions in the 1960s (see 9.4).

In February 1950 Iowa State's WOI-TV at Ames, Iowa, became the first nonexperimental educationally owned television station. Taking some programs from the networks and selling advertising, the station was able to support a variety of educational programming without expense to the university. WOI-TV soon sent material to other schools for placement on commercial stations until they could have their own educational channels.

For the first time in years, since they allowed AM licenses to slip from their fingers in the late 1920s and early 1930s, educational broadcasters had something to work and plan for—expansion into FM and television. The allocation of specific reserved channels, in the early 1940s for FM and in 1952 for television, saved educators from having to compete for outlets with potential commercial broadcasters. After three decades of commercial broadcasting, nonprofit licensees and potential licensees now had a chance to show what *they* could do.

7•5   Radio Advertising Supports Television

The end of the war saw the end of the excess profits tax and ten-cent-dollar advertising (see 6.5). But now consumer advertising for goods and services would expand as industry reconverted to civilian needs. Advertising time and space sales more than doubled from 1945 to 1952, from just under $3 billion to well over $7 billion. Newspapers continued to receive about 35

percent of the expenditure, with broadcasting in second place with 15 percent. The percentages changed little, but from 1945 to 1952 broadcast advertising volume increased from $425 million to more than $1,078 million. While television got little of that prior to 1950, by 1952–1953 television and radio divided the ever larger broadcast advertising pie about evenly.

However, these overall figures tend to hide a number of important—and, for some broadcasters, serious—internal developments.

7•51   The Changing Economics of Radio

While advertising revenues generally supported FM and television as well as AM, major shifts were occurring in radio advertising. First, advertising agencies had less control of programs, especially after CBS moved in 1946 to take more control of network programs. Criticism about the role of agencies in radio may have been involved, but the rationale for the switch was that it gave the networks more of radio's potential profits, which they needed for their expansion into television. The agencies, on the other hand, while willing to risk capital on developing new radio programs to sell to advertisers, refused to risk the amounts that would be necessary for television programming and reduced all their broadcast programming activities (see 7.52). Another change in advertiser support of AM network radio was that, as audience and advertiser interest in television waxed, interest in network radio waned each year.

While radio advertising revenue was rising, the network share of it, including O & O stations, fell from $23 million to just over $11 million—a drop of more than 50 percent in seven years. The four networks' share went from 47 percent in 1945 to 26 percent in 1952. As early as 1948, more and more programming became sustaining and networks repeatedly cut their time charges, but to no avail. Advertisers changed to local spot radio and other media, including television. Once network radio started to slip, it went fast.

Locally, two conflicting trends spelled financial trouble for many postwar AM stations. As radio went from a national to a local advertising medium, its competitive stance changed. The local radio station proportion of radio income increased from one-third of radio's revenues in 1945 to well over one-half just seven years later. Although the increased revenue was welcome—and overall radio advertising was up too—the pot had to be split among more stations than before and competition with other media was fierce. Whereas up to and during the war radio competed mostly against magazines and a few major newspapers for a national or regional audience, after 1950 it competed directly with the well-entrenched chief local advertising medium: newspapers. There were, of course, twice as many daily newspapers as radio stations at first, but the postwar growth of radio balanced these numbers by 1949, and the gap continues to widen.

The very growth of radio was one of its worst problems, since more stations meant more operators scrambling for available advertising dollars. New stations commonly operated in the red for a longer period, with perhaps one-third of *all* stations losing money in any given year. Stations allowed on the air only during daylight hours suffered in their search for advertisers, as did those with low power or especially restrictive directional antenna patterns. Early in 1947, the FCC issued *An Economic Study of Standard Broadcasting*, which suggested that the financial outlook for radio was dim because the increasing

number of new stations would get ever smaller pieces of the advertising pie. The FCC report suggested that "old" radio markets would have the most difficulty, with new stations taking advertising from old ones; whereas in "new" radio towns the first station would have only the local paper as competition.

Amid these internal changes, however, even though *network* radio was dying, at no time prior to 1953 did *overall* radio revenues fail to grow each year (see Appendix C, table 4). AM radio's share of all advertising income dropped from 15 percent in 1945 to 9 percent in 1952, but the total dollar value for revenue kept increasing.

While AM radio had problems in distributing income, at least it had the income to distribute. The FM station operator usually had little or no income at all. The reasons for FM's failure to attract money during its period of growth were several and serious, and, as will be seen in future chapters, none of them was easily overcome.

Foremost was that advertisers saw FM radio merely as another kind of radio. They were spending on AM, and frequently on television (see 7.52), and could not figure any gain by adding FM. To a large degree, they were right; most FM stations merely duplicated the programming of their sister AM stations, making the FM audience, such as it was, a free bonus. This mass giveaway of FM time was almost fatal to the few independent FM stations that tried to sell advertising. In addition, few FM operations could obtain and show to advertisers information as to how many listeners in the market owned FM receivers. Advertiser analysis of FM receiver sales (see 7.71) suggested a small audience. Stations not duplicating AM programming soon earned a reputation for "fine music" programming, which, although admirable to their faithful listeners, attracted far too few people to attract advertising. Of those stations trying to sell time, few published rate cards, making it clerically hard for prospective purchasers.

Total FM revenues did not pass $1 million until 1948, and at no time during this period was the FM industry collectively even close to the black. A few big independent stations did fairly well in major markets—thanks to loyal audiences providing some direct support for the programming—but most were a drain on their owner's finances. Chiefly because of this drain, in the face of radical adjustments in AM radio, and the continuing demand of television expenses, hundreds of FM stations folded after 1950. Unable to bolster a system that obviously had peaked and now was in decline, broadcasters cut their losses and concentrated on AM and television.

7•52   Video Commercialism

Though soon to become the leading national advertising medium, television began in this country in a limited, local setting, and advertising revenues did not begin to cover programming and technical expense. Thanks to the precedent of more than two decades of radio advertising, advertising promised from the start to become television programming's prime support. The major question was: when would television reach enough big city audiences to make network television worthwhile—for advertisers feared its huge cost. As one research report put it late in 1949, "We seriously doubt that television will ever become a truly nationwide medium (as compared with present radio patterns and service) if it has to depend on the economics of advertising alone."

Television costs in the late 1940s generally ran ten times higher than those for radio. Construction of a station without live production facilities, equipped only for reproducing movies or programs from another station, cost much more than the typical radio station. Construction of a fully equipped station with at least one studio, a film and slide chain, and network capability cost considerably more. Running such a station took many more trained technical and business personnel. A typical network prime-time program cost between $6,000 and $8,000, and even the far less costly local programs ran much higher than radio's finest show. The visual demands of television—sets, lighting, costumes, makeup—and more personnel, the costs of buying, maintaining, and operating television cameras and other studio equipment—all added up. Finally, the costs of laying coaxial cable or setting up microwave links—even in 1949–1950 when the network reached only from the eastern seaboard to the Midwest—led AT&T to raise its hourly charges to at least ten times the comparable charge for radio network lines. These initial construction and continually rising operational costs kept the television broadcasting industry in the red until 1952, and many stations were money losers long afterwards.

Faced with time charges high enough to cover such costs, advertisers moved into television very cautiously, and some agencies stayed out completely, fearing that their standard commission would never cover the work and costs of getting into television. The agencies also abandoned the field of network program development, which they had dominated since the late 1920s. Companies that began to advertise in 1946–1948 aimed to secure a time slot on a given station, to obtain rights to talent or program ideas, to gain experience while the rates were comparatively low, or just to experiment with the new medium. Polled after initial advertising stints, most sponsors had little idea of the impact of their messages, especially since audiences were so limited. Advertisers without radio advertising experience were extra cautious.

Early commercials ran from the "standard" minute format to occasional *pitches* or advertising "programs" of 15 or 30 minutes. Early television commercial experiments sought an effective combination of visual and aural appeal at the least cost. The simplest advertisements were merely signs held before a television camera while an announcer off camera voiced the brief message. Slightly more involved ads combined slides and announcer talk. Even more complex was the silent film with live announcer—the first format to use movement in a commercial. The sound film, especially with animation and other visual sleights of hand, quickly became popular with sponsors, despite its costs. Many sponsors chose the lower costs but greater simplicity and greater risks— particularly if something went wrong during a demonstration—of live television. A television commercial could cost as little as $50 or as much as $10,000 to *produce*—before buying time on which to show it to an audience. Product identification became of utmost importance, and symbols or animated characters introduced on television spread the advertising message by word of mouth and other media. Gillette continued to back sporting events on radio while moving into television. It sponsored the Joe Louis–Billy Conn heavyweight fight of June 1946—the first interconnected "network" program. Bristol-Myers sponsored a series of travel films, becoming the first sponsor of any television series.

During these early years most advertisers sponsored entire programs and became identified with the program and

its stars. For example, Texaco's identification with *Texaco Star Theater*—the Milton Berle show, a Tuesday night institution— sold a lot of gasoline (see 7.63). Although the network often owned the program, full sponsorship allowed the advertiser considerable control. As rising costs made partial sponsorship or spot buying necessary, the advertiser's influence on the program faded.

Television advertising was placed with individual stations until 1949 when the eastern and midwestern branches of the networks were connected. Network advertising became possible as interconnected stations supplied a widespread audience for the same program at the same time. Network advertising accounted for at least half of the 1949–1952 television advertising (see Appendix C, table 5), as local advertising dropped from one-third to less than one-quarter and national and regional spot ads rose in importance. Thus the emphasis of television advertising was set nationally from the start. The first network rate card, issued by NBC in June 1949, offered advertisers 19 interconnected stations for $7,000 an hour; New York alone was $1,500. By adding other noninterconnected stations, which would insert the ad by film, NBC charged around $10,000 an hour for its 34 affiliates. These rates appeared astronomical to advertising agency and advertiser personnel used to radio's rates, but in a few short years they would seem amazingly cheap.

7·6   Programming: Both Heard and Seen

No startling new types of programming appeared in the immediate postwar years. Strong internetwork rivalry in both radio and television marked the difficult transition of many programs from

Network Radio Programming: Fred Allen and "Stop the Music"

Two developments in this period epitomize what was happening to radio network programming—and both affected radio comedian Fred Allen. For 15 seasons Allen's Sunday night hour (later a half-hour) on NBC had been one of the ten most highly rated shows. His first problem was more a public relations man's dream than anything else. One of Allen's key joke targets had been the many NBC vice presidents: Allen noted that their job, on finding a molehill on their desk in the morning, was to make it a good-sized mountain before they left that afternoon. Things came to a head, however, when Allen ran overtime on the April 27, 1947 show and his comment about NBC having a vice president in charge of program ends—who saved minutes and seconds of program time until he had two weeks' worth, at which time he took a vacation—was cut off the air. The problem snowballed the following week when NBC cut off Bob Hope and Red Skelton when each tried to joke about Allen's hassle. Newspaper stories and ads indicated that ratings of all the affected programs were going up. It was a tempest in a small teapot, but the enmity between Allen and NBC brass did not help him later when he was in trouble.

In 1948, ABC began *Stop the Music,* a national music quiz program starring Bert Parks. It placed telephone calls at random across the country. When a person answered, Parks would call to the show's orchestra to "stop the music!," and the caller who could name the tune being played—the assumption was that he or she would have been listening to the program—won big prizes. ABC put this program opposite Allen's Sunday night slot with bad results for the comedian. His show dropped from the top 10 to number 38 while the new quiz show went to the number 2 slot within a few weeks. Genuinely concerned about the effect of the competing show on his audience, Allen posted a bond to guarantee a $5,000 prize to anyone listening to his program who missed an opportunity to answer a *Stop the Music* call correctly. There were several fake attempts to collect, but no genuine payoffs. But the result was that Allen went off the air in June 1949 as the quiz show mania took over much of radio's network audience.

Radio Drama at Its Height

Since all new entertainment media seem to draw from the content of older media (television from the movies, and so on), it is no surprise that early radio featured a great deal of aural drama in addition to other programming.

An entire new art form developed, with its writers (such as Norman Corwin and Arch Oboler), directors (50 years later, Orson Welles's 1938 "War of the Worlds" broadcast still was important news), and actors (many of who later made their mark in the movies or on television). Although long rehearsals were a rare luxury, these programs melded words, voices, music, and sound effects (a new art form in itself!) into audience-gripping experiences.

While some programs (such as the Columbia Workshop) experimented with new forms of radio drama—including the use of blank verse—most dramatic radio programs used more conventional material. Some programs, such as the *Lux Radio Theatre,* used familiar plots and well-known stars from the stage or motion picture screen. Many of these programs later had life on television, but there still are some who would claim that the audio-only *Lights Out* or *Suspense* was more frightening than most recent big-screen horror films, that *X-Minus-One* was better science fiction than its television counterparts, or that an evening soap opera of the caliber of *Those We Love* has never been equaled.

Many programs had extraordinarily loyal audiences. Soaps like *One Man's Family* and *Those We Love,* adventure programs like *I Love a Mystery,* and sitcoms like *Vic and Sade, Myrt 'n' Marge,* and *Easy Aces* all had their fans.

Of special interest during World War II and after was an increase in radio "thriller" programs, aimed primarily at school-age boys (see Appendix C, table 6). Popular programs were *Challenge of the Yukon* (with Sergeant Preston of the Royal Canadian Mounted Police and his dog King,

around the turn of the century), *Sky King* (a modern rancher using his airplane, the "Songbird," as well as a convenient pair of young relatives with whom the audience could identify), *Roy Rogers* (the singing cowboy star), *Straight Arrow* (a western with an Indian point of view), *Mark Trail* (as much nature education as adventure), and *Space Patrol* (young cadets learning the ropes in a future century). Traditionally, the thrillers were "stripped" or "across the board" at the same hour five days a week after school and had the serial element of suspense—hanging from one episode to the next. They were often the focus of radio and cereal package premium offers or items enclosed in cereal boxes. Some of the programs made the transition to television quite well—*Sky King, Roy Rogers, Superman, Lone Ranger*—while others—*Jack Armstrong, Captain Midnight*—either lasted on video briefly or did not make the move at all.

Several programs for parents and older children also soon transferred to television. Crime-detective drama included *Sam Spade, Dragnet* (low-key police realism in Los Angeles), and *Lineup* (police work in San Francisco). Comedy was also strong, especially the new *Our Miss Brooks* (Eve Arden as a long-suffering high-school teacher who loves a biology instructor from afar). While most of these shows were off radio by 1952 or 1953, a few went to television for lengthy runs. Then, they faded out for years, only to be revived for a new audience in the 1970s fascinated by nostalgia. Recordings were sought by collectors, and old radio programs played in the evening, usually on selected stations in larger markets, drawing sizable audiences, especially college students, from prime-time television. As noted in Chapter 9, a few original dramatic presentations for radio appeared in the 1970s, but the late 1940s marked the height, and 1970s drama was mostly not-so-instant replay.

radio to television, and the decline of national radio and the rise of network television produced some programming changes and trends.

7·61   Decline of Network Radio

Before radio networks disappeared from the scene, they had two or three very good years—and before they succumbed had a lively knockdown fight over top stars and their shows. Television helped instigate the radio "talent raids" of 1948–1949. CBS started them when it realized that it was left behind in the race for television affiliates.

Always with a bent for showmanship, CBS, realizing that radio stars might also become popular on television, came up with a novel interpretation of the tax laws. If a star formed a corporation with himself or herself as the major asset, employee, and stockholder, the network could then purchase control of the program from the corporation for a great deal of money and the star would pay a tax on capital gains rather than on straight income, which was more heavily taxed. The first major acquisition came in September 1948, when CBS "stole" *Amos 'n' Andy* from NBC in a $2 million deal with stars Freeman F. Gosden and Charles Correll. CBS then enticed Jack Benny and Edgar Bergen ("Charlie McCarthy") from NBC, and Bing Crosby from ABC. The *Ozzie and Harriet* show and Red Skelton also went over to CBS before other stars started getting better deals from their own networks. Many of the CBS contracts were personally negotiated by CBS Chairman William Paley. The networks tried to counter one another's gains with lawyers and also with advertising and promotional battles in the press. Most of these changes took place in the 1948–1949 sea-

son—coincidentally, the first network TV season—but continued into the following year, when NBC came back with offers to CBS stars and managed to hire away Groucho Marx, Bob Hope, Kate Smith, and Ed Wynn with their respective shows. To prevent further migrations, the respective networks hurriedly placed under long-term contracts each program and star then working for them. Ironically, none of this had a lasting effect on network radio, all but defunct within five years, but strengthened CBS's financial and programming resources for television.

Radio's trend toward cheaper music and quiz shows, as opposed to drama, in prime time was one indication of increasing psychological pressure from television. *Stop the Music* (see page 273), a big money show based on music, was followed by *Break the Bank, Hit the Jackpot, Sing It Again* on the networks and similar programs on local stations. While most network variety and straight music shows used live bands, the local stations, and soon ABC, began to use transcriptions, breaking the old taboo on recorded music over network radio. Music, which always had been strong in local radio, now penetrated daytime network programming. The late 1940s saw development of the *musical clock* format of music, weather, time checks—hence the format's name—news on the hour, and commercials. A local *disc jockey* ad-libbed chatty background material. Indeed, the concept of the disc jockey as opposed to the anonymous, regimented studio announcer began to grab hold in local radio in these years, as declining network programming left stations to their own devices. From a mere announcer playing records, making commercial announcements, and introducing news and other program segments, the *jock* began to build his own on-air personality, reaching informally out to the audience, tailoring

Types of Radio Programs Broadcast in 1946 / Shown below are the program types broadcast by 85 sample radio stations representing all types of AM stations in all sizes of markets, for a week in November 1946. Compare this table to the slightly different data for 1932 (page 120), and 1925 (page 73) to see the continuing major role of music, the increase in drama on the air, and the great increase in news and public affairs programs. This table includes both networks and local programs.

Program Types and Subtypes	Percentage of Time	
Music		**41%**
Old familiar and western	7%	
Popular and dance	26	
Classical and semiclassical	8	
Drama		**16**
Daytime serials	6	
Mystery	3	
Comedy	2	
Other	5	
Other Entertainment		**14**
Women's (homemaking)	1	
Comedy and variety	7	
Quiz and audience participation	6	
Information		**23**
News and commentators	13	
Sports of all types and formats	4	
Talks	3	
Farm programs	2	
Forums and panels	1	
Other		**8**
Religion and religious music	6	
Unclassified miscellaneous	2	
Total	**102%** (error due to rounding)	

For large stations, about one-third of the schedule was local and live, about one-quarter was recorded or transcribed, and the remainder was network material. Non-network stations devoted nearly two-thirds of their schedules to recorded material, chiefly music. Of the full sample of 85 stations, about one-third of the time on the air was sustaining, with little variation by station size. For all but the largest stations, most news came from the networks.

Source: After Kenneth Baker, Table 4 "An Analysis of Radio's Programming," in Paul F. Lazarsfeld and Frank N. Stanton, eds. *Communications Research 1948–1949* (New York: Harper & Row, 1949), pages 51–72, mainly page 58.

music and other elements to build that personality. Though the heyday of such a role was yet to come, the basic idea was set. On New York stations such programs as *Milkman's Matinee* and Martin Block's *Make-Believe Ballroom* were popular. On smaller stations, to the unhappiness of unions and the joy of station management, disc jockeys ran their own control boards and played their own turntables, without the help of an engineer—a combination or *combo* of duties that was to become the rule for radio.

Much of the music on networks replaced faltering daytime serials. While ratings of the long-running titles remained strong, attempts to begin new serials met with little success. Loyal audiences kept this type of program on the air, but fewer people listened than before and during the war. Competing with the soap operas was an increasing number of music, quiz, and human interest programs. One of them, which ran for years on radio and later on television, was *Queen for a Day*, which started on Mutual in 1945. Host Jack Bailey would pick women from the audience who had sad tales to tell, and the audience would applaud according to how miserable a particular life was. The woman garnering the loudest applause measured on a volume meter was crowned queen for that day, and got prizes and, to the extent feasible, whatever she had requested to make her life happier. This sort of participation by the studio audience was not new, but the human interest element of *Queen for a Day* was unusual.

Realizing that it would be hard to support radio programming as advertisers left for television, broadcasters toyed briefly with the idea of direct audience support —or pay-radio. Under this scheme, listeners would pay a nickel a day, $18 a year, to hear programming without advertising. There was strong opposition, and

the plan was shelved when one of its proponents, William Benton—founder of the major advertising agency of Benton & Bowles—became U. S. Senator from Connecticut. The concept of pay-radio was revived briefly in 1947–1948 when several stations expressed interest in a home music service based on patents of the Muzak Corporation, but opposition and lack of favorable interest killed the idea.

The only noticeable trend in radio programming during this period was the slow decline in total network programs and the increase in sustaining programs. A typical network affiliate now originated more programming than it took from the network—a reversal of the two-decades-long trend of network domination. The conviction that television would soon make all radio programming obsolete gave the radio business a general feeling of foreboding. Bright young, and not so young, programming executives looked for opportunities to move over to the newer medium. A straw in the wind was the increase in *simulcast* programs in the 1950s, in which popular radio programs became television programs, with the audio portion carried on radio. Radio listeners reacted with annoyance to unexplained references or disconcerting studio laughter. Many of these programs gave the impression of waiting for the time when they could abandon radio completely.

7•62   FM: Fine Music and Duplication

FM did not offer much that was new (see 7.71). Ever since the standard (AM) broadcasters had convinced the FCC in the 1944–1945 debate that FM would develop much faster if it could duplicate AM shows, the FCC had allowed unlimited

AM-FM duplication. To protect AM advertisers from discrimination, the networks and many local AM stations took this one step farther: co-owned FM stations could duplicate AM programming only if they carried *all* AM programs and advertisements. Since about 80 percent of the FM stations going on the air in the late 1940s were owned by AM stations in the same market, most FM stations carried AM programs. This sharply reduced the motivation of the public to buy FM receivers.

The independently owned-and-operated FM stations—fewer than 90 of the more than 700 on the air—opted for inexpensive musical programs, either background music hardly ever marred by talk or ads, or classical music and commentary. They also started issuing monthly program guides, which detailed the station's offerings for the coming month and often community events as well. In some cases these guides made more money through subscriptions and advertising than advertising carried on the FM station itself.

In many ways, FM was temporarily out of the running. Whether or not it was a "conspiracy," the AM radio broadcasting industry effectively throttled FM development by making the new medium sound just like existing radio but without static and costing more for a receiver. Lacking sufficient unique appeal, FM—not surprisingly—did not attract audiences (see 7.71) and stations began to leave the air (7.22).

7•63   *Early Television Entertainment*

Of all the periods in broadcasting history, two share the excitement of audience expectancy that the American public felt toward broadcasting. The first was in the early 1920s when radio was getting underway, the second was the period when television was beginning to reach across the country. While radio programs continued to attract large audiences, attention was now focused on the generally unexperienced television medium.

In 1945 the few television stations that had started in 1940–1941 returned to the air after wartime suspension with only a few hours of broadcasting a day, mostly on weekday evenings. Much early television programming was radio material with the addition of limited visual elements. Except for some theatrical or short subject films, most programming was live. From 1946 to 1952 television spread into daytime and weekend hours, started to use many different kinds of programming, mostly entertainment formats that had developed on radio, and became dominated by the networks.

As new stations increased competition in a few large markets, and as more television receivers were sold (see 7.72), stations began to offer programs in the afternoons. By the early 1950s, most stations were on the air in the morning and on weekends as well. The increased air time called for more programming material—again, usually local and live. Every station had its cooking expert; a late afternoon children's program host, usually a cowboy or a clown; a general interview host for daytime shows; and a small local news staff. Local programming filled daytime hours and weekend mornings, and networks filled evening hours.

Prior to fall 1948, however, all television programming was local, with only an occasional special event being carried by more than one station at a time. Even network-owned stations operated as local independents. But, thanks to the operators' experience with radio's formats and talent, program variety, even on local stations, quickly approximated radio's, with music, variety, drama and comedy, quiz and other audience-participation shows, newscasts, and special events.

At the same time, video experimented with format, as radio had in the 1920s. Even early limited-length schedules had program hours to fill, and nearly anything could be tried as long as it did not cost too much; television was losing money in this period. Technicians, creative programmers, and performers had an exciting time trying, changing, and discarding formats. There were few restrictions or regulations. The twin aims were to fill air time and to see what would work best.

One format many television executives considered a natural was the motion picture, once the technical problem of converting 24 pictures a second to 30 was solved. But what they had in mind was the short; many doubted that the feature film would ever be available for home television. The pattern of television programming, except for sports and public events, fell into 10- and 20-minute segments rather than radio's 15-minute program pattern. Indeed, until the influx of ex-radio executives in the late 1940s, television scheduled programs in multiples of 20 minutes —long enough for two film reels of 1,000 feet on 35mm and a couple of commercials. Television programmers were uncertain as to how long audience attention could be held. With radio one could use imagination, but with television the audience had to pay total attention, which they believed any program an hour or longer could not command. In addition, the motion picture industry, alarmed over the growth potential of television, refused to sell any post-1948 and very few earlier movies for television showing. This visual media competition increased in the 1950s (see 8.6 and 8.91).

Network programming dominated most evening hours on television from the start, and gradually expanded to daytime and weekends. Program managers quickly learned to fill local off-hours with the least expensive fare they could find—usually short films or off-network or independently produced and syndicated programs. They also ran old network output in fringe hours—a trend which was to increase in importance during the 1950s and 1960s as more old programs on film or videotape became available for reruns.

There was no question that advertiser-supported entertainment would be the basis of television programming just as it had been in radio. Because of its higher costs, getting the largest possible audience was even more important to video than radio, as the key to attracting advertiser money. The NAEB survey of a week on New York's seven stations in January 1951 (see box, page 282) showed that of 564 hours telecast, 25 percent was drama (including 10 percent police/crime and 6 percent western), 14 percent was variety and vaudeville, 13 percent was entertainment for children, 10 percent each was sports, homemaking, and interviews/news, while only 4 percent was informational apart from news. The week covered offered little important programming and only one hour of serious music. Advertising was heavy, especially in the daytime and particularly on the Dumont and NBC stations. A year later the researchers found that crime shows had increased to 15 percent of the total for New York, thus giving 25 percent of the programs over to what the NAEB termed portrayals of lawlessness—crime and western combined—while variety shows had declined. The NAEB later found basically similar conditions in Los Angeles and Chicago television: predominantly entertainment with emphasis on action-adventure drama. Advertising took up about 20 percent of the broadcast time in Los Angeles compared to about 15 percent in New York, including some program-length pitches.

The industry's own major awards stressed entertainment too. The annual Emmy Awards, named after the image orthicon television camera tube, or *immy*, were first made in 1949 for the previous season. They covered only Los Angeles stations for three years and honored entertainment programs only. Six awards were made in 1949 and 11 in 1950. In February 1952 the awards attained coast-to-coast coverage and applied to national content. Six awards that year went to entertainment programs and one to Senator Estes Kefauver (see 7.64).

With the single exception of sports broadcasts (see below), variety programs were more abundant on network television evening prime time than any other type during this period. And, just as radio networks had prospered with *Amos 'n' Andy*, so did television expand on the antics of Milton Berle. Labeled by extensive publicity as "Mr. Television," or "Uncle Miltie," Berle was the host and chief screwball of *Texaco Star Theater*, which began on June 8, 1948, and was amazingly popular—far more popular than the Fred Allen radio program with the same name for the same sponsor—for the next five years. Berle knew how to use the visual "sight gags" possible only on television and was happy to make a fool of himself. He delivered one-liners and topical jokes, used weird costumes and settings, and had top-flight guest stars who joined in the antics. For an audience becoming used to television, the combination was highly entertaining.

A calmer version of the variety show—actually, closer in spirit to vaudeville—was *Toast of the Town*, which began on June 20, 1948, with Broadway gossip columnist Ed Sullivan as host and lasted more than two decades as the *Ed Sullivan Show*. Sullivan was wooden and ill at ease in front of a crowd, but he had a talent for selecting stars, potential stars, and other acts for his program. The very first program featured the then little-known comedy team of Dean Martin and Jerry Lewis, making their television debut amidst a classical pianist, the Broadway composer-author team of Richard Rodgers and Oscar Hammerstein II, and a boxing referee. This mixture of high culture, popular interest, and three-ring circus became the hallmark of several television shows, all modeled to some extent on Sullivan's.

Many other long-lasting television stars started in these early years of network television. Garry Moore began a daytime variety show in 1950 and was on television in various capacities for decades. In Chicago, *Garroway at Large* began in 1949, a low-key program epitomizing the "Chicago School" of television and reflecting the low profile approach of Dave Garroway. Three years later, Garroway was the initial host on NBC's *Today* show. Suffering at first from its early hour of 7 A.M. (ET) and perhaps excessive gimmicks, this live two-hour combination of news, weather, features, interviews, and some performances, programmed with short lengths of viewer attention in mind, made *Today* a lasting fixture. *Today,* and its sister *Tonight* show, hosted over the years by Steve Allen, Jack Paar, and Johnny Carson, are good examples of unique television formats—both devised by NBC's brilliant network chief of the early 1950s, Sylvester "Pat" Weaver.

Another rapidly accepted staple of early television was the talent contest, a radio holdover made more interesting to both performer and listener by the addition of sight. In 1949 television won over the long-running *Original Amateur Hour* (see 5.61), now under the direction of Ted Mack, and radio personality Arthur Godfrey's *Talent Scouts*. Both programs were to last a decade or more on network television, spurring some local station copies.

A common musical format of early television was the 15-minute or half-hour *filler* show—though few called it that then—featuring a singer or orchestra playing popular music interspersed with ads. Local stations offered such programs because they were simple and inexpensive to produce, with few or no guest stars or other gimmicks. Some programs were built around well-known orchestras—Paul Whiteman, Wayne King—and singers—Vaughn Monroe, Kate Smith—but other programs created stars. One was a former Pennsylvania barber named Perry Como, whose relaxed informality—he looked out of place in a necktie—brought him a network program in 1950 after two years as a featured personality in a variety show. However, some well-known performers did not "make it" on the intimate medium of television. One was Frank Sinatra, fresh from a spectacular recording and radio career, who did not do well in television in 1950–1952.

A musical program built more on an idea than on its stars—one of whom was Sinatra—was *Your Hit Parade*, which had run for 15 years on radio when it moved to television in 1950. The program played the top-selling tunes of the week selected by a "survey," plus a few extras. Extensive sets and dances helped maintain interest, especially when the same tunes were in the "top ten" for weeks. When the faster paced rock music came in, often instrumental and dependent for success on the styling of a particular artist or group, this type of program went into decline.

As on radio, little "serious" or classical music appeared on television. *Voice of Firestone*, beginning in 1950, was one of the few such programs regularly shown. Although it was attractive to its sponsor and audience, the network killed the program because the audience was too small to provide audience flow to adjacent programs. A cultural highlight of television's early years was Gian Carlo Menotti's opera, *Amahl and the Night Visitors*, which was commissioned by NBC and first shown on Christmas Eve 1951. An estimated five million viewers, at that time a sizable audience, viewed it in the first of many Christmastime showings.

Music and variety formats were important from the start but never dominated the medium as they did radio. Although they were "good television," they were expensive and not specially suited to the visual element of television. The particular advantage of variety and musical programs in the early days of television was that they could be simulcast on radio with little or no loss in content.

The situation comedy rapidly became a mainstay of television programming. A number of such programs came directly from radio in 1948 and 1949, with others following later. Among the most popular programs were the *Life of Riley* with William Bendix, one of the earliest programs dealing with a blue-collar worker; *Our Miss Brooks*, a wisecracking teacher played by Eve Arden; *The Goldbergs*, written by and starring Gertrude Berg in a Jewish, New York setting; and *Amos 'n' Andy*, with black actors playing the leads instead of originators Gosden and Correll. The last left the air finally in 1966 because blacks resented the stereotypes and whites never related to it as they had to the radio version.

I Love Lucy appeared in 1951 and set a standard for television comedy for decades to come. On the surface, it was just another situation comedy, but the

Changing Patterns of Television Programming: 1951–1954 / The most extensive analyses of early television programming were the series of programming studies conducted and published by the National Association of Educational Broadcasters. Here are the major findings of those content analyses.

Program Type	New York 1951	New York 1954	Los Angeles 1951	Chicago Summer 1951	New Haven 1952
Drama	25%	38%	26%	26%	24%
Comedy	3	9	3	3	4
Crime-detective	10	13	8	5	9
Western	6	4	6	6	—
Domestic/romance	5	4	5	1	9
Other drama	1	8	4	11	2
Music and Variety	18	15	16	12	19
Serious (classical)	1	1	—	} 3	} 4
Popular and light music	3	6	6		
Variety programs	14	8	10	9	15
Other Entertainment	12	8	8	15	11
Personalities	5	3	2	8	1
Quiz shows	7	5	6	7	10
Information	31	24	39	39	36
News	5	6	12	5	12
Weather	—	1	—	1	—
Public discussions and events	2	3	2	3	1
Other information	4	2	4	2	6
Sports	10	5	5	21	11
Homemaking	10	7	16	7	6
Other	14	14	11	8	9
Religion	1	2	1	—	1
Children's shows of all types	13	12	10	8	8
Total	100%	99%	100%	100%	99%
Number of stations:	7	7	8	4	1

Source: Los Angeles Television: May 23–29, 1951, by Dallas W. Smythe and Angus Campbell. (Urbana, Ill.: NAEB, 1951), pages 6, 79; The Purdue Opinion Panel, *Four Years of New York Television: 1951–1954* (Urbana, Ill.: NAEB, 1954), pages 69–75; Donald Horton, Hans O. Mauksch, and Kurt Lang, *Chicago Summer Television: July 30–August 5, 1951* (Urbana, Ill.: NAEB, 1951), pages 15, 25, 27, 55; and Dallas W. Smythe, *New Haven Television: May 15–21, 1952* (Urbana, Ill.: NAEB, 1953), page 106. © National Association of Educational Broadcasters. By permission.

combination of the zany Lucille Ball, her Cuban husband Desi Arnaz (until they were divorced in real life), and a fine supporting cast instantly gave it a high rating. Under varied titles and with changes of cast, the show stayed on the air until the 1970s. One show was particularly memorable—when nature and art combined to have Lucille Ball and "Lucy Ricardo" give birth during the same week. Many years later, the son joined the cast. Another long-lasting situation comedy reflected something of a real life marriage. *Ozzie and Harriet,* formerly a radio program (see 6.65) starred the real family of bandleader Ozzie Nelson.

Other comedy also caught on, particularly programs such as Jack Benny's, or (George) *Burns and* (Gracie) *Allen.* On television, these programs were a mixture of situation comedy and variety. One of the best was *Your Show of Shows,* a variety format with inspired sketches by Sid Caesar, Imogene Coca, and a supporting cast that included Carl Reiner. The unusual 90-minute format focused on Caesar's satiric commentary on everyday life, and became such a classic that a film put together from old kinescopes was successful in the 1970s. Bob Hope did stand-up humor and slapstick sketches on several programs before his own *Bob Hope Show* debuted in 1952. Except for some of the longer variety formats, the television comedy show dealt for a half-hour with a narrow range of predictable, but often funny, situations fea-

Radio to Television: The Goldbergs / Running on CBS television from January 1949 to September 1953, *The Goldbergs* was based on the long-running radio series about the daily lives of a poor Jewish family in the Bronx. The program was built around the character of Molly, played by program creator Gertrude Berg, shown here with Eli Mintz playing Uncle David. Photo credit: Culver Pictures, Inc.

The Great TV Comedy Teams / Two mainstays of network television programming in the 1950s were the situation comedy—epitomized by Lucille Ball (shown here in the original *I Love Lucy* with then husband Desi Arnaz and William Frawley as Fred Mertz)—and the comedy-variety show, one being *Your Show of Shows,* in which Sid Caesar and Imogene Coca brightened television with sophisticated team humor.

Photo credit: Culver Pictures, Inc.

Photo courtesy of National Broadcasting Company, Inc.

turing actor-comedians, frequently unknowns, of varying quality.

Another early television genre was the half-hour crime-detective show, long a radio staple. The best known was *Dragnet*, which began on television in 1951 with a low-key, starkly realistic portrayal of a Los Angeles police team at work. Its musical theme became instantly recognizable, and its approach, use of jargon, and true-to-life characters became a model for many police-based series. Most other early shows, some of which had transferred from radio, were low-budget and relied on violence, before it was of much concern, rather than on plot or characterization.

However, these first years of network television are perhaps best remembered for their path-breaking work in prestige anthology drama. In the 1948–1949 season *Studio One, Philco Playhouse,* and *Kraft Theater* all went on the air live for a half-hour or more each week. "Anthology" programs used a different cast and story each week, staying away from the stereotyping and restrictions of the weekly serial or situation series. Many present television stars, and a number of film and stage personalities, entered television in these programs. Slightly less prestigious were anthology series hosted by a movie star; Ronald Reagan for *Death Valley Days* or Loretta Young, who might play a role in several shows a year. *Studio One*, on CBS, programmed adaptations of novels, stories, or plays, while *Philco Playhouse* aired original drama. These and other drama programs provided a valuable outlet and training ground for stage or radio actors and new plays; the legitimate theater and television were much closer at this time than the motion picture industry and television, partly because most television production was in Broadway's backyard. By 1951 16 anthology series, each presenting a different live drama each week, made

up 12 percent of prime-time programming. While such programs had great audience appeal at first, partly due to the higher income and education of early set owners, anthology audiences began to drop off as program costs doubled from 1949 to 1952 and a larger audience wanted diversion rather than serious drama.

Most early programming for children of school age also used the dramatic format. One popular format was the western program—there were no "adult westerns" until the mid-1950s—including *Hopalong Cassidy, The Lone Ranger,* and *The Cisco Kid*. Originally network programs, they have returned over and over again in syndication. A few of these, produced by far-seeing creators, were shot in color and had a revival in later years, when color telecasting came along. Another children's program type was the science-fiction thriller such as *Captain Video, Tom Corbett, Space Cadet*, or in modified form, the first (1950) television version of *Superman*. This series, based on the hero of radio, comics, and films, was another example of the universality of a good archetype or gimmick.

A favorite of the youngest audiences was the children's equivalent of the variety show: circus, puppet, or animal. Some of them were *Super Circus* (1949), with music, circus acts, animals, and, of course, clowns; the immensely popular *Howdy Doody*, which began in New York in 1947; and the appealing *Kukla, Fran, and Ollie*, a Chicago product with the very human Fran Allison and two Burr Tillstrom puppets. Although attracting adults as well as children, *Kukla, Fran, and Ollie* did not have the audience size of *Howdy Doody*, which featured a western puppet character, host Buffalo Bob Smith, Clarabelle the clown, and a "peanut gallery" of children in the studio. It was a late afternoon "must" until 1960, and Buffalo Bob Smith was able to tour colleges successfully in the early

1970s, reaching the same audience. In 1952 a program aimed at the youngest preschoolers, *Ding Dong School*, offered the conversation, low-key instruction, commercials, and entertainment of Miss Frances, a former professional teacher.

The remaining important format as to time on the air and audience size was sports programming. Boxing, basketball, and bowling were most common in 1948–1949 but dropped sharply within four years. The Wednesday and Friday night prizefight telecasts, together with baseball's World Series and special events in golf and racing, enlarged television's audience in neighborhood bars more than almost any other format. Throughout this period, wrestling and roller derby matches offered more spectacle than sport, and their stars became well-known personalities. These programs, often scripted, were not intended as pure sports contests; wrestling, in particular, was often played as melodrama.

Quiz and panel programs came over from radio as mainstays of both evening and daytime television programming. One of the first was the Goodman-Todson production firm's *What's My Line?*, which began in 1950 and was still showing in syndicated form decades later. Somehow, its panel of articulate celebrities trying to guess a contestant's occupation has held audience interest all this time. Others of this genre were *I've Got a Secret*; the *Quiz Kids,* featuring child prodigies and playing more on human interest than knowledge; *Beat the Clock*; *Strike It Rich*—the show with a "heart line" for announcement of donated special prizes for those with tearjerking problems; *Truth or Consequences*; and *Queen for a Day* (see 7.61). Groucho Marx's *You Bet Your Life* was more a vehicle for Groucho's talk and gags than a true quiz show. Appealing to many who like quiz programs was *This Is Your Life*, where

host Ralph Edwards surprised a famous personality by confronting him or her with persons from the past, who would tell the personality's life story and engage in tearful reunion.

7•64   Rise of Television Journalism

Radio news in the 1946–1952 period was dominated by the newsmen who had reported World War II. Edward R. Murrow, the best known, became a CBS network vice president and member of the board—positions he soon gave up for full-time news work on both radio and television. Network and local newscasts, a legacy of the immediate prewar and war years, continued although reduced in number of hours from the wartime peak. The audience still turned to radio for fast-breaking news. News veterans who broadcast into their second and even third decades were Drew Pearson; Edwin C. Hill; Fulton Lewis, Jr.; Gabriel Heatter; Lowell Thomas, whose nightly news program on NBC and later CBS lasted from 1930 to 1976; and Walter Winchell, who often spoke more gossip than solid news. One of the more famous and long-running news interview programs, *Meet the Press*, began during this period, and so did *Capitol Cloakroom*, which presented interviews with senators and representatives.

Both NBC and CBS televised daily 15-minute newscasts in the networks' first season. The NBC *Camel News Caravan* had John Cameron Swayze narrating clips of newsreel film, while *Douglas Edwards with the News* did the same on CBS. Swayze was to last until 1956 and Edwards until 1962.

Supplementing regular newscasts was a series of special events. In 1951 television covered the welcome given General Douglas MacArthur after President

Truman had relieved him of command in Korea, and the closing ceremonies of the San Francisco peace conference that officially ended the war with Japan. Perhaps the televising of the 1950–1951 Senate hearings into organized crime in the United States made the greatest audience impact. As the little-known Tennessee Senator Estes Kefauver chaired hearings for weeks in various parts of the country, viewers saw the world of organized crime unfold. The high point was the testimony of reputed gangster leader Frank Costello, who demanded that the cameras stay off his face—so they focused on his hands instead. The nervous movement of the hands, tied to what he was saying, clearly portrayed a man under extreme pressure. These hearings informed the country about organized crime—and catapulted Kefauver into the limelight in time for the 1952 presidential race.

The first television public-affairs series on a network was *See It Now*, hosted by Edward R. Murrow and produced by Fred W. Friendly, the same team that had created radio's *Hear It Now*. Beginning in 1951, this weekly half-hour program usually focused on a newsworthy and often controversial (see 8.64) person or news event.

7•65   Election Broadcasting

Another indication of the passing of an age was the 1948 election campaign. That radio still could make or break candidates was demonstrated in a Portland, Oregon, debate between Harold Stassen, former governor of Minnesota, and front-running Governor Thomas E. Dewey of New York, both Republican presidential candidates. The two men debated whether the Communist party should be outlawed. Stassen, soundly trounced for his poorly

expressed liberal views, subsequently lost the primary to Dewey. Given the political realities of that year, at the height of the cold war with the Soviet Union, both Dewey and the polls figured he had the November election in the bag. But on radio, although Dewey certainly was the "better" speaker, with a more traditional "radio voice" than his opponent, President Harry S Truman, he tended to speak over the heads of his audience. Truman had the difficult task of offsetting minority party incursions from Progressive Party nominee Henry Wallace on the Democratic left and States' Rights Party nominee J. Strom Thurmond on the right. Truman's radio talks were sometimes abruptly cut off for lack of funds to pay for the entire program. Both sides relied heavily on spot announcements and short political programs. Truman won a famous political upset and by 1951 became the first President to allow audio recording of his news conferences—at first just for checking reporters' notes but a few months later for direct broadcasts.

The 1952 presidential campaign was the first to be televised nationally and made available to a majority of the population, although some politicians had appeared on camera as early as 1928 and the 1948 campaign had been covered in cities with television. Both conventions were broadcast, and reporters covered preconvention primaries. However, the highlight of the election year—ironic in relation to the events that occurred 22 years later—was the September 23, 1952 nationally televised address of the GOP vice-presidential candidate, Senator Richard M. Nixon of California. Nixon had been accused of having access to a multi-thousand-dollar secret "slush fund" given him by supporters. General Eisenhower, the Republican presidential nominee, was ready to dump Nixon, but the latter asked for a chance to clear himself. That night Nixon, speaking without notes, explained his financial condition in a half-hour, emotional address later called the "Checkers" speech, because of its reference to a pet dog his daughters had been given and which they were going to keep "no matter what." Listeners reacted to the speech with telegrams and calls urging the GOP leaders to keep Nixon on the ticket. The rest of the election was predictable, although neither major candidate came across well on television: Eisenhower because he bumbled and often misspoke or mispronounced words, and Illinois Governor Adlai Stevenson because he often spoke over the heads of his listeners. In Massachusetts, Congressman John F. Kennedy won a Senate seat against incumbent Henry Cabot Lodge after a series of televised debates. The television networks provided detailed election-night coverage for the first time. Nationally, the 1952 campaign proved the value of television spot advertisements for making voters aware of candidates rapidly and was the start of politicians' concern with television *image.*

In five years or so, television networks and stations had developed most of the program formats the medium would use for decades to come. The prior existence of radio had enhanced the growth of television, which used many of the same shows and performers—particularly in these transitional years when many shows were presented on both media at the same time.

7•7 The Increasing Demand for Broadcast Services

Audience attention immediately after the war focused not on television but on radio. Television was no closer in 1946 to most Americans than it had been in 1941

when only a few cities had stations and a few thousand people had receivers. Readers of magazine and newspaper stories knew about television, but immediate ownership was beyond most people. Far more concern centered on radio—how to get those old sets repaired or replaced. After four years of war there was a tremendous demand for radio receivers—and everything else.

7•71 Meeting the Continuing Demand for Radio

As can be seen in Appendix C, table 8, the number of radio families increased by nearly 10 million in the seven years under discussion. In the same period, the number of cars with radios more than doubled so that, for the first time, by 1951–1952 a majority of cars had radio. These bare figures hide a number of interesting developments.

Virtually all manufacturing effort was put into the AM market in the postwar 1940s. More than 50 million AM receivers were made in 1946–1948 alone, to replace older sets and satisfy the major immediate postwar demand. The phenomenon of the multiset household bloomed: as radio prices came down, the number of sets per household increased. Bedrooms and kitchens now contained small $15 table model receivers with plastic cases and simplified internal circuitry, in addition to larger sets in living rooms.

For FM radio, the story was different. Two things combined to hold down receiver production: the 1945 allocation change for FM, which forced major reengineering by the manufacturers, and the great demand for AM sets. Naturally, with all major companies tooled up for the ready-made AM radio market, it got precedence. While more than 50 million inexpensive AM sets came off the lines, FM production was limited to only 2.9 million units in the 1946–1948 period—less than 6 percent of AM production. Furthermore, FM sets cost $50 or more, as they were more complicated and manufacturers had start-up costs to recover.

Much FM production was limited to large and expensive console radios and television sets. Because the new FM band was located just above VHF television channel 6, and because television's sound system was FM, about one-third of the television sets made in the late 1940s had FM radio reception capability built in. This proportion dropped to 20 percent by 1952 and disappeared a few years later. As FM's fortunes waned, FM trade groups and set makers tried to promote FM receiver purchases, but few urban areas had more than 10 percent FM set penetration by 1952. Caught between the lack of audience and too few stations to attract any, FM broadcasting found itself unable to break the vicious circle before the 1960s (see 8.21).

7•72   *Trends in Television Receivers*

Unlike AM and FM radio, television had to build its postwar audience from scratch. Of the perhaps 8,000–10,000 receivers in use before the war, only part were still working when peace came. In 1946, some 6,500 were made and sold in New York, Los Angeles, Chicago, Philadelphia—communities that had stations on the air at that time. Television set manufacture started slowly because of lack of facilities due to AM demand, supply bottlenecks—picture tubes, for example— uncertainty over final spectrum allocations (see 6.82) and the possibility of black-and-white obsolescence due to color, and the chicken-or-egg relationship between high prices and consumer demand. Picture tubes, blown and shaped by hand at first, could not be made in quantity. Some early sets were sold in kit form to meet demand and reduce price. Dumont announced the first postwar television receivers for sale in May 1946, followed several weeks later by RCA. Philco came into the market in 1947 and many others by 1949, although the sales process was confused and unorganized.

A television set was a sizable investment. The typical 5-inch to 7-inch receiver cost from $375 to $500 in mid-1948 —several weeks' pay for the average worker. In addition, the buyer paid an installation fee ranging from $45 to $300, depending upon antenna requirements, and usually invested in a one-year service contract and a roof-top antenna, especially in cities more than 30 miles from the transmitter. Fully three-fourths of early receiver production went to East Coast cities; half to New York. The small screen sizes led to a brisk market in large magnifiers, costing from $10 to $60 each, set in front of the receiver to enlarge the picture. In 1949 and 1950, larger screen sizes were made, with the 10-inch set becoming the standard, although Dumont, long a leader in this area, offered a $500, 20-inch tube (not complete set) as early as 1947. Zenith introduced a set with a circular picture—actually almost all tubes were circular but covered with a rectangular mask—and garnered a good portion of the market in 1949–1950 before rectangular tubes were marketed. Although the screen looked larger, the circular shape chopped off much of the sides of the rectangular picture being transmitted. As set sales increased and competition became stronger, the cost of receivers dropped so that a typical small-screen set cost only $200 by the early 1950s. Manufacture was slightly limited after 1951 by the Korean War military equipment demands (see 7.821).

TV Receivers from the Early 1950s / As noted in the text, the earliest (1947–1950) television receivers were expensive, often costing several hundred dollars. These newspaper ads of the early 1950s taken from metropolitan papers give an idea of what was available then for what price. All sets then were black and white.

9-PC-41
Projection $795
model
Plus $3.61
Fed. Tax

Motorola

TABLE
MODEL
TELEVISION
WITH
BIG 16-INCH
PICTURE!

- Big-as-life pictures on 16-inch rectangular tube!
- Easy to operate. Just two simple controls!
- Built-in antenna gives powerful performance!
- "Performance Tested" to insure you long, dependable service!
- Beautifully styled, modern, walnut-effect bakelite cabinet!
- Pictures clearer than ever, just as the TV camera "sees" them!

MODEL 17-T-3

$219.95
Plus
Tax and
Warranty

Big 12½-Inch Television!

new
"BROADVIEW"
SCREEN
gives 25% more
picture area

SIMPLIFIED
CONTROLS
even a child
can operate it!

Brighter,

clearer, steadier pictures

by *Motorola*

Here's a big screen permitting an entire roomful of people to see comfortably. Features the new BILT-IN-TENNA—no installation in "good signal" areas. Here's cabinet beauty to complement your lovely furniture. Hand rubbed to satin-smooth "piano finish." Mahogany or blond. See it, hear it, *compare* it today. CONVENIENT TERMS.

New Zenith TV Console

Model 2438R. 165 sq. in. "2-in-1" screen. 18th century cabinet, mahogany veneers and hardwoods. Only

$319.95
Plus Fed. Tax

Model
Shown
Only
$279.95
$6.00 in-
cludes 1 year
parts warran-
ty and tax.

Still, the television audience increased (see Appendix C, table 9) from almost zero to more than one-third of the nation's homes in the few years covered in this chapter. As the number of set owners grew, the market became more organized and inadequate manufacturers and sales organizations were squeezed out. The installation charge came down sharply or was eliminated. In 1952 not only was a television receiver a far better product, with a much larger screen, but it sold for perhaps half of its 1948 price. Most people saw their first television program in a public place, either a store window or a neighborhood bar—"We have TV" signs were a surefire come-on, especially just before a major sports event. With that initial exposure and increasing advertising by television stations and sales outlets, a few families made the plunge—and then more followed.

The receiver soon dominated the early television home. It usually went into the living room, relegating radio to another room, and became the center of attention for the family, and their non-television-owning friends. Some families without sets installed outside antennas in order to keep up with their neighbors. For the first week or two the family looked at virtually every program and marveled at the phenomenon. Slowly, the fascination declined, and individual family members began to watch specific programs. In a very short time, television replaced most radio, reading, and weekend movies—to the detriment of the other media.

Television's expansion was much faster than radio's: radio had taken a decade to reach a 33 percent penetration, but television managed it in only seven years. Initially, the large cities and the Northeast generally had more sets than elsewhere. Although people in rural areas without stations, particularly in the South and

Midwest, went to great lengths to receive distant signals, these regions naturally had the slowest rate of television set sales.

7•73 Developments in Audience Research

In the late 1940s, the last years of AM radio hegemony over broadcasting, two excellent major surveys of public attitudes toward radio and its content appeared, both under the direction of Paul Lazarsfeld. *The People Look at Radio* (1946) showed that the vast majority of persons surveyed in 1945 thought the radio did a good or excellent job, ranking higher than the churches, newspapers, schools, or local government. An expanded and updated survey published in 1948 as *Radio Listening in America* showed that, while television was just getting underway, the majority of listeners still liked radio, but it had slipped in favor of newspapers as the prime source of news now that the war was over. These volumes provide a useful picture of the radio audience just before television radically changed audience habits and views.

Prior to 1950, radio ratings were dominated by C. E. Hooper's "Hooperratings," based on coincidental telephone call surveys. With the coming of television, A. C. Nielsen's meter-produced ratings (see 5.73 and 6.72) began to cut into Hooper's near-monopoly. Clients endlessly debated the merits of the two systems. Advertisers and broadcasters complained about having to pay for two different services doing the same job, and Hooper began losing clients to Nielsen. Early in 1950 Nielsen purchased the other's national rating service, leaving Hooper free to work in local individual markets but giving Nielsen a virtual monopoly over national television ratings. Nielsen has provided meter-based national television ratings ever since, although other companies later came into the field (see 8.72).

Until 1952 most research into television viewing habits was eminently practical: who owned sets, how much they watched, and what products and services they bought. A New York advertising agency began systematically and periodically to poll a New Jersey town of 40,000 people (dubbed "Videotown") near New York City to see how television was changing the population's lives. The surveys showed high satisfaction with television and increasing amounts of time spent watching it daily. Families tended to stay together more of the day because of television, but researchers realized after a while that a family watching television together did not necessarily communicate more; they just sat in silence and watched, sometimes with their television-less visitors.

Television was recognized as different in many ways from radio. For one thing, since it required less imagination than radio, it focused attention more than radio. Television made personalities appear more human when seen as well as heard, gave the viewer a sense of sharing in events, and appealed to young children. These capabilities forewarned social scientists of its potential impact on families and American life.

Each of the networks issued research reports for agencies and affiliates, and these today make excellent snapshot views of television's progress. They show that the early television-owning American household was not typical but had a higher income, needed for the purchase of expensive receivers, and above-average education. Early audience profiles also showed that television-owning families were larger and younger, spent more time every day with television than with all other media

combined, and bought more products in general and cars and appliances in particular. But most Americans, especially those removed from large cities or the Northeast, probably did *not* own a television set.

At least one concern of the 1970s cropped up in the first days of television: its effect on young children. Suddenly the home environment harbored a medium with sound and pictures less easily controlled than other media and attractive to very young children. Television critic Robert Lewis Shayon's *Television and Our Children* suggested that the answer to such problems lay in family control over their children's viewing habits and in organized community action to encourage better children's programming and less violence on the air. Such arguments grew louder in the decades to come (see 8.73 and 9.72).

7•8   Regulating Expansion

The Federal Communications Commission found itself in the thick of the broadcasting transition that marked the 1945–1952 period. Probably the most important and certainly the most time-consuming controversy was television allocation—how to apportion sufficient channels to allow a choice of content in most regions without sanctioning interference from or to stations already on the air. At the same time, the commission issued its clearest statement yet on "public service responsibility" for broadcast licensees; the commission's staff fretted over the increasing number of radio stations trying to divide a relatively static advertising pie; a Chicago union leader was tying broadcasters into knots; and the industry was acquiescing in the blacklisting of entertainers accused of communist sympathies.

7•81   *Mess in the Making:*
        1945–1948

As the war ended, there were enough television channels and enough skepticism about television's future in the smaller markets that an applicant could easily obtain a license for a frequency. However, in larger markets, particularly in the crowded Northeast, there were not enough channels. The FCC engineering staff tried to apply sound engineering standards in assigning channels to the various cities and to avoid co-channel interference by allowing sufficient geographical distance between stations on the same channel. Their plan, based on the May-June 1945 decisions (see 6.82), specified the locations at which stations could be licensed, market-by-market, and the number of stations, or channels, at each location. This would ensure some coverage for rural areas and would ease the administrative burdens on both commission and applicant, since expensive engineering surveys would be unnecessary. The only alternative would have been a grab bag analogous to the unsatisfactory AM radio solution: letting applicants fight for what they considered the best channel in the best location, no matter how many stations in other towns thereby could not be started. Since the number of channels, 13, had been determined, the only other major variable was the distance between stations operating on the same or adjacent channels. Power and antenna height were less important variables (see Appendix B, Waves, etc.). Although FCC engineers hoped to allow a margin for safety against interference by 200-mile co-channel spacing, such spacing would give New York City only four channels if the rest of the congested portion of the Eastern Seaboard was to get adequate service. This meant that New York City—always in need of more stations because it was the nation's largest market—would not have three of the total seven channels available. (Since adjacent channels would give interference if used in the same market, only 7 of 13 could be used in any one city.) The FCC quickly found itself in a political box: New York *had* to have the maximum number of stations, yet, with Congress still dominated by rural interests, service had to be provided to smaller communities.

The compromise solution, reached after several trials, gave New York its seven channels by eliminating two of the three "community" (low-power) channels and, among other compromises, by locating (in the FCC's own words) "television stations . . . somewhat closer together in the eastern part of the United States than was done in the original Commission proposal." No allocation plan gives something for nothing. In this case, the price of seven channels in New York was neglect of the safety factors previously deemed necessary to protect television against tropospheric interference. Instead of the 200-mile separations proposed originally, the plan adopted by the commission toward the end of 1945 (see 6.82) called for separations of only 150 miles. This distance took care of anticipated interference but made no provision for the possibility, particularly at the height of the sunspot cycle, of radio waves traveling, as Armstrong and others had warned, through the lower atmosphere (troposphere) and causing very bad interference between stations on the same channel.

The FCC took steps in 1947 to solve two other problems with the 1945 television allocation plan. First, only one community channel was used solely by television; the other 12 channels were shared with the safety and special services. Although the assignments were based on mutual noninterference, this was obviously an impossible standard. Second, establishment of television in Canada and Mexico conflicted with U.S. television.

After a number of revisions, the commission decided in May 1948 to delete channel 1 (44–50 MHz) and turn it over to the safety and special services. In exchange, the other television channels would be free of fixed and mobile services sharing. Although the television industry made a protest as a matter of form at the loss of channel 1, it generally agreed that 12 *exclusive* channels were preferable to 13 channels if 12 of them were subject to sharing. The safety and special services also were pleased at this compromise—until they outgrew channel 1 and were permitted to share some lower UHF television channels in the most congested areas and take over—together with common carriers—the upper 15 UHF channels in 1970. The border station problem was solved by international agreements governing assignments of channels to cities within 250 miles of the border with Mexico in 1951 and Canada in 1952.

The chief problem remained. As television grew in popularity, the demand for new stations became insistent. The Television Broadcasters Association pushed for the seven channels in New York City. The commission, apparently unable to foresee the consequences of its actions, repeatedly narrowed the mileage separations between stations on the same or adjacent channels. Although broadcasters were pleased to receive grants of the new channels, safety factors had been thrown away.

By fall 1948—less than three years after the television broadcasters and potential broadcasters started putting pressure on the FCC through the public and individual congressmen to get stations for *their* city—it was obvious that a major error had been made. As more stations went on the air, and as the sunspot cycle reached its zenith, the shortcomings of the 1945 allocation table became unbearable. For example, mutual interference between stations in Detroit and Cleveland, a little more than 90 miles apart, was making reception impossible well into the heart of each city. The situation called for drastic action, of a sort not seen since the FRC acting as "traffic policeman of the airwaves" had cleaned up the AM band using the Radio Act of 1927.

In September 1948, with only 50 or so stations on the air but with an additional 50-plus construction permits outstanding, the effect of narrow separations, heightened by the sunspot phenomenon, led to a flood of complaints from broadcasters and the public that the FCC could not ignore. After hearings, on September 29 the commission "ordered applications for new TV stations placed in the pending file." They remained there, not for the six to nine months suggested by FCC Chairman Wayne Coy, but for nearly four years. The reasons for instituting the now-famous *television Freeze* were not the only reasons it took four years to lift. The Freeze provided time for RCA and CBS to continue their fight over color television, committees to resolve the use of UHF frequencies, pressures for an educational channel reservation system to mount, and interference problems to be settled.

7·82   The Television Freeze: 1948–1952

The "temporary" Freeze on new television stations lasted until April 14, 1952. Although the FCC acted upon no new applications, it allowed stations holding construction permits to go on the air. The people that had television enjoyed expanded programming, but people in other areas looked forward to the end of the Freeze as ardently as the potential licensees.

Arrayed against those wishing access to a competitive television structure were the 108 "pre-Freeze" stations, including the outlets owned and operated by the networks. This group worked in various ways to maintain the Freeze and hold off potential competition, while promoting scarcity and inequality of television channels to ensure the least competition when the Freeze eventually lifted. Manufacturers, too, were glad to sell millions of sets, using well-understood prewar technical standards, to viewers of pre-Freeze stations.

The maneuverings of the haves and have nots focused on a lengthy series of commission hearings, which determined the eventual end of the Freeze and future shape of television. These hearings covered five substantive issues, related chiefly by their differential values to the two groups involved. The issues, not in any special order, were (1) color television standards, (2) reduction of tropospheric interference, (3) possible spectrum locations for additional channels, (4) city-by-city assignment of channels and criteria for these assignments, and (5) educational television channel reservations.

7•821 Color Television Standards Hindsight tells us that color television standards might better have been considered separately from the main Freeze hearings. Regardless of the motives of participants in the imbroglio, the color phase of the hearings delayed the end of the Freeze by more than a year. The color controversy was incorporated into the general hearings partly because it raised problems of spectrum allocation until 1949, when both CBS

and RCA managed to make their respective systems work within the 6 MHz–channel bandwidth in use for black-and-white television.

Although CBS had lost round one of its fight for a wide-band color system during the 1944 hearings (see 6.82), the setback did not stop the firm for long. While CBS's main field of endeavor had been radio broadcasting, it recognized the potential of television and wanted a place of leadership in the new medium similar to RCA's. Despite the conclusion of most electronic manufacturers and engineers that commercial color television was years in the future, CBS sought to marshal public opinion behind the notion of "color now." In doing so, it may only have confused prospective set buyers. RCA, in order to protect its own extensive investment in color research, was forced into a public demonstration of its admittedly outmoded (1941) system. By showing its system, although RCA protested that a good electronic color system—as contrasted to the mechanical CBS system—was at least five years away, RCA admitted that there was something to the CBS claims after all.

During the hearings, CBS had to bear the burden of proof not only against the public's growing investment in the VHF black-and-white system but against RCA's improved all-electronic compatible color system. Because the CBS system was not compatible, viewers with black-and-white sets would be unable to pick up color telecasts in monochrome. Another drawback was the large, noisy, and hard to synchronize and maintain mechanical color wheel used to filter, transmit, and reconstitute the primary colors in sequence, but CBS said that could be overcome by further engineering work. In spite of repeated public statements that RCA would sell its color kinescope (picture playback) tubes to any-body, CBS never was able to purchase any in order to demonstrate that electronic rather than mechanical color reconstitu-tion devices could be used at the receiver end.

RCA, in addition to publicizing the advantages of all-electronic compatible color, which it continued to perfect over the next several years, questioned CBS's motives in asking for immediate color standards. RCA representatives main-tained that the industry, happily making black-and-white sets, should agree on new standards before the public heard about them. This was, of course, a complete re-versal of RCA's position during the 1940 standards fight, when RCA tried to force through its own standards for commercial use in the face of violent opposition from the industry.

In hearings over its petition, the fringes of the industry supported CBS and the major established firms such as Du-mont and Philco supported RCA. The FCC tended to depend on older elements of the industry in preference to CBS, with its lim-ited experience in engineering and man-ufacturing. The same established compa-nies also supplied most of the leadership for the RTPB and RMA committees, which the FCC continued to follow.

However, after long and acrimoni-ous hearings and demonstrations, the commission approved the CBS color sys-tem in October 1950, over the entries of RCA and Color Television, Inc. Neither RCA, which appealed the FCC decision up to the Supreme Court and an 8-0 decision in 1951 upholding the commission, nor the rest of the manufacturing industry would accept this decision. John Crosby, col-umnist for the *New York Herald Tribune*, summed up the color decision in his Oc-tober 24, 1950, column:

And God said, Let there be light: and there was light.

And God saw the light, that it was good: and God divided the light from the darkness.

And the FCC saw color and said, "Let there be color," and there was color. Or at least there was an edict decreeing color. And the public tried to divide the black and white from the color and discovered only confusion. Next to the FCC's, God's problem was com-paratively simple.

Few CBS-standard color sets ever were made, although the company pur-chased some manufacturing facilities to make its challenge of RCA credible. While manufacturers were balking at the idea of constructing noncompatible, clumsy small-screen television sets and paying CBS a royalty for the privilege, RCA worked hastily to improve its own system. CBS rec-ognized that its meager support would soon evaporate, since the new compatible RCA system would not disrupt existing television broadcasting, stop the profitable manufacture of black-and-white sets, cause public resentment over sets that would become obsolete overnight—even though CBS proposed that monochrome televi-sion on the VHF band be continued, for a while, at least—or cost the manufacturing industry additional royalties. Accordingly, the decision by the National Production Administration (NPA) in October 1951 that color television was "nonessential" to the stepped-up Korean War effort had the ef-fect of getting CBS off the hook. The FCC also learned that it was unable to exercise practical control over the manufacturing industry and force the innovation of some-thing the industry did not want.

Although the FCC rescinded its 1950 order approving the CBS system and in December 1953 approved RCA color—

in the slightly improved and modified version recommended by the National Television System Committee—manufacturers showed almost as little inclination to go ahead with RCA as with CBS color. The industry had no reason to consider color until the vast market for monochrome sets became saturated, and the cost was too high—$1,000 and up per set—and there were too few color programs for the public to buy many of the complicated RCA sets.

The war between CBS and RCA really had ended with the NPA decision to halt production of CBS color-standard sets. After some bitter words between RCA's Sarnoff and CBS's Stanton, even CBS joined the NTSC effort to perfect a compatible color system. Although CBS had not been able to innovate its color system, in a sense it had won the war. Not only had the NPA order saved it from incurring serious loss, but it had gained the time needed to compete with RCA in the television broadcasting field. RCA inherited the mantle of possessing the color system but, as we shall see later, could not persuade the broadcasting and manufacturing industries to accept color fully for more than a decade. As a footnote to the CBS system's demise, it should be noted that specialized medical closed-circuit television units used the slightly better color rendition of the CBS system for many years and that color pictures transmitted from the moon in the early 1970s came from CBS-type cameras—built by RCA! There were a number of self-satisfied smiles around CBS when the moon pictures came through.

7•822 Interference Reduction Since the most obvious cure for tropospheric interference is increased mileage between stations on the same channel, this problem

could be and was solved within a few months, although the specific solution was not promulgated until the Freeze ended in 1952. Technical developments, such as *off-set carrier*, by making it easier to tune stations also would alleviate the problem without affecting home reception. Instead of the 150-mile or less separations it had approved in 1945–1947, the commission toyed in 1949 with extremely rigid standards of 220-mile VHF co-channel separations. In its 1952 *Sixth Report and Order*, the FCC actually imposed 190-mile co-channel separations over most of the country. In the Gulf states, where propagation characteristics were different, the new standard was 220 miles. In the crowded Northeast, the FCC had to compromise, with a 170-mile standard. No station had to leave the air, but several were moved about on the VHF band in order to eliminate the worst examples of interference, such as in the Detroit-Cleveland area (see 7.81).

The commission held firmly to these new standards after they were established. Having once been burned, it was unwilling to reduce safety margins again, even though many of its prediction formulas came under attack as being inconsistent with measured characteristics of signals. To provide a third channel for Pittsburgh, it created a complicated new rule allowing a shift in assigned channel to a community within 15 miles of a listed major community rather than supporting a co-channel situation short-spaced by little more than a half-mile.

Most observers applauded the greater separations, particularly the 108 "pre-Freeze" stations, which would face less competition from new licensees. However, parties that wished to obtain VHF channels after the Freeze objected, claiming that a bit of interference was a small price to pay for healthy competition and multiple program sources, since increases in separation would mean fewer local stations.

7·823   *Obtaining Additional Channels*   To provide for a competitive nationwide television system, the commission had to find more channels for television. Increasing co-channel mileage separations reduced the number of stations possible on the 12 remaining VHF channels and made the problem worse. However, even those in favor of greater access were not in favor of starting in the untried UHF band, with its concomitant problem of receiver conversion. Accordingly, the FCC made unsuccessful attempts for a number of years to obtain additional VHF channels from the military and the FM band. Although for a while in the mid-1950s FM, then in the doldrums, had to fight hard to retain the 88–108 MHz band (see 8.21), the FCC was unable to overcome the political support FM enjoyed as a legacy from Armstrong's efforts. The military flatly refused to turn over a substantial part of its spectrum to television, even after several requests and studies. The Department of Defense argued that the "national security" required the reservation of these frequencies, even if they were not in full use.

The "outs" made some proposals that would have shoehorned in additional stations through less than maximum power, directional antennae, and reduced mileage separations. The FCC, with the growing administrative problem of allocation of the AM band as a warning, and also with a tender regard for the established service areas of the pre-Freeze stations, turned down these proposals.

Of necessity, the question became not *whether* to utilize the UHF band (470–890 MHz) set aside in 1945 for television experimentation and future broadcasting

but, rather, *how much* of it to use. Proposals ranged from a half-dozen channels up to the maximum possible, 70. To counteract the advantages enjoyed by the established pre-Freeze stations, it was suggested that *all* television be moved to the UHF band. The commission rejected this proposal, because of the already huge investment in VHF transmitters and receivers and because the propagational characteristics of the UHF band were such that some persons in rural areas would lose reception if the bands were changed.

The commission decided to allocate the entire 70 UHF channels to television but then restricted the upper end (channels 70–83) to low-power translators and other devices that provide television service inexpensively to smaller communities, and eventually turned it over to other services (see 9.22). Of extreme importance, the commission made no move to transfer all television from the VHF to the UHF bands, in spite of vague proposals to that effect that it had made in the mid-1940s (see 6.82).

One interesting experiment, with some implications for later proposed use of space satellites for direct broadcasting, was *Stratovision*. This system, originally proposed by Westinghouse and the Martin aircraft company, consisted of a standard television transmitter built into a transport airplane, which circled at 30,000 feet while sending out television signals. Tests conducted in 1946 and afterward (see 7.42) showed that transmission of this kind could achieve reliable coverage over a circle of from 50 to 200 miles in diameter. Once, the aircraft was used to link up the eastern and midwestern isolated segments of AT&T's coaxial cable network so that the Midwest could enjoy the World Series. Stratovision saved money over the equivalent ground transmitters, but it interfered with assignments of frequencies to ground-based stations and did not accommodate differences in population density. Analogous to AM clear-channel stations and eliminating much of the need for both coaxial cables or microwave linking stations and the many small stations otherwise needed to cover the nation, Stratovision must have seemed attractive to the FCC. However, the same small station operators and members of Congress who earlier had managed to restrict clear-channel AM stations to 50,000 watts objected on the grounds that Stratovision might be monopolistic. The commission dropped the idea when it found that some 20 channels would be needed to supply the entire nation with four signals and that the necessary perturbations of the aircraft would disastrously affect the principles of "fair, efficient and equitable distribution of television facilities to the various communities." Westinghouse donated the equipment to a university, and the principle was ignored until Midwest Program on Airborne Television Instruction (MPATI) started flying in the 1960s using nonbroadcast channels (see 9.4), and proposals for direct-to-home space satellite broadcasting became more frequent in the 1970s (see 9.1).

7·824 City-by-City Assignments Despite the pleas of potential broadcasters hoping for equality of access to a given community and of ABC and Dumont, the FCC finally assigned channels to communities by a system of priorities. These priorities ignored population density, the key to successful advertiser-supported station operation, and adopted a strict interpretation of Section 307(b) of the Communications Act, which calls for a fair geographic apportionment of channels to the several states and to the United States as a whole. Multiple services or programming choices for the public were only a secondary priority.

The published priorities were to provide (1) at least one television service to all parts of the United States; (2) at least one outlet for local expression (station) to each community; (3) a choice of at least two services to all areas; (4) at least two program outlets or stations to each community. Assignments of channels which remained unassigned would follow the same pattern. Educational reservations (see 7.825) would be assigned to major educational centers, and to larger cities in a proportion of one educational for every four commercial assignments. Above all, the boat would not be rocked if possible: no existing station would be moved from a VHF to a UHF channel, or even from a lower (channels 2–6) to a higher (channels 7–13) VHF channel. However, under the FCC plan, almost all cities would be intermixed with both UHF and VHF channels assigned in the same community.

Channels would be assigned through an *assignment table**—a technique devised by the commission in the mid-1940s for both television and FM. Without such a table, an applicant for a station in an eastern state would be in competition with all applicants east of the Mississippi. The FCC had successfully defended this technique in court and further strengthened it in the preliminary (1951) and final (1952) reports ending the Freeze, by holding that applicants for a channel not specified in the table would have to secure an

---

*Although the FCC originally referred to a television "allocation table" when distributing channels city-by-city, it really meant "assignment table," the term used in the United States for many years but replaced in the early 1980s by "allotment." This chapter will use the term *assignment* for the earmarking of a channel for a given community or user, and the term *allocation* for the setting apart of a group of channels for a given service, such as television. (See Appendix B.)

amendment through lengthy and costly rulemaking proceedings—a major deterrent to making such changes. The only flexibility was to permit unlisted cities to apply for UHF "flexibility" channels and, as mentioned earlier, to allow an applicant in an unlisted town within 15 miles of a listed city to apply for assignment of a channel that met the mileage separation rules for the town in order to serve the city. Los Angeles joined New York in having seven VHF channels and several UHF channels assigned, largely because most of the VHF channels were already on the air. No other cities had as many VHF channels assigned.

The maneuvering among applicants for real or imaginary advantages of channel assignment or speed of obtaining a license could fill another book. City fought city, existing station fought applicant, and applicant fought applicant—but all parties grew weary and accepted most commission decisions, even Dumont, which had proposed its own nationwide assignment scheme based on different separation standards. The adopted assignment table, as amended in some cases, still determines local availability of channels.

7•825 *ETV Reservations* Educators hailed a suballocation within both the UHF and VHF bands to noncommercial educational television broadcasting, but it further restricted the number of channels assigned for commercial use in a given community. Reservation of educational channels in the assignment table was an advance over the practices on the AM band, where some 200 stations licensed to educational institutions in the 1920s had shrunk to a bare two dozen in the 1950s (see 3.4, 4.4, 5.4). However, it did not go as far as the FM separate educational allocation (see 5.4) of 20 specifically inviolate channels contiguous to the commercial FM band, which any FM set could receive.

The ETV suballocation, or rather assignment, criterion was promoted almost singlehandedly by Commissioner Frieda Hennock who, with the aid of various educational organizations (see 7.42), persuaded the commission to adopt a reservation principle for educational television. Educators gradually realized that this might be their only chance to obtain broadcast channels and soon became an effective lobby. First enunciated in 1951, the criteria for establishing a reservation were explained in the FCC's *Sixth Report and Order* of April 1952 (see 7.83): When more than three VHF channels were assigned to a city, one would be for education. Forty-six educational centers also would receive a reservation, 23 of them the only VHF channel in the community. A UHF channel would be reserved where a given market, not an educational center, had *fewer* than three VHF assignments or where all VHF channels already were in use. Unlike FM, the reservations could be for any of the 82 television channels.

Opposition to these reservations was strong but unsuccessful. It came chiefly from Dumont and others who were fearful of establishing channel scarcity in major markets. Other objectors included the NAB, which suggested—much as in 1934 (see 5.4)—that "voluntary cooperation" between broadcasters and educators would be satisfactory to both, and Senator Edwin Johnson (D-Colorado), who had led a congressional fight for the approval of CBS color and a speedy end to the Freeze, and whose desires for competitive broadcasting led him to suggest that commercial licensees be required to give a certain amount of time each day to educators. The commission rejected the latter proposal on legal grounds, as well as proposals by educational institutions to make ETV stations partly commercial so that they would be self-sustaining.

In a final move, possibly inspired by President Truman's emphatic support of ETV, the FCC refused to place a definite time limit on using the educational reservations, although procedures for protesting them or changing them to commercial channels were to have been established after a year. Slow-moving educational institutions still had an opportunity to obtain a television license three decades later. By 1988, more than 330 ETV—or, as they have since come to be called, *public television*—stations were on the air, roughly one-quarter of the television stations in the United States. Their existence allows commercial stations to ignore to some extent the discriminating ETV audience and also helps restrict potential commercial broadcasters from some markets.

7•83   The Sixth Report and Order: Seeds of Future Problems

On April 14, 1952, more than 42 months after the start of the Freeze, the decisions described above were made public and formal as the FCC issued its *Sixth Report and Order*. That it took the commission *six* "Reports and Orders" to reach final decisions suggests the complexity of the issues. The FCC had to deliberate in the face of strong urging by manufacturers, smaller networks, new station applicants, and the public in unserved or underserved communities to lift the Freeze at the earliest possible moment. Having incorporated virtually all its television problems into one omnibus hearing docket, the FCC was not inclined to loosen the leash on new television stations until it had made decisions on *all* problems. Thus,

we have the spectacle of selection of a color television system holding up consideration of UHF use, technical standards, allocation, and assignment. The group seriously interested in retaining the Freeze for its own sake, the pre-Freeze broadcasters, did not have to come into the open. As a matter of fact, their heterogeneity was such as to make unanimity impossible, since each of the 15 network owned-and-operated stations would favor the objectives of its parent network, to gain more affiliates and increase its nationwide salable "circulation." Much of the delay was due to people like Senator Johnson, who insisted that the color issue be decided before the allocation phase could come to a hearing. Such political pressure counterbalanced the efforts of manufacturers and organized labor to lift the Freeze and provide more television-related jobs, and the importunings of communities with limited or no television. When the FCC refused to lift the Freeze for such relatively unserved areas as Hawaii and Alaska, Senator Johnson grew nervous over the growing public pressure and assured his constituents that they would have television in time for the 1952 World Series. They did.

As with any FCC decision of this magnitude, the *Sixth Report and Order* included compromises that were to plague the industry, the public, and the commission in later years. Two of the most important were intermixture and the methods for serving smaller communities.

Under the *Sixth Report and Order*, cities would be intermixed with both VHF and UHF channels. Opponents of this scheme pointed out the grave disparity between the service the two bands could offer, and the economic disadvantage for a UHF station in a city with VHF stations assigned. If the VHF station had been operating during the Freeze, and the public had been saturated with VHF-only receivers, the problem would be compounded. Dumont's rejected plan provided at least some equality of outlets for the four networks in a majority of larger communities able to support television. Other organizations urged upon the FCC their own assignment plans, some of which tried to avoid intermixture. Even the report of the President's Communications Policy Board, issued a year before the *Sixth Report and Order*, clearly foresaw drawbacks to intermixture:

> *The proposed plan of the FCC contemplates the allocation of both VHF and UHF stations to the same community. There is little possibility that a UHF station can compete successfully with a VHF station. Within practical limits of power, a UHF station cannot serve as large an area as can a VHF station. For a considerable period after the UHF stations commence operation, particularly in cities where there are VHF stations, there will probably be few UHF receivers and consequently a limited audience.*

. . . and also consequently a limited amount of advertising agency interest in buying time on the station.

However, because of theoretical propagation characteristics and equipment availability, the commission decided to support the fiction of equivalence of VHF and UHF. As a result, UHF stations in intermixed markets had ever increasing financial problems, forcing hundreds off the air (see 8.81). In the mid-1960s the commission and Congress belatedly took remedial action, after more than a decade of agonizing and conducting hearings (see 9.22).

Although the FCC understood the political power of rural and small-town areas of the nation in Congress, the *Sixth Report and Order* did not serve those areas adequately. It was recognized that small towns rarely could generate advertiser revenues high enough to support a full-fledged station and that propagation characteristics of both VHF and UHF were such that many areas of the country could not be served by a television equivalent to a clear-channel radio station. But the FCC did not do anything substantive to supply the desired service.

However, even before the Freeze was well underway, people in some underserved communities had taken matters into their own hands. The first community antenna, now cable, television (CATV) in the United States was developed in 1949. In numerous isolated mountainous regions, particularly in Pennsylvania and Oregon, cooperating citizens or businesses established for the purpose placed antennas on neighboring peaks and strung wires from the antennas to homes in the valleys. In other isolated communities, clever electronics experts rigged the receiving antenna to receive the distant station and fed the signal into a homemade *repeater* or *booster* transmitter of low power in the valley. Such boosters gave good service to the valley community but, since all transmitters can cause interference farther than they can give service, caused widespread interference to the "parent" station.

At first, the FCC ignored cable and tried to close down the boosters—but they were too hard to track down and too easy to establish again virtually overnight, and had too much political support. Governor —former Senator—Edwin Johnson of Colorado appointed booster operators to his personal communications staff and successfully defied the FCC to act against them. The FCC attempted to provide alternatives—*satellite* stations with no original programming, and *translators* to move the received signal high into the little-used UHF channels—but failed (see 8.81). Although cable is now in most big cities as well as small towns, it primarily provided service to communities with poor off-the-air reception into the late 1970s. Distant signal importation and specialized "pay-cable" services were for the future. All that has changed is the commission's regulatory stance toward it, and the belief of many people in its future (see 9.83).

Although the *Sixth Report and Order* was the result of much thought, work, and argument, its intended effect has not been realized. Because of its imperfections —and the imperfections of other policy statements by the commission and other government agencies—the number of television signals available today in a given community is far below the expectations engendered by the allocation and assignment plans. Television's growth in the United States has been phenomenal, but it has not been smooth. The inertia of political and economic force has aborted many possible organizational patterns for the medium. The shortage of television broadcast stations or, perhaps, cable outlets today restricts the viewing fare of the average citizen, sharply reduces the potential number of nationwide program sources (networks), and creates conditions of monopoly or near-monopoly in many communities, raises costs beyond the reach of the local advertiser, and restricts opportunity for new talent. At the same time, there is a critical shortage of space in the radio spectrum for services other than television.

7•84   *Public Service Responsibility*

On March 7, 1946, the FCC issued what may be its single most important programming policy document. Entitled *Public Service Responsibility of Broadcast Licensees* but bearing a deep blue paper cover that gave it its popular title, the "Blue Book" contained five major parts. First, it gave examples of station promises on programming—providing local live public

service programs, limiting advertising—versus their performance—inexpensive recorded music and a heavy proportion of ads. The second section provided the legal rationale for the FCC to act in the area of programming, chiefly in the process of choosing between competing applicants. Part three outlined what the FCC thought of as public service factors. These included the need for sustaining programs to (1) provide a balance to advertiser-supported material, (2) offer programs whose nature would make them unsponsorable, (3) serve minority tastes and interests, (4) cater to the needs of nonprofit organizations, and (5) allow experimentation with new types of programs. Charts and tables were used to show that networks usually aired sustaining programs at hours when few could listen, reserving the prime hours for advertiser-supported programming. The commission noted that when networks did provide public service material, most of their affiliated stations rejected it for a locally sponsored show. The third part of the "Blue Book" also outlined local station practices in programming and advertising that made it difficult to hear discussion of public issues on the air. Part four provided tabular statistical data to show how broadcast profits had increased from 1937 to 1944, which presumably would have allowed broadcasters to pay for some of the suggested improvements. The last part of the "Blue Book" was a summary that reiterated the importance of the station licensee in policing his own product. The FCC would favor renewal applications from stations that had met their public service responsibilities, defined as: sustaining programs, local live shows, discussion of public issues, and no excessive advertising. The "Blue Book" conclusions were described as neither regulations nor proposals for new rules but rather as a codification of FCC thinking to help licensees and regulators alike. Yet, this *was* the first major report on FCC consideration of broadcast programming policy, although the commission previously had acted against specific stations on specific matters.

Initial reaction of the broadcasting industry to the "Blue Book" was calm but predictable; it claimed that the government was violating radio's freedom of speech since the Communications Act forbid the FCC to censor. A month later the issue heated up with the publication of *Radio's Second Chance* (1946) by Charles A. Siepmann, who was thought to be chief writer of the "Blue Book." Actually, although Siepmann—a former British broadcaster accustomed to the public service philosophy of the BBC—had been a consultant on the "Blue Book" project for a short while, FCC economist Dallas Smythe and others had put most of the report together. In *Radio's Second Chance* Siepmann criticized American broadcasting and brought down on the FCC, and himself, the wrath of an industry fearing that the commission was planning specific programming rules and regulations. Newspapers were divided over the FCC report, some defending it and others fearing a government takeover of radio. The trade press—particularly the business weekly, *Broadcasting*—attacked it mercilessly, although no station was ever taken to hearing or off the air for not meeting "Blue Book" standards. Baltimore station WBAL, held up as a bad example in the "Blue Book," won its license renewal over a competing application from columnist Drew Pearson.

Still, the report had some solid results over time: the NAB strengthened its self-regulatory radio code, broadcasters had a clearer notion of what the FCC was looking for in comparative license renewal and application hearings, the FCC showed that it had the backbone for once to speak

out if not act in a controversial area, and the "Blue Book" still provides the commission with a useful precedent and the industry with a rallying point.

A specific area of public service received special attention in 1948–1949, when the FCC reversed itself over the right of stations to editorialize on the air. In 1941, while passing on a competing challenge to Boston radio station WAAB's license renewal, the FCC decided that "the broadcaster cannot be an advocate" or, in other words, that a licensee should not use the airwaves he controls to propagate his own opinions. A few broadcasters, and others claiming that it would limit the free speech rights of broadcasters, attacked this "Mayflower Decision," named after the competing applicant, the Mayflower Broadcasting Corporation. But, although a few stations ignored the rule, no licensee challenged the FCC in court. Most broadcasters did not editorialize anyway, and disliked antagonizing sponsors and segments of the audience by taking sides on any question. Some broadcasters avoided any mention of labor unions on the air because the topic was "controversial."

After hearings in which the NAB took a leading role, the FCC issued a report in 1949, *In the Matter of Editorializing by Broadcast Licensees*, which "clarified" the 1941 decision. It stated that "Only insofar as it is exercised in conformity with the paramount right of the public to hear a reasonably balanced presentation of all responsible viewpoints on particular issues can such editorialization be considered to be consistent with the licensee's duty to operate in the public interest." That decision generally was hailed as allowing broadcasters more of the rights enjoyed by print media under the First Amendment. The way was opened for editorializing, which started slowly in the 1950s. Even more important, the precedent was set for what was later called the Fairness Doctrine (see 9.82).

An important case in this area opened in February 1948, when the Radio News Club of Southern California formally charged that G.A. Richards, president and controlling stockholder of stations KMPC in Los Angeles, WJR in Detroit, and WGAR in Cleveland, had ordered his news employees to slant the news—against President Roosevelt and his family in particular. Voluminous hearings began in 1950, but Richards' death in May 1951 rendered the matter moot in the opinion of the FCC Hearing Examiner. After Richards' heirs "rejected" the earlier practices, the commission closed the case without penalty, and the stations were soon sold.

7•85   The Petrillo Affair
         (continued)

To add to broadcasting's economic complications in the postwar years, the American Federation of Musicians was still making demands (see 6.83). In October 1945 it ordered networks to hire duplicate orchestras or forgo use of network programs on FM. A month later it gave local stations the same order, helping speed the end of studio orchestras at all but the largest stations, as most turned to recorded music completely. Congress reacted to the AFM pressure by passing the Lea Act (after Congressman Clarence F. Lea, D-California, its sponsor) in April 1946, which made it unlawful to force a broadcast licensee to, among other things, hire unneeded personnel, pay salaries in lieu of those unneeded personnel, pay more than once for a single service, or pay for services which were not performed. After a series of court appeals, the Supreme Court of the United States upheld the act in June 1947. Further weakening the power of unions was the

passage six months later of the Taft-Hartley Labor Relations Act. Faced with these restraints, AFM President Petrillo agreed in 1948 to a two-month trial of using one orchestra for AM-FM programming—and then caved in on the issue for good. In the meantime, radio stations had begun to rely more on recorded music and disc jockey programming, further weakening the ties between broadcasting and live music.

7•86   Self-Regulation and
         Blacklisting

The roles of trade and professional groups in broadcasting reflected the confusion of the period. There seemed to be a trade group for every kind of station—FM, television, would-be educational stations, new stations, old stations, and, of course, the National Association of Broadcasters. NAB, essentially a conservative association of members of the broadcast station establishment, working hand-in-glove with Sol Taishoff, the publisher-editor of *Broadcasting* magazine, had to reevaluate its functions with the coming of television. In 1951, to eliminate the rival Television Broadcasters Association, it changed its name—for seven years anyway—to the more cumbersome National Association of Radio and Television Broadcasters. (*Broadcasting* became *Broadcasting • Telecasting* at around the same time.) NAB's temporary shift in title helped pacify new television license holders who felt the organization was overly beholden to old-line AM radio operators. All groups spent as much time bickering with one another about roles and priorities as they did educating the public and politicians to their point(s) of view.

The NAB directed its major attention toward what it saw as government encroachment on programming decision-making. As a result of the "Blue Book," oft-repeated threats of specific legislation, and public pressure to improve radio and television program standards, the NAB completely revised the 1939 radio code. "Standards of Practice," issued in 1948, was more stringent on limitations on advertising time. Although many stations adhered to them, they were still unenforceable. As more stations went on the air, especially in sparsely populated rural areas or urban regions with great competition, the struggle for economic survival often prevented adherence to the NAB code standards. "Standards of Practice" and the motion picture code served as models when the NARTB issued its first Television Code early in 1952, basically an unoriginal, proscriptive recitation of things the licensees should *not* do. The single means of enforcement was not much of a threat: NAB's right to prevent the station's display of the Television Code Seal on the air and in advertising.

The period of the communist scare and blacklisting—in which the industry, through fear and cowardice, let others control it—was a grim era in broadcasting and film and the arts generally. Blacklisting was the process of secretly refusing to employ someone, usually in this case a creative talent—actor, writer, producer, director—solely because of a frequently unsupported claim that he or she was a communist, had communist, "fellow traveler," or ultraliberal left-wing inclinations, or had been duped by communists. The vicious thing about blacklisting is suggested by its name. It was done by small groups of self-appointed investigators who made surreptitious reports to advertisers, agencies, stations, and networks indicating that someone either should not be hired because of his or her political beliefs or was "cleared" for employment. Potential employers who did not pay attention to these

messages could expect to have their own patriotism impugned. Potential employees not cleared were seldom told why, and no executive ever admitted the existence of the blacklists. Blacklisting worked, from about 1948 until the early 1950s, because its organizers hit the broadcast system at its weakest point: the advertiser. Under threats of product boycotts, advertisers pressured agencies and broadcasters not to hire someone for fear of losing sales, or at least creating controversy, which all advertisers shun. With advertisers representing the broadcasting industry's source of income, no one in broadcasting would speak out against the practice or even admit it existed—only persons who had been blacklisted themselves, and they were no longer in broadcasting.

Perhaps the most successful and ironically, considering its secretive nature, the most visible blacklisting group was American Business Consultants, based in New York. Consisting of three former FBI agents, it issued a newsletter called *Counterattack* and often published special monographs. On June 22, 1950, it issued *Red Channels: The Report of Communist Influence in Radio and Television*, some 200 pages of detailed background information on 151 broadcast personalities, whom it suggested were at least sympathetic to communist thinking. *Red Channels*, carefully avoiding outright accusations, reprinted reports from the House Un-American Activities Committee and other official and unofficial groups, using the umbrella of official sources—mixed with some "guilt by association" and innuendo—to brand persons as undesirable. An accident of timing made *Red Channels* particularly effective: three days after it was published, North Korea invaded South Korea and the United States entered the Korean War or "police action." Other than this one report, which was widely distributed, black-

The Big Red Scare: 1950

If the Communist Party USA exacts a heavy financial toll of its members and dupes, it has been no less energetic in seeing to it that they get ahead in show business, while articulate anti-Communists are blacklisted and smeared with that venomous intensity which is characteristic of Red Fascists alone. . . . Those who are "right" are "boosted" from one job to another, from humble beginnings in Communist-dominated night clubs or on small programs which have been "colonized" to more important programs and finally to stardom. Literally scores of our most prominent producers, directors, writers, actors and musicians owe their present success largely to the Party "boost" system, a system which involves not only "reliable" producers and directors, but also ad agency executives, network and station executives, writers, fellow-actors and critics and reviewers. In turn, the Party member or "reliable" who has "arrived" gives the "boost" to others who, the Red grapevine whispers, are to be helped. . . . Contrary-wise, those who know radio and TV can recite dozens of examples of anti-Communists who, for mysterious reasons, are *persona non grata* on numerous programs, and who are slandered unmercifully in certain "progressive" circles.

The purpose of this compilation is three-fold. One, to show how the Communists have been able to carry out their plan of infiltration of the radio and television industry. Two, to indicate the extent to which many prominent actors and artists have been inveigled to lend their names, according to . . . public records, to organizations espousing Communist causes. This, regardless of whether they actually believe in, sympathize with, or even recognize the cause advanced. Three, to discourage actors and artists from naively lending their names to Communist organizations or causes in the future.

Excerpts from *Red Channels: The Report of Communist Influence in Radio and Television* (New York: Counterattack, 1950), pages 4–5, 9.

It is quite clear that whereas the editors and publishers of *Red Channels* and *Counterattack* do not consciously strive for the same objectives as the agents of Communism, their methods and techniques are very similar and so are their standards of morality and their respect for the essential "Blessings of Liberty" guaranteed by the Constitution and the Bill of Rights. As the vigorously anti-Communist *Saturday Review of Literature* has said, "*Red Channels* accepts Red Doctrine: to accuse is enough." It would be difficult to imagine any doctrine more profoundly un-American.

Playwright Robert E. Sherwood's reaction as he introduced an American Civil Liberties Union report on the subject, Merle Miller's *The Judges and the Judged* (New York: Doubleday, 1952), page 9.

listing remained institutionalized behind closed doors. Advertising and package agencies and networks soon assigned a "security checker" to make certain that anyone hired was "clean" with the black-listers. Some stations and networks even required new employees to take a loyalty oath. Actors and writers who "confessed" their associations and informed on their colleagues before the House Un-American Activities Committee or prominent unofficial groups usually could be expunged from the blacklist. The insidious process continued until a celebrated case (see 8.85) helped break the system.

7·9   The Impact of Television

That radio and television listeners and viewers were becoming more concerned about broadcasting's role in their daily lives was demonstrated by the rising clamor of complaints that helped lead to the 1948 revision of the NAB code, and in group action. In the late 1940s radio listener councils that sought programming of more value to the local community reached a peak. These councils were active in New England, the Midwest, often sparked by university activists, and California. They issued lists of good programs, conducted audience surveys, held informational meetings, produced special programs in cooperation with some stations, and generally encouraged greater educational use of radio. Although in Europe such groups often met for communal listening to special programs, that pattern did not develop here. Some councils organized around program production, frequently in association with a university, while others merely studied the industry and its problems and then pressured or at least advised local station managers to improve their programming. None of these groups

covered a wide enough area or lasted long enough to have a lasting impact on the industry.

Many critics and professional broadcasters became increasingly concerned that radio was changing from a varied format, with something for everyone, to a stereotyped format of popular music and news with high advertising saturation. The increase in radio stations and expansion of television put such a financial strain on most radio broadcasters that they could not afford to accommodate many community requests for change.

7·91   Television's Domestic Effect

Of concern to all other mass communication media, as well as operators of any means of recreation or entertainment, was the impact of television. Two media that felt the immediate brunt were radically changed—radio and the movies. We have already discussed radio's loss of drama, variety, other entertainment—and advertisers—to television, and radio networks dried up to little more than news services with some sustaining entertainment programming (see 7.61). As radio in the 1950s became more a local advertising medium, concentrating on recorded music, television became the evening-in-the-home entertainer and national advertising medium.

Hollywood, however, seemed in some ways totally unprepared. This was understandable, since the movie industry was fighting two important battles not directly connected with television. It lost the battle with the federal government over the right of large production studios to own chains of theaters. When the Paramount studio was forced in 1948, after a decade of antitrust litigation, to divest itself of its theater chain, panic set in. All major studios had to sell their theaters, keeping the production studios and distributing organizations, and with the sale went the benefits of vertical integration and a guaranteed market for the hundreds of feature films made each year. The motion picture industry also encountered blacklisting, although here it often surfaced in public, during emotional congressional and other hearings where actors and other movie people fell over one another in informing—with or without evidence—on old friends and enemies. Some of the accused took the Fifth Amendment, or refused to testify—at the cost of a jail term in a number of cases. The scars are still evident.

After 1950, television provided another punch to an industry no longer secure in its role or its profits. As early as 1949 motion picture attendance was off by 20 percent and employment was down by 25 percent, with lower-ranking workers, and not the top-heavy management, being laid off. As fewer films were made, more people were out of work. The former film audience was staying home, or going for a ride now that wartime transportation shortages had ended, and the movie audience soon dwindled from a family affair to an opportunity for teenagers to date. After 1950 the abandoned motion picture theater became a common sight. Hollywood unfairly blamed everything on television and tried to boycott the video medium. Stars under contract were not allowed to appear on television, old films were not released to networks or stations for television showing, and television workers were shunned in the movie colony. It was an ostrich act, which had to change radically when the American feature film industry faced even greater problems in later years.

Professional sports promoters also worried about the effects of television on game attendance. Televised sports events often had the direct result, according to team management's perceptions of the data, of reducing the gate receipts. Team owners were caught between the lure of substantial income from selling rights to a game to a network or station and the sight of empty seats and reduced parking and concession income as the fans stayed home to watch in comfort. Research sponsored by a number of professional teams showed that television had little effect on attendance over a season. Still, local game *blackouts* date from those early years, with many variations depending on the personal opinions of team owners. Only in 1973 did Congress impose restrictions on the blacking out of sold-out games in pro football (see 9.63).

Television affected other institutions as well. Advertisers began to shift vast sums of money into television that had once gone to radio or the print media. Likewise, television was radically changing the process and appearance of national elections and between-campaign politics (see 7.64). There were rumors and reports of changes in family life-styles, sleeping habits, children's entertainment and activity preferences—it was a lot more fun and easier to watch the *Lone Ranger* than to go outside and play cowboys and Indians—eyesight problems, juvenile delinquency. However, many of these developments were merely hinted at during the late 1940s and early 1950s; television's impact on children would not be readily observed in the United States until later (see 8.73 and 9.72).

7•92   Postwar Broadcasting Abroad

While television preoccupied most of this country right after World War II, radio remained the preeminent broadcast medium abroad. Even by late 1952, few countries outside the United States had television, and most of the transmitters and approximately 85 percent of the world's television sets were American—even though the country had only a little more than 5 percent of the world's population. The major foreign countries using television regularly were Canada, Cuba, Mexico, and Brazil in the Western Hemisphere and using U.S. technical standards, and France and Great Britain in Europe, each using different technical standards.

In the United Kingdom, the BBC resumed television transmissions in June 1946 by including in the opening program the same film cartoon that had been the last thing seen when BBC television left the air at the outbreak of the war in 1939. The French had conducted some experimentation and programming in Paris under German occupation during the war, and had continued transmissions after the war. But television in most other countries was limited to one or two transmitters and a few hundred or few thousand receivers —about where American television had been before the war.

With radio, a far more important and widespread medium, the main postwar job abroad was rebuilding and replacing transmitters, systems, and receivers. Since radio was easy to reconstruct and immediately useful once rebuilt, many countries put their mass communications effort in radio. German radio, under Allied occupation, was restructured along local and regional lines with no national radio organization whatever—in reaction to the Nazi centralized control of broadcasting and other media. In Japan the American occupation forces held strict control over radio at first, gradually easing it in the late 1940s to permit NHK to resume as the principal broadcasting organization. The

United States allowed some Japanese international broadcasting early in 1952, expanded it when Japan's utility as a base during the Korean War became apparent, and then ended the occupation.

International broadcasting after 1945 became a weapon in the cold war with the Soviet Union and its allies, which intensified after 1947. For the first time, the United States was active in such communication in "peacetime." The Voice of America had started with the wartime operations of the OWI (see 6.61) but had moved to the State Department. It operated in many languages and beamed news, music, and other programming to most areas of the world. In addition, the United States government set up three radio services *in* Europe. Radio Free Europe, which for years claimed to be privately supported when it was in fact supported clandestinely by the CIA, tailored its programming to the nations of Eastern Europe that the Soviets had occupied in 1945. Radio Liberty, also U.S. government–supported although declaring its private status, broadcast directly to the Soviet Union. Radio in the American Sector of Berlin (RIAS) was overtly run by the State Department, and was heard throughout East Germany. Much of the programming was music and "straight" news, with little direct propaganda, although the services varied—Radio Free Europe, for instance, at first held out hope of freedom to the European satellites of the Soviet Union and was largely programmed by refugees from the Communists—and *any* content, even if not directly controlled by the government, might be called propaganda. The Soviets spent huge sums building transmitters to send out noise to "jam" the incoming signals in urban areas. Penalties were imposed for listening to foreign broadcasts, although much "radio" broadcasting in the Soviet Union was wired or "rediffusion" much like CATV, and thus the audience could not select programs. Other nations broadcast to the world on the international shortwave bands as well, particularly the BBC, which had been doing so since the 1930s, and the Soviet Union.

After much preliminary work a major International Telecommunications Union meeting was held in Atlantic City in 1947 to revise the international frequency allocation table. Few changes in American broadcasting were necessary, but it was desirable to allocate the frequencies that had been opened up by wartime research. This conference, like other ITU meetings, showed that international cooperation *could* be achieved in the telecommunications field.

7•93   Period Overview

As the length of this chapter attests, summarizing the important events and trends of 1945–1952 is not easy. Overall, the period contained the transition from the AM radio–only broadcast industry, which had been around since the early 1920s, to a system incorporating AM and FM radio and VHF and UHF television, with such services as CATV and pay-TV in the wings. The industry was far bigger and more complex in 1952 than in 1945. The radio establishment helped pave the way for the new television network establishment; indeed the ownership of the new medium came essentially from the groups that had controlled prewar radio. The organization and operation of early television is the overriding theme of this period.

This short space of time also saw the fortunes of educational broadcasting rise as reserved frequencies became available first in FM and then in television. These decisions paved the way for the spectacular expansion of educational, later "public," broadcasting in the decades af-

ter 1950. But in the rush to television, some things were given short shrift. FM radio, the chief initial loser, entered a long period of decline after a short burst of postwar growth. Even television met problems as a result of the complicated FCC allocations proceedings during the Freeze. Although intended to correct earlier FCC mistakes, the 1952 *Sixth Report and Order* created UHF television stations as second-class citizens —a condition that soon would be abundantly clear.

Television expanded far more rapidly than radio simply because it built on the existing radio structure. Thus television used radio program formats with added video, networks were operated along radio lines, the role of advertisers was never in doubt, and radio set makers learned to make television sets. With its rapid growth and more complicated organization, the overall pattern of expanding television was the same as existing radio. Compared to radio's initial impact on American society (see 3.91), television's effects on motion pictures, sports, and leisure patterns were felt in less than half the time. The new medium quickly dominated America's life-style.

The 1945–1952 period brought such radical changes that today's broadcasting can almost be said to date from this era rather than from the pioneering of the 1920s. While FM radio and television suffered from growing pains, they benefited from the lessons of AM radio. The greatest growth of both new broadcast services, and the transformation of AM radio's functions, were to come in the Eisenhower years—between 1952 and 1960.

Further Reading

There are several fine reviews of radio at its peak, up to 1948 or so: Landry's history and description (1946), Llewellyn

White's highly critical overview of radio development and regulation (1947), Bryson's review of major problems facing radio (1948), Waller's textbook (1950) describing network and station operations, and Siepmann's text (1950) reviewing the role of broadcasting and society in a way timely today. Social history of this era, with broadcasting emphasis, is to be found in Barnouw (1968) and Lichty and Topping's reader (1975).

The FCC's *Network Broadcasting* (1958) offers one of the best overviews of early regulatory and organizational development in network television. The commission's *Economic Study* (1947) details the pretelevision economic plight of the expanding number of AM stations. Midgley (1948) gives a cogent review of pre-TV station and network operations, Wolfe (1949) deals with the same material in greater depth, and Diamant (1971) describes early television commercials. The struggle for educational television is detailed in Powell (1962), and Blakely (1979).

The transition of CBS from radio to

Key Broadcasting Indicators: 1950 / This is the fifth of 12 tables offering comparable information over a 60-year period (to 1985), presented at five-year intervals. Sources for items 1–6 and 11 are the tables in Appendix C, while other information comes from sources indicated below. Most data are for January 1.

Indicators	AM	FM	TV
1. Number of commercial stations	2,061	733	98
2. Number of noncommercial stations	± 25	48	—
3. Total stations on the air	2,086	781	98
4. Number of network-affiliated stations	1,170	na	96
5. Percentage of commercial stations affiliated with networks	56%	na	98%
6. Total industry revenue (add 000,000)	$605.4	$2.8	$170.8
7. One-hour station rate (New York)	$1,200	na	$1,500
8. One-minute station rate (New York)	na	na	na
9. One-hour network rate, evening	$20,400	na	$17,425
10. Number of broadcasting employees	.... 52,000		14,000
11. Percentage of families with sets	94.7%	na	9%
12. Broadcasting regulatory budget (FCC)	.... $6,729,345		
13. Total FCC personnel	.... 1,285		

Notes (see Appendix D for full citations)

na = not applicable or not available.

2. The one educational TV station (WOI-TV in Ames, Iowa) was operating on a commercial channel as there was no educational allocation until 1952.

7. WEAF (NBC radio, New York) and WNBT (NBC television, New York).

9. NBC radio network (172 affiliates) and television network (50 affiliates).

10. Radio figure is for 1949, while TV figure is for 1952. Radio includes both AM and FM stations and networks. Lichty and Topping (1975), page 290, table 23.

11. The comparable FM figure would have been no more than 1 percent nationally, though it approached 10 percent in the bigger cities.

12–13. FCC figures for fiscal year 1950, ending June 30.

television, including views of the famous "talent raid" on NBC, are in Metz (1975) and in Paley's (1979) memoirs. Campbell offers a pictorial and text 50-year history of NBC radio and television (1976). See also the special 60th-anniversary reports on NBC issued by *Broadcasting* and *Television/Radio Age* (both 1986). Bergreen (1980) is a good history of all the radio and television networks. Halberstam's (1979) best-seller relates the rise of the media and their journalistic role in the United States as seen in descriptions of CBS, *Time*, and two newspapers.

Programming for radio is best covered in the books noted in chapter 5. Critical views of radio and television programs of this period can be found in Crosby (1952) and Gross (1970). A good feeling of the transition from radio to television news is found in the three biographies of Murrow—Kendrick (1969), Sperber (1986), and Persico (1988).

The literature on television programming gets larger every year, and there is now a considerable amount of both reference and anecdotal material. The discussion that follows relates to chapters 7–10 of the present history (but see the books noted in those chapters for period-specific items). There are several good pictorial histories of television: Blum (1959), the first, consists of hundreds of small photos; Shulman and Youman (1966) combines considerable descriptive text with the pictures appearing in sections by genre; Settel (1969) and Settel and Laas (1969) offer a continuing narrative with photos; Greenfield (1977) is by far the largest and most useful of the lot because of a critical text and substantial content; Goldstein and Goldstein (1983) has a season-by-season approach covering prime-time shows; and Marschall (1986) includes a chapter on British programming. Combining more text with fewer photos in a season-by-season

approach is Castleman and Podrazik (1982). Wilk (1976) relates the "golden age" of television in the 1950s.

Major reference works on all network television programs from 1947 to date include Brooks and Marsh (1988), by far the most inclusive guide to prime-time shows; McNeil (1980), which covers daytime and weekend as well as prime-time shows; Terrace (1979), which in two volumes offers cast lists but little text; Brown (1982), which covers major programs but also key figures and institutions and events in television history; and the five-volume Gianakos (1978–1987), which gives details for every episode of all drama series on television from 1947 through 1984. Rose (1985) is an invaluable handbook of television program genres, with history, comment, and guides to readings and recordings.

Works on specific programs or program types are becoming more common. The earliest years of television drama (up *to* 1947) are related in Hawes (1986). Rose (1986) provides one of the few guides to the development of dance, classical music, opera, and theater on American television. Glut and Harmon (1975) recall the heroes of early-day television shows, especially those aimed at children. The television western is reviewed in MacDonald (1987). Comedy shows are well covered in book form: one of the better books by a broadcast star is Steve Allen's (1956) study of his fellow comedians on radio and television. Sennett (1977) provides text, photos, and script excerpts on *Your Show of Shows*; Blythe and Sackett (1986) tell the story of Burns and Allen; Andrews (1976) relates the phenomenon of *I Love Lucy*; and Fates (1978) tells of the long-running *What's My Line* quiz show.

The major national radio audience surveys of the period are those of Lazarsfeld and Field (1946) and the lengthier follow-up by Lazarsfeld and Kendall (1948), as discussed on page 292. Lowery and De Fleur (1988) covers several important audience studies of this period.

Regulatory events of this era are best described in the FCC's annual reports, in Warner (1948 and 1953), and in the FCC "Blue Book," officially titled *Public Service Responsibility of Broadcast Licensees* (1946). For blacklisting, see *Counterattack's Red Channels* (1950), Cogley's interpretive and critical analysis of 1956, and Vaughn's (1972) history. A good summary of industry views on amending the Communications Act can be found in the NAB's *Broadcasting and the Bill of Rights* (1947). The FCC's seminal *Sixth Report and Order* discussed on pages 302–304 was printed officially in 41 FCC 148 and by both *Broadcasting* and *Television Digest*.

Most early books on television look at the medium with awe, but the following titles are useful: Kempner (1948) and Abramson (1955 and 1987) for technical development, Dunlap (1947) for a forecast of the medium's future, and both Eddy (1945) and Hutchinson (1950) for early production methods and station operations. Dupuy (1945) provides a very early handbook on production based on five years of work at GE's WRGB television station.

World communications are described in most detail in the Unesco series *Press, Film, Radio* (1947–1951), which assays media systems of nearly all countries and territories of the world, beginning with the war-torn countries of Europe. Likewise, Unesco's *Television: A World Survey* (1953 and 1955) details the rise of that medium around the world. See also the first editions of Unesco's *World Communications* (1950 and 1951). The postwar-euphoria-backed attempt to export American ideals of press freedom is detailed in Blanchard (1986).

**The Age
of Television
(1952–1960)**

8

"On the evening of March 7, 1955, one out of every two Americans was watching Mary Martin play Peter Pan before the television cameras. Never before in history had a single person been seen and heard by so many others at the same time. The vast size of the audience was a phenomenon in itself as fantastic as any fairy tale. The age of television had arrived."—Leo Bogart, The Age of Television, page 1

The Age
of Television
(1952–1960)

8

". . . we are convinced that the UHF band will be fully utilized, and that UHF stations will eventually compete on a favorable basis with stations in the VHF."—FCC <u>Sixth Report and Order</u> (1952), paragraph 197

"[potential UHF operators] had better study astronomy to figure up their balance sheets and buy lots of red ink."—Commissioner Jones in dissent to the <u>Sixth Report and Order</u>

Radio seemed to fade into the wallpaper during the 1952–1960 period, and television came to the fore. This chapter takes us from the end of the FCC Freeze on television station construction in 1952 to the quiz show and payola scandals in 1959–1960, which caused a shakeup in the FCC and new public awareness of the business of broadcasting. For television the period opened with growth and excitement but ended with questions and recriminations.

The 1950s were the Eisenhower years—a time of conflicting images. After two decades of Democratic administrations, General Dwight D. Eisenhower won the 1952 Republican presidential nomination from the more conservative Ohio Senator Robert A. Taft and then won the elec-

Outline:
The Age of Television (1952–1960)

tion from Adlai E. Stevenson (see 7.64). Since the Freeze had ended early in 1952 (see 7.83), plans for building hundreds of television stations were well advanced by the time "Ike" moved into the White House. Viewers absorbed the political turnover and subsequent shifts in international relations, particularly after the death of Stalin in March 1953. Wisconsin's Senator Joseph McCarthy, riding high in his witch hunt for communists everywhere, had a rendezvous with television that ended his power in American political life. The Supreme Court issued its famous school desegregation decision, which led to political and social crises aired in detail on the nation's television screens. In New York, the United Nations headquarters was completed with provision for television and radio coverage of important events.

The 1950s had many fads—the Davy Crockett craze, inspired by a television show; tail fins on Detroit cars; small kids writing the letter Z on everything in sight, just like the hero of the Walt Disney television series *The Mark of Zorro*; hula hoops; silly putty; rushing home from school to catch the five-minute episode of *Crusader Rabbit*; evangelists Billy Graham and Oral Roberts on television; the sack dress, which made a woman look like a chic sack of potatoes; rock 'n' roll music; telephone booth stuffing; swooning over pop singer Elvis Presley. The few fads that were not based on or inspired by television shows were at least reported widely by the medium.

People had more leisure time, and television quickly became the most popular way to spend it. Families had much larger incomes since the war had ended the Great Depression, while workers spent less time on the job. The work week very slowly shrank to less than 40 hours by 1960. Additional leisure came with increasing purchases of washing machines,

dishwashers, garbage disposals, dryers, and power mowers. As people spent many hours a day watching television, audiences dwindled for nearly every other kind of entertainment. The television audience grew faster than that for any other medium or means of recreation. By 1958 more homes had television than the 1939 number of radio homes; that is, though far more expensive, television achieved near-saturation in half the time it took radio.

Virtually all the developments in radio and television were predictable from occurrences of the revolutionary 1946–1952 period, since television built upon and expanded the industry established by radio. AM continued to grow and change, despite fears that it was doomed by television; interest in FM radio faded away until it began a slight upturn at the end of the decade; and television's growth, problems, and promise filled the news of broadcasting. The 1952–1960 period was in nearly every way an age of television, more so than any time before or since.

8·1   Stereo and Videotape Technology

Two developments in broadcast technology in this period soon proved of immense value. The first was single-station stereophonic radio broadcasting, and the second was the perfecting of the videotape magnetic recording process for television.

8·11   Stereo and Multiplexing

The idea of stereo was not new. There had been lab experiments with stereophonic sound in the early 1900s, and in the 1920s stereo radio binaural broadcasts had been made from the stage of the Berlin Opera House, using six microphones in

three pairs, half of each pair fed to a separate AM transmitter. In this country, some
AM stations, especially those that played
classical music, experimented with two-
station AM stereocasting, with one station
broadcasting the right channel and the
other the left. The difficulties were that listeners to only one of the stations got but
half a signal, and offering the same program on two different wavelengths wasted
spectrum space.

The same limitations were present
in 1952 when the *New York Times*–owned
WQXR tried AM-FM two-station stereocasts, using AM for the right sound channel and FM for the left. In 1954 Boston's
WCRB began four hours a week of such
programming, boosting it to 40 hours a
week by 1959. These early broadcasts were
nearly always of live music, as there were
few sources of stereophonically recorded
music even on tape. After 1958 commercially recorded stereo records became
available and recorded music could be
readily broadcast in stereo. Even the networks got into the act when NBC broadcast the *Bell Telephone Hour* stereophonically in 1958 over its four O & O AM and
FM stations. CBS followed suit, and television also was used when ABC stereocast
the Lawrence Welk program on television
and AM. Other experiments or demonstrations intermixing AM, FM, and television channels brought out another problem: FM stations offered such better sound
reproduction quality that, when one station was an AM, the two channels sounded
very different. In addition, since the coverage area of these broadcasts obeyed the
propagation laws of the frequency bands
on which the two services operated, the
AM half of the signal reached out much
farther. The obvious notion of FM-FM two-
station stereo was impracticable since few
people had a single FM receiver, let alone
two.

Faced with these technical limitations but responsive to audience interest
in stereo broadcasts, broadcasters, particularly the hard-pressed FM operators, began to petition the FCC for commercial use
of experimental single-station stereo
broadcasting. Common technical standards would be needed so that all stations
would broadcast the same sort of signal
and all stereo receivers could pick up any
stereo signal.

Meanwhile, some FM stations (see
8.21) had discovered a way of making
money. While it made use of their transmitters, it was not broadcasting. In the late
1940s, stations in urban areas had developed *storecasting*—the sending of music
directly into stores and offices over special
receivers that, upon transmission of a special tone, automatically cut out talk, leaving only the background music. Income
came from rental of these receivers to business establishments. Although recognizing the stations' need for income, the FCC
ruled against such use of the broadcast signal in the early 1950s, claiming that these
customers had a stronger say in selection
of music to be broadcast than regular listeners, a contravention of the 1934 Communications Act.

The commission ruled in 1955 that
FM stations, instead of shutting off the
special receivers with a simple tone in a
process called *simplexing*, could storecast
only by *multiplexing*—a more complicated
process whereby the station transmitter
sent out two different but simultaneous
signals, one to the stores, one to the general public. Although broadcasters objected to the expense that this would en-
tail, the FCC stuck to its guns. But
storecasting and single-station FM stereo
came into conflict, because both processes
required some form of multiplexing. In the
mid-1950s, broadcasters did not know how
to transmit more than one FM subcarrier

signal at a time. Yet, because storecasting was a ready money-maker, and stereo offered FM a way out of its downward slide in audience appeal, broadcasters wanted to be able to provide both services at once.

At the start, 17 technical systems were proposed for stereo broadcasting. Unfortunately, few of them allowed simultaneous storecasting. To try to sort out the conflicting systems, the industry resorted to an approach used earlier for television allocations and standards (see 6.81): it set up a committee of engineering experts from the industry to eliminate inferior systems by a series of comparative tests. In 1959–1960, this National Stereophonic Radio Committee (NSRC), working with FCC engineers, cut the number of competing systems to seven. Easily eliminated were those that did not allow storecasting and stereo at the same time, since by now some 250 stations were engaged in storecasting. While the tests dragged on, many stations kept using AM-FM two-station stereo.

Finally, in April 1961, the FCC set as the industry standard one that combined the Zenith and General Electric systems. Of the 15 other proposals, some had come from firms that merely wanted to promote stereo or FM, but most, of course, came from individuals or companies that wanted to exploit strong patent positions. As will be seen in the next chapter, this 1961 decision contributed to a new era of FM expansion through stereo while preserving storecasting and other Subsidiary Communications Authorizations (SCA) multiplexed services.

8•12   Videotape Recording

In the 1950s a magnetic tape recording process for television achieved broadcast quality. Since commercial television broadcasting took hold in 1948, pro-gramming had been of three types: live, film, or kinescope recording (see 7.13), which was noticeably fuzzier and grainier than live or regular film. The search to replace the kinescope recording process had begun after the war, and a magnetic videotape system had been publicly demonstrated in 1951–1952. Late in 1953, shortly after FCC approval of color television standards (see 7.821), RCA demonstrated a videotape recording (VTR) system for both color and monochrome television. The system, like earlier ones, showed promise but had serious technical problems.

The unveiling of a practical VTR took place in April 1956 at the NAB convention in Chicago. Ampex, a small California-based firm which had worked on audio tape recorders for Bing Crosby in the early 1950s, demonstrated a working black-and-white VTR system. Within days, Ampex took in $4.1 million in orders, even though these models, using a two-inch tape moving at 15 ips, cost about $75,000 each. Now, finally, West Coast stations had a high-quality, practical means of delaying East Coast broadcasts without having to use film or kinescopes, or simply having New York repeat the show live. CBS apparently was the first broadcast organization to make this use of videotape recording, in November 1956.

In 1957 Ampex and RCA pooled their patents and knowledge so both could build compatible systems for color and black-and-white. Ampex, being first with a workable system, had sold more than 600 by early 1960, more than two-thirds of them to networks. After the introduction of the VTR, the networks rarely used the "kine." Because of the many network orders and high unit cost, fewer than 200 television stations had bought a VTR by 1960, and these naturally were the bigger stations in the larger markets.

The arrival of tape led to some

changes in television programming and production. It made editing much faster than with film because the tape did not have to be processed. It made special effects possible with the push of a button, and far cheaper than on film. It produced higher quality than either kinescope recordings or 16mm film. Hollywood makers of film for television had to find ways of paring down their costs to compete with videotape, particularly with respect to series programs. Using an erase/rerecord (make /remake) system, one could easily remove a mistake in an original production. Audience participation shows, during which producers always worry about an obscenity or libel going over the air, could now be taped beforehand. Although shot-by-shot editing was a difficult and expensive procedure until new electronic devices were invented in the late 1960s, VTR gave the programmer greater flexibility. Some critics claimed, however, that actors rarely gave performances with the same intensity as in the "live" days, since they knew that a *fluff* or mistake could be removed, however expensively, before it went on the air. Above all, program production was no longer tied to air dates and hours. Although it took years for the full benefits of VTR to be felt, its potential was obvious from the start.

8·2   The Spurt in Station Population

Until 1958 or so, broadcasting was characterized by growth of AM and television and decline of FM radio. For the first time, growth in itself was questioned: How many AM stations could be accommodated without unacceptable interference? Was UHF anywhere near as good as VHF for television? Should stations in the same service—radio or television—in the same market have roughly equal power and range? Was there enough advertising income to cover all the new stations? These were the have versus have-not arguments of previous decades, but now increasing numbers of three different kinds of broadcasting stations complicated the fray.

8·21   AM Growth and FM Adjustment

In 1945 radio engineers agreed that the spectrum could take only about 900 AM stations without undue interference. But, as the result of FCC relaxation of engineering standards for prospective station licensees after World War II (see 7.21), the number of AM stations grew to 2,400 by 1952. Again, many engineers thought that was the limit. But more than 100 stations were added to the list each year of the 1950s. As small stations went on the air in smaller towns, and more were shoehorned into the cities, the number of AM stations rose to 3,500 by 1960, and an average of 30 stations was operating on each frequency in the United States. This is misleading of course, as Class IV (local) channels had hundreds of stations squeezed on each, and a few of the Class I (clear) channels had only one or two stations on each.

This growth of AM was achieved at some cost. First, an increasing proportion—one-third in 1952, nearly one-half in 1960—of AM stations was restricted to daytime operation so that these stations did not conflict with other, usually older, stations at night, when radio waves travel farther (see Appendix B). More stations also had to use directional antennas to reduce interference. At the same time, power used by AM stations continued to climb, so that the 100 watt station became the exception rather than the rule. Local stations had to increase power—within

FCC set limits—simply to maintain adequate power in relation to other stations on the same frequency that had acquired higher power. By 1960, 18 percent of the 3,456 AM stations were on clear channels with all, except for a handful of Class I stations, using lower power, directional antennas, or going off the air at night; 54 percent were regional outlets using 5,000 or 10,000 watts of power; and 27 percent were low-powered (250–1,000 watts) local stations.

If nothing else, the addition of one thousand AM stations in the 1950s showed that, although network radio was dying (see 8.3), radio stations still were thought of as successful business opportunities. By 1960, virtually every American town of respectable size, and most suburbs of major cities, had their own AM radio station or stations.

On the other hand, more FM stations went off the air than went on. The 616 FM stations on the air in 1952 had shrunk to 530 five years later. Most were owned by AM stations, which duplicated their programming over the FM outlets and hung onto them in case FM should ever amount to anything. In several large cities, their owners kept FM stations on the air in order to hold what might become a valuable frequency. Few FM stations made money and most lost substantial sums. But the FM audience kept about the same size—mostly devotees of the few classical music stations that broadcast in the largest cities.

Other groups needing radio spectrum space soon began to eye the FM allocation. In 1955, for example, the National Association of Manufacturers petitioned the FCC to share the FM band with land mobile and other services with pressing needs. Two years later there was a similar attempt at spectrum "raiding," and even television made a pitch for ad-

ditional VHF channels at the expense of FM (see 8.81). In each instance, the majority of the industry stood fast, and the FCC decided to leave the FM band alone. Still, the threat to reduce its number of channels was implicit if FM's fortunes did not change for the better.

Then in April 1957 the trade weekly *Broadcasting* noted that, for the first time since the late 1940s, applications for new FM stations outnumbered stations going off the air. Several group owners of stations announced plans to set up separate programming for their FM stations and talk of an FM network was heard. Something was relighting FM's fire. By mid-1958 there were 548 stations on the air, the first increase in a decade, and two years later there were nearly 750 commercial FM operations—an all-time high. Applicants were competing for the same channels in cities where shortly before no one had cared.

Subsidiary Communications Authorizations (SCA) for services such as storecasting were proven money-makers for FM outlets, but they could not alone explain what was happening. More important, especially in major cities, was the increasingly crowded AM spectrum. Since there was practically no room for a new AM station in any sizable city by the late 1950s, the only way to get a new radio signal on the air, especially at night, was to use FM. In addition, when television's first major growth spurt (see 8.22) slowed down, investment money and labor became available for FM. The country was going through a cultural boom, and people discovered the independently programmed minority of FM stations that specialized in classical music. The production of FM receivers had picked up, with lower-cost imports from Germany and later from the Far East (see 8.71). Finally, transistor AM-FM radios, introduced in the mid-

1950s, had AFC (automatic frequency control) to prevent the annoying *drift* of tube-type receivers. All these factors helped break the vicious circle of no audience/no advertisers/no money for stations/no stations/no programs/no audience and finally produced the growth in FM which had been expected when it was approved for commercial operation in 1941. FM radio was still a secondary radio service, but the increasing number of stations on the air and growing audience suggested that it was here to stay.

8•22   *Rapid Expansion of Television*

When after four long years instead of the expected six months, the Freeze ended in April 1952 with the *Sixth Report and Order* (see 7.82 and 7.83), the effect was much like unplugging a pipe. The television industry almost exploded, growing from the 108 pre-Freeze stations in 1952 to more than 530 in mid-1960. Distribution, which had been very irregular with six or seven stations in New York and Los Angeles but no service in many areas of the country, evened out as many medium-size towns got their own television station. The number of single-station markets dwindled within a few years. No longer could one station carry the best or most profitable programs of all four networks—ABC, CBS, NBC, and until 1955 Dumont—plus its own local programming and make a huge profit from pitting advertisers and networks against each other. With the coming of a second and third station in many areas, each with a network affiliation—invariably, the last stations in a market of four stations wound up with ABC or Dumont—television competition in the modern sense began.

The end of the Freeze led to stations being established on the UHF band. Initially, hope was expressed—except by engineers, who knew better—that the new UHF allocations would provide universal television service, with a wide choice of programming. What too many applicants forgot, however, was that UHF stations had nowhere near the coverage of their VHF competitors—partly due to poor receiver design.

Station operators and advertisers soon recognized that the typical VHF station on channels 2–6 would give reliable coverage to 65–70 miles, channels 7–13 traveled about five miles less—and UHF stations were lucky to reach much past 30–40 miles (lower-numbered channels giving better service) even if sets had UHF tuners or converters. The FCC had tried to solve this problem by allowing channels 7–13 to use 316 kw of power as contrasted to the 100 kw allowed on channels 2–6; the UHF stations were allowed 1,000 kw (later 5,000 kw or 5 megawatts). Even with this adjustment, coverage differences remained—and canny advertisers placed most of their business with VHF stations. Compounding the problem, few UHF-capable receivers were produced in the early 1950s and even fewer after 1956. All pre-1952 sets, and about five-sixths of those manufactured between 1952 and 1963 could receive only VHF channels. If a UHF station was started in a town, owners of sets would have to buy new ones—and few did—or an *outboard* conversion device that cost $30 to $50 and attached to the antenna terminals. Since antenna placement was more critical for UHF, and since the converter rarely gave a picture as good as the picture from channels the set was engineered to provide, there was little stimulus for people to watch UHF stations if they had a choice. When there were more VHF than UHF channels in a market, the network affiliations and the better programs went to the VHFs, and most of the audience did not even know about the UHFs. There had to be at least a two-to-one ratio of UHF to VHF for a majority of the potential audience to invest in all-channel sets or converters. Thus the typical UHF station could not compete, since it had a smaller coverage area and, within that, a meager audience. The combination was to prove almost fatal to UHF, and did result in more than 100 UHF stations going dark.

The FCC had decided to intermix VHF and UHF stations in the same market (see 7.83), supposedly to assure even competition. More than 100 stations started on UHF channels as soon as they could after the Freeze, each hoping to do as well as the pre-Freeze VHF stations. But shortly, after having spent hundreds of thousands or even millions of dollars, they found that few advertisers cared about UHF stations and their tiny audiences, and networks were uninterested in affiliating a UHF station, unless it was the only one in town—and even the network would switch to a nearby VHF station when given the chance. Within months, UHF operations were failing for lack of operating funds and audience interest.

Although VHF and UHF were regulated as one service, while they were not really equal, and FM as a separate service from AM, there was a strong parallel between UHF television and FM radio. Both services came after a sister service— VHF television and AM radio—had become entrenched. Both started strongly— FM in the late 1940s and UHF in the mid-1950s—only to fall quickly on bad times and decline in number of stations on the air. Both services lacked network affiliations and advertiser interest. Audiences were small because neither radio nor television owners cared to spend extra money for converters or new receivers. In both services, broadcasters with ownership interests in the older, competing service had little concern for the newer service. In both cases, the best urban markets initially were filled with the older services, leaving only smaller markets, with less economic and political clout, as building areas for the newcomers. There were increasing threats in the 1950s that FM and UHF spectrum allocations would be divided with other services, as they were not fully being used by broadcasters.

Ironically the FCC and various congressional committees stated that FM and UHF were to be favored services. There were constant comments in official reports and hearings about moving the older radio and television operations over to FM and UHF frequency assignments, which were technically better and would at least put all operators on an even footing. At times the commission appeared like the nervous doctor who cannot pinpoint the ailment but is sure that further ministrations will help. FM started an upturn after 1957 but economic factors within the broadcasting industry caused UHF to continue sliding slowly downhill throughout the 1950s. New rules and legislation of the 1960s would give both secondary services a shot in the arm.

Thus, during the 1950s, television's commercial growth took place in the VHF band. The 108 VHF stations in 1952 had grown to 344 in 1956 and 440 by 1960, but the number of commercial UHF stations was only 97 in 1956—and 75 by 1960 (see 8.81).

8•23   *To Pay or Not to Pay: The Debate Intensifies*

To a number of struggling UHF operators and some who had gone off the air, there appeared to be one salvation: pay-television. In the postwar years (see

7.24), debates over the idea and some ex- perimentation had started something of a battle between those in favor, led by Ze- nith, and those against, led by the broad- casting networks, motion picture produc- ers, and theater owners.

Through the 1950s there were sev- eral developers of pay-television systems. Zenith's "Phonevision" system, which had been tested in Chicago in 1951 (see 7.24), sent a scrambled audio and visual signal over the air, and used a separate telephone wire to decode or unscramble it. The cus- tomer was to secure "decoding" informa- tion by mail, phone, or vending machine and set a five-number "code translator" attached to his home receiver to unscram- ble the transmitted signals. Zenith sug- gested that stations devote 15 percent of their time to pay operations and 85 per- cent to normal, advertiser-supported, programming. A second firm, Skiatron, planned to send its signals by wire, not over the air, and unscramble them by use of a printed electric circuit on a punch card, purchased at a neighborhood store, inserted into a box attached to the viewer's set. Though this system could be used over the air, Skiatron concentrated on es- tablishing programming companies that would distribute programs only by wire. Telemeter also used a wire system, de- coded by inserting the proper sum into a coin box on the home set. Various other companies, changing from year to year, used similar technology—although one proposed simply sending the unscrambled audio by telephone wire. Each firm claimed that pay-TV would provide new kinds of programming—cultural events, plays, sporting events then not seen on tele- vision, first-run films—and would do it without interruptions for advertising.

Arrayed against the pay-TV pro- ponents were the broadcasting and most of the film industries. They claimed that pay operations would spell the end of "free," advertiser-supported television. The pay operators would be able to siphon off whatever kinds of programming they wanted, since even a small sum per view- ing home would amount to millions of dol- lars. In addition, pay-TV would inflate tal- ent costs. It could pay higher fees than regular television did because it could pass all costs on to the viewers without worry- ing about pricing itself above rival adver- tising media. Finally, pay-TV would raise the cost of advertising since it would leave fewer viewers for commercially sponsored programs—at a higher cost-per-thousand to the advertisers.

Agitation for pay-TV grew follow- ing the 1951 Zenith demonstration and a later, six-month test by Telemeter, owned by Paramount Pictures, in the exclusive desert community of Palm Springs, just outside the Los Angeles market. The test was limited to 200 subscribers, and few results ever were announced. In Septem- ber 1954 Skiatron—following Zenith's ex- ample of 1952—formally asked the FCC to approve regular pay-TV operations, invit- ing support by suggesting that only UHF stations could be pay stations—for the first three years, anyway. In spring 1955, the FCC held hearings on the proposal, and government policy makers and the public were inundated with petitions, newspaper editorials, booklets, reports, and other propaganda on both sides. Many public opinion polls, other than those commis- sioned by broadcasters, favored giving pay- TV a chance. But opponents convinced some powerful figures in Congress that what seemed attractive to some would mean less "free" television to many. This produced several bills to outlaw pay-TV, but none reached a vote.

In spring 1956, the FCC proposed

a two-to-five year test to determine the viability of pay-TV. It would limit the test to programs other than those then aired over commercial television, to cities with at least three operating stations, and to UHF outlets. This proposal merely inflated the debate. In October 1957 the commission issued its First Report on pay-TV, providing specifications for putting the test into practice. Any of the various pay-TV techniques could be used, only 20 markets could be affected at one time, and a given system could be tried in up to three cities.

In the meantime, an extensive test of pay-TV by wire was taking place over a Bartlesville, Oklahoma, cable system. Making use of two different channels, and offering programs from noon to midnight at $9.50 a month, this system depended heavily on first-run films shown repeatedly over a short period. The Bartlesville operation started with 800 subscribers, but after the novelty wore off the number dwindled and the form of payment was changed from a monthly fee to a per program charge. When the operation closed down in April 1958, it was losing $10,000 a month. Operators blamed the loss partly on the release of newer films to commercial television (see 8.62). Pay-TV enemies heralded this failure as proof that people given a choice between regular television and pay-TV would shun the latter. (Although there are similarities between this experiment and the pay-cable operations of today, there was no attempt in the 1950s to identify CATV with pay-TV, particularly as the few CATV systems could not carry many signals and had not yet entered the larger cities where pay operations would be most profitable.)

Just as the Bartlesville test was proving too expensive to continue, a House committee held hearings and in February 1958 issued a "sense of the Committee" resolution asking the FCC to delay application of its 1957 rules until Congress was able to consider and act. In the face of this pressure and a huge flow of mail, the FCC hastily issued a Second Report postponing pay-TV. But there was little movement in Congress, and the FCC's Third Report of February 1959 provided specifications for a more limited test of pay-TV. After more FCC and congressional hearings, only three applications were filed and only one of these resulted in an actual test in the United States (see 9.22).

One test market was explored in the late 1950s. Telemeter offered pay-TV programs to Etobicoke, a suburb of Toronto, Canada. The 1,000 subscribers paid a $5 installation charge and a per program fee for use of any of three channels, two of which carried only movies. Telemeter claimed to have 3,000 families on a waiting list and estimated that it might reach 5,000 homes by late 1960.

Indicating the validity of warnings by commercial broadcasters that pay-TV would funnel off popular programming, Skiatron contracted with the Giants and Dodgers baseball teams, then recently moved to California from New York, to telecast only on pay-TV. This scheme failed when the Los Angeles City Council refused to sanction a pay-TV system in the city.

And there pay-TV stood—about where it had in 1952 insofar as hard data on its potential was concerned. But the passing of time worked against the on-air pay-TV proponents. As commercial television expanded and offered more feature films, the financial and programming rationales for pay-TV faded. Backers of pay systems tired of fighting other industries, FCC bureaucracy, and congressional indecision. And the audience did not seem to care, judging from the nebulous success of the pay-TV tests.

8·24 *The Expansion of Cable Television*

Cable television did not create much controversy initially (see 7.83), and it grew fairly quickly in the mountain areas of Pennsylvania and the Far West. By 1952, some 70 systems served 14,000 subscribers. Typically, for an installation fee and then a monthly charge of about $5, a subscriber got one or more signals "imported" from afar. By 1960 more than 650,000 television set owners were reported to be subscribing to 640 fairly small and local cable systems. Television stations in this period usually welcomed the cable operations because they provided more listeners for a station's programming.

At this time *cable* and *pay* television were very different. Cable subscribers paid a set fee for being hooked to the system and a monthly charge for reception of some or all the stations they could not receive directly off the air. Pay-TV viewers paid "per program" and usually could receive "free" programs as well. The line between these two types of service was to merge in the late 1960s when, ironically, over-the-air pay-TV had faded in potential importance while the innocent-appearing CATV systems had become one of the broadcast industry's major problems (see 9.83).

8·3 The Domination of Network Television

The broadcasting trends apparent in the late 1940s continued to the point where the radio webs had shrunk to little more than AM news outlets by 1960 and television networks were almost entirely VHF affiliates.

In 1952, half the AM stations on the air were affiliated with one or more networks, but by 1960, although there were 1,000 new stations, only one-third of AM stations maintained affiliation, including less than 10 percent of the stations beginning in this eight-year period. Clearly, the networks no longer dominated radio programming and economics in an era when all attention—including that of network personnel—was turned to television. In the early 1950s, network radio cut its rates in an attempt to retain advertisers, but most sponsors preferred television or spot advertising on individual radio stations. Many major stations gave up network affiliation to program on their own rather than be tied to a system that failed to attract listeners. The Westinghouse Broadcasting Corporation, a major group owner, pulled four stations out of NBC in August 1956 to go to fulltime local programming. Many other stations stayed with the networks but only for their news services and those daytime programs that retained some following (see 8.61).

What had been the largest network in affiliates, Mutual, fell on hard and scandalous times. From 1956 to 1959, ownership of the network changed six times, with one management convicted of stock manipulation and another accused of selling a guarantee of favorable mention on its news programs to Dominican Republic dictator Rafael Trujillo. As a consequence of all these factors, more than 130 stations dropped their Mutual affiliation.

The other radio networks drifted along in the wake of television. Ironically, some "new" radio network programs derived from television shows. The only real program innovation of lasting importance in the period was NBC's *Monitor*, which began in 1955 as a 40-hour over-the-weekend "magazine" program. The combination of talks, interviews, news, music, comedy, and sports was a hit with listeners and advertisers.

The only major attempt at FM-only networking, the Continental Network (see 7.31), was unable to expand beyond the East Coast, except for mailing recordings to other affiliates. This limited experiment ended early in 1954 with the suicide of FM inventor Edwin H. Armstrong, who had been quietly paying for telephone line interconnection of these FM stations. Several regional FM interconnection arrangements dried up at the same time. Even at their peak, they too had been limited to the Northeast.

More than anything else, the middle and late 1950s were marked by the domination of network television—and that meant NBC and CBS. But this period also saw the demise of one nationwide network and the bare survival of another.

The first was Dumont, the only television network not built on radio. Although it was fragile from the start, the network did not stop operations entirely until late summer 1955. Dumont's chief problem was always being number four at a time when most markets had fewer than four stations. CBS or NBC had first pick of affiliates, with ABC or Dumont clutching at the leftovers. Stations with more than one network affiliation—common in the 1950s—hardly ever chose to carry Dumont programming, and advertisers understandably shied away from placing ads few would see. Thus Dumont made only one-third to one-tenth of the revenue of the other networks. In January 1955 Dumont was feeding only 21 hours a week—the three prime time hours each night—and by August, although it claimed to have 160 affiliates, it was down to just over

five hours a week. Dumont then sold its profitable Pittsburgh station and withdrew to manufacturing and research activities, later selling its stations in New York and Washington, D. C.

The network that barely survived during this period was ABC, which had had many financial crises and always seemed to arrive at a television idea just after CBS and NBC had been there and cleaned up. The end of Dumont cleared time on some stations for ABC programming, and the ABC–Paramount Theaters merger (see 7.32) provided money needed to pay debts and update facilities of their O & O stations. But ABC lacked a star vehicle on which to build audience popularity, something analogous to NBC's early use of Milton Berle. All networks wanted such a boost, and for once ABC was the winner. Early in 1954, ABC signed a contract with Walt Disney Productions to air some of the "appeal to the whole family" Disney films and a new Disney-developed family television program. That show, premiering in fall 1954, was *Disneyland*, which was followed a year later by *The Mickey Mouse Club* afternoon children's program. The popularity of these programs improved ABC's image and appeal to advertisers as they promoted Disney's new amusement park. This and the increase in number of three-station markets following the Freeze improved ABC's competitive position with CBS and NBC by the late 1950s.

All television networks went through important evolutionary changes in these years. Probably most important, the networks were increasingly producing and controlling their own programs. This trend away from sponsor or agency programming control was to come to a head with the quiz show scandals (see 8.63 and 8.84). Second, after 1954 the networks relied less on half-hour or hour series programs and offered more *specials*, one-shot plays and documentaries of longer duration (see 8.62). Third, the networks were making initial investment in color equipment and programming, although only NBC, on behalf of its parent RCA, was actively promoting color (see 7.821). Like the special programming, the move to color was mainly for the sake of prestige. Hence, NBC consistently offered most color hours, followed by a reluctant CBS, with ABC not even in the running until 1958. From a total of 68 hours transmitted in 1954, color programming rose to nearly 500 hours in 1956 and more than 650 hours two years later. Nearly all the color shows were specials and most were live or on film, as color videotape recording was not yet perfected.

There were few color productions—650 hours a year is less than two hours a day —because color equipment and color broadcasting were costly, CBS and ABC were reluctant to support RCA's manufacturing adventures, and not many expensive color television receivers were being sold (see 8.71).

In the early years, most network productions had originated in New York or Chicago. By 1955–1957, however, nearly all production activity had moved to the West Coast, as television drew more heavily on Hollywood's hungry film (see 7.91) production talent pool. The shift left administrative and fiscal control in New York and creative work in Hollywood.

In these years the networks had

Sarnoffs and Weaver: NBC's Executive Team / David Sarnoff (left), operating head of RCA almost from its start in 1919, is seen talking with NBC/TV Network (1949–1953) and NBC president (1953–1955) Pat Weaver (center)—creator of the concept of "spectaculars" and the *Today* and *Tonight* shows—and his son Robert Sarnoff (then NBC chairman), who was to lead RCA after the senior Sarnoff's retirement in 1969. The younger Sarnoff was fired in 1975. Their CBS competitors are shown on page 261. Photo credit: Indelible, Inc.

their greatest influence over television development, for without an affiliation a local station was almost doomed to failure. NBC had the most affiliates, although its proportion dropped from more than 55 percent to about 42 percent of all stations between 1953 and 1960. CBS started the period with half as many affiliates as NBC but ended with nearly the same number. ABC was one-third to one-half the size of its two competitors (see Appendix C, table 3).

NBC's programming was dominated at first by network president Sylvester "Pat" Weaver, the driving force behind the radio network's *Monitor* (see above) and such television innovations as *Today* and the specials. But the real power in NBC was synonymous with the power in RCA, and soon RCA Chairman David Sarnoff's son Robert, who had earned his programming spurs as producer of the award-winning documentary series *Victory at Sea*, took over the operation of NBC. CBS continued under the leadership of Chairman William S. Paley and President Frank Stanton and a succession of television network presidents. Both networks had to face almost continuous investigation by Congress and the FCC (see 8.82) into monopolistic tendencies of networks in general and these two in particular.

After the Dumont demise, each network owned its full complement: five VHF stations. Not wishing to enter the unprofitable markets, each concentrated on the largest cities and shunned ownership of the two permitted UHF stations, although both CBS and NBC owned one or two for short periods. Ironically, ABC, the weakest of the networks, had the best O & O lineup: a station in five of the top seven markets (albeit on channel 7), with ABC as the original licensee. CBS and NBC, on the other hand, bought and sold several stations in the 1950s, jockeying for ownership of the most stations in the top five or six markets (see box on page 266).

This led to a strange deal between group owner Westinghouse and NBC. In 1955, NBC offered to buy KYW-TV, Westinghouse's Philadelphia station, in exchange for NBC's stations in Cleveland plus $3 million. Westinghouse probably would not have considered the deal except for NBC's threat to withdraw television network affiliations from other Westinghouse stations if Westinghouse did not accept. The swap took place in 1955. A year later, the Justice Department accused NBC of coercing Westinghouse with the threat of affiliation cancellations. After several years of FCC and court actions and appeals—and the intervention of other parties who hoped to gain from the situation —the FCC decided on *status quo ante:* to put everything back where it was before. In 1964 Westinghouse returned to Philadelphia, keeping the $3 million, and NBC went back to Cleveland. Observers who saw the initial deal as an example of raw network power concluded that concentration of network ownership of stations in the country's largest markets might be against the public interest.

8·4   The First ETV Stations

A small number of groups and individuals had lobbied to get channel reservations for educational television (see 7.42 and 7.825) and had succeeded with the *Sixth Report and Order's* reservation of 242 channels. Lobbying effort then switched from national to state and local governing bodies and other sources to obtain money for such stations quickly, for the FCC had reserved the educational allocations for only one year, after which commercial applications might be accepted. Though later extended indefinitely, the deadline provided the impetus to get stations on the air. The Ford Foundation, working mostly through the Fund for Adult Education (FAE) and the Fund for the Advancement of Education (also FAE), provided seed money for the campaign. The National Citizen's Committee for Educational Television was formed to convince the public of the potential values of educational stations. Their job was (1) to sell the notion of educational television to universities and other groups which would serve as licensees; (2) to gain public interest and organized action in favor of such stations for alternative programming; (3) to convince community leaders that such stations would be outlets for local talent and local government and other agencies in action; and (4) to save the ETV channel reservations from commercial pressure for reallocation.

A milepost was reached when the first educational channel on a reserved frequency took to the air—the University of Houston's KUHT, in May 1953. (WOI-TV, at Ames, Iowa, was on a pre-Freeze non-reserved channel.) The second station was KTHE on channel 28 in Los Angeles. However, its sponsors, the University of Southern California and the Alan Hancock Foundation, had financial and other difficulties, and after several months it went dark—the first ETV outlet forced to close down. Los Angeles was without an ETV station until KCET, Community Television for Southern California, reactivated channel 28 in 1964. Station growth was slowed in the process of raising tax monies, foundation support, or aid from other sources. In many cases, commercial broadcasters donated help and equipment to educational stations—sometimes in the nick of time. These altruistic-seeming donations also prevented or discouraged new competing commercial stations, since an ETV station in a market occupied a channel but

rarely attracted a large audience. Also, the ETV station provided cultural and special-interest programs to small audiences and reduced the pressure on commercial stations to carry such programs. In mid-1955, there were 12 ETV stations on the air, by 1958 there were 35, and by 1961 there were 51, but half the states had none. As with commercial channels, most of the reserved frequencies were UHF—182 of the 274 reservations the FCC had made by 1960—but as with the commercial outlets, most of the early ETV stations were on the VHF band.

Once on the air, the educational broadcasters had to fill their operating hours. Having no network to provide programming, and being unable to use ordinary television fare, most ETV stations operated for only a few hours a week. Some of these were devoted to in-school broadcasts, sometimes paid for by school districts, and others, to cultural and entertainment programs. Even by 1959, the typical ETV station was on the air for only 35 hours a week, half the time of the typical commercial station, and used mostly local productions. However, in May 1954 the National Educational Television and Radio Center was established in Ann Arbor, Michigan—it later moved to New York City—and began to provide several hours of programs to the four stations then on the air. By 1958, 30 stations were getting a minimum of six hours a week from this cooperative, chiefly as kinescope recordings or film. By 1959, having lost interest in radio, it supplied members with eight hours of programming a week—a quarter of all ETV programs. Major producing stations were WGBH (Boston), WQED (Pittsburgh), WTTW (Chicago), and KQED (San Francisco). The programs were distributed by mail, in a bicycle network from one station to the next.

Most ETV stations were under the control of a single educational institution, usually a college or university, although some school boards were interested. A few were genuine community stations, managed by nonprofit associations, with representatives from appropriate educational and civic agencies. Alabama was the first to establish a state network of several educational outlets offering concerted programming (see 9.82). Other states followed suit as funding became available.

Educational stations generally offered two separate types of programming: programs with general cultural content—adult education, foreign films, public affairs, general educational material, concerts—and instructional television (ITV). ITV was designed for the classroom (broadcast or closed circuit), or for individual viewing as a series of instructional units from kindergarten through college, for which credit could be given. The first purely instructional effort by a commercial national network was NBC's *Continental Classroom*, which began in October 1958, airing from 6:30 to 7:00 A.M.(!) It began with a series of lectures on nuclear physics and dealt over the years with many other subjects. This program obviously was not aimed at everyone, although some of its loyal viewers were able to arrange local college credit for the work done via television.

8·5   Advertising: Local Radio and National Television

There is a myth among broadcasters and students of broadcasting that radio began to lose money in the 1950s as television was beginning to make it. While the importance of radio and particularly radio networks in national advertising did decline, its income increased during this period. However, as the pie was sliced in more pieces, radio and television ex-

changed positions until in 1960 television was receiving twice the advertising dollars of radio—but radio kept making money.

What *did* decline was the economic clout of radio networks. In 1952, the webs still took in 25 percent of radio advertising revenues, but as more unaffiliated stations went on the air and advertiser interest in radio networks declined, that share plunged to 6 percent in 1960. In the same period local advertising revenues, already 52 percent of radio income in 1952, increased to 62 percent by 1960. NBC was hit harder and faster than CBS, partly because many NBC shows had lower ratings—a possible result of the 1948 CBS "talent raid" (see 7.61).

Individual stations adjusted to the changing advertising pattern as it was affected by the audience size and interest pattern. In the 1950s, evening prime time, which formerly drew the biggest radio audiences, gave way to morning and evening "drive time," when people in autos were on their way to and from work. In larger cities drive time was more easily sold and brought in greater revenue. Some local stations took over their own programming and sold their own advertising so that they could retain all the income, rather than the small fraction passed on under network arrangements. Still, roughly one-third of the AM stations, particularly new ones, were losing money in 1960. Broadcasters found out again that the advertising pie could be successfully divided just so far.

This problem was especially acute for the independent FM station operators. As an industry, FM radio didn't make money and almost all stations were in the red, though total FM income jumped from $2.6 million in 1952 to $9.4 million in 1960.

Overall, radio as an advertising medium declined from 9 percent of all advertising dollars in 1952 to 6 percent in 1960. But, as advertising in general increased throughout the Eisenhower years, radio's total revenues increased from $624 million in 1952 to $692 million in 1960. So the economic changes in radio were mainly changes in pattern. Most radio stations operated with an adequate profit margin, and the larger clear-channel stations made excellent profits.

Television's income increased spectacularly in these eight years, growing from $454 million in 1952—about 6 percent of all advertising expenditures—to over $1,600 million—13 percent of all advertising—by 1960 (see Appendix C, table 5). But television pattern changes were opposite to radio's. Local advertising declined—from 23 percent of television revenue in 1952 to 17 percent in 1960—as did network advertising—from 57 percent to 50 percent—while spot advertising increased from one-fifth to one-third of all television income. The networks' own income increased, but their proportion of the pie dropped as many non-network-owned stations came on the air.

It has been suggested by both broadcasters and their critics that a television license was, in effect, "a license to print money." A VHF station with a network affiliation, as nearly all had, usually was in the black within a couple of years of going on the air even though establishing it frequently took $1 million or more. Unfortunately, and not unexpectedly, this profitable picture did not extend to UHF stations. Although only about half the operating UHF stations were losing money in 1960, many others had failed for lack of income or operating capital. With their more limited range and often without network affiliation, UHF stations had too small an audience to interest national and regional advertisers. They attracted only local advertising, aside from some national spot business, and some independent UHFs had a reputation for low standards

of advertising acceptance. Quarter- and half-hour programs that consisted of advertisements with a bit of entertainment thrown in to hold viewers were common. Many UHF stations did not subscribe to the NAB Television Code (see 8.85) simply because they had to sell all the commercial time they could, regardless of how many spots were aired in an hour, or type of products advertised. Although UHF rates were lower than competing VHF station rates, UHF stations could not attract more business and thus make up for the lower rates per spot because advertisers wanted to reach the largest possible audiences in each market.

On the networks, and to some extent on local stations, an important change was taking place in sponsorship patterns. In 1952, one advertiser normally sponsored an entire program, just as in radio. Some major manufacturers of consumer goods controlled several programs, particularly daytime shows. In 1951, for example, Procter & Gamble had become—and still is—the biggest television advertiser, as it had been in radio, with several daytime soap operas and evening programs. But as the television audience increased, as programs got more complex, and as talent and technical personnel demanded larger salaries, programming costs went up sharply (see 8.62). Networks, being able to cover their increased expenses without having a cost-per-thousand greater than competing media, raised their advertising rates until, by the late 1950s, half-hour or hour network programs were beyond the reach of many advertisers.

Starting with longer programs, and then with shorter series episodes, networks began to develop new types of advertiser support. First appeared alternating or shared sponsorship, where two noncompeting firms would share the sponsorship of a single program by alternating weeks or some other segment. In this way they cut their costs while maintaining a regular identification with the program and exposure to potential buyers. One of the first programs to make this approach popular was the Arthur Godfrey radio variety program, which was sold in 15-minute segments to participating advertisers. Television's *Today* operated the same way. Daytime and then prime-time programs required shared sponsorship as costs continued to rise. By 1957–1958, about half the network shows were still fully sponsored by one firm, while 28 percent were under an alternation arrangement, and 20 percent used a participating format, where advertisers regularly purchased time for their spots in a particular show. By 1960 this was the standard for specials and hour-long series, while full or alternating sponsorship still was prevalent for half-hour shows. (*Participating* advertising was placed within a designated program, and *spot* advertising was placed anywhere in the station's schedule according to the class of time, based on audience size, purchased by the advertiser.) Both spot and participating advertisers paid a rate that covered the advertising time, a *pro rata* share of the program adjacent to the spot, and a profit for the program packager, usually a network. When advertising agencies relinquished television programming control to program packagers and networks, spots were sold without sponsorship, and the two-decades-long relationship between sponsor and program, amounting to sponsor control of programming, broke down.

Television time rates and the cost of production became prime issues with advertisers. In the late 1950s, production of a one-minute commercial cost between $3,000 and $15,000, depending on the degree of production difficulty. In the years under discussion, talent costs went up 60 percent to 85 percent, a major part of an overall 20 percent cost increase. On top of the production cost and the cost of duplicating and distributing the filmed commercials themselves—which was, of course, spread over a number of airings—the advertiser had to buy network time. Full sponsors had to absorb costs that for a prime-time hour rose from $33,000 in 1952 to more than $87,000 by 1960, and spot advertisers had to absorb their share of the costs. These expenses, even with good results in sales, drove many smaller firms out of television advertising and back into radio or print, while big national firms made heavy use of national and regional television. But numerous television advertisers grew from almost nothing to highly profitable size in a few years because of their sponsorship of a popular program. Probably the best example was relatively unknown cosmetics maker Revlon, which grabbed a major portion of the cosmetics market through its sponsorship of highly popular quiz shows during that format's heyday of the late 1950s. While some such successes later evaporated, Revlon held its improved product position despite the quiz show scandals (see 8.63). On the other hand, when research demonstrated that many children watched the Lucille Ball program, a tobacco company sponsor dropped the program. Although it was the most popular show on the air, it did not reach enough *smokers* to pay off.

8·6 Programming Trends in the Fifties

While advertiser and audience interest was centered on television programming developments, radio—even network radio—did not dry up and blow away. The rise in revenues during most of this period (see 8.5) suggested that radio stations had to be doing something right; neither the influx of new radio stations nor program competition from television was killing them. Television was firmly established by 1952, and was falling into recognizable program cycles much like those radio had experienced.

8•61   Revival of Local Radio and Coming of Top 40

The late 1950s marked the end of network radio. Even in the early and mid-1950s network schedules resembled the great days of the two previous decades in that a variety of sponsored programs were available day and night. Interestingly, at no time before or after the 1953–1954 season have the radio networks presented so many programming hours per week. But by 1956, the total began to drop off sharply. The first signs were (1) simulcasting of popular shows on radio and television, and eventual transition to television alone, and (2) the continuing broadcast of sustaining programs for prestige and to create the semblance of a going operation.

In the evening hours, formerly prime time, only variety and musical programs and various types of talk shows increased in hours per week after 1952. The light music format, which had not been popular on network radio since the 1930s, returned in the late 1950s with 15- and 30-minute filler programs built around singers—similar to television offerings of the same period. The only markedly different radio format was NBC's *Monitor* (see 8.3).

This is not to say that all creative talent had left radio for television. A variety program, the *Big Show*, was one of the most ambitious ever attempted of its type. NBC produced an adult science-fiction program called *Dimension X* (later retitled *X Minus One*). Two decades later, when NBC rebroadcast many of the orig-

inal episodes, they played well—even in an era of space flight. A major evening program format in the late 1950s was news, and by 1956 there were more hours of news broadcast than any other type of network program. Today, of course, news is the main if not only reason for the existence of radio networks.

Soap operas continued to dominate daytime radio, although they were heard for one-half and then for only one-third of their previous hours per week. The soaps were one of the last bastions of advertiser support in network radio at a time when most network shows had become sustaining, partly because many soap operas were owned and produced by their sponsors. Another lasting network radio daytime program format was the general talk variety program, including Arthur Godfrey on CBS and Don McNeill's *Breakfast Club* on ABC.

But total radio network hours on the air dropped drastically in the late 1950s. Local affiliates first dropped sustaining musical programming because they wanted to go their own ways, and then most of the remaining sponsored programs except news because they made insufficient income to warrant network costs. Many affiliates no longer automatically cleared time for network shows. The last radio soap operas and evening dramatic programs died in 1960. *Gunsmoke*, one of the latter, was converted to an extraordinarily popular television program that lasted more than two decades. Present to the end was a version of the show that had given network radio its first impetus—*Amos 'n' Andy*. The blackface program had converted in the late 1950s from situation comedy to musical variety with short comedy bits between popular tunes, but it too was eventually dropped. In place of these vestiges of big-time radio, CBS announced a new programming plan, intended to pre-

The End of Radio's Daytime Serial: 1960

Friday, November 25, 1960, 2 p.m. Eastern Standard Time, marked the conclusion of one of the most distinctive eras in domestic mass communications; after nearly thirty consecutive years of broadcasting the radio soap operas had reached a conclusion. "Goodbye, and may God bless you," Ma Perkins told her loyal audience as she finished her 7,065th and final broadcast. Young Dr. Malone also bid "a sad goodbye" to his audience. The Second Mrs. Burton did the same, introducing members of her cast for quick goodbyes. Local radio stations along the CBS network line continued with their transcribed spot announcements, time signals and station breaks as radio moved relentlessly forward, never pausing to mourn the departed nor, indeed, even heeding their loss. . . .

A major drop-off began in 1955 when only nineteen serials were renewed for the Fall season. Among those which did not return were such veterans as "Lorenzo Jones," "Stella Dallas" and "Just Plain Bill." The total dropped to sixteen in 1956, ten of which were on CBS and the remainder equally divided between NBC and ABC. They were discontinued altogether by ABC the following season. There were virtually no changes in 1958 but the 1959–60 season represented another serious diminution. NBC listed but one serial, "True Story," and CBS, dropping "Backstage Wife," "Our Gal Sunday" and "Nora Drake," was down to seven titles. NBC discontinued its only serial, along with its other entertainment programming, at the end of the season and "Helen Trent" was dropped from CBS.

The 1960–61 season began with a total of six serials, all on CBS and all on borrowed time. The programs were owned by sponsors who were no longer interested in using them. Rather than discontinue the serials entirely, CBS chose to lease the properties by paying royalties to Procter and Gamble and other owners. Other sponsors were then sought to fill the four commercial positions within the programs. No regular pattern was followed in this application of spot advertising and there was none of the earlier commercial identification with a particular serial. Only half-sold through most of 1960, they dropped to 25% sold toward the end of the year. "Best Seller" was introduced by the network in a final attempt to instill new vitality in the daytime serial by dramatizing novels but it was too late. Affiliated stations increased their efforts to force discontinuance of the serials altogether, determined to obtain release of the time for local sales and operations. In mid-August CBS announced that the last Friday in November would be the final broadcast date for the remaining serials. Each program thus had time to tie all of its loose ends together and to resolve its current complications. Significantly, none closed with such finality that the plot could not be resumed on a moment's notice.

Source: George A. Willey, "End of an Era: The Daytime Radio Serial," *Journal of Broadcasting* 5:97-115 (Spring 1961), pages 97, 102–103. By permission.

serve the physical network for prestige, emergency, and news: 10 minutes of news on the hour supplemented with five-minute feature shows during the day, and a loosely formated Arthur Godfrey show. Period.

In the 1950s the networks changed from controlling their affiliates to merely supplying them with part of their program input. By 1960–1961, radio networks were set in a mold which was to survive into the 1970s: news on the hour and little else. But in a changing and frightening world, special news events were to remain radio's forte, as it could deliver flash or bulletin stories faster than television or any other medium. Almost any other program carried on radio—political conventions, sporting events—also was carried on television, albeit with different commentators. Radio networks became vestigial. Stations without network affiliations offered a minimum of "rip 'n' read," or "yank 'n' yell," newscasts, composed of the wire services' five-minute summaries read by a disc jockey. However, in times of great stress or national disaster the networks often allowed independent stations free use of their coverage.

With radio networks no longer providing programs or income to local stations, by the late 1950s radio stations had to use their own resources for the first time since the 1920s. Most stations followed the networks with a music and news format, soon known as standard (later MOR—middle-of-the-road), which usually meant trying to program a bit of something for everyone, with emphasis on vocal and orchestral popular music. Traditional radio sound lingered in such operations, which offered recorded music about half the time, sometimes adding local talk or variety programs, and in general aimed for the widest and largest possible audience.

While a majority of radio stations followed an MOR format in the 1950s, a new trend was developing. Freed from the restraints of network shows and schedules, and seeking ways of attracting listeners in markets with increasingly competitive radio stations, stations in several cities began to specialize in a particular kind of music. This was not new; there had been classical music stations, usually FM, and, in some rural areas, country-and-western (C & W) music stations. Now stations in markets with a substantial black population began to program to that audience with "rhythm and blues." There were perhaps 20 such stations in 1952 and about 50 by the end of the decade. Stations that went to a background orchestral "good music," or *wallpaper*, format with little or no talk frequently were engaged in storecasting (see 8.11), and were among the first to adopt automation for assembling and playing the day's programming.

The format that was almost to take radio by storm began slowly. Looking at sales of phonograph records, program directors in several stations decided to emphasize the tunes that were selling well, either as records or sheet music. Station owner Todd Storz in Omaha and theater and station owner Gordon McLendon in Dallas are often given credit for originating what quickly was to become known as *Top 40* radio by the late 1950s. Storz tried the idea as early as 1949, bringing it to full force by 1953–1954. He operated in major markets while McLendon adopted the format in smaller and medium-sized markets because the formula was relatively inexpensive. Essentially, they created a tightly controlled, fast-paced format that usually involved playing each hour a certain number of what program directors, disc jockeys, and a growing number of "tip sheet" newsletters expected to become hits, three or four "top ten" tunes as measured by record sales, an old favorite—as time went on, "old" might mean anything out more than a few months—and fast-paced orchestrals and vocals. The tunes were divided by spot commercials, frequently delivered by the disc jockey, weather forecasts, time announcements, and news on the hour. Strong station identification became more important than selling the network or a local or network program. The process of station identification became an art far beyond the mere repetition of station call letters and city required by the FCC. The jingle, used extensively for commercials in the past, was revived to give a station a specific image. Identity built on call letters, frequency location on the dial, or key talent, was constantly repeated until listeners knew it by heart. Directly tied to station identification were the station's on-air staff, who grew from mere announcers into *disc jockeys* (DJs) or, after station publicity people got involved, *personalities*. Their stock in trade was to create a specific approach to the music, intermixed with talk, jokes, and comment usually delivered at a rapid pace with little or no "dead" air space or silence.

Thus was born *formula* or *Top 40* or *rock* radio in 1952–1954. It expanded from about 20 stations in 1955 to hundreds by 1960, although most imitators copied the outward format of the pioneers without really understanding the formula. It was a unique format that only radio could accomplish. It was aimed at teenagers, who were the fastest growing segment of the population, had growing disposable income, and had plenty of time to listen. Time and time again, an MOR-format station would take the plunge and achieve dramatic increases in listeners and income. When one rock station played the same music as another, with much the same sound, the personalities on the air contributed tremendously to a station's success. An unknown announcer named Alan

Freed came out of Ohio to become one of the most important jocks on a New York radio station, and soon worked himself into a commanding position in the music world. Another, Dick Clark, became almost an industry unto himself first in radio and then television, in Philadelphia (see 8.62). Similar radio personalities soon were affecting everyday life and manners of the youth of most major cities, and attracting negative comment from persons who disapproved of those manners and that music.

While radio always had been an important adjunct to sheet music and phonograph record sales, Top 40 radio personalities now developed virtual life-or-death power over popular music record makers and sellers. If a song was played, it usually meant instant success and profit, and even an excellent record was doomed to failure if it could not get an airing on one of the key Top 40 stations. Thus, the jocks (and sometimes even program managers) at the 50 kw rock 'n' roll stations in New York, Chicago, St. Louis, Los Angeles, and Philadelphia suddenly found themselves waited on hand and foot not only by their fans but by recording groups and record salesmen who depended on radio. Many disc jockeys responded to this adulation and flattery by accepting payments, gifts, and favors in return for playing specific records, always asserting however that they played only those records they had judged to be good. The *payola* business became a public scandal (see 8.84) at the end of the decade to match that of the television quiz shows, and a degree of cleaning up was instituted.

For most of the 1950s, the important thing was combining records and radio to create instant events in the minds of listeners—the task of the disc jockey. Reflecting the times, the DJ had to get popular stars and music on the air without making radio sound Negro-oriented, even

The Rise of Formula Radio / With formula or Top 40 radio, radio became more than a carrier of media content originating elsewhere; it became central to a type of entertainment.

Rock's radio and record orientation is critical in distinguishing the music as a folk idiom. Although rock was not the first folk music style to *use* records and radio, it was the first to express itself *primarily* through these mechanical, impersonal media. Before rock, popular records and radio shows were inspired by live situations—Broadway shows, nightclub performances, and other personal appearances of a group or individual. Radio tried to duplicate these situations; Pop disk jockeys like Al Jarvis and Martin Block described "make-believe ballrooms" which created the atmosphere of a large dance hall, and in which songs were experienced as if a particular musician were performing in person instead of on records. Similarly, folk music traditionally emerged from live situations—from groups sharing a common experience of work or play, or from an individual singing to his people. With rock, however, records became the primary, common bond among artists and listeners, and radio shows provided the primary, common situation in which the music was experienced. Without consciously describing a hootenanny or trying to elicit the atmosphere of one, the rock radio show generated the experience of a folk gathering. The unique feature of this experience was that it existed only in the mind and emotion of the individual listener; he did not pretend that the records he heard were anything but records, because the sounds he absorbed were realities in themselves.

The rock disk jockey played an instrumental role in this experiential folk reality. Because he spontaneously participated in the event—rather than structuring it and separating it from himself by assuming the role of a detached "master of ceremonies"—he encouraged the listeners to react in equally spontaneous and personal ways. Moreover, when the disk jockey audibly hammered the beat to one of his favorite songs, or sang a few of its lyrics, and when he breathlessly read the news, weather and sports, he gave the radio show a pace which—to listeners accustomed to an older radio style—caused everything to blend indiscriminately together. But this style also surrounded the show with a total atmosphere that was typical of rock. In the dense fabric of sounds which characterized the radio event, the records assumed the imprint of performances and the show assumed the immediacy—although not the illusion—of a live folk gathering.

With rock, the radio and record media assumed lives of their own. They became ends in themselves instead of means to other ends.

Source: Carl Belz, *The Story of Rock* (New York: Oxford University Press, 1972), pages 46–47. By permission.

though much of the impetus for what Alan Freed titled *rock 'n' roll* was the blacks' rhythm and blues. Program directors were concerned that too much "black" sound would alienate their basically white suburban listeners, and thus the early rock stars, except for Chuck Berry, were all white. The first star was Bill Haley and his Comets, who mixed country and western with the new rhythm. In 1956 the first rock superstar arrived—Elvis Presley, a former C & W singer whose career rose dramatically after he appeared on the Ed Sullivan television show. The cameras were limited to shooting him from the waist up, since his pelvic gyrations were deemed too hot for television—or at least for Sullivan. Viewers of the show heard little singing as the girls in the audience screamed with excitement, reminding many of the similar reaction to Frank Sinatra at his concerts a decade earlier. Before 1960 Presley had 18 records each selling more than one million copies. Fan magazines turned to radio again, as it was the rock stars' major medium. Formula format continued with modifications as the mainstay of radio for many years.

The country and western boom came on the heels of rock 'n' roll popularity. After 1957, C & W records were heard on many stations, and C & W specialty stations began to appear in the Northeast, heretofore out of reach for country stars and songs whose "natural" audience was in the South and Midwest. Another type of music allied to both C & W and rock was the folk music of the Kingston Trio and similar well-rehearsed groups whose songs were musically enjoyable and had much less "bite" than the socially significant folksongs of the 1930s and before. By the late 1950s rock was being recycled, stations playing "oldies but goodies" or "golden oldies" several years after they left the Top 40 list.

8·62　The Age of Television Entertainment

In the 1950s as quiz shows and westerns filled evening prime time, sponsors produced fewer and fewer programs. As late as 1957, sponsors or advertising agencies still produced about one-third of the network shows, especially daytime programs, while networks produced another third. The remainder came from the *packagers*, companies that combined talent, production facilities, and ideas for specific programs or series under contract to a network. Typically, a packager developed or bought the program idea and, if the network was interested, produced a *pilot* or sample program. If the network and a potential sponsor were still interested, the packaging company would then produce series episodes. For each program, the packager would assemble talent, technical facilities—sometimes rented from the network—and personnel, so that the network would purchase a finished film or tape package. By 1960 these companies produced about 60 percent of television network programming, networks about 20 percent, chiefly news and documentaries, and sponsors about 14 percent. The packagers made much of their profit from syndication to individual stations of programs no longer aired on the network. Frequently, however, the networks acquired a financial interest in the programs produced by the packagers—a system that developed further in the 1960s.

Another important trend was the change from live to recorded programs. In 1953, 80 percent of the network shows were done live before television cameras at the time of televising so that any mistakes went out over the air—actors forgetting their lines, "dead" bodies getting up and walking off a scene, a stagehand walking outside a window that was supposed to be 25 stories high. The remaining 20 percent of programs were on film, including a few kinescopes. By 1960, the VTR (see 8.12) had taken hold on the networks, and one-third of their programs were taped—a process even then so good that most viewers could not tell the difference between live and tape. Live network shows were down to 36 percent of the total —and continued to drop sharply in the early 1960s—with the remaining third being filmed. The kinescope virtually disappeared from network use.

Stations had used syndicated, filmed programming for their off-network hours from the beginning. At first it had consisted of some original material and old theatrical films. By 1955 a good part of syndicated offerings was off-network material —programs that had finished their first runs on the networks. But in 1960, after a short-lived attempt in 1957–1958, the networks began showing feature films, which were not available for syndication until the networks were finished with them. As a result, the stations expanded their network television schedules, typically from 48 percent to 61 percent, and reduced local live and syndicated film material, from 22 percent down to 11 percent for local live and from 14 percent to 13 percent for theatrical film available for station use.

That television made voracious use of program material was demonstrated by its rapid turnover. From 1955 to 1959, the networks averaged 46 new programs each season. Only about 20 of these returned for a second year, and many failed to make it through their first season. Such short runs were costly for networks and packagers. Furthermore, a program that had been in active production for less than a year was unattractive for syndication. Why some programs last and others do not never has been clearly understood, but in the mid-1950s observers suggested four

reasons: sponsor satisfaction, personality continuity of the host or characters, a low-pressure format, and familiar situations. Certainly another influence on program selection if not longevity was program cycles, for as soon as a format became popular, other networks or producers aired their own versions, rapidly satiating public interest until the format began to decline for lack of material and viewer following. The television *adult western* format (see below) is an excellent example.

Another trend was the gradual lengthening of programs. Whereas in the early years program directors had been concerned about holding interest for longer than 15 or 20 minutes, the half-hour show had become standard by the early 1950s. As the decade wore on, the hour-long program became prevalent, and 90- and even 120-minute special programs became almost common. Some program types, such as situation comedies, stayed with the half-hour period. The general trend was to lessen the lock-step progression of programs on all networks at the same hour. For instance, a very popular hour-long program might be scheduled so that its second half would overlap the start of a program on another network.

One of the most interesting developments of this period was the *spectacular*. Beginning in 1954, with the coming of limited colorcasting by NBC, the special or spectacular program made lavish use of settings and costumes, color, and major names to attract an audience from the humdrum of series formats, even though they often emphasized spectacle over content. As noted at the head of this chapter, one of the most important shows of this type was *Peter Pan*, telecast by NBC for two hours, live, in color, in early March 1955. Mary Martin's bravura performance was seen by nearly 70 million Americans, making it the largest audience for any single event in history up to that time. Early specials marking major anniversaries of the Ford Motor Company or the electric light were telecast on two or three networks at a time. The specials were expensive to produce, and programmers at first were unsure of their possible effect on viewers used to regular programs in scheduled slots week after week. In the 1954–1955 season, there were only 41 hours of specials, but in 1959–1960 there were six times as many. NBC broadcast more of these programs than the other networks, thanks to the prodding of "Pat" Weaver; CBS was second, although similar in approach; and ABC seldom was in the running. Content varied from lavish variety specials to documentaries and drama, which usually appeared in inverse proportions—more drama, less documentary, and so on. All were intended for large audiences.

Another important program was NBC's *Tonight* variety show, which began on September 27, 1954, with Steve Allen as host. This 90-minute agglomeration of talk, guests, music, sketches, and jokes began at 11:30 P.M. (ET) and took network programming into the wee hours of the morning. *Tonight*, with Jack Paar taking over as host in 1957, quickly attracted a following of night owls.

Straight musical programming consisted of former radio orchestral shows, including the semiclassical *Voice of Firestone* and the popular *Your Hit Parade* (see 7.61), and light music shows. The latter, generally 15-minute filler programs built around a single singer, faded from television after 1954 in favor of general variety shows. The rock music format came to television in 1957 with *American Bandstand* on ABC, hosted by Dick Clark for two hours late every afternoon. This program, begun in Philadelphia in 1952, became a nationally televised teenage dance party with guest star visits. To save rehearsals and to give the audience the sound they were used to, the singers merely moved their lips in synchronization (*sync*) to a record. Youthful fans responded to the dancers and new dances as much as the music itself. Building on this program and his radio popularity, Clark built an interlocking, highly profitable empire of music publishers, production, and other companies. Many local stations had similar programs, which were relatively easy to produce, but they never had the impact of rock radio.

Four major kinds of drama dominated network television in the 1950s: daytime soap operas, general and anthology drama, situation comedy, and, at the end of the decade, adult westerns. The familiar housewife-pointed serial drama grew slowly after 1953, until it reached 20 hours a week by 1960. This increase came partly from extending the programs from 15 to 30 minutes in the middle of the 1950s and partly from new shows coming on the air. Prestige anthology drama flourished. During the 1953–1956 period it was at its height, with some 20 programs per week on the three networks. After 1958 such programs were presented as specials, comprising between one-quarter and one-third of all special programming. In either category, the shows usually ran an hour or longer, although there were a few half-hour programs in the 1950s; were presented live or, toward the end of the decade, on tape; used changing characters and actors in different stories; and presented adaptations as well as original plays.

Playhouse 90, started by CBS in fall 1956, probably typified the best of television anthology drama. This weekly, 90-minute, live, original drama series allowed optimal development of characterization and plot. Programs such as *Studio One*, *Kraft Theater*, and the *U.S. Steel Hour* had proven very successful as early as 1953.

Rod Serling's "Patterns," on the *Kraft The-ater* program, had so much response that it was repeated, live, a few weeks later. It was later made into a movie, as were his "Requiem for a Heavyweight" and Paddy Chayefsky's low-key but warmly satisfying "Marty." For the first time people on the street talked about television theater —plays written by Chayefsky, Serling, Reginald Rose, and others, and produced and directed by people like John Frankenheimer, Delbert Mann, and Franklin Schaffner. These creative people, many of whom moved to the feature film industry in later years, understood the television medium and concentrated on images that would move from the small screen into the minds and emotions of the television audience. Some programs used major stars in substantial dramatic roles, but others used "unknown" actors, including many from radio drama, with great success. One program, dealing with the death of Stalin, precipitated an international incident and rebounded on Soviet attitudes toward network newsmen stationed in Moscow.

Naturally, with the pressure of weekly deadlines, the quality was uneven —something that is often overlooked in reviewing the "golden age" of television drama. Many programs were thoroughly panned by critics. Although new series aired—CBS's suspenseful *Climax* and shorter programs like *Death Valley Days* and the *Jane Wyman Theater*—rising costs and declining ratings reduced the anthology format to an occasional special.

A continuing staple through the 1950s was the half-hour situation comedy. Paced by the long-running Lucille Ball program under the title of *I Love Lucy* and other labels, this type peaked in 1954 and 1955 and then dropped with the onslaught of the western adventure show. But this drop may be misleading, for the televised situation comedy is one of the most long-

lasting formats ever devised for broadcasting. Though it fluctuates, it continues strong. Usually built on a "typical" but actually very atypical American family, it spawned subgenre such as the rural situation comedy, first successful with *The Real McCoys*.

Another situation comedy subgenre saw humor in confidence men. Robert Cummings appeared as a leering photographer surrounded by beautiful models, and hopelessly pursued by his eminently sensible but very plain assistant. This program, which ran for five years, was familiar to moviegoers who had seen Cummings play similar parts in films. Comic Phil Silvers created one of television's unique characters, Army Sergeant Ernie Bilko, in the last part of the 1950s. Sergeant Bilko ran rings around his camp commander, most of his men, and his noncommissioned colleagues but often got his comeuppance while trying to make money in slippery ways.

Another television staple that dwindles but never disappears is the crime-adventure-detective genre. The most successful of the television crime fighters of the 1950s was lawyer *Perry Mason* played by Raymond Burr, who brought the Erle Stanley Gardner character to life in 1958. In 1956 film director Alfred Hitchcock brought his suspense and macabre sense of humor to television. His half-hour thrillers with weird twists were famous almost more for the director's opening and closing monologues than for the dramas themselves. Crime à la Chicago's bootlegging days showed up on *The Untouchables*, with a machine-gun narration by gossip columnist Walter Winchell and a wonderful cast of old automobiles. Despite protests from Italian-Americans that all the villains appeared to be Italians, the program had high ratings for years. *Peter Gunn*, a series notable for its improvisational jazz theme and background, had a detective who, like most television heroes, usually won but often took a beating in the process. Running through the 1950s and, after a break, again in the late 1960s was the archetype *Dragnet*, created by and starring Jack Webb in a realistic account of police operations in Los Angeles. Another show with a California setting was *77 Sunset Strip*, which had a good theme, fast cars, Hollywood living, and a new idol for teenage girls, Edd "Kookie" Burns. It and other Warner Brothers productions, such as *Hawaiian Eye*, were so formula-written that, during a writers' strike, they exchanged old scripts and merely changed the characters' names. David Janssen, later to star in several other popular series, was *Richard Diamond, Private Eye,* whose telephone-answering service operator "Sam" —only her attractive legs were seen on the screen—was Mary Tyler Moore. Every television season most networks offered a couple of detective or police-related programs, usually in realistic half-hour formats.

In the late 1950s, the western became the most popular type of television series drama. There always had been westerns on television—even one produced live each day in a station backyard in Philadelphia—but like *The Lone Ranger* and other radio westerns, they were aimed at younger listeners. *Hopalong Cassidy*—originally a series of inexpensive movies —was tremendously popular among youngsters. *The Cisco Kid* and other westerns were major television syndication items. The *adult western*, with three-dimensional characters, arrived in fall 1955, with *Gunsmoke*, a former radio show, serving as the archetype. The four continuing characters—a frontier U.S. marshal, his assistant, the female saloon owner, and the grizzled doctor—anchored two decades of episodes that concentrated on

character and incident rather than on the old action-adventure, good versus bad, of children's programs. Although the cast changed, *Gunsmoke* became one of television's longest running programs. The growth in western-located programs was rapid: from six shows in 1955–1956 to 18 in 1957–1958 and 30 in 1959–1960, the year in which *Bonanza*, the second most successful western program, made its debut. This hour-long show was built around a ranch-owning patriarch played by Lorne Greene—formerly a top announcer for the Canadian Broadcasting Corporation—and his four, later three, sons. The episodes on the Ponderosa Ranch were to fill television screens for 14 seasons and then continue into endless years of syndication. Many other westerns did too, such as *Have Gun — Will Travel*, which set a high standard for acting, as its cultured gunman-hero, Richard Boone, roamed the West for hire. The overwhelming popularity of the western format was brief but some programs achieved ratings of more than 40, when a rating in the low 20s was considered good, for weeks at a time. The American West of the late 1800s had long been a major theme of the movies and printed fiction, and it fascinated television audiences steadily through the 1960s, although with diminishing popularity.

Most of Hollywood's feature films were not available to television in the 1952–1960 period. Films made prior to 1948 often were syndicated to local stations, but most film producers and distributors kept the classics and post-1948 production away from television. Their reasons were economic. Films made after August 1948 were bound by a contractual requirement that performers be paid additional income for television showings. In addition, film producers were afraid that, if they sold their product to their chief competing medium, old films showing on local stations would cut into the potential theater audience for new films or re-releases. The major producers held this front tenuously through the 1950s and then agreed to a common release date for most of their old productions, holding on only to classics and recent films still valuable for theatrical release. Thus in 1956–1957, thousands of Hollywood feature and short-subject films flooded into television, usually as "packages" of good and not-so-good films from a given studio. Why the sale in 1956 after years of holding off? Simply because Hollywood was hurting financially and needed the capital badly enough to cause the studios to sell their own heritage and ignore the potential disadvantages. Interestingly, in light of later events, feature films appeared in *network* schedules in 1956 and 1957 only in limited numbers, and did not return until the early 1960s. At the time, it still was economically more feasible for networks to prepare and present original material. The network also feared that theatrical films would not attract large audiences, since many people already had seen them.

A number of innovations were made in children's programs, reducing reliance on *Hopalong Cassidy*. In 1956 CBS began a morning show for preschoolers, *Captain Kangaroo*—a mixture of songs, education, fun, and a bit of light philosophy. Bob Keeshan, who was actually in his thirties, played the easygoing elderly sea captain in such a way as to charm parents and children alike. Once in the late 1950s, when CBS contemplated taking *Captain Kangaroo* off the air, brief mention of these plans in the trade press and newspaper television columns brought thousands of letters from outraged parents, many of them connected with the broadcasting industry. CBS executive Hubbell Robinson promised that the program would remain. However, this outpouring of support attracted the pre-

viously missing advertisers to the point that many parents sighed for the days of fewer commercials and more program content. Most network programming for children consisted of action-adventure shows and cartoons presented in the late afternoon or on Saturday or Sunday morning. The ABC-Disney deal led to *Disneyland* for all ages and to the *Mickey Mouse Club*, which in 1956 practically owned the grade-school audience in the late afternoon. Soon the cast's wearing of caps with Mickey Mouse ears caused a nationwide fad, and the show's theme song became a camp hit among older children. The Disney organization again syndicated the original shows in the 1970s, long after many of the young performers had risen in show business or sunk to obscurity. The success of this revival led to a later—unsuccessful—version, featuring a cast that better reflected American cultural and ethnic diversity.

8•63   The Quiz Shows: Success and Scandal

Even more emphatically but more briefly than westerns, big money quiz shows grabbed the nation's fancy. The *$64,000 Question,* under the sponsorship of Revlon cosmetics, began on CBS on June 7, 1955, and within a month was the most popular program on the air, with a Nielsen rating of 41.1. It was based on an old radio quiz program that doubled the ante as the contestant answered each succeeding question, up to $64. The *$64,000 Question* was a triumph of psychological appeal—vast sums of money—and format, with quickly famous isolation booths, bank-guarded questions developed by a team of university researchers, and participants in everyday occupations who apparently often had expert knowledge in unlikely fields. So the nation saw a Marine captain who was a cooking expert, a grandmother fascinated with baseball statistics, a woman psychologist knowledgeable about boxing (Dr. Joyce Brothers, who had deliberately memorized boxing data to get on the show, and who later had her own broadcast advice program), a shoemaker who knew grand opera, and a ten-year-old math whiz. The show's producers received 15,000–20,000 applications a week, and cut that number to about 500 "possibles." Of those they actively considered half, but selected only about 15 each week. Louis Cowan, whose organization developed the idea for the program, became a high CBS executive. The *$64,000 Question* became so popular that it was followed by the *$64,000 Chal-lenge*, where winners from the first show were challenged by other contestants. At one point *Question* and *Challenge* were one-two in the ratings, and Revlon had to change its advertising because it had run out of product!

These programs were soon followed by *Twenty-One*, in which harder questions received more points and it took 21 to win a match; *Dotto*, trying quickly to identify a face that gradually emerged as dots were slowly connected; and others in both evening and daytime hours. The prize money made weekly headlines. Several contestants won more than $100,000, and even the losers earned a new Cadillac as consolation.

But this success did not continue.

TV's Isolation Booth Era / The format was fairly similar on all the big money quiz shows before the end came, in a blaze of cheating and scandal—curtains, the sponsor's name in evidence, the ubiquitous isolation booths presumably precluding hanky-panky for the competitors, and the velvet-chained stands for the contestants before the questions were asked. This shot is from *$64,000 Challenge*, the program for successful contestants from *$64,000 Question*. Photo credit: Indelible, Inc.

By late 1957 and early 1958, ratings were falling off and some newer shows aired only briefly. It was difficult to maintain a fever pitch of interest among viewers. But much more serious were the mutterings from various quarters that the shows had been rigged—an accusation that program producers and contestants vigorously denied. But the denials were false and the dam had to break: too many people knew what was going on. The first news of something seriously wrong came in August 1958 when *Dotto* was abruptly canceled from its CBS morning slot and its NBC evening position. Several contestants had claimed that the program had been rigged, and one had written to the FCC. Within days, some 20 quiz programs left the air in television's first major programming scandal. Network officials claimed ignorance of rigging, program producers said that people did not understand commercial television's purposes and practices, and advertisers said nothing. In 1959 a New York grand jury investigated the matter, but its final report in July was not made public. Responsibility for investigation—which the public demanded, particularly after popular winner Charles Van Doren had admitted complicity in cheating on *Twenty-One*—then devolved on Congress and the FCC. The shock waves that went through the industry as a result of the quiz show and payola scandals made many persons wonder about the merits of the high pressure and stakes of broadcasting and especially of the demand for high ratings to please advertisers (see 8.84).

8•64   Development of Television Journalism

News programming on most television stations and networks changed little during this period. The networks each of-fered a 15-minute early evening roundup, which by the late 1950s contained more network reporting and newsfilm shooting than the simple newsreel of the early 1950s. NBC ended John Cameron Swayze's news anchor job in 1956, replacing him with a team of reporters first assembled for reporting the 1956 elections (see 8.65), Chet Huntley and David Brinkley, both experienced broadcast journalists. Douglas Edwards continued to hold down the CBS evening news, and John Daly anchored the ABC program. Local stations usually scheduled a half-hour of news, weather, and sports—often in the form of three ten-minute programs—prior to the network news and then offered a recap at the end of network programming at 11 P.M.—10 P.M. in the midwestern and mountain states. This format did not change until 1963, when the CBS and NBC programs were lengthened to a half-hour (see 9.64).

Supplementing the regular network news programs were many special events. There is space here for only some of the highlights. The June 1953 coverage of Queen Elizabeth II's coronation in London was a technical tour-de-force. The time differential of six hours between London and New York, the transatlantic distance, and the desire of people in North America to see what transpired as soon as possible offered interesting problems. The time differential and the need to transport film actually helped, for what happened in London up to 1 P.M. would have shown up in the United States too early for viewing if direct electronic transmission of video signals across the Atlantic had been available. Still photographs transmitted from London by wirephoto were telecast in New York within ten minutes of being taken. But film coverage of the day's events, photographed mostly by the BBC, or taken from their television coverage, was carried by special airplane flights to the nearest

North American cities on the network lines and fed into the vigorously competing commercial networks and into Canada's CBC. By late afternoon and evening of Coronation Day, Americans were seeing the events, within 12 hours of their occurrence. The television networks also moved rapidly to cover President Eisenhower's illnesses in 1955 and 1956. The Suez fighting and Hungarian uprising of late 1956, coming toward the windup of an American political campaign, tested television news, which attempted to cover complicated events in three areas at once. In 1959, Soviet leader Nikita Khrushchev visited the United States for several days and was followed by a mob of reporters. The televised scenes of Khrushchev banging his shoe on a desk at the United Nations gave a peculiar image of international politics. Television also covered the rise of Fidel Castro in Cuba, from early network specials on the rebels in the Sierra Maestra in 1957–1958 to lavish coverage of Castro's 1959 triumph and takeover. For the most part such news events were carried on regular newscasts rather than as specials.

8•65   Political Broadcasting

The exception was, of course, politics. The era saw three major political events: the Army-McCarthy Hearings in 1954, and the 1956 and 1960 election campaigns. In addition, the presidency came

A Pioneering TV Documentary Team / Top CBS reporter Edward R. Murrow (left) teamed up in the late 1940s with producer Fred Friendly (right) to do a series of radio and record documentaries. In 1951, the two created *See It Now* as the first continuing television documentary series—best remembered for the attack on Senator McCarthy discussed in the text. Friendly later headed CBS news. Photo courtesy of Edwin Ginn Library, Tufts University.

a bit closer to the people when President Truman in 1951 permitted excerpts from recordings of presidential news conferences to be aired, and President Eisenhower in 1953 allowed filming, and later videotaping, of news conferences for delayed, censored broadcast. Before, reporters could only paraphrase, and later quote, the President's remarks from stenographic, and later recorded, transcripts.

Joseph McCarthy (R-Wisconsin) was riding high in 1953 when he began an investigation of communism in the U.S. Army. Due to a number of events too involved to relate here, this culminated in a series of televised hearings before McCarthy's investigative subcommittee from late April to early June 1954. For television, it was the most important long-term live reporting since the Kefauver crime hearings of 1951 (see 7.64). But shortly before the hearings started, on March 9, 1954, CBS newsman Edward R. Murrow had used one of his weekly half-hour *See It Now* broadcasts to expose the senator's vicious tactics—and did it by showing films of the senator's own speeches. Keeping in mind the political mood and the usual lack of aggressive investigative reporting or commentary on television, the broadcast took considerable courage, as well as some of Murrow's and program producer Fred Friendly's money. They advertised it in selected newspapers because the network was worried about any controversy and particularly controversy of this sort. The program together with a later one created a storm of reaction, with thousands of calls and letters, most of them favorable to Murrow's stand. A short time later, when McCarthy was given the chance to respond, he used the time to attack Murrow.

These broadcasts roused interest in the Army–McCarthy hearings that followed. For nearly eight weeks, the networks, particularly ABC, which had the least revenue to lose, scrapped morning programs to carry all or part of the hearings and, to their surprise, saw daytime ratings increase by 50 percent. Soon all viewers became familiar with the pounding questioning by McCarthy and his chief aide, Roy Cohn, and the gentlemanly effective cross-examination by Army counsel Joseph Welsh, who, over the weeks, revealed McCarthy as a bully who played with facts, people's reputations, and important issues for his own political gain. Much of the American public turned from McCarthy in disgust, and he soon faded from prominence, after being censured by the Senate. To a great degree, television had destroyed McCarthy's public esteem merely by showing intensively what happened—even though television's regular news programs had helped build him up. One unfortunate lasting effect of the McCarthy hearings coverage was identification, in the public mind, of the Constitutional right of "taking the Fifth Amendment" with guilt.

The 1956 presidential race was something of a replay of the 1952 campaign, with the same candidates but a more important role for television. For one thing, there were now four times as many television stations and twice as many home receivers. Second, as President Eisenhower had been seriously ill, television was used as the primary means of getting his image and message to the people. This saved his strength and let him concentrate more on the Suez and Hungarian crises. There was a greater use of five-minute programs at the end of shortened popular entertainment programs, rather than the half-hour political broadcasts of 1952, which alienated many viewers whose favorite shows had been pre-empted. That television had become of primary importance in broadcast political campaigning, reporting, and advertising was shown by television political revenues surpassing radio's for the first time.

The 1960 campaign featured two very different men and two quite different approaches to television. John F. Kennedy brought a relaxed, modern style to television, born of his need to overcome the handicap of being a member of a wealthy Catholic family not well known to the national public. Vice President Richard Nixon often ignored ideas of his television advisers, apparently feeling that his 1952 "Checkers" speech had proved his television skill.

The highlight of the campaign was four "Great Debates," the first such face-to-face confrontation of candidates for presidential office. In summer 1960, Congress had suspended, for that campaign and for the offices of President and Vice President only, Section 315 of the Communications Act, which required that candidates for a given political office be given equal opportunity to use broadcasting facilities. Relieved of the "equal time" obligation to fringe candidates, the three major networks offered, and the Nixon and Kennedy camps accepted, time for four or five debates. The first, televised live on September 26 on all three networks, may have cost Richard Nixon the election. He looked haggard, owing partly to a light suit against a light background and also to a tired and furtive look he seemed to have on television—partly due to an unwillingness to take network technicians' advice on

The "Great Debates" of 1960 / The four debates between Vice President Richard M. Nixon and Senator John F. Kennedy in the fall of 1960 probably decided the election—for in the first debate Nixon came across as gray (in several ways) and evasive compared to the crisp Kennedy style. In part because incumbents dislike giving exposure to challengers, the next national television debates were not held until President Ford and Governor Carter met in 1976. Photos courtesy of State Historical Society of Wisconsin and the *Milwaukee Journal*.

makeup—while Kennedy appeared confident and outgoing. Interestingly enough, listeners on radio thought that the candidates were about even or that Nixon did better. But more persons saw the program than heard it, and Kennedy got exposure he could not have got in any other way. Nixon, who had been leading in public opinion polls, lost much of his carefully cultivated aura of experience and leadership. Nixon fared somewhat better in the three subsequent debates in October, with varied formats, but the damage had been done. Plans for a fifth debate fell through at the last minute, and both candidates relied instead on election eve *telethons* from their respective headquarters. Some historians believe that the debates provided the less well-known Kennedy with the narrow margin by which he won in November. On election night, the networks introduced the use of computers to predict winners. They flopped. Early in the evening, CBS predicted a Nixon landslide victory about the time NBC was saying that Kennedy would take the election by a wide margin. Only early the following morning did the true thin margin of the Kennedy victory become clear.

8•7   Viewing Trends and Research

As in every period discussed thus far, the broadcast audience increased in the 1950s. The proportion of homes with television sets rose from just over one-third in 1953 to nearly 90 percent by 1960—a truly phenomenal increase. The radio audience also grew, with even FM receivers selling well by the end of the decade. But as audiences increased so did concern about the effects of broadcasting, especially about the effects of television program content on young viewers.

8•71   *Cheaper Receivers—and More of Them*

AM radios in the 1950s were smaller than earlier sets and, in the latter part of the decade, truly portable. People still bought console radio-phonograph combinations, but the volume market in radio was in table, clock, portable (with batteries), and other smaller-size sets for every room of the house. Plastic cases and tube sets were the rule; transistor portable radios—lightweight and using inexpensive batteries—did not appear until the cost of transistors lowered in the last half of the decade. The typical home radio sold for $20 to $30, and the typical purchaser was a radio owner who wanted an extra set. In another potential audience area of AM radio, the proportion of automobiles with radios increased in these eight years from 55 percent to 68 percent.

For most of the decade, the FM receiver market remained low and stagnant. Each year from 1953 through 1958, no more than 700,000 sets were sold; for four of these years, fewer than 300,000. At the same time, 10–15 million AM radios and 5–7 million much more expensive television sets were sold each year. The least expensive FM receiver sold for about $50, more than double the price of a typical AM set, and distribution of FM sales and service outlets was inadequate. Then, in late 1958 and 1959, for the first time in eight years, more than one million FM receivers were sold. In 1960, nearly two million FM receivers were sold, about 10 percent of them imports from Germany and Japan, where war-devastated electronics industries had been rebuilt into advanced-technology, highly efficient operations. The average FM-AM set price came down to about $30, only $10 to $15 above the cost of an AM-only radio. The use of transistors and circuit innovations that prevented frequency "drift" as sets warmed up made FM receivers far more attractive. Other reasons for the growth of FM broadcasting have been discussed above (see 8.21), but public awareness and advertising of sets helped a great deal.

Television continued to absorb the most attention and the most money. In 1952–1953, the typical set had a 12-inch, 14-inch, or 16-inch screen and cost about $250 plus installation. When you could buy a 21-inch set, it cost more than $400. Virtually all sets were American-made and black-and-white; only 500,000 color sets were manufactured between 1953 and 1960, as contrasted to more than 52 million monochrome sets. While volume production continued to lower prices, it took the arrival of small portables in 1956 to bring the cost of a television set to less than $100. Television expanded across the country: 45 percent of U.S. homes had sets in 1953, although many markets in the Northeast had more than 80 percent set saturation, and some in the South had only a scattering. By 1960, however, regional variations had evened out considerably: the northern states were running about 90 percent and the southern states less, but the national average was 87 percent. But, even in 1960, less than 75 percent of homes in isolated rural areas had television, due to receiver cost and distance from transmitters.

The television market was influenced by two post-1952 developments. The first was the establishment of UHF stations, bringing about a need for UHF reception capability. Some receivers offered both VHF and UHF tuners built in, but the number of such sets declined annually from 1.4 million in 1954 to 400,000 in 1958—a small fraction of the 6–7 million sets sold yearly. Set manufacturers claimed that there was insufficient demand for the more complicated and $10 to $30 more expensive all-channel sets, while UHF operators

and some potential viewers countercomplained that the manufacturers wanted to concentrate on the more lucrative VHF market. The only way to get UHF reception in a receiver built without UHF tuning was to purchase an externally mounted converter costing $30 to $50. The converter did not sell well; its quality was uneven, usually no better than "fair," and it could cause interference to other sets on the same or different channels. The limited sale of UHF reception equipment increased the inequality between stations on the two television bands and placed further pressure on the FCC or Congress to relieve it (see 8.81).

The other new element in television, color, took hold slowly for technical and economic reasons. Color adjustment on early sets was very difficult, with blue faces and green lips particularly common; color programming was scarce; and color sets cost at least $800 for a number of years. The first 1953–1954 color sets had 12-inch to 14-inch screens, and at $1,000 it is not surprising that only 5,000 were sold. But as the sets improved and as color programming on the networks, mainly NBC, increased, so did interest in color receivers, sparked by the enthusiastic reviews of color programs by newspaper television columnists. Between 1956 and 1960, from 80,000 to 120,000 color sets were sold each year, and prices crept downward into the $500–$800 range. RCA built 90 percent of color sets made. By late 1959, less than 1 percent of American homes had color. As these households relegated the old black-and-white set to stand-by or bedroom service, and as others bought newer black-and-white receivers, television homes with more than one set rose to 10 percent. To stimulate set sales, color programming rose from 68 hours in 1954 to nearly 700 hours in 1959. Most was on NBC; in 1959 CBS offered only 6½ hours of color and financially pressed ABC offered none and said that it had no plans for color. Obviously, NBC's color programming was tied to parent RCA's manufacturing role, and CBS saw no reason, after the torpedoing of its own color plans earlier in the decade (see 7.821), to put money in RCA's pocket. Color was only an expensive toy for a small minority. The pundits who claimed that color television would "make it big this year" constantly had to backtrack.

8•72   Broadcast Viewing and Listening Trends

By the late 1950s, the A.C. Nielsen company clearly dominated the national television rating field despite competition from the American Research Bureau (ARB, now Arbitron), its closest rival, The Pulse, Trendex, and others. The Nielsen meter, placed in a sample of 1,200 homes across the nation, provided the audience data often responsible for changing network programs from season to season. In addition to regular ratings reports sent to customers, Nielsen published related research showing that by 1960 the average television household had the set on for roughly six hours a day. Most daytime viewing was done by *heavy viewers*, households that used the set for 10 or more hours a day.

The methods of testing audience preferences and habits had been weighed since the early 1930s. ARB depended on listener diaries, little booklets in which test families, changed for each *sweep*, kept track of their viewing and some demographic factors. In the 1950s, Trendex tried to revive the system of coincidental telephone calls for given programs rather than for all shows on the air, but advertiser and agency interest was insufficient to support this expensive service. Its main appeal was

overnight readings on specific programs, so that decision-makers would not have to wait two weeks or more to act on a special program or a show in trouble. In 1958 ARB borrowed Nielsen's meter idea but tied a small sample by telephone line to a central processing computer to derive overnight "Arbitron" ratings for New York. Again, expense limited this operation. All methods had drawbacks: the diary suffered from errors and nonresponses; the meter measured tuning rather than viewing.

An important development in the 1950s was the increasing demand by advertising agencies for demographic information. Knowing that a large number of people had looked at a given show was no longer enough. Advertisers wanted to know the ages and sex of viewers, their income, and other factors believed crucial to product sales decisions. The Home Testing Institute made the first attempt to supply these figures with its "TVQ" or "Television Quotient" service, and other market research organizations, including the rating services, attempted to provide similar information, adding to the higher costs of the stations and networks. One can argue that this was a sign of what some social scientists later called the decline of the *mass* media concept. For now, instead of focusing on a maximum size undifferentiated audience, advertisers sought a specific audience for specific products or services. The result was a series of programs and supporting advertisements aimed carefully at a specific mini-audience and not at a mass one. This trend was to continue.

The ratings services fell into public disfavor as a result of the quiz show scandals, although it did not stop their use. For the loss of favorite programs the public blamed the ratings services rather than the decision-makers who used the data the services provided, and now the quiz show situation added a moral dimension. Time and again in subsequent regulatory proceedings (see 8.84), the argument was raised that the need for high ratings had caused the quiz show deceptions. Growing concern about the derivation, validity, reliability, and role of ratings led in the 1960s to major congressional and industry investigations of methods used.

Amidst the television hoopla, radio was overshadowed but not forgotten. The first in-depth look at radio in more than five years, widely reported in the trade press, was a 1953 Politz study. It showed that, while the *pattern* of radio listening had changed with the coming of television, the increase of radio listening in cars, in daytime, and away from the home had kept total radio listening high.

8·73   Children and Television: Phase One

From the start, families with children were among the first to buy television sets—at the urging of the children. Television became a natural babysitter, freeing parents and older children. Parents soon learned what researchers later found out: children as young as three were regular and heavy users of television. Parents worried that their children might be getting ideas from television that they were ill-equipped to handle—first apparent in the child's loud urging to buy some television-advertised product. A more serious concern was the constant action and violence seen on many cartoon shows, slapstick comedies such as *The Three Stooges*, and westerns aired when young children could see them. The number of fights, shootings, and killings broadcast in any week made viewers wonder what young children were learning. This concern had been expressed to some degree over radio

and motion pictures in the 1930s and 1940s, and over comic books later, but people had worried then about radio's overtaxing the child's imagination. Now, they feared that *any* child, of any age, seeing mayhem on television day after day would become desensitized and accustomed to this behavior, even to the extent of adopting such values in his or her own life.

This concern led Senator Estes Kefauver (D-Tennessee) to hold hearings in 1952 into the causes of juvenile delinquency. The hearings touched often on the potential lessons to be found in daily television fare. The same committee looked into the problem again in 1954–1955, when witnesses cited examples of behavior models shown in adult action-adventure programs often watched by children. They associated the child's habit of imitating older people with the opportunity for young television viewers to follow violent examples. Some experts' testimony at the hearings suggested, however, that televised violence might be good for children as catharsis, which implies that *watching* violence takes away the need for *doing* violence. Most observers and researchers disagreed—and continued to disagree (see 9.72 and 10.72)—with one another.

The first two in-depth research studies on the interaction of children and television appeared in the late 1950s. The first, by Himmelweit, Oppenheim, and Vince (1958), was based on observations and interviews of several thousand children in England, while the second, by Schramm, Lyle, and Parker (1961), reported results of research in ten American cities during the 1958–1960 period. The chief finding of both studies was something parents long had known: that from its arrival in the home, television dominated other media and family activities. Its great novelty appeal lasted a few weeks and then, like another toy, it became part of the child's daily input. No physical effects showed up, although parents had worried about posture and eyesight in the early years of television, and about an increase in passivity—the *narcotizing· dysfunction* of the mass media. The effect of television on school progress varied so much from child to child that generalizations were hard to make. The medium seemed to open children's eyes to the adult world faster, and in many youngsters sparked great interest in new things, but others simply sat in front of the set for hours, looking at whatever was on the tube. The determining factor seemed to be not the television set or its content but the background and emotional or psychological makeup of the child before he or she ever saw television. Both studies showed that sixth-grade children, about eleven years old, watched television the most—about four hours a day.

8·8   Crises of Regulatory Confidence

More than at any time since the Cox-Lea investigations during World War II (see 6.86), the regulatory picture was filled with investigations, soul-searching, and a feeling of smashed standards in broadcast content and operation. Members of the FCC testified on Capitol Hill more than they minded their own shop. One possible explanation for the events of 1952–1960 discussed below is that mistakes of the first decade of television had to be shaken out to make way for a fresh approach. That certainly happened!

8·81   *The UHF Mess*

Throughout this chapter we have mentioned the plight of UHF stations.

When the FCC issued the *Sixth Report and Order* in April 1952, it did not create the competition it claimed to desire (see 7.83). At best, the commission could create conditions and facilities for competition, hoping that new broadcasters would provide the competition and service to the public. However, the FCC established *unequal conditions*, which necessarily meant unequal competition. As the first UHF stations went on the air, they discovered that the stated FCC policy of equality of facilities in a given market did not exist in practice.

When UHF stations had to compete with VHF stations in the same market —a condition called *intermixture*—they were in trouble, particularly if the VHF station or stations had been operating for some time. In addition to the preponderance of VHF-only sets in such communities, the viewing habits of the audience, and the network affiliation contracts with pre-Freeze stations, a UHF operator had to neutralize or overcome the greater coverage area or range of VHF transmission. Both networks and advertisers relied on the concept of unduplicated population coverage or "circulation" in awarding affiliations and contracts. This basic inequality was aggravated by FCC moves to permit many VHF stations to increase antenna height and power, at a stage when the transmitter manufacturers were unable to construct high-powered UHF transmitters. Also, despite promises by receiver manufacturers to the contrary, only a small proportion of television receivers was able to pick up any UHF channels (see 8.71); all-channel set production peaked at 35 percent in the first half of 1953 and dropped below 9 percent by 1958, although field conversions raised the total proportion of UHF-capable receivers to more than one-fifth.

The FCC was too busy processing

applications and issuing construction permits to worry about UHF operators for some years. Congress made it clear that the FCC's first priority was to meet the needs of television-hungry constituents. Surviving UHF operators lived on hope alone. The seriousness of their plight was indicated by the nearly 55 percent of the 165 UHF stations that went on the air between mid-1952 and mid-1959 later going dark. The high point of 127 UHF stations came in March 1954; five years later there were fewer than 80.

The FCC's hope—or, in light of the commission's penchant for ignoring engineering advice, fantasy—that UHF and VHF were equal was not immediately obvious from the *Sixth Report and Order*. Of the 1,275 communities to which channels were assigned, 110 were to be VHF only, 910 UHF only, and only 255 (20 percent) intermixed. Also not immediately apparent from the *Sixth Report and Order* was the fact that of the top 162 markets 8 were to be VHF only, 31 UHF only, and 123 (76 percent) intermixed. Considering the cost of establishing even the smallest station, it is no wonder that only 308 communities out of 1,275 had stations in operation in June 1958, and that virtually no UHF station was doing well against entrenched competition in the larger markets.

The loud complaints of UHF operators against the manufacturers, advertisers, networks, competition, and commission were to a large extent justified. Manufacturers were not interested in designing better all-channel sets or in promoting them, although their argument that there was little demand for UHF sets has pragmatic merit. Advertisers went where the people were, and VHF operators could hardly be expected to nurture their competition. The networks gave lip service to UHF but tended to give affiliations to VHF stations. Each established a plan—CBS's

"Extended Market Plan" and NBC's "Program Service Plan"—to provide network programs to some isolated UHF stations at practically no cost. This would give advertisers a few thousand more viewers and help the station sell spots before and after the network programs. After the FCC declared new multiple-ownership rules in fall 1954, allowing a single entity to hold five VHF and two UHF stations at the same time, both NBC and CBS bought two UHF stations apiece. Two were in the Hartford area and the others were in Milwaukee (CBS) and Buffalo (NBC), but all had been sold by early 1959 (see box on page 266).

The predicament of UHF stations stemmed mainly from three problems: (1) the technical inequality of UHF stations with respect to coverage, (2) intermixture, and the vast inertia of millions of VHF-only receivers, and (3) lack of confidence in the capabilities of and need for UHF television. None of these would easily yield to wishful thinking, persuasion, or the market place.

It was recognized fairly early that solutions to these problems might lie in one or a combination of (1) deintermixture, or unscrambling the egg so that each community would be *either* VHF *or* UHF; (2) converting to an all-UHF system, which would make all stations equal but would be very expensive for existing VHF stations and would reduce the number of signals that rural areas could pick up; (3) converting to an all-VHF system, discarding the UHF band for television and picking up a probably limited number of channels from FM or government; (4) promoting the manufacture and sale of all-channel sets by removing excise taxes or—in an analogy found in the Wireless Ship Act of 1910 (see 2.4)—forbidding the transport of VHF-only receivers in interstate commerce; (5) making unspecified but major changes in the relationships between networks and affiliates; or (6) somehow reducing the coverage of VHF stations so that they would be comparable to UHF. Another industry-staffed engineering group, the Television Allocation Study Organization (TASO), was established under FCC auspices to study technical ramifications of these and similar proposals—an act that delayed FCC decisions for another few years. Meanwhile, 75 percent of UHF stations showed losses.

Some of the proposals would not provide sufficient help and some were politically or technically infeasible. Neither FM broadcasting, which was starting to grow again (see 8.21), nor the military, who were asked several times up through 1958, was willing to give up VHF spectrum space. UHF operators, although many had little confidence and staying power, saw no advantage in abandoning their toehold in the television industry. Broadcasters and the commission supported the idea of all-channel sets but recognized that any addition to consumer costs would be unpopular with Congress. Since range was affected more by antenna height than by power at these frequencies, reducing VHF power would seem to be ineffective, and allowing UHF stations to go to 5 million watts would not necessarily give a farther-reaching signal—if a transmitter could be made to deliver that power, and anyone could afford to buy it.

Because the UHF situation became caught up in the larger and politically more urgent issue of getting television to small communities, it received more and more congressional attention. At this time, before the Supreme Court "one man–one vote" decisions, rural areas and small communities had disproportionate political clout and representation in Congress. As a result, political rather than technological factors often ruled FCC decisions,

and indecision, in respect to CATV; then-illegal on-channel *boosters*, which retransmitted, causing considerable interference, on the same channel as the orginal signal; translators, which picked up a signal and retransmitted it on a high-UHF channel in a small community; and satellites, essentially regular stations that originated no programming (see 7.823).

The FCC, under considerable pressure from Senator Charles Potter's (R-Michigan) Communications Subcommittee of the Senate Commerce Committee and recognizing the political pressures and the unlikelihood of a radical solution, started a series of hearings in 1955. It grasped at every straw, including the possibility of obtaining military spectrum space, "drop-in" of VHF channels without doing violence to the mileage-separation standards set forth in the *Sixth Report and Order*, and selective or total deintermixture.

The hearings gave UHF backers a platform from which to operate, and they tried to make the most of it; moving all television to the UHF band, limiting color to UHF, adding channels—all were proposed. They gave deintermixture limited support as a compromise but applauded removal of excise taxes on all-channel receivers. Although VHF operators, aided perhaps overly much by the NARTB, gave their views and the networks, led by CBS, indicated their lukewarm approval of UHF, the hearings bogged down in politics.

As with most political decisions, what emerged after FCC hearings in 1955, 1956, and 1958 was a compromise: selective—that is, in as few communities as possible—deintermixture in markets where it could be achieved without disrupting many existing stations and their audiences. Although a few markets were successfully deintermixed in the late 1950s, particularly in California's San Joaquin Valley, the UHF situation sat on almost dead center until the mid-1960s. The TASO final report advocated that the UHF be abandoned and television stick with a degraded, due to drop-ins, VHF system. In February 1959, shortly after the TASO report, the commission proposed several alternatives for further study, coordination, and discussion: (1) a 50-channel VHF system, retaining the present 12 VHF channels, (2) a continuous 50-channel VHF system, abandoning channels 2–6 but moving farther in the spectrum above channel 13, (3) a contiguous 25-channel VHF system retaining channels 7–13, (4) the existing 82-channel VHF-UHF system, and (5) a 70-channel all-UHF system. These proposals needed further study, and each had its proponents among the commissioners. Although deintermixture and slight degradations of the VHF spectrum were believed to be practical and acceptable, the FCC said that they would not solve the problem.

The FCC requested and received $2 million to test UHF propagation characteristics—especially in large cities—about which there were much disagreement and little data. Using for the study the channel assigned to New York's Municipal Broadcasting System station WNYC-TV (which managed to have the test transmitter donated to it at the conclusion of the experiment some years later), the commission prodded dormant UHF construction permit holders, and waited noisily for Congress to agree on the best course. Senator Potter's investigation had merged into a study of network operations by Senator John Bricker (R-Ohio) and, after the Democrats took over the Senate Commerce Committee in 1955, by Senator Warren Magnuson (D-Washington). Magnuson, who was very interested in television policy, covered a tremendous amount of ground, in the course of his Television Inquiry of 1956–1958 (see 8.83). Congress

made most of the FCC's policy decisions, and until members of Congress and their constituents resolved their conflicting viewpoints, it was improbable that any commission decision in the UHF area would stick. More than a decade went by from the end of the Freeze to the first real legislative action—and the UHF was still a troublesome issue more than a decade after that (see 9.22).

8•82   The FCC Investigates the Networks—Again

In fall 1955, somewhat in response to Senator Bricker, the FCC decided that, because of the many changes in broadcasting, it was time for another look at the roles and practices of networks. Although the investigation was announced as covering both radio and television, money and staff limitations and recognition of the reduced role of radio networks allowed it to concentrate on television. Under the direction of University of Cincinnati Law School Dean Roscoe Barrow, extensive research was conducted in and about the networks—network-affiliate relations, option time, program sources, network ownership of stations, advertising revenues. The first report, issued in October 1957, provided a detailed review of commercial television and the organization and economic status of the major networks, with a brief chapter on the radio industry. It also provided recommendations that shook the industry.

Most important, the Barrow report urged that the networks be put under direct FCC regulation. The long-standing FCC regulation of network-owned or affiliated stations was considered insufficient for the complicated role and importance of television networks, which dominated television far more than radio networks had dominated radio. In addition, the report recommended: (1) a ban on option time—specific times during the day when by contract the network had priority on station time; (2) limits on network ownership of stations; (3) a ban on *must-buy* stations—a technique that required an advertiser to pick his lineup of stations so that a minimal nationwide network identity would be preserved at all times; (4) publication of affiliation agreements; (5) a right of nonaffiliates to obtain network programs when the local affiliate rejects the network feed, and (6) penalties such as fines and forfeitures for breaking these or other rules. While the industry immediately complained that such rules would destroy the structure of broadcasting—a familiar lament (see 5.83)—the FCC took these initial recommendations under advisement.

In June 1960, the network study staff issued its second report, focusing on network program procurement. Described as an interim report, it covered months of FCC hearings with testimony from broadcasters, producers, critics, and others. It described current network practices in getting and using programming, including standards for program development and acceptance. It made some very tentative conclusions about public service programming and issued two further interim and detailed studies—without recommendations—in 1963 and 1965.

This examination of networks was unlike the 1939–1941 investigation in several ways. For one thing, none if its recommendations promised changes as fundamental as the chain broadcasting rules upheld by the Supreme Court in 1943. Second, it was far more intensive and exhaustive than the 1941 Chain Broadcasting Report, yet it dealt with but a decade of television network operation. Finally, the 1957 report was the first in a series pre-

pared by a regular, not *ad hoc,* part of the commission staff, showing that the networks could expect continuing scrutiny.

However, the two investigations were also alike. Both came up with specific recommendations to temper business practices that appeared to restrain competition. Both were undertaken under congressional pressure, for the 1957 network study grew out of several years of House and Senate hearings on networks and the FCC. In both cases the final rule changes instituted by the FCC stuck, despite strong industry opposition (see 5.83 and 9.3).

8•83   . . . and Congress
          Investigates the FCC—
          Again

In March 1957 the House Committee on Interstate and Foreign Commerce formed a Subcommittee on Legislative Oversight to look into problems of certain regulatory agencies, which this committee was to "oversee" or supervise. The subcommittee was chaired at first by Congressman Morgan Moulder (D-Missouri) and later by full committee chairman Oren Harris (D-Arkansas). Almost from the start, the FCC became a prime target for the subcommittee chief counsel, New York University law professor Bernard Schwartz. Schwartz had little patience for diplomatic convention and made a habit of leaking to the press his latest findings on real and imagined shortcomings of the FCC. Those leaks led to Schwartz's firing in January 1958. He promptly wrote a book charging a political cover-up of regulatory commission shenanigans. In spring 1958 the committee began hearings into the qualifications and activities of FCC commissioners, concentrating on their use of free industry-provided television sets and travel and on their *ex parte* (outside the normal forum for adjudication) contacts.

On March 3, 1958, FCC Commissioner Richard Mack resigned under fire, after it became known that he had accepted a sizable bribe to vote for an applicant for a Miami television channel. Mack was the first commissioner forced from office but not the last. Congress, concerned about chumminess between segments of the broadcasting industry and its regulators, focused on the Mack case. In April 1958 the subcommittee issued its report, calling for a code of ethics for administrative agency personnel, and the right of the President to remove commissioners for neglect of duty.

The subcommittee also investigated fairness in comparative application cases and the possible need for antitrust action against some broadcast owners. During the summer and fall of 1958, hearings continued into *ex parte* contacts, trafficking in licenses, mergers, and pay-offs —all actions considered to be not in the public interest. The quiz show scandals and the payola problem (see 8.84) took up most of the subcommittee's time in 1959 and 1960. A 1959 Attorney General report to the President called for legislation to strengthen and clean up the operations of the FCC and the FTC, and also dealt with the ethics of commissioners and staff members. This aspect received more attention just a few months later.

Early in 1960, pressure built up to get rid of FCC Chairman John C. Doerfer. He had used very poor judgment, especially in light of the ongoing investigations, had taken pleasure trips on a broadcaster's yacht, and had submitted double and triple billing for official trips. When he took yet another trip on group station owner George B. Storer's yacht, President Eisenhower asked for his resignation.

Doerfer was dissuaded from going on television with his side of the story, and resigned. The black eye on the regulator, the FCC, naturally eased congressional pressure on the regulated, the broadcasters.

Early in 1961 the Subcommittee on Legislative Oversight ended its activities before the hearings resorted to personality battles or vendettas like the Cox investigation of the early 1940s (see 6.86). This time, the FCC clearly had ethical problems that needed airing as well as the dismissal of Mack and Doerfer.

For more than a decade after 1950, there was almost always at least one congressional hearing or staff study of FCC activities underway in either the House or Senate or both. This period of investigation involved not only the commission's internal operations but also problems of the broadcasting industry. Although some broadcasting investigations may have been the proddings of a publicity-hungry congressman on a commerce, small business, or appropriations committee, the hearings of the late 1950s were more useful and less emotional than those of the early 1940s. The Senate Commerce Committee maintained a watchful eye on the FCC, and the commission knew it. Specific legislation and rule changes resulted, unlike the fizzle of earlier investigations.

8•84 The Quiz and Payola Investigations

Investigations of network quiz shows (see 8.63) drew most of the regulatory, congressional, and public attention. In late 1959, the focus shifted from New York and its grand jury proceedings to Washington where both a congressional committee and the FCC held hearings. The highlight, or low point, of the congressional hearings came when the *Twenty-*

Charles Van Doren on How the Quiz Shows Were Rigged / After considerable soul-searching, the popular quiz show winner finally appeared before the House committee investigating the quiz programs and told the shocked audience how he had been co-opted:

[*Twenty-One* Producer Albert Freedman] told me that Herbert Stempel, the current champion, was an unbeatable contestant because he knew too much. He said that Stempel was unpopular, and was defeating opponents right and left to the detriment of the program. He asked me if, as a favor to him, I would agree to make an arrangement whereby I would tie Stempel and thus increase the entertainment value of the program. I asked him to let me go on the program honestly, without receiving help. He said that was impossible. He told me that I would not have a chance to defeat Stempel because he was too knowledgeable. He also told me that the show was merely entertainment and that giving help to quiz contestants was a common practice and merely a part of show business. . . . Freedman guaranteed me $1,000 if I would appear for one night. . . .

I met him next at his office, where he explained how the program would be controlled. He told me the questions I was to be asked, and then asked if I could answer them. Many of them I could. But he was dissatisfied with my answers. They were not "entertaining" enough. He instructed me how to answer the questions: to pause before certain of the answers, to skip certain parts and return to them, to hesitate and build up suspense, and so forth. On this first occasion and on several subsequent ones he gave me a script to memo-

rize, and before the program he took back the script and rehearsed me in my part. This is the general method which he used throughout my fourteen weeks on "Twenty-One." He would ask me the questions beforehand. If I could not answer them he would either tell me the answers, or if there was sufficient time before the program, which was usual, he would allow me to look them up myself. . . . When I could answer the questions right off he would tell me that my answers were not given in an entertaining and interesting way, and he would then rehearse me in the manner in which I was to act and speak.

After the first program, on which I tied Stempel three times, Freedman told me that I would win the next evening and be the new champion. My guarantee was increased to $8,000. I again agreed to play, and I did defeat Stempel. . . . I asked [Freedman] several times to release me from the program. . . . He told me I had to be defeated in a dramatic manner. A series of ties had to be planned which would give the program the required excitement and suspense.

Source: House Committee on Interstate and Foreign Commerce, Special Subcommittee on Legislative Oversight. *Investigation of Television Quiz Shows*. Hearings, 86th Cong., 1st Sess., 1960. Volume II, pages 625–626.

One winner Charles Van Doren confessed his complicity in the rigging process, thus admitting that he had committed perjury before the New York grand jury. Van Doren's confession shocked the nation, more so because he was a relative of author-scholars Carl and Mark Van Doren and a faculty member of Columbia University. Former contestants, network officials, advertisers, agency representatives, and others also appeared before both the committee and the FCC and testified to the rigging story, giving a good picture of the pressures that brought about such unethical behavior. A rigged contest or quiz was a fraud on the public. Van Doren resigned his post at Columbia, and he and others fell into public disgrace although they did not go to jail. It was several years before he could publish again under his own name. The networks established stringent procedures for supervision of the few quiz shows still on the air and hoped that the worst was over.

But just as the quiz show situation was settling down, corruption in radio arose in the form of *payola*. Record manufacturers had recognized the importance of the disc jockey (see 8.61) in selling records. A few plays of a new tune on an important market's top rock station could spell the difference between wild success and failure. To persuade programmers and disc jockeys that a given record had Top 40, or Top 10, qualities required salesmanship as well as sending the DJ a sample record.

But the persuasion soon moved past consideration of the record's merit to gifts of money, liquor, and even women and occasionally drugs. In short, bribery. Important disc jockeys enriched themselves while accepting "guidance" in evaluating new records—a payola process dating back to the era of big bands. But in the late 1950s, concern over this illicit business

practice—a fraud because the public counted on the DJ's professional judgment and not his self-interest in selecting records—combined with the older generation's distaste for and impatience with rock music to put the whole issue before Congress. A House investigating subcommittee heard testimony from many famous disc jockeys, including Alan Freed and Dick Clark. Freed's disclosure that he had freely partaken of payola stopped his career cold, while Clark's admission of his widespread and interlocking business interests, which obviously entailed conflict of interest if not outright payola, marred his reputation. These revelations led to legislation intended to curb commercial bribery in record selection, and to reaffirm the licensee's responsibility for whatever went on the air.

The congressional committee and the FCC also discussed the practice of radio or television *plugola,* closely related to payola. This involved programmers or show hosts deliberately mentioning the name of a product or service. In due course the plugger would receive some of the product, or a case of whiskey, or cash. This was not sponsorship, because the station or network received no revenue from it, but the on-air personality received a welcome boost in effective annual income. This practice infuriated station management, which saw its employees undercutting its advertising rate card.

In December 1959, Attorney General William Rodgers reported to President Eisenhower on the need for legislation to eliminate false and deceptive programming and advertising. At about the same time, FCC Chairman Doerfer announced a plan for expanding network public service programming—a form of penance, although it was not announced as such. It called for minimal public service programming on each network, rotating in prime time. The networks had previously relegated such programming to fringe hours, but, desperate to regain viewers' respect, they agreed to Doerfer's plan and announced several new documentary and public affairs programs for the following season. Thus, by 1959–1960, action by the FCC (hearings into quiz show and payola scandals), Congress (more hearings, and some legislation), and the Attorney General (a report with recommendations)—all coalesced into amendments to the Communications Act that made rigged or otherwise deceptive programming punishable by law rather than merely admissible as possible evidence of unfitness of licensees at renewal time. The rigged programs left the air for good. Payola and plugola, however, while diminished, have continued to exist more or less underground. The various scandals, a failure of self-regulation, tarnished the image of broadcasting and paved the way for stronger governmental regulation.

8•85   Self-Regulation: Improving Television's Image

To undo some of the damage of the quiz show debacle, the National Association of Broadcasters set up a concerted public relations campaign. In October 1959, it created the Television Information Office (TIO), headquartered in New York and sponsored by television stations and networks, to give the public favorable information about all aspects of television. Its initial project was an Elmo Roper survey on public reactions to television following the quiz investigations—the first in a long series of similar, well-publicized reports. TIO also organized a library, provided study guides on specific television programs and series for elementary and secondary schools, and ran full-page ads in such prestige magazines as the *New Yorker*

and *Saturday Review* to convince opinion leaders that television could be beneficial.

One industry wound continued to fester during the 1950s: the blacklisting of talent for their political beliefs (see 7.86). In 1953 several members of the American Federation of Television and Radio Artists (AFTRA, the performers' and announcers' union) and individuals with American Legion and advertiser connections created Aware, Inc., which attacked alleged communist influences in broadcasting. Feeding on the anticommunist mood spearheaded by Senator Joseph McCarthy, this self-appointed group formalized the process of "clearing" performers whose background had been questioned—often by Aware itself. By competing for jobs with those it attacked, Aware members had at least one possible conflict of interest other than that of union members engaging in what might be considered a management activity. Aware's officers created a 12-step process through which an accused performer could publicly declare his rehabilitated thinking and once again become employable. That Aware was operating in several guises became obvious when, after the New York AFTRA chapter held elections, Aware began investigations of the candidates it had opposed. Only after a long and emotional fight did a group of independents capture control of AFTRA in 1955, ending the relationship between a union and a minority of its members operating on ideological grounds.

In the meantime, a candidate for AFTRA office found himself in deepening trouble. John Henry Faulk, a very popular New York radio personality, lost his CBS radio job in fall 1957 and suddenly found himself unemployable. His dismissal followed initiation of a lawsuit against Aware, which he accused of having caused an end to his radio sponsorship. CBS kept mum. But here the typical blacklisting case took an unusual turn. Faulk decided to fight and, with the financial aid of CBS's Ed Murrow and other friends, took the matter to court. Aided by celebrated lawyer Louis Nizer, Faulk won a series of important preliminary decisions, only to be faced with dwindling financial resources. By 1960 the case grew progressively more complicated with the addition of other defendants who had allegedly organized a boycott or otherwise affected Faulk's and others' employment. Finally, in summer 1962, Faulk won and was awarded more than $3.5 million—a record in libel judgments (although, because of the death of the chief defendant, he collected only a small portion of it). The decision was upheld on appeal two years later, effectively putting an end to the blacklisting movement. Blacklisting not only lost credibility but was exposed as the product of a few self-appointed—and often self-serving—extralegal guardians of political morality. In addition, of course, relations between the United States and the Soviet Union as well as the political tenor of the country had changed substantially between 1953 and 1962. Although numerous books, plays, and movies have been written about blacklisting, including Faulk's own, dispassionate chronicles are rare; too many of the persons hurt as both victims and prosecutors are still alive. But there is little doubt that the blacklisting decade was a fearsome time in which to work in broadcasting and other media; one never knew when all jobs would suddenly close up or when one would be disavowed by one's friends, without warning or explanation.

8·9   The Age of Television

By the late 1950s researchers knew that television focused individual (and national) attention more than radio had, and

that it was more concrete. But both media had a neutral point of view and a limited program choice, and both were essentially universal, with common symbols and approaches readily understood by the audience. Radio apparently stimulated the imagination more than television, but television was more glamorous and live television could provide a sense of "here and now" that was unmatched by any other medium. Like radio and sometimes more than radio, television seemed official and highly credible. But few viewers noticed these distinctions; they simply looked at and enjoyed television, and found new uses for radio's music and news.

The nation's colleges and universities paid little attention to television at first. It might be used as a tool (see 7.4 and 8.4), but, except for the work of a few social scientists, it was not studied formally as a medium (see 7.73). This was partly because professional training requires costly equipment and also because of the typical academic wait-and-see-if-it-is-more-than-a-fad approach to new things. It has been said that an academic discipline is identified by a professional association and a scholarly journal. The small University Association for Professional Radio Education (UAPRE) was organized in 1948, nearly died for lack of specific activities, and reorganized in 1956 as the Association for Professional Broadcasting Education (APBE). APBE, which changed its name in 1974 to the Broadcast Education Association (BEA), began publication of the quarterly scholarly *Journal of Broadcasting* in the winter of 1956–1957. The organization's purpose was to combine broadcasters, through an affiliation with the NAB, and educators in the common goal of solid career and liberal arts education in broadcasting. It now has approximately 350 colleges and universities—and some 450 individuals—as members.

8·91   Television and Other Media

By 1960 television was no longer a fascinating toy for the few; it was nearly universal. Thus, when households spent more time with television, other media sometimes suffered.

By and large the print media were not affected, though both newspapers and magazines sometimes catered to public interest in television at the same time that they downgraded the medium with which they were competing for advertising revenue. In the 1950s, television and print co-existed successfully, and such durable magazines as *TV Guide*, directly related to the growth of interest in television, *Sports Illustrated, Playboy,* and *American Heritage* all got their start. Many newspapers and general magazines published a television column, to join the few remaining radio columns. It can be argued that reviews or esthetic comment had little effect on audiences, since most reviews appeared after the public had seen the program. One critic said, in an aphorism long credited to comedian Jackie Gleason, that "television reviewing is like describing an accident to the victims." But such discussions helped raise the level of some programming by influencing television policy makers. Reviews by *New York Times's* Jack Gould and *New York Herald Tribune's* John Crosby, and other critics of stature, were frequently quoted and discussed in television circles, in colleges and universities and, less frequently, by other readers and viewers.

The relationship between motion pictures and television was another story, since television was one of three main causes of the decline of the feature film (see 7.91). By 1953, 25 percent of the nation's theaters had closed, with only drive-ins continuing to expand in number. Unemployment in Hollywood was up, while those still working feared both the film

blacklist and industrywide economic uncertainty. However, the filmmakers, undaunted, put out more color films—remember, most television was black-and-white—and experimented with wide-screen techniques impossible to reproduce on the home screen. The first of these was the three-dimensional (3-D) film, for which the audience wore cardboard and plastic glasses that converted a blurry picture to striking realism. The fad lasted for about 18 months and two or three dozen 3-D films. In its place came Cinemascope and similar processes which used a new wide film stock and special projection lenses to provide a picture about half again as wide as the normal movie. In 1956, a few theaters—some later were specially built for the process in major cities—were converted for Cinerama, which used three cameras and three projectors for a 165° wide picture with stereo sound. This gave a larger-than-life, startling, realistic, and spectacular three-dimensional effect but was expensive and required major modification to the theaters and very careful adjustment. Less expensive wide-screen techniques such as Cinemascope, however, rapidly became common even though they required special lenses for showing and subsequent cropping of the picture when later shown on a television screen.

The other prong of the film industry's response to television was to withhold all older films from television showings. But the film companies could not keep a united front past early 1956 (see 8.62), and before long thousands of old Hollywood films were appearing on individual stations, further depressing business at the neighborhood movie house. Having given in to television to this extent, Hollywood experienced a slow takeover by television in the late 1950s. By 1960–1961, when feature films were still scarce on the networks, a good proportion of the film industry's employment and production was in filming series for network television showing. Although feature film workers decried the "takeover" of the film industry by television, live television workers in New York, now out of their jobs, wondered whether Hollywood had not taken over television! Some unusual developments occurred within this relationship; although many television series were inspired by hit movies, now some television programs (see 8.62) were made into films for release in theaters.

8·92   Television around the World

The worldwide expansion of television had been delayed by World War II and its aftermath, but by the 1950s many countries were building television systems. A "buy at home" philosophy, and the opportunity to build a state-of-the-art system by starting from scratch, led to a variety of technical standards, particularly in Europe, since Latin America and Japan had adopted the 525-line system used in the United States. France had an 819-line system and Great Britain had a 405-line system, but Europe eventually settled on two slightly different 625-line systems, one for eastern Europe and one for western. By 1960 eight countries each had more than one million television receivers in use: the United States, Great Britain, France, West Germany, Italy, Canada, Russia, and Brazil. In several of these countries, receivers were in public places, as in the United States in the late 1940s and early 1950s when there seemed to be more sets in bars and store windows than in homes. Because of these publicly located sets, the television audience in many of these countries was larger than the number of receivers might imply. In the United Kingdom,

the high cost of the "telly" was overcome through monthly receiver rentals rather than purchases.

Countries in the Western Hemisphere generally followed the United States model of private ownership and commercial operation, except for Canada, which had a BBC-modeled Canadian Broadcasting Corporation (CBC) as well as many private stations. In other countries, television was directly or indirectly operated by the government, even though costs sometimes led to commercial but not private operation. In Great Britain, the BBC had operated television as a monopoly since it started in 1936 except for a shutdown during the World War II period ending in 1946. But in 1954, after a long, involved parliamentary and behind-the-scenes debate, a commercially supported television system was established as an alternative to the BBC. Supervised by the Independent Television Authority (ITA), which franchised regional program production companies ("programme contractors") to use ITA-owned transmitters, the new service was supported by advertising rather than receiver license fees as was the BBC—although license revenues were diverted to aid ITA in its formative years. Program sponsorship is not allowed, in the *magazine* system of television advertising, with advertisers buying spots but having no control over their placement. The best programs were put "on the network" and aired by other contractors. Japan and Canada developed similar competing systems in which one channel or network was operated by the government and another privately. Most major foreign cities had only one to three channels of television fare, compared to the three to seven in the larger American cities.

Considering the high cost of television programming and the short geographical distances in Europe, it is not surprising that the nations belonging to the European Broadcasting Union decided to exchange programs. This exchange, called "Eurovision," also permitted efficient pooling of effort for coverage of important sporting and other events. In eastern Europe, the International Radio Television Organization (OIRT) started a similar venture, "Intervision." After settling political and technical difficulties, the two systems occasionally exchanged nonpolitical programs.

In 1953 the U.S. Information Agency (USIA) was established to operate the Voice of America and print, film, and television propaganda activities of the United States government. Except for overseas operations directly under the control of an ambassador, it took over most State Department operational information functions and operated most overseas information and propaganda activities. Although the USIA distributed some material to be shown on foreign television systems, most American television programs went abroad through the efforts of commercial networks and program packagers. Foreign television systems provided an additional market for an American product, following the long-standing example of the feature film industry, as well as a new means of intercultural communication. Some commentators wondered what a constant fare of *I Love Lucy* would do to foreign opinions of the United States, and what effect it might have on the customs of foreign countries.

In Canada, regular television programming began from CBC stations in Toronto and Montreal in September 1952. A few months later, the government allowed expansion of the government-controlled CBC as well as privately operated television stations. By 1956, there were nine CBC and 30 commercial television outlets. As mentioned before, Canada used U.S.

technical standards, and operated only on the VHF channels. About half the Canadian population also could and did tune in to stations in the United States, since Canadian cities are located largely in a narrow band just north of the border. The CBC stations were supported by the proceeds of a 15 percent excise tax on receiver sales. By 1960 private stations had increased to 38, while CBC stations remained at nine, including three that broadcast in French. Few Canadian cities had more than one channel until after 1961. Television viewing was divided almost evenly between U.S. and Canadian channels, and much of the fare on the Canadian channels was American.

Mexican television began in the early 1950s when commercially run channels went on the air from Mexico City under authority of licenses that were good for 25 years. In 1953, the two major station operators combined to form Telesistema Mexicano S.A., which in the 1950s was to control the content of virtually all television in the country. By 1960 there were 25 stations on the air, all on VHF channels. A few stations located near the U.S. border programmed in English, very profitably directing their broadcasts to the north. For domestic consumption, most program content was produced in Mexico but was like the American fare—with the substitution of bullfights for baseball. Having got into television quite early, Mexico quickly became one of the chief program suppliers for the rest of Latin America, and later expanded into the United States with affiliated stations in markets with large Spanish-speaking populations such as Los Angeles and New York.

8•93 *Period Overview*

This space of eight years can be thought of as the evolution that followed the 1945–1952 revolution. There were no fundamental changes in the industry; radio and television expanded within the patterns set in the immediate postwar years. AM radio and VHF television led this growth, with television networks becoming dominant in the broadcasting industry. FM radio had started out of its long decline by 1960, in part through subsidiary services and stereo; but UHF television was in serious trouble with small audiences and limited advertising income and usually no network affiliation. There was growth in educational television and FM, but the audiences were very small and funding was a paramount problem.

To many observers in later decades, these were the golden years of television programming—primarily because most network programming was live and often spontaneous, and high-quality anthology drama was plentiful, since television production was cheaper than the movies or Broadway and thus more hospitable to young playwrights. Some of this perceived quality was actually present, but

---

Key Broadcasting Indicators: 1955 / This is the sixth of 12 tables offering comparable information over a 60-year period (to 1985) at five-year intervals. Sources for items 1–6 and 11 are the tables in Appendix C, while other information comes from sources indicated below. Most data are for January 1.

Indicators	AM	FM	TV
1. Number of commercial stations	2,644	552	411
2. Number of noncommercial stations	± 25	122	11
3. Total stations on the air	2,669	674	422
4. Number of network-affiliated stations	1,355	na	374
5. Percentage of commercial stations affiliated with networks	50%	na	91%
6. Total industry revenue (add 000,000)	$545.0	$1.9	$1,035.0
7. One-hour station rate (New York)	$1,200	na	$6,200
8. One-minute station rate (New York)	$200	na	na
9. One-hour network rate, evening	$26,000	na	$101,000
10. Number of broadcasting employees	.... 45,300		32,300
11. Percentage of families with sets	96.4%	na	64.5%
12. Broadcasting regulatory budget (FCC)	.... $6,911,769		
13. Total FCC personnel	.... 1,094		

Notes (see Appendix D for full citations)

na = not applicable or not available.

7–8. WRCA radio (later WNBC) and WRCA-TV (later WNBC-TV) in New York.

9. NBC radio (208 affiliates) and TV (186 affiliates) networks.

10. Radio figure covers both AM and FM, and networks. Lichty and Topping (1975), page 290, table 23.

11. FM figure would have been on the order of 1 percent or 2 percent.

12–13. FCC figures for fiscal year 1955, ending June 30.

part was due to the audience, which in the early 1950s had more income and education—due to cost of television receivers—than the general population. Yet the medium's problems were evident in growing concern about television violence, the quiz scandals, and so on. Many persons in the industry, in government, and among the public felt that television had grown too fast to develop ethics commensurate with its huge role in society. Part of the problem was that the impact of television was becoming hidden by its very ubiquity.

No longer was the television set a novelty. No longer would programs seen the night before be the main topic of conversation at work or at play. Now television was merely something one sat in front of in the living room, and radio was something that provided music and news in the car, the bedroom, or the kitchen. There are many who believe that we are the poorer

---

Key Broadcasting Indicators: 1960 / This is the seventh of 12 tables offering comparable information over a 60-year period (to 1985) at five-year intervals. Sources for items 1–6 and 11 are the tables in Appendix C, while other information comes from sources indicated below. Most data are for January 1.

Indicators	AM	FM	TV
1. Number of commercial stations	3,431	688	515
2. Number of noncommercial stations	± 25	162	44
3. Total stations on the air	3,456	850	559
4. Number of network-affiliated stations	1,153	na	496
5. Percentage of commercial stations affiliated with networks	33%	na	96%
6. Total industry revenue (add 000,000)	$692.4	$9.4	$1,627.0
7. One-hour station rate (New York)	$1,200	na	$9,200
8. One-minute station rate (New York)	$175	na	na
9. One-hour network rate, evening	$12,100	na	$151,500
10. Number of broadcasting employees	51,700	1,300	40,600
11. Percentage of families with sets	95.6%	10%	87.1%
12. Broadcasting regulatory budget (FCC)	. . . .$10,550,000		
13. Total FCC personnel	. . . . .1,396		

Notes (see Appendix D for full citations)

na = not applicable or not available

7–8. WRCA radio and TV (NBC flagship stations) in New York.

9. NBC radio (202 affiliates) and TV (192 affiliates) networks.

10. AM radio figure covers both AM stations and networks. Lichty and Topping (1975), page 290, table 23.

12–13. FCC figures for fiscal year 1960, ending June 30.

for that change—when the excitement died, broadcasting became ordinary and familiar. Ed Murrow, in a 1958 speech to his colleagues in the Radio-Television News Directors Association, summed it up with "This instrument can teach, it can illuminate; yes, and can even inspire. But it can do so only to the extent that humans are determined to use it to those ends. Otherwise it is merely wires and lights in a box."

Further Reading

The best single book describing broadcasting in the late 1950s is the first edition of Head (1956), along with Bogart's discussion of early television research (1956 and 1958), Wylie's (1955) examination of industry problem areas, the last volume of Barnouw's history (1970), and the articles and data in Lichty and Topping (1975). The developing network structure of television is described in CBS's *Network Practices* (1956) and in the extensive U.S. Senate Commerce Committee's *Television Inquiry* hearings the same year. The FCC's *Network Broadcasting* (1958), together with its interim reports on the program procurement process (1963 and 1965), offer invaluable details on network decision making in this period. The best survey of broadcast advertising practice in the 1950s is Seehafer and Laemmar (1959).

The early years of educational television are related in Powell (1962) and Blakely (1979), while instructional applications are reviewed in Saettler (1968). Hill (1965) and Alford (1966) describe the development of the NAEB. Placing events of the 1950s in context with later developments is Wood and Wylie (1977).

For pictorial and reference material on television programming, see pp. 314–315; books on television commercials and specific program types are at the end of chapter 9. For the changing musical sound of radio, see Passman (1971) and Eberly (1982). Chester (1969) tells television's early political role, while Bluem (1965) assesses early television documentaries. The changing role of Murrow is found in Friendly (1967), Kendrick (1969), Sperber (1986), and Persico (1988).

In addition to Bogart (above), major television audience studies include Elliott (1956) and the Steiner (1963) report of a national survey of attitudes toward television. The two seminal studies of children and television noted on page 355 are Himmelweit, Oppenheim, and Vince (1958) and Schramm, Lyle, and Parker (1961).

Regulation in this period is best described in Smead (1959), Coons (1961), and Emery (1971), the FCC's annual reports, and the Fall 1957 and Winter 1958 issues of *Law and Contemporary Problems*. Schwartz (1959) discusses the role of commissions and Congress; Anderson (1979) is the definitive word on the quiz show scandals (including several full program scripts); and the end of blacklisting is described grippingly in Faulk (1964) and Vaughn (1972). Baughman (1985) is an insightful assessment of FCC program regulation in this era.

For worldwide developments, see notes at end of chapters 7 and 9.

Accommodation and Adjustment (1961–1977)

9

"I invite you to sit down in front of your television set when your station goes on the air and stay there without a book, magazine, newspaper, profit-and-loss sheet or rating book to distract you—and keep your eyes glued to that set until the station signs off. I can assure you that you will observe a vast wasteland."—FCC Chairman Newton N. Minow to NAB convention, 1961

Accommodation
and Adjustment
(1961–1977)

"... there always will be, of necessity, a TV wasteland. The three TV networks must produce 10,950 hours of entertainment per year, in contrast to only 600 hours demanded of the entire moving picture industry of our country and the 125 hours per year demanded of the Broadway theater."
—Ed Sullivan testifying before the FCC, 1961

Despite Minow's observations, television was not *all* wasteland. For special events, it was the medium to which everyone tuned. Perhaps the most dramatic occasion was the four days starting November 22, 1963, when radio and television served as the ears and eyes of the American people, bearing witness to the shocking assassination of President John F. Kennedy. For these four days almost all at home watched solemn and terrible events, listened to attempts to make them meaningful, and finally found some relief in the tributes from the nation's performing artists. It made no difference that most people got the first news by word-of-mouth, or whether they saw the shooting of the suspected assassin on their screens two days

Outline:
Accommodation and Adjustment (1961–1976)

later—broadcasting brought the American people together through those days.

Another FCC Commissioner, Lee Loevinger, has called the journalistic function of the media "essential." Just a year before President Kennedy's assassination, listeners and viewers had stayed close to radio and television for ten days as the United States and the Soviet Union stood on the brink of nuclear war over Russian placement of missiles in Cuba. News and special programs gave a gripping portrayal of the crisis, and President Kennedy delivered clear warning over the air of his intentions. After 1965 the steady buildup of American troops and commitment to South Vietnam was covered in the "living room war"—perhaps the most frustrating war this country has ever fought. The dramatic peak and possible turning point of American public opinion may have been the 1968 Tet offensive and the summary execution of a communist suspect on a Saigon street before NBC cameras. In 1968 there also were domestic assassinations and a violent demonstration outside the Democratic national political convention in Chicago. A year later, the nation and much of the world were watching when Neil Armstrong became the first man to walk on the moon. Toward the end of this period, the nation watched the fall of a President, as the Watergate scandal finally led to Nixon's resignation, the brief administration of the first nonelected president, Gerald R. Ford, and the second set of "great debates" before the start of President Jimmy Carter's administration.

The 15 years from the cold winter day when John Kennedy was inaugurated to the warm summer evening when Richard M. Nixon resigned were increasingly complicated and tension-filled. The country careened from domestic problem to foreign crisis and back again. In a world where many people wanted simple black-and-white answers, even the gray alternatives were getting harder to find.

Many Americans understandably retreated, when possible, to another world —a world of small pictures that provided hours of entertainment. Millions found *Perry Mason, The Beverly Hillbillies,* and *The Lucy Show* a welcome respite from the harsh truths of news programs. Daily serials and game shows on television, and music and talk on radio, helped pass the hours for housewives and youth. Radio, liberated by the transistor from the weight and expense and fragile tubes of earlier models, appeared everywhere. It was soon a standard accessory of the nation's urban youth—to carry a blaring radio on the street was the symbol of being "with it" and "tuned in." For the first time, the general public listened to an academic theorist, Canadian Marshall McLuhan, who spoke fluently, if sometimes confusingly, of the degree to which broadcasting, and to a lesser extent other media and elements in society, had become an integral part of modern life (see 9.9).

But behind the scenes, generally unknown to the public, were the tensions of an industry beset with growth and change. More stations, particularly FM, went on the air, dividing the audience and the advertising pie into ever smaller pieces with sometimes devastating results for the newcomer. The television industry feared mounting competition from cable television, and the FCC was caught in the old problem of how much to protect an existing industry in the face of a new one. Public concern about violence on the air and its effect on youth pushed Congress into sponsoring the biggest research effort ever connected with broadcasting (see 9.72), and questions about fair treatment of controversial issues plagued broadcast management. Government concern, sometimes politically inspired, about concentration of ownership added to the industry's headaches.

9•1   Changing Technologies

In 1960–1961, most broadcasting equipment—home receivers and station and studio equipment—used electronic tubes similar in principle to those manufactured in the 1920s. The invention of the transistor by scientists in the Bell Labs in 1948 did not have an effect on broadcasting until the early 1960s, when their cost fell low enough to allow their widespread use. Transistors permitted more compact construction, cooler operation and thus longer life, and use of much less electric power. By the late 1960s transistors were giving way to even more compact successors, which were direct outgrowths of the nation's space research. First came printed circuits that reduced a series of tubes, resistors, capacitors, and other components to a sheet of plastic with many of the components literally painted or printed thereon and with sockets for transistors studded about. Then came truly microscopic integrated circuits, which were grown in a solution and then cut apart, and which incorporated the equivalent of transistors as an integral part of the tiny structure. The trend to smaller and more rugged, if somewhat sensitive to heat and humidity, components made automatic assembly of virtually all electronic equipment possible and therefore easier, quicker, and less expensive.

There had been rather unsuccessful automated radio programming experiments as early as the 1940s. But now, with more reliable electronics, timing units could be connected to long-running tape playback machines, allowing a station to be prerecorded and run automatically for hours. FM stations, short of cash to pay

personnel—always the largest part of any broadcasting station's operating costs—often were the first to use automation. Their music-and-little-talk formats of the 1950s and early 1960s lent themselves to this approach. Several companies specialized in offering both the equipment *and* the programming suitable for automated operations. While this led to distant stations sounding almost alike, companies rarely sold a given programming service to more than one station in a market, thus maintaining the appearance of program format competition.

Coming at the same time as automation, and, indeed, forming part of most automation systems, was the tape cartridge. Reel-to-reel magnetic tape recordings had increasingly replaced disc records until about 1960. In that year a small plastic-enclosed *single hub* self-contained cartridge of tape, activated by a shove into the slot of a special tape player, was developed. Foolproof; no need to set up the reels or find a starting place on the tape—just grab the cart and shove it in. This made the fast-paced formula or Top 40 station far easier to operate. Cartridges were used mainly for commercials and other segments from 15 seconds, or even less for station IDs, to about 10 minutes. As carts became available in half-hour and hour lengths, their use in radio broadcasting grew, with much programming originally in other formats transferred to carts. From the studio the cartridge spread to the consumer in the form of playback machines, and radio-recorders, in automobile and home.

By 1964, however, the cartridge had competition from the even smaller and lighter *two hub cassette,* developed by Philips (Norelco in the United States), the giant Netherlands electrical manufacturing company. While the cassette did not have the impact of the cart in broadcasting, other than providing reporters with small and lightweight recorders, it made rapid gains in the consumer market. Philips wisely made it cheap and easy for any manufacturer to make cassettes, not restricting it to their own companies, which led to rapid adoption of the technology. Cassette-radio combinations became increasingly popular.

The next home audio development seemed likely to be four-channel or quadraphonic hi-fi systems. But disagreement over standards for the new service between advocates of the *matrix* and the *discrete* systems, and the high cost, virtually doubling the cost of a stereo system, led to very slow adoption. Although the first quadraphonic broadcasts had been aired in Boston and New York in 1968, using two cooperating FM stereo stations in each city, true *quadraplex* (four channels over one station) transmissions were not tried until the early 1970s. Because such transmissions required dropping any Subsidiary Communications Authorizations (SCA) the station was operating, few stations had an incentive to inaugurate four-channel broadcasting.

These problems of audio standards seemed almost simple when contrasted to video variations. By the late 1960s, two roads for video expansion seemed possible: cable television or home video recording systems. Some crystal ball gazers saw both in the cards: cable now, and home video systems later. Cable, having grown slowly since 1949 (see 8.24), was already present on the broadcast scene. By the early 1970s some people predicted that CATV would oust over-the-air broadcasting. Possibilities included store purchases by cable, doctors' visits by closed-circuit television via cable, two-way interconnection with computers using a telephone as the home terminal, meter-reading and home protection devices activated through

cable, and other *wideband communications* devices leading to the "wired nation." But in a couple of years cable seemed to have lost momentum, and the economic recession of the mid-1970s shelved most of these ideas (see 9.22), although the number of homes served by cable continued to grow.

Economics and burgeoning technology also played a large part in delaying home video systems that could play whatever a person selected whenever he or she wanted. Programming would be for the individual. The first home videotape recorders, essentially the same as the relatively inexpensive helical-scan VCR machines used by industry and education, had little impact when they appeared in 1965, although they cost far less than quad-head broadcast-quality VCRs. Laboratories also were developing new systems based on videotape, film, and even lasers, and promising them first for industry and education and shortly afterwards for the home market. In the late 1960s, CBS Laboratories promoted, but later sold, its Electronic Video Recording system (EVR). This heralded combination of film and television was supplanted by another possible pot of gold at the end of the rainbow, the video disc. Developed first by Philips, the video disc, on its own special machine, could provide both picture and sound for a half-hour or so on a side. Other companies were developing their own, incompatible technologies. The benefits of the disc over a cassette videotape system, several of which also were being developed, were analogous to those of the phonograph disc over the cylinder; countless copies could be stamped out at very low cost per unit. But this market too was held back by unsettled standards and the economic downturn of the mid-1970s.

Late in 1975, a premonition of the future appeared on a few store shelves.

Sony "Betamax"* system videocassette recorders (VCRs) were first reaching the market, initially in a console including a 19-inch color television monitor for $2,295. The price dropped (to about $1,300) when the first Betamax tape decks were placed on sale in February 1976. Even these first relatively limited machines (the tapes had only a one-hour capacity) allowed the television viewer to become something of a programmer—recording material off the air for playback at a later time, or *time-shifting*. Several months later, the Universal and Disney film studios sued to stop sales of the machines for fear their copyrights would be imperiled by home tapers of movies shown on television. Publicity about the suit and initial ads for the machine led to half the country's population telling pollsters they knew what a Betamax was barely a year after its introduction. The introduction of the VCR would create a significant watershed in the history of broadcasting in the space of remarkably few years (see 10.1).

A major development in long-distance communication, threatening to destroy AT&T's long-held monopoly on network interconnections and making remote pickups possible from almost everywhere in the world, is the communications satellite. Predicted in detail as early as 1945, the technology for these devices was developed after 1957 when the Soviet Union launched the first artificial orbital satellite. It took only a few years to progress from placing a tape recorder aboard a satellite to broadcast a Christmas message from President Eisenhower (1958) and bouncing signals off a passive orbiting balloon named *Echo* (1960) to using active satellites that could receive messages and retransmit them on another frequency. Most early satellites were in orbits from a few hundred to a few thousand miles high, including AT&T's pioneering *Telstar,* launched in July 1962, which was capable of relaying television pictures across the Atlantic when in the proper orbital position. Later ones were placed in equatorial geosynchronous orbit 22,300 miles high. At this altitude a satellite maintains its position relative to the earth, appearing to be stationary and thus providing an easy target for transmitting and receiving antennas on the ground.

These satellites, starting with *Early Bird* and going through various more sophisticated *Intelsats*, were generally launched by the National Aeronautics and Space Administration (NASA) for the Communications Satellite Corporation (COMSAT), a corporation created by Congress after considerable debate. COMSAT not only handled the United States side of international satellite circuits but managed the global network for the multinational International Telecommunications Satellite Organization, INTELSAT. Although AT&T owned *Early Bird* and *Telstar* and, originally, a large portion of COMSAT stock (which was divided roughly 50-50 between the general public and U.S. common carriers such as AT&T and Western Union), it sold most of its interest in COMSAT in the early 1970s. The FCC had approved a domestic satellite policy which effectively limited the Bell System to providing local ground connections at transmitting and receiving stations. Although the Soviet Union in the 1960s and Canada in the early 1970s had established domestic communications satellite systems, the rush in the United States did not occur until Western Union's *Westar* was launched in 1974. Several companies leased channels on *Westar* and then retailed access to them at a considerable saving over AT&T land-line tariffs.

---

*The word "beta" refers to a Japanese brush stroke that completely covers the surface underneath it—just as the Betamax VCR uses the entire tape surface for a signal. See Lardner (1987).

The networks began to investigate interconnection by communications satellites in what might be thought of as the first breach in the 1926 agreements between RCA and AT&T (see 3.23). The development of mobile ground stations—such as the one President Nixon took on his trip to China in 1972—together with satellites permitted full telecommunications facilities, including several television channels, almost anywhere.

One creative contribution of the communications satellite to television, however, awaited the late 1975 announcement by Home Box Office, a Time-Life pay-cable subsidiary, that it planned to use a Satcom I *transponder* to deliver its movies to participating cable system *head ends* nationwide. Systems that purchased a television receive-only (TVRO) antenna could now carry a pay-cable service, charge subscribers an additional fee, and share the proceeds with HBO. Early in 1976, a then little known (outside of yachting and sports circles) entrepreneur named Ted Turner announced that he too was going to make the programming of his Atlanta UHF station available to cable systems, using a transponder on the same Satcom I satellite. Coining the term "superstation" to describe his concept, Turner figured that a diet of movies and sporting events (especially those of the professional teams he owned, the Atlanta Braves baseball and Hawks basketball) carried on his independent channel 17 would be a good supplement for the many television markets hitherto restricted to network fare. By the end of 1976, Turner's station was being carried by 20 cable systems in different parts of the country.

Together, the HBO and Turner moves pioneered a dramatic expansion in the role of cable television. Use of satellite transponders solved the age-old problem of expensive and time-consuming expansion of terrestrial networking by substituting instant nationwide distribution of a signal. Cable systems would have to buy a receiving antenna. However, once that step was taken, they would be able to provide Turner's and HBO's programs—and other signals promised for the late 1970s—as added incentives for cable subscribers.

9•2   Station Population Explosion

Broadcasting station growth continued into the 1970s, but the pattern was different. Despite FCC efforts to slow this growth (see 9.21), AM stations increased from about 3,600 early in 1961 to approximately 4,500 by 1976—even though engineers had considered the AM band crowded with only 950 stations in 1945. But radio's most prominent growth—a surprise to long-time industry observers—was in FM. Commercial FM stations increased from about 800 in early 1961 to more than 2,100 by late 1976. Even more dramatic, educational FM stations increased from just 170 to more than 800. All told, there were nearly 3,700 FM stations on the air by late 1976—a dramatic turnaround for a one-time "loser" service. Television grew somewhat more slowly—from 560 commercial stations, mostly on VHF, in 1961 to more than 700 commercial stations, all but 200 of them VHF, by late 1976. Educational TV station growth was substantial—from just 52 outlets in 1961 to more than 250 (many of them merely repeater transmitters) 15 years later.

From such figures (see Appendix C, table 1 for details) come three interesting conclusions: (1) FM was now the fastest-growing broadcast service; (2) educational FM and television grew very rapidly, finally providing educational and cultural interests with the coverage they had wanted for so long; and (3) even by 1976, use of UHF channels was slight, with only 352 UHF stations actually on the air, nearly half of them educational, versus more than 600 VHF stations, only 97 of them educational, even though the FCC had made far more UHF channels available. The VHF-UHF problem (see 8.81) had obviously not been resolved even after a quarter century. At the same time, the sustained growth of other services led to problems of spectrum crowding.

9•21   Slowing AM and Expanding FM

It is hard to believe, from data in Appendix C, table 1, that for nearly half of the period 1961–1976 there was a freeze on new AM license awards. From May 1962 to July 1964, and again from July 1968 to February 1973, the FCC stopped most licensing of new AM stations while seeking rule changes to limit growth on that band. The problem had technical, economic, and political aspects, all interrelated. Most stations starting after 1961 were limited to daytime operation. Although most regions, particularly metropolitan ones, did not need another daytime station, adding nighttime stations would have caused massive interference elsewhere. By the mid-1970s, the largest markets were served by from 20 to 70 different AM or FM radio stations. In some places there were too many stations to divide the available advertising dollars effectively; 40 percent of the radio stations were already marginal or losing money. Television had taken much of the audience, and salable program formats were few. But politically, it was difficult to persuade persons wanting to get into the radio industry and smaller communities that desired more outlets that AM growth had to stop. Finally, at the end of the second AM freeze in 1973, the FCC issued stringent rules for

considering a request for a new AM station. Such a station would have to provide a first service—that is, for a community in which at least 25 percent of the coverage area or 25 percent of the population had no radio service at all. If an unused FM channel was available in the area to be served, no AM grant would be made.

Earlier, in fall 1961, the commission had decided to resolve the question of clear channels, which had been dragging on since the allocation hearings of 1944. Complaints about the inherent unfairness of the clears, originally established by the FRC in 1928 (see 4.82 and 5.22), and the desire to make room for even the lowest-power AM station had finally overcome the arguments for their retention. The FCC decision was to "break down" 13 of the 25 1-A channels in the United States. Naturally, the high-powered stations on these channels fought this move through the final judicial decision of November 1963 upholding the FCC. By the early 1970s, very few clear stations were still clear, or operating alone on that channel day and night. Some remained clear, or protected by the width of the continent, at night, but many new low-power or daytime-only stations had been squeezed in to provide local service.

As the number of FM stations grew, the commission found it had to improve its assignment structure. To avoid the first-come first-served shoehorning typical of AM since broadcasting's start, both FM and television channels eventually were assigned to specific communities to permit orderly and efficient growth and to avoid concentration of facilities in the largest cities. In July 1962 this resulted in the establishment of three main classes of FM station plus provision for 10 watt noncommercial educational stations: Class A, low power (100 watts to 3,000 watts), and a restriction on antenna height to 300 feet above average terrain leading to a service radius of about 15 miles, and a distance between stations on the same channel of 65 miles; Class B (5 kw to 50 kw), 500-foot limit, 40-mile service radius, and 150-mile co-channel spacing; and Class C, high power (25 kw to 100 kw), 65-mile service radius, and 180-mile co-channel spacing. Using these standards, the commission assigned nearly 3,000 potential stations to about 1,800 communities. Classes A and B were to be used primarily in the crowded Northeast and in Southern California, while Class C would be allowed only in other parts of the country. Most existing stations were "grandfathered."

This reassignment ended several years of concern and a short freeze on issuance of new FM licenses. With the thaw, and with the stereo standards decision (see 8.11), FM stations began to increase rapidly. Most new stations were equipped for stereo broadcasting, so that, as older stations slowly developed stereo capability, about one-quarter of the FM stations were broadcasting in stereo by 1965 and about two-fifths by 1971. These studio and transmitter changes were costly, and for a while there were too few stereo-equipped receivers to make the decision pay off. But with the increasing availability of stereo, and later four-channel, sound in tapes, records, and broadcasting, more and more stations took the plunge. By the mid-1970s, a large majority of FM outlets could broadcast in stereo.

As FM stations approached AM stations in service area and size of audience, FM channels assumed greater value to broadcasters. The commission, taking full notice of their potential equality, considered separating AM and FM ownership in the same community. A 1963 rule led to partial nonduplication of programs between the two radio services (see 9.61) in all but the smallest markets. The FCC

was constantly considering eventual breaking up of AM-FM ownership and programming combinations in the same market. FM stations were bringing steadily higher prices, with the first million-dollar sale taking place in 1968. Soon, the majority of FM licensing cases required comparative hearings, as would-be broadcasters competed for channel assignments. In addition, the unusual loyalty of FM audiences caused problems as stations changed hands and new managers tried to change format. A classical music FM station in Chicago (WFMT) was sold to the *Chicago Tribune's* WGN and ran into a well-organized public complaint campaign fearing it planned to adopt a different music format. WGN finally gave the station to an educational operator who would continue the classical music format. A New York classical music station (WNCN) changed hands and went to a pop format in 1974, raising an outcry from its listeners. Political considerations of "concentration of power" gave strength to these protests. Despite, or because of all this, FM stations in some markets achieved respectable audience ratings in competition with AM stations for the first time (see 9.61 and 9.71).

The multiplicity of broadcasting stations—approximately 9,000 by 1976—made heavy paperwork for both the commission and the stations. Smaller stations especially complained bitterly to Congress and the commission. Finally, in 1973, the FCC cautiously started a process initially called "re-regulation" to simplify and loosen some technical and record-keeping requirements.

9•22   *Television: UHF, STV, and CATV*

In the 1960s, many of the parallels between UHF television and FM radio disappeared. While FM grew and even prospered, UHF television grew so slowly that even a 1962 law requiring UHF and VHF reception capability on all new sets sold in the United States did not immediately help (see 9.7). Few new UHF stations went on the air, few UHF-equipped sets were made before the mid-1960s, and broadcasters, advertisers, and viewers showed little interest in UHF (see 8.81). It was a circle that UHF was unable to break. However, in the decade after the 1964 effective date of the all-channel receiver law, UHF added 111 stations while VHF added only 47, largely because of a shortage of desirable channels. Probably both the legislation and the increasing scarcity of desirable VHF channels helped UHF growth.

VHF scarcity was implicit in the 1952 *Sixth Report and Order* (see 7.83), and became evident with the 1965–1966 reassignment and reallocation of television frequencies. While the original plan offered a total of 551 commercial VHF assignments, only about 40 of these, mostly in very small western towns, were not on the air by late 1976. On the other hand, of 590 commercial UHF assignments, nearly 400 were still vacant. Much the same pattern existed for educational television (see 9.4), although a much higher proportion of UHF assignments was in use. In 1952, 242 educational channel reservations had been established, a number raised to 615—508 on UHF—in 1966. In 1966 the FCC stopped assigning channels above channel 69, although the 1952 *Sixth Report and Order* allocation included UHF channels through 83. For various reasons, television stations on the top 14 channels had poorer coverage capability than stations lower in the spectrum, and most higher numbered channels were used only for low-power translators. This waste of spectrum space, combined with other options for its use—translators or the growing and aggressive land mobile, safety, and special radio ser-

vices—led to the FCC's decision to remove these 84 MHz permanently from television broadcasting in May 1970.

This reallocation plus the earlier all-channel receiver legislation effectively ended FCC plans for deintermixture or any other 1950s proposals for rescuing UHF (see 8.81). The general hope now was that natural replacement of sets would increase the number of UHF homes and that the growing audience would attract advertising money and improve station finances.

Another major matter at least temporarily laid to rest in this period was pay or subscription broadcast television (STV). The focus of long debate in the 1950s (see 8.23) and a battle with Connecticut film theater owners that went all the way to the Supreme Court, pay-TV was given a test from 1962 to 1968 in Hartford. Like so many other earlier tests, it was inconclusive.

The biggest operational attempt at pay-TV took place in California, using wires to provide three programs besides those received off the air and maintaining free on-air television channels. Former NBC president Sylvester "Pat" Weaver led the Subscription Television company, whose 1964 venture had $25 million in capital, the backing of major corporations, and several important sports and entertainment contracts, including the Giants and Dodgers baseball teams. Movie theater owners led the fight against pay-TV. Pay-TV made a midsummer debut in the Santa Monica section of Los Angeles with about 4,000 subscribers paying to see new—but often not as new as hoped—films, educational and cultural features, and sports. Although STV briefly expanded to San Francisco, the costs of a public opinion fight forced the Weaver group to curtail operations. In November, voters killed pay-TV by a nearly two-to-one margin on a ballot referendum initiated by the motion picture industry. The vote later was declared unconstitutional, but by then the company was out of money and out of business.

In Congress bills were introduced to outlaw pay-TV, and both sides sent out heavy propaganda. Finally, the battle centered on three areas: the House Commerce Committee, which continued to hold hearings and ask the FCC to delay a decision; the FCC, which said it was ready to establish rules allowing regular STV operation under very controlled conditions; and the experiment on Channel 18 in Hartford, which was approved in 1968 for three more years, having already run for six. However, Zenith took the experiment off the air due to the impending FCC decision and the need to convert to color.

In December 1968 the FCC adopted rules allowing broadcast pay-TV but delayed implementing them until Congress had time to react. To be shown for pay, movies had to be less than two years old and sports events could not have appeared on free television in the previous two years; no continuing series could be shown. Over-the-air pay-TV could be established only in cities with more than four operating commercial stations and would have to operate a minimum of 28 hours a week. There could be no commercials, and at least 10 percent of the offerings had to be other than sports or movies. Technical standards were announced in fall 1969. A 1971 "antisiphoning" rule extended the ban on pay-TV use of sporting events to five rather than two years, and banned special sports events like the Olympic Games for ten years after their last network or free television showing. By 1974 three technical systems had been approved for operation, the first being Zenith's pioneering "Phonevision." Applications for stations in different markets had been received, and several approved

by the FCC; but the first two over-the-air pay stations (one in Los Angeles, the other in a New Jersey suburb of New York City) did not get on the air until spring 1977 (see 10.22).

Most of the then very limited pay-TV in the United States was a service of some cable systems rather than broadcast. By mid-1976 more than 750,000 subscribers paid to receive programs on special channels of 250 cable systems. The ability of these systems to charge for special programming made their operation far more attractive to investors.

Cable television had grown very slowly during the 1950s and early 1960s. By the mid-1960s, more than one million homes out of more than 60 million were on the cable, and more than 1,200 systems were operating (see Appendix C, table 10). Systems continued to increase in number and size, so that by late 1976 more than one in six of the nation's homes were hooked up to one of more than 3,700 cable systems, mostly in rural and suburban areas, particularly of the West. Cable's fortunes improved in 1965–1966 partly as a result of increased regulatory activity (see 9.83). Some cable systems began to originate programming, most provided far better reception of color programs, and many larger towns began to see cable television. This last development reminded the FCC of past experiences with uncontrolled growth in big cities, and it put a freeze on signal importation into the nation's 100 top markets.

But cable was growing in other ways, although probably not as fast as industry publicity would have one believe. As equipment improved, systems expanded their capacity from three to five channels to ten or more, and the technology allowed 20 or more at a time, although only 12 percent of systems had this capability by 1976. As the investment required to build systems increased, the traditional "Mom and Pop" cable companies gave way to the better financed and managed Multiple System Operator (MSO). With this development the FCC became concerned over concentration of ownership, and in early 1970, it prohibited cable system ownership by telephone companies or television stations in the same market area, and of cable systems anywhere by national television networks. As more cable systems became program originators, the FCC tried various ways to prevent undue concentration of control.

This FCC action had, as a side effect, established contention among cable systems and broadcasters and some telephone companies, which charged cable high—perhaps exorbitant—rates to rent space on their poles. Skirmishes between broadcasters and cable operators sometimes led to decreased service to the public. By the late 1960s, the National Cable Television Association (NCTA) was facing off against the National Association of Broadcasters in arguments over copyright, program carriage, signal importation, and other regulatory issues of economic and political importance to both sides. Because of the potential effects of cable on the public, Congress took an increasing interest in cable. Broadcasters were not united, since cable provided larger audiences for many stations, especially the hard-pressed UHF outlets, and because many broadcasters owned cable operations in communities outside the range of their stations.

But the public was being told that cable was the greatest invention since the zipper with its new programming and new outlets for people with political, social, and economic interests not served by the broadcast system. New York and other large cities, already well served by on-air stations, acquired their first major cable systems. Unfortunately, the high cost of wiring in the city and insufficient new programming to interest potential subscribers left many cable operators—some of whom made money from tax loopholes rather than from any concern for the public interest—with a hand-to-mouth livelihood. The recession of the mid-1970s and the natural caution of many MSOs, particularly in light of the failure of the New York systems to make a substantial profit, seemed to dim cable's promise for the time being.

9·3   A Continuing Network Pattern . . . Ripe for Change

The basic pattern of network operation continued into the 1970s. The FCC finally banned option time agreements in mid-1963, an action first proposed in the 1941 Chain Broadcasting Report (see 5.83 and 8.82), but by this time most industry observers felt it would have little effect, as FCC rule changes and competitive pressures had made network and affiliate relations more flexible. Early in 1965 the commission proposed limiting the financial control by networks to 50 percent of the programs they carried, with no part of syndication. The ostensible point was to enhance competition and possibly other points of view by allowing other production sources to enter the network television market. This rule aroused such strong opposition that the commission withdrew it but returned in May 1970 with another approach to the same end. This would limit network programming in the top 50 markets between 7 P.M. and 11 P.M. (6 P.M. to 10 P.M. in the Central and Mountain Time Zones) to three hours—in effect, removing a half-hour the networks had programmed for their affiliates for years. The commission allowed syndicated "off-network" shows for the first year of the rule and then insisted on either station-produced shows or independently syndicated material, with the expressed hope that stations would use the time for local public affairs programming. The unfortunate result was a flood of inexpensive syndicated entertainment material—game shows, travelogues, some cheap variety and adventure programs—that was little different from network programs. The Prime Time Access Rule (PTAR) was debated, modified slightly, nearly modified again, and debated some more. In 1972 the Justice Department filed antitrust suits against the networks in a possibly politically motivated attempt to further diversify program control. The suits were later dismissed and still later (1974) reinstated, leading many to predict a lengthy court battle ahead. However, as discussed in 10.32, although this lawsuit was settled out of court late in 1976, it was only one of the pressures on the network-station relationship of the time.

The long-lasting Yankee and Don Lee regional radio networks both folded in 1967. All networks changed their top management, retiring pioneers in television and bringing in younger people, some with little or no broadcasting experience. Network broadcasting stopped being special and began to approximate other businesses. In 1967 a national labor dispute took most performers and live programs off the air. The American Federation of Television and Radio Artists (AFTRA), a performers union, called a strike over the wages paid announcers at network-owned FM stations. It quickly got out of hand, and CBS viewers tuning in the first night of the strike heard a bespectacled young man introduce the evening news with "This is Arnold Zenker substituting for Walter Cronkite." Except for a few like NBC's Chet Huntley who felt newsmen had no business on picket lines, news and

entertainment figures respected the strike, and live shows were replaced with reruns or other canned programs. The dispute was settled just two hours before the scheduled beginning of the motion picture academy "Oscars" telecast, a major viewing event each year. Cronkite came back on that night deadpanning "This is Walter Cronkite, substituting for Arnold Zenker." Temporary news anchor Zenker, a lowly CBS executive, went to an on-air role in Boston and later in Baltimore on the strength of this sudden thrust into the spotlight.

ABC had particular problems that almost led to a controversial merger. By the 1964–1965 season, ABC had become competitive in ratings with both CBS and NBC. Long a distant third in popularity and advertising billings, ABC had gathered large audiences through the Disney program (see 8.62) and formula-ridden action-adventure shows. One year later, its new position of strength was in danger as the other two networks, led by NBC, began to program major amounts of time in color. ABC lacked sufficient capital to purchase color cameras, VTRs, and other equipment necessary for equal competition. While NBC prime time was nearly all color and CBS about half-color, ABC trailed into the season with 60 percent of prime-time programming still in black-and-white. Its ratings and its reputation with advertising time buyers suffered.

ABC, casting about for new investment funds, and International Telephone and Telegraph (ITT), looking for new acquisitions, found each other late in 1965. Because ABC owned stations, such a merger would be subject to approval by the FCC and the Justice Department, whose antitrust division already was concerned with conglomerate ITT. The FCC held hearings on the proposed merger in September 1966 and approved the ITT takeover 4–3, even though the Justice Department had requested a delay. In January 1967, Justice requested that the FCC reopen the hearings. ABC stock dropped 14 points at the news. Faced with low ratings and consequent low income, ABC asked ITT for a $25 million loan. It did this partly to show how ITT would put money *into* the network rather than financially milking it, as some critics had anticipated. In March the FCC reheard the issues and on June 22, 1967, approved the merger a second time, by the same split vote. But a month later the Justice Department appealed the matter to the courts. Faced with further delay, ITT in January 1968 canceled the merger agreement. Those who felt that ABC would have been forced to temper its news coverage of ITT's many connections were delighted. ABC was left back in third place among the networks. That summer, recluse billionaire Howard Hughes tried to buy controlling interest in ABC for $150 million, but ABC management was not interested.

As hopes for the ITT merger died, ABC took an innovative plunge into networking during this period—but in radio and not television. On January 1, 1968, it replaced the old ABC Radio Network with four separate networks: Personality (soon renamed Entertainment), Information, Contemporary, and American FM. Using the single ABC network line leased from AT&T, the four shared each broadcast hour in a set pattern, one network getting the first 15 minutes, the next network the second, and so forth. This kept costs down and, perhaps more important, allowed the FCC to waive the duopoly rule by using an obscure section of the 1941 Chain Broadcasting rules (which were not dropped until 1977). For the first time, networks were to be tailored to specialized station formats. *Each* network in a single market

could have one affiliate. In a year ABC had twice as many radio affiliates as before the changeover, and soon more than 1,200 stations were assigned to one of the four networks, making ABC by far the largest radio network operation, with about 30 percent of all radio stations. Mutual, formerly the largest radio network, suffered from the competition in the smaller markets which it had controlled. It brought a law suit on the basis of alleged violation of the duopoly rule to enjoin ABC from the plan, but the suit was dismissed. That the Information network was, from the first, the largest of the four networks indicates the desire of stations for national news.

In 1972 Leonard Goldenson, the chief figure at ABC since the merger with Paramount Theaters in 1953, moved up to chairman of the parent company, and Elton Rule, manager of KABC-TV Los Angeles before his move to network headquarters in New York in the late 1960s, became president.

CBS had many changes in operating personnel. At the end of the quiz show scandals, CBS Television President Louis Cowan, who was closely identified with the genre, was eased out in favor of young executive James Aubrey. Aubrey ruled CBS with a steel hand early in the 1960s, earning the sobriquet "Smiling Cobra" for his cold-blooded decision-making, and was highly successful at first in selecting network programs. His sudden dismissal in February 1965 in favor of another former station manager, John Schneider, mystified the television world. Aubrey offered no explanation, and neither did CBS President Frank Stanton or Board Chairman William Paley. In general, Aubrey did not fit the CBS image of quality so dear to Paley and Stanton. Some of his programming decisions apparently were based on cronyism rather than judgment, and by 1965 their ratings were wearing thin. After leaving CBS, Aubrey moved to other entertainment enterprises.

In 1973 Stanton, who by then was vice-chairman of the CBS board, retired on schedule (to run the American Red Cross), and the broadcasting industry lost its most respected spokesman. Stanton would have liked, and expected, to move up to chairman, but Paley was not about to give up power in the corporation he had built. Stanton's finest moment had come the year before, when CBS was attacked for its *Selling of the Pentagon* documentary (see 9.64) and Stanton had successfully stood up to the committee chairman seeking to cite him and CBS for contempt of Congress. Many regarded his defense of the network on First Amendment grounds as a capstone to a distinguished career. CBS went "outside" for his replacement—first to a former ITT vice president, who died within a year of his appointment while Stanton was still available, and then in mid-1972 to thirty-seven-year-old Arthur Taylor. Like ABC, CBS was beginning to rely on younger executives although Paley was unwilling to give up overall control of his network. In a pattern common to other companies in which the strong founding executive remains active, Paley over the next decade went through several heirs apparent, finding each wanting in some respect. Apparently Taylor and Paley did not hit it off personally, for while the network was doing well financially late in 1976, Taylor was suddenly relieved of his duties. Named in his place was a man with no broadcasting experience, John D. Backe, who had headed up CBS's publishing arm.

A highly successful company throughout this period, CBS began in the late 1960s to diversify its holdings. Although it could "beat" NBC in television

ratings, it was a very small company compared to RCA. CBS Laboratories under Peter Goldmark developed important electronic devices, but CBS did not become a manufacturing concern. Instead, it purchased such diverse firms as Creative Playthings, Fender Guitars, and Holt, Rinehart and Winston and other publishing firms. CBS's strong artistic style and sense of image, credited to Stanton, showed in everything from the design of their new headquarters, to CBS stationery, to their television network programming (see 9.63).

At NBC, the retirement in 1969 and death in 1971 of long-time RCA head David Sarnoff cut an important string to the past. His son Robert took over active direction of RCA until he suddenly was fired late in 1975. Economic reverses of the 1960s and 1970s caused the parent company to drop out of space and computer activities to concentrate on electronics. In the early 1970s RCA briefly tried to sell NBC's radio O & O stations together with the radio network but could not find an acceptable buyer willing to take the package. In 1975 the NBC radio network replaced the long-running weekend *Monitor* with the first 7-day, 24-hour, live, all-news network service. The News and Information Service (NIS) would be available to any station, not just NBC affiliates, that cared to purchase it, and would run 50 minutes of each hour, leaving 10 minutes for NBC network or local news and features. An insufficient number of affiliates ended the venture early in 1977.

There was a serious attempt to form a fourth commercial television network in the mid-1960s. After the Du Mont network collapsed in 1955, most observers claimed that too few major markets had a fourth commercial television channel to permit a successful fourth network. Kaiser Broadcasting, a group owner and operator of UHF stations, kept announcing that it would start a UHF-based network if it could get its O & O stations in the black (which it had not managed by 1977 when it sold out to Field Enterprises). Then in July 1966 Ohio warehouse owner Daniel Overmyer, who had several UHF construction permits, announced plans to launch a fourth network with an eight-hour nighttime service, including two of news and two of a live show from Las Vegas. With former ABC-TV president Oliver Treyz to head the operation, the Overmyer Network (ON) signed up 85 affiliates by fall and then appeared to drift while it sought more affiliates. In March 1967 ON became the United Network when a West Coast syndicate gained control, and in May the United Network went on the air with a two-hour program from Las Vegas fed to 125 stations with 13 advertisers defraying most of the costs. This effort collapsed after 31 days when the network was unable to pay AT&T line interconnection charges. Various attempts to restart the network were made throughout the year, but none succeeded.

Several broadcast networks for special occasions—a harbinger of what was to come late in the decade with the new cable networks—were established. The most successful was the Sports Network, purchased by Howard Hughes in late 1968 after his abortive attempt to purchase ABC. The Hughes Sports Network operated on a special program basis, with various stations acting as affiliates depending on the events covered. UPI, AP, and Group W (Westinghouse) each offered audio news services to purchasers, and there were video (film) news services, but these were not full networks in the generally accepted sense. This is not to say that entrepreneurs did not think about establishing new conventional networks, but projected costs and the limited number

of markets, with more than three operating commercial television stations, led to the shelving of these dreams.

9•4   Educational Broadcasting Goes Public

Until 1967, educational radio and television developed differently from earlier years in one important respect: the number of educational stations increased each year. Although only a couple of dozen noncommercial AM stations remained, educational FM stations rose in number from 186 in 1961 to 291 in 1966 and 804 a decade later, nearly a quarter of all FM stations, while ETV outlets doubled from 52 in 1961 to 114 in 1966 and again to 252 in 1976, more than one-quarter of all television stations. But the watchwords of these educational stations remained "local" and "inexpensive"; there was little national programming and very little money. The National Educational Television and Radio Center changed its name to National Educational Television (NET) in 1963 and eventually was providing up to ten hours a week of programming on film or tape. But, as Sydney Head has pointed out, "Despite remarkable progress, considering the odds, the course of educational television during the 1960s seemed dangerously parallel to that of educational radio—curving downward from a peak of high promise and fervent enthusiasm toward a plateau of mediocrity and neglect."* Some important help had come in 1962 with the first federal grants, requiring 25 percent local matching funds, to educational television. The NAEB sponsored studies on the problems of educational broadcasting, usually

*Sydney W. Head, *Broadcasting in America*, 3rd ed. (Boston: Houghton Mifflin Company, 1976), page 182.

arriving at the obvious conclusions that money and a national image were needed.

Funded primarily by the Ford Foundation, the Midwest Program on Airborne Television Instruction (MPATI) in 1961 revived the Stratovision notion (see 7.823). MPATI provided instructional television to schools in Indiana, most of Ohio and Illinois, and parts of Kentucky, Michigan, and Wisconsin from airborne transmitters on two UHF channels. Due to costs, scheduling problems, and the failure of some users to pay, MPATI finally sold its two airplanes and its transmitters in 1968, although it continued for a few years to produce and distribute programs on videotape.

A turnaround in the fortunes of ETV began in January 1967 with two important events. The first was the provision of several hours per week of interconnected live evening programming, with the Ford Foundation covering the interconnection costs. Later in the year NET, again with Ford Foundation backing, presented the *Public Broadcasting Laboratory*, a two-hour news and feature program on Sunday evenings. The first program included a one-hour drama by blacks in whiteface, which bored and puzzled many viewers and which many southern ETV stations did not carry. Between 1951 and 1977, the Ford Foundation pumped $292 million into educational television stations, networks, and other operations.

The second, and most important, ETV event of 1967 was publication of the report of the Carnegie Commission on Educational Television, *Public Television: A Program for Action*. The commission had been established in 1965 by the Carnegie foundation. Its first decision was to distinguish between commercial television, entertainment for large or mass audiences; instructional television, generally in-class educational material; and public television,

virtually everything else, with a large helping of public affairs, that was not supported by advertising. Among their final recommendations were (1) that a Corporation for Public Television be created to receive and disburse funds from government and other sources, (2) that it support at least two national and many more local production agencies, (3) that it seek ways to encourage interconnection of stations, and (4) that sufficient funds, not subject to the annual appropriation process, be provided through a 2 percent to 5 percent excise tax on television receivers.

This report sold 50,000 copies in a few days, received wide attention, and led to rapid action. President Johnson specifically mentioned public television—a term that caught on rapidly over the objections of some commercial broadcasters—in his 1967 State of the Union address and shortly afterwards proposed legislation along the lines of the Carnegie proposals. Eight months later, in November, the Public Broadcasting Act of 1967 became law. It created a Corporation for Public Broadcasting (CPB), as radio had been added at the congressional hearings. Unfortunately, the new corporation had to compete with the rising fiscal priorities of the Vietnam War, with a new Republican administration, which soon conveyed disinterest in a national system of public television, and with disagreement among educators as to whether the public television system should be centralized or station based and funded.

CPB could not legally operate stations or engage in program production. From March 27, 1968, to June 30, 1976, it received $376.2 million in income and gave out $310.7 million in grants, awards, and programs; its first federal appropriation had been $5 million in fiscal year 1969. CPB worked on four major areas of system development in its first months: grants to

Carnegie Commission and the 1967 Act: The Creation of "Public" Television / The first few paragraphs of the Carnegie Commission's 12 recommendations (the key ones are noted in the adjacent text) and part of the resultant 1967 act's "Congressional Declaration of Policy" make clear a substantial new role for public television.

The Carnegie Conclusions . . . The Carnegie Commission on Educational Television has reached the conclusion that a well-financed and well-directed educational television system, substantially larger and far more pervasive and effective than that which now exists in the United States, must be brought into being if the full needs of the American public are to be served. This is the central conclusion of the Commission and all of its recommendations are designed accordingly.

———————————

The programs we conceive to be the essence of Public Television are in general not economic for commercial sponsorship, are not designed for the classroom, and are directed at audiences ranging from the tens of thousands to the occasional tens of millions. No such system now exists to serve us as model, and hence we have been obliged to develop a suitable new arrangement to bring this kind of television to the country. The Commission's proposal deals primarily with that new arrangement.

Although it provides for immediate assistance to existing stations, this is a proposal not for small adjustments or patchwork changes, but for a comprehensive system that will ultimately bring Public Television to all the people of the United States: a system that in its totality will become a new and fundamental institution in American culture.

This institution is different from any now in existence. It is not the educational television that we now know; it is not patterned after the commercial system or the British system or the Japanese system. In the course of our study, we examined all those and others: members of the staff visited

Canada, England, Italy, Germany, and Sweden, and papers were commissioned on the Japanese and Russian systems. We found in many countries serious and skillful attempts to provide superior television programming, and in some countries highly successful attempts. But when such a system was successful it met the special needs of society in terms of that society's culture and tradition, and there was little or nothing we could expect to import. We propose an indigenous American system arising out of our own traditions and responsive to our own needs.

The 1967 Act . . . Sec. 396. (a) The Congress hereby finds and declares—(1) that it is in the public interest to encourage the growth and development of noncommercial educational radio and television broadcasting, including the use of such media for instructional purposes; (2) the expansion and development of noncommercial educational radio and television broadcasting and of diversity of its programming depend on freedom, imagination, and initiative on both the local and national levels . . . (5) that it is necessary and appropriate for the Federal Government to complement, assist, and support a national policy that will most effectively make noncommercial educational radio and television service available to all the citizens of the United States; (6) that a private corporation should be created to facilitate the development of [such] broadcasting and to afford maximum protection to such broadcasting from extraneous interference and control.

Source: Carnegie Commission on Educational Television, *Public Television: A Program for Action* (New York: Harper & Row, 1967), pages 3–4 and 47 U.S.C. 396(a).

local stations with an immediate disbursement of $10,000 to all stations and the understanding that future grants would apply to individual needs and plans; interconnection of public television stations; underwriting national programs; and national publicity and research for public television.

A key problem present from the beginning was to plague public broadcasting well into the 1970s. Upon approving CPB, Congress had appropriated a few million dollars in seed money, much of it for facilities rather than for programs, without providing for long-term financing. The Carnegie report had made clear that isolation from the political process was crucial, and President Johnson had promised to furnish a long-range funding plan, which would permit CPB to plan ahead. He left office before this was done, and the Nixon administration, with its growing dislike for nationally oriented public television and unhappiness with what many Republicans perceived as excessive liberalism and independence in news and public affairs programming, dispensed annually a fraction of the recommended funds. This prevented long-range planning and hamstrung national development of public television. The problem was exacerbated as the Nixon Administration proposed funding directly to local stations instead of the centralized programming agencies. The local stations were eager to augment their woefully inadequate funds and pick and choose among the national programs. Many local stations reflected their conservative populations and the business community, which provided most local voluntary financial support; and giving them the power to determine what programs they would "buy" from program suppliers would encourage programming that was politically safe.

Early in 1969, PBS (Public Broad-casting Service) was added to the alphabet soup, to oversee the interconnection process, then mainly funded by the Ford Foundation, and other kinds of program distribution. It was not a program producer itself. It soon was controlled, however, by the station managers of public television stations, many of whom had long resented the national program monopoly of NET and were just as unhappy over the centralized funding power of CPB, which now supported them to a large extent. From its start, PBS got into a wrangle over the control of funds for producing programs, which soon enveloped CPB, the stations, other program producers and supporters, and the Ford Foundation, until the OTP made it clear that federal funding under the Nixon administration would depend upon the system staying decentralized. Politically motivated bills appeared in Congress to ban programs on public affairs and news events on public television, using the reasoning that federal funds should not be used to support a governmental propaganda organ. Many congressmen objected to the high salaries of several on-air news people. Congress was nibbling around the edge, holding off funding until CPB would come around to the stations' and the administration's point of view. President Nixon vetoed a two-year funding bill, but a series of one-year authorizations for CPB passed. Congress was beginning to take an interest in public television (PTV), because substantial segments of the public had begun to watch.

PTV's adult audience increased to the point where some programs showed up in commercial rating service reports. Julia Child's *The French Chef*, produced by WGBH, Boston—one of the most prolific of the production centers for PTV, like KCET, Los Angeles; WNET, New York; and WTTW, Chicago—achieved great popularity. Perhaps most prominent were several British television programs, whose production and storytelling qualities far surpassed the run-of-the-mill commercial American situation comedies and adventure shows. The first of these was *The Forsyte Saga*, based on the Victorian-Edwardian novels of John Galsworthy. The 26 BBC-produced segments held audiences enthralled and increased listener donations. This was followed by *Masterpiece Theatre*, an all-inclusive title for other British series and miniseries produced by the BBC or the commercial IBA's program contractors, and hosted by English-American commentator and columnist Alistair Cooke. Some of these series dealt with historical subjects—*Elizabeth R* and *The Six Wives of Henry VIII*—but others dealt with less impressive subjects. *Upstairs, Downstairs*, to some extent a weekly soap opera but also social history, depicted life in a London town house in the early 1900s as seen by the family and its servants. This series won several American Emmy awards. Public stations also made heavy use of classic and foreign films. NET public affairs programs such as William F. Buckley's *Firing Line*, the debate program *The Advocates*, *Black Journal*, *The Banks and the Poor*, and *The Great American Dream Machine* brought audience attention and more controversy, including the displeasure of the Nixon administration and other conservatives. Essentially, public television was casting off its staid image and collecting larger and more varied audiences. Major companies frequently supplied funding for PTV series in exchange for a one-line credit: *"Masterpiece Theatre* is brought to you by a grant from Mobil Oil Corporation." These companies also often paid for newspaper advertising, which attracted larger audiences. Neither action was greeted with enthusiasm by commercial broadcasters.

In fall 1969, PTV took a giant step forward in children's programming with the first airing of *Sesame Street*. Planned since the formation of the Children's Television Workshop (CTW) early in 1968, with Ford and Carnegie foundation and U.S. Office of Education funding, *Sesame Street* was quite different from such traditional PTV children's programs as *The Friendly Giant* or *Mister Rogers' Neighborhood* and commercial television's Saturday morning cartoons and adventure shows. It used modern commercial television techniques for education, having programs "sponsored" by different letters of the alphabet or numbers each day, having the show set on a city street, relying on very short animated cartoons with live and puppet segments, and breaking the show into many rapidly moving parts to keep the interest of preschool children. The show was an instant outstanding success, to the chagrin of the commercial networks that had turned down the idea before it had been offered to public television. *Sesame Street* was supported by a continuing research program, and changes were made in the format from time to time reflecting the results of that research. The CTW soon supplemented the preschool *Sesame Street* with *The Electric Company*, a half-hour program for older children that concentrated on words, spelling, and other concepts. CTW attempted an adult medical program using entertainment elements in 1974, but it was soon withdrawn for major changes and, even after drastic surgery, ran only briefly.

By late 1976, concern over the future of public broadcasting centered on two important sets of questions: how the expanding system was to be adequately financed, and how the increased interorganizational squabbles (especially those between CPB and PBS) were to be resolved.

9•5 Advertising Clutter and Consumerism

Perhaps more than in any other period of broadcasting's development, advertising itself was controversial. Advertiser demand for air time continued to increase, while costs and public concern about advertising effects also rose.

9•51 Trends: Clutter

The major trend toward local radio advertising continued during these 15 years, with the proportion rising to 70 percent. Total radio revenues more than doubled, but inflation in the mid-1970s and the increased number of stations on the air hid the effects of that increase from the individual station. FM's advertising revenue position improved, but the industry remained in the red. While overall FM revenues rose from less than $10 million to more than $308.6 million between 1962 and 1975, many more stations reported losses than profits. FM's problems were the same as in previous decades: compared to AM, there were too little data, audience, station services. But with increased specialization and improved ratings for some FM stations, some of this old refrain wore down. Station owner Gordon McLendon, often an innovator, tried broadcasting nothing but classified ads on FM stations KADS in Los Angeles in 1966–1967—no programs, just ads. This experiment was not successful, and KADS reverted to a "normal" musical format.

In television, full sponsorship nearly disappeared as participating or shared advertising spread through both daytime and prime-time hours. This change came fairly quickly; from the 1964–1965 season when only 48 percent of network ads were participating to 95 percent four seasons later. The long-standard one-minute commercial gave way to the 30-second spot. About 40 percent of spots were "30s" in 1964–1965; more than 80 percent four years later. Network advertising was so expensive that few advertisers could afford the steady weekly costs of full sponsorship, or even many one-minute spots—and research showed that the 30-second spots sold goods and services almost as well at less—but not half—cost. Thus cost-spreading shorter ads became popular throughout prime-time and day time schedules. Unfortunately, their brevity resulted in a new pattern that audiences found irritating: the clustered or piggyback ad break. While the total time devoted to advertising did not increase, the number of commercial messages rose sharply as two 30s replaced one 60, or sometimes 20- and 10-second spots were strung together with 3-second quickies at station identification time. A prime-time viewer often would see four or five ads in a row in the middle of a program, and the (in)famous midnight break on the late night network shows was usually cluttered with three to five minutes of national and local ads, promos (promotional announcements), and station breaks in a row. A survey showed 30 different products presented in the typical daytime hour. The public was not the only complainer; advertisers, concerned that their 30-second message in the middle of such clutter would never stick in the viewer's mind, spent more effort and money on the design of commercials. By the late 1960s the most clever were getting "Clio" awards in annual industry self-recognition. Listeners also accused the stations or networks of playing the audio of commercials louder than the program—often a bum rap; really a case of *more* audio, electronically compressed, than *louder* sound. Devices, such as the "blab-off," that enabled viewers to cut audio had a brisk sale.

But clearly television was doing something right. In the 1961–1976 period, its share of all advertising rose from 14 percent to 20 percent and total revenues increased more than 300 percent. Local advertising started to grow in importance again, rising from 15 percent to 25 percent of all television advertising. Non-network affiliated stations grew from 24 in 1961 to 97 in 1976 (see Appendix C, table 3).

During the late 1960s the practice of advertising discounts became a concern within the industry. For a long time stations and networks had provided volume discounts for major advertisers to encourage large buys of time over long periods. The network discount practice came under investigation by the Federal Trade Commission, the courts, and Congress in the late 1960s, not so much for the discounts as for the allegedly unfair market advantage they gave major companies, creating difficulties for new products and smaller companies. In 1960, an FTC case taken to court prohibited Procter & Gamble from retaining the recently acquired Clorox company. The court had based its decision largely on Procter & Gamble's eligibility for massive discounts, due to the volume of its multiproduct advertising on the networks, and the unfair discrimination this position might exert on its competitors in the bleach field. This precedent made everyone more cautious and conglomerate mergers less attractive. The problem began to work itself out during the 1960s for several reasons. First, discounts for participating advertising were far smaller than for full sponsorship. Second, as television became a cause of antitrust actions against advertisers, discounts sometimes were eliminated. Finally, the increasing demand for television time did away with the net-

works' need to offer advertisers massive discounts.

All of the above, plus inflation, led to steadily rising prices for advertising time. The typical network prime-time minute went from $30,000 in the early 1960s to over $100,000 by 1976. Special events, like the annual Super Bowl football game, brought upwards of $225,000 for each minute, although network costs for rights to the game also were huge. Television was not a medium for advertising by most small businesses.

9•52   *A Question of Fairness*

For most of the 1960s, the most acute broadcast advertising question was whether cigarette advertising would be banned and, by extension, whether the government had the right to ban the advertising of any legal product. The issue opened with the 1964 report of the Surgeon General, which declared, on the basis of scientific and statistical research, that cigarette smoking might be dangerous to the health of the smoker. In mid-1965, the FTC demanded that all cigarette advertising include a warning notice, a move blocked in Congress by tobacco-growing-state congressmen. Many critics saw the matter as one of fairness: since smoking cigarettes entailed controversy and public health, opposing views to cigarette commercials should be aired.

The first effective attempt to use this approach came late in 1966 when New York lawyer John Banzhaf requested WCBS-TV to provide some time for anti-smoking spots. When the station refused, he appealed directly to the FCC. Most observers expected the complaint to disappear in the sea of bureaucracy, but they were surprised. On June 2, 1967, the FCC decided that the Fairness Doctrine (see

9.82) did apply in this case, and that the public should hear the antismoking point of view. Informally, FCC General Counsel Henry Geller said that one antismoking spot for every three smoking commercials would be a fair proportion. The Court of Appeals in Washington upheld the FCC decision. Various governmental and voluntary health organizations made extremely creative spots and provided them to stations. Although the commission declared that the Surgeon General's report made this foray into commercial fairness unique, and thus not precedent-setting, advertisers, consumer advocates and environmentalists, and some lawyers were not so sure.

The increasingly active FTC and FCC proposed an outright ban on cigarette advertising on radio and television—the FTC wanted to include all media—and congressional hearings began to explore that idea. Broadcasters, alarmed because cigarette advertising accounted for about 10 percent of network advertising billings, offered many alternative plans, such as limiting ads to late evening and eliminating appeals to youth. Finally, under heavy pressure, the cigarette industry and the broadcasters split: the broadcasters suggested a four-year phaseout of cigarette advertising, and the cigarette people, concerned that FTC action might restrict them from other media, favored a quick and voluntary break with broadcast advertising. Indeed, if *all* tobacco companies were to drop television advertising at the same time, they could save a lot of money and no company would hold an advantage. They suggested termination in fall 1970 if broadcasters would forgo contract provisions on canceled ads. The broadcasters—except for some who had voluntarily dropped tobacco advertising earlier—refused, and Congress then banned advertising by law.

After January 1, 1971—a date selected so that cigarettes could sponsor New Year's Day football bowl games one last time—no cigarette advertising would be allowed on radio or television. That last day was heavy with smoke, and during the late evening on January 1 tobacco company commercials filled the air as they used their expensive spots for the last time. From that date, $200 million in annual billings was lost to the broadcasters, who claimed the new law was unfair in that it did not affect the rival print media. They also pointed out that similar bans in other countries had done little to lower cigarette smoking. They apparently were right, but that made little difference. In fall 1973, Congress closed a loophole in the law by outlawing ads for "little cigars," which had been heavily advertised on the air during the previous year.

The cigarette matter was only the beginning of new FTC activity. Six months later, the FTC proposed an advertising claim substantiation program, whereby product makers would have to be able to support any and all claims made in print or broadcast advertisements. In broadcasting, this meant that erring sponsors would have to make "corrective" ads and telecast them for a specified time to counteract misleading ad claims. The heavy use of broadcasting by large multiproduct advertisers, even with diminished discounts, led to antitrust actions. Early in 1972, the FTC proposed that the four major cereal makers be broken up because of their market control, achieved chiefly through television ads concentrated in children's week-end programming.

This activity came to a head in February 1972 when the FTC proposed to the FCC that broadcasters should provide air time for *counteradvertising* to balance the views of commercial sponsors. The FTC felt that, if necessary, free time should be offered. The FCC demurred. A few test spots were produced, using the donated talents of Burt Lancaster to speak against Bayer's claims for aspirin superiority and to remind drivers of a massive recall of recent model Chevrolets, but very few stations used them. Proponents of counteradvertising said that it would enhance freedom of speech and that commercial advertisers, often notorious for false claims, should not have a monopoly on the publicly owned airwaves. Broadcasters and advertisers united against this idea, as might be expected, because counteradvertising would (and here comes a familiar claim!) "ruin the industry." They believed that advertisers faced with counterads on the air would leave broadcasting and go to print media, where no such threat waited. Proponents of counteradvertising noted that the antismoking spots of the late 1960s had not driven cigarette firms from the air; no one firm could afford to leave the field to others, and joint action would have violated antitrust laws. Broadcasters further claimed that arguments would fill the air and that free time was unfair to broadcasting since it was not required from other media. By 1976 it appeared unlikely that the counteradvertising concept would attain the force of law, although some stations accepted such advertising and law suits were started demanding such a right. The issue became one aspect of the battle for public access under the Fairness Doctrine (see 9.82), which included court suits against "misleading" ads.

9•6   Program Specialization and Cycles

Programming in both radio and television after 1960 was a matter of slow evolution of types, with program cycles of invention-imitation-decline being more important than any revolutionary change. A common phenomenon in broadcasting was rapid copying of any program approach that showed it could gain an audience.

9•61   Radio Specialization

Until the late 1960s, the trend in AM radio was toward increased specialization of formats. A new all-news format spread to a few of the largest markets in the late 1960s. Their manpower requirements made all-news stations expensive, but they did very well in the ratings. Many more stations adopted all-talk formats that included, but did not depend on, news. Telephone call-in programs, discussions, interviews, news, and public affairs were the hallmarks of radio without music.

Stations continued to specialize in music, although the Top-40 station, together with what had been rock music, slowly changed its sound. It is difficult to summarize briefly the changes in music over 15 years, although these changes were directly reflected in radio. Music prior to 1964 changed little from that of the late 1950s; Top-40 formula radio persisted. But the music of the Beatles drastically changed the sound of popular music after 1964; and after the Vietnam War became an issue in 1965–1966, college students' folk music turned into songs of protest. Singers were identified as much with their cause as with their music, and emphasis shifted from "sound," music and beat, to an appreciation of lyrics. Judy Collins and others made great music—sometimes with serious messages. Because certain lyrics seemed to glorify drug usage, the FCC warned management that it should clearly understand lyrics before airing a number; licensees would be held responsible for glorification of illegal actions. Another change of the mid-1960s was the increasing presence of black popular music artists on the air. Where in the 1950s, whites had performed rhythm and blues, which had originated as black music, new black soloists and groups turned their rhythm and blues into *soul music*. The center of this activity was Motown ("Motor town" = Detroit) Record Co., controlled by blacks, and having under contract a number of groups popular with both blacks and whites—notably Diana Ross and the Supremes. What became known as the *Detroit sound* of strong instrumental background to rhythmic music was reminiscent of the music of the 1950s.

Stations in the 1960s increasingly specialized in particular kinds of music. Some stations concentrated on programming music and other content by and for blacks, especially in the larger markets with sizable black populations, even though almost all licensees were white. Country and Western music spread from its southern home to the rest of the country, including the supposedly sophisticated Northeast. By the 1970s, every major market had at least one C & W operation. Other stations specialized in rock, the most popular; "middle-of-the-road" music; or "golden oldies."

Some stations appealed to even smaller specialized audiences—religious or ethnic groups, classical music fans, and listeners to a handful of listener-supported "underground" stations, such as those of the Pacifica Foundation, whose programming is too eclectic to categorize. As the fragmentation of audiences produced a fragmentation of advertising revenues, inexpensive and often automated formats became very desirable.

In May 1963 the FCC proposed that AM-FM operations in the same market and under the same ownership be required to program separately some of the time. This would reduce duplicated programming, which had characterized most FM stations since the late 1940s. The industry predictably claimed that any such action would harm FM by taking away popular programs. But the FCC was insistent and issued a rule in July 1964 specifying that, in markets of 100,000 or more, such stations must offer separate programming at least half the time. There was considerable legal wrangling, and whole classes of stations were given delays of execution, but by 1967 most FM stations had come under the ruling. The rule was expanded to include smaller markets in the 1970s. The result was predictable: FM began to specialize as much as AM, and soon the air was filled with FM rock stations, FM Country and Western stations, as well as "progressive jazz" and the more traditional FM "beautiful music" and classical music stations. By the late 1960s the specialization had changed the decades-old idea that "FM is special," to the view that "FM is radio." An increasing number of receivers capable of receiving FM testified to the resulting audience appeal.

Nonmusical entertainment programming did not disappear. Catering to nostalgia buffs, returns of old radio drama and comedy programs appeared, first on stations appealing to college students in evening hours and then spreading to other stations for an hour or so a week at different hours of the day. In 1973, NBC began to broadcast repeats of *X-Minus-One*, a series of science fiction dramas from the early 1950s. Mutual offered several old shows, and a few specialty companies bought up broadcast rights to old series— *The Lone Ranger, The Shadow,* and some comedies—to syndicate them on tape to local stations. National Public Radio, the radio arm of CPB, funded several radio drama workshops, including one specializing in the use of stereo in radio drama.

Beginning in 1974, CBS broadcast *Mystery Theater,* an hour-long original drama each night. Hosted by noted actor E. G. Marshall, the series provided the first network outlet for writing and acting talent in radio in more than two decades and was a success with listeners and advertisers alike. A child-oriented *Adventure Theater* followed two years later.

"Old radio" sound of another sort was the fare of the "golden oldie" stations of the 1970s, which based their appeal on the replaying of hit music from the past—six months to a decade or two. These stations generally aimed at adults in the advertiser-desired ages between eighteen and thirty-five who had listened to this music on radio as teenagers.

9•62   *Economics of Television Programming*

The most obvious differences between television programs of 1961 and the 1970s were the addition of color and the virtual elimination of live programming, although tape—using live television studio techniques—largely supplanted film. Color had languished after its 1954 introduction by RCA because of receiver and studio cost and lack of support from the rest of the industry with investments in monochrome. Only RCA's subsidiary NBC had programmed much color, while CBS had only occasional color shows and ABC had none.

By fall 1965 all three networks had adopted color; NBC announced that its prime-time schedule would be about 95 percent in color, CBS would produce half its programs in color, and ABC hoped to achieve 40 percent. Black-and-white television had reached nearly every home, and many sets purchased during the boom years were due for replacement. Color set

quality had improved and prices had dropped. Advertisers and some far-seeing program packagers had been preparing commercials and programs in color for some time.

Surveys had shown that color caused increased viewing and more attention to commercials, and for a time stations broadcasting more color had a ratings edge. But the cost of that edge was heavy. It was estimated that the networks spent $30 million to $40 million to purchase color equipment and add the required graphics, costumes, sets, and so on. Station costs also were high, since color cameras cost three times as much as monochrome cameras. To go "full color" was prohibitively expensive for most stations, but it cost them little to carry network programs and not too many thousands of dollars more to show color film. Hence, during that first color season, 97 percent of the stations could carry network shows in color, 60 percent had color film and slide capacity, while only 15 percent could originate programs in color. The 1965–1967 period saw stations scrambling for color equipment—and for the money to pay for it. By January 1966, 70 percent of commercials were shot in color, and a year or so later monochrome commercial spots were rare, at least on a network. By December 1966, more color than black-and-white sets were being sold for the first time. Lower receiver prices led to more set production and importation and still lower prices. It was estimated that one-sixth of the nation's homes had color by 1967, and three-quarters by 1976 (see Appendix C, table 9).

A major change in television programming's source also was apparent. Prior to the quiz show scandals (see 8.63), advertisers and their agencies produced about one-third to one-quarter of network programming, package agencies or companies produced about 45 percent, and the networks themselves made up the difference—around 20 percent in typical years, much of it news. By the late 1960s and early 1970s, advertisers had almost disappeared as program producers, providing less than 3 percent of network shows, mostly daytime. Packagers now produced 80 percent of network programming and nearly all of prime time, although the networks often had a financial stake in the product. Programs produced by the networks themselves accounted for only 8 percent of a typical season's programming. This change was due only partly to the outcry for tighter network control and responsibility after the quiz show scandals. The most important factor was cost: up to a million dollars for a one-hour pilot and perhaps two-thirds that sum for a half-hour program pilot by 1976. Regular program costs were up as well, from $100,000 per hour in the early 1960s to about $300,000 for the same kind of show by late 1976. With packaging, networks could control their daily programming patterns better than when advertising agencies controlled many productions. Advertisers were naturally more concerned with a single program than with an overall pattern, but the package agencies had to cater to network needs and demands.

In the 1950s, most programs had been live or on film. But by the mid- to late-1960s the development of videotape recordings (see 8.12) did away with most live programs except news on the three networks and many local stations. Comedy and drama programs usually were shot on film so that syndication to smaller stations or overseas, which used different VTR standards, could help recoup costs. Tape often was used for music and variety programs, because its slightly sharper image and the pace permitted by "live" multicamera television practice gave it a more immediate look, and for talk pro-

grams and daytime serials, whose lower cost usually could be recouped in a single showing. In addition, of course, tape made use of existing, expensive television production facilities and could be shown without a delay for film processing.

Programs were running longer. The 15-minute format disappeared, the 30-minute format remained for situation comedies, while 60-, 90-, and even 120-minute dramatic or special programs became fairly common. Once in a while, a network would present a special program lasting the entire evening. There were more and more news and entertainment special programs and feature movies on network television (see 9.63) that ran an hour or two—or longer. In order to hold viewers over normal program switching periods, a few of these longer programs avoided ending an act or segment on the half-hour.

Then there was the problem of reruns. In the days of live shows, there had been few program repeats, as shows either were produced year-round or had summer replacements. Beginning in the 1960s, filmed and taped programs began to offer progressively fewer original episodes and more reruns each year, until, by the mid-1970s, some series had reruns for more than half the year. Unemployment in talent and craft unions in Hollywood spearheaded pressure to change this situation. By 1972 the problem had attracted White House activity, since President Nixon not only had no love for the networks but had promised economic aid for the film workers in his home state of California. The Office of Telecommunications Policy, a White House agency, suggested that reruns cheated viewers and created much of the unemployment afflicting the movie industry. The networks replied that to reduce or eliminate reruns would cost so much that (1) they would have to program a heavier dose of inexpensive game and variety shows, (2) much program production would be forced out of the country to places with cheaper labor, and (3) reduced network profit ratios would mean fewer network news and public affairs programs, traditionally paid for by entertainment show profits. All of these would further reduce employment in the program production studios. The issue died with tacit recognition that reruns probably would stay. Since audience research showed that the audience for a rerun often was almost as large as for the original showing, it was said that they did serve the public interest.

As the number of new programs in a given series in a year shrank from 39 to 26 or less, the use of *miniseries* with four to ten program episodes became attractive as *fill-ins* for canceled programs or as specials. This followed the British practice of making no more programs than could be made well, considering the long lead time for scripts and the fatiguing effect of a long-running series on performers and crew. The success of British miniseries on PBS (see 9.4) paved the way for their use on commercial television, as did the rapidity with which networks would "kill" a series that did not initially do well in the ratings. A number of novels were serialized in this way starting in 1976, including Alex Haley's *Roots,* which achieved record ratings—as many as 80 million viewers—when it was aired for 12 hours over eight nights on ABC in January 1977.

Programming cycles became common by the early 1960s. Program types were invented, were imitated, and then declined. Some observers have suggested that after the early 1950s no new program types appeared—only adaptations of format, stars, and producers. New ideas were quickly exploited and imitated; a new show was built on a minor character in an earlier show, or merely followed a similar

line. A prime reason for these *spin-offs* was cost. As a popular program lasted through several seasons, its creative or *above-the-line* costs, covering talent, direction, script, and music, increased far faster than the technical or *below-the-line* costs, partly because stars demanded a larger piece of a successful show. When the network could no longer make a profit on the cost per episode—although foreign sales and other factors had to be considered—it would cancel the show for a less expensive replacement as soon as ratings began to dip. Imitations of successful program types came in roughly three-year cycles, which helped this process along: there were periods for westerns, situation comedies, crime and detective, and action-adventure shows.

9•63   Television Entertainment Formats

The number of variety programs doubled after 1961 but then declined rapidly in the 1970s. Ed Sullivan finally left the CBS lineup in 1972, due to declining ratings and an aging audience, after a record run in his Sunday evening prime-time slot. Other shows, built around singers—Dean Martin, Andy Williams—or comedians—Carol Burnett, Flip Wilson—came on, but had nearly disappeared by 1976. Quiz and audience participation programs also nearly disappeared in the network evening hours, although they remained popular during the daytime and on local stations.

In 1961 NBC started a trend with *Saturday Night at the Movies,* playing fairly recent theatrical films in prime time. The ratings were so high that the other networks joined in. In 1967 prime-time movies played 12 hours a week on the networks and soon at least one network had one every night of the week. Films of all sorts—comedy, drama, musicals—were used; in the long run they were less expensive, better produced, and earned higher ratings than most comparable network series programs. Their popularity kept up until the the 1975–1976 season.

For prime-time showing, the networks needed more films appropriate for television than Hollywood could provide. They had exhausted recent feature films—production was drastically less than pre-1948 output—and most older films were too overshown or too unimportant for further syndication. Again, NBC led the way to a solution with *World Premiere* in 1966, presenting "made for television" movies—90- or 120-minute films shot on a television schedule of days rather than months. The speeded-up shooting schedule kept costs down, still put more entertainment values into a program than most series offered, and often led to better ratings than regular series. Once again, the other networks followed suit; in the 1971–1972 seasons, 100 such films were shown on all three networks. They were not cheap—about $400,000 for a 90-minute film in 1974—but when played twice, once as a rerun, they could recoup costs with good ratings and advertiser response. By the early 1970s, television films were doubling as series pilots or even as feature movies abroad. Earlier, when a pilot did not sell as a series, the half-hour or hour film had little sales appeal. But expanded to 90 or 120 minutes, such a pilot could be shown as a film, without a series sale, and its track record would contribute tremendously to its salability as a series.

Television comedy was consistently strong in prime-time network programming. Situation comedies were particularly prone to the cyclical spin-off process. The long-running *Andy Griffith Show*—a comedy about a rustic sheriff—began in the 1961–1962 season and ran on network and in reruns through the decade, eventually spinning off *Gomer Pyle* (about a naive Marine Corps recruit from Andy's hometown), which in turn spun off *Mayberry R.F.D.* before CBS dropped rural programs in the early 1970s because they appealed to too old an audience to attract advertisers. In the same category was the immensely popular *Beverly Hillbillies* (about a hillbilly family, suddenly oil-rich, moving to Beverly Hills but keeping their country ways and clothes). This 1962 program spun off *Petticoat Junction* and Eva Gabor, Eddie Albert, and Arnold the pig in *Green Acres* (about rich city folks trying to make good in the country). Comedies of the mid-1960s featuring a monster, witch, or genie, included the long-running *Bewitched* (about a wife and her mother who were goodhearted witches), possibly the best of this lot; shows with talking cars or horses, and a program based on the weird cartoon characters of Charles Addams.

Some comedy shows stressed gimmick, some stressed plot, and many of the longest lasting featured a personality: Lucille Ball, Dick Van Dyke, and others. Van Dyke did not repeat the popular success of the award-winning *Dick Van Dyke Show* of the mid-1960s, but his co-star, Mary Tyler Moore, did. Her subsequent show—one of several successes packaged by her MTM Productions, under the leadership of her then-husband, Grant Tinker—was one of the few with a broadcasting milieu—a local television station's news department, *not* in Hollywood or New York.

The most important comedy program factory of the 1970s was Norman Lear and Bud Yorkin's Tandem Productions. They broke many barriers by adapting two successful British television program ideas, which became *All in the Family* (about "lovable bigot Archie Bunker" and family) and *Sanford and Son* (about a black junk dealer). *Family* spun off *Maude* (about a middle-aged liberated woman), *The Jeffersons* (about Archie Bunker's black neighbors who move to a new, mainly white neighborhood), and others. Their short run in 1975 of *Hot l Baltimore* (from the play about a sleazy hotel with a letter missing from its sign), which depicted two homosexuals, several prostitutes, and numerous older people in a comic light, and their syndicated *Mary Hartman, Mary Hartman* (an adult soap opera spoof that the networks would not touch, although many local stations snapped it up, opening a new market for packagers and doing very well when scheduled against the late night news on other stations) showed that the barriers on subject matter were coming down. The change had been swift. As late as 1967, some socially and politically oriented skits in the Smothers Brothers' comedy-variety show contained language and topics that bothered the CBS continuity acceptance staff. Rising costs, slipped ratings, and alleged contract problems gave CBS the excuse to drop the program. The brothers sued CBS successfully but were not able to revive their show on a regular schedule until 1975 (on ABC). It was a dismal failure; their humor had been passed by as television and public taste changed.

A comedy program departing from the usual situation formula was *Rowan and Martin's Laugh-In*. Starting in January 1968 after some tryouts, it offered extremely rapid pacing, blackout comedy lines, a zany and inventive acting troupe of relative unknowns, and topical humor held together by comedians Dan Rowan and Dick Martin. It was reminiscent of the innovative Ernie Kovacs show of 1955–1956 and subsequent specials before Kovacs's death in a 1962 auto crash. Several programs tried unsuccessfully to imitate *Laugh-In's* format, including one that

succumbed after a single showing to affiliates' complaints about its bad taste. *Laugh-In* itself folded in mid-1973.

The hours devoted to western action-adventure programs diminished after 1961, with none scheduled for the 1976–1977 season. Only two had very long and successful lives: *Bonanza*, which lasted 14 seasons, and *Gunsmoke*, which lasted for 20. A flurry of war programs marked the early 1960s, nearly all of which replayed World War II. Some played it straight, like *Combat* or *12 o'Clock High*, and some tried an odd comedy form like *Hogan's Heroes*, which took place in a German prison camp; but most disappeared with the heating up of the real Vietnam War.

The fantastic and tongue-in-cheek approach to action-adventure was best epitomized by *The Man from U.N.C.L.E.*, started in 1964, which showed intrepid agents of a mythical anticrime organization trying to outsmart a global underworld organization. It was a spoof on the popular "James Bond" spy films, and after a season or two it became more obviously comic. The bumbling spy reached new heights in the long-running *Get Smart* half-hour comedy, which first aired in 1965. Straight-faced television parodies of comic-strip character *Batman* and old radio character *The Green Hornet* on ABC created a short-lived student cult in 1966–1967. Fantastic but deadly serious was *Mission Impossible*, beginning in 1966 and going into syndication after 1972. It had a stock opening scene of the lead character retrieving from some out of the way place a cheap tape recorder which would "self-destruct in five seconds" after giving him instructions. Complicated mechanical and electronic gimmicks and plots were typical of this series, which ran for many years on the network and had healthy reruns and syndication with a 1988 sequel.

A limited science fiction movement peaked after 1966 with *Star Trek,* which depicted the "five-year voyage of the Starship *Enterprise*" and her diverse and stereotyped crew, including a pointed-eared alien executive officer. The voyage lasted only three years on network television, but the program plays in seemingly endless reruns. Its fans, known as "Trekkies," have created a cult, complete with annual conventions and the lobbying ability to force NASA to change the name of the first U.S. space shuttle to *Enterprise.* None of the other science fiction shows— the childish *Lost in Space* or *The Invaders* or the British syndicated *Space: 1999* had the attraction or lasting power of *Star Trek,* which later spawned feature films, a cartoon series, and, in 1987, a sequel featuring a new generation of actors.

Crime and detective programs were prevalent in the early 1960s and the mid-1970s. General formats of these two periods were frequently similar. *The Lineup,* a late 1950s show about veteran San Francisco police officers, was followed in the 1970s by *Streets of San Francisco;* the successful New York–based police detective *Kojak* of the 1970s reminded many of the superbly done *Naked City* of 1959–1963. Not all crime detective shows could be repeated, however. After nearly a decade, *Perry Mason* left the network lineup in 1966; although it had highly profitable reruns and star Raymond Burr's *Ironside,* about a wheelchair-bound police chief, was another long-term success—a revival of *Perry Mason* in 1973 was unsuccessful. However, until the 1970s television seemed unable to handle the uncompromisingly realistic look at police work of former Los Angeles Police Sergeant Joseph Wambaugh's *Police Story.* Most crime and detective programs continued their pot-boiling emphasis on action rather than on character and depth. For obvious production and audience distribution reasons, most shows of the genre took place supposedly in New York City or California. Recently, the "good guys" were seen to lose occasionally, but familiar plot lines, themes, and characters remained, more so in the police and private detective programs than in lawyer-centered programs such as *The Defenders* (a 1960s program about a father-son team defending unpopular causes) and a mid-1970s special and miniseries, *The Law.*

Between *Ben Casey* and *Dr. Kildare,* which started in 1961, and *Medical Center* and *Marcus Welby, M.D.* in the early 1970s, few medical programs had prime-time popularity, but hospitals, doctors, and their adventures and love lives never left the networks, particularly the daytime soap operas, which often drew on medical locales or themes. By the early 1970s, medical dramatic programming was dealing more and more with controversial themes—abortion, euthanasia, costs of medical service, malpractice—in starker portrayals of hospital personnel, medical problems, and human character.

Regularly scheduled dramatic programs with little action but deep thinking did not last. George C. Scott as a concerned social worker in *East Side, West Side* was well reviewed by critics but insufficiently watched by the public, which wanted entertainment rather than conscience. Later shows about state legislators, *Slattery's People,* and even a U.S. senator, *The Senator,* met the same fate. Serious drama was limited in the late 1960s to the occasional special. The only regular anthology dramas of this period were on public television, and most were British imports.

The rise in public consciousness of racial and ethnic minorities in society was making television programming more complicated. Falling ratings and complaints from Italian-American groups about the preponderance of villains with Italian names forced the popular *Untouchables* off the network. Even though names were carefully changed during the last year of the show, the protest had achieved a life of its own. Mexican-Americans had the same effect on the "Frito Bandito" commercial cartoon character and, by the early 1960s, black concern about the lily-whiteness of television shows and commercials was bearing fruit. Though some network shows had starred blacks in the 1950s and 1960s, none lasted until *I Spy* in 1965 combined white Robert Culp and black Bill Cosby (then little known) as U.S. undercover agents. Their warm relationship and

repartee as equals together with an awakening racial consciousness helped bring on more programs with black stars. The first series of the 1960s with one black star was *Julia*, a comedy about a divorced black nurse. Although a breakthrough, it received criticism for being too middle-class. By the early 1970s, blacks were present in about one-third of all commercials and in many television shows. For a time, Flip Wilson's variety show won top ranking in the ratings. The color bar seemed broken.

In daytime hours, television drama consisted of reruns of situation comedies, soap operas, or quiz and other human-interest programs. All of these had low budgets and high profits, which often

Talk, Talk, Talk . . . Morning and Night / Both *Today* and *Tonight* began in the 1950s, the brainstorms of then NBC president Pat Weaver. The *Today* show combined news and features for its early morning listeners—and in early programs the camera panned outside of the ground floor studio to show watching New Yorkers. The *Tonight* show has been hosted since 1962 by Johnny Carson, shown here with his announcer-foil Ed McMahon. Earlier hosts included Steve Allen (1952–1957) and the mercurial Jack Paar (1957–1962). Photos courtesy of National Broadcasting Company, Inc.

helped offset network losses from expensive, prime-time television programs. Soap operas were thriving and expanding, with several becoming hour-long programs by 1976. Plot development remained lethargic, and differences between shows seemed slight except for *Dark Shadows*, telecast live with heavy gothic overtones, including a vampire. ABC briefly telecast *Peyton Place*, based on the best-selling novel, twice a week in prime time, but serials did not do well in the evening. In the early 1970s, although the serials maintained a certain decorum—no swearing, for example—they dealt increasingly directly with adultery, drugs, and other current controversies.

The game shows became a daytime staple, and for a time in the late 1960s they outrated the serials. Game programs had three basic formats: audience participation, panels—*Hollywood Squares*, for example, used entertainers or other "professionals" to participate in a quiz, often with scripted repartee—and human interest—or perhaps greed, as with *Let's Make a Deal*, in which studio audience members tried to get as much money or goods as possible. Local television stations adapted many of these and also used short features like *Dialing for Dollars* as audience-building and advertising vehicles.

Talk programs now ran through the day on both network and local television. The magazine format of NBC's morning *Today* program (see 7.63), built around news and features, had many local station midday imitations aimed mainly at housewives. NBC was unsuccessful with another daytime talk program, the lavish *Home* of the early 1950s. Many men and women stars hosted talk or variety hours. Among the few who made national reputations were Dinah Shore and Mike Douglas. He began a low-key talk and variety program for Westinghouse's KYW, Philadelphia, in 1965 and had a syndicated solid hold on large daytime audiences a decade later. Merv Griffin had a similar show—in content and in ratings—in some markets.

The late evening hours became the domain of Johnny Carson after the former daytime quiz show MC took over Jack Paar's host job on the *Tonight* show in 1962. With band leader Skitch Henderson (and later "Doc" Severinsen), many guests, and announcer Ed McMahon, Carson expanded a late night, highly profitable institution on NBC that successfully and almost effortlessly fought off competing network programs with talk hosts such as Joey Bishop or Dick Cavett (ABC), or movies (ABC and CBS).

Sports programming was a staple of weekend and some other daytime hours. The last of the pre-scripted television wrestling programs left major stations early in 1964. By then television had revitalized professional football as the development of videotape and videodisc "instant replay," starting in 1963, greatly added to audience interest. New Year's Day now belonged to football, much as Guy Lombardo and his orchestra was the expected harbinger of midnight on New Year's Eve. After 1967 the annual January Super Bowl earned enormous ratings and advertiser per-minute charges. The popularity and pitfalls of sports programs were illustrated in 1969 when NBC cut the last few seconds of a game to start a special children's program (*Heidi*) on time. In an unbelievable nine seconds, one team scored two touchdowns and won the game—but the enraged and frustrated television football fans saw none of it. The networks learned their lesson: stay with the sports coverage no matter how long the game might go. In 1975, as a result, a network stayed with a major game for 45 minutes into another children's special— and was roasted by enraged and frustrated parents.

ABC was more innovative in sports than the other networks. Its *Monday Night Football*, beginning in 1970, brought in audiences not reached by normal entertainment programming on the other networks. Its *Wide World of Sports*, on the other hand, attracted many viewers not normally interested in sports. Coverage of the 1964, 1968, 1972, and 1976 Olympics showed television technical ingenuity at its best, as ABC provided detailed and well-narrated coverage, usually by ex-athletes. The 1972 event in Munich became a tragedy, with terrorist murder of Israeli athletes, and the sports-suddenly-turned-news team reported the story well. ABC's sports chief, Roone Arledge, was promoted to head of ABC News in 1977.

As the popularity of sports programs became evident and all three commercial networks bid for the rights to sporting events, television revenues became as important as gate or box office receipts to the various clubs and leagues. Sports fans had long objected to club contracts that required television blackouts for the area in which a contest was being played, even when the seating was sold out. This practice was stopped in 1973 when federal legislation banned such blackouts for football games sold out three days in advance.

9•64   *Growing Independence of
          Television News*

For most of the 1960s, before and after evening network newscasts were lengthened from 15 minutes to a half-hour in September 1963, CBS's Walter Cronkite competed with the NBC team of Chet Huntley and David Brinkley for audience, while ABC ran a series of newsmen through its anchorman slot. It found long-term success in 1970 when Harry Reasoner left CBS and joined Howard K. Smith, another ex-CBS correspondent, to create a team. However, the Smith-Reasoner team broke up in 1975, with Smith becoming a commentator, such as Eric Sevareid was at CBS until his 1977 retirement and Brinkley was at NBC, and Reasoner becoming sole anchorman. In 1976 ABC hired Barbara Walters from the NBC *Today* show to be co-anchor in a million-dollar deal. At NBC, with Huntley's retirement in 1971, the anchor position reverted to John Chancellor, a veteran NBC news correspondent and the head of the Voice of America from 1965 to 1967. During and after the 1976 political campaigns, NBC teamed Chancellor with Brinkley.

Daytime network newscasts also increased greatly during the late 1960s, partly under the pressure of news from Southeast Asia. Local stations frequently programmed more news than the networks, with short noontime programs, half-hour late evening shows, and up to an hour and a half adjoining the network news at the dinner hour. By 1976, the networks were running up trial balloons for increasing their evening newscasts to 45 or 60 minutes, against the strong opposition of their affiliates, who would lose revenue as a result.

Spurred by the need to cover events in other continents—the Vietnam War, the Olympics—broadcasting networks turned to space communication satellites. Although each satellite use cost several thousand dollars, it permitted live coverage of some events and eliminated the complexities and red tape of air transport of film from overseas. Broadcast journalists also had, by the mid-1970s, a wide range of such electronic news-gathering (ENG) equipment as portable color cameras and videotape recorders, whose flexibility and ability to deliver live pictures led many television stations to replace their newsfilm equipment with a true television system.

A watershed of American history and of broadcast journalism occurred a few months after the networks lengthened their evening newscasts to a half-hour. Almost everyone old enough to remember can tell you exactly where he or she was on November 22, 1963, when the news came of President Kennedy's assassination in Dallas. The authors of this book both happened to be standing by UPI teletype machines, one in Madison, Wisconsin, and the other in Los Angeles. Although radio could respond immediately, the television networks had to take a few minutes to warm up cameras, insert a few hasty words into the normal programming, and switch over to four extraordinary days of news, commentary, and tribute. Although broadcasters, like the rest of the nation, were in shock, they somehow solved the logistic problems and produced the necessary pictures: preparations for the funeral, the first hours of the Johnson administration, varied tributes, the further shock of Jack Ruby shooting alleged assassin Lee Harvey Oswald, telecast live on NBC, and finally the almost unbearable emotion of the funeral and burial at Arlington National Cemetery. For all four days Americans remained glued to their sets. CBS research showed 93 percent of the nation's homes tuned in during the burial, and the average home having a set in use for more than 13 consecutive hours. By the end of these four days, broadcasters could stand down from a job well done and commiserate with the rest of the country about the senseless assassination and the terrible feeling of loss—not just of a President but of purpose and enthusiasm.

Unfortunately, the shooting in Dallas was but the first of a series of political assassinations and attempted assassinations. In April 1968 television covered riots that broke out in black ghettos all over the country after Martin Luther King, Jr's assassination in Memphis. Two months later, Senator Robert Kennedy was killed on the night of his California presidential primary victory. Live television did not catch the shooting itself—late at night in Los Angeles—but the networks stayed on the air to report the senator's condition and eventual death in a hospital. For both Kennedy funerals, television was an integral part of impressive and symbol-laden ceremony. Through television, as it followed the train carrying the senator's body from New York to Washington, millions of Americans, whether political supporters or foes of Kennedy, joined vicariously with the hundreds of thousands who lined the tracks. Watching these events helped to achieve catharsis. The 1972 election process was similarly marred when a man shot Alabama Governor George Wallace at a rally. Television cameras covered the shooting and, in subsequent years, per-

---

And now . . . the evening news with . . . / From 1963 until 1981, the CBS evening news was anchored by Walter Cronkite. A UP reporter until after World War II, Cronkite became one of the most trusted men in America. Although well known for his interest in the space program of the 1960s, his influence was most visible after he became a "dove" on the Vietnam war following a lengthy visit to Saigon. The photo here shows Cronkite in the 1960s. His chief competitor was the NBC team of Chet Huntley and David Brinkley (see picture on the first page of Chapter 8) from 1956 to 1971, then John Chancellor for several years. During and after the 1976 elections Chancellor and Brinkley teamed together—and are shown here in the network booth above the floor of the Democratic convention that nominated Jimmy Carter for President.

Photo credit: Indelible, Inc.

mitted the paralyzed Wallace to present his political message to the public. The horror of assassination loomed again in fall 1975 when attempts were made in California on the life of President Gerald Ford.

Some of the most exciting positive moments on television occurred in the "space race" of the 1960s with the Russians, after President Kennedy promised to put a man on the moon within the decade. Even the manned suborbital flights of 1961 were exciting when all that the viewer could see was the blast-off. With John Glenn's first orbital trip in February 1962, the nation hung on every minute of the several hours of coverage, although it was largely in the studio, with mockups and animation and interviews. In May 1963 Gordon Cooper used live television from space to show us what Earth looked like from orbit. Television covered the first space walk in 1965, showed the *Gemini* recovery live later that same year, and covered the disastrous flash fire in January 1967 that killed three *Apollo* astronauts about to make the first flight of their three-man spacecraft. On Christmas Eve the mission commander of *Apollo 8* read passages from Genesis on live television while the spacecraft orbited the moon and we got our first closeup of the moon's surface. Seven months later, *Apollo 11* placed man on the surface of the moon itself. All the networks geared up with science reporters, ex-astronauts, explanatory animation, and models to explain the lengthy and

Photo courtesy of National Broadcasting Company, Inc.

complicated mission from lift-off to splash-down. On July 20, 1969, at 4:17 P.M. (EDT), the lunar module landed on the moon and even normally restrained CBS anchorman Walter Cronkite could not contain his joy. At 10:56 P.M., Neil Armstrong became the first man to walk on the moon, and a small television camera covered the event live for Americans and millions of others who watched via satellite relay. For the next hours the world watched while the astronauts wandered over the surface, talked by telephone with the President, planted the American flag, and cavorted and worked. There also were live telecasts from the returning spacecraft, and live coverage of the splashdown and delivery of the astronauts to a germ-proof quarantine station.

Color television added great visual interest to later missions. The most suspenseful flight was that of *Apollo 13*, which aborted on the way to the moon because of a fuel cell explosion. Television kept the nation informed of emergency procedures to bring the crew safely home. Some viewers complained that space coverage was overdone, even during the *Apollo 11* and *Apollo 13* missions—they missed their favorite programs or resented the public relations exposure for the space program—but most viewers, judging from the ratings, were fascinated by every minute of it.

Television also provided momentum for the civil rights movement of the 1960s, in news reports, documentaries, and other programming. It also covered—

CBS News Covers Man's First Landing on the Moon: July 1969 / Sunday, July 20, 1969, about 4 P.M. (EDT). The three national television networks have scrapped normal program schedules to cover the initial moon landing by Astronauts Neil Armstrong and Edwin Aldrin on the *Apollo 11* mission. Here is how CBS's Walter Cronkite, assisted by former Astronaut Walter Shirra, reported the landing. (*Houston* is the Manned Spaceflight Center at Houston, Texas; *Capcom* is the capsule communicator at Cape Kennedy; *Eagle* is the landing craft; *Tranquility Base* was the name used by *Eagle* after the landing.)

Capcom: Eagle, you're looking great, coming up on nine minutes. We're now in the approach phase, everything looking good. Altitude 5200 feet.

Cronkite: *5200 feet. Less than a mile from the moon's surface.*

Eagle: Manual altitude control is good.

Capcom: Roger. We copy. Altitude 4200 and you're go for landing. Over.

Eagle: Roger, understand. Go for landing. 3000 feet. Second alarm.

Cronkite: *3000 feet. Um-hmmm.*

Eagle: Roger. 1201 alarm. We're go. Hang tight. We're go. 2000 feet. 2000 feet, into the AGS. 47 degrees.

Cronkite: *These are space communications, simply for readout purposes.*

Capcom: Eagle looking great. You're go.

Houston: Altitude 1600. 1400 feet. Still looking very good.

Cronkite: *They've got a good look at their site now. This is their time. They're going to make a decision.*

Eagle: 35 degrees. 35 degrees. 750, coming down at 23. 700 feet, 21 down. 33 degrees.

Schirra: *Oh, the data is coming in beautifully.*

Eagle: 600 feet, down at 19. 540 feet down at 30—down at 15...400 feet down at 9...8 forward...350 feet down at 4...300 feet, down 3½...47

and some would say caused or at least abetted—much of the urban racial and campus political and social unrest of the mid-1960s. In August 1965 television cameras covered the burning and looting by residents of large parts of the Los Angeles black community of Watts. A helicopter-borne KTLA camera provided amazing coverage, but television crews also went into the ghetto—many for the first time, residents complained—only to discover that they, too, were targets for frustration and rage. Riots in other cities, notably Washington, D.C., also occurred during this "long, hot summer." Some blamed the riots on unfulfilled expectations of blacks who had swallowed television's glamourized version of upper-middle-class white

life. By the time of the massive riots in 1968 in Washington, Philadelphia, and other cities following Martin Luther King, Jr.'s assassination, broadcasters had learned what *not* to do. News teams, in addition to feeling like targets, had frequently encouraged violent, or more violent, action or confrontation simply by showing up at a protest with cameras and lights; and persons or groups who wanted to publicize their cause often alerted the news media to potential clashes.

After the racial conflict, the most important violence and protest that persisted in this period was the war in Vietnam. Beginning with coverage of American "advisers" participating in small unit actions in the early 1960s, the nightly eve-

---

forward...1½ down...70...got the shadow out there...50, down at 2½, 19 forward...altitude-velocity lights...3½ down...220 feet...13 forward ...11 forward, coming down nicely...200 feet, 4½ down...5½ down... 160, 6½ down...5½ down, 9 forward...5 percent...quantity light 75 feet. Things still looking good, down a half...6 forward...lights on...down 2½...forward...40 feet, down 2½, kicking up some dust...30 feet, 2½ down...faint shadow...4 forward...4 forward, drifting to the right a little...6...drifting right...

Cronkite: *Boy, what a day.*

Capcom: 30 seconds.

Eagle: Contact light. O.K. engine stopped...descent engine command override off...

Schirra: *We're home!*

Cronkite: *Man on the moon!*

Eagle: Houston, Tranquility Base here. The Eagle has landed!

Capcom: Roger, Tranquility. We copy you on the ground. You've got a bunch of guys about to turn blue. We're breathing again. Thanks a lot.

Tranquility: Thank you.

Cronkite: *Oh, boy!*

Capcom: You're looking good here.

Cronkite: *Whew! Boy!*

Schirra: *I've been saying them all under my breath. That is really something. I'd love to be aboard.*

Cronkite: *I know. We've been wondering what Neil Armstrong and Aldrin would say when they set foot on the moon, which comes a little bit later now. Just to hear them do it. Absolutely with dry mouths.*

Capcom: Roger, Eagle. And you're stay for T-1. Over. You're stay for T-1...

Tranquility: Roger. We're stay for T-1.

Capcom: Roger. And we see you getting the ox.

Cronkite: *That's a great simulation that we see here.*

Schirra: *That little fly-speck is supposed to be the LM.*

Cronkite: *They must be in perfect condition...upright, and there's no complaint about their position.*

Schirra: *Just a little dust.*

Cronkite: *Boy! There they sit on the moon! Just exactly nominal wasn't it...on green with the flight plan, all the way down. Man finally is standing on the surface of the moon. My golly!*

Capcom: Roger, we read you Columbia. He has landed. Tranquility Base. Eagle is at Tranquility. Over.

Source: 10:56:20 PM EDT 7/20/69 (New York: CBS Television News, 1970), pages 76–78. © 1970 CBS, Inc. By permission.

ning newscasts brought to millions of American homes the "living room war"— day-to-day life and death in battle. For more than seven years, families sat down to dinner in front of the television set and watched Americans and Asians shooting and being shot at in the longest war in our history. It was a war of small actions, and this is what television and cameramen, anxious to make their marks as Murrow, Sevareid, and others had done in an earlier war, showed best. Critics contended that television's incomplete, piecemeal coverage had converted many Americans from a prowar or "hawk," or neutral, stand to an antiwar or "dove" stand during or after the early 1968 Vietcong and North Vietnamese Tet offensive. Coverage of peace marches on Washington and other such demonstrations by an expanding group of Americans led many to support this cause. Unrest on many campuses was strong, partly due to the war and partly due to Vietnam-related policies and politics. Starting at Berkeley, and spreading rapidly to Columbia, Wisconsin, and other campuses, the climax of this movement was the killing by Ohio National Guardsmen in early 1970 of four students during a protest at Kent State University.

Many television reporters who went to Vietnam—and most did—came away feeling that the United States was backing a string of dictatorships, that the war was morally wrong, and that it was being mishandled. ABC for several years offered a documentary overview of the week's events in Vietnam, but most other network coverage was restricted to evening newscasts and occasional special documentaries. Although reporters claimed that military control of their reporting, especially in countries like Thailand and Cambodia, made it difficult to get and transmit a true picture of what was happening, no previous war has been so ac-

cessible to reporters. The lazy reported the war from Saigon by relying on the military briefings known locally as the "Five o'Clock Follies"; the brave, ambitious, or foolhardy went out on combat patrols, where a number of them were killed or listed as missing. But there was little depth to the coverage. It is an unanswered question whether the steady coverage of wartime violence deadened Americans to reality or whether the reporting showed the forest behind the trees and changed American thinking. It is too early to conclude more than that television *did* play an important part in its first war.

Television news and documentary units, especially those of CBS and NBC, were taking on increasingly tough subjects and saying something of value or importance about them. But controversy surrounding the television documentary was increasing. The 1960s began with the last of Edward R. Murrow's documentaries, *Harvest of Shame*, dealing with problems of migrant farm workers. When Murrow later was serving as head of USIA for President Kennedy, he tried to suppress export of the program, but to no avail and much criticism. Programs such as *Biography of a Bookie Joint*, with films of gambling operations going on without police intervention and *Battle of Newburgh* (about a town that cut off funds for many welfare recipients) led to public outcry and threats of legal action against the network responsible. Howard K. Smith's ABC documentary on *The Political Obituary of Richard Nixon*, just after Nixon lost the California gubernatorial election in 1962, raised sparks when Alger Hiss gave his views on his old tormenter. (Nixon, as a congressman, had been instrumental in sending former State Department official Hiss to jail for perjury for denying that he had been a communist agent.) Nixon supporters and other complainers and victims accused television of political bias and unfair reporting. CBS got into trouble with its "Pot Party at a University" segment of a Chicago local news show when it became known that the event had been set up for the cameras. Not only was the use of marijuana illegal but news "created" by the broadcaster was, at best, misleading to the public.

Perhaps the biggest complaint—and a congressional hearing—resulted from CBS's 1971 telecast of *Selling of the Pentagon*, a hard-hitting discussion of military public relations, which questioned spending large amounts of tax money in this way. The documentary angered conservative congressmen, though many admitted they had not seen the program, and they engineered a full-scale hearing on documentary practice, film splicing, editing of shows, and *out-takes* (unused film material). CBS refused to supply any materials not actually aired on the program, contending that such action would violate First Amendment freedoms and stifle all investigative reporting. An attempt to cite CBS and president Frank Stanton for contempt of Congress failed in what most broadcasters regarded as a victory. But several important points had been raised, and some documentary production methods were changed and controls of viewpoint tightened. What seemed acceptable and normal to a documentary maker might not appear so to a concerned viewer. Prior to 1964, the networks themselves had produced all news and news documentary programs. In 1963, ABC opened the door to other producers a bit by showing the David Wolper production of *Making of the President: 1960*. As television became the most commonly used and trusted source of information by the American public, its responsibilities increased.

The networks' news coverage received the strongest—generally politically inspired and planned—criticisms in the very late 1960s and early 1970s. In a televised speech to a Republican group in Iowa in fall 1969, Vice President Spiro T. Agnew complained that three major networks had a stranglehold on the nation's news and thinking. He asked rhetorically who had selected the small group of network officials, editors, and anchormen who made news decisions. A week later he offered another complaint, and soon similar remarks from other politicians joined in a well-orchestrated campaign and safety valve for long-standing resentments. The broadcast industry responded with its usual defensiveness, emphasizing the dangers of governmental control of news. Agnew's comments ostensibly had been sparked by the network practice of commenting on a presidential speech immediately—what he called "instant analysis." That the networks usually had copies of presidential speeches to study hours in advance did not placate those who believed that the President should not be interpreted in this way. For a time in 1970–1971, CBS eliminated any post-speech analysis.

Many local stations joined in the clamor over network news control. They either had different political viewpoints, station owners frequently being more conservative than network news officials in New York and Washington, or wanted to avoid controversy that might interfere with sales of advertising time. The months-long confrontation, part of the Nixon administration's battle with a more or less independent center of information and power, the press, was useful in many ways. Broadcasters had to consider their own actions and policies, explain them, tighten up sloppy practices, and improve their professionalism. Viewers had been directly exposed to critically important differences between government and media, and government and media both had reevaluated their roles and assumptions. These struggles between media and government, including the release of the "Pentagon Papers" and the resulting legal clash between the *New York Times* and the government, and further disillusionment over Vietnam culminated in the biggest domestic news event in decades: Watergate.

Television did not play a strong role for the first year of the Watergate scandal of 1972–1974, which started with a "third rate burglary" and ended with the resignation of President Nixon. From discovery of the burglars in the Democratic Party offices in June 1972 through the election the following November, most investigative research was by the printed press, notably the *Washington Post*. Television stories and special programs became more common in 1973, but television's greatest value was its coverage of the Senate Watergate Committee hearings. Running from May through August 1973, and chaired by North Carolina's crusty Sam Ervin, these hearings were a fascinating live exposition of the political process in America, and were "must" television watching as a parade of witnesses told—or evaded telling—what they knew of the broad conspiracy to assure the re-election of Nixon and then to cover up the conspiracy itself. The members of the Senate committee soon became household names and faces, as the various witnesses supplied their pieces of the puzzle. For a time, the networks alternated coverage so that they and the viewers would have a choice between the hearings and regular entertainment programming. The more the viewers watched the hearings the more important the Watergate issues became in national affairs.

Newscasts and special news programs punctuated the course of the tottering administration. In October 1973 Vice President Agnew had to resign because of his acceptance of kickbacks when he was a Maryland official—to be replaced by Congressman Gerald Ford. Shortly afterward, when Nixon chose to fire the special prosecutor investigating Watergate, there was a "Saturday Night Massacre" that included several resignations and firings of top Justice Department officials and the firing of the special prosecutor. The story continued to build. Nixon professed innocence of the coverup, gave edited tape transcripts of his White House conversations to Congress—with the transcripts, in large binders, impressively piled behind him as he spoke on television. There were court battles over access to the tapes by Congress and by the new special prosecutor, arguments over a deleted 18½-minute portion of one tape, and further arguments over executive privilege and the right of Congress to subpoena the tapes. When the House Judiciary Committee in mid-1974 recommended impeachment, and the Supreme Court said that the President could not withhold the tapes, it was all over. On August 9, 1974, television and radio presented President Nixon's resignation speech to a startled public as well as the swearing in of Vice President Gerald Ford the next day. The story finally ended with Ford's pardon of Nixon some weeks later.

9•65   Election Broadcasting

There were few changes in political campaign coverage in the 1964, 1968, and 1972 elections—but 1976 was different. The 1964 election fight between President Lyndon B. Johnson and Senator Barry Goldwater saw some of the strongest—some would say dirtiest—political ads ever aired. A soon famous—though aired only once—Johnson spot intimated that Goldwater was likely to start an atomic war, and a Goldwater spot virtually accused Johnson of immorality. For election night, the networks and wire services joined together for the first time to coordinate reporting of election returns. The resulting Network Election Service (later, News Election Service) was to become permanent. The networks each took nine states, and the wire services split the rest. Although all "raw vote" tabulations were now common to all media, each network still used its own sample areas and computerized prediction techniques for forecasting or "declaring" winners—sometimes before polls closed in western states. This caused such an outcry that the networks had to delay "declarations" until the last polls had closed, although surveys commissioned by the networks indicated this action was not warranted.

The 1968 election was most notable for the debacle outside the Democratic convention in Chicago. Mayor Richard Daley tightly controlled the city and the location of cameras by the networks. It was not enough. When his police and the youthful antiwar and antiestablishment demonstrators clashed in front of the convention hotels several nights running, home viewers were treated to the dichotomy of calm inside the hall, as Vice President Hubert Humphrey became the nominee, and riots outside. Several reporters were arrested or roughed up inside the hall as well as outside, as the Daley forces sought to retain control in what was called a "police riot" in one official report. There were bitter post-convention attacks that television had biased viewers by covering the riots while neglecting the scheduled convention events. The networks replied that both were news events worthy of coverage. Daley supporters also claimed that the presence of the television cameras

stimulated the rioting. The entire event was a prime hunting ground for researchers and contributed to Humphrey's subsequent loss at the polls.

Convention coverage differed from previous years. ABC did away with its daytime and evening-long gavel-to-gavel coverage and concentrated its report into the late evening hours. ABC thus gained a ratings advantage by preserving its entertainment programs and gathering some political watchers later on.

The 1968 campaign and the off-year elections of 1970 brought the talents of the professional image-makers fully into focus. Joe McGinniss' devastating *The Selling of the President 1968* exposed the media campaign behind Nixon, and many other candidates were accused of having been packaged and sold like consumer goods. Debate raged over the effects of television and other media usage, and experts analyzed the massive amounts of money that had been spent in the past in mass media in attempts to persuade or even "buy" voters. By 1972, however, it was clear that television and image-building alone would not do the trick, and the image merchants lost some of their glamour and appeal. Expenditures on radio and television in the 1972 campaign, however, came to $60 million as compared to only $14 million spent on broadcasting in the 1960 race. Nixon, whose Committee to Reelect the President (CREEP) greatly outspent Democratic candidate Senator George McGovern, won by a landslide. As a result, a new federal law was passed that was designed to crimp the costs and style of campaigns after 1972.

The 1976 election campaign featured an old wrinkle—the "great debate" format pioneered in 1960 (see 8.64). Late in 1975, in response to a petition from the Aspen Institute, the FCC revised its interpretation of Section 315. Its "Aspen ruling" held that debates and other coverage of candidates would be exempt from the equal opportunities provisions of the law if such political events were arranged by groups other than the candidates or the broadcasters, and if that broadcast coverage was "incidental" to the event taking place.

Gerald Ford, in accepting the GOP nomination in August (after a tightly fought battle with former California Governor Ronald Reagan), challenged the Democrat's Governor Jimmy Carter to a series of debates—an unusual action for a sitting President, but taken because Ford was then far behind in the polls and was a bit unsure of himself, never having run in a presidential campaign before. There eventually were three debates between the presidential candidates, plus one (this was a new turn) between the vice-presidential candidates, Senators Walter Mondale and Robert Dole. All were sponsored by the League of Women Voters, which had gotten some practice with Democratic primaries during the spring, to comply with the FCC ruling. As in the 1960 debates, when Nixon's appearance in the first debate cost him heavily, so did the debates affect the 1976 campaign. In the second debate, President Ford asserted quite clearly, and repeated when questioned, that Eastern Europe was not under Soviet domination. His campaign lost 10 days in trying to explain that statement away, and the lost momentum likely cost him the election. Carter had appeared weak in the first debate (which had its audio cut off the air for 28 minutes due to a technical failure), but Ford's error in the second appeared to have greater impact in the end. Carter won the election. The 1976 elections were the first to be heavily covered using flexible electronic news-gathering (ENG) equipment, at both national and local levels.

9•7   Audience Ratings and Research

As much as the 1950s had been depicted as the Age of Television, it was not until the 1960s that we really began to determine how television was affecting us. Much research centered on the effects of television on children and youth, but there also was concern over its broader consequences.

Radio was in 96 percent and television in 90 percent of American homes at the beginning of this period, so growth in number of television homes slowed although the number of sets increased as people bought their second and third receivers. Three-quarters of American homes had color sets by 1976. Transistors made radio and television sets smaller and lighter, and more and more sets were imported each year, first from Germany and then increasingly from the Far East (to the extent that Japan and the United States signed an agreement in 1977 to limit Japanese color television set exports to the United States). By the late 1960s, largely due to the labor economics of manufacturing abroad, virtually no radio receivers and very few black-and-white television receivers were manufactured in the United States, although U.S. firms had some foreign plants. In 1961, only 70 percent of cars had radios, but by the mid-1970s nearly 90 percent had, a substantial minority had added short-range transceivers in the Citizens Band, and even more had FM. Digital clock radios were popular in the 1970s, and very tiny transistor radios could be bought for as little as $5, with novelties—radios built into earphones or toilet paper holders—easily made.

Most homes of the early 1960s did not have the ability to receive UHF telecasts (see 8.81) and therefore UHF stations could not compete adequately with VHF stations in the same market. But in July 1961 the FCC proposed requiring all television sets be able to receive all channels. Congress approved the proposal in return for the commission's dropping all consideration of deintermixture (see 8.81), and President Kennedy signed the bill in July 1962, to take effect in mid-1964. Thanks to the steady market in portable and, after 1965, color television, the proportion of homes capable of receiving UHF broadcasts increased sharply from about 10 percent in 1961 to 90 percent in 1976. This act finally brought the UHF stations into the club, even though UHF tuners did not measure up to VHF tuners in quality in the same set until the manufacturers were pushed by the FCC in the late 1970s. The all-channel act was not the whole answer, but it helped immensely.

Noting the success of television's all-channel bill, those concerned with FM radio's lack of financial success tried but failed to get a bill passed that would require AM and FM capability in all radio, including automobile, receivers. The cost differential and manufacturer-dealer indifference held automobile FM radio sales down in the 1960s, preventing FM stations from cashing in on AM radio's big audiences in morning and evening drive time. By the early 1970s, FM saturation was about 60 percent compared to UHF's almost non-existent capability when the 1962 all-channel television bill was being considered—thus reducing the need for all-channel radio legislation.

9•71 Viewing Trends and Ratings Problems

By 1961, 89 percent of the nation's families had a television set—47.2 million families. By late 1976, 97 percent owned television, but that small percentage increase covered a growth of more than 22 million families as the population rose. Thanks largely to the coming of color in the mid-1960s, retention of first-generation sets, and the relatively low cost of black-and-white portables, the proportion of multiset homes rose from 13 percent in 1961 to more than 45 percent by 1976. This is a far cry from the corner tavern announcing with great excitement in the late 1940s: "We have television!"

The basic pattern of television viewing remained as it had in the 1950s: Viewing was higher in winter than in summer and peaked between 8 P.M. and 10 P.M. Color-set owners viewed about seven hours a week more television than monochrome-set owners. Average daily household viewing slowly increased from about five hours in 1961 to about 6¼ hours in 1976. Roper (1977) collected data for TIO that showed median individual viewing rose from 2:17 in 1961 to 2:53 in 1976. Naturally, families with children made heavier use of the set, and overall viewing decreased somewhat as education and income increased; to 2:24 for the college educated and 2:40 for individuals in upper economic brackets. Women did the most viewing and teenagers the least, while persons over 55 of either sex did the most viewing of all.

Viewership information, constantly updated, was generated by the two chief national ratings firms: the A.C. Nielsen Company, which had dominated national television ratings since 1949, and the American Research Bureau (ARB), later called Arbitron. After 1964 radio was measured only in local markets. At that point, radio was in 94 percent of American homes, sets were in use about 15 hours a week—down sharply from pretelevision days—and home receivers were giving way to portable and automobile sets, which were hard to measure. The radio pattern of listening remained the reverse of television—steady, except for a peak in the early morning, a brief spurt during afternoon drive time, especially in large cities, and a drop during television prime time.

The ratings themselves were in and out of trouble (see 8.84). Rumors of fraud and overdependence on ratings led to investigations in 1960–1961 by Congress, which commissioned an intensive investigation of ratings methods and statistics. The resulting report noted several important shortcomings in ratings sampling and survey techniques, statistical standards, and use. In 1963–1964, the House Commerce Committee held hearings on ratings, which included a ten-day grilling of top A.C. Nielsen personnel and uncovered shortcuts and skimping in research techniques that could cause significant differences in the results. Other firms also were examined, including a small company that faked much of its data in the back room, but the importance and problems of Nielsen took up much of the long hearings. From this investigation and its aftermath came several organizations intended to clean up the ratings and their image. The Broadcast Ratings Council combined representatives of networks, broadcasting organizations, and advertisers to oversee ratings operations, making sure—for the benefit of advertisers as well as public relations—that gathering and reporting methods for ratings were accurate and met acceptable standards. The Committee on Nationwide Television Audience Measurements (CONTAM) was created by and for the networks to conduct a series of studies to find more valid and reliable ways of deriving program ratings. In the 1970s, both organizations became more and more involved with generating positive publicity and information on the ratings system on which networks, advertisers, and stations mutually survive. Statisticians agree that ratings firms now use generally sound methods, although the publicity they engender in station and network promotion efforts might be questioned, and some advertisers and ad agencies place far more reliance upon them than is warranted.

Just as the Lazarsfeld studies in the 1940s described the peak period of radio listening and Bogart's 1956 volume showed the rise of television, two books after 1960 demonstrated television's increasing hold on the American public. The first was Gary Steiner's *The People Look at Television* (1963), based on a 1960 nationwide survey (with a substudy of New York viewers) underwritten by CBS. It showed that television generally had replaced other means of socialization, and that its popularity and use were high in nearly all sectors of the population except for those of high education and income. Interestingly, although viewers nearly always claimed to want more cultural or educational programming when asked about program balance, they usually would pick more entertainment content when given a choice of material. Reactions to overall programming and advertising were highly positive; television was the one nonessential item in the typical home that was regarded as nearly essential.

A decade later this study was repeated, again with support from CBS, in Robert Bower's *Television and the Public* (1973). This update generally supported the earlier findings, although the public's fascination with television had worn off—it no longer was a constant topic of conversation and viewers were more critical of it. Television's impact as a news source was greater than in 1960, and parental concern and control over children's viewing were stronger than a decade earlier. Here the specific market surveyed was Minneapolis–St. Paul, and again viewers spoke of desiring more educational and cultural programming, while generally ignoring that choice when it was available. Researchers suggested that in both surveys viewers may have considered cultural programming a "proper response," regardless of their viewing preferences.

Issued about every two years, starting just after the quiz show scandals, were the Roper studies sponsored by the Television Information Office, an arm of the NAB, on what the public thought of television vis-à-vis other media. Early editions drew newspaper criticism for using a method whereby multiple responses showed television as far and away the most believed and most used news medium. Some of the questions used in these studies dated back to Lazarsfeld's work in the early 1940s, providing a longitudinal look at public reaction to broadcasting.

9•72 Television and Children: Phases Two and Three

The Kefauver investigation into television and juvenile delinquency in the mid-1950s (see 8.73) led to an even more intensive investigation in the early 1960s. The new probe came about because people were increasingly concerned over violence in the streets, juvenile delinquency, and the possibility that this behavior was related to violence in television programs. Some senators and staff members felt that broadcast self-regulation was not reducing violence on the air; others were well aware of the publicity value of hearings on this subject. In addition, some new research had suggested a direct cause-and-effect relationship between media violence and

violent activities by viewers. In June 1961, Senator Thomas Dodd (D-Connecticut) opened what became nearly three years of intermittent hearings. In addition, the results of three committee staff monitoring reports of television content in 1954, 1961, and 1964 showed incidents of violence—a very difficult concept to define validly—on television to be increasing, especially at hours when children might be watching.

This second phase of concern over children and television ended late in 1964 with the publication of the hearings and a mimeographed interim report of what had been learned. That the final report never appeared and the interim report had limited distribution spoiled the potential effect of the hearings. The subcommittee suggested greater prime-time network efforts in programming for children, revision of the FCC station application form to clarify the minimal public service and children's program requirements, addition of sanctions to give teeth to the NAB code, a mechanism for the public to voice its opinions of television, and the need for further research. The implied threat was congressional action if the industry did not police itself as it had promised in 1954.

These issues simmered until 1968. That year, in response to the assassinations of Senator Robert Kennedy and the Reverend Martin Luther King, Jr., President Lyndon Johnson created a Commission on the Causes and Effects of Violence with Milton Eisenhower as chairman. The commission's report contained a chapter on media violence and, more importantly, a lengthy staff report in book form on the issues and questions of media and violence. Other staff reports, accusing broadcasters of failing to clean up violence on the tube, led to Senate action some months later. Senator John Pastore (D-Rhode Island), powerful chairman of the Communications Subcommittee of the Senate

Commerce Committee, wrote to the Surgeon General in March 1969 requesting creation of a research panel to evaluate the research literature and conduct original studies on the relation between television and violent behavior. Within six weeks, a research program had been created and funded with $1.5 million from existing budgets—something of a record for this sort of government action.

Unfortunately, both politics and industry pressure worked against constructive results. The 12 researchers appointed to the panel included five from the networks, three from the academic research community, and "the naive four" with no background in the subject. Having been given a *de facto* veto power, the networks blackballed several well-known television-violence researchers as being no longer impartial since their opinions were well known—and allegedly antinetwork. The 12-member committee let contracts for 23 laboratory and field studies by a wide variety of researchers, as well as some literature review and synthesis. The results were in by late 1971, and the report of the committee, issued in January 1972, appeared to have been written quickly and under pressure. Its inconclusive conclusion was that television violence can affect some of the viewers some of the time. This was not a new notion. Some of the studies themselves, however, published in full shortly after the report, pointed far more strongly to the conclusion that television violence does indeed help stimulate violent actions by some viewers in both short and long run. Controversy boiled in the trade and public press, and in hearings held by Pastore to sort out what the research expenditure and effort really meant. There was criticism of the networks' role in the formation of the panel and writing of the report. Broadcasters hailed the report as clearing them of a never-admitted responsibility for causing violence. Critics said, "Ignore the report and look at the studies." Academicians worked over the data and strove to improve the methodologies as well.

And there it probably would have died, like the earlier studies, except for one key difference. The 1970s was a period of vocal citizens' action groups (see 9.85), and one of the most vocal was Action for Children's Television. ACT had been formed by a group of Boston area mothers concerned about violence on the air and excessive commercialism aimed at children, both on Saturday mornings and in other hours when children were likely to be viewing. ACT and other groups helped arouse public opinion to the extent that the industry and the commission, particularly after Richard Wiley became chairman in 1974, finally took action. The networks agreed to the suggestion from CBS president Arthur Taylor that, starting in fall 1975, prime-time network programming, except for news, before 9:00 P.M. (Eastern and Pacific time) would be for "family viewing" (see 9.85) with limits on the depiction of violence. In addition, after 1972 violent cartoons substantially were removed from children's morning and weekend programming. Critics agreed that the amount of violence was diminishing in the 1970s, but the disagreement over the definition of violence was illustrated in disputes over the findings by George Gerbner of the University of Pennsylvania, who regularly issued new editions of an "index" (later dubbed a "profile") that reported the incidence of violence on all network television programming. ACT, Pastore, and many researchers, critics, and other politicians kept this matter in the public eye—now that the incidence of real-life violence (coverage of the Vietnam War) no longer occupied as much of the evening news before "family viewing."

Television Violence: The Surgeon General's Committee Reports (January 1972) / The following conclusions of the best-funded research program into the effects of television are a good example of the imprecision of much social science research. Newspaper accounts of the cautious qualifications contained in the committee reports naturally varied widely. See 10.72 for the similar conclusions reached a decade later.

... there is a convergence of the fairly substantial experimental evidence for *short-run* causation of aggression among some children by viewing violence on the screen and the much less certain evidence from field studies that extensive violence viewing precedes some *long-run* manifestations of aggressive behavior. This convergence of the two types of evidence constitutes some preliminary indication of a causal relationship, but a good deal of research remains to be done before one can have confidence in these conclusions.

The field studies, correlating different behavior among adolescents, and the laboratory studies of the responses by younger children to violent films converge also on a number of further points.

First, there is evidence that any sequence by which viewing television violence causes aggressive behavior is most likely applicable only to some children who are predisposed in that direction. . . .

Second, there are suggestions in both sets of studies that the way children respond to violent film material is affected by the context in which it is presented. Such elements as parental explanations, the favorable or unfavorable outcome of the violence, and whether it is seen as fantasy or reality may make a difference. Generalizations about all violent content are likely to be misleading.

Thus, the two sets of findings converge in three respects: a preliminary and tentative indication of a causal relation between viewing violence on television and aggressive behavior; an indication that any such causal relation operates only on some children (who are predisposed to be aggressive); and an indication that it operates only in some environmental contexts. Such tentative and limited conclusions are not very satisfying. They represent substantially more knowledge than we had two years ago, but they leave many questions unanswered.

Source: The Surgeon General's Scientific Advisory Committee on Television and Social Behavior, *Television and Growing Up: The Impact of Televised Violence.* (Washington: Government Printing Office, 1972), pages 17–19.

9•8   Regulatory Confusion

The regulatory scene became much more complicated in the 1960s and early 1970s for several reasons. First, conflicting views arose because there were more participants involved: new broadcasting stations, new groups familiar with and involved in the regulatory process, and new media—cable systems and potential operators of pay-TV and cable systems. Second, events had forced participants to look at problems in new ways. Earlier they had discussed the Fairness Doctrine, cable and broadcast television relationships, and ownership and control, but now these issues became much more salient and controversial and often intractable. Third, the proliferation of stations and services, such as FM and public television, together with pressures from such closely related media as audio and video recordings, produced greater competition within the industry. Fourth, and increasingly evident in the years to follow, was the beginning of a fundamental rethinking of the role of regulation in electronic media. The very increase in means of program delivery seemed to some observers (especially some conservative economists and politicians) to negate the traditional conception of broadcasting as a "bottleneck" with a small and finite technological limit on number of outlets in a given locality. If technology's promise of a future of many channels and more choice came true, would traditional regulation be necessary any longer? This question was first faced with respect to cable television (see 9.83).

9•81   Changing Cast of Regulators

On the regulatory scene, older groups changed and newer ones arrived. The FCC was shaken up to an extent not

seen since the days of James Lawrence Fly in the 1940s. In 1961, after the conflict of interest scandals involving Commissioners Doerfer and Richard Mack, President Kennedy appointed thirty-four-year-old Newton Minow to the FCC chairmanship. Minow early served notice of his displeasure with much of what was broadcast when he spoke before the NAB of television as a "vast wasteland" (see this chapter's opening quotations) requiring more high quality television programming. The phrase caught on with the public. While the industry fretted over the newly critical FCC, Minow helped provide a Kennedy "New Frontier" activism to commission decisions. However, he was hamstrung by more conservative holdover appointees and, soon frustrated, he returned to private law practice in 1963. Minow was replaced by an even younger activist chairman, E. William Henry, until 1966. After Henry's departure, veteran Commissioner Rosel Hyde became chairman but could not readily control Commissioner Nicholas Johnson's highly public consumer activism (see below). President Nixon named conservative GOP leader Dean Burch as chairman in 1969. Serving until 1973, when he joined the White House staff, Burch was considered one of the FCC's better administrators, with the commission arriving at decisions in several controversial areas (particularly CATV) just before his departure. He also kept the FCC's factions communicating. Burch and Johnson both left in 1973, and General Counsel Richard Wiley was elevated to commissioner and in 1974 to the chairmanship. Wiley proved to be an even better administrator than Burch, establishing an atmosphere of hard work and more timely decision-making.

During much of the 1960s, the team of Kenneth Cox and Nicholas Johnson issued reports and dissents attacking broadcasting organizations and practices, persuaded the commission to hold a couple of well-publicized citizens' gripe sessions outside of Washington, and supported greater citizen action to upgrade public service broadcast programming. Their approaches were different; Cox was generally low key, but the youthful Johnson quickly took his campaign to the public. He built a constituency with books like *How to Talk Back to Your Television Set* (1970), many articles and speeches, and detailed dissenting opinions to FCC decisions. He sometimes shot from the hip, but he awakened public interest and concern and made people feel that they had a voice on the commission. At the opposite end of the political spectrum was Commissioner Lee Loevinger, one of the brightest men ever to serve on the FCC, a strong conservative whose well-honed legal mind generally matched the liberalism of Cox and the more radical opinions of Johnson. Both Johnson and Loevinger had been appointed to the FCC because they had ruffled too many feathers on earlier governmental jobs; Loevinger as head of the antitrust division of the Justice Department and Johnson as head of the Maritime Commission.

President Nixon soothed the broadcasting industry with his appointment of commercial broadcasters Robert Wells and James Quello but aroused the ire of consumer and minority groups. Yet Nixon also appointed the first black on the FCC, Benjamin Hooks. Hooks started quietly but by 1974 was making stronger statements on the place of minorities in broadcasting—and probably stepping on toes by insisting on enforcement of equal employment opportunity rules, even for PTV stations. Nixon also named the second woman to serve on the FCC, Charlotte Reid, who was much less important to the commission's deliberations than the first (see 7.42 and 9.825). For much of the

period, the commission was ideologically divided.

By the late 1960s the FCC, designed in 1934, was beginning to suffer from overload, but in the 1970s it was nearly swamped. Controlling interstate telephone and telegraph as well as broadcasting, it spent an increasing amount of time on complicated safety and special service rules, communication satellite policy, cable television, and processing paperwork for more than 9,000 broadcast and millions of other licenses. It had to act on everything: from the millions of letters insisting that a petition to require fairness on religious-body-owned stations was a "petition against God"—an attempt to remove all religion from the air, to the occasional complaint about obscene programming, particularly on educational stations—the Pacifica Foundation's WBAI, the University of Pennsylvania's WXPN—since few commercial broadcasters would risk their licenses. As new technology and innovations made long-range policy questions more insistent, the FCC had even less time than in the 1930s to consider them.

Two kinds of studies had been undertaken to examine the FCC's policies and efficiency, particularly in the decision-making process. First were those concerned with organization—one conducted for the 1949 Hoover Commission on executive branch organization, one prepared under Judge Landis's direction for President Kennedy, and one prepared under Roy Ash's direction for President Nixon. Second were those concerned with telecommunication policy—the President's Communications Policy Board established by President Truman, and the President's Task Force on Communications Policy, which reported to President Johnson at the very end of his term.

In response to some of these analyses and the shortcomings of the FCC in the late 1960s, and in order to accumulate more immediate power, President Nixon proposed to Congress early in 1970 that the Office of Telecommunications Management, a White House staff agency primarily concerned with government agency spectrum use and assignment, be converted to an Office of Telecommunications Policy (OTP). It would have a broader purview, including supervision of the more than 50-year-old Interdepartmental Radio Advisory Committee, and would be located within the Executive Office of the President to show its power to speak for the executive. The plan was activated in April, and Rand Corporation researcher Clay T. Whitehead was named to head the OTP. It quickly became clear that, while OTP would provide needed long-range policy planning and research, using facilities of the Office of Telecommunications in the Department of Commerce, its function was more actually political than technical.

OTP's first major coup was engineering a compromise between NAB and NCTA in fall 1971 that led to the 1972 FCC cable rules (see 9.83). Soon it was involved in seeking five-year license terms for broadcasters, a major broadcaster goal for most of this period; VHF channel drop-ins in large markets ostensibly to broaden competition; limiting program reruns, brought about by administration concern for unemployment in the West Coast entertainment production unions; financing for public broadcasting; and limiting the Fairness Doctrine. After the demise of the Nixon administration in 1974, OTP almost dropped from sight and Whitehead resigned. Although it was kept alive by members of Congress who realized the potential value of long-range policy and research, after 1973 OTP had little of the strength of its earlier years, when the FCC, broadcasters, and many citizens had become increasingly concerned about

White House encroachment onto commission regulatory territory.

A third participant in the regulatory arena, in addition to the FCC and OTP, was the U.S. Court of Appeals for the District of Columbia, which the 1934 Communications Act had designated to hear all appeals from FCC decisions. Until the 1960s it usually had backed up FCC decisions on appeal, seldom taking it to task unless procedures had been badly mismanaged, and many broadcasters looked on it as the enforcement arm of the commission. Changing membership on the court, which has nine members—three of whom normally sit on a given case—and changing public pressures, however, changed the court's view of the FCC and the industry. This new view was brought home with a vengeance in March 1966 when a three-judge panel overturned an FCC decision which had refused to let a citizens' group stand as a participant in a license-renewal case. The Office of Communications of the United Church of Christ, headed by Everett Parker, had sought to speak for the 45 percent black population of Jackson, Mississippi, for the purpose of denying license renewal to WLBT. The panel of judges, in what became a landmark case, held that the public was entitled to participate (or have "standing") in such proceedings. Hitherto, such matters had been between broadcasters and the FCC, claiming to act on behalf of the public, and sometimes other broadcasters with an economic interest. Over the next several years, by granting other citizen groups the right to be heard before the FCC, the court expanded public access to the decision-making process. In 1969, the court went further in the same case, ordering the FCC to lift WLBT's license and assign it to an interim operation—a *very* rare action—until a new "permanent" licensee could be selected. The decision spoke of the FCC's "curious neutrality in favor of an existing licensee." By 1970 some industry observers were referring to this increasingly independent and anti-FCC court as "broadcasting's preemptive court." Public interest groups rapidly understood that, if the FCC denied them standing or access, they could often obtain it on appeal. The preemptive role of the court seemed to expand into the mid-1970s.

Major concern for long-range broadcast policy in Congress switched from the Senate side (where longtime Communications Subcommittee head John Pastore retired late in 1976) to the House Communications Subcommittee under Torbert Macdonald (D-Massachusetts) and then Lionel Van Deerlin (D-California). With a professional and knowledgeable staff, the subcommittee held a series of hearings into many aspects of communications, expressed concern about the limited role of cable versus broadcasting, and looked into the varied interrelationships of point-to-point communications and the broadcast-cable media. Late in 1976, Van Deerlin announced the subcommittee's most extensive project yet, aimed at a complete review and possible rewrite of the 1934 act (see 10.81).

9•82   Fairness on the Air

The FCC's Fairness Doctrine (see 7.84) caused growing controversy during the 1960s and 1970s. Politics, cigarette advertising, the Vietnam War, and other matters were reflected in the growing body of case law. Congress had perhaps inadvertently provided a seeming statutory base for the Fairness Doctrine in 1959, when it amended Section 315 (the political "equal opportunity" section of the Communications Act) to note that nothing in

the revised section would exempt broadcasters from their responsibility ". . . to afford reasonable opportunity for the discussion of conflicting views on issues of public importance." The Supreme Court's *Red Lion* decision in 1969 (see box on page 427) firmly supported the idea that the concept of fairness, which was intended to benefit the average citizen and viewer and which previously had been included under the "public interest" standard, now had its own statutory authority. The FCC published specific regulations on the "personal attack" aspects of fairness in 1967 and 1968, and public notices which codified the case law and defined proper and improper adherence to the "controversial issues" aspects of the Fairness Doctrine. Many broadcasters, and others who opposed FCC intervention in programming because of the First Amendment, were unhappy about these steps.

The 1964 notice included rigid rules for broadcasting editorials—the station would have to seek out opposing views—and even more rigid rules for informing, providing texts, and providing rebuttal opportunities for persons attacked.

A landmark case began with a 15-minute recorded program in which right-wing preacher Billy James Hargis attacked Fred Cook, author of a book critical of Senator Barry Goldwater, the Arizona conservative Republican candidate for President in 1964. Around two hundred stations carried the program, and Cook, apparently with some support from the Democratic Party, claimed time to reply from all of them. Most offered him the free time required under FCC fairness rules. But WGCB—in the small town of Red Lion, Pennsylvania, 75 miles west of Philadelphia, which had broadcast the program in November 1964—sent him a rate card offering to *sell* reply time. Cook

Rise of the Fairness Doctrine: 1941–1974

January 16, 1941 Radio can serve as an instrument of democracy only when devoted to the communication information and the exchange of ideas fairly and objectively presented. A truly free radio cannot be used to advocate the causes of the licensee. It cannot be used to support the candidacies of his friends. It cannot be devoted to the support of principles he happens to regard most favorably. In brief, the broadcaster cannot be an advocate.

FCC, Mayflower Decision, 8 FCC 333.

June 1, 1949 To recapitulate, the Commission believes that under the American system of broadcasting the individual licensees of radio stations have the responsibility for determining the specific program material to be broadcast over their stations. This choice, however, must be exercised in a manner consistent with the basic policy of the Congress that radio be maintained as a medium of free speech for the general public as a whole rather than as an outlet for the purely personal or private interests of the licensee. This requires that licensees devote a reasonable percentage of their broadcasting time to the discussion of public issues of interest in the community served by their stations and that such programs be designed so that the public has a reasonable opportunity to hear different opposing positions on the public issues of interest and importance in the community. The particular format best suited for the presentation of such programs in a manner consistent with

the public interest must be determined by the licensee in the light of the facts of each individual station. Such presentation may include the identified expression of the licensee's personal viewpoint as part of the more general presentation of views or comments on the various issues, but the opportunity of licensees to present such views as they may have on matters of controversy may not be utilized to achieve a partisan or one-sided presentation of issues. Licensee editorialization is but one aspect of freedom of expression by means of radio. Only insofar as it is exercised in conformity with the paramount right of the public to hear a reasonably balanced presentation of all responsible viewpoints on particular issues can such editorialization be considered to be consistent with the licensee's duty to operate in the public interest. For the licensee is a trustee impressed with the duty of preserving for the public generally radio as a medium of free expression and fair presentation.

FCC, "In the Matter of Editorializing by Broadcast Licensees," 13 FCC 1246, paragraph 21.

September 14, 1959 Nothing in the foregoing sentence [a modification of the "equal opportunities" for political candidates clause in Section 315 of the Communications Act of 1934] shall be construed as relieving broadcasters, in connection with the presentation of newscasts, news interviews, news documentaries and on-the-spot coverage of news events from the obligation imposed upon them under this Act to operate in the public interest and to afford reasonable opportunity for the discussion of conflicting views on issues of public importance.

Public Law 86-274, 86th Congress (amending the 1934 Communications Act).

June 9, 1969 It is the right of the viewers and listeners, not the right of the broadcasters, which is paramount . . . It is the purpose of the First Amendment to preserve an uninhibited marketplace of ideas in which truth will ultimately prevail, rather than to countenance monopolization of that market, whether it be by the Government itself or a private licensee . . . It is the right of the public to receive suitable access to social, political, esthetic, moral, and other ideas and experiences which is crucial here. . . .

In view of the scarcity of broadcast frequencies, the Government's role in allocating those frequencies, and the legitimate claims of those unable without governmental assistance to gain access to those frequencies for expression of their views, we hold the regulations [Public Attack Rules] and ruling [Fairness Doctrine] at issue here are both authorized by statute and constitutional.

Supreme Court decision in *Red Lion Broadcasting Co.* v. *FCC*, 395 U.S. 367.

May 29, 1973 If broadcasters were required to provide time, free when necessary, for the discussion of the various shades of opinion on the issue . . . the affluent could still determine in large part the issues to be discussed. Thus . . . a right of access . . .

would have little meaning to those who could not afford to purchase time in the first instance.

If the Fairness Doctrine were applied to editorial advertising, there is also the substantial danger that the effective operation of that doctrine would be jeopardized. To minimize financial hardship and to comply fully with its public responsibilities a broadcaster might well be forced to make regular programming time available to those holding a view different from that expressed in an editorial advertisement. . . . The result would be a further erosion of the journalistic discretion of broadcasters in the coverage of public issues, and a transfer of control over the treatment of public issues from the licensees who are accountable for broadcast performance to private individuals who are not. The public interest would no longer be "paramount" but rather subordinate to private whim. . . . The congressional objective of balanced coverage of public issues would be seriously threatened.

Supreme Court decision in *Columbia Broadcasting System, Inc.* v. *Democratic National Committee*, 412 U.S. 94.

June 25, 1974 The clear implication has been that any such a compulsion to publish that which "'reason' tells them should not be published" is unconstitutional. A responsible press is an undoubtedly desirable goal, but press responsibility is not mandated by the Constitution and like many other virtues it cannot be legislated.

Supreme Court decision in *Miami Herald Publishing Co.* v. *Tornillo*, 418 U.S. 241.

appealed to the FCC, which ordered the station to give the time. On WGCB's refusal, the issue entered the courts, with the station losing at all levels, and eventually reached the Supreme Court of the United States. There, it was combined with another case, in which the Circuit Court of Appeals in Chicago had upheld the attempt of the Radio Television News Directors Association to modify or loosen the editorializing and personal attack rules which they thought had restricted broadcast journalism. The two opposing decisions helped make these cases a fit subject for Supreme Court adjudication. The *Red Lion Broadcasting Co.* v. *FCC* decision in June 1969 was the most important broadcast-related court decision since the 1943 network case (see 5.83). The court upheld the FCC's editorializing and personal attack rules and its right to enact a Fairness Doctrine, reaffirming the paramount importance of the listener or viewer under the 1934 Communications Act. In the early 1970s, two cases showed some limits to the Fairness Doctrine. The Business Executives Move for Peace in Vietnam (BEM) and the Democratic National Committee (DNC) tried separately to get broadcasters to sell them advertising time to comment on current issues of public importance. The broadcasters turned them down. In a 1973 decision, the Supreme Court upheld the commission's refusal to overturn broadcasters' judgment, suggesting that to allow such sales might undermine the licensees' decision making and responsibility for content aired over their stations.

The ostensible purpose of the Fairness Doctrine was to give the public access to more than one side of a controversial issue. Although a branch of the doctrine giving an individual who has been subject to a personal attack an opportunity to reply was codified into the FCC rules, most controversial issue cases have been

decided on their merits in accord with the principle that the public deserves to receive opposing views on controversial matters of public importance.

The FCC's decisions on controversial issue cases became increasingly involved and confusing to both broadcasters and the public. Many mistakenly thought that only the two most salient points of view on any given issue needed to be aired, or that carefully measured "equal time" was required, or that broadcasters should have no say in how different points of view were to be expressed. To help guide licensees, the FCC issued a primer in 1964, conducted a dialogue from 1971 through 1974 on all aspects of the doctrine, and issued a long public notice in 1974. Many still misunderstood what was required. Some critics complained that the doctrine was still too vague and that it involved government meddling in key areas of programming. They suggested that its requirements often kept broadcasters from doing any discussion of controversial issues for fear of having to defend themselves before the FCC. Communications attorney Jerome Barron, among others, believed that the public interest would be served better by unlimited *access* to the airwaves by all who want it than by *fairness* left in the hands of the broadcaster. Bills to abolish the Fairness Doctrine were often introduced, reverting to an absolute view of the First Amendment stricture that "Congress shall pass no law" in this area. Yet many others, notably members of minority groups, rely on the doctrine for the opportunity to air their views on controversial issues of public importance. A decade later, in the late 1980s, all of this debate had escalated substantially (see 10.82).

Although not part of the Fairness Doctrine as such, during the early and mid-1970s the FCC became active in supporting equal employment opportunity in the broadcasting industry, by requiring stations regularly to submit data on minority and female employment, and by considering such matters in comparative and license renewal hearings. The WLBT case (see 9.81), in fact, involved claims of discrimination against blacks, both in employment and in program content, as did the FCC's 1975 action refusing to renew the licenses of eight stations of the Alabama educational television network. The latter decision marked the first time a public television license had been lifted— though after extended litigation the chastened Alabama authority resumed control.

9•83   The Cable Conundrum

Although cable systems had provided limited television service—from one to three channels—to small communities since 1949 (see 8.24), their competition with television stations was not immediately apparent. In the late 1950s, broadcasters began to object seriously to cable picking broadcast programs off the air free and selling them to subscribers, with broadcast stations and program originators getting nothing for the use of their product. But there was little local or state regulation of cable until the early 1960s, and the FCC was contending that it could not federally regulate cable under the 1934 act because it was not a broadcasting service and was intrastate in nature.

In 1959, the FCC issued its first analysis of the relationship between CATV and broadcasting, focusing on three former UHF stations that claimed cable had helped force them off the air by not carrying their signals. Some leading cable operators pushed for federal regulation so as to avoid a confusion of local and state

rules, while others wished to maintain the local orientation of their industry. In a 1962 case, the commission decided to take limited regulatory control over systems that used microwave relay to bring in distant signals (beyond off-air pickup range) to the *head end*, and imposed carriage and non-duplication rules to protect broadcast licensees from economically damaging conditions.

In 1965 the FCC expanded its microwave rules to cover both intra- and inter-state systems, and required that they carry any television station within 60 miles when requested to, and that they refrain from showing the same shows from a distant station for 15 days before or after the local television station airing. Less than a year later, another order limited CATV growth in the country's top 100 markets by requiring such systems to get specific approval for carrying distant signals. This was based on the belief that both cable and UHF would grow best in urban areas, because of the density of the population and lower costs of reaching that audience and that, if cable were unrestricted, financially weak local UHF stations might be forced off the air. The likelihood that cable would serve only *parts* of a given urban area, certainly not for as many miles radius as a station, made it less in the public interest.

The Supreme Court upheld the FCC's authority to regulate cable if that authority was related in some way to the commission's statutory regulatory power over broadcasting in *Southwestern Cable Co. v. United States* (1968). The next year, the FCC proposed that cable systems with more than 3,500 subscribers be required to originate some programming over one of the six to eight channels they carried. Court challenges delayed the effective implementation of this order, and it was eventually dropped.

The so-called definitive FCC rules on cable appeared in 1972. Cable systems were freed to expand in the top 100 markets, although with restrictions on the number and kind of signals they could carry. They had to offer channels to municipal governments and educational institutions and provide access for members of the public with something to say. New systems had to have at least 20 channels and existing ones had to have them by 1977—although these requirements were later postponed. Systems in smaller markets could import fewer signals, as the popu-

lation was smaller and the harm to over-the-air local television stations might be greater. Older systems could continue to operate under the original, simpler regulations, but newer systems had to follow a maze of carriage and protection rules. Pay-TV over cable, which even by the late 1960s appeared more likely than pay-TV over the air, was officially permitted in the late 1960s. Specific rules on content, to prevent loss to over-the-air television of series programs and sporting events like the World Series, were included in the 1972 rules. Most of the restrictions were chal-

The Cable Regulatory Cycle / Unlike the much longer trek of broadcasting from virtually no regulation in the 1920s to pervasive regulation just a few years later, cable television passed from no regulation to severe restrictions—and back to virtually no regulation—in just under two decades. The later events on this chart are discussed in Chapter 10.

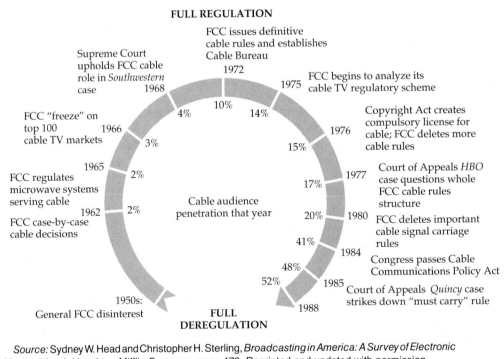

Source: Sydney W. Head and Christopher H. Sterling, *Broadcasting in America: A Survey of Electronic Media*, 5th ed. Houghton Mifflin Company, page 473. Reprinted and updated with permission. Copyright © 1987.

lenged, and the courts and the commission had dropped or modified many of them by 1977.

Yet, by 1977, the predicted cable revolution or "wired nation" was not happening. The downturn in the economy after the Vietnam War caused older systems to have increasing economic difficulties and discouraged expansion and construction of new systems. The largest cable MSO (multiple system operator), Tele-PrompTer, had serious reverses, and its president went to jail for bribing city officials to obtain a franchise. Expectations of the big cities becoming fertile markets for CATV were not borne out, and the "public access" channel did not take hold in New York, where it first was tried. Only a few "video freaks" and persons who wanted to see how far they could go with pornographic programming made full use of the channel, and the audience was tiny.

Although the cable industry gained friends by offering free service to 1974 political candidates, the operators claimed that the three-level regulatory situation—federal, state, and city or other local franchising authority—in some states was stifling development and asked that legislatures "shed a tier" of regulation. The 1972 requirements for 20-channel capacity and originating various services made starting and operating a cable system so expensive that a fair return seemed doubtful, particularly since many of the best potential markets, underserved by broadcast television, had already been wired. Cable adherents claimed that the FCC was restricting cable to protect broadcasting, while broadcasters objected to the lack of reimbursement from CATV's "unfair" use of their programs. By 1976, faced with this confusion, and beginning to reassess its whole cable regulatory approach, the FCC decided to postpone implementation of many 1972 rules, including rebuilding.

Congress had been holding hearings on revisions of the 1909 Copyright Law for years, with little result, and a firm decision on cable's copyright liability had to wait until the law was changed, which it was late in 1976, to take effect a year later. Since, under FCC rules from the late 1960s, television broadcasters could not own cable systems within their primary coverage area, the battle lines were drawn, and the NCTA and NAB could find little to agree upon—even when forced to "agree" on copyright liability and licensing under pressure from the FCC and the OTP. In the meantime, as seen in Appendix C, table 10, cable continued to expand slowly, but the wired city or nation was a long way away.

9•84   Who Shall Own the Stations?

Monopoly control of broadcasting became an important issue again in the 1960s. The major concern was over the control of television stations, because they attracted by far the largest audience and showed up consistently as the major source of news. The slowly increasing power of group owners—firms, not networks, owning stations in several different markets—became apparent to Congress and the FCC by the early 1960s. Revived fears of newspaper dominance of broadcasting led to denial of one license renewal and new rules to keep television networks from controlling any CATV systems or local stations from controlling cable systems in the station's coverage area. The Justice Department intervened in several "concentration of control" cases. Whether or not a changing cast of commissioners was willing to go so far is uncertain, but the trend was toward "one station to a customer." Complicating these issues after

1970, members of minority groups became increasingly vocal about their lack of media ownership.

The commission's first major move, in 1965, was to propose that ownership of television stations in the top 50 markets be limited to three, only two of which could be VHF. Rather than promulgate such a rule, the FCC proceeded case by case, but it waived the proposed rule in every case and finally killed the idea early in 1968. That year (1965), however, the FCC implemented a new comparative license procedure for use when two or more applicants desired the same broadcast channel. Key criteria were the applicant's capacity to attune to local concerns, to favor local control rather than group ownership, to avoid connections with local newspapers or other broadcast stations. Unlike the 50-market ruling, this procedure was upheld on court review as was the requirement that licensees survey the public and community leaders in order to ascertain the community's needs.

A cold wind blew on broadcasters in 1969 when the FCC voted not to allow the *Herald Traveler* newspaper to retain the license for WHDH, channel 5 in Boston, apparently on grounds of cross-media ownership. Although technically the action stemmed back to the original 1957 grant for the station, which had been challenged because of *ex parte* contacts (which were later termed the "$100,000,000 lunch" by author Sterling Quinlan) and remanded by a court to the FCC for reconsideration, most broadcasters felt that their own licenses now were insecure, no matter how well the station had been programmed or for how long. In 1972, after appeals failed, the *Herald Traveler* gave up channel 5 to an independent, locally owned consortium and soon went out of the newspaper business, keeping only a radio station. It was a convincing demonstration of the importance of television to the financial well-being of a newspaper-station combination. The new licensee of channel 5, operating as WCVB, demonstrated something else: programming many hours of locally produced programs a day can be profitable.

The unique WHDH decision not only shocked the industry, it also increased the number of petitions to deny renewal and caused many licensees to fear renewal time—once a simple formality. Their reaction led to FCC concern, triggered by congressional pressure, about the economic and psychological stability of the industry. As a result, it ill-advisedly issued a public notice early in 1970 on comparative broadcast proceedings, stating that the incumbent licensee would be relicensed every three years *unless* its programming and public service could be shown to have been less than adequate. Until such showing was made, competing applicants would not be considered. Most of the industry naturally liked this idea, but newly vitalized public interest groups and law firms protested. They claimed that the ruling was against the intent of the 1934 act, since it essentially gave indefinite licenses to incumbents. The Court of Appeals for the District of Columbia overturned the FCC proposal within a year, leaving some confusion, since the commission had repeatedly said that WHDH would *not* be a precedent. Parallel developments helped dispel the confusion to some degree.

In April 1968, the FCC initiated a rule-making docket on ownership during the hearings on which it would consider most of the arguments and controversies. The commission adopted a one-to-a-customer rule in 1970, prohibiting common control of more than a single AM, FM, or television station in the same market. Since many major market operations were

based on full or partial AM-FM-TV combinations, existing combinations could be
retained until the stations were sold. AM-
FM combinations could continue, but
radio-television combinations had to be
divested when sold.

In 1970 the commission undertook
a long rule-making procedure concerning
newspaper-broadcast station cross-ownership in the same market (see 5.83). Early
in 1975, a rule was issued essentially
grandfathering the many existing cross-
media combinations, but requiring divestiture in several small markets where the
only paper and the only broadcast station
were under common ownership (see
10.85).

9•85   Self-Regulation and Citizen Action

The broadcasting industry after
1960 faced the worst heat in its history.
While most viewers and listeners were satisfied with their program fare, many public service and special interest groups pressured the broadcasting industry to change
its ways in respect to advertising, especially in commercials for children, amount
of advertising time, and types of products
advertised; program violence; ownership
patterns; access for minority views and talent; portrayal of various ethnic and religious groups; and minority and female
employment. It was not an easy time to be
a defender of broadcasting.

Much of television's public relations effort was shouldered by the Television Information Office (see 8.85), which
continually issued reports, analyses,
newspaper editorial reprints, slide presentations extolling American television, and
its well-known survey series on what the
public thought about television and other
media (see 9.71). TIO's parent, the
National Association of Broadcasters, was

affected by internal dissension caused by
the wide range of broadcasting services,
viewpoints, and goals. After the death of
a broadcaster-president, the NAB tried to
achieve political visibility by replacing him
in 1961 with former Florida governor
LeRoy Collins. Collins was a man of con-
victions, and his sympathetic view of those
who would limit cigarette advertising and
other issues brought him powerful enemies within NAB, and a relatively short
tenure as president. He was succeeded by
NAB staff member Vincent Wasilewski,
whom the membership liked more,
although while he was in office NAB lost
many campaigns before the public and
Congress. It fought hard against the ban
on cigarette advertising and lost heavily,
since even the tobacco companies knew it
was time to quit and had retired grace-
fully—and profitably, since advertising
costs went down and sales remained
steady—leaving broadcasters holding the
bag. The association then focused on
lengthening the broadcast license period
to five years and presuming that a license
would be renewed unless there were
strong reasons for refusing it. That campaign had not borne fruit by the end of
this period. The NAB may have raised the
First Amendment flag too often—every
time somebody suggested the smallest
change in American commercial broadcasting. As congressional committees tired
of this line, the increasingly vocal minority
and public interest groups became more
effective.

NAB had to become defensive.
The radio and television codes were frequently revised, but the revisions usually
weakened them—except in instances
where Congress had shown that tighten-
ing of standards was politically essential.
The most serious problem was that the
codes had no teeth. A station that violated
their provisions only lost its right to show

the code seal—surely a doubtful deterrent. Such long-banned products as personal hygiene products and hemorrhoid
treatments found their way onto the
nation's screens and loudspeakers as commercial standards came down in the wake
of the cigarette advertising decision and
the economic recession of the 1970s.

An example of the "Catch 22"
problem in self-regulation arose in the
1975–1976 "Family Viewing Time" case.
Although accounts differ (and those differences became very important), apparently FCC Chairman Wiley strongly
encouraged the networks and the NAB to
institute a policy of limiting violence in
programs telecast before 9 P.M. (8 P.M. in the
Central and Mountain zones). Then-CBS
President Arthur Taylor championed this
move, and the industry climbed on the
bandwagon—except for the West Coast
package companies making about 80 percent of all television programs. Led by producer Norman Lear, they claimed that
Wiley had violated the First Amendment
by advocating such a provision in the NAB
code, that the networks had violated the
antitrust laws by agreeing to it, and that,
even more important to the packagers, it
cut into their potential revenues from syndication, as programs deemed violent and
played on the networks only after 9 P.M.
were similarly limited when played on
local stations adhering to the NAB code.
The program packagers took the issue to
court. Late in 1976, a federal district judge
in Los Angeles ruled that the "Family
Viewing Time" self-regulatory rules were
mainly due to excessive behind-the-scenes
pressure from the FCC on the networks
and the NAB. The decision, a long and
important one, was appealed, but it put
the whole self-regulatory process in doubt
when it said that an industry's attempt to
self-censor all its members was unfair,
regardless of the purpose. Each licensee

had to make its own final decisions on
programming.

Making NAB's job tremendously
harder were the new activist groups concerned with broadcasting. They had
gained impetus from FCC commissioner
Nicholas Johnson, who, in his 1966–1973
term, had called for reforms and greater
public input into broadcasting decisions.
While listening groups had existed since
the 1930s, few had made an impact on
broadcasters or the general public. One of
the most active of the new breed of public
interest groups in the 1960s was one of the
oldest—the Office of Communications of
the United Church of Christ. It was the
prime mover in the Jackson, Mississippi
(WLBT) case (see 9.81), which helped open
the regulatory process to public input. It
continued to be active in other license
cases, in studying the role of minority hiring in broadcasting, and in putting out
useful publications on how to get the public involved in radio and television.

After several years of effective
grassroots action, Action for Children's
Television (see 9.72) forced NAB code
changes on commercialism and violence
and an FCC hearing on the topic, and
found funding for research studies. In the
mid-1970s, ACT began to create local community groups with the same goals. The
National Citizen's Committee for Broadcasting (NCCB), originally a public broadcasting support group in New York in the
late 1960s, under ex-commissioner Johnson moved to Washington in 1974, started
a bi-weekly magazine (access) and began to
seek active input into broadcast decision-
making by connecting local groups with
public service law firms, sources of financial support and necessary information.
Other nonbroadcast-oriented national
groups—from the American Medical
Association to the Parent-Teacher Association—became interested in, commented

upon, and even, in the case of the PTA, threatened a boycott of advertisers' products because of violence on television.

Many smaller groups concentrated on the employment and the portrayal of women in television and radio; ethnic programming—usually working to remove such negative images as *The Untouchables* (Italian-Americans), the television version of *Amos 'n' Andy* (blacks), the "Frito Bandito" commercials (Mexican-Americans); and blacks in broadcast ownership and programming. This last cause was aided in 1972 with the appointment of black Benjamin Hooks to the FCC (see 9.81). Many of these groups were very activist, applying for a license up for renewal or petitioning for its denial in order to get the broadcaster's attention, and then bargaining for whatever the group wanted, such as employment or more programming time. The beleaguered broadcasters thought of this as blackmail, but it was effective— although the FCC warned that the broadcaster could not delegate his authority to decide what should be aired. Broadcasting became a battleground of lobbyists, advocates, and pressure groups—all somewhat encouraged by the courts, a more open FCC, foundation-supported national organizations, and foundations themselves such as Markle and Ford.

Another factor, if only as a yardstick or precept, was the loosely organized groups of listener-supported radio stations—the Pacifica stations in Berkeley, Los Angeles, New York, and Houston; the "KRAB Nebula" stations, and some very independent independents in Seattle, San Jose, San Francisco, Dallas, St. Louis, Yellow Springs, and elsewhere. Several of these were established or otherwise nurtured by Lorenzo Milam, who put a substantial financial legacy and much time into many of these stations. His philosophy is best expressed in *Sex and Broadcast-*

ing, a handbook on how to start a community radio station that poses seldom asked questions about the purpose of broadcasting.

Of particular interest were the first feeble attempts toward increased professionalism and self-policing by newsmen, both broadcast and print. In the late 1960s spurred by overt antagonism toward the press at the Democratic National Convention in Chicago in 1968 and by the Nixon administration's attacks on the media, several journalism reviews were established. These ranged from the prestigious *Columbia Journalism Review* to infrequently published magazines in a dozen other cities, and provided a much-needed public washing of dirty linen as well as seminars on journalistic ethics. Journalism had no professional organization with the prestige and moral authority to establish and *enforce* a code of ethics in the way that law and medicine policed their memberships, although the Radio Television News Directors Association and the Society of Professional Journalists/Sigma Delta Chi tried. Accordingly, attempts were made, with foundation help, to establish a national "press council," the National News Council, to adjudicate claims of unfairness made against broadcasting and the printed press. Some of the complaining groups, such as Accuracy in Media, and individual complainants were vulnerable to charges of bias themselves, but most wanted to improve the social responsibility of the media.

9•9   The Impact of Broadcasting (1960–1976)

Broadcasting, despite its growing diversity in programming, brought the nation together from time to time. Most of these occasions were tragic, such as the assassinations of John F. Kennedy, Martin Luther King, Jr., and Robert F. Kennedy, and the resignation of Richard M. Nixon. But, more positively, in 1969 most of mankind watched Neil Armstrong step onto the moon.

9•91   Crises for Media Competing with Television

Television, it must be remembered, had captured the entertainment function of the mass media almost completely by 1960. Motion pictures had felt the pinch in the 1950s and, until the networks began heavy use of feature films in the early 1960s, the film industry was surviving on a few blockbuster films, a few dependable stars, and by making television programs. Most television series were shot on film in Hollywood as well as many of the "made for television" feature films (see 9.63), which were developing in the late 1960s. Although there was a new generation of moviegoers, and films for them, much of Hollywood's income in the early 1970s came from prime-time network showings of recent movies. Still, unemployment in the creative trade unions in Hollywood was so high that the Nixon administration condemned the increasing use of reruns on television, which limited the need for original program material. In spite of this threat to the networks, Hollywood remained television-dominated, in both ownership and output. The independent producers—often successful directors or stars who could convince the banks that they were a good risk for a production loan—continued to turn out more important films than the major studios, although the surviving majors made enough nota-

ble blockbusters to cover the costs of less successful films.

Magazines felt the full brunt of television in the 1960s. The once popular *Colliers* died in 1957. By the mid-1960s, the *Saturday Evening Post* was in deep economic and editorial trouble, and after publishing bi-weekly for several years, the Curtis Publishing Company stopped publishing it in 1969. Many people said that television had stolen the audience for the mixture of fiction and fact that had made the *Post* a popular giant for over four decades. Then the two major picture magazines, which had started within a year of each other in the mid-1930s, ceased publication within a year of each other three decades later. *Look* went first, followed in 1971 by *Life*. The circulation was there nearly till the end, but advertisers had lost confidence in national general circulation magazines and thought that television would do them more good at less cost. Some national magazines tried to appeal more to advertisers by not renewing subscribers in poorer rural counties, much as CBS had killed its rural-oriented programs in 1971 (see 9.63), but to no avail. Magazines became specialized, with the *Reader's Digest* being the only general circulation non-newsweekly magazine to survive into the mid-1970s. *TV Guide*, with its many regional editions and 1977 weekly circulation of approximately 20 million, was the nation's most popular magazine.

Newspapers faced increasing economic problems, only partly caused by radio and television taking away their late-breaking news role—the "extra" edition had virtually disappeared by the end of the 1950s—and television taking much of the entertainment function. In city after city, dailies died—New York's seven metropolitan dailies of 1961 had shrunk to three by 1968—generally to the benefit of advertisers who with one or two papers could cover the audience that once had been split among many. The soaring demands by labor unions, justifiably worried over technological unemployment, and the escalating costs of newsprint discouraged many publishers and investors. Business-oriented publishers raised their papers' daily price to readers and advertisers and then, as circulation and net profits dropped, killed them off or merged them. Some new suburban dailies and weeklies bucked this trend.

The increasing media competition and the corollary cost rise contributed to a trend to media conglomerates in the 1961–1976 period, particularly in the book publishing industry, which had been generally removed from group ownership in the past. By the mid-1970s, several media empires had major holdings in print and broadcast media and often in film as well. It was argued that it took economies of scale to meet competition from other huge media empires, demands of large advertising agencies, inflation, and the costs of labor. The cost was loss of diversity in content, fewer outlets for advertising of new products or services unable to meet the price, and fewer jobs.

9•92   Television around the World

Two major developments were the coming of color and the use of communications satellites for news transmissions (see 9.1 and 9.64). By the 1970s, most of the developed nations of the world had color television. Unfortunately, three systems were in competition for adoption: the American NTSC, the German PAL, and France's SECAM. The Western Hemisphere and Japan adopted the U.S. standard; Great Britain and most of Western Europe adopted the German system; and France, the USSR, and much of Eastern Europe, partly for political reasons, took the French system. Great Britain began color transmissions late in 1967. Canada had begun the year before, although an estimated 50,000 Canadian sets had been tuned to colorcasts from south of the border before this. Japan and other Far Eastern countries quickly became the major sources for the world's television receivers. By the 1970s, more television sets were in use outside the United States than in it.

Transistors and then integrated circuits made radios smaller and more rugged, and their low cost and lack of need for power lines brought domestic broadcasting to many underdeveloped countries for the first time. Radio's low cost and ready access to rural areas made it a widespread ingredient in successful developmental communication in Africa, Latin America, and Asia. Developing nations that introduced television frequently supported it by advertising, and typically placed a single station in the capital city more for prestige and the pleasure of the ruling elite than for service to the public. American television programs and radio shows were popular, but toward the end of this period some countries established regulations limiting the showing of foreign import programs in order to protect their own artists, industry, and cultural independence. Even Canada passed strong laws to limit U.S. television advertising, programs, and other media influences that were considered harmful to the Canadian culture and media industry. Because of the language difference, Mexico was not as directly affected as Anglophone parts of Canada by U.S. stations. Indeed, Mexico had by the late 1960s become a major program source for the rest of Latin America and even for Spanish-language television stations in the United States.

9•93   Period Overview

As the title of this chapter suggests, this 15-year period saw more evolution than revolution for the media. FM radio and cable television grew to importance. Yet, at the same time, commercial television and AM radio also continued to grow. Public (formerly educational) broadcasting became a matter of national policy and achieved national impact for the first time. UHF and pay-TV continued as discussion topics, although diminished in importance.

Major issues in the 1960s and 1970s included financing of public broadcasting, the amount of advertising on both radio and television, the content of ads specifically aimed at children, violent program content, bias or suspected bias in

---

Key Broadcasting Indicators: 1965 / This is the eighth of twelve tables offering comparable information over a 60-year period (to 1985), presented at five-year intervals. Sources for items 1–6 and 11 are the tables in Appendix C, while other information comes from sources indicated below. Most data are for January 1.

Indicators	AM	FM	TV
1. Number of commercial stations	4,019	1,270	569
2. Number of noncommercial stations	ca 25	255	99
3. Total stations on the air	4,044	1,525	668
4. Number of network-affiliated stations	1,302	na	516
5. Percentage of commercial stations affiliated with networks	32%	na	91%
6. Total industry revenue (add 000,000)	$917	$25	$2,515
7. One-hour station rate (New York)	$600	na	$10,200
8. One-minute station rate (New York)	$175	na	$3,000
9. One-hour network rate, evening	$12,587	na	$146,400
10. Number of broadcasting employees	.... 62,207		47,753
11. Percentage of families with sets	97%	ca 40%	93%
12. Broadcasting regulatory budget (FCC)	.... $16,911,000		
13. Total FCC personnel	.... 1,502		

Notes (see Appendix D for full citations)

na = not applicable or not available

7–8. WNBC radio and television stations in New York.

9. NBC radio (209 affiliates) and television (197 affiliates) networks.

10. Radio figure covers both AM and FM stations and networks. Lichty and Topping (1975), page 290, table 23.

12–13. FCC figures for fiscal year 1965, ending June 30.

broadcast journalism, responsibility for regulating broadcasting, political influence in the regulatory process, the increasing potential of cable television, all the issues surrounding the Fairness Doctrine, economic—and political and social class—concentration of ownership in broadcasting and other media, and a gnawing concern that broadcasting would serve the public's needs better if the public would express some interest. Few of these issues were clearly resolved by 1976, as the number of "players" in the broadcast issues arena and the economic stakes kept increasing.

The era began with an obvious major change in the FCC, as it went from years of complacency and even acquiescence to a period of strong regulatory activity. Relatively few issues were decided, however; diversity and confusion typically won out over clear-cut decisions and trends.

Key Broadcasting Indicators: 1970 / This is the ninth of twelve tables offering comparable information over a 60-year period (to 1985), presented at five-year intervals. Sources for items 1–6 and 11 are the tables in Appendix C, while other information comes from sources indicated below. Most data are for January 1.

Indicators	AM	FM	TV
1. Number of commercial stations	4,267	2,184	677
2. Number of noncommercial stations	ca 25	413	185
3. Total stations on the air	4,292	2,597	862
4. Number of network-affiliated stations	2,165*	na	568
5. Percentage of commercial stations affiliated with networks	50%*	na	84%
6. Total industry revenue (add 000,000)	$1,308	$85	$3,596
7. One-hour station rate (New York)	na	na	na
8. One-minute station rate (New York)	$200	na	$6,000 [30 sec]
9. One-hour network rate, evening	$1,450	na	$163,600
10. Number of broadcasting employees	65,000	6,100	58,425
11. Percentage of families with sets	98%	74%	95%
12. Broadcasting regulatory budget (FCC)	. . . . $24,562,000		
13. Total FCC personnel	. . . . 1,537		

Notes (see Appendix D for full citations)

na = not applicable or not available

4–5. *The increase in radio network affiliates was due to the 1968 inception of four ABC networks. While one was for FM stations, a separate FM figure is not shown here as many FM stations were affiliated with other networks. There is no consistent source for such information.

7. By this time, station rate cards seldom listed such a price. Full hours were sold only by special arrangement.

8. WNBC radio and television stations, New York.

9. NBC radio (220 affiliates) and television (215 affiliates) networks.

10. Radio figures cover both AM and FM stations, and networks. Lichty and Topping (1975), page 290, table 23.

12–13. FCC figures for fiscal year 1970, ending June 30.

Further Reading

Good contemporary views of broadcasting in this period are found in Summers and Summers (1966 and 1978), Head (1972 and 1976), Mayer's 1972 discussion of television issues and problems, and Cole's 1970 collection of 69 articles from *TV Guide*. Other works based on that weekly publication are Harris's 1978 collection of material from the magazine's first 25 years and Johnson's 1979 author and subject index. Two wide-ranging anthologies reflecting controversies and problems are White and Averson and Skornia and Kitson (both 1968). The one-volume history of television by Barnouw (1975) covers a lot of this period. Development of cable is related in Smith (1972) and Le Duc (1973), while early pay-TV schemes are described in Kamen (1973). The early rise of the VCR is best told in Lardner (1987). The inception of HBO is related in Mair (1988).

Key Broadcasting Indicators: 1975 / This is the tenth of twelve tables offering comparable information over a 60-year period (to 1985), presented at five-year intervals. Sources for items 1–6 and 11 are the tables in Appendix C, while other information comes from sources indicated below. Most data are for January 1.

Indicators	AM	FM	TV
1. Number of commercial stations	4,407	2,636	711
2. Number of noncommercial stations	ca 25	717	241
3. Total stations on the air	4,432	3,353	952
4. Number of network-affiliated stations	2,458	na	617
5. Percentage of commercial stations affiliated with networks	55%	na	87%
6. Total industry revenue (add 000,000)	$1,980	$309	$5,263
7. One-hour station rate (New York)	na	na	$10,700
8. One-minute station rate (New York)	$250	na	$6,000 [30 sec]
9. One-hour network rate, evening	$1,600	na	$163,615
10. Number of broadcasting employees	68,800	12,900	62,300
11. Percentage of families with sets	98%	na	97%
12. Broadcasting regulatory budget (FCC)	.... $46,759,000		
13. Total FCC personnel	.... 2,022		

Notes

na = not applicable or not available.

4–5. The great increase in radio network affiliates was due to the continued expansion of the four (post-1968) ABC radio networks. While one of those was for FM stations, a separate FM figure is not shown as such stations were increasingly affiliated with all networks. A consistent source for such data is lacking.

7. Full hours were sold only by special arrangement.

8. WNBC radio and television stations in New York.

9. NBC radio (232 affiliates) and television (219 affiliates) networks.

12–13. FCC fiscal year figures for 1975, ending June 30.

Broadcast management in this era is described in Quaal and Brown (1975), television business practices are discussed in Roe (1964), and changes in radio are evident by comparing Reinsch and Ellis (1960) with Johnson and Jones (1972). A good review of network developments is found in Bergreen (1980)—for CBS, see Paley (1979) and the more insightful biography of him by Paper (1987). Quinlan (1979) offers an informal history of ABC. A scholarly analysis of the economic constraints and policy concerns in television is in Noll, Peck, and McGowan (1973). Television commercials are treated in historical fashion in Barnouw (1978), while Diamant reviews the first decade of network commercials (1971) and studies in-depth production of a specific commercial (1970). Two anthologies of the best commercials, combining pictures, scripts, and supporting text, are Price (1978) and Hall (1984), both of which range over many years. Arlen (1980) offers insightful critiques. Sterling (1984) provides statistics.

Koenig and Hill (1967) assesses educational television on the eve of great change, while the first Carnegie Commission report (1967) is crucial to an understanding of that transition to public broadcasting. Macy (1974) discusses the early years and problems of public television development, while the annual reports of the Corporation for Public Broadcasting (1970–1975) are valuable in tracing trends. An assessment of the difficult Nixon administration–public broadcasting relationship is found in Stone (1985). Schramm, et al. (1963) is the first national study of the educational television audience.

There is a wealth of material on television programming—see pages 314–315 for the major pictorial and reference books. Overviews of television in this period include Brown's 1971 discussion of a television season from a network point of view; Owen, Beebe, and Manning's 1974 economic study of the program business; Cantor's 1972 study of the role of the Hollywood television producer; Miller and Rhode's funny but true story of the trials of getting a show on the air (1964); and a collection of critical pieces in *The Eighth Art* (1962). The annual "Fall Preview" issues of *TV Guide* give an excellent sense of the new shows each year.

Books on specific types of television program are increasingly common. See Rose (1985) for the best single survey of television genres. The television serial drama or soap opera is placed in context best in Stedman (1977), while popular historical treatments are found in the books by LaGuardia (1983) and Schemering (1985). Three books providing insight into the appeal of that genre include Cantor and Pingree (1983), Allen (1985), and the content analyses in Cassatta and Skill (1983). A study of adult female characters in prime-time television is in Meehan (1983). Science-fiction programs, popular in this period, are described and illustrated in Gerani and Schulman (1977) and in the two books about the original *Star Trek* television series, Whitfield and Roddenberry (1968) and Gerrold (1973), both of which give good insight into the process and problems of developing network shows. The situation comedy is traced season by season in Mitz (1980), while specific episode data for 153 series are found in Eisner and Krinsky (1984). Adler (1979) assesses the top comedy show of the period, *All in the Family*. The development and operation of the television game show is told in Fabe (1979), while a directory of movies made for television (beginning in 1964) is found in Marill (1984). The television series of two specific production firms have been chronicled: Warner Brothers in Woolley, et al. (1985) and Universal in Perry (1983).

Children's television is reviewed season by season in text and pictures in Fischer (1983), along economic and content-analysis lines in Turow (1981), and in definitive detail by series in the two volumes by Woolery (1983 and 1985). The symbiotic relationship of television and professional sports is explored in Johnson (1971) and in Sugar (1978), which deals with the special role played by ABC Sports.

Television journalism is amply covered with descriptive and critical works. Barrett (1969–1980, eight volumes) is an excellent survey of annual developments. Gates (1978) describes changes in CBS news. Bluem (1965) and Hammond (1981) tell the story of the television documentary through 1975. Epstein (1973) is a reasoned assessment of behind-the-scenes factors in television news, balanced to some degree by Small (1970), a network executive's viewpoint. Coverage of the Vietnam War on television is the topic of several books: MacDonald (1985) reviews television coverage of the military *before* the war; Hallin (1986) provides a content analysis of television coverage from 1965 to 1973; and Braestrup (1977) gives a detailed analysis of television and print coverage of the Tet offensive of 1968. Political broadcasting is covered in Chester (1969), Gilbert (1972), and MacNeil (1968) and in McGinniss's classic account of the 1968 "selling" of Richard Nixon (1969). Minow, et al. (1973) assesses the use of television by presidents once in power. Diamond and Bates (1988) reviews the rise of the television political spot. Two books cover the role of media in the Watergate affair—Lang and Lang (1983) and Lashner (1984), the latter specifically dealing with television coverage, limitations, and "chilling" effects.

Material on the television audience is more limited. Beville (1988) traces changing methods and findings. Steiner (1963)

and Bower (1973) provide useful contrasting national survey reports done a decade apart. Glick and Levy (1962) suggests useful points on viewing habits and audience types. Reports of the various studies of television violence include the official report of the Surgeon General's committee (1972), Cater and Strickland (1975), and Rowland (1983), the latter two providing reviews of the political process behind the research, and the National Institute of Mental Health (1982).

Regulatory issues are covered in Johnson's 1970 guide for consumer activists; Levin's 1971 description of allocation issues and options; Emery (1971), which is a broad text survey; the first edition of Krasnow and Longley (1973); and Jones's casebook (1976). Cole and Oettinger (1978) gives a sense of pre-deregulation FCC operations, while Graham and Kramer (1976) tells the controversial story of FCC nominations and their congressional approvals. The Fairness Doctrine is reviewed in Simmons (1978) and Rowan (1984). A novel-like telling of the "Red Lion" case is found in Friendly (1976). The best history of early cable regulation is Le Duc (1973). Material on ownership is found in Compaine, et al. (1982); Rucker (1968); Baer, et al. (1974), reviewing research on the topic; Cherington, Hirsch, and Brandwein (1971); and Seiden (1974), the latter two providing more industry-oriented viewpoints. Quinlan (1974) tells the story of the WHDH decision.

World broadcasting is described in Unesco (1964 and 1975); world television patterns are discussed in Green (1972) and Dizard (1966). Emery (1969) is a pioneering survey of radio and television in selected countries. Smith (1973) provides a good comparison of several European broadcasting systems and how they came to be that way. Broadcasting in Africa is detailed in Head (1974), while Paulu (1967 and

1974) discusses broadcasting in Europe. British broadcasting is well covered: Briggs (1986) takes the story of the BBC to 1972; Sendall (1982 and 1983) relates the development of commercial television; the annual handbooks of both the BBC and IBA are invaluable; and Harris (1970) describes the rise of pirate stations. Peers (1969 and 1979) discusses the rise of Canadian broadcasting.

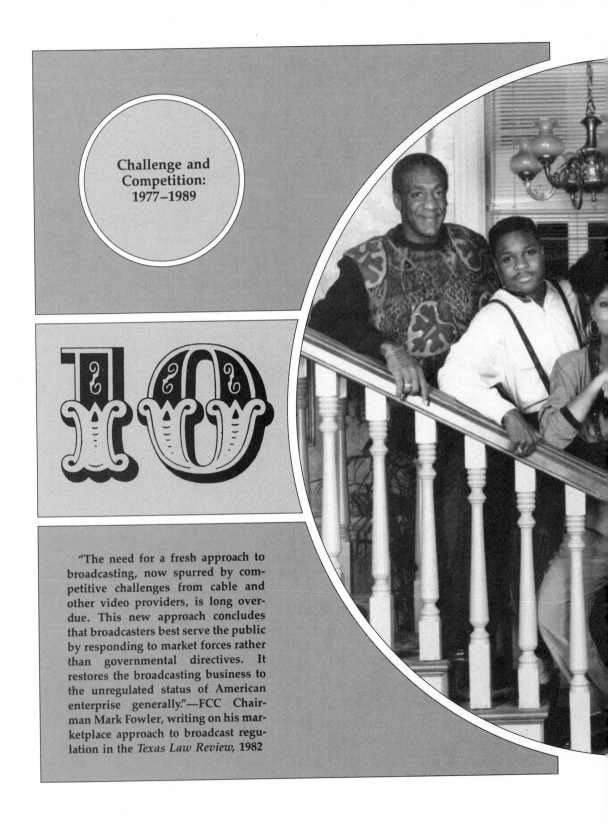

Challenge and Competition: 1977–1989

10

"The need for a fresh approach to broadcasting, now spurred by competitive challenges from cable and other video providers, is long overdue. This new approach concludes that broadcasters best serve the public by responding to market forces rather than governmental directives. It restores the broadcasting business to the unregulated status of American enterprise generally."—FCC Chairman Mark Fowler, writing on his marketplace approach to broadcast regulation in the *Texas Law Review,* 1982

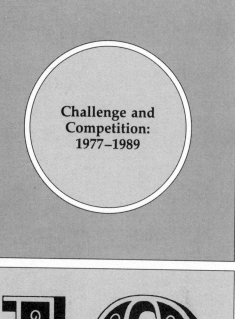

10

"No one doubted five years ago that
. . . television would be altered quite
drastically in this decade. Cable had
already exceeded 30 percent penetration and HBO . . . was being spoken
of as the likely fourth network. . . .
Although no one can deny the impact
of these technologies, the sweeping
predictions about their inevitable
progress were, as it turns out, overly
optimistic. . . . Few of the early promises of the new media have been realized." —Television critic Les Brown,
summing up the mid-1980s in *Channels Field Guide 1987*

Jimmy Carter took office as the 39th President of the United States at the beginning of 1977. His decision to walk the length of Pennsylvania Avenue during his inaugural ceremonies made for exciting television. A few weeks later, wearing a sweater and seated next to a White House fireplace, he appeared in an informal televised "fireside chat" much like those of President Roosevelt on radio four decades earlier. Carter tried to appear new and folksy at the same time—promising a continuation of past Democratic philosophy with few changes in government operation. In contrast, just over a decade later, as Ronald Reagan ended his two terms and George Bush took office, the relationships of government and business (including the industry

Outline:
Challenge and Competition 1977–1988

of broadcasting) that the United States had known for most of the twentieth century had undergone drastic changes as a result of rapid technological innovation combined with adoption of radical economic and political ideological views.

Increasingly after 1980, broadcasting's institutions were challenged more than in any other period discussed so far in this volume. Technological innovations and competitive pressures that began to develop in the late 1970s forced broadcasters to adjust to an evolving—and soon mostly deregulated—marketplace of communication. For the first time, nonbroadcast electronic media began to dictate the direction of traditional over-the-air broadcasting. The dramatic changes that became

increasingly evident in the 1980s had been gestating for years, as noted in chapter 9. As with most revolutions, however, these changes seemed to come—or we became aware of them—suddenly and often in combination, and they began to alter drastically the role of "broadcasting."

Perhaps these shifts were exacerbated by changes in the cast of characters. Manufacturing moved overseas. The young veterans who had returned from World War II to go into broadcasting were now contemplating the ends of their careers, and the first generation of broadcasters from the 1920s and 1930s had long since stepped down. Broadcasting was becoming a commodity, something to be bought or sold rather than a calling or a profession—and this attitude, reflected in the enrollment growth of business and law schools, fit right in with a growing trend toward economic conservatism in Washington.

The era covered in this chapter can be divided into two periods by the year 1980. The 1977–1980 period (the Carter years) marks a kind of calm before the storm. There was the excitement and uncertainty of widespread predictions about the possible demise of broadcasting as a result of the proposed introduction of as yet experimental new services such as broadband cable with unlimited capacity (the "wired city" concept) and direct broadcast satellites. Still, even though there were some initial moves toward deregulation, broadcasting largely continued operating as it had before, ignoring promised but not yet practical new competitors.

Indeed, some would argue that broadcasting stood at the peak of its performance on the eve of its 60th anniversary in 1980. Certainly, that year marked a gap in, if not an end to, the straight line of growth that had started in the 1920s. Before 1980, much of television was still run by the station and network leaders who had helped to develop it and who still believed broadcasting had a concern with, and continuing responsibility to serve in, the public interest. The FCC continued to play a strong role in regulating broadcasting, despite the start of deregulation when Charles Ferris became chairman in early 1977. Only after 1980 did the long-promised new technologies begin to make a real difference. The increasing penetration of cable and videocassette recorders (VCRs) made these technologies a part of everyday life for their audiences, with both in more than half the country's households by 1987 (see 10.7). At the same time, under Reagan-appointed commissioners, the FCC began to back away—and then run—from decades of public interest regulation, relying on the politically popular (in a conservative administration) but unproven theory that marketplace competitive pressures would regulate broadcasting and other electronic media for the public good.

The changes that technology and the deregulators brought about after 1980 require a broader definition of such traditional terms as "broadcasting," "network," and "local station." "Broadcasting" has become a generic reference to any electronic means of delivering entertainment and information-news content to consumers, while the term "network" no longer is restricted to a system in which local affiliates have to present the same content at the same time. In addition, delivery of programming of affiliates now is almost entirely by space communications satellite rather than terrestrial wires or microwave relays. And "local station," by the 1980s, includes cable systems and other small-area distribution channels as well as individual stations. To members of the public, of course, the way a program reaches them is of little importance.

As this chapter will show, the expansion of delivery options and new economic pressures had substantial impact on the industry. However, programs—the content of broadcasting—were little changed (with rare exceptions), although they were subject to ever-tighter budget limitations. Alterations in broadcasting were not unique. They were occurring against a background of change elsewhere. For example, the once tightly regulated airline industry was thrown on its own competitive resources after 1978. This led to a mix of lower prices but often far poorer service from a lot of new, merged, and often short-lived airline companies, most trying to skim the cream of large market service, ignoring or overcharging many intervening cities and changing prices so rapidly that even travel agencies' computers had difficulty keeping track. The potential for deregulation of broadcasting and telecommunications services often was compared to the hypothetical and presumed benefits of a more competitive airline market, but the public was not as aware of all of the ramifications of this change.

The biggest telecommunications industry story of the early 1980s started when the Justice Department moved against AT&T with an antitrust suit in 1974, a case that finally went to trial in 1981. However, early in 1982, AT&T and the Justice Department settled out of court, subjecting AT&T and its operating companies to the continuing supervision of federal judge Harold Greene. The Bell System was broken up, with AT&T divested of its local, regulated operating companies and freed—in part—to engage in new, often unregulated ventures in the information and computer fields. The operating companies were reorganized at the beginning of 1984 into seven independently owned regional holding firms. The most radical changes insofar as consumers were concerned were in how they now obtained telephones (generally by purchase), chose a long-distance carrier (where there had been little choice before 1980, now AT&T competed with lower-cost firms like MCI and Sprint), and paid their increasingly complicated phone bills. This restructuring of what had been one of the largest institutions on earth, and a paragon of technological efficiency, was thought by many to be another indicator of fundamental changes in the American economic system, which was becoming service oriented rather than manufacturing oriented, harder to enter against entrenched firms, and subject to many formal and informal controls because of worldwide influences. Broadcasters and cable operators alike kept a wary eye on this now partially unshackled colossus that might at any moment try to move back into the field it had left in 1926 (see 3.23).

10•1   New Technologies

The years since World War II have been marked by an accelerating pace of technological change in most fields. Cycles of innovation have shortened because of the competitive pressure to market new ideas before someone else does. Sometimes shoddy "novelty" has been substituted for progress, leading to equipment designed to be thrown away by the consumer and replaced rather than repaired; sometimes bold new products have been embraced by the public. Yet the same competitive pressure can harm technological progress in the long run. In 1987, for example, under pressure to increase its short-term profits, CBS closed its research labs in Connecticut, where Peter Gold-

mark had developed CBS's early color television and LP record projects in the 1940s. RCA's David Sarnoff Research Center in Princeton, deemed unnecessary by its new owner, General Electric, was given to another research company for a tax write-off in the same year. Changes in federal tax laws, often good indicators of real, as contrasted to rhetorical, public policy changes, removed much of the financial incentive for investing in research and development. While some inventions and innovations still came out of American laboratories, telecommunications manufacturing increasingly moved abroad, and the United States became a more service oriented economy. Only time will tell if these losses are to be made up in other ways.

Broadcasting's once unique role has been altered most because of the increasing availability of competing delivery technologies. But, as will become evident, most of this technological change has improved the production and distribution process rather than enhanced program content quality and variety. The dramatic changes of the 1980s, while based on years of earlier technical innovation, also were due to a substantial degree of regulatory reconsideration. The increasing availability of new technologies contributed to arguments both for and against deregulation, as discussed in 10.8.

10•11   Delivery: Getting Here from There

Put simply, many of the so-called new technologies are largely duplicate means of delivering similar programming from producer to consumer rather than a whole new system of communication, as was radio broadcasting in the 1920s. Until the early 1980s, with the exception of the relatively few homes wired for cable (see

Appendix C, table 10-A), radio and television retained their monopoly on electronic delivery of news and entertainment to households. But after that, other means of delivery, especially cable, VCRs, and (indirectly) communications satellites, became increasingly important.

Developed in the 1960s (see 9.1), the geostationary- (geosynchronous-) orbit space communications satellite finally ended AT&T's lucrative monopoly of wire and, later, microwave broadcast network interconnection, which dated back to 1926 (see page 68). Broadcasting's use of this improved means of program distribution was pioneered by public, not commercial, broadcasters. In 1978, the Public Broadcasting Service began distributing programming to its 280 television affiliates by means of transponders (satellite devices that receive signals beamed up to them from earth and transmit back to earth on a different frequency over a wide area known as a "footprint") on the *Westar I* domestic communications satellite rather than using AT&T's terrestrial links. The new system allowed better-quality transmission, more flexibility in sending programs east or west or within time zones or regions, and a greater choice of programs for stations—which could now choose among four channels of material instead of one—and it was cheaper. By 1980, with prices of television receive-only antennas (TVROs or "dishes") dropping, National Public Radio joined the satellite hookup and dropped its terrestrial interconnection. It is interesting that the last commercial television networks to switch to satellites were those that had been around the longest: NBC in 1985, followed soon by ABC and CBS. (But AT&T, after monopolizing this function since the start of radio networking, had not given up and demonstrated its fiber-optic circuits to the networks in mid-1988.) In addition, the 1980s saw the rise of many satellite-delivered cable networks (see 10.34).

Use of similar but more powerful satellites allowing direct service to the home was a bold idea given solid form in 1980 by the Communications Satellite Corporation (COMSAT). COMSAT's specially formed subsidiary, Satellite Television Corporation (STC), applied in December 1980 to the FCC for permission to design and launch the country's first direct broadcast satellite (DBS) service designed to reach rural areas and inner cities, both inadequately served by cable and over-the-air stations. (Of course, the satellite's coverage footprint would also cover wealthier areas.) STC's plan for DBS was but the first of many filed with the FCC in 1980–1982. The potential of DBS seemed bright, much to the consternation of traditional broadcasters, who feared instant obsolescence. They need not have worried. Though the FCC proceeded with spectrum allocations for possible DBS service, none of the many applicants survived, and only STC actually built satellites. The costs (estimated at $700 million through the first year of STC's operation) were too high for the limited potential audience. Further, none of the DBS applicants ever resolved the central problem of programming—what to provide that was different from or better than what most consumers already had from over-the-air broadcasting, cable, and videocassettes.

One DBS operator did, briefly, show what could be done. United Satellite Communications, Inc., with substantial financial backing from the Prudential Insurance Company, provided service to portions of the Midwest and Northeast in late 1984 using a Canadian ANIK satellite transponder. Expecting to serve several tens of thousands of homes, but actually reaching fewer than 11,000, USCI closed up early in 1985 owing some $47.6 million.

By the late 1980s, a few companies, notably Hubbard Broadcasting of Minneapolis, were still expressing interest in a possible DBS service in the United States. But despite ever more efficient satellite technology, the daunting costs of design and launch and the inability to create programming sufficiently different from that already available made DBS in the United States seem unlikely for some years to come . . . although European and Japanese systems (often proposing high-definition television—see 10.124) seemed more likely to succeed. A bootleg version of DBS was to be found in nearly a million American homes—often in localities with poor broadcast or cable service—that equipped themselves at high cost to pick up material from the low-powered communications satellites used by broadcast and cable networks. However, by the fall of 1987, several large users of satellites—the commercial networks, under pressure from local affiliates, and most cable networks—had "scrambled" their signals, in some cases willing (for a monthly fee approximating that of cable) to supply decoders to those with TVRO dishes at home.

While many electronic media looked to the skies for improved delivery systems, one terrestrial technology brought things back to earth. Developed in laboratories of several companies in the 1970s, optical fiber or glass cables modulated by lasers began to spread across the country in the 1980s. Optical fiber has high signal reliability and a huge bandwidth capacity, thus lowering costs of delivery. Telephone companies first used it for high-density trunk circuits, and the first transatlantic fiber cable for voice and video communication went into service in mid-1988. Domestic communications satellite operators and telephone or other telecommunications systems now saw optical fiber links

as competition for many kinds of point-to-point communication, though for broadcast and cable services, satellite delivery remained essential. In the future, when the costs of wiring individual homes with fiber optics declines, it may replace some present broadcast and cable services using the electromagnetic spectrum, raising the political and economic question of why we need to pay for two broadband (cable television and telephone-data) connections to our homes.

Several other delivery technologies also played minor roles in the expanding electronic media delivery marketplace. Widely discussed and debated, but having limited audience impact, were low-power television stations (LPTV) and "wireless cable" MMDS microwave broadcasting systems (see 10.22). But in both cases, their programming was largely conventional broadcast fare, underlining our earlier point that the new delivery technologies were largely duplicate means of achieving the same end: getting news and entertainment from one producer to many homes—the essence of broadcasting.

10•12   New Technologies at Home

After 1980, an increasingly intense battle was fought for the loyalty and wallets of consumers seeking the latest in electronic communication gadgets. By the late 1980s, the most expensive (and potentially useful) of these gadgets was the home or personal computer (PC), which brought information, often in an interactive mode, through telephone lines using modem ("modulator-demodulator") devices. With game programs, PCs took up some leisure time people might otherwise have spent watching television. A second commonly purchased gadget might be a cordless (radio) telephone or a telephone answering machine, both technically more reliable

Changing Transmission Modes / Broadcast, cable, and auxiliary services used an increasing variety of delivery systems in addition to over-the-air transmission by the 1980s. The major ones are compared here.

Medium	Description	Capacity/Use	Cost
Twisted-wire pair	Two insulated copper wires	Usually voice grade; typically one audio circuit; used for radio networks	Least expensive
Coaxial cable ("coax")	Insulated hollow copper cylinder with signal wire conductor	TV networks (until 1985) and cable systems; typically one video channel, but may carry more than two dozen	More expensive than twisted-wire
Optical fiber ("fiber optics")	Glass fiber strands carrying light beams within a protective cable	Multiple TV or radio channels or cable relay; very high capacity	Usually much more expensive than wire or coax
Microwave relay	Ultra-high frequency point-to-point radio carrier	Multiple TV or radio signals, linking cable systems, MMDS, and ENG relay; capacity similar to coax	Less costly than optical fiber
Satellite relay	Radio transponders on satellite receive from uplinks and transmit to downlinks	TV channel or multiple audio signals per transponder (usually 24 transponders per satellite); also SNG	Most expensive, but highly efficient for national or regional coverage

to more people than the dwindling CB (Citizens Band) radio craze of a few years before, and a great deal cheaper than the full-scale cellular car phones being installed by many business executives in the late 1980s.

While electronic devices were filling the average home, the electronic innovations we are most interested in can be divided into four categories: audio recording, video recording, video text services, and improved video quality. Certainly the dominant trend in 1980s consumer electronics was to ever-better means of home recording and playback, for both audio and video. The recording industry's "battle of the speeds" in the late 1940s (see 7.11) was but a precursor to a never-ending stream of rapidly introduced innovations in the 1980s, each seeking at least a niche of consumer acceptance. The struggle was complicated by the FCC's abandonment of its traditional role of selecting technical standards for broadcast services, leaving the success or failure of several technologies to an ill-defined marketplace (see 10.83).

10•121 Home Audio Recording

Although the audiocassette continued to be improved to the point where it made major inroads into sales of LP records (and 45-rpm records and eight-track units had joined 78-rpm records as historical novelties), near perfection of sound recording resulted from development of a digital recording system modulated by a laser, called the "compact disc" or CD, which offered great advantages over the traditional analog means of music recording. The CD, named for its just-under-five-inch size rather than the totally different means of recording, was first introduced in 1983, offering fine sound reproduction at an initially stiff $800 for a player and at

least $20 per disc. The discs were said to be indestructible and could be played endlessly without wear and resulting sound deterioration (though by the late 1980s there was concern about how long CDs would really last due to shortcuts taken by some CD makers). As with traditional record players, the CD player could not be used to record. But its superiority in quality of sound and absence of hiss or noise over analog-based reel-to-reel or cassette tape or disc systems made it a hit with audiophiles. Rising demand led to increased production of players, and costs dropped so that players could be had for $150 or so by 1987, and some CD discs were list priced under $12 and discounted below that. By 1986, a CD boom had developed, and what had been a niche market took on the trappings of a widespread consumer product, with home, portable, and automobile versions, stimulated by radio stations' increasing use of CDs on the air. By 1987, thousands of titles were available on CD (about half popular and half classical), cassettes were being relegated to a small section in music stores, and the traditional LP looked as if it also might be on the way out.

By 1988, the inability to record CDs at home was their only major limitation. That limitation paved the way for a major policy debate about allowing American sales of yet another technology, the digital audiotape (DAT) recorder and player. Developed in Japan and carrying initial retail prices hovering around $2,000 per player-recorder machine, the DAT was seen as a menace by record companies concerned that consumers (or well-organized pirates) with a DAT could, for the first time, make copies of CDs without losing any of their vaunted sound quality. (To record from a borrowed CD onto a conventional cassette tape, besides being a possible violation of the copyright law,

The Consumer Digital Era / In the late 1980s, digital technology was increasingly common in radio and recordings and was beginning to make headway in television. By 1989, compact discs were in about 10 percent of American homes, while the digital audiotape recorder (DAT) was the next potential product on the market. Videodiscs made an abortive market push in the early 1980s, and in laser form they seemed likely to make a comeback in the early 1990s. All relied on digital rather than analog recording and sound generation.

A. How a Laser CD or Videodisc Works

Information is etched into microscopic "pits" arranged in spiral tracks on the surface of the disc. Rather than being contained in the visible undulating grooves of the analog recording system used in vinyl LPs, data on a CD or laser videodisc are stored digitally as a sequence of 1s and 0s in the pits and "lands" of the disc surface. A focused laser beam "reads" the information in the reflected pits and lands. The signal is transferred to a prism, then directed into a photo detector for conversion into sound signals in CDs and video signals in videodiscs. A transparent plastic coating protects the information on the disc from damage and also carries the record label. The laser beam scans for information without physically wearing down the surface—thus laser-read discs, video or audio, theoretically should never wear out. (CD-ROMs for computers work in a closely similar fashion.)

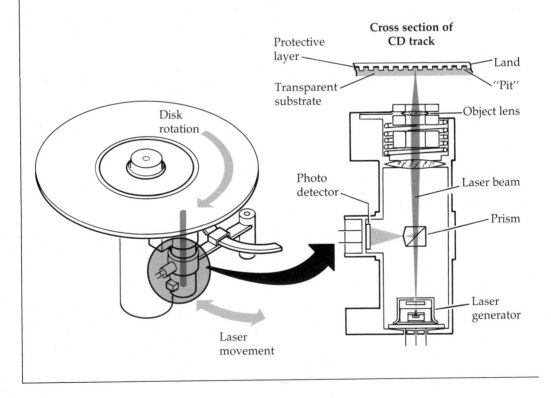

B. How Digital Audiotape Works

A digital audiotape machine uses a cassette of audiotape that is smaller than that used in an analog machine, but otherwise it is similar in operation. The tape records data in helical, or slanted, tracks, using two recording heads. Data on track one are oriented differently from those on track two, allowing a tight squeezing together of tracks without danger of interference. As with CDs (above), DAT machines "read" digital signals, 1s and 0s, which are then converted into analog sound for playback. Unlike CDs, DAT machines can be used to record and play back material.

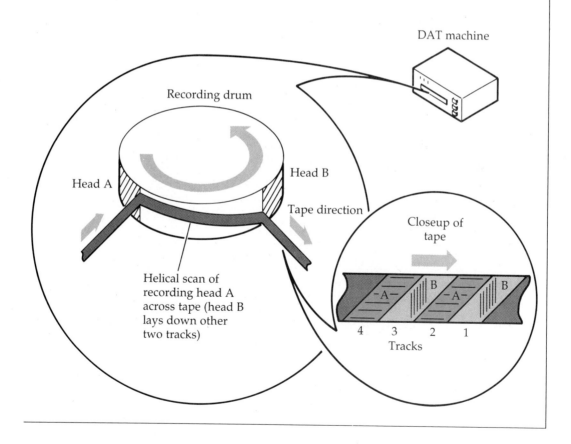

DAT machine

Recording drum

Head A

Head B

Tape direction

Helical scan of recording head A across tape (head B lays down other two tracks)

Closeup of tape

B   B
-A-   -A-

4   3   2   1
Tracks

introduced hiss and other noise that even the best cassettes could not escape.) Fearful of heavy sales losses if DAT machines took hold, the recording industry pressured Congress to ban DATs, or, failing that, to require some means of limiting their ability to record copyrighted material. Columbia Records, the largest record company in the world, spearheaded the move toward a "notch" system of recording that would ruin any attempted DAT dubbing. The notch system, however, was found to deliver inferior sound and to be easily circumvented in a study by the National Bureau of Standards. (Columbia Records may not have been too disturbed, however, for early in 1988 CBS sold its record company to Sony—a major backer of DAT technology—for some two billion dollars. Sony was no doubt pleased by the failure of the Columbia-developed notch system.) Nevertheless, until Congress acts, or indicates that it will not act, it seems unlikely that any major Asian manufacturer will risk tariff-free retaliation by exporting DAT equipment to the United States.

10•122   Home Video Recording

Leading the parade of home video products for most of the decade was the videocassette recorder (VCR), heralded as a true mass medium. Introduced in 1965 (see 9.1), the VCR made hardly a dent in consumer interest until the early 1980s because of initially high average unit prices ($785 in 1978). Heating up competition and thus contributing to lower prices (down to $388 by 1986) was the fact that the Japanese producers of VCRs backed two conflicting standards—Sony's pioneering Beta format and Matsushita's competing VHS, introduced in 1977, which a decade later seems to have won the war, at least in the United States. The differences were minor on the screen, but the cassettes were of different

sizes and thus were incompatible. The public was attracted to buy as first VHS and then Beta increased the amount of recording time from an hour to as much as eight hours per ever-cheaper cassette. Increasingly complicated machines were capable of being programmed to record on a timer, without the need for someone present to push the buttons. VCRs with video cameras attached (known as *camcorders*) also took over most of the home movie business. As shown in Appendix C, table 9-B, the penetration of VCRs rose sharply in the mid-1980s, reaching half of all television homes in 1987, the first broadcast-related service to achieve such a plateau since color television 15 years before.

For the viewer, a VCR brought a large degree of viewing control into the home and away from the broadcaster or cable system owner. With such machines, viewers could practice time-shifting—recording of programs to watch when convenient rather than when scheduled by the network or station (see 10.71). Further, libraries of video material could be developed and saved. Now everyone could become his or her own television programmer, a fact that made life much more difficult for the ratings services (see 10.71). This ability to duplicate freely broadcast and cablecast programming, especially motion pictures, led to adverse film industry reaction and eventually to unsuccessful legal actions to control VCR use (see 10.86). It led as well to businesses aimed specifically at VCR owners—rental (and sometimes sale) of cassette recordings of feature films and video programming was highly competitive but largely successful, due to low overhead and ability to meet a public desire. On the other hand, an attempt to cash in on the growing popularity of VCRs by ABC-TV's "TeleFirst" service from Chicago failed in just six months

Keeping Up with Technology / With rapid improvements in studio and transmission technology and increased interest by foreign manufacturers in sales to American business, the annual equipment exhibition of the National Association of Broadcasters (NAB), the biggest of its kind in the United States (and, some say, in the world), has taken on increased importance. Until the early 1970s, this annual exhibition was held in Chicago or Washington, D.C., where hotel exhibition halls were sufficient to hold all the equipment demonstrations. As the industry grew, the NAB was forced to move to Las Vegas (where these photos were taken, at the 1988 exhibition) or Dallas, which have exhibition halls large enough to hold the several hundred exhibitors, who occupy more space each year. Electronic media engineers count on this four-day exhibit and related convention technical sessions to get a sense of larger industry trends and to order new equipment. While the NAB's is by far the largest, other industry groups also have technical exhibitions. Photos courtesy of the National Association of Broadcasters.

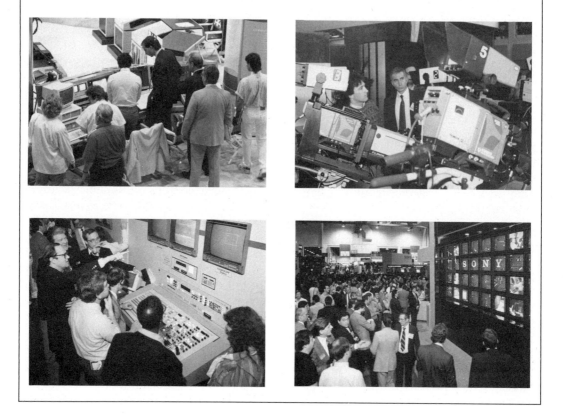

in 1984. ABC offered a subscription service of films telecast in early morning hours to preset VCRs. It signed up only 5,000 subscribers and lost some $15 million. The complications of setting VCRs for later recording, and the ready—and cheaper—local availability of rental tapes, doomed the venture. (Had it worked, many likely would have watched the previous night's recorded movie rather than prime-time television, a factor ABC may not have thought through!)

The success of the half-inch VHS format in this country, and the desire of supporters of the Beta format to regain its market share, have led to the development of new formats, such as Super-VHS and Beta II. While of higher pictorial quality, some of these machines are unable to play the tapes recorded on their less expensive relatives, and, of course, vice versa.

Many VCRs have been sold in association with camcorders, television camera-recorder combinations, which have all but replaced the home movie camera. While a plethora of different standards often limited playback to the home VCR for which the camera was bought, all of these units capture images in color and with sound. Some camcorders—either half-inch (VHS or Beta) or 8 mm—are evolving to a quality level that may find them a role in nontheatrical or news production.

The application of the familiar record format to video—the videodisc—did not initially fare as well. First marketed by Magnavox in 1978 to sell copies of popular theatrical films to consumers, and given a big push by RCA after 1981, the videodisc was sold as a cheaper but nonrecording (playback-only) alternative to the VCR. The videodisc industry also was plagued by several incompatible technologies, some based on lasers, others (like RCA's) based on mechanical (stylus-in-groove)

techniques. Sharply lower VCR prices in the early 1980s, plus the videodisc's inability to record off the air, doomed the various videodisc systems, though many felt the disc's picture tended to be better than the VCR's, and it had significant uses in education and industry. RCA finally gave up on its unwanted product in 1984, after a loss of more than $500 million.

In the late 1980s, interest in the videodisc idea revived, thanks to the parallel, and far more successful, development of the audio compact disc (CD). Already available by 1987 was what seemed the best of all possible record worlds: machines that would play—but not record—audio CDs and laser videodiscs interchangeably. Paced by sales of music video discs, the videodisc market showed signs of new life. Further, development of the CD-based read-only-memory (CD-ROM) computer memory technology paved the way for machines able to play any kind of disc: audio, video, or computer memory. Publishing ventures looked forward to placing enormous amounts of data—such as the complete Bible or U.S. Census—on a CD-ROM disk, with any section, page, or even word retrievable almost instantly with the proper computer commands. (The major cost is in preparing the content for recording, since existing automatic scanning devices for converting print to a computer storage medium are not perfect.) Industrial and training uses of CDs, videodiscs, and CD-ROM were paving the way, said many observers, for major consumer product breakthroughs in the 1990s.

10•123 Video Text Devices

Despite much promotional hoopla and investment by several large media firms, two closely related new technologies, teletext and videotex, seemed unable to find a consumer market in America. Introduced first in Britain in the 1970s, then in Canada and France (using, as you might by now expect, differing technical standards), both of these are means to allow the viewer to select "pages" of printed information rather than the television picture being transmitted at the same time.

Teletext is a means of sending text and diagrams to a properly equipped television screen by use of one of the "vertical blanking interval" lines that together form the dark band dividing pictures horizontally on the television screen. The communication is one-way, with the station transmitter sending one screen or "page" of information after another and able to store perhaps 200 at a time.

Videotex looks the same on the screen but reaches the home or office by cable and has an interactive ability (you can select any of possibly thousands of specific screens by punching up numbers on a push-button telephone or similar control). Both of these techniques could provide useful data—news headlines, airline schedules, weather reports, goings-on in town—to the subscriber. In France, a similar system was being phased into use that would, for example, do away with the need to publish telephone directories.

The 1980s saw considerable policy debate about such systems, and massive loss of money on them. Videotex attracted the most attention because it offered the ability to make thousands of pages of information, advertising, or entertainment available on a subscription basis at the push of a button. The Knight-Ridder newspaper chain introduced its "Viewtron" videotex experiment in Coral Gables, Florida, in October 1983 and spent nearly $30 million in programming and promoting the system in its first 14 months. In Southern California, the Times Mirror Company

tried a similar system. By March 1986, both projects were wound up, with losses of $50–$60 million and $20 million, respectively. The public seemed confused by what was offered, disliked having to buy or rent decoding devices to receive the videotex signals, and was not very interested in the limited information made available.* It seemed clear that, as had been the case in Britain, videotex was best suited for business rather than home use. Newspapers were in the business of supplying content to consumers, so it is no wonder that they were early experimenters, just as they were when facsimile was proposed as a broadcast medium in the 1940s. By the late 1980s, the formerly AT&T owned Bell operating companies (BOCs) were arguing in federal court that they should be allowed to provide such information services, a new wrinkle for a delivery-oriented, rather than content-oriented, industry. And, as again might be expected, newspaper chains (such as Knight-Ridder, which sold its television stations to provide capital for its own videotex plans) and other existing information providers were opposing any Bell market entry.

A similar technology was of particular value and interest to a special minority of viewers. On March 16, 1980, NBC and ABC began to provide some of their programming with "closed captions," a teletext-like service that provides subtitles for the hearing impaired. Broadcast on line 21 of the vertical blanking interval, the captions (termed "closed" because they

*French Telecom's "Minitel" may illustrate a better path to success. Minitel is a videotex system widely available in France. The French government's posts-telephones-telegraphs ministry, seeking to avoid the cost of constantly revising telephone directories, provided free terminals to homes requesting them, and, using electronic yellow pages as the chief lure, developed a broad audience base for other service providers—nearly 5,000 by 1988.

require special equipment to see) are decoded and put on the screen by a device (sometimes built into the set) that for some years only Sears, Roebuck was willing to sell. ("Open" captioning for the deaf was used for a few years on PBS's late-night rebroadcasts of the *ABC Evening News*, and some religious services and other programs insert a sign-language version in a corner of the picture.)

Closed captioning grew slowly from 10 hours of ABC and NBC and 20 hours of PBS programming in 1980; CBS was promoting a form of teletext that included captioning among other services and did not join until 1984. By 1989, 200 hours a week— virtually all—of network prime-time programs, all CPB-funded programming, and some daytime children's programs, sports, and even soap operas were being captioned. Many producers now insist on captioning. The U.S. Department of Education alone pays more than $6 million a year for captioning to nonprofit organizations (such as the National Captioning Institute and WGBH) and another $1 million to subsidize the manufacture of decoders. Captioning requires much time and skill, since only a few of the words spoken in the time available can be shown, making "instant captioning" of events rather rare.

10•124   *High-Definition Television*

Another potentially far reaching technology is the development in the 1980s of several competing systems of "high-definition television" (HDTV). The idea of HDTV is not a new one—the definition of "high" has simply climbed higher over the years.

Considered in its modern context, however, HDTV dates from a 1,125-line, wide-screen, stereophonic system of television developed by the Japanese network

NHK and first shown in the United States in 1981 (see box). While HDTV offered a tremendous improvement in both picture and sound, it did so, as usual, at a price. When first demonstrated in 1981, the HDTV system required six normal 6 MHz television channels to send only one signal! By the late 1980s, band compression and other techniques had cut this to 8.1 MHz—still too much to be compatible with the American system of television allocation but workable for satellite or cable transmission, assuming receivers were available to consumers.

For this reason, the Japanese proposed leaving their conventional television system alone and reserving HDTV for a direct broadcast satellite (DBS) system. This "you can get the high quality of HDTV only if you buy new equipment" approach clearly differs from the quest in the United States for compatible systems (see 7.8) but would open vast new potential markets for equipment manufacturers.

Partially out of fear of contributing to yet another Japanese consumer electronic product influx, and in a desire to control their own technical standards, by 1987 several European countries had begun cooperative development of their own high-definition television tied to their 50 Hz electrical system, thus making synchronization between transmitter and receiver easier to achieve. And in the United States, several "advanced" television systems (ATVs) suggesting a kind of middle ground—higher-definition pictures compatible with existing sets—were announced and initially demonstrated in 1987–1988. In mid-1988, the FCC bowed to political reality and decided that any broadcast HDTV system in the United States would have to accommodate the need to continue to supply programming to the nearly 90 million homes with NTSC-standard sets. But it had taken the British

HDTV: Improving the Picture / By the late 1980s, the major technical issue in broadcast and cable television was the eventual adoption of one or more systems of high-definition television (HDTV). Companies—and countries—vied to have their product adopted as *the* system in order to reap the huge potential patent, manufacturing, and trade benefits of worldwide use by the late 1990s. Many systems and approaches were suggested—this table illustrates only some of the major systems projected.

System	Country (firm)	Bandwidth Required*	NTSC Compatible?	Aspect Ratio (wide : high)	Number Scan Lines	Comments
For Comparison: The Current American Standard						
NTSC	United States	6 MHz	Yes	4 : 3	525	Present American TV system in use since 1941; with color since 1953
A. Single-Channel Systems						
ACTV I	United States (David Sarnoff Research Center)	6 MHz	Yes	5 : 3	525	Two-stage system: first would enhance existing NTSC (ACTV II is found below)
Super NTSC	United States (Faroudja Laboratories)	6 MHz	Yes	4 : 3	525/ 1,050	Improved system for current receivers
HD-NTSC	United States (Del Rey Group)	6 MHz	Yes[#]	5 : 3	525	Higher-definition version of current NTSC TV
MUSE-6	Japan (NHK)	6 MHz	Yes[#]	16 : 9 or 4 : 3	525	Improved current system (one of several "narrow" MUSE options)
B. Dual-Channel/Wideband Systems						
MUSE	Japan (NHK)	9.+ MHz	No	16 : 9	1,125	The pioneering system, demonstrated in United States in 1981. Four digital sound channels
Eureka	European Consortium	na	No	16 : 9	1,250	Designed around European 625-line, 50-field system; prototypes promised 1989–1990
Vista (Glenn)	United States (New York Institute of Technology)	6 + 3 MHz	Yes	16 : 9	1,125	Would use two separate channels: receivers and VCRs would be cheaper
ACTV II	United States (David Sarnoff Research Center)	6 + 3 MHz	No	5 : 3	1,125	Two-channel full HDTV
HDS-NA	United States (North American Philips)	6 + 3 MHz	Yes[#]	16 : 9	1,050	

*6 MHz is NTSC channel width—any system showing more would have to use an additional spectrum and would require a converter to allow viewing on an NTSC-standard set.
[#]There will be some picture degradation of an advanced signal when shown on current NTSC receivers, and the wider aspect ratio will be either lost or shown only by masking the top and bottom of screen.
na = not available

Sources: *HDTV: Planning for Action* (Washington, D.C.: National Association of Broadcasters, 1988), page 45; *Business Week* (January 30, 1989), page 59; Walter S. Baer, "New Communications Systems and Services," in Paula Newberg, ed., *Working Papers in Telecommunications Policy* (New York: Markle Foundation, December 1988), page 27.

more than two decades to make a similar switch-over from their pre–World War II 405-line system to a 625-line one, and that conversion was speeded by providing color telecasts only on the newer system. By the end of the 1980s it appeared that some means of supplying higher-definition pictures was on the way, though whether this was to be accomplished over the air or by other means was not clear. Many members of Congress—and Pentagon officials—felt that it would be necessary to support U.S. industry in this endeavor to prevent yet another part of the domestic electronics industry from moving production overseas.

However, even though receivers were not available, as early as 1987 some farsighted producers were using HDTV as a production medium; very expensive prototype cameras and other equipment were snapped up for the production of commercials and theatrical "films," with conversion to NTSC or 35 mm film making them available to those using existing standards.

This was not the only new production device. Other equipment had evolved, particularly field cameras and recorders that no longer required weight lifters to carry and needed less light for a good picture; mobile satellite transmission equipment (used for news coverage in most larger markets by the end of the decade); highly sophisticated character generators for inserting graphics on the screen; and computerized animation or "paint boxes" affordable by larger stations. The latter two permitted an operator sitting at a PC keyboard to replace a studio full of carefully painted backgrounds and mechanical counters during election or sports coverage. At the equipment exhibits of the National Association of Broadcasters' convention, almost every other booth now show a use of computers. A cou-

ple of generations of broadcast videotape recorders had come and gone, with smaller, better-quality, lighter, and electronically controlled one-inch machines replacing the original two-inch, four-head broadcast VTRs for entertainment, and a whole family of half-, three-quarter, and one-inch portable equipment for electronic field production (EFP) and news-gathering (ENG) was now in use. Solid state CCD cameras were lighter and more rugged than those using pickup tubes, although they initially did not have studio quality. While one could no longer expect a studio camera to last more than a decade—as was the case with early generations of television equipment—the additional bells and whistles produced by manufacturers each year often were used to persuade budget managers that planned obsolescence was not altogether bad if one gained new capabilities—and if one's competition had just bought that same new piece of gear.

10•13   Technology Overview

At the simpler, cheaper, and smaller end of the spectrum of consumer devices were ever-smaller radio and audiotape cassette machines with tiny earphones, allowing radio listening, often with surprisingly high fidelity (some devices had five-band graphic equalizers), in private in the midst of public places. Often called "walkmen" (after a Sony trade name), these radios were miniature throwbacks to the earliest days of radio listening, when earphones were a limitation rather than a benefit, but they also threatened the shiny, large "boom box" stereo radio-cassette players, except where seeing—and hearing—one's media had a social role to play. As discussed in 10.83, the FCC's unwillingness to set technical standards for AM stereo radio has led that development to stagnate, even though its proponents' belief that stereo would enable AM once again to become more popular than FM ignores both the higher fidelity of FM broadcasting and the pivotal place of programming in listener preferences (see 10.62).

Where broadcasters had been sharply concerned by the rising number of competing delivery systems early in the 1980s, by the end of the decade they were considerably calmer, possibly more nimble, and perhaps more resigned to added competition. It appeared that only cable television among delivery systems, and VCRs among consumer electronics devices for the home, had broken into the magic circle of electronic media reaching a majority of homes, and both relied heavily on broadcast programming. Many other delivery options were of little interest to audiences and advertisers alike (see 10.52).

Still at the center of it all, as had been the case since the late 1940s, were the family television receivers. They were larger now (26 inches was a common screen size, and projection screens up to several feet in diameter were selling briskly by the late 1980s) and were mostly in color. They were also increasingly augmented by improved sound—including some programs in stereo—and related systems such as a "picture-in-picture" circuit that enabled a viewer to watch at least part of two programs at once. Television receivers were as common in the bedroom as in the living room, and multiple sets could be found almost anywhere in the home. Remote control devices could be used to change channels, adjust sound volume, and control VCRs without having to leave one's chair. No matter what delivery system was used, the home (and, increasingly, portable) receiver still was needed to interface between the program supplier and the viewer.

10•2   Stations and Systems

From the very beginning of radio broadcasting in the 1920s, the local service nature of the medium had been central in the way stations were owned and operated, the type of programming they provided their listeners (at least some of the time), and the advertisers to whom they appealed. This was a national policy, declared most clearly in the language of the Communications Act of 1934. Early television followed suit, though national programming took hold far earlier in the history of that more expensive medium. Yet, certainly by the late 1970s if not before, the once-local nature of radio and television had fundamentally changed, with a variety of implications for both older and newer media. In the ever-tighter competitive search for programming, advertiser support, and audiences, broadcast stations had evolved from locally programmed media often reflective of their community of license to mere local outlets for one or more national networks (television stations and cable systems) or formats (radio). A major force driving this change was the high cost of local production of any kind of program compared with the ability of networks and syndicators to spread their production costs across many outlets.

To some extent, this shift was due to the increased number of stations on the air—nearly 13,000 by early 1989 (not counting LPTV and other minor services), compared with fewer than 1,000 at the end of World War II—all competing for the same audiences and advertisers. But the change was also the result of deregulation (see 10.82) that saw the FCC pulling back from imposing any kind of local service requirements. Stations became more like any other businesses in the eyes of most broadcasters—who were rapidly entering managerial ranks from business schools and other industries rather than from lower operational positions in broadcasting—and in the eyes of their regulators, thus making a once unique service with special "protections" more vulnerable to competition from unexpected quarters.

A strong indicator of the shift in role of broadcasting was the rapid change in ownership, causing ever-higher station prices, that characterized the 1980s. This increase in mergers and takeovers was sparked by the FCC's relaxation of long-standing multiple ownership and "trafficking" rules (see 10.85) combined with a perception that many broadcasting companies were worth far more than their stock prices indicated. The most important rule change was the lifting of the number of stations any one entity could own from the 7 AM–7 FM–7 television limit set in the 1950s to a new 12-12-12 rule in 1985 (see 10.85). The first of the cross-media megadeals in the 1980s was the Westinghouse Broadcasting takeover of TelePrompTer, then the largest cable MSO, for $646 million in 1981. Westinghouse sold off its cable acquisition just four years later (by then 115 systems serving 2.1 million subscribers) for a substantial profit by dividing its systems among several previously competitive cable MSOs. The widespread buying and selling of cable systems, usually noted only by the communities served (and those lending money for the purpose), obscured the slow movement of more and more systems into the control of the top 100 (or top 10) MSOs, another change from theoretical local control to control by national corporations.

Other major deals concerned network control (see 10.3) and the purchase of stations for breathtaking prices. Australian press baron Rupert Murdoch purchased the highly successful Metromedia chain of seven television stations (reaching about a fifth of the nation's population, close to the limit established in the 12-12-12 rule) in 1985 for $2 billion—and he had to become an American citizen before the FCC would allow him to take over the station's licenses. (This action put him in some difficulty in his native country.) The buy was a key part of his plan to develop a fourth over-the-air network (see 10.33).

Desperate for a toehold in the second largest market in the country, Tribune Broadcasting (WGN in Chicago and WPIX in New York) paid out $510 million for the license of Los Angeles independent television station KTLA in 1985—a record price for any single broadcast outlet. KTLA had been purchased for $245 million just two years before by Golden West Broadcasters, so the station had, in effect, increased in value by about $300,000 for each day Golden West owned it before the sale to Tribune. Critics of deregulation pointed to such transfers as proof that an important "scarcity" still existed when demand for stations could lead to such prices.

As with many industries, there seemed to be an almost frantic tendency for media organizations to merge with, buy out, or otherwise acquire other media firms in order to grow larger, often at the expense of potential competition (see box on page 469). While most media companies are quite small when compared with America's manufacturing and service giants, recent large acquisitions have involved big money. Rupert Murdoch bought *TV Guide* for $3 billion. Warner Communications, already a major supplier of television programming (Warner Brothers studio), bought one of the most successful production houses, Lorimar Telepictures, in 1988, and then almost immediately announced a proposed merger with Time Inc. (a large MSO, owner of HBO and other cable networks, and magazine and book publisher) early in 1989. If the merger goes through, Warner and Time will have an annual revenue of approximately $10 billion and will be the largest worldwide television producer, the largest magazine publisher, the largest record company, the second largest cable operator, the largest pay-TV programmer, and the largest direct marketer of books in the United States.

10•21   FM Pulls Ahead

The radio business faced an increasingly difficult competitive situation after 1977 as a steadily larger number of stations fought for a more slowly expanding advertising market and listener pool. In most cities, radio stations had to make do with a smaller proportion of both. Some stations could not find formats to increase audiences quickly enough and either changed hands (some stand-alone AM stations were sold at a loss in the 1980s) or went off the air. But the decade after 1977 is mainly the story of a historical reversal, with the longtime second service, FM, finally coming out on top. Although the numbers of both types of stations were roughly the same, by the late 1980s FM radio stations collectively had about three-quarters of the nation's radio audience.

There were no surprise reasons for this change. For decades, it had been known by broadcasters and advertisers that FM stations aired music with higher fidelity, were not subject to most natural and man-made static, could now be easily tuned, had a dependable and calculable service area, and could stay on the air 24 hours a day—unlike AM stations, which usually could meet only one or two of these standards. Further, by the late 1970s FM receivers in all sizes and price ranges were universally available. Now the public

realized all of this, and its infatuation with stereo high-fidelity music naturally caused it to gravitate toward FM. Although most FM channel assignments had been applied for by the mid-1980s, the FCC completed a proceeding that allocated an additional several hundred channels, potentially causing the audience-advertiser pie to be split even more ways. Because of the FM signal's line-of-sight range, however, this step caused less interference on the FM band than adding more AM stations would have caused on its band.

The FCC's halfhearted support of AM stereo (see 10.83—actually, the commission avoided the decision on which system to adopt, leaving it to the marketplace, which had kept its hands off the decision as well), its allowing of higher power for the smallest stations, and its arranging with Canada and Mexico for more U.S. AM stations to stay on the air for more hours helped AM, but not much. International plans to expand the standard broadcast band some 10 channels beyond its present 1605 kHz upper boundary would only provide more competition for the beleaguered existing AM broadcasters . . . but it would also supply a toehold in the business for newcomers who could wait until most people had radios that would tune that high. The real reason for AM's decline, although each of the factors mentioned above is real, was programming (see 10.61).

10•22   Is More Television Better?

Although some new television receivers have the ability to show more than one picture at a time, and the more than half of the public with VCRs can record one program while watching another, it is nevertheless true that one can pay attention to only one program at a time—

and that there is a finite amount of programming talent available.

The need for more programming became evident in the late 1970s. The pressure came, in part, from a growing number of independent television stations, many on UHF. There were 78 such stations in 1980 and more than 250 by early 1989, strengthening their political clout to the point where the Independent Television Association (INTV) was able to schedule a dinner on the same night as the NAB's—and draw an equally impressive lineup of congressmen and regulators. The FCC had spent a lot of time and money in the 1970s on a variety of studies, reporting to Congress on how to improve UHF television transmission and reception, so that UHF, the proverbial second-class service, could compete more equally with VHF, though always subject to the basic spectrum propagation limitations imposed by nature.

The growing number of independent stations (from 120 in 1980 to nearly 300 in 1988) tended to be "lean and mean," willing to experiment with programming, technology, and other new ideas. Because the independent stations are able to move fast, it is probable that when higher picture definition becomes feasible they will jump faster than most network affiliates, if they can afford to. But the outlook is not all favorable. Most independent stations, except for a handful in the largest markets—such as WGN (Chicago), WPIX (New York), KTLA (Los Angeles), and WTBS (Atlanta), which are serving as superstations supplying programming to cable systems around the country—are constantly on the thin edge of bankruptcy. Programming costs are kept as low as possible—few have any news staff—and only nimble counterprogramming (for example, running entertainment programs while the network affiliates are airing news)

brings in a large enough audience to attract advertisers. In markets where specialization pays off, independent stations tend to air older feature films, some sporting events, game shows, children's cartoons, and hour after hour of old network reruns. Even though independent stations brag about their status, there are few that would not jump at a network affiliation (even with as new an entity as struggling Fox— see 10.33) if one were offered.

Network affiliates (the number of which varied little in this period), on the other hand, often have fallen into a rut. Programming relies on the network and on tried-and-true syndicated programs. Even news, where the most competition occurs, tends to cloning of content and personnel. The number of affiliates of the three major commercial networks is unlikely to grow substantially, since no more than one station is affiliated in a given market. A fourth commercial network, such as Fox, would have to draw its affiliates from the ranks of independent stations, although as one network's programming goes down in popularity and another's goes up, there are occasional defections of strong stations from the weaker to the stronger network. This sort of change, of course, has a ripple effect through an entire market.

One attempt to broaden the variety of people able to own and operate television stations was the well-intentioned but apparently misguided attempt by the FCC to launch a low-power television (LPTV) system in the early 1980s. Based on results of some Canadian experiments, the FCC late in 1980 announced its intention to establish potentially thousands of spectrum allotments for tiny television stations. Most would be UHF outlets, using up to 100 watts of power (or in some cases VHF, with only 10 watts) for a coverage area with a radius of up to five or six miles. These new stations would be dropped into the existing allocation structure of full-power stations but with the new LPTV outlets forced to shield the larger stations from interference. The FCC claimed to be looking forward to a new age of neighborhood television stations and rural services where none existed thus far, and for outlets owned by members of minority groups and women, for a (relatively) low construction price of perhaps $200,000. Naturally, legislators representing the communities where the new stations would go were all in favor of the plan—and the goodwill the FCC got at first was perhaps its only reward.

Two problems arose immediately. For one thing, the FCC was so impressed with its brainchild that it allowed applications to be filed even before final forms and rules had been developed. Some individuals, groups, and firms (such as Sears, Roebuck and Co., which planned a network of more than 100 LPTV stations) filed literally hundreds of applications, and consulting engineers and lawyers cranked them out in assembly-line fashion. Belatedly calling for a freeze on new applications, the commission began to dig through the pile of paper, the processing of which had become more legally complicated than getting the new service on the air. The pressure from impatient LPTV applicants was one reason the FCC approached Congress requesting permission to select applicants by means of a lottery rather than by expensive and time-consuming comparative hearings. In 1982, Congress agreed, and, helped by new computers, the commission began to process applications, allowing the first stations to go on the air.

The other problem was more serious and long lasting—how to support such tiny stations. Advertisers were not usually interested in their miniscule audiences, and few stations could afford the fees to secure programming for pay-TV (already available on cable in most cases). While new networks of LPTV stations were a possibility, most knowledgeable broadcasters (and, eventually, many nonprofit or alternative media groups) decided that there was little to gain from LPTV. By the end of 1988, 455 LPTV stations were on the air (with call letters that included their channel number), mainly in rural and some suburban areas, and another 1,359 had been granted construction permits. But the dream of a viable new television service seemed as far away as ever, and the total LPTV audience was miniscule.

Another minor entry into the television outlet business was a service oddly named "wireless cable" to try to make its function more understandable to the public. More formally known as a multichannel multipoint distribution service (MMDS) or a multipoint distribution service (MDS), this is a microwave broadcast (rather than point-to-point) delivery system, originally created by the FCC in the 1960s for business-related common carrier use. With channels widened to carry video signals in the 1970s, and then with a total of eight channels allotted to each of the top 50 markets in 1983, MMDS took on the potential of competing with cable in some unwired urban areas. Being a "broadcast" service (although the FCC vacillated between regulating it as a common carrier or as a broadcast service), MMDS was far less expensive to build (just a transmitter and special antennas and receivers that the subscriber would have to pay for) than the wired connections between a cable system's headend and each home served. But its operators suffered limited growth in the face of the cable industry's reluctance to sell them cable-controlled programming. By 1988, MMDS served only a small proportion of the national audience and faced a bleak future as the number of cities without cable service dwindled.

A variation of MMDS, keeping costs low, used leased time in the evenings on the instructional television fixed-service (ITFS) channels in the same band as MMDS that were owned and operated by educational or religious organizations for educational programming during the rest of the day. The payments from MMDS operators were very welcome to the educational licensees, and the MMDS operators benefited by not having to apply or pay fully for their own stations. As the 1980s drew to a close, the future of this service was unclear.

An older television service saw a brief period of marginal success from 1977 to the early 1980s and then succumbed to newer competition. As noted in 9.22, though the FCC had approved a new system of subscription television (STV) in 1968, the first two channels (in New York and Los Angeles) did not air until 1977 because of regulatory constraints. By 1983, about 27 pay stations were in operation, most offering scrambled pay signals at night and regular "in the clear" broadcasts during the day. Another 20 outlets were announced as being in various stages of planning. But the surface success was misleading, and the licensees knew it. Pay-cable, with multiple channels, was rapidly expanding and closing down opportunities for STV stations providing but a single channel of premium programming. By 1987, only two STV outlets remained in business, both of them LPTV stations. The former STV stations had nearly all converted to regular (independent) broadcast operations, some of them specializing in "home-shopping" programming, which became popular and profitable in the late 1980s.

10•23 Cable—The New Basic Distributor

One of the most important single changes in electronic media in this era was the expansion of cable television from a minority service to a majority distributor of video. As is evident in Appendix C, table 10–B, the number of cable systems and subscribers increased substantially in this period. Cable penetration soared from just under 18 percent in 1977 to more than 52 percent in 1988. A variety of factors contributed to this rapid expansion after several decades of slow growth to the late 1970s.

Perhaps most important was the coming together of several kinds of demand. Television viewers were interested in getting clearer reception of local stations even in well-served markets and wanted some distant (usually independent) stations for their movies and sports. By the late 1970s, demand for pay-cable services by viewers interested in a new way to see films, and by cablecasters eager for a piece of additional income, helped to lead the way to cable expansion. After 1980, desire for the specialized new services (see 10.34), especially news and sports, attracted viewers who did not care about movies. Important too was the rapid deregulation of cable (see 9.83 and 10.82) by the courts and the FCC after the mid-1970s. This had the effect of reducing uncertainty about what programming cablecasters could carry and settling the nagging question of copyright (see 10.86).

As cable systems increased in importance nationally, they also became more controversial in many markets. The late 1970s were a time of frantic competition for long-term (usually 15-year) franchises in the last cities and suburban areas to be wired. The cost of applying for a major franchise, often several hundred thousand dollars, was a factor in industry consolidation, for smaller companies could not compete in the face of such financial pressures. Several scandals resulted from cable company payoffs to city officials, and plenty of perfectly legal but less than ethical means were used to obtain franchise agreements. Most popular was the technique of giving a small portion of the stock of an applicant to various officials and community leaders in return for their backing. Sometimes the fault lay with the city's excessive demands—in one case, a successful applicant had to promise to plant several thousand trees in the community. In what was logically an adversarial relationship, the main cable trade group, the National Cable Television Association (NCTA), constantly faced several associations of city officials, especially the National League of Cities, as each tried to get the upper hand in persuading Congress and the FCC. Until the late 1980s, cable did consistently well in these policy and legal face-offs, in part because of strong congressional support. Cable played on its "local" nature and often donated time to incumbent officials to curry favor.

As with broadcasting and other media, cable's expansion was fueled in part by a growing trend toward consoli-

---

Cable Concentration / The motion picture and broadcast industries tried to focus congressional and FCC attention on the increasing concentration of ownership of cable television systems by the major multiple system operators (MSOs). Broadcasters argued that rules limiting station ownership were unfair compared to a lack of any multiple system (or proportion of national audience served) limits on cable.

Percentage of All Cable Subscribers Served by Largest

Year	4 firms	8 firms	25 firms	50 firms
1970	17.2%	28.0%	50.3%	64.0%
1975	26.4	38.1	58.5	69.8
1980	25.8	38.6	62.1	74.5
1985	26.1	38.8	62.3	74.8
1988*	25.6	37.5	66.1	81.8

*Figures for this year depend on how cable subscribers controlled by the biggest MSO, Tele-Communications Inc., are counted. If all partnerships and percentage interests in other cable companies are included, TCI subscribers increase from about 4.2 million to just under 9 million. The percentage shown here assumes the *lower* figure. For more detail, see *Channels Field Guide 1989*, page 117.

Sources: Yale Braunstein, *Recent Trends in Cable Television Related to the Prospects for New Television Networks* (Washington, D.C.: FCC Network Inquiry Special Staff, January 1980), page 14; and *Television Digest*, Special NCTA Supplement, 1980, as reprinted in Sterling (1984), page 72 (see Appendix D for full citation). Data for 1985 and 1988 calculated by authors from basic MSO data supplied by NCTA.

dation of ownership. Where the business had been characterized by "Mom and Pop" small-town community antennas into the 1960s, by the 1970s cable showed signs of both needing and attracting big money. Needing cash because of the capital-intensive nature of building new systems before any income was forthcoming, cable owners found that larger systems were more attractive to lenders. Cable became a more impersonal business as a result. By the late 1980s, Tele-Communications Inc. (TCI) was the largest multiple system operator (MSO), with about 20 percent of all cable subscribers. Its president, John Malone, constantly defended his firm's success while others held up TCI as an example of corporate greed and a portent of where cable was headed. Neither Mom nor Pop remained part of the cable picture.

For a brief time (1977–1984) many eyes were on Columbus, Ohio, as the Warner-Amex cable franchise there operated its "Qube" system featuring five interactive channels. Widely publicized across the country, the interactive channels allowed viewers to vote on simple questions in talk shows and the like. Many predictions were made about the potential for wide adoption of such technology for future polls and shopping. But Warner found that few subscribers used the feature after the novelty wore off, and Qube's interactive channels were closed down in 1984 after a loss of some $30 million. Some pessimists felt the end of Qube might spell the real end of the wired city concept (in which homes would be connected by cable networks and computers rather than by broadcast channels) that had been discussed and debated for almost 20 years.

One final but always faithful indicator of cable's increasing importance among electronic media was the competitive reaction of other media. Jack Valenti, longtime Washington lobbyist for the motion picture industry, seemed to build his speeches in the 1980s around attacks on cable, describing it as a monopoly menace controlling a bottleneck delivery system into the nation's homes. The National Association of Broadcasters, too, was constantly bickering with the NCTA about such concerns as must-carry and cross-ownership rules (see 10.85).

By late in the 1980s, it seemed that cable's success curve in both the marketplace and the policy arena was likely to turn downward. For one thing, most initial franchise construction was finished, leaving only system enlargement by reconstruction and, more likely, takeovers of small companies by larger ones. There was some concern that cable "overbuilds" (a hitherto rare situation in which a second company installs a parallel network in a given community, competing directly for subscribers) might result. For another, over half of the audience owned VCRs and often used them rather than watching either over-the-air or cable television.

10·3   Networks: A New Age

In the mid-1980s, American commercial broadcasting networks underwent more changes than they had since their establishment 40 to 60 years before. They changed ownership; they did not exactly welcome a great deal of competition; and even the definition of "network" changed. No longer was a network "two or more stations interconnected by some means or associated for the often simultaneous transmission of the same messages or programs." With VCRs and round-the-clock cable services such as CNN, the need for simultaneous transmission to the public disappeared, and the medium serving the public often was a cable system that carried the local affiliate broadcasting station.

Interconnections now were by satellite links rather than wire or microwave circuits.

10•31   New Entrants

The worlds of broadcasting and cable networking were made more exciting, less predictable, and perhaps riskier by the activities of worldwide press baron Rupert Murdoch and broadcast and cable entrepreneur Ted Turner. Able to command the power of millions of dollars of their own and of other investors, both men moved to take important ownership positions in broadcasting and cable services. Turner came first with what became his "superstation," WTBS-TV in Atlanta, followed by the Cable News Network (see 10.64) and Turner Network Television (TNT!) in 1988.

Turner specialized in ideas that others had not thought of or had rejected. For example, his synergistic ownership of a small Atlanta UHF television station and the Atlanta Braves led to an attractive package for cable system operators when it was made available (for a small sum per month per subscriber) via satellite. In addition, Turner could charge advertisers national advertising prices for what originally was a small UHF station! Some of Turner's later investments—in companies owning feature films, such as MGM, for example— were to ensure plenty of "product" for WTBS to distribute. Turner, whose ability to plan and take risks led to his being captain of more than one America's Cup sailboat racing defender, at one time also tried to purchase CBS (see 10.33). His establishment of CNN, thought by many to be a financially foolish move, turned out to be a success. Although the bankers achieved stronger control over Turner's empire when he needed cash to start new ven-

tures, his ability to come up with successful ideas has seldom been matched in broadcasting's history.

Rupert Murdoch, whose life story parallels those of other press magnates, such as the Canadian-born Lord Thomson of Fleet, started his career buying and operating newspapers in his native Australia. Soon he owned a major share of Australian commercial television broadcasting and expanded his activities to other continents, buying newspapers, magazines, and broadcasting stations. His interest in starting a fourth network—the first since the abortive Overmyer Network (see 9.3) 20 years before—predated his purchase of the Metromedia group of seven stations (see 10.2). In 1984, Murdoch had taken a half-interest in 20th Century-Fox, buying the rest in 1985. He announced his plans to combine the production capacity of the film studio with the former Metromedia stations, and future affiliated stations, to create the Fox television network. He planned to begin his new network slowly, with a late-evening program, and then expand into prime time, adding a day or so each year. In 1988, he added to his broadcasting-related properties with the $3 billion purchase of Triangle Publications, including the immensely popular (and profitable) weekly *TV Guide*—which might be a useful vehicle with which to publicize the Fox network.

In the United States, Murdoch had to become an American citizen (at some legal risk to his Australian broadcasting holdings) in order to buy television stations. In the 1986–1988 period, he owned both television stations and major daily newspapers in the same cities—WNYW and the *New York Post,* and WFXT and the *Boston Herald.* Although such cross-ownership of media in the same market was against FCC rules, the commission traditionally granted waivers for a year or two until one or the other medium could be sold. Murdoch decided to fight the rule and showed himself to be a master of political public relations when he went on the offensive after a clause was inserted by Senator Ted Kennedy at the last minute into a Senate appropriations bill that forbade the FCC to drop the rule or grant indefinite waivers under the guise of "deregulation." It so happened that Murdoch's stations were the only ones waiting for such waivers, and he went a long way toward establishing himself as an underdog. Later, he tried to place some of his holdings in trust, but even that had to be modified to include a firm commitment to sell one or the other. Meanwhile, as all-channel (VHF-UHF) receivers became universal, and as more UHF stations were established in larger cities, the Fox television network found many more independent stations hoping for a network affiliation than had been available to Overmyer (or Kaiser or Du Mont before him; see 7.32). By keeping a close eye on expenses, Murdoch seemed more likely to succeed than his predecessors (see 10.33).

As discussed later (see 10.61), new radio networks appeared in the 1980s for the first time in decades as satellite delivery made provision of specific kinds of music and talk formats less expensive.

10•32 *Competitive Pressures*

Broadcast networks flourished—as did the American economy, for the most part—in the late 1970s. The antitrust suits brought in 1972 (see 9.3) were eventually settled—NBC's in 1976, with ABC and CBS falling into line in 1980. But while the overall pattern of network dominance of television continued, traditional over-the-air networks saw their audiences (in terms

of percentages, if not absolute numbers fed by population growth) dwindle slightly every year after the mid-1980s as a result of competition from both VCRs and cable. An excellent snapshot of the television networks both at the peak of their power and on the brink of decline is found in the 1980 report of the third FCC network inquiry.

Following the Barrow report (see 8.82), the FCC did not again assign a special staff to report on network television for two decades. An Office of Network Study reviewed network programming practices (see 9.3) but had little impact on policy and faded from sight in the late 1960s. A few years later, however, affiliates' displeasure with the tiny amount of then-huge network profits being paid to them began to reach the ears of the commission as well as stockholders. Specifically, Westinghouse Broadcasting and Cable Inc., which had stations affiliated with each of the three networks, filed a formal petition with the FCC in 1976 asking for an investigation of affiliate compensation and other network practices. Pressure from Congress contributed to the FCC's formation of a Network Study Special Staff in 1978.

Codirected by an attorney and an economist (an indication of how much the latter field had caught up with the former in helping to shape regulation of business), the inquiry developed or contracted for 18 staff reports issued in 1979–1980 examining both traditional broadcasting and the developing new services. Taken together, the studies, issued in only limited numbers, provide an excellent view of the industry as it existed at that time and how it was expected to develop. The final report took a very different approach from its 1941 and 1957 predecessors. It strongly criticized most existing commission rules limiting network behavior, saying that they usually did not work and, at any rate, that their economic cost was far higher than any social gain. The development of cable and other competing services sparked the network staff to urge on the commission a welcoming approach to newer services seeking to compete with the traditional networks rather than the generally restrictive approaches taken thus far.

But when the FCC moved to act on the study's recommendations, voices of the competition—those now "in" rather than those trying to gain a foothold—were heard loud and clear. A plan to drop the Prime Time Access Rule led to heavy pressure from the program-producing industry based in Hollywood, which had been given new life by the rule when it was first instituted in 1974. Similarly, a 1983 attempt to drop some complicated and somewhat arcane rules banning networks' financial interest in the entertainment programs they carried, or in their subsequent syndication, also brought Hollywood pressure groups out in strength. FCC chairman Mark Fowler was called in for an unprecedented dressing down (press releases spoke of a "briefing") by President Ronald Reagan, who may have thought back to his movie actor days when he made it clear that the FCC was to leave the network-limiting rules in place. Despite these careful studies showing the television networks to have less power than they once did, old rules set up to protect then-defenseless programmers from network controls would not be easily dropped, even after the ratings services and headlines showed everyone that the day of the all-powerful networks was done. In 1988, the FCC turned to another of the now-eight-year-old recommendations of its network study and announced plans to ease rules banning network ownership of cable systems.

10•33   Network Upheaval

"In a matter of months during 1986 the television industry was transformed beyond recognition. All three of the commercial networks—against which the progress of the other media inevitably is measured—came under new ownership or leadership. Each of the acquirers pledged to run these huge television machines in a more businesslike fashion than before, with fewer frills and executive perquisites, less staff, greater cost control and strict attention to the bottom line. So the networks have lost during the past year not only their near total domination of the television market but also their swagger, their corporate identities and perhaps also their hallowed traditions."—Les Brown, writing in Channels Field Guide 1987, *p. 9*

The upheaval that longtime television critic Brown reports was sudden— it cracked open a closed network shop that had operated with unchanged ownership and surprisingly static management since 1953. The revolution began with the industry-stunning announcement in March 1985 that group owner Capital Cities Communications was taking control of the American Broadcasting Companies, operator of the ABC radio and television networks, in a $3.5 billion deal. ABC chairman Leonard Goldenson, who had taken over ABC in 1953 (see 7.32), had, on the eve of his retirement, decided to sell his shares. The FCC approved the sale in November (a marked contrast to the months of proceedings concerning ABC in 1953–1954). The company changed its name to Capital Cities/ABC. Cap Cities, as it was known, and its chairman, Thomas Murphy, had a well-deserved reputation for attention to the bottom line, and ABC was merely the first of the networks to resort to layoffs to prune overexpanded staffs and improve short-term profitability.

In contrast to the friendly takeover of ABC, Atlanta-based Ted Turner announced just a few months later a brash attempt at an unfriendly (his target was clearly not interested) bid for control of the much larger CBS. While given little chance of success by most Wall Street experts, the takeover attempt was in the headlines for weeks as both sides maneuvered. CBS chairman Thomas Wyman (he had replaced John Backe in 1980 and had become chairman when founder William Paley retired in 1983) headed the network's defense while overseeing its now widely diversified assets. Late in 1985, Turner withdrew his offer—having sold his own CBS stock back to the network for a tidy profit. In fighting off Turner, however, CBS had gone deeply into debt to buy back a fifth of its own shares. Thus weakened and needing cash, CBS had to sell off its St. Louis owned and operated station KMOX-TV and accept the friendly purchase of a large minority of its shares (just under 25 percent) by Loew's Inc. (chiefly hotels and movie theaters) chairman Laurence Tisch.

Late in 1986, after a boardroom tussle in which Tisch and Paley collaborated, Wyman was eased out and Tisch became the chief operating officer of the network. William Paley was brought back into the now largely ceremonial position of chairman. The Tisch era at CBS began with a new (for CBS) era of austerity, with extensive personnel layoffs, low resultant morale at CBS News (even an offer to buy the news division by several of its key employees), and the selling of many of the network's nonbroadcast interests. One of these sales, in early 1988, was of Columbia Records to Sony for $2 billion (see 10.121). The changes at CBS were reflected in its unaccustomedly poor audience ratings—

the network ended the 1987–1988 season in third place for the first time in its history. A much smaller company than either of its competitors after all these sales, CBS in the late 1980s seemed ready to use its hoard of several billion dollars to expand its self-defined sphere of broadcasting (and possibly cable) operations. Late in 1988, CBS bought control of a VHF station in Miami, increasing its O & O holdings to five (see page 266).

Change came as well to NBC. In January 1978, the network announced a substantial coup—it had hired away ABC program chief Fred Silverman to become its new president. Silverman was then an industry wunderkind who could do no wrong and who seemed to have a magic touch with programming. He had propelled longtime number three ABC to the top of the ratings heap. But this final shift (Silverman was the only executive to have had senior programming positions with all three networks) was one too many. NBC floundered through a series of expensive program disasters and stayed in the ratings basement. Finally, in June 1981, RCA's chairman Thornton Bradshaw replaced Silverman with a widely respected programming figure, MTM Productions' chief, Grant Tinker. Tinker wrought wonders for NBC with his quiet, relaxed California style of management and sure sense of the right balance between high quality and popularity in programming. NBC moved to first place in network ratings in 1983 and stayed at or near the top for the rest of the decade.

But dramatic change was also coming for the senior network. Late in 1986, the broadcasting community was surprised to hear that NBC's parent, RCA, had been taken over by General Electric in a $6.28 billion deal—and that thus NBC would be under new ownership. The sale represented an ironic return to its origins by RCA—for, as detailed in 3.12, General Electric had created RCA in 1919. A year later, Tinker retired as NBC's president to return to his first love, Hollywood program development, and the network was taken over by a GE official. One of Robert Wright's first decisions, in July 1987, was to sell off the NBC Radio Network (for $50 million to Westwood One), thus giving up on radio networking to concentrate on the more lucrative television service and then selling the NBC owned and operated radio stations piecemeal. The pioneering radio network was no longer in the radio business.*

As mentioned earlier (see 7.32 and 9.3), the possibilities of a fourth commercial television network had been discussed and even attempted several times. But that inveterate acquirer of media properties, Rupert Murdoch, appeared in the late 1980s to be making the best try yet at establishing a fourth network in 1986 with the Fox (named after movie studio 20th Century-Fox, which he also owned) television network (see 10.31).

This is not to say that the Fox network found easy sailing: its first big show, a late-evening attempt to compete with the venerable *Tonight* show starring Johnny Carson, featured Joan Rivers (a frequent Carson vacation substitute). In only a matter of weeks, Rivers and Fox came to a parting of the ways, probably due to the program's low ratings—and Carson's resentment over her defection seemed likely to put a crimp in her future career. Fox then presented several prime-time original (but inexpensive) series programs for two evenings a week. Ratings were

poor, however, and by 1988, some affiliated stations were reverting to the independent mode of playing movies and off-network reruns rather than sticking with a ship only half afloat. But after Fox obtained the rights to popular specials such as the 1988 Emmy Awards, stations found the economics of affiliation with Fox more favorable. In June 1988, Fox's editing out of all political content of a multihour rock concert in honor of black South African leader Nelson Mandela raised a great deal of protest, particularly from performers in the concert. Nevertheless, Fox's plans remained on schedule, with a third evening of prime-time programming scheduled to start in mid-1989. Fox reported losses of $80 million in fiscal 1988—an indication of just how expensive starting up a fourth network could be.

Radio networking—or, in 1980s terms, national distribution of program formats—revived to some extent in the 1980s, thanks to both satellite technology (see 10.11) and more competition among the increasing number of stations. Following television's example, use of a satellite transponder allowed a radio program service to reach hundreds of potential subscriber radio stations (many of them fully automated) without the need for expensive wired interconnections. By the late 1980s, despite some consolidation, there were more than 20 services, most delivered by satellite. Transtar Radio Network and Satellite Music Network, for example, together produced 15 different 24-hour music formats. National Public Radio and American Public Radio were early and successful users of satellite technology for program distribution.

At the same time, traditional radio networks—music and news services—changed hands. ABC had the most affiliated stations, as was the case for nearly two decades (see Appendix C, table 2-A).

---

*RCA suffered further dismemberment when its consumer electronics division was sold to a French company. By this time, only one major American company—Zenith—still manufactured television receivers in the United States.

Westwood One, a California-based syndicated program service, purchased the Mutual network from Amway in 1985 for $39 million and, as noted earlier, added the NBC radio network to its growing holdings to broaden its role as a provider of middle-of-the-road features and music services. Westwood, then the second largest network operation, continued to operate as NBC, Mutual, and the original Westwood One program service.

10•34   Coming of Cable Networks

Although space communications satellites became increasingly important in both television and radio broadcasting program distribution in the 1980s, this was old hat to cable programmers. As shown in the chart (see box), the pioneering efforts of HBO and Turner (see 9.1) started a bandwagon of new services, all seeking to differentiate their content from rivals

---

Auxiliary Television Services Since 1977 / While over-the-air pay broadcasting (STV) had a fairly short life span, multichannel multipoint distribution services (MMDSs) and low-power television (LPTV), especially the latter, appeared to offer a niche service option to full-power television stations by the end of the 1980s. For the success of competing cable, see Appendix C, Table 10-B.

Year	STV		MDS/MMDS		LPTV Stations on Air
	Stations	Subscribers (thousands)	Systems	Subscribers (thousands)	
1977		5	27	65	
1978	2	59	29	91	
1979	3	260	44	207	
1980	6	520	54	352	
1981	14	1,082	73	479	
1982	24	1,747	99	570	na
1983	29	1,823	na	570	na
1984	12	1,203	na	490	252
1985	6	622	na	440	316
1986	3	187	na	270	383*
1987	2	118	na	240	407
1988	2	100	na	200	346
1989	na	na	na	na	457

*1986 data as of February 25.

Sources: STV and MMDS data through 1982 from Paul Kagan Associates, "Census of Pay TV Population," in *MDS Databook 1982*, page 13, as listed in Sterling (1984), pages 33 and 255 (see Appendix D for full citation), showing data as of June 30 (MDS) and December 31 of *previous* year for STV stations. STV and MDS data since 1982 from *Kagan Media Index* (May 17, 1988), page 8, citing data for last day of *previous* year. All LPTV data directly from FCC, showing outlets licensed (not all are on the air) as of December 31 of the *previous* year.

and all seeking to secure use of a transponder on one of the few satellites to which early cable system TVROs were aimed. Indeed, until TVRO costs declined after 1980, allowing a system operator to install multiple dishes aimed at different birds, it was important for cable program services to be on the same satellite as their competitors. Cable's demand for satellite transponders was equaled by the demand of other users (the military and telecommunications carriers, for example), but it took several years to translate the demand into new satellite capacity in orbit.

Beginning with HBO's pioneering use of *Satcom I* in 1976, and lasting into the early 1980s, the driving force in cable networking—and hence in the overall growth of the cable industry—was the appeal of pay-cable services to the public. Pay pioneer HBO was always the largest in number of subscribers (page 663). This

The Networks' Eye in the Sky / An artist shows how the Westar VI satellite is able to cover the continental United States with "spot beams" aimed at Hawaii and Alaska (over the horizon in this view) from its geosynchronous orbit, 22,300 miles out in space above the equator. Communication satellites so located allowed broadcast and cable networks in the 1980s to efficiently cover the entire country, moving electronic media from reliance on terrestrial wire, cable, and microwave links to application of space age technology. Photo courtesy NASA.

Time Inc. service first faced competition after March 1978 when Showtime, another first-run movie oriented service begun two years earlier in California, started satellite distribution. Other services started in the next two years included The Movie Channel, which became the first to provide movies 24 hours a day; Cinemax, also owned by Time Inc. and counterprogrammed with HBO; The Playboy Channel, carrying soft-core adult material; and several short-lived rivals, including at least two that attempted to provide more highbrow arts and performance content.

All of these pay-cable networks worked in much the same way. The pay service bought pay-cable rights to theatrical films or other content and sometimes produced special events itself. It then persuaded the cable system operator to carry and promote its service. The cable system operator then set about collecting money from the subscribers. First, there was a flat monthly fee for "basic" service (originally just on-air stations, and later inexpensive national services, such as superstations in Atlanta, Chicago, Los Angeles, and New York, for which the operator paid a few cents per subscriber per month). With pay-cable, the operator also could charge an additional flat monthly fee (usually $7 to $10 by the mid-1980s) for everything carried by pay-cable services. (Usually, half of this fee was remitted to the pay-cable service.) Toward the end of the decade, many systems also offered "pay-per-view" (PPV), which brought in money for each showing ordered by the subscriber (see below). Each service offered a monthly menu of movies and specials, repeated on different days and at different times. Eventually, most cable operators had two or three tiers of service, each adding to the subscriber's cost.

By the mid-1980s, the pay-cable boom had flattened as the number of sub-scribers giving up service ("churn" in cable parlance) about equaled those signing up. Among the factors blamed were the increasing use of home VCRs (see 9.1 and 10.12), the ever-rising prices charged subscribers (particularly after the 1984 Cable Communications Policy Act (see 10.84) allowed cable operators to ignore restrictions in their franchises), and the limited amount of high-quality programming. The average cost per cable household per month had tripled to nearly $30, but the psychological limit still had not been reached. More than half of American households now subscribed to cable, and the cable MSOs looked around for additional ways to profit even while they engaged in wheeling-and-dealing consolidation. One way was a new version of an old idea—the notion of paying to see a specific program rather than subscribing to everything carried over a channel or tier. This would be analogous to buying a single issue of a magazine at the newsstand rather than subscribing for a year at a much lower price per issue. Over-the-air pay-TV proponents of the 1950s originally had planned to charge for specific programs (see page 326) but had been unsuccessful.

In the late 1970s, cable or MMDS operators in several major markets regularly transmitted scrambled pictures of special sports events. To receive an unscrambled picture, viewers could telephone the system and agree to pay a one-time charge to clear up the picture. Dubbed pay-per-view (PPV), the system's first regular national nonsports services aired in November 1985 when Viewer's Choice, owned by Showtime/The Movie Channel, and Request Television began. PPV could be offered only on cable systems with computer-addressable decoder boxes, allowing instant descrambling of the PPV channel when viewers called to order a specific showing. The charges of $3 to $5 for each movie or event were very profitable for the cable operator, the PPV company, and the original supplier of the programming. PPV differed from HBO and other pay-cable channels by providing only a few first-run movies (often while they were still in theatrical release) or sporting events per month heavily promoted and repeated at different times to catch all possible viewers. Much as the earliest television sets were to be found in public places like taverns, many members of the public first became aware of the possibilities of PPV by its availability in many hotel rooms.

Following the path of the pay services (but much less expensive to the supplier) came advertiser-supported basic cable networks, some of which charged systems to carry their service but were designed to be free of additional cost to viewers. However, speculation in the 1970s that there would be a flood of highly specialized cable services providing narrowcasts to targeted audiences, as a counter to the broadcast business, did not materialize. The costs of developing specific programming delivered by satellite to relatively small numbers of viewers were just too high. Some observers believed that the amount of talent needed to produce such programming also was near its limit. Thus, much of cable television increasingly began to resemble broadcasting in its content, even on services designed specifically for cable. Several cable networks tried to repeat the old radio approach of being all things to all viewers (such as the USA Network beginning in 1980, which relied heavily on broadcast reruns), while others took a specific programming niche (for example, Christian Broadcasting Network (CBN), one of the first and most widely successful conservative religious/family-oriented cable services; MTV, the first 24-hour music video service, beginning in

1981; C-SPAN, Cable Special Public Affairs Network, which, among other things, carried all proceedings from the House of Representatives and later the U.S. Senate, and The Weather Channel, starting in mid-1982). And, as discussed further in 10.64, Ted Turner's Cable News Network helped to change television journalism practice—and audience viewing habits—after 1980.

By the late 1980s, the impact of cable networks was being felt at the broadcast networks, each of which had lost audience and income from the competition, and in homes across the country, where the notion of "network" now included dozens of satellite- and cable-delivered services. One indicator of cable's increasing importance was the development of concern over concentration among cable programmers and system operators. MSOs got larger, and independent system operators grew fewer (see 10.85). Another indication was the steady increase in space devoted to cable program listings in *TV Guide*.

10•4   Public Broadcasting (Still) Seeks Its Place

Public broadcasting both progressed and regressed in the years after 1977. This should come as no surprise. As noted in 9.4, interorganizational squabbles and questions of long-range funding pervaded the system in the mid-1970s—as they still did in the late 1980s. The problem was partially organizational politics, but underlying the malaise was a continued search for the right role . . . and an audience. Public television still lacked a cohesive sense of what its mission should be. Even public radio, always more focused, had troubles in the 1980s. As one wag put it, if public broadcasting officials were armed and asked to form a firing squad, they would stand in a circle!

One timely indicator of the problems was the report of a second Carnegie commission (Carnegie II). Those frustrated by many years of confusion centered their hopes on this effort, remembering the impact of the first commission a decade earlier (see 9.4). But times had changed. The second report, *A Public Trust,* issued in January 1979 after a year and a half of study, included a detailed accounting of what had been accomplished in public broadcasting's first decade and described the continuing problems of inadequate long-range funding and of insulation of programming from political pressures. Unfortunately, its call for substantially higher federal funding reached Congress in the midst of recession and belt-tightening. And its emphasis on a substantial restructuring of public broadcasting organizations—replacement of the Corporation for Public Broadcasting by a Public Telecommunications Trust—was largely ignored. Carnegie II was an interesting document, but it had nothing of the effect of the landmark first Carnegie report.

10•41   Politics As Usual

Carnegie II's relative lack of impact was due in part to entrenched factions in the various national organizations in public broadcasting. The battles of the 1970s involved hardened points of view, but the 1980s can be seen as one long and continuing struggle for both internal and external control of the Corporation for Public Broadcasting. This political infighting would be of mere parochial interest except that public broadcasting's establishment was thus ill prepared to face the Reagan administration's continued attempts in the 1980s to cut drastically (if not eliminate) federal funding of station facilities building, and operation of CPB. Although the policy of distributing CPB funds to local stations rather than centralizing production ensured that PBS programming was unlikely to be as offensive to the White House as that of a truly independent public broadcasting system would be, control of the corporation would ensure that this situation would continue.

The battle for control of the corporation centered on its 15-member board of directors, all appointed by the president. No matter who serves in the White House, CPB appointments are not a high priority, and thus the CPB board often was short of members. In addition, political appointees often have strong political views, which led to board battles over policies and personnel. For nearly a year in 1987, for example, the board considered a controversial content analysis of its own programming advocated by a right-wing Reagan appointee. When the board finally decided against the research, the member lost interest and resigned. The sharpest disagreements came while Reagan appointee Sonia Landau served as chair (1984–1987). Wife of a *New York Times* television columnist, Landau clearly had a political assignment—to bring CPB to heel by increasing its corporate underwriting and reducing federal funding. Policy and personality disagreements led in 1985 to the firing of CPB president Edward Pfister and the most severe public break between local stations and the Washington power structure in some years. The CPB board then fired Pfister's successor after only 10 months. His successor, Donald Ledwig, became CPB's sixth president in late 1987.

In the early 1980s, a financial crisis and scandal nearly ended National Public Radio. NPR had begun to seek means of self-support as funding from CPB seemed increasingly uncertain. Under Frank Mankiewicz, its president since 1977, NPR announced in 1982 an ambitious plan of further underwriting and sale of various services to allow total independence from the creaky federal funding process by 1988. The plans were too large and the base was too small—and by 1983 Mankiewicz was out and NPR was reeling from more than a $6 million deficit due to poor fiscal controls over expense accounts and expansive hiring practices. Congress investigated (some of the funds were federal), and things looked dark until CPB came through with a loan to allow operations to continue. For the first time, many individuals contributed to this national programming source in order to preserve their own listening choices. Nearly 100 employees were let go. The loan was paid back to CPB on schedule—but NPR lost some of its cherished independence from the political influences controlling CPB.

10•42   The Programming Dilemma

The audience knew little of the behind-the-scenes agony over finance and control, for it rarely directly affected what was on the air. Radio, particularly, continued to carve out a small but important audience interested primarily in news, public affairs, and the arts. Less than a third (about 280) of the more than 1,300 public radio stations (see Appendix C, table 1-B) were "CPB qualified" and able to secure any of the dwindling pot of CPB funding. This meant also that only a small fraction of all public radio stations were carriers of NPR programming, with the remainder trying to attract local or specialized audiences, perhaps serving as a training ground for college or high school students of broadcasting or just indulging the preferences of whomever was in charge of programming.

But in almost every market of any size, at least one station carried National Public Radio. NPR's *Morning Edition* transported the low-key news and features approach of *All Things Considered* to a morning drive-time audience beginning in 1979, and *Weekend Edition* had its debut in 1985. Major congressional hearings, such as the Iran-Contra investigation, and inquiries into the fitness of nominees to the Supreme Court, were carried live by NPR as a matter of record. The fiscal crisis had eased sufficiently early in 1987 that *Performance Today* was begun (to mixed reviews) on a five-day-a-week basis.

In May 1980, Garrison Keillor's *A Prairie Home Companion* was first offered by Minnesota Public Radio. The weekly two hours of Keillor's creatively off-brand strain of humor quickly attracted a large (for public radio) and fanatically faithful late Saturday afternoon audience in most communities. The show typically was in three parts: an eclectic selection of musical performers (often folk or bluegrass), dramatic sketches, and a monologue about the doings in a mythical town called Lake Wobegon, Minnesota, with its strange yet familiar population of misfits, mixed with humorous "commercials" (for Powdermilk Biscuits, Bob's Pretty Good Grocery, Bertha's Kitty Boutique, The Side Track Tap, Hoo-Hah! Hot Sauce, and the like). Keillor, a talented fiction writer for *The New Yorker* magazine, each week softly delivered a lengthy monologue about what was happening in Lake Wobegon and to its citizens (who reminded us of slightly larger-than-life reflections of people we knew). The program evoked a gamut of emotions in its audience, much as the *Vic and Sade* network radio program had in the 1930s and 1940s. The show was carried live from an old theater in the Twin Cities, although it occasionally went on the road and was simulcast on television a few times.

The popularity of *A Prairie Home Companion*—more people may have listened to it than to any other public radio program—helped Minnesota Public Radio create a new national organization, American Public Radio (APR), in 1981. Keillor finally became tired of the punishing creative requirements of *Companion* (it had been on the air in one form or another for 13 years), and production ceased in mid-1987. APR, meantime, had become an important program distributor and provided an option to NPR's material by carrying *MonitoRadio* (produced by the *Christian Science Monitor*, which was also edging into commercial radio and television) and other programs. Thanks to the availability of a satellite system, other programming was distributed nationally by stations with the funds to produce it, such as the jazz programming welcoming in the New Year from every time zone or Robert J. Lurtsema's unique blend of music and commentary on *Morning Pro Musica*, which originated in New England but had spread across the country.

Most public radio stations, even those controlled by school boards, were carrying less classroom instructional material (often under two percent by the mid-1980s), a sad end to the high goals worked toward for decades by the National Association of Educational Broadcasters (which itself went out of existence by 1981).

Public television also became less overtly instructional and more of a general appeal medium. Indeed, except for a little during school hours, most "educational" programming also appealed to a general audience. Among those programs that might be classified in this way were *Sesame Street*, *Nova*, numerous nature programs, and other specials and miniseries. (Of course, such programming also existed on commercial television, but the commercial stations and networks would never label it "educational" for fear of audience turning off.)

The first regularly scheduled national evening newscast on public TV was the *Robert MacNeil Report*, starting in 1976 and expanded in 1983 as *The MacNeil/ Lehrer NewsHour*, to become the country's only nightly hour-long newscast–interview-documentary (the format depended on the topic), although ABC's *Nightline* had similar content in a shorter time frame. Likewise, public television often seemed the only congenial home for controversial documentaries. *Frontline*, which often used the products of independent documentary filmmakers or video producers, was the only regularly scheduled documentary program in the mid-1980s. *Vietnam: A Television History* offered 13 hour-long episodes produced in 1983 by Boston's WGBH in association with British and French television companies to tell the entire story of the Vietnam wars from the 1940s to the 1970s. Because of the importance of television's on-the-spot coverage of that war, which affected (and was in turn affected by) public opinion (see 9.64), the series was in part a study of the video medium itself and raised considerable controversy. It was not as controversial, however, as a multipart idiosyncratic view of black history titled *The Africans*, which raised the hackles of some Americans who objected to the left-wing approach of the program and demanded (and received) the opportunity to prepare a rebuttal.

PBS viewers still were attracted by old staples such as Sunday evening's *Masterpiece Theatre*, which continued to present British television dramas introduced by the urbane Alistair Cooke (and continued to make viewers wonder why American television could rarely do as well). A similar compilation of mostly British miniseries under the title of *Mystery!* did almost as well, extending the career of its host, one-time film horror star Vincent Price; Children's Television Workshop's *Sesame Street* was well into educating its third generation when it celebrated two decades on the air in 1989; *American Playhouse* presented U.S. productions from a consortium of public television stations beginning in 1982; and there were many documentaries dealing with nature and adventure. A number of the miniseries featured on these programs—such as *Jewel in the Crown,* about India during World War II and its achievement of independence—attracted audiences of extraordinary loyalty. Weekly current events programs like *Washington Week in Review* and *Wall Street Week* also had large and loyal audiences.

One indicator of the identity problem public television seemed to have was the blurring of lines dividing commercial entertainment from public television programming. A few public stations, seeking broader audiences at lowest cost, began to provide reruns of former commercial fare. The airing of movies, once intended to expose the audience to rare art films, started to concentrate on musicals and other popular fare—often to the annoyance of independent commercial broadcasters. In 1980, the critically acclaimed but low-rated *Paper Chase* series, which realistically portrayed law school students and practices (featuring veteran director-actor John Houseman as the senior professor) was rerun on public television after being canceled by CBS after only one season (1978–1979). (In 1983, the Showtime pay-cable service produced new episodes with much of the old cast, keeping the program alive for another year.) Similarly, *National Geographic Specials* and *Smithsonian,* among other series, often appeared on higher-paying commercial networks after their initial airing on PBS, carrying on a tradition ranging back to *The Finder* in the 1950s. Individuals also moved in both

directions: Larry Grossman of PBS was president of NBC News for several years; movie critics Siskel and Ebert moved over to the better-paying commercial world; network newsmen Daniel Schorr and Roger Mudd moved from commercial to public television (which may have allowed more latitude, if less cash); and Bill Moyers went from PBS to CBS and back again in the 1980s as he sought an outlet for his documentaries and interviews that would allow him to say what he felt needed to be said.

10•43   Financing: A Gordian Knot

The financial crisis—almost a normal state of affairs for noncommercial radio and television stations—continued throughout the 1980s. Unfortunately, many felt that money itself was the chief problem, losing sight of the fact that disagreement on the basic mission (or at least on how best to accomplish that mission) contributed strongly to the continuing dearth of funds.

Lack of any action on the second Carnegie commission's recommendations (see 10.41) laid the ground work for the first major congressionally supported review of funding options. In a 1981 funding bill, Congress established the Temporary Commission on Alternative Funding for Public Telecommunications (TCAF), made up of both public- and private-sector representatives, to study and experiment with options. TCAF operated through 1983 with support from the FCC and, under the authority of the 1981 act, conducted an 18-month experiment with overt advertising on 10 public television stations (public radio did not participate).

Following this experiment, TCAF recommended against advertising as an answer to public television's fiscal problems for fear that only major stations in large markets would receive sufficient revenue to justify added expense of sales staffs and higher union costs, and because acceptance of advertising and its implied search for larger audiences might well undermine the whole rationale of PBS as an alternative to commercial broadcasting. Although public television has always trumpeted its "commercial-free" status, most programs—since they often are prepared without knowledge of whether they will appear on public or commercial television—tend to be of the same length. As a result, PBS stations typically have four or five minutes at the end of each program to fill with promos and other material.

But it was clear to TCAF that the powerful commercial broadcasting industry would not sit still for continued spectrum reservations and other special benefits for a system supported by advertising in competition with regular commercial stations. Instead, after assessing several ideas, TCAF concluded that a system of "enhanced underwriting," or more extensive announcements at the beginning and end of each program by corporations providing support for the program (and hardly distinguishable from short commercials in some cases) would be of greatest value. The FCC subsequently modified its rules and regulations to allow such an approach.

Still, enhanced underwriting, membership drives, and auctions were not enough, and public broadcasters trekked to Capitol Hill every year, seeking additional funding for the system. Budget pressures on Congress and the Reagan administration's lack of support in the 1980s led to a new threat—"recisions" of money previously allocated. This situation made a hash of advance program financial commitments and other long-range planning—and effectively undid the whole rationale of three-year funding cycles.

State contributions to public stations, once a major factor in overall funding levels, also declined under similar budgetary pressures.

On the local level, stations had little choice but to undertake on-the-air auctions and "membership" pledge week "begathons" to increase viewers' participation in financial support of "their" stations. While the $35–$50 basic membership category hardly paid for itself, since fund-raising is not cheap and a program guide had to be published and distributed, the stations felt that commitments of any amount would lead to larger audiences, a selling point for enhanced underwriting, and the opportunity to seek more contributions from members throughout the year. On the other hand, public stations that did on-the-air fund-raising knew that they often alienated much of their audience during the campaign, but saw no alternative in a time of reduced federal funding.

10•5   Advertising: Money and Motives

Outside of public broadcasting, advertising revenues remained the lubricant of the electronic media and one reason for the merger mania noted earlier (see 10.2). While network television continued to be the country's prime national mass advertising medium during this period, changes in the old order clearly were in sight as early as the 1970s.

10•51   Broadcast Advertising: A Continuing Relationship

More than a few industry experts in the late 1970s were questioning how long a mass advertising–supported system of broadcasting could last amidst the growing number of delivery options and increasing specialization of content that then was just beginning to divide the audience. More than half a century of experience in reaching large, heterogeneous listening audiences seemed to be in jeopardy. Yet, ten years later, broadcasting's major advertisers still were largely loyal to the national television networks, though they experimented widely with other options. The declining rate of growth in radio and television advertising revenues (see Appendix C, tables 4 and 5) was due to changes in listening and viewing and to a slower-growing audience divided among more and more different services, as discussed further in 10.7.

For the first time, a substantial number of American homes had other ways to get electronic entertainment, chiefly videocassettes (often carrying promos for other films, if not actual advertising messages) and cable (a competitor for advertising itself). The growing number of independent stations also cut into the networks' revenues. In part, the ever-higher costs of television time and production lost it some advertisers. Newspapers still were the medium of choice for local retail and classified advertising, and other media, such as direct mail, grew in sophistication.

Still, through the 1980s, broadcasting remained an immensely successful advertising medium. The years after 1977 saw FM radio slowly develop into an important advertising medium for the first time in its varied history. AM's audience decline (see 10.7) translated in the mid-1980s into a parallel decline in its importance to advertisers. While the number of advertiser dollars put into any form of radio nearly tripled from 1970 to 1980 and almost doubled again during the first seven years of the 1980s, most of this was apparent rather than real, as a result of the monetary inflation of the period, and was

matched by other media. (Between 1970 and 1985, television advertising revenues grew fivefold, as compared with radio's nearly fourfold increase and newspapers' better than threefold rise—though inflation accounted for more than half of these increases.) For both radio and television, local advertising revenues grew substantially faster than national "spot" advertising during this period, while network revenues climbed proportionately faster for radio than for television. During these 15 years, radio advertising constituted approximately 7 percent of all advertising, while television advertising's share grew from 18 to 22 percent.

Several threats to broadcast advertising arose in this period but disappeared without impinging on broadcasters' incomes. Early in the 1980s, bills were introduced in Congress to eliminate all advertising of wine and beer on television. ("Hard" liquor advertising always had been voluntarily refused by the industry as a public relations gesture.) Advertising of legal over-the-counter drugs also was questioned in mid-decade, with critics arguing that children and others seeing any pill-taking as acceptable might translate that image to the use of illicit drugs. Although the analogy of the law eliminating cigarette advertising in 1971 was raised, none of these limitations became law, in part because of effective lobbying by the wine, beer, drug, and broadcasting industries.

More fractious was the debate over advertising in children's programming. As a part of its radio deregulation decision (see 10.82), the FCC removed its limits on the amount of advertising time allowed in programs aimed at children. Action for Children's Television and other groups petitioned the commission and courts for reinstatement of those guidelines. In 1988, Congress passed, but President Reagan vetoed, guidelines similar to those dropped by the commission. Concerns over so-called program length commercials (often cartoon shows with close tie-ins with commercial products) and selling by hosts of children's programs continued to trouble many critics. Indeed, it had troubled some broadcasters, as was evidenced in the advertising guidelines found in the now-abandoned (see 10.8) National Association of Broadcasters' code.

Often raised and always successfully beaten back were attempts by various states to tax advertising receipts, including, of course, radio and television (and cable) advertising revenues. In 1987, Florida's governor pushed through legislation to tax services, including advertising. Soon national advertisers were pulling their campaigns off Florida stations to avoid the tax hassles—and moving trade association meetings from Florida to drive home the point. Pressure from those stations, other services affected, and Florida's tourism industry got the law rescinded in 1988.

10•52   New Media, Limited Appeal

As cable penetrated half of all homes in the country, glowing talk of the wired medium as a mass advertising vehicle was heard again. Cable's potential as an ad medium had been touted for years, but for several reasons the potential had never become practice. Cable's very success in providing more channels for its audience was at the core of the problem, for each new channel further divided the audience, making it harder to sell any one channel or program to a given advertiser. Individual cable networks often rose and fell on the results of their selling sufficient adver-

tising time to cover costs. Cable systems' main revenue source had always been subscribers' fees, making the need for advertising secondary. While radio and television combined carried more than a quarter of all advertising in the country by the mid-1980s, cable television accounted for less than 1 percent. However, some analysts expected the networks' proportion of television advertising to continue to decline (from roughly half) while cable's might rise to nearly 5 percent, with most of the network loss flowing to local stations and syndicated programming rather than cable.

Not quite advertising in the accepted sense, but certainly a way of moving products, was the cable home-shopping craze of the mid-1980s. The notion of direct selling over the air was not new—it dated back at least half a century to early radio experiments, and numerous products had been sold on a "per-inquiry" basis (with a commission going to the station). Also similar have been pitches for "greatest hits" records and tapes. In 1977, an AM station in Clearwater, Florida, offered home listeners a chance to call in directly and order products described on the air. It did this for several years before moving the concept to the local cable system in 1982. In July 1985, as the Home Shopping Network, the operation began national satellite distribution to cable systems across the country, offering system operators a small portion of the income received from their coverage area as an encouragement to carry the signal. A changing cast of hosts offered dozens of products during the course of a day at what were touted as deep discount prices, while cameras lovingly portrayed the item of the moment and constantly displayed a toll-free "800" number for viewers to use in placing their orders. In March 1986, a second HSN channel came on line to meet viewer demand. Other shopping services soon crowded on the air, some on cable and some on local UHF stations desperate for programming and revenue. Some of these stations eventually were purchased by one of the shopping networks. The process was the same in each case—products being shown constantly and huge batteries of telephone operators standing by to take orders and credit card numbers. Programming and advertising had merged to become one and the same.

Of the many other television delivery options offered in the 1980s, none except cable was large enough to garner much advertiser interest, although once in a while an advertiser would make videotapes of popular movies available at a drastic price reduction in order to be able to use the first few minutes of the tape for a commercial. Home VCRs actually were a threat to television advertisers because of the viewers' habit of "zipping" ahead through prerecorded ads, or else "zapping" (not recording) them in the first place. Surveys showed that a substantial proportion of those who recorded programs off the air generally skipped over the accompanying advertisements.

10•6   Programming

A television viewer at the end of the 1980s saw programming not much different from that aired a decade or two earlier. There was more use of computer graphics and somewhat more attention paid to sound quality, but most programming was still unpretentious entertainment. Some more attention was paid to "reality" (often defined as—or at least with—sex and violence), and there was a frantic search for successful formats to imi-

tate. Poorly rated shows tended to leave the networks much faster by the late 1980s than a decade earlier—both because of better research and because of the risk involved in keeping an expensive show on the air. Radio formats tended to be aimed at those who liked either popular rock music or telephone-in talk, with hardly discernible differences between stations.

10•61   Radio's Survival

Radio programming changed remarkably little in the 1977–1988 period. Virtually no major unique format was developed. AM and FM stations continued to fragment the existing music and talk formats in search of specific audience niches as more stations crowded the airwaves. A "nostalgia" format appealed to more stations by the 1980s, but then there was more "golden oldie" rock music on which to base such an approach. Further, radio's audience was slowly aging and carrying its radio format preferences with it. More stations on the air simply meant that each station had a smaller piece of the pie—and seeking and holding that segment became both harder and more important.

The most important radio shift was the decline of AM in the face of FM. As indicated in 10.21, almost all new portable or automobile radios were AM-FM, and, with free choice, the audience tended to gravitate toward the better-sounding medium. In 1976, FM had about 40 percent of the audience and perhaps half that proportion of total radio income. A decade later, FM's audience and revenue shares both hovered at 70 percent. Crucial to the switch had been the FCC's nonduplication programming decisions of the mid-1960s (see 9.61), which forced FM stations to develop their own sound, which in turn gave about half the national radio audience to FM stations by 1980. In the early 1980s, country, adult contemporary, Top 40 (usually called "contemporary hit radio" or CHR), album-oriented rock (AOR), and the old middle-of-the-road (MOR) format (combining talk, features, and some music) were the leaders, with country music being the single most common radio format. These same formats were strong at decade's end. With major markets often having 30 to 50 stations competing for listeners, focusing on specific demographic groups became more common. Some stations went for smaller audiences concentrated in demographic categories appealing to advertisers, such as men and women in the 18–45 age category or even women 18–35, rather than teens with less money to spend.

AM stations, to survive, looked to more specialized formats, including all-news, talk, and sports (all programs not helped by FM's better sound quality) and also specifically focused on ethnic minorities. All-talk stations, which featured telephone-in programs hosted by opinionated and controversial figures, attracted appreciable audiences. Several of these individuals, including Morton Downey, Jr., moved on to television. A few major market AM outlets struggled to survive with MOR formats not much different from radio three and four decades earlier. In small markets, of course, the limited number of outlets gave any radio station substantial flexibility in choosing its format. The traditional mix of news, personality, features, and some music had strong appeal, especially among older listeners. Likewise, especially in the South and Midwest, religious stations programming a mixture of conservative talk and features plus religious music and sermons (with monetary appeals) held a loyal audience.

10•62 Rising Risks in Television Programming

The arrival of VCRs and cable in a majority of homes by the late 1980s made those new media more important to the actors, writers, other creative people, and technicians who make television programs. The same was true with foreign rights to American programs as more countries found it popular and profitable to show American material. In 1981, and again in 1988, the start of the fall television season was delayed by strikes. The 1981 delay was caused by a July–September strike by the Screen Actor's Guild and the American Federation of Television and Radio Artists, who wanted more residual income from use of their programs on new media. This lack of a strong start contributed to a drop-off in network viewing levels for the entire season. The 22-week 1988 strike, which lasted until mid-August, saw the writers of television programs strike over similar issues plus a larger part of income from overseas sales. The new season was delayed into November, and fears were expressed again about pushing viewers tired of reruns to other services. While the "summer" (actually, September) Olympic Games and the presidential election campaign somewhat camouflaged the effect of the strike, the networks justifiably feared the potential for long-term negative effects. In the short term, of course, the strike concerned those striking and the companies struck (and the many ancillary industries, from restaurants to accountants, that depended largely on television production). Nevertheless, the strikes were an indicator of the growing recognition by others besides those in the executive suites of the changing economics of television programming.

The chief change, of course, was the ever-higher cost of making television shows. Program costs climbed, due in part to inflation and in part to improved production values (computer animation; location costs; a willingness to pay almost anything to secure the services of actors who were "bankable," or so popular that they could command a large audience no matter what the program; and so on). A typical one-hour prime-time drama that would have cost about $100,000 to produce in 1965 was up to about $300,000 a decade later, and to about $900,000 by the late 1980s, in spite of such cost-cutting practices as making programs in less-expensive Canada or using nonunion crews to the extent possible. As the cost of production rose, so did the risks attendant in making programs for television. Networks balked at paying more for their license to show a program (usually twice, before all rights reverted back to the independent program concern) so that by the late 1970s, network payments covered only 90 to 95 percent—at best—of the per-episode cost of production. The production company was thus taking at least a temporary loss and the very real risk that the network would not renew the program for additional seasons, which would mean there would not be enough episodes to make the series attractive for eventual syndication.

By the late 1980s, successful syndication (domestic and often foreign) was required for a program merely to break even, let alone to make a profit. Until the 1970s, syndication nearly always provided profit over and above income from the network, which usually paid all actual production costs. There was little "first-run" (made for syndication) material. Passage of the Prime Time Access Rule (see page 385), the establishment of nearly 300 independent television stations by the late 1980s (see 10.22), plus the increasing interest in recent (and even older) programming by basic cable networks changed that. In

1980–1981, 25 first-run syndicated shows aired at the start of the season. By 1986–1987, that number had jumped to 96. New companies developed to meet the demand, but there were problems as well. All production costs were up sharply, increasing the risk of program making and buying.

Syndication's image was of a steady diet of game shows and interview programs. Indeed, *Wheel of Fortune* (with the handsome Vanna White turning the letters) and *Jeopardy* were the top-rated syndicated shows of the late 1980s, followed closely by the Oprah Winfrey and Phil Donahue daytime interview shows (Merv Griffin having gone into big-time real estate). The cost of both formats was only a fraction of that of dramatic or variety programming. In 1988, *Wheel* cost about $8 million a year to make—but this daily program earned some $100 million!

To secure the rights for sufficient programming, many networks and producers went to measures that might not have been attempted in the past. International co-productions, involving money from one or more countries and creative talent from others, became common. WGBH (PBS) no longer had a monopoly of the many programs produced in England, with both good and bad programming going to the highest bidder (or the co-producer). Entrepreneurs like Ted Turner might go so far as to purchase the films of an entire major Hollywood studio in order to be able to feed the always-demanding channels that he programmed. HBO frequently produced major programs with its own money, and consortia of stations or other cable program services did the same, although less often. Indeed, the expectations engendered by pro-cable publicity in the 1960s and 1970s, which held out hope that cable would become a source of tremendous amounts of higher-quality programming than the commercial broad-cast networks, appeared to be ill founded.

10•63 Television Entertainment: Imitation and Evolution

In the late 1980s, prime-time television remained a search for ratings success amidst slight variations of previously successful shows or stars. There was little that was new or different, for the risks in taking such a path were too great considering the costs of production, let alone the pressures of competing cable and VCR offerings. Of course, once in a while (as with *Hill Street Blues*) a new program so intrigued the audience (and other producers) that it was quickly imitated—but the process of innovation itself never really caught on. During other parts of the day, there was even less change. Soap operas and interview shows occupied most of the day, with morning programs such as the *Today* show and *Good Morning, America* starting off and NBC's *Johnny Carson* celebrity and variety show (and ABC's *Nightline*) serving as a nightcap after the local station's 11 o'clock news.

Although formulas remained the same, some genres changed more than others. Science fiction became less common, although fans of the long-running— it went through at least four actors in the title role—British import *Dr. Who* on PBS were a force to be reckoned with. In 1987 *Star Trek: The Next Generation* was aired (still without seat belts in the control room), and *ALF* began in 1986 on NBC. The latter could be considered either a throwback to earlier animal-centered comedy series featuring a "typical" television family or science fiction, since ALF was an "alien life form" from outer space with a smart-aleck mouth and a taste for cats (to eat). Paralleling the fate of feature films on the home

screen, the western had almost disappeared from television, though the mini-series *Lonesome Dove* achieved very high ratings for CBS early in 1989.

10•631 Network Jockeying

In the mid-1970s, ABC briefly was the highest-rated network, thanks to the programming success of Fred Silverman (see 9.6). CBS moved back into its accustomed top spot in the 1979–1980 season. And then, in 1986, for the first time in television history, NBC nudged into top position and CBS slipped to third–a reversal of three decades' pattern. Later still, ABC slipped back down the mountain. No longer could a network plan a season's programs and then stick with them for several months to see if the audience would start to grow, as had happened often in the past. Now, if a program did not do well in the "overnight" weekly ratings, it was cut at once without compunction, since the advertisers could read the ratings just as easily as the networks. Each program not only had to build its own audience but had to deliver an audience to the programs that followed it later in the evening.

As before, all three networks would trot out special programs, typically made-for-television movies and mini-series, during the three ratings "sweep weeks" each year to try and bolster their image and ranking. To some extent, this occasional break with the regular pattern of weekly series added to the debate over whether to provide programming people merely watch or that which they watch and talk about. While conventional wisdom has it that few series (let alone most individual episodes) stay in viewers' minds, it is believed that specials—and the commercial spots they contain—often do. Networks were thus also able to capitalize on popular topics, stars, movies, or books without committing themselves to a full season's series (see also 10.42).

In early 1983, for example, ABC offered 16 hours of *The Winds of War* (based on the popular Herman Wouk novel of World War II and featuring veteran movie actor Robert Mitchum in his first television role) and *The Thorn Birds* for nine hours (largely set in the Australian outback and exploring the pressures on an ambitious priest who falls in love). Both were highly successful audience-grabbers. Indeed, ABC came back with a *Winds* sequel (*War and Remembrance*) five years later that ran even longer (18 hours in November 1988 and 12 more early in 1989—said to be the most costly program ever made for television, at a cost of over $100 million!). ABC found, however, that the program had marginal audience appeal, which made it likely that it would be the last miniseries this expensive. Also popular were "docudrama" specials, which retold history with a bit of license: biographies of John F. and Robert Kennedy and Lyndon Johnson; recreations of the life and work of Sam Houston and George Washington; refighting of various portions of the Civil War; famous recent murder cases; and visits back to the times of Napoleon, Peter the Great, and Columbus. A tendency to recycle became evident in the late 1980s, as "reunion" or "what do they look like now" specials featuring the original casts of frothy programs such as *Leave it to Beaver* and *Gilligan's Island* were presented to a nostalgic audience.

Some specials had substantial impact. Building on ABC's 1977 success with *Roots* (see page 400), NBC offered a four-night dramatization of the life and death of the Jewish families during World War II in *Holocaust,* creating substantial controversy and widespread interest here and overseas (the series was eventually shown in West Germany, raising even more controversy in that country). Several programs dealing with the aftermath of a nuclear war (*Testament, The Day After*) generated strong reactions. More than half the country's adult population tuned in to *The Day After,* a several-hour view of a family in Lawrence, Kansas, after a nuclear exchange. Antiwar groups found that the program reinforced their message; "hawkish" groups claimed it was antidefense propaganda; all viewers found the images horrible and long lasting.

Another form of special reverted to former days of television music and variety, for a good cause. In July 1985, top music groups and individuals appeared free on a 17-hour marathon concert televised from London and Philadelphia to raise money for starving people in Africa. Dubbed *Live Aid,* some $75 million was raised in this series of musical acts seen by millions. The show used 14 satellites and was seen in 110 countries live (and in another 40 on tape). In later months, similar though less ambitious domestic versions sought to raise money for relief for economically distressed and weather-battered American farmers and other causes.

10•632   *New Dramatic Techniques*

Not all serious television programs were specials. *Hill Street Blues,* which began as a mid-season replacement in January 1981 on NBC, focused on the members of a local police station in a depressed area in a large city. The characters were realistic, and so was the constant pressure of dealing with societal dregs and getting on with life. The viewer saw humor, pathos, and violence as he or she followed fully formed characters in a semi-serial fashion from week to week. Each episode took place in a single day, from the early morning roll call to late evening, with rapid cutting between multiple story lines and a cast of more than a dozen principals to keep track of. *Hill Street Blues* characters appeared as real (if somewhat larger than life) people, and it seemed appropriate to allow the line between the real (and ultimately fatal) health problems of the actor playing the precinct sergeant and the health of the fictional character to become fuzzy. The black humor of the fictional conditions of death of "Sergeant Esterhaus" became a posthumous tribute to the actor who portrayed him.

Another dramatic series that sometimes covered important topics but did not take itself too seriously was *St. Elsewhere*. On NBC from 1982 to 1988, the program at first took a realistic warts-and-all approach to life and death in a struggling urban teaching hospital, where more seemed to go wrong than right and where not all days were good ones. The title came from the mythical "St. Eligius Hospital" in Boston's slums, to which all sorts of people needing help came—including Governor Dukakis (sprained ankle) and the medical staff itself. As with *Hill Street Blues*, the comedy was often submerged in the trauma of trying to cope, interpersonal relationships could resemble a soap opera's, and the many intertwining plot lines and cast members were not easy to sort out.

Toward the end of its run, some of *St. Elsewhere's* programs dealt with unlikely events such as an out-of-body experience and a husband and wife ex-CIA team (Steve Allen and his wife, Jayne Meadows) who could disappear at will. A final program (which received a "jeer" from *TV Guide*) indicated that the entire series existed merely in the imagination of an autistic child who was a minor character. *St. Elsewhere* had a penchant for "in" jokes, in which actors would be addressed by the name of a character they played in some

other program, and one episode contained a brief, unheralded scene in which almost the entire cast of the old Steve Allen show briefly gathered around a piano.

A similarly constructed program from the same production house (MTM), *Bay City Blues,* dealing with a minor league baseball club, ran out of story lines and audience early in its first year, but *L.A. Law,* which started in 1986, proved to be the same sort of success as *Hill Street Blues* and *St. Elsewhere,* appealing to a very loyal audience with its combination of good writing, action, tragicomic drama, and fine acting. Its multiple story lines told of the professional and private lives of associates and partners in a Los Angeles general practice law firm. A realistic (on the whole, greed outbalanced altruism) approach to the pressures of the job, combined with stereotyping of characters (the fatherly senior partner, the grasping managing partner, the philandering divorce lawyer, the sharp and ambitious women, black and Hispanic associates in the firm, and even the mentally retarded messenger) rapidly built the program to top ratings.

Many of these programs were created by Steven Bochco and produced under MTM (Mary Tyler Moore) Productions' auspices. The head of MTM when *Hill Street Blues* was first produced was Grant Tinker, ex-husband of Mary Tyler Moore, who went on to be president of NBC until shortly after it was sold to GE (see 10.3).

The differences between these programs and conventional ones were subtle. Whereas a *Barney Miller* or a *Night Court* brought a couple of intersecting and predictable plots to a location (few of these programs had more than a couple of sets) populated by permanent members of the cast, a *Hill Street Blues* or *L.A. Law* took the cast out into the streets or to other locations and let them interact with a large group of other actors and a large number of unpredictable parallel plots, few of which would be tidily resolved by the end of the program.

10•633   The Unusual . . .

The 1980s saw some of the last barricades against sensitive topics crumble. Homosexuality and even AIDS frequently were the subjects of story lines, as were drug abuse, the posttraumatic stress disorder affecting Vietnam veterans, child abuse, alcoholism, and other problems. The Vietnam War finally arrived on the same screen in programs such as *Tour of Duty* and *China Beach. Golden Girls*, starting in the fall of 1985, showed with good humor one of the most overlooked minorities in America as it followed the lives of four clearly over-50 (or -60) single women living in Miami and still seeking men and/ or happiness. The mixture of personalities and situations was a rare case of television not focusing exclusively on youth and beauty, and we laughed with, not at, the Golden Girls.

There seemed to be a new "problem" theme or two each year that appeared in some guise in almost every series. Some of this was due to the typical "copycat" approach to developing new program series, but some also was due to low-key efforts by the federal government to sensitize the creative forces of television to what Washington thought was the problem of the year. Sometimes the creative heads of studios, networks, and production houses were brought to the White House to receive a briefing—and then went back to their typewriters (or, more likely, word processors) to prepare and produce scripts giving their own view of the matter. While the effect of this strategy usually was benign, some were concerned that it might lead to having television pre-

sent only one approach to political, as well as medical or social pathological, matters, which in the future might enable an unscrupulous government and an unwary television industry to brainwash the public.

A stand-out "conventional" series was *M*A*S*H*, which had begun on CBS in 1972 and lasted for 11 years. Its combination of humor and empathy set against the activities of an army medical unit in Korea during the early 1950s' war built on an antiwar ethic growing out of the frustrating Vietnam War. The humane and antimilitary messages of Gene Reynolds and Larry Gelbart (producers and writers) and Alan Alda (the principal actor, who moved into directing) were positive and aroused resentment only among brass hats and stuffed shirts. While most regular comedies used a laugh track, it was noteworthy that *M*A*S*H*'s laugh track was never used in the operating room scenes. Alda's character of Hawkeye Pierce was the essential glue that kept things together, surrounded by the psychiatric-discharge-seeking Corporal Klinger in nylons, the naive yet shrewd Corporal "Radar" O'Reilly, and the professional and sexy chief nurse Major "Hot Lips" Houlihan. Over the years, the program survived many cast changes: new M.D. sidekicks for Hawkeye; a new commanding officer in the form of commonsensical Colonel Sherman Potter (played by *Dragnet* veteran Harry Morgan) to replace the somewhat fey reservist Lieutenant Colonel Blake (played by McLean Stevenson); and the switch from one broadly buffoonish foil to a more urbane one. Some of the programs were unique: in one, the entire half-hour was shot in black-and-white as a television documentary might have looked in the 1950s, with the actors ad-libbing in character. In another, three generations of the Alda family were featured, and in one episode the camera showed only what an injured soldier would have seen. Some episodes were downright sad and insightful rather than funny. The two-and-a-half-hour final episode of M*A*S*H, telecast on February 28, 1983, was the most-watched television show in history, with a 60.3 rating and a 77 share of those watching television at that hour! Naturally, M*A*S*H continued in syndicated reruns.

Another ground-breaking situation comedy started in the fall of 1984 when Bill Cosby returned to prime time as a New York doctor married to an attorney. The relationships between the couple and their five children remind one of *Father*

The Vietnam War as Television Drama / The 1972–1983 CBS hit M⋆A⋆S⋆H, set during the Korean War (1950–1953), helped make wartime comedy/drama popular. In 1988 network television ventured into the far more controversial waters of the Vietnam War with *China Beach* on ABC and *Tour of Duty* on CBS. *China Beach* stories centered on the women (nurses, entertainers, enlisted personnel and their commanding officer) and the men they work and live with at a military rest and recreation center and base hospital in 1968, the peak year of American fighting in Vietnam. Unlike M⋆A⋆S⋆H, *China Beach* was serious drama in an hour-long format. Like the earlier program, *Beach* and *Tour* focused on the various personal impacts of a far-off and unpopular war. Photo © 1988 Warner Bros. Inc. All rights reserved.

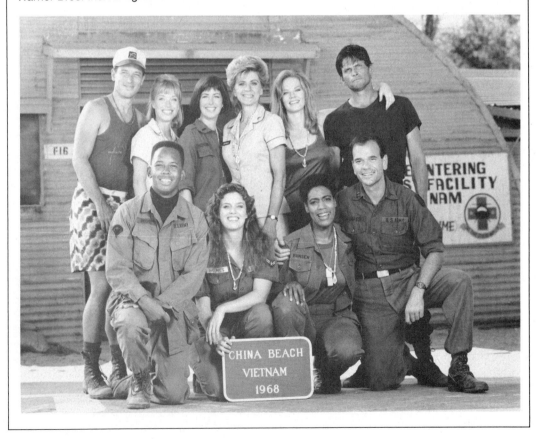

Knows Best, but this family happened to be black. *The Cosby Show* quickly helped carry NBC to the top of the ratings heap as Cosby's impeccable timing (honed by many years as a stand-up comic), recognizable family situations, and supporting cast maintained a broad appeal. Other "family" sitcoms tended to appeal to one demographic group or another—but Cosby was universal.

10•634   . . . and the More Usual

More typical television drama built around people (as opposed to situations or action-adventure) thrived in these years. The crusty but credible Lou Grant character (played by Ed Asner) went from being a television news director on the old *Mary Tyler Moore Show* to an editor on the mythical "*Los Angeles Tribune*" newspaper on the

Cosby—Comedy Success / Bill Cosby portrays New York obstetrician Dr. Cliff Huxtable, who applies gentle common sense in the raising of his son and daughters, is shown here with Rudy, his youngest child. (See the chapter opening photo for the whole group.) Showing the trials and joys of parenthood—for which Cosby always has just the right response—*The Cosby Show* first aired in the fall of 1984 and helped propel NBC to ratings leadership for the first time in history. Photo courtesy of the National Broadcasting Company, Inc.

Lou Grant program, which ran on CBS from 1977 to 1982. Its opening titles were notable in the first season for providing a half-minute music-and-film documentary on how newspapers are made—and end up as the absorbent lining for a bird cage! Both programs provided dramatic backgrounds for presenting the ethical problems of journalism. A decade later, the yuppie generation became the focus of ABC's *thirtysomething*, which combined humor and drama in an hour-long slice of life of young married professionals coping with new child, new job, or new home. Each week, the program offered more insight than situations in the accepted comedy sense, although those viewing over a generational gap might find trivial some of the problems faced by the cast. *The Days and Nights of Molly Dodd* appealed to many of the same critics and audience members, but not enough to find it a permanent network slot.

"Evening soap opera" was one term describing CBS's *Dallas*, which first aired in the spring of 1978 as a made-for-television film and began series telecasts that fall. It seemed that everyone was following the nefarious affairs (literal and figurative) of J. R. Ewing, Jr., played with a wonderful sense of evil by Larry Hagman. A huge audience was hooked by the last episode of the 1979–1980 season when J. R. was shot—and all summer, fans of the show had to await the new episodes in the fall to answer the question "Who shot J. R.?" Nearly 80 percent of all those watching television that night saw the November 21, 1980, program, which answered the question. Beginning in 1981, CBS followed up with *Falcon Crest*, starring veteran actress Jane Wyman as the domineering matriarch of a California vineyard. *Crest* built its success on the same manipulative types of characters and stories as *Dallas*. Over on ABC, beginning in January

1981, John Forsythe played Blake Carrington on *Dynasty*, the story of still another greedy big-money (oil) family, this time set in the Denver area. Much of the program built around the rivalry of Carrington's gorgeous past (Joan Collins) and present (Linda Evans) wives, all set against the glamour of luxurious settings and costumes and devious plots. Other programs, such as *Knotts Landing*, reached a similar audience. All of these programs also were popular abroad and were extremely profitable. Of course, daytime soap operas also retained their popularity (and their low production costs), moving further and further into story lines that featured explicit sex. A remarkably broad range of viewers, from college students to army trainees to retirees, were devoted to soap operas and had to get their "fix" each day.

Even without the deeper insights into the human condition provided by programs focusing on the individual rather than the situation, the action-adventure drama category, another longtime television staple format, continued to draw audiences in the 1980s. Some drama labeled action-adventure also focused on fantasy. *Charlie's Angels* professed to be about three female investigators working for a heard but never seen boss (played by John Forsythe when he was not on *Dynasty*). In fact, it was a vehicle for fast action and beautiful women during its ABC run (1976–1981) and was often criticized for its possibly sexist exploitation of "the girls" as they constantly hid their detective roles within an undercover disguise (which often hid little else). *Fantasy Island* also ran on ABC, from 1978 to 1984, building each one-hour episode around the arrival of new guests at a mysterious resort island where a lifelong dream could come true. As the series went from season to season, the plots seemed ever more unlikely.

Any setting could be home to programs of different types. The world of law had *Paper Chase* (law school), *L.A. Law,* and *Night Court* (a warm comedy program). Medicine had programs ranging from comedy to the macabre. The military, big business, police forces, college, and almost any other professional setting could house a television program of some sort. About the only rare subject was the kind of daily work done by most Americans from nine to five. True, Flo was a waitress in Mel's Diner, "Ski" worked for a brief time in a steel mill, *Taxi's* drivers seemed to do some work, and Jackie Gleason achieved fame as a bus driver. Yet the life of the "working stiff" was rarely portrayed on television.

One program that may be thought of as an exception was *Cheers,* which was set in a Boston neighborhood bar. This program, which ran on NBC from 1982 to 1989, grew steadily in popularity for several of these years. Plots were subordinated to character, and audiences felt that they knew a real Sam Malone (a jock—former baseball player—who owned the bar and had a large ego about his attractiveness to the opposite sex and not too many brains); Diane (a mousy blonde know-it-all who seemed his direct opposite and with whom he fought for the first years of the show—the culmination of their relationship in bed coinciding with a major ratings drop); barflies Cliff (a postman who knew nothing) and Norm (an overweight, henpecked accountant); and sharp-voiced waitress Carla. When the actor playing "Coach," the bartender, died, the audience at home grieved with the cast on the screen.

Conventional situation comedy clearly remained a prime-time staple throughout these years, as it had been for decades. And the overall format varied little—half an hour, usually with a laugh track and a regular cast. Some programs were superficially like others in terms of setting, but there was a big difference between the unconventional *Hill Street Blues* and the conventional *Barney Miller.* This is not to deprecate *Barney Miller,* which was a literate and low-key half-hour ABC sitcom from 1975 to 1982. Although it too followed big-city cops in the station house, it was a comedy (with some serious moments) that looked to the past for its production values rather than to the future.

Even more traditional were programs like *Love Boat.* In 1976, ABC ran several two-hour specials about life and love on a cruise ship. There was enough audience-pleasing fantasy and light romance in the two or three independent short stories in each "cruise" that ABC decided to commission Aaron Spelling to bring the idea back as a series in the fall of 1977. The program ran into the mid-1980s, benefiting ABC and the Princess cruise ship line, which always sold out when it could announce that *Love Boat* filming would take place on a particular voyage. Actors portraying the ship's crew provided continuity, while guest stars (who got a free tropical cruise as well as pay) appeared in the vignettes, which were all based on some aspect of the love story formula.

Over the years, the networks have presented programs that purported to show (humorously) what goes on in the broadcasting industry. Feature and made-for-television films like *Network, Broadcast News, Special Bulletin* (another nuclear disaster drama), and *11 o'Clock News* took care of the serious end. Even radio programs from the 1940s like the *Jack Benny Show* used this approach, as did television programs like the *Mary Tyler Moore Show* and *Good Morning Beantown.* One of the zaniest of the genre was CBS's 1978–1982 *WKRP in Cincinnati.* A flashy sales director, a zonked-out jazz DJ and a hip black DJ, a takes-himself-too-seriously news director, a sexy front office secretary, a slightly confused general manager, and a "normal" new program director made up the cast.

10•635   Among the Missing

What was missing from television in the 1980s? Reviewing popular network programs of past decades, you find few or no variety programs in prime time after the late 1970s. Likewise, despite several attempts to revive the genre, the "adult western" remained a staple of the distant past, finding little audience interest in the 1980s. Music was mainly a matter of themes and background—even popular singers like Dolly Parton could not make a go of prime-time television. On the other hand, old programming (even in black-and-white) had new life on cable and independent stations, and those wanting pop music could always listen to radio or watch MTV on cable.

10•64   More News at All Times

Television news became both more available and more watched by the late 1980s . . . but not always on the networks. Local stations had realized with a vengeance the desirability of having the reputation of being "first'" in news, and cable services like CNN and C-SPAN cut into network news audiences. PBS, with its *MacNeil/Lehrer NewsHour,* became a player. Overall, television news now showed it could attract audiences and thus advertisers and revenues. In the early 1960s, network news programs were 15 minutes long (on weekdays only), and local stations typically provided no more than a half-hour divided into news, sports, and weather. By the late 1970s, network news was half an hour long (often with a 15-minute program

on Sunday night), and most stations provided half an hour or possibly an hour of local news. Cable originated nothing. But ten years later, the situation had radically changed. The networks supplied short news breaks throughout the day in addition to their flagship news programs in the early evening and the soft features and news of the *Today* show and its competition often took over the agenda-setting role previously held by daily newspapers. A large number of people (including many news-makers, who previously had gotten into the habit of watching the networks' weekly news interview programs, such as the long-running *Meet the Press*) tuned in at 11:30 P.M. to watch ABC's *Nightline;* and local television stations might present news programs in the early morning, at noon, wrapped around the network news in the early evening for a total of as many as two hours, and at the end of the network entertainment schedule at night. "News junkies" who were still unsatiated could listen to all-news radio in many markets, view one of the Cable News Network's (CNN's) two channels, find numerous radio outlets that aired sports or financial news all day, and even buy a special radio receiver to obtain U.S. Weather Service forecasts directly without having to wait for them on The Weather Channel on cable.

To some extent, the increase in amount of news was based on expanding technological options. As noted in 10.124, by the 1980s most television stations had converted from use of news film (which, while less expensive at first, required developing and could not be reused) to videotape, usually gathered by mobile or even portable video units collectively labeled as electronic news-gathering equipment (ENG). Live telecasts could be made from remote sites so long as the signal could be microwaved back to the station. If it was not necessary to have the signal live, it could always be videotaped in the field and brought back to the station for editing. In a competitive market, one might see reporters and crews anywhere. However, microwaves were of use only where one had a clear line of sight to the receiving station, and the demand for channels seemed never to end. If a station wanted to cover a story in another city, it had to accept delays and pay through the nose for a connection through the telephone company or a satellite common carrier. Although some stations with helicopters for news and traffic coverage used them as relays for distant ENG microwave signals, this was uneconomical and often technically difficult—and dangerous. (Several helicopters owned or leased by stations for reporting on traffic conditions have crashed over the past twenty-five years.)

In the mid-1980s, a new solution, satellite newsgathering (SNG), allowed major market station news crews to operate from trucks housing a satellite transmission antenna. Such vehicles, substantially larger than the vans in which conventional ENG crews could travel, often cost several hundred thousand dollars. SNG combined with ENG placed stations more in control of their own news coverage and lessened their traditional reliance on network news department outtakes to supplement local news. By the late 1980s, several SNG networks, notably CONUS (for "continental U.S.," set up by Minneapolis-based Stanley Hubbard), interconnected stations across the country on an ad hoc basis depending on the news story and its location. Since members of this association agreed to provide service to other members if their equipment was not tied up, a station sometimes found itself feeding a news event to affiliates of a rival network that would in turn feed it

back to the originator's competition! All of this spelled more news options for local news directors.

These additional options were mixed blessings. Since the station with the highest-rated local news typically retained that lead throughout the evening's schedule, the news department came under much closer scrutiny by station management. The high costs of new hardware (such as computers for the weathercasters or SNG trucks) did not carry over to higher salaries for news personnel—except, of course, for anchors, who were able to charge as much as the traffic would bear but whose tenure often ran from rating book to rating book, since they acted, and were treated, as entertainers.

The cable industry finally jumped on the news bandwagon in the 1980s. Considerable expectations surrounded the start-up of Ted Turner's Cable News Network (CNN), which was announced in 1978 and began operation in June 1980. Turner offered to provide something that only all-news radio stations had supplied before—24 hours of news and features. Based in Atlanta, CNN was thought by some (especially those in broadcasting) to be a joke or gimmick that would not last. How could a video news service sustain itself without the backing of a network or some other existing news organization? And would Turner fiscally be able to afford a true news service? But starting with fewer than two million cable homes, CNN quickly established itself as a lasting player. Because of its constant availability, its effective tie-in with European news agencies, and its reliance on young and hungry staff members whose apparent interest was in getting out the news and not in gaining a few minutes of air time to benefit their own careers, CNN grew in importance. At the beginning of 1982, CNN provided a second channel, CNN

Headline News, with half-hour updates. The clear audience success of the service brought competition. ABC and Westinghouse set up their Satellite News Channel in 1982 and marketed it to cable systems. Both CNN and SNC lost money, which discouraged ABC and Westinghouse more than Turner, who was able to buy out the competition for $12.5 million in October 1983. CNN showed the networks that a lot of people clearly wanted access to national news at times other than the traditional six o'clock. The networks responded by giving *Nightline* (ABC) a regular time period and by trying an all-night all-news service (NBC's *Overnight*) for a short while. As one result, Linda Ellerbee, the outspoken and down-to-earth co-host of that and several other programs over the years, finally decided to try to produce her own shows—from which she could not be fired when network strategies changed.

When longtime ABC sports chief Roone Arledge was given the network's news portfolio in 1977 and instructed to get the third-ranking news operation up to competitive status with CBS and NBC, he experimented with several formats in the evening newscast. One unsuccessful approach had three or four anchors in as many cities. Finally, Arledge settled on Peter Jennings, who had anchored for ABC in the early 1970s but admittedly had done a miserable job then, in part because of lack of experience. After several years of foreign reporting, Jennings made a far more appealing and creditable anchor for ABC in the 1980s, frequently coming out on top in the weekly ratings wars.

Another bright ABC star was Ted Koppel, who was assigned to a nightly series of programs starting at 11:30 dealing with "America Held Hostage" by Iran's imprisonment of American embassy officials in 1979. As the captivity of the American diplomats extended into 1980 (they were released the day Ronald Reagan was sworn in as President in 1981), other topics were covered. The program's name was changed to *Nightline* and its length was regularized, dropping to half an hour (with the authority to extend beyond that if needed). Koppel, a superb interviewer, was one of the few in the news business who had the background, intelligence, and insight to hold his own against news-makers with their own agendas and thus obtain useful and revealing information. ABC created short documentaries on a few hours' notice to set the stage for each program. *Nightline* provided a regular outlet in addition to the weekend interview programs (such as *Meet the Press*) for people with important things to say. While many of the subjects covered on *Nightline* (and on a long-form version of the program aired several times a year) were picked in advance, it always seemed able to provide a perspective on important events that had taken place the same day. The program became increasingly influential, and not only as a late-evening tonic for those stuffed with entertainment programming and CNN during the day. Koppel's staff was particularly good at obtaining people with opposing points of view to debate their positions face-to-face (or, since they might be facing cameras at affiliated stations all over the country, face-to-monitor), and Koppel had the ability usually to keep them on the subject, although half an hour was hardly enough to cover a topic in depth.

CBS News went through years of internal agony in the 1980s as the network with the Murrow tradition and the Cronkite image fell on bad times, poor judgment, and worse luck. It began with the retirement in 1981 of longtime anchor Walter Cronkite (see page 408), eased out by network management worried about losing up-and-coming Dan Rather to the

Network Anchors . . . The Next Generation / In the early 1980s, all three broadcast networks changed anchors from those who had long held the posts (see pages 408–409). Dan Rather replaced Walter Cronkite on CBS early in 1981, Tom Brokaw moved from the early-morning *Today Show* to replace NBC's John Chancellor (who stayed on to deliver editorials once or twice a week), and Peter Jennings returned to ABC, where he had briefly anchored in the late 1960s. The ratings seesawed back and forth among the three networks through the decade.

Photo by Anthony Edgeworth

Photo courtesy of Tom Brokaw

Photo courtesy of Capital Cities/ABC News

competition as well as by the increasingly older demographics of the *CBS Evening News* audience. Ratings dipped when the sometimes overly intense Rather took over. More serious was a combination of changing CBS news directors and the growing pressure from headquarters to cut costs—particularly after Laurence Tisch assumed effective control (see 10.33). While Rather rebuilt the show according to his own agenda (Cronkite was not even allowed to participate in the 1984 election coverage, though he did play a role in 1988, when Rather felt more settled in his post), he made some mistakes. One was an apparently petulant several minutes of dead air when a sporting event ran overtime, and another was allowing himself to be manipulated by Vice President George Bush in an interview early in 1988. Layoffs and political infighting severely hurt CBS's image and performance, and a number of veterans moved on to other jobs. The level of internal conflict was reflected in several books (typically written by the losers) about executive turnover and the decline of news division independence and prestige during that period. At one point, some of the present and past members of the staff offered to buy CBS News from the parent company. Nevertheless, by the time Douglas Edwards (whose network anchoring assignment had started 40 years before) retired in 1988, CBS News was quite different from the organization it had been during its glory years.

NBC's new generation came on board with less fuss as longtime *Today* host Tom Brokaw replaced John Chancellor in 1982. David Brinkley left after more than 30 years at NBC to become a commentator on ABC News. NBC's prime-time ratings success helped to propel the quiet-spoken Brokaw to the top of the evening news ratings heap. Networks increasingly were willing to accept (or recruit) those who had

been successful elsewhere and even hire those who had not made their previous career in broadcast journalism. When Larry Grossman was eased out of the NBC News presidency in 1988, the network went to the newspaper industry for Grossman's successor.

In spite of all the new technology and changes in personnel, network news was still only 30 minutes long at the end of the 1980s—the same length it had been for a quarter of a century, and occupying the same period. The networks had tried several times to persuade their affiliates to accept longer evening network broadcasts, but the money being made on local news and syndicated shows continued to limit network news feeds to half an hour. Further, network documentary production was down sharply in the 1980s from levels of years before. The number of documentaries and news specials on the three major networks shrank to a total of 31 in 1987—versus 51 in 1977 and 100 in 1967. Many of the surviving documentaries were more entertainment or soft news features than hard-hitting investigative reporting. Few hard-nosed documentaries or similar programs remained—and they often attracted legal problems (see 10.86). The small audiences and advertiser dislike of controversy in documentaries all but did in the genre, except for an occasional special dealing with the problem of the year and PBS's *Frontline*. The networks closed down their documentary units and concentrated on 90-second reports for the evening newscasts.

A "softer" format did successfully survive. CBS's *60 Minutes* thrived and stayed among the top-ten-rated programs for decades. Its formula of offering three or four stories a week and some important and many softer features brought imitations like ABC's *20/20*. When the costs of entertainment programming rose, several networks looked to their news divisions for relief—spawning such programs as CBS's *West 57th*. This development was exacerbated by the 1988 Hollywood writers' strike, since newswriters were not affected. Syndicated feature programs under such names as *Chronicle, PM Magazine,* and *Evening Magazine* occupied the profitable "prime-time access" period between the network news and the start of entertainment programming at 8 P.M. (7 P.M. CST) for those stations that wished to counterprogram game shows such as *Jeopardy* and *Wheel of Fortune*. Even the often-parodied *Lifestyles of the Rich and Famous* fit into this category.

During this period, the Middle East replaced Vietnam as the hot spot most often shown on home television screens. No longer was this oil-rich region simply the scene of conflict between Jews and Arabs, for now Americans were intimately involved. On November 3, 1979, in the aftermath of the Ayatollah Khomeini's ouster of the Shah of Iran, a mob of "students" stormed the American embassy in Tehran, taking several dozen prisoners from among the staff. While the Carter administration made fruitless and apparently weak efforts to free the captives (including an abortive rescue attempt by helicopter), the networks covered the Islamic Shiite revolution in Iran and its overflow into once-peaceful Lebanon. Night after night, scenes of the civil war in Beirut or interviews with often veiled spokespersons of one sect or another were shown on network newscasts—often making no more overall sense to American viewers than the recently abandoned Asian war, which also lacked clear reasons, sides, and lines of fighting. The taking of a number of individual hostages in Beirut in the 1980s and the blowing up of both the American embassy and a barracks (killing more than two-hundred Marines) kept the story hot. Critics expressed concern about network coverage of terrorists, since some terrorists seemed to engage in deadly acts solely to facilitate access by their spokespersons to American television screens.

To some extent, the story was "terrorism" rather than "the Middle East." Such stories as the bombing of Pan Am Flight 103 over Scotland at the end of 1988 and American attacks on Libyan aircraft and cities all could fit into this framework. The hijacking of TWA Flight 847 in July 1985 and the two-week drama that ensued illustrated the problems of trying to balance hostage and family concerns with the public's demand for news, any news, of progress in negotiations for the hostages' freedom. (This dilemma was given a reprise when a made-for-television movie on the hijacking was shown in 1988, shortly before one of the hijackers was brought to trial.)

Television faced severe problems of access to other stories. The military had learned its lesson in Vietnam: allowing reporters independent access to an armed conflict would open more doors to questions about the wisdom of engaging in the conflict in the first place. The almost farcical invasion of the Caribbean island of Grenada in 1984 was poorly covered at first because the Pentagon would not allow reporters near the island for several days. Criticized by all media, the Pentagon suggested guidelines for future "pool" reporting. These were tested in the 1987–1988 crisis in the Persian Gulf, when gunboats and aircraft tried to sink oil tankers of neutral nations during the dragging Iran-Iraq war and a large force of U.S. Navy ships was sent to the area. Twice in less than a year, American ships were attacked, and one American ship shot down an Iranian airliner by mistake, killing all aboard. The media found—not to their surprise—that they were almost totally at the mercy of what the military would allow in coverage. Some reporters operated independently, and the monitoring of radio transmissions (honed to a fine extent during the Israeli-Arab conflicts of the previous decades) also proved useful. But without "credentials," it was impossible for the news media to prevail against the curtain of military might dropped over the region.

Many viewers and listeners were reminded of the assassination of President John F. Kennedy when, early in 1986, the space shuttle *Challenger* blew up just over a minute after launch. Only CNN had been carrying the launch live—we had become that used to routine and safe space travel—but the networks soon joined in the coverage. Over and over we watched the videotape of the exploding shuttle. For days, the media badgered the families of the astronaut crew and besieged the National Aeronautics and Space Administration for more information. Only slowly did the full story of equipment defects come out, and nearly three years were to pass before NASA again sent a shuttle into orbit, in late September 1988. In the meantime, broadcasters as well as other industries and the military worried about their inability to place new or replacement communications satellites in orbit, since the United States had allowed its rocket booster capability to deteriorate, expecting to be able to use the shuttles whenever needed. Some satellites eventually were launched into orbit using vehicles produced by other countries. Even the USSR and China offered to launch for others—for a price.

Domestic news—disasters, scandals, government hearings—also received substantial coverage, made easier by the new news-gathering technologies. But ability to show pictures did not always mean that the full story was being told.

When the Three Mile Island nuclear power plant near Harrisburg, Pennsylvania, vented radioactive waste into the air in mid-1979, the media (so said a later investigating commission) stressed more "what if" stories about a potential meltdown than factual "what is" material about the hour-by-hour events inside the plant—adding to the audience's concern with, and stress over, events. (Of course, the power company and government spokespersons provided as little information as they could—a foolish move in light of the success of an entertainment film, *The China Syndrome*, which had opened that month and had almost the same scenario as TMI.) When a Soviet nuclear plant at Chernobyl burned and let loose a huge amount of radioactivity over much of Europe in 1986, television reports seemed to fall into the same trap, partially—again—for lack of definitive official information.

10•641   Sports

Sports on television continued to fascinate for many Americans. Two of the five largest audiences in U.S. television history were for Super Bowl football games—and the other games in this series were right behind. The jokes about "couch potato" fans of televised football (especially on weekend afternoons) seemed perennial. Some of the most profitable cable program services, such as ESPN, provided the viewer with nothing but sports. As a result, it was far easier to pry money and new equipment (such as stop-action videotape recorders) from managers for sports than for news.

Sports coverage during the past 15 years continued to be punctuated by the quadrennial Olympic Games, covered in this period mostly by ABC. The 1980 Winter Games were highlighted by an emotional win by the U.S. hockey team against a more experienced Soviet team. The Summer Games never came off on U.S. television, as NBC was faced with a U.S. government boycott of the Moscow-based games due to the Soviet invasion of Afghanistan the year before. NBC had paid $85 million for the rights to televise the games and lost about $25 million even after insurers paid up. In 1984, with the Summer Games in Los Angeles, ABC provided 180 hours of coverage from 30 locations as much as 190 miles apart all over the Los Angeles area. The ceremonial opening and closing sessions, staged by impresario David Wolper and held in the old 1932 Olympic Stadium, harked back to the massed entertainment of old Busby Berkeley musical movies from the 1930s. Some 80 million viewers from all over the world watched. ABC covered the 1988 Winter Games in Calgary in a visual feast but found that the audience numbers were down as the U.S. athletes did not do well in the nationalistic or chauvinistic race for medals. The 1988 Summer Games in Seoul, South Korea, covered by NBC, which had paid a record $300 million for the rights, were held under some of the tightest security arrangements ever seen. While the 14-hour time difference between Seoul and the eastern United States was a factor, many observers felt that one reason for a severe drop-off in audience size and interest was the lack of audience familiarity (and, perhaps, level of experience) of NBC's on-air crew.

Television coverage of a professional sport often meant the difference between financial success and failure. Tennis and golf tournament winners moved into the big money because of increased television attention to their playoff games. Virtually all professional baseball and football teams, and players of other sports such as basketball and hockey, signed coverage contracts with one or more stations

or networks, and the resulting television income was considerable. Even college teams got into bidding wars. In 1988, the Chicago Cubs, the last major league baseball team to restrict itself to the traditional afternoon contests at home, began to play under lights at Wrigley Field. This came about when the other organized baseball owners exerted pressure because their clubs were losing gate receipts by not playing televised night games in Chicago. By the late 1980s, cable was flexing its muscles and seemed likely to play a more important role in covering some sports events, including perhaps the Olympics, before the 1990s would draw to a close.

10•65   Media/Politics; Politics/Media

Television played an expanding role in American politics in the decade covered here, in part because of the development of new services. Chief among them was the cable industry sponsored and supported C-SPAN (Cable Special and Public Affairs Network), developed initially to cover the U.S. House of Representatives after that body approved television access in 1979. C-SPAN took its feed from the House-controlled cameras and thus became a visual record of debates on the floor. C-SPAN also covered some hearings. In 1984 a political controversy arose when the House Speaker, Democrat Tip O'Neill, allowed the cameras to pan the floor of the House to show how few members were present for some late-afternoon GOP speech-making. The Speaker was slapped on the wrist, and the cameras were ordered to remain focused on the podium—but the coverage continued, however little it was used by the commercial networks.

The Senate took much longer to decide that the benefits of coverage outweighed the disadvantages. In 1978, radio was allowed to carry the floor debate on the ratification of the Panama Canal treaty, and NPR carried the entire three days, while CBS and NBC aired only the first day. Otherwise, television coverage was limited to various Senate committee hearings, which over the years have created substantial video drama—the 1951 Kefauver crime hearings, the Army-McCarthy hearings of 1954, and the investigations of the teamsters in the late 1950s (see 8.65). Both houses had long recognized that the public expected to see some congressional events on their screens, including ceremonial proceedings such as the annual presidential State of the Union address, and matters of major importance such as the House of Representatives' proceedings leading toward impeachment of President Nixon or the Iran-Contra hearings. When the House of Representatives decided to allow television coverage, the Senate agonized in a series of hearings and reports. By the 1980s, it was clear that the lower house was getting more publicity and news coverage thanks to the presence of the cameras—and that finally tipped the balance for the politicians in the Senate. After an experiment with limited coverage, the Senate finally opened its floor to full-time cameras under control of the presiding officer, causing C-SPAN to set up a second channel.

Television covered three presidential elections in this period: 1980, 1984, and 1988. In the first two, an incumbent president was running for office. In all three, television played the dominant role in carrying the candidates' images and messages to the voters.

President Jimmy Carter (serving from 1977 to 1981) made effective use of the medium, doing well in debates with President Gerald Ford, including one in which a technical bobble caused both candidates to stand silently behind their podiums for nearly 20 minutes. Carter won the election and started his term with the inaugural-day walk down Pennsylvania Avenue with which this chapter began. He held regular news conferences and appeared on talk shows. But despite his successes in such things as bringing Egypt and Israel to an agreement, Carter carried with him a public perception of ineptitude.

Former California governor Ronald Reagan, his opponent in 1980, was a master of the media, even gaining approval for "taking charge" with an "I paid for this microphone!" comment during a New Hampshire primary campaign debate that Reagan had, in fact, paid for. It had been expected by the Carter camp that there would be several one-on-one televised debates with Reagan. But Representative John Anderson's third-party quest for the job gave broadcasters equal-time problems, so only one debate took place. The October 28 face-off was in Cleveland, was produced, as before, by the League of Women Voters, and was carried by all three networks. The debate did not seem to play any pivotal role this time. On election night, Reagan was declared winner early—by NBC at 8:15 P.M. EST—rekindling the old debate about the impact of such early declarations on voters in states where polls were still open. West Coast voters had several hours left to vote, and some later research argued that thousands had remained home, with resultant impacts on many local and statewide races.

Reagan ironically made more limited use of television than did Carter, despite the new President's theatrical film background and reputation as "the great communicator." While he continued his weekly radio program throughout his two terms in office, Reagan seldom held traditional press conferences, forcing reporters to yell questions at him during "photo opportunities" in hopes of some give-and-take. Although part of this was blamed on the need for security—Reagan had been seriously wounded in an attempted assassination early in his first term—much of it was due to the universal desire of politicians to control news. Reagan came over well, folksy but seemingly in charge, in televised Oval Office speeches. His personal popularity insulated him from attack and even from sharp questioning by reporters such as ABC's Sam Donaldson, who assumed the mantle worn by CBS's Dan Rather in the Nixon administration. Other Republican candidates and policy issues tended to fade out of sight, as did Reagan's own penchant for making errors in public utterances (a tendency that seems to have afflicted many Presidents of recent years).

In late 1983, the FCC revisited its policies on televised political debates. It reversed several previous decisions and held that broadcasters could produce debates without fear of equal-time requests from excluded minor party candidates. No longer would the networks have to go through the charade of covering a debate as if they were mere bystanders rather than the reason the debate took place. Despite the rule change, the League of Women Voters managed to retain its role in 1984 by sponsoring two debates featuring presidential candidates and a third featuring vice presidential candidates.

Ever since the 1950s, political campaign managers had been controlling more and more of what the public could see of a campaign, although it was impossible for them to control everything. For example, the 1984 campaign will be remembered for having the first woman on a major party's

Covering the Conventions / Television coverage of political conventions continued to dominate the quadrennial rituals in the 1980s (this is the 1988 Republican National Convention.) The formation of Cable News Network (CNN) in 1980 led to its playing an important role, often providing the "gavel-to-gavel" coverage that was once the hallmark of network television. In 1988 the traditional networks limited their coverage to a few prime-time hours into which convention planners had moved all important events. Even less coverage was predicted for the conventions of the 1990s as primary elections took away the suspense of the party gatherings by preselecting candidates. Photos courtesy of National Association of Broadcasters.

national ticket as New York Congress-woman Geraldine Ferraro ran for Vice President on the losing Democratic ticket with Senator Walter Mondale. Many felt that she more than held her own in the vice presidential debate with Republican George Bush, and the media focused on her—and on her husband's financial prob-lems—more than it had on most vice pres-idential candidates in the past. An obscure 80-year-old Chicago manicurist named Clara Peller who had played in a television commercial as a fast-food customer won-dering "Where's the beef?" found her question underlining the Mondale theme that the Reagan administration lacked sub-stance. On election night, due in part to pressure from Congress, the networks tried to avoid jumping the predictive gun that had raised so much controversy in 1980 and were somewhat more cautious in making early predictions.

The 1988 race seemed to start ear-lier than ever—as far back as 1986, when the first candidates declared for both par-ties in what was seen as a wide-open race without an incumbent for the first time since 1968. On the Republican side, long-time television evangelist Pat Robertson declared for the GOP nomination, and for a time it appeared that those years of preaching might translate into votes. After a strong showing in early primaries, Rob-ertson was undone, in part, by television tapes of some of his earlier religious claims. (Scandals involving other televi-sion evangelists such as Jimmy Swaggart and Jim Bakker also did not help Robert-son's cause with the average voter.) Former Colorado Senator Gary Hart was the Dem-ocratic front-runner until reporters, acting almost on Hart's dare, discovered his apparent dalliance with a model. Jesse Jackson, building on his 1984 race, made a creditable showing in early primaries and

electrified the drawn-out process with his televised oratory.

More than in earlier elections, the 1988 race was called a "media campaign" as press and television "horse race" stories made and broke candidates until the first primary votes were counted. The net-works jumped to conclusions, and the pol-iticians and public followed. There were televised network-sponsored debates among the initially long list of candidates (six or seven for each party) before most primaries. By the time the Democrats met in convention in Atlanta, it was clear that the electorate found the drawn-out process boring. Consequently, the networks con-tinued their practice, started in the sum-mer of 1984, of not carrying the proceed-ings of each political convention "gavel to gavel." Indeed, even with the coverage abbreviated to two hours or so per evening (not including CNN and C-SPAN, which, by carrying the entire convention, gave the networks an excuse not to bother), the network coverage tended to consist as much of reporters roaming the halls to try to find a delegate or official with some-thing to say than of presenting on the screen the carefully scripted convention itself. This was particularly true during the Republican convention, when Senator Dan Quayle's military record became a subject of controversy just prior to his nomination as George Bush's running mate. The han-dlers of both presidential candidates, Mas-sachusetts governor Michael Dukakis and Vice President Bush, groomed their men to deliver outstanding acceptance speeches—and both did. But audiences for the net-work's abbreviated coverage were lower than ever before—cable and independent stations saw huge ratings jumps, even for grade B movies. It appeared likely that the traditional four-day convention coverage was doomed to further streamlining, with television paying attention only to high-lights . . . and any real news (or rumor) they could garner in spite of the best efforts of the political party managers to script the event.

The 1988 debates—two for presidential and one for vice presidential candidates—took place on schedule, one under auspices of the League of Women Voters, which refused publicly to do more because of the tight control of the political parties. Unlike the situation in 1960, few people changed their minds as a result of the debates—and many stations did not even bother carrying them. Still, Dukakis's weaker presentation and stiff personal style, especially in the second debate, helped cost him the election. Even more important to Bush's win, however, was his campaign's masterful establishment of a media agenda through orchestrated attacks on the media, short negative commercials, and his being sure to provide "sound bites" (a few seconds of slogan or pithy quote rather than a detailed presentation of the issues) to the news media (particularly television) in time to make the evening news on a daily basis.

10·7   Audience Changes and Constants

One important basis for assessing the impact of broadcasting and other technologies has been the comparative pace with which the potential audience purchased the product (such as a receiver or player) and the resultant "penetration" of service into American homes at any given time. Optimistic talk of new technologies in the 1970s usually stumbled over the crucial detail of just how many or how few Americans could (or would) use the new option. For example, despite the hoopla, only 13 percent of American homes had

CD players at the start of 1989, whereas 11 percent had home security alarm systems and 21 percent had home computers (many of them not used), according to the Electronic Industries Association.

Cable television, though first developed in the late 1940s, took until 1972 or 1973 to reach even 10 percent of the nation's homes (see Appendix C, table 10-B) and reached half the homes only in 1988—40 years after first appearing. Radio took a decade to reach 50 percent penetration (see Appendix C, table 8-A). But the videocassette recorder took only 12 years from the first sales of the Betamax in 1975 (see 9.1) to reach the 50 percent of homes standard (see Appendix C, table 9-B), helped along by falling prices and the VCR's relation to expanding cable and other services worthy of home recording. It also led to a new retail business—the rental of videocassettes of feature films at some store in almost every neighborhood. The growth of VCR usage contributed more to the decline in movie theater attendance than anything had since television itself burgeoned in the 1950s. In the more distant future, we may look back and see 1987 as a watershed year, when these two "new" electronic media—cable and VCRs—became more important to the average member of the audience than the radio and television stations that had provided so much for so many years.

Continued expansion of television receiver ownership naturally provided outlets for the new services as well as for broadcast television. By the start of 1989, 95 percent of American homes had color, and 60 percent had more than one receiver (see Appendix C, table 9-A). More than 98 percent of homes had some form of television and some form of radio set. Because of intense competition, television set prices actually fell during this period, particularly if the high rates of inflation in the late 1970s and early 1980s are taken into account. In 1988, a 19-inch color receiver for the living room might have been bought for as little as $250, and one of the many black-and-white sets purchased for other rooms of the house, or even for portable use, for as little as $69.

A small but growing minority of homes had top-of-the-line television receivers with stereo sound (about 15 percent early in 1989, with another 11 percent that could be adapted for stereo), pictures-within-pictures, built-in digital tuners for cable, displays indicating which channel was being viewed, or large display screens. These ranged in size from about 40 inches to several feet diagonally—and were in perhaps 2 to 5 percent of homes and a much larger proportion of taverns, following the pattern of usage set in television's earliest days. Some home projection television receivers could cost as much as $3,500. Most television sets were made in the highly competitive Far East—first in Japan and then (as Japanese costs rose) in Korea, Singapore, Hong Kong, Taiwan, and elsewhere. By 1987, only Zenith among major manufacturers still made television receivers in the United States, and the number of American-made television sets exported was only half a million. Although American manufacturers made and sold another six million sets in the United States, these figures are small when compared with the 15.11 million sets made abroad and imported that year. (In 1977, the equivalent figures were about 340 thousand, nearly 4 million, and 7.5 million—showing both a near-doubling in total number of television sets sold in the United States and a faster rate of growth in the proportion of imports.) Almost three-quarters of all VCRs, which barely existed in 1977, were manufactured abroad in 1987.

Television usage—or, more precisely, the number of hours any television set was turned on in the average home, a figure that had regularly climbed several minutes per week for years—began to dip slightly in the late 1980s, down from a peak seven hours and eight minutes of daily use recorded in 1983–1984. Homes with pay-cable service generally viewed more per week than did homes with only basic cable or those with only off-air broadcast service. Since these figures included all family viewing (see Appendix C, table 9-C), they should not be confused with figures for the amount of time that given individuals—male and female adults and children—watched.

Likewise, radio-listening patterns changed perceptibly in the late 1970s. After years of bringing up the rear, FM radio stations reached larger national audiences than AM stations in 1979, and soon the top-rated stations in most markets were all FM outlets—except for all-news AM stations, which reached more people but for only a few minutes a day. The reasons for the belated success of FM were varied, including the usually fewer advertisements, better sound quality (including stereo), and more musical format variety (see 10.61). By the late 1980s, AM stations collectively shared only a quarter of the national radio audience (see 10.21).

Both radio and television were forced to share ever more audience time with prerecorded materials: rented or purchased videocassettes and audiocassettes (now available everywhere and accessible at any time through tiny, lightweight portable players and earphones) or compact discs. Whatever the source of the sounds, more than a few critics—and long-suffering parents—argued that whatever kind of music teens listened to, especially with earphones, the audio levels were usually so high that serious hearing losses would likely result in later years.

10•71   New Methods, New Media

That the audience generally continued to be pleased with the service given them by television was evident in the biennial Roper Organization surveys done for the television industry (see 9.71). Overall public opinion changed little from year to year after 1976, with 68 to 74 percent of the audience feeling that television was doing an excellent or good job and only 29 to 23 percent feeling that the job was fair or poor. Television ranked better, overall, than did newspapers. As the source of the typical person's news, television had consistently outranked newspapers and radio since about 1970. Although the television industry pays for this professionally conducted survey, the consistency of findings at least argues television's prominent place in American life for more than three decades—nearly twice as long as network radio had held this position.

Suggesting some degree of dissatisfaction, however, were the findings of a 1980 national survey that built on related studies tracing back two decades (see 9.71). Robert Bower's *The Changing Television Audience in America* (1985) concluded that there were both consistencies and changes in audience reactions to television. While overall public reactions to television had, Bower reported, "drifted from high enthusiasm to modest appreciation" from 1960 to 1980, this was due in part to increased education ("higher education decreases admiration for television as an institution") and in part to a wearing off of the novelty of the medium after 35 years. But viewing was up about 27 percent from 1960 to 1980, pointing out again that pub-

licly expressed attitudes toward the medium are often poor predictors of actual viewing behavior. Parents' favorable reaction toward "the big babysitter," children's television, rose until 1970 but has declined since, as more is learned—and expressed in competing media, such as newspapers and magazines—about television's sometimes negative impact on children's development (see 10.72).

Yet another "effect" of the media might be measured in the increasingly successful campaigns by politicians and special interest groups to discredit the traditional watchdog role of the mass media. The messenger was attacked rather than whatever it was that the media had uncovered, making some wonder if the eleventh commandment ("thou shalt not get caught") was not becoming more important in America than the other ten (see 10.73).

Ratings firms were put under increasing pressure from advertising agencies to update their techniques because of the expanding number of channels delivering programs into the home, the growing sophistication of advertisers, and improved methodologies developed by academic and commercial researchers. Until 1987, "the ratings" were not substantially different in approach or form from those of three decades before. The costs of this audience research to the networks, stations, and advertising agencies that paid for it continued to rise, however, since it was essential to the commercial broadcasting system. That was one of the factors that led to takeover of the two largest ratings companies by larger, well-funded new parents. Arbitron had become a part of Control Data in 1967, while the A.C. Nielsen Company was purchased by Dun & Bradstreet in 1984. A new player and method entered the scene in late 1984 mitted to Congress late in 1981. Specifically, he argued that Congress should eliminate Section 315 and Section 312(a) requirements on political broadcasting. Congress, aware of the value of broadcasting to its own campaigns, demurred. The commission began to build a record, arguing the fact that the huge and growing number of broadcast stations, plus additional services, made the 1927 political broadcasting clause and 1949 Fairness Doctrine no longer necessary. (A further supporting factor was that an ever-growing proportion of the population now lived in or near large cities, weakening congressional interest in rural areas with few stations.) While most citizens' groups felt the Fairness Doctrine was the only entrance ticket for their opinions to be heard over the air, a number of other groups—such as the Radio-Television News Directors Association (RTNDA)—felt that the doctrine actually reduced broadcast controversy because station owners preferred to eliminate all controversy rather than donate time for mandated rebuttals. At first, under some pressure from Congress and other critics, the FCC backed off any attempt at outright repeal, given the general belief that Congress had codified the doctrine into law with its 1959 amendments to Section 315 and that the Supreme Court had endorsed this with the 1969 *Red Lion* decision (see 9.82). But in 1985, the commission sent a major policy report to Congress arguing for repeal. Facing little likelihood of action there, in August 1987 the FCC took the final step and unilaterally eliminated the Fairness Doctrine, using as a vehicle a fairness case remanded to it by the Court of Appeals for further action (see box on pages 524–525).

Despite the trend to deregulation, enforcement of existing rules and regulations continued. The most controversial decisions concerned RKO General, a group owner of radio and television stations and a subsidiary of General Tire. In mid-1980, the FCC denied renewal of three RKO television station licenses, citing serious rule violations and misrepresentation to the commission. On appeal, one of the denials was upheld (for a Boston television station), while the others were thrown, together with 12 remaining licenses, into a massive legal process while the commission tried to determine RKO's fitness to be a broadcaster. Dozens of applicants vied for the licenses in question. In mid-1987, a tentative decision found RKO unfit and recommended lifting of all RKO licenses. By late 1988, it appeared the FCC would allow RKO to sell off the remaining stations, but at a fraction of their normal worth. The case illustrated one of the worst examples of length and cost of regulatory proceedings and added to the pressure for substantial streamlining of FCC investigative and legal procedures.

10•83   Technical Standards

Until the 1980s, the FCC played a consistent and essential role in determining, testing, and enforcing technical standards for broadcast services. This role had developed in part because of the limited technological knowledge about transmission and other aspects of radio when the 1927 and 1934 acts were drawn up. Technical standards for equipment and broadcast signal quality were needed to ensure uniform (or at least minimum) quality and as a support to interference-free allocation of the spectrum. This position often helped establish an industry, as, for example, in the shaping of modern television during the 1940s (see 6.8 and 7.8). But during the Fowler regime at the FCC, this role of the commission as a national technical overseer was strongly questioned for the

so high that serious hearing losses would likely result in later years.

10•71   New Methods, New Media

That the audience generally continued to be pleased with the service given them by television was evident in the biennial Roper Organization surveys done for the television industry (see 9.71). Overall public opinion changed little from year to year after 1976, with 68 to 74 percent of the audience feeling that television was doing an excellent or good job and only 29 to 23 percent feeling that the job was fair or poor. Television ranked better, overall, than did newspapers. As the source of the typical person's news, television had consistently outranked newspapers and radio since about 1970. Although the television industry pays for this professionally conducted survey, the consistency of findings at least argues television's prominent place in American life for more than three decades—nearly twice as long as network radio had held this position.

Suggesting some degree of dissatisfaction, however, were the findings of a 1980 national survey that built on related studies tracing back two decades (see 9.71). Robert Bower's *The Changing Television Audience in America* (1985) concluded that there were both consistencies and changes in audience reactions to television. While overall public reactions to television had, Bower reported, "drifted from high enthusiasm to modest appreciation" from 1960 to 1980, this was due in part to increased education ("higher education decreases admiration for television as an institution") and in part to a wearing off of the novelty of the medium after 35 years. But viewing was up about 27 percent from 1960 to 1980, pointing out again that publicly expressed attitudes toward the medium are often poor predictors of actual viewing behavior. Parents' favorable reaction toward "the big babysitter," children's television, rose until 1970 but has declined since, as more is learned—and expressed in competing media, such as newspapers and magazines—about television's sometimes negative impact on children's development (see 10.72).

Yet another "effect" of the media might be measured in the increasingly successful campaigns by politicians and special interest groups to discredit the traditional watchdog role of the mass media. The messenger was attacked rather than whatever it was that the media had uncovered, making some wonder if the eleventh commandment ("thou shalt not get caught") was not becoming more important in America than the other ten (see 10.73).

Ratings firms were put under increasing pressure from advertising agencies to update their techniques because of the expanding number of channels delivering programs into the home, the growing sophistication of advertisers, and improved methodologies developed by academic and commercial researchers. Until 1987, "the ratings" were not substantially different in approach or form from those of three decades before. The costs of this audience research to the networks, stations, and advertising agencies that paid for it continued to rise, however, since it was essential to the commercial broadcasting system. That was one of the factors that led to takeover of the two largest ratings companies by larger, well-funded new parents. Arbitron had become a part of Control Data in 1967, while the A.C. Nielsen Company was purchased by Dun & Bradstreet in 1984. A new player and method entered the scene in late 1984

services in Europe before its introduction here), the people meter promised more information of interest to advertisers, though at some risk to broadcasters, since some people—particularly children—failed to indicate their presence when queried by the people meter, thus reducing overall ratings. A.C. Nielsen had the strength and advertising agency support to start phasing out its Audimeter-diary methods and move to people meter techniques, finally replacing its traditional procedures in September 1987. In 1989, Nielsen reported initial development of a scanning device—rather than push buttons—to determine who was in the room.

The networks, already under pressure from cable and other services, were very unhappy with what they called a rush to the new system. They complained about the sample size (initially 2,000 homes, as compared with the national Nielsen meter sample of 1,700—but planned for an increase to 5,000) and composition (too many cable and pay-cable homes were included for the networks' taste) of the people meter national sample. Critics argued that the frequent button-pushing called for by the new system would quickly bore or tire audiences, thus skewing results. The new means of measurement showed that television viewing overall was off by about 10 percent, while many specific program ratings were sharply different from ratings obtained in the older way. Columns of trade magazines were filled with arguments and conflicting data as to why this drop occurred and whether it was an artifact of the technique. However, since the advertisers were pleased, the conversion to people meters seemed assured.

Arbitron also proposed a new technique, engaging in an extensive experiment in Denver called "ScanAmerica," which combined a Universal Product Code reader (able to interpret those thick and thin lines found on almost all packages nowadays) with a people meter so that sample households could easily report product purchases. Researchers presumably could now compare actual viewing behavior with resultant buying decisions—the kind of research connection that advertisers had wanted for years and that had been enjoyed only by some small marketers who took orders only by telephone and kept track of which commercial had aired immediately before the call.

The researching of local market television audiences was not directly affected by people meters in the late 1980s. The comparatively high cost of these electronic devices continued to restrict local market researchers to written diaries and (sometimes) telephone calls.

Measuring the audiences for newer and still-developing electronic media, especially cable and VCR use, posed another major methodology problem in the 1980s. Researchers wondered about the effect of increasing remote control usage on viewers' behavior (more channel switching and thus less "loyalty"?), whether cable and VCR use added to or took away from time spent with broadcast services (a bit of both, with more hours viewed overall, but nearly all of the added time went to the new services), how to measure delayed viewing by means of VCR time-shifting, and whether wholly new methods were needed to portray fairly and accurately the audience for the newer, often multichannel, services. By the mid-1980s, Nielsen was issuing regular ratings reports for the major advertiser-supported and pay-cable networks. A fair bit of information on patterns of VCR use was also emerging—including the fact that a substantial proportion of material recorded was never viewed!

Audience research had gone a long way along the road from estimating set-tuning to estimating individual viewing. But it had to be acknowledged that the amount of attention paid to the set while "viewing," and the amount of commercial information comprehended and retained, were studied only in the laboratory. Still largely ignored by the commercial industry was any possible system of qualitative ratings that would regularly seek data on viewers' reactions to, if not the effects of, what they watched. Even such a seemingly simple bit of information as what kind of radio-listening went on in automobiles was on shaky methodological grounds. And to go from these figures to deciding that a given commercial reached a given member of an audience *and* caused him or her to buy a particular product or service clearly was not justified. The ratings (see Appendix B) were the only game in town for the advertisers, and they were improving— but they most decidedly were not yet perfected.

Advertising agencies constantly improved their own tools for assessing potential consumers, spending large sums on such techniques as "psychographics" (categorizing people in psychological rather than demographic terms) and "focus groups" (which were subject to intensive interviewing and debriefing). Assisting in defining these problems and finding means to overcome them was the industry supported and directed Electronic Media Ratings Council (EMRC), formerly the Broadcast Ratings Council (see 9.71), whose research concerns extended in 1982 to cable and VCRs. As with its predecessor, the EMRC performed a combination auditing and accrediting function, helping to ensure that ratings surveys met at least minimal—and common—standards of reliability, although shying away from many questions of validity.

10·72   Kidvid (Phase Four)

The late 1970s saw what may have been the peak of serious government interest in improving television programming for young children. The effort came in parallel actions at two federal agencies. First, an FCC task force study issued late in 1979 found that broadcasters were not in compliance with the FCC's 1974 policy statement, which called for voluntary action to increase educational programming and for less advertising in children's television (see 9.72). The staff recommended mandatory program quotas for school-age and preschool children's programming. At the same time, a Federal Trade Commission staff study strongly recommended limiting or eliminating all advertising in programming aimed primarily at children, calling it "inherently unfair." Numerous members of Congress found these reports excellent public relations vehicles on which to stand, while others declared them to be antibusiness and moved to oust the FTC chairman.

But the election of Ronald Reagan, and the resultant change in personnel and deregulatory priorities at both commissions (see 10.8), stopped these recommendations in their tracks. Late in 1983, after an FCC hearing on the policy issues involved, the commission issued a new statement that once again rejected any mandatory children's programming requirements and simply restated the commission's 1974 call for voluntary action. That weak action was insufficient for the activist views of Action for Children's Television (see 9.72), which took the FCC decision to court. The U.S. Court of Appeals upheld the FCC's decision, arguing that the agency had changed its thinking on children's programming, an action certainly within the commission's power. When the FCC later deregulated television

advertising time guidelines, including those for children's programs, ACT appealed again, and this time the Court of Appeals agreed, noting that the FCC had not adequately justified its deregulatory action. In 1987, the FCC reluctantly was forced to reopen the question of the amount of advertising in children's shows.

Concern over the hypothesized impact on children of violent behavior portrayed on television was fed by several legal cases in the late 1970s. In 1977, 15-year-old Ronnie Zamora went to trial in Florida, accused of murdering the elderly lady next door when he was surprised during an attempted theft. His attorney tried a novel defense: he argued that Ronnie could not tell the difference between the real world and television due to his addiction to—the lawyer said "intoxication" with—such programs as *Kojak* and *Police Woman*. The jury was not convinced, and young Zamora received a life sentence. (Interestingly, this case was the first covered by television cameras after Florida allowed television news to record in its courtrooms.)

The murder-after-watching television argument, however, merely gave ammunition to those concerned about television's effects. That concern was further fed just a year later, when an NBC made-for-television movie, *Born Innocent*, simulated a brutal rape in a women's prison. Just days after the showing, a young girl was similarly attacked by several others. Her parents sued the network for having shown the program that "caused" the attack on their daughter. A California court, however, concluded that NBC had not tried to incite the rape, and thus the First Amendment protected the network from any findings of responsibility.

A more definitive statement of television's impact came in a two-volume 1982 National Institute of Mental Health report titled *Television and Behavior: Ten Years of Scientific Progress and Implications for the Eighties,* an assessment of research conducted during the decade after the famous Surgeon General's report (see 9.72). Given the huge body of research in this field (some 3,000 studies issued after 1972—90 percent of all research publications on the influence of television on human behavior ever produced), the new report synthesized what was already known rather than reporting on original research or proposing more. The report took a broader view, reviewing violence studies (now found to conclude that televised violence did have a fairly direct effect on subsequent real-life behavior) but going beyond that to include broader social impacts. Noting that by 1982 half of all Americans had never known life without television, the report claimed that the medium had become an embedded part of daily life, with deep and only partially understood impacts on our perceptions of social groups and issues, health concerns, and the role of the family. Television was an informal educator of considerable importance.

Although most (not all) researchers agreed that the evidence supported the report's conclusions, it should be noted that the majority of the studies reviewed were content analyses of one kind or another, as opposed to the more conceptually and methodologically difficult studies of the impact of that content.

At least one important theoretical concept emerged in this period—the study of mass communication's role as the prime agenda-setting means for society. Researchers in many universities noticed that concern with a given issue rose in opinion polls after coverage of that issue in print and broadcast media. A 1977 book by Donald Shaw and Maxwell McCombs raised the notion of such agenda-setting to a more practical level by providing many

examples. A stellar example (in both senses of the term) was the mid-1985 worldwide telecast of the Live Aid concert discussed in 10.631. While initial news reports helped place the famine on the public agenda, the concert enabled millions to try to help solve the problem.

10•73   Other Audience Effects and Criticism

The legal quibbling in the Zamora and *Born Innocent* cases did not deter further attacks on the medium from those who saw television as something that could subvert society. A growing number of people, particularly Protestant religious fundamentalists and the "Moral Majority" group organized by the Reverend Jerry Falwell, joined by political conservatives who objected to television news's coverage of things they would rather not have covered (such as U.S. involvement in Central America), felt that television itself was evil and that its content should be regulated (few called for its abolition) on moral grounds. Many broadcasters were timid about responding to these attacks, but producer-writer Norman Lear (*All in the Family, Maude*) organized a counter group, People for the American Way, to combat head-to-head those who would restrict television's ability to reflect changing social mores and provide progressive political and economic views.

Yet the impact of television continued to attract the anger of those who felt harmed or limited by its power. Conservative television evangelists claimed to reach huge audiences in the 1980s and began to flex their political muscle in the elections of 1984 and 1988, attacking television even while using it (although their power waned by 1988 as first Jim and Tammy Bakker and then Jimmy Swaggart were alleged to have committed improper

acts). The right and the left both complained about the coverage of their organizations by the national networks. Former evangelist Pat Robertson on the right and ex-Colorado senator Gary Hart on the left both ran antimedia campaigns during the primaries of the 1988 election. Senator Jesse Helms started a weak attempt to take over CBS in the mid-1980s, calling on his right-wing followers to "become Dan Rather's boss," thus controlling the network's news output to their liking. As the primary provider of news for most Americans, television news was constantly battered—as is the historical fate of most messengers bearing bad news—from all sides, even though repeated reputable studies of television news content generally showed no clear pattern or evidence of bias. However, more and more, by one means or another, the independence of the mass media was under attack . . . and the public joined in with glee. This tendency was far more destructive than the traditional polarization between the tending-to-be-more-liberal editorial staffs and the tending-to-be-more-conservative managers and owners. Of course, the increasing tendency of all news media to provide entertainment rather than the information citizens in a democracy need in order to make valid decisions made some observers feel that the crime was suicide, not murder, whenever the news media lost public respect.

10•8   Rethinking Regulation

During the 1980s, the continuing political debate over the proper relationship between government regulators and the electronic media industry heated up. While much of the focus was on FCC chairman Mark Fowler's clearly stated ideological bias in favor of marketplace solutions to industry problems, a small but vocal

minority kept alive a more traditional view of regulation's benefits. And the FCC was not the only arena—Congress played an extremely active role in deciding on electronic media policy matters.

The policy debate after 1977 was chiefly defined by two schools of thought in continuous collision. On the one hand, "traditional liberals" argued that the "public interest, convenience, and/or necessity" wording of the 1934 act meant that government had to continue playing an important central role in charting the direction and operations of electronic media to make sure the industry served the public, and that the success of the current system in serving the public showed the wisdom of that course. On the other side, "marketplace conservatives" claimed that government regulation cost far more than the limited value derived from it (for either the industry or consumers) and thus that years of past regulatory precedents were now merely baggage to be discarded so that the public could benefit from the effects of highly motivated competition. Both sides relied on ideological argument more than on reliable data, and neither side was willing to carry its argument to the extreme. Sometimes—as with the conservatives' dismissal of the "spectrum scarcity" argument—any attempt to analyze the matter objectively would run afoul of very slippery definitions of such basic terms as "market" and "competition."

Deregulation in broadcasting had begun in the mid-1970s under FCC chairman Richard Wiley (from 1972 to 1977) and accelerated under Charles Ferris (mid-1977 to early 1981). Serving both Republican and Democratic presidents, Wiley (a Republican) and Ferris (a Democrat) both believed that changes were necessary and proposed regulatory trade-offs for broadcasting. In return for retaining and even expanding such structural regulation as ownership limits and employment guidelines, the FCC would back away from consideration of more direct content controls, such as specific program or advertising guidelines. The latter type of proposals suffered constant attack on First Amendment grounds anyway and were by far the most controversial measures considered by the commission over the years. So regulators worked under an increasingly clear compromise premise in the late 1970s: government should help to set a broad structural arena within which broadcasters could operate freely.

Extreme deregulation, aimed at "getting the government off industry's back," came with Mark Fowler's chairmanship of the FCC from 1981 to early 1987. The compromise was abandoned, together with all but the most generalized support of the "public interest, convenience, and/or necessity" standard. The cast of regulatory players also changed in this period. Members and committees of Congress, with their own agendas and with membership changes from every election, exercised closer control over what they considered to be their creature, the FCC. Initially, Fowler had the backing of Congress for the FCC's deregulatory push. But after the mid-1980s, Fowler, and his successor, Dennis Patrick, found fewer supporters on Capitol Hill, in part because Congress felt the FCC was moving too far too fast and in part simply because Congress, with more substantial staff backing, wanted to play a more direct role in the policy sandbox.

The executive branch was not idle. Presidents ignored questions of telecommunications policy at their own political peril. Joining the fray early in 1978 was the National Telecommunications and Information Administration. NTIA was the lineal descendant of the once-powerful Nixon White House–based Office of Tele-

communications Policy. Now a part of the Department of Commerce, NTIA had the functions of advising the executive branch on telecommunications issues, representing the President's telecommunications policies, and keeping peace among federal government users of the electromagnetic spectrum (through IRAC). As international meetings of the ITU and other organizations became more common and more central to domestic electronic media developments, the Department of State also took a more active role.

The industry continued to play in all the Washington arenas, although the entry of new players based, in part, on new technology tended to splinter points of view as the 1980s wore on. The National Association of Broadcasters continued to play the umbrella organization role, trying to represent the many different parts of the industry, from large networks to tiny market radio stations. (Indeed, the National Radio Broadcasters Association, an expansion of an FM radio trade group of the 1960s, merged into the NAB early in 1986, much as had the Television Broadcasters Association more than 30 years before.) But the points of view on regulatory issues grew more disparate, and the NAB found itself criticized loudly from all directions. Specialized groups spoke up increasingly for independent stations, large stations, daytime operators, and newer media, such as cable, all of which disagreed with NAB positions at one time or another.

The NAB's position as the industry spokesman and leader was not helped any when, in June 1979, the Justice Department filed an antitrust suit against the NAB's radio and television codes. Justice claimed that the code guidelines served to restrict the market for advertising (by limiting the amount of advertising per hour)—thus driving up costs for sponsors.

After a March 1982 decision on one small part of the advertising code went against the NAB, the government and trade association signed a consent decree effectively ending both the advertising and program guideline codes, which had been around since 1939 (radio) and 1952 (television). Although the demise of the codes was greeted with a sigh of relief from those who had been skirting and violating them, there was significant negative public relations fallout from the unseemly haste with which the NAB dropped the entire idea of program standards, particularly those dealing with children's programs.

The networks, which had always relied on their own "standards and practices" offices rather than the NAB code, and many stations continued to enforce programming and advertising codes of their own. By making it desirable for advertisers to meet one fairly high standard rather than different standards for each station, the networks and conscientious stations thus prevented the anticipated flood of substandard and even harmful programming and advertising.

On the other hand, although citizens' groups such as Action for Children's Television remained active, the desire of the networks to cut costs, and the FCC's abdication of responsibility for content in the name of "deregulation," led to a substantial reduction in staffing in the network standards and practices departments in the late 1980s. The Television Information Office, founded by the industry as a public relations arm in the aftermath of the quiz show scandals at the end of the 1950s (see 8.63 and 8.85), was eliminated early in 1989.

The 1980s were not a settled time for broadcasters. Although many welcomed the fruits of deregulation, Congress made it clear that sooner or later there would be a price, perhaps in the form of

rent (called a "spectrum use fee") for a channel. Broadcasters were frequently reminded that they could not have it both ways: if they were "special" because of their role in meeting the public interest, they probably should be subject to at least some generalized content-service guidelines. If, on the other hand, they were just like any other business, they should be subject to the charges that the federal government makes for use of public resources.

Broadcasting, although in the public eye, was an ever-smaller part of the larger telecommunications scene in the 1980s. Fundamental structural and service changes in the telephone industry, fed in part by the need to provide cheap and efficient computer communication networks (outside the scope of *Stay Tuned*), were causing far more fundamental changes to the common carrier telecommunications industries than were changes in broadcast regulation, although the latter were more likely to be noticed by the general public.

10•81 Congress Tries to Rewrite the 1934 Act

From 1977 until 1982, Congress was deeply involved in its most serious attempt thus far to review and replace completely the half-century-old Communications Act of 1934. Driven by changing technology (see 10.1) and a belief that the spectrum scarcity argument accepted by the Supreme Court in the 1969 *Red Lion* decision should be overcome by such a rewrite, as well as a rapidly changing common carrier regulatory scene, members of first the House and later the Senate moved through several generations of hearings and bills in what was touted as a "basement-to-attic" review of American domestic communications policy.

The process began with an ill-conceived attempt by AT&T in 1976 to persuade Congress to amend the 1934 act essentially to reinstate its by-then crumbling telephone monopoly status.* Initially backed by many members of both houses, the bill never came to hearing, let alone a final vote. For, despite its title as the "Consumer's Communications Reform Act," the hands of special interests were all over its provisions, and it was soon seen as far too narrow and reactionary. (One later bill was numbered S. 611—the same digits as the Bell System's repair service telephone number.)

Congressman Lionel Van Deerlin (D-California), one of an increasing number of congressmen with a broadcasting background, took over the chairmanship of the House Communications Subcommittee concerned that the issues raised in the "Bell bill" needed resolution—but so did many other long-hanging controversies in broadcast and cable regulation. Perhaps it was time to reinvent the wheel.

In May 1977, armed with special appropriation support, the Van Deerlin subcommittee staff issued an 800-page set of Options Papers outlining the current regulatory status of all services regulated by the FCC, along with the options Congress might consider in changing those relationships. Among the possible changes discussed were almost total deregulation

---

*The Department of Justice had brought suit to break up AT&T in late 1974. Even by 1976, it was evident that the legal procedures would drag on for years. AT&T also was troubled by a series of FCC and court decisions that had introduced competition into long-distance service by specialized common carriers, such as MCI and Sprint, and into the customer premises equipment market (the *Carterfone* decision of 1968 allowed others to connect to "Ma Bell's" lines). Yet AT&T was still closely regulated and required to provide service on a near-universal basis, no matter how expensive that was to accomplish.

of radio content requirements, different funding mechanisms for public broadcasting, and ways of having licensees pay for the right to use the spectrum. The papers were designed to stimulate and crystallize thinking, one staff member even assuring a group of academics that the committee would consider all ideas, even "crazy ones." Instead, they often stimulated fear and opposition.

A year later, Van Deerlin introduced H.R. 13015, hopefully titled the "Communications Act of 1978." Among other things, the huge bill, which was designed to supersede the 1934 act, called for replacement of the FCC with a five-member Communications Regulatory Commission, which would regulate "only to the extent marketplace forces are deficient" and would thus do away with the "public interest, convenience, and/or necessity" standard in the existing legislation. For electronic media, the bill envisioned the total deregulation of radio, no federal regulation of cable (leaving that to state and local authorities), lengthening the television station license period from three to five years and extending it to "indefinite" after a decade, no more multiple ownership of stations in the same market (though "grandfathering" of the many existing radio-television combinations would be allowed), and limiting of one person's or firm's ownership to no more than 10 radio and 10 television stations (instead of the existing 7-7-7 limit, or 21). To replace the Fairness Doctrine, the bill proposed a more general "equity principle" that called for balanced treatment of controversy but did not require coverage of issues in the first place. The "equal-time" political broadcasting requirements would be eliminated on radio for national and statewide races. It sounded too good to be true—and there was a kicker, which broadcasters instantly rallied against. All licensees (not just broadcasters) were to pay a spectrum license fee to operate, the funds going to defray the cost of regulation and to serve public, minority, and rural telecommunication needs. Extensive hearings in Washington's July heat received testimony from a divided industry and a divided FCC—several commissioners were firmly against the radical changes proposed. Van Deerlin was forced to agree that the rewrite needed rewriting.

In March 1979, Van Deerlin introduced H.R. 3333, which carried broadcast deregulation even further. It provided that there would be no enforcement of Fairness Doctrine and EEO requirements for radio. In addition, the bill proposed indefinite licenses for the aural broadcast services and elimination of comparative hearings and substitution of random selection—lotteries—for new stations. There would be no radio ownership rules, and public stations would be allowed to carry some commercials. But the new bill still contained the spectrum license fee as a trade-off. And Broadcasting editorialized that with the new rewrite, "Van Deerlin threatened to steal the all-purpose security blanket"—the 1934 act—which, despite its faults, the players clearly understood. Other critics attacked the lottery provision, suggesting that giving a license to the luckiest rather than the best qualified was a concept that should stay in the Las Vegas casinos. (Another proposal, not in the bill, that proposed that licenses be auctioned off, was met with approval only by those with lots of money.)

By then, as the subcommittee headed into further weeks of hearings, positions had hardened and there was clearly too much controversy and disagreement among and within the many industries involved. Van Deerlin thus reluctantly agreed that his staff would concentrate on common carrier matters,

Rewrites and Deregulation / This chart compares and contrasts the existing requirements of the Communications Act of 1934, the proposals of early rewrite bills in 1978–1979, and the status a decade later of those same requirements.

1934 Act	1978–1979 Proposals	Deregulation by 1989
Regulation needed to: Promote the public interest, convenience, or necessity	"To the extent marketplace forces are deficient"	As in 1934 act
The Regulatory Agency FCC, with 7 members	Communications Regulatory Commission, with 5 members	FCC, with 5 members
Fees No provision	Spectrum fee on all licenses, to be used to pay for FCC, public broadcasting	Application fees for all services
License Terms 3 years	Indefinite for radio; 10 years for TV	7 years for radio, 5 years for TV
Renewals Okay if in public interest; comparative hearing if competing applications	Lottery proceeding for competing applications with minority preferences	Comparative process intact for radio-TV; lottery for new services with some minority preferences
Program Regulations None: gives FCC limited discretion	Eliminate program guidelines, limits on advertising, Fairness Doctrine, ascertainment	All proposals later adopted in modified form by FCC
Political Broadcasting Original Section 315	Would continue for TV, might be eliminated for radio. Would exempt some campaigns	Section 315, though modified, still in place
Public Broadcasting None: added in 1967	Eliminate CPB and set up a program endowment; allow editorializing	CPB still in place; stations can now editorialize
Ownership Limits None: FCC can adopt; FCC set 7-7-7 in 1954	One station per market; otherwise no limit on number of stations	Still one per market, but 12-12-12 nationwide
Cable Regulation None	Would eliminate then-existing FCC rules, require cable systems to get consent of broadcasters before carrying signal	Most FCC rules gone; cable enjoys retransmission consent under copyright act. 1984 cable act largely deregulatory

which seemed to need the most fixing, rather than a complete rewrite.

After the 1980 elections, the focus shifted to the Senate. Van Deerlin, surprisingly, had lost his bid for re-election (his opponent said the congressman was away in Washington doing his best to raise constituents' telephone bills!). Representative Timothy Wirth (D-Colorado) took over the House subcommittee chair. The Senate bills of the next two sessions focused mainly on common carrier matters, and though S. 611 and S. 622 did drop the call for a spectrum fee while proposing longer broadcast license periods, they still called for a lottery for new licenses and for some regulation of cable. These bills were stalled in committee and went nowhere. A final attempt in the House, delayed for more than a year while the subcommittee held extensive background briefings with experts to hone its knowledge, came to grief under lobbying pressure from AT&T.

While no new comprehensive act resulted, the rewrite process was not a total waste of time and energy. Members of Congress were now more knowledgeable about communications issues. While the initial rewrite had been radical in its departure from existing institutions and practices, subsequent versions looked more and more like the existing FCC and national telecommunications policy. Congress realized that without any clear industry agreement on the makeup of a replacement, the existing act, amended as needed, would have to continue to serve.

Congress focused as well on FCC membership and practices. Several commissioners who served in this period, among them chairman Ferris and commissioners Fogarty and Dawson, had moved up from congressional staff jobs. (Despite the fact that the President may nominate anyone as a commissioner, the chief executive often uses such posts as a way of gaining congressional favor.) That certainly helped Congress keep an eye on the commission! Further, several of the provisions in the defunct rewrite bills did see the light of day. A massive budget reconciliation bill in mid-1981 slipped in an extension of broadcast licenses from three years to five for television and seven for radio—something long sought by the industry. And cable was largely deregulated in a 1984 act (see 10.84).

But the 1980s are perhaps best seen as a time of increasing tension between Congress and the FCC. Mark Fowler took his strong ideological views to the Hill again and again in hearings, where they did not always sit well with those skeptical of his reliance on marketplace regulation. He appeared to flout congressional interests—as when the commission proposed elimination of the Section 315 political broadcasting provisions dear to all candidates, particularly incumbents. He seemed unwilling to compromise with Congress until forced. The tension came to a peak in 1982 over President Reagan's appointment of Stephen Sharp, the commission's general counsel, as a commissioner. Fowler strongly urged the appointment, angering several in the Senate who thought the seat had been promised to someone else. Sharp got his seat—but at the same time, the commission was reduced from seven to five commissioners (now serving five-year terms), and Sharp served for less than a year. In 1983, congressional displeasure with the FCC's generally independent policy direction led to a change in the commission's legal status from a permanent government agency to one that had to be, in effect, recreated every two years! The idea was to get the FCC's attention and force it to toe the congressional line more closely. Fowler's successor in 1987, former White House personnel officer Dennis Patrick, seemed

more conciliatory in manner but just as confrontational and ideological in intent. When the FCC unilaterally declared in mid-1987 that it would no longer enforce the Fairness Doctrine (see 10.82), members of both houses angrily sought ways to "punish" the commission and to insert congressional endorsement of the doctrine in a "veto-proof" bill so that President Reagan or his successor would have to approve it, in a scenario reminiscent of congressional ire at then-chairman Fly in the 1940s.

10•82   Broadcast Deregulation

A content analysis of material written about American broadcasting in the decade 1978–1988 would show deregulation as one of the most discussed topics. The move to lift some requirements and restrictions from broadcasting had been coming for a long time. It was obvious that many rules were honored in the breach rather than the observance and that far too many waivers and exemptions were granted. If rules were not enforced, they were useless. Further, for reasons already explored in this chapter, the place of broadcasting amidst its rising competitors was clearly changing. No longer was radio or television the only game in town. The introduction of new media, especially cable, that were unfettered by the limitations of the electromagnetic spectrum increasingly called into question some of the basic underpinnings of past regulation. Scarcity of channels was politically—if not physically—removed from the argument. In an administration that showed little sign of defending public ownership of natural resources and parks, the idea that public ownership of the airwaves justified regulation was laughable.

A step in the right direction, from the FCC's point of view, came in a March 1981 Supreme Court decision that held that the commission need not become involved in decisions over which radio music or talk formats might best serve a given market. The court opinion resolved a controversy that had rumbled through the 1970s, culminating in a 1979 lower court decision holding that the FCC did have to play a role when a station wanted to switch away from a "unique" format desired by some members of the public in a given market. The Supreme Court held that the First Amendment clearly left such decisions to station owners, not regulators.

More widely seen as the real watershed of deregulation, however, was the elimination of four requirements dealing with radio proposed late in 1978 during the Ferris regime. The FCC had initially planned to limit the deregulation to major markets in which many stations competed. By the time the FCC held two days of oral hearings in September 1980, the plan had been expanded to cover all commercial radio stations and had become highly controversial. Critics felt the FCC was abandoning its proper role as an overseer of the airwaves. Some were misinformed— hundreds of letters expressed fears that religious, agricultural, or other service programming might disappear if no longer "required" (it never had been).

The FCC's 1981 decision dropped "ascertainment," which required applicants to go through a complicated process to determine or ascertain just what the "city of license" (the community where the station was located by terms of its license) needed or wanted from its radio stations, especially in public service programming. Further, stations would no longer have to maintain detailed program logs and keep them open for public inspections. Those

complaining about radio content would now have to keep their own records to back up complaints, making it extremely hard for them or the commission to determine if the stations had indeed been operating in the public interest. And the FCC did away with two "processing guidelines" that guided staff decisions on applications: no longer would stations have to promise even minimal public service programming or specify maximum amounts of advertising to be aired. Both would be left to the as-yet-unproven concept of "marketplace competition." The commission had come a long way from its abortive 1963 attempt to limit the amount of advertising content on the air (see 9.71)! After these rules were lifted (and similarly abandoned for commercial television and public broadcast stations in mid-1985), the FCC retained but two program areas of concern: political programming and obscenity.

Many other attempts at reregulation and deregulation followed, most of them dealing with control of industry ownership, entry, and structure (see 10.84

Fall of the Fairness Doctrine / Compare these quotes with those on pages 426–427, which describe the "rise of the Fairness Doctrine." These excerpts from FCC inquiries and decisions, several court decisions, and a failed legislative attempt to codify the doctrine show the changing thinking about the doctrine in the 1980s in the face of an increase in stations and competing services—and substantial shifts in regulatory ideology.

June 9, 1969 "... If experience with the administration of these doctrines indicates that they have the net effect of reducing rather than enhancing the volume and quality of coverage, there will be time enough to reconsider the constitutional implications."—Supreme Court in *Red Lion Broadcasting Co.* v. *FCC*, 395 U.S. 367, at 393.

July 2, 1984 "The prevailing rationale for broadcast regulation based upon spectrum scarcity has come under increasing criticism in recent years. ... We are not prepared to reconsider our longstanding approach *without some signal from Congress or the FCC that technological developments have advanced so far that some revision of the system of broadcast regulation may be required.*"—Supreme Court in *FCC* v. *League of Women Voters of California,* 468 U.S. 364, at 376–377, footnote 11, emphasis added.

August 7, 1985 "Based on the voluminous record compiled in this proceeding, our experience in administering the doctrine and our general expertise in broadcast regulation policy determinations, we believe that as a policy matter the fairness doctrine no longer serves the public interest. ... Notwithstanding these conclusions we have decided not to eliminate the fairness doctrine at this time. The doctrine has been a longstanding administrative policy and a central tenet of broadcast regulation in which Congress has shown a strong ... interest."—FCC, *Report* on Gen. Docket No. 84-282, "Inquiry into ... Fairness Doctrine Obligations of Broadcast Licensees," 102 FCC 2d 145, at 246–247.

September 19, 1986 "We do not believe that the language adopted in 1959 made the fairness doctrine a binding statutory obligation; rather it ratified the commission's longstanding position that the public interest standard authorizes the fairness doctrine. The language, by its plain import, neither creates nor implies any obligation, but

mitted to Congress late in 1981. Specifically, he argued that Congress should
eliminate Section 315 and Section 312(a)
requirements on political broadcasting.
Congress, aware of the value of broadcasting to its own campaigns, demurred.
The commission began to build a record,
arguing the fact that the huge and growing
number of broadcast stations, plus additional services, made the 1927 political
broadcasting clause and 1949 Fairness Doctrine no longer necessary. (A further supporting factor was that an ever-growing
proportion of the population now lived in
or near large cities, weakening congressional interest in rural areas with few stations.) While most citizens' groups felt the
Fairness Doctrine was the only entrance
ticket for their opinions to be heard over
the air, a number of other groups—such as
the Radio-Television News Directors Association (RTNDA)—felt that the doctrine
actually reduced broadcast controversy
because station owners preferred to eliminate all controversy rather than donate
time for mandated rebuttals. At first,
under some pressure from Congress and
other critics, the FCC backed off any
attempt at outright repeal, given the general belief that Congress had codified the
doctrine into law with its 1959 amendments to Section 315 and that the Supreme
Court had endorsed this with the 1969 *Red
Lion* decision (see 9.82). But in 1985, the
commission sent a major policy report to
Congress arguing for repeal. Facing little
likelihood of action there, in August 1987
the FCC took the final step and unilaterally
eliminated the Fairness Doctrine, using as
a vehicle a fairness case remanded to it by
the Court of Appeals for further action
(see box on pages 524–525).

Despite the trend to deregulation,
enforcement of existing rules and regulations continued. The most controversial
decisions concerned RKO General, a
group owner of radio and television stations and a subsidiary of General Tire. In
mid-1980, the FCC denied renewal of three
RKO television station licenses, citing serious rule violations and misrepresentation
to the commission. On appeal, one of the
denials was upheld (for a Boston television
station), while the others were thrown,
together with 12 remaining licenses, into a
massive legal process while the commission tried to determine RKO's fitness to be
a broadcaster. Dozens of applicants vied
for the licenses in question. In mid-1987, a
tentative decision found RKO unfit and
recommended lifting of all RKO licenses.
By late 1988, it appeared the FCC would
allow RKO to sell off the remaining stations, but at a fraction of their normal
worth. The case illustrated one of the
worst examples of length and cost of regulatory proceedings and added to the
pressure for substantial streamlining of
FCC investigative and legal procedures.

10•83   Technical Standards

Until the 1980s, the FCC played a
consistent and essential role in determining, testing, and enforcing technical standards for broadcast services. This role had
developed in part because of the limited
technological knowledge about transmission and other aspects of radio when the
1927 and 1934 acts were drawn up. Technical standards for equipment and broadcast signal quality were needed to ensure
uniform (or at least minimum) quality and
as a support to interference-free allocation
of the spectrum. This position often
helped establish an industry, as, for example, in the shaping of modern television
during the 1940s (see 6.8 and 7.8). But during the Fowler regime at the FCC, this role
of the commission as a national technical
overseer was strongly questioned for the

and 10.85). Overshadowed were hundreds of technical changes consolidating duplicate requirements and the like.

But it was not quite that easy. "Re-regulation," not "deregulation," was still the buzzword for several years. Broadcasters, initially pleased at the elimination of ascertainment, discovered that beginning in 1985 they would have to file a quarterly "problems and programs" list, specifying key community problems and the programs that were broadcast to deal in some way with those problems. Gone were the old but fairly specific guidelines that broadcasters could easily meet and know the FCC would not bother them. Now, managers had to make daily determinations on coverage of public affairs, knowing such a listing had to be prepared four times a year.

Getting the most attention in the mid-1980s, however, was a growing FCC campaign to end the Fairness Doctrine. FCC chairman Mark Fowler had hinted at such an action in his first package of proposed amendments to the 1934 act sub-

seeks to make it clear that the statutory amendment does not affect the fairness doctrine obligation as the Commission had previously applied it. The words employed by Congress also demonstrate that the obligation recognized and preserved was an administrative construction, not a binding statutory objective."—U.S. Court of Appeals for the District of Columbia Circuit, *Telecommunications Research and Action Center* v. *FCC*, 801 F 2d 501, at 517.

April 2, 1987 "(7) For more than thirty years, the Fairness Doctrine and its corollaries, as developed by the Federal Communications Commission . . . have enhanced free speech by securing the paramount right of the broadcast audience to robust debate on issues of public importance; and . . . (8) the Fairness Doctrine (A) fairly reflects the statutory obligation of broadcasters under th[e] Act to operate in the public interest, (B) was given statutory approval by the Congress . . . in 1959, and (C) strikes a reasonable balance among the first amendment [sic] rights of the public, broadcast licensees, and speakers other than owners of broadcast facilities."—Last two "findings" of H.R. Bill 1934, 100th Cong., 1st Sess., proposing new Section 315(a) to the Communications Act, passed by Congress in June 3, 1987, but vetoed by President Reagan June 19.

August 6, 1987 "We find that the fairness doctrine chills speech and is not narrowly tailored to achieve a substantial government interest. We therefore conclude . . . that the fairness doctrine contravenes the First Amendment and thereby disserves the public interest. . . . Accordingly, we . . . conclude that the Constitution bars us from enforcing the fairness doctrine. . . ."—FCC, Memorandum Opinion and Order in Complaint of Syracuse Peace Council against Television Station WTVH, 2 FCC Rcd 5043, at 5057–5058, paragraph 98.

when the British company AGB introduced the "people meter" with an experiment in Boston. While AGB did not last (it stopped operation after just 11 months, unable to get the networks and major advertising agencies to support its attempt to compete with Nielsen), people meters did.

People meters are electronic devices that measure when a television receiver is on, to what channel it is tuned, and—unlike traditional meters—just who is actually watching (see box). Developed independently by several firms during the 1980s (and actually used by regular ratings

---

People Meters / The "people meter" machines used by Nielsen and Arbitron in the late 1980s did not look very special, but they heralded a vastly improved system of audience ratings. Here are the three devices that form the Arbitron system: (right) the large box contains the measurement devices and sits atop the home television set; (below, left) the "joy stick" device, called a Scan Wand by Arbitron, is used to scan universal product codes after purchase and is then returned to its base unit so the code information can be tallied with television watching; and (below, right) the small hand-held unit allows the viewer to punch in a number assigned to each member of the household (up to eight), plus up to nine guests. A viewer "prompt" (a question mark in the upper left-hand side of the screen) appears every half hour if no new audience information has been entered by the hand-

held unit. In the early morning hours, each ScanAmerica household's people meter is "read" by the national computer to help form overnight and national ratings and product purchase reports.

Source: Arbitron, ScanAmerica Press Office, 142 West 57th St., New York, NY 10019.

first time. In August 1981, the commission did away with the first-, second-, and third-class radiotelephone licenses, which had been issued for generations as indicators of varied levels of expertise for station engineering personnel, replacing them with a new "general" license. The commission then blandly announced that high technical quality was still required of all station licensees—but how they ensured that quality was going to be up to them, in an era of shrinking government resources.

The next stage in the commission's departure from the setting of technical standards came about when it was faced with establishing standards for AM stereo broadcasting. Not a crucial decision in itself (except to AM station owners, who were hoping stereo would help counteract FM's growing success in attracting large audiences), it became a watershed in FCC technical thinking. At first, after several years of consideration, the FCC in April 1980 selected, by a vote of 5-to-2, one of five proposed standards then in competition for AM broadcasters desiring to transmit stereo signals. Radio engineers ridiculed the technical basis for the decision, and the commission withdrew it shortly thereafter. Two years later, by then a very different body in both membership and political thinking, the FCC voted 6-to-1 to allow AM stereocasts, but without selecting one of the five systems. The commission claimed that the marketplace would do the selecting, though there was some doubt even as to what the marketplace was in this case (radio manufacturers? broadcast stations? the general set-purchasing and listening public?). The FCC also argued that by not selecting a system, it was avoiding years of delay that would be caused by legal challenges. The result? By the late 1980s, AM stereo was only a minor factor in the AM business, with perhaps 10 percent of all stations using one system or

another (by 1989, only two systems were left, and the Motorola system was winning a *de facto* victory, especially after General Motors selected that system for installation in its cars). Despite several revisits to the issue, the FCC stuck by its guns, claiming that government had no business making such a decision, both for lack of money and facilities to do so and because of the dominant deregulatory philosophy, which said that this was not a fit subject for regulatory action.

The AM stereo precedent was applied in March 1982 when the commission approved a low-power television service, with few restrictions on it save a strict requirement not to interfere with full-power television stations (a necessary rule in a political sense, since the viewers of the existing full-power stations would be sure to generate congressional action if interference developed). In June of the same year, in approving a system of DBS (see 10.1), the FCC set no technical rules, merely requiring no interference with other services and even said PBS "wasn't broadcasting." This decision had the further effect of eliminating any early possibility of using DBS to introduce a system of HDTV (see 10.124) broadcasts directly to American homes. In March 1983, the FCC declined to pick specific standards for teletext, allowing television stations to transmit teletext signals so long as they did not cause interference with other signals. With television stereo, the commission in 1984 decided to "protect" an industry-agreed-on standard but did not, again, specifically require one approach. It was clear that in the future this FCC would generally approach any new service with the assumption that no standard would be selected other than a requirement that the new service not interfere with older services already in place . . . and even that practical rule was not sacrosanct.

While deregulating at home, the FCC, other government agencies (especially the Department of State and NTIA), and private telecommunications carriers and manufacturers were playing a far more active role in international standard-setting bodies such as the International Standards Organization and the International Consultative Committee for Radio, both based in Geneva, Switzerland, the latter a part of the International Telecommunication Union. With increasing trade in consumer and industry electronics, worldwide participation in developing agreements on standards became progressively more important in the 1970s. Different countries often rallied behind their standards because of the tremendous potential profits to be made, as had happened with color television (see 9.92). France, Britain, and Canada all backed conflicting standards for teletext early in the 1980s, while Japan and Europe (and, belatedly, the United States) were squaring off on standards for systems of high-definition television later in the decade (see 10.124).

10•84   Entry and Equity

Fundamental policy questions of market entry and of equity of treatment across services faced the FCC throughout this period, often stimulated by new services made possible by new technologies. In a search for "a level playing field" for competition, the commission generally tried to avoid regulating new services at the same time it largely deregulated existing services. Cable television became caught in the middle of the switch in regulatory policy and came full circle in less than 20 years (see page 430). The first important question, however, dealt with a class of people, not media.

There was little disagreement by the 1970s that American minorities owned far fewer media outlets than would be suggested by their proportion of the nation's population. In response to petitions from several government and minority groups, and in an attempt to increase the number of stations in the hands of members of minority groups, in May 1978 the FCC agreed to two new methods of transferring licenses. If a station were sold to a minority-controlled licensee, the seller would receive a tax certificate that would cut or delay his or her capital gains tax. If an existing station was in trouble with the commission, that station could change hands (prior to the start of any formal FCC hearing on the problem) in a "distress sale to a minority group" for no more than 75 percent of the fair market price of the property. In April 1979, a Rhinelander, Wisconsin, television station was the first to transfer under the distress sale rule. In 1982, the policy was extended to members of minorities who had controlling roles but as little as 20 percent equity interest. By early 1989, 160 stations had passed into minority hands by means of tax certificates alone. In 1986, the commission began to reconsider the constitutionality of such minority preferences. It initiated a public inquiry and suspended granting of both tax certificates and distress sales while a hearing was pending. This angered Congress, which in proceedings for the FCC's 1987 appropriation successfully demanded that the inquiry be abandoned and both policies reinstated.

Facing continued demand for more broadcasting stations from all sides (except from existing stations and the NAB, which wondered if more were always better), the FCC during this decade examined many ways to squeeze more traditional broadcast operations into the existing spectrum space allotted for each service. For AM, the FCC considered, approved, and then reconsidered and rejected a change from the long-existing 10 KHz channel bandwidth to 9 KHz spacing, as is used in Europe and Asia. This change might have allowed 400 or more additional AM stations to squeeze onto the air. Pressure from existing AM stations fearful of the costs of the change, as well as of more competition, killed the idea in 1981. In another action, Western Hemisphere spectrum allocation changes, agreed to in meetings of the International Telecommunication Union beginning in 1979, called for extending the upper limit of the AM band from 1605 to 1705 KHz late in the decade, the first such expansion since 1952 (see box, page 86). Although this band was used by broadcasting elsewhere, its use in the United States first required the moving of police transmissions to another band. The first of several hundred new stations in the United States and Canada is expected to be on the air by 1990. Likewise, the squeezing of more stations into the FM band was the result of FCC Docket 80–90 (the numbers indicated the 90th proceeding initiated during 1980), which may allow as many as 800 new FM stations to take to the air. All of this expansion would be made possible primarily by improved technology and interference-reduction techniques.

More controversial have been attempts to expand the number of television stations on the air. For many years, the commission had attempted to solve the shortage of television channels by planning to "drop in" as many as several hundred channels into the assignment table on a case-by-case basis. Naturally, existing broadcasters in those communities objected. The debate was vigorous, with some government agencies supporting the idea (to take some of the pressure off those who wanted to enter the television broad-

casting business without the cost of buying an existing station) and others opposing it. Eventually the plan fizzled, with only four such VHF drop-in channels added in a 1980 decision.

While initially the cause of less debate and more promise, the FCC's creation of a low-power television (LPTV) service described in 10.22 led to more headaches in the early 1980s as the application process bogged down. Part of the problem was that this was the FCC's first serious attempt to get a new service on the air with a minimum of regulatory paperwork. The commission's approach to totally new services now was generally quite simple— when in doubt about regulation, don't. Perhaps the best example from the mid-1980s was the short life of direct broadcast satellites (DBSs). First seriously proposed in a detailed six-volume filing by COMSAT's subsidiary, Satellite Television Corporation, to the FCC in December 1980, the notion of DBS briefly took the policy world by storm. Here was a potential system that seemed to suffer few of the limits of terrestrial broadcasting, would bring in a new player (thus presumably adding to the diversity of program sources), and would specifically be aimed at underserved rural, and later inner city urban, viewers. Once the satellite was in orbit, most costs, except for programming, would be paid by the consumer. The FCC moved with the regulatory speed of light, and in a series of decisions over the next two years decided to move an existing microwave service out of the 12.2–12.7 GHz (gigahertz—one GHz = 1,000 MHz) spectrum space assigned by international agreement to DBS. FCC rules were generous—applicants could decide whether they wanted to be regulated as broadcasters or as common carriers. There were no ownership, financial, or technical regulations. Obviously, there would be no requirement for local service. The only requirement laid on the many applicants (more than a dozen by 1982) was to show "due diligence" in planning and ordering satellites and launch capacity. But as "due diligence" deadlines approached in 1982 and 1983, the DBS balloon quickly sprang a leak. None of the prospective operators had resolved the old problem of programming—what to provide potential viewers that they did not already have. Further, when all the numbers were in, the costs of satellite design, launch, and operation quickly surpassed any estimates of revenue. By 1983–1984, DBS was back to the blue sky category—for an indefinite time. But no one could blame the FCC for regulatory delay in this case! Of course, whether the public interest was best served by this concentration of FCC resources and attention is open to argument.

When other prospective technologies were proposed in the 1980s, the commission again moved quickly and provided few regulatory impediments. Teletext services were authorized with few restrictions of any kind. MMDS grew out of a common carrier service first set up in the early 1960s (see 10.22).

Subscription television, the existing over-the-air single-channel pay system originally approved in 1968, also benefited from the FCC's retreat from regulation. STV had languished in a morass of regulatory red tape so soggy that no stations went on the air until 1977 (see 9.22). Beginning in 1979, the STV rules were slowly unraveled to allow more flexibility in station assignment and operation. Rules eliminated over the next several years included those allowing no more than one STV station to a market, a minimum of 28 hours of "conventional" (nonsubscription) programming per week, and a special FCC application process. By 1983–1984, regu-

lation was no longer the key impediment to STV's future. The problem lay with STV's single-channel limitation and, once again, the need for programming.

More complicated and dragged out, and with the courts playing a major role, is the story of the FCC's deregulation of cable television, partly summarized in the box on page 430. This story had more positive results for the service in question. Under pressure from several groups, including recommendations from Congress and independent business groups, the FCC had begun to re-examine its cable policy as early as 1975, just three years after issuing so-called definitive regulations clearly restricting cable to ancillary status, behind broadcast television. In March 1977, an appeals court decision overturned many of the FCC's pay-cable rules as unduly restrictive or protective of broadcasting. After 1977, many relatively minor restrictions were lifted by an FCC steadily moving toward a lower regulatory profile. In the summer of 1980, the FCC deleted two important and related rules that had limited the broadcast signals cable systems could carry. In 1984, after years of hearings but little action, Congress passed the Cable Communications Policy Act, which added a new title (Title VI) to the 1934 Communications Act. The cable act, the first federal legislation devoted to the medium, was a clear victory for the cable business. It generally limited regulation to a few local rules and lifted virtually all controls on cable programming and subscription rates, as well as limiting fees to be paid to cities and other franchising authorities—to their dismay and annoyance. The National League of Cities was the clear loser in this law, while the NCTA and the NAB struck an uneasy truce under the congressional gun. While some provisions called for various types of local "access" channels for school, government, and public use, many argued—correctly—that those requirements would be challenged on the basis of the First Amendment. The FCC and the courts also chipped away at the last vestiges of local control by allowing a second cable operator to come into a community to offer competition (called "overbuilding") and by making it very difficult for a municipality to refuse to renew a franchise when its term was up.

The longest-lasting FCC headache with cable concerned the must-carry rules, which soon became entwined with the "syndication exclusivity" (syndex) rules applied to television stations. First established in 1965, the must-carry rules required cable systems to carry all "significantly viewed" television stations within their system's coverage area. The rule, which dated from the period when cable was seen as supportive of broadcasting, was designed to ensure local stations equal access to viewers who might be cable subscribers. There was little controversy over this requirement, even from cable operators, until the late 1970s and early 1980s, when the number of cable networks mushroomed (see 10.34). The increase in cable networks put pressure on older systems with limited channel capacity, which had to carry broadcast signals in place of much more profitable pay-cable or other cable networks. Further, with deregulation of other content requirements, and the 1984 legislation, the must-carry rules seemed to many to be out of sync with the changing view of cable. In the 1985 *Quincy Cable TV Inc. v. FCC* decision, the Court of Appeals for the District of Columbia Circuit held that the must-carry rules violated the intent of the First Amendment by limiting cable system program choice because of an ill-supported FCC fear of cable's impact on broadcasting. In 1986, after considerable

wrangling among broadcast and cable industry trade groups, the FCC established a new must-carry rule. The new rule was to run for five years and was supposedly designed not to protect broadcasters but to maximize the viewer's variety of choice of channels. The new approach still did not survive court review—late in 1987, the revised rules were struck down again, on largely similar grounds, by the same court.

Broadcasters, especially newer independent stations and public broadcast outlets, were fearful about how long they would continue to be carried on nearby cable systems. During the same period, the broadcasters lost almost every court battle to prevent cable from carrying superstations and other outlets that also were running the syndicated programming that now cost those stations so much—and that originally had been sold with the assurance that no other station could air it in that community. The sniping grew intense, with both sides looking to the courts as well as the commission. One development that was particularly annoying to broadcasters, who had spent a great deal to make their channel numbers well known, was the arbitrary move of many stations to cable channels with unfamiliar numbers. Clearly, the pendulum had swung to the other side—and it was cable that seemed to be winning every fight against the older medium of on-the-air television in every forum.

10•85   Regulating Competition

With the FCC's structural rather than behavioral or content approach to regulation, questions of ownership, mergers and acquisitions, and concentration of control arose frequently in this period. To the commission, at least until the early 1980s, constraints on the media's "urge to merge" were a primary means of attempting to preserve some diversity in points of view in the local community. (The FCC never really wanted to come to grips with determining if there really was any relationship between diversity in ownership and diversity in content.) But the economic pressures supporting increased concentration, especially the ever-higher costs of buying and programming for stations and systems, led to many changes in the FCC's ownership rules in the 1980s.

The FCC's rule banning all but existing newspaper-broadcasting cross-ownership, promulgated in 1975 (see 9.84), came under court review late in that decade. The Court of Appeals for the District of Columbia Circuit overturned the FCC in the spring of 1977, contending that if cross-ownership was bad, as the court felt the commission's record suggested, all cross-ownerships in the same market should be divested. Ironically, although this court tended to have a conservative bent, this was the same conclusion sought by President Franklin D. Roosevelt in the 1930s in an attempt to counter the power of newspaper owners who tended to oppose him. The industry faced a draconian situation: forced breakup of several dozen station-newspaper combinations across the country. On appeal in 1978, the Supreme Court ruled 5-to-4 that the FCC's original plan of forcing the divestiture of only a select few egregious cases was preferable. Most existing station-newspaper combinations could continue—at least until their sale, when a breakup would be mandatory.

Cable cross-ownership rules, set up in 1970, also were examined in the 1980s. The economic tension between telephone companies and cable systems were kept alive by the debate over an FCC rule, carried over into the 1984 cable act, that prevented telephone companies from operating cable systems in their franchise area. The telephone companies argued that cable would never get to some rural areas unless telephone companies, with their engineering skills and tradition of "universal service," supplied it. But many feared the concept of a single company controlling both telephone and cable lines into homes and remembered the bitter battles CATV systems had to wage in order to secure space on telephone poles for their wires. For somewhat similar potential conflict of interest reasons, the ban on co-owned and co-located television stations and cable systems stayed in force. By 1988, the FCC was investigating whether cable cross-ownership rules could be lifted, arguing that cable as a mature medium could operate and expand with less structural control.

Rules limiting regional concentration of broadcasting stations faded as a result of deregulation. Rules limiting any single licensee to no more than one VHF station in the top 50 markets (a rule never enforced while on the books), regional concentration rules, and even limitations on "trafficking" (sale of a license in less than three years, considered to be *prima facie* evidence that the owner was interested more in buying and selling than in serving the public) were all swept away by the Fowler FCC—and helped contribute to the merger and takeover activity of the mid-1980s discussed in 10.2 and 10.3

The number of stations any one entity should be allowed to own in the nation had been argued for half a century. For some three decades, the FCC rule on broadcasting was to allow no more than 7 in each service (AM, FM, and television—but only 5 of the television stations could be on VHF), for a possible maximum of 21.

Even though only one licensee actually did acquire the maximum, in 1985 the commission raised that limit, first for radio and then for television, to 12 stations of each type. (The television limit, however, had the additional restriction that no more than 25 percent of the nation's population may be served by a given licensee, even if reached with fewer than 12 stations.) The commission acted after failing to get Congress to agree that no ownership limits whatsoever should be imposed on radio. Furthermore, Congress would not support a commission proposal to drop all ownership limits by 1990. On the other hand, none of the newer media had ownership limits. LPTV, DBS, and other broadcast services established in the 1980s had no artificial or noneconomic ownership ceilings. The motion picture industry, among others, constantly pushed the FCC and Congress to set up broadcast-comparable ownership limits on the number of cable systems or subscribers any one MSO company could control (see table on page 469). But by 1988, there was still no rule limiting ownership of either cable systems or cable networks.

One cable venture did run up against antitrust law, however. In 1980, Getty Oil and four film studios (Columbia, MCA, Paramount, and 20th Century-Fox) agreed to cooperate in a new venture called Premiere, which would compete with HBO in the thriving pay-cable market. The film studios were unhappy with what they felt were low rates paid by HBO, and thus each agreed to supply a nine-month exclusive license for its films to be shown on Premiere. Announced in April, the venture was in trouble six months later when the Department of Justice filed suit to halt it, arguing that Premiere would be a restraint of trade. Premiere initially continued planning, but a New Year's Eve injunction to stop its planned start-up two days later killed the venture.

10•86 Regulating Rights

The post-1976 period was a tumultuous one in several areas of law affecting media's relationship to individual rights, as reflected in copyright, libel, and obscenity legislation and litigation. Feelings that the media had become too big and intrusive clashed with beliefs of those who felt that First Amendment freedoms were being threatened. Only a few highlights of a contentious period of often confusing trends can be noted here, since the courts became quite inconsistent and the number of law cases involving the media expanded to the point where several publishing services are devoted solely to indexing and abstracting them.

Two-thirds of a century after its predecessor, a new copyright act finally passed in 1976, to be effective at the beginning of 1978 (see 9.83). It quickly came under pressure from constantly changing technology—and some old controversies as well. The act took into account, said its authors, both cable and broadcast interests. Cable would now have a "compulsory license" right to carry any broadcast signal without having to ask permission or pay the station directly. In return, cable systems had to pay a copyright royalty, based on cable system revenue and the number of distant signals carried. Congress established the Copyright Royalty Tribunal to set the royalty rates, collect the fees, and decide how they should be allotted. Each year, the collection and payout decisions were subject to legal appeals and dragged-out proceedings. Broadcasters said that the fees paid were far too low given the value of the programming carried, while cable systems claimed that broadcasters were being given an expanded audience at no cost to them. Payouts typically took three to four years, given all the legal hassles—and most of the money wound up in the pockets of the motion picture production companies. A decade later, Congress was considering doing away with the cumbersome royalty tribunal process altogether.

Another hotly contested question of competing rights concerned the authority of home videocassette recorder owners to record material from broadcast and cable channels. Part of the issue was resolved in the 5-to-4 Supreme Court decision in January 1984 in the "Betamax" (*Universal Studios* v. *Sony*) case. After a highly unusual two sessions of oral argument, the court ruled that the recording of material off the air for private home usage was not a violation of the filmmakers' copyright. The court held that most recording was for time-shifting purposes, not for any money-making reason . . . and demonstrated thereby an awareness of the political furor that would have resulted had it decided the other way. (Delays in litigation make a difference: a year earlier, only half as many VCRs were owned by the public, and the Supreme Court's hands would not have been so tied.) The film industry, later joined by the music business, turned to another forum and urged Congress to amend the Copyright Act to require those selling VCRs and blank tapes to collect a small royalty fee to be turned over to various copyright holders. This proposal did not get very far, since much blank tape is used for camcorder making of home movies and recording of other noncopyright material.

A related concern by the mid-1980s was the right of satellite-delivered program services to protect their signals from unauthorized reception. Led by HBO in January 1986, cable networks began to scramble their satellite signals to prevent backyard television receive-only antenna owners from getting programs free. The commercial television networks, for var-

ious reasons—including the embarrassment of unplanned, unscripted, and incomplete "back channel" transmissions designed only for communication with affiliate stations being seen by the public—also started to scramble. Sales of the ever less expensive backyard dishes, which had been running in the tens of thousands per month before scrambling began, dropped sharply as the once free signals disappeared into a haze of electronic noise. Owners of backyard dishes descended on Congress demanding access to the satellite signals, and a few highly publicized incidents of breaking briefly into network signals with signs of protest highlighted the argument. By 1989, however, nearly all satellite-delivered cable services had scrambled their signals, though many would provide service to individual homes equipped with decoder boxes for a monthly fee. Sales of backyard and rooftop dishes began to move upward again. Although this development was encouraging to those touting DBS, it was recognized that there was a vast difference between access to one or a few DBS program sources and access to more than a hundred satellite transponders—even if the equipment one had to buy for the latter was large, unsightly, and complex and made the neighbors complain of zoning law violations!

One of the first legal issues faced by radio broadcasters in the 1920s—payment for music used on the air—was still contentious six decades later. Every three to five years, as contracts from ASCAP and BMI came up for renewal, committees representing the radio and television stations would argue that royalty rates demanded by the music-licensing agencies were too high, or that television stations were hit unfairly when forced to buy blanket music licenses covering thousands of songs just to get the rights to use a few bits of sound track or theme music. A March 1985 Supreme Court decision held that such blanket licensing for television stations did not violate antitrust law. The negotiating process usually managed to convince broadcasters that they had fought successfully, but the basic tension between the music and broadcast industries remained.

Countless times in the late 1970s and into the 1980s, people famous or unknown sued a broadcast station, cable system, or network for harm, real or imagined. Most of these cases alleged libel— that the person's reputation had been harmed by broadcast of some falsehood. The networks and stations fought back vigorously, generally preferring to fight rather than apologize or voluntarily pay damages. As the law of defamation, and that of privacy, grew ever more complicated, the only sure thing that could be said was that a lot of lawyers were getting rich.

Two of the more widely discussed cases resulted from programs aired on CBS. Both dealt with aspects of the Vietnam War, and both were interviews conducted by Mike Wallace. In a *60 Minutes* profile, a highly decorated army officer, Anthony Herbert, was interviewed by Wallace about his attacks on the army's role in the war. Then the program questioned some aspects of his record. Herbert sued, claiming that the edited segment was defamatory and had injured his reputation. Though the case was eventually dismissed, along the way the Supreme Court issued a landmark—and to media journalists, dangerous—precedent. In its 1979 opinion in the case of *Herbert* v. *Lando* (Barry Lando was the segment's producer), the Supreme Court ruled 6-to-3 that Lieutenant Colonel Herbert's lawyers could probe the producers and reporters involved to determine their "state of mind" at the time the interview and edit-

ing took place. The court reasoned that since public figures had to prove "actual malice" (a legal term that really translates as having "knowledge that something was untrue, or with reckless disregard as to whether it was true or not") on the part of the media before winning a libel judgment, such questioning was a legitimate way to determine if such malice had been present.

The other case never went to a jury for final verdict (a large fraction of cases are settled or dismissed beforehand, but not until each party has spent a great deal of money in lawyer's fees), but it received even closer attention. In January 1982, CBS broadcast *The Uncounted Enemy: A Vietnam Deception,* a documentary alleging a high command cover-up of enemy force figures in the late 1960s. A few months later, the former U.S. commander in Vietnam, General William Westmoreland, sued the network for what he and other "hawks" called character assassination, claiming that Mike Wallace's interview with him was edited in a way that distorted his true views and specific answers. The case went to trial in New York in October 1984, at the same time as a similar case involving an Israeli political figure and *Time* magazine, the juxtaposition garnering wide attention as once-powerful figures relived their key decisions. Just before the case would have gone for the jury's assessment—almost certainly in favor of CBS—the general abruptly withdrew his suit and CBS issued a statement of correction and amplification of Westmoreland's role no different from that promised before the trial. Both sides claimed victory, although in the end Westmoreland had nothing to show for two years of effort (fortunately for him, his legal fees were donated by a conservative public interest law firm). Even so, CBS News's careful internal self-examination (the Benjamin

Report) of its editing process showed that operational improvements were necessary. The case appeared to show that the "actual malice" standard a public figure or public official had to demonstrate was a very steep cliff indeed. (Private figures, however, merely had to prove negligence—that the material defamed the identified victim, and the media couldn't prove that it was true—in most states.)

Obscenity has seldom been a serious problem for broadcasters, though some audience members decry what they perceive as widespread portrayal of sexual activity. One incident, however, led to a landmark decision. Comedian George Carlin's nightclub monologue on "seven dirty words you can't say on the air" was aired by a New York FM station on a serious program dealing with language at 2 P.M. one October afternoon in 1973, repeating no-no terms no fewer than 106 times in 12 minutes. A listener driving into the city with his teenage son heard the segment and complained to the station and the FCC. The FCC, some of whose members apparently were looking for a chance to condemn breaches of their standard of morality (one commissioner frequently took issue with the lyrics of rock music), immediately invoked an obscure section of law (dealing with "indecency," not "obscenity") and took the station to court. Ironically, this was the same licensee (the Pacifica Foundation, a listener-supported nonprofit organization that had several stations) about whose programming an earlier FCC had issued a ringing declaration that the airwaves were not to be restricted to the "wholly inoffensive, the bland." After a lower court decision in favor of the station, the Supreme Court in June 1978 reversed on a 5-to-4 vote and upheld the FCC's fine levied against the station, arguing that broadcasting's First Amendment rights were limited because

of its availability in the home and especially its ready accessibility to children. Thus, the court held, the FCC had taken the right approach in telling stations to "channel" possibly objectionable broadcasts to hours when children were less likely to be present in the audience (informally, after 10 P.M.). As was typically the case, the commercial broadcasting industry did not rally to Pacifica's support. Also as might be expected, the FCC refused to define "indecency," leaving stations the choice of risking sanctions—or making almost all such programming less offensive and blander. Some stations, of course, took the risk with "topless radio" and telephone-in and interview programs that were quite explicit when it came to sexual matters. Predictably, it took the FCC until 1987 to bring action against these "indecent" commercial programs. However, in April and again in December 1987, in cases against three stations, the FCC issued public policies setting up a more general definition of indecent material and setting aside the midnight to 6 A.M. time period, when parents could be assumed to have control of the set, if not the children, for stations to have somewhat more latitude in what they broadcast to adults. The decision seemed both to free broadcasters (in the six-hour period after midnight—a so-called safe haven that was removed by Congress in 1988 in a law not yet tested in the courts) and to tie them to a somewhat vague standard (for the other 18 hours of the day), to the concern of First Amendment purists.

On the other hand, even the commission could not overlook the changes in American mores, where four-letter words were used in situations hardly dreamed of a decade or two before and where "jiggle" or "T&A" portrayals of well-endowed women and men, and steamy encounters between them, were a staple attraction in prime-time—as well as daytime and late-night—programming.

The 1984 cable act made illegal the cable transmission of obscene material (while preempting local regulation of content for any other reason, including indecency—a concern of many, given the content of some pay-cable channels). Several states, notably Utah, tried more specific restrictive laws—the very existence of the Playboy Channel was offensive to some legislators—but were defeated on court appeal, since the 1984 federal cable law preempted state action in this area as well as others.

10•87   Regulation Overview: Abandoning the Trust

By 1988, the electronic media could look back on more than a decade of confusion, competition, and courtroom and congressional pressure—and substantial progress in deregulation. Licenses now ran for longer periods and it was harder for a challenger to petition to deny a station's license renewal; the FCC played a much-diminished role in content; the Fairness Doctrine was dead (at least until Congress was able to override a presidential veto); and citizens' action groups typically were demoralized and ineffective. The FCC had come to be perceived by the industry as cooperative and market oriented, not as a regulator or critic. On the other hand, many citizens felt that the commission had abdicated its responsibilities.

10•9   Impact

Long before the 1980s, broadcasting had become an integral part of every American's daily landscape. We awoke to radio news and weather and traffic reports. We switched on one of the network morning shows to have some light news and entertainment while getting dressed and eating breakfast. We drove to and from work with four- (or six- or eight-) speaker AM and FM stereo and tape decks in our cars. After watching the evening's prime-time fare, or a rented videocassette, we might go to sleep after a late-evening television news wrap-up . . . or stay up with a late-night show or cable movie rerun. We denied that the derogatory term "couch potato" applied to us and pointed to our careful selection of programs from TV Guide or the newspaper.

A radio receiver was nearly always within reach—even when traveling on mass transit, thanks to featherweight earphones of superb quality. While 2-inch portable television sets were only a novelty item in the 1980s, who was to say what they might become in the 1990s? The 1980s may be another period of consolidation, simply underlining this universal availability of receivers and programming with improved technology. We had more options from which to choose and somewhat more control over what we watched and heard—so long as it was chosen from what the station licensee or cable system operator made available to us.

10•91   Competing for the Consumer

Other media continued to respond to the changing challenges of broadcasting and its newer brethren. Newspapers increasingly took on the short and snappy story approach of television news, perhaps best epitomized by the rise of USA Today, the first attempt at a truly national American newspaper designed as such from the ground up. Published by the huge Gannett chain based in Washington, D.C., and printed in plants all over the country, USA

Today first appeared in selected sample markets in 1981 and was soon sold across the country from ubiquitous sales boxes designed to look like television sets. *USA Today* made creative use of color (becoming perhaps the first newspaper best known for its weather page!), short stories from every state, and focused writing backed up with photos and clear diagrams and tables. Although deprecatingly called "McPaper" (a reference to the homogenized food to be found across the nation at the sign of the golden arches), *USA Today* met and exceeded all of its financial and circulation predictions. (A televised version launched in the fall of 1988, however, received terrible reviews and seemed destined to failure, since the very appeal of the print *USA Today*—the reader's ability to turn to the page that interested him or her—was lost in the necessarily linear presentation of television.) Other papers followed suit. At the same time, newspapers also provided more soft and entertainment news as their hard news function diminished further in the face of competition from round-the-clock radio and television news availability.

Although newspapers remained the medium of choice for some types of advertising—local department stores, for example—the handwriting was on the wall: the overall circulation of newspapers in this country had remained steady while the population grew. Younger generations were finding newspapers more and more irrelevant, except for some advertisements and entertainment features such as sports, the comics, and even horoscopes. Yet another trend, similar to that found in most industries, was the ever-growing concentration of ownership in the newspaper business. Between 1963 and 1988, the number of daily newspapers in the United States dropped by 6 percent to 1,645—but the proportion of those owned by a group or chain more than doubled,

from 31 percent to 74 percent. In some cases, editorial quality was improved, but in almost all cases, since these companies tended to be publicly traded on the stock exchanges, decisions were increasingly made for the sake of short-term profits. In order to support the ideal of editorial diversity, Congress passed the Newspaper Preservation Act (known to the more polite of its many detractors as the "failing newspaper act"), allowing supposedly independent papers to engage in joint operating agreements (JOAs) that would save both papers enormous sums in printing and advertising sales costs—and make it harder for new competition that was not part of the JOA to enter the market.

Magazines continued to proliferate and specialize. Consumers in the 1980s were hit with a flood of computer magazines of all types, one of which could claim that its hundreds of pages (mostly advertising) made it the largest magazine in history—until the next month saw that record broken. Color became universal in advertising and editorial material except for small-circulation "serious" periodicals. *Life*, which had folded in 1977 in the face of competition from television for its advertisers, was brought back as a glossy monthly with limited editorial content. *Life*'s publisher, Time Inc., did not fare so well with a short-lived national cable television guide, dropping millions in an ill-planned venture marked by a lack of understanding of the multichannel medium (despite the fact that Time Inc. owns the HBO and Cinemax services, plus a large cable MSO). A sign of the changing composition of the American public was the rise of *Modern Maturity*, a membership publication of the American Association of Retired Persons aimed at senior and retired citizens, to the top of the circulation charts, where it joined other magazines with more than 10 million subscribers: *National Geographic, Reader's Digest,* and *TV Guide. TV Guide* itself continued to flourish and was sold with two other magazines for $3 billion to media tycoon Rupert Murdoch in mid-1988.

Perhaps most affected by changes in the electronic media was the Hollywood movie community. Buffeted by television's onset in the 1950s, and down in the dumps economically because of shrunken audiences by the 1960s, Hollywood regained some of its old production power in the 1970s—though producing more for television networks than for theaters. Box office blockbusters remained rare, and the sure-fire ones often were co-financed and co-produced with European companies, reflecting the motion picture industry's century of experience of finding profits in distribution abroad. But a much more substantial revival of production developed after 1980, sparked by the expanding program needs of the two new services, cable and VCRs. The latter made effective use of both old films and often substandard "exploitation" films of various kinds (terror and horror films were big among teen renters in the mid-1980s), which had heretofore had few outlets. Cable networks and the expanding channel capacity of individual cable systems created an almost insatiable demand for product, which breathed new life into film and tape program production.

Independent and "runaway" (to other, cheaper locations) production, using portable equipment rather than big 35 mm and 70 mm studio cameras, abounded. Some started to experiment with HDTV for feature films, with the edited product to be dubbed to 35 mm film for release. Cable pay-per-view services developed in the mid-1980s often showed top new films just after their initial theatrical showings—and provided a substantial increase in movie industry revenues even as the number of theaters in separate locations shrank. The number of theater "screens" (a more accurate figure than the number of "theaters," since many old movie palaces had been divided and almost all of the new shopping mall film centers had multiple screens) rose in the 1980s for the first time in decades, perhaps a result of the fact that the cost of seeing a film in a theater had soared.

Many creative figures in Hollywood unsuccessfully objected to the computerized coloration of old black-and-white films for use by television (particularly Ted Turner's superstation, WTBS), even while many farsighted observers suspected that HDTV would soon replace celluloid. Directors and actors accused the newer medium of bastardizing the product of the old in pursuit of increased revenue and of ignoring the effects of colorization on the original intent of the films' creators. But the larger questions of art versus commerce took a back seat to the ever-growing need for more talent and for that talent's own economic concerns. These concerns were epitomized by a lengthy strike of television writers in 1988 against producers and production houses (which delayed the 1988–1989 television season), chiefly over the question of increases in residual payments to writers for programs being rerun.

Hollywood expanded in more traditional ways as well. By the late 1980s, perhaps epitomized by Rupert Murdoch's takeover of 20th Century Fox to make films (and shows for his Fox network), came a return to vertical integration (the big studios controlling chains of first-run theaters as guaranteed outlets for their product). This practice had been banned by the Justice Department in a series of consent decrees in the 1940s and 1950s (see 7.91), but by the late 1980s, theatrical film had sufficient competition from television, cable, and home video that the government no longer seemed concerned about such ownership concentration. The metamorphosis of several studios into rental facilities for independent producers also appeared to reduce their power. But regardless of the number of feature films and theaters, the new kings of Hollywood were the television program producers, some of whom also made movies, reflecting a tendency for actors, directors, and producers to work in both media.

10•92   Changing Electronic Media
         Worldwide

Just as newer electronic media modified broadcasting's role in the United States, so did they change radio and television elsewhere. In Britain, by the mid-1980s the long-revered BBC was under pressure more severe than any seen since the days of John Reith. Commercial radio had joined commercial television to offer British listeners a greater choice. The Conservative government, thanks to the fact that its leader, Margaret Thatcher, was enjoying the longest term as prime minister in this century, was able to push the BBC into being more a carrier of other producers' material than the closed shop of high quality and elitist goals it had been for decades. New networks ("channels") were devised with careful spectrum allocation planning, giving the commercially supported Independent Broadcasting Authority parity (and then some) with the BBC's two main channels. Cable appeared; local radio flourished; VCRs became popular in the United Kingdom before they did in the United States (given the few over-the-air channels in Britain). DBS was on the horizon—and the choice of programs included a growing proportion (previously restricted to 14 percent) of popular shows from the United States.

Critics argued that one of the world's premier broadcasting organizations was being threatened with reversion to "just another broadcaster" status. Clearly the public service image of the BBC was being forced to change to a more entertainment-based one.

Deregulation of broadcasting slowly spread overseas from the U.S. model, without necessarily the same amount of intellectual ferment but with an equal chance for those involved to make a great deal of money. French broadcasting, for example, underwent a revolution. Long a government operation, French television became a privately operated entity in the early 1980s. On the horizon was a potential competitor of considerable clout as the French telephone authority installed thousands of "Minitel" videotex terminals in homes across the country in a bid to leapfrog over the existing limits of poor French telephone service and telephone books.

In Canada, by the end of the decade, an overwhelming proportion of the population received its television via cable. The CBC continued to serve the two primary language groups—English (a favorite service of many radio listeners on this side of the border) and French—across the nation, but it maintained a wary eye on the cultural and economic colossus to its south. Canadian cable systems, to the dismay and anger of U.S. stations located near the border, were authorized to delete U.S. commercials from American entertainment television. At the same time, Canadian manufacturers could not deduct from their taxes any payments for advertising on U.S. stations. Nevertheless, Canadian talent increasingly made its way to Hollywood—only to return in order to shoot "Hollywood" films in the much cheaper surroundings of our neighbor to the north.

Complicating life for many Americans was the growing 1980s deficit in the balance of trade. The formerly robust American dominance of trade in telecommunications began to reverse by the late 1970s, led by offshore (foreign-based, but often American-owned) manufacturing and imports of radio and television equipment. The consumer electronics market had become largely an import sector even by the late 1960s. Costs of labor and parts were lower in the Far East (initially Japan and more recently Korea, Taiwan, Hong Kong, and Singapore). By the end of the 1980s, virtually no radios or VCRs and very few television sets were being made in America by U.S. firms—or had been for years. After 1981, however, even industrial telecommunications equipment markets became import rather than export centers. Protectionist pressures grew in organized labor and its congressional allies. Only one American export product remained strong, despite active protectionist moves by other countries: American television programming.

Partially due to the interest in increasing sales abroad, American companies became more active in international meetings held to set technical standards and make spectrum allocation decisions. Because these meetings usually were held under the auspices of the International Telecommunication Union or one of its constituent bodies, planning for such meetings had to take place under State Department auspices (with help from the NTIA and the FCC) and required a great deal of debate before the U.S. delegation could decide on a national position. Emerging technologies, such as HDTV (see 10.124), were particularly problematic. European countries (and the United States) were not enchanted with the idea of giving over the future of television to a Japanese-developed technology that would threaten their own still-viable consumer electronics industries.

International meetings, attended by often sizable U.S. delegations made up of both government and private sector personnel, also worked for improved spectrum efficiency (crowding of more services into the same space) and debated questions of equal access by all nations to the important geostationary communications satellite orbit 22,300 miles out in space. The loss of launch capacity caused by suspension of U.S. space shuttle flights for nearly three years following the 1986 *Challenger* disaster and some mishaps in European space rocket launches added spice to the situation—particularly after the USSR and China offered to loft our satellites for a not-unreasonable price.

Sometimes these meetings were confrontational. American response to an increasingly politicized Unesco was very negative. Long a center of important research and action on communications, especially for developing nations, by the late 1970s this Paris-based U.N. specialized agency, under the direction of Secretary General M'Bow, had become increasingly obsessed with Third World social and political issues. This had caused discomfort for many Western countries that felt that the educational, scientific, and cultural emphasis for which Unesco had been designed was being buried in political controversy. Of most concern to American media was Unesco's support of a "New World Information Order" (NWIO), a scheme calling for greater Western support for Third World communication concerns. These included training (no problem there); access to the worldwide telecommunications networks, including satellites—which, it was pointedly emphasized, passed directly over the territory of many Third World nations (also acceptable); control over information that leaves a nation, to include licensing of reporters and other government oversight of media, such as a willingness to punish one's own reporters who offend another country (all of this repugnant to Americans used to operating under the First Amendment); and control by a country over what information comes into its territory (which most Americans would call "censorship"). The 1980 Unesco publication of an extensive report on the NWIO by a commission headed by Ireland's Sean MacBride brought American unhappiness with Unesco's direction to a new peak. Finally, after several more years of attempting to work change from within, the United States pulled out of Unesco membership (thus depriving the organization of about a quarter of its income) in an attempt to apply pressure to change Unesco's goals back to research and support of educational and cultural activities (it had been less involved in scientific matters). If nothing else, this debate helped to illustrate the growing central role of communications in the lives of most countries—and the growing interdependence of the United States with the rest of the world.

10•93 Period Overview

If the 1961–1976 period discussed in chapter 9 was one of evolution, the 1977–1989 period was clearly more revolutionary. Broadcasting no longer had a huge consumer market largely to itself as cable and VCRs developed as majority service providers. The networks, dominant in the late 1970s, faced a declining audience by the 1980s, as well as a host of cable network competitors. Programming looked and sounded much the same throughout this period—there simply was more of it produced for cable and VCR audiences, as

well as a still-growing number of broadcast stations.

The relationships of government and the electronic media underwent a fundamental shift in the 1980s, a shift likely to outlast any short-term political changes. The FCC no longer was seen as a "national nanny," as Mark Fowler once called it. Instead, television was no longer perceived as something special—it now was, to use another Fowler phrase, simply a "toaster with pictures" and thus should be regulated no more or less than most other businesses. There was general agreement in Congress and the FCC that past days of close regulation and guidelines were gone for good. Just as clearly, there also was disagreement about some important details of the trend toward less regulation, especially concerning ownership limitations, the Fairness Doctrine, and programming for or received by children. The pace of deregulation had slowed by the late 1980s, partly due to congressional unhappiness with the commission and partly due to a dwindling number of things left to deregulate, but indicating that a period of consolidation and consideration was at hand.

In the end, the public was receiving technically better quality material by the end of the 1980s, though largely more of the same so far as content was concerned. Yet surveys showed that the audience was generally pleased with—or, at least, did not want to discard—electronic media. As broadcasting approached its three-quarter-century mark in the mid-1990s, it appeared to maintain its central role in the lives of most Americans.

Further Reading

As the number of media options for most Americans increases, so, it seems, does the number of books about electronic media. The 1980s has seen a steadily increasing stream of publications.

Among the several useful surveys of "new" technologies are Gross (1986) and Singleton (1986), which both assess technology, applications, and likely developments. Rogers (1986) is the best theoretical essay to date. Winston (1986) suggests that satellites, the computer, and television have not changed society as much as many argue. Williams (1989) looks at the overall impact of changing means of communication. Braun and Macdonald (1982) and Reid (1984) provide useful overviews of the rise of semiconductors. Antebi (1982) is historical but concentrates with photos and charts on recent breakthroughs. One good history of satellite development is in Smith (1976), while Cook and Vaughan (1983) focuses more on home TVRO reception. "Electronic publishing" is explored in Greenberger (1985) and Compaine (1984). A very good history of the VCR's increas-

---

Key Broadcasting Indicators: 1980 / This is the 11th of 12 tables offering comparable information over a 60-year period (to 1985) presented at five-year intervals. Sources for items 1–6 and 11 are the same as for the tables in Appendix C, while other information comes from sources indicated below. Most data are for January 1.

Indicators	AM	FM	TV
1. Number of commercial stations	4,534	3,155	734
2. Number of noncommercial stations	ca 25	1,038	277
3. Total stations on the air	4,559	4,193	1,011
4. Number of network-affiliated stations	3,110	na	615
5. Percentage of commercial stations affiliated with networks	na	na	84%
6. Total industry revenue (add 000,000)	$3,206	$863	$8,808
7. One-hour station rate (New York)			
8. One-minute station rate (New York)	na	na	na
9. One-hour network rate, evening			
10. Number of broadcasting employees	98,000		78,300
11. Percentage of families with sets	98.6%	95%	98%
12. Broadcasting regulatory budget (FCC)		$75,992,000	
13. Total FCC personnel		2,094	

Notes
na = not applicable or not available.

4–5. It is not possible to isolate FM network affiliation data.

6. These were the last official FCC figures issued.

7–9. In the 1980s, many stations stopped publishing their rate cards.

10. This is for networks and stations only—it excludes cable (FCC reported 39,300 for cable systems) and ancillary/manufacturing.

11. Homes-with-receivers data are from Electronic Industries Association.

12. FCC figures for fiscal year ended June 30.

ing role in American life is in Lardner (1987). Ganley and Ganley (1987) focuses more on the international impact of VCRs. Graham (1986) reviews the rise and fall of the RCA videodisc.

Expansion of the electronic media is traced in the descriptive statistical tables and supporting text in Sterling (1984). Turow (1984) provides the structural context for the production of news and entertainment, while an insightful study of the whole Hollywood milieu of television production is found in Tunstall (1981). For modern station operation, see Keith and

Krause (1986), O'Donnell, et al. (1989), and NAB (1985) for radio and Marcus (1986), McCavitt and Pringle (1986), and Sherman (1987) for broader perspectives.

The rise of UHF is detailed in *Independent Thinking* (1986). The changing role of networks amidst competition is told in the third network inquiry by the FCC (1980). Quinlan (1979) tells the story of the pre–Cap Cities/ABC, while Bedell (1981) discusses network television as reflected in the career of Fred Silverman at CBS, ABC, and then NBC. The cable industry and its operation is best described in Baldwin and

---

Key Broadcasting Indicators: 1985 / This is the last of 12 tables offering comparable information over a 60-year period (to 1985) presented at five-year intervals. Sources for items 1–6 and 11 are the same as for the tables in Appendix C, while other information comes from sources indicated below. Most data are for January 1.

Indicators	AM	FM	TV
1. Number of commercial stations	4,729	3,176	904
2. Number of noncommercial stations	ca 25	1,172	290
3. Total stations on the air	4,754	4,888	1,194
4. Number of network-affiliated stations	na	na	621
5. Percentage of commercial stations affiliated with networks	na	na	69%
6. Total industry revenue (add 000,000)	$6,563		$20,298
7. One-hour station rate (New York)			
8. One-minute station rate (New York)	na	na	na
9. One-hour network rate, evening			
10. Number of broadcasting employees		177,981	
11. Percentage of families with sets	98.6%	95%	98.1%
12. Broadcasting regulatory budget (FCC)		$95,441,000	
13. Total FCC personnel		1,825	

Notes
na = not applicable or not available.

4–5. It is not possible to isolate FM network affiliation data.
7–9. In the 1980s, many stations stopped publishing their rate cards.
10. This is 1986 data for networks and stations only—it excludes cable (FCC reported 80,235 for cable systems in 1986) and ancillary/manufacturing.
11. Homes-with-receivers data are from Electronic Industries Association.
12. FCC figures for fiscal year ended September 30.

McVoy (1988) and Roman (1983), while Webb (1983) discusses cable economics. Garay (1988) is a combination narrative and bibliographic guide to all aspects of cable television. The main movers and shakers in the electronic media are covered in biographies: Turner in a book by Williams (1981) and Murdoch in biographies by Kiernan (1986) and Leapman (1983). Paper's 1987 biography of CBS founder William Paley tells the good and the bad about a long career. The context for HBO's development is found in the third volume of the corporate history of *Time* by Prendergast and Colvin (1986) as well as in Mair (1988).

The high-water mark of projected federal input into public television is found in the report of the second Carnegie commission (1979). Changing priorities within public broadcasting show up in the CPB's annual reports (1969–date) and in the work issued by the National Association of Public Television Stations (1984). The reports of the Temporary Commission on Alternative Financing for Public Telecommunications (1982–1983) are a fine survey of funding options and the advertising experiment. Witherspoon and Kovitz (1987) provides a brief overview concentrating mainly on the previous decade's developments on the national level.

Advertising in the 1980s is reviewed in Heighton and Cunningham (1984) and described in Arlen (1980), while promotion is covered in Eastman and Klein (1982). Poltrack (1983) reviews electronic media marketing, and Warner (1986) concentrates on cable and broadcast selling. Means of financial assessment of media are covered in Vogel (1986).

Programming is traced best in periodicals for this period. For general reference works, see the titles discussed in chapter 7 and the genre works listed in chapter 9. A good overview of the process,

written by industry experts, is Eastman, et al. (1989), covering radio, television stations, and networks and cable. Levin (1987) details the content and appeal of talk radio. How programming worked in the 1980s on the network level is found in Christensen and Stauth (1984) and Gitlin (1983). Two reviews of a single television season are found in Eliot (1983) and Sklar (1980). The rising role of religion on television is brought out in Horsfield (1984), Frankl (1986), and Hadden and Shupe (1988). Sports coverage is assessed in Rader (1984) and Powers (1984), both of which are critical of the tube's impact on professional teams, and Klatell and Marcus (1988), which takes a broader contextual view of television and money in sports. Winship (1988), in a "companion book" to a PBS series (both series and book were better in their English originals), assesses several decades of television programming.

Electronic journalism is controversial and thus is widely covered. Barrett's biennial reviews of broadcast journalism (1977–1982), though now discontinued, are useful for trends. Powers (1977) scathingly attacks the quality of local television news. Matusow (1983) details the behind-the-scenes scramble to be a network evening news anchor. Madsen (1984) is the best material on the top documentary of this era, *60 Minutes*. The continuing soap opera story of CBS News after 1981 is engagingly told in Boyer (1988), while the Westmoreland libel suit is covered in Benjamin (1988), among several other sources. News coverage of crises is reviewed in case studies by Nimmo and Combs (1985). The long struggle to achieve television coverage of Congress is reviewed in Garay (1984). Swerdlow (1984) sums up thinking on televised debates—see Kraus (1979) and Bishop, et al. (1978) for the 1976 resumption of debates after a 16-year lapse. The 1980 campaign is content-ana-lyzed in Robinson and Sheehan (1983). Changes in the 1984 race are discussed in Blume (1985) and Robinson and Ranney (1985), and there is a very good study of television spot advertising in politics in Diamond and Bates (1988).

The most comprehensive review of what is known of the television audi-ence is Comstock (1978), while Meyrowitz (1985) is a good popularized statement of recent thinking. Methods of audience research are detailed in Beville (1988) for the commercial services and in Wimmer and Dominick (1987) for broader research approaches. Bower (1985) and Frank and Greenberg (1980) report on the most recent national surveys of audience atti-tudes. The fourth phase of the investiga-tion into the role of television on children is related in the staff reports from the FTC (1978) and FCC (1979), in Adler's 1980 sur-vey of research on advertising and chil-dren, and in the National Institute of Men-tal Health's 1982 literature review.

The trend to deregulation is sur-veyed best in articles in legal journals and in the trade press. A good introduction, with case studies, is Krasnow, et al. (1982). Some of the basis for deregulation is laid out in Levin (1980). A sense of how much things have changed is found in Cole and Oettinger (1978), which discusses the reg-ulatory situation just before most deregu-lation. Powe (1987) and Le Duc (1987) do a good job of showing the recent impact of deregulation on both broadcasting and cable. More on the family viewing case is in Cowan (1979). Policy toward cable and related media is exhaustively analyzed in the three volumes by Ferris, et al. (1983–1989) and in Brenner and Price (1986). "Where Things Stand," appearing quarterly and, more recently, weekly in *Broadcasting*, is another good way to stay current or trace recent developments. A collection of brief case annotations through the history of broadcasting is found in Bensman (1983 and 1985), while Kahn (1984) provides full texts of crucial docu-ments. The complications of copyright are sorted out in Johnston (1982) and Strong (1984). Pool (1983) questions the impact of changing technology on some basic free-doms and rights.

Electronic media worldwide are analyzed in depth in Head (1985), the best single-volume survey of patterns. Unesco (1980) is the seminal document in the world news flow debate. Annual issues of the *World Radio-TV Handbook* are good for patterns of who is broadcasting to whom and when. Katz and Wedell (1977) is still the best assessment of broadcasting in the development process. Specific regions covered by books are Asia by Lent (1978), the Arab world by Boyd (1982), Latin America by Alisky (1981), and Africa by Head (1974). There is an increasing num-ber of books—far more than we can include here—on electronic media in indi-vidual countries around the world. Pro-pagandistic use of international radio is reviewed best in Browne (1982) and in Soley and Nichols (1987), a study of revolutionary and counterrevolutionary uses of radio. Codding and Rutkowski (1982) reviews the structure and operation of the ITU.

For further information on current American electronic media, see the anno-tated bibliography in Head and Sterling (1990) and the annual issues of *Broadcasting Yearbook*, and *Television Factbook*.

Lessons from the Past for the Future

II

"Those who cannot remember the past are condemned to repeat it."—George Santayana, *Life of Reason*

Lessons
from the Past
for the Future

"Let us judge of what can be done by
what has been done."—Jean Jacques
Rousseau, *Social Contract*

In more than a century of technological development and nearly 70 years of actual American broadcasting, some patterns have become evident. These patterns, principles, and trends should be useful to anyone who wishes to face the future with some grounding in the past, whether the broadcasting of tomorrow resembles the broadcasting of yesterday any more than the health care of tomorrow resembles the medical practice of yesterday.

Broadcasting, whether considered as a business or industry, an art, an application of technology, an embryonic profession, a force shaping our culture, an establishment or institution, or a social phenomenon—and it is all of these, and more—has roots in the past that we can use as precedent. Yet all too often, since broadcasting started, potentially valuable decisions, actions, and general lessons have been ignored or forgotten in the heat of new controversy.

Our purpose in this final chapter is twofold: (1) to identify patterns, themes, and concepts from the past that help explain *why* things happened as they did and (2) where possible, to suggest implications, guidelines, and lessons for the future. We are aware of the potential pitfalls of prediction, particularly in a rapidly changing field such as this, since history is not truly cyclical, and we intend to err on the side of caution. We have been told that the first edition of *Stay Tuned* has helped some of its readers to cope with the massive changes of the past decade. This has given us the right to hope that this second edition also will prove useful.

This chapter parallels the internal structure of most previous chapters: the difficulties and opportunities caused by technological innovation; the linking of local outlets into national services (networks); the evolution of educational (later, public) broadcasting; advertising and

Outline:
Lessons from the Past for the Future

other financial support and economic competition; program cycles and programming; the changing size and behavior of the audience; government policy and regulation (including self-regulation); and the reason for the study of broadcasting in the first place: the social roles and impact of American radio and television.

11·1 Technological Innovation

Not all aspects of technological development or innovation are strictly technological. One must consider the differences between invention and innovation, which often indexed the success or failure of important pioneers; the interwoven concepts of "not invented here," national security, and economic nationalism; the battles over a finite amount of usable spectrum space; the industrial or government research team as contrasted to the individual inventor; the search for common standards for any new device; the varied roles of government; the economic and marketing system into which an innovation is introduced; and the different goals of manufacturers and users.

The first theme is the difference between conceiving something, which requires creativity and imagination; its development, using engineering or scientific skills and luck; and successful introduction of that invention into use, which requires financial, promotional, legal, and marketing skills—and more luck. The number of inventors in this field who died broke—one even died of starvation—testifies to the need for a sound business head at the innovation stage. Armstrong, an inventor of outstanding talent, also was a successful innovator until he tangled with RCA over FM. Marconi and Alexander Graham Bell had good business

managers, but Fessenden, de Forest, Stubblefield, Farnsworth, and others never had enough good fortune or entrepreneurial skill to innovate successfully.

Another principle is "NIH," the "not invented here (so forget it!)" syndrome that has led to the disregard of inventions from other countries, or even from other domestic laboratories, and the consequent wasted motion of duplicated effort. While less important since U.S. manufacturers abdicated in favor of their Asian competition, it still crops up in the form of agitation for "U.S." standards for high-definition television.

Allied to NIH is the desire of each country to control its own telecommunications systems, for both national security and economic nationalistic reasons. This attitude can have technological or regulatory effects as well as economic ones, as in the U.S. Navy's objection to sale of the Alexanderson alternator to British Marconi or the parallel development of telecommunications devices in various countries. Analogous to this early radio policy—which has been modified because of the need to coordinate frequency usage around the world—is the current frustration of most countries over their inability to secure self-sufficiency in sources of energy. Since profit-motivated economics alone would lead to failure of this "go it alone" policy—as demonstrated by the move of most American consumer electronics manufacturing to countries where costs are lower—governments often establish tariff protections or subsidies. Governments of Third World countries also have supported political initiatives—such as the Unesco-sponsored New World Information and Communications Order in the early 1980s—that would give each nation equal access to the world telecommunications networks regardless of investment or technological contributions.

Yet a third principle also is concerned with political realities as well as technology. The need of radio communication services for frequency spectrum space has led to many trade-offs between technical efficiency and fiscal economy. At first, equipment could be imprecise, inefficient, and inexpensive, because spectrum space was plentiful. As demand rose and spectrum space grew scarce, communication services required more sophisticated and expensive equipment. But with broadcasting, the investment by the general public in receivers designed for older frequency bands or standards interfered with technological advances. No congressman seeking re-election could allow the FCC to render obsolete all those expensive receivers in his constituents' living rooms! As a result, television is still "frozen" into essentially 1941 technical standards.

In most instances, a new standard allowed an older one to continue in use, as in the case of FM stereo serving older receivers monaurally. However, if the new standard was important or cheap enough, the public could be persuaded to relegate the older form to another room, to relatives who might find it useful, or to the discard pile. The replacement of black-and-white television sets in the living room by color took two decades, but it did eventually happen (although only 85 percent of all sets sold as late as 1987 were color). The British needed even longer to move all television from the VHF to the UHF band, even with the "carrot" of allowing color only on the UHF, an important lesson as we contemplate the innovation of HDTV. Over the years, a number of new standards for musical recordings have come and gone, such as 78-rpm and 45-rpm disks and eight-track tapes. The life span of each standard seems to be growing shorter; the compact disk (CD) was still new to the public when DAT (dig-

ital audiotape) reached a level of development that caused its backers to suggest that DAT would soon replace CDs. Manufacturers have become aware that there is a small but profitably significant portion of the public that can be depended on to buy any consumer electronics product so long as it is "new" and "better," even if there is no longer a single standard accepted by consumers.

The "throwaway" quality and pricing of many products, which are difficult to repair even by the few repairers left, is reflected in the frantic—and in financial terms, impractical—desire to achieve either a home reception or a television production facility that is truly "state of the art" in terms of its equipment. A visit to any of the major showings of new hardware—the EIA Consumer Electronics Show or exhibitions at the National Association of Broadcasters or the Society of Motion Picture and Television Engineers—is an opportunity to see how quickly manufacturers issue new models with bells and whistles to attract people to buy them. When coupled with the shorter life expectancy of such equipment—studio cameras once could be counted on for a decade's service but now must be replaced much more frequently—it is no wonder that accountants in the broadcasting industry find it accurate (as well as advantageous for tax reasons) to "write off" most production equipment as quickly as possible.

In most technical fields in the past half-century, invention has increasingly come from industrial or government laboratory teams rather than individual inventors. Such radio inventors as Fleming and Alexanderson worked for large corporations even in the early 1900s, but others—Marconi, Fessenden, Farnsworth, de Forest, and Armstrong—worked essentially alone or with a few subordinate helpers. The increasing complexity of civilian telecommunication technology and the enormous cost of continuing research now favor team effort supported by large companies. The planned obsolescence desired by marketers often places a premium on styling rather than solid technical advances. While there still is a place for the small company with an excellent product—if financing can be found—it is no accident that the transistor came from Bell Telephone Laboratories and color television in its present configuration from RCA. The videotape recorder, first produced by then very small Ampex, nevertheless required more than a decade of financial support by a variety of foundations and corporations for its development. Very few companies can now afford to manufacture, let alone design and develop, a full line of broadcasting equipment, and even fewer are willing to take the risk. Economic pressures on even the largest companies—particularly with respect to current demand for short-term profits rather than long-term investments—seem to have steered them toward applied rather than pure research. Even this applied research rarely is applied to items that would not be immediately profitable, such as high-quality UHF tuners for television sets, until attention is focused by government regulation or other external factors. In recent years, with the removal of most consumer electronics production to the Far East and deletion of tax advantages, research and development by American firms in this field has dropped substantially.

Two interconnected principles guide the adoption of inventions. First is a search for common standards or specifications for any new device; second is the drive by each major company to have a commanding patent control position for products built to that standard. Sometimes this latter strategy is rejected, as when N.V. Philips of the Netherlands allowed all manufacturers to use its audiocassette patents in an attempt to build up that industry, but the more common pattern is demonstrated by the drawn-out battles over patents for the telephone (Bell versus several others), the vacuum tube (Fleming versus de Forest), the regenerative circuit (de Forest versus Armstrong), FM radio (Armstrong versus RCA), television camera tubes (RCA versus Farnsworth), audio recording speeds (RCA versus CBS), video recording speeds (a battle royal), and so on.

These battles sometimes shaped entire industries: examples are the attempt to innovate standards for mechanical scanning television before electronic scanning was perfected, the development of color television, and the plethora of standards for disc and magnetic recording. The buying public is wary of multiple standards and often shies away from the product (as in the case of AM stereo) rather than let the marketplace decide. On the other hand, the market made VHS a *de facto* videocassette recording standard in this country, beating out Beta. Because the legal, laboratory, and public relations battles are so expensive and lengthy, only the largest corporations are able to join in. The risks are large, but so are the rewards: once the FCC, the public, or some international or industry body puts a stamp of approval on a technical standard, it is extremely difficult for a new technical approach to enter the market. Only when the government intervenes on the side of innovation, or a company decides not to exploit a patent position, or a new device (such as television itself) catches the public's fancy, does the field open up.

The role of the government in technological innovation is many faceted and important. In addition to its more obvious roles as both regulator and user of communication services, it also is a facilitator. Congress appropriated the money that enabled Morse to build the first electrical telegraph line, and, more than a century later, through NASA, it financed the development of space communications satellites, and is becoming involved with HDTV. The government administers the patent system. During both world wars, the government created the conditions for a tremendous burst of activity in industrial laboratories designing and building war-related devices. The navy-administered patents pool during World War I showed how industrial cooperation might be established in peacetime, and World War II research opened up vast reaches of the electromagnetic spectrum. At the end of World War I, the navy, already a major radio equipment customer, was instrumental in the establishment of RCA by GE and others. Sometimes the government acts *against* technological innovation by yielding to the greatest pressure, frequently from those groups already in place in that industry, as during the periods when the FCC benefited AM and later VHF television station owners by using regulatory activity or inactivity to delay innovation of FM radio, UHF, and cable television.

The innovation of broadcasting equipment in the studio and at the transmitter was more conservative than in most telecommunications fields, principally because the public was satisfied with the status quo and offered no financial incentive to change. Hence, transmitters grew larger and more efficient but not essentially different. Studio control equipment became more flexible and more complex as both a reflection and a precursor of programming flexibility and complexity in both radio and television. Adoption of solid state equipment was speeded only when broadcast station management realized the cost savings inherent in it. The advent of color programming in the late 1960s required the purchase of new and expensive equipment but did not lead to many programming ideas. The substitution of digital for analog equipment seems to be following the same route, bringing the viewer only a marginally improved picture along with important-to-the-engineers but nearly invisible improvements in reliability and noise reduction. Even though we now expect to see "reporting live via satellite" on our news programs, the use of space communications satellites for program production really is very limited, although satellites have found an important economic niche in program distribution.

The story of technical innovation in the broadcast studio is replete with production people enjoying new toys while wondering how they could use them to communicate more effectively. One exception, for which everyone had a use, was magnetic recording. In radio, recordings progressed from inferior techniques banned from the networks to virtually omnipresent means of programming. Tape permitted nearly random access to program segments not possible with discs. In television, while film could be edited, until the advent of videotape all nonfilm programming was live. With VTR, the programmer could edit, store, and rearrange at will—although losing some of the spontaneity of live production. The home VCR now permits the consumer to accomplish some of the same functions. When wedded to lightweight, portable color television cameras, the new generation of VTRs permitted electronic news-gathering (ENG).

The broadcasting receiver industry also has been cautious about adopting new technologies, but for political as well as economic reasons. Billions of dollars' worth of receivers in millions of voters' homes causes tremendous political inertia. However, manufacturers also are rarely willing to sponsor research or tool up for production unless they see a chance to steal a march on the competition or must catch up with it, whether in the United States or (as is the case with almost all receivers produced today) in the Far East. Voluntary industry research and development of UHF tuners that would meet standards of quality more easily obtained on the VHF has been minimal, even with government prodding. The expansion of color television came only after black-and-white television had reached nationwide saturation. High-definition television (HDTV), although experimentally demonstrated by CBS in the 1940s, also would require a saturated low-definition receiver market before the "smart money" started to back it. The unwillingness of American business to take risks also may be reflected in the fact that the logical union of direct broadcast satellites (DBSs) and HDTV is already taking place in Europe and Japan, while it is merely being talked about in the United States.

The broadcasting field has demonstrated evolution and not revolution in its technology. The trials of FM radio after World War II illustrated how little happens when backers of an innovation (FM) try to label an existing industry and its technology (AM) as obsolete. Success for any future innovation will take either powerful economic backing and acceptance of its standards by most of the industry for economic reasons or strong political pressure to allow a direct approach to the public, as in pay-TV by cable. New technology is most likely to come from big companies, here or abroad, able to support generally conservative approaches to research. Some small companies have built "better mousetraps," but the investment in manufacturing design and assembly lines is almost prohibitive. The public may benefit from innovation and from economies of scale and production—solid state receivers are cheaper to repair and require less electricity than vacuum tubes, permitting the development of high-quality, battery-operated, portable equipment at a reasonable cost—but generally, technological innovations per se make little difference in the content and effects of broadcasting. As a rule, the public tends to hold on to obsolescent devices while they are still usable (and not embarrassingly old if seen by visitors), so it requires decades for the new to replace the old—even with the recent wave of devices that cannot be repaired, the careful metering out of small changes and cosmetic improvements, and the design of appliances with "built-in obsolescence" intended to speed the replacement cycle.

Although the future shape of broadcasting is unknown, it seems likely to be evolutionary. Revolutions—as when transistors made truly portable radio receivers available to all, or as the integration of computers into most aspects of life significantly yet subtly changes our culture—are rare. So there will be more bells and whistles, such as remote control tuners with memory, and HDTV already is being used for initial production even though its future in home delivery of programming is cloudy. The general public presumably will grow to demand better television audio (in stereo), and specialized uses of the television channel—closed captioning for the deaf, interactive video games for children, or interfacing with home computers—will burgeon. Manipulation of signals by internal computers may permit receivers to fool eyes and ears into believing they are experiencing higher quality without using an inordinate amount of the electromagnetic spectrum.

Spectrum-greedy techniques such as DBS have become political rather than technological problems. Broadcasters already benefit from inexpensive time base correctors that permit use of cheap VTRs on broadcast channels, while at the other end of the economic spectrum, production houses are installing terribly expensive computer-controlled tape editing devices. New types of cameras, such as the CCD, require no alignment, last for years, need little light, and are so small that the lens is larger than the rest of the camera. Digital probably will replace analog transmission systems, leading to a "cleaner," noise-free picture. Stereophonic music is the hallmark of most radio stations, and many television stations are transmitting in stereo. The long-held dream of television receivers thin enough to hang on a wall is almost realized, and "picture-in-picture" and large-screen television sets are now for sale. Home VCRs permit everyone to be his or her own programmer, through off-air recordings or rentals from the local store. Almost all networks now use space communications satellites for distribution.

We cannot know whether we will find a substantially different world about us by the turn of the century. It is (fortunately) unlikely that all entertainment media will be replaced by the frightening specter of direct electrical stimulation of the pleasure center of the brain, but some more likely technologically oriented decisions probably will be made. We know from the past what is likely to happen in the camera and receiver field. But, more fundamental, the race between cable television (which ties television sets to a fixed wire) and the ability to make miniature portable television sets still has to be decided. The home VCR took less than a decade to reach the number of homes cable took forty years to reach. For the first time, we may have more channels available through cable than we have worthwhile (defined as you will) programming to fill them. Although they may not affect programming, each of these devices—and those not mentioned or even dreamed of—will affect broadcasting politically as well as economically.

11·2   A Local Station Service . . .

From the start, the FCC's practice of granting licenses to *local* radio and television stations has been basically inconsistent with the *national* economic character of network advertising and the theoretical ability of networks to cover the nation instantly. Responding to the American political principle of sovereign states and local electorates, the FCC not only licenses the local station to provide service to a specific community but has made almost every broadcast transmitter a separate "station," applying regulation to this level rather than to the national networks and advertisers. A similar fiction considers every cable system as a separate unit, without regard to the multiple system operator (MSO) who typically controls it. The FCC has limited the number of stations a licensee can own in order to ensure local expression, furnish advertising facilities for local businesses, and assuage congressional fear that a handful of companies might dominate the media. All of these factors have tended to make the local station a force in its geographic or social community. In times of crisis or disaster or local political activity, only local newspapers or local broadcasting stations can provide the necessary communication. Other media, such as cable, are technically capable but rarely have the will, equipment, or personnel for local reporting and programming. "Local," however, may mean a station that gives service over a legally, politically, and technologically determined area that often is far larger than the area that can be economically served by any other medium.

Although economies of scale led radio broadcasting from wholly locally owned and programmed stations to a system of control by national networks in the late 1920s, after World War II the pendulum swung back. With network executives preoccupied with television and thousands of AM and FM stations on the air for the first time, local radio programming control resurged. Actually, the demise of network radio has given only an illusion of local programming, since formulas, imitation, and a limited number of national music program sources predominate. Although there is some news and talk, particularly in markets large enough to accommodate such minority programming profitably, radio today—even with 10 times the number of outlets as at the end of World War II—*is* what David Sarnoff called a "music box" some seventy years ago.

Television stations air the same programs at similar times in most areas, and most television programming is dominated by the networks. The 20 percent or so of stations that are independent (non-network affiliated) usually use old network programs now in syndication for much of their programming, making the material on the screen look older rather than local or original. The result, for both radio and television, is a few similar national services from lots of local transmitters. In addition, the FCC has permitted absentee and group ownership of stations, which means that station ownership is not always the same as local community management. Those who control stations in what is now as many as 12 different markets per service (AM, FM, and television) do not have to owe special loyalty or service to any single

community, although many hundreds of stations, usually smaller ones in smaller markets, have conscientious operators who are as much a part of their community as the traditional small-town newspaper publisher supposedly is. Usually, the result of this pattern is diversity in number but not necessarily diversity in programming service.

A similar pattern has evolved with respect to cable television. But on the other hand, the primary programming fare on cable systems is anything but "local." It consists of rebroadcasts of network affiliates, feature films or sports such as those found on HBO or ESPN, superstations from elsewhere in the country with independent programming of the same sort, and a few cable-only services like Cable Network News (CNN) or religious programming. The number of locally originated cable programs is tiny, and CATV operators during the 1985–1987 period, when the FCC's must-carry rules were not in effect, often made local independent stations pay for carriage. Sometimes, local network affiliates were dropped when a big-city affiliate of the same network already was being carried. Hence, even the small amount of local programming on the typical television station was not available to cable subscribers in that community.

Videocassette recorders (VCRs) clearly are not transmitting stations, but they might be considered as the ultimate in local programming control. They allow the viewer to become his or her own programmer, choosing from a variety of rented, purchased, and home-recorded content.

Another important theme is the continuing tension between the haves and the have-nots among broadcasting stations. Since broadcasting is a business, those already on the air and prospering have little economic reason to encourage competition. AM radio and VHF television station licensees became the broadcasting "establishment." AM radio resisted both FM and television, but when the financial potential of television became evident, far-sighted AM licensees often started television stations. Pre-Freeze VHF stations epitomized this development. Both AM and VHF shared several attributes: they generally had been successfully established long before the directly competing FM and UHF services were introduced; they received the most revenue; and they controlled the industry's trade associations—and to a great extent, still do. Advertiser acceptance, network status, and audience belonged to the older and generally more powerful AM and VHF services as late as the mid-1970s. Although UHF television still works under a technical handicap (except where delivered by cable), FM, because of its better sound quality and more careful programming, became the more audience appealing and profitable segment of radio, in spite of AM's attempts to use stereo to compete. Any new competing service—FM radio, UHF television, on-air pay-TV, or cable television—or government regulation threatening the livelihood of existing stations is strongly attacked. The older media logically try to keep newer competitors from full development by political action (local representatives are very sensitive to the wishes of any medium that helped elect them and helps them reach their constituents) and economic pressures, or by themselves becoming involved in the newer medium, thus learning its weaknesses and containing the potential competition by occupying one of a limited number of channels.

In recent years new classes of have-nots have appeared outside broadcasting and wanting to get in. These include minority groups that either lack funding to purchase a station or, because of the startling growth in number of stations—elevenfold in the past 40 years—suffer from a shortage of channels on which to build a new station. Local community-supported stations and cable systems often are looked down on by more traditional and larger profit-oriented broadcasting stations. A move to allow establishment of very low power television stations, with very small coverage areas, predictably has not been very effective. A surprising number of stations have gone bankrupt, and others jump for any income source, such as home-shopping services. To launch a *new* service successfully against an entrenched and uncooperative industry is even more difficult than gaining a foothold in the existing service.

The truism that "them that has, gets" holds particularly true in broadcasting. Many stations founded early on by those willing to take the risk of pioneering achieved financial success; and their resulting economic status led to local and national political power often used to perpetuate it. Later owners of these stations, often large conglomerates willing to enter any industry so long as it might be profitable, benefited from the struggles of their predecessors. In such circumstances, both the haves and the have-nots feel ill used. The clear implication is that any new service can succeed only by overcoming the opposition of the existing industry. Frequently, economic resources, talent, and programming are hard to get, and the new service struggles for public recognition and acceptance. Without such acceptance, manufacturers of consumer electronics are unwilling to bend and advertisers ignore the new medium. Other means of financial support may be sought, but rarely have they been successful on a national scale, with the possible exception of the on-air appeals for funds conducted by public broadcasting stations and some television evangelists.

Some experienced media people have suggested that American radio and television, as they evolved over sixty years, already are obsolete and will disappear within a decade or two. They suggest that broadband—probably fiberoptic—wired connections (already in place for cable and—a frightening specter to both broadcaster and cable operator—being installed by telephone companies looking for new services to market) or degeneration of broadcasting into a service feeding programs and movies automatically into home VCRs previously programmed by the householder will occur. Probably this will not come about in the next decade; the investment in the status quo by both the public and broadcasters is too great for the existing system to be junked overnight. But *if* some new and exotic service fills a public need or wish, change probably will come slowly, marked by some accommodation between the new service and the existing industry. If it does not fill a public need or desire, no matter how much ballyhoo is engendered, the new medium is unlikely to succeed, as broadcast facsimile and some newer services have learned.

11·3 . . . with National Program Suppliers

The most important thing about the three older commercial networks is their long-term dominance of broadcast programming, economics, and public image. This is true even though cable, VCRs, and independent stations have made inroads into network audience levels during prime time. Over the years we have seen problems of haves and have-nots among networks (at least one network, ABC, has made the circuit between these poles twice), their varied roles as carriers of others' programming, their increasing use of Hollywood product, their great caution in accepting change, the difficulties of establishing new networks, and some usurpation of the networks' program distribution role by cable and VCRs.

But since their formation in the late 1920s, networks have dominated audience loyalty. Their chief strategy, economy of scale—more affiliates, in larger markets, with which to reach larger audiences and thus command greater advertiser income at no increase in production cost—has led to bland programming designed to appeal to the largest possible audiences and to please cautious advertisers. Each network tries to be all things to all viewers or listeners, and each is extremely wary of innovative programming but is willing to jump on the bandwagon when another has a successful venture. In this way, cycles of programming, spin-offs, and an occasional successful programming innovation—such as careful scheduling of an entire evening of similar programs to attract and retain a similar audience, or the miniseries—develop and are copied. As long as national advertisers are attracted, networks are content. This successful strategy has become a model for local stations to follow in programs, formats, and advertising, although some profitably counterprogram.

Radio networks in their heyday (the 1930 and 1940s), and television networks since then, have repeated the old motion picture industry pattern of centralized financial control in New York with production facilities in Hollywood. This split has led to many of the same money-versus-creativity conflicts that affected the major Hollywood film studios. Networks have more control over their product, since they essentially control the national distribution system, even though most programs—for financial reasons, and as the result of an FCC edict—technically are produced by independent packaging agencies or production houses. While New York and Chicago also were major production centers for national programming in radio and early television, today the Los Angeles area is the center for almost all production except news, public affairs, and some serials, although actual filming or taping may be done wherever costs are lowest.

The two oldest networks, NBC and CBS, are traditionally the strongest. In television, they quickly dominated the industry and continued to do so for a quarter-century. ABC, founded later, was the weakest financially and, until it briefly jumped into first place in the mid-1970s, was the weakest in programming as well. But by the middle 1980s, NBC was way ahead, and ABC once again was bringing up the rear. For various reasons, the Du Mont network did not survive past the mid-1950s, the attempt to establish Overmyer as a fourth network failed in 1967, and the jury is still out on Murdoch's Fox Television Network. In radio, Mutual and other networks were either regional in concentration or generally affiliated with smaller stations. CBS usually could move faster than NBC in such matters as the "talent raids" in the late 1940s because broadcasting was the keystone of the corporation's business, whereas NBC was only a small part of the much larger RCA. On the other hand, a talented programming chief could make a big difference: Fred Silverman brought ABC from behind to parity in the 1970s (only to fail dismally when he later took over NBC's programming); but innovative programming modeled on his experience with the MTM production

house helped Grant Tinker when he moved NBC into the number one spot in the mid-1980s.

Until the 1980s, network ownership was remarkably stable. True, the Mutual Broadcasting System changed hands more than once, NBC radio had to divest itself of the Blue Network (which became ABC) in 1943, and ABC merged with Paramount in 1953 (see 9•3). But for more than 30 years there was little change in ownership of the three major commercial television networks.

In the mid-1980s everything happened all at once. Encouraged by FCC deregulation, liberalized limits on station ownership, Wall Street's realization of the profit potential of broadcasting, the death or retirement of many network executives, and the frenzied national climate of merger and acquisition, all three networks changed hands in less than two years. Capital Cities, a very successful group station owner, bought and merged with ABC in 1985. RCA (and, hence, its subsidiary, NBC) was purchased by General Electric in 1986, bringing the story of RCA full circle (see 3•12). CBS technically remained independent, but, partly because of William Paley's inability to find a successor to whom he was willing to entrust what was called "Paley's candy store," in 1986 the network fell under the financial and operational control of Laurence Tisch, the chairman of Loews Inc., a major corporation with entertainment and hotel interests. Their rivalry remained, but leadership and corporate goals had changed. Layoffs, sell-offs, and other belt-tightening measures showed that the new owners considered networks to be businesses like any others—requiring that the "bottom line" be served above all else.

There are regulatory, technological, and economic reasons for the limited number of television networks. There are fewer markets with four commercial channels assigned than there are with three channels, placing the fourth-place network (usually Fox) in a position of playing endless "catch-up." Any fourth network has a much smaller potential audience than the three major networks, since fourth channels frequently are on UHF with less range and coverage than their VHF competitors. Although the networks often are blamed for encouraging this scarcity of competition by fighting against dropins of additional VHF channels into top markets, national policy has long reflected the need to keep potential interference low in order to avoid irritating viewers of existing stations. Since the networks had the foresight to build or buy stations in the largest markets (see page 266), this reasonable policy has been a source of economic benefit to them. While the networks as such rarely made much profit until the 1970s, the handful of network-owned-and-operated stations in large cities were extremely profitable all along.

Although often overlooked by commercial broadcasters, there *is* another major network: PBS (Public Broadcasting Service). In most markets, the FCC has reserved approximately one in four channels for noncommercial educational television. The majority of these channels are now occupied by stations, and most are affiliated with PBS, which supplies programs in a manner roughly similar to the way the other networks operate. But decisions on *which* programs will be produced are made by the stations through a complicated bidding-commitment procedure made necessary by the fact that federal funding is supplied to stations and not to PBS or CPB. In public radio, as in commercial radio, the networks are of limited importance, with only about one-sixth of

noncommercial FM stations being affiliated with NPR (National Public Radio). Nevertheless, some NPR news and public affairs programs, and even entertainment programs (from NPR or APR, a group of stations organized by Minnesota Public Radio, which does not have the overhead of NPR) have large and fanatically loyal audiences.

Because the Communications Act of 1934 does not provide for direct FCC regulation of the networks, they have been regulated through their affiliated stations. For many years, a network could control its affiliates' programming through a one-sided contract giving the network an option on the station's time. In the early 1940s, the FCC limited radio option time; two decades later, television option time was eliminated; and in the 1970s, the FCC promulgated the Prime Time Access Rule (PTAR)—but the networks remained strong.

Until the 1970s, network affiliation was almost a lifetime relationship, with few stations ever switching, although in the days when a market might have only one or two stations, the less desirable network might have to accept secondary status until another outlet went on the air. However, when ABC became a strong competitor, several stations switched from one of the then-weaker networks. This precedent led to less permanent affiliations, as had the likelihood that a group may have stations affiliated with two or three networks and thus be familiar with their strengths and weaknesses. Although many object to the concentration of national programming in so few hands, it may also be argued that the networks are the only institutions—other than a tiny handful of newspapers, the two national news wire services (AP and UPI), and CNN—that have the fiscal and political strength to support national news-gathering operations.

Until the early 1950s, radio and, later, television networks acted almost as common carriers, distributing programs produced or controlled by advertising agencies and often having only a limited say in program content or scheduling. Although this was a comfortable relationship during radio network days, the networks had to take over the programming function when rising television costs made developing and producing programs too risky for advertisers or advertising agencies. This trend quickened as escalating costs led to a drop in sole sponsorship, and the development of alternate or multiple sponsorship led to an even greater loss of advertiser control. Eventually, the networks found it cheaper to farm out most program production to packagers and production houses, notably West Coast movie studios suffering from a decline in feature film attendance that was partly caused by television. A 1970 FCC decision made it official, restricting the networks' ability to be the production source for most of their prime-time programming—and limiting their ability to benefit from after-network-run syndication income. The exception was network news and public affairs. For the above reasons, as well as for prestige and for supervision of content for fear of libel suits, the networks themselves had always controlled news. By World War II, network radio news had become a major means to inform the public. Television news, starting as little more than a newsreel introduced by a talking head, quickly became the most used and believed national news medium.

During the late 1970s and 1980s, a new type of national program distributor began to affect the viewing habits of Americans. Cable, no longer content to be a mere carrier of on-the-air stations that could not be picked up in remote areas, started selling a second tier of cable-only programming services. One of these was Cable News Network (CNN), which was started as television's first all-news network by Ted Turner, whose independent Atlanta superstation WTBS already was a staple source of cable system programming. CNN evolved into a service that "news junkies" and those who need to know what is going on will turn to, even though it does not provide any local news. The entertainment cable services are epitomized by Home Box Office, which supplies uncut and uninterrupted feature films in exchange for a monthly subscription fee. Roughly half of those with cable also subscribed to this second (or even a third) tier of pay-cable programming. All are transmitted by satellite to cable system head ends and, until suppliers started to scramble their satellite signals, to viewers who had installed small satellite receiving dish antennas in their yards in order to tune in for free.

The cautious broadcasting networks often are accused of running a closed shop, encouraged by several decades' general economic success achieved by appealing to a low common denominator in programming. They are rarely interested in program ideas from outside that do not fit into a mold developed in their own headquarters. The competitive scheduling of network programs has become an art with the trappings of a science. The programming chiefs rely not only on rating services but also on the track records of major packagers such as MTM (*The Mary Tyler Moore Show, Rhoda, Hill Street Blues, St. Elsewhere*), Lorimar (*Dallas, Falcon Crest, Knots Landing, Perfect Strangers, ALF*), Warner Brothers (*Growing Pains, China Beach, Night Court*), which announced a merger with Lorimar in 1989,

Desilu (*The Lucille Ball Show*), and Tandem (*All in the Family, Sanford and Son, The Jeffersons*). Padiagev's spin-offs from successful series are preferred by networks to new program ideas from new sources. It is unlikely that this pattern will change until channels are provided to support more than four or five on-air (ABC, CBS, NBC, Fox, and PBS) programming services or unless new means of distributing programs are further developed. Such new means of distribution might include temporary sports networks or first-run syndication of serials (such as *Mary Hartman, Mary Hartman*), miniseries, and occasional dramatic programs distributed over ad hoc networks consisting of both independent and network affiliated stations. Cable networks tend to seek out independent, specialized (such as sporting events), and inexpensive off-network programming to distribute, with only HBO regularly (but not often) producing special dramatic programming of its own.

Although the networks are the obvious target for critics of broadcasting's real or imagined shortcomings and are prone to complain at the slightest interference in their activities, they (and their owned-and-operated stations) have done extremely well financially, which is one reason why they are now being bought and sold. But not everything has gone their way. They lost one-tenth of their income—perhaps $200 million—when cigarette advertising was banned; citizens' group pressures reduced the income from children's programs; the Prime Time Access Rule forced them to return some prime-time inventory to their affiliates; cable, PBS, and VCRs made inroads on their prime-time audiences (the major commercial networks now share only 70 to 80 percent of the audience rather than the 90 percent of the recent past); election campaign reforms substantially reduced

election time revenues; and costs of acquiring sports events such as the Olympic Games and covering major news events kept rising. They are greatly restricted in their ownership of programs, including a ban on syndicating them in the United States. Yet they still make huge profits, and the symbiotic relationship between network and affiliated station has proven to have more merits than demerits for all concerned. However, without the profits of their O & O stations, it is doubtful whether the networks could do as well for themselves, advertisers, program producers, affiliates, and the public.

11•4   The Public Broadcasting Alternative

The development of educational radio, and later of public television, took place in the face of limited public knowledge of or support for such a system, the indifference and even hostility of commercial broadcasters, regulatory caution based on political concerns, and the overriding and interrelated questions of the exact mission of such a system and its financial support—and consequent probable control of content.

The key theme running through this story is the continuing lack of agreement on what public broadcasting was to do for its listeners and viewers. From the start, educational broadcasting was held up as a great potential educational force. Such a platitude has currency, particularly as the common definition of education has broadened. But should public broadcasting be an alternative to commercial radio and television? A chance for education in the home or expansion of adult education programs at the college level? An adjunct to in-class instruction? A general cultural service? A locally oriented service or a national one? Controlled by the community, the educational establishment, or counterculture organizations? Should it emphasize opportunities for minority interest programming, or should it be a fourth national network in competition with the three commercial networks? All of these questions remain active, and the goals of this kind of broadcasting have been as varied as the names applied to it: instructional, educational, and public—or cultural, community, and alternative.

This vagueness of national purpose and consequent dearth of financial capitalization have intimidated and confused the leaders of public broadcasting. From the beginning, educators have failed to grasp opportunities; they often set their sights too low and were subservient to those in government and elsewhere, who might have been good allies but turned out to be less helpful as masters.

Approximately two hundred noncommercial AM radio stations in the 1920s shrank to a couple of dozen by the late 1930s. Apparently once the glamour of the new medium wore off, fiscal caution and the apprehension of classroom teachers who feared for their jobs were sufficient, in a depression, to choke off funds needed to upgrade facilities to FRC standards and continue operating. During the 1930s and 1940s, a few educational broadcasters kept alive the dream of regaining access to broadcast channels in every community. Commercial broadcasters were using most of the AM channels previously and briefly occupied by the educators, and, in spite of commercial broadcasters' assurance to Congress that adequate time for educational programming would be provided, fulfillment of the dream had to wait until educators won reservations on FM channels in 1940 and on television channels in 1952. Although the initial beneficiaries were equipment manufacturers rather than

students or the general public, educational broadcasting, still confused about its purposes, slowly grew out of the demonstration stage. For the past several decades, the number of noncommercial FM and television stations (including those operated by religious groups) has approximated a quarter of the total of all FM and television stations, and the audiences have grown to the point where the programs often show up well in the ratings and are listened to or viewed at least once a week by the majority of American households.

The lack of common goals led to a corresponding lack of public concern. As a result, political and economic pressure was never mobilized to support ETV; lack of money was a symptom more than a cause of its malaise. Despite all the rhetoric, ETV never has attempted to be an alternative to commercial entertainment. Only with movies or high-quality drama, much of the latter from Britain, some music, comedy, and satire, and some children's programs have public television stations been able to garner substantial audiences. Listeners and contributors have continued to come largely from a narrow spectrum of society. One can argue that these are the decision-makers and movers of society, but this group already is well served by other media. Public broadcasting is just barely a medium for the general public.

In Great Britain and many other countries, the publicly controlled broadcasting system was established as an instrument of national policy long before commercial broadcasting was allowed. In the United States, commercial broadcasting began first and remains primary while educational broadcasting has had to subsist on crumbs. This existence was self-defeating because there never was enough money to produce the programming and promotion that could lead to general public support. Similarly, in the 1980s, after federal funding was reduced, public television stations were allowed to give "underwriting credits," virtually indistinguishable from commercials, to firms that contributed to a program's production costs—and as a result were strongly attacked by those who appreciated receiving programming *without* commercial interruptions. A few municipalities, school districts, and universities provided minimal support for educational broadcasting each year until the late 1950s, when outside agencies offered help. The Ford Foundation had demonstrated cultural programs to the general public first over commercial channels and then through the National Educational Television and Radio Center affiliates. In 1967 the Carnegie foundation's report proposed a new name, "public television," and a new vision and generated enough pressure on Congress for the government to establish the Corporation for Public Broadcasting, with some tax support for equipment and programming.

Yet, public broadcasting still is hampered by restricted funding, lack of a consistent long-range funding plan, and political influence on decision-making. Members of Congress and other politicians object to tax monies going to independent programming supporting various political and social views they may not favor themselves. Accordingly, noncommercial educational radio stations were legally prevented from editorializing or endorsing political candidates, and local pressure frequently is even more severe. This is true even though only about one in six noncommercial FM stations is a member of National Public Radio and eligible for federal grants. It is significant that many years passed before an educational broadcaster challenged the constitutionality of this provision. Educational broadcasters, will-

ing to do almost anything for money, have discovered that "he who pays the piper calls the tune." They also have found that a promise to fund is not proof of money forthcoming. Two decades after the first Carnegie Commission report, and a decade after the second, a long-range funding plan isolated from short-term political pressures is still only in the offing. Proposals for "dedicated" funding from excise taxes on receiver or station sales remain unpopular. Internal dissension is rampant. Public television is called elitist, yet its role of providing programming not generally supplied by commercial television is recognized—and some of it is very good. Cautious governing boards of local public television stations are at loggerheads with the alphabet soup of national organizations. Government remains ambivalent, although no recent President seems to have wanted another "real" or effective network to have to parry and has ensured this condition by directing the dribble of federal funding to local rather than national organizations. Finally, public television's success, though limited, in attracting underwriting funds from commercial firms has alienated many commercial stations—which now view it as competition to be fought rather than as a public service to be supported.

The long-term future of public broadcasting is unclear. With the support of tax and foundation money, there is little danger that it will blow away. But without that support, and with fewer and fewer apparent differences between public and commercial television programming, even the minority that now supports public broadcasting may turn away, removing the last stimulus for congressional support. When PBS carries the congressional Iran-Contra hearings live, in their entirety, a public service is being performed—but there are always many who would rather be viewing the originally scheduled entertainment programs instead.

The immediate future appears to hold few programs with the wide public appeal of *Sesame Street,* more bickering over a limited financial pie, a struggle with cable television operators who have little interest in carrying PBS stations, and continued infighting among competing organizations. When those in public broadcasting can confidently sell a substantial portion of the general public on clearly defined goals and aims, receive support with fewer strings attached, and stop the nearly constant internal and political bickering, then will this medium become more than a stepchild to commercial radio and television.

11•5   Dollars and Sense

In spite of initial attempts to find other means of financing broadcasting, strong debate over the propriety of broadcast advertising in the mid-1930s, and concern over some aspects of it since, advertising has been the chief support of American broadcasting since the late 1920s, and radio and television, in turn, have become major advertising media. This situation has affected program content and production, widened the differences between the ever-present haves and have-nots, and helped establish different roles for today's radio and television.

Because most U.S. broadcasting is advertising supported, programs are only a means to an end: attracting consumer audiences to sell to advertisers. Programs become bait to gather audiences, which stations and networks then sell to advertisers. Thus programs tend to be mass entertainment, with education and information—news and public affairs—receiving just enough time to ensure a good pub-

lic image. Mass programming generally is bland and politically neutral, aiming to offend as few while entertaining as many as possible. Program content appeals to a low common denominator so that the largest number can enjoy it—and attend to the supporting commercials. To the advertiser, so long as the "cost per thousand" remains the same and the audience's demographic mix is desirable, it does not matter if the message appears in the form of a 30-second spot or an "informational" underwriting identification at the open and close of a popular program on "non-commercial" PBS.

In the United States, following the initial sale of commercial time in 1922, the rush to adopt this method of financing carried all before it. Other possible approaches for securing operating income had abounded: annual license fees on receivers, as levied in Great Britain but never seriously considered in the United States; general tax revenues, which support some municipal and university stations today; special taxes; annual subscriptions, received currently by many ETV and some radio stations; donations in addition to or replacing subscriptions, received by community-sponsored public television stations or religious broadcasters; or operation of stations as auxiliary enterprises by receiver manufacturers. All of these are far less common than commercial sponsorship, both here and abroad. A few stations have been supported out of the pockets of an individual or firm for altruistic, political, religious, or public relations reasons, or to save on federal taxes, since one can reduce one's taxes on a profitable enterprise by losing money supporting an unprofitable one. But by 1928, radio had become a mass advertising medium, and through the 1940s the larger advertising agencies controlled radio network programming.

On the other hand, the high (and rising) costs of producing television programs turned off advertising agencies, so the networks had to take over this function themselves when television burgeoned in the late 1940s. Until the late 1950s, when the quiz show scandals forced networks to supervise programming more strictly to protect their affiliated stations from FCC sanctions, advertisers still could veto the content of most sponsored programs. At the same time, the cost of sponsoring an entire program had risen beyond the capacity of most corporate sponsors. As a result, broadcasting slowly adopted, in part, a modified "magazine concept," which allowed advertisers to buy national or local spots without sponsoring programs—allowing advertiser support without complete advertiser control.

This system has shaped American broadcasting. Most national advertising goes to larger stations and to the networks partly because of the convenience to the advertiser of using only one large outlet instead of many smaller ones. Local advertisers, unable to afford the prices charged national ones, must use smaller and less efficient independent stations or fringe time on larger ones. Independent stations, often with poorer UHF technical facilities, must handle the same large, fixed operating costs on the smaller amounts of money generated by local ads, and hence often are willing to "break" their published rates or arrange barter deals in order to have enough income flow to pay their bills.

Competition in radio and television is restricted by the interaction of advertisers' desires for efficiency and the technological factors that limit the number of networks and make most smaller stations inherently and permanently inferior as advertising media. New systems of distributing entertainment and information to the American public—FM, UHF television, cable, pay-TV, and home video recording—are automatically and immediately under attack by existing industries and their supporting trade organizations and press, co-opted government officials, and others anxious to retain the status quo. Once a new medium or approach has won a long, expensive struggle to get public or government support or approval—such as, for example, the 1962 all-channel receiver bill that helped UHF—the battle has just begun. Now it must start the *marketing* fight against those stations or other institutions that hold an economic advantage.

Although one-quarter of all television stations are licensed to be noncommercial, most broadcasting will continue to be supported by advertising in the near future. But cable television has discovered that large potential profit is to be gained from a form of subscription (payment by the month for unlimited use of "basic" advertiser-supported programming) and from direct "pay-per-view" programming.

Many early commercial cable operators—other than those established by retailers or repair shops in rural areas who merely wanted to supply programming so that they could sell sets—made money only when they sold the system. This was largely a function of the tax laws, which allowed deductions for financing as well as operating expenses and levied low-rate capital gains taxes on profits from the sale. Then the new owner would go through the same process. If the monthly subscription fees paid out-of-pocket costs, much of the rest was pure profit, and a substantial number of multiple system operators (MSOs) stayed in the business only because they could profit from investing the large and regular cash flow now and could hope for even larger profits when the system later was sold.

However, this changed in the late 1970s, when the first "cable only" programming, such as recent feature films on HBO, was distributed by satellite to local systems. Suddenly there was an opportunity for the system operator to profit every month, by sharing in an extra monthly fee charged the subscriber. Since much of the wiring was already in place, pay-cable was a money-maker for cable operators from its inception. By the mid-1980s, a "tiering" pattern had emerged. Of American homes with the CATV trunk line running down their street ("passed by cable"), roughly half subscribed. Of those who subscribed, about half also took one or more "tiers" of pay-cable. The average income per subscriber per month climbed rapidly from $5 or less to $30 or more for many cable systems. The larger audiences attracted an increasing amount of local and national spot advertising to the cable system as additional revenue. However, many large cities still did without cable for economic, political, or technological reasons because the costs of providing cable service to a large city are high—as are public expectations of quality, since urban audiences already are well served by on-the-air broadcasting. By 1987, however, the magic "half of American television households subscribe to cable" figure had been reached. Television manufacturers touted "cable ready" tuning, and *TV Guide* successfully eliminated potential competition by covering cable as well as broadcast television in its pages. Television networks, still immensely popular, nevertheless saw their proportion of the total television audience dwindle. The public still watched television—but now it was seeing a non-network program supplied by cable, or a rented film played on a VCR, or even a pickup from a backyard satellite receiving dish. Because of U.S. population growth, the networks and stations are not suffering

as much as they would if the population were stagnant—but it is a far more competitive world than it was in 1975.

While most national advertisers still find television to be the medium of choice, the "pie" that their expenditures creates now has to be cut in ever smaller wedges. Viewers with twenty or more advertising-supported cable channels to choose from are harder for advertisers to reach than viewers with only three on-air network affiliates. The growth of advertising-free cable, PBS, and rented cassette channels among those competing for the viewer's attention makes the advertising agency's job more difficult. The old concept that a television station license was a license to print money is obsolete, even though the outrageously high price tags on stations and cable networks indicate that they still are considered extremely valuable properties. The money is still there, but it has to be earned rather than picked up off the ground.

11•6   Programming

The programming that has resulted from increased competition in the mid-1980s is neither as bad as some critics who decried the tendencies toward consensus, timidity, and the lowest common denominator would claim nor as good as some idealogues touting the virtues of competition and diversity would have us believe. Much of it is "more of the same," produced as inexpensively as practicable. Even highly profitable programs such as *60 Minutes* keep a close eye on costs. Something "new" tends to be merely a gimmick or something to titillate the audience rather than a carefully crafted artistic advance. Since broadcasters sell people to advertisers, programs are the bait or lure used to attract viewers. As a result, programming is a reflection of demands from advertisers; pressures from government regulations, which, in turn, reflect congressional and public concerns; varied audience preferences; and the profit-and-loss interests of station owners and managers. Out of this background comes programming standardization and a cyclical, largely imitative, development of program types and themes.

The needs of networks as well as the time constraints imposed by early recording media led to standardized program lengths, generally in 15-minute increments, in the United States. Radio of the early 1920s and then since 1960 has been more free-form. Program formats usually are restricted by the need of networks to insert into the program a certain number of commercials at exact times, often determined by computer or previously distributed schedule. If the particular "availability" has not been sold, the network may insert an unpaid program promotion or public service announcement so that the schedule is maintained and the public is further conditioned to expect program interruptions. Even PBS programs originally produced abroad without the straitjacket of commercial scheduling generally adhere to this pattern, with regular climaxes written into scripts to motivate public viewing during the commercial interruption.

Similarly, success of early programs led to standardization of program types. Musical, variety, drama, comedy, sports, and game formats all were common by the late 1930s, and most radio and television programming since then is but modification and adaptation. For most of broadcasting's history, prime-time programming generally has been aimed at housewives from 18 to 45, who determine most consumer purchases.

For many reasons, there has been little program experimentation. First, this medium, which constantly reaches and presumably inspires so many people, has a shortage of real talent and new ideas. Vaudeville performers were shocked to see routines that might have pleased stage audiences for a lifetime gobbled up by radio's national listenership in days or weeks. Broadcasting's appetite for content, especially with 18- to 24-hour programming days, is prodigious. Second, few advertisers wish to risk supporting nonconventional programs, since the stakes are so high. They generally must appeal to the largest possible audience without antagonizing parts of it. Third, costs and thus risks are always rising. Radio programs seemed cheap to produce; even television of the late 1940s rarely cost more than a few thousand dollars a week for a network show. But by the mid-1980s an hour of dramatic prime-time programming often required more than three-quarters of a million dollars before it could be sent to the home screen. When these risks are added to the tendency of networks, advertising agencies, and production studios to play it safe with accepted methods and formats, it is no wonder that programmers follow conventional ideas and copy successes rather than innovate creatively. Another effect of these high costs is the reduction in number of shows produced for a season from the 39 of network radio's day to less than half that number today. Performers, always on the lookout for residual payments for reruns, now hope that their programs run for four or five seasons, not just one or two, so that there will be enough episodes to make the show attractive for syndication.

But, every so often, frequently in unsponsored sustaining time, on public television, or in another country or medium, one program or idea that is a bit different from others of its genre becomes popular; less often, a producer will support a program that is substantially different; and once in a while, the gamble pays off. Most recently this happened with music videos, and a few years ago self-contained miniseries were in vogue, possibly reflecting apparent reductions in audience attention spans. (This latter effect also is evidenced by fast-moving programs such as *Sesame Street* and the practice that restricts network television news stories to about 90 seconds.) Norman Lear showed that current controversies could be the subject of situation comedies such as the late-1970s *All in the Family*. Immediately, close copies were produced, in a process of imitation that continued until the ratings for that type of program began to decline. By then, another program format or genre would be on the upswing of *its* cycle. Generally, it takes from one to four seasons for a program type to run its course, and some types have returned to popularity every "TV generation" of 10 to 15 years. (Indeed, a look at Appendix C, tables 6 and 7, shows a remarkable similarity between television programming today and radio programming of half a century ago.) It is possible to "milk" or extend the life of a program or format by making changes in cast, changing from a serial format to a story-contained-in-one-episode approach, or emphasizing some aspect of the program (such as sex and violence) until it is virtually a parody of itself. But some of the best program series of recent years, like *M*A*S*H, Hill Street Blues,* and the *Mary Tyler Moore Show,* decided to retire voluntarily while still popular, often wrapping up many of the loose ends in their story lines in the final show. Of course, these programs had produced enough episodes that they were bound to be highly profitable in later syndication, and some of the talent in them would receive large residual payments for the rest of their lives.

It has been said that there are only 15 major literary plots, and television and radio drama have used and reused them so often that they have become nearly as conventionalized—with stock characters, pacing, and plot—as the lengths or genres of the programs themselves. Most avid television watchers can predict the outcome of a program or subliminally know when the plot is building in suspense and interest toward a commercial interruption. This familiarity becomes a comfort to persons who use television strictly as entertainment or companionship. Since even those who turn to television for more than relaxation and entertainment are unwilling to do so *all* the time, low audiences for public television's varied approach and sugarcoated commercial programs result.

Hence, the very sameness of broadcasting seems to be one of its greatest strengths. Rather than responding to the presumed or possible needs of the audience, broadcasting tends to cater to the public's desires, which are reduced to the limited choice of programming aired. Since much of the audience finds change uncomfortable and stability welcome, broadcasters and advertisers use these attitudes to establish continuing audience preferences and habits. About the only change is in the amount of information that today's audience seems to be able to absorb. The 20-second spots of today, with improvements in message construction and production, seem to be as effective as the one-minute commercials of two decades ago.

Locally produced programming is rare, in spite of the efforts of organizations like the National Association of Television Program Executives and the overseas examples of cooperative program exchanges. When the networks were established, local formats for both radio and television rarely could compete except by copying network programs. A half-dozen radio formats of today have no network counterparts—since radio networks no longer provide large amounts of programming—but have a similarity from market to market that cannot be blamed solely on the success of program consultants. In television, in spite of the Prime Time Access Rule, the term "local origination" generally is a misnomer. It really means that nationally syndicated programs (particularly game shows like *Jeopardy* or *Wheel of Fortune* or, sometimes, "soft" or feature "magazine" news programs) or films are being selected by local stations to be shown with local commercials.

The chief exception to this is news programming. Not only do broadcasters still believe that the FCC and Congress look with favor on programming news and public affairs "in the public interest," a sizable minority of the public feels a need to be well informed on local matters—a need that cannot be satisfied by the networks or CNN. Therefore, local broadcast news often supplies a major share of local, as opposed to national, spot revenues. Indeed, there is evidence to indicate that a strong local news program in the early evening will lead an audience to that evening's prime-time programming. This suggests that money spent on the 6 o'clock local news program will pay off by helping that station "win" the entire evening in the ratings. But even here the approach is standardized. In radio, it may be "rip 'n' read" superficiality torn from the AP or UPI wires; on television, network newscasts may be virtually indistinguishable except for their individual, highly paid anchors and gimmicks suggested by consultants, such as "happy talk" interaction among on-air presenters.

The changing of its news anchor by a network is occasion for much nervousness (and coverage by other media), as when Dan Rather moved into Walter Cronkite's chair at CBS in 1981. The last few holdovers from World War II radio network commentary days have retired, and so today caution and "objectivity" are rigorously maintained. Editorials, if presented, are bland; limits on time and cost restrict what might be aired on evening newscasts; and negative reactions to infrequent controversial documentaries usually make it harder for network news executives to get permission from their programming chiefs to budget future documentaries. Success in conventional terms *is* possible, although rare. Networks have the examples of CBS's *60 Minutes'* long membership in the list of top 10 programs in terms of ratings, and ABC's unexpected success with *Nightline,* to show that news can attract audiences and advertiser support.

There is some justice to the complaint that the networks spend huge amounts of money for sophisticated hardware and personnel to report news, political events, sporting events such as the Olympics, political assassinations, and other disasters but spend very little time or money on interpretations or implications of the news—the depth of information a citizen in a democracy needs in order to make valid decisions. In fact, the documentary has been debased and confused in the public mind by the networks' entertainment divisions, which show fictional presentations of (sometimes) real events in "docudramas." Although the amount of time devoted to straight and "soft" news has grown, after six decades the question remains: what is the proper balance between the industry's legitimate interest in a reasonable profit and the public's legitimate interest in news and public affairs?

The propaganda from those wanting a piece of the pie who claim that an increase in number of channels will automatically lead to "class" rather than "mass" programming is misleading. However, it has been accepted by some people, who believe that their programming wants would be better served if there were more outlets. However, if the undifferentiated size of a mass audience has profitable economic implications for advertiser-supported broadcasting, sheer size also is attractive to media supported by direct subscription or purchase. The name of the industry is *broad*casting, not *narrow*casting. Will cable, pay-TV, DBS, videocassettes, videodiscs, and the like really give us a golden age of program diversity? Unlikely. What evidence we have indicates that it will become more profitable to continue commercial broadcasting's pattern of mass entertainment programming intended to attract the most potential buyers at the least per-unit cost.

11·7   And What of the Audience?

The public interest, as reflected in the desires and needs of listeners and viewers, is paramount in American broadcasting—according to politicians, the Supreme Court in its 1969 *Red Lion* decision, broadcasters speaking at public hearings and meetings, and almost everyone else. Yet, because of the commercial orientation of most broadcasting, pleasing the advertisers often comes first when determining program schedules.

The audience itself generally is passive, with a few exceptions in the form of small activist citizens' groups like Action for Children's Television (ACT). Voluntary feedback—phone calls or letters—is rare but frequently is effective, sometimes even when trying to bring back a canceled program. Some audience groups work to persuade the FCC and Congress that action is needed, although now that the FCC no longer requires stations to retain program logs and has made it more difficult to challenge a license renewal, the political or legal approach seems less likely to succeed.

Research shows that most viewers are content to let the experience wash over them with little overt reaction. Even channel switching seems to be more a result of boredom than a conscious decision to change. Discussion of a program the next day with relatives, friends, or co-workers is ever more rare. Broadcasters and advertisers have relied on "head-counting" research—the ratings—to determine the success of the programming they supply and make it the criterion for retaining or dropping a program. The claim that the majority of the public is satisfied with current broadcast fare has some validity, even though the public has no choice beyond that which networks, stations, and cable systems provide. Of course, in a country of nearly 250 million people, even a small minority may contain millions of citizens!

The growing sophistication of advertisers and the increase in number of stations and cable systems over the years has led to a redefinition of "mass communication," particularly as applied to radio. The many highly specialized stations of today have loyal but relatively small audiences for very specific types of programming. Advertisers, realizing that a "class" audience with interest in their product or service might be more desirable than a much larger but indifferent "mass" audience, have geared their time-buying accordingly.

Although most programming is directed to a mass audience, increasingly sophisticated advertisers are well aware of *demographics*—data on audience composition for a given program—and *psychographics*—data on the likes and dislikes of that audience—which will allow them to groom and aim their messages at a particular target. Ratings and other research services have developed techniques, such as "people meters," to determine the characteristics of an audience, even on the still mass oriented networks, so that advertisers may match their efforts to potential customers.

Researchers and other observers do not agree on the effects broadcasting has on its audience, although virtually everyone agrees that there *are* effects. Since the mid-1950s, concern about the effect of televised violence on children has elicited a series of congressional hearings, millions of dollars' worth of research, and two important government reports, resulting in several schools of thought on the issue. But the research had to be stimulated from "outside," by nonindustry groups; broadcasters were unwilling or unable to determine broadcasting's impact. People spend more time with radio and television than with almost any other activity, but the theoretical constructs and objective data to determine the effects of such attention are only slowly becoming available. Broadcast time salesmen cite a great deal of research, much of it self-serving, to convince advertisers that radio or television would be the most persuasive medium for selling goods and services, but very little definitive research on passivity, violence, or other hypothetical or real effects has been done. Broadcasting can provide a learning experience, but just what is learned, by whom, and with what effect is not well understood even after decades of speculation and a growing amount of research.

The industry, fearful of change,

recognizes that if the public becomes truly aroused by programs emphasizing violence and sex and the problems they may cause for children, it is bound to lead to government restrictions or possible public relations–conscious advertiser boycotts. The few cases of an imitative violent act in real life following a violent act on the screen rarely show a direct cause-and-effect relationship on close analysis. In cases that seem to show a relationship, it usually can be shown that the person had exhibited abnormal tendencies previously and that Wilbur Schramm's conclusion that "some kinds of stimuli have some kinds of effect on some kinds of people sometimes" still holds. Yet this does not satisfy those who believe that the mass media are to blame for most of the world's evils. To forestall more onerous regulations, for many years broadcasters advocated self-regulation, which culminated in 1975 with the "family viewing" restriction on airing violent programs in the early evening. Although some broadcasters blamed this development for a drop in prime-time ratings, and there is a general disregard of the millions of children who watch television after nine o'clock and of the many violent scenes on the evening news, self-regulation was not the last word. When an antitrust legal challenge to the NAB's self-regulatory code on advertising was successful, the NAB quickly abolished *all* program standards, leaving it up to the networks' and stations' own self-interest to parry public objections. On the other hand, in the mid-1980s the FCC seemed to disown its 1964 Pacifica decision that the airwaves are not wholly for the inoffensive and bland when it came to "indecency," responding to a handful of complaints and relegating serious (as well as possibly prurient) content to the middle of the night, when children might be expected to be in bed.

"Media-bashing" tends to be a favorite pastime of critics and politicians, and there is a tendency to blame the media (film, radio, comic books, television, and records, in that general order, over the years) for anything that goes wrong with our children. But to the general public, getting higher-quality receivers at reasonable prices and being able to get a distant signal over the air or through cable with an entertaining program were far more important. Static mattered more than sociology, and big-name sports and entertainment was more important than high culture. This self-generating cycle supported the economic rationale for limiting programming experimentation. Most people wanted to be entertained; even at the height of World War II or during a moon shot, complaints flowed into stations about news cutting into favorite shows. News and documentaries had low ratings, and when combined with the unpopularity of the war in Vietnam or the unpleasantness of the Iran-Contra affair, it is no wonder that the networks often shunned such special public affairs programming.

Furthermore, in an interrelationship with technology, the public generally demands programming service *before* investing in receivers, VCRs, and other expensive home entertainment devices. During the 1950s and 1960s, whenever there was special scheduled programming—*Peter Pan*, the Olympics, the Academy Awards—people rushed out to buy their first sets. Later, people bought color sets to see special programs transmitted in color. Although free-enterprise purists suggest that competing devices or standards be allowed to fight it out in the marketplace, neither the public nor the manufacturers are willing to take much risk by investing in devices that might not be adopted. So, everyone usually waits until the government or a united industry

determines technical standards and specifications. The FCC now seems to favor deferring to an ill-defined market, and various media—audio disks, AM stereo—have fought out their standards there. But even today, questions on standards for HDTV or AM stereo, or on whether higher-quality VCR formats will be successful, are open—waiting, in the final analysis, for the public to commit itself.

"The public" actually consists of many publics, as was recognized decades ago by advertisers. Boredom, overfamiliarity with a given program or format, and increasingly limited attention spans must all be taken into account. Further, the average person today does not remember a time before television but has completed more formal education than his or her forebears, is growing older, and some may have more leisure time.

The audience's role, although passive, is essential. It supports the advertisers who support programming. Although there is more research and increasing congressional interest and there are a few activist groups trying to improve the system, most citizens, virtually addicted to media that did not exist a generation or two ago, relax and watch and listen. The only major change on the horizon is development of the recent ability to program one's own entertainment through the use of VCRs for time-shifting, the playback of rented movies, and the availability of dozens of cable channels. Although the negative effects of broadcasting have rarely bothered most people, the public is aware that there are many things that are pathological about today's society and world. Consequently, it considers broadcasting—the messenger telling us about the world's problems—as an obvious and vulnerable target. On the one hand, broadcasting is condemned as *causing* social ills; on the other hand, radio and television are attacked for not doing something to cure them.

11·8   Regulation and Policy

Running through most of the history of American broadcasting is a search for the meaning of the elusive "public interest, convenience, and/or necessity." Promulgated in the Radio Act of 1927 and continued under the Communications Act of 1934, this is the criterion against which all regulation of broadcasting is measured, yet it never has been satisfactorily defined either by Congress, which thought it up, the FCC, which has to administer under its terms, or the courts, which have to deal with the result. This may have some advantages in that it permits interpretations that reflect current reality rather than an idealized and rigid fiction. Surprisingly, recent proposals to do away with the public interest standard in the interests of allowing the broadcaster more freedom actually tend to be far more rigid.

Part of the problem is the FCC's traditional reluctance to regulate. This is not just a recent development, although the emphasis in the 1980s on deregulation and marketplace ideology indicates that this reluctance has reached such an extreme that one wonders if members of the FCC believe in any of the principles spelled out in the Communications Act. Never possessed of clear jurisdiction, sufficient information on which to base decisions, or the power to enforce them, this politically sensitive body traditionally has ignored problems—and no wonder. In recent years, the Court of Appeals for the District of Columbia Circuit has overturned many FCC decisions, further reducing the incentive to make them. Although many participants in the regulatory arena practice delaying tactics in

order to maintain the status quo for their own advantage, at the commission delay seems virtually a goal in itself. Even so, the trend, from the first enactment of radio laws in 1910 and 1912 until the end of the 1970s, was toward greater government supervision. Growing case law precedent, congressional interest in anything that affects the interests of its constituents, and the accretion of cases and policies into formal doctrines established a situation in which many broadcasters felt themselves narrowly circumscribed.

Except at the very beginning, the broadcasting industry has always agreed that the less regulation there was, the better. The chaos caused by unrestricted competition prior to 1927, in a field inherently limited by the strictures of the electromagnetic spectrum, was ended when Congress passed the Radio Act of 1927—with the enthusiastic approval of both the listening public *and* broadcasters. So long as the federal role was limited to such technical matters as clearing the airwaves of interference, most broadcasters had little objection to the new agency. But soon, in the self-perpetuating nature of most bureaucracies, the FRC and, later, the FCC moved into programming areas to serve better that ill-defined "public interest." From then on, a low-grade war was waged between private enterprise and government bureaucracy, punctuated by moments of high drama as dirty laundry—the quiz show, payola, and plugola scandals, for example, or the behavior of incompetent or dishonest commissioners—was washed in public and pious promises were made about doing better in the future.

In its first four and a half decades, the commission varied between "leaning tower of Jell-O" accommodation with, or even subservience to, the industry and mutual antagonism, which built to one peak with the 1946 "Blue Book" and to another during the several years of FCC activism that started with Chairman Minow's "vast wasteland" speech in 1961. Although no major revisions in law or regulation resulted from these activities, the climate changed after Minow was appointed, and broadcasters no longer possessed the informal control over the commission they had long held. In recent years, broadcasters and most members of the now-five-member commission have been on the same side of the ideological fence—but, unfortunately for broadcasters, their most important adversary has become the cable industry, and Congress and the FCC have leaned toward cable's favor.

In evaluating the government's role in broadcasting, it is good to remember that the several agencies involved—Congress, the FCC, the OTP and its successors, and the courts—are not monolithic. They are composed of a changing cast of people with varied goals. Commissioner Johnson's interest in eliminating cross-media ownership had a very different philosophical base from President Nixon's attack on the ownership of television stations by the *Washington Post,* which opposed him. Most FCC members were appointed because of their earlier activities and views, with some getting the position because of old political debts, some because of outstanding service as a staff member of either the FCC or Congress, and some because a President wanted someone who thought as he did. Most recently, the nod often has gone to individuals who have the backing of influential members of Congress—and who fit into an unwritten quota system for women and members of minority groups.

Behind the scenes, however, were "the staff"—the generally unknown congressional committee aides, FCC senior civil servants, and politically oriented technocrats of the OTP—who had their own goals and a great deal more continuity than their elected or appointed superiors—and who often were not averse to arguing with their masters. Most of these people worked conscientiously in the public interest, but their length of tenure often froze their points of view, including a tendency to protect the status quo.

Although current controversies occupy our attention, they are seldom truly current. Most regulatory problems have been around for a long time; some took two decades to reach a decision. Precedent often becomes so encrusted that various sides in a dispute often have difficulty finding new approaches to long-standing issues. Nevertheless, identification of some of the themes underlying today's problems may help explain them.

One such theme is concern over concentration of ownership of broadcasting stations and cable systems. This concern typically was stimulated and pushed on the FCC by populist members of Congress. Restrictions were slowly instituted on multiple ownership of stations in a given market, on cross-ownership between media, and on particular combinations such as television station–cable ownership within a station's coverage area. The courts generally supported this FCC and Justice Department activity, starting with the Supreme Court's 1943 upholding of the commission's network rules and similar actions in programming and economics. Existing combinations have been allowed to continue, and some no-holds-barred attempts have been launched to persuade the FCC to grant waivers, notably by Rupert Murdoch, who wanted to own both newspapers and television stations in New York and Boston in 1988. Changes in corporate ownership also have led to such extremes as pioneer NBC having to divest itself of its owned-and-operated radio stations in order to retain television stations in the same markets after purchase of its parent, RCA, by GE in 1985.

The commission's relaxation of the multiple ownership rules in the past decade—permitting a given licensee to own 12 AM, 12 FM, and 12 television stations (in different markets) or reaching a specified proportion of the American public, rather than the 7-7-7 limit prescribed for 30 years—predictably led to a large increase in station sales, abetted by relaxation at the same time of rules against "trafficking" in station licenses. This was a triumph of the ideology of deregulation, which had started late in the Carter administration under the label of reregulation, billed as removing only outmoded and technical clauses from the rules. By allowing stations to be bought and sold for short-term gains, it removed one of the last regulations that was based on the concept that the broadcast media were "special" and subject to the public interest standard.

Perhaps the FCC's most important and longest-running policy donnybrook is the Fairness Doctrine, which started simply enough when the FCC decided in the 1941 *Mayflower* case that the broadcaster should not be an advocate. The FCC then changed its mind in 1949, arguing that a broadcaster *could* be an advocate if he or she provided an opportunity for opposing views to be heard. As the doctrine evolved case by case over the years, it split into two parts: the right of the public to hear opposing views on controversial matters of public importance was incorporated in Section 315 of the Communications Act in 1960, and the right for time to reply of those personally attacked during such a presentation was incorporated in the FCC rules in 1967. The Supreme Court, in the 1969 *Red*

Lion decision, upheld the Fairness Doctrine's personal attack rules.

The Fairness Doctrine, which was intended to benefit the public by permitting airing of various opinions on matters of public concern, was a rallying point for activist citizens' groups after 1964. When it was used in 1967 to require that stations broadcasting cigarette commercials provide free antismoking spots, the broadcasting industry felt that this was an extremely dangerous precedent since the requirement did not affect nonelectronic media, and different groups seized on the decision to demand time to respond to other commercials on consumerism or environmental grounds. The FCC, with the aid of the courts, later managed to put the lid back on this Pandora's box, and Congress later banned all broadcast cigarette advertising.

This did not stop citizens' groups from pressuring for increased access. They tried to use the Fairness Doctrine and other regulations to achieve something different from fairness: *access* to the airwaves for persons who had something to say—in the way they (and not the broadcaster) wanted it said. Argued best by attorney Jerome Barron, this concept led to little-used public access channels for CATV in the FCC's 1972 rules, to parts of the 1984 cable act, and to continuing pressure on broadcasters in the form of petitions to deny license renewal.

Congress and the commission, both now believing that the Fairness Doctrine had been pushed too far, instigated hearings, revision proposals, and court tests of the doctrine's procedures—and even of its basic desirability. Post-Watergate election reform laws and rapid changes in the case law of libel in the 1970s further confused relationships among public officials, the general public, broadcasters, and fairness. Supported by a coalition of broadcasters, the FCC became loath to apply the Fairness Doctrine. In 1985 the commission let it be known that it was looking for a way to dump the doctrine as unconstitutional. While this would please conservatives in and out of government, as well as broadcast journalists and others who felt that the doctrine interfered with their First Amendment rights, a majority in Congress felt so strongly that the doctrine should be retained that when the FCC dropped it in 1987, Congress passed a bill to restore it—only to have the bill vetoed by President Reagan. The final act in this saga has not yet been written.

Broadcasters, supposedly held accountable by the Communications Act, came to distrust the FCC's continual investigations and rule changes and "harrassment" by citizens' groups, many of which had financial support from tax-exempt foundations or government agencies. Until this trend was reversed during the Reagan administration, the government increasingly seemed to guide and limit the licensee's authority over station operations. The FCC, itself under pressure and subject to almost continual investigations by Congress since the early 1940s, at first tried to walk in the middle of the road, refereeing confrontations between broadcasters and listener groups, to the dissatisfaction of both sides. The commission's usual tactic of delay proved ineffectual as citizens' groups found their way to the usually more receptive courts, a not-surprising development in an ever more litigious society. When the WLBT decision of the late 1960s (see 9•81) gave some types of citizens' groups standing before the FCC, it permanently expanded the list of participants in the regulatory arena. While some proceedings grew more involved, these newcomers, like other players, soon found it advisable to negotiate their concerns directly with broadcasters rather

than take the long road through the commission and the courts.

Throughout the period from the mid-1960s on, broadcasters often found that their own causes were not doing well. This was partly due to an inability to lobby Congress as effectively as the rival motion picture and cable industries. Cable, in particular, steadily improved its ability to lobby both Congress—particularly pleased by "free time" each week—and the FCC. The FTC, the antitrust division of the Justice Department, and other agencies developed popular antibroadcast ideas for increasing regulation of broadcast advertising and building intramarket media competition until the laissez-faire atmosphere of the 1980s buried these efforts. Congress made increasing demands on broadcasters for the carriage of political campaigning at bargain prices. Anti–job discrimination laws—one of the few areas under active FCC regulation during the Reagan era—and a requirement that broadcasters survey community leaders and the public to ascertain the community's needs as part of the license renewal process added to the mound of paperwork required of each broadcaster. On the other hand, Congress in 1981 finally lengthened license terms and made it much harder to challenge an existing licensee.

Although these increasingly complex regulations led broadcasters to think that the commission was firmly in the citizens' group ("enemy") camp during the 1960s and 1970s, such was not the case. Some regulations were mandated by Congress, some were the product of normal bureaucratic expansion, and others were the consequence of court decisions or were in response to real abuse of the public interest. The increasing number of multimillion-dollar libel suits reflected the case law of defamation, not a policy of the commission. The FCC's policy of delay fitted in well with the goals of those broadcasters who were economically powerful at a given time. Commission action or inaction—as contrasted to commission rhetoric—generally favored broadcasters over outsiders, AM over FM, VHF over UHF, and television broadcasters over cable until the newly found political strength of the cable industry caused a flip-flop. Only when the need for new services or technologies became apparent did the commission approve stereo and nonduplication rules to help FM, support the all-channel receiving set law to help UHF television, and loosen restrictions on pay-TV and cable. The courts—in decisions on cable television, or on the copyright law, as in the "Betamax" case—showed careful attention to political winds but settled into this same pattern. Even then, the new regulations seldom were even handed. Usually they protected the existing service; sometimes, as with cable in the mid-1970s, they favored the new service; but always they claimed to be serving the "public interest, convenience, and/or necessity."

"Self-regulation" in broadcasting is one barometer of public concern over radio and television's role in society. Like most such industry self-regulatory efforts, the NAB codes were intended to influence public opinion. They had little policing effect, no matter how much effort was devoted to their wording. With some exceptions—the ban on hard liquor advertising and provision for "family viewing" time are two—the codes were platitudes, often ignored if the industry was in economic difficulty. Most important, not all stations were members of the codes, many did not feel bound by them, and the only enforcement penalty was withdrawal of permission to use the code's symbol or seal. Consequently, when a federal court decision struck down television code lim-

itations on the amount of commercial time allowed per hour, the NAB and the broadcasters readily eliminated any pretense of maintaining industry-wide programming and commercial time standards. Apparently today only the carefully honed ability of networks to avoid controversial material and congressional and political interest in the protection of young children from sexually explicit or other "indecent" programming prevent anything-goes programming.

However, broadcasters are subject to laws, regulations, and policies that are not within the purview of the FCC. For example, a federal shield law protecting the confidentiality of reporters' sources has never gotten anywhere, although many states now allow cameras and microphones in the courtroom. The successful coverage of the Nixon impeachment proceedings in 1974 led to the allowing of gavel-to-gavel coverage of the House of Representatives' proceedings after 1979 over C-SPAN, a public affairs cable service that, ironically, was not available in the District of Columbia. The more conservative Senate followed suit in 1986. Even with a Freedom of Information Act, journalistic access to government information—particularly in the courts and in those parts of the executive branch that used the excuse of "security"—became more difficult each decade since its passage in 1966.

Finally, it should be noted that there never has been a consistent long-range communications policy for the United States, except as inadequately sketched out in the 1934 act. Attempts by Congressman Lionel Van Deerlin to rewrite completely the Communications Act in the late 1970s foundered. The pressures of budget and day-to-day duties have restricted the FCC's long-range vision; some members of the FCC and Congress would like to abolish it altogether; Congress is too concerned with politically inspired hearings and lacks the continuity for such planning; and broadcasters are running businesses, not research centers. In 1951 and 1968, presidential commissions examined American telecommunications policy, but most of their quite-different recommendations were ignored. When the OTP was formed in 1970, it seemed to be a step toward continuing policy research at a high government level, but it quickly became mired in politics and short-range goals. It is this lack of long-range, policy-oriented thinking that has led to government *reaction* to recurring problems rather than *anticipation* of their recurrence, even with an increase in telecommunications policy research in the 1970s. In the 1980s, doctrinaire conservative economists dominated policy that previously had taken account of technical constraints and broad political economy theory. Much of the agenda of the Reagan administration was determined by ideological economic principles, and the administration preferred to develop new policies within conservative think tanks rather than in the give-and-take of traditional policy-making procedures.

After more than 65 years of broadcasting, and nearly 60 years of broadcast regulation, the controlling phrase "public interest, convenience, and/or necessity" remains undefined beyond what the current political situation says it means, with resultant regulatory confusion and lack of goals. Not only does the half-century-old Communications Act respond slowly to change, it often is administered by people who seem to have little loyalty to its principles. This uncertainty ensures that philosophical and operational regulatory problems will remain with us in the future.

The swings from regulation to reregulation to deregulation and back

again ensure that the current situation will not remain stagnant. It might be said that the debate is between those who believe "that government is best which governs least" and those who believe "that government is best which governs best." At one time, both sides cited the public interest standard as backing their positions. Today, with this standard in eclipse, there appears to be little appeal to the idea that broadcasting is unique and important in our society and that it should be carefully nurtured—or restrained, if necessary.

The time is past for continual application of ad hoc solutions to seemingly permanent problems. As both the industry and government are understandably looking out for themselves, the public interest suffers as a result. Concerted action by knowledgeable and impartial citizens could change this pattern but would require preparation, popular support, and funding. Past experience suggests that it would be desirable to have solid, impartial research and policy initiatives supported by funds generated outside of either bureaucratic or industry control. The potential for such a "third force" in the electronic media is great.

11•9   And if There Were *No* Broadcasting?

In this book we have discussed the development and some of the effects of broadcasting in America. But what if radio and television broadcasting had never developed? How would life in this country differ? The answers to such questions suggest the overall impact of nearly two-thirds of a century of broadcasting.

Clearly, life without broadcasting would be a throwback to the days before the early 1920s so far as mass communication is concerned. Yet without broadcasting the world would not have stood still, and we cannot look back almost 70 years and say, "That's how it would be today, without broadcasting." We can only resort to a guessing game, a form of reverse futuristics, similar in some ways to taking the data in this book and extrapolating into the twenty-first century *with* broadcasting.

Some things would be obvious, others more obscure to those who were born in the second half of this century. Even the smallest unit of social life, the family, would offer a substantially different milieu in which to grow up. Without broadcasting's socializing effect, the family would have a far more important social role than it has today. Family members probably would fill their ever-longer hours of leisure with activities less passive than watching television. They might even do more things together. Our entertainment media would be very different: the film industry would be thriving, and newsreel theaters might be popular. Vaudeville would have remained both a major entertainment medium and a way for aspiring legitimate theater and motion picture performers to hone their acts and their abilities—which would have more than satisfied "father of radio" Lee de Forest, who reportedly fought against networks in favor of a circuit of vaudeville performers moving on from station to station! Recreational reading of magazines and books of all types would be greater. Even with twentieth-century transportation and the telephone, localism would be more important for more of us. Home, school, church, and immediate community might play larger roles in the absence of pictures of the "greener grass" elsewhere. Our personal and collective identities would be with our community, city, state, or region rather than with the nation or world, which probably would have major conse-

quences for the distribution and sale of retail goods. Education would concentrate more on improving literacy.

When we take away broadcast journalism, with its ability to tell us almost instantly what is happening anywhere at any time, we are left with newspapers or magazines (and perhaps motion picture newsreels) that take hours or days to publish admittedly more complete news, even when the event warrants speed. We would find it much harder to identify with happenings far away when it took so long for the news to reach us. Lacking the cohesive force of broadcasting, regions of the country, let alone of the world, would be far more different from one another than they are today. Fads and information on living and social styles would travel more slowly and penetrate less deeply when passed on only by print, film, and word of mouth. Even our language would be different, as there would be no broadcast media to help override regional dialects. Our knowledge of other areas would be limited to memories of personal travel or to images from the printed page, still photographs, and movies. Results of international diplomatic and sports meetings would take at least a day to reach us, and the latter would lose much of their thrill when reduced to print rather than conveyed live or on videotape by satellite. The old familiar sports, as played by local teams rather than distant national leagues, would be preferred over accounts of exotic events, such as many Olympic activities, that have to be seen to be understood. In fact, without television coverage to pay for team transportation and huge player salaries, the organization of national sports would be very unlike that with which we are familiar.

In addition to changes in lifestyle—generally, a slowing down of the introduction of new fashions and ideas—there would be substantial political and economic impacts from the absence of broadcasting. No longer could a political idea or a national leader mobilize or galvanize an entire populace—particularly persons who cannot or will not bother to read—in a day. The civil rights movement for minorities and women would have progressed much more slowly without the constant broadcast coverage of recent decades. If we had been engaged in a war in Vietnam without television, our views of it would probably have changed more slowly—if at all. Other Presidents might have been elected or Watergate more easily covered up. This alternative world would be unimaginably different.

In the economic sphere, some products and services would suffer from the lack of broadcast advertising, and advertisers would be forced to use print or perhaps film for national advertising, while—as is true today—direct mail and point-of-purchase displays and billboards continue to receive the most advertising dollars. Naturally, the consumer electronics industry—and the related trade deficit with Japan—would be *much* smaller. The larger general circulation magazines, most of which went out of business in the 1950s and 1960s, still would be thriving as mass audience advertising vehicles, with circulations in the tens of millions. Advertisers probably would want to have more say about the content of such magazines in order to avoid offending potential consumers. Careers of show business personalities would rise and decline much more slowly. The recording industry would boom, although stars of the music field would develop more slowly than today's overnight sensations. Many performing arts groups would have larger live audiences than they now do.

But, of course, since radio and television *were* invented and successfully innovated, we need to look backward a bit

in order to forecast the future intelligently. The coming of radio in the 1920s took the nation by storm and had substantial effects on print, film, and phonograph records—as well as on the family, economics, and politics. But, unlike the complete displacement of the horse and buggy by the automobile, competing media, particularly records, came back part of the way and lived in symbiosis with radio. Radio has taken over the role of the newspaper extra, but it is not suited to disseminate the comic strip or the political cartoon or to serve as a medium of record. When television arrived in the late 1940s and early 1950s, this dislocation was repeated. Radio, after less than twenty-five years, was virtually eclipsed as a national (but not as a local) medium. The film industry was shattered for decades, expanding output in the 1980s only because of demand from cable and VCRs.

For more than a third of a century, television has been the dominant mass medium in the United States, with other media scrambling for significant and profitable niches. It has carried an increasing proportion of national advertising and has given a majority of citizens most of their news. The motion picture industry is primarily its handmaiden, and the newsreel and the national weekly picture magazine have died. Minor league sports have all but disappeared in the face of major league television coverage; indeed, many teams and leagues have been established solely because of expected television income.

But broadcasting is more than a mere economic institution. Television and radio have given us moments of laughter and high and low drama—including wars, the death of one President, and the resignation of another—and have extended our eyes and ears to the entire world and even to the moon. Those born since 1950 have grown up with television. They spend several hours each day in front of the set and will spend more time with television than with almost any other activity. They make up the first television generations. Those born since 1970 missed the exciting and rapid growth of the early years, and by not remembering anything different and accepting television as it is, they unfortunately may be unaware of much possibility for improvement. The violence and sex, the beauty and laughter, the emotion and reason provided by society's ambiguous mirror, which both reflects and projects, have affected and will affect them. They, in turn, will change American society, including, in full circle, the electronic media. The impact of broadcasting may not always have been beneficial, but it has been deep. To understand what has been heard and seen over radio and television over the past two-thirds of a century is to understand American life better. As for the future—

Stay tuned . . .

A Short Chronology of American Broadcasting

A Short Chronology of American Broadcasting

This *very* selective chronology of highlights is divided into periods paralleling the chapters in the text and is restricted to what we feel are the most important events of each year. The material has been gathered and condensed from (see bibliography for full citations) Kempner (1948), Dunlap (1951), *Broadcasting* (1970, 1976), Barnouw (1966, 1968, 1970, 1975), Head (1976), and several unpublished sources of which the most useful was L. W. Lichty's "A Chronology of American Television to 1966" (unpublished).

The Prehistory of Broadcasting (to 1919)

1725 Gray (England) discovers the principle of conduction by observing electricity carried several hundred feet through a hemp thread.

1753 An anonymous published letter (England) suggests wired communication with a wire connection for each letter of the alphabet.

1794 Chappe (France) devises optical telegraph system using signals on towers between major French cities.

1832 Morse (United States) develops basic sense of what will become his telegraph system and code.

1840 Morse receives telegraph patent applied for in 1837.

1843 Bain (Scotland) devises basic principles of transmitting pictures (later known as *facsimile*), much of it applicable later to television.

1844 First telegraph circuit, between Washington and Baltimore, is officially opened with message "What Hath God Wrought?"

1858 First underwater telegraph cable is laid across the Atlantic but works for only a few months.

1861 Coast-to-coast telegraph lines put 18-month-old Pony Express out of business.

1862 Caselli (France) transmits a crude image by wire between two towns.

1864 Clerk Maxwell (Scotland) theorizes existence of electromagnetic waves.

1865 International Telegraph (later Telecommunication) Union is founded.

1866 Atlantic cable is successful on third major attempt. • Loomis (United States) conducts wireless telegraph experiments in Virginia and sends signals about 15 miles.

1872 Loomis acquires world's first patent on a wireless system but fails to commercialize it for lack of funds.

1873 May (England) discovers that selenium can produce electricity in direct relation to amount of light received.

1876 Bell (United States) applies for patent on telephone device, then demonstrates same at Philadelphia Centennial Exposition.

1877 Edison (United States) succeeds in first audible reproduction of recorded sound—basis of phonograph and subsequent recording methods. Carey (United States) proposes bank of selenium cells, each with wire conductor to similarly arranged bank of lights on reception end, for crude means of picture transmission.

1880 Leblanc (France) suggests the principle of scanning to allow faster transmission of pictures using only one wire.

1884 Nipkow (Germany) patents the scanning disc with spiral of holes with which to scan and later reproduce pictures.

1885 American Telephone and Telegraph (AT&T) is formed from several earlier phone companies.

1887 Hertz (Germany) proves Clerk Maxwell theories in series of laboratory experiments.

1888 First photocell is developed, later of great importance to television.

1892 Stubblefield demonstrates his wireless telephone system.

1894 Jenkins (United States) begins experimentation with television system using mosaic system. Lodge (England) introduces and improves Branly (France) coherer as a wireless detector. It becomes the standard for two decades.

1895 Marconi (Italy) sends wireless telegraph messages approximately a mile on his father's estate during initial experiments.

1896 Marconi arrives in England, demonstrates his improved system, and leads in formation of what will become in 1900 the "British Marconi" firm.

1897 Braun (Germany) develops cathode-ray oscilloscope as crude electronic display tube.

1899 Marconi sends wireless signal across English Channel. British and American navies experiment with several wireless systems. American Marconi, British-controlled subsidiary of main firm, is founded. • Wireless calls for aid bring about first rescues of crew and passengers from vessels in distress in European coastal waters.

1901 Marconi and aides send letter *S* across the Atlantic Ocean, suggesting long-range communication applications of wireless.

1903 Berlin is site of first international radio conference, which proposes greater cooperation in ship-to-shore communication.

1904 United Fruit Company begins to build its network of radio stations in Central America and Caribbean countries to coordinate banana shipping. • Fleming (England) patents two-element vacuum tube, or valve.

1906 Fessenden (United States) transmits voice and music program from transmitter at Brant Rock, Massachusetts. • De Forest (United States) develops three-element tube, called triode or Audion. • Pickard and Dunwoody (United States), among others, develop crystal detector—first inexpensive and easily duplicated detecting device. • Berlin is site of second international radio conference, which adopts "SOS" call and demands all companies and ships equipped with apparatus from various manufacturers to communicate with one another in emergencies.

1907 Rosing (Russia) receives a faint television signal by using Braun tube and adding photocells.

1908 Campbell Swinton (England) suggests a completely electronic system of television.

1909 Herrold begins broadcasts from San Jose, California, and schedules them regularly shortly thereafter.

1910 First United States radio law, Wireless Ship Act of 1910, calls for radio and operator on all oceangoing passenger vessels.

1912 *Titanic* disaster dramatically shows value of wireless as 700 of 2,200 persons are saved in midatlantic iceberg collision. • Second United States Wireless Ship Act requires two radio operators on all vessels at sea. A month later, Radio Act of 1912 provides first regulations for land radio stations and amateur operators. • De Forest discovers amplification potential of triode, which leads to AT&T purchase of telephone rights to three-element tube.

1915 Coast-to-coast telephone service established. • American Radio Relay League set up as association of amateur operators. • General Electric and British Marconi tentatively agree that GE will sell Alexanderson alternators exclusively to Marconi.

1916 De Forest broadcasts presidential election returns in Wilson-Hughes race. • Sarnoff files "radio music box" memo with officials of American Marconi, who are interested only in international and ship radio for private messages.

1917 United States enters World War I. The navy takes over radio transmitters—especially the Alexanderson alternators, the only reliable long-distance wireless transmitters—for the duration, or closes down facilities; establishes system until 1920 of indemnifying companies for patent infringement—essentially a patents pool—so that best equipment can be made for wartime use.

The Beginnings of Broadcasting (1919–1926)

1919 Navy continues control of radio facilities after war as battle rages over government's role in future of wireless; Congress holds hearings (May–June). • British Marconi resumes negotiations with GE for alternator, still demanding monopoly rights, but after navy intervention, GE forms RCA to safeguard American radio interests. RCA acquires rights to alternator (October) and assets of American Marconi, and enters into first patent cross-license agreement with GE (November).

1920 President Wilson orders navy to relinquish control of amateur and all other nongovernment radio facilities (March). • AT&T joins RCA-GE cross-licensing agreement in step leading to postwar civilian-controlled patents pool (July). • To outflank position of RCA, Westinghouse purchases two key receiver patents from Armstrong (October). To encourage sales of radio receivers, Westinghouse establishes KDKA in East Pittsburgh, based on experimental station 8XK run by their engineer Frank Conrad. Initial KDKA broadcast is of Harding-Cox presidential election returns (November).

1921 Westinghouse attempt to compete in international radio collapses as RCA has tied up most foreign contacts. Westinghouse joins RCA patents pool, splitting receiver manufacturing rights with GE 60–40. United Fruit joins pool (June). • Thirty broadcasting stations go on the air, including six owned by Westinghouse and others operated by GE and RCA. Only two frequencies (channels) are in use for broadcasting.

1922 Hoover hosts first radio conference in Washington, which calls for government regulation of radio technology, limited advertising, and classes of stations based on kind of service (February). With hundreds of new stations, Hoover adds new frequency for stations of higher power and high quality programming. First use of four-letter station calls (August). • AT&T enters broadcasting, seeing it as extension of toll telephone operation. First paid-for commercial announcement on WEAF (August).

1923 Jenkins transmits unmoving facsimile silhouettes from Washington to Philadelphia by wireless (March). Zworykin (United States) patents iconoscope camera tube, key to an electronic television system. • Second radio conference reiterates suggestions and calls for temporary licensing guidelines until Congress will act (March). • Planning meeting in Chicago leads to formation of National Association of Broadcasters, to fight ASCAP demand for payment from radio stations for all music used on the air and to seek government technical regulation. • Hoover announces three classes of stations and assigns greatly increased frequency spectrum, about two-thirds of current AM band, to two of them (June). • RCA enters broadcasting by taking over programming of Westinghouse's New York outlet and building a station in Washington and another in New York. The New York stations, WJY and WJZ, become major competition for AT&T's WEAF. • First multiple station hookup combines WEAF (New York), WGY (Schenectady), KDKA (Pittsburgh), and KYW (Chicago) (June). First lasting hookup between WEAF and Massachusetts station comes a month later. • Federal Trade Commission report, aimed mainly at RCA, criticizes monopoly in radio equipment and patents (December).

1924 First coast-to-coast radio program demonstrates use of telephone-line circuits and lays groundwork for planned national AT&T network, using WEAF as originating station (February). • Third and largest radio conference in Washington calls for broadcasting use of entire 550–1,500 kHz band and urges research into monopoly and station interconnection (October). • Competition between Telephone Group (WEAF and allied companies and stations) and Radio Group (RCA, GE, Westinghouse, and others and their stations) affects decisions on programming, station interconnection, patents, and equipment manufacture.

1925 Baird (England) gives public demonstration of mechanical (Nipkow disc) system of television by transmitting silhouettes (April). Jenkins (United States) sends first filmed (moving) images by wireless using mechanical television system (June). • Fourth and last radio conference in Washington agrees that limit on number of stations may be required, radio is not a public utility, and limited advertising is acceptable (November).

1926 Zenith case shows limits of 1912 act when federal court holds Secretary of Commerce cannot prevent firm from changing station frequency, thus wiping out Hoover's voluntary regulatory scheme. U.S. Attorney General releases opinion that Secretary of Commerce can only process license applications and not regulate them. With all controls ended, licensing of 200 new stations adds to interference chaos on the air (fall).

The Coming of Commercialism (1926–1933)

1926 Internal strife within industry is resolved as Telephone and Radio groups sign three-part agreement including provision that AT&T will drop business of broadcasting station operations (July). • RCA forms National Broadcasting Company (NBC) (September). NBC purchases WEAF from AT&T for $1 million and begins regular broadcasting on NBC-Red, based on old AT&T chain of stations (November).

1927 NBC-Blue network, based on New York's WJZ, begins operations with 1927 Rose Bowl broadcast (January). • President Coolidge signs Radio Act of 1927, which creates Federal Radio Commission (FRC) (February). • New FRC orders stations back to frequencies assigned by Hoover and sets broadcast band at 550–1,500 kHz (April). • Columbia Broadcasting System (CBS) goes on the air with 16 stations for a long and shaky start-up period (September). • Ives (United States) transmits both still and moving pictures, as well as synchronized sound by wire. Farnsworth (United States) transmits first electronic television pictures. • Millions listened to radio coverage of Lindbergh solo transatlantic flight (May).

1928 Baird transmits television picture across the Atlantic and later demonstrates mechanical color television. Zworykin develops and patents a much-improved iconoscope tube. The FRC allocates several 10 kHz channels in the standard (AM) band for television. • Congress passes Davis Amendment to Radio Act, which calls for equality of radio service in five regions in the country (March). • Radio generally is becoming accepted as advertising medium, though it carries only 2 percent of all advertising this year. • FRC announces plan to allocate clear, regional, and local AM channels (August). • Paley buys control of CBS; is named president in early 1929. • NBC begins fulltime (but not 24-hour) coast-to-coast operation.

1929 In the Great Lakes case, the FRC analyzes what the public interest means for a broadcasting station. • National Association of Broadcasters issues a code of radio advertising and programming ethics (April). • Crossley's Cooperative Analysis of Broadcasting offers first system of network program ratings. • FRC becomes permanent body after several short-term extensions (December).

1930 Formation of conflicting National Advisory Council on Radio in Education and National Committee on Education by Radio. • Lowell Thomas begins national daily newscast, on NBC-Blue (and broadcasts regularly until May 1976). • RCA takes over GE and Westinghouse efforts in television as part of the reorganization of roles of each firm following antitrust action.

1931 Court upholds FRC denial of license renewal to Brinkley's KFKB because of past programming and personal attacks on the air (February). Appeals court dismisses appeal of FRC denial of Schaeffer license because of profanity uttered by candidate for public office; saying licensee is responsible (March). FRC rescinds license of Baker's KTNT in Iowa for personal attacks and other program matters (June) and of Shuler's Los Angeles station for personal attacks (November). The last decision is later upheld as not being improper government censorship. These four cases help solidify the FRC's right to examine programming for public interest. • Metropolitan Opera Broadcasts begin with Milton Cross as announcer (until his death in 1974).

1932 Radio reports the Lindbergh kidnaping, one of first tragedies covered on the air (March). • University of Iowa begins scheduled educational broadcasting with mechanical television (the station staying on the air to 1939). RCA initiates 120-line electronic television field testing. • GE and Westinghouse end long legal wrangle with agreement to sell all RCA stock; RCA, now fully independent, competes with former owners (November).

1933 First of President Roosevelt's famous "Fireside Chats" (March). • As newspaper-radio tensions rise, Associated Press limits sale of news to local stations. CBS gathers network news on its own (April). • Biltmore Agreement between networks and news agencies eliminates independent radio reporting by networks (December). • RCA initiates use of Zworykin's iconoscope-kinescope combination and raises picture definition to 240 lines. • Armstrong receives the four key patents to new FM radio system (December).

Radio's Golden Age (1934–1941)

1934 Three independent organizations are established to gather and sell news for radio in fight against Biltmore Agreement (March). • Station WLW begins experimentation with 500,000 watts (until mid-1939) (May). • Roosevelt signs Communications Act of 1934 replacing FRC with Federal Communications Commission (June). • A new network, first called Quality and then Mutual, is started by owner and joint operator stations WOR, WGN, WLW, and WXYZ (September).

1935 RCA and Armstrong end cooperation over FM radio. Armstrong announces his FM system, and RCA achieves 343-line interlaced television scanning and announces million-dollar television research program (May). Armstrong demonstrates his FM system (November). • United Press and International News Service agree to sell news to radio stations and networks, marking effective end of Biltmore Agreement (May).

1936 Congress repeals Davis Amendment requiring equal radio service in five zones, thereby allowing for more stations and greater power in areas of high population (June). • FCC holds engineering conference and hearings on future of FM and television (June). • BBC (England) initiates regular television broadcasts comparing Baird mechanical with EMI-Marconi electronic systems (November). • New York to Philadelphia coaxial cable is tested (December).

1937 American Federation of Radio Artists (originally "Artistes"), a union for announcers and performers (later known as AFTRA), is formed (July). • In wake of chaotic Hauptmann

(Lindbergh kidnaping) trial, American Bar Association adopts Canon 35, banning radio, recordings, and photography in courtrooms (September). • FCC allocates 19 channels for experimental television (October), and Philco demonstrates 441-line television pictures.

1938 FCC makes first educational allocation in broadcasting, 25 channels in 40-MHz band (January). • First FM station, Armstrong's W2XMN in New Jersey, goes on the air (April). • Wheeler-Lea Act gives Federal Trade Commission right to curb false and misleading advertising (April). • Radio's reporting of month-long Munich crisis is first major use of shortwave for live coverage of international event (September). • Orson Welles's production of *War of the Worlds*, the most famous single broadcast, scares many listeners (October).

1939 Associated Press begins to supply news without charge for sustaining programs on NBC (February) and later begins to sell news (June), thus finally ending the Press-Radio war. • FCC issues a memorandum on 14 types of objectionable programming (March). • Unable to buy his patents, RCA signs television patent license agreement with Farnsworth. NBC starts regular television programming with opening of New York World's Fair (April). • New NAB code goes into effect: disallows liquor advertising or paid controversial ads, and limits all advertising to 10 percent of each hour (July). • Facing rising pressure from ASCAP for higher royalties, NAB establishes its own music licensing organization, Broadcast Music, Incorporated (BMI) (September). • BBC suspends television operations for the duration of World War II (September).

1940 FCC gives go-ahead for limited commercial television as of September, using 441-line standard (February), but rescinds order after RCA pushes receiver sales against FCC desires and understandings (March). • Radio correspondents provide regular reports from Europe at war, especially eye-witness accounts from Murrow in London, Shirer in Berlin and France. • CBS demonstrates its color television system—a mixture of electronic and mechanical methods (August). • Justice Department prepares antitrust action against ASCAP, BMI,

and radio networks for music monopoly (December); settled by consent degree in February 1941.

1941 Commercial FM radio operations are authorized (January). • FCC issues "Mayflower" decision, which is understood to eliminate licensee editorializing (January). • Nearly all stations change frequencies, many only slightly, as the North American Regional Broadcasting Agreement (NARBA) goes into effect between the United States, Canada, Mexico, and Cuba (March). • FCC issues Chain Broadcasting Report with eight important recommendations; most upsetting to the industry is requirement that NBC give up either Red or Blue network (May). • FCC approves commercial television with 525-line standard and FM sound—effective July 1. • CBS and NBC stations operate stations by the first day. • FCC begins two and one-half year investigation of press ownership of radio stations (August).

Radio Goes to War (1941–1945)

1941 Largest radio audience to date, estimated at 90 million, hears Roosevelt declare war. Amateur stations are closed down, and weather forecasts are limited for the duration (December).

1942 Wartime code bans man-on-the-street and ad-lib interviews, and most quiz shows (January). FCC bans construction of broadcasting stations in areas with primary (local) service (February) and freezes all station construction except for operations underway, to conserve war material. Receiver production is ended, and shellac, used in records, is sharply limited for civilian use (April). • President Roosevelt creates Office of War Information (OWI) and names newsman Elmer Davis to head it (June). • American Federation of Musicians, under new president Petrillo, announces no musicians will play for recording sessions—beginning of a long strike (August).

1943 Supreme Court upholds FCC's chain broadcasting regulations, forcing NBC to shed one network, forbidding exclusivity, and curtailing option time (May). • Congressman Cox begins lengthy House investigation of the FCC (June). • E. J. Noble purchases the Blue network from RCA for $8,000,000, and the FCC approves the transfer (October).

1944 FCC ends newspaper-broadcasting ownership investigation without drawing up new rules (January). • Networks allow FM stations to carry AM programs without extra charge to sponsors (January). • FCC holds major allocations hearings on spectrum above 30 MHz, concerned especially with future of FM and television (September–November). • Networks sign with Petrillo's AFM, on his terms, after an appeal from President Roosevelt fails to end strike. Two-and-a-half-year-old recording ban is ended (November).

1945 Blue Network becomes American Broadcasting Company (April). • FCC delivers television allocation of 13 VHF channels (May) and FM service is moved up to 88–108 MHz band (June). • The war ends, and the FCC begins to process backed-up station applications; receiver production is resumed; OWI is abolished (August); amateur bands are released to civilians (November).

Era of Great Change (1945–1952)

1946 FCC's "Blue Book" makes strongest statement yet on licensee's responsibility in public service programming (March). • BBC reestablishes television broadcasting with 405-line prewar standards (June). • RCA publicly demonstrates all-electronic system of color television (November).

1947 Strong anticommunist attacks on broadcasting include *Counterattack* newsletter and early blacklisting. • Zenith announces Phonevision system of pay-TV by wire, setting off two decades of experimentation and intense debate (July). • Over a period of several months, interconnection of television stations by both microwave and coaxial cable develops, connecting stations in both the East and Midwest (late 1947 through spring 1948).

1948 AFM lifts ban (begun in late 1945) on musicians playing for television or on AM-FM

simulcast programs (March). • Broadcast and nonbroadcast sharing of television channels is eliminated, but channel 1 deleted for other uses (May). • Scientists at Bell Telephone Labs demonstrate transistor (June). • NBC and CBS announce plans for major television network expansion by 1950. First ABC television station goes on air in New York (August). Midwestern AT&T coaxial cable network opens, linking existing stations from St. Louis to Buffalo (September). • After hearings on allocations (June–September), FCC orders Freeze on stations license applications for television, while it attempts to solve problems of interference and expansion space (September).

1949 Eastern and midwestern television networks are connected, linking 32 stations in 14 cities. First televising of presidential inaugural (January). • FCC releases report which allows stations to take editorial positions if they treat opposing views fairly—later seen as birth of Fairness Doctrine (June). • FCC disallows (after October 1) certain giveaway shows with jackpots as violations of the U.S. Criminal Code prohibition on lotteries. • FCC begins television hearings, initially concentrating on choice of color processes (September).

1950 FCC allows Zenith to test Phonevision for 90 days in Chicago (February). • Editors of *Counterattack* issue *Red Channels*, which leads to more blacklisting in radio and television (June). • Korean War leads to restrictions on civilian construction, including radio and television sets, although reduced production continues. • FCC approves CBS mechanical-electronic color system (October).

1951 Televised sessions of hearings on crime by Senate committee catapult Tennessee's Senator Kefauver into prominence (January). • ABC and United Paramount Theaters merge, with UPT's Leonard Goldensen becoming top man at network (April). • First coast-to-coast live television broadcast features President Truman's address to Japanese peace treaty conference in San Francisco, uses AT&T microwave facilities costing $40,000,000 (September). • Manufacture of color television equipment is stopped for duration of Korean War (October).

1952 NBC begins the *Today* show (January). • FCC issues *Sixth Report and Order* on television allocation, ending Freeze and opening UHF band to television broadcasting (April). • First major amendments to Communications Act of 1934 become law; allow FCC to issue cease and desist orders as well as revoke licenses; require lower time charges for political ads (July). • First commercial UHF station takes to the air in Oregon (September). • Bing Crosby Enterprises demonstrates magnetic videotape recording machines to replace kinescopes (films) previously used for permanent television record (December).

The Age of Television (1952–1960)

1953 After two-year legal wrangle, required because station licenses were involved, FCC approves merger of UPT and ABC (January). • RCA and then NTSC ask FCC to adopt RCA compatible system of electronic color; and even CBS announces it will telecast with the system in the fall (June–July); FCC approves (December). • Armstrong demonstrates multiplexing system for FM—the basis of later storecasting and stereo operations (October). • FCC extends license period of television stations from one to three years, and limits ownership of stations for single owner to: five television (later extended to seven with addition of two UHF), seven AM, and seven FM stations (November).

1954 ABC and Disney studios sign a long-term contract, which generates the famous *Disneyland* and greatly strengthens ABC's competitive position (April). • Weeks of televised Army–McCarthy hearings mark the beginning of the downfall of Senator Joseph McCarthy.

1955 President Eisenhower opens news conference to first television newsfilm coverage, with films shown later after both White House approval and editing (January). • House and Senate Commerce committees issue reports critical of network monopolies, calling for major changes in regulation (February). • FCC authorizes Subsidiary Communications Authorizations (SCAs) for FM stations to trans-

mit music into stores and other business places, providing badly needed source of FM station income (March). • NBC announces *Monitor* weekend radio network program, which lasts into 1975. • Dumont television network switches over to film presentations with live coverage only for special events and sports. Network disappears altogether in September. • First major congressional investigation of television effects on juvenile delinquency ends, calling for FCC program censorship, stronger NAB code, and other changes (August). • Commercial television starts in England (September).

1956 Major film companies sell rights to "post-'48" films for television showing (January). • Ampex shows successful black-and-white videotape recorder (April).

1957 Major test of pay-TV begins in Bartlesville, Oklahoma (September). • FCC study of television network development and practices recommends more than 30 rules changes (October).

1958 FCC Commissioner Mack resigns for accepting bribes to vote for station applicant in the Miami channel 10 case (March). • FCC decides that regulation of cable television is beyond its authority because that service is not broadcasting (April). • United Press and International News Service merge to form UPI. (June). • Rumors of television quiz show rigging turn out to be true—programs are taken off the air, and investigation begins in New York (summer).

1959 In amending Section 315 of 1934 Act, exempting newscasts from equal opportunity for political candidate roles, Congress gives statutory backing to Fairness Doctrine. • Mutual network undergoes several changes of control to reduce financial pressures. • At congressional hearings, former quiz show contestants admit complicity in rigging process (October–November). To improve its image, industry forms Television Information Office, surveys audience reaction to the quiz and other scandals; networks promise more prime-time news programming.

1960 Attorney General Rogers says FCC and FTC have power to regulate payola and plugola problems, as well as quiz show rigging (January). • FCC Chairman Doerfer resigns under fire for failing to maintain arms-length distance from broadcasters he is regulating (March). • Daytime serials and most other radio network entertainment programming ends, leaving news and special events coverage. • In first basic programming statement since 1946 "Blue Book," FCC outlines the responsibilities of licensees in public interest programming. • Congress suspends Section 315 for the 1960 election of national officials, paving way for four televised "Great Debates" between Nixon and Kennedy. Those debates, especially first one, probably change course of election. • Program of airborne television transmission for educational use in the Midwest (MPATI) begins after 15 years of plans and experiments (December).

Accommodation and Adjustment (1961–1977)

1961 Minow is named FCC chairman by President Kennedy (January). He sets tone for commission by depicting television as a "vast wasteland" at NAB meeting (May). • First presidential news conference covered live by radio and television (January). • Edward R. Murrow leaves CBS to head USIA (January). • FCC approves standards for FM stereo broadcasting (April), and stations begin using new means of transmission (June). • First man-in-space television special coverage is for suborbital flight of Alan Shepard (May). • FCC ends a 16-year controversy by breaking down 13 of 25 Class I-A (clear channel) frequencies to allow more local AM stations (September).

1962 John Henry Faulk wins libel judgment of $3.5 million blacklisting case, helping to end blacklisting era (June). • Government begins financial grants to help support construction and facilities of educational television stations. • Telstar, first means of relaying television signals by space satellite, is launched into orbit for AT&T by NASA (July). • Comsat, the Communications Satellite Corporation, is formed after long congressional hearings (Sep-

tember). • Legislation is passed calling for all new television sets by early 1964 to have UHF reception capability (September).

1963 CBS and NBC begin half-hour evening newscasts, up from 15-minute length (September). • Television covers four days of tragedy following assassination of President Kennedy (November).

1964 Release of Surgeon General's report on dangers of smoking increases pressures for cigarette advertising limitation (January). • Supreme Court, in *New York Times* v. *Sullivan* case, makes conviction for libel unlikely in reporting of public officials' duties and character (March). • Networks and wire services set up election reporting service to pool results in upcoming fall election (June). Previous election campaign had brought complaints over television ads. • Subscription Television begins to provide pay-TV to homes in California cities (July), but referendum—later held to have been unconstitutional—rejects STV, and forces system to close down (November).

1965 First commercial synchronous communications satellite, Early Bird, goes into orbit and allows constant Europe–to–United States television (April).

1966 FCC takes over regulation of cable systems, calling for carriage of all local signals, same-day nonduplication, limited distant signal importation (February). • Television coverage of Vietnam War expands as fighting increases and United States becomes increasingly embroiled. • Court of Appeals for the District of Columbia says in WLBT case that audiences of stations have a right to be heard in FCC legal proceedings (March). • ABC applies to FCC for permission to merge with ITT (April), FCC twice approves on split votes, but Justice Department pressure kills merger at end of 1967. • Overmyer Network is announced as a fourth commercial chain of television stations, claiming 85 stations to take a two-hour nightly feed from Las Vegas (October).

1967 Thanks to Ford Foundation grant, NET offers first coast-to-coast network interconnected educational telecasts (January). That same month, Carnegie Commission report offers many recommendations, helping to start era of *public* television and radio. • Overmyer (now named United) Network goes on the air (May) but soon stops operations due to lack of funds (June). • FCC, in first commercial application of Fairness Doctrine, announces that antismoking spots are needed to balance cigarette ads (June). • ABC announces (August) and gets FCC approval for (September) plan for four radio networks operating on a single telephone interconnection line, each network to cater to a different type of radio program format. • Corporation for Public Broadcasting is created by Public Broadcasting Act of 1967, based on Carnegie Commission recommendations (November).

1968 ABC splits radio operation into four separate networks (January). • Heavy coverage of aftermath of Martin Luther King, Jr., assassination shows major riots in some cities, helps to prevent others (April). Two months later television covers shooting and funeral of Senator Robert Kennedy (June). • Supreme Court, in *Southwestern Cable Co.* case, upholds FCC regulatory authority over all cable television systems (June). • Television networks receive many complaints over coverage of violence in Chicago streets during Democratic convention (August). • President's Commission on Telecommunication policy issues report, sees cable supplementing broadcasting services (December).

1969 FCC resolves long-controversial status of channel 5 in Boston by lifting license from *Herald-Traveler* newspaper and awarding it to local group with no other media holdings (January). • Senator Pastore requests Surgeon General to investigate effects of television violence on viewers, especially children (March). • Public Broadcasting Service is formed to operate public television station interconnection (April). • In *Red Lion* decision, Supreme Court upholds FCC's Fairness Doctrine noting that needs and rights of viewers to diversity of views are more important than rights of broadcasters (June). • Apollo 11 mission puts man on the moon, and television takes the story around the world, with live tele-

vision from surface of moon (July). • FCC requires program origination by cable systems with more than 3,500 subscribers, but rule not effectively enforced (October). • *Sesame Street,* product of Children's Television Workshop, begins daily telecasts on public television stations and quickly wins critical and children's acclaim. • In speech at Des Moines, Iowa, Vice President Agnew attacks television news and its perceived bias. This marks beginning of Nixon administration's antimedia campaign (November).

1970 FCC adopts rule to disallow AM–FM–TV or radio-television station ownership combinations in the same market in the future, while grandfathering (allowing to stand) existing combinations (March). • FCC limits network prime-time television programming to three hours a night—the Prime Time Access Rule, or PTAR—and effectively eliminates network control of syndicated programming (May). • Television UHF channels 69–83 reallocated to nonbroadcast uses (May). • President Nixon names Clay Whitehead as first director of his new Office of Telecommunications Policy (June).

1971 Ban on radio-television advertising of cigarettes begins after Congress passes restrictive legislation (January). • *Selling of the Pentagon* documentary on CBS creates wrangle between Congress and networks, and near contempt citation for CBS' Stanton, over television documentary and general news methods (January). • FCC releases rules for license applicants to follow, defining community ascertainment process (March)—seen by some as expanding "public access" movement in broadcasting, now five years old.

1972 Surgeon General's committee report on children and television viewing suggests there may be a causal relationship between video violence and some children's subsequent actions (January) • FCC issues definitive rules for cable television, allowing but restricting scope of cable in top 100 markets (February) • Justice Department files antitrust suit against three television networks, charging excessive control of programming and advertising (April) • Administration-sponsored reorganization of public broadcasting begins, stressing local stations rather than national service—partly as a result of President Nixon's dislike of independent public affairs programming on PBS.

1973 FCC begins "re-regulation," or lessening of some administrative requirements, mainly for local radio stations. • Supreme Court rules, in BEM and DNC cases, that broadcasters are not required to sell time for editorial advertisements—a setback for advocates of greater media access (May). • Senate (Ervin) Watergate Committee hearings are carried on television for several weeks and help focus national attention on the scandal (spring and summer).

1974 Westar, first U.S. domestic communications satellite, is launched. • Television covers impeachment hearings against Nixon in first video coverage of House (July). Television covers the last days of Nixon administration, including first presidential resignation speech (August).

1975 FCC adopts rule restricting future newspaper ownership of local market radio stations (January). • Expansion of Citizens Band radio begins to create administrative headache for FCC and interference in other services, including broadcasting. • Electronic newsgathering—ENG, or use of videotape and live portable television cameras rather than film—expands rapidly among local stations. • Beginning of substantial pay-cable television operations, including Home Box Office (HBO). • NBC radio network drops *Monitor* and other programs and begins first national fulltime radio news service (June). • FCC interprets Section 315 to add more exemptions (September). • RCA Chairman Robert Sarnoff, son of David Sarnoff, is forced to resign by board of directors because of RCA's financial performance (November).

1976 After nearly two decades of discussion, Congress passes a new copyright bill to replace the 1909 act. Among many other things, it requires cable operators carrying signals to pay fees to broadcasters (October). • For the first time since 1960, presidential candidates "debate" one another (October). • In a sudden move, CBS fires Arthur Taylor as president, naming John Backe as successor and likely

eventual replacement for network founder William Paley, who announces his own plans to step down early in 1977 (October). • Federal judge in Los Angeles finds "Family Viewing Time" standard of networks and the National Association of Broadcasters TV Code to be illegal, partially because of findings of undue FCC pressure on the industry to adopt this self-regulation move. Decision places effect and impact of entire NAB radio and television code structure in doubt (November). • House Communications Subcommittee announces plans for total revision of the Communications Act of 1934 (December).

Challenge and Competition (1977–1988)

1977 Alex Haley's *Roots* is serialized in ABC miniseries with huge audience and great impact (January). • NBC ends experiment with an all-news radio network service as too few stations affiliate (May). • Congress begins an unsuccessful five-year effort to rewrite the Communications Act (May). • The first two STV (over-the-air pay-TV) stations air. • OTP is disbanded, with most functions going to the Department of Commerce (October). • "Qube" interactive cable experiment begins (it will end in 1984) in Columbus, Ohio (December).

1978 New copyright law, the first complete revision since 1909, goes into effect (January). • Showtime begins satellite distribution and becomes HBO's chief rival (March). • FCC approves distress sale and tax certificate policies to increase minority station ownership (May). • First of "rewrites" of 1934 act introduced in House (June). • Second Supreme Court "Pacifica" decision upholds FCC concern over indecent and obscene programming (June). • Magnavox markets first videodiscs.

1979 "Carnegie II" report urges vast infusion of federal funds into public broadcasting (January). • House of Representatives sessions are regularly shown by C-SPAN (March). • First station is transferred to a minority group under "distress sale" policy of FCC (April). • FTC staff recommends elimination of advertising on children's television while an FCC task force calls for enforcement of program quotas for young children's fare (November). • FM surpasses AM in size of total national radio audience.

1980 NBC and ABC begin to offer closed captions for the deaf on some programs (March). • Cable News Network (CNN) begins 24-hour news service (June). • FCC drops most of its remaining cable television rules (July). • Third FCC broadcast network inquiry completed (December). • COMSAT announces extensive DBS plans, beginning two-year push for authorization (December). • "Premiere" pay-cable network stopped by Justice Department's antitrust action (December).

1981 Complicated news day as Ronald Reagan is sworn in as President and U.S. embassy hostages return from Iran (January). • HDTV is first demonstrated in the United States. • FCC begins a "freeze" on new LPTV applications (April). • Mark Fowler becomes chairman of FCC and implements strong deregulation policy (May). • Radio licenses extended to seven years, television to five in congressional budget bill (August).

1982 Radio deregulation drops several rules for commercial stations (March). • FCC formally approves new low-power television service rules (March). • NAB drops its self-regulatory codes in a consent decree with the Justice Department (March). • Ten-year review of television violence studies released by the National Institute of Mental Health finds clear connection between what is viewed and subsequent actions.

1983 Final episode of *M*A*S*H* is most-watched program in television history (February). • FCC is changed from permanent agency to one requiring reauthorization every two years. • NPR experiences financial crisis due to overexpansion and loose management. • FCC creates MMDS or "wireless cable" service (May). • Compact discs first introduced to consumer market.

1984 Supreme Court issues "Betamax" decision allowing home taping of off-air signals (January). • As part of its settlement of a government antitrust suit, AT&T divests its local operating companies (January). • Congress passes Cable Communications Policy Act. •

Radio deregulation is expanded to cover television and public broadcasting (July). • United Satellite Communications, Inc. begins brief DBS operation using a Canadian satellite but closes up early in 1985. • RCA pulls out of videodisc market after a half-billion-dollar loss. • National candidates debate election issues on television (September–October).

1985 Seventeen-hour-long "Live Aid" concert is broadcast by satellite from Philadelphia and London to 100 countries in famine fund-raiser (July). • Home Shopping Network begins national service—first of a host of competing services (July). • Capital Cities takes over ABC network—first to change hands since 1953 (November). • First pay-per-view cable services air (November). • GE announces plans to take over RCA and its NBC networks (December). • NBC is first of commercial television networks to begin using satellite rather than land-line distribution. • FCC increases number of stations one entity can own from 21 (7 AM–7 FM–7 TV) to 36 (12-12-12).

1986 Space shuttle *Challenger* explosion is covered by television (January). • HBO is first cable service to scramble its signals to limit piracy (January). • Knight-Ridder and Times Mirror close down their videotex marketing efforts begun in 1983–84—with a combined $80 million loss (March). • NBC wins seasonal ratings race for first time in televison history (April). • Coverage by radio and television of Senate proceedings begins (June). • Laurence Tisch takes effective control of CBS (September). • Fox Broadcasting Company airs first show on way to becoming a fourth network (October). • NBC changes hands as RCA is bought by General Electric (December).

1987 NBC Radio Network is sold to Westwood One (July). • FCC drops Fairness Doctrine (August). • People meters are first used to provide Nielsen ratings (September). • Cable and VCR penetration both pass the 50 percent mark. • FCC's attempt to retain must-carry rules for cable systems is overturned in court (December).

1988 CBS sells Columbia Records, world's largest record company, to Sony. • Twenty-two-week writer's strike, ending in August, delays fall television season. • Rupert Murdoch buys *TV Guide* (August). • FCC decides that any future broadcast HDTV system must be compatible with existing receivers and will have to use no more than present broadcast spectrum (September). • Ending more than 65 years of history, WNBC (AM), the former AT&T station WEAF, is sold and becomes an all-sports outlet. • National candidates debate election issues on television (September–October). • There are more than 12,000 radio and television stations on the air.

This glossary has an essay form in preference to the typical circular set of definitions. Most terms deal with technology, although some deal with business and economics or broadcast programming. The technical basis for broadcasting is a subject for a book in itself, but it is also important as a factor in the development of electrical-electronic communication, together with politics, economics, the arts, and the social structure. Indeed, technology is less flexible than but fully intertwined with these other factors. Sometimes we can find a way around apparent technical or physical barriers—for example, by sacrificing quantity for speed, or by accepting less-than-perfect reproductions—but we can never ignore them.

Most words not found in this glossary can be readily found in a dictionary or are explained in context in the text. When a term has more than one meaning, the one most pertinent to broadcasting is used. We have tried to limit the brief explanations that follow to specialized terms and their interrelationships. Internal cross-references are supplied except where they would be unduly duplicative or easily found as, for example, within the entries for *Broadcasting* and *Broadcast Media*. Terms that are mentioned in an entry but which are discussed in fuller scope elsewhere in this glossary are printed in **boldface,** but internal cross-references are listed as (*see* Such-and-so). The most efficient way to absorb this technical terminology rapidly may be to read the entire glossary as if it were a textbook.

ABC (American Broadcasting Company. Now merged to become Capital Cities-ABC.) *See* Network.

Actors Equity *See* Unions.

Aerial *See* Antenna.

af (audio frequency) *See* Receiver.

Affiliation, Affiliates *See* Network *and* Ownership.

AFM (American Federation of Musicians) *See* Unions.

AFTRA (American Federation of Television and Radio Artists)   *See* Unions.

AGVA (American Guild of Variety Artists)   *See* Unions.

Allocation, Assignment, Allotment, Licensing   Because all radio transmissions can cause *interference* in the form of man-made *static* or degradation of signal over a greater distance than they can give service, and since different frequencies (*see* Waves) have different characteristics, the FCC must apportion certain bands of frequencies or channels to a given service, such as television broadcasting or ship-to-shore or amateur radio—*allocation;* divide an allocated frequency band to reserve designated frequencies or sub-bands for use by certain users or in specified geographical areas—*assignment;* and authorize a given user to operate a radio transmitter on a discrete frequency at a particular location or locations under specified conditions—*licensing.* In recent years, the FCC and NTIA (see below) often have used the word *allotment* rather than *assignment* for the second stage (and sometimes the first stage) of this process, and NTIA has added to the confusion by using the word *assignment* for what the FCC would call *licensing.* (For a period in the 1950s and 1960s, the FCC itself confused "allocation" and "assignment" in some public documents.) Because federal government agencies use about half the radio spectrum, allocation, which is circumscribed worldwide by international agreements and treaties (*see* ITU), and assignment for these stations is done by the *Interdepartment Radio Advisory Committee (IRAC),* now a part of the *National Telecommunications and Information Administration* of the U.S. Department of Commerce. The FCC standards for granting a broadcast station license involve citizenship, character, financing, and technical competence or facilities. Before a license is issued, a *construction permit (CP)* gives the potential licensee authority to build the station. Licenses are granted for distinct periods—three years until recently, now five (television) or seven (radio), in broadcasting—and may be revoked for cause. Sometimes, when the FCC has many applications for the same channel, it holds *comparative hearings.* When unexpected demand or unexpected technical difficulties arise with a given service or allocation to it, the FCC institutes a *freeze* on new licenses until the problem is resolved. In choosing between competing applicants—particularly between different services applying for the same band of frequencies, as in the recurrent conflict between television broadcasting and land mobile for the UHF television band—the FCC must make its decision in light of the touchstone criterion set forth in the Communications Act: the *public interest, convenience, and/or necessity.*

Alternating Currents (AC)   *See* Vacuum Tube.

Alternators   *See* Transmitter.

Amateur (also known as a *ham*)   An individual interested in radio technique solely with a personal aim and without pecuniary interest, characterized by self-training and technical investigations. To become an amateur operator, a person must pass tests of technical knowledge and ability to communicate in **Morse code,** as contrasted to the simpler requirements for **Citizens Band** (CB) operators. In exchange, amateurs may, depending on their class of skill, use much higher power than CBers may, a variety of frequencies, some permitting very long range communication and techniques forbidden to CBers. Many amateurs build or modify their own equipment. Amateurs frequently provide outstanding public service in times of disaster; their spectacular breakthroughs in technological and operational development contributed particularly to early broadcasting; and the military and naval forces, especially during World War I, eagerly recruited their services as trained radio operators. The frequencies allocated to amateurs throughout the spectrum permit them to communicate with other amateurs around the world. Amateurs communicate "person-to-person"—although they may start a conversation by calling "CQ," a general call to anyone who may be listening. They do *not* "broadcast" intentionally to the general public, but anyone with the proper receiving equipment may listen.

AM Channels   On the standard (AM) broadcast band, 107 channels are divided into three categories with five classes of stations operating on them. A *clear channel* is one on which only one *dominant station* operates at night for several thousand miles, although a number of low to medium power *secondary stations* may share it with the dominant station during the day. The United States, Canada, Mexico, and other North American countries are signatories to the North American Regional Broadcasting Agreement (*NARBA*), negotiated in 1937 and revised in 1950. Each country has channels on which one of its stations is dominant. The treaty also provides that each dominant station use at least 50,000 watts of power; in the United States, 50 kw is also the upper limit because of a "Sense of the Senate" resolution in the late 1930s. (*See also* Waves *and* Bandwidth.)

The following are the ways in which standard broadcast (AM) channels are presently classified in the United States:

60 **Clear channels**—one dominant station in most instances.
   24 Class 1A—one U.S. dominant station on each, with only 1–7 other, lower power stations sharing the channel by day and none by night.

   17   —dominant station in Canada, Mexico, Cuba, etc., may be used by some U.S. lower power stations by day.

   19 Class 1B—two or, in some cases, more stations sharing each channel at night, with from 1 to 40 or more Class II U.S. stations and others in other countries sharing the channel during the day.

41 **Regional channels** (Class III)—each generally used by from 20 to 70 or more stations spaced several hundred miles apart, using 5 to 50 kw of power.

6 **Local channels** (Class IV)—each generally used by 150 to 175 stations using low power (250 watts at night, 1 kw during the day), often spaced only a few tens of miles apart so that their tower lights sometimes can be seen farther than the signal reaches.

107 Channels from 540 through 1,600 kHz. Since each channel is 10 kHz wide, the total standard broadcast band is from 535 through 1,605 kHz. Additional channels soon may be added between 1,605 and 1,705 kHz.

Amperes *See* Circuit.

Amplification *See* Receiver *and* Vacuum Tube.

Amplitude Modulation (AM) *See* Modulation.

Antenna, Aerial A metallic device used for the sending and receiving of electromagnetic waves; often in the form of a tower or series of towers but frequently a horizontal length of wire, often a *parabolic reflector* or *dish*, and sometimes a short vertical *whip*. Most broadcasting stations use vertical antennas; shipboard stations string antennas between the vessel's masts. For efficiency, an antenna must bear a relationship to the wavelength (*see* Waves) of the frequency for which it is designed, usually one-half or one-quarter wavelength. If it does not bear such a relationship, the antenna will not *resonate* properly to the transmitted or received wave. Hence, since wavelength increases as frequency diminishes, we find that standard (AM) broadcast stations use their entire tower as an antenna, whereas FM broadcast stations, on a much higher frequency, have only a small antenna on top of the tower. The international radiotelegraph distress frequency, 500 kHz, is very short to use as a wavelength for long-range use over water, but it was chosen many years ago because antennas for that frequency could fit physically between the masts of the typical oceangoing ship. A VHF television or FM receiving antenna is roughly five feet wide, whereas a UHF television antenna—of higher frequency and thus shorter wavelength—is less than two feet wide. At even higher frequencies, precisely aimed *dishes* from 2 to 100 feet in diameter are used to focus the extremely short waves precisely onto the antenna element located at their focal point. It is also possible to "aim" huge antenna arrays on the shortwave (high-frequency) band and even to construct a directional system with towers to reinforce and cancel one another so that a standard broadcast (AM) station causes minimal interference in one or more directions. *Directional antenna (DA)* installations are particularly useful for AM today, since the FCC has put a large number of stations on almost every **channel.** Transmitting antennas can be oriented to supply *horizontal, vertical,* or *circular polarization,* the first two of which require similarly oriented receiving antennas for efficient reception. These techniques generally permit a reduction in interference so that stations on the same frequency can be located closer together.

AP (Associated Press)   *See* News.

ASCAP (American Society of Composers, Authors and Publishers)   *See* Copyright.

Aspect Ratio   *See* Television Signals.

Assignment   *See* Allocation.

ATV   *See* HDTV.

Audience   *See* Communication.

Audio   Of or pertaining to audible sound, or its broadcasting, or recording and reproduction.

Audion   *See* Vacuum Tube.

Automation   The totality of mechanical and electronic techniques and equipment used to achieve control of a process, equipment, or system. Many automated radio stations use automatic playing of music tapes and recorded commercials to cut down on use of engineers and other personnel. In its favor, automation cuts down the boring, repetitious, and complex tasks that often lead to on-air errors, particularly at station-break time ("panic periods"). More and more broadcast equipment, including transmitters, is operated by unattended automation. Most automated devices today are computer controlled.

Bandwidth   The bandwidth, the amount of electromagnetic *spectrum* space efficiently occupied by a **channel,** depends on the amount of information that one wants to transmit. For example, a dot in Morse code takes an appreciable fraction of a second to form but requires only one "bit" of information: the telegraph key is momentarily depressed, and a brief spurt of electricity is sent down the line or to the transmitter. In a radiotelegraph system, such a signal requires only about 50 *Hz* of bandwidth. (A *Hertz*, or Hz, is equivalent to one cycle per second of alternating current; a kiloHertz [kHz] to one thousand cycles per second, a megaHertz [MHz] to one million cycles per second. The terms kilocycle [kc] or megacycle [mc] were used until the 1960s, when it was internationally agreed to honor Heinrich Hertz, one of the earliest wireless experimenters.) Voice requires more: although your hi-fi system may state on its nameplate that it handles audio frequencies

from "20 to 20,000 Hz," the human voice rarely requires more than 5,000 Hz (or 5 kiloHertz or 5 kHz) of bandwidth. In fact, the typical telephone system transmits only some 2,500 Hz, accounting for the tinny sound of a telephone conversation, which has lost its highest and lowest voice frequencies. This is all that is needed for maximum intelligibility, although radio stations using telephone lines for networking or picking up programs from remote locations have special equipment at both ends to extend the response of the telephone system to 5 kHz or, in the case of high-fidelity FM, as much as 15 kHz. A single picture on a television set, requiring only a tiny fraction of a second to form, contains a great deal of information—but requires 4.5 MHz (*see* Television Signals). High-definition television (HDTV) requires even more bandwidth, one of the reasons for its slow rate of adoption in many countries.

   If the necessary bandwidth is not available, it is possible to transmit the information by sampling—the human eye and ear can "remember" through such processes as persistence of vision, which makes it possible to perceive motion in a series of still pictures on a film—or by presenting the information in sequential rather than simultaneous form, as in television *scanning*. For example, some early experimenters with the telegraph used a separate wire **circuit** for each of the 26 letters of the alphabet, a logical although inefficient and expensive configuration. One of Morse's and his associates' contributions was the use of a code for sending the letters of the message one after the other as electrical pulses through one wire. (*See also* Television's Early Technological Development.)

Base   *See* Land Mobile.

Bell System   The former name for the American Telephone & Telegraph Company and its operating companies, Long Lines Department, and manufacturing arm (Western Electric). In 1984, the Bell System (familiarly known as *Ma Bell*) was broken up as the result of an antitrust agreement with the Justice Department. While AT&T is still in the long-distance, manufacturing, and computer fields, there are now seven independent "Baby Bells" or regional Bell operating companies (*RBOC*); competition in long-distance carriage; manufacturing; new technologies such as integrated service digital networks (ISDNs), and so on, at all but the level of the local operating companies . . . which themselves want to get into cable television.

Beta *See* Recordings.

Binaural *See* Modulation.

Blanking Interval *See* Television Signals.

BMI (Broadcast Music, Inc.) *See* Copyright.

Boosters *See* Satellite.

Broadcasting A radiocommunication service of transmissions intended to be received directly by the general public. This service may include transmissions of sounds—**radio broadcasting**—or transmissions by **television, facsimile,** or other means. Broadcasting—to everyone—should be distinguished from two-way or point-to-point communication, which was called *narrowcasting* in the early 1920s. *Narrowcasting* now refers to the programmer's focus on a specific audience rather than on the public as a whole or on a technical bandwidth limitation. (*See* Mass Communication.)

Broadcast Journalism *See* News.

Broadcast Media In the United States, standard broadcast (AM) stations; frequency modulation (FM) stations, both commercial and noncommercial educational; television stations, both commercial and noncommercial educational; international (shortwave) stations; and experimental facsimile and other classes of service.

Cable (also *CATV* or *Community Antenna Television*) Although the word "cable" was used after the mid-1850s to refer to underwater telegraph lines, particularly between continents, and still has that connotation, since the 1950s it has been used as a shortened form of "cable television," a system for distributing television (and sometimes radio) to homes in an area by means of wire rather than radiocommunication. Although systems from the late 1940s into the 1960s typically provided very few channels and were sometimes a cooperative or nonprofit public service, modern systems can provide

from 35 to 120 or more channels and operate as profit-making businesses. In addition to providing interference-free reception of local stations, modern systems bring in signals from distant cities and sometimes provide *local origination*, government, educational, and *public access* channels and *pay-cable* service (*see* Pay-TV). The *"wired city"* is a proposal that telecommunication services in the United States, including television and access to computers, will and should eventually be distributed by a *wideband* (great information-carrying capacity) cable directly to individual homes. Telephone companies and CATV operators both are eyeing this possibility of a new line of business.

A CATV system typically consists of a *head end*—the location where signals from local stations or microwave (*see* Waves) or **satellite** signals are picked up and amplified for retransmission through the system—several miles of *trunk lines* either on poles or underground, and individual *service drops* or wired connections to individual subscribers, together with the various amplifiers and other devices that are needed to push the signal through the system. A *two-way cable system* permits some signal transmission from the subscriber's home back to the head end—for remote reading of utility meters, information as to whether a *pay-cable* or **pay-TV** signal is being used, and so forth. In the 1970s some experimentation and planning went on for *interactive cable systems* allowing a complete two-way voice and picture communication process. Most CATV systems charge subscribers a monthly fee for each *tier* (such as basic or pay) of service. A trend is toward multiple system operators (*MSOs*), who own or operate cable systems in several communities. Most regulation of cable is through municipal *franchising*, although some states and the federal government (FCC) have promulgated some regulations and standards. In the 1980s, the FCC pre-empted much local regulation but did not install its own. In Europe, CATV would be called *rediffusion*, a term applied to wired radio (particularly in the United Kingdom and the Soviet Union) as well as wired television. A *master antenna system (MATV)* typically serves only a single institution or apartment house and rarely offers the auxiliary services mentioned above. An *SMATV* system is an MATV that receives its programming directly from a satellite dish.

Call Letters Combinations of letters and sometimes numbers used to identify radio stations over the air. Blocks of initial letters are assigned to a particular country, a practice started as a result of the London International Radiotelegraph Conference of 1912. The United States has been assigned all of the blocks with the initial letters W, K and N, and much of A, although both A and N calls tend to be used mostly by the armed forces. Several N (for Navy) stations were used for early radio experimentation. In broadcasting, W is generally used east of the Mississippi and K west, with a few exceptions—usually older stations such as KYW, Philadelphia, and KDKA, Pittsburgh. An X following a number generally means an experimental station (9XM, 8XK, W2XR) with numbers in these early calls, and in amateur licenses, representing geographical districts. Some calls (FM in the early 1940s, LPTV today) used two digits to indicate the assigned channel. Although some pioneer stations still have three-letter call signs, most are four-letter, with many FM and television stations using those suffixes to create five- and six-letter calls (WNYC-TV). Stations may select their own call signs, within FCC guidelines and rules, leading to ingenious acronyms (WIOD, Miami = Wonderful Isle of Dreams; WGN, Chicago = World's Greatest Newspaper, the original licensee the *Chicago Tribune*) or associative meanings (KOP = Detroit Police Department; WILK = Wilkes-Barre, Pennsylvania).

Camcorder *See* Recordings.

Carrier Wave *See* Modulation *and* Transmitter.

Cartridge *See* Recordings.

Cassette *See* Recordings.

Cathode *See* Vacuum Tube.

CATV (community antenna television) *See* Cable.

C-Band *See* Satellite.

CBS (Columbia Broadcasting System) *See* Network.

CCD (controlled capacitance discharge) *See* Television Camera Tubes.

CD (compact disc) *See* Recordings.

Cellular Telephone *See* Land Mobile.

Chain Broadcasting *See* Network.

Channel A channel is an arbitrarily defined group of radio frequencies occupying a segment of the spectrum wide enough to permit operation of a station of a given service. For example, a channel for a standard (AM) broadcasting station is 10 kHz wide, but one for a television broadcasting station is 600 times wider (6 MHz) in order to handle the additional information of a picture.

Character Generator A device (often called a *Chyron*, for a popular brand name) for inserting titles and other words and material into a television picture.

Chicago School A laid-back approach to television variety and drama, as typified by much network programming from Chicago in the 1950s and 1960s.

Chip *See* Vacuum Tube.

Circuit A pathway which ends at the same place it began. In *electrical circuits*, electricity flows from the source, through a switch or other control device and a *load*, and back to the source. The source may be a *generator*, a rotating machine that produces electricity when spinning; a *battery*, a chemical source of electricity; or, as in the case of radio, a *transmitter*. The load may be a lamp, a motor, a heater, or something similar that does a certain amount of work—produces light, motion, heat, and so on. If there is no load, there is also no *resistance*—an electrical property measured in *ohms* related to the amount of energy (*watts*) the load requires to do work; and, if a conducting path, a wire, connects one side of the source to the other without a load, we have a *short-circuit*, a condition demanding an infinite amount of electricity, which quickly results in a burned-out wire or generator—or fuse, if such a protection was inserted in the circuit. There are two basic electrical circuits: *series*, which is like a chain, through each link of which all the *current* flows;

and *parallel,* which requires both sides of the source to be linked to each load, as, for example, all outlets in a house must have two wires connected to them. With a parallel circuit, one part of the load may be disconnected without having any effect on the others; with a series circuit, the removal of any part of the circuit "breaks the chain." Current is measured in *amperes,* calculated by dividing the *voltage* in the circuit (the amount of "pressure," measured in *volts*) by the resistance.

In a simple electrical telegraph circuit, the elements consist of batteries (the source), a key (a switch which can be manipulated on and off very rapidly), the wire connecting the sending and receiving stations, a relay at the receiving **station,** and a *return wire* to the other terminal of the battery. (Actually, since the *ground* will conduct electricity, in most cases the earth itself is used for the return part of the circuit, with both the return wire from the relay at the receiving station and one terminal from the battery at the sending station connected to it.) The *relay,* or *sounder* in early telegraph language, consists of a fine coil of wire wound around a piece of soft iron, the thinness of the wire providing some resistance in the circuit. Electricity passing through the coil converts the iron core into an *electromagnet,* which is set up to attract or repulse another piece of iron or steel that hits it with an audible "click" and then is pulled away by a spring as soon as the current is off. These clicks form the dots and dashes of **Morse code.**

A radio circuit is comparable: the source of electricity is a **transmitter,** which is "keyed" or "modulated" much as the electrical telegraph circuit is keyed manually. However, instead of needing a wire conductor to connect sending and receiving stations, radio **waves** can be sent through the atmosphere from an antenna connected to the transmitter and through the ground for a return. A circuit, in radio terms, generally if a little loosely applies to a two-way pathway using a particular frequency or **channel.** It may also refer to the arrangements of components within a transmitter, receiver, or other electronic device—the design of the unit, in electronic terms. This latter usage is derived from the fact that *electrons,*

tiny units of energy, must travel in a circuit from source back to source to do any work.

Citizens Band (CB)   A two-way radio service that any member of the public, not just truckers, may use. Simple to operate, CB consists of low-power fixed and mobile stations intended for personal or business communication, radio signaling, control of remote devices, and almost anything else not prohibited. It differs from broadcasting in that it is a short-range point-to-point service, and it differs from amateur radio in that amateurs have technical skills and use radio more as a hobby than for personal or business communication. CBers may not engage in technical experimentation. Some channels have been formally or informally assigned to special uses: channel 9 for emergencies, channel 19 for truckers. Citizens Band radio was established by the FCC in 1958 but grew slowly until the mid-1970s, when suddenly millions of units were sold, perhaps sparked by the desire of motorists to avoid traffic police ("smokey") enforcing speed limits during a gasoline shortage, and the service assumed the status of a fad complete with its own songs and movies and references on comedy television shows. In 1977 the number of CB channels was increased from 23 to 40 because of demand for more space. (*See also* Amateur.)

Clear Channel   *See* Channel.

Closed Caption   *See* Modulation.

Closed-circuit   Not broadcast; availability intentionally restricted as to location through use of wired circuits or radio frequency band used.

Coaxial Cable   A cable consisting of two concentric metallic conductors—a thin wire or pipe in the middle and, separated by a carefully and evenly sized insulator, an outer conductor of woven metal mesh or a larger pipe. Most coaxial cable is flexible with an outer plastic sheath for insulation and mechanical protection; the kind that has rigid piping generally is restricted to short runs carrying high current, such as from a powerful transmitter to an antenna. Coaxial cable can carry a tremendous **bandwidth** and has made long-distance—beyond the range of off-the-air pickup—television transmission or program distribution practical. Much of the intercity television (and telephone) network (and, indeed, most video signals carried by wire within a studio or in a **cable** system) requires coaxial cables, since ordinary wires do not carry a television signal satisfactorily. The rest of the intercity network uses wideband *microwave* (*see* Waves) point-to-point transmission and reception systems. Although modern practice has produced cables utilizing several coaxial conductors independently covered by the same outer sheath, permitting very wide bandwidths to be carried, the new *fiber optic,* an extremely fine thread of fiberglass modulated with light waves by a **laser** and capable of carrying a tremendous amount of information, is being increasingly used in their stead.

Coherent   *See* Laser.

Coherer   *See* Receiver.

Coincidental   *See* Ratings.

Color, Colorburst, Color Wheel   *See* Television Signals.

Common Carrier   A transportation or communication activity—bus lines, telegraph and telephone companies—which undertakes to accept for transmission at published nondiscriminatory rates all correspondence—freight, passengers, messages—tendered by members of the public. A common carrier is often a *public utility,* an organization operating under a franchise from a government and charged with certain activities necessary for the public welfare, that accepts regulation of rates in exchange for monopoly or near-monopoly status. By law, broadcasting is not considered a common carrier and is not regulated as such for rates or program content. On the other hand, while cable might better fit under the "common carrier" label, it actually fits into both classifications (or neither one) because of special legislation, FCC rules, and court decisions.

Communication   The transmission and reception of information through any medium between and among humans and/or machines and/or animals (*see also* Mass Communication, Mass Media). *Information,* according to the theory developed by Shannon, Weaver, and

others, is anything (particularly, but not exclusively, knowledge and intelligence) that someone desires to have transmitted, together with any intelligence transmitted—intentionally or not. *Intelligence* is an old word for "news," information of military value, as well as information understandable to or capable of being deduced by the recipient or *audience,* the eventual recipient(s) of a message. A *message* is intentionally coded (into speech or some other form) and transmitted as information. Most messages have *meaning,* which means that there is a sharing of concepts between a communicator and the audience. A *symbol* or *sign* or code has meaning to the extent that its connotations and denotations are mutually understood by communicator and audience. (*See also* Signal.)

Community Antenna Television   *See* Cable.

Comparative Hearings   *See* Allocation.

Compatible   A new technological advance is said to be compatible if it will *not* render existing receivers or other equipment obsolete.

Conduction   *See* Radiation.

Conductivity   *See* Waves.

Conglomerate   *See* Ownership.

Construction Permit (CP)   *See* Allocation.

Continuous Wave (CW)   *See* Modulation.

Copyright, Performing Rights Societies   Literally, the power to control the right to copy a literary work (such as books or plays), music, paintings. The copyright system was established in Article I, Section 8 of the U.S. Constitution (*see* Invention, Innovation, Patents). Although one copyrights a piece by labeling it, prior to publication or distribution, with a © or the word "copyright," the name of the copyright owner, and the year, it is wise to *register* the copyright with the U.S. Register of Copyrights in order to have dated proof of notice of copyright. *Infringement* of copyright—copying without permission—is a federal offense. A 1976 copyright law (effective January 1, 1978) puts obligations on CATV for the first time, and grants copyright for the author's life plus 50 years. *Performing rights societies* such as *ASCAP* (American Society of Composers, Authors and Publishers) and *BMI* (Broadcast Music, Incorporated) administer the copyrights held on most music for the benefit of the copyright holder(s); some European music is controlled by *SESAC*, Incorporated. Started in 1914 when composer Victor Herbert objected to the playing of his music in a restaurant, benefiting the restaurant but not Herbert, ASCAP licenses performance of all music owned by persons for whom it acts as agent. (Recording, dramatic, and other rights are licensed case by case.) Each station pays a percentage of its gross revenues for the right to play all ASCAP music. Each year, ASCAP distributes these monies to its members according to a complex formula and following a sample survey of actual renditions of each piece of music. In 1939–1940, ASCAP raised its rates to the point where broadcasters rebelled and organized a rival organization, BMI. Today, most stations have contracts with both organizations—although the relationship is never placid and is presently complicated by court supervision.

Counterprogramming *See* Programming.

Cross-media Ownership *See* Ownership.

Crystal Control *See* Transmitter.

Crystal Set *See* Receiver *and* Vacuum Tube.

Current *See* Circuit.

DAT (digital audiotape) *See* Recordings.

DBS (direct broadcast satellite) *See* Satellite.

Decoherer *See* Receiver.

Deregulation Policy of FCC (and other government agencies) after 1980 to remove existing regulations and rely on market forces such as competition for control of potential excesses.

Detection *See* Vacuum Tube.

Diaries *See* Ratings.

Digital/Analog Digital signals are a series of discrete "on" or "off" conditions, based on rapid sampling rather than a continuously varying one as in an analog signal. Digital inherently is able to ignore static and other interference and is capable of very high quality reproduction (as in audio *CD* or *DAT* recordings), but it requires a far greater bandwidth than does an analog signal. Almost all computers use digital signals, and the newest (and most expensive) models of all types of other devices

are now designed for digital processing.

Diode *See* Vacuum Tube.

Diplexing *See* Modulation.

Direct Current (DC) *See* Vacuum Tube.

Direct Wave *See* Waves.

Directional Antenna (DA) *See* Antenna.

Discrete *See* Laser *and* Modulation.

Dish *See* Antenna.

Dominant Station *See* Channel.

Dot Sequential *See* Television Signals.

Downlink *See* Satellite.

Duopoly *See* Ownership.

DX-ing A hobby, quite popular in the first decades of radio, of attempting to receive stations far beyond normal reception range. Most stations in a given city cooperated by going off the air one night a week, the *"silent night,"* so that listeners could pick up stations elsewhere in the country. Silent nights had stopped by the late 1920s as more stations went on the air, competition increased, and broadcasting became more familiar, but DX-ing continues today among amateur and some broadcasting listeners, particularly of FM and television near the height of the 11-year sunspot cycle when freak reception is more common.

Edison Effect *See* Vacuum Tube.

Editorials *See* News.

Educational Television *See* ETV.

Electrical Circuit *See* Circuit.

Electrical Transcription *See* Recordings.

Electromagnet *See* Circuit.

Electromagnetic Energy A class of phenomena such as radio waves, heat (infrared) waves, light waves, X-rays, gamma rays, and cosmic rays. These waves are propagated at the speed of light—approximately 186,300 miles per second, or 300,000,000 meters per second—and differ chiefly in the degree to which waves of various frequencies or lengths are reflected from or pass through different physical media. The electromagnetic spectrum is composed of all types of waves, from electrical and radio waves alternating a few times per second through light waves with frequencies measured in billions of Hertz (cycles per second) and even beyond. (*See* Waves.)

Electrons   *See* Circuit.

ENG (electronic news-gathering), **EFP** (electronic field production), **SNG** (satellite news-gathering).   *ENG* uses portable, battery-operated electronic equipment—microphones, television cameras, VTRs—for acquiring television **news,** in contrast to the use of portable film cameras for this purpose. In the process, tapes are taken back to the station or sent by means of a mobile or portable transmitter, as a **remote.** Editing may be done in the field or at the station, and the coverage may be aired "live" if the signal can be sent back to the station by microwave or by helicopter or other relay. *EFP* is the use of similar equipment for the field production of more complex programs or commercials. *SNG* is the use of a space *satellite,* rather than microwave, transmitter truck, with the signal received at the station. With SNG, the station or network can receive news program content from almost any place on earth. ENG became dominant in many markets in the 1970s after development of portable color equipment (including *time base correctors* permitting the use of less expensive videotape recorders over the air), in spite of its high initial cost, partly because it permitted immediate replay of pictorial material without film processing delays.

ETV, ITV, PTV (*educational, instructional,* and *public* television)   Originally *educational* broadcasting was the generic term for classroom instructional, adult education, and cultural programming, particularly when aired over non-commercial educational stations. *Public* broadcasting, popularized by a 1967 Carnegie Commission report, generally refers to broadcasting on noncommercial stations. *Instructional* television generally has been restricted to in-class or other **closed-circuit** or videotaped uses. The same descriptive words can be applied, with suitable modification, to radio.

Ex Parte   Contact with a regulatory body or court by one party only to a dispute.

Facsimile   A system of **telecommunication** for the transmission of fixed images (*television* transmits moving or transient images) with a view to their reception in a permanent (paper) or semipermanent form. Includes the *wirephoto* process used by wire services to send pictures to newspapers. Experiments with broadcast facsimile were conducted in the 1940s, and industrial interest in the technique was being exploited into the 1970s. Systems using blank lines in a television picture to transmit "pages" of information to the home video screen, such as Britain's CEEFAX, are **teletext,** not facsimile. In the late 1980s, inexpensive and reliable equipment made "FAX" transmissions over regular dial telephone circuits very popular among businesses of all sizes. (*See also* Television's Early Technical Development.)

Family Viewing   *See* Programming.

FAX   *See* Facsimile.

Feedback   Feedback is any situation whereby a portion of the output of any process or system influences the input into the system in the future. *Negative feedback* is used to control or "dampen" the process; *positive feedback* reinforces the ongoing process and is usually detrimental. In **mass communication,** any means of responding to a particular message (letters to the editor, sales, audience ratings) is an example of feedback.

Fiber Optic   *See* Coaxial Cable.

Fields   *See* Television Signals.

Field Sequential   *See* Television Signals.

Filament   *See* Vacuum Tube.

Film Chain   *See* Television Camera Tubes.

Fixed   *See* Land Mobile.

Fleming Valve   *See* Vacuum Tube.

Formats (Program)   *See* Programming.

Formats (Videotape)   *See* Recordings.

Frames   *See* Television Signals.

Franchising   *See* Cable.

Freeze   *See* Allocation.

Frequency   *See* Waves.

Frequency Modulation (FM)   *See* Modulation.

Galvanometer *See* Receiver.

Generations *See* Recordings.

Generator *See* Circuit.

Geostationary Orbit (GSO) *See* Satellite.

Grandfathering Allowing existing situations to continue regardless of new rules.

Grid *See* Vacuum Tube.

Ground *See* Circuit.

Groundwave *See* Waves.

Guard Bands *See* Television Signals.

Ham *See* Amateur.

HBO (Home Box Office) A major pay-cable service. *See* Cable.

HDTV (high-definition television) Any of several means of improving television to the quality level of 16 mm or even 35 mm film. While far advanced in Japan *(MUSE)* and Europe using *DBS*, HDTV may become a production standard in the United States (for television programs and feature "films") rather than a direct-to-home delivery system in the foreseeable future. For a number of reasons—primarily the political urgency of ensuring that existing NTSC-standard sets (*see* Television Signals) are not rendered obsolete—the United States is experimenting with **ATV** (advanced television), which is *compatible* rather than incompatible with existing sets, even though it may not be capable of true high definition.

Head End *See* Cable.

Helical Scan *See* Recordings.

Hertz (Hz) *See* Bandwidth.

Heterodyne *See* Receiver.

High Band *See* Recordings.

Holography *See* Laser.

IATSE (International Alliance of Theatrical Stage Employees) *See* Unions.

IBEW (International Brotherhood of Electrical Workers) *See* Unions.

Iconoscope *See* Television Camera Tubes.

Image Dissectors *See* Television Camera Tubes.

Image Orthicon *See* Television Camera Tubes.

Incoherent *See* Laser.

Induction *See* Radiation.

Information *See* Communication.

Information Theory *See* Morse Code.

Infringement *See* Copyright.

Innovation *See* Invention.

Instructional Television *See* ETV.

Integrated Solid State Circuits *See* Vacuum Tube.

Intelligence *See* Communication.

Interactive Cable Systems *See* Cable.

Interference *See* Allocation.

Interlaced *See* Television Signals.

Intermediate Frequency (IF) *See* Receiver.

International Telecommunication Union (ITU) A specialized United Nations agency, founded in 1865 as the International Telegraph Union, particularly concerned with radio frequency *allocation* matters.

Invention, Innovation, Patents *Invention* is the act or process of developing something new—a device, a process, a thing—through study and experimentation. *Innovation* is the introduction of an invention into use or into the marketplace. The U.S. Constitution (Article I, Section 8) empowers the federal government to issue *patents,* which guarantee to the inventor exclusive rights for 17 years to manufacture, or to *license* the manufacture of the invention, in exchange for monetary *royalties.* In exchange, the invention goes into the public domain after that period, or it may be renewed once. The intent of a patent system is to encourage both invention and use of that invention widely, rather than keep it as a *trade secret* for an indefinite period. (*See also* Copyright.)

Ionosphere *See* Waves.

IRAC (Interdepartment Radio Advisory Committee) Now part of **NTIA.** *See* Allocation.

ITFS (instructional television fixed service) Channels set aside in the 12 GHz band for televised school instruction; channels are often leased to MDS operators at night.

Kinescope Recorder (Kine) *See* Recordings *and* Television Camera Tubes.

Ku-Band *See* Satellite.

Land Mobile A family of radiocommunication services, generally the **safety and special services**—police, forestry—but sometimes the **common carrier** services such as mobile telephone. Includes **cellular** telephones that enable one to keep in touch over a wide geographical area, with no loss of quality, because of continuous computer-directed assignment of the call to the closest transmitter-receiver site from which the call can be connected to the wire network. Mobile units in cars and airplanes may be associated with *fixed* or *base* stations that communicate with a number of mobile units. Since the late 1940s, the growth of land mobile has clashed with the growth or preservation of television broadcast frequency bands, since both services need vast amounts of spectrum space with similar characteristics.

Laser An acronym for *l*ight *a*mplification by *s*timulated *e*mission of *r*adiation. Any one of a number of devices that can convert incident electromagnetic radiation of mixed frequency *(incoherent)* energy to one or more very specific or *discrete* frequencies of highly amplified and *coherent* visible radiation. Can be used for carrying great amounts of information or, because of the coherent nature of the radiation and its sharply aimed focus, for cutting materials; also for *holography,* a technique for recording and reproducing three-dimensional "pictures."

License *See* Invention *and* Allocation.

Licensee *See* Ownership.

Licensing *See* Allocation.

Line-of-Sight *See* Waves.

Lines *See* Television Signals.

Local Oscillator *See* Receiver.

Local Origination *See* Cable.

Long Playing (LP) *See* Recordings.

Longwave *See* Waves.

LPTV (low-power television) A television service designed to service extremely small areas. Supposedly intended for minority groups and others with a programming affinity. Since there effectively are no multiple ownership restrictions, some large corporations applied for hundreds of channels in various localities.

Mass Communication Simultaneous (or nearly so) process of essentially one-way communication from a single source addressed to a mass audience. The message usually is reproduced in quantity through mechanical or electronic devices. A *mass audience* is more than two undifferentiated persons voluntarily engaged in the same communications behavior or activity, but not necessarily interacting in other ways. **Feedback,** often economic, may alter the content of mass communication but does not alter the one-way nature of a given mass communication event. (*See* Communication.)

Mass Media The means or channels of mass communication: primarily newspapers, magazines, radio (sound) broadcasting, television broadcasting, motion pictures, and, secondarily, the theater, recordings, and books. Heterogeneity of content within the medium, but not necessarily any specific item or example, and voluntary attention by the audience are common characteristics of the mass media.

Master *See* Recordings.

Master Antenna (MATV) *See* Cable.

Matrix *See* Modulation.

MDS or **MMDS** (multipoint distribution service or multichannel multipoint distribution service) A microwave service, sometimes using channels leased from *ITFS,* typically used to provide *HBO* and other pay-cable services in cities where cable is not yet fully installed. The MDS operator generally leases special *downconverter* tuning devices that pick up the microwave signal and convert it to the television frequencies expected by the television set.

Meaning *See* Communication.

Mechanical Scanning *See* Television's Early Technological Development.

Message *See* Communication.

Microgroove *See* Recordings.

Microwave *See* Waves.

Modulated Continuous Wave (MCW) *See* Modulation.

Modulation A radio signal generally consists of a *carrier wave* and one or two *sidebands.* [Sophisticated systems such as *single sideband* do not strictly follow this pattern, but they are not used for broadcasting, except for television's *vestigial sideband* (*see* Television Signals).] The carrier wave **signal** generally is on the center frequency of the **channel** on which the **transmitter** is operating and, unless used in an "off-on" manner to transmit **Morse code,** carries no intelligence itself. The *information* or intelligence or *message* is carried in the form of *modulated* sidebands. Sometimes the modulation is a variation in the strength or *amplitude* of the sideband; sometimes it is a swing of *frequency* within the channel; sometimes it has other forms, such as *pulses.* The first two (amplitude modulation, or AM, and frequency modulation, or FM) are used for broadcasting. AM takes up less spectrum space but is more prone to interference on most bands. Television uses FM for sound and AM for picture. Some radiotelegraph systems use the modulation of a tone, interrupted to produce dots and dashes, on a *continuous wave (CW)* or *modulated CW* transmitter. Within each channel there may be space to put additional information; a telegraph signal, using very little **bandwidth,** can generally be added to a telephone channel, with the telegraph sound being filtered out at the telephone. In addition, the bandwidth of a channel can often be divided and made more useful by *diplexing* or *multiplexing*—inserting two or more signals on the same channel in such a way that each may be retrieved independently at the receiving end. The FCC has allowed FM broadcast stations to obtain a *Subsidiary Communications Authorization (SCA)* that will permit it to use one or more *subcarriers* within the total channel bandwidth of 200 kHz but outside the modulated frequency swing of the main program channel.

These subcarriers generally are used for *stereophonic (stereo)* music transmissions. In a *binaural* system, the human condition of two ears feeding one brain is extended backward from ears to two loudspeakers, two amplifiers, two signals from the receiver, and two microphones. Stereo permits listeners with proper equipment to hear the music stereophonically and other listeners to hear it *monaurally.* In recent years *quadrasonic* systems, which give the illusion of four sound sources surrounding the listener, have been developed, some using the *discrete* system—four separate isolated channels fed to four speakers—and others the *matrix* system—reduction and encoding of four channels into two, and decoding back into four at the receiver or player, a less expensive but slightly less efficient process. Other FM stations use their subcarriers for *storecasting* or *transitcasting* or for even more specialized services such as **facsimile** or special programming to the blind or, using teletypewriters, the deaf. (*See* Waves.) *Transitcasting* is an SCA service supplied to trains, buses, and similar conveyances by FM stations. Since the driver or crew usually controls the receiver, the riding public becomes a captive audience to the broadcast station and its music, and sometimes commercial messages. After some public outcry and the decline in public transit use after the early 1960s, transitcasting became rare. A similar service is *storecasting*, in which a music service—sometimes labeled *Muzak* after the franchised trademark used by the largest of such firms—is delivered over a subcarrier or over leased wire lines to stores, doctors' offices, and other business places. If broadcast, special receivers able to pick up the subcarrier are supplied for a monthly fee.

Television multiplexing is less common, although an audio program cue and intercom for station personnel in the studio or field, called *IFB (interruptible foldback)*, stereo sound, or a *secondary audio service (SAP)* such as a simultaneous language translation can be found.

Particularly common are means of providing printed captions for the deaf on a **closed caption** basis, in which a special receiver or decoder must be purchased to pick up the *character-generated* captions on a line of the **VBI** or *vertical blanking interval* between pictures. *Open captioning* may be seen by everyone, without the need for a special receiver, but it is deemed by programmers to be disruptive to those with normal hearing and is not common. The open use of sign language, usually shown in an insert in the picture, is chiefly found in telecasts of religious services.

Monaurally   *See* Modulation.

Morse Code   Code that permits transmission of the alphabet as a series of short and long pulses of electricity or signal: "dots and dashes." It was invented by Samuel F. B. Morse and his associates (especially Alfred Vail) in the 1830s for use with the electrical **telegraph.** Because it made use of the fact that some letters are more common in English than others, it was an unconscious use of some of the principles of *information theory* (*see* Communication) to achieve greater efficiency—the letter *e*, for example, is very common and is coded as one quickly and easily transmitted dot, whereas the infrequently used letter *z* requires two dashes and two dots.

MOS   *See* Television Camera Tubes.

Mosaic   *See* Modulation.

Motion Pictures   A visual record of a story or event, stored in the form of images, and usually the associated sound, on film, for later projection at such speed as to give an audience an illusion of motion; also, the projection of same. In a television studio, films generally are projected in a film chain (*see* Television Camera Tubes).

MSO (multiple system operator)   *See* Cable.

MTV   A cable programming service specializing in short *music videos*.

Multiple Ownership   *See* Ownership.

Multiplexed   *See* Modulation *and* Television Camera Tubes.

Must-Carry Rules   *See* Cable.

Mutual Broadcasting System (MBS)   *See* Network.

NAB   (National Association of Broadcasters)

Television Code   *See* Programming.

NABET (National Association of Broadcast Employees and Technicians)   *See* Unions.

NARBA (North American Regional Broadcasting Agreement)   *See* AM Channels.

Narrowcasting   *See* Broadcasting.

Network   Two or more stations, often broadcasting stations, interconnected by some means, or associated for the often simultaneous transmission of the same messages or programs. When one station picks up the signal off the air from another, it is a *relay*. Broadcasting networks were referred to as *chain broadcasting* in the 1920s and 1930s, and colloquially are known as *webs* or *nets*. Since the late 1970s, various pay-cable program services, such as *HBO* (Home Box Office), *Showtime*, and *CNN* (Cable News Network), and *"superstations,"* such as WTBS in Atlanta, WPIX in New York, and others that provide programming by satellite to cable system operators, have been referred to as "networks," further confusing the issue. In 1989, there were five broadcast national television networks in the United States—American Broadcasting Company (ABC), now merged with Capital Cities Broadcasting; Columbia Broadcasting System (*CBS;*) National Broadcasting Company *(NBC)*, a subsidiary of RCA, which in turn is owned by General Electric; the *Fox* broadcasting network (owned by Rupert Murdoch and still not in full operation); and the Public Broadcasting Service *(PBS)*, funded in part by the *Corporation for Public Broadcasting*. National radio networks include ABC (which supplies four separate services), CBS, NBC (which actually was sold to and is operated by Westwood One), the *Mutual Broadcasting System*, and National Public Radio *(NPR)*. Most television stations and just over half the country's radio stations are affiliated with networks. In the United States, a network generally consists of the program-producing and central administering organization, a small number of *owned-and-operated (O & O)* stations (*see* Ownership), and a greater number of independently owned but *affiliated* stations. The network generally produces, or buys from independent producers or *packagers*, programs that are beyond the resources of a single station and "sells" them to national advertisers for program production costs and the aggregate sum of the time charges of all affiliates airing the program. Stations may refuse to carry network programs, since the station licensee is legally responsible for everything aired over the station. The affiliates receive only 25 to 35 percent of their normal time charges but gain in other ways. They can sell *spots*—commercial advertisements—immediately before and after the program, during *station break* or *station ID* (identification) periods, for high prices because of advertiser desire to reach the large audiences attracted by the expensive network programs. The networks also supply affiliates with some *sustaining*—not *sponsored* by commercial advertisers—programs without cost, as well as with prestigious news programming. Until the last decade, networks usually paid for interconnecting the stations by microwave or **coaxial cable** facilities supplied by AT&T, but in recent years most networks lease relay facilities on space communications **satellites** for that purpose.

News   The timely report of an event of interest to a number of people, often obtained through the *wire services* or *news agencies*—organizations that gather news and transmit it, usually by *tele-type*writer, to media clients for dissemination to the public by various means. The main wire services used in the United States are the Associated Press *(AP)*, United Press International *(UPI)*, and *Reuters*, an English firm. Frequently considered part of *broadcast journalism* are *public affairs* programs, which consist of news and feature material dealing with government and public issues that help citizens make reasoned decisions on such matters, and *editorials*, which are clearly identified, on-the-air expressions of opinion by a station licensee or his representative on a topic of public interest and concern. (*See* ENG *and* Remote.)

Nipkow Disc   *See* Television's Early Technological Development.

Noise   *See* Signal.

NTIA   National Telecommunications and Information Administration of the U.S. Department of Commerce.

NTSC (National Television Standards Committee)   *See* Television Signals.

O & O (owned and operated)   *See* Network.

Off-network   *See* Programming.

Ohm   *See* Circuit.

Optical Fiber   *See* Fiber Optic.

Orthicon   *See* Television Camera Tubes.

Outside Broadcast (OB)   *See* Remote.

Ownership   Although physical facilities and goodwill may be owned, the Communications Act of 1934 (and the Radio Act of 1927 before it) reserves title to the entire electromagnetic spectrum in the hands of the people of the United States, with the government administering it. Hence, although someone may own a transmitter, the public owns the channel on which it is operating. The broadcaster merely has a permit to use it in the public interest for a few years; in practice, licenses are renewable and have rarely been revoked during or at the end of their term. The FCC has frequently investigated the possibility of concentration of control and has issued reports, orders, and rules frowning on *cross-media ownership*, overlapping ownership of a newspaper and a broadcasting station in the same market; prohibiting *duopoly*, one licensee from controlling more than one station of the same service in a single market; and limits *multiple ownership*, currently the number of stations an individual or company may own in the broadcasting services to 12 standard (AM), 12 FM, and 12 television. For many years the limits were 7-7-7, with no more than five of the television stations VHF. In addition, the commission no longer routinely approves AM-FM-TV combinations in the same market, although those already licensed to a single individual or company may continue until a change of ownership occurs. Many multiple or group owners have stations in different towns; in recent years *conglomerate* companies—firms that own or control numerous companies in different fields—have entered the field of broadcasting. **Network** *affiliation* is *not* the same as ownership; many group owners have one station affiliated with one network, a second station with another network, and so on. The *licensee*, or station "owner," is responsible for everything broadcast over the station since, at least in theory, he or she is a trustee for the public.

Package, Packager   *See* Network *and* Programming.

PAL (Phase Alternation by Line)   *See* Television Signals.

Parabolic Reflector   *See* Antenna.

Parallel   *See* Circuit.

Patents   *See* Invention.

Pay-TV, Pay-Cable   A television distribution plan in which members of the audience pay a special charge for particular programs. Originally planned as an over-the-air service, and the subject of a number of demonstrations and experiments from 1951 on, most pay-TV is now in the form of separate *pay-cable* channels (such as HBO, Showtime and The Movie Channel) for which additional monthly charges are levied. Sometimes, pay-TV charges are on the basis of pay-per-view (PPV), the cost to the viewer varying depending on the individual program, using a variety of hardware to prevent nonpaying viewers from descrambling or obtaining the pay program(s). *Scrambling* is a process that mixes up picture or sound elements during transmission but permits normal reception on a set with the proper equipment attached. Home Box Office was the first to establish a system to provide pay-cable programs to the head ends of cable systems using space communications satellites or, in some instances, microwave. Most "free" or pay national programming services, including PPV, distribute in the same way. The few on-air pay-TV stations tend to be independently programmed.

People Meters   *See* Ratings.

Performing Rights Societies   *See* Copyright.

Phosphor   *See* Television Signals.

Picture Elements or **Pixels**   *See* Television Signals.

Plate   *See* Vacuum Tube.

Plumbicon   *See* Television Camera Tubes.

Polarization (horizontal, vertical, or circular) *See* Antenna.

PPV (pay-per-view)   *See* Pay-TV.

Precision Offset Carrier   *See* Transmitter.

Prime Time Access Rule (PTAR)   *See* Programming.

Production House   An organization, sometimes associated with a motion picture studio, that specializes in *packaging* and producing television programs or commercials. Examples of the former are MTM and Lorimar.

Programming   Among terms needing definition are *family viewing* (FV) *time*, the period from 7 P.M. to 9 P.M. in most parts of the country which, starting in 1975, was to contain only content suitable for the entire family. This standard was written into the *NAB Television Code* after pressure from Congress and others concerned about the possible effect of violence and sex content on children. FCC chairman Wiley's "encouragement" was a factor in a federal judge's decision late in 1976 that individual stations should control their own programming; concerted or mandatory (NAB code) advertising restrictions were illegal. The NAB promptly dropped the entire code idea: program content as well as advertising; radio as well as television. *PTAR*, or the *Prime Time Access Rule*, was a 1974 FCC action that required affiliated stations to program at least one hour during prime time, 7 P.M. to 11 P.M. in most areas, from non-network sources, to encourage a diversity of programming and programming sources. A *format* is a type of program (or *genre*) such as a soap opera; the term may also refer to the specific organization of content of a particular show. A program *stripped* or *across the board* is scheduled at the same time each weekday. When a different program is shown at the same time each weekday, the strategy is called *checkerboarding*. *Counterprogramming* is the scheduling of material usually not aired by competitors at that hour, e.g., entertainment when most stations are airing local news. *Station* or *affiliate time* is the prime-time period (usually from 7 P.M. to 8 P.M.) not programmed by the network. Many non-network programs are *syndicated*— either *off-network*, having been shown on a network in the past, or original—and sold to individual local stations. A *spin-off* is a program developed around a character or a situation in a successful program. A program *package* is the program idea, writers, stars, director, and so forth assembled by a *packager* for production or sale to a network or for syndication.

Propagation   *See* Waves.

Public Access   *See* Cable.

Public Affairs   *See* News.

Public Broadcasting Service (PBS) *See* Network.

Public Interest, Convenience and/or Necessity   *See* Allocation.

Public Television   *See* ETV.

Public Utility   *See* Common Carrier.

Pulse Modulation (PM)   *See* Modulation.

Quad Head (Quadraplex)   *See* Recordings.

Quadrasonic   *See* Modulation.

Radiation, Conduction, Induction   Electricity can travel from one point to another in a variety of ways. *Conduction* requires a conductor, usually a piece of wire, to carry the current. However, something not specially prepared as the conductor can also serve, as, for example, the earth, salt water, or some other common **circuit** ground. *Induction* uses the principle that an object may be electrified, magnetized, or given an induced voltage by exposure to a magnetic field. During the 1800s several experimenters, particularly Nathan B. Stubblefield, arranged two loops of wire a distance apart and sent an electrical signal through one of them. The resulting magnetic field was picked up by the other loop, some distance away—up to three miles in some cases. Although the method was generally used for **Morse code,** speech could be transmitted in this way. Most of the energy in an induction field is, however, contained in the vicinity of the transmitting loop. At higher frequencies, it is possible to *radiate*—diffuse from a center, as when a balloon is blown up—the signal for great distances. Generally radio communication requires frequencies above those used for telegraph or voice, although any radio frequency may undergo **modulation** with the audio frequencies of speech and allow the code or the speech to ride piggyback on the radio frequency wave. *See* Waves.

Radio, Radiocommunication   A general term applied to the use of electromagnetic, or Hertzian, waves to communicate. An earlier term was *wireless*.

Radio Broadcasting   Strictly speaking, multiple-address radio telephony (*see* Broadcasting).

Radiotelegraphy   *See* Telegraphy.

Radiotelephony   *See* Telephony.

Radio Television News Directors Association *See* Unions.

Ratings   Estimates of audience size and composition used to measure the popularity of programs. Ratings are compiled by a *rating service* such as A.C. Nielsen or Arbitron or, in earlier years, the Cooperative Analysis of Broadcasting, C. E. Hooper, and others. Methods include telephone calls that are *coincidental* with the program, *diaries*, and various kinds of recorders, including *people meters*, which require each viewing member of the household periodically to push a button that is recorded at the ratings company, but do quickly secure information about individual (rather than household) viewing. The results are expressed either as *ratings*—proportion of all television homes that are tuned to a given program—or *share*—proportion of homes using television at that time that are tuned to the particular program—and frequently include additional demographic data of value to advertisers. Advertising agencies also use many other kinds of research data, such as *psychographics.*

Receiver   A device for the reception of electromagnetic waves carrying modulated radiocommunication signals, generally including (or attached to) an antenna; tuning components; a detector; and enough amplification stages to permit use of a loudspeaker. Among the earliest devices for detecting radio waves were the *galvanometer*, a sensitive meter which would show, by deflection of the meter's pointer, when a signal was present, and the *coherer*, a glass tube containing metallic filings that would clump together or cohere when an electric current passed through. A *tapper* or *decoherer* would disperse the filings between each dot or dash. Later, the *crystal set* (*see* Vacuum Tube) was employed, since electric current could flow only in one direction through it and it did not need decohering. The diode vacuum tube supplanted the galena or other crystal for this purpose. Greater and greater *selectivity*—the ability to choose between competing signals—and *sensitivity*—the ability to receive weak signals—

were obtained with the *regenerative, superregenerative, heterodyne,* and *superheterodyne* receiver circuits. Receiving sets using the last named circuits worked most efficiently at a single frequency, the *intermediate frequency* or *IF,* no matter what the frequency of the station being received. In essence, this type of receiver used a *local oscillator* to generate a "local" radio frequency signal within the set, which would be a certain number of kiloHertz—the value of the IF—above or below the frequency of the station to which the receiver was tuned. In tuning to the frequency of the desired station, one would automatically change the local oscillator or transmitter since the same knob controlled both tuning condensers. The two frequencies would "beat" against one another, leaving the resultant intermediate frequency, the difference between the two signals, which would always be the same. The generally relatively low IF— a common frequency used in AM radios today is 455 kHz—permits simple and rugged design of components and, beyond the tuning stage, use of only one frequency. The equipment can be designed for that one frequency rather than to correspond with the broad range of frequencies used by the various transmitting stations within range. As a result, almost all radio receivers today combine tuning or radio frequency *(rf)* stages, a detector stage, and a number of intermediate frequency and audio frequency *(af)* stages of *amplification*—boosting the signal without otherwise changing its characteristics. The word "receiver" is now commonly used for high-fidelity tuner-amplifier combinations that are attached to external loudspeakers, with the word "radio" used for cheaper self-contained units. A television receiver is similar to a radio receiver in function: the desired channel is tuned in much as in the radio receiver and the resulting signal is eventually fed to the picture tube (kinescope) and loudspeaker for reproduction of the picture and sound.

Receiving Station *See* Station.

Record Communication A term to distinguish nontransient communication. For example, the telegraph is a record communication; the telephone is not. Film is a record communication; "live" television is not.

Recordings Reproduction of musical or other performances stored in the form of magnetic patterns in tape, or grooves in plastic discs. A number of other forms of recording—even writing falls in the category—are used in broadcasting. The earliest sound recordings were made on wax cylinders. Later, discs, usually 10 or 12 inches in diameter, running at 78.26 rpm, were used. The *electrical transcription (ET),* used for broadcast programming for many years, consisted of a 15-inch or 16-inch disc revolving at 33⅓ rpm, which gave 15 minutes of playing time per side using standard width grooves. In the late 1940s, Peter Goldmark and a CBS Laboratories team developed the *LP (long-playing)* record for home use. It was 10 or 12 inches in diameter and revolved at 33⅓ rpm but used an extremely fine *microgroove* that enabled one side to hold more than 20 minutes of music. RCA attempted to market a 7-inch, 45-rpm microgroove disc with an oversize center hole, but after a long struggle it was restricted to popular music, one tune to a side, and the 78-rpm disc was phased out. Most recently, the highest-quality audio reproductions have come from **CD**s or *compact discs,* which are computer controlled, using **digital** rather than **analog** signals that virtually eliminate hiss or *noise.* A similar system, called *CD-ROM* (compact *d*isk–*r*ead *o*nly *m*emory), is used interactively with computers for the storage and retrieval of vast amounts of data. *Reel-to-reel* magnetic tape recording derived from magnetic wire recording machines and from steel tape continuous loop recording machines used for such things as telephone weather forecast announcements in the early 1940s. Reel-to-reel sound recordings are being replaced in homes with easier to handle, self-contained devices that give good sound reproduction. The most common such device is the twin hub *cassette,* in which the tape is permanently threaded on supply and takeup reels and the entire unit is placed over shafts driven from the motor. For some years, there also was the single hub *cartridge,* which, although a bit bulkier and more complex, plays multichannel music with higher fidelity and is even easier to insert in the playback device than the cassette. A new digitalized system, *DAT* (digital *audiotape*), which can make perfect copies (or *dubs*) of CDs or other DATs, is technically available but has been held up in this country because of the apprehension of record companies and other copyright holders.

Television or video recording originally consisted of the *kinescope* (television picture tube) *recorder*, in which a motion picture camera photographed the images on a television picture tube. The quality of the resulting *kine* was not high, partly because our television system scans 30 complete pictures per second but a sound movie camera photographs only 24 frames per second. In the late 1950s, magnetic *videotape recording (VTR)* was developed, revolutionizing the industry. The first bulky *quad head* or *quadraplex* videotape recorders used a revolving assembly of four record-playback heads over which 2-inch tape was transported at 15 or 7½ inches per second (ips), with the heads briefly overlapping as they turned at

Some Audio Recording Formats

	Medium	Speed	Usual Size (diameter)	Frequency Response (Hz)	Usual Playing Time (minutes, one side)	Notes
Standard	Mechanical	78.26 rpm	10″, 12″	100–6,000	7 (12″)	Standard groove
Transcription (ET)	Mechanical	33⅓ rpm	16″	70–8,000	15	Standard groove broadcasting programs
Wire recorder	Magnetic		2″	100–6,000	60	.01″ thick wire
Long-playing (LP)	Mechanical	33⅓ rpm	10″, 12″	20–18,000	25 (12″)	Microgroove
45-rpm (RCA)	Mechanical	45 rpm	7″	100–8,000	5	Microgroove for popular music; later 60–16,000 Hz
Reel-to-reel	Magnetic	1⅞ to 15 ips	7″	20–15,000	60 (3¾ ips) 15 (15 ips)	¼″ wide magnetic tape; consumer can record
Cassette (micro size)	Magnetic	1⅞ and 15⁄16 ips	2½″ × 4″ 1¼″ × 2″	20–14,000	30–60	Original frequency response was low; consumer can record
Compact disc (CD)	Laser optical		120 mm	15–20,000	70	Digital; playback only
Digital audiotape (DAT)	Magnetic	8.15 mm/sec	2″ × 3″	15–22,000	120	Digital cassette; record or playback

Note: This is not an exhaustive list. It is arranged chronologically. Some formats—like magnetic wire recorders and eight-track cassettes—have come and gone; others, such as 16-rpm records, never really had much use. Others were used for specialized purposes: 10″ reels for professional audiotaping, reel-to-reel speeds as high as 60 ips, early field recordings on motion picture film, audio cartridges (carts) for broadcast commercials, and so on. Playback time for magnetic tape depends on the thickness of the tape and how much can be put on a reel or into a cassette. Some reel-to-reel and cassette formats permit multiple tracks of recording. Improvements were made to each format during its existence that enhanced audio fidelity, particularly to the audiocassette and the 45-rpm record, which now exists in a 12″ format for high-fidelity professional use as well as in the format familiar to consumers.

high speed, providing a picture almost indistinguishable from "live." Later, the *high band VTR*, which used a high-frequency—10 MHz—carrier, yielded a very high signal-to-noise ratio, and its excellent interference-free picture enabled more *generations* (successive duplicates) to be made from the original recording, or *master*. Color recording and electronic editing to the exact frame desired are now possible on even the relatively inexpensive *helical scan* VTRs used for industrial and educational purposes. In these VTRs the tape is wrapped in a spiral (helix) around a large-diameter, fixed drum within which a record-playback head revolves. Helical scan VTRs and U-Matic cassette VCRs are much less expensive than the obsolete quad head machines or 1" professional models but at the expense of image quality. In the 1980s, the home VCR *(videocassette recorder),* in a variety of formats, such as *VHS* and *Beta,* became a very popular consumer item. VCRs usually are used for *time-shifting* (recording for later playback) or for the playing of videocassettes of motion pictures rented or purchased from a variety of retail

Some Video Recording Formats

	Medium	Reel, Cart, Cassette, or Disc	Usual Width	Usual Playing Time (minutes)	Notes
Kinescope	Optical (film)	Reel	16 mm or 35 mm	60	Poor quality; now obsolete
Quadruplex	Magnetic	Reel	2"	30–60	Broadcast use
Helical scan	Magnetic	Reel	2"	30–60–120	Industrial, broadcast use
Helical scan (types A, B, C)	Magnetic	Reel	1"	10–180	Mostly broadcast, some industrial use
Cartridge	Magnetic	Cart	2"	5–20 ⎫	Carts and cassettes used by stations for commercials
Cassettes	Magnetic	Cassette	2"	5–20 ⎭	
U-Matic (color under)	Magnetic	Cassette	.75"	20–60	Limited broadcast use
Beta	Magnetic	Cassette	.50"	270	Primarily home use
VHS	Magnetic	Cassette	.50"	360	Primarily home use
Betacam VHS-C	Magnetic	Cassette	.50"	20	Used for ENG and as camcorders
ED Beta	Magnetic	Cassette	.50"	360 ⎫	Higher quality, but not compatible with earlier designs; nonbroadcast
S-VHS	Magnetic	Cassette	.50"	270 ⎬	
Video 8	Magnetic	Cassette	8 mm	120 ⎭	
Videodisc	Optical or mechanical	Disc	7" diameter	120+	Usually playback only
D-1, D-2, etc.	Magnetic	Reel	1"	60	Digital, broadcast use

Note: Literally dozens of formats have been used for video recording. Most are mutually incompatible. Above are those most commonly found in television broadcasting stations, listed chronologically. When magnetic videotape recording (VTR) became possible in the late 1950s, kinescope recordings became obsolete—but they may be the only source for programs aired before 1960. The many motion picture film formats used by television news departments are not included here. Although some broadcasting stations use home videocassette recorders (VCRs) for their news operations, these machines do not meet the FCC's technical broadcasting standards.

outlets. Some of these, combined with a small camera, are called *camcorders* and have replaced the home movie camera and projector. First used for stop-action recording during sporting events, the various kinds of *videodiscs* now being developed—thin, flexible plastic discs used to record and play back video and audio material by magnetic, **laser,** or other complicated processes—may eventually be used in the home in the same way as musical recordings. Since there is no agreement on technical standards, even with videodisc's many potential advantages—inexpensive materials, simple duplication processes—it has not yet replaced videotape *cartridge* and *videocassette* systems for short—and even long—messages in home machines. Although the use of *time based correctors* now permits relatively inexpensive VTRs to be used, particularly in **ENG** and **EFP** applications, it seems probable that the broadcast industry soon will settle on a new 1-inch digital professional machine as its standard, although new professional *formats* appear almost as frequently as home VCR formats. One difficulty with the lack of agreement on *compatible* VTR and VCR formats is that it frequently is virtually impossible to *dub* (or copy) from one to another unless the signal is separated into its *luminance* (monochromatic brightness) and *chrominance* (color) components, known as Y and C. Even then, dubbing often is quite difficult because of nonstandardized plugs, cables, and electronic parameters.

Rectifier   *See* Vacuum Tube.

Rediffusion   *See* Cable.

Reel-to-Reel   *See* Recordings.

Regenerative   *See* Receiver.

Register   *See* Copyright.

Relay   *See* Network.

Relay, Sounder   *See* Circuit.

Remote   A broadcast or part of a broadcast that originates from outside the studio. In the United Kingdom, a remote is called an *outside broadcast (OB)*. In the early days of radio, such a broadcast was called a *Nemo*, presumably reflecting telephone company usage—"not emanating main office"—although possibly associated with the "Little Nemo" comic strip about fanciful dreams off in the middle of nowhere. (*See* ENG *and* News.)

Resolution   *See* Television Signals.

Resonating Frequency   *See* Waves.

Return Wire   *See* Circuit.

Reuters   *See* News.

rf (radio frequency)   *See* Receiver.

Rotary Arc   *See* Transmitter.

Royalties   *See* Invention.

Safety and Special Services   The FCC traditionally divides the radio stations under its supervision into **broadcasting, common carrier,** and safety and special services—a term that includes every other kind of user, from amateur to police.

SAG (Screen Actors Guild)   *See* Unions.

Satellite   A body in orbit around another, larger body. Often used in a political sense ("the Soviet Union's satellites of Poland, East Germany . . ."), the word has two meanings that concern broadcasting. First, artificial *space communications satellites* are launched by rocket into an orbit approximately 22,300 miles above the equator. This height and orbit enable them to remain stationary *(synchronous)* with respect to one spot on the earth's surface and high enough to "see" roughly one-third of that surface. Hence, line-of-sight radio frequencies can be used to cover entire continents or oceans. Typically, each channel requires a separate *transponder* (a receiver picking up the signal from earth, which responds by changing its frequency and retransmitting the signal to many terrestrial television receive-only *(TVRO)* dishes located at television stations and cable system head ends). The signal from earth to satellite is called an *uplink;* the return signal—particularly when used for *SNG* (satellite newsgathering) is called a *downlink*. Most satellite relays operate on SHF microwave frequencies, such as the *Ku-* and *C-bands* (nomenclature originally applied to radar). These satellites can *relay* virtually any kind of electronic signal—telephone, television—point to point from one large earth station to another. They also are successfully used with small receive-only dish **antennas** at pay-cable (*see* Pay-TV) installations, network affiliates, and remote villages and towns and by more than a million private citizens in areas where over-the-air and cable signals are hard to get. *DBS,* or direct satellite-to-home broadcasting, appears to be some years away because of the need to increase power in the satellite and provide special antennas on rooftops, but is being introduced abroad. In reaction to the many dishes in private hands, networks and pay-cable companies have taken to *scrambling* their signals so their programs cannot be viewed without a special decoder. Second, a satellite is a television station that does not originate its own programming but retransmits the programs of a parent station. Satellite television stations operate on a channel regularly assigned to their community and not on the parent station's channel, as do *boosters,* or on one of the upper UHF television channels with very low power, as do *translators,* which "translate" the parent station's signal up to the high UHF.

Scanning   *See* Television's Early Technological Development *and* Television Signals.

Scrambling   *See* Pay-TV.

Screen Directors Guild   *See* Unions.

SECAM (Séquential Couleur à Mémoire)   *See* Television Signals.

Secondary Station   *See* Channel.

Selectivity   *See* Receiver.

Selenium   *See* Television's Early Technological Development.

Semaphore   A device for sending coded signals visually by means of flags, lights, or mechanically moving arms. Developed to a high degree of efficiency in the century before introduction of the electrical telegraph, semaphore today survives to a limited extent in the navy, where signal lamps using Morse code have taken over from the sailor who holds two small flags and moves them to a different position for each letter, and in railroading, which uses a simple code based on the position, ranging from vertical to horizontal, of short paddles on towers.

Sensitivity   *See* Receiver.

Series   *See* Circuit.

SESAC (originally Society of European Stage Authors and Composers)   *See* Copyright.

Service Drops   *See* Cable.

Share   *See* Ratings.

Short-circuit   *See* Circuit.

Shortwave   *See* Waves.

Sidebands   *See* Modulation.

Sign   *See* Communication.

Signal   Sometimes referring to any transmission (including one without intentionally encoded information or desire for **communication**), the term generally refers either to a message or to the actual electromagnetic wave propagated from a **transmitter.** The mere presence of a carrier wave signal indicates the important fact that a transmitter exists, but, technically, information is carried in the **modulation** of the signal, not in the signal itself. *Noise* in a channel is that which can interfere with reception of a message. Generally, noise is either electrical/mechanical (such as *static*) or semantic (imperfect agreement on the connotations and denotations of symbols or signs). The *signal-to-noise ratio (S/N)* is often used to describe the relative amount of interference in a given channel.

"Silent Night"   *See* DX-ing.

Single Sideband (SSB)   *See* Modulation.

Skip   *See* Waves.

Skywave   *See* Waves.

SMATV   *See* Cable.

Solid State, Transistor, Chip   *See* Transmitter *and* Vacuum Tube.

Space Communications Satellite   *See* Satellite.

Spark Gap   *See* Transmitter.

Spectrum   *See* Waves *and* Bandwidth.

Spin-off   *See* Programming.

Sponsored   *See* Network.

Spots   *See* Network.

Static   *See* Allocation *and* Signal.

Station The place or position from which a service is provided or operations are directed; in other words, a *transmitting station* in a given radiocommunication service. A *receiving station* is the place—the home, the car—where a receiver is located. In recent years, the general public has mistakenly taken to calling their cable systems "stations."

Station Break, Station ID *See* Network.

Stereophonic *See* Modulation.

Stereoscopic *See* Television Signals.

Storecasting *See* Modulation.

Subcarriers *See* Modulation.

Subsidiary Communications Authorization (SCA) *See* Modulation.

Superheterodyne *See* Receiver.

Superpower In the United States, any standard (AM) broadcast station that uses more than 50 kw of power. Only one such station, WLW (Cincinnati), has operated here, from 1935 to 1939, when the U.S. Senate frowned on superpower. However, the proposal remains active, and such stations operate in other countries, notably Mexico. In the 1920s, the term referred to lesser amounts of power.

Superregenerative *See* Receiver.

Superstation One of a half-dozen independent (non-network-affiliated) broadcasting stations (the first was Ted Turner's WTBS in Atlanta) whose programs are uplinked to a satellite and then made available to cable system operators for a small sum per subscriber per month. Generally, these stations (WGN in Chicago, WPIX and WWOR in New York, and KPIX in San Francisco, for example) feature movies, old reruns, and sporting events.

Sustaining *See* Network.

Symbol *See* Communication.

Synchronizing *See* Television Signals.

Synchronous *See* Satellite.

Syndicated *See* Programming.

Talent A generic term referring to a person or persons appearing on radio or television as actor, announcer, singer, performer, on-air news reporter, and so forth. This meaning is the one most commonly used in broadcasting; it probably is derived as a sarcastic extension of the dictionary definition, which refers to persons with gifts, aptitudes, or abilities of a superior quality.

Tapper *See* Receiver.

Telecine A *film chain;* a facility at a station or network used for the projection of motion picture film over a television system. Consists of a projector or projectors, an optical multiplexer and a television camera.

Telecommunications Any transmission, emission, or reception of signs, signals, writing, images, and sounds or intelligence of any nature by wire, radio, visual, or other electromagnetic systems of communication. An implication from the first part of the word (*tele-* = far, distant) is that the communication takes place over a substantial distance.

Telegraphy A telecommunication system for the transmission of written matter by a signal code, through a wire channel unless the term *radiotelegraphy* is used to signify use of a **radiocommunication** channel.

Telephony A telecommunication system for the transmission of speech or other sounds, through a wire channel unless the term *radiotelephony* is used to signify use of a **radiocommunication** channel.

Teletext, Videotex Techniques for sending numerous "pages" of data to the home, generally using a television set as the display device. Teletext uses a *vertical blanking interval (VBI)* line, is one-way, and sends up to 200 pages in sequence, over and over again. Videotex is transmitted over a wider cable channel and is interactive to the extent that the viewer can select which of thousands of pages of news, weather, sports scores, airline schedules, menus, and so forth, are desired. Early systems have been available in the United Kingdom and France for several years, while there still is some doubt as to its potential utility and profitability in the United States. This is one vital component of the broadband "wired city" concept.

Teletype *See* News.

Television A telecommunication system for the transmission of transient images of fixed or moving objects; also the broadcast service of the same name, which includes both the picture and the accompanying sound.

Television Camera Tubes Although the original television pickup devices, which converted light energy into electrical energy, were mechanical (*see* Television's Early Technological Development), all-electronic camera tubes were devised and introduced in the late 1930s. These were generally of a storage-discharge type, storing the light falling on the tube face and then discharging it into the system by scanning the storage element with an electron beam. The all-electronic camera tubes included the *Iconoscope* of Vladimir Zworykin (RCA) and the *Image Dissector* of Philo Farnsworth. These were combined into the *orthicon* and *image orthicon* tubes by RCA engineers in the early 1940s. The image orthicon (*IO* or *orth*) tube, in use for more than a quarter-century, was replaced for high-quality broadcast uses by the *Plumbicon,* which used a lead oxide—Pb is the symbol for lead—for a key part, and for industrial and other nonbroadcast uses by the lower resolution quality (*see* Television Signals) and less sensitive—needing more light for a good picture—*vidicon* tube. The vidicon is used in *film chains*—motion picture and slide projectors are *multiplexed* through an optical device that focuses two or more sources of program material at a small vidicon television camera—in television studios because light levels from film or slide *projectors* are high and can be controlled. A *kinescope* is either a television picture tube used at the receiver end of the system or a kind of television **recording.** The solid state *CCD* or *controlled capacitance discharge* device is becoming popular for **ENG, EFP,** and **camcorder** use. It is rugged and very lightweight, although it needs some picture quality improvement before it replaces tubes in studio cameras. While the better CCD devices are getting close to comparability with three- or four-tube cameras, even newer solid state *imaging devices* such as *MOS* are in the wings.

Television's Early Technological Development Television's first practical technological development was recorded when English telegraph engineer Joseph May discovered in 1873 that the element *selenium* was capable of producing small amounts of electricity in direct response to the amount of light falling on it. His supervisor, Willoughby Smith, notified the prestigious Society of Telegraph Engineers in England, and today both men are given credit for the discovery.

Within a couple of years, various inventors designed methods for putting this discovery to work in a television system. Although the actual devices were imperfect, the principles were straightforward. G. R. Carey of Boston in 1877 proposed a crude imitation of the human eye: a bank of selenium cells and lamps that could be used for breaking up pictures and sending the elements over wire. Three years later English scientists Ayrton and Perry tried out such a mosaic device. Fournier and Rignoux first transmitted actual images in France in 1906. Following the telephone's invention by Alexander Graham Bell, who had also experimented with the use of light waves rather than wire to transmit voice, inventors in several countries proposed or demonstrated a rash of television—or still-picture, nonmoving, **facsimile**—devices.

Some of these, like today's animated advertising signs, used a wire to connect each selenium cell—the pickup device, analogous to one facet of the eye—with a small electric lamp—the reproduction device, in a *mosaic.* The more lamps, the more detail could be put into the picture. In some versions the lamps simply were "on" or "off," while in others their intensity varied in direct response to the different intensities of light projected on each cell. This approach, experimented with for many years, required an impractical amount of wiring and a mechanically awkward arrangement of cells and lamps. To reproduce a picture equal in detail to a 23-inch television screen of today would require more than 350,000 lamps, each not more than one-fortieth of an inch in diameter!

French scientist Maurice Leblanc developed a technique in 1880 to avoid this quandary, using the principle of *scanning,* in which each picture element was viewed successively rather than all at once as in the mosaic devices. Each picture was divided into lines and each line into minute segments. His approach was analogous to the solution of a similar **bandwidth** problem in telegraphy.

By 1884 basic principles of scanning had been incorporated in some *mechanical* devices. L. B. Atkinson's apparatus employed a drum fitted with tangential mirrors, each successive mirror being oriented through a small angle so that, as the drum rotated, the picture would be scanned in a series of lines that would be projected on a single selenium cell. The resulting electrical output of the cell could be transmitted over a wire circuit, as at this time there were no wireless transmission devices. As with all television systems, rotating drums at both ends of the circuit had to be *synchronized* in order to transmit the image successfully. No full description of Atkinson's device was published, and many writers give credit for the mirror drum to a European, Lazare Weiller, who proposed a similar system in 1889. The scanning disc and other devices quickly overshadowed the *mirror drum*, although experimenters used it for many years—E. F. W. Alexanderson of General Electric as late as 1927.

The scanning disc, basis for almost all mechanical scanning systems for several decades, was invented in 1883 and patented in early 1884 in Germany by Paul Nipkow. Lacking the money to extend the patent on his "electrical telescope," he allowed it to lapse and worked for the next 32 years as an engineer for a German railway signal company. Although he lived until 1940 and is generally recognized as the inventor of the system that could reproduce moving objects, Nipkow never built a working model of a complete transmission-reception system, since he lacked means of synchronizing the discs, adequate light sources, amplifiers, photocells, and all the sensitive and increasingly complicated tools of later experimenters.

The *Nipkow disc* looked like a phonograph record, perforated with a single spiral of small holes, each hole a fraction of an inch closer to the center of the disc and a fraction of an inch farther along the rim of the disc than the preceding one. When the disc was placed directly between a narrow-beam light source

(although sunlight and gas lamps were used, the electric lamp was the most common) and an object and then rotated, the light would shine through only one hole at a time. In one complete turn, the narrow beam would illuminate every part of the object, moving across it in what appeared, because of the speed of rotation and the persistence of vision, as slightly curved lines or streaks. In practice, the light merely illuminated the object, and a selenium cell—after 1888, a more sensitive device called a *photocell*—"looked" at the scene through each hole as the disc revolved. At the receiving end, a neon lamp varied rapidly in brightness in response to the current produced by the photocell, and the viewer observed it through a Nipkow disc rotating in synchronization with the disc at the other end of the circuit. A mask, of the same size at both ends of the circuit, blocked out part of the disc and focused both the cell and the viewer's eye at the same relative place. Persistence of vision caused the combination of varying-intensity neon lamp and rapidly spinning disc to reproduce a crude picture of the original object in the viewer's brain. The picture, at first, was only an inch or two wide, being limited chiefly by the size of the holes, the diameter of the disc, and the speed of rotation—each of which led to mechanical problems. (*See also* Bandwidth, Television Signals, *and* Television Camera Tubes.)

Television Signals   The *resolution* or sharpness of a television picture is measured in terms of *picture elements,* or *pixels.* In gross terms, the resolution of a picture is the product of the number of horizontal *lines* scanned for each picture times the number of complete pictures, sometimes called *frames,* analogous to frames of a motion picture film, per second. However, not only are some cameras, recorders, and receivers incapable of providing maximum resolution, but the 525 lines used in an *NTSC* (National Television Standards Committee) system are *interlaced*—much as one interlaces his or her fingers by placing those on one hand between those on the other. First the odd-numbered lines are transmitted and then the even-numbered so that in one second we actually see

60 pictures or *fields* of 262½ lines each. Because of the persistence of vision in human beings, transmission of 60 half-fields produces a moving picture with better resolution, particularly when something on the screen is moving rapidly, than a 30-frame noninterlaced system. The use of 60 pictures per second originally permitted locking or *synchronizing* the picture in the studio to the picture at home through the 60 Hz power line frequency. (In much of the world, 50 Hz power is used, resulting in 50-field, 25-frame television in those countries.) A strong synchronizing signal, produced by a synchronizing or *sync* generator at the studio or transmitter, does most of the work in keeping the picture at home in step with the one in the studio. In *scanning* a scene, the beam of electrons in a television camera tube sweeps across the target, onto which the scene is focused by a lens, from left to right and then, during the *blanking interval*, returns to the left without generating a signal, drops down two lines because of interlacing, and sweeps across again. The *aspect ratio*, or the ratio of horizontal to vertical size, of a television picture is 4:3. Although *three-dimensional (3-D)* or *stereoscopic* television was experimented with as early as 1926, it is not now in use. (*See* HDTV.)

Now common, *color* was also the subject of experiments in the 1920s. In early times the image was focused through a spinning *color wheel* that fed each primary color in turn to one pickup tube. A modern studio color television system uses a system of filters to feed primary colors—red, green, blue, or sometimes their complements—to each of three camera tubes. Less expensive industrial systems use one-tube cameras. Very little additional bandwidth is required for the *colorburst* signal component of a television signal, since it is merely an instruction to the receiving set to produce various strengths of color signal at a given instant. Standards differ for television around the world; some countries use our NTSC (525 lines, 30 frames); eastern Europe uses one form of 625/25 and western Europe a slightly different one. The British have closed out the 405/25 system they had used since the 1930s in favor of 625/25, and the French also have dropped their 819/25 system. Other standards were used prior

to World War II. Three color systems—*NTSC*, *PAL*, originally a German system, and the French *SECAM*, also used in Soviet Russia—are in use. Fortunately, it is now possible (but complex and often expensive) to convert programming made on one standard to another. The *field sequential* system was the original color system, since the lower speeds (60 fields rather than 15,750 lines per minute) were easier to use with mechanical color wheels. The *dot sequential* system is presently in use, since color picture tubes are now made with hundreds of little triangles consisting of red, green, and blue chemical *phosphor* dots that glow when hit by the focused electrons from the *guns* in the tube. However, the camera actually used by the astronauts during moon landings in the early 1970s was field sequential.

The channel for a 525/30 system is 6 MHz wide, but the actual picture needs only approximately 4 MHz. The rest of the channel is taken up with the sound portion of the transmission, *guard bands* to reduce interference from stations on adjoining frequencies, and a *vestigial sideband*—when present television transmission standards were adopted in 1941, NTSC engineers attempted to save frequency space by using only one sideband and a carrier, but the state of the art forced them to "waste"

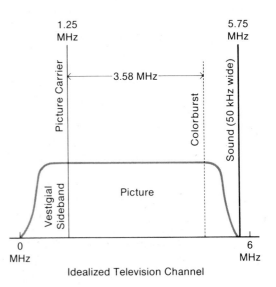

Idealized Television Channel

1.25 MHz by providing a second sideband of reduced size and no appreciable value.

Time-shifting   *See* Recordings.

Trade Secret   *See* Invention.

Transceivers   *See* Transmitter.

Transducer   A device for converting one form of energy to another (as a microphone transduces sound energy into electrical energy).

Transistor   *See* Vacuum Tube.

Transitcasting   *See* Modulation.

Translators   *See* Satellite.

Transmitter   A device for radiating signals that might be received at a distant location. (The term is also used for the portion of a telephone that is spoken into). It is fed or controlled by a microphone or other speech input equipment, or a telegraph key, or some other source of signal, and feeds to an antenna a composite signal that usually consists of a *carrier wave, modulated* by (has superimposed on it) the intelligence that one desires to transmit or send.

The earliest radiotelegraph transmitters employed the *spark-gap* principle whereby a high current or voltage jumps across a gap in a wire or other conductor. This spark will radiate over a wide band of frequencies, much as a bolt of lightning does. But when tuned to some extent and fed into an antenna of a certain wavelength, the spark cannot be detected over nearly as wide a band as lightning, thus conserving spectrum space. In the earliest transmitters, the spark was controlled by a telegraph key to produce dots and dashes. The *rotary arc* transmitters, developed later, were motors designed to produce an almost continuous arc, which could be fed to the antenna by a key. Because arcs offered a gentler approach to radiotelegraph than the spark gap, they—particularly the Poulsen arc—continued in use into the 1930s, generally aboard ships needing medium-range transmissions. The Alexanderson and other *alternators* (alternating current generators) were often pickup-truck-sized rotary electrical generators driven by motors at speeds, and hence frequencies, so high that they could send energy a long distance by

radiation from an antenna without using wires. The Alexanderson alternator spun so fast that the output was of a frequency of alternations more than one thousand times that of the 60 Hz power supplied to houses today. Designed for transoceanic communication from fixed installations on shore, it was very reliable, efficient, and expensive. The current from the alternator could be fed to an antenna much more efficiently than could the broader signal from an arc transmitter, and attempts to secure exclusive use of the Alexanderson machine played an important role in establishing radio in this country.

Just before World War I the first practical high-powered *vacuum-tube transmitters* were tried, and a few years later they were placed in commercial service. **Vacuum tubes** permitted virtually silent operation, voice transmissions, and smaller, even mobile or portable, size. Although many low-power transmitters and *transceivers—trans*mitter and re*ceiver* combined in a single unit, such as a walkie-talkie or a Citizens Band set—have used *solid state* technology for years, high-power broadcast transmitters with solid state devices rather than vacuum tubes were not available until the mid-1970s.

Early broadcast transmitters did not have many features we take for granted, such as limiters to prevent overloading or overmodulating the transmitter. Until 1925 or so transmitters were *tuned*, much as a radio receiver is tuned, and often drifted off frequency and caused interference to other stations. Eventually, *crystal control* was perfected—a technique based on the capacity of a quartz crystal of a given thickness to force a current flowing through it to vibrate at a certain, determined frequency. When mounted in an enclosure that kept the crystal at an even temperature and prevented heat expansion or contraction, the unit held the station at a specified frequency. Transmitters with crystal control for broadcast and other uses caused less interference. One of the FRC's first orders of 1927 required crystal control and other standards for broadcast transmitters. A technique known as *precision offset carrier* permits television stations on the same channel to be located a few miles closer to each other without interference. (*See also* Modulation, Waves.)

Transmitting Station   *See* Station.

Transponder   *See* Satellite.

Triode   *See* Vacuum Tube.

Tropospheric Forward Scatter   *See* Waves.

Trunk Lines   *See* Cable.

TVRO (television receive-only satellite earth station)   *See* Satellite.

Two-way Cable System   *See* Cable.

Unions   Labor unions are plentiful in broadcasting and even more plentiful in the motion picture industry, which provides so many television programs. Among the most prominent are *AFTRA*, the American Federation of Television and Radio Artists (formerly AFRA), which serves announcers, actors, and other talent; *AFM*, the American Federation of Musicians, which has jurisdiction over virtually all musicians and a small number of turntable operators in Chicago radio stations; *IATSE*, the International Alliance of Theatrical Stage Employees and Moving Picture Machine Operators of the United States and Canada, whose members range from stagehands on Broadway and motion picture projectionists to television technical crews (camera operators and so forth), particularly in New York; *IBEW*, the International Brotherhood of Electrical Workers, which also represents many technicians; and *NABET*, the National Association of Broadcast Employees and Technicians. Originally *NABET* stood for National Association of Broadcast Engineers and Technicians; the change from "engineers" to "employees" marked the trend in many unions to represent a broad range of job categories in a given station. A number of actors and singers belong to either *Actors Equity* or *AGVA*, the American Guild of Variety Artists. The Screen Actors Guild *(SAG)*, the *Writers Guild of America* (West and East), and the *Screen Directors Guild* also have jurisdictions in broadcasting, but only the larger stations, networks, and program packagers, particularly those based in Hollywood, have direct connections with them. Although the networks may deal with dozens of different unions, most stations contract with only one or two or even none, with the technical and clerical staffs often represented by the same union. A few union contracts may affect the entire industry, but most are negotiated for the individual market. A professional association, such as the *Radio Television News Directors Association (RTNDA)*, is not, strictly speaking, a union organized for collective bargaining purposes.

UPI (United Press International)   *See* News.

Uplink   *See* Satellite.

Vacuum Tube   Before the *transistor* and *integrated solid state circuits* and devices came into almost universal use in the 1960s and 1970s, respectively, the vacuum tube performed the essential functions of electronic *detection* and *amplification*. Today, only the picture tube in a television set is still a vacuum tube. Modern solid state devices—the *transistor* and later developments such as integrated circuit *chips*—are essentially grown in laboratories and then cut apart, rather than manufactured, but fill the same functions as the vacuum tube.

   Yet, without some kind of one-way *valve*—still the name for the vacuum tube in Great Britain and elsewhere—to permit only the positive half of each cycle of radio-frequency alternating current waves to pass, it would be impossible to *demodulate* or permit the audio-frequency signal superimposed on the radio-frequency waves to be detected. (A *rectifier*, used to convert *alternating current [AC]* to *direct current [DC]* for power supplies and other uses, works the same way, whether vacuum tube or solid state.) The *crystal set*, used as a **receiver** from the earliest days of radio until the 1930s, was a primitive *solid state* device that used as a *detector* a piece of galena or some other crystalline ore that would allow current to pass in only one direction.

   The other major function of the vacuum tube, one that permitted today's selectivity and sensitivity, is **amplification,** the strengthening of a signal or current without otherwise changing its characteristics—much as power steering in an automobile amplifies the turning motions of the driver.

   The principles of vacuum-tube theory are simple: opposites attract and likes repel, just as with a pair of bar magnets; electrons are negative by definition; and the amount of repelling or attracting is roughly proportional to the voltage applied to that part of the tube. Thomas Alva Edison first noticed the actions of electrons within a glass tube evacuated of air. The *Edison effect* is the blackening of the glass wall of a tube caused by the electrons boiling off the glowing wire of the *filament* within an electric light bulb and striking the glass hard enough to blacken it. Ambrose Fleming inserted a second element, known generally as the *plate*— although technically it was an *anode* and the filament a *cathode*—in the glass bulb and discovered that when a positive charge was placed on the plate, a current would flow between the filament and the plate but that no current would flow when a negative charge was applied. The device converted the weak AC radio currents picked up by an antenna attached to the plate to a pulsating DC and delivered the audio component that had been used to modulate the radio waves as sounds—dots and dashes or speech—in a pair of earphones. His device was known as the *diode* (two electrodes) or *Fleming valve*.

Lee de Forest, in the first decade of the twentieth century, discovered how to amplify weak electronic signals. If a grid or mesh of fine wire was placed in the tube between the filament and the plate, a weak negative voltage on that grid would repel the electrons coming from the filament. A condition of no voltage on the grid would permit the maximum current to flow between the filament and the plate. Varying voltage on the grid would permit varying current flow in the main circuit. Accordingly, a weak current flow from an antenna or microphone or other source fed into the grid in such a way as to vary from zero to slightly negative would cause the extremely strong current flow in the main circuit to vary in precisely the same way—or, in other words, the weak input current was "amplified." De Forest called his tube an *Audion*, but the generic name is *triode*—a three-element or three-electrode vacuum tube.

Although there have been improvements—a separate *cathode* wrapped around the filament that acts as an oven, permitting a more even flow of electrons; increased complexity:

two or three separate circuits within the same tube, generally operating with the same filament source of electrons; smaller sizes; and more rugged construction: sometimes metal or ceramic instead of glass—all vacuum tubes use the same basic principles.

Vacuum Tube Transmitters   *See* Transmitter.

Valve   *See* Vacuum Tube.

Vertical Blanking Interval (VBI)   *See* Modulation and Television Signals.

Vestigial Sideband   *See* Television Signals.

VHS   *See* Recordings.

Video   Of, or pertaining to, the visual or picture portion of television.

Videocassettes and Videocassette Recorders (VCRs)   *See* Recordings.

Videodiscs   *See* Recordings.

Videotape Recording (VTR)   *See* Recordings.

Videotex   *See* Teletext.

Vidicon   *See* Television Camera Tubes.

Volts   *See* Circuit.

WARC (World Administrative Radio Conference)   *See* International Telecommunication Union.

Watts   *See* Circuit.

Waves, Propagation, Frequency, Wavelength   All *electromagnetic waves* or *electromagnetic energies* travel at 300,000 kilometers per second in free space, roughly 186,300 miles per second, and a fraction slower in wire or other materials. What distinguishes these waves or parts of the *electromagnetic spectrum*—radio, infrared, visible light, ultraviolet, X-rays—from one another is their length, the actual distance from crest to crest or trough to trough. If one uses the analogy of water waves traveling at a constant speed breaking on a seacoast, it becomes obvious that as the wavelength grows, the number of waves per unit of time will drop proportionally, and vice versa. Hence, *longwave* = low frequency; *shortwave* = high frequency; *microwave* = upper ultrahigh frequency or beyond. (See chart, page 628.) Further, since wavelength, measured in meters, times frequency, measured in thousands of cycles per second, equals 300,000—the

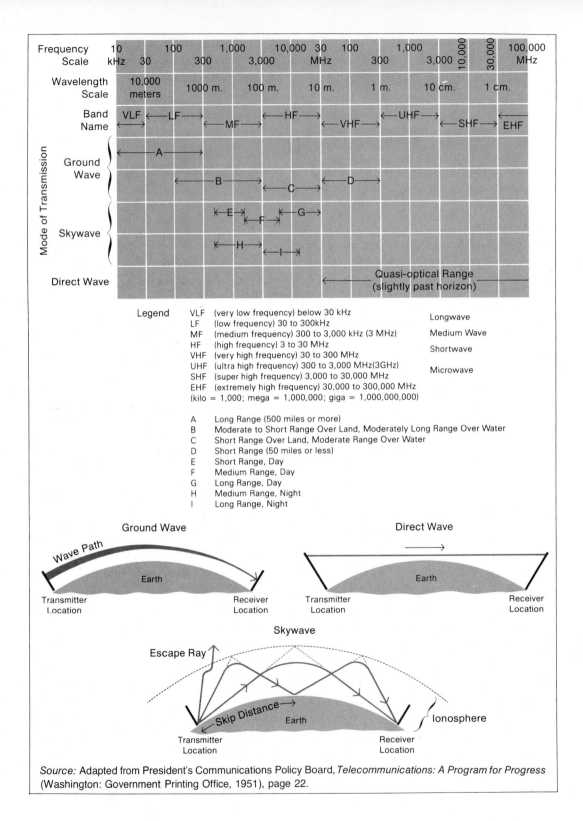

Frequency Scale	10 kHz	100	1,000	10,000	30	100	1,000	10,000	30,000	100,000

Source: Adapted from President's Communications Policy Board, *Telecommunications: A Program for Progress* (Washington: Government Printing Office, 1951), page 22.

speed of light or electromagnetic radiation in kilometers per second—we find that the wavelength of frequencies used in the standard (AM) broadcast band ranges from more than 555 meters (approximately six football fields) long at 540 kHz down to only 187 meters at 1,600 kHz. As discussed under **antenna,** this has implications for equipment; a half-wave antenna in the middle of the very high frequency (VHF) band used for FM radio is only five feet long. Because of the small size of tuning components at VHF or UHF frequencies (much as a combination of thickness and length of a musical tuning fork determines its pitch, so does a combination of two electrical values, capacitance and inductance, determine the *resonating frequency* of a piece of radio apparatus), the equipment is prone to drift off frequency as it heats up and metal expands. This is why early FM sets needed to be retuned after a period of use. Later sets avoided this problem with a combination of compensating circuits known as *automatic frequency control (AFC)* and the nonheating characteristics of most transistors.

Different wavelengths have different characteristics. Some—visible light—can be perceived directly by our senses but do not penetrate solid objects in the way that X-rays can. Some need a pathway, such as the wire used for 60 Hz electrical power, while others—radio and light—can travel or radiate in free space or atmosphere. Some will *attenuate*—that is, lose strength—very rapidly with distance, while others, if aimed or focused or guided carefully, will lose very little strength. Within that part of the electromagnetic spectrum used for radiocommunication, standard nomenclatures and characteristics apply (see box on page 628).

Radio waves occupy the electromagnetic spectrum below 100,000 MHz (megahertz, formerly designated mc, or megacycles per second). Above that part of the electromagnetic spectrum are infrared waves or rays, visible light (roughly 10^9 Hz), ultraviolet rays, X-rays, gamma rays, and cosmic rays.

The standard (AM) radio band runs between 535 and 1,605 kHz (kiloHertz). FM radio broadcasting runs between 88 and 108 MHz; noncommercial educational FM is between 88 and 92 MHz. VHF television is in three segments: 54–72, 76–88, and 174–216 MHz (channels 2–4, 5–6, and 7–13). UHF television (and some other services near the upper end) occupies the band between 470 and 890 MHz. AM radio now uses a bandwidth of 10 kHz, FM radio a bandwidth of 200 kHz, and television a bandwidth of 6 MHz.

Radio waves have three major means of *propagation,* and the efficiency of each varies with the frequency of the wave. *Groundwave,* for example, which hugs and travels along the earth's surface, is good for long-distance communication—up to worldwide in some cases—particularly when the ground *conductivity* near the transmitter is high, as is the extreme case with salt water, on frequencies from ELF into the medium-wave standard (AM) broadcast band. From about the middle of the standard broadcast band through the shortwave band, to about 30 MHz or even a little beyond, the most effective long-range mode is *skywave.* These wavelengths are such that signals bounce off the ionized layers that surround the earth, the *ionosphere,* at between 50 and 250 miles of altitude, much as a flashlight beam will bounce off a mirror. The bounce or *skip* may be calculated—the angle of incidence is equal to the angle of reflection, and the height is known—and the desired target area pinpointed by directional antenna arrays—a technique used for international shortwave but not for domestic broadcasting. Skywave useful range varies with time of day, season, and sunspot cycle. At high frequencies and above, groundwave is limited to only a few miles under normal conditions. Above the frequencies at which skywave is reliable, radio propagation is limited to about 125 percent of the distance to the optical horizon or *line-of-sight.* This *direct wave* propagation is the reason for the limited range of FM and television stations, whose antennas are rarely tall enough to send good signals more than 100 miles. A fourth transmission mode, *tropospheric forward scatter,* can be used for extensive distances in very expensive and huge military point-to-point systems at VHF frequencies and beyond. It scatters and bounces through the troposphere, which extends downward to the earth's surface. Space communication **satellites** use frequencies in this *quasi-optical* range because, although far away in distance, they have an unobstructed line of sight to the earth station antenna—over one-third of the globe. Since on almost any band, the lower the frequency, the higher the practical range—partly due to greater ease of designing equipment for frequencies that are familiar and easier to work with—television channels 2–6 often may be received for a greater distance than channels 7–13, and much farther away than frequently more powerful UHF television stations. This inequality in technical facilities for the same category or service of stations on the same band leads to economic, and consequently political, problems, particularly with respect to the standard (AM) band, where stations at the low end can expect more reliable groundwave coverage over a radius of around 100 miles than those at the high end. (*See also* Bandwidth, Channel, *and* Modulation.)

"Webs"   *See* Network.

Whip   *See* Antenna.

"Wired City"   *See* Cable.

Wireless   *See* Radio.

Wirephoto   *See* Facsimile.

Wire Services   *See* News.

Writers Guild of America   *See* Unions.

Historical
Statistics on
Broadcasting

Historical
Statistics on
Broadcasting

The tables on the following pages provide an overall view of many aspects of broadcasting history. Many of these data originally were assembled by L. W. Lichty and Sterling in 1967–1968. Some were published in different form in Lichty and Topping (1975), and more extended information on all of these categories except radio network programming appears in Sterling (1984). Specific sources are shown for all tables, with a brief form used if the item is listed in the bibliography (Appendix D), or a full citation if not.

Two points concerning all the tables: First, we have not noted all the exceptions or special cases that may occur in these tables but have pinpointed the more important. Second, where no information is shown, we have used the following system:

blank space	Indicates no such information (i.e., no television stations in 1921).
—	Zero or none.
na	Data unavailable, though theoretically the item or service did exist or may have existed.

Table 1 Number of Stations: 1921–1989

Table shows the number of stations actually on the air (regardless of license status) as of January 1 each year unless otherwise noted. Commercial and educational FM and VHF television were authorized in 1941, with UHF and noncommercial educational television appearing first in 1953. These figures should be used with some caution, as methods of counting varied with original source (Department of Commerce, FRC, FCC, or one of the commercial data firms). Basic station data here match that used in network affiliate tables 2 and 3 in this appendix.

1-A / AM Radio Stations through 1940

1921	5	1931	612
1922	30	1932	604
1923	556	1933	599
1924	530	1934	583
1925	571	1935	585
1926	528	1936	616
1927	681	1937	646
1928	677	1938	689
1929	606	1939	722
1930	618	1940	765

1-B / Broadcasting Stations since 1941

Year	AM Radio	FM Radio		Television		Total
		Commercial	Educational	Commercial	Educational	
1941	831	18	2	2 (July 1)		853
1942	887	36	7	4		934
1943	910	41	8	8		967
1944	910	44	8	8		970
1945	919	46	8	8		981
1946	948	48	9	6		1,011
1947	1,062	140	10	12		1,224
1948	1,621	458	15	16		2,110
1949	1,912	700	27	51		2,690
1950	2,086	733	48	98		2,965
1951	2,232	676	73	107		3,088
1952	2,331	637	85	108		3,161
1953	2,391	580	98	126		3,195
1954	2,521	560	112	354	2	3,549

1-B / Broadcasting Stations since 1941 (continued)

Year	AM Radio	FM Radio Commercial	FM Radio Educational	Television Commercial	Television Educational	Total
1955	2,669	552	122	411	11	3,765
1956	2,824	540	123	441	18	3,946
1957	3,008	530	125	471	23	4,157
1958	3,196	537	141	495	28	4,396
1959	3,326	578	151	510	35	4,600
1960	3,456	688	162	515	44	4,865
1961	3,547	815	175	527	52	5,116
1962	3,618	960	194	541	62	5,375
1963	3,760	1,081	209	557	68	5,675
1964	3,854	1,146	237	564	85	5,886
1965	4,044	1,270	255	569	99	6,237
1966	4,065	1,446	268	585	114	6,478
1967	4,121	1,643	296	610	127	6,797
1968	4,190	1,753	326	635	150	7,054
1969	4,265	1,938	362	662	175	7,402
1970	4,292	2,184	413	677	185	7,751
1971	4,343	2,196	472	682	199	7,892
1972	4,374	2,304	511	693	213	8,095
1973	4,395	2,411	573	697	230	8,306
1974	4,407	2,502	652	697	241	8,499
1975	4,432	2,636	717	706	247	8,738
1976	4,463	2,767	804	710	252	8,996
1977	4,497	2,873	870	728	256	9,224
1978	4,513	3,001	926	716	266	9,419
1979	4,549	3,107	982	724	274	9,636
1980	4,558	3,155	1,038	734	277	9,762
1981	4,589	3,282	1,092	756	282	10,001
1982	4,634	3,349	1,118	777	288	10,166
1983	4,685	3,421	1,090	813	293	10,304
1984	4,733	3,527	1,122	862	287	10,571
1985	4,754	3,716	1,172	904	290	10,836
1986	4,718	3,875	1,231	941	300	11,065
1987	4,863	3,944	1,261	999	296	11,363
1988	4,902	4,041	1,301	1,017	325	11,586
1989	4,948	4,174	1,383	1,062	338	11,905

Sources: Most data on Tables 1-A and 1-B are derived from FCC records, many of which are reported only in secondary sources. Data for earlier years (1921–1959) taken from *Broadcasting Yearbook 1977*. For many years, *Broadcasting Yearbook* and *Television Factbook* published different figures. We have chosen to follow *Television Factbook* for the 1960–1975 period, with supplementary data, including 1976–1977, from *Broadcasting* magazine and/or *Broadcasting Yearbook*. Data from 1978 through 1983 are as reported in Sterling (1984), pp. 5–7 and 18–19, citing FCC data as provided in *Television Digest* and/or *Broadcasting*. Data for 1984–1989 are as reported by FCC for stations licensed on the last day of the *prior* year (so, December 31, 1987 data is shown here as representing January 1, 1988), with 1985 and 1988 figures as printed in *Broadcasting*, and 1986 data showing stations licensed as of February 25. Other sources or exceptions: (1) AM radio column includes educational stations, which dwindled in number from as many as 200 in the mid-1920s to approximately 25 in 1941 and since; (2) data for 1921–1926 include "total authorized" stations, those for 1927–1947 include "authorized" and/or "licensed," not necessarily stations actually on the air as reported for later years (1923 data for March 1, 1924 data for October 1, 1925 data for June 20, and 1926–1932 data for June 30); (3) educational FM figures through 1973 from Corporation for Public Broadcasting, *Status Report on Public Broadcasting* (Washington: CPB, 1974), p. 8, with remainder from the FCC; and (4) educational television stations, 1941–1947 gathered by Lichty and Sterling from FCC.

Table 2 Commercial Radio Network Affiliates: 1927–1988

Figures in the next three tables show the growth of national commercial radio networks over six decades, with most figures as of January 1 of each year. In table 2-A, NBC figures include both Red and Blue networks (see table 2-C for details of NBC's two networks) until 1943, when Blue became independently owned (and was renamed ABC in 1945). Table 2-B details radio networks since 1965, which have increasingly included FM stations as affiliates. Total percentage of network stations is approximate, as many stations were affiliated with more than one network at a time. In 1968, ABC broke into four specialized networks, presaging the radio network specialization of the 1980s. All percentage columns refer to all commercial stations (AM only in table 2-A, AM and FM in table 2-B), not just network affiliates.

2-A / Commercial Radio Networks: 1927–1964

Year	NBC Number	NBC Percentage	CBS Number	CBS Percentage	Mutual Number	Mutual Percentage	ABC Number	ABC Percentage	Total AM Stations	Network Stations Number	Network Stations Percentage
1927	28	4.1%	16	2.3%					681	44	6%
1928	52	7.6	17	2.5					677	69	10
1929	58	9.6	49	8.1					606	107	18
1930	71	11.5	60	9.7					618	131	21
1931	75	12.3	76	12.4					612	159	25
1932	86	14.2	84	13.9					604	170	28
1933	88	14.7	91	15.2					599	179	30
1934	88	15.1	92	15.8	4	.7%			583	184	32
1935	88	15.0	97	16.6	3	.5			585	188	32
1936	89	14.4	98	15.9	39	6.3			616	226	37
1937	111	17.2	105	16.3	80	12.4			646	296	46
1938	142	20.6	110	16.0	107	15.5			689	359	52
1939	167	23.1	113	15.7	116	16.1			722	396	55
1940	182	23.8	112	14.6	160	20.9			765	454	59
1941	225	27.1	118	14.2	166	20.0			831	509	61
1942	136	15.3	115	13.0	191	21.5	116	13.1%	887	558	63
1943	142	15.6	116	12.7	219	24.1	143	15.7	910	620	68
1944	143	15.7	133	14.6	245	26.9	173	19.0	910	694	76
1945	150	16.3	145	15.8	384	41.8	195	21.2	919	874	95
1946	155	16.4	147	15.5	384	40.5	195	20.6	948	881	93
1947	161	15.2	157	14.8	488	46.0	222	20.9	1,062	1,028	97
1948	167	10.3	162	10.0	519	32.0	256	15.8	1,621	1,104	68
1949	170	8.9	167	8.7	526	27.5	269	14.1	1,912	1,132	59
1950	172	8.2	173	8.3	543	26.0	282	13.5	2,086	1,170	56
1951	180	8.1	183	8.2	552	24.7	295	13.2	2,232	1,210	54
1952	191	8.2	194	8.3	560	24.0	302	13.0	2,331	1,247	53
1953	207	8.7	203	8.5	560	23.4	348	14.6	2,391	1,318	55
1954	212	8.4	205	8.1	560	22.2	360	14.3	2,521	1,337	53
1955	208	7.8	207	7.8	563	21.1	357	13.4	2,669	1,335	50
1956	205	7.3	204	7.2	558	19.8	342	12.1	2,824	1,309	46
1957	199	6.6	201	6.7	525	17.5	334	11.1	3,008	1,259	42
1958	203	6.4	200	6.3	431	13.5	299	9.4	3,196	1,133	36
1959	209	6.3	198	6.0	441	13.3	286	8.6	3,326	1,134	34

2-A / Commercial Radio Networks: 1927–1964 (continued)

Year	NBC Number	NBC Percentage	CBS Number	CBS Percentage	Mutual Number	Mutual Percentage	ABC Number	ABC Percentage	Total AM Stations	Network Stations Number	Network Stations Percentage
1960	202	5.8%	198	5.7%	443	12.8%	310	9.0%	3,456	1,153	33%
1961	201	5.7	195	5.5	428	12.1	339	9.6	3,547	1,163	33
1962	200	5.4	206	5.6	510	13.8	342	9.3	3,618	1,258	34
1963	200	5.4	207	5.6	510	13.9	366	10.0	3,760	1,283	35
1964	202	5.2	227	5.8	500	12.8	353	9.1	3,854	1,282	33

2-B / Commercial Radio Networks: 1965–1988

Year	NBC Number	NBC Percentage	CBS Number	CBS Percentage	Mutual Number	Mutual Percentage	ABC Number	ABC Percentage	Total Commercial AM-FM Stations	Network Stations Number	Network Stations Percentage
1965	209	3.9%	237	4.5%	501	9.4%	355	6.7%	5,314	1,302	24.5%
1966	215	3.9	239	4.3	520	9.4	361	6.6	5,511	1,265	23.0
1967	216	3.7	240	4.2	na	na	337	5.8	5.764	na	na
1968	217	3.7	243	4.1	515	8.7	500	8.4	5,943	1,457	24.5
1969	222	3.6	245	3.9	492	7.9	1,013	16.3	6,203	1,972	31.8
1970	220	3.4	247	3.8	523	8.1	1,175	18.1	6,476	2,165	33.4
1971	230	3.5	249	3.8	538	8.2	1,074	16.4	6,539	2,091	30.9
1972	231	3.5	242	3.6	545	8.2	1,169	17.5	6,678	2,187	32.7
1973	233	3.4	243	3.6	568	8.3	1,246	18.3	6,806	2,290	33.6
1974	230	3.3	248	3.6	632	9.1	1,293	18.7	6,910	2,403	34.8
1975	232	3.1	247	3.5	657	9.3	1,322	18.7	7,068	2,458	34.8
1976	223	3.1	257	3.6	684	9.5	1,353	18.7	7,230	2,517	34.8
1977	236	3.2	266	3.6	755	10.2	1,546	21.0	7,370	2,803	38.0
1978	245	3.3	270	3.6	800	10.6	1,554	20.7	7,514	2,869	38.2
1979	268	3.5	278	3.6	950	12.4	1,561	20.4	7,656	3,057	39.9
1980	281	3.6	321	4.2	934	11.9	1,574	20.4	7,713	3,110	40.3
1981	315	4.0	400	5.1	902	11.5	1,591	20.2	7,871	3,208	40.8
1982	370	4.6	425	5.3	876	11.0	1,631	20.4	7,983	3,302	41.4
1983	363	4.5	na	na	860	10.6	1,750	21.6	8,106	na	na
1984	318	3.8	na	na	841	10.2	1,745	21.1	8,260	na	na
1985	355	4.2	na	na	847	10.0	1,726	20.4	8,470	na	na
1986	478	5.6	na	na	na	na	1,893	22.0	8,593	na	na
1987	389	4.4	na	na	na	na	2,133	24.2	8,807	na	na
1988	475	5.3	na	na	731	8.2	2,251	25.2	8,943	na	na

Sources: For total number of stations: FCC. For number of their affiliates: the radio networks. NBC data after 1982 are for various dates, usually September, October, or November, and are from both the radio network and "The Source." Mutual data are from *Broadcasting Yearbook*.

2-C / NBC Red and Blue Radio Networks: 1927–1941

Year	Red (WEAF)	Blue (WJZ)	Alternates
1927	22	6	na
1928	17	11	24
1929	22	14	22
1930	22	17	32
1931	23	18	34
1932	28	22	36
1933	28	24	36
1934	28	20	40
1935	27	20	41
1936	26	18	45
1937	30	33	48
1938	36	44	62
1939	48	55	64
1940	53	60	69
1941	74	92	59

Source: NBC.

Table 3 Commercial Television Network Affiliates: 1947–1988

Figures show growth of television networks over a 40-year period, with all data as of January 1 of each year. Because the Du Mont network left the air in October 1955, and as most of its affiliates held a primary affiliation with another network, its figures are presented in the footnote. Through the 1950s, the separate network affiliation listings may not add to the number of network stations shown: multiple affiliations were more common in the days of fewer television outlets per market.

Year	NBC Number	NBC Percentage	CBS Number	CBS Percentage	ABC Number	ABC Percentage	Total Stations	Network Stations Number	Network Stations Percentage
1947	2	16.7%	1	8.3%	1	8.3%	12	4	33%
1948	9	56.3	3	18.8	6	37.5	16	17	100
1949	25	49.0	15	29.4	11	21.6	51	50	98
1950	56	57.1	27	27.6	13	13.3	98	96	98
1951	63	58.9	30	28.0	14	13.1	107	107	100
1952	64	59.3	31	28.7	15	13.9	108	108	100
1953	71	56.3	33	26.2	24	19.0	126	125	99
1954	164	46.3	113	31.9	40	11.3	354	317	90
1955	189	46.0	139	33.8	46	11.2	411	374	91
1956	200	45.4	168	38.1	53	12.0	441	421	95
1957	205	43.5	180	38.2	60	12.7	471	445	94
1958	209	42.2	191	38.8	69	13.9	495	469	95
1959	213	41.8	193	37.8	79	15.5	510	485	95

3 / Commercial Television Network Affiliates: 1947–1988 (continued)

Year	NBC Number	NBC Percentage	CBS Number	CBS Percentage	ABC Number	ABC Percentage	Total Stations	Network Stations Number	Network Stations Percentage
1960	214	41.6%	195	37.9%	87	16.9%	515	496	96%
1961	201	38.1	198	37.6	104	19.7	527	503	95
1962	201	37.2	194	35.9	113	20.9	541	508	94
1963	203	36.4	194	34.8	117	21.0	557	514	92
1964	212	37.6	191	33.9	123	21.8	564	526	93
1965	198	34.8	190	33.4	128	22.5	569	516	91
1966	202	34.5	193	33.0	137	23.4	585	532	91
1967	205	33.6	191	31.3	141	23.1	610	537	88
1968	207	32.6	192	30.2	148	23.3	635	547	86
1969	211	31.9	190	28.7	156	23.6	662	557	84
1970	215	31.8	193	28.5	160	23.6	677	568	84
1971	218	32.0	207	30.4	168	24.6	682	593	87
1972	218	31.5	209	30.2	172	24.8	693	599	86
1973	218	31.3	210	30.1	176	25.3	697	604	87
1974	218	31.3	212	30.4	181	26.0	697	611	88
1975	219	30.8	213	30.0	185	26.0	711	617	87
1976	218	30.7	213	30.0	182	25.6	710	613	86
1977	212	29.1	210	28.8	190	26.1	728	612	84
1978	213	29.3	208	28.6	195	26.8	716	616	86
1979	213	29.3	208	28.6	202	27.5	724	623	86
1980	213	28.6	200	26.8	202	27.1	734	615	84
1981	213	28.3	200	26.6	207	27.5	756	620	82
1982	215	27.8	200	25.8	206	26.6	777	621	80
1983	na	na	202	24.8	207	25.4	813	na	na
1984	206	23.8	202	23.3	210	24.3	862	618	72
1985	205	22.7	205	22.7	211	23.3	904	621	69
1986	207	22.0	204	21.7	214	22.7	941	625	66
1987	207	20.7	184	18.4	215	21.5	999	606	61
1988	208	20.4	na*	na*	222	21.8	1,017	na	na

*CBS reported its affiliates merely as "over 200."

Note: Figures above do not include the Du Mont network, as most affiliations were secondary or tertiary after prime affiliation with one of the networks above. Du Mont figures (from *Broadcasting Yearbook*) were: 1949 (45), 1950 (52), 1951 (62), 1952 (62), 1953 (133), 1954 (195), 1955 (158). Du Mont suspended network operations late in 1955. In early 1967, the United (Overmyer) Network broadcast an evening program to 106 stations. The Fox network, discussed in 10.3, began with 111 affiliates in 1986 and had 122 by March 1989. All percentages are based on total number of commercial stations.

Sources: For total number of stations: FCC. For number of their affiliates: the television networks. Data for 1978–1982 from Sterling (1984), page 24, citing the networks; 1983–1988 from the networks to the authors.

Appendix C

Table 4 Radio Advertising: 1927–1988

Figures show amount of advertising revenue accruing to national radio networks (including program, talent, time, commercial, and agency commission costs), national and regional spot (including commissions), and local advertising (including discounts and agency commissions). Discounts are excluded for networks and spots. Last column is radio percentage of all advertising expenditure. Dollar figures are in millions; add 000,000.

Year	Network Dollars	Network Percentage	National Spot Dollars	National Spot Percentage	Local Dollars	Local Percentage	Total Dollars	Percentage of All Advertising
1927	$ 3.8	79.0%	$ .9			19.0%	$ 4.8	na
1928	10.3	73.0	3.9			28.0	14.1	na
1929	19.2	72.0	7.6			28.0	26.8	na
1930	27.7	68.0	12.8			32.0	40.5	2%
1931	37.5	67.0	18.5			33.0	56.0	3
1932	39.1	63.0	22.8			37.0	61.9	5
1933	31.5	55.0	25.5			45.0	57.0	5
1934	42.6	59.0	30.0			41.0	72.8	6
1935	62.6	55.6	$ 14.9	13.2%	$ 35.1	31.2%	112.6	7
1936	75.6	61.8	22.7	18.6	24.0	19.6	122.3	7
1937	88.5	53.8	28.0	17.0	48.1	29.2	164.6	8
1938	89.2	53.4	34.0	20.3	43.9	26.3	167.1	9
1939	98.6	53.6	35.0	19.0	50.2	27.3	183.8	9
1940	113.3	52.6	42.1	19.5	60.2	27.9	215.6	10
1941	125.4	50.7	52.3	21.2	69.5	28.1	247.2	11
1942	128.7	49.5	58.8	22.6	72.5	27.9	260.0	12
1943	156.5	49.9	70.9	22.6	86.2	27.5	313.6	13
1944	191.8	48.7	87.4	22.2	114.3	29.0	393.5	14
1945	197.9	46.7	91.8	21.7	134.2	31.7	423.9	15
1946	199.6	43.9	98.2	21.6	156.6	34.5	454.4	14
1947	201.2	39.7	106.4	21.0	198.8	39.3	506.4	12
1948	210.6	37.5	121.6	21.7	229.9	40.9	561.6	12
1949	203.0	35.5	123.4	21.6	245.0	42.9	571.4	11
1950	196.3	32.4	135.8	22.4	273.3	45.1	605.4	11
1951	179.5	29.6	138.3	22.8	288.5	47.6	606.3	10
1952	161.5	25.9	141.5	22.7	321.1	51.5	624.1	9
1953	141.2	23.1	145.6	23.8	324.4	53.1	611.2	8
1954	114.4	20.5	134.9	24.1	309.4	55.4	558.7	7
1955	84.4	15.5	134.1	24.6	326.4	59.9	544.9	6
1956	60.5	10.7	161.0	28.4	345.5	60.9	567.0	6
1957	63.5	10.3	186.9	30.2	367.5	59.5	617.9	6
1958	57.8	9.3	189.7	30.6	371.7	60.0	619.2	6
1959	44.1	6.7	206.4	31.4	405.8	61.8	656.3	6

4 / Radio Advertising: 1927–1988 (continued)

Year	Network Dollars	Network Percentage	National Spot Dollars	National Spot Percentage	Local Dollars	Local Percentage	Total Dollars	Percentage of All Advertising
1960	$ 43.1	6.2%	$ 221.6	32.0%	$427.7	61.8%	$ 692.4	6%
1961	42.8	6.3	220.0	32.2	420.0	61.5	682.8	6
1962	45.8	6.2	233.0	31.7	457.0	62.1	735.8	6
1963	56.4	7.1	243.0	30.8	490.0	62.1	789.4	6
1964	59.1	7.0	256.0	30.3	531.0	62.8	846.1	6
1965	60.0	6.5	275.0	30.0	582.0	63.5	917.0	6
1966	63.5	6.3	308.0	30.5	638.5	63.2	1,010.0	6
1967	64.0	6.1	313.5	29.9	670.5	64.0	1,048.0	6
1968	63.0	5.3	360.0	30.3	767.0	64.5	1,190.0	7
1969	59.0	4.6	368.0	29.1	837.0	66.2	1,264.0	7
1970	56.0	4.3	371.0	28.4	881.0	67.4	1,308.0	7
1971	63.0	4.4	395.0	27.3	987.0	68.3	1,445.0	7
1972	74.0	4.6	402.0	24.9	1,136.0	70.5	1,612.0	7
1973	68.0	3.9	400.0	23.2	1,255.0	72.8	1,723.0	7
1974	69.0	3.8	405.0	22.0	1,363.0	74.2	1,837.0	7
1975	83.0	4.2	436.0	22.0	1,461.0	73.8	1,980.0	7
1976	105.0	4.5	518.0	22.2	1,707.0	73.3	2,330.0	7
1977	137.0	5.2	546.0	20.7	1,951.0	74.1	2,634.0	7
1978	147.0	4.8	620.0	20.3	2,285.0	74.9	3,052.0	7
1979	161.0	4.9	665.0	20.1	2,484.0	75.0	3,310.0	7
1980	183.0	4.9	779.0	21.0	2,740.0	74.0	3,702.0	7
1981	230.0	5.4	879.0	20.8	3,121.0	73.8	4,230.0	7
1982	218.0	4.8	909.0	20.3	3,365.0	74.9	4,492.0	7
1983	254.0	5.0	1,023.0	20.4	3,739.0	74.6	5,015.0	7
1984	288.0	4.9	1,184.0	20.1	4,412.0	75.0	5,884.0	7
1985	328.0	5.0	1,319.0	20.0	4,915.0	75.0	6,563.0	7
1986	380.0	5.4	1,332.0	19.0	5,313.0	75.6	7,026.0	7
1987	413.0	5.7	1,330.0	18.5	5,463.0	75.8	7,206.0	7
1988	420.0	5.6	1,425.0	18.4	5,900.0	76.2	7,745.0	7

Note: Readers should be aware that ".0" has been added to parts of this table for typographical consistency—on percentages from 1927 through 1934, and on dollar figures from 1961 through 1988.

Sources: Research Department, McCann-Erickson (data reprinted in several sources, including *Television Factbook*) for data since 1935. Earlier information refers to estimated gross radio billings (and is thus not directly comparable to the post-1935 data) and comes from *Broadcasting Yearbook 1951*, page 12, table V. These represent advertising volume at the one-time rate, ignoring discounts. McCann-Erickson has provided rounded and corrected data for several earlier years. Data for 1976–1981 from Sterling (1984), page 85, citing McCann-Erickson; 1982–1986 from Radio Advertising Bureau, *Radio Facts 1987–1988*, page 43; 1987–1988 from McCann-Erickson to authors.

Appendix C

Table 5 Television Advertising: 1949–1988

Figures show amount of advertising revenue accruing to national television networks (including program, talent, time, commercial and agency commission costs), national and regional spot advertising (including commissions), and local advertising (including discounts and agency commissions). Discounts are excluded for networks and spots. Last column is television percentage of all advertising expenditure. Dollar figures are in millions; add 000,000.

Year	Network		Nat.-Reg. Spot		Local		Total	Percentage of All
	Dollars	Percentage	Dollars	Percentage	Dollars	Percentage	Dollars	Advertising
1949	$ 29.4	50.9%	$ 9.2	15.9%	$ 19.2	33.2%	$ 57.8	1%
1950	85.0	49.8	30.8	18.0	55.0	32.2	170.8	3
1951	180.8	54.4	69.9	21.0	81.6	24.6	332.3	5
1952	256.4	56.5	93.8	20.7	103.7	22.8	453.9	6
1953	319.9	52.8	145.5	24.0	140.7	23.2	606.1	8
1954	422.2	52.2	206.8	25.6	180.2	22.3	809.2	10
1955	550.2	53.1	260.4	25.2	224.7	21.7	1,035.3	11
1956	643.1	52.5	329.0	26.9	252.6	20.6	1,224.7	12
1957	690.1	53.7	351.6	27.4	243.6	19.0	1,285.3	12
1958	742.0	53.5	397.0	28.6	248.4	17.9	1,387.4	13
1959	776.0	50.7	486.4	31.8	266.8	17.4	1,529.2	13
1960	820.0	50.4	526.7	32.4	280.5	17.2	1,627.3	13
1961	887.3	52.5	548.0	32.4	256.0	15.1	1,691.0	14
1962	976.0	51.4	629.0	33.2	292.0	15.4	1,897.0	15
1963	1,025.0	50.4	698.0	34.4	309.0	15.2	2,032.0	16
1964	1,132.0	49.5	806.0	35.2	351.0	15.3	2,289.0	16
1965	1,237.0	49.2	892.0	35.5	386.0	15.3	2,515.0	17
1966	1,393.0	49.3	988.0	35.0	442.0	15.7	2,823.0	17
1967	1,455.0	50.0	988.0	34.0	466.0	16.0	2,909.0	17
1968	1,523.0	47.1	1,131.0	35.0	577.0	17.9	3,231.0	18
1969	1,678.0	46.8	1,253.0	35.0	654.0	18.2	3,585.0	19
1970	1,658.0	46.1	1,234.0	34.3	704.0	19.6	3,596.0	18
1971	1,593.0	45.1	1,145.0	32.4	796.0	22.5	3,534.0	17
1972	1,804.0	44.1	1,318.0	32.2	969.0	23.7	4,091.0	18
1973	1,968.0	44.1	1,377.0	30.9	1,115.0	25.0	4,460.0	18
1974	2,145.0	44.2	1,497.0	30.8	1,212.0	25.0	4,854.0	18
1975	2,306.0	43.8	1,623.0	30.8	1,334.0	25.3	5,263.0	19
1976	2,857.0	42.6	2,154.0	32.0	1,710.0	25.4	6,721.0	20
1977	3,460.0	45.4	2,204.0	29.0	1,948.0	25.6	7,612.0	20
1978	3,975.0	44.4	2,607.0	29.1	2,373.0	25.5	8,955.0	20
1979	4,599.0	45.3	2,873.0	28.3	2,682.0	26.4	10,154.0	20
1980	5,130.0	45.0	3,269.0	28.6	2,967.0	26.0	11,416.0	20
1981	5,540.0	43.5	3,746.0	29.4	3,368.0	26.5	12,729.0	21
1982	6,144.0	42.6	4,364.0	30.3	3,765.0	26.1	14,423.0	22
1983	6,955.0	42.3	4,827.0	29.4	4,345.0	26.5	16,427.0	22
1984	8,318.0	43.1	5,488.0	28.4	5,084.0	26.3	19,310.0	22

5 / Television Advertising: 1949–1988 (continued)

| Year | Network | | Nat.-Reg. Spot | | Local | | Total | Percentage of All |
	Dollars	Percentage	Dollars	Percentage	Dollars	Percentage	Dollars	Advertising
1985	$8,060.0	39.6%	$6,004.0	29.6%	$5,714.0	28.2%	$20,298.0	21%
1986	8,342.0	37.9	6,570.0	29.8	6,514.0	29.6	22,026.0	22
1987	8,500.0	37.1	6,845.0	29.8	6,514.0	29.6	22,026.0	22
1987	8,500.0	37.1	6,845.0	29.8	6,835.0	29.8	22,941.0	21
1988	9,435.0	36.9	7,600.0	29.6	7,725.0	30.1	25,635.0	21

Note: Readers should be aware that ".0" has been added to parts of this table for typographical consistency, particularly for dollar figures for the years from 1961 through 1988.

Sources: Research Department, McCann-Erickson (data reprinted in several sources, including *Television Factbook*). McCann-Erickson has provided rounded and corrected data for several earlier years. McCann-Erickson data for 1976–1988 as reported to the authors from that company.

Table 6 Commercial Radio Programming: 1927–1988

The first four tables, based on data in Summers (1958), show trends in programming on the national radio networks from their inception through the mid-1950s, when television had drastically changed the role of network radio. Noncommercial radio programming is excluded. Data for 1927 refer only to NBC's Red network, while data after that year include NBC-Blue and CBS and data after 1934 include Mutual. NBC-Blue became independent in 1943 and was renamed ABC in 1945.

The figures shown are the number of quarter-hours of that program type on the air for all networks for a single week—typically, the third week in January. Thus the data are indicative of that "season's" programming but are no more than that, especially as the "season" concept did not become important for the networks until well into the 1930s.

The tables cover (A) evening programs, or those on the air after 6 P.M., any day of the week, (B) weekday daytime programs on the air Monday through Friday before 6 P.M., (C) a total program summary combining the data in A and B plus weekend daytime figures, and (D) a percentage summary for selected years showing trends in program types. For convenience, the programs in the first three tables are divided into four major categories: variety, music, drama, and talk. Each is further subdivided into specific program types. Note the following in the set of tables:

Other than children's variety, programs directed at children are included in totals with adult programs.

Recorded music and magazine variety, to name the two most obvious types, do not appear in network schedules until the 1950s.

Under *drama*, "general" refers to anthology and prestige dramatic programs, while "light" is a catchall for series not covered in other categories.

Under *talk*, "human interest" means a program type concentrating on personalities and occupations and activities, though the nominal format of such programs was often audience-participation, panel, or quiz show in style.

Under *music*, all the programs shown were live except those labeled "recorded."

Note: Tables 6-A through 6-D are copyrighted by L. W. Lichty and are used with permission. Table 6-E details radio station formats since 1964 and is drawn from many different surveys, as listed in the footnote.

6-A / Evening Network Radio Programs: 1927–1956
(number of quarter-hours on commercial networks)

	1927	1928	1929	1930	1931	1932	1933	1934	1935	1936	1937	1938
Variety												
Vaudeville and Comedy	—	4	6	12	9	5	28	32	30	28	38	36
Semi-Variety	—	—	—	8	18	37	8	23	18	16	16	6
Amateur and Talent	—	—	—	—	—	—	—	—	2	9	4	4
Hillbilly, Country & Western	—	—	2	2	—	2	7	9	10	20	10	8
General and Talk Variety	4	10	12	10	16	12	14	14	23	22	24	30
Children's Variety	—	—	—	—	—	—	—	—	—	3	—	—
Magazine Variety	—	—	—	—	—	—	—	—	—	—	—	—
Music												
Musical Variety	30	34	55	90	75	87	57	64	99	70	56	52
Light Music	8	28	34	46	37	60	44	27	29	34	25	20
Concert Music	39	76	68	62	62	33	44	48	47	49	36	48
Recorded Music	—	—	—	—	—	—	—	—	—	—	—	—
Drama												
General	—	—	—	—	—	—	—	2	2	6	8	6
Light	—	8	16	22	20	13	15	13	18	17	11	17
Women's Serial	—	—	—	—	—	16	15	15	13	5	—	—
Comedy, Comedy Situation	—	—	—	11	18	17	16	8	10	22	34	16
Thriller	—	—	2	6	9	19	38	34	35	22	25	23
Documentary, Information	—	4	—	2	—	3	4	4	4	7	8	12
Talk												
Human Interest	—	—	—	—	—	—	—	6	7	5	16	16
Quiz	—	—	—	—	—	—	—	—	—	—	6	8
News	1	4	2	4	13	12	19	27	28	31	34	23
Public Affairs, Forums	—	2	2	5	5	8	7	—	12	5	8	8
Talk	4	4	2	4	14	12	13	14	15	26	14	18
Sports Play-by-Play	—	—	—	—	—	—	—	—	—	—	—	2
Religion	2	2	2	4	14	4	2	5	5	5	5	5
Total Quarter-Hours	88	176	203	288	310	340	331	345	407	402	378	358

6-A / Evening Network Radio Programs: 1927–1956 (continued)
(number of quarter-hours on commercial networks)

1939	1940	1941	1942	1943	1944	1945	1946	1947	1948	1949	1950	1951	1952	1953	1954	1955	1956
38	32	18	32	34	38	32	30	38	34	30	24	22	26	18	6	8	12
6	16	6	9	2	5	2	—	4	2	2	4	4	4	2	2	10	10
4	4	4	4	2	2	2	—	—	4	8	7	7	9	6	2	2	2
12	12	8	8	6	8	10	4	6	4	10	4	4	4	12	12	11	5
32	16	28	24	21	29	22	22	18	4	4	8	4	4	2	8	25	7
—	—	—	—	—	—	—	—	—	—	—	—	—	—	—	—	—	—
—	—	—	—	—	—	—	—	—	—	—	—	—	—	—	—	—	30
48	59	58	69	60	63	70	63	40	44	52	51	33	29	56	52	76	51
12	24	4	11	7	5	13	9	3	4	2	7	6	15	23	26	28	37
28	28	34	37	22	29	29	24	18	22	23	21	26	32	30	38	27	24
—	4	—	—	—	—	—	—	—	—	—	—	—	10	12	10	4	15
14	14	14	16	12	16	8	18	16	18	20	14	20	16	16	12	6	—
28	24	20	17	14	11	8	17	19	12	22	12	9	25	15	22	7	5
—	—	—	—	—	—	—	—	—	—	—	—	—	—	—	—	—	—
18	21	17	27	20	23	32	40	44	41	35	53	39	33	36	41	16	13
33	40	30	41	35	56	48	57	79	78	68	91	95	91	79	71	62	37
8	4	4	9	12	16	16	6	6	10	4	2	12	9	10	11	6	18
13	10	19	12	10	16	9	11	12	12	8	10	12	6	—	6	2	9
18	30	37	28	30	30	32	38	27	36	48	34	32	16	36	25	19	12
33	56	45	62	65	88	73	77	49	65	50	77	82	83	96	103	82	85
12	13	18	14	12	11	10	14	17	9	13	13	12	10	12	17	17	23
23	38	23	26	8	5	9	21	23	14	22	19	19	18	25	32	21	27
2	3	3	2	—	—	2	3	3	3	3	5	6	6	3	3	26	—
7	5	9	7	11	9	5	5	5	5	3	7	—	—	—	2	10	10
389	453	399	455	383	460	432	459	427	421	427	463	444	446	489	501	465	432

6-B / Daytime Network Radio Programs: 1927–1956
     (number of quarter-hours on commercial networks)

	1927	1928	1929	1930	1931	1932	1933	1934	1935	1936	1937	1938
Variety												
Vaudeville and Comedy	—	—	—	—	—	—	2	—	5	4	—	—
Semi-Variety	—	—	—	—	—	—	—	—	—	—	—	—
Amateur and Talent	—	—	—	—	—	—	—	—	—	—	—	—
Hillbilly, Country & Western	—	—	—	—	—	—	—	—	—	—	—	—
General and Talk Variety	—	—	—	—	—	—	—	20	27	20	30	40
Children's Variety	—	—	—	11	8	15	25	—	12	10	7	4
Magazine Variety	—	—	—	—	—	—	—	—	—	—	—	—
Music												
Musical Variety	—	—	—	2	—	9	5	—	6	—	8	—
Light Music	—	10	27	18	30	62	54	92	49	87	45	42
Concert Music	—	—	4	8	4	6	9	20	16	13	18	16
Recorded Music	—	—	—	—	—	—	—	—	—	—	—	—
Drama												
General	—	—	—	4	4	4	8	8	4	4	4	4
Light	—	—	—	—	—	2	4	—	—	—	5	—
Women's Serial	—	—	—	—	—	—	20	43	48	88	154	240
Comedy, Situation Comedy	—	—	—	—	—	6	5	9	15	—	5	7
Thriller	—	—	—	—	—	5	14	13	18	25	27	41
Documentary, Information	—	—	1	—	10	10	10	10	12	10	12	10
Talk												
Human Interest	—	—	—	—	—	—	—	5	5	16	12	17
Quiz	—	—	—	—	—	—	—	—	—	—	—	—
News	—	—	—	—	—	—	6	—	—	10	29	18
Public Affairs, Forums	—	—	—	—	—	—	—	—	—	—	—	1
Talk	3	31	89	51	96	134	79	91	80	70	83	88
Sports Play-by-Play	—	—	—	—	—	—	—	—	—	—	—	—
Religion	—	—	—	—	—	—	—	—	—	—	—	5
Total Quarter-Hours	3	41	121	94	152	253	241	311	297	357	439	533

6-B / Daytime Network Radio Programs: 1927–1956 (continued)
(number of quarter-hours on commercial networks)

1939	1940	1941	1942	1943	1944	1945	1946	1947	1948	1949	1950	1951	1952	1953	1954	1955	1956
—	—	—	—	—	—	—	10	—	—	—	—	—	—	10	5	—	—
—	—	—	—	—	—	—	—	—	—	—	—	—	—	—	—	—	—
—	—	—	—	—	—	—	—	—	—	—	—	10	10	10	—	—	—
—	—	—	2	—	2	10	—	35	30	30	35	35	15	24	19	—	—
40	42	40	32	62	70	30	55	40	30	55	80	95	65	110	101	121	126
3	4	5	—	—	—	—	—	—	—	—	—	10	5	14	5	—	—
—	—	—	—	—	—	—	—	—	—	—	—	—	—	—	—	—	95
—	—	—	4	5	9	—	10	10	10	20	30	25	10	15	20	41	48
65	46	38	35	4	13	30	29	24	6	21	16	15	25	53	43	23	23
16	10	11	14	2	4	—	—	—	—	2	2	—	—	—	5	5	5
—	—	—	—	—	—	—	—	—	40	15	20	10	30	25	36	28	35
—	—	—	—	—	—	—	—	—	—	—	—	—	—	—	—	—	—
3	—	—	—	—	15	14	14	9	13	15	20	20	10	15	28	33	23
225	305	300	275	200	220	195	200	165	180	165	160	135	175	140	135	130	95
—	5	5	5	—	5	5	10	10	10	10	10	—	—	—	—	5	5
30	20	26	35	25	30	40	50	45	45	40	42	35	35	15	12	12	8
20	19	10	10	10	10	10	10	10	10	—	—	—	—	—	—	—	—
6	4	—	—	—	10	30	45	58	70	85	70	50	50	44	53	35	28
—	—	5	5	—	15	15	15	41	50	50	31	50	60	45	35	35	13
—	10	20	41	49	50	50	51	50	50	35	35	40	30	51	73	63	55
—	—	—	—	—	—	—	—	—	—	—	—	—	—	—	—	—	—
75	68	68	76	33	37	42	44	37	36	54	45	55	40	48	15	18	25
—	—	—	—	—	—	—	—	—	—	—	—	—	—	—	—	—	—
5	5	—	—	—	—	—	5	—	—	5	5	5	5	5	5	—	—
488	538	528	534	390	490	471	548	534	580	602	591	590	565	624	595	544	584

6-C / Network Radio Programs: Summary 1927–1956
(number of quarter-hours on commercial networks)

	1927	1928	1929	1930	1931	1932	1933	1934	1935	1936	1937	1938
Evening												
Variety	4	14	20	32	43	56	57	78	83	98	92	84
Music	77	138	157	198	174	180	145	139	175	153	117	120
Drama	—	12	18	41	47	68	88	76	82	79	86	74
Talk	7	12	8	17	46	36	41	52	67	72	83	80
Daytime												
Variety	—	—	—	11	8	15	27	20	44	30	37	44
Music	—	10	31	28	34	77	68	112	71	100	71	58
Drama	—	—	1	4	14	27	61	83	97	127	207	302
Talk	3	31	89	51	96	134	85	96	85	96	124	129
Weekend Daytime												
Variety	—	—	—	—	—	4	6	10	8	8	10	12
Music	—	2	10	14	27	56	55	66	ꜱ8	62	65	55
Drama	—	—	2	2	2	15	12	19	16	7	16	11
Talk	16	22	15	21	25	26	24	22	23	35	38	36
Total by Type												
Variety	4	14	20	43	51	75	90	108	135	136	139	140
Music	77	150	198	240	235	313	268	317	304	315	253	233
Drama	—	12	21	47	63	110	161	178	195	213	309	387
Talk	26	65	112	89	167	196	150	170	175	203	245	245
Total Quarter-Hours	107	241	351	419	516	694	669	773	809	867	946	1,005

6-C / Network Radio Programs: Summary 1927–1956 (continued)
(number of quarter-hours on commercial networks)

1939	1940	1941	1942	1943	1944	1945	1946	1947	1948	1949	1950	1951	1952	1953	1954	1955	1956
92	80	64	77	65	82	68	56	66	48	54	47	41	47	40	30	56	66
88	115	96	117	89	97	112	96	61	70	77	79	65	86	121	126	135	127
101	103	85	110	93	122	112	138	164	159	149	172	175	174	156	157	97	73
108	155	154	151	136	159	140	169	136	144	147	165	163	139	172	188	177	166
43	46	45	34	62	72	40	65	75	60	85	115	150	95	168	130	121	221
81	56	49	53	11	26	30	39	34	56	58	68	50	65	93	104	97	111
278	349	341	325	235	280	264	284	239	258	230	222	190	220	170	180	175	131
86	87	93	122	82	112	137	160	186	206	229	186	200	185	193	181	151	121
24	16	12	15	14	30	18	20	12	10	12	14	22	24	23	58	66	90
56	63	64	66	51	60	43	69	63	53	47	47	50	52	108	83	78	80
18	16	17	18	14	36	30	34	39	39	35	39	38	36	36	27	22	16
35	53	58	65	50	62	60	70	69	58	77	79	90	77	107	99	92	92
159	142	121	126	141	184	126	141	153	118	151	176	213	166	231	218	243	377
225	234	209	236	151	183	185	204	158	179	182	194	165	203	322	313	310	318
397	468	443	453	342	438	406	456	442	456	414	433	403	430	362	364	294	220
229	295	305	338	268	333	337	399	391	408	453	430	453	401	472	468	420	379
1,010	1,139	1,078	1,153	902	1,138	1,054	1,200	1,144	1,161	1,200	1,233	1,234	1,200	1,387	1,363	1,267	1,294

6-D / Network Radio Programs:
Percentages 1929–1956 (every three years)

	Percentage of All Quarter-Hours:						
Year	Variety	Musical	Drama	Interview, Human Interest, Quiz	News, Sports, Forums, Talks	Other* Programs	Total Quarter-Hours Broadcast per Week
1929	5%	56%	6%	—	28%	5%	351
1932	11	46	15	—	26	2	694
1935	18	39	25	2%	11	5	809
1938	15	24	38	4	16	3	1,005
1941	10	20	42	6	18	4	1,078
1944	16	16	38	7	19	4	1,138
1947	14	15	33	14	21	3	1,144
1950	13	15	36	13	19	4	1,233
1953	15	25	28	8	20	10	1,387
1956	31	23	16	5	19	6	1,294

*Includes Farm, Religious, Miscellaneous, and Unclassified.

Sources: Data in this table derived from tables 6-A through 6-C.

6-E / Radio Station Formats: 1964–1988

Year and Size of Market	Number of Stations	Percentage of Total								
		Middle of the Road	Top 40/ Contemporary	Beautiful and Background	Country/ Western	Black/ Soul	Progressive Rock	News and Talk	Classical	Other
1964										
(AM and FM)										
Large, Multiple-Station Markets	na	12%	10%	22%	6%	5%	—	—	—	45%
Single-Station Markets	1,400	22	9	21	12	1	—	—	—	35
1966										
(FM only)										
Top 50 Markets	244	49	15	30	—	—	—	—	—	6
Other Markets	564	64	4	23	5	—	—	—	—	4
1968										
(AM and FM)										
Top 50 Markets	1,076	40	15	13	11	7	—	—	—	14
1970										
(AM and FM)										
All Markets	1,365	35	17	22	11	1	4%	1%	—	9
1971										
(AM and FM)										
Top 100 Markets										
AM Stations	955	21	27	17	18	—	—	—	—	17
FM Stations	643	18	25	39	10	—	—	—	—	8
1973										
(AM and FM)										
All Markets	4,193	22	26	8	21	14	3	3	3%	—
1975										
(AM and FM)										
Top 40 Markets										
AM Stations	600	26	17	5	16	10	2	9	2	13
FM Stations	475	13	21	24	9	5	10	2	6	10
1976										
(AM and FM)										
Top 50 Markets	500	14	27	18	6	5	—	8	1	22

6-E / Radio Station Formats: 1964–1988 (continued)

Year and Size of Market	Number of Stations	Percentage of Total									
		Middle of the Road	Rock/ Contemporary	Beautiful Music	Country	Black/ Urban	News and Talk	Religion	Classical	Other
1978										
AM Stations	1,479	26%	24%	3%	21%	6%	5%	6%	1%	11%
FM Stations	1,174	6	41	26	11	4	—	4	3	5
AM/FM Combined	2,653	17	32	13	17	5	3	5	2	6
1980										
AM Stations	1,474	29	19	3	21	7	6	7	1	7
FM Stations	1,293	5	45	23	12	6	—	5	2	2
AM/FM Combined	2,767	18	32	12	17	6	3	6	1	5
1982										
AM Stations	1,530	29	8	2	21	11	6	9	1	13
FM Stations	1,374	11	39	18	17	6	—	4	2	3
AM/FM Combined	2,904	19	23	9	19	8	3	7	1	9
1984										
AM Stations	1,430	29	6	2	20	8	9	11	1	16
FM Stations	1,437	18	35	13	18	6	—	5	2	2
AM/FM Combined	2,867	24	20	7	19	7	4	8	1	10
1986										
AM Stations	1,323	30	3	1	18	9	9	11	1	18
FM Stations	1,551	24	33	11	15	6	—	5	2	4
AM/FM Combined	2,874	27	19	6	16	8	4	7	1	11
1988										
AM Stations	1,311	29	4	2	16	8	10	12	1	20
FM Stations	1,628	24	32	9	15	6	—	4	2	7
AM/FM Combined	2,939	26	19	6	15	7	5	7	1	13

Notes: The percentages for 1964 refer only to musical content and therefore are not strictly applicable to later figures. Blank spaces generally indicate that the programming category has been included under "Other." In some cases, however, the particular programming format was not broadcast that year. Figures for 1976 are based on the top 10 stations in the top 50 markets. Thus, while the listing encompasses the top 50 markets, it excludes many stations in these markets that feature minority-taste programming. "Black/Urban" represents black and disco music combined. "Other" represents a variety of formats, including jazz, religious, nostalgia, Spanish, other ethnic (except black), and other/unknown categories.

Sources: Sterling (1984), pages 180–181 for data through 1982. Original sources include the following: 1964–1973 data: Lichty and Topping (1975), page 435, table 32. 1975 data: *Cox Looks at FM Radio: Past, Present, and Future* (Atlanta, Ga.: Cox Broadcasting Corporation, 1976), page 55, exhibit 16. 1976 data: *Broadcasting* (September 27, 1976), "The Many Worlds of Radio, 1976," page 46. 1978, 1980, and 1982 data all from James Duncan, using Arbitron ratings. 1984–1986 data from James Duncan, *American Radio: Tenth Anniversary Issue, 1976–1986* (Indianapolis, Ind., 1986), page A-29. Percentages calculated by authors; 1988 data from Duncan to authors.

Table 7 Commercial Network Television Programming: 1949–1988

The first three tables show trends in programs on the national commercial television networks from their inception in 1948 to either 1988 (prime time) or 1973 (daytime). *Not* shown here is any noncommercial or (after 1967) "public" television programming, including that of the Public Broadcasting Service. Except for table 7-A, these tables show the number of quarter-hours of each program type on the air for a single week, typically the third week in January—parallel to tables 6-A through 6-D. The data are thus indicative of that television season; that is, 1954 data refer in a general sense to the whole 1953–1954 television season.

The tables show (A) evening programs on the air after 6 P.M. (listed by hours rather than quarter-hours, and with somewhat different program categories from the other tables); (B) weekday daytime programs on the air Monday through Friday before 6 P.M.; (C) a total programming summary of number of quarter-hours and percentages, allowing a direct comparison of prime-time and daytime information plus that for weekend programming, and also including cost and other measures of program change; and (D and E) detailed major network format types in both prime-time and daytime hours summarized from data provided by A.C. Nielsen. Tables 7-D and 7-E differ from tables 7-A through 7-C not only in source but because (1) they include only programs carrying advertising (the vast majority) and (2) they cover only 10 A.M. to 4:30 P.M. as "daytime."

The program types for these television tables are more refined than those for radio, making direct comparisons a bit difficult. For example, "thriller" in the radio tables includes crime-detective, action-adventure, westerns, and suspense programs in television. Note also:

Children's programs are grouped together under a single entry, "other types."

Under *music*, "light music" indicates a program of singing or instrumental music only, typically a 15-minute filler program used in television's early years but seldom since.

Under *drama*, "general" includes anthology and prestige dramatic presentations primarily, but also a few programs not readily classified in the other categories shown.

Note: Tables 7-A through 7-C are copyrighted by L. W. Lichty and are used with permission.

7-A / Evening Network Television Programs: 1949–1988
(number of hours on commercial networks)

	Variety	General Drama	Movie	Action-Adventure	Crime-Detective	Western	Situation Comedy	Quiz and Panel	News and Information	Talk, Sports, Religion
1949	22	6	9	—	1	—	1	3	12	28
1950	21	11	2	4	3	1	4	5	7	32
1951	42	16	3	6	4	2	4	5	6	33
1952	30	14	—	7	7	2	6	5	7	19
1953	20	11	—	5	6	2	9	5	11	14
1954	19	15	—	7	5	2	13	6	9	15

7-A / Evening Network Television Programs: 1949–1988 (continued)
(number of hours on commercial networks)

	Variety	General Drama	Movie	Action-Adventure	Crime-Detective	Western	Situation Comedy	Quiz and Panel	News and Information	Talk, Sports, Religion
1955	25	20	—	2	3	2	15	6	9	7
1956	28	18	3	5	2	4	10	7	7	4
1957	26	19	3	7	2	4	9	6	7	3
1958	20	13	—	6	5	10	10	6	8	3
1959	17	9	11	5	8	16	7	2	8	3
1960	18	8	—	8	12	18	8	2	6	2
1961	9	7	11	8	10	14	13	1	14	2
1962	11	9	2	8	12	12	13	2	13	1
1963	17	14	4	9	5	9	12	1	12	1
1964	19	15	4	8	5	9	10	2	13	2
1965	20	9	6	11	2	6	16	1	13	—
1966	16	5	8	14	3	9	18	—	11	—
1967	12	2	12	19	3	10	13	1	13	—
1968	15	1	13	18	6	9	10	2	12	—
1969	17	3	14	8	10	10	11	2	13	—
1970	18	9	18	5	6	6	14	2	12	—
1971	17	9	16	2	12	6	13	1	12	—
1972	9	5	18	3	12	4	10	—	11	—
1973	13	6	25	5	11	3	11	—	12	—
1974	5	6	23	4	16	3	7	—	11	—
1975	6	7	19	4	20	2	9	—	11	—
1976	5	9	14	3	25	—	13	1	12	—
1977	8	8	12	9	19	—	14	—	13	—
1978	10	9	14	7	12	—	15	1	12	—
1979	8	15	14	9	10	1	14	1	13	—
1980	6	14	14	7	11	2	13	—	14	1
1981	5	14	13	8	10	—	13	—	14	3
1982	5	12	17	6	8	1	13	—	14	2
1983	1	14	16	11	8	—	14	—	13	3
1984	1	12	17	10	11	—	11	—	14	5
1985	1	11	15	11	14	—	11	—	13	2
1986	—	10	16	11	14	—	12	—	13	1
1987	—	12	15	10	12	—	13	—	15	—
1988	1	13	13	3	20	—	13	—	14	—

Note: "Variety" includes comedy, music, country, and talk variety formats and miscellaneous (or varied). "Movie" includes made-for-television movies. "Action-Adventure" includes suspense–psychological thriller, crime-detective, and situation comedy. "Quiz" includes panel, audience participation, and human interest. "'News" includes network evening news program as well as documentary, forum, and other information formats. "Talk" includes all sports programs and religion.

1948–1949 to 1976–1977 based on sample week of programming, third week in January; 1977–1978 to 1988–1989 based on "regular" (not special, one-time, or miniseries) programs during 26-week season. Figures are rounded to whole hours.

7-B / Daytime Network Television Programs: 1949–1973
  (number of quarter-hours on commercial networks)

	1949	1950	1951	1952	1953	1954	1955	1956	1957	1958
Variety										
Special, Variety	—	—	—	—	—	—	—	—	—	—
Comedy	—	—	—	35	—	—	—	—	—	—
Amateur, Talent	—	—	—	—	—	—	—	—	—	—
Country and Western	—	—	—	—	—	—	—	—	—	—
General, Talk	10	10	13	129	79	86	166	166	114	76
Music										
Musical Variety	5	—	20	20	40	50	30	10	10	55
Light Music	10	5	5	5	—	—	—	—	—	—
Drama										
General	—	—	—	—	—	—	—	20	20	30
Motion Pictures	—	—	—	—	—	—	—	40	30	—
Women's Serials	—	—	5	30	20	45	84	40	55	65
Action-Adventure	20	—	—	—	—	—	—	—	—	10
Crime-Detective	—	—	—	—	—	—	—	—	—	—
Suspense	—	—	—	—	—	—	—	—	—	—
Westerns	—	—	15	—	—	10	—	—	—	—
Comedy, Situation Comedy	—	—	—	—	—	—	—	—	30	10
Animated Cartoons	—	—	—	—	—	—	—	—	—	—
Quiz and Panel										
Audience Participation	20	30	24	28	42	44	40	40	50	80
Human Interest	15	5	8	1	25	25	20	30	35	45
Panel Shows	—	—	10	—	—	—	—	—	5	—
News and Information										
Newscasts	—	—	—	10	5	5	—	—	5	5
Forums, Interviews	—	—	—	—	—	—	—	—	—	—
Documentary, Information	—	—	—	—	—	20	—	—	—	—
Other Types										
Religion	—	5	—	—	—	—	—	—	—	—
Talk	15	90	28	11	—	—	27	—	—	—
Children's Shows	10	40	30	15	21	35	32	70	40	25
Sports	—	—	—	—	—	—	—	—	—	—
Miscellany	—	—	—	—	—	—	—	—	—	—
Total Quarter-Hours	105	185	158	284	232	320	399	416	394	401

7-B / Daytime Network Television Programs: 1949–1973 (continued)
   (number of quarter-hours on commercial networks)

1959	1960	1961	1962	1963	1964	1965	1966	1967	1968	1969	1970	1971	1972	1973
—	—	—	—	—	—	—	—	—	—	—	—	—	—	—
—	—	—	—	—	—	—	—	—	—	—	—	—	—	—
—	—	—	—	—	—	—	—	—	—	—	—	—	—	—
—	—	—	—	—	—	—	—	—	—	—	—	—	—	—
70	60	40	50	70	45	40	40	40	40	40	50	50	50	60
50	30	30	20	20	10	10	10	20	—	—	—	—	—	—
—	—	—	—	—	—	—	—	—	—	—	—	—	—	—
20	50	50	50	40	20	—	20	20	20	—	—	—	—	—
—	—	—	—	—	—	—	—	—	—	—	—	—	—	—
70	80	100	70	60	70	120	150	110	108	138	158	180	160	160
—	20	20	—	—	—	—	—	—	—	—	—	—	—	—
—	50	—	—	—	—	—	—	—	—	—	—	—	—	—
—	—	—	—	—	—	—	—	—	—	—	—	—	—	—
—	50	10	10	—	20	20	—	—	—	—	—	—	—	—
10	40	50	20	40	50	60	60	50	50	50	60	60	70	20
—	10	—	—	—	—	—	—	—	—	—	—	—	—	—
140	80	100	140	110	120	100	100	128	128	114	68	70	90	130
40	40	50	30	20	20	10	10	20	20	8	—	—	—	—
—	—	—	10	20	20	10	10	10	18	10	28	20	10	10
5	5	9	22	16	24	24	24	22	18	18	26	24	25	25
—	—	—	—	—	—	—	—	—	—	—	—	—	—	—
—	—	—	—	—	—	—	—	—	—	—	—	—	—	—
—	—	—	—	—	—	—	—	—	—	—	—	—	—	—
50	20	20	30	40	10	10	10	10	12	12	10	10	10	10
25	15	15	40	20	20	20	20	20	20	20	20	20	20	20
—	—	—	—	—	—	—	—	—	—	—	—	—	—	—
—	—	—	—	—	—	—	—	—	—	—	—	—	—	—
480	550	494	492	456	429	424	454	450	434	410	420	434	435	435

7-C / Network Television Programs: Summary 1949–1973 (every third year)
(number of quarter-hours on commercial networks)

	1949	1952	1955	1958	1961	1964	1967	1970	1973
All Programming: **Quarter-Hours**									
Variety	66	249	278	161	95	134	116	195	150
Music	45	64	52	99	50	42	40	28	16
Drama	87	196	266	309	468	400	478	518	483
Quiz	68	93	108	167	170	180	174	102	142
News / Information	45	56	60	62	77	94	88	83	94
Other	166	145	157	75	97	88	74	84	86
Total	477	803	921	873	957	938	970	1,010	971
All Programming: **Percentage**									
Variety	14%	31%	30%	18%	10%	14%	12%	19%	15%
Music	9	8	6	11	5	4	4	3	2
Drama	18	24	29	35	49	43	48	51	50
Quiz	14	12	12	19	18	19	18	10	15
News / Information	9	7	7	7	8	10	9	8	10
Other	35	18	17	9	10	9	8	8	9
Total	99%	100%	101%	99%	100%	99%	99%	99%	101%
Average Production Cost: **Prime-Time Programs**									
90 min. Drama	na	na	na	na	na	$181,000	$200,000	$300,000	$342,500
60 min. Variety	$ 5,900	$35,900	$67,700	$84,000	$110,000	115,700	182,170	193,210	204,286
60 min. Drama	10,800	21,100	34,100	65,450	86,640	120,810	176,520	203,610	213,636
30 min. Variety	3,800	16,700	24,600	44,100	63,000	65,000	na	100,000	na
30 min. Drama	3,500	13,200	26,100	36,200	42,270	59,030	88,690	103,960	104,194
30 min. Quiz	1,730	9,640	11,400	29,330	28,200	45,500	71,000	35,000	na
Movies	na	na	na	na	180,000	200,000	380,000	750,000	750,000
Movies for TV	na	na	na	na	na	na	na	400,000	418,333
Live-VTR or Film **(percentage of quarter-hours in prime time)**									
Live-VTR	34%	78%	65%	42%	17%	25%	19%	22%	12%
Film	na	25	40	69	81	54	67	51	58

Source: Lichty and Topping (1975), Table 36, pages 439–440. Information in the last two sections (average production cost and live-VTR or film) is *only* for prime-time programs broadcast 7–11 P.M. Average production cost is actually the lease (rental) payment for all showings (usually two) for "Movies" while referring to production costs for all other categories. The percentage figures for live-VTR and film are based on prime-time quarter-hours—and may not add to 100 percent due to rounding.

7-D / Network Television Prime-Time Program Types: 1973–1987
(number of quarter-hours per week)

Year	Variety	Drama/ Adventure	Film	Mystery	Situation Comedy	Other	Total
1973	20	40	64	68	48	12	252
1974	8	68	58	76	30	12	252
1975	16	68	40	84	44	12	264
1976	28	52	46	66	50	22	264
1977	16	60	48	48	64	28	264
1978	12	72	48	48	58	26	264
1979	—	48	56	56	68	36	264
1980	18	60	56	28	70	32	264
1981	16	76	40	48	60	24	264
1982	12	76	40	48	64	24	264
1983	8	104	48	28	52	24	264
1984	6	84	48	84	48	22	284
1985	4	90	40	82	48	20	284
1986	—	78	48	58	56	24	264
1987	4	72	36	74	58	20	264

Sources: All data derived from A.C. Nielsen. 1973–1982 from Sterling (1984), page 198; 1983–1984 from *Television Audience 1984* (Northbrook, Ill.: A.C. Nielsen Co., 1984), page 40; 1985–1987 from *Television Audience 1987* (Northbrook, Ill.: A.C. Nielsen Co., 1987), page 43. Figures are quarter-hour averages calculated by the authors from Nielsen data for the fall of each indicated television season. Totals may not add due to rounding. "Film" means feature films. 1987 data do not include figures for Fox Broadcasting Company, for purposes of comparative continuity. The available figures for Fox are as follows (in quarter-hours):

Sitcom: 14; Mystery: 6; Total: 20

7-E / Network Television Daytime Program Types: 1973–1987
(number of quarter-hours per week)

Year	Daytime Drama	Situation Comedy	Quiz/Audience Participation	News/Other	Total
1973	148	20	158	13	340
1974	138	10	188	3	340
1975	158	10	168	3	340
1976	180	30	130	20	360
1977	180	50	120	10	360
1978	200	30	100	20	350
1979	210	20	120	10	360
1980	220	40	60	20	340
1981	220	30	80	10	340
1982	230	20	80	—	330
1983	210	30	90	10	340
1984	230	20	80	20	350
1985	220	10	110	—	340
1986	200	10	90	10	310
1987	220	20	100	—	340

Sources: All data derived from A.C. Nielsen. 1973–1982 from Sterling (1984), page 198; 1983–1984 from *Television Audience 1984* (Northbrook, Ill.: A.C. Nielsen Co., 1984), page 40; 1985–1987 from *Television Audience 1987* (Northbrook, Ill.: A.C. Nielsen Co., 1987), page 43. Figures are quarter-hour averages calculated by the authors from Nielsen data for the fall of each indicated television season. Totals may not add due to rounding. Some data for 1977–1982 are estimated from Nielsen data by the authors.

Table 8 Ownership of Radio Receivers: 1922–1988

Though radio production was frozen during World War II (1942–1945), the number of radio households grew as extra sets were dis-

tributed to those with none. As cars were junked during that period, however, car radios in use obviously declined. While household radios continued to increase in numbers with population growth after 1960, the percentage of homes with radio and typical cost changed little.

8-A / Ownership of Radio Receivers: 1922–1959

Year	Radio Households	Percentage of All Households	Average Receiver Cost	Cars with Radio	Percentage of All Cars
1922	60,000	0.2%	$50	na	na
1923	400,000	1.5		na	na
1924	1,250,000	4.7		na	na
1925	2,750,000	10.1	83	na	na
1926	4,500,000	16.0		na	na
1927	6,750,000	23.6		na	na
1928	8,000,000	27.5		na	na
1929	10,250,000	34.6		na	na
1930	13,750,000	45.8	78	30,000	.1%
1931	16,700,000	55.2		100,000	.4
1932	18,450,000	60.6		250,000	1.2
1933	19,250,000	62.5		500,000	2.4
1934	20,400,000	65.2		1,250,000	5.8
1935	21,456,000	67.3	55	2,000,000	8.9
1936	22,869,000	68.4		3,500,000	14.5
1937	24,500,000	74.0		5,000,000	19.7
1938	26,667,000	79.2		6,000,000	23.8
1939	27,500,000	79.9		6,500,000	24.9
1940	28,500,000	81.1	38	7,500,000	27.4
1941	29,300,000	81.5		8,750,000	29.6
1942	30,600,000	84.0		9,000,000	32.3
1943	30,800,000	83.6		8,000,000	30.9
1944	32,500,000	87.6		7,000,000	27.5
1945	33,100,000	88.0	40	6,000,000	23.4
1946	33,998,000	89.9		7,000,000	24.9
1947	35,900,000	93.1		9,000,000	29.3
1948	37,623,000	94.2		11,000,000	33.1
1949	39,300,000	94.8		14,000,000	38.6
1950	40,700,000	94.7	26	18,000,000	49.6
1951	41,900,000	95.5		21,000,000	52.3
1952	42,800,000	95.6		23,500,000	55.3
1953	44,800,000	98.2		25,000,000	57.3
1954	45,100,000	96.7		26,100,000	56.4
1955	45,900,000	96.4	20	29,000,000	60.0
1956	46,800,000	96.3		30,100,000	57.9
1957	47,600,000	96.2		35,000,000	64.6
1958	48,500,000	96.3		36,500,000	65.5
1959	49,450,000	96.7		37,200,000	65.7

Sources: For radio households: National Association of Broadcasters (to 1950) and Radio Advertising Bureau (1950 to 1959). For cars with radio: Electronic Industries Association (to 1954) and Radio Advertising Bureau (1955 to 1959). Average receiver cost from Lichty and Topping (1975), page 521, table 41. Otto Schairer, in *Patent Policies of Radio Corporation of America* (New York: RCA Institutes Press, 1939, page 57), reports an average retail price for radio receivers of $120 in 1929 and $43.60 in 1937.

8-B / Development of Home Audio Market since 1960

Year	FM Receivers as Percentage of			Households with		
	All Radios Sold	All Households	Automobile Radios Sold	Cars with Radio	Component Audio	Compact Disc
1960	8%	na	na	68%	na	
1965	15	na	6%	79	na	
1970	48	74%	14	93	na	
1975	65	93	38	95	na	
1980	78	95	78	95	na	
1985	na	na	na	95	39%	2%
1988	na	na	90	95	44	8

Sources: All data through 1980 as reported in Sterling (1984), pages 225–226, citing Electronics Industries Association estimates for all but household penetration of FM, which is from Pulse Inc. for data through 1975 and from Radio Advertising Bureau for data since 1975. Data since 1980 from Electronic Industries Association and Radio Advertising Bureau.

Table 9 Television Receiver Ownership and Use: 1946-1988

9-A / Ownership of Television Receivers: 1946–1988

Year	Television Households	Percentage of All Households	Television Homes			Average Receiver Cost	
			Percentage with Multiple Sets	Percentage with UHF	Percentage with Color	B & W	Color
1946	8,000	.02%	—				
1947	14,000	.04	—			$279	
1948	172,000	.4	1%				
1949	940,000	2.3	1				
1950	3,875,000	9.0	1			190	
1951	10,320,000	23.5	2		na		
1952	15,300,000	34.2	2	na	na		
1953	20,400,000	44.7	3	na	na		
1954	26,000,000	55.7	3	na	na		
1955	30,700,000	64.5	3	na	.02%	138	$500
1956	34,900,000	71.8	5	na	.05		
1957	38,900,000	78.6	6	9.2%	.2		
1958	41,925,000	83.2	8	8.1	.4		
1959	43,950,000	85.9	10	8.0	.6		

9-A / Ownership of Television Receivers: 1946–1988 (continued)

			Television Homes				
Year	Television Households	Percentage of All Households	Percentage with Multiple Sets	Percentage with UHF	Percentage with Color	Average Receiver Cost B & W	Color
1960	45,750,000	87.1%	13%	7.0%	.7%	$132	$392
1961	47,200,000	88.8	13	7.1	.9	125	381
1962	48,855,000	90.0	14	7.3	1.2	128	352
1963	50,300,000	91.3	16	9.6	1.9	118	346
1964	51,600,000	92.3	19	15.8*	3.1	109	348
1965	52,700,000	92.6	22	27.5	5.3	106	356
1966	53,850,000	93.0	25	38.0	9.7	98	371
1967	55,130,000	93.6	28	47.5	16.3	92	362
1968	56,670,000	94.6	29	57.0	24.2	74	336
1969	58,250,000	95.0	33	66.0	32.0	78	328
1970	59,700,000	95.2	34	73.0	39.2	75	317
1971	61,600,000	95.5	36	80.0	45.1	81	324
1972	63,500,000	95.8	38	81.0	52.8	79	319
1973	65,600,000	96.0	41	86.0	60.1	77	308
1974	66,800,000	96.1	42	89.0	67.3	79	316
1975	68,500,000	96.3	43	91.0	70.8	84	341
1976	70,500,000	96.4	45	92.0	73.3	89	349
1977	71,200,000	97.4	47	92.0	76.0	89	350
1978	72,900,000	97.6	48	na	81.0	85	350
1979	74,500,000	97.7	48	na	83.0	86	350
1980	76,300,000	97.9	50	95.0	85.0	89	367
1981	79,900,000	98.1	51	96.0	85.0	89	370
1982	81,500,000	98.1	53	na	88.0	88	364
1983	83,300,000	98.1	55	na	89.0	81	350
1984	83,800,000	98.1	55	na	90.0	83	334
1985	84,900,000	98.1	57	na	91.0	82	331
1986	85,900,000	98.1	57	na	92.0	81	328
1987	87,400,000	98.1	59	na	92.0	83	333
1988**	88,600,000	98.1	60	na	94.0	75	336

*The all-channel receiver requirement passed by Congress in 1962 took effect in 1964.
**Estimates

Sources: NBC Corporate Planning data as reprinted annually in *Television Factbook*, except for UHF penetration data, which are from NBC Research, based, in turn, on studies by the Advertising Research Foundation (to 1968) and U.S. Census reports. Average set prices taken from *Television Digest* (17:27:9) for 1960–1976, inclusive, using Electronic Industries Association data. Estimates for earlier years from Lichty and Topping (1975), page 522, table 42, and authors. Column on multiple sets is a compromise by the authors due to extensive disagreement on this statistic between various original sources (which is why figures are rounded to nearest whole number). Through 1963, the figures are those of NBC Research as published in *Television Factbook*—data closely paralleled by other sources. After 1963, the figures are a compromise most closely following data supplied by A. C. Nielsen Co. 1976 television household and color penetration data derived from estimates in Blair's 1977 *Statistical Trends in Broadcasting*. 1977 data supplied by *Television Factbook* staff. Color and UHF data generally from Nielsen fall survey of the previous year. Set prices for 1978–1988 from *Television Digest* (28:13:11 and 27:22:9), with black-and-white television prices reported to authors by *Television Digest* based on information from EIA *Consumer Electronics*. Television households 1978–1986 from *Broadcasting Yearbook 1988*, page G-16. Data for multiple-set and color households 1978–1988 from annual issues of *Television Audience* (Northbrook, Ill.: A. C. Nielsen Co.).

9-B / Growth of Home Video Market since 1975

	Sales to Dealers (in thousands of units)				VCR Households (thousands)	Percentage of TV Homes with VCRs
Year	VCRs	Videodisc Players	Video Cameras	Projection TVs		
1975	30	—	—	—	—	—
1976	55	—	—	—	—	—
1977	160	—	—	—	—	—
1978	402	—	—	—	200	0.3%
1979	475	—	61	29	400	0.5
1980	805	—	114	57	840	1.1
1981	1,361	157	190	139	1,440	1.8
1982	2,035	223	296	117	2,530	3.1
1983	4,091	307	414	144	4,580	5.5
1984	7,616	200	489	195	8,880	10.6
1985	11,853	200	517	266	17,660	20.8
1986	13,174	200	1,169	304	30,920	36.0
1987	13,306	220	1,604	293	42,560	48.7
1988	14,500	250	2,000	300	51,390	58.0

Sources: All unit sales figures from Electronic Industries Association, *Consumer Electronics Annual Review,* various issues. VCRs for 1975–1977 are estimates based on import figures from *Television Digest* (February 1, 1988), page 15. Video cameras for 1985–1988 and VCRs for 1988 from *EIA Consumer Electronics US Sales* (June 1988), page 7. VCR households and percentage of television homes with VCRs: *Trends in TV* (March 1988), Television Bureau of Advertising, page 5.

9-C / Hours of Radio-Television Use: 1931–1986 (selected years)

	Daily Hours per Household	
Year	Radio	Television
1931	4:04	—
1935	4:48	—
1943	4:48	—
1946	4:13	na
1950	4:06	4:35
1955	2:12	4:51
1960	1:53	5:06
1965	2:27	5:29
1971	2:52	6:02
1976	3:25	6:18
1981	3:19	6:45
1986	na	7:08

Sources: Sterling (1984), pages 219–220, for data through 1981, citing diverse sources that are not strictly comparable but are still useful for trends. Specifically: **1931:** Lumley (1934), page 196, reporting on a survey of some 14,000 listeners in 10 cities; **1935:** CBS, *Radio in 1937* (New York: CBS, 1937), page 30, reporting on research in communities of 2,500 persons and over; **1943:** C. H. Sandage, *Radio Advertising for Retailers* (Cambridge, Mass.: Harvard University Press, 1945), page 140, citing Nielsen Radio Index research for January of total listening in cities over 100,000; **1946** and **1965:** Lichty and Topping (1975), page 523, citing A.C. Nielsen; **1950, 1955, 1960:** A.C. Nielsen; **1971** radio figure from *CBS Radio Network: Affiliate Research/Promotion Reference Guide* (New York: CBS, 1972), citing RADAR studies; television figure from A.C. Nielsen; **1976** radio figure from *Encyclomedia: Radio 1978* (New York: Decisions Publications, 1978), page 6; television from *Broadcasting* (April 3, 1978), page 48, citing Nielsen. **1981** radio from Radio Advertising Bureau, citing RADAR; television from Nielsen. **1986** from Television Bureau of Advertising, citing Nielsen.

Table 10 Growth of New Media: 1952–1988

Data below, for various dates (usually in the fall or January 1) of each year, show estimates of the number of cable systems, total number of cable subscribers, percentage of television homes with cable, and the average number of subscribers per system. The latter figure may mislead, since even in 1977 only 22 percent of all reporting systems had 3,500 or more subscribers and only 10 systems had 50,000 or more.

10-A / Cable Television Systems: 1952–1969

Year	Number of Systems	Number of Subscribers (thousands)	Percentage of Homes with Cable Service	Average Number of Subscribers per System
1952	70	14	0.1%	200
1953	150	30	0.2	200
1954	300	65	0.3	217
1955	400	150	0.5	375
1956	450	300	0.9	667
1957	500	350	0.9	700
1958	525	450	1.1	857
1959	560	550	1.3	982
1960	640	650	1.4	1,016
1961	700	725	1.5	1,036
1962	800	850	1.7	1,063
1963	1,000	950	1.9	950
1964	1,200	1,085	2.1	904
1965	1,325	1,275	2.4	962
1966	1,570	1,575	2.9	1,003
1967	1,770	2,100	3.8	1,186
1968	2,000	2,800	4.4	1,400
1969	2,260	3,600	6.1	1,593

Source: Original estimates from *Television Factbook* and *Television Digest*.

10-B / Cable Television Systems since 1970

Year	Number of Systems	Number of Subscribers (thousands)	Percentage of Homes with Cable Service	Average Number of Subscribers per System	Number of Channels Offered	
					Up to 12	20 or more
1970	2,490	4,500	7.6%	1,807	89.9%	na
1971	2,639	5,300	8.8	2,008	89.3	na
1972	2,841	6,000	9.6	2,112	85.0	na
1973	2,991	7,300	11.1	2,441	83.0	na
1974	3,158	8,700	13.0	2,755	83.7	na
1975	3,506	9,800	14.3	2,795	77.6	11.2%
1976	3,651	10,800	15.5	2,958	76.1	12.0
1977	3,800	11,900	17.3	3,132	75.0	12.8
1978	3,875	12,500	17.1	3,355	73.7	13.9
1979	4,150	13,600	18.3	3,398	70.4	26.7
1980	4,225	15,200	19.9	3,787	na	na
1981	4,375	17,830	22.3	4,183	59.8	35.2
1982	4,825	24,290	29.8	4,352	na	na
1983	5,600	28,320	34.0	5,057	41.4	46.0
1984	6,200	32,930	39.3	5,311	36.4	54.6
1985	6,600	36,340	42.8	5,506	19.2	71.7
1986	7,500	39,160	45.6	5,221	23.6	63.3
1987	7,771	41,690	47.7	5,365	20.7	66.1
1988	8,413	43,790	49.4	5,205	17.7	67.3

Sources: For data through 1983, Sterling (1984), pages 28 and 206, citing information gathered by *Television Digest* and *Television Factbook,* which are also the sources for the 1984–1988 data, as reprinted in the NCTA's *Cable Television Developments* (December 1988).

10-C / Basic Cable Service Subscribers since 1980

Programming Service	Start-up Date	Number of Subscribers (in millions) in				
		July 1980	Sept. 1982	Oct. 1984	Mar. 1986	Aug. 1988
ACTS Satellite Network	5/84			na	4.0	6.6
Arts and Entertainment Network	4/81		8.0	12.0	18.0	34.2
Black Entertainment Television	1/79	3.7	2.0	8.0	13.0	20.0
Cable Health Network	6/82		na	na	—	—
Cable News Network (CNN)	6/80	2.3	15.3	28.5	33.5	46.9
CNN Headline News	1/82		1.9	12.6	18.0	32.7
Christian Broadcasting Network	4/77	7.5	18.2	25.1	30.1	41.6
C-SPAN (I)	3/79	5.8	10.5	19.3	24.0	39.2
C-SPAN (II)	6/86					15.7
Country Music Television	3/83			5.5	5.3	8.0
Daytime	1/82		7.2	na	—	—
Discovery Channel	6/85				6.2	33.8
Entertainment and Sports Programming Network (ESPN)	9/79	4.0	18.8	34.0	36.9	47.8
Eternal Word Television Network	8/81		.6	na	4.0	10.0
Financial News Network	11/81		.8	17.0	21.0	30.5
GalaVision	10/79			.1	na	3.0
Home Shopping Network	7/85				7.0	15.7
The Learning Channel	10/79	.3	1.8	5.0	6.3	12.8
Lifetime	2/84			20.1	24.0	39.8
Modern Satellite Network	1/79	2.3	5.7	10.4	—	—
Movietime	7/87					7.0
MTV Networks, Inc.	8/81		6.8	22.6	28.0	42.7
The Nashville Network	3/83			17.9	23.8	41.1
National Christian Network	6/80		1.4	1.2	—	—
National Jewish Television Network	5/81		2.1	5.0	5.6	na
Nickelodeon	7/79	2.5	9.0	20.1	26.0	41.2
NICK at Night	7/85				na	36.9
Nostalgia	5/85				.8	4.0
PTL—The Inspirational Network	4/78	3.0	6.5	10.0	12.5	na
Satellite Program Network	1/79	2.8	4.8	11.5	12.0	na
SCORE	5/85				11.0	20.0
Spanish International Network (became Univision in 1/87)	9/76	na	3.8	3.5	4.3	4.7
Tempo TV	1/79	na	na	na	na	8.0
Travel Channel	2/87					9.3
Trinity Broadcasting Network Inc.	5/78	3.5	2.3	4.5	6.1	8.0
USA Network	9/80	4.8	13.0	28.0	31.0	45.2
Video Hits-1	1/85				14.1	27.9
The Weather Channel	5/82		6.0	12.0	20.2	36.0
Superstations						
WTBS (Atlanta)	12/76	8.9	23.3	31.0	36.1	45.7
WGN (Chicago)	11/78	3.9	9.4	14.2	17.7	24.7
WOR (New York)	4/79	2.8	4.3	4.9	5.4	12.3
WPIX (New York)	6/84			.8	1.4	9.7

Notes: All figures are rounded to nearest 100,000. Excluded are text-only services such as AP News Cable and Reuters News Views. A&E began as ARTS in 1981 and became Arts and Entertainment Network in February 1984. Nostalgia began as a pay network and converted to basic status.

Sources: 1980 and 1982 from Sterling (1984), pages 207–208, citing *Cablevision* (January 12, 1981), page 28, and (November 1, 1982), page 119; 1984 from *Channels Field Guide 1985*, pages 53, 54, and 58; 1986 from *Cablevision* (March 31, 1986), page 40; 1988 from *Broadcasting* (August 22, 1988), pages 32–33.

10-D / Pay-Cable Service Subscribers since 1980

Programming Service	Start-up Date	Number of Subscribers (millions) in				
		June 1980	June 1982	Oct. 1984	Oct. 1986	Aug. 1988
American Movie Classics	10/84			na	.7	12.0
Bravo	12/80		na	.7	.3	1.1
Cinemax	8/80		na	2.5	3.7	5.1
The Disney Channel	4/83			.3	2.6	3.8
Home Box Office (HBO)	11/72	8.1	19.9	12.5	14.6	15.9
Home Theatre Network (HTN)	9/78	na	na	.2	.3	—
The Playboy Channel	11/82		na	.5	.7	.5
SelecTV of California, Inc.	10/85			na	.2	—
Showtime	7/76	1.2	3.1	4.5	5.2	6.3
Warner/The Movie Channel	1/80	.4	2.3	2.5	3.0	2.6
Pay-per-View Services						
Choice	10/84			na	4.0	3.5
Playboy Private Ticket	7/85				.1	—
Request Television	11/85				1.4	3.2
Viewer's Choice	11/85				1.2	3.5
World Video Library	12/86				.3	—

Notes: HBO was the first national pay-cable network (late 1975 inception of satellite service) and reported 475,000 subscribers in 1976 and 1.5 million in 1978. Showtime in 1978 reported 154,000 subscribers. Several services for which no subscriber data are shown for 1988 appear to have ended service (Playboy pay-per-view now markets as Playboy on Demand and reported 2.2 million subscribers late in 1988).

Sources: 1980 and 1982 from Sterling (1984), page 74, citing Paul Kagan Associates' data; 1984 from *Channels Field Guide 1985*, page 62; 1986 from *Channels Field Guide 1987*, pages 81 and 83; 1988 from *Broadcasting* (August 22, 1988), pages 32–33.

10-E / Television Station Signals Received: 1964–1986
(over the air or by cable)

Number of TV Stations Receivable per Household	Percentage of All Households						
	1964	1968	1972	1976	1980	1982	1986*
1 to 3	22%	7%	6% ⎫	12%	9%	6%	3%
4	19	11	11 ⎭				
5	14	13	12	11	10	7 ⎫	9
6	19	9	10	12	10	10 ⎭	
7	12	20	18	18	10	9 ⎫	17
8	6	11	12	9	7	10 ⎭	
9	4	9	11	11	11	11 ⎫	71
10 or more	4	17	20	27	43	47 ⎭	
Average Received	na	na	na	7.7	na	9.8	11.2

*Data for 1986 are grouped differently from previous years. 1–4, 5–6, 7–8, 9–10 (22 percent), 11–14 (27 percent), 15–19 (17 percent), and 20 or more (5 percent). Figures show only broadcast station signals received, not other (cable) channels, though cable-carried broadcast station signals *are* included here.

Sources: Nielsen Television Index, as found in annual issues of *Television Audience*. Data for 1964–1982, also from Nielsen, are reproduced here as summarized in Sterling (1984), page 22.

10-F / Growth of Satellite Distribution: 1975–1987

Year	Domestic Satellites (U.S. only)	Total Transponders Carried	Cable Services (using satellites)			Earth Stations			
			Basic	Pay	Total	Radio	TV	Cable	Home
1975	3	48	—	1	1	na	na	na	na
1977	6	120	3	1	4	na	na	161	na
1979	8	156	14	4	18	na	150	1,579	na
1981	8	156	19	8	27	1,200	300	3,100	20,000
1983	19	420	30	11	41	4,856	970	8,000	300,000
1985	29	504	45	20	65	*	*	*	1,500,000
1987	26	524	53**	17**	70	*	*	*	1,980,000

*While specific numbers of TVROs are hard to come by, by the mid-1980s virtually all cable systems and television stations had access to at least one. According to the NAB, 85 percent of radio stations in 1985 and 90 percent by 1987 used TVROs. Most broadcast stations and cable systems had more than one to allow use of the increasing number of different satellites used to distribute video signals. SNG facilities not included.

**1987 cable service data include home-shopping services within basic services and pay-per-view within pay services.

Sources: For 1975–1983 data, except home earth stations, see Sterling (1984), page 34, which cites data from a variety of sources, most reported by the National Association of Broadcasters and the National Cable Television Association. See also Compaine, et al. (1982), page 416. All home earth station figures from Paul Kagan Associates, *The Kagan Media Index* (May 17, 1988), page 8. Data for 1985 and 1987 satellites and broadcast use from the NAB, *Many Roads Home: The New Electronic Pathways* (Washington, D.C.: National Association of Broadcasters, 1988), pages 72–91. 1985–1987 cable data taken from *Channels Field Guide 1987*, pages 108–121.

Table 11 Years to Reach 34 Million Homes

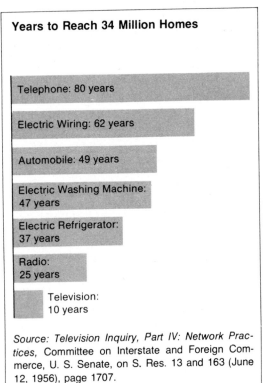

Years to Reach 34 Million Homes

Telephone: 80 years

Electric Wiring: 62 years

Automobile: 49 years

Electric Washing Machine: 47 years

Electric Refrigerator: 37 years

Radio: 25 years

Television: 10 years

Source: Television Inquiry, Part IV: Network Practices, Committee on Interstate and Foreign Commerce, U. S. Senate, on S. Res. 13 and 163 (June 12, 1956), page 1707.

**A Selected
Bibliography**

**A Selected
Bibliography**

This listing, which stresses American broadcasting, is selective—a complete bibliography, even one restricted to books, would fill a volume itself. What follows is designed to support the "Further Reading" annotations following each chapter. Publications not designed to be historical when published are included for the light they shed on a particular period or phase of broadcasting. Some titles are of marginal quality and are included only because of a paucity of material on a given topic.

Postpublication reprint editions and bibliographies of special value are noted. (The New York Times Company closed down Arno Press in the early 1980s, but many of the books so annotated below, gathered into collections by the authors of this volume and others, are still available from Ayer Company Publishers, 382 Main St., P.O. Box 958, Salem, N.H. 03079.) Periodical entries include years of publication, frequency of appearance, and a brief line of description. For all books, the year shown is that of original publication unless a later edition is specified. American editions of books published originally in Britain are usually listed under the American publisher. Generally omitted are script collections, histories of individual stations, special material on old radios, and broadcasting in specific other countries. As a rule, the latest edition of a title is cited.

While some of this material is in print or has been reprinted for the library market, most of it is not currently available outside of libraries. We have intentionally omitted most materials, including dissertations, that cannot be found in libraries—no matter how good they may be. Likewise, we list few periodical articles due to space limitations. The listing is current as of early 1989.

Abramson, Albert H. *Electronic Motion Pictures: A History of the Television Camera.* Berkeley: University of California Press, 1955 (reprinted by Arno Press, 1974).

———. *The History of Television, 1880–1941.* Jefferson, N.C.: McFarland, 1987.

Adler, Richard P., ed. *All in the Family: A Critical Appraisal.* New York: Praeger, 1979.

Adler, Richard P., et al. *The Effects of Television Advertising on Children*. Lexington, Mass: Lexington Books, 1980. Bibliography, pp. 325–361.

Aitken, Hugh G. J. *Syntony and Spark: The Origins of Radio*. New York: Wiley/Interscience, 1976.

———. *The Continuous Wave: Technology and American Radio, 1900–1932*. Princeton, N.J.: Princeton University Press, 1985.

Alford, W. Wayne. *History of the NAEB: 1955–1965*. Washington, D.C.: NAEB, 1966. (For the earlier period, see Hill, Harold, below.)

Alisky, Marvin. *Latin American Media: Guidance and Censorship*. Ames: Iowa State University Press, 1981.

Allen, Fred. *Treadmill to Oblivion*. Boston: Little, Brown, 1954.

Allen, Frederick Lewis. *Only Yesterday*. New York: Harper, 1931.

———. *Since Yesterday*. New York: Harper, 1940.

Allen, Robert C. *Speaking of Soap Operas*. Chapel Hill: University of North Carolina Press, 1985.

Allen, Steve. *The Funny Men*. New York: Simon and Schuster, 1956.

Aly, Bower, and Gerald D. Shively. *A Debate Handbook on Radio Control and Operation*. Norman: University of Oklahoma, 1933. Bibliography, pp. 7–43.

Anderson, Kent. *Television Fraud: The History and Implications of the Quiz Show Scandals*. Westport, Conn.: Greenwood, 1979.

Andrews, Bart. *Lucy & Ricky & Fred & Ethel: The Story of "I Love Lucy."* New York: Dutton, 1976.

Annals of the American Academy of Political and Social Science. Philadelphia: the Academy, bimonthly, 1890–date (in the 1980s, Sage Publications became the publisher for the Academy). The following issues (reprinted in a volume by Arno Press, 1971) deal exclusively with broadcasting: Stewart, Irwin, ed., "Radio," Supplement to No. 142 (March 1929); Hettinger, Herman S., ed., "Radio: The Fifth Estate," No. 177 (January 1935); Hettinger, Herman S., ed., "New Horizons in Radio," No. 213 (January 1941).

Antebi, Elizabeth. *The Electronic Epoch*. New York: Van Nostrand Reinhold, 1982.

Appleyard, Rollo. *Pioneers of Electrical Communications*. London: Macmillan, 1930 (reprinted by Books for Libraries).

Archer, Gleason L. *History of Radio to 1926*. New York: American Historical Society, Inc., 1938 (reprinted by Arno Press, 1971).

———. *Big Business and Radio*. New York: American Historical Company, Inc., 1939 (reprinted by Arno Press, 1971).

Arlen, Michael J. *Living-Room War*. New York: Viking, 1969.

———. *Thirty Seconds*. New York: Farrar, Straus & Giroux, 1980.

Arnheim, Rudolf. *Radio*. London: Faber and Faber, 1936 (reprinted by Arno Press, 1971).

Arnold, Frank A. *Broadcast Advertising: The Fourth Dimension—Television Edition*. New York: Wiley, 1933.

Atkinson, Carroll. *American Universities and Colleges That Have Held Broadcast License*. Boston: Meador, 1941.

———. *Radio Network Contributions to Education*. Boston: Meador, 1942a.

———. *Broadcasting to the Classroom by Universities and Colleges*. Boston: Meador, 1942b.

———. *Radio in State and Territorial Educational Departments*. Boston: Meador, 1942c.

———. *Radio Programs Intended for Classroom Use*. Boston: Meador, 1942d.

Baer, Walter S. *Cable Television: A Handbook for Decision Making*. New York: Crane, Russak, 1974. Bibliography, pp. 221–230.

Baer, Walter S., et al. *Concentration of Mass Media Ownership: Assessing the State of Current Knowledge*. Santa Monica, Calif.: Rand Corp., 1974. (P) Bibliography, pp. 173–202.

Baker, John C. *Farm Broadcasting: The First Sixty Years*. Ames: Iowa State University Press, 1981.

Baker, W. J. *A History of the Marconi Company*. New York: St. Martin's Press, 1972.

Baldwin, Thomas, and D. Stevens McVoy. *Cable*

Communications. 2nd ed. Englewood Cliffs, N.J.: Prentice-Hall, 1988.

Balfour, Michael. *Propaganda in War 1939–1945: Organizations, Policies, and Publics in Britain and Germany.* London: Routledge & Kegan Paul, 1979. Bibliography, pp. 446–457.

Bannerman, R. LeRoy. *Norman Corwin and Radio: The Golden Years.* University of Alabama Press, 1986.

Banning, William Peck. *Commercial Broadcasting Pioneer: The WEAF Experiment, 1922–1926.* Cambridge, Mass.: Harvard University Press, 1946.

Barnouw, Erik. *A Tower in Babel: A History of Broadcasting in the United States to 1933.* New York: Oxford University Press, 1966. Bibliography, pp. 317–328.

———. *The Golden Web: A History of Broadcasting in the United States, 1933–1953.* New York: Oxford University Press, 1968. Bibliography, pp. 349–369.

———. *The Image Empire: A History of Broadcasting in the United States from 1953.* New York: Oxford University Press, 1970. Bibliography, pp. 355–373.

———. *Tube of Plenty: The Evolution of American Television.* New York: Oxford University Press, 1975. Bibliography, pp. 479–494.

———. *The Sponsor: Notes on a Modern Potentate.* New York: Oxford University Press, 1978. Bibliography (in the form of "Notes"), pp. 185–205.

Barrett, Marvin, ed. *The Alfred I. DuPont–Columbia University Survey of Broadcast Journalism.* New York: Grosset & Dunlap (1969–1971), Crowell (1972–1980), Everest (1982). (Note: main title varies; published annually to 1972 and biennially to 1982.)

Barron, Jerome A. *Freedom of the Press for Whom? The Right of Access to Mass Media.* Bloomington: Indiana University Press, 1973.

Barry, Gerald, et al., eds. *Communication and Language: Networks of Thought and Action.* New York: Doubleday, 1965.

Batson, Lawrence D. *Radio Markets of the World, 1930.* Washington, D.C.: Department of Commerce Trade Promotion Series No. 109, 1930 (reprinted by Arno Press, 1971).

Baudino, Joseph E., and John M. Kittross, "Broadcasting's Oldest Stations: An Examination of Four Claimants," *Journal of Broadcasting* 21:61–83 (Winter 1977).

Baughman, James L. *Television's Guardians: The FCC and the Politics of Programming 1958–1967.* Knoxville: University of Tennessee Press, 1985. Bibliography, pp. 265–302.

BBC. *War Report: A Record of Dispatches Broadcast by the BBC's War Correspondents with the Allied Expeditionary Force 6 June 1944–5 May 1945.* London: Oxford University Press, 1946.

BBC Handbook. London: BBC Publications, 1928–1987. (Title varies: "Handbook" 1928–1929, "Yearbook" 1930–1934, "Annual" 1935–1937, "Handbook" 1938–1954, "Yearbook" 1943–1952, not published in 1953–1954, "Handbook" 1955–1980, and "Annual Report and Handbook" 1981–1987.) Publication ceased in 1987.

Bedell, Sally. *Up the Tube: Prime-Time TV in the Silverman Years.* New York: Viking, 1981.

Beniger, James R. *The Control Revolution: Technological and Economic Origins of the Information Society.* Cambridge, Mass.: Harvard University Press, 1986. Bibliography, pp. 439–476.

Benjamin, Burton. *Fair Play: CBS, General Westmoreland and How a Television Documentary Went Wrong.* New York: Harper & Row, 1988.

Bennett, Jeremy. *British Broadcasting and the Danish Resistance Movement, 1940–1945.* Cambridge: Cambridge University Press, 1966.

Bensman, Marvin R. *Broadcast Regulation: Selected Cases and Decisions.* Lanham, Md.: University Press of America, 1983, 1986.

Bergreen, Laurence. *Look Now, Pay Later: The Rise of Network Broadcasting.* New York: Doubleday, 1980.

Beville, Hugh Malcolm, Jr. *Social Stratification of the Radio Audience.* Princeton, N.J.: Princeton University Press, 1939.

———. *Audience Ratings: Radio, Television, Cable.* 2nd ed. Hillsdale, N.J.: Lawrence Erlbaum, 1988.

Bilby, Kenneth. *The General: David Sarnoff and the Rise of the Communications Industry.* New York: Harper & Row, 1986.

Billboard (1894–date; monthly, then weekly). Trade periodical, mainly of the music industry, with a good deal of information on radio music.

Bishop, George E., et al. *The Presidential Debates: Media, Electoral and Policy Perspectives.* New York: Praeger, 1978.

Blake, George G. *History of Radio Telegraphy and Telephony.* London: Chapman and Hall, 1928 (reprinted by Arno Press, 1974). Bibliography, pp. 353–403.

Blakely, Robert J. *To Serve the Public Interest: Educational Broadcasting in the United States.* Syracuse, N.Y.: Syracuse University Press, 1979.

Blanchard, Margaret A. *Exporting the First Amendment: The Press-Government Crusade of 1945–1952.* New York: Longman, 1986.

Bliss, Edward, Jr., ed. *In Search of Light: The Broadcasts of Edward R. Murrow, 1938–1961.* New York: Knopf, 1967.

Bluem, A. William. *Documentary in American Television: Form, Function, Method.* New York: Hastings House, 1965. Bibliography, pp. 297–301.

Blum, Daniel. *A Pictorial History of Television.* Philadelphia: Chilton, 1959.

Blume, Keith. *The Presidential Election Show: Campaign '84 and Beyond on the Nightly News.* South Hadley, Mass.: Bergin & Garvey, 1985.

Blythe, Cheryl, and Susan Sackett. *Say Goodnight, Gracie! The Story of Burns and Allen.* New York: E. P. Dutton, 1986.

Boettinger, H. M. *The Telephone Book: Bell, Watson, Vail and American Life: 1876–1983.* New York: Stearn Publishers, 1983.

Bogart, Leo. *The Age of Television.* New York: Ungar, 1956, 1958, 1972. Bibliography, pp. 481–501. (1972 edition is a facsimile reprint of the 1956 edition, with extensive added notes.)

Boorstin, Daniel J. *The Americans: The Democratic Experience.* New York: Random House, 1973. Bibliography, pp. 605–682.

Bower, Robert T. *Television and the Public.* New York: Holt, Rinehart and Winston, 1973.

———. *The Changing Television Audience in America.* New York: Columbia University Press, 1985.

Boyd, Douglas A. *Broadcasting in the Arab World: A Survey of Radio and Television in the Middle East.* Philadelphia: Temple University Press, 1982.

Boyer, Peter J. *Who Killed CBS? The Undoing of America's Number One News Network.* New York: Random House, 1988.

Braestrup, Peter. *Big Story: How the American Press and Television Reported and Interpreted the Crisis of Tet 1968 in Vietnam and Washington.* Boulder, Colo.: Westview, 1977. (Several shorter versions of this title were published.)

Braun, Ernest, and Stuart Macdonald. *Revolution in Miniature: The History and Impact of Semiconductor Electronics.* 2nd ed. Cambridge: Cambridge University Press, 1982.

Brenner, Daniel L., and Monroe E. Price. *Cable Television and Other Non-Broadcast Video.* New York: Clark Boardman, 1986.

Briggs, Asa A. *The Birth of Broadcasting: The History of Broadcasting in the United Kingdom* [to 1926]. London: Oxford University Press, 1961. Bibliography, pp. 407–409.

———. *The Golden Age of Wireless: The History of Broadcasting in the United Kingdom* [1926–1939]. London: Oxford University Press, 1965. Bibliography, pp. 660–663.

———. *The War of Words: The History of Broadcasting in the United Kingdom* [1939–1945]. London: Oxford University Press, 1970. Bibliography, pp. 727–732.

———. *Sound and Vision: The History of Broadcasting in the United Kingdom* [1945–1955]. London: Oxford University Press, 1979. (Note: a further volume in this series is expected to bring the story into the 1970s.)

———. *The BBC: The First Fifty Years.* London: Oxford University Press, 1986.

Bright, Charles. *Submarine Telegraphs: Their History, Construction and Working.* London: Crosby, Lockwood and Son, 1898 (reprinted by Arno Press, 1974).

Brindze, Ruth. *Not to Be Broadcast: The Truth about the Radio*. New York: Vanguard, 1937 (reprinted by Da Capo, 1974).

Broadcasting (1931–1941, biweekly; 1941–date, weekly). The most important trade journal of the broadcasting industry, with news, special analyses, statistics, and reviews of all aspects of radio and television, especially advertising, programs, the networks, and regulatory trends. The following special issues are of special value in broadcasting history: "Two Exciting Decades" (October 16, 1950), pp. 67–168; "Radio at 40 Enters Its Critical Years" (May 14, 1962), pp. 75–140; "Broadcasting at 50: Can It Adapt?" (November 2, 1970), pp. 65–154; "The First Amendment and the Fifth Estate" (January 5, 1976), pp. 44–100; "The First 50 Years of NBC" (June 21, 1976), pp. 29–92; "CBS: The First Five Decades" (September 19, 1977), pp. 45–116; "The 50th Anniversary Issue: On the Road to 2001," (October 12, 1981), pp. 115–311; "Sixty Years of NBC," (June 9, 1986), pp. 49–119, and "Cable: The First Forty Years," (November 21, 1988), pp. 35–49.

Broadcasting Yearbook (1935–date). Title has varied. Standard directory of broadcasting stations and other elements of the industry, with useful tables of data.

Brock, Gerald W. *The Telecommunications Industry: The Dynamics of Market Structure*. Cambridge, Mass.: Harvard University Press, 1981.

Brooks, John. *Telephone: The First Hundred Years*. New York: Harper & Row. 1976.

Brooks, Tim, and Earle Marsh. *The Complete Directory to Prime Time Network TV Shows, 1946–Present*. 4th ed. New York: Ballantine, 1988.

Brown, Les. *Televi$ion: The Business Behind the Box*. New York: Harcourt Brace Jovanovich, 1971.

———. *Les Brown's Encyclopedia of Television*. 2nd ed. New York: Zoetrope, 1982.

Brown, Ronald. *Telecommunications: The Booming Technology*. New York: Doubleday, 1970.

Browne, Donald R. *International Radiobroadcasting: The Limits of the Limitless Medium*. New York: Praeger, 1982.

Bruce, Robert V. *Bell: Alexander Graham Bell and the Conquest of Solitude*. Boston: Little, Brown, 1973.

Bryson, Lyman. *Time for Reason about Radio*. New York: George Stewart, 1948.

Buehler, E. C. *American vs. British System of Radio Control*. New York: H. W. Wilson "Reference Shelf" Series, VIII:10, 1933. Bibliography, pp. 25–50.

Bulman, David. *Molders of Opinion*. Milwaukee: Bruce, 1945.

Burlingame, Roger. *Don't Let Them Scare You: The Life and Times of Elmer Davis*. Philadelphia: Lippincott, 1961.

Burns, R. W. *British Television: The Formative Years*. London: Peter Peregrinus, 1986.

Burrows, A. R. *The Story of Broadcasting*. London: Cassell, 1924.

Buxton, Frank, and Bill Owen. *The Big Broadcast: 1920–1950*. New York: Viking, 1972. Bibliography, pp. 266–270.

Byron, Christopher M. *The Fanciest Dive: What Happened When the Media Empire of Time/Life Leaped Without Looking into the Age of High-Tech*. New York: W. W. Norton, 1986.

Campbell, Robert. *The Golden Years of Broadcasting: A Celebration of the First 50 Years of Radio and TV on NBC*. New York: Charles Scribner's Sons, 1976.

Cantor, Muriel G. *The Hollywood TV Producer: His Work and His Audience*. New York: Basic Books, 1972. Bibliography, pp. 242–249.

Cantor, Muriel, and Suzanne Pingree. *The Soap Opera*. Beverly Hills, Calif.: Sage, 1983.

Cantril, Hadley, with the assistance of Hazel Gaudet and Herta Herzog. *The Invasion from Mars: A Study in the Psychology of Panic*. Princeton, N.J.: Princeton University Press, 1940.

Cantril, Hadley, and Gordon W. Allport, *The Psychology of Radio*. New York: Harper, 1935 (reprinted by Arno Press, 1971).

Carnegie Commission on Educational Television. *Public Television: A Program for Action*. New York: Harper & Row, 1967.

Carnegie Commission on the Future of Public Broadcasting. *A Public Trust*. New York: Bantam Books, 1979.

Carter, Samuel, III. *Cyrus Field: Man of Two Worlds*. New York: Putnam, 1968. Bibliography, pp. 363–367.

Cassata, Mary, and Thomas Skill. *Life on Daytime Television: Tuning-in American Serial Drama*. Norwood, N.J.: Ablex, 1983.

Castleman, Harry, and Walter J. Podrazik. *Watching TV: Four Decades of American Television*. New York: McGraw-Hill, 1982.

Cater, Douglass, and Stephen Strickland. *TV Violence and the Child: The Evolution and Fate of the Surgeon General's Report*. New York: Russell Sage Foundation, 1975.

Chappell, Matthew N., and C. E. Hooper. *Radio Audience Measurement*. New York: Stephen Daye, 1944.

Chase, Francis, Jr. *Sound and Fury: An Informal History of Broadcasting*. New York: Harper, 1942.

Cherington, Paul W., Leon V. Hirsch, and Robert Brandwein. *Television Station Ownership: A Case Study of Federal Agency Regulation*. New York: Hastings House, 1971.

Chester, Edward W. *Radio, Television, and American Politics*. New York: Sheed and Ward, 1969. Bibliography, pp. 313–334.

Childs, Harwood L., and John B. Whitton, eds. *Propaganda by Short Wave*. Princeton, N.J.: Princeton University Press, 1942 (reprinted by Arno Press, 1972).

Christensen, Mark, and Cameron Stauth. *The Sweeps: Behind the Scenes in Network TV*. New York: Morrow, 1984.

Clarke, Arthur C. *Voice Across the Sea*. Rev. ed. New York: Harper & Row, 1975.

Coates, Vary T., and Bernard Finn. *A Retrospective Technology Assessment: Submarine Telegraphy—The Transatlantic Cable of 1866*. San Francisco: San Francisco Press, 1979.

Codding, George A., and Anthony M. Rutkowski. *The International Telecommunication Union in a Changing World*. Dedham, Mass.: Artech House, 1982.

Codel, Martin, ed. *Radio and Its Future*. New York: Harper, 1930 (reprinted by Arno Press, 1971).

Cogley, John. *Report on Blacklisting II: Radio-Television*. New York: Fund for the Republic, 1956 (reprinted by Arno Press, 1971).

Cole, Barry G., ed. *Television: A Selection of Readings from TV Guide Magazine*. New York: Free Press, 1970.

———. *Television Today: A Close-Up View: Readings From "TV Guide."* New York: Oxford, 1981.

Cole, Barry G., and Mal Oettinger. *Reluctant Regulators: The FCC and the Broadcast Audience*. Reading, Mass.: Addison-Wesley, 1978.

Cole, J. A. *Lord Haw-Haw and William Joyce*. New York: Farrar, Straus & Giroux, 1964.

Collins, Robert. *A Voice from Afar: The History of Telecommunications in Canada*. Toronto: McGraw-Hill Ryerson, 1977.

Columbia Broadcasting System. *Crisis*. New York: CBS, 1938.

———. *Radio and Television Bibliography*. New York: CBS, 1942. First 32 pages cover books and pamphlets, 15 pages deal with periodical articles, and another 15 pages detail early CBS radio publications.

———. *From D-Day through Victory in Europe*. New York: CBS, 1945a.

———. *From Pearl Harbor into Tokyo*. New York: CBS, 1945b.

———. *Network Practices*. New York: CBS, 1956.

———. *10:56:20 pm EDT, 7/20/69: The Historic Conquest of the Moon as Reported to the American People by CBS News over the CBS Television Network*. New York: CBS, 1970.

Compaine, Benjamin M., ed. *Understanding New Media: Trends and Issues in Electronic Distribution of Information*. Cambridge, Mass.: Ballinger, 1984.

Compaine, Benjamin M., et al. *Who Owns the Media? Concentration of Ownership in the Mass Communications Industry*. 2nd ed. White Plains, N.Y.: Knowledge Industry Publications, 1982. Bibliography, pp. 497–513.

Comstock, George, et al. *Television and Human Behavior*. Santa Monica, Calif.: Rand Corp., 1975 (three volumes, all annotated bibliography).

————. *Television and Human Behavior*. New York: Columbia University Press, 1978.

Connah, Douglas. *How to Build the Radio Audience*. New York: Harper, 1938.

Cook, Rick, and Frank Vaughan. *All About Home Satellite Television*. Blue Ridge Summit, Pa.: TAB, 1983.

Coons, John E., ed. *Freedom & Responsibility in Broadcasting*. Evanston, Ill.: Northwestern University Press, 1961.

Cooper, Isabella M. *Bibliography on Educational Broadcasting*. Chicago: University of Chicago Press, 1942 (reprinted by Arno Press, 1971). Coverage of 1,800 items is far broader than title suggests, covering all of broadcasting in well-organized and annotated indexed guide.

Cooper, Kent. *Barriers Down: The Story of the News Agency Epoch*. New York: Farrar & Rinehart, 1942 (reprinted by Kennikat, 1969).

Corporation for Public Broadcasting. *Annual Report*. Washington, D.C.: CPB, 1969–date.

————. *Public Television Program Content*. Washington: CPB, 1974–date (biennial).

————. *Status Report on Public Broadcasting*. Washington: CPB, 1973, 1977, 1980 (title varies).

————. *Summary Statistics of CPB-Qualified Public Radio Stations*. Washington: CPB, 1970–date (irregular; title varies).

————. *Summary Statistics of Public Television Licensees*. Washington: CPB, 1970–date (irregular; title varies).

Counterattack, editors of. *Red Channels: The Report of Communist Influence in Radio and Television*. New York: American Business Consultants, 1950.

Covert, Catherine L., and John D. Stevens, eds. *Mass Media Between the Wars: Perceptions of Cultural Tension*. Syracuse, N.Y.: Syracuse University Press, 1984.

Cowan, Geoffrey. *See No Evil: The Backstage Battle over Sex and Violence on Television*. New York: Simon and Schuster, 1979.

Crosby, John. *Out of the Blue: A Book about Radio and Television*. New York: Simon and Schuster, 1952.

Csida, Joseph, and June Bundy Csida. *American Entertainment: A Unique History of Popular Show Business*. New York: Watson-Guptill, 1978.

Culbert, David Holbrook. *News for Everyman: Radio and Foreign Affairs in Thirties America*. Westport, Conn.: Greenwood, 1976. Bibliography, pp. 211–229.

Czitrom, Daniel J. *Media and the American Mind from Morse to McLuhan*. Chapel Hill: University of North Carolina Press, 1982.

Dalton, W. M. *The Story of Radio*. London: Adam Hilger, 1975 (three volumes).

Danielian, N. R. *AT&T: The Story of Industrial Conquest*. New York: Vanguard, 1939 (reprinted by Arno Press, 1974).

Davis, Henry B. *Electrical and Electronic Technologies: A Chronology of Events and Inventors*. Metuchen, N.J.: Scarecrow, 1981–1985 (three volumes).

Davis, Stephen B. *The Law of Radio Communications*. New York: McGraw-Hill, 1927.

de Forest, Lee. *Father of Radio: The Autobiography of Lee de Forest*. Chicago: Wilcox and Follett, 1950.

Delfiner, Henry. *Vienna Broadcasts to Slovakia: 1938–1939—A Case Study in Subversion*. New York: Columbia University Press, 1974.

DeLong, Thomas A. *The Mighty Music Box: The Golden Age of Musical Radio*. Los Angeles: Amber Crest, 1980.

Desmond, Robert W. *World News Reporting*. Iowa City: University of Iowa Press, 1978–1984 (four volumes).

DeSoto, Clinton B. *Two Hundred Meters and Down: The Story of Amateur Radio*. West Hartford, Conn.: American Radio Relay League, 1936.

Diamant, Lincoln. *The Anatomy of a Television Commercial: The Story of Eastman Kodak's "Yesterdays."* New York: Hastings House, 1970.

————. *Television's Classic Commercials: The*

Golden Years, 1948–1958. New York: Hastings House, 1971.

Diamond, Edwin, and Stephen Bates. *The Spot: The Rise of Political Advertising on Television.* 2nd ed. Cambridge, Mass.: MIT Press, 1988.

Dibner, Bern. *The Atlantic Cable.* New York: Blaisdell, 1964.

Dill, Clarence C. *Radio Law: Practice, Procedure.* Washington, D.C.: National Law Book Company, 1938.

Dinsdale, A. A. *First Principles of Television.* New York: Wiley, 1932 (reprinted by Arno Press, 1971).

Dizard, Wilson P. *Television: A World View.* Syracuse, N.Y.: Syracuse University Press, 1966. Bibliography, pp. 321–333.

Douglas, Susan J. *Inventing American Broadcasting 1899–1922.* Baltimore: Johns Hopkins University Press, 1987.

Dreyer, Carl. *Sarnoff: An American Success.* New York: Quadrangle, 1977.

Dryer, Sherman H. *Radio in Wartime.* New York: Greenberg, 1942.

Dummer, G. W. A. *Electronic Inventions 1745–1976.* Oxford, England: Pergamon Press, 1977.

Dunlap, Orrin E., Jr. *Radio in Advertising.* New York: Harper, 1931.

——. *The Outlook for Television.* New York: Harper, 1932 (reprinted by Arno Press, 1971).

——. *Marconi: The Man and His Wireless.* New York: Macmillan, 1937 (reprinted by Arno Press, 1971).

——. *The Future of Television.* New York: Harper, 1942, 1947.

——. *Radio's 100 Men of Science: Biographical Narratives of Pathfinders in Electronics and Television.* New York: Harper, 1944.

——. *Communications in Space: From Marconi to Man on the Moon.* 3rd ed. New York: Harper & Row, 1970.

Dunning, John. *Tune in Yesterday: The Ultimate Encyclopedia of Old-Time Radio, 1925–1976.* Englewood Cliffs, N.J.: Prentice-Hall, 1976.

Dupuy, Judy. *Television Show Business.* Schenectady, N.Y.: General Electric, 1945.

Dygert, Warren B. *Radio as an Advertising Medium.* New York: McGraw-Hill, 1939.

Eastman, Susan, and Richard Klein. *Strategies in Broadcast and Cable Promotion.* Belmont, Calif.: Wadsworth, 1982 (reprinted by Waveland Press, 1988).

Eastman, Susan, et al. *Broadcast/Cable Programming: Strategies and Practices.* 3rd ed. Belmont, Calif.: Wadsworth, 1989.

Eberly, Philip K. *Music in the Air: America's Changing Tastes in Popular Music, 1920–1980.* New York: Hastings House, 1982.

Eckhardt, George H. *Electronic Television.* Chicago: Goodheart-Willcox, 1936 (reprinted by Arno Press, 1974).

Eddy, William C. *Television: The Eyes of Tomorrow.* New York: Prentice-Hall, 1945.

Edelman, Murray. *The Licensing of Radio Services in the United States, 1927–1947: A Study in Administrative Formulation of Policy.* Illinois Studies in the Social Sciences, vol. 31. Urbana: University of Illinois Press, 1950 (reprinted by Arno Press, 1979).

Edmonson, Madeleine, and David Rounds. *From Mary Noble to Mary Hartman: The Complete Soap Opera Book.* New York: Jove/HBJ, 1977 [a paperback reprint and updating of *The Soaps* (New York: Stein & Day, 1973)].

Education on the Air. Annual proceedings of conference on educational broadcasting. Columbus: Ohio State University, 1930–1953, 1959.

Educational Broadcasting Review (1967–1973; bimonthly). Official journal of the NAEB; in earlier years was published as *NAEB Journal* and *AERT Journal*; for later years, see *Public Telecommunications Review.*

The Eighth Art: Twenty-Three Views of Television Today. New York: Holt, Rinehart and Winston, 1962.

Eisner, Joel, and David Krinsky. *Television Comedy Series: An Episode Guide to 153 TV Sitcoms in Syndication.* Jefferson, N.C.: McFarland, 1984.

Electronic Media. (1981–date, weekly).

Eliot, Marc. *Televisions: One Season in American Television*. New York: St. Martin's Press, 1983.

Elliott, Philip. *The Making of a Television Series: A Case Study in the Sociology of Culture*. London: Constable, 1972.

Elliott, William Y., ed. *Television's Impact on American Culture*. East Lansing: Michigan State University Press, 1956.

Emery, Michael, and Edwin Emery. *The Press and America: An Interpretive History of the Mass Media*. 6th ed. Englewood Cliffs, N.J.: Prentice-Hall, 1988.

Emery, Walter B. *National and International Systems of Broadcasting: Their History, Operation and Control*. East Lansing: Michigan State University Press, 1969. Bibliography, pp. 723–738.

———. *Broadcasting and Government: Responsibilities and Regulations*. 2nd ed. East Lansing: Michigan State University Press, 1971. Bibliography, pp. 545–559.

Eoyang, Thomas T. *An Economic Study of the Radio Industry in the United States of America*. New York: Columbia University Press, 1936 (reprinted by Arno Press, 1974).

Epstein, Edward Jay. *News from Nowhere: Television and the News*. New York: Random House, 1973.

Erickson, Don V. *Armstrong's Fight for FM Broadcasting: One Man vs Big Business and Bureaucracy*. University: University of Alabama Press, 1973.

Ettlinger, Harold. *The Axis on the Air*. Indianapolis: Bobbs-Merrill, 1943.

Everson, George. *The Story of Television: The Life of Philo T. Farnsworth*. New York: Norton, 1949 (reprinted by Arno Press, 1974).

Ewen, Stuart. *Captains of Consciousness: Advertising and the Social Roots of the Consumer Culture*. New York: McGraw-Hill, 1976.

Ewen, Stuart, and Elizabeth Ewen. *Channels of Desire: Mass Images and the Shaping of American Consciousness*. New York: McGraw-Hill, 1982.

Fabe, Maxene. *TV Game Shows*. New York: Doubleday, 1979.

Fahie, J. J. *A History of Electric Telegraphy to the Year 1837*. London: Spon, 1884 (reprinted by Arno Press, 1974).

———. *A History of Wireless Telegraphy*. 2nd ed. Edinburgh: Blackwood, 1901 (reprinted by Arno Press, 1971).

Fang, Irving E. *Those Radio Commentators!* Ames: Iowa State University Press, 1977.

Fates, Gil. *What's My Line? The Inside Story of TV's Most Famous Panel Show*. Englewood Cliffs, N.J.: Prentice-Hall, 1978.

Faulk, John Henry. *Fear on Trial*. New York: Simon and Schuster, 1964.

Federal Communications Commission. *Annual Report*. Washington, D.C.: GPO, 1935–date (1935–1956 reports reprinted by Arno Press, 1971).

———. *Reports* (1935–1986). Washington, D.C.: GPO (official texts of decisions, reports, and orders). Replaced in 1987 by *Federal Communications Commission Record* (biweekly).

———. Engineering Department. *Report on Social and Economic Data Pursuant to the Informal Hearing on Broadcasting*. Washington, D.C.: GPO, 1938 (reprinted by Arno Press, 1974).

———. *Investigation of the Telephone Industry in the United States*. U.S. House of Representatives Document 340, 76th Cong., 1st Sess., 1939 (reprinted by Arno Press, 1974).

———. *Report on Chain Broadcasting*. Washington, D.C.: GPO, 1941 (reprinted by Arno Press, 1974).

———. *Public Service Responsibility of Broadcast Licensees*. Washington, D.C.: GPO, 1946 (most of the text was reprinted in Kahn, Frank J., below, and fully reprinted by Arno Press, 1974).

———. *An Economic Study of Standard Broadcasting*. Washington, D.C.: FCC Mimeo, 1947 (reprinted by Arno Press, 1974).

———. The Children's Television Task Force. *Television Programming for Children*. Washington, D.C.: FCC, 1979 (five volumes).

———. Network Inquiry Special Staff. *New Television Networks: Entry, Jurisdiction, Ownership*. Washington, D.C.: GPO, 1980 (two volumes).

————. Office of Network Study. *Network Broadcasting*. U.S. House of Representatives Report 1297, 85th Cong., 2nd Sess., 1958.

————, Office of Network Study. *Television Network Program Procurement*. U.S. House of Representatives Report 281, 88th Cong., 1st Sess., 1963.

————, Office of Network Study. *Television Network Program Procurement, Part II*. Washington, D.C.: GPO, 1965.

Federal Communications Law Journal (1937–date, thrice yearly). Legal and scholarly articles, mainly on broadcast regulation. (Note: Was *Federal Communications Bar Journal* until 1977.)

Federal Radio Commission. *Annual Report*. Washington, D.C.: GPO, 1927–1933 (reprinted by Arno Press, 1971).

————. *Commercial Radio Advertising*, U.S. Senate Document 137, 72nd Cong., 1st Sess., 1932 (reprinted by Arno Press, 1974).

Federal Trade Commission. *Report on the Radio Industry*. Washington, D.C.: GPO, 1924 (reprinted by Arno Press, 1974).

————. *Staff Report on Television Advertising to Children*. Washington, D.C.: FTC, 1978.

Fejes, Fred. *Imperialism, Media, and the Good Neighbor: New Deal Foreign Policy and United States Shortwave Broadcasting to Latin America*. Norwood, N.J.: Ablex, 1986.

Felix, Edgar. *Using Radio in Sales Promotion*. New York: McGraw-Hill, 1927.

————. *Television: Its Methods and Uses*. New York: McGraw-Hill, 1931.

Ferris, Charles, et al. *Cable Television Law: A Video Communications Practice Guide*. Albany, N.Y.: Matthew Bender, 1983 (updated twice a year, three volumes).

Fessenden, Helen. *Fessenden: Builder of Tomorrows*. New York: Coward-McCann, 1940 (reprinted by Arno Press with a new index, 1974).

Fifty Years of A.R.R.L. Newington, Conn.: American Radio Relay League, 1965.

The First 50 Years of Broadcasting. Washington, D.C.: Broadcasting Publications, 1982.

Fink, Donald G. *Television Standards and Practice: Selected Papers of the Papers of the National Television System Committee and Its Panels*. New York: McGraw-Hill, 1943.

Fischer, Stuart. *Kids' TV: The First 25 Years*. New York: Facts on File, 1983.

Fleming, John A. *The Principles of Electric Wave Telegraphy*. London: Longmans, Green, 1906, 1910, 1916, and 1919. (First two editions are most detailed in their historical treatment.)

Fowler, Gene, and Bill Crawford. *Border Radio*. Austin: Texas Monthly Press, 1987.

Fox, Stephen. *The Mirror Makers: A History of American Advertising and Its Creators*. New York: Morrow, 1984.

Frank, Ronald E., and Marshall G. Greenberg. *The Public's Use of Television*. Beverly Hills, Calif.: Sage, 1980.

Frankl, Razelle. *Televangelism: The Marketing of Popular Religion*. Carbondale: Southern Illinois University Press, 1986.

Franklin, Marc A. *Cases and Materials on Mass Media Law*. 3rd ed. Mineola, N.Y.: Foundation Press, 1986.

Friendly, Fred. *Due to Circumstances Beyond Our Control. . . .* New York: Random House, 1976.

Frost, S. E., Jr. *Education's Own Stations*. Chicago: University of Chicago Press, 1937a (reprinted by Arno Press, 1971).

————. *Is American Radio Democratic?* Chicago: University of Chicago Press, 1937b.

Ganley, Gladys D., and Oswald H. Ganley. *Global Political Fallout: The VCR's First Decade*. Norwood, N.J.: Ablex, 1987.

Garay, Ronald. *Congressional Television: A Legislative History*. Westport, Conn.: Greenwood, 1984.

————. *Cable Television: A Reference Guide to Information*. Westport, Conn.: Greenwood, 1988.

Gates, Gary Paul. *Air Time: The Inside Story of CBS News*. New York: Harper, 1978.

Gerani, Gary, with Paul H. Schulman. *Fantastic Television*. New York: Harmony, 1977.

Gerrold, David. *The World of Star Trek.* New York: Ballantine, 1973.

Gianakos, Larry James. *Television Drama Series Programming: A Comprehensive Chronicle.* Metuchen, N.J.: Scarecrow, 1978–1987 (five volumes, covering 1947–1984).

Gibson, George H. *Public Broadcasting: The Role of the Federal Government, 1912–1976.* New York: Praeger, 1977.

Gilbert, Robert E. *Television and Presidential Politics.* North Quincy, Mass.: Christopher Publishing, 1972.

Gillmor, Donald M., and Jerome A. Barron. *Mass Communication Law: Cases and Comment.* 4th ed. St. Paul, Minn.: West, 1984.

Gitlin, Todd. *Inside Prime Time.* New York: Pantheon, 1983.

Glick, Ira O., and Sidney J. Levy. *Living with Television.* Chicago: Aldine, 1962.

Glut, Donald F., and Jim Harmon. *The Great Television Heroes.* New York: Doubleday, 1975.

Goldmark, Peter C. *Maverick Inventor: My Turbulent Years at CBS.* New York: Saturday Review Press, 1973.

Goldsmith, Alfred N., and Austin C. Lescarboura. *This Thing Called Broadcasting.* New York: Holt, 1930.

Goldstein, Fred, and Stan Goldstein. *Prime-Time Television: A Pictorial History from Milton Berle to "Falcon Crest."* New York: Crown, 1983.

Graham, Margaret B. W. *RCA and the VideoDisc: The Business of Research.* New York: Cambridge, 1986.

Gramling, Oliver. *AP: The Story of News.* New York: Farrar & Rinehart, 1940 (reprinted by Greenwood, 1969).

Grandin, Thomas. *The Political Use of the Radio.* Geneva, Switzerland: Geneva Research Centre (*Studies* X:3), 1939 (reprinted by Arno Press, 1971).

Green, Timothy. *The Universal Eye: The World of Television.* New York: Stein and Day, 1972.

Greenberger, Martin, ed. *Electronic Publishing Plus: Media for a Technological Future.* White Plains, N.Y.: Knowledge Industry Publications, 1985.

Greenfield, Jeff. *Television: The First Fifty Years.* New York: Abrams, 1977.

Gross, Ben. *I Looked and I Listened: Informal Recollections of Radio and TV.* 2nd ed. New Rochelle, N.Y.: Arlington House, 1970.

Gross, Lynne Schafer. *The New Television Technologies.* 2nd ed. Dubuque, Iowa: Wm. C. Brown, 1986.

Guide to Independent Television. London: Independent Television (later Broadcasting) Authority, 1963–date, annual. (Note: title has been changed from year to year; *Television and Radio* was common in 1980s.)

Hadden, Jeffrey K., and Anson Shupe. *Televangelism: Power and Politics on God's Frontier.* New York: Henry Holt, 1988.

Halberstam, David. *The Powers That Be.* New York: Knopf, 1979.

Hale, Julian. *Radio Power: Propaganda and International Broadcasting.* Philadelphia: Temple University Press, 1975.

Hall, Jim. *Mighty Minutes: An Illustrated History of Television's Best Commercials.* New York: Harmony, 1984.

Hallin, Daniel C. *The "Uncensored War": The Media and Vietnam.* New York: Oxford, 1986.

Hammond, Charles M., Jr. *The Image Decade: Television Documentary, 1965–1975.* New York: Hastings House, 1981.

Hancock, H. E. *Wireless at Sea: The First Fifty Years.* Chelmsford, England: Marconi International Marine Communication Co., 1950 (reprinted by Arno Press, 1974).

Harlow, Alvin F. *Old Wires and New Waves: The History of the Telegraph, Telephone, and Wireless.* New York: Appleton-Century, 1936 (reprinted by Arno Press, 1971). Bibliography, pp. 527–538.

Harmon, Jim. *The Great Radio Heroes.* Garden City, N. Y.: Doubleday, 1967.

———. *The Great Radio Comedians.* Garden City, N.Y.: Doubleday, 1970.

Harris, Jay S. *TV Guide: The First 25 Years.* New York: Simon and Schuster, 1978.

Harris, Paul. *When Pirates Ruled the Waves.* Aberdeen, Scotland: Impulse Press, 1970.

Hawes, William. *American Television Drama: The Experimental Years.* University: University of Alabama Press, 1986.

Hawks, Ellison. *Pioneers of Wireless.* London: Methuen, 1927 (reprinted by Arno Press, 1974).

Head, Sydney W. *World Broadcasting Systems: A Comparative Analysis.* Belmont, Calif.: Wadsworth, 1985. Bibliography, pp. 423–438.

Head, Sydney W., ed. *Broadcasting in Africa: A Continental Survey of Radio and Television.* Philadelphia: Temple University Press, 1974. Bibliography, pp. 415–440.

Head, Sydney W., and Christopher H. Sterling. *Broadcasting in America: A Survey of Electronic Media.* Boston: Houghton Mifflin, 1956, 1972, 1976, 1982, 1990. (Head was sole author until 1982; subtitle has varied.) Bibliography (in last edition), pp. 547–581.

Heighton, Elizabeth, and Don R. Cunningham. *Advertising in the Broadcast Media.* Belmont, Calif.: Wadsworth, 1976, 1984.

Henck, Fred W., and Bernard Strassburg. *A Slippery Slope: The Long Road to the Breakup of AT&T.* Westport, Conn.: Greenwood, 1988.

Herring, James M., and Gerald C. Gross. *Telecommunications: Economics and Regulation.* New York: McGraw-Hill, 1936 (reprinted by Arno Press, 1974).

Hettinger, Herman S. *A Decade of Radio Advertising.* Chicago: University of Chicago Press, 1933 (reprinted by Arno Press, 1971).

Hettinger, Herman S., and Walter J. Neff. *Practical Radio Advertising.* New York: Prentice-Hall, 1938.

Hill, Harold. *NAEB History, 1925–1954.* 2nd ed. Washington: NAEB, 1965. (For continuation, see Alford, W. Wayne.)

Himmelweit, Hilde T., A. N. Oppenheim, and Pamela Vince. *Television and the Child.* New York: Oxford University Press, 1958.

Hogben, Lancelot. *From Cave Painting to Comic Strip: A Kaleidoscope of Human Communication.* New York: Chanticleer Press, 1949.

Horsfield, Peter G. *Religious Television: The American Experience.* New York: Longman, 1984.

Hosley, David H. *As Good as Any: Foreign Correspondence on American Radio, 1930–1940.* Westport, Conn.: Greenwood, 1984.

Howeth, L. S. *History of Communications-Electronics in the United States Navy.* Washington, D.C.: GPO, 1963.

Hubbell, Richard W. *4000 Years of Television: The Story of Seeing at a Distance.* New York: Putnam, 1942.

Husing, Ted. *Ten Years Before the Mike.* New York: Farrar & Rinehart, 1935.

Hutchinson, Thomas H. *Here Is Television: Your Window to the World.* New York: Hastings House, 1946, 1948, 1950.

Huth, Arno. *La Radiodiffusion Puissance Mondiale.* Paris: Librairie Gallimard, 1937 (reprinted by Arno Press, 1972). Bibliography, pp. 466–482. (In French.)

———. *Radio Today: The Present State of Broadcasting.* Geneva, Switzerland: Geneva Research Centre (*Studies* XII:6), 1942 (reprinted by Arno Press, 1971).

Independent Thinking: An Overview of the Independent Television Industry. Washington, D.C.: Frazier Gross & Kadlec Inc., 1986.

Inge, M. Thomas, ed. *Handbook of American Popular Culture.* Westport, Conn.: Greenwood, 1979–1981 (three volumes, each with extensive bibliographies).

Instant World: A Report on Telecommunications in Canada. Ottowa: Information Canada, 1971.

Johnson, Joseph S., and Kenneth Jones. *Modern Radio Station Practices.* Belmont, Calif.: Wadsworth, 1972, 1978.

Johnson, Katherine E., ed. *TV Guide 25 Year Index.* Radnor, Pa.: Triangle, 1979.

Johnson, Nicholas. *How to Talk Back to Your Television Set.* Boston: Little, Brown, 1970.

Johnson, William O. *Super Spectator and the Electric Lilliputians.* Boston: Little, Brown, 1971.

Johnston, Donald F. *Copyright Handbook*. New York: Bowker, 1982.

Jolly, W. P. *Marconi*. New York: Stein & Day, 1972.

Jome, Hiram L. *Economics of the Radio Industry*. Chicago: A. W. Shaw, 1925 (reprinted by Arno Press, 1971).

Jones, William K. *Cases and Materials on Electronic Mass Media: Radio, Television and Cable*. Mineola, N.Y.: Foundation Press, 1976, 1979.

Journal of Broadcasting (1956–date, quarterly; added *and Electronic Media* to title effective with vol. 29 in 1985). Major source of scholarly research and reference on radio and television; many historical research articles and bibliographies, 15 reprinted in Lichty and Topping (see below). A 25-year index was issued in spring 1982.

Journal of Law and Economics (1958–date, now twice yearly). Has published important articles on FCC, IRAC, media economics.

Journalism History (1973–date, quarterly).

Journalism Quarterly (1924–date, quarterly). General mass communications research. Published by the Association for Education in Journalism and Mass Communication. Cumulative indexes are published periodically.

Kahn, Frank J., ed. *Documents of American Broadcasting*. 4th ed. New York: Appleton-Century-Crofts, 1984. (Earlier editions also are useful.)

Kaltenborn, H. V. *I Broadcast the Crisis*. New York: Random House, 1938.

———. *Fifty Fabulous Years: 1900–1950*. New York: Putnam, 1950.

Kamen, Ira. *Questions and Answers about Pay-TV*. Indianapolis: Howard W. Sams, 1973.

Katz, Elihu, and George Wedell. *Broadcasting in the Third World: Promise and Performance*. Cambridge, Mass.: Harvard University Press, 1977.

Keith, Michael C., and Joseph M. Krause. *The Radio Station*. Stoneham, Mass.: Focal Press, 1986.

Kempner, Stanley. *Television Encyclopedia*. New York: Fairchild, 1948. Bibliography, pp. 401–415. Chronology, pp. 3–42.

Kendrick, Alexander. *Prime Time: The Life of Edward R. Murrow*. Boston: Little, Brown, 1969.

Kiernan, Thomas. *Citizen Murdoch*. New York: Dodd, Mead, 1986.

King, W. James. *The Development of Electrical Technology in the 19th Century: The Telegraph and the Telephone*. Washington, D.C.: U.S. National Museum (Bulletin 228), 1962 (reprinted by Arno Press, 1977).

Kirby, Edward M., and Jack W. Harris. *Star-Spangled Radio*. Chicago: Ziff-Davis, 1948.

Kittross, John M., ed. *Documents in American Telecommunications Policy*. New York: Arno Press, 1977 (2 volumes).

———. *Administration of American Telecommunications Policy*. New York: Arno Press, 1980 (2 volumes).

Klatell, David A., and Norman Marcus. *Sports for Sale: Television, Money, and the Fans*. New York: Oxford University Press, 1988.

Knightley, Phillip. *The First Casualty—From the Crimea to Vietnam: The War Correspondent as Hero, Propagandist, and Myth Maker*. New York: Harcourt Brace Jovanovich, 1975.

Koch, Howard. *The Panic Broadcast: Portrait of an Event*. Boston: Little Brown, 1970.

Koenig, Allen E., and Ruane B. Hill, eds. *The Farther Vision: Educational Television Today*. Madison: University of Wisconsin Press, 1967.

Krasnow, Erwin G., and Lawrence D. Longley. *The Politics of Broadcast Regulation*. New York: St. Martin's Press, 1973, 1978, 1982. (With Herbert Terry in 3rd ed.)

Kraus, Sidney, ed. *The Great Debates: Background, Perspectives, Effects*. Bloomington: Indiana University Press, 1962.

———. *The Great Debates: Carter vs. Ford 1976*. Bloomington: Indiana University Press, 1979.

Kris, Ernst, and Hans Speier. *German Radio Propaganda: Reports on Home Broadcasts During the War*. London: Oxford University Press, 1944.

LaGuardia, Robert. *Soap World*. New York: Arbor House, 1983.

Landry, Robert J. *This Fascinating Radio Business.* Indianapolis: Bobbs-Merrill, 1946.

Lang, Gladys Engel, and Kurt Lang. *The Battle for Public Opinion: The President, the Press, and the Polls During Watergate.* New York: Columbia University Press, 1983.

————. *Politics and Television Re-Viewed.* Beverly Hills, Calif.: Sage Publications, 1984.

Lardner, James. *Fast Forward: Hollywood, the Japanese, and the VCR Wars.* New York: W. W. Norton, 1987.

Lashner, Marilyn A. *The Chilling Effect in TV News: Intimidation by the Nixon White House.* New York: Praeger, 1984.

Lasswell, Harold D., et al., eds. *Propaganda and Communication in World History.* Honolulu: University of Hawaii Press, 1979–1980 (three volumes).

Law and Contemporary Problems (1933–date, quarterly). Journal of the School of Law, Duke University. See, especially, "Radio and Television" (22:4, 1957, and 23:1, 1958) and "Communications," (34:3–4, 1969).

Lazarsfeld, Paul F. *Radio and the Printed Page.* New York: Duell, Sloan & Pearce, 1940 (reprinted by Arno Press, 1971).

Lazarsfeld, Paul F., and Harry N. Field. *The People Look at Radio.* Chapel Hill: University of North Carolina Press, 1946 (reprinted by Arno Press, 1975).

Lazarsfeld, Paul F., and Patricia L. Kendall. *Radio Listening in America: The People Look at Radio—Again.* New York: Prentice-Hall, 1948.

Lazarsfeld, Paul F., and Frank N. Stanton, eds. *Radio Research 1941.* New York: Duell, Sloan & Pearce, 1941.

————. *Radio Research 1942–1943.* New York: Duell, Sloan & Pearce, 1944.

————. *Communications Research 1948–1949.* New York: Harper, 1949.

Lean, Tangye. *Voices in the Darkness: The European Radio War.* London: Secker and Warburg, 1943.

Leapman, Michael. *Barefaced Cheek.* London:

Hodder & Stoughton, 1983. (A biography of Rupert Murdoch.)

Le Duc, Don R. *Cable Television and the FCC: A Crisis in Media Control.* Philadelphia: Temple University Press, 1973. Bibliography, pp. 265–282.

————. *Beyond Broadcasting: Patterns in Policy and Law.* New York: Longman, 1987. Bibliography, pp. 195–207.

Lee, Alfred M. *The Daily Newspaper in America.* New York: Macmillan, 1937.

Leinwoll, Stanley. *From Spark to Satellite: A History of Radio Communication.* New York: Charles Scribner's Sons, 1979.

Lent, John A., ed. *Broadcasting in Asia and the Pacific: A Continental Survey of Radio and Television.* Philadelphia: Temple University Press, 1978. Bibliography, pp. 397–416.

Lessing, Lawrence. *Man of High Fidelity: Erwin Howard Armstrong.* Philadelphia: Lippincott, 1956 (revised edition, Bantam Books, 1969).

Levin, Harvey J. *Broadcast Regulation and Joint Ownership of Media.* New York: New York University Press, 1960.

————. *The Invisible Resource: Use and Regulation of the Radio Spectrum.* Baltimore: Johns Hopkins Press, 1971.

————. *Fact and Fancy in Television Regulation: An Economic Study of Policy Alternatives.* New York: Russell Sage Foundation, 1980.

Levin, Murray B. *Talk Radio and the American Dream.* Lexington, Mass.: Lexington Books, 1987.

Lewis, C. A. *Broadcasting from Within.* London: George Newnes, 1924.

Lichty, Lawrence W., and Malachi C. Topping, eds. *American Broadcasting: A Source Book on the History of Radio and Television.* New York: Hastings House, 1975. Bibliography, pp. 693–708.

Lingel, Robert. *Educational Broadcasting: A Bibliography.* Chicago: University of Chicago Press, 1932.

Lodge, Oliver J. *Signalling through Space without Wires: The Work of Hertz and His Successors.* 3rd ed. New York: Van Nostrand, 1900 (reprinted by Arno Press, 1974).

Lohr, Lenox. *Television Broadcasting: Production, Economics, Technique.* New York: McGraw-Hill, 1940.

Lowery, Shearon, and Melvin L. De Fleur. *Milestones in Mass Communication Research.* 2nd ed. New York: Longman, 1988.

Lumley, Frederick. *Measurement in Radio.* Columbus: Ohio State University Press, 1934 (reprinted by Arno Press, 1971). Bibliography, pp. 293–309.

Lyons, Eugene. *David Sarnoff: A Biography.* New York: Harper & Row, 1966.

Mabee, Carleton. *The American Leonardo: A Life of Samuel F. B. Morse.* New York: Knopf, 1943 (reprinted by Octagon Books, 1969).

MacDonald, J Fred. *Don't Touch That Dial! Radio Programming in American Life from 1920 to 1960.* Chicago: Nelson-Hall, 1979.

———. *Blacks and White TV: Afro-Americans in Television since 1948.* Chicago: Nelson-Hall, 1983.

———. *Television and the Red Menace: The Video Road to Vietnam.* New York: Praeger, 1985.

———. *Who Shot the Sheriff? The Rise and Fall of the Television Western.* New York: Praeger, 1987.

Maclaurin, W. Rupert. *Invention and Innovation in the Radio Industry.* New York: Macmillan, 1949 (reprinted by Arno Press, 1971).

MacNeil, Robert. *The People Machine: The Influence of Television on American Politics.* New York: Harper & Row, 1968.

Macy, John, Jr. *To Irrigate a Wasteland: The Struggle to Shape a Public Television System in the United States.* Berkeley: University of California Press, 1974.

Madsen, Axel. *60 Minutes: The Power & The Politics of America's Popular TV News Show.* New York: Dodd, Mead, 1984.

Maine, Basil. *The B.B.C. and Its Audience.* London: Thomas Nelson, 1939.

Mair, George. *Inside HBO: The Billion Dollar War Between HBO, Hollywood and the Home Video Revolution.* New York: Dodd, Mead, 1988.

Marconi, Degna. *My Father, Marconi.* New York: McGraw-Hill, 1962.

Marcus, Norman. *Broadcast and Cable Management.* Englewood Cliffs, N.J.: Prentice-Hall, 1986.

Marcus, Sheldon. *Father Coughlin: The Tumultuous Life of the Priest of the Little Flower.* Boston: Little, Brown, 1973.

Marill, Alvin H. *Movies Made for Television: The Telefeature and the Mini-Series, 1964–1984.* New York: New York Zoetrope, 1984.

Marland, E. A. *Early Electrical Communication.* London: Abelard-Schuman, 1964.

Marschall, Rick. *History of Television.* New York: Gallery Books, 1986.

Martin, James. *The Future of Telecommunications.* 2nd ed. Englewood Cliffs, N.J.: Prentice-Hall, 1976.

Matusow, Barbara. *The Evening Stars: The Making of the Network News Anchor.* Boston: Houghton Mifflin, 1983.

Mayer, Martin. *About Television.* New York: Harper & Row, 1972.

McCavitt, William E., and Peter K. Pringle. *Electronic Media Management.* Stoneham, Mass.: Focal Press, 1986.

McGinniss, Joe. *The Selling of the President 1968.* New York: Trident Press, 1969.

McMahon, A. Michal. *The Making of a Profession: A Century of Electrical Engineering in America.* New York: IEEE Press, 1984.

McNamee, Graham, in collaboration with Robert Gordon Anderson. *You're On the Air.* New York: Harper, 1926.

McNeil, Alex. *Total Television: A Comprehensive Guide to Programming from 1948 to 1980.* New York: Penguin, 1980.

McNeil, Bill, and Morris Wolfe. *Signing On: The Birth of Radio in Canada.* Toronto: Doubleday Canada, 1982.

McNicol, Donald. *Radio's Conquest of Space.* New

York: Murray Hill Books, 1946 (reprinted by Arno Press, 1974).

Meehan, Diana M. *Ladies of the Evening: Women Characters of Prime-Time Television.* Metuchen, N.J.: Scarecrow, 1983.

Merton, Robert K. *Mass Persuasion: The Social Psychology of a War Bond Drive.* New York: Harper: 1946 (reprinted by Greenwood, 1971).

Metz, Robert. *CBS: Reflections in a Bloodshot Eye.* Chicago: Playboy Press, 1975.

Meyrowitz, Joshua. *No Sense of Place: The Impact of Electronic Media on Social Behavior.* New York: Oxford University Press, 1985.

Michael, Paul, and James R. Parish. *The Emmy Awards: A Pictorial History.* New York: Crown, 1970.

Michelis, Anthony. *From Semaphore to Satellite.* Geneva, Switzerland: International Telecommunication Union, 1965.

Midgley, Ned. *The Advertising and Business Side of Radio.* New York: Prentice-Hall, 1948.

Milam, Lorenzo. *Sex and Broadcasting: A Handbook on Starting a Radio Station for the Community.* 3rd ed. Los Gatos, Calif.: Dildo Press, 1975 (reprinted by MHO and MHO Works, 1988).

Miller, Merle, and Evan Rhodes. *Only You, Dick Daring! Or, How to Write One Television Script and Make $50,000,000. A True-Life Adventure.* New York: William Sloane Associates, 1964.

Minow, Newton N., et al. *Presidential Television.* New York: Basic Books, 1973.

Mitz, Rick. *The Great TV Sitcom Book.* New York: Richard Marek, 1980.

Morris, Joe Alex. *Deadline Every Minute: The Story of the United Press.* New York: Doubleday, 1957.

Moseley, Sydney A. *John Baird: The Romance and Tragedy of the Pioneer of Television.* London: Odhams, 1952.

Mott, Frank Luther. *The News in America.* Cambridge, Mass.: Harvard University Press, 1952.

———. *American Journalism: A History 1690–1960.* 3rd ed. New York: Macmillan, 1962.

Murrow, Edward R. *This Is London.* New York: Simon and Schuster, 1941.

Murrow, Edward R., and Fred W. Friendly, eds. *See It Now.* New York: Simon and Schuster, 1955.

National Association of Broadcasters. *Broadcasting in the United States.* Washington, D.C.: NAB, 1933.

———. *Broadcasting and the Bill of Rights.* Washington, D.C.: NAB, 1947.

———. *Radio in Search of Excellence: Lessons from America's Best-Run Radio Stations.* Washington, D.C.: NAB, 1985.

National Association of Public Television Stations. *Public Television and Radio and State Governments.* Washington, D.C.: NAPTS, 1984 (two volumes).

National Broadcasting Company. *The Fourth Chime.* New York: NBC, 1944.

National Institute of Mental Health. *Television and Behavior: Ten Years of Scientific Progress and Implications for the Eighties.* Washington, D.C.: GPO, 1982 (two volumes).

Newcomb, Horace. *Television: The Critical View.* 4th ed. New York: Oxford University Press, 1987.

NHK (Nippon Hoso Kyokai). *The History of Broadcasting in Japan* and *50 Years of Japanese Broadcasting.* Tokyo: NHK, 1967 and 1977.

Nimmo, Dan, and James E. Combs. *Nightly Horrors: Crisis Coverage in Television Network News.* Knoxville: University of Tennessee Press, 1985.

Noll, Roger G., Merton J. Peck, and John McGowan. *Economic Aspects of Television Regulation.* Washington, D.C.: Brookings Institution, 1973.

Norman, Bruce. *Here's Looking at You: The Story of British Television 1908–1939.* London: BBC, 1984.

Nye, Russel B. *The Unembarrassed Muse: The Popular Arts in America.* New York: Dial Press, 1970.

O'Donnell, Lewis B., et al. *Radio Station Operations: Management and Employee Perspectives.* Belmont, Calif.: Wadsworth, 1989.

O'Hara, J. C., and W. Pricha. *Hertz and the Maxwellians: A Study and Documentation of the Dis-*

covery of Electromagnetic Wave Radiation, 1873–1894. London: Peter Peregrinus, 1987.

Owen, Bruce M. *Economics and Freedom of Expression: Media Structure and the First Amendment.* Cambridge, Mass.: Ballinger, 1975. Bibliography, pp. 193–197.

Owen, Bruce M., Jack H. Beebe, and Willard Manning, Jr. *Television Economics.* Lexington, Mass.: Lexington Books, 1974.

Paley, William S. *As It Happened: A Memoir.* New York: Doubleday, 1979.

Paper, Lewis. *Empire: William S. Paley and the Making of CBS.* New York: St. Martin's Press, 1987.

Passman, Arnold. *The Deejays.* New York: Macmillan, 1971.

Paulu, Burton. *Radio and Television Broadcasting on the European Continent.* Minneapolis: University of Minnesota Press, 1967. Bibliography, pp. 277–283.

———. *Radio and Television Broadcasting in Eastern Europe.* Minneapolis: University of Minnesota Press, 1974. Bibliography, pp. 573–581.

———. *Television and Radio in the United Kingdom.* Minneapolis: University of Minnesota Press, 1981. Bibliography, pp. 449–465. (See also the same author's two earlier studies on the same topic from the same publisher: *British Broadcasting* [1956], and *British Broadcasting in Transition* [1961].)

Pawley, Edward. *BBC Engineering: 1922–1972.* London: BBC, 1972.

Peers, Frank W. *The Politics of Canadian Broadcasting: 1920–1951.* Toronto: University of Toronto Press, 1969.

———. *The Public Eye: Television and the Politics of Canadian Broadcasting: 1952–1968.* Toronto: University of Toronto Press, 1979.

Pegg, Mark. *Broadcasting and Society 1918–1939.* Dover, N.H.: Croon Helm, 1983.

Perry, Armstrong. *Radio in Education: The Ohio School of Air and Other Experiments.* New York: Payne Fund, 1929 (reprinted by Arno Press, 1971).

Perry, Jeb H. *Universal Television: The Studio and Its Programs: 1950–1980.* Metuchen, N.J.: Scarecrow, 1983.

Persico, Joseph E. *Edward R. Murrow: An American Original.* New York: McGraw-Hill, 1988.

Peterson, Theodore. *Magazines in the Twentieth Century.* 2nd ed. Urbana: University of Illinois Press, 1964.

Phillips, Vivian J. *Early Radio Wave Detectors.* New York: Peter Peregrinus, 1980.

Poindexter, Ray. *Golden Throats and Silver Tongues: The Radio Announcers.* Conway, Ark.: River Road Press, 1978.

Pollay, Richard W., ed. *Information Sources in Advertising History.* Westport, Conn.: Greenwood, 1979.

Poltrack, David F. *Television Marketing: Network, Local, Cable.* New York: McGraw-Hill, 1983.

Pool, Ithiel de Sola, ed. *The Social Impact of the Telephone.* Cambridge, Mass.: MIT Press, 1977.

———. *Technologies of Freedom.* Cambridge, Mass.: Harvard University Press, 1983.

Pope, Daniel. *The Making of Modern Advertising.* New York: Basic Books, 1983.

Porterfield, John, and Kay Reynolds, eds. *We Present Television.* New York: W. W. Norton, 1940.

Powe, Lucas A., Jr. *American Broadcasting and the First Amendment.* Berkeley: University of California Press, 1987.

Powell, John Walker. *Channels of Learning: The Story of Educational Television.* Washington, D.C.: Public Affairs Press, 1962.

Powers, Ron. *The Newscasters.* New York: St. Martin's Press, 1977.

———. *Supertube: The Rise of Television Sports.* New York: Coward, McCann, 1984.

Prendergast, Curtis, with Geoffrey Colvin. *The World of Time Inc: The Intimate History of a Changing Enterprise 1960–1980.* New York: Atheneum, 1986.

Presbrey, Frank. *The History and Development of Advertising.* New York: Doubleday, Doran, 1929.

President's Task Force on Communications Policy. *Final Report.* Washington, D.C.: GPO, 1968.

Price, Jonathan. *The Best Thing on TV: Commercials*. New York: Penguin, 1978.

Prime, Samuel I. *The Life of Samuel F. B. Morse*. New York: Appleton, 1875 (reprinted by Arno Press, 1974).

Public Opinion Quarterly (1937–date, quarterly). Scholarly research on public opinion, polls, and media audiences.

Public Telecommunications Review (1973–1980, bimonthly). Topical research and comment on public radio-TV. Official journal of the National Association of Educational Broadcasters. See also *Educational Broadcasting Review*.

Quaal, Ward, and James A. Brown. *Broadcast Management*. 2nd ed. New York: Hastings House, 1975.

Quinlan, Sterling. *The Hundred Million Dollar Lunch*. Chicago: O'Hara, 1974.

———. *Inside ABC: American Broadcasting Company's Rise to Power*. New York: Hastings House, 1979.

Rader, Benjamin G. *In Its Own Image: How Television Has Transformed Sports*. New York: Free Press, 1984.

Radio Annual (1937–1964, annual). Trade directory with statistics, information on stations and networks, and review of previous year.

Radio Broadcast. (1922–1930, monthly). Popular discussion of the industry combined with technical advice for home receiver makers.

The Radio Industry: The Story of Its Development. Chicago: A. W. Shaw, 1928 (reprinted by Arno Press, 1974).

Radio Regulation. Washington, D.C.: Pike and Fischer, 1948–date (loose-leaf reporting service of FCC and court decisions).

Reid, James D. *The Telegraph in America: Its Founders, Promoters and Noted Men*. New York: Derby, 1879 (reprinted by Arno Press, 1974).

Reid, T. R. *The Chip*. New York: Simon and Schuster, 1984.

Reinsch, J. Leonard, and Elmo I. Ellis. *Radio Station Management*. 2nd ed. New York: Harper & Bros., 1960.

Rhodes, Frederick Leland. *Beginnings of Telephony*. New York: Harper, 1929 (reprinted by Arno Press, 1974).

Rivkin, Steven R. *Cable Television: A Guide to Federal Regulations*. Santa Monica, Calif.: Rand Corp., 1973.

Robinson, Michael J., and Austin Ranney, eds. *The Mass Media in Campaign '84*. Washington, D.C.: American Enterprise Institute, 1985.

Robinson, Michael, and Margaret Sheehan. *Over the Wire and on TV: CBS and UPI in Campaign '80*. New York: Russell Sage Foundation, 1983.

Robinson, Thomas Porter. *Radio Networks and the Federal Government*. New York: Columbia University Press, 1943 (reprinted by Arno Press, 1979).

Roe, Yale. *Television Station Management: The Business of Broadcasting*. New York: Hastings House, 1964.

Rogers, Everett. *Communication Technology: The New Media in Society*. New York: Free Press, 1986.

Rolo, Charles J. *Radio Goes to War: The "Fourth Front."* New York: Putnam, 1942.

Roper Organization, Inc. *Changing Public Attitudes toward Television and Other Mass Media*. New York: Television Information Office, 1959–1989. Title varies; issued approximately every 18 months for a total of 16 published reports. (When the TIO closed down in 1989, publication of this series was passed to the National Association of Broadcasters.)

Rose, Brian G., ed. *TV Genres: A Handbook and Reference Guide*. Westport, Conn.: Greenwood, 1985.

———. *Television and the Performing Arts: A Handbook and Reference Guide to American Cultural Programming*. Westport, Conn.: Greenwood, 1986.

Rose, Cornelia B., Jr. *National Policy for Radio Broadcasting*. New York: Harper, 1940 (reprinted by Arno Press, 1971).

Rose, Oscar. *Radio Broadcasting and Television: A Bibliography*. New York: H. W. Wilson, 1947.

Rosen, Philip T. *The Modern Stentors: Radio Broadcasters and the Federal Government*,

1920–1934. Westport, Conn.: Greenwood, 1980.

Rosewater, Victor. *History of Cooperative News-Gathering in the United States*. New York: Appleton, 1930 (reprinted by Greenwood, 1970).

Rothafel, Samuel L., and Raymond Francis Yates. *Broadcasting: Its New Day*. New York: Century, 1925 (reprinted by Arno Press, 1971).

Rowan, Ford. *Broadcast Fairness: Doctrine, Practice, Prospects*. New York: Longman, 1984.

Rowland, Willard. *The Politics of TV Violence: Policy Issues of Communication Research*. Beverly Hills, Calif.: Sage, 1983.

Rowman, James W. *Cablemania: The Cable Television Sourcebook*. Englewood Cliffs, N.J.: Prentice-Hall, 1983.

Rucker, Bryce W. *The First Freedom*. Carbondale: Southern Illinois University Press, 1968.

Saettler, Paul. *A History of Instructional Technology*. New York: McGraw-Hill, 1968. Bibliography, pp. 371–384.

Sarnoff, David. *Network Broadcasting*. New York: RCA, 1939.

———. *Looking Ahead: The Papers of David Sarnoff*. New York: McGraw-Hill, 1968.

Schechter, A. A., with Edward Anthony. *I Live on Air*. New York: Stokes, 1941.

Schemering, Christopher. *The Soap Opera Encyclopedia*. New York: Ballantine, 1985.

Schmeckebier, Laurence F. *The Federal Radio Commission: Its History, Activities and Organization*. Washington, D.C.: Brookings Institution, 1932. Bibliography, pp. 135–157.

Schramm, Wilbur, Jack Lyle, and Edwin B. Parker. *Television in the Lives of Our Children*. Stanford, Calif.: Stanford University Press, 1961. Bibliography, pp. 297–317.

Schramm, Wilbur, et al. *The People Look at Educational Television*. Stanford, Calif.: Stanford University Press, 1963.

Schubert, Paul. *The Electric Word: The Rise of Radio*. New York: Macmillan, 1928 (reprinted by Arno Press, 1971).

Schwartz, Bernard. *The Professor and the Commissions*. New York: Knopf, 1959.

Seehafer, Eugene, and J. W. Laemmar. *Successful Radio and Television Advertising*. New York: McGraw-Hill, 1951, 1959.

Seiden, Martin H. *Cable Television U S A: An Analysis of Government Policy*. New York: Praeger, 1972.

———. *Who Controls the Media? Popular Myths and Economic Realities*. New York: Basic Books, 1974.

Sendall, Bernard. *Independent Television in Britain: Origin and Foundation, 1946–62*. London: Macmillan, 1982.

———. *Independent Television in Britain: Expansion and Change, 1958–68*. London: Macmillan, 1983.

Sennett, Ted. *Your Show of Shows*. New York: Collier, 1977.

Settel, Irving. *A Pictorial History of Radio*. 2nd ed. New York: Grosset & Dunlap, 1967.

Settel, Irving, and William Laas. *A Pictorial History of Television*. New York: Grosset & Dunlap, 1969.

Sevareid, Eric. *Not So Wild A Dream*. New York: Knopf, 1946 (reprinted by Atheneum, 1976).

Shayon, Robert Lewis. *Television and Our Children*. New York: Longmans, Green, 1951.

Sheldon, H. Horton, and Edgar Norman Grisewood. *Television: Present Methods of Picture Transmission*. New York: Van Nostrand, 1929.

Sherman, Barry L. *Telecommunications Management: The Broadcast and Cable Industries*. New York: McGraw-Hill, 1987.

Shiers, George, ed. *Technical Development of Television*. New York: Arno Press, 1977.

Shiers, George, with May Shiers. *Bibliography of the History of Electronics*. Metuchen, N.J.: Scarecrow, 1972. (Concentrates on electrical communications, both wired and wireless.)

Shirer, William L. *Berlin Diary: The Journal of a Foreign Correspondent 1934–1941*. New York: Knopf, 1941.

Shulman, Arthur, and Roger Youman. *How Sweet It Was: Television—A Pictorial Commentary*. New York: Shorecrest, 1966.

Shurick E. P. J. *The First Quarter-Century of*

American Broadcasting. Kansas City: Midland, 1946.

Siepmann, Charles A. *Radio's Second Chance*. Boston: Little, Brown, 1946.

————. *Radio, Television, and Society*. New York: Oxford University Press,1950.

Simmons, Steven J. *The Fairness Doctrine and the Media*. Berkeley: University of California Press, 1978.

Singleton, Loy A. *Telecommunications in the Information Age*. 2nd ed. Cambridge, Mass.: Ballinger, 1986.

Sivowitch, Elliot. "A Technological Survey of Broadcasting's 'Pre-History,' 1987–1920," *Journal of Broadcasting* 14:1–20 (Winter 1970–1971). Also in Lichty and Topping (above).

Sklar, Robert. *Prime-Time America: Life Behind the Television Screen*. New York: Oxford University Press, 1980.

Skornia, Harry J., and Jack William Kitson. *Problems and Controversies in Television and Radio*. Palo Alto, Calif.: Pacific Books, 1968.

Slate, Sam J., and Joe Cook. *It Sounds Impossible*. New York: Macmillan, 1963.

Slater, Robert. *This . . . Is CBS: A Chronicle of 60 Years*. Englewood Cliffs, N.J.: Prentice-Hall, 1988.

Slide, Anthony. *Great Radio Personalities in Historic Photographs*. New York: Dover, 1982.

Small, William. *To Kill a Messenger: Television News and the Real World*. New York: Hastings House, 1970.

Smart, James R., comp. *Radio Broadcasts in the Library of Congress: 1924–1941*. Washington, D.C.: Library of Congress, 1982.

Smead, Elmer E. *Freedom of Speech by Radio and Television*. Washington, D.C.: Public Affairs Press, 1959.

Smith, Anthony. *The Shadow in the Cave: The Broadcaster, the Audience, and the State*. Urbana: University of Illinois Press, 1973.

————. *The Geopolitics of Information*. New York: Oxford University Press, 1980.

Smith, Delbert D. *Communication via Satellite: A Vision in Retrospect*. Boston: Sijthoff, 1976.

Smith, George David. *The Anatomy of a Business Strategy: Bell, Western Electric, and the Origins of the American Telephone Industry*. Baltimore: Johns Hopkins University Press, 1985.

Smith, Myron J., Jr. *U.S. Television Network News: A Guide to Sources in English*. Jefferson, N.C.: McFarland, 1984.

Smith, R. Franklin. *Edward R. Murrow: The War Years*. Kalamazoo, Mich.: New Issues Press (Western Michigan University), 1978.

Smith, Ralph Lee. *The Wired Nation: Cable TV— The Electronic Communications Highway*. New York: Harper & Row, 1972.

Smythe, Dallas W. *Structure and Policy of Electrical Communications*. Urbana: University of Illinois Press, 1957 (reprinted by Arno Press, 1977).

Sobel, Robert. *RCA*. New York: Stein & Day, 1986.

Socolow, A. Walter. *The Law of Radio Broadcasting*. New York: Baker, Voorhis, 1939 (two volumes).

Soley, Lawrence C., and John S. Nichols. *Clandestine Radio Broadcasting: A Study of Revolutionary and Counterrevolutionary Electronic Communication*. New York: Praeger, 1987.

Spalding, John W., "1928: Radio Becomes a Mass Advertising Medium," *Journal of Broadcasting* 8:31–44 (Winter 1963–1964). Also in Lichty and Topping (above).

Sperber, A. M. *Murrow: His Life and Times*. New York: Freundlich Books, 1986.

Sponsor (1946–1968, weekly, then monthly). Broadcast advertising trade magazine. See special issues on "40 Year Album of Pioneer Radio Stations" (May 1962); "CBS: Documenting 38 Years of Exciting History" (September 13, 1965); and "NBC: A Documentary" (May 16, 1966).

Stedman, Raymond. *The Serials: Suspense and Drama by Installment*. 2nd ed. Norman: University of Oklahoma Press, 1977. Bibliography, pp. 538–553.

Steiner, Gary. *The People Look at Television: A Study of Audience Attitudes.* New York: Knopf, 1963.

Sterling, Christopher H. *Electronic Media: A Guide to Trends in Broadcasting and Newer Technologies, 1920–1983.* New York: Praeger, 1984. Bibliography, pp. 311–335.

Sterling, Christopher H., and Timothy R. Haight, eds. *The Mass Media: Aspen Guide to Communication Industry Trends.* New York: Praeger Special Studies, 1978. Bibliography, pp. 429–448.

Stokes, John W. *70 Years of Radio Tubes and Valves.* Vestal, N.Y.: Vestal Press, 1982.

Stone, David M. *Nixon and the Politics of Public Television.* New York: Garland, 1985.

Storey, Graham. *Reuters: The Story of a Century of News-Gathering.* New York: Crown, 1951 (reprinted by Greenwood, 1970).

Strong, William S. *The Copyright Book: A Practical Guide.* 2nd ed. Cambridge, Mass.: MIT Press, 1984.

Studies in Broadcasting. Cambridge, Mass.: Harvard Radiobroadcasting Project, 1940–1948 (reprinted by Arno Press, 1971).

Sturmey, S. G. *The Economic Development of Radio.* London: Duckworth, 1958.

Sugar, Bert Randolph. *"The Thrill of Victory": The Inside Story of ABC Sports.* New York: Hawthorne, 1978.

Summers, Harrison B., ed. *Radio Censorship.* New York: H. W. Wilson, 1939 (reprinted by Arno Press, 1971). Bibliography, pp. 285–297.

———. *A Thirty-Year History of Programs Carried on National Radio Networks in the United States, 1926–1956.* Columbus: Ohio State University, Department of Speech, 1958 (reprinted by Arno Press, 1971).

Summers, Robert E., and Harrison B. Summers. *Broadcasting and the Public.* Belmont, Calif: Wadsworth, 1966, 1978. (With John Pennybacker in 2nd ed.)

Surgeon General's Scientific Advisory Committee on Television and Social Behavior. *Television and Growing Up: The Impact of Televised Violence.* Washington, D.C.: GPO, 1972.

Swerdlow, Joel L. *Beyond Debate: A Paper on Televised Presidential Debates.* New York: Twentieth Century Fund, 1984.

Swift, John. *Adventure in Vision: The First 25 Years of Television.* London: John Lehmann, 1950.

Tebbel, John. *The Media in America.* New York: Crowell, 1975.

Television (1944–1968, monthly). Feature articles on the television industry.

Television Digest (1945–date, weekly). Detailed and informed newsletter of broadcasting and electronics industries.

Television Factbook (1945–date, biennial to late 1950s, then annual). Major reference directory of entire television industry—with useful data and statistics.

Television Quarterly (1962–date, quarterly, though issued irregularly in mid-1970s). Official journal of the National Academy of Television Arts and Sciences.

Television/Radio Age (1953–date, biweekly), covers programming and advertising. See NBC 60th Anniversary Issue, May 1986.

Temin, Peter, with Louis Galambos. *The Fall of the Bell System.* New York: Cambridge University Press, 1987.

Temporary Commission on Alternative Financing for Public Telecommunications (TCAF). *Report to the Congress.* Washington, D.C.: TCAF/FCC, 1982–1983.

Terrace, Vincent. *The Complete Encyclopedia of Television Programs, 1947–1979.* 2nd ed. Cranbury, N.J.: A. S. Barnes, 1979.

———. *Radio's Golden Years: The Encyclopedia of Radio Programs, 1930–1960.* San Diego: A. S. Barnes, 1981.

Thompson, Robert L. *Wiring a Continent: The History of the Telegraph Industry in the United States (1832–1866).* Princeton, N.J.: Princeton University Press, 1947 (reprinted by Arno Press, 1972). Bibliography, pp. 518–526.

Toll, Robert C. *The Entertainment Machine: American Show Business in the Twentieth Century.* New York: Oxford University Press, 1982.

Tunstall, Jeremy, and David Walker. *Media Made in California: Hollywood, Politics and the News.* New York: Oxford University Press, 1981.

Turow, Joseph. *Entertainment, Education, and the Hard Sell: Three Decades of Network Children's Television.* New York: Praeger, 1981.

————. *Media Industries: The Production of News and Entertainment.* New York: Longman, 1984.

TV Guide. (1953–date, weekly). See especially the Fall Preview Issue each September.

Tyler, Tracy F. *An Appraisal of Radio Broadcasting in the Land-Grant Colleges and State Universities.* Washington, D.C.: National Committee on Education by Radio, 1933.

Tyne, Gerald. *Saga of the Vacuum Tube.* Indianapolis: Howard W. Sams, 1977.

Udelson, Joseph H. *The Great Television Race: A History of the American Television Industry, 1925–1941.* University: University of Alabama Press, 1982.

United Nations Educational, Scientific, and Cultural Organization (Unesco). *Many Voices, One World: Communications and Society Today and Tomorrow.* Paris: Unesco, 1980 (the "MacBride Commission" report).

————. *Press, Film, Radio: Reports on the Facilities of Mass Communication.* Paris: Unesco, 1947–1951 (seven volumes reprinted in three by Arno Press, 1972).

————. *Television: A World Survey,* and *Supplement.* Paris: Unesco, 1953, 1955 (reprinted in one volume by Arno Press, 1972).

————. *World Communications: A 200 Country Survey of Press, Radio, Television, Film.* Paris: Unesco, 1950, 1951, 1956, 1964, and 1975. (Subtitle varies.)

United States, Congress, House of Representatives. *Radio Laws of the United States.* Washington, D.C.: GPO, 1972 (revised from time to time with varied titles).

United States, Congress, House of Representatives, Committee on Interstate and Foreign Commerce. *Regulation of Broadcasting.* 85th

Cong., 2nd Sess., 1958. (Prepared by Robert S. McMahon.)

————. *Investigation of Television Quiz Shows.* Hearings. 86th Cong., 1st Sess., 1960 (two volumes).

————. *Responsibilities of Broadcast Licensees.* Hearings. 86th Cong., 2nd Sess., 1960 (two volumes).

United States, Congress, Senate, Committee on Interstate and Foreign Commerce. *Television Inquiry.* Hearings in Six Parts, with several interim and special reports. 84th and 85th Congs., 1956–1958.

United States, Department of Commerce. "Recommendations of the [Second] National Radio Committee," *Radio Service Bulletin* (April 2, 1923), pp. 9–13 (reprinted, with next five items, in Kittross, 1977, above).

————. *Recommendations for Regulation of Radio Adopted by the Third National Radio Conference.* Washington, D.C.: GPO, 1924.

————. *Proceedings of the Fourth National Radio Conference and Recommendations for Regulation of Radio.* Washington, D.C.: GPO, 1926.

————. *Annual Report of the Commissioner of Navigation to the Secretary of Commerce.* Washington, D.C.: GPO, 1921–1926.

————. *Annual Report of the Chief of the Radio Division to the Secretary of Commerce.* Washington, D.C.: GPO, 1927–1932.

Variety (1905–date, weekly). Major trade weekly of show business.

Vaughn, Robert. *Only Victims: A Study of Show Business Blacklisting.* New York: Putnam, 1972. Bibliography, pp. 340–348.

Vogel, Harold L. *Entertainment Industry Economics: A Guide for Financial Analysis.* New York: Cambridge University Press, 1986.

Waldrop, Frank C., and Joseph Borkin. *Television: A Struggle for Power.* New York: Morrow, 1938 (reprinted by Arno Press, 1971).

Waller, Judith C. *Radio, the Fifth Estate.* 2nd ed. Boston: Houghton Mifflin, 1950.

Warner, Charles. *Broadcast and Cable Selling.* Belmont, Calif.: Wadsworth, 1986.

Warner, Harry P. *Radio and Television Law* and *Radio and Television Rights*. Albany, N.Y.: Matthew Bender, 1948, 1953.

Webb, G. Kent. *The Economics of Cable Television*. Lexington, Mass.: Lexington Books, 1983.

Wedlake, G. E. C. *SOS: The Story of Radio Communication*. Newton Abbot, England: David & Charles, 1973.

Weinberg, Meyer. *TV and America: The Morality of Hard Cash*. New York: Ballantine, 1962.

Wertheim, Arthur Frank. *Radio Comedy*. New York: Oxford University Press, 1979.

White, David Manning, and Richard Averson, eds. *Sight, Sound, and Society: Motion Pictures and Television in America*. Boston: Beacon, 1968.

White, Llewellyn. *The American Radio*. Chicago: University of Chicago Press, 1947 (reprinted by Arno Press, 1971).

White, Paul W. *News on the Air*. New York: Harcourt, Brace, 1947. Bibliography, pp. 374–392.

Whitfield, Stephen E., and Gene Roddenberry. *The Making of Star Trek*. New York: Ballantine, 1968.

Wilk, Max. *The Golden Age of Television: Notes from the Survivors*. New York: Delacorte, 1976.

Williams, Christian. *Lead, Follow or Get Out of the Way: The Story of Ted Turner*. New York: Times Books, 1981.

Williams, Frederick. *The New Communications*. 2nd ed. Belmont, Calif.: Wadsworth, 1989.

Wilson, Geoffrey. *The Old Telegraphs*. London: Phillimore, 1976.

Wimmer, Roger D., and Joseph R. Dominick. *Mass Media Research: An Introduction*. 2nd ed. Belmont, Calif.: Wadsworth, 1987.

Winkler, Allan M. *The Politics of Propaganda: The Office of War Information 1942–1945*. New Haven: Yale University Press, 1978.

Winship, Michael. *Television*. New York: Random House, 1988.

Winston, Brian. *Misunderstanding Media*. New York: Oxford University Press, 1986.

Witherspoon, John, and Roselle Kovitz. *The History of Public Broadcasting*. Washington, D.C.: Current, 1987.

Wolfe, Charles H., ed. *Modern Radio Advertising*. New York: Funk and Wagnalls, 1949.

Wood, Donald N., and Donald G. Wylie. *Educational Telecommunications*. Belmont, Calif.: Wadsworth, 1977.

Woolery, George W. *Children's Television: The First Thirty-Five Years, 1946–1981*. Metuchen, N.J.: Scarecrow, 1983, 1985 (two volumes).

Woolley, Lynn, et al. *Warner Bros. Television: Every Show of the Fifties and Sixties Episode-by-Episode*. Jefferson, N.C.: McFarland, 1985.

World Radio-TV Handbook. New York: Billboard Publications, annual.

Wylie, Max. *Clear Channels: Television and the American People*. New York: Funk and Wagnalls, 1955.

Yates, Raymond Francis, and Louis Gerard Pacent. *The Complete Radio Book*. New York: Century, 1922.

The Year Book of Wireless Telegraphy and Telephony. London: The Wireless Press, 1913–1923 (annual). Each volume includes a detailed bibliography.

Finding Out More About the Development of Broadcasting

Following are just a few of the more important groups, museums, archives, libraries, and sources of program scripts.

1.   *Museums/Libraries/Archives*

American Advertising Museum, 9 NW Second Ave., Portland, Ore. 97209
Excellent exhibit and extensive collection on print and broadcast advertising with screening of classic television ads.

ATAS-UCLA Television Archive, University of California, Melnitz Hall, Room 1438, Los Angeles, Calif. 90024
One of the larger collections of television programs on both film and videotape.

Broadcast Pioneers Library, 1771 N St. NW, Washington, D.C. 20036
One of the largest archives of books, papers, documents, recordings, photos, and so on for the entire history of broadcasting. Issues a newsletter and offers research assistance. Formed in 1971.

A Directory of Broadcast Archives by Donald R. Godfrey (published by Broadcast Education Association, 1983) is now out of print but may be found in many libraries. It offers 90 pages listing collections by state with details on each.

Division of Electricity and Nuclear Energy, National Museum of American History, Smithsonian Institution, Washington, D.C. 20560
Owns the massive Clark "Radioana" collection of paper memorabilia from radio's early days, plus premier collection of electrical communication devices and related archives.

Mass Communications History Center, State Historical Society of Wisconsin, Madison, Wisc. 53705
Formed in 1955 around the papers of newscaster H. V. Kaltenborn and now covers all media. Holds most of NBC archives.

Motion Picture and Sound Recording Branch, National Archives, Washington, D.C. 20408
Many catalog aids are available for this huge collection of thousands of news, documentary, and government radio, television, and film programs.

Museum of Broadcasting, 1 East 53rd St., New York, N.Y. 10022
Collects, preserves, and exhibits radio and television programs, issues valuable catalogs of programs and stars, and holds exhibitions on radio and (especially) television.

Vanderbilt Television News Archive, Vanderbilt University, Nashville, Tenn. 37203
Keeps videotapes of all network newscasts and special events since 1968; has published index since 1972.

2.   Old-Time Radio Groups/Archives

The Friends of Old Time Radio, Jay Hickerson, P.O. Box 4321, Hamden, Conn. 06514
Has run an annual convention since 1976 with workshops, re-creations of radio shows, dealer tables, and so on. Hickerson has long issued a bimonthly newsletter called *Hello Again* on programs available on tape.

North American Radio Archives, P.O. Box 118781, Cincinnati, Ohio 45211
Lending library of open-reel and cassette tapes plus large collection of scripts and books. Quarterly newsletter.

Radio Historical Association of Colorado (RHAC), P.O. Box 1908, Englewood, Colo. 80150
Formed in 1975 and operates both a lending tape library and a printed reference library. Monthly newsletter.

Society to Preserve and Encourage Radio Drama, Variety, and Comedy (SPERDVAC), P.O. Box 1587, Hollywood, Calif. 90078
Largest group in the country, formed in late 1974. Has two tape libraries: one from original source material, the other from a variety of sources. Monthly newsletter and meetings in Los Angeles area, plus national convention.

3.   Sources of Scripts and Sound Tracks

Published Radio, Television, and Film Scripts: A Bibliography by G. Howard Poteet (Troy, N.Y.: Whitson Publishing, 1975) is the only guide of its kind and is divided into sections on each of the listed media.

Radio Soundtracks: A Reference Guide, 2nd ed., by Michael R. Pitts (Metuchen, N.J.: Scarecrow Press, 1986) offers details on more than 1,000 programs and series available on tape or records.

Index